Annual Review of Environment and Resources

EDITORIAL COMMITTEE (2003)

PAMELA A. MATSON (EDITOR)
ASHOK GADGIL (ASSOCIATE EDITOR)
DANIEL M. KAMMEN (ASSOCIATE EDITOR)
WILLIAM C. CLARK
PETER H. GLEICK
DONALD KENNEDY
DIANA LIVERMAN
DAVID S. SCHIMEL

RESPONSIBLE FOR THE ORGANIZATION OF VOLUME 28 (EDITORIAL COMMITTEE, 2002)

PAMELA A. MATSON (EDITOR)
ASHOK GADGIL (ASSOCIATE EDITOR)
WILLIAM C. CLARK
PETER H. GLEICK
DANIEL M. KAMMEN
DONALD KENNEDY
DIANA LIVERMAN
DAVID S. SCHIMEL

Production Editor: JESSLYN S. HOLOMBO
Bibliographic Quality Control: MARY A. GLASS
Electronic Content Coordinator: SUZANNE K. MOSES
Subject Indexer: BRUCE TRACY

ANNUAL REVIEW OF ENVIRONMENT AND RESOURCES

VOLUME 28, 2003

PAMELA A. MATSON, *Editor*
Stanford University

ASHOK GADGIL, *Associate Editor*
Lawrence Berkeley National Laboratory

DANIEL M. KAMMEN, *Associate Editor*
University of California, Berkeley

www.annualreviews.org   science@annualreviews.org   650-493-4400

ANNUAL REVIEWS
4139 El Camino Way • P.O. Box 10139 • Palo Alto, California 94303-0139

ANNUAL REVIEWS
Palo Alto, California, USA

COPYRIGHT © 2003 BY ANNUAL REVIEWS, PALO ALTO, CALIFORNIA, USA. ALL RIGHTS RESERVED. The appearance of the code at the bottom of the first page of an article in this serial indicates the copyright owner's consent that copies of the article may be made for personal or internal use, or for the personal or internal use of specific clients. This consent is given on the condition that the copier pay the stated per-copy fee of $14.00 per article through the Copyright Clearance Center, Inc. (222 Rosewood Drive, Danvers, MA 01923) for copying beyond that permitted by Section 107 or 108 of the US Copyright Law. The per-copy fee of $14.00 per article also applies to the copying, under the stated conditions, of articles published in any *Annual Review* serial before January 1, 1978. Individual readers, and nonprofit libraries acting for them, are permitted to make a single copy of an article without charge for use in research or teaching. This consent does not extend to other kinds of copying, such as copying for general distribution, for advertising or promotional purposes, for creating new collective works, or for resale. For such uses, written permission is required. Write to Permissions Dept., Annual Reviews, 4139 El Camino Way, P.O. Box 10139, Palo Alto, CA 94303-0139 USA.

International Standard Serial Number: 1543-5938
International Standard Book Number: 0-8243-2328-9

All Annual Reviews and publication titles are registered trademarks of Annual Reviews.

⊚ The paper used in this publication meets the minimum requirements of American National Standards for Information Sciences—Permanence of Paper for Printed Library Materials, ANSI Z39.48-1992.

Annual Reviews and the Editors of its publications assume no responsibility for the statements expressed by the contributors to this *Annual Review*.

TYPESET BY TECHBOOKS, FAIRFAX, VA
PRINTED AND BOUND BY MALLOY INCORPORATED, ANN ARBOR, MI

Preface

Many have called the twenty-first century the "century of the environment." In a similar vein, others have identified sustainable development as the central challenge of this new millennium and emphasized the dual goals of meeting human needs while (or by) preserving the life support systems of the planet. These perspectives are at the heart of our concept for the *Annual Review of Environment and Resources*. This series will focus on the interactions between nature and society and between environment and development. The *Annual Review of Environment and Resources* will include reviews on the scientific, policy, and technological issues related to Earth's life support systems, sectors of human activities, and human dimensions of environmental change and management.

Beginning with this volume, the *Annual Review of Environment and Resources* replaces the *Annual Review of Energy and Environment*. Energy systems will still be an important focus of the journal, but we are now including in-depth reviews in a wider field of view. We want these reviews to provide scholars and practitioners in a range of fields with a thorough, fundamental analysis of the most critical and integrative issues and controversies in the environment and resource arena. We hope too that the journal will be an essential guide within a number of disciplines and a unique resource for interdisciplinary thinking, education, and research.

It is our intention that each volume will provide peer-reviewed syntheses of current literature in most of the following categories:

I. Earth's Life Support Systems
  Climate
  Atmosphere
  Marine and Terrestrial Ecosystems
  Biogeochemistry

II. Human Use of Environment and Resources
  Energy
  Water
  Agriculture
  Settlements
  Industry and Manufacturing
  Living Resources
  Land Use

III. Management and Human Dimensions
  Governance
  Methods

Observations/Monitoring/Indicators
Health and Well-being
Population and Consumption
Ethics/Values/Justice

IV. Emerging Integrative Themes

Who should read the *Annual Review of Environment and Resources*? This journal will be a useful resource for researchers and practitioners working on nature-society interactions who want and ought to know the current state of affairs on topics such as those listed above, but who do not have the time to cover the individual articles in each of the dozen or so high impact journals that would need to be read to keep up to date. We also hope this annual review will be useful to faculty and students presently using textbooks in environmental science and policy. It will update and provide the most recent take on many of the same issues covered more generally in such texts. In effect, we intend that this journal be used as a rolling textbook or desk reference about environment, resources, and society. Finally, we hope that this journal will count among its readership nonscientists who are professionally charged with making sense of changing environmental issues—for example, journalists, congressional and agency staff, and international organization analysts. We believe that the authoritative, up-to-date reviews will provide key background information at the intersections of science and policy.

Volume 28 is an exciting beginning. The reviews collected here provide analysis, review, and guides to the emerging literature in fast moving and diverse fields. A theme that runs through many of the reviews in the life support systems category reflects on the growing scientific understanding of the linkages among spatially separate parts of the earth system. Guiling Wang and David Schimel address an area of research that has yielded tremendous progress over the past decade. They review the state of knowledge concerning dynamical climate modes that result in synchronized climate behavior in regions that are geographically far apart. The chapter illustrates the ecological and biological impacts of modes and discusses the evidence for relationships between mode changes and global climate change. Several chapters in this category explore atmospheric processes and include the use of new measurement capabilities and dynamical models for analysis of change. In his synthesis of the rapidly growing literature on the oxidizing and cleansing capacity of the atmosphere, Ronald Prinn provides a primer on tropospheric and stratospheric oxidation chemistry and then explores global change in chemistry due to natural and human processes, the progress made with in situ measurement, as well as the role of chemical transport models in testing knowledge. James Fine, Laurent Vuilleumier, Steve Reynolds, Philip Roth, and Nancy Brown discuss the sources and importance of uncertainties in photochemical air quality simulation modeling for use in local and regional regulatory planning. Although mixing and transport in the atmosphere have been long recognized, the synthesis presented by William Reiners and Kenneth Driese illustrates the intrinsic importance of a number of less well recognized transport vectors in connecting the biosphere at all scales; they conclude their rich review and synthesis with a discussion of the extent to which human actions have altered these vectors.

Ecosystems, the species that inhabit them, and the biogeochemical processes that link them with other systems locally and globally are also critical elements of Earth's life support systems. The state of global biodiversity and its loss due to human activities are themes that have garnered considerable public and scientific attention over the past decade. Rodolfo Dirzo and Peter Raven examine the nature and distribution of Earth's biodiversity today and summarize the knowledge about extinction rates and the factors that most critically drive them. With a focus on forest ecosystems, Stith Gower summarizes the state of knowledge on the regulation and controls on carbon cycling and the influence of disturbances and human-caused global changes, such as elevated CO_2, nitrogen deposition, and climate change, on carbon storage and processing in forests. His review concludes with a brief analysis of forests in the context of greenhouse gas management schemes, a topic addressed in greater depth in a later chapter by Lisa Dilling and her colleagues.

Our second major category delves into the patterns and consequences of human uses of environment and resources. Eric Lambin, Helmut Geist, and Erika Lepers explore the dynamics of land-use change, provide recent change estimates for different land-uses (such as cropland, tropical forests, pastures, and urban land covers), and illustrate how a finite set of pathways interact to drive land-use decisions. Although the growth of urban centers is just one element of land-use change, it has tremendous import in terms of meeting the needs of the human population as well as in environmental impact. Gordon McGranahan and David Satterthwaite review the scale and nature of urban change and the consequences for environment and sustainability, emphasizing the tight coupling between urban systems and the resources and sinks outside their boundaries.

Water resources research has traditionally focused on water supply and flow to users. In his review and synthesis, Peter Gleick refocuses our attention on the questions of how societies use water and how efficiency and productivity of water use can and are being improved. Issues of efficiency and productivity are also the focus of a chapter on changing agricultural yields, written by Kenneth Cassman, Achim Dobermann, Daniel Walters, and Haishun Yang. The authors explore the potential for increasing yields of major cereal crops while reducing environmental consequences. Ray Hilborn and his coauthors likewise tackle sustainable resource use in their chapter on the state of the world's marine fisheries and the communities and institutions that interact with them; the review ends with a discussion of two contrasting futures for fisheries, one sustainable and one of continued collapse, that are unfolding in different regions. The final chapter in this section discusses the issue of sustainability perspectives in manufacturing. Anne Marteel, Julian Davies, Walter Olson, and Martin Abraham summarize the state of thinking on green chemistry and engineering, including a discussion of drivers and metrics, and then focus in on a specific example (the hydroformylation processes) to illustrate how some of the principles of green chemistry are used in real life.

In the third major category of this volume, six chapters explore several dimensions of the management and measurement of environment and resources. The first of these delves into governance structures and approaches through a review and synthesis of international environmental agreements. Ronald Mitchell provides a survey of the hundreds of international legal agreements that address environmental issues and reviews research on the factors that influence negotiation and performance. Two chapters analyze critical tools and methods for measuring and monitoring aspects of resource use and environmental change. Thomas McKone and Matthew MacLeod review the development and use of multimedia mass-balance models to evaluate pollutant fate and human and ecosystem exposure at a range of spatial scales; they end with a discussion of evaluation strategies and uncertainties in these approaches. Michael Goodchild follows with a synthesis of the recent advances in the uses, capabilities, and operability of geographic information systems for analysis and modeling of environmental data. In a review that addresses an issue central to climate change policy, Lisa Dilling and her coauthors briefly summarize carbon sequestration and disposal options and then evaluate current scientific observational and measurement capacity to provide the information necessary for the application of carbon management strategies and policies. They conclude that there is a significant mismatch between scientific understanding and measurement capabilities and the needs of managers and policy makers in this realm. Measurement capacity is also addressed in the analysis, by Thomas Parris and Robert Kates, of the state of practice for characterizing sustainable development. The authors examine the similarities and differences among a subset of the hundreds of efforts focused on indicators and measures of sustainability; they identify problems with terminology, data, and methods and propose an analytical framework that could reduce the confusion and improve the usefulness of sustainability indicators.

In the final chapter in this volume of *Environment and Resources*, Dara O'Rourke and Sarah Connolly use an environmental justice framework to examine the distribution of costs and benefits of oil production among countries, communities, and individuals. They conclude that oil's adverse impacts are widespread but that they appear to disproportionately affect groups such as indigenous communities, migrant workers, and communities living near refineries, pipelines, and gas stations. They note, however, the very limited availability of information concerning the overall distribution, cumulative impacts, or demographic impacts from oil; this limitation makes a complete analysis of trade-offs resulting from oil production and consumption impossible for policy makers and the public alike.

Trade-offs are a subtext of many of the chapters in this volume. These reviews grapple with the challenges and conflicts inherent in meeting people's needs while protecting the resources and environment that we, and future generations, must share. The authors who wrote for this volume are pragmatists; their analyses are focused on what we know and what we can learn from the research efforts that have gone before. We hope that their reviews foster communication not only among the disciplines that carry out research on issues of environment, energy, and resources but also with the managers, policy makers, and public who must depend on such information to assist decision making.

Pamela Matson, William Clark, Ashok Gadgil, Peter Gleick, Daniel Kammen, Donald Kennedy, Diana Liverman, Rosamond Naylor, and David Schimel

June 2003

Annual Review of Environment and Resources
Volume 28, 2003

CONTENTS

I. EARTH'S LIFE SUPPORT SYSTEMS

Climate Change, Climate Modes, and Climate Impacts, *Guiling Wang and David Schimel*	1
The Cleansing Capacity of the Atmosphere, *Ronald G. Prinn*	29
Evaluating Uncertainties in Regional Photochemical Air Quality Modeling, *James Fine, Laurent Vuilleumier, Steve Reynolds, Philip Roth, and Nancy Brown*	59
Transport of Energy, Information, and Material Through the Biosphere, *William A. Reiners and Kenneth L. Driese*	107
Global State of Biodiversity and Loss, *Rodolfo Dirzo and Peter H. Raven*	137
Patterns and Mechanisms of the Forest Carbon Cycle, *Stith T. Gower*	169

II. HUMAN USE OF ENVIRONMENT AND RESOURCES

Dynamics of Land-Use and Land-Cover Change in Tropical Regions, *Eric F. Lambin, Helmut J. Geist, and Erika Lepers*	205
Urban Centers: An Assessment of Sustainability, *Gordon McGranahan and David Satterthwaite*	243
Water Use, *Peter H. Gleick*	275
Meeting Cereal Demand While Protecting Natural Resources and Improving Environmental Quality, *Kenneth G. Cassman, Achim Dobermann, Daniel T. Walters, and Haishun Yang*	315
State of the World's Fisheries, *Ray Hilborn, Trevor A. Branch, Billy Ernst, Arni Magnusson, Carolina V. Minte-Vera, Mark D. Scheuerell, and Juan L. Valero*	359
Green Chemistry and Engineering: Drivers, Metrics, and Reduction to Practice, *Anne E. Marteel, Julian A. Davies, Walter W. Olson, and Martin A. Abraham*	401

III. MANAGEMENT AND HUMAN DIMENSIONS

International Environmental Agreements: A Survey of Their Features, Formation, and Effects, *Ronald B. Mitchell*	429

Tracking Multiple Pathways of Human Exposure to Persistent Multimedia
    Pollutants: Regional, Continental, and Global Scale Models,
    Thomas E. McKone and Matthew MacLeod   463

Geographic Information Science and Systems for Environmental
    Management, *Michael F. Goodchild*   493

The Role of Carbon Cycle Observations and Knowledge in Carbon
    Management, *Lisa Dilling, Scott C. Doney, Jae Edmonds,*
    Kevin R. Gurney, Robert Harriss, David Schimel, Britton Stephens,
    and Gerald Stokes   521

Characterizing and Measuring Sustainable Development,
    Thomas M. Parris and Robert W. Kates   559

Just Oil? The Distribution of Environmental and Social Impacts of Oil
    Production and Consumption, *Dara O'Rourke and Sarah Connolly*   587

INDEXES
Subject Index   619
Cumulative Index of Contributing Authors, Volumes 19–28   649
Cumulative Index of Chapter Titles, Volumes 19–28   653

ERRATA
An online log of corrections to *Annual Review of
Environment and Resources* chapters may be found
at http://environ.annualreviews.org

Related Articles

From the *Annual Review of Anthropology*, Volume 32 (2003)

Environmental Pollution in Urban Environments and Human Biology, Lawrence M. Schell and Melinda Denham

Resource Wars: The Anthropology of Mining, Chris Ballard and Glenn Banks

Sustainable Governance of Common-Pool Resources: Context, Methods, and Politics, Arun Agrawal

Urbanization and the Global Perspective, Alan Smart and Josephine Smart

Complex Adaptive Systems, J. Steven Lansing

From the *Annual Review of Astronomy and Astrophysics*, Volume 41 (2003)

Evolution of a Habitable Planet, James Kasting and David Catling

From the *Annual Review of Earth and Planetary Sciences*, Volume 31 (2003)

Is El Niño Sporadic or Cyclic? S. George Philander and Alexey Fedorov

Production, Isotopic Composition, and Atmospheric Fate of Biologically Produced Nitrous Oxide, Lisa Y. Stein and Yuk L. Yung

The Effects of Bioturbation on Soil Processes and Sediment Transport, Emmanuel J. Gabet, O.J. Reichman, and Eric W. Seabloom

From the *Annual Review of Ecology, Evolution, and Systematics*, Volume 33 (2002)

Saproxylic Insect Ecology and the Sustainable Management of Forests, Simon J. Grove

The Causes and Consequences of Ant Invasions, David A. Holway, Lori Lach, Andrew V. Suarez, Neil D. Tsutsui, and Ted J. Case

Gulf of Mexico Hypoxia, a.k.a. "The Dead Zone," Nancy N. Rabalais, R. Eugene Turner, and William J. Wiseman Jr.

Homogenization of Freshwater Faunas, Frank J. Rahel

The Renaissance of Community-Based Marine Resource Management in Oceania, R.E. Johannes

Effects of UV-B Radiation on Terrestrial and Aquatic Primary Producers, Thomas A. Day and Patrick J. Neale

Disturbance to Marine Benthic Habitats by Trawling and Dredging—Implications for Marine Biodiversity, Simon Thrush and Paul K. Dayton

Stable Isotopes in Plant Ecology, Todd E Dawson, Stefania Mambelli, Agneta H. Plamboeck, Pamela H. Templer, and Kevin P. Tu

The Pacific Salmon Wars: What Science Brings to the Challenge of Recovering Species, Mary H. Ruckelshaus, Phil Levin, Jerald B. Johnson, and Peter M. Kareiva

From the ***Annual Review of Fluid Mechanics***, Volume 35 (2003)

Flow and Dispersion in Urban Areas, R.E. Britter and S.R. Hanna

The Flow of Human Crowds, Roger L. Hughes

From the ***Annual Review of Public Health***, Volume 24 (2003)

Public Health, GIS, and Spatial Analytic Tools, Gerard Rushton

One Foot in the Furrow: Linkages Between Agriculture, Plant Pathology, and Public Health, Karen-Beth G. Scholthof

ANNUAL REVIEWS is a nonprofit scientific publisher established to promote the advancement of the sciences. Beginning in 1932 with the *Annual Review of Biochemistry*, the Company has pursued as its principal function the publication of high-quality, reasonably priced *Annual Review* volumes. The volumes are organized by Editors and Editorial Committees who invite qualified authors to contribute critical articles reviewing significant developments within each major discipline. The Editor-in-Chief invites those interested in serving as future Editorial Committee members to communicate directly with him. Annual Reviews is administered by a Board of Directors, whose members serve without compensation.

2003 Board of Directors, Annual Reviews

Richard N. Zare, *Chairman of Annual Reviews*
  Marguerite Blake Wilbur, Professor of Chemistry, Stanford University
John I. Brauman, *J.G. Jackson–C.J. Wood Professor of Chemistry, Stanford University*
Peter F. Carpenter, *Founder, Mission and Values Institute*
Sandra M. Faber, *Professor of Astronomy and Astronomer at Lick Observatory,*
  University of California at Santa Cruz
Susan T. Fiske, *Professor of Psychology, Princeton University*
Eugene Garfield, *Publisher*, The Scientist
Samuel Gubins, *President and Editor-in-Chief, Annual Reviews*
Daniel E. Koshland, Jr., *Professor of Biochemistry, University of California at Berkeley*
Joshua Lederberg, *University Professor, The Rockefeller University*
Sharon R. Long, *Professor of Biological Sciences, Stanford University*
J. Boyce Nute, *Palo Alto, California*
Michael E. Peskin, *Professor of Theoretical Physics, Stanford Linear Accelerator Ctr.*
Harriet A. Zuckerman, *Vice President, The Andrew W. Mellon Foundation*

Management of Annual Reviews

Samuel Gubins, President and Editor-in-Chief
Richard L. Burke, Director for Production
Paul J. Calvi, Jr., Director of Information Technology
Steven J. Castro, Chief Financial Officer and Director of Marketing & Sales

Annual Reviews of

Anthropology
Astronomy and Astrophysics
Biochemistry
Biomedical Engineering
Biophysics and Biomolecular
  Structure
Cell and Developmental
  Biology
Earth and Planetary Sciences
Ecology, Evolution, and
  Systematics
Entomology

Environment and Resources
Fluid Mechanics
Genetics
Genomics and Human Genetics
Immunology
Materials Research
Medicine
Microbiology
Neuroscience
Nuclear and Particle Science
Nutrition
Pharmacology and Toxicology

Physical Chemistry
Physiology
Phytopathology
Plant Biology
Political Science
Psychology
Public Health
Sociology

SPECIAL PUBLICATIONS
Excitement and Fascination of
  Science, Vols. 1, 2, 3, and 4

CLIMATE CHANGE, CLIMATE MODES, AND CLIMATE IMPACTS

Guiling Wang[1] and David Schimel[2]

[1]*Department of Civil and Environmental Engineering, University of Connecticut, Storrs, Connecticut 06269; email: gwang@engr.uconn.edu*
[2]*Terrestrial Science Section, National Center for Atmospheric Research, Boulder, Colorado 80307; email: schimel@ucar.edu*

Key Words North Atlantic Oscillation, El Niño-Southern Oscillation, Pacific Decadal Oscillation, ecosystem response, global warming

■ **Abstract** Variability of the atmospheric and oceanic circulations in the earth system gives rise to an array of naturally occurring dynamical modes. Instead of being spatially independent or spatially uniform, climate variability in different parts of the globe is orchestrated by one or a combination of several climate modes, and global changes take place with a distinctive spatial pattern resembling that of the modes-related climate anomalies. Climate impact on the dynamics of terrestrial and marine biosphere also demonstrates clear signals for the mode effects. In this review, we view modes as an important attribute of climate variability, changes, and impact and emphasize the emerging concept that future climate changes may be manifest as changes in the leading modes of the climate system. The focus of this review is on three of the leading modes: the North Atlantic Oscillation, the El Niño-Southern Oscillation, and the Pacific Decadal Oscillation.

CONTENTS

INTRODUCTION	2
CLIMATE MODES AND CLIMATE VARIABILITY	3
Climate Modes: Phenomena	3
Impact of NAO on Global Climate Variability	7
Climatic Impact of ENSO and PDO	8
CLIMATE CHANGES: RELATIONSHIP WITH THE LEADING MODES	9
Observed Changes in the Recent Past	10
Causes for Changes: A Modeling Perspective	12
CLIMATE MODES AND ECOLOGICAL IMPACTS	16
Population and Reproductive Responses	17
Biogeochemistry, Disturbance, and the Global Carbon Cycle	19
Summary	21
FINAL REMARKS	21

INTRODUCTION

Climate can be defined by the long-term statistics that describe the behavior and structure of the Earth's atmosphere, hydrosphere, and cryosphere. Life on the Earth depends on the hospitality of its climate. Any change in the Earth's climate will have an immediate impact on humankind, on biodiversity, and on the health and services delivered by ecosystems around the globe, and it will alter the ability of the earth system to support socioeconomic development. For adaptation to and mitigation of climate changes, it is essential to understand the natural variability of climate, why and how climate changes, and how changes of climate impact the Earth's ecosystems. Recent historical data indicates that the Earth's climate is changing, and such changes tend to take place with a distinctive spatial pattern(s) that may be characterized by one or several modes (repeating patterns of time-space variability) of the climate system. In this review, we discuss climate modes as an important way of understanding climate variability, changes, and impact.

Mode patterns are common and important features of complex dynamical systems. They represent low-dimensional features of high-dimensional systems and provide a better predictive capacity. In meteorology and climatology, "mode" is often used to describe a spatial structure with at least two strongly coupled centers of action. Its polarity and amplitude are represented by the index of the mode, and the temporal variation and changes of the mode index are more predictable than climate anomalies at individual stations. Within the Earth's atmosphere-ocean system, the variability of primary climate variables (e.g., pressure, temperature, and precipitation) gives rise to an array of important, naturally occurring dynamical modes. These include, among many others, the North Atlantic Oscillation (1–3), the Arctic Oscillation and its Southern Hemisphere counterpart, the Antarctic Oscillation (also known as the northern and southern annular modes, respectively) (4–6), the El Niño-Southern Oscillation (1, 2, 7), and the Pacific Decadal Oscillation (8).

Dynamical modes of the climate system result from fundamental physical processes such as "instabilities of the climatological mean flow, large-scale atmosphere-ocean interaction, or interactions between the climatological mean flow and transients" (9). Instead of being spatially independent, large-scale climate variability is often orchestrated by one or several climate modes, which results in synchronized behavior in regions that are geographically far apart. In addition, various data analyses indicated that observed climate changes in the past several decades are statistically related to trends in some of the leading modes, with modal changes explaining a major part of the recent temperature warming. Moreover, numerical modeling studies suggested that future climate changes are likely to occur with a distinctive spatial pattern and are likely to occur as changes in the polarity, frequency, and/or intensity of naturally occurring modes of the climate system.

Modal behavior of the climate system is also manifest in ecological variability and changes over various regions around the globe. In fact, as the first intensively studied climate mode, El Niño was originally noticed in the late nineteenth century by fishermen along the coasts of Ecuador and Peru as a biological phenomenon in fishery fluctuations, which we now know is caused by El Niño-related oceanic circulation changes resulting in fluctuations of nutrient availability. Climate modes influence the dynamics of both the terrestrial and marine biosphere at levels ranging from individual organisms to communities to ecosystems. In face of the expected anthropogenic climate changes, it becomes critical to understand and predict how the biosphere will respond. Studying the effects of climate modes on the biosphere is crucial to understanding the physical climate system and its coupling to life on planet Earth.

In the following, we will first review the phenomena and climate anomalies associated with various climate modes. The relationship between mode changes and global climate changes will then be analyzed based on both observational data and numerical modeling results. Finally, the ecological and biological impact of climate modes will be reviewed.

CLIMATE MODES AND CLIMATE VARIABILITY

Climate Modes: Phenomena

An important method to define the dominant modes of variability for a certain climate anomaly field is the empirical orthogonal function (EOF) analysis (10), also known as the principal component (PC) analysis, of grid data. For example, the first EOF (EOF1) of a meteorological field defines the spatial pattern of the leading mode for this field in the region of analysis, and the associated PC time series provides an index for the temporal variation of the mode. The spatial patterns of leading EOFs have a certain degree of dependence on the shape of the analysis domain. For example, Arctic Oscillation (5, 6, 11) and its Southern Hemisphere counterpart Antarctic Oscillation (4, 12) correspond to the EOF1 of the sea level pressure (SLP) field of the Northern and Southern Hemispheres, respectively, while North Atlantic Oscillation is identified as the EOF1 of the SLP field over the Atlantic sector (13). Similarly, El Niño Southern-Oscillation and Pacific Decadal Oscillation can be derived from the EOF1 and EOF2, respectively, of the SST field over the entire Pacific Basin (14), and Pacific Decadal Oscillation can also be derived from the EOF1 of North Pacific sea surface temperature (8). Many of the mode indices used later in this chapter are derived from EOF/PC analysis, the fundamental technique in defining and analyzing climate modes. Whenever such a mode index is used, the domain of analysis will be specified.

The distribution of SLP in the Atlantic sector of Northern Hemisphere features a subtropical high-pressure center around 35°N and a high-latitude low-pressure center around 55°N, which cause westerly winds across the midlatitude Atlantic throughout the year. Although the exact location of the pressure centers varies from season to season and from year to year, the high-pressure system is generally centered around the Azores, and the low-pressure system is centered around the Iceland. The North Atlantic Oscillation (NAO) represents a north-south oscillation in atmospheric mass between the Icelandic low and Azores high (1). During the positive phase of NAO, lower-than-normal surface pressure over the Icelandic to Arctic regions and higher-than-normal surface pressure over the subtropical Atlantic together yield a larger than normal meridional pressure gradient, causing stronger than normal midlatitude surface westerlies across the Atlantic onto Europe. The opposite occurs during the negative phase of NAO. This oscillation system gives rise to the leading mode of climate variability in the Northern Hemisphere. A frequently used index for the NAO variation is the PC time series corresponding to the EOF1 of the extended winter (December through March) SLP field over the Atlantic sector in the Northern Hemisphere. An alternative NAO index is defined as the difference in normalized SLP anomalies between individual stations such as that between Lisbon, Portugal, and Stykkisholmur/Reykjavik, Iceland (3). Figure 1a plots the normalized anomalies of both the PC time series and the station-based NAO index, which shows negligible difference between these two.

NAO is sometimes considered as the regional manifestation of the Northern Hemisphere annular mode. The annular modes Arctic Oscillation (AO) and Antarctic Oscillation (AAO) refer to a highly zonally symmetric, north-south oscillation in atmospheric mass and momentum between the polar region and temperate latitudes in each hemisphere (5). These modes are most distinctive in the hemispheric SLP fields and are characterized by a primary center of action over the polar caps and anomalies of opposite polarity in midlatitudes. The opposing anomalies in midlatitudes split into two centers of action: For the AO, one is located in the Atlantic sector, and one is over the Pacific; for the AAO, one is in the western Pacific-Indian Ocean sector, and one is near the tip of South America (15). The positive phase features abnormally low pressure over the polar cap and the surrounding regions and higher-than-normal pressure in the midlatitudes with particularly strong anomalies around the centers of actions. The polarity of SLP anomalies reverses during the negative phase. In the Northern Hemisphere, the strongest teleconnectivity between the Arctic basin and midlatitudes occurs over the Atlantic sector, and the teleconnectivity between the Atlantic and Pacific midlatitudes is weak. A similar lack of strong sectoral coherency is documented for the Southern Hemisphere as well. This raises the possibility that the annular modes may have resulted from the large areal extent and the zonal symmetry of their primary centers of action in the Arctic/Antarctic, rather than coordinated behavior between the centers of action in different sectors. As a result, there has been no consensus in the literature regarding whether they represent dynamically significant modes of variability of the hemispheric circulation (6, 9, 13, 15) or are artifacts of EOF analysis. This is particularly the case in the Northern Hemisphere, where the objectively derived NAO and AO indices are nearly indistinguishable and the climate regression with the NAO and AO indices are remarkably similar (except over the northern Pacific where the impact of other climate modes dominates). In this review, we will not treat the annular modes separately and will refer the leading climate mode of the Northern Hemisphere as NAO, with the understanding that NAO and AO may represent two paradigms of the same phenomenon (9).

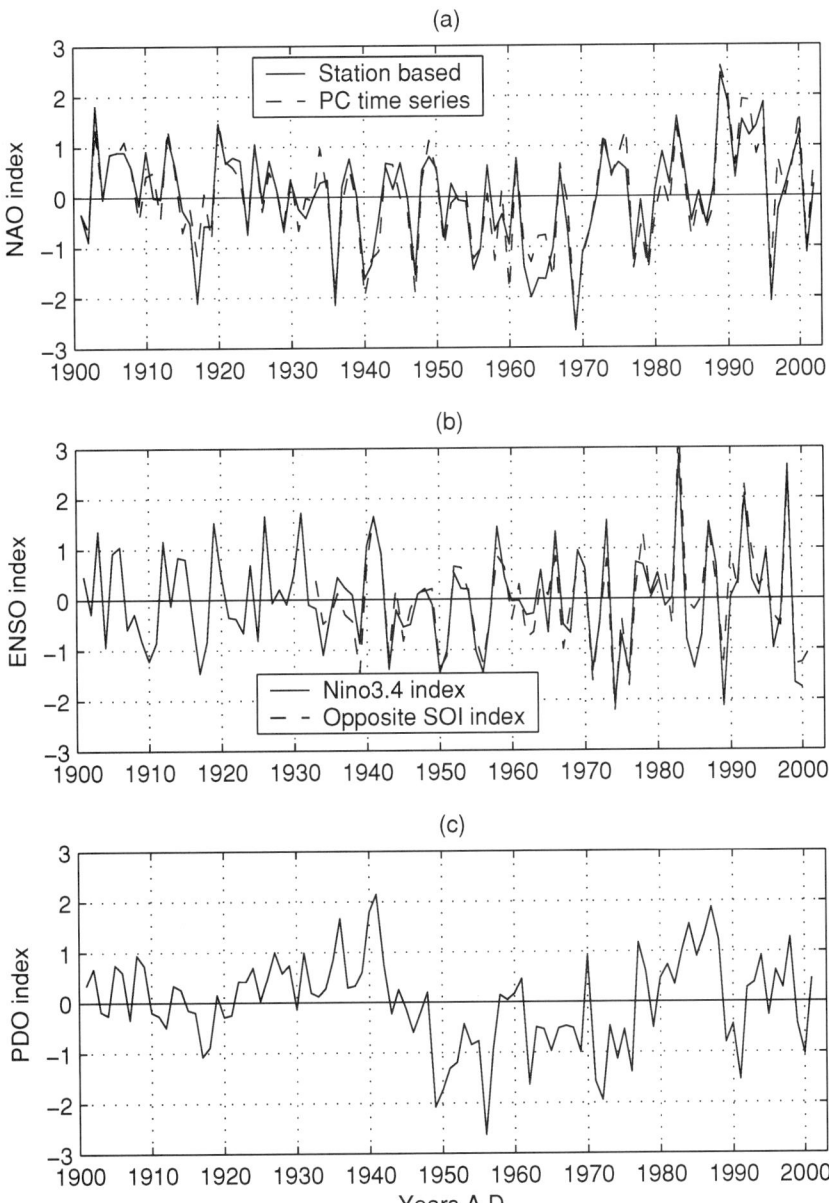

Figure 1 Normalized time series of (*a*) the NAO index, based on Hurrell (3); (*b*) the ENSO index, based on Trenberth (17) and Trenberth & Hoar (16); (*c*) the PDO index, based on Mantua et al. (8) and Zhang et al. (18).

El Niño-Southern Oscillation (ENSO) is a natural phenomenon arising from the unstable interactions between the tropical Pacific Ocean and the atmosphere. Its oceanic component El Niño (EN) refers to the warm phase of sea surface temperature oscillation in the tropical Pacific Ocean, with the cold phase referred to as La Niña (7). Its atmospheric component the Southern Oscillation (SO) describes a seesaw in atmospheric mass between Eastern and Western Hemispheres in tropical and subtropical latitudes with centers of actions over Australia-Indonesia and the tropical southeastern Pacific (16). Manifestation of ENSO can be found in various meteorological fields across the tropical Pacific, including SLP, trade wind, seas surface temperature, and precipitation, to name a few. Under normal conditions, the trade winds across the tropical Pacific blow toward the west, piling up warm surface water in the West Pacific and causing upwelling of cold water from the ocean depth in the East Pacific off the coast of South America. As a result, sea surface temperature is 6–8°C higher in the west, and convective activities over the warm water bring abundant rainfall to the west. During El Niño, SLP is above normal in the Australia-Indonesia region and below normal in the southeast Pacific; trade wind across the equatorial Pacific relaxes or even reverses; sea surface temperature in central and eastern equatorial Pacific rises significantly; and the major area of precipitation follows the warm water eastward and causes drier-than-normal conditions in the west and wetter-than-normal conditions in the east. The opposite conditions occur during La Niña. Although an index for the ENSO variation can be defined using objective EOF analyses of the Pacific SST field (14), other ENSO indices based on more localized conditions are frequently used. Examples include the Niño3.4 index, defined as the normalized SST anomalies averaged over the Niño3 (5°N-5°S, 150°W-90°W), and Niño4 (5°N-5°S, 160°E-150°W) regions in the equatorial Pacific and the SO index, defined as the difference in the normalized pressure anomalies between Tahiti (T) in the South Pacific and Darwin (D) in northern Australia (i.e., T-D) (16, 17). As such, the warm phase of Niño3.4 (i.e., El Niño) corresponds to the negative phase of the SO (Figure 1b). As evidenced in Figure 1b, the average timescale of ENSO is approximately four years, with the actual length of cycle ranging from two to seven years.

The Pacific Decadal Oscillation (PDO) refers to a mode of Pacific variability that resembles the ENSO pattern but is dominated by variations at longer timescales (8). The spatial pattern of PDO is qualitatively similar to that of ENSO, with large SST anomalies of one sign in the tropical and northeastern Pacific and anomalies of opposite sign in the central North Pacific (14, 18, 19). The PDO signal is most obvious in the extratropics over North Pacific/North America and weaker in the tropics, as opposed to the ENSO signal that is stronger in the tropics than extratropics. The PC time series corresponding to the EOF1 of Pacific SST poleward of 20N (Figure 1c) has been used as a PDO index (8), which shows a preferential timescale of several decades. Due to the difference in their dominant timescale of variations, ENSO is more important in interannual climate variability, and the impact of PDO is more evident in decadal climate variability.

Impact of NAO on Global Climate Variability

Although the NAO is evident all year long, its impact is particularly strong during boreal winter (20), with NAO-related patterns of temperature and precipitation variability "extending from Florida to Greenland and from northwestern Africa over Europe far into northern Asia" (21). To further demonstrate this, we plot in Figure 2 (see color insert) the correlation coefficient between NAO index and global surface temperature as well as precipitation during Northern Hemisphere winter (December-March). Here, the station-based NAO index as shown in Figure 1a (i.e., the difference between the normalized SLP anomaly during winter at Lisbon, Portugal, and Stykkisholmor, Iceland) is used. The global surface temperature dataset (22) has a resolution of 5 degrees in both latitudinal and longitudinal directions and comprises surface air temperature over land and SST over ocean. The correlation analysis was conducted for the time period 1951–2000. For precipitation data, we use the CAMS-OPI data (23), a merged precipitation dataset based on both rain gauge measurements and satellite estimates for the period 1979–2001 with a resolution of 2.5 degrees.

Surface temperatures over much of the Northern Hemisphere are significantly correlated with the NAO index, as is evident in Figure 2a. During the positive phase of the NAO, the enhanced high-pressure system over midlatitudes and low-pressure system over Iceland cause both the cyclonic and the anticyclonic winds to become stronger than normal, which leads to enhanced midlatitude westerly winds across the North Atlantic, enhanced southerly winds in the eastern United States and northwestern Europe, and enhanced northerly winds over the Mediterranean, western Greenland, and its surrounding regions (24). The strong westerlies carry mild air from the ocean downwind, causing warmer winter conditions across Europe all the way to northern Asia. At the same time, the enhanced northerlies (southerlies) bring cold (warm) air southward (northward). As a result, colder-than-normal winter conditions occur over Greenland, northeastern Canada, northwest Atlantic, North Africa, and the Middle East, while the majority of the United States and the region poleward from the northwest Europe experience warmer-than-normal winters (Figure 2a). A relatively strong cold anomaly develops during the positive phase of the NAO over the Atlantic Ocean between the equator and 30°N, due to the stronger-than-normal northeasterly wind that increases the heat loss from ocean surface to atmosphere. The NAO impact on temperature beyond the Northern Hemisphere is generally weak, with an exception over the midlatitude Southern Hemisphere ocean where summer is warmer than normal during the positive phase of the NAO.

Atmospheric circulation changes associated with the NAO variability lead to pronounced shift of the winter storm track as well as changes of storm frequency in the Euro-Atlantic sector, which is accompanied by changes in precipitation distribution as demonstrated in Figure 2b. Specifically, during the positive phase of the NAO, winter storm activities shift toward the northeast, which causes precipitation to decrease in the south and west and increase in the north and east (25). As a result, drier-than-normal winter conditions are observed over southern Europe, the northern Mediterranean region, part of North Africa, Greenland, and the northeast North America, while more snow falls over the region from Iceland to Scandinavia and northern Europe where winters are stormier during the positive phase of the NAO (3, 26–28). Such NAO-related changes of precipitation are also evident in the swing of river runoff (29) and in the advance and retreat of glaciers (30) and sea ice (31).

Climatic Impact of ENSO and PDO

Although its primary centers of action are located over the tropical Pacific, ENSO has significant climatic effects over the globe. In fact, most of the interannual variability in the tropics and a substantial portion of the extratropics over both hemispheres are orchestrated by ENSO. Using as the ENSO index the standardized PC time series corresponding to the EOF1 of tropical Pacific SSTs (positive index corresponding to SST warming/El Niño), Figure 3 (see color insert) [modified from Plate 1 and 2 in Diaz et al. (32)] shows the correlation coefficient between the ENSO index and global surface temperature as well as precipitation in different seasons. During the warm phase of ENSO, a general tropical-wide warming is observed all year long, except over part of the Maritime Continent where cooler-than-normal condition occurs during the ASO season (Figure 3a,c). In the Pacific Ocean, strong tropical warming is flanked by extratropical cooling during all seasons. The southeastern United States experiences cold anomalies in El Niño years, especially during Northern Hemisphere winter. In the extratropics, the strongest correlation between ENSO index and surface temperature occurs in the North Pacific-North America region, where northwestern North America and northeastern Pacific experience significant El Niño-induced warming while cooling occurs over the rest of the North Pacific.

Compared with its impact upon surface temperature, the impact of ENSO on precipitation demonstrates greater spatial variability (Figure 3b,d). Rainfall increase in the narrow equatorial belt across the Pacific is significantly correlated with El Niño. This is accompanied by rainfall decrease over both the South and North Pacific. Over land, strong drought anomaly in response to El Niño is evident in the Central America, northeastern South America, the Maritime Continent, Australia, and the Indian monsoon region, while wet anomaly occurs over the southern part of both North and South Americas. The ENSO signal over the above-mentioned regions is either seasonally persistent or most pronounced during the local rainy season (32), which leads to a similarity between the relation of ENSO index with seasonal rainfall amount (as shown in Figure 3b,d) and that with the annually accumulated rainfall amount (33). Substantial seasonal contrast in the response of precipitation to ENSO is observed in part of East Africa (approximately over the Nile River Basin) and South Africa; each features drier-than-normal conditions in the corresponding rainy season and wetter-than-normal conditions in the corresponding dry season during El Niño years (Figure 3c,d). The impact of ENSO on precipitation is also reflected by consistent relationships between ENSO and river discharges. For example, during or immediately following El Niño years, stream flow tends to be abnormally low in the Nile River (34, 35), Ganges River (36), Amazon River (37), and River Murray (38, 39), and abnormally high in rivers across the southern United States (40).

The correlation coefficients between the PDO index and global surface temperature and precipitation during the Northern Hemisphere extended winter (December–March) are presented in Figure 4 (see color insert). These correlation analyses use the global surface temperature data of Jones et al. (22) during 1951–2000 and the CAMS-OPI precipitation data (23) during the period 1979–2001; the PDO index used here is the PC time series corresponding to the EOF1 of the Pacific SST poleward of 20°N as shown in Figure 1c. The length of data record used in analyzing the correlation of PDO with each climate variable is comparable to that used in the ENSO-climate correlation analysis done by Diaz et al. (32) (and shown in Figure 3). It is clear from Figures 3a,b and 4a,b that, compared with the ENSO signal, the PDO signal is stronger in the extratropics and weaker in the tropics. Most noticeable in Figure 4 is the strong correlation between PDO index and temperature in the Pacific-North America region that features cooling in central North Pacific and warming over northwestern North America during the positive phase of PDO.

In summary, from studies reviewed in the two previous sections, it is clear that climate variability in different regions around the globe is not spatially independent. Instead, it tends to be orchestrated by one or the combination of several leading dynamical modes. Except over the North Pacific where the PDO signal is extremely strong, climate variability in the middle- and high-latitudes of Northern Hemisphere is dominated by the NAO. In the tropics and Southern Hemisphere extratropics, ENSO is the dominant forcing of climate variability.

CLIMATE CHANGES: RELATIONSHIP WITH THE LEADING MODES

Global mean climate in the twentieth century features a significant decadal trend. This is most manifest in temperature warming (22) and to a lesser degree in the intensification of the hydrological cycle (41). Much of this trend is attributable to the rapid changes observed over the past two to three decades. Figure 5 plots the departure of global average temperature from its 1951–1980 mean (42), which shows a dramatic warming trend since the 1970s. Proxy data indicate that the 1990s was likely to be the warmest decade during the past 1000 years (43). The rapid warming in the last three decades of the twentieth century coincides with

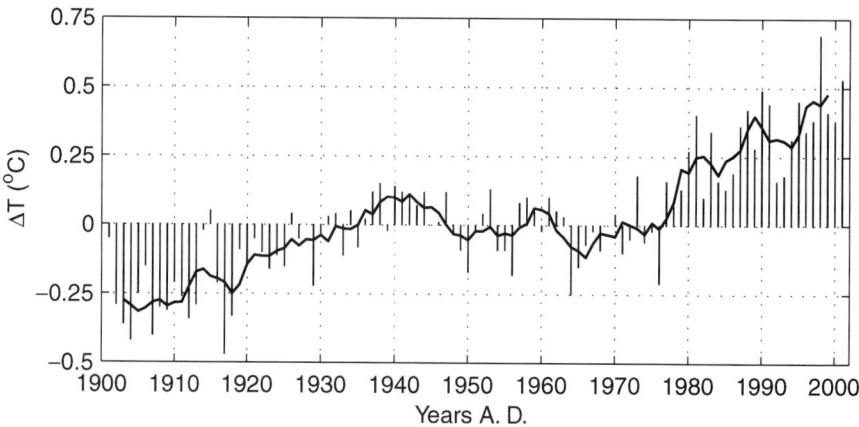

Figure 5 Global-average surface temperature anomaly with respect to the 1951–1980 climatology, based on the meteorological station analysis of the Goddard Institute for Space Studies by Hansen et al. (42). The heavy solid line plots the 5-year moving average.

a trend or phase shift in several leading modes of climate variability. Since the 1970s, both the NAO and PDO have been developing toward a more positive phase (Figure 1a,c), and El Niño events have become more frequent (or persistent) and intense (Figure 1b). This raises an interesting perspective that climate changes may be expressed as a phase shift or structure change of naturally occurring modes of climate variability and suggests that modes may be a crucial attribute of global climate changes.

Observed Changes in the Recent Past

Although climate changes are often described by global mean trend, these changes, instead of being uniform in time and space, take place with considerable seasonality and distinctive spatial patterns (44). During the last two decades of the twentieth century, the strongest warming has been observed during the winter and spring seasons in the mid- and high-latitudes of Northern Hemisphere continents, which include the northwestern part of North America, northern Eurasia, and Siberia (20). Little warming or even slight cooling has taken place in part of the northern oceans, including the central North Pacific and northwestern North Atlantic. Most of the Mediterranean region and part of North Africa also witnessed slight cooling impact. This spatial pattern is evident in Figure 6a (see color insert), which shows the departure of surface temperature averaged during 20 recent winters (1981–2000) from the previous 20 winters (1961–1980). In the Southern Hemisphere, little warming has been observed.

The spatial patterns of recent temperature changes are associated with climate anomalies related to changes in the primary modes of atmospheric and/or oceanic variability, mainly the NAO and to a lesser degree ENSO and PDO. Figure 6*b* and 6*c* present the linear regression of local surface temperature upon the winter NAO and PDO indices, respectively, based on data during the 50-year period 1951–2000. In Figure 6*b*, the largest temperature anomalies associated with the NAO variation occur over the northern Eurasia and Siberia, with a warming of approximately 0.6–1.2°C attributable to a unit increase of the normalized NAO index. The same change of the NAO index accounts for a moderate warming (mostly under 0.6°C) over North America and moderate cooling (mostly under 0.6°C) in eastern Canada, northwest North Atlantic, the Mediterranean, and North Africa. On the other hand, as shown in Figure 6*c*, a strong warming with the magnitude exceeding 1.2 degree centigrade in northwest North America and a moderate cooling in central North Pacific are attributable to a unit increase of the normalized PDO index. Temperature variations accounted for by a unit deviation of the ENSO index (not shown here) and those associated with a unit PDO deviation are broadly similar in their spatial pattern; this indicates that ENSO and PDO explain much of the same climate anomalies. Overall, the spatial distribution of the observed recent climate changes is remarkably similar to that of the NAO-related climate anomalies in Northern Hemisphere except over the Pacific-North America sector where it resembles the spatial distribution of PDO- and ENSO-related climate anomalies.

From the period 1961–1980 to the period 1981–2000, the average of NAO index increases by 1.2 times of its standard deviation and of PDO index by 0.9 (Figure 1). With the correlation coefficient between the NAO and PDO indices not exceeding 0.1, these two time series can be treated as linearly independent. Following the approach of Hurrell (20), subtracting the linear impact of NAO and PDO from the observed temperature changes yields the residual temperature anomalies (Figure 6*d*) that cannot be explained by the variation of these two climate modes. Despite the similarity between climate anomalies associated with PDO and ENSO, PDO is chosen in this analysis because climate over the extratropical Northern Hemisphere is more strongly correlated with the PDO index, as evident in Figures 3 and 4. Replacing the impact of PDO with that of ENSO in this analysis does not cause significant changes in the results. Comparison between Figure 6*a* and 6*d* suggests that most of the observed rapid warming during the past several decades in the extratropical Northern Hemisphere can be accounted for by changes in the naturally occurring modes of climate variability such as the NAO, PDO, and ENSO.

Analysis of global precipitation changes is difficult due to the lack of high-quality data. No precipitation data over the global ocean existed prior to 1980 when satellite-based measurement became available; long-term (multi-decadal) station records of precipitation over land, where they do exist, suffer from various factors such as gauge undercatch and instrumental and technique discontinuity. Therefore, global precipitation changes cannot be estimated with the same level of confidence as temperature changes. Nevertheless, collection of gauge data over the global land does indicate a general, though unsteady, trend of precipitation increase during the twentieth century (26, 45); this is consistent with the temperature warming that promotes a more intense hydrological cycle. It is noteworthy that the increasing trend of global land precipitation is small relative to its interannual and multi-decadal variability. Although the type of global analysis for precipitation changes similar to the one done for temperature changes shown in Figure 6 is not conducted here due to limited spatial and temporal data coverage, localized analyses suggest the link of precipitation changes with observed trends of climate modes, of the NAO and ENSO in particular, as shown below.

In the past two to three decades, most of the precipitation increase has been observed in the Northern Hemisphere mid- and high-latitudes. Conditions over the majority of North America, northern Europe, and Scandinavia have become significantly wetter than normal (44–46), while a general drying trend has been noticed in the Mediterranean region, North Africa, southern Europe, part of northeast Canada, and south Greenland (47, 48). For example, above-normal winter precipitation over Scandinavia is considered responsible for the positive mass balance of the local maritime glaciers (30), snow depth and duration of snow cover over the Alps in the 1990s are at the lower end of their record (49), and severe drought has also been documented for part of Spain and Portugal. Such an increasing trend of precipitation in northern Europe and Scandinavia and decreasing trend to the south as well as over the land mass surrounding northwest Atlantic Ocean are consistent with the northeastward shift of Atlantic storm track resulting from changes of the NAO toward a stronger positive polarity. Precipitation increase in North America, especially over the south and southeast United States, may be related to the development of ENSO and/or PDO toward a more positive phase.

Precipitation data from islands in tropical oceans indicate a coherent decreasing trend over large parts of the tropical oceans but with considerable spatial variability. In particular, most of the eastern Pacific islands exhibit an increasing trend of precipitation, while the western Pacific islands have a decreasing trend (45). This east-west contrast in precipitation changes over the tropical Pacific, which resembles the El Niño-induced anomalies in precipitation distribution, is likely to be related to the increase in the frequency and/or intensity of El Niño events during the recent past (Figure 1*b*).

Causes for Changes: A Modeling Perspective

It has long been speculated that observed climate changes, the rapid surface warming in particular, during the last two to three decades of the twentieth century may have resulted from the accumulation of anthropogenic greenhouse gases in the atmosphere. On the other hand, as evidenced from the above review, most climate anomalies in the recent past can be accounted for by the observed trend in the natural modes of atmospheric (and oceanic) circulation. This raises the possibility that the recently observed rapid temperature warming may be due to natural climate variability instead of related to the increased greenhouse gas concentration. However, another possibility, which reconciles the above two perspectives, is that increase of greenhouse gas concentration may have caused the observed decadal trend in the naturally occurring modes of climate variability, and that anthropogenic climate changes may be manifest as changes in the preferred modes of low-frequency climate variability. If this is true, observed modal trends (e.g., the upward trend of the NAO and ENSO indices) are expected to continue into the future as greenhouse gas concentration keeps rising. Currently, due to the short period of record, it is difficult to assess based on observational data whether these trends are anthropogenically induced or are part of the natural decadal variability that coincide with the increase of greenhouse gas concentration. Climate models can be a useful tool to gain some insight regarding possible causes of recent modal changes and their implication for future climate.

Many studies on the response of global climate to past and projected future CO_2 concentration increase, which used different coupled atmosphere-ocean general circulation models (AOGCM), found an El Niño-like pattern in CO_2-induced climate changes, including changes in surface temperature, precipitation, and SLP (50–54). This pattern is characterized by a larger degree of SST warming in the central and eastern tropical Pacific than in the West, an eastward shift of the precipitation zone in equatorial Pacific resulting in precipitation reduction in western Pacific and increase in central and eastern Pacific, higher pressure over Australasia, and lower pressure over the tropical eastern Pacific. Such climate change patterns reflect changes of the model-simulated ENSO system as CO_2 concentration increases and include more frequent and/or more intense El Niño events than La Niña events. These modeling results support the argument that observed changes in ENSO occurrence during the past several decades may include contributions from human impact. However, several other studies on CO_2-induced climate changes found no evidence of El Niño-like warming. For example, Meehl et al. (55) documented the lack of SST east-west gradient changes across the equatorial Pacific in a 1% per year transient CO_2 experiment using the National Center for Atmospheric Research climate system model (CSM); Washington et al. (56) showed a similar lack of El Niño-like warming in a set of transient CO_2 experiments using the Department of Energy (DOE) Parallel Climate Model (PCM). It is interesting to note that the PCM used in Washington et al. (56) and the version of CSM used in Meehl et al. (55) share the same atmospheric component. Discrepancy between different studies may have risen from differences in the parameterization of certain physical processes such as cloud feedback (54) between different climate models.

While the NAO phenomenon and its climatic impact are largely constrained in the extratropics, a recent modeling study by Hoerling et al. (57) found that the observed trend of NAO toward its positive phase in the past several decades may be of tropical origin. Using an atmospheric general circulation model driven with observed SST forcing, this study showed that progressive warming in the tropical Indian and Pacific Oceans modifies the magnitude and spatial pattern of tropical rainfall and thus atmospheric latent heating, which then cause changes in extratropical atmospheric circulation, including the trend of NAO toward a more positive phase in the past several decades. As the observed tropical SST warming is very likely a result of CO_2 concentration increase, the Hoerling et al. study provides a piece of evidence, although indirect, that the upward trend of

NAO and the associated warming in mid- to high-latitude Northern Hemisphere constitute an anthropogenic signal. Using coupled AOGCM driven with realistic greenhouse gas forcing, Shindell et al. (58) reproduced the observed trend of the AO (the hemispheric scale counterpart of NAO) when stratospheric dynamics was included in the model. Their results directly demonstrated that the recent trend in AO/NAO and the surface temperature warming associated with it should be attributed to human activities instead of to climate natural variability. It is also indicated in their study that stratospheric dynamics is important to the simulation of anthropogenically induced climate changes. Another study using a different suite of coupled AOGCMs, carried out by Paeth et al. (59), documented that both the NAO mean and its variance are sensitive to greenhouse gas forcing; the former increased while the latter decreased with the increase of CO_2 concentration. It was suggested that these two contrasting responses may serve as an indicator for greenhouse gas–induced regional climate changes. However, similar to the simulated ENSO response, not all models agree on how the NAO may respond to CO_2 concentration changes. For example, Fyfe et al. (60) argued that the upward trend of the AO/NAO simulated in their coupled AOGCM with greenhouse gas forcing reflects essentially unchanged mode variations superimposed on a forced climate change pattern.

Modal changes related to the greenhouse gas forcing involve more than changes in the polarity, frequency, and/or intensity. They can also be manifest in the spatial pattern of climate anomalies associated with a specific mode. For example, in a transient greenhouse gas experiment using the DOE PCM (B04.29) where CO_2 concentration increases by 1% per year from 355 ppmv to 710 ppmv (Figure 7*a*), the NAO develops toward a less negative (or more positive) phase (Figure 7*b*). Figure 8 (see color insert) shows the correlation coefficient between the NAO index and climate anomalies in the Northern Hemisphere winter, based on model simulation for the 30 years right before the onset of CO_2 increase in PCM (i.e., concentration fixed at 355 ppmv, labeled as Control) (Figure 8*a–c*) and the 30 years after the stabilization of CO_2 concentration at 710 ppmv (labeled as $2 \times CO_2$) (Figure 8*d–f*). For the control simulation, the correlation between the model NAO index and temperature (T) as well as precipitation (P) broadly resembles that based on observations (Figure 2*a,b*). The freshwater flux (i.e., P-E, where E stands for evaporation or evapotranspiration), which impacts ecological responses by controlling salinity in the ocean and plant water availability over land, correlates with the NAO in essentially the same manner as precipitation does. Relative to the control, the NAO-climate correlation at $2 \times CO_2$ is generally weaker. In some regions, the spatial pattern of the correlation coefficient at elevated CO_2 is considerably different than at the control CO_2 level. For example, over the southern United States, wetter-than-normal conditions correspond to the positive phase of the NAO in the control, but drought is expected during the positive phase of the NAO in the $2 \times CO_2$ experiment. The opposite occurs in the northwest United States. Such spatial pattern changes in mode-related climate anomalies are potentially more important than the rather gradual changes in the modal polarity and may pose dramatic impact on regional environment and resources.

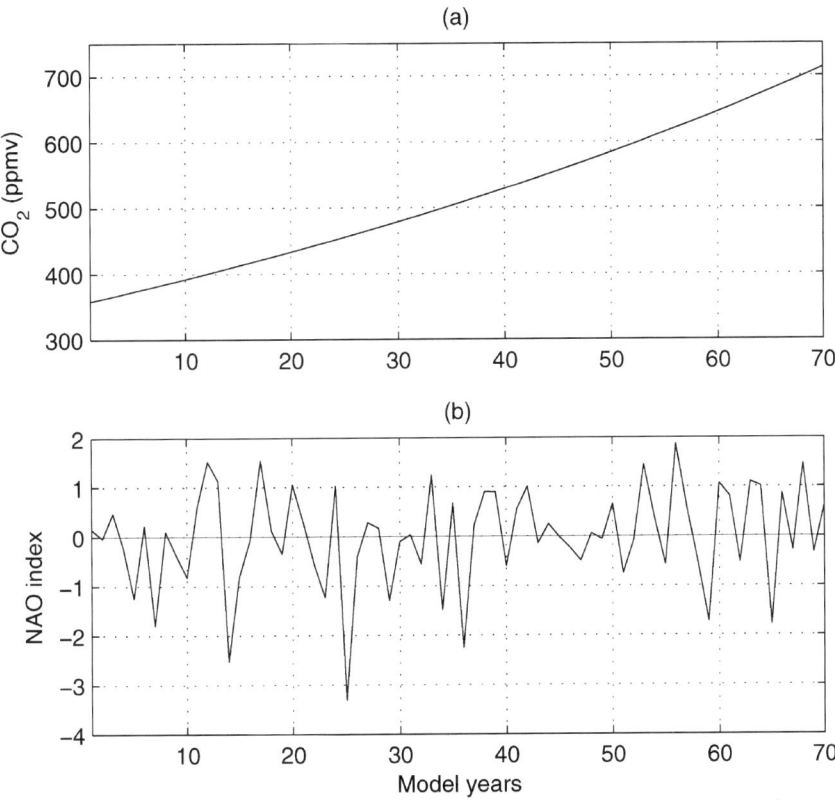

Figure 7 (*a*) CO_2 concentration increase (at 1% per year) and (*b*) the simulated NAO index in the DOE PCM transient CO_2 experiment B04.29. Here the NAO index is defined as the difference in normalized anomalies of simulated SLP between Azores and Iceland.

Overall, there exists ample evidence from both observations and numerical modeling studies that anthropogenic climate changes may occur through changes in the preferred modes of atmospheric and/or oceanic circulation. At the same time, it is important to recognize that no conclusive remarks can be made before a longer observational record becomes available, and the model dependence of the simulated modal response to greenhouse gas forcing cannot be overlooked. Further intercomparison study involving multiple global climate models is necessary in order to address such model dependence and to improve our understanding of the modal response to CO_2 concentration changes. However, despite the documented discrepancy between different studies, the notion that anthropogenic climate changes may take place as changes in the preferred modes of atmospheric/oceanic circulation represents a potentially significant concept, i.e., greenhouse gases, in addition to their direct radiative effects, may cause significant climate changes through dynamical effects as well.

CLIMATE MODES AND ECOLOGICAL IMPACTS

Variations in climate modes tend to produce correlated changes in physical variables. For example, ENSO produces spatially structured changes in temperature, precipitation, and cloud cover. Changes in westerly winds associated with the NAO not only change heat transport, they alter patterns of water vapor transport and lead to hydrological cycle changes (24). First-order changes in atmospheric circulation associated with mode changes that produce changes in heat and water transport often result in changes to smaller-scale events in the climate system, and they may change storm frequency, droughtiness, and the frequency of high wind events (see above). Climate modes thus produce correlated changes in multiple physical variables, which include temperature, rainfall, and solar radiation, and also in statistical variables, such as storm frequency and severity as well as precipitation frequency and intensity.

Most literature on climate change impact has focused on the impacts of a single variable (e.g., temperature), or on several variables changing independently in a sensitivity analysis, or on a correlation structure derived from a climate model (61–64). These approaches differ significantly from the syndromes of changes associated with changes to climate modes. In fact, analyses using ecosystem models suggest that biological and hydrological systems are more sensitive to changes in energy balance and water balance (65) arising from changes to heat and water budgets than to temperature or precipitation per se (66). For example, correlated increases in both temperature and rainfall can have a qualitatively different effect than changes in each variable separately. Anti-correlated changes can have complex effects: increases in rainfall (and cloudiness) are often accompanied by decreases in solar radiation for photosynthesis-producing counteracting effects (67, 68). If temperature also decreases (due to reduced radiation), this will affect both photosynthesis and radiation. Effects of changing physical variables on plant and animal phenology and reproduction can also be influenced by these changes, again in complex ways (69). Furthermore, some of the strongest evidence for links between modal variability and ecological responses comes from marine systems in which effects of modes are propagated not only through temperature, but also through ocean circulation changes (70).

Studying the response of the living parts of the earth system to modal variability has two advantages. First, mode shifts provide a geophysical experiment in which climate variables and correlations change systematically, regionally, and with persistence. Second, as discussed above, future climate change may manifest itself partly as changes in the frequency of certain model patterns (for example, a persistently strengthened NAO or more frequent ENSO), and so examining responses to present-day mode shifts is intrinsically useful (71). Below, we review the literature on responses of ecological processes to changes in modal patterns with a focus on reproductive and population responses, seasonality, phenology, productivity, disturbance, and biogeochemistry.

Population and Reproductive Responses

It has become apparent that climate variability can have a major influence over ecological processes. Modes such as the ENSO, NAO, or PDO can be used as proxies for the actual climate drivers affecting ecosystems and produce clear correlations with biological responses at individual, community, and ecosystem levels. Variation due to climate modes often significantly affects the timing of ecological events. For example, plant phenology is often influenced by modal variation. Williamson & Ickes (72) showed that fruiting of mast-fruiting tropical trees (Dipterocarpaceae) in Southeast Asia was triggered by ENSO events, so that fruiting tended to be synchronized. ENSO events produce significant mortality, which creates a favorable environment for seedling success. In addition, synchronized mass fruiting may increase survivorship by satiating frugivores. They suggest that ENSO-synchronized fruiting may be an evolutionary response to the combination of seedling environment and predator response. Because these trees live far longer than the typical ENSO cycle and are themselves hosts of a wide range of organisms, the ENSO cycle can create periodic phenomena that are triggered by the ENSO cycle but have far longer periods. The linkage between ENSO and mast-fruiting of tropical trees was also reported by other studies (73). The spatial correlation in climate anomalies created by modes has been demonstrated in a wide range of environments. Post & Forchhammer (74) showed populations of musk oxen and caribou on opposite coasts of Greenland were synchronized because the population dynamics were entrained by the same environmental variation. In this case, the driving mode was the NAO that caused coupled population dynamics between groups of organisms separated by a 1000 km of inland icecap. Post & Stenseth (75) showed detailed links between the NAO, plant phenology, and the population dynamics of ungulates in North America and northern Europe. They analyzed 137 time series for plant phenology and showed significant correlation between the NAO and the timing of early blooming. Although there were differences in sensitivity between different functional groups of plants (woody vs. herbaceous and early vs. late bloomers), most species phenology showed correlations with the NAO. In the same study, they analyzed time series of ungulate populations and found strong correlations between NAO and ungulate body size and fecundity. They identified differences between inland and maritime populations. The trigger associated with most NAO effects seemed to be warmer and wetter winters, and surprisingly, they found much stronger effects of wintertime temperatures on animal than plant populations.

Interannual variability due to climate modes can have rather indirect effects. The global decline and local extinctions of amphibians is a well-known phenomenon. Kiesecker et al. (76) showed a potential link to ENSO variability. They found correlations between pathogen outbreaks, amphibian mortality, and the ENSO cycle in the western United States. It was suggested in their study that climate (ENSO drought) conditions in the Pacific Northwest reduced water depths at oviposition sites, which increased UV-B exposure and thus increased susceptibility to the pathogen *Saprolegnia ferax* and hence mortality. The link between *Saprolegnia ferax* susceptibility and UV-B exposure is established, and the correlation between water depths and the Southern Oscillation index is statistically significant in this region. This provides another example of the potential cascading complex of effects between global climate modes, the biophysical environment, and organismal responses. In a rather different study, Morrison & Bolger (77) found effects of both El Niño and La Niña on avian reproductive success. They found relationships between rufous-crowned sparrows and rainfall, with rainfall linked to the ENSO cycle. However, while effects in El Niño years were due to direct effects of rainfall on food, effects in La Niña years were due to altered activity by predators (snakes).

Marine ecosystems show strong links to climate variations. ENSO-induced fluctuation in fishery productivity in the East Pacific is a very well known example, first noticed centuries ago by fishermen along the coasts of Peru and Chile. During El Niño, easterly trade winds across the tropical Pacific slacken or reverse, which slows down the upwelling of cold, nutrient-rich water from the ocean depth in the tropical eastern Pacific. As a result, phytoplankton production drops, which works up the marine food web to eventually reduce fishery productivity (78). Salmon in the North Pacific are influenced by both temperature and circulation changes linked to ENSO and the PDO (shifting fisheries north or south, depending on the phase) and are also affected by drought conditions on land (79). Warmer ocean conditions during El Niño adversely affect chinook and coho salmon. El Niño and PDO also affect the riverine systems used by salmonids for part of their life cycle (8, 80). For example, warmer river water poses a barrier to upstream migration, but low stream flow reduces barriers (such as rapids) that exist at higher flows.

Another important fishery, that of skipjack tuna, is also linked to the ENSO cycle. The skipjack inhabits the Pacific warm pool region, where productivity is low and sea surface temperatures are high. The distribution of skipjack populations is linked to the position of the warm pool and follows it during ENSO years. Interestingly, little is known about the trophic relationships of skipjack, a zooplankton feeder with high energetic demands, and the ecosystem that supports this species. However, hypotheses center on westward transport of plankton communities into a zone of oceanic convergence. The linkage of this trophic system to large-scale transport in the ocean suggests that further research will reveal additional and complex links between pelagic food webs and climate modes. Atlantic fisheries are also linked to climate modes. The NAO appears to be a significant control over recruitment and survival in Atlantic cod. Sirabella et al. (81) showed links between the NAO, temperature, and cod recruitment in the Barents Sea and North Sea. The patterns of correlation suggest a temperature optimum for cod, because in the cold Barents Sea recruitment is directly correlated to temperature (and temperature to the NAO), yet in the warmer North Sea, the correlation is inverse. Chan et al. (82) analyzed a long time series of cod-landing data from Scandinavia in areas where artificial supplementation of larval cod populations had been practiced. They found little evidence for an effect of cod releases on cod populations beyond 6 months of age, but they did find significant dependence across the Norwegian coast of cod populations on the NAO and temperature consistent with the Sirabella et al. (81) findings.

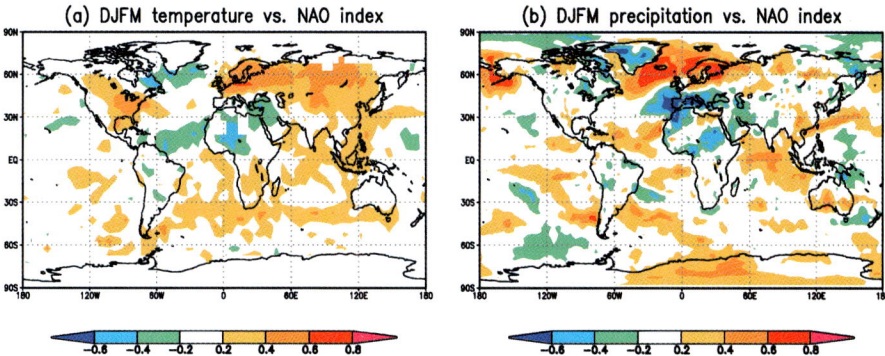

Figure 2 (*a*) Correlation coefficient between the NAO index and global surface temperature in extended boreal winter December–March (DJFM), based on data during 1951–2000; (*b*) Correlation coefficient between the NAO index and global precipitation in DJFM, based on data during 1979–2001. The 5% significance level corresponds to a correlation coefficient of approximately 0.28 in (*a*) and 0.42 in (*b*).

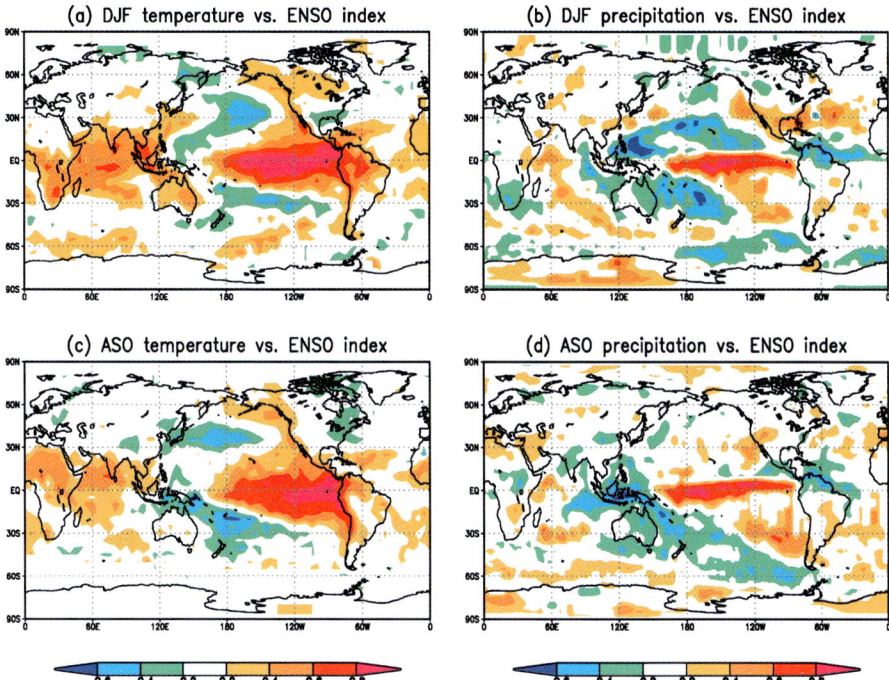

Figure 3 Correlation coefficients between the ENSO index and (*a*) global temperature in December–February (DJF); (*b*) global precipitation in DJF; (*c*) global temperature in August–October (ASO); (*d*) global precipitation in ASO. Figures are modified from Diaz et al. (32).

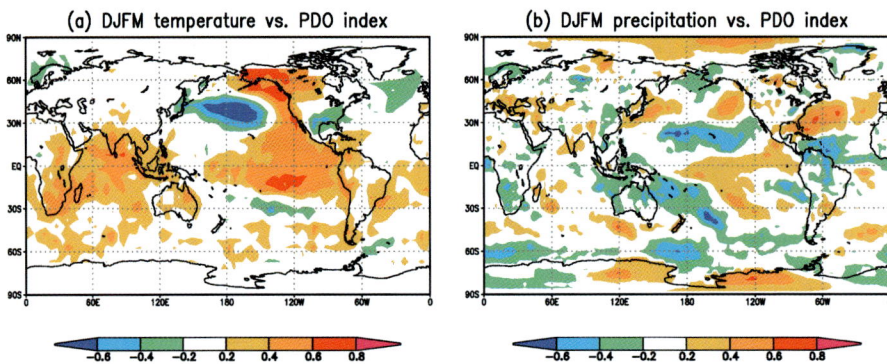

Figure 4 Same as Figure 2, but for the PDO index. Figure 4*a* uses data from the period 1951–2000, and Figure 4*b* uses data from the period 1979–2001.

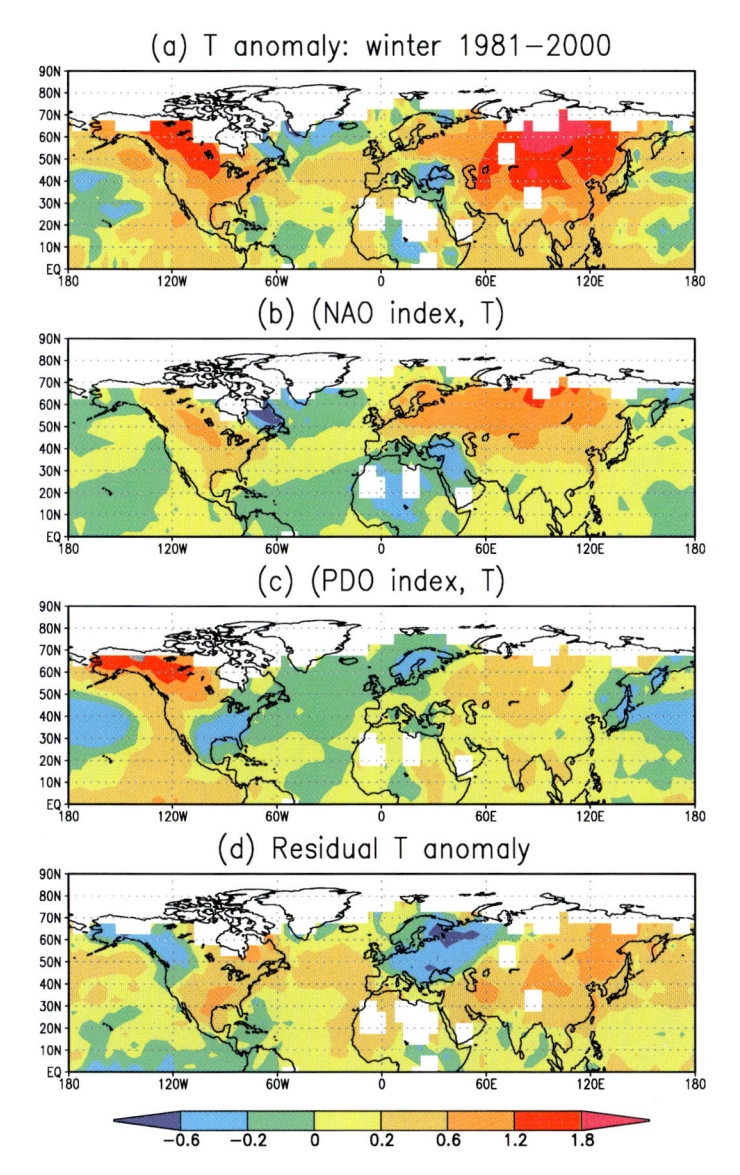

Figure 6 (*a*) Departure of the winter (December–March) surface temperature averaged during 1981–2000 from the preceding 20-winter average (1961–1980); (*b*) winter temperature anomalies corresponding to a unit increase of the normalized NAO index; (*c*) winter temperature anomalies corresponding to a unit increase of the normalized PDO index; and (*d*) residual temperature anomaly in (*a*) that cannot be explained by the NAO and PDO. The regression analysis in (*b*) and (*c*) are based on data during the period 1951–2000. All temperature units are °C.

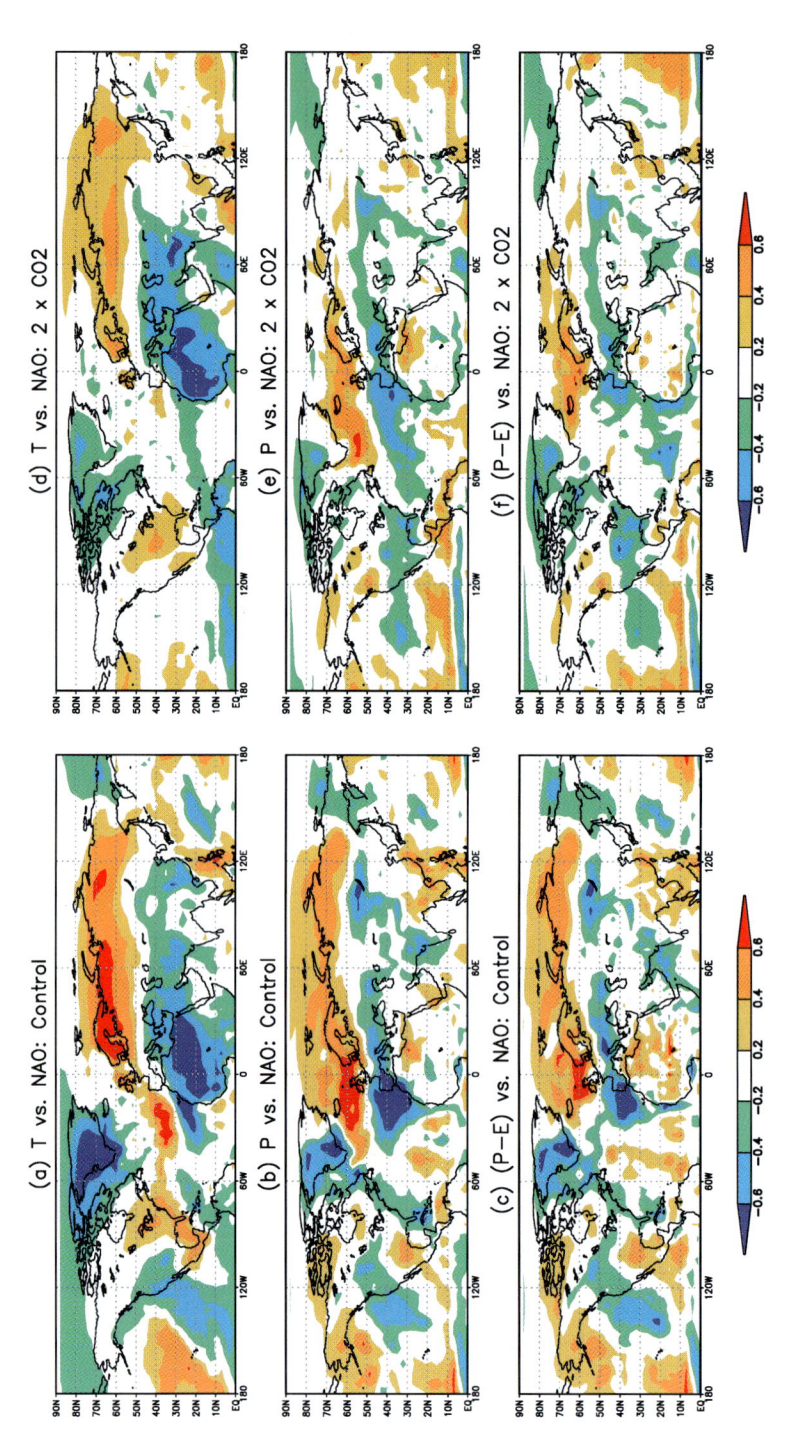

Figure 8 Correlation coefficients between the NAO index and surface temperature (T), precipitation (P), and fresh water flux (P-E) based on DOE PCM simulations (B04.10 and B04.29). Left panels present results based on a 30-year episode of model integration in the control simulation (B04.10) where CO_2 concentration was fixed at 355 ppmv; right panels present results based on the 30-year model integration after the stabilization of CO_2 concentration at 710 ppmv in the transient CO_2 experiment B04.29. For a sample size of 30, the 5% significance level corresponds to a correlation coefficient of about 0.36.

Terrestrial-marine links also exhibit modal variability. Stapp et al. (83) studied island food webs using stable isotopes off Baja California. In these systems, carbon and nutrients from the sea, transported by seabirds and in detritus, support terrestrial communities. In normal years, food webs are based on allochthonous inputs transported from marine sources. In wet El Niño years, rainfall supports flushes of vegetation, and the food webs switch to a terrestrial primary productivity base. In these island ecosystems, climate modes switch the ecosystems from being based on inputs from the sea to being based on in situ terrestrial photosynthesis.

Some of the most complex interactions triggered by modal shifts are in human-environment systems. There now exist a significant number of suggestive case studies linking climate anomalies, ecosystem responses, and human systems (84). In East Africa, a semiarid region, El Niño tends to trigger unusually high rainfall, and this was well documented during the large El Niño of 1997–1998. A complex of cascading effects was documented there (85, 86) in which ENSO-induced changes in vegetation led to significant changes in livestock dynamics. This was of great importance to the semi-traditional pastoral economies of the region with effects that differed, however, by region and elevation. The modulation of the global ENSO phenomenon, first by topographic and ecological differences and then by social systems, resulted in the translation of a common regional process into a host of synchronized but diverse local responses. Increases in precipitation are an anomaly in the drier areas of East Africa and can actually be a stress to human-environment systems well adapted to the prevailing drought conditions (87). Case studies during the 1997–1998 El Niño suggest that negative effects of colder and wetter conditions may actually dominate in parts of East Africa, with increases in both animal and human disease. In Southern Africa, increases in African Horse Sickness (AHS) were found, a disease that affects horses and zebra (88). The virus vector, the biting midge *Culicoides imicola*, breeds in moist soil and can increase dramatically in years of heavy rainfall. Epizootics of AHS occur, typically in ENSO years, but especially in ENSO years when initial drought is followed by heavy rain. The authors suggest that drought causes susceptible animals to congregate near remaining water sources, where, once rains begin, they can both infect vectors and be infected more readily. The El Niño cycle is also linked to human disease. For example, cholera in Bangladesh follows the ENSO cycle closely, probably because of links between disease processes and temperature, but it is also possibly because of changes to the large-scale hydrological cycle (89).

Biogeochemistry, Disturbance, and the Global Carbon Cycle

The first mention of a link between climate modes (El Niño) and biogeochemistry was probably in Bacastow et al. (90) in which they noted a significant relationship between the Mauna Loa CO_2 record and the El Niño cycle, suggesting a link between the ocean carbon cycle and atmospheric CO_2. This link is one of the most useful and important pieces of evidence for strong effects of climate on the carbon cycle (71), together of course with the ice core record.

Although the link between ENSO and carbon was first thought to be an oceanic phenomenon (90) due to the marine origins of the El Niño, work in the 1990s showed that the variations were too large to be explained exclusively by marine circulation or temperature changes (91, 92), a conclusion since supported by isotopic analyses (93). Expansion of the tropical warm pool reduces upwelling of cold, CO_2-rich water in the tropics during El Niño and should cause an apparent increase in global ocean carbon uptake. Feely et al. (91) supported this argument but showed the observed changes in marine CO_2 to be too small to explain the atmospheric variations. Oceanic changes during El Niño may not explain the global carbon cycle correlation, but time-series data from marine process studies suggest profound effects of ENSO on marine biogeochemistry (94), which was also suggested implicitly in fisheries studies, above.

In the 1990s, terrestrial explanations for El Niño-CO_2 correlations began to emerge. The Amazon basin experiences droughts during El Niño years. Using a model, Tian et al. (95) suggested that reductions in soil moisture caused increases in respiratory carbon release relative to photosynthetic uptake. Despite model-based analyses, satellite-based studies of terrestrial biosphere primary productivity do not show a clear global signature although regional changes were observed, which suggests that productivity and respiration may not be the only terrestrial process contributing to El Niño-related CO_2 variations. Nepstad et al. (96) showed that biomass burning associated with forest clearing was linked to El Niño droughts, due to the flammability of slash. They argued that Amazon basin emissions could double in strong El Niño years.

Vukicevic et al. (97) fit a simple model of the responses of photosynthesis, respiration, and nitrogen cycling to interannual temperature variability. They showed that a significant amount of interannual biogeochemical variability could be explained by ecosystem responses to temperature but that large residuals were associated with El Niño periods. The residuals were negative (uptake) early in the El Niño period and large and positive (emissions) later. This pattern is consistent with ocean uptake early in the El Niño and emissions following as ENSO droughts take hold. New evidence suggests that El Niño droughts may play a major role in the carbon cycle and interact with wildfire. Langenfelds et al. (93) used atmospheric measurements of CO_2, $^{13}CO_2$, and several chemical tracers of fire. They found a high degree of correlation between changes to the growth rates of pyrogenic compounds (H_2, CH_4, and CO) and that of CO_2 during time periods in which $^{13}CO_2$ suggested a primarily terrestrial origin for the CO_2. Langenfelds et al. (93) concluded that a significant fraction of the interannual variability in carbon cycling during the 1990s was due to wildfire. In parallel studies, several groups began to focus on the extremely large wildfires in Indonesia during the 1997–1998 El Niño. Page et al. (98) estimated that emissions from these fires were between 0.8 and 2.6 Gt of carbon, an amount equal to 13%–40% of global fossil emissions, and similar to total global biospheric storage in a typical year (99). The emissions were large because of the size and intensity of the fires, and also because they burned through peatlands, where vast amounts of carbon were stored in the soil. While these wildfires were triggered by the El Niño drought, the fires were most severe in regions that were recently logged, where large amounts of flammable material were available and where roads and drainage channels had lowered the water table and allowed the peat soils to burn as well as vegetation. The Indonesian emissions were very large and produced a clearly detectable signal in atmospheric CO_2, but additional analysis suggests that other tropical regions were also sources in that El Niño year (100).

Summary

Recent research has revealed roles for the climate modes in controlling ecosystems at scales ranging from growth, reproduction, and survival of individual organisms through the global carbon cycle. Although the diversity of organisms and ecological processes with documented links to climate modal variation is enormous, a few themes emerge. First, many regional variations in climate are associated with climate mode shifts. These large regional climate shifts are important ecologically for two reasons. First, they tend to produce regional synchrony in biological and/or biogeochemical processes over large regions. Regional synchrony can have population or even evolutionary links (72) due to interactions with density-dependent population processes (75). Regional synchrony can also produce large biogeochemical fluxes as is evident in the ENSO cycle-global carbon cycle correlation. The second, and coupled, theme is the link between climate mode shifts, climate extremes, and ecological responses. Many climate extremes of drought and heavy precipitation are linked to phases of the climate modes. Human and livestock health are linked to El Niño flooding in East Africa (87), barriers to salmon migration are linked to El Niño precipitation variation in the U.S. Pacific Northwest (80), and wildfire impacts on the carbon cycle are linked to El Niño droughts (98). In anticipating the future, climate change impacts are likely to be significantly mediated via changes to the intensity, spatial pattern, or frequency of climate modes. Entirely new impacts could occur if climate change produces new modes or if the spatial domain affected by an existing mode shifts. Research on the impacts of climate modes, typically described as producing variation on seasonal to decadal timescales, is extremely complementary to research on climate change typically thought of as occurring on decadal to centennial timescales.

FINAL REMARKS

Variations in the Earth's atmospheric and oceanic circulations generate an array of important dynamical modes, which provide an efficient way to study large-scale climate variability, climate impact, and even anthropogenically induced climate changes. Our review was limited to several of the leading modes, which included the NAO, ENSO, and PDO. These modes were chosen either because of the extensive spatial coverage of their impact or because of their strong impact on a specific region. In addition, ENSO and NAO are also among the most intensively studied modes of the climate system and are therefore better understood than others.

Long-term observational data produced evidence for strong and statistically significant correlations between dynamical modes and regional-global climate variability. The relationships between modes and certain ecological processes in both terrestrial and marine environments are also well established. For both climate variability and ecological impact, the NAO effects dominate over the majority of the Atlantic sector that includes eastern North America, North Atlantic, and Eurasia; the ENSO signal is prominent over the tropics and the majority of Southern Hemisphere extratropics; the PDO plays a significant role in North Pacific and a major part of North America. Therefore, examining the temporal variation of modes may lead to important predictive information for many aspects of regional and global environment and resources, such as winter severity, storminess, water resources, agriculture and fishery productivity, and timing and length of growing season. In particular, the persistence of some climate modes and their link to slowly varying ocean conditions create an opportunity for limited prediction of seasonal climate (101). For example, information from seasonal predictions based on the El Niño cycle is now made available regularly by the International Research Institute for Climate Prediction (http://iri.columbia.edu/) and has significant value for preparing for climate impacts (102, 103). In addition, several studies have demonstrated the potential use of ENSO index as a predictor for the discharge of some major rivers (34–40).

The linkage between modes and climate changes is less definitive. The secular trend found in the global mean surface temperature during the past century is mainly due to the rapid warming since the 1970s, and the majority of these temperature changes can be explained by the trend of NAO and PDO toward a more positive phase and by the more frequent/persistent occurrence of El Niño during the past two to three decades. This suggests that CO_2-induced climate changes may manifest through changes in the naturally occurring modes of the climate system. However, before a longer record becomes available, one cannot exclude the possibility that recent modes anomalies might be just part of their long-term variability. Although there has been no consensus among numerical modeling studies, many climate models indicated that increasing greenhouse gas concentration changes the naturally occurring modes of the climate system and supported the linkage between modes and anthropogenic climate changes.

It has long been established that CO_2 impacts the global climate through its direct radiative effects. More recent studies indicated that indirect effects through plant physiology and vegetation structure changes are also important (104–106). The perspective that CO_2-induced climate changes may take place through changes in the primary dynamical modes implies the potential existence of a third type of effects, i.e., through changes in the atmospheric and oceanic circulation patterns. This potential linkage between modes and climate changes will also make modes a useful tool for evaluating the regional and global impact of future climate changes.

Although this review focused on recent historical data, information about climate modes is preserved in the paleo-record as well and demonstrates that at least some modern modes are ancient (107). Paleo-record and archeological data also show that modal variability has long had environmental and human consequences (108). Modes are an important factor to consider for climate variability and changes, and their impacts are not limited to modern times.

The *Annual Review of Environment and Resources* is online at
http://environ.annualreviews.org

LITERATURE CITED

1. Walker GT, Bliss EW. 1932. World weather V. *Mem. R. Meteorol. Soc.* 4:53–83
2. Wallace JM, Gutzler DS. 1981. Teleconnections in the geopotential height field during the Northern Hemisphere winter. *Mon. Weather Rev.* 109:784–812
3. Hurrell JW. 1995. Decadal trends in the North Atlantic Oscillation: regional temperatures and precipitation. *Science* 269:676–79
4. Limpasuvan V, Hartmann DL. 1999. Eddies and the annual modes of climate variability. *Geophys. Res. Lett.* 26:3133–36
5. Thompson DWJ, Wallace JM. 1998. The Arctic Oscillation signature in the wintertime geopotential height and temperature fields. *Geophys. Res. Lett.* 25:1297–1300
6. Thompson DWJ, Wallace JM. 2001. Regional climate impacts of the Northern Hemisphere annual mode. *Science* 293:85–89
7. Philander SGH. 1985. El Niño and La Niña. *J. Atmos. Sci.* 42:2652–62
8. Mantua NJ, Hare SR, Zhang Y, Wallace JM, Francis RC. 1997. A Pacific interdecadal climate oscillation with impacts on salmon production. *Bull. Am. Meteorol. Soc.* 78:1069–79
9. Wallace JM. 2000. North Atlantic Oscillation/annular mode: Two paradigms– one phenomenon. *Q. J. R. Meteorol. Soc.* 126:791–805
10. Jolliffe IT. 2002. *Principal Component Analysis*. New York: Springer. 502 pp.
11. Thompson DWJ, Wallace JM, Hegerl GC. 2000. Annual modes in the extratropical circulation. Part II: trends. *J. Clim.* 13:1018–36
12. Rogers JC, van Loon H. 1982. Spatial variability of sea level pressure and 500-mb height anomalies over the Southern Hemisphere. *Mon. Weather Rev.* 110:1375–92
13. Ambaum MHP, Hoskins BJ, Stephenson DB. 2001. Arctic Oscillation or North Atlantic Oscillation? *J. Clim.* 14:3495–3507
14. Barlow M, Nigam S, Berbery EH. 2001. ENSO, Pacific decadal variability, and U.S. summertime precipitation, drought, and stream flow. *J. Clim.* 14:2105–28
15. Deser C. 2000. On the teleconnectivity of the "Arctic Oscillation." *Geophys. Res. Lett.* 27:779–82
16. Trenberth KE, Hoar TJ. 1996. The 1990–1995 El Niño-Southern Oscillation event: longest on record. *Geophys. Res. Lett.* 23:57–60
17. Trenberth KE. 1984. Signal versus noise in the Southern Oscillation. *Mon. Weather Rev.* 112:326–332
18. Zhang Y, Wallace JM, Battisti DS.

1997. ENSO-like interdecadal variability: 1900–93. *J. Clim.* 10:1004–20
19. Mantua NJ, Hare SR. 2002. The Pacific Decadal Oscillation. *J. Oceanogr.* 58:35–44
20. Hurrell JW. 1996. Influence of variations ion extratropical wintertime teleconnections on Northern Hemisphere temperature. *Geophys. Res. Lett.* 23:665–68
21. Visbeck MH, Hurrell JW, Polvani L, Cullen HM. 2001. The North Atlantic Oscillation: past, present, and future. *Proc. Natl. Acad. Sci. USA* 98:12876–77
22. Jones PD, Osborn TJ, Briffa KR. 2001. The evolution of climate over the last millennium. *Science* 292:662–67
23. Janowiak JE, Xie PP. 1999. CAMS-OPI: a global satellite-rain gauge merged product for real-time precipitation monitoring applications. *J. Clim.* 12:3335–42
24. Hurrell JW, Kushnir Y, Ottersen G, Visbeck M, eds. 2003. *The North Atlantic Oscillation: Climate Significance and Environmental Impact*. Geophys. Monogr. Ser. 134. Washington, DC: Am. Geophys. Union. 279 pp.
25. Hurrell JW, van Loon H. 1997. Decadal variations in climate associated with the North Atlantic Oscillation. *Clim. Change* 36:301–26
26. Dai AG, Fung IY, Genio ADD. 1997. Surface observed global land precipitation variations during 1900–88. *J. Clim.* 10:2943–62
27. Hartley S, Keables MJ. 1998. Synoptic associations of winter climate and snowfall variability in New England, USA, 1950–1992. *Int. J. Climatol.* 18:281–98
28. Dickson RR, Osborn TJ, Hurrell JW, Meincke J, Blindheim J, et al. 2000. The Arctic Ocean response to the North Atlantic Oscillation. *J. Clim.* 13:2671–96
29. Perreault L, Hache M, Slivitzky M, Bobee B. 1999. Detection of changes in precipitation and runoff over eastern Canada and US using a Bayesian approach. *Stoch. Environ. Res. Risk Assess.* 13:201–16
30. Siggurdson O, Jonsson T. 1995. Relation of glacier variations to climate changes in Iceland. *Ann. Glaciol.* 21:263–70
31. Deser C, Blackmon ML. 1993. Surface climate variations over the North Atlantic Ocean during winter: 1900–1989. *J. Clim.* 6:1743–53
32. Diaz HF, Hoerling MP, Eischeid JK. 2001. ENSO variability, teleconnections and climate change. *Int. J. Climatol.* 21:1845–62
33. Dai AG, Wigley TML. 2000. Global pattern of ENSO-induced precipitation. *Geophys. Res. Lett.* 27:1283–86
34. Eltahir EAB. 1996. El Niño and the natural variability in the flow of the Nile River. *Water Resourc. Res.* 32:132–37
35. Wang GL, Eltahir EAB. 1999. Use of ENSO information in the medium- to long-range forecasting of the Nile flood. *J. Clim.* 12:1726–37
36. Whitaker DW, Wasimi SA, Islam S. 2001. The El Niño-Southern Oscillation and long-range forecasting of flows in the Ganges. *Int. J. Climatol.* 21:77–87
37. Richey JE, Nobre C, Deser C. 1989. Amazon River discharge and climate variability: 1903–1985. *Science* 246:101–3
38. Simpson HJ, Cane MA, Herczeg AL, Zebiak SE, Simpson JH. 1993. Annual river discharge in southeastern Australia related to El Niño-Southern Oscillation forecasts of sea surface temperature. *Water Resourc. Res.* 29:3671–80
39. Simpson HJ, Cane MA, Lin SK, Zebiak SE. 1993b. Forecasting annual discharge of River Murray, Australia, from a geophysical model of ENSO. *J. Clim.* 6:386–90
40. Piechota TC, Dracup JA. 1996. Drought and regional hydrologic variation in the United States: associations with the El Niño Southern Oscillation. *Water Resourc. Res.* 32:1359–73
41. Hulme M, Osborn TJ, Johns TC. 1998. Precipitation sensitivity to global warming: comparison of observations with HadCM2 simulations. *Geophys. Res. Lett.* 25:3379–82

42. Hansen J, Ruedy R, Glascoe J, Sato M. 1999. GISS analysis of surface temperature change. *J. Geophys. Res.* 104:30997–1022
43. Mann ME. 2001. Climate during the past millennium. *Weather* 56:91–101
44. Intergov. Panel Clim. Change. 2001. *Climate Change 2001: The Scientific Basis—Contribution of Working Group I to the Third Assessment Report of the Intergovernmental Panel on Climate Change*, ed. JT Houghton, Y Ding, DJ Griggs, M Noguer, PJ van der Linden, et al. New York: Cambridge Univ. Press. 881 pp.
45. New M, Todd M, Hulme M, Jones P. 2001. Precipitation measurements and trends in the twentieth century. *Int. J. Climatol.* 21:1899–922
46. Hanssen-Bauer I, Forland E. 2000. Temperature and precipitation variations in Norway 1900–1994 and their links to atmospheric circulation. *Int. J. Climatol.* 20:1693–708
47. Piervitali E, Colacino M, Conte M. 1998. Rainfall over the central-western Mediterranean basin in the period 1951–1995. Part I: precipitation trends. *Nuovo Cimento Della Soc. Italiana Di Fis. C—Geophys. Space Phys.* 21:331–44
48. Romero R, Guijarro JA, Ramis C, Alonso S. 1998. A 30-year (1964–1993) daily rainfall data base for the Spanish Mediterranean regions: first exploratory study. *Int. J. Climatol.* 18:541–60
49. Beniston M. 1997. Variation of snow depth and duration in the Swiss Alps over the last 50 years: links to changes in large-scale climatic forcings. *Clim. Change* 36:281–300
50. Knutson TR, Manabe S. 1995. Time-mean response over the tropical Pacific to increased CO_2 in a coupled ocean-atmosphere model. *J. Clim.* 8:2181–99
51. Meehl GA, Washington WM. 1996. El Niño-like climate change in a model with increased atmospheric CO_2 concentrations. *Nature* 382:56–60
52. Meehl GA, Washington WM, Arblaster JM, Bettge TW, Strand WG Jr. 2000. Anthropogenic forcing and decadal climate variability in sensitivity experiments of twentieth- and twenty-first-century climate. *J. Clim.* 13:3728–44
53. Boer GJ, Flato G, Ramsden D. 2000. A transient climate change simulation with greenhouse gas and aerosol forcing: projected climate to the twenty-first century. *Clim. Dyn.* 16:427–50
54. Timmermann A, Oberhuber J, Bacher A, Each M, Latif M, Roeckner E. 1999. Increased El Niño frequency in a climate model forced by future greenhouse warming. *Nature* 398:694–97
55. Meehl GA, Collins WD, Boville BA, Kiehl JT, Wigley TML, Arblaster JM. 2000. Response of the NCAR climate system model to increased CO_2 and the role of physical processes. *J. Clim.* 13:1879–98
56. Washington WM, Weatherly JW, Meehl GA, Semtner AJ Jr, Bettge TW, et al. 2000. Parallel Climate Model (PCM) control and transient simulations. *Clim. Dyn.* 16:755–74
57. Hoerling MP, Hurrell JW, Xu TY. 2001. Tropical origins for recent North Atlantic climate change. *Science* 292:90–92
58. Shindell DT, Miller RL, Schmidt GA, Pandolfo L. 1999. Simulation of recent northern winter climate trends by greenhouse-gas forcing. *Nature* 399:452–55
59. Paeth H, Hense A, Glowienka-Hense R, Voss R, Cubasch U. 1999. The North Atlantic Oscillation as an indicator for greenhouse-gas induced regional climate change. *Clim. Dyn.* 15:953–60
60. Fyfe JC, Boer GJ, Flato GM. 1999. The Arctic and Antarctic oscillations and their projected changes under global warming. *Geophys. Res. Lett.* 26:1601–4
61. Schimel DS, Parton WJ, Kittel TGF, Ojima DA, Cole CV. 1990. Grassland biogeochemistry—links to atmospheric processes. *Clim. Change* 17:13–25
62. Schimel DS, Braswell BH, McKeown R,

Ojima DS, Parton WJ, Pullian W. 1996. Climate and nitrogen controls on the geography and timescales of terrestrial biogeochemical cycling. *Glob. Biogeochem. Cycles* 10:677–92
63. Schimel D, Melillo J, Tian H, McGuire AD, Kicklighter D, et al. 2000. Contribution of increasing CO_2 and climate to carbon storage by ecosystems in the United States. *Science* 287:2004–6
64. Melillo JM, Borchers J, Chaney J, Fisher H, Fox S, et al. 1995. Vegetation ecosystem modeling and analysis project—comparing biogeography and biogeochemistry models in a continental-scale study of terrestrial ecosystem responses to climate-change and CO_2 doubling. *Glob. Biogeochem. Cycles* 9:407–37
65. Schimel DS, Emanuel W, Rizzo B, Smith T, Woodward FI, et al. 1997. Continental scale variability in ecosystem processes: models, data, and the role of disturbance. *Ecol. Monogr.* 67:251–71
66. Bachelet D, Neilson RP, Lenihan JM, Drapek RJ. 2001. Climate change effects on vegetation distribution and carbon budget in the United States. *Ecosystems* 4:164–85
67. Tian H, Melillo JM, Kicklighter DW, McGuire AD, Helfrich J. 1999. The sensitivity of terrestrial carbon storage to historical climate variability and atmospheric CO_2 in the United States. *Tellus B* 51:414–52
68. Tian H, Melillo JM, Kicklighter DW, McGuire AD, Helfrich J, et al. 2000. Climatic and biotic controls on annual carbon storage in Amazonian ecosystems. *Glob. Ecol. Biogeogr.* 9:315–35
69. Ottersen G, Planque B, Belgrano A, Post E, Reid PC, Stenseth NC. 2001. Ecological effects of the North Atlantic Oscillation. *Oecologia* 128:1–14
70. Sugimoto T, Kimura S, Tadokorol K. 2001. Impact of El Niño events and climate regime shifts on living resources in the western North Pacific. *Prog. Oceanogr.* 49:113–27

71. Cox PM, Betts RA, Jones CD, Spall SA, Totterdell IJ. 2000. Acceleration of global warming due to carbon-cycle feedbacks in a coupled climate model. *Nature* 408:184–87
72. Williamson GB, Ickes K. 2002. Mast fruiting and ENSO cycles—does the cue betray a cause? *Oikos* 97:459–61
73. Curran LM, Caniago I, Paoli GD, Astianti D, Kusneti M, et al. 1999. Impact of El Niño and logging on canopy tree recruitment in Borneo. *Science* 286:2184–88
74. Post E, Forchhammer MC. 2002. Synchronization of animal population dynamics by large-scale climate. *Nature* 420:168–71
75. Post E, Stenseth NC. 1999. Climate variability, plant phenology, and northern ungulates. *Ecology* 80:1322–39
76. Kiesecker JM, Blaustein AR, Belden LK. 2001. Complex causes of amphibian population declines. *Nature* 410:681–84
77. Morrison SA, Bolger DT. 2002. Variation in a sparrow's reproductive success with rainfall: food and predator-mediated success. *Oecologia* 133:315–24
78. Caviedes CN, Fik TJ. 1992. The Peru-Chile eastern Pacific fisheries and climatic oscillations. In *Climate Variability, Climate Change and Fisheries*, ed. MH Glantz, pp. 355–76. Cambridge, UK: Cambridge Univ. Press
79. Francis RC, Hare SR, Hollowed AB, Wooster WS. 1998. Effects of interdecadal climate variability on the oceanic ecosystem of the NE Pacific. *Fish. Oceanogr.* 7:1–21
80. Miller KA, Munro G, McKelvey R, Tyedmers P. 2001. Climate, uncertainty and the Pacific salmon treaty: Insights on the harvest management game. In *Microbehavior and Microresults: Proceedings of the Tenth Biennial Conference of the International Institute of Fisheries Economics and Trade*, ed. RS Johnston, AL Shriver. Corvallis: IIFET
81. Sirabella P, Giuliani A, Colosimo A, Dippner JW. 2001. Breaking down the

climate effects on cod recruitment by principal component analysis and canonical correlation. *Mar. Ecol. Prog. Ser.* 216:213–22
82. Chan K-S, Stenseth NC, Kittilsen MO, Gjoseter J, Lekve K, et al. 2003. Assessing the effectiveness of releasing cod larvae for stock improvement with monitoring data. *Ecol. Appl.* 13:3–22
83. Stapp P, Polls GA, Pinero FS. 1999. Stable isotopes reveal strong marine and El Niño effects on island food webs. *Nature* 401:467–69
84. Glantz MH. 2000. *Currents of Change: Impact of El Niño and La Niña on Climate and Society.* Cambridge, UK: Cambridge Univ. Press. 272 pp. 2nd ed.
85. Boone RB, Galvin KA, Smith NM, Lynn SJ. 2000. Generalizing El Niño effects upon Maasai livestock using hierarchical clusters of vegetation patterns. *Photogramm. Eng. Remote Sens.* 66:737–44
86. Galvin KA, Boone RB, Smith NM, Lynn SJ. 2001. Impacts of climate variability on East African pastoralists: linking social science and remote sensing. *Clim. Res.* 19:161–72
87. Little PD, Mahmoud H, Coppock DL. 2001. When deserts flood: risk management and climatic processes among East African pastoralists. *Clim. Res.* 19:149–59
88. Baylis M, Mellor PS, Meiswinkel R. 1999. Horse sickness and ENSO in South Africa. *Nature* 397:574
89. Pascual M, Bouma MJ, Dobson AP. 2002. Cholera and climate: revisiting the quantitative evidence. *Microbes Infect.* 4:237–45
90. Bacastow RB, Adams JA, Keeling CD, Moss DJ, Whorf TP, Wong CS. 1980. Atmospheric carbon dioxide, the Southern Oscillation, and the weak 1975 El Niño. *Science* 210:66–68
91. Feely RA, Wanninkhof R, Takahashi T, Tans P. 1999. Influence of El Niño on the equatorial Pacific contribution to atmospheric CO_2 accumulation. *Nature* 398:597–601
92. Lee K, Wanninkhof R, Takahashi T, Doney SC, Feely RA. 1998. Low interannual variability in recent oceanic uptake of atmospheric carbon dioxide. *Nature* 396:155–59
93. Langenfelds RL, Francey RJ, Pak BC, Steele LP, Lloyd J, et al. 2002. Interannual growth rate variations of atmospheric CO_2 and its ^{13}C, H_2, CH_4, and CO between 1992 and 1999 linked to biomass burning. *Glob. Biogeochem. Cycles* 16: Artic. 1048;10.1029/2001GB001466
94. Karl D, Letelier R, Tupas L, Dore J, Christian J, Hebel D. 1997. The role of nitrogen fixation in biogeochemical cycling in the subtropical North Pacific Ocean. *Nature* 388:533–38
95. Tian HQ, Melillo JM, Kicklighter DW, McGuire AD, Helfrich JVK, et al. 1998. Effects of interannual climate variability on carbon storage in Amazonian ecosystems. *Nature* 396:664–67
96. Nepstad DC, Verissimo A, Alencar A, Nobre C, Lima E, et al. 1999. Large-scale impoverishment of Amazonian forests by logging and fire. *Nature* 398:505–8
97. Vukicevic T, Braswell BH, Schimel D. 2001. A diagnostic study of temperature controls on global terrestrial carbon exchange. *Tellus B* 53:150–70
98. Page SE, Siegert F, Rieley JO, Boehm HDV, Jaya A, Limin S. 2002. The amount of carbon released from peat and forest fires in Indonesia during 1997. *Nature* 420:61–65
99. Schimel DS, House JI, Hibbard KA, Bousquet P, Ciais P, et al. 2001. Recent patterns and mechanisms of carbon exchange by terrestrial ecosystems. *Nature* 414:169–72
100. Schimel DS, Baker D. 2002. Carbon cycle: the wildfire factor. *Nature* 420:29–30
101. Goddard L, Mason SJ. 2001. Sensitivity of seasonal climate forecasts to persisted SST anomalies. *IRI Tech. Rep. 01–04.* Int.

Res. Inst. Clim. Predict., Columbia Univ., Palisades, NY
102. Glantz MH. 2001. Once Burned, Twice shy: lessons learned from the 1997–98 El Niño. Tokyo, Jpn: United Nations Univ. Press, 294 pp.
103. Phillips JG, Deane D, Unganai L, Chimele AB. 2002. Changes in small-holder grain production in Zimbabwe using seasonal climate forecasts. *Agric. Syst.* 74:351–69
104. Betts RA, Cox PM, Lee SE, Woodward FI. 1997. Contrasting physiological and structural vegetation feedbacks in climate change simulations. *Nature* 387:796–99
105. Levis S, Foley JA, Pollard D. 2000. Large-scale vegetation feedbacks on a doubled CO_2 climate. *J. Clim.* 13:1212–325
106. Wang GL, Eltahir EAB. 2002. Response of the biosphere-atmosphere system in West Africa to CO_2 concentration changes. *Glob. Change Biol.* 8:1169–82
107. Eltahir EAB, Wang GL. 1999. Nilometers, El Niño, and climate variability. *Geophys. Res. Lett.* 26:489–92
108. Sandweiss DH, Maasch KA, Burger RL, Richardson JB, Rollins HB, Clement A. 2001. Variation in Holocene El Niño frequencies: climate records and cultural consequences in ancient Peru. *Geology* 29:603–6

THE CLEANSING CAPACITY OF THE ATMOSPHERE

Ronald G. Prinn
*Massachusetts Institute of Technology, Cambridge, Massachusetts 02139;
email: rprinn@mit.edu*

Key Words atmospheric oxidation, troposphere, trace gases, hydroxyl free radical, human influences

■ **Abstract** The atmosphere is a chemically complex and dynamic system that interacts significantly with the land, oceans, and ecosystems. Most trace gases emitted into the atmosphere are removed by oxidizing chemical reactions involving ozone and the hydroxyl free radical. The rate of this self-cleansing process is often referred to as the oxidation capacity of the atmosphere. Without this process, atmospheric composition and climate would be very different from what we observe today. The fundamental chemistry involved and the influence of human activity on oxidation capacity are reviewed. Both the current measurements designed to determine rates of oxidation and evidence for changes in oxidizing capacity over recent decades are critically discussed.

CONTENTS

1. INTRODUCTION	29
2. FUNDAMENTAL REACTIONS	33
2.1. Troposphere	33
2.2. Stratosphere	38
3. HUMAN INFLUENCES	39
3.1. The Natural Atmosphere	40
3.2. Industrial Revolution	41
3.3. Forecasts	42
4. MEASURING THE HYDROXYL RADICAL	45
4.1. Direct Measurement	45
4.2. Indirect Measurement	48
4.3. Comparing Models and Observations	51
5. CONCLUSIONS	52

1. INTRODUCTION

The atmosphere is the recipient of a vast array of chemical compounds emitted by natural processes and, in recent times, increasingly emitted by human activity. The oxidation of this wide variety of chemical compounds is a key process proceeding in our oxygen-rich atmosphere. The compounds undergoing oxidation include hydrocarbons (RH), carbon monoxide (CO), sulfur dioxide (SO_2), nitrogen oxides (NO_x), ammonia (NH_3), hydrofluorocarbons, and hydrochlorofluorocarbons. A summary of the present-day composition of the atmosphere is given in Table 1. Without an efficient oxidation process, levels of many emitted gases could rise to such high levels, relative to Table 1, that they would radically change the chemical nature of our atmosphere and biosphere and, through the greenhouse effect, our climate. Hence, oxidation reactions are sometimes referred to as nature's atmospheric "cleansing" process. The overall rate of this cleansing process is a measure of the "oxidation capacity" of the atmosphere.

The key role of OH as a removal mechanism for atmospheric trace gases is illustrated in Table 2, which shows the global emissions of each gas and the approximate percentage of each of these emitted gases that is destroyed by reaction with OH (3).

From the last column in Table 2, OH removes a total of about 3.65×10^{15} grams of the listed gases each year or an amount equal to the total mass of the atmosphere every 1.4 million years. Without OH, our atmosphere would have a very different composition dominated by these otherwise trace gases.

There are also significant connections between atmospheric oxidation processes and climate. This is because ozone (O_3) is a powerful infrared absorber and emitter (a greenhouse gas) and because many other greenhouse gases, notably CH_4, are destroyed principally by reaction with OH. Also, the first step in production of aerosols from gaseous SO_2, NO_2, and hydrocarbons is almost always reaction with OH. Aerosols play a key role in climate through absorption and/or reflection of solar radiation. Oxidation processes involving O_3 and OH are also dominant in the chemistry of air pollution in which the occurrence of harmful levels of ozone and acidic aerosols depends on the relative and absolute levels of urban emissions of NO, CO, hydrocarbons, and SO_2.

The atmospheric oxidation process depends on the abundant presence of molecular oxygen. This O_2 photodissociates in the atmosphere to give O atoms, which combine with O_2 to form ozone (O_3). When O_3 absorbs ultraviolet light at wavelengths less than 310 nm, it produces excited oxygen atoms [$O(^1D)$] that can attack water vapor to produce the hydroxyl free radical (OH). It is the hydroxyl radical that, above all, defines the oxidative capacity of our O_2- and H_2O-rich atmosphere (3, 5, 6). Its global average concentration in the present atmosphere is only about 10^6 radical cm^{-3} or about 6 parts in 10^{14} by mole in the troposphere (7), but its influence is enormous. Typically, it reacts with CO, usually within about 1 second, to produce CO_2 (and also an H atom that quickly combines with O_2 to form hydroperoxy free radicals, HO_2). Another key player is nitric oxide (NO), which can be produced by lightning, combustion, and nitrifying and denitrifying bacteria in soils, sediments, and water. NO can react with either O_3 or HO_2 to form NO_2. The reaction of NO with HO_2 is special because it regenerates OH. Thus there are two major sources [$O(^1D) + H_2O \rightarrow 2OH$ and $NO + HO_2 \rightarrow NO_2 + OH$] for this key oxidizing species. The NO_2 is also important because

TABLE 1 Chemical composition of the atmosphere and major sources of constituents (1, 2) (1 ppt = 10^{-12}, 1 ppb = 10^{-9}, 1 ppm = 10^{-6})

Atmospheric constituent	Chemical formula	Mole fraction in dry air	Major sources
Nitrogen	N_2	78.08%	Biogenic
Oxygen	O_2	20.95%	Biogenic
Argon	Ar	0.93%	Inert
Carbon Dioxide	CO_2	360 ppm	Anthropogenic and biogenic
Neon	Ne	18.18 ppm	Inert
Helium	He	5.24 ppm	Inert
Methane	CH_4	1.7 ppm	Biogenic and anthropogenic
Hydrogen	H_2	0.55 ppm	Biogenic, anthropogenic, and photochemical
Nitrous Oxide	N_2O	0.31 ppm	Biogenic and anthropogenic
Carbon Monoxide	CO	50–200 ppb	Photochemical and anthropogenic
Ozone (troposphere)	O_3	10–500 ppb	Photochemical
Ozone (stratosphere)	O_3	0.5–10 ppm	Photochemical
Nonmethane Hydrocarbons	C_xH_y	5–20 ppb	Biogenic and anthropogenic
Sulfur dioxide	SO_2	10 ppt–1 ppb	Photochemical, volcanic, and anthropogenic
Dimethyl sulfide	CH_3SCH_3	10–100 ppt	Biogenic
Carbon disulfide	CS_2	1–300 ppt	Biogenic and anthropogenic
Carbonyl sulfide	OCS	500 ppt	Biogenic, volcanic, and anthropogenic
Hydrogen sulfide	H_2S	5–500 ppt	Biogenic and volcanic
Chlorofluorocarbon 12	CF_2Cl_2	540 ppt	Anthropogenic
Chlorofluorocarbon 11	$CFCl_3$	265 ppt	Anthropogenic
Methyl chloroform	CH_3CCl_3	65 ppt	Anthropogenic
Carbon tetrachloride	CCl_4	98 ppt	Anthropogenic
Nitrogen oxides	NO_y	10 ppt–1 ppm	Biogenic, lightning, and anthropogenic
Ammonia	NH_3	10 ppt–1 ppb	Biogenic
Hydroxyl radical	OH	0.05 ppt	Photochemical
Hydroperoxyl radical	HO_2	2 ppt	Photochemical
Hydrogen peroxide	H_2O_2	0.1 ppb–10 ppb	Photochemical
Formaldehyde	CH_2O	0.1–1 ppb	Photochemical

TABLE 2 Estimates of the global emission rates of tropospheric trace gases (Tg) and the fraction and absolute amounts removed by reaction with OH according to Ehhalt (3). The mean global OH concentration was taken as 1×10^6 cm^{-3} (4) and 1 Tg = 10^{12} g

Trace gas	Global emission rate (Tg/yr)	Removal by OH (%)	Removal by OH (Tg/yr)
CO	2800	85	2380
CH$_4$	530	90	477
C$_2$H$_6$	20	90	18
Isoprene	570	90	513
Terpenes	140	50	70
NO$_2$	150	50	75
SO$_2$	300	30	90
(CH$_3$)$_2$S	30	90	27

it photodissociates even in violet wavelengths to produce O atoms and thus O$_3$. Hence, there are also two major sources of ozone (photodissociation of both O$_2$ and NO$_2$).

Levels of OH in the atmosphere change rapidly on a wide variety of space and timescales. Ultraviolet radiation fluxes and water vapor concentrations are largest in the tropics and in the summers in the Northern and Southern Hemispheres. Hence, the levels of OH generally have their maxima in the lower troposphere in these regions and seasons (Figure 1). Also, because much ozone is produced in and exported from industrialized areas, its concentrations generally have maxima in the Northern Hemisphere midlatitude summer (Figure 1). In the lower atmosphere, OH sources can be decreased or turned off by lowering ultraviolet radiation (e.g., nighttime, winter, increasing cloudiness, and thickening stratospheric ozone layer), lowering NO emissions, and lowering H$_2$O (e.g., in a cooling climate). Its sinks can be increased by greater emissions of reduced gases (CO, RH, and SO$_2$). But because natural or anthropogenic combustion of biomass or fossil fuel is a primary source of gases driving the oxidation processes, and because CO and NO are both products of combustion with (usually) opposite effects on OH levels, the system is not as unstable as it could otherwise be.

Here we review the fundamental chemical reactions involved and the influences of meteorology and human activity on atmospheric oxidation. Several key questions are addressed. What controls the levels of OH and other oxidizing chemicals? How has human activity altered the natural OH budget since preindustrial times? With industrialization continuing, how will the oxidizing capability of the atmosphere change over the next century? How are OH concentrations measured and are there discernable current trends? How well do theoretical models

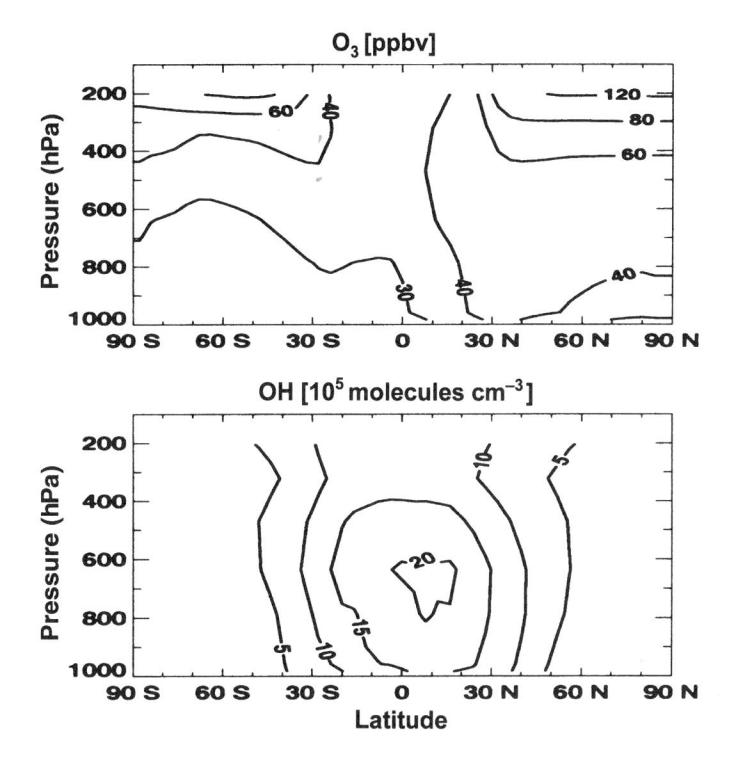

Figure 1 Calculated mole fractions of ozone (in parts per 10^9, upper graph) and concentrations of hydroxyl radicals (in 10^5 radical cm^{-3}, lower graph) as functions of latitude and pressure (hPa) from a model of the present-day atmosphere (8).

explain OH behavior? And finally, what are the major unanswered questions or controversies?

2. FUNDAMENTAL REACTIONS

The oxidation processes in the troposphere (the layer between the surface and 16 km above in the tropics and 8 km above at high latitudes) are distinctly different from those in the stratosphere (which lies above it). The fundamental reactions in these two regions are therefore discussed separately below.

2.1. Troposphere

The ability of the troposphere to chemically remove trace gases depends on complex chemistry driven by the relatively small amount of solar ultraviolet radiation that penetrates through the stratospheric ozone layer (3, 5, 6, 9–11). This chemistry is also driven by emissions of nitrogen oxides, carbon monoxide, and hydrocarbons and leads to the production of ozone, which is one of the indicators of the oxidizing capacity of the atmosphere. The most important indicator, however, is the hydroxyl free radical (OH). More specifically, it is widely recognized that a key measure of the capacity of the atmosphere to oxidize trace gases injected into it is the local concentration of hydroxyl radicals. Figure 2 reviews, with much simplification, the chemical reactions involved in production and removal of O_3 and OH (12). This chemistry is also very significant because it involves compounds that help govern climate, local air pollution, and acid rain.

In Figure 2, H_2O, CH_4, and ozone (O_3) are all important greenhouse gases. Hydrocarbons (RH), carbon monoxide (CO), and nitrogen oxides (NO, NO_2) are all important air pollutants emitted mainly as a result of human activity (including fossil-fuel combustion, biomass burning, and land use). Reactive free radicals or atoms are in two forms: the very reactive species, such as $O(^1D)$ and OH, and the less reactive ones, such as HO_2, $O(^3P)$, NO, and NO_2.

Figure 2 shows that when OH reacts with a hydrocarbon (RH), the RH is oxidized in several steps mostly to carbon monoxide (CO). These steps consume

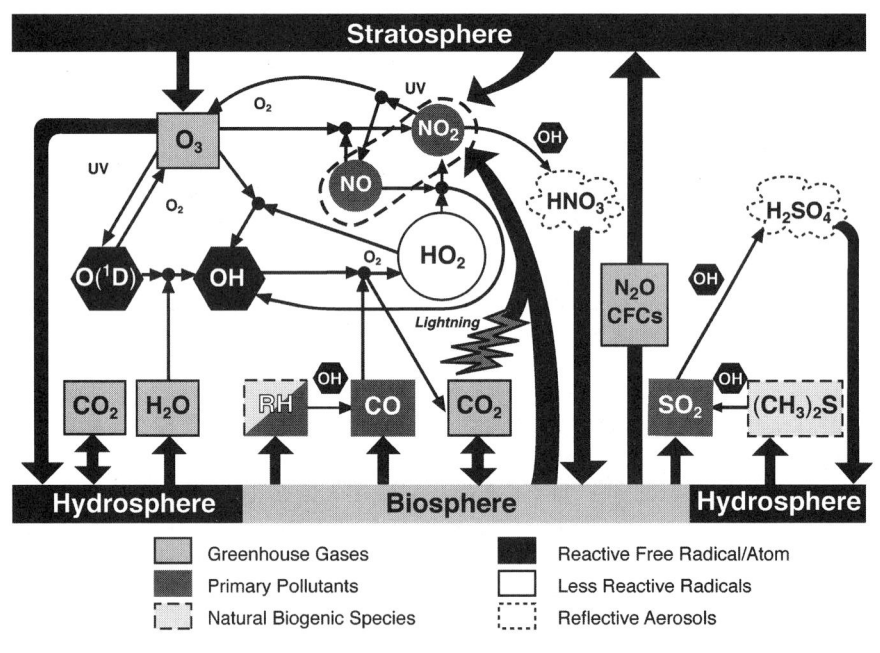

Figure 2 Summary of the main oxidation processes in the troposphere in NO_x-rich air (12). In NO_x-poor air (e.g., remote marine air), recycling of HO_2 to OH is achieved by reactions of O_3 with HO_2 to form OH and $2O_2$ or by conversion of $2HO_2$ to H_2O_2 followed by photodissociation of H_2O_2. Note also that nonmethane hydrocarbons (RH) also react with OH to form acids, aldehydes (e.g., CH_2O) and ketones in addition to CO.

OH and can also produce HO_2. The OH oxidizes CO to CO_2, and it also oxidizes the gases NO_2 and SO_2 (sulfur dioxide) to nitric (HNO_3) and sulfuric (H_2SO_4) acids, respectively. The primary OH production occurs when water vapor reacts with the very reactive singlet oxygen atom, $O(^1D)$, that comes from photodissociation of ozone by solar ultraviolet radiation at wavelengths less than 310 nm. Within a second of its formation, on average, OH oxidizes other compounds either by donating oxygen or removing hydrogen leaving an H atom or organic free radical (R). R and H then attach rapidly to molecular oxygen (O_2) to form hydroperoxy radicals (HO_2) or organoperoxy radicals (RO_2), which are relatively unreactive. If there is no way to rapidly recycle HO_2 back to OH, then levels of OH are kept low. Adding the nitrogen oxides (NO and NO_2), which have many human-related sources, significantly changes the outcome. Specifically, nitric oxide reacts with the HO_2 to form nitrogen dioxide (NO_2) and reform OH. Ultraviolet radiation then decomposes NO_2 at wavelengths less than 430 nm to form O_3 and reform NO. Hence, the nitrogen oxides are catalysts and are not consumed in this reaction. The production rate of OH by this secondary path involving NO is 5.3 times faster than the above primary path involving $O(^1D)$, according to a study of relatively polluted air in Germany by Ehhalt (3). The reaction of NO with HO_2 does not act as a sink for odd hydrogen (the sum of the H, OH, and HO_2 concentrations). Instead it determines the ratio of OH to HO_2. In the above Ehhalt study (3), the [HO_2] to [OH] ratio was 44 to 1. This is due to, and symptomatic of, the much greater reactivity of OH compared to HO_2. To review, the principal catalyzed reactions creating OH and O_3 in the troposphere are

(a)
$$O_3 + \text{ultraviolet} \rightarrow O_2 + O(^1D)$$
$$O(^1D) + H_2O \rightarrow 2OH$$

Net effect: $O_3 + H_2O \rightarrow O_2 + 2OH$,

and

(b)
$$OH + CO \rightarrow H + CO_2$$
$$H + O_2 \rightarrow HO_2$$
$$HO_2 + NO \rightarrow OH + NO_2$$
$$NO_2 + \text{ultraviolet} \rightarrow NO + O$$
$$O + O_2 \rightarrow O_3$$

Net effect: $CO + 2O_2 \rightarrow CO_2 + O_3$,

and

(c)
$$OH + RH \to R + H_2O$$
$$R + O_2 \to RO_2$$
$$RO_2 + NO \to RO + NO_2$$
$$NO_2 + \text{ultraviolet} \to NO + O$$
$$O + O_2 \to O_3$$

Net effect: $OH + RH + 2O_2 \to RO + H_2O + O_3$.

In computer models, the global production of tropospheric O_3 by the above pathway beginning with CO is typically about twice that beginning with RH. For most environments, it is these three net processes (a, b, and c) that produce the majority of the OH and O_3 in the troposphere. If the concentration of NO_2 gets too high, however, its reaction with OH to form HNO_3 ultimately limits the OH concentration.

Hough & Derwent (13) estimate the global production rate of tropospheric ozone by the above reactions to be 2440 Tg/year in preindustrial times. A comparison of several tropospheric ozone models for present-day conditions showed a chemical production rate range for ozone of 3425 to 4550 Tg/year (14) with the increase over preindustrial times caused by human-made NO_x, hydrocarbons, and CO. Because the troposphere contains about 350 Tg of ozone (3), the chemical replenishment time for ozone (defined as the tropospheric content divided by the tropospheric chemical production rate) is 28–37 days. This is much longer than the replenishment time for OH, which is about 1 second and illustrates the much greater reactivity of OH relative to O_3.

The oxidative power of the atmosphere is also affected by meteorology. Convective storms can carry short-lived trace chemicals from the planetary boundary layer (the first few hundred to few thousand meters above the surface) to the middle and upper troposphere in only a few to several hours. This can influence the chemistry of these upper layers in significant ways by delivering, for example, reactive hydrocarbons (RH) to high altitudes. Conversely, the occurrence of very stable conditions in the boundary layer can effectively trap chemicals near the surface for many days leading to polluted air. Larger scale circulations serve to carry gases around latitude circles on timescales of a few weeks, between the hemispheres on timescales of a year, and between the troposphere and stratosphere on timescales of a few years.

Moist convection also directly affects the oxidizing reactions in the atmosphere, besides being a vigorous vertical transport mechanism. First, lightning and thunderbolts serve to thermally convert atmospheric N_2 and O_2 to 2NO and leads to a very important natural source of NO_x. Second, the formation of cloud droplets is aided by (and consumes) aerosols (as cloud condensation nuclei), and the cloud droplets then serve as sinks for soluble species like H_2O_2, HNO_3, NO_x, SO_2, and H_2SO_4. For some oxidation reactions, for example oxidation of SO_2 to H_2SO_4, this dissolution leads to an additional nongaseous pathway for oxidation generally considered comparable to the gas-phase processes for SO_2. Third, the formation of convective clouds and particularly the extensive anvils leads to reflection of solar ultraviolet radiation enhancing the photooxidative processes above the clouds and inhibiting them below (15).

The relative timescales associated with meteorology and chemistry are very important. A convenient measure of the stability of a trace chemical is its local chemical lifetime, which is defined as its local concentration (e.g., in mole liter^{-1}) divided by its local removal rate (e.g., in mol/liter^{-1}/s^{-1}). Concentrations of chemicals whose lifetimes (due to chemical destruction or deposition) are comparable to or longer than the above transport times will be affected profoundly by transport. As a simple example, in a steady (constant concentration) state with a horizontal wind u, the concentration $[i]$ of chemical i whose lifetime is t_i decreases downwind of a source region (located at horizontal position $x = 0$) according to:

$$[i](x) = [i](0) \exp[-x/(ut_i)].$$

Note that the concentration of i decreases by a factor of e over the distance scale ut_i. Note also that, if the transport time x/u is much less than t_i, the concentration remains essentially constant, and the species can be considered as almost inert. For oxidation by OH of NO_2 and SO_2 to form the acids HNO_3 and H_2SO_4, the time t_i is about 3 days (2.6×10^5 s), so the e-folding distance ut_i is only about 800 km for a typical u of 3 ms^{-1}. Alternatively for the oxidation of CO by OH to form CO_2, t_i is about 3 months (7.9×10^6 s), so $ut_i = 24{,}000$ km for the same u. In a simple way, this illustrates why NO_2 and SO_2 are local or regional pollutants, whereas CO is a hemispheric pollutant.

From the above equation, if the chemical lifetime t_i is much less than the transport time x/u, then we could ignore transport and simply consider chemical sources and sinks to determine concentrations. However, for the chemicals controlling oxidation reactions, care must be taken in defining t_i. Specifically, sometimes members of a chemical family are converted from one to another on very short timescales relative to transport, whereas the total population of the family is produced and removed on longer timescales. For example, in the family composed of NO and NO_2 (called the NO_x family) the reactions

$$NO + O_3 \rightarrow NO_2 + O_2,$$

$$NO_2 + \text{ultraviolet} \rightarrow NO + O, \text{ and}$$

$$O + O_2 + M \rightarrow O_3 + M$$

rapidly interconvert NO and NO_2 on timescales much less than typical transport times and do so without affecting the total $[NO_x] = [NO] + [NO_2]$. However, the removal of NO_x by the reaction

$$NO_2 + OH + M \rightarrow HNO_3 + M$$

is much slower (e.g., about 3 days). Hence, we can use the chemical steady-state approximation (which equates chemical production to chemical loss only) to define the ratio of NO to NO_2. We must however take full account of transport in calculating $[NO_x]$. Similar arguments hold for the "odd oxygen" ($[O_x] = [O] + [O_3]$) and "odd hydrogen" ($[HO_x] = [H] + [OH] + [HO_2]$) families.

2.2. Stratosphere

Stratospheric ozone is maintained by a very different set of chemical reactions than the troposphere. Figure 3 shows that the driving chemicals, such as water vapor, chlorofluorocarbons, and nitrous oxide, are transported up from the troposphere to the stratosphere where they produce chlorine-, nitrogen-, and hydrogen-carrying free radicals that destroy ozone. Interestingly, the nitrogen oxide free radicals, which destroy a significant fraction of the ozone in the stratosphere, are the same

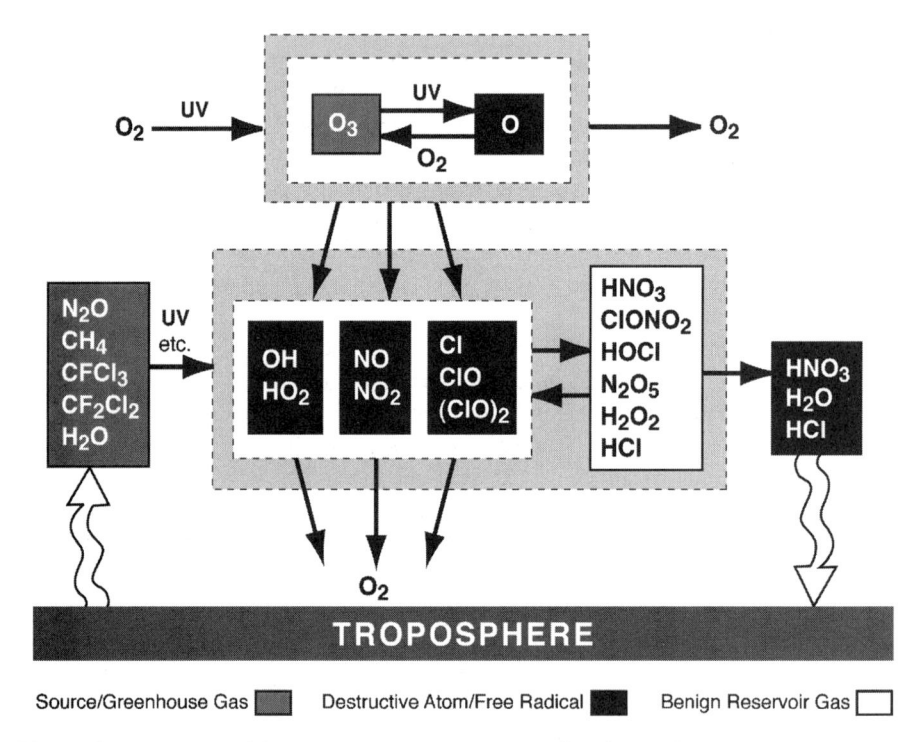

Figure 3 Summary of the major chemical processes forming and removing ozone in the stratosphere (12). Ultraviolet (UV) photodissociaton of largely natural (N_2O, CH_4, and H_2O) and exclusively human-made ($CFCl_3$ and CF_2Cl_2) source gases leads to reactive HO_x, NO_x, and ClO_x free radicals that catalytically destroy ozone. The catalysts reversibly form reservoir compounds (e.g., HNO_3), some of which live long enough to be transported down to the troposphere to complete the chemical cycles.

free radicals that produce ozone in the troposphere through the chemistry outlined earlier (Figure 2). When the ratio of nitrogen oxide free radicals to ozone is low, as it is in the stratosphere, the net effect of NO_x is for ozone to be destroyed overall. In contrast, if this ratio is high, as it is in much of the troposphere, then the net effect is for ozone to be produced overall (16).

Due to its high ozone and ultraviolet (UV) levels, the stratosphere is chemically very active. But the densities and usually temperatures are much lower in the stratosphere than in the lower troposphere so that only a small fraction of the destruction of the gases listed in Table 2 occurs in the stratosphere. The stratosphere contains about 90% of the world's ozone and exports about 400–846 Tg/year of ozone to the troposphere to augment the local chemical production of ozone discussed in Section 2.1 (14).

The precursor gases for the destructive free radicals in the stratosphere are also greenhouse gases, as is stratospheric ozone itself. Therefore, although increases in the concentrations of the source gases for ozone-depleting chemicals will increase radiative forcing of warming, these increases will, at the same time, lead to decreases in stratospheric ozone, which lowers the radiative forcing. As in the troposphere, there are important feedbacks between chemical processes and climate through the various greenhouse and ozone-depleting gases. It is not just human-made chemicals that can change stratospheric ozone. Changes in natural emissions of N_2O and CH_4 and changes in climate that alter H_2O flows into the stratosphere undoubtedly led to changes in the thickness of the ozone layer over geologic time even after O_2 levels reached near-present-day levels.

Because $O(^1D)$ can only be produced from O_3 at wavelengths less than 310 nm, and the current ozone layer effectively absorbs all incoming UV radiation at less than 290 nm, there is only a very narrow window of 290–310 nm radiation that is driving the major oxidation processes in the troposphere. Decreasing stratospheric ozone, as has occurred in recent decades, can therefore increase tropospheric OH by increasing the flux of radiation less than 310 nm reaching the troposphere to produce $O(^1D)$ (17). By the same arguments, if the stratospheric ozone layer were very much thicker in the past, it would have removed a great deal of the oxidizing capacity of the Earth's troposphere potentially leading to much higher levels of gases like CO and CH_4. Hence, there is also a strong link between the thickness of the stratospheric ozone layer and concentrations of OH in the troposphere.

3. HUMAN INFLUENCES

How stable is the oxidizing power of the troposphere? How might it have changed even after oxygen reached near today's levels? What is the human influence on atmospheric composition and chemistry? What are the likely future trends? If emissions of gases that react with OH, such as CH_4, NMHC, CO, and SO_2, are increasing then, keeping everything else constant, OH levels should decrease. Conversely, increasing NO_x emissions from combustion (of biomass in the past, augmented by fossil fuel today) should increase tropospheric O_3 (and thus the primary source of

OH), as well as increase the recycling rate of HO$_2$ to OH (the secondary source of OH). Climate change will also affect OH. If the oceans are increasing in temperature, we expect increased water vapor in the lower troposphere. Because water vapor is involved in the primary source of OH, climate warming thus increases OH. This increase could be lowered or raised due to changes in cloud cover accompanying the warming and lead to more or less reflection of UV radiation back toward space. Rising temperature also increases the rate of reaction of CH$_4$ with OH thus lowering the lifetimes of both CH$_4$ and OH. Opposite conclusions apply if trace gas emissions increase or the climate cools. Finally, decreasing stratospheric ozone can also increase tropospheric OH as discussed earlier.

3.1. The Natural Atmosphere

To provide the context for a discussion of our current (human-perturbed) atmosphere, it is useful to review the evolution of oxidation processes in the natural atmosphere. Before evolution of photosynthetic bacteria, which provided the first biological source of O$_2$ over 2 billion years ago, the atmosphere was relatively chemically neutral or even reducing. Its cleansing capacity would have depended significantly on the quantities of reduced gases produced from volcanic sources (e.g., sources in which primordial Fe, S, C, and organic compounds were thermally oxidized by H$_2$O and CO$_2$ producing H$_2$, CO, and CH$_4$) (18, 19). Small amounts of O$_2$ can be produced from H$_2$O photodissociation (20), and small quantities of NO can be formed by shock heating by lightning and large asteroidal collisions (21–23) in these prebiotic atmospheres. However, it is reasonable to conclude that the evolution of the powerful oxidizing processes involving O$_3$ and OH in the present atmosphere had to await the evolution of photosynthetic O$_2$. Before that, atmospheric chemical transformations were likely driven by simple photodissociation, dissolution reactions, and episodic processes like lightning and collisions. The transformation from reducing/neutral to oxidizing atmosphere was itself a long-term competition between abiotic sources of reduced gases, anaerobic microbial processes, and finally the aerobic biological processes that came to dominate the biosphere.

Even under the approximately constant levels of atmospheric O$_2$ in the past few hundred million years, we expect that OH and O$_3$ changed. For example, the glacial-interglacial cycles should have significantly changed atmospheric H$_2$O (inferred to be low in ice ages) and CH$_4$ (observed to be low in ice ages). But these particular changes would have partially offsetting effects on OH (by lowering both OH production from H$_2$O and OH removal by CH$_4$ in ice ages). Unfortunately, the lack of direct information about the abundances of the key short-lived gases CO, NO$_x$, nonmethane hydrocarbons (NMHC), and stratospheric ozone in paleoenvironments makes it difficult to be quantitative about past OH changes (24). In this respect, one observational record over the past millenium that is useful is the analysis of hydrogen peroxide (H$_2$O$_2$) in Greenland permafrost, which indicates approximately constant H$_2$O$_2$ from 1300 to 1700 followed by a 50% increase through to 1989 (most of the increase occurs in the last 20 years and is not seen in Antarctic permafrost) (25, 26). Increases in H$_2$O$_2$ during industrialization could signal a decrease in OH due to net conversion of HO_2 to H_2O_2 rather than recycling of HO_2 back to OH. Staffelbach et al. (27) have used CH_2O measurements in Greenland ice cores to suggest that preindustrial OH levels were 30% higher than present (CH_2O is a byproduct of hydrocarbon oxidation by OH). Model studies, which assume low preindustrial emissions of CO, NO_x, and NMHC compared to the present, imply OH levels in the years 1200–1800 were about 10%–30% higher than present (24). Ozone levels in the 1880s can be inferred from iodometric measurements (28, 29) and indicate mole fractions as low as $(7-12) \times 10^{-9}$, which are lower by a factor of three or more from those observed today. Such low levels of ozone are difficult to reconcile with CO measurements in ice cores (30) indicating CO mole fractions of about 60×10^{-9} (Antarctica) and 90×10^{-9} (Greenland), which are not much less than those observed today. As discussed in Section 2, oxidation of each CO molecule ought to produce one ozone molecule, so that presuming similar OH levels in the 1880s to those today implies similar ozone production rates from CO both then and now.

3.2. Industrial Revolution

The industrial revolution in the past 150 years, together with increased biomass burning associated with human land use, has led to significant increases since preindustrial times in the global emissions of NO_x, CO, NMHC, and methane (8, 31). Also, the observed temperature increase of $0.6 \pm 0.2°C$ in this time period (32) should have led to increases in tropospheric H_2O and possibly changes in global cloud cover (of unknown sign). Anthropogenic aerosols, both scattering and absorbing, have also increased due to human activity (33). These aerosol increases should decrease UV fluxes below the cloud tops due to both their direct optical effects (absorbing or reflecting sunlight) and their indirect effects as cloud condensation nuclei, which should increase the reflectivity and lifetime of water clouds. Finally, depletion of stratospheric ozone, which has occurred due to human-made halocarbons, will increase tropospheric UV levels (17).

Each of these changes to the natural (preindustrial) state should have affected O_3 and OH concentrations, sometimes offsetting and sometimes augmenting each other as discussed earlier. Table 3 summarizes expected changes in OH and O_3 relative to preindustrial times. Where quantitative estimates are not available, the signs only of expected changes are indicated. For OH, note in particular that the positive effects of NO_x increases have been more than offset by the negative effects of CO, NMHC, and CH_4 increases so the net change in OH is a modest 10% decrease (8, 34). Because combustion is a common and (except for CH_4) a dominant source for all these gases affecting OH, the offsetting increases of NO_x, CO, and hydrocarbons mean that OH levels are not very sensitive overall to past increases in combustion. However, if future air pollution controls lower NO_x emissions more than CO and hydrocarbon emissions, then OH decreases should result.

In contrast to OH, the effects of NO_x, CO, and hydrocarbon emission increases are additive for O_3 and, in sum, are calculated to have caused about a 63% increase in O_3 (8). The actual increase may be even larger because observations (albeit

TABLE 3 Calculated or hypothesized effects of observed or expected human-driven changes in trace gas emissions, concentrations, or meteorological variables between preindustrial and present times on the oxidizing power of the atmosphere (expressed where available as percentage changes (δ) in [OH] or [O_3] from preindustrial to present)

	Present ÷ preindustrial	δ [OH] ÷ [OH]	δ [O_3] ÷ [O_3]
NO_x[a]	4.7	+36%	+30%
CO[a]	3.2	−32%[b]	+10%[b]
NMHC[a]	1.6	—	—
CH_4[a]	2.1	−17%	+13%
Combined[a]	—	−10%[c]	+63%[c]
H_2O(T)	>1	>0	>0
Clouds[d]	>1, <1	<0, >0	<0, >0
S-cat. Aero[e]	>1	<0	<0
Abs. Aero[f]	>1	<0	<0
Strat. O_3[g]	<1	>2%	>0

[a]Individual effect of each specific chemical computed in sensitivity runs with preindustrial conditions except for the specific chemical, which is at present levels (8).
[b]CO and NMHC effects combined.
[c]CO, NMHC, CH_4, and NO_x effects combined. Total effect not equal to sum of individual effects due to interactions.
[d]Cloud cover changes unknown. Effects shown for either an increase or a decrease.
[e]Specifically scattering aerosols with high single scattering albedos (e.g., sulfates) that reflect UV radiation back to space.
[f]Specifically absorbing aerosols with low single scattering albedos (e.g., black carbon) that absorb UV radiation.
[g]Specifically decreases in stratospheric ozone allowing more UV to drive formation of OH (17, 65).

not very accurate) of ozone during the 1800s (29) suggest even lower values than computed by Wang & Jacob (8).

3.3. Forecasts

Because of the importance of oxidation processes in climate, the Intergovernmental Panel on Climate Change (IPCC) investigated the effects on O_3 and OH of 11 IPCC scenarios for future anthropogenic emissions of the relevant O_3 and OH precursors (31). In all of the scenarios, except one, OH was projected to decrease between 2000 and 2100 by 3% to 18%, and O_3 was projected to increase by 2.6% to 46% (Table 4). As expected, the smallest decrease in OH and smallest increase in O_3 were seen in the scenario in which emissions of NO_x, CO, NMHCs, and CH_4 were projected to change by only +3.4%, −8.3%, +2.0%, and +9.2%, respectively, between 2000 and 2100. Also as expected, the greatest OH decreases were seen in two scenarios in which small increases or even decreases in NO_x emissions (decreasing the OH source) were accompanied by relatively very large increases

TABLE 4 Percentages by which either emissions of NO_x, CO, NMHC (plus oxidized NMHC), and CH_4, or concentrations of tropospheric OH, or column amounts of tropospheric O_3 are projected to change between 2000 and 2100 for various IPCC scenarios (31)

Scenario	NO_x emission	CO emission	NMHC emission	CH_4 emission	OH concentration	O_3[a] column
A1B	+26%	+90%	+37%	−11%	−10%	+7.7%
A1T	−12%	+137%	−9.2%	−15%	−18%	+5.5%
A1FI	+243%	+193%	+198%	+128%	−14%	+47%
A2	+241%	+165%	+143%	+175%	−12%	+46%
B1	−42%	−59%	−38%	−27%	+5%	−8.6%
B2	+91%	+128%	+21%	+85%	−16%	+23%
A1p	+27%	+138%	+15%	−13%	−18%	+11%
A2p	+238%	+140%	+133%	+163%	−12%	+46%
B1p	+3.4%	−8.3%	+2.0%	+9.2%	−3%	+2.6%
B2p	+86%	+100%	+13%	+46%	−11%	+19%
IS92a	+124%	+64%	+125%	+95%	−11%	+29%

[a]Ozone changes decreased by 25% to account for modeling errors as recommended by the IPCC.

in CO emissions (increasing the OH sink). The largest O_3 increases were seen in two scenarios in which emissions of all four ozone precursors increased very substantially. Finally, the one anomalous scenario (in which OH increased by 5%, and O_3 decreased by 8.6%) involved significant decreases in emissions of all four precursors, which is a very improbable sequence of events.

It is very clear from the results in Table 4 that forecasts of the future oxidation capacity of the atmosphere depend critically on the assumed emissions. While the IPCC did not assign probabilities to its emission scenarios, it is clear that a few of these scenarios are highly improbable estimates for oxidant precursor emissions. This is because these emissions are dependent on fuel and agricultural choices and technological developments, which are tightly linked to projections about economic development in developed and developing countries. Integrated assessment models, which couple global economic and technological development models with natural earth system models, provide an alternative approach to the IPCC scenario approach with the added advantage that objective estimates of individual model uncertainties can be combined with Monte Carlo approaches to provide more objective ways of defining means and errors in forecasts. To illustrate this approach, one such model (35) integrates a computable general equilibrium economics model with a coupled chemistry and climate model and an ecosystem model. The economics model automatically accounts for the strong correlations between emissions of air pollutants (gases and aerosols) and greenhouse gases because of their common production processes (e.g., combustion of coal, oil, gasoline, gas, and biomass). Results from this model for a (high probability) reference emissions forecast and (for lower probability) high and low emissions

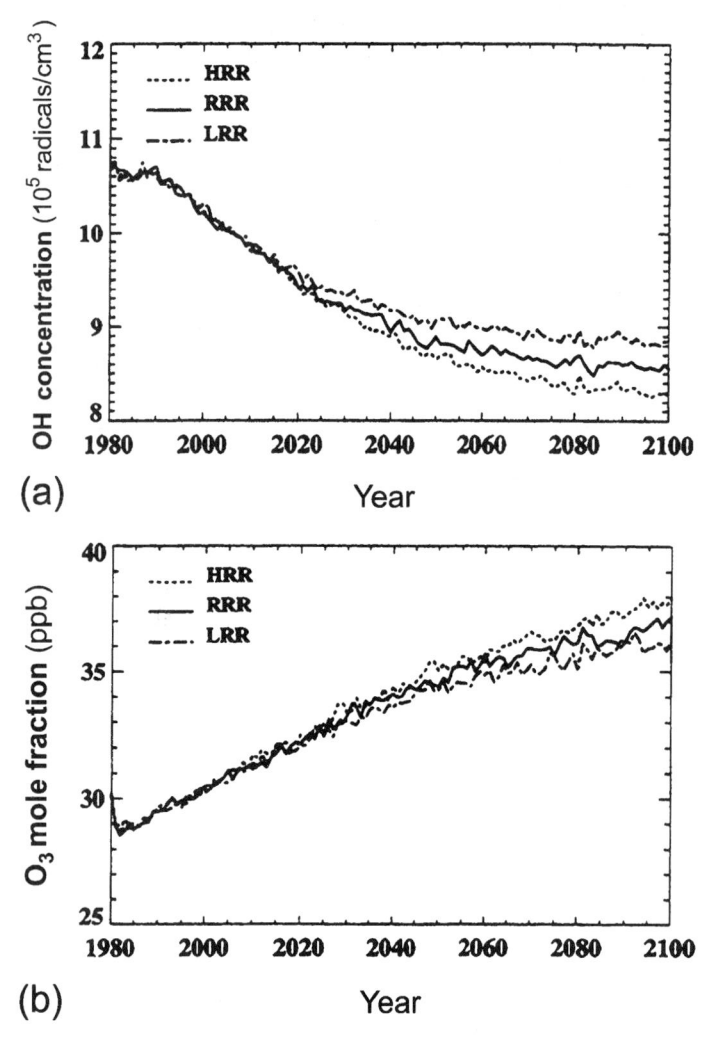

Figure 4 (a) Present and future tropospheric average concentrations of OH (in 10^5 radical cm^{-3}) and (b) mole fractions of ozone (in parts in 10^9) calculated for three scenarios [reference (RRR), high (HRR), and low (LRR)] of future emissions of ozone and OH precursors (as well as greenhouse gases) predicted in an economics model (35). The system model driven by these emissions includes simultaneous calculations of atmospheric chemistry and climate (36).

forecasts are shown in Figure 4 (36). The emissions driving these projections are summarized in Prinn et al. (35). The reference anthropogenic CO, NO_x, and CH_4 emissions increase by about 18%, 95%, and 33% between 2000 and 2100 in these projections. It is apparent that these emissions projections from the economics model (which consistently models all of the relevant industrial and agricultural sectors producing these gases) led to projections of significant depletion of OH and enhancement of O_3 between 2000 and 2100 with magnitudes comparable to the larger of the changes predicted from the IPCC scenarios (Table 4).

4. MEASURING THE HYDROXYL RADICAL

Do observations suggest that the cleansing capacity of the atmosphere is changing? Given its importance as the primary oxidizing chemical in the atmosphere, a great deal of effort has been placed on measuring OH concentrations and trends. Two approaches, direct and indirect, have been taken to address this measurement need.

4.1. Direct Measurement

Direct and accurate measurements of local OH concentrations have been one of the major challenges in atmospheric chemistry over the past 20 years. This goal was first achieved in the stratosphere (37), but the troposphere has proven more difficult. Despite the difficulties, early long-baseline absorption methods for OH were adequate to test some of the basic theory outlined in Section 2 (38). Successful direct methods at the present time include differential optical absorption near-UV spectroscopy with long baselines (39–41), laser-induced fluorescence after expansion of air samples (42–44), and a variety of chemical conversion techniques (45–47).

Utilization of the long-baseline spectroscopic techniques requires path lengths in air of 3–20 km. This can be achieved by a single pass through air [e.g., (39) uses a 10.3 km path to achieve a sensitivity of 5×10^5 radical cm^{-3}], or multiple reflections in long cells [e.g., (40) uses 144 passes through a 20 m cell to observe 6 OH absorption lines around 308 nm]. In the laser-induced fluorescence methods, either 282 or 308 nm photons are used to excite OH, which then subsequently emits at 308 to 310 nm [e.g., (48) and (44) use 308 nm laser light and achieve detection limits of $(1–3) \times 10^5$ radical cm^{-3}].

Chemical conversion techniques generally use a flow reactor in which ambient OH reacts with isotopically labeled SO_2 or CO to yield observable products [e.g., (45) uses ^{14}CO with radioactive $^{14}CO_2$ detection, and (49) uses $^{34}SO_2$ with $H_2^{34}SO_4$ detection by ion-assisted mass spectrometry].

Critical tests of current theoretical models of fast photochemistry are achieved using these varied direct OH measurement techniques. These tests involve simultaneously measuring NO, NO_2, CO, H_2O, O_3, hydrocarbons, and other relevant trace species, UV fluxes, the frequency of photodissociation of O_3 to produce $O(^1D)$, and the concentrations of OH (and sometimes HO_2). Then a model incorporating the best estimates of the relevant kinetic rate constants and absorption coefficients is used, along with the trace gas and photodissociation rate measurements, to predict OH concentrations for comparison with observations. The Mauna Loa Observatory Photochemistry Experiment (MLOPEX) and Photochemistry of Plant-Emitted Compounds and OH Radicals in North Eastern Germany Experiment (POPCORN) illustrate the nature of these tests and sample results are shown in Figures 5 and 6.

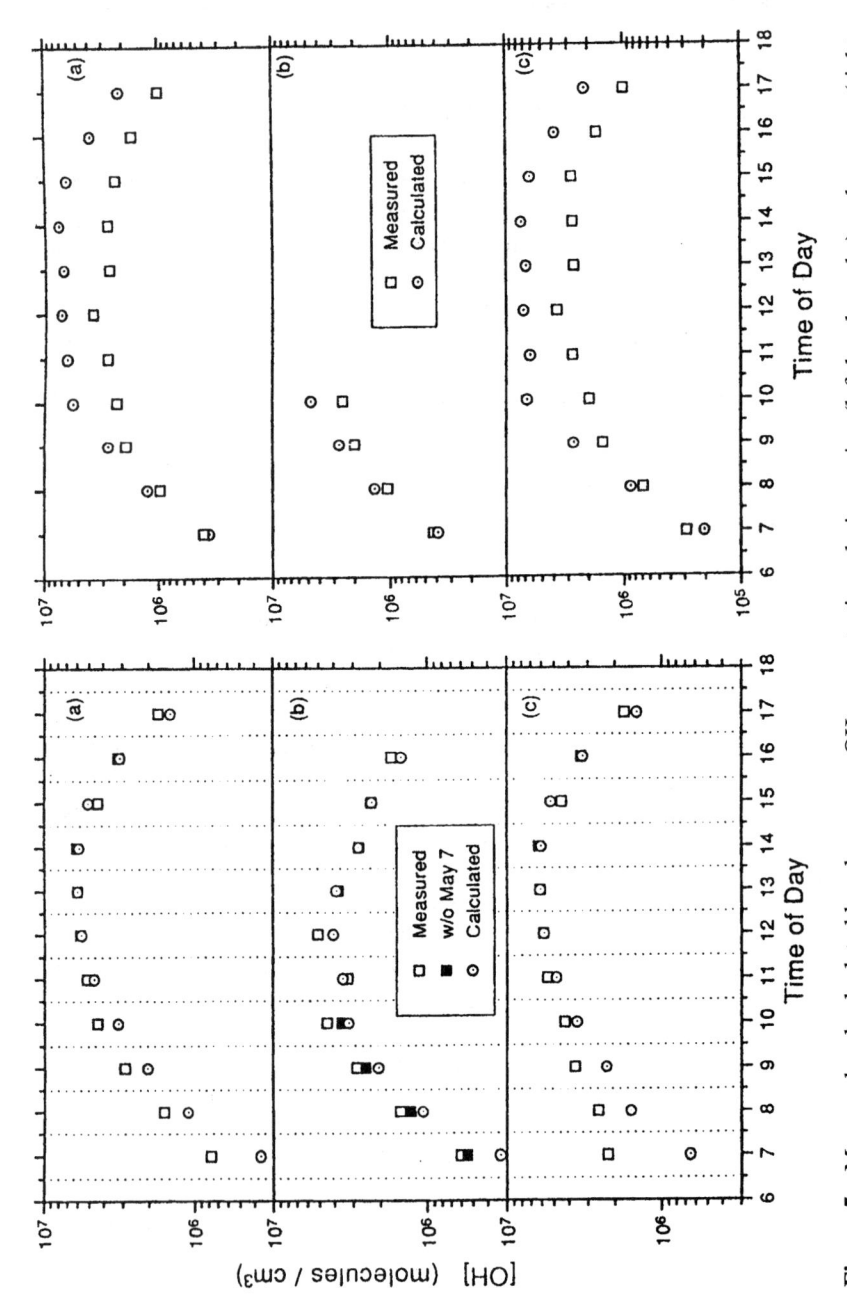

Figure 5 Measured and calculated hourly average OH concentrations during spring (left-hand graphs) and summer (right-hand graphs) of 1992 in MLOPEX: (*a*) all times, (*b*) free tropospheric air only, and (*c*) boundary layer air only (50). The measurements on May 7 were excluded because they were anomalous.

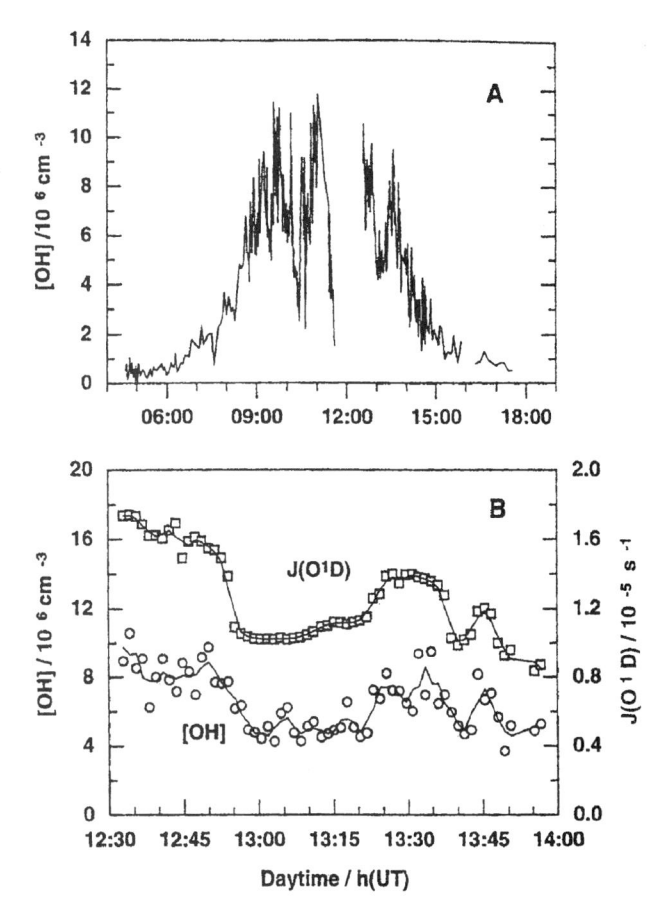

Figure 6 (A) Variation of OH concentrations during the daytime in POPCORN (August 16, 1994). (B) Version of (A) with higher time resolution showing fast response of OH concentrations to J(O^{1}D) variations (solid lines are 3-point running averages) (51).

Both free tropospheric air (associated with downslope winds at this high mountain station) and boundary layer air (upslope winds) were sampled during the 1992 MLOPEX experiment. Figure 5 makes it evident that agreement between observed (using the $^{34}SO_2$ method) and calculated OH concentrations was always good in the free troposphere, but in the summer, the calculated boundary layer OH was about twice that observed (50). This suggests a missing OH sink in their model because the measurement accuracy was argued to be much better than a factor of two. They suggest the missing sink might involve unmeasured hydrocarbons from vegetation or undetected oxidation products of anthropogenic compounds.

Measurements of OH using laser-induced fluorescence were compared to calculations in a regional air chemistry model during the 1994 POPCORN experiment in rural Germany. The measured OH concentrations as a function of time are shown in Figure 6. Very evident is the expected strong diurnal variation in OH due to the daily cycle in UV radiation. In Figure 6B, there is also a demonstration of the expected strong correlation between the measured frequency of photoproduction of O (^{1}D) from O_3 [J(O^1D)] and the measured OH (see Section 2.1). The large high frequency variations in OH evident in Figure 6A are real and due to strongly correlated variations in solar UV fluxes caused by transient cloud cover. Observed and calculated OH agreed quite well during POPCORN, but as in MLOPEX, there was also a tendency for the model to overpredict OH (3, 51). The discrepancy may be attributable in part to the combined effects in the modeling of rate constant errors and measurement errors in the observed hydrocarbons CO, NO, NO_2, O_3, and H_2O used in the model. Poppe et al. (52) estimate this modeling error to be ±30%.

The great importance of the in situ direct measurement is that in conjunction with simultaneous in situ observations of the other components of the fast photooxidative cycles, they provide a fundamental test of the photochemical theory. Considering the difficulties in both the measurements and the models, the agreements between observation and theory are encouraging at least for the relatively clean and clear air environments investigated in the above experiments. However, the very short lifetime and enormous temporal and spatial variability of OH, which was emphasized earlier, make it practically impossible to use these direct techniques to determine regional to global scale OH concentrations and trends. These large-scale averages are essential to understanding the regional to global chemical cycles of all of the long-lived (>few weeks) trace gases in the atmosphere that react with OH as their primary sink. An indirect integrating method is needed for this purpose.

4.2. Indirect Measurement

In principle, the large-scale concentrations and long-term trends in OH can be measured indirectly using global measurements of trace gases whose emissions are well known and whose primary sink is OH. To date, the best trace gas for this purpose is the industrial chemical 1,1,1-trichloroethane (methylchloroform, CH_3CCl_3). First, there are accurate long-term measurements of CH_3CCl_3 beginning in 1978 in the Atmospheric Lifetime Experiment/Global Atmospheric Gases Experiment/Advanced Global Atmospheric Gases Experiment (ALE/GAGE/AGAGE) network (2, 7, 53) and beginning in 1992 in the National Oceanic and Atmospheric Administration/Climate Monitoring and Detection Laboratory (NOAA/CMDL) network (54). Second, methyl chloroform has fairly simple end uses as a solvent, and voluntary chemical industry reports since 1970, along with the national reporting procedures under the Montreal Protocol in more recent years, have produced fairly accurate emissions estimates for this chemical (55).

Another useful OH indicator is ^{14}CO, which is produced primarily by cosmic rays (56–58). The accuracy of the ^{14}CO emission estimates, and especially the frequency and spatial coverage of its measurements, do not match those for CH_3CCl_3, but its lifetime (2 months) is much shorter than for CH_3CCl_3 (4.9 years), so it provides estimates of average concentrations of OH that are more regional than CH_3CCl_3. Also useful is the industrial chemical chlorodifluoromethane (HCFC-22, $CHClF_2$), which yields OH concentrations similar to those derived from CH_3CCl_3 but with less accuracy due to greater uncertainties in emissions and less extensive measurements (59). Although the industrial gases CH_2FCF_3 (HFC-134a), CH_3CCl_2F (HCFC-141b) and CH_3CClF_2 (HCFC-142b) are potentially useful OH estimators, the accuracy of their emission estimates needs to be improved (60, 61).

Inverse methods infer information about causes from their observed effects (in contrast to forward methods that compute effects given their causes). For estimating OH, we define the changes in concentration of a trace gas (which reacts with OH) as the effect and the concentrations of OH as the cause. Mathematically determining OH concentrations from trace gas observations involves solution of an inverse problem in which the observables are expressed as Lagrangian line integrals (along back trajectories) and the unknown OH concentrations (expressed as functions of space and time) are contained in the integrands. The inverse problem of interest consists of determining an optimal estimate (in the Bayesian sense) of the unknown OH concentrations from imperfect concentration measurements of say CH_3CCl_3 over space and time. Given the discrete time series nature of CH_3CCl_3 measurements, it is convenient (but not essential) to solve for OH using a discrete recursive optimal linear filter, such as the discrete Kalman filter (DKF). The DKF is particularly useful because it provides an objective assessment of the uncertainty in estimates of OH as each CH_3CCl_3 measurement is used and thus of the usefulness of each measurement. Application of the DKF, or any other inverse OH estimation method, requires an accurate chemical transport model, because the value of each observation in improving and lowering the errors in the OH estimates depends sensitively on both observational errors and chemical transport model errors (62). This inverse approach using the DKF was the one adopted for analysis of CH_3CCl_3 data by the ALE/GAGE/AGAGE scientists from the inception of the experiment (2, 53).

Using CH_3CCl_3, it has been established that the global weighted average OH concentration in the troposphere is currently about 10^6 radical cm^{-3} (4, 7, 54, 63–65). Formally, the weighting factor for this average is the rate constant k (which is temperature dependent) of the reaction of OH with methyl chloroform, multiplied by the CH_3CCl_3 concentration, $[CH_3CCl_3]$. This means that the average is weighted practically toward the tropical lower troposphere. A similar average OH concentration is derived from ^{14}CO (58), although the weighting in this case is not noticeably temperature dependent.

The average OH concentration appears quite well defined by this method. However, the temporal trends in OH are more difficult to discern because they require long-term measurements, very accurate calibrations, realistic model transports, and, above all, a very accurate time series of CH_3CCl_3 emissions (64). In the first attempt at trend determination, Prinn et al. (64) derived an OH trend of $1.0 \pm 0.8\%$ yr^{-1} between 1978 and 1990. Primarily owing to a subsequent recalibration of the ALE/GAGE/AGAGE CH_3CCl_3 measurements, the estimated 1978–1994 trend was lowered to $0.0 \pm 0.2\%$ yr^{-1} (4). In a later reanalysis of the same measurements (but not with the same emissions), Krol et al. (65) derived a trend of $0.46 \pm 0.6\%$.

Several possible reasons for this difference, including differences in models, data processing, emissions, and inverse methods, have been debated (66, 67). However, when the Prinn et al. (4) method is used with the same emissions as Krol et al. (65), it yields a trend of 0.3% yr^{-1} in reasonable agreement with their value (66).

Prinn et al. (7), in the latest published analysis applied to the entire 1978–2000 ALE/GAGE/AGAGE CH$_3$CCl$_3$ measurements, showed that global OH levels grew by 15 ± 22% between 1979 and 1989. The growth rate was decreasing, however, at a statistically significant rate of 0.23 ± 0.18% yr^{-2} so that OH began slowly declining after 1989 to reach levels in 2000, 10 ± 24% lower than 1979 values (see Figure 7). The weighted global average OH concentration overall was

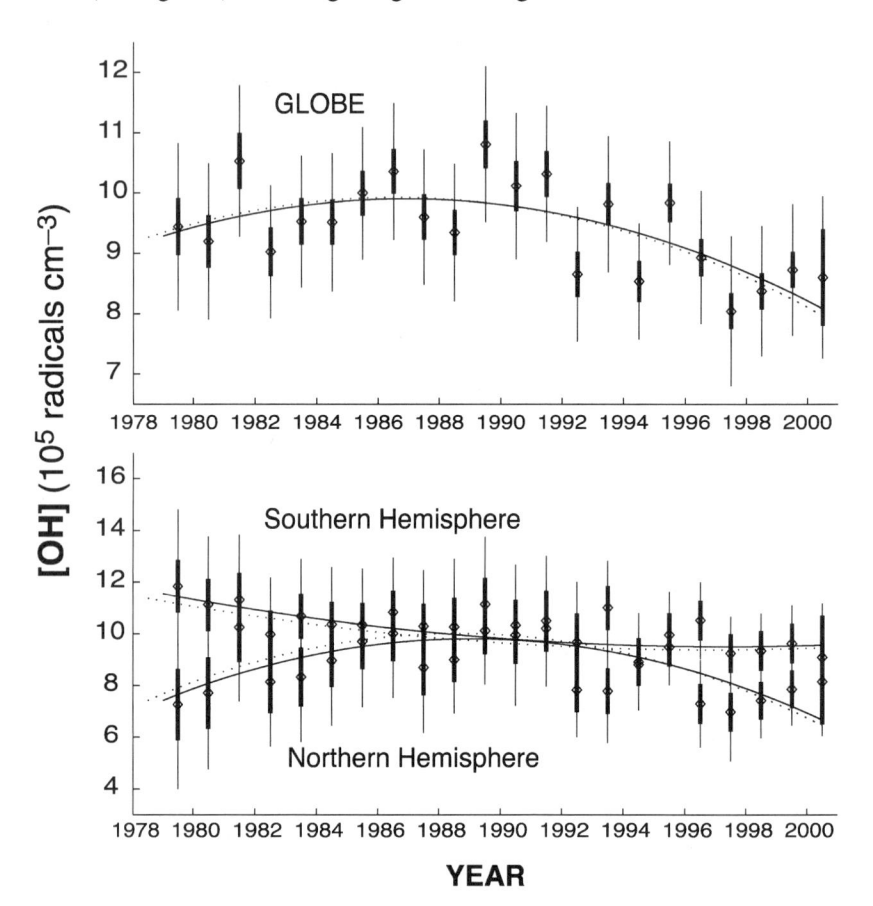

Figure 7 Global annual average (*upper graph*) and hemispheric annual average (*lower graph*) OH concentrations estimated from CH$_3$CCl$_3$ measurements (7). Uncertainties (one sigma) due to measurement errors are indicated by thick error bars and uncertainties due to both measurement, emission, and model errors are shown by thin error bars. Polynomial fits to these annual values (*solid lines*) and polynomials describing OH variations, which were estimated directly from CH$_3$CCl$_3$ measurements, (*dotted lines*) are also shown.

$[9.4 \pm 1.3] \times 10^5$ radical cm^{-3} with concentrations $14 \pm 35\%$ lower in the Northern Hemisphere than the Southern Hemisphere. In addition to the measurement errors, the Prinn et al. (7) analysis included a full Monte Carlo treatment of model errors (transport and chemistry), emission uncertainties, and absolute calibration errors with the last two being the dominant contributors to OH trend errors.

The substantial variations in OH were not expected from current theoretical models. Therefore, these results have generated much attention and scrutiny. Prinn et al. (7) recognized the importance of their assumed emissions estimates in their calculations and also estimated the emissions required to provide a zero trend in OH. These required emissions differ by many standard deviations from the best industry estimates particularly for 1996–2000 (55). They are also inconsistent with estimates of European and Australian emissions obtained from measurements of polluted air from the two continents reaching the ALE/GAGE/AGAGE stations (7). Interestingly, if the required zero-trend emissions are actually the correct ones, then the phaseout of CH$_3$CCl$_3$ consumption reported by the party nations to the Montreal Protocol must be seriously in error. The accuracy of the emissions used for OH estimations is expected to be studied intensively in the future. The good news is that the influence of these emission errors on OH determinations becomes negligible as the emissions of CH$_3$CCl$_3$ go to essentially zero (as they almost are today).

The above positive and negative OH trends, presuming they are correct, are not simply explained by the measured trends in trace gases involved in OH chemistry. There is no clear negative or positive global-scale trend in the major OH precursur gases O$_3$ and NO$_x$ between 1978 and 1999. Also, levels of the dominant OH sink CO decreased rather than increased in the Northern Hemisphere (31). Concentrations of another OH sink, CH$_4$, have at the same time risen significantly from 1978–1999. Prinn et al. (7) suggest that in tropical and subtropical countries increases of hydrocarbons and SO$_2$ that react with OH, along with a decrease of NO$_x$ emissions in developed countries, could be involved. A growth in levels of anthropogenic aerosols could also increase heterogeneous OH destruction. Such a growth in both absorbing and reflecting aerosols may also lower UV fluxes through direct and indirect reflection and absorption, thus lowering OH. The reason why the higher OH levels inferred in the Southern Hemisphere are not simulated in many current models may also be due to neglect of these aerosol effects, as well as urban-scale chemistry that can remove NO$_x$ locally.

Further study on possible causes of OH variations of the type suggested from the CH$_3$CCl$_3$ analysis is obviously necessary. On this subject, the lack of long-term global-covering measurement of O$_3$, NO$_x$, SO$_2$, hydrocarbons, and aerosols is a very serious impediment to the understanding of OH chemistry.

4.3. Comparing Models and Observations

Another important method for testing our knowledge of atmospheric oxidation processes (including OH) has involved a careful comparison between trace gas and free radical observations and the predictions from three-dimensional (3D) chemical transport models (CTMs) that incorporate the latest understanding of homogeneous and heterogeneous fast photochemstry. These 3D-CTMs simulate qualitatively many features of the observations, but there are discrepancies that point out the need for additional research. Some illustrative examples are briefly reviewed.

Berntsen et al. (68) report that their 3D-CTM runs indicate increases in upper tropospheric ozone in the 1980s, whereas observations show a leveling off or a decrease. They suggest that unmodeled stratospheric ozone changes might explain this discrepancy. To provide a test of their CH_4 emissions assumptions and OH concentrations, Houweling et al. (69) compared their 3D-CTM simulations of CH_4 and CH_3CCl_3 with observations. They conclude that further work is needed on realistic models for seasonal CH_4 emissions from wetlands and rice paddies. Spivakovsky et al. (70) extensively tested their OH calculations using CH_3CCl_3, $CHClF_2$, and other trace gas data. They concluded that this 3D-CTM gave good agreement except in the two tropical winters (possibly due to underestimated OH) and southern extratropics (possibly due to overestimated OH). The authors also emphasize the greater utility of CH_3CCl_3 observations for regional OH tests now that emissions of this gas are becoming negligible.

Computer models have also been tested using paleo data as noted in Sections 3.1 and 3.2. Wang & Jacob (8) found that they significantly overestimated ozone levels in the 1800s. They discussed the possible effects of incorrectly modeled surface deposition and troposphere-stratosphere exchange in producing this discrepancy. Mesoscale three-dimensional models that couple the dynamics of convection with cloud microphysics and fast photochemistry have also been tested against observations. Wang & Prinn (15), for example, concluded that NO_x produced from lightning can deplete O_3 in the tropical Pacific upper troposphere, which has often been observed. However, there were difficulties in simulating the observed high O_3 concentrations in the middle troposphere in these same regions. These tests of our understanding are made possible by a large number of observational experiments using surface, aircraft, balloon and satellite platforms and range from short-term campaigns to multi-decadal measurement networks. Some of the relevant experiments focused on tropospheric oxidants; these were reviewed by Lelieveld et al. (14) and Ehhalt (3). They note the advances made in direct NO_x and HO_x observations that enabled careful testing of photochemical models. Thompson et al. (71) discuss the gaps in tropospheric ozone observations and present an important new data set for the Southern Hemisphere tropics, which will provide new tests of chemical models.

5. CONCLUSIONS

Oxidation processes have been a major influence on the evolution of Earth's atmosphere. Fundamental information about these processes are provided by observations of trace gases and free radicals in the present atmosphere and of chemicals in ice cores and sediments recording the composition of past atmospheres.

Basic laboratory studies of chemical kinetics, although not reviewed here, have also played an essential role in defining mechanisms and rates. Computer models have been developed for fast photochemistry and for coupled chemical and transport processes that encapsulate current laboratory and theoretical understanding and help explain some of these atmospheric observations. However, there are important discrepancies between models and observations for OH and O_3 (both locally and globally) that still need to be resolved.

Looking to the future, there is urgent need for more observations to further our understanding. To improve and ultimately validate models, we need to measure much more extensive global three-dimensional distributions for many shorter-lived trace gas species (O_3, CO, NO_x, reactive hydrocarbons, and H_2O_2) and to obtain many more measurements of key reactive free radicals (e.g., OH and HO_2) in the present atmosphere. More attention is needed, in both modeling and observational programs, to the roles of aerosols and clouds in determining UV fluxes and rates of heterogeneous chemical reactions. Refinement of existing methods for determining long-term trends in OH (especially resolving uncertainties in CH_3CCl_3 emissions) along with development of new independent approaches (e.g., alternative trace gases to augment CH_3CCl_3 and ^{14}CO as OH estimators) are also clearly important.

We need more innovative methods for discerning the composition of past atmospheres. Such information tests current understanding and helps elucidate the process of atmospheric evolution. Finally, human and natural biospheric activities serve as the primary net emitters of both oxidant precursors and oxidant sink molecules. The past, present, and possible future trends in these emissions need to be much better quantified if we are to fully understand oxidation processes in our atmosphere.

The *Annual Review of Environment and Resources* **is online at**
http://environ.annualreviews.org

LITERATURE CITED

1. Brasseur GP, Orlando JJ, Tyndall GS. 1999. *Atmospheric Chemistry and Global Change*. Oxford, UK: Oxford Univ. Press. 654 pp.
2. Prinn R, Weiss R, Fraser P, Simmonds P, Cunnold D, et al. 2000. A history of chemically and radiatively important gases in air deduced from ALE/GAGE/AGAGE. *J. Geophys. Res.* 105:17751–92
3. Ehhalt DH. 1999. Gas phase chemistry of the troposphere. In *Global Aspects of Atmospheric Chemistry, Topics in Physical Chemistry 6*, ed. R Zellner, pp. 21–109. Germany: Springer-Verlag-Darmstädt-Steinkopff
4. Prinn R, Weiss RF, Miller BR, Huang J, Alyea FN, et al. 1995. Atmospheric trends and lifetime of CH_3CCl_3 and global OH concentrations. *Science* 269:187–92
5. Levy H. 1971. Normal atmosphere: large radical and formaldehyde concentrations predicted. *Science* 173:141–43
6. Chameides WL, Walker JCG. 1973. A photochemical theory of tropospheric ozone. *J. Geophys. Res.* 78:8751–60
7. Prinn RG, Huang J, Weiss RF, Cunnold DM, Fraser PJ, et al. 2001. Evidence for

substantial variations of atmospheric hydroxyl radicals in the past two decades. *Science* 292:1882–88
8. Wang Y, Jacob DJ. 1998. Anthropogenic forcing on tropospheric ozone and OH since pre-industrial times. *J. Geophys. Res.* 103:31123–35
9. Crutzen PJ, Zimmerman PH. 1991. The changing photochemistry of the trophosphere. *Tellus AB* 43:136–51
10. Ehhalt DH, Dorn H, Poppe D. 1991. The chemistry of the hydroxyl radical in the troposphere. *Proc. R. Soc. Edinburgh* 97:17–34
11. Logan J, Prather M, Wofsy S, McElroy M. 1981. Tropospheric chemistry: a global perspective. *J. Geophys. Res.* 86:7210–54
12. Prinn R. 1994. The interactive atmosphere: global atmospheric—biospheric chemistry. *Ambio* 23:50–61
13. Hough AM, Derwent RG. 1990. Changes in the global concentration of tropospheric ozone due to human activities. *Nature* 344:645–48
14. Lelieveld J, Thompson AM, Diab RD, Hov O, Kley D, et al. 1999. Tropospheric ozone and related processes. In *Scientific Assessment of Ozone Depletion: 1998*, ed. D Albritton, pp. 8.1–8.42. Geneva, Switz.:World Meteorol. Organ.
15. Wang C, Prinn RG. 2000. On the roles of deep convective clouds in tropospheric chemistry. *J. Geophys. Res.* 105:22269–97
16. Crutzen PJ. 1979. The role of NO and NO_2 in the chemistry of the troposphere and stratosphere. *Annu. Rev. Earth Planet. Sci.* 7:443–72
17. Madronich S, Granier C. 1992. Impact of recent total ozone changes on tropospheric ozone photodissociation, hydroxyl radicals, and methane trends. *Geophys. Res. Lett.* 19:465–67
18. Prinn R. 1982. Origin and evolution of planetary atmospheres: an introduction to the problem. *Planet. Space Sci.* 30:741–53
19. Lewis J, Prinn R. 1984. *Planets and their Atmospheres: Origin and Evolution.* New York:Academic. 470 pp.
20. Levine JS. 1985. The photochemistry of the early atmosphere. In *The Photochemistry of Atmospheres*, ed. J Levine, pp. 3–38. New York:Academic. 518 pp.
21. Chameides WL, Walker JCG. 1981. Rates of fixation by lightning of carbon and nitrogen in possible primitive atmospheres. *Orig. Life* 11:291–302
22. Prinn R, Fegley B. 1987. Bolide impacts, acid rain, and biospheric traumas at the Cretaceous-Tertiary boundary. *Earth Planet. Sci. Lett.* 83:1–15
23. Fegley B, Prinn RG, Hartman H, Watkins GH. 1986. Chemical effects of large impacts on the Earth's primitive atmosphere. *Nature* 319:305–8
24. Thompson AM. 1992. The oxidizing capacity of the Earth's atmosphere: probable past and future changes. *Science* 256:1157–65
25. Sigg A, Neftel A. 1991. Evidence for a 50% increase in H_2O_2 over the past 200 years from a Greenland ice core. *Nature* 351:557–59
26. Anklin M, Bales RC. 1997. Recent increases in H_2O_2 concentrations at Summit, Greenland. *J. Geophys. Res.* 102:19099–104
27. Staffelbach TA, Neftel A, Stauffer B, Jacob DJ. 1991. Formaldehyde in polar ice cores: a possibility to characterize the atmospheric sink of methane in the past? *Nature* 349:603–5
28. Volz A, Kley D. 1988. Evaluation of the Montsouris Series of ozone measurements made in the nineteenth century. *Nature* 332:240–42
29. Marenco A, Gouget H, Nedelec P, Pages JP. 1994. Evidence of long-term increase in tropospheric ozone from Pic du Midi data series, consequences and positive radiative forcing. *J. Geophys. Res.* 99:16617–32
30. Haan D, Martinerie P, Raynaud D. 1996. Ice core data of atmospheric carbon monoxide over Antarctica and Greenland during

the last 200 years. *Geophys. Res. Lett.* 23: 2235–38
31. Prather M, Ehhalt D, Dentener F, Derwent R, Dlugokencky E, et al. 2001. Atmospheric chemistry and greenhouse gases. In *Climate Change 2001: The Scientific Basis*, ed. JT Houghton, pp. 239–88. Cambridge, UK:Cambridge Univ. Press
32. Folland CK, Karl TR, Christy JR, Clarke RA, Gruza GV, et al. 2001. Observed climate variability and change. See Ref. 31, pp. 99–181
33. Penner J, Andreae M, Annegarn H, Barrie L, Feichter J, et al. 1999. Aerosols: their direct and indirect effects. See Ref. 31, pp. 289–348
34. Levy H, Kasibhatla PS, Moxim WJ, Klonecki A, Hirsch A, et al. 1997. The global impact of human activity on tropospheric ozone. *Geophys. Res. Lett.* 24:791–94
35. Prinn R, Jacoby H, Sokolov A, Wang C, Xiao X, et al. 1999. Integrated global system model for climate policy assessment: feedbacks and sensitivity studies. *Clim. Change* 41:469–546
36. Wang C, Prinn RG. 1999. Impact of emissions, chemistry and climate on atmospheric carbon monoxide: 100-year predictions from a global chemistry model. *Chemosphere Glob. Change* 1:73–81
37. Stimpfle RM, Anderson JG. 1988. In situ detection of OH in the lower stratosphere with a balloon borne high repetition rate laser system. *Geophys. Res. Lett.* 15:1503–6
38. Poppe D, Zimmerman J, Bauer R, Brauers T, Bruning D, et al. 1994. Comparison of measured OH concentrations with model calculations. *J. Geophys. Res.* 99:16633–42
39. Mount GH. 1992. The measurement of tropospheric OH by long-path absorption. 1. Instrumentation. *J. Geophys. Res.* 97:2427–44
40. Dorn HP, Brandenburger U, Brauers T, Hausmann M. 1995. A new in situ long-path absorption instrument for the measurement of tropospheric OH radicals. *J. Atmos. Sci.* 52:3373–80
41. Brandenburger U, Brauers T, Dorn H-P, Hausmann M, Ehhalt DH. 1998. In-situ measurement of tropospheric hydroxyl radicals by folded long-path laser absorption during the field campaign POPCORN in 1994. *J. Atmos. Chem.* 31:181–204
42. Hard TM, O'Brien RJ, Chan CY, Mehrabzadeh AA. 1984. Tropospheric free radical determination by FAGE. *Environ. Sci. Technol.* 18:768–77
43. Hard TM, George LA, O'Brien RJ. 1995. FAGE determination of tropospheric HO and HO_2. *J. Atmos. Sci.* 52:3354–72
44. Holland F, Hessling M, Hofzumahaus A. 1995. In-situ measurement of tropospheric OH radicals by laser-induced fluorescence. A description of the KFA instrument. *J. Atmos. Sci.* 52:3393–401
45. Felton CC, Sheppard JC, Campbell MJ. 1990. The radiochemical hydroxyl radical measurement method. *Environ. Sci. Technol.* 24:1841–47
46. Chen X, Mopper K. 2000. Determination of tropospheric hydroxyl radical by liquid-phase scrubbing and HPLC: preliminary results. *J. Atmos. Chem.* 36:81–105
47. Tanner DJ, Jefferson A, Eisele FL. 1997. Selected ion chemical ionization mass spectrometric measurement of OH. *J. Geophys. Res.* 102:6415–25
48. Brune WH, Stevens PS, Mather JH. 1995. Measuring OH and HO_2 in the troposphere by laser-induced fluorescence at low pressure. *J. Atmos. Sci.* 52:3328–36
49. Eisele FL, Tanner DJ. 1991. Ion-assisted tropospheric OH measurements. *J. Geophys. Res.* 96:9295–308
50. Eisele FL, Tanner DH, Cantrell CA, Calvert JG. 1996. Measurements and steady state calculations of OH concentrations at Mauna Loa Observatory. *J. Geophys. Res.* 101:14665–79
51. Hofzumahaus A, Aschmutat U, Hebling M, Holland F, Ehhalt D. 1996. The measurement of tropospheric OH radicals by

laser-induced fluorescence spectroscopy during the POPCORN field campaign. *Geophys. Res. Lett.* 23:2541–44
52. Poppe D, Zimmerman J, Dorn HP. 1995. Field data and model calculations for the hydroxyl radical. *J. Atmos. Sci.* 52:3402–7
53. Prinn R, Rasmussen R, Simmonds P, Alyea F, Cunnold D, et al. 1983. The atmospheric lifetime experiment 5. Results for CH$_3$CCl$_3$ based on three years of data. *J. Geophys. Res.* 88:8415–26
54. Montzka SA, Spivakovsky CM, Butler JH, Elkins JW, Lock LT, Mondeel DJ. 2000. New observational constraints on atmospheric hydroxyl on global and hemispheric scales. *Science* 288:500–3
55. McCulloch A, Midgley P. 2001. The history of methyl chloroform emissions: 1951–2000. *Atmos. Environ.* 35:5311–19
56. Volz A, Ehhalt DH, Derwent RG. 1981. Seasonal and latitudinal variation of ^{14}CO and the tropospheric concentration of OH radicals. *J. Geophys. Res.* 86:5163–71
57. Mak JE, Brenninkmeijer CAM, Tamaresis J. 1994 Atmospheric ^{14}CO observations and their use for estimating carbon monoxide removal rates. *J. Geophys. Res.* 99:22915–22
58. Quay P, King S, White D, Brockington M, Plotkin B, et al. 2000. Atmospheric ^{14}CO: a tracer of OH concentration and mixing rates. *J. Geophys. Res.* 105:15147–66
59. Miller BR, Weiss RF, Prinn RG, Huang J, Fraser PJ. 1998. Atmospheric trend and lifetime of chlorodifluoromethane (HCFC-22) and the global tropospheric OH concentration. *J. Geophys. Res.* 103:13237–48
60. Simmonds PG, O'Doherty S, Huang J, Prinn R, Derwent R, et al. 1998. Calculated trends and the atmospheric abundance of 1,1,1,2-tetrafluoroethane, 1,1-dichloro-1-fluoroethane, and 1-chloro-1,1-difluorethane using automated in-situ gas chromatography-mass spectrometry measurements recorded at Mace Head, Ireland, from October 1994 to March 1997. *J. Geophys. Res.* 103:16029–37
61. Huang J, Prinn R. 2002. Critical evaluation of emissions for potential gases for OH estimation. *J. Geophys Res.* 107: No. D24, 4784; doi: 10.1029/2002JD002394
62. Prinn RG. 2000. Measurement equation for trace chemicals in fluids and solution of its inverse. In *Inverse Methods in Global Biogeochemical Cycles*, Geophys. Monogr 114, ed. P Kasibhatla, pp. 3–18. Washington, DC: Am. Geophys. Union
63. Prinn RG, Cunnold DM, Rasmussen R, Simmonds PG, Alyea FN, et al. 1987. Atmospheric trends in methylchloroform and the global average for the hydroxyl radical. *Science* 238:945–50
64. Prinn R, Cunnold D, Simmonds P, Alyea F, Boldi R, et al. 1992. Global average concentration and trend for hydroxyl radicals deduced from ALE/GAGE trichloroethane (methyl chloroform) data for 1978–1990. *J. Geophys. Res.* 97:2445–61
65. Krol M, van Leeuwen PJ, Leileveld J. 1998. Global OH trend inferred from methyl chloroform measurements. *J. Geophys. Res.* 103:10697–711
66. Prinn R, Huang J. 2001. Comment on "Global OH trend inferred from methyl chloroform measurements." by Maarten Krol et al. *J. Geophys. Res.* 106:23151–57
67. Krol M, van Leeuwen PJ, Lelieveld J. 2001. Reply to comment by RG Prinn and J Huang on "Global OH trend inferred from methyl chloroform measurements." *J. Geophys. Res.* 106:23158–68
68. Berntsen TK, Myhre G, Stordal F, Isaksen ISA. 2000. Time evolution of tropospheric ozone and its radiative forcing. *J. Geophys. Res.* 105:8915–30
69. Houweling S, Dentener F, Lelieveld J. 2000. The modeling of tropospheric methane: How well can point measurements be reproduced by a global model? *J. Geophys. Res.* 105:8981–9002

70. Spivakovsky CM, Logan JA, Montzka SA, Balkanski YJ, Foreman-Fowler M, et al. 2000. Three dimensional climatological distribution of tropospheric OH: Update and evaluation. *J. Geophys. Res.* 105:8931–80
71. Thompson AM, Witte JC, McPeters RD, Oltmans SJ, Schmidlin FJ, Logan JA, Fujiwara M, et al. 2003. The 1998–2000 SHADOZ tropical ozone climatology: comparison with TOMS and ground-based measurements. *J. Geophys. Res.* 108: No. D2, 8238; doi:10.1029/2001JD000967

EVALUATING UNCERTAINTIES IN REGIONAL PHOTOCHEMICAL AIR QUALITY MODELING*

James Fine,[1] Laurent Vuilleumier,[1,2] Steve Reynolds,[3] Philip Roth,[4] and Nancy Brown[1]

[1]*Atmospheric Sciences Department, Environmental Energy Technology Division, Lawrence Berkeley National Laboratory, Berkeley, California 94720-1740; email: jdfine@usfca.edu, njbrown@lbl.gov*
[2]*MeteoSwiss, Aerological Station, Les Invuardes, CH-1530 Payerne, Switzerland; email: laurent.vuilleumier@meteosuisse.ch*
[3]*Envair, 12 Palm Avenue, San Rafael, California 94901; email: steve@sreynolds.com*
[4]*Envair, 836 Fawn Drive, San Anselmo, California 94960; email: pmr9@attbi.com*

Key Words ozone, emissions controls, simulation models, atmospheric transport

■ **Abstract** This review evaluates analyses that are or may be performed to estimate uncertainties associated with air quality modeling used in regulatory planning to meet National Ambient Air Quality Standards for ozone. The sources of uncertainties in photochemical air quality simulation models (PAQSMs) are described. Regulatory requirements for evaluating PAQSM performance and uncertainty concerns not addressed through standard performance evaluations are discussed. Available techniques for evaluating uncertainties are presented. Experiences with analyses conducted most commonly are reviewed, as are those that might be used in a cohesive model uncertainty evaluation. The review concludes with a call for renewed emphasis on applying current techniques complemented by heretofore sparsely used diagnostic, corroborative, and alternative approaches and enhanced observational databases.

CONTENTS

I. INTRODUCTION 60
   Purpose and Organization of the Review 61
   Importance and Uses of Model Uncertainty Information 61
II. PAQSM AND THEIR UNCERTAINTIES 63
   PAQSM Defined 63
   PAQSM Uncertainties 67
   Experiences with PAQSM Uncertainties 73
III. FRAMEWORK FOR UNCERTAINTY ANALYSES 75

---

*The U.S. Government has the right to retain a nonexclusive, royalty-free license in and to any copyright covering this paper.

Uncertainty Analyses Defined 75
Operational Performance Evaluation 76
Framework for Developing Uncertainty Information 78
IV. SENSITIVITY ANALYSES 78
  Overview 78
  Methods 83
  Applications 87
  Summary 87
V. DIAGNOSTIC ANALYSES 90
  Overview 90
  Limitations of Available Measurement Data 91
  Examples of Diagnostic Analyses 91
  Future Needs 93
VI. CORROBORATIVE/ALTERNATIVE MODELING AND
  SUBJECTIVE JUDGMENT 94
  Overview 94
  Subjective Judgment 94
  Corroborative Analyses 95
  Potential Uses Within Current Regulatory Context 97
VII. LOOKING TO THE FUTURE 98

I. INTRODUCTION

Tropospheric ozone forms on hot, sunny days via photochemistry that involves nitrogen oxides and hydrocarbons emitted from both human and natural sources. The complexity of ozone formation compels air quality managers to use a photochemical air quality simulation model (PAQSM) system to plan how to bring nonattainment areas into compliance with health-based National Ambient Air Quality Standards (NAAQS) of the Federal Clean Air Act (FCAA). Progress in attaining ozone standards has been slow. According to monitoring data gathered in 2000, approximately 52 million people lived in 30 metropolitan statistical areas where the highest second daily maximum concentration violated the ozone NAAQS threshold of 0.12 ppm averaged over one hour (1). Nonattainment areas include many major cities and rural/suburban settings, such as Houston, Los Angeles, and the San Joaquin Valley, in California. The new federal ozone NAAQS promulgated by the U.S. Environmental Protection Agency (EPA) in 1997 is another challenge. The new standard threshold concentration of 0.08 ppm averaged over eight hours was exceeded by the highest fourth daily maximum measured in over 100 areas encompassing a population of 119 million people (1).

The "discouraging and perplexing" (2) inability to reduce peak urban ozone concentrations inspired three federal studies (2–4) and a privately sponsored review (5). All reports noted significant modeling inaccuracies and called for their evaluation and reduction.

Purpose and Organization of the Review

This review describes analyses that are performed or may be developed to evaluate uncertainties in modeling results used to support emissions control plans to meet ozone NAAQS.[1, 2] A description of PAQSMs and the sources of uncertainties in their results is provided in Section II. Section III defines uncertainty and sensitivity analyses, summarizes regulatory requirements for model performance evaluation, and introduces the techniques available for evaluating uncertainties in modeling.

Experiences with uncertainty analyses conducted most commonly, as well as those that might be used in a cohesive modeling uncertainty evaluation, are reviewed in Sections IV through VI; these include uncertainty evaluations using sensitivity (Section IV), diagnostic (Section V), and corroborative/alternative modeling and subjective judgment (Section VI). The review closes with suggestions for improving uncertainty analysis estimation capabilities.

Importance and Uses of Model Uncertainty Information

Uncertainty information is needed by planners who must decide what emissions controls to implement in pursuit of air quality standards. The fundamental question underlying a plan to meet ozone standards is: How much must current and anticipated future nitrogen oxides (NO_x) and volatile organic compound (VOC) emissions be reduced to meet the ozone NAAQS by a specified deadline? Models are used explicitly to generate information to meet the needs of the planner. Most important is the ability to simulate the interactions of complex chemical, meteorological, and pollutant emissions processes and to estimate air quality in the future. If used wisely, simulation is an "indispensable tool for predicting the outcomes of alternative policies" (6).

During SIP development, PAQSM are used to simulate an observed violation of the NAAQS concentration threshold for ozone. Once the base case simulation meets performance criteria specified by oversight agencies[3], the PAQSM is rerun with scenarios representing emissions reductions from hypothetical controls. The modeling is said to "demonstrate attainment" when modeling results indicate that planned controls will reduce ozone concentrations to below the standard if the meteorological conditions in the simulated episode are experienced again. Similarly, changes in distant, upwind emissions sources may be simulated to evaluate the

---

[1] An air quality improvement plan required by the FCAA when an area violates a NAAQS is a State Implementation Plan (SIP).
[2] Most emissions are associated with the production of energy; hence, control strategy design and air quality modeling are of consequence for national energy policy.
[3] EPA sets performance criteria to be met before using a modeling simulation for SIP planning [see (7)]. In California, additional criteria are set by California Air Resources Board (CARB) [see (8)].

significance of pollutant transport. As discussed below, modeling output may also be used to characterize uncertainties.

If model capabilities fall short of demands, decision makers still need information. They may rely on judgments to span information gaps and to justify decisions. This subjective aspect of planning often leads to controversy. There is also legal impetus to use models to demonstrate that decisions are neither arbitrary nor capricious. For example, in *Chevron U.S.A. versus Natural Resources Defense Council (NRDC)*, NRDC challenged the EPA approach for applying emissions controls to meet the requirements of the Clean Air Act Amendments of 1977. The U.S. Supreme Court supported EPA, stating, "the EPA should have broad discretion in implementing the policies of the 1977 Amendments [of the FCAA]" (467 U.S. 837). The opinion further states, "If Congress has explicitly left a gap for the agency to fill, there is an express delegation of authority to the agency to elucidate a specific provision of the statute by regulation. Such legislative regulations are given controlling weight unless they are arbitrary, capricious, or manifestly contrary to the statute." Planners rarely have other tools or information available to provide the bases for decisions. Model uncertainty information can reduce the need for judgment and make judgments explicit for the purposes of public debate.

Depending on the decision criteria,[4] decisions may be facilitated by more complete model uncertainty information. Making decisions under uncertainty, planners should consider the likelihood that their plans will yield air quality goals once implemented. They need to assess risk, which is the chance of suffering harm or loss. The question that comes to mind is: What is the likelihood that ozone NAAQS will actually be met when the model indicates that planned emissions reductions will yield attainment?

The answer to this question is a probabilistic statement. Using modeling output as well as information about output uncertainty facilitates risk assessment. In addition to risk assessment and management, there are at least six uses for model uncertainty information:

1. Satisfy the regulatory requirement to demonstrate acceptable model performance.
2. Enable planners to estimate the probability of not meeting goals even though model projections indicate the goals will be met.

---

[4]Examples of decision criteria given by Morgan & Henrion (9), include:

1. *cost-benefit*, deterministically comparing the costs and benefits of alternatives or doing so probabilistically by incorporating uncertainty and then comparing expectations of costs and benefits;
2. *cost-effectiveness*, choosing least cost routes to goals that are not necessarily based on economic considerations; and
3. *zero or bounded risk*, decisions reducing or altogether prohibiting undesirable outcomes without consideration of costs or benefits.

3. Identify situations in which model uncertainties are greater than the needed air quality improvement. For example, when interpreting modeling results, it is important to know if changes in modeled ozone concentration due to changes in emissions are of the same magnitude, or less, than accompanying uncertainties.
4. Suggest alternative control plans that may produce comparable air quality improvement within the range of uncertainty of the modeling results.
5. Inform general planning and resource allocation. For example, guide the planning of large field studies by identifying what data to gather, as well as where and when to gather them.
6. Set research priorities to improve the characterization of complex atmospheric processes by using both uncertainty and sensitivity information to identify key PAQSM components that need improvement.

II. PAQSM AND THEIR UNCERTAINTIES

PAQSM Defined

A photochemical air quality simulation model is an attempt to "... describe a dynamic, physical phenomenon by mathematical relationships which, when combined with accurate input data, imitate the real system" (11). A PAQSM is a mathematical representation of physical and chemical processes occurring in the atmosphere and at the atmosphere/land interface; the model includes emissions, diffusive and advective transport, chemical transformation, and deposition. A PAQSM integrates our knowledge of the spatial and temporal evolution of gaseous and particulate constituents in the atmosphere. In addition to emissions and atmospheric processing, it represents the physical system comprised of topography (e.g., mountains), surface characteristics (e.g., land use and land cover), and meteorology (e.g., winds, temperatures, and clouds). The PAQSM domain may range from an urban airshed to a regional to a continental-scale area.

MODELS OF A PAQSM   The key components of PAQSM are shown in Figure 1. They are meteorological, emissions, and air quality models. (The entire photochemical air quality simulation modeling system is referred to as a PAQSM and the embedded components within the PAQSM as models.)

The meteorological model uses pertinent information to generate meteorological "fields"—wind speed and direction, temperatures, and humidity—that are inputs to the emissions and air quality models. The emissions model calculates emissions from natural and anthropogenic sources. The air quality model contains descriptions of physical and chemical transformations, transport, and numerical solution algorithms.

Many tiers and types of models are embedded in the components of the PAQSM depicted in Figure 1. For example, the emissions model component will include

```
┌─────────────────┐      ┌─────────────────┐
│ Meteorological  │─────▶│    Emissions    │
│     model       │      │     model       │
└─────────────────┘      └─────────────────┘
         │                        │
         │    ┌──────────────┐    │
         └───▶│ Air quality  │◀───┘
              │    model     │
              └──────┬───────┘
                     ▼
              ┌──────────────┐
              │ Post-processor│
              │     and      │
              │graphical display│
              └──────────────┘
```

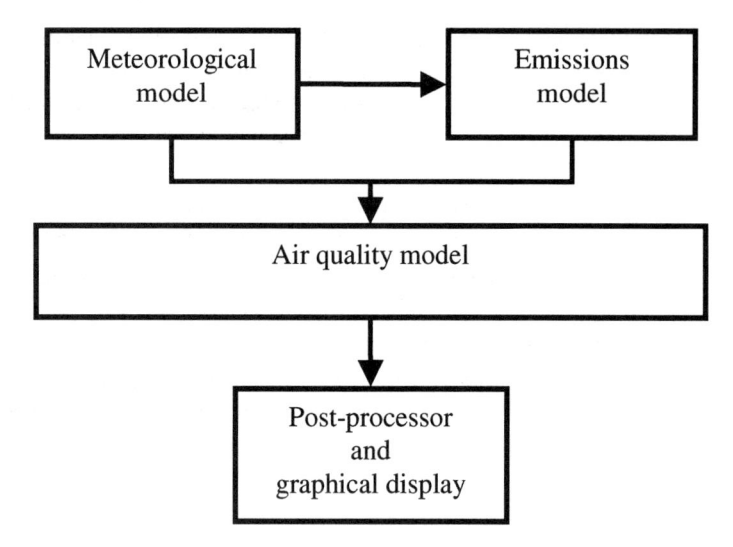

Figure 1 Component models of a photochemical air quality modeling system.

formulas for estimating emissions from stationary point, area, on- and off-road mobile, and biogenic emissions. In addition, a geographic information system may be used to organize and manipulate spatially resolved data, and post-processing systems may summarize and display results graphically.

Mathematical description of the dynamics of gases and aerosols in the atmosphere is achieved using conservation equations for mass, momentum, and energy. Pollutant transport and transformation is tracked temporally and spatially using the advection-diffusion equation (ADE):

$$\frac{\partial c_i}{\partial t} = -\frac{\partial}{\partial x_j}(u_j \partial c_i) + \frac{\partial}{\partial x_j}\left(K_{jj}\frac{\partial c_i}{\partial x_j}\right) + R_i + S_i + L_i \qquad 1.$$

$$= \text{advection} + \text{turbulent diffusion} + \text{reactions} + \text{sources} + \text{removal}.$$

$$j = \text{x, y, z dimensions}.$$

$$i = 1, \ldots, \text{n pollutant species}.$$

The ADE describes how the time rate of change of concentration, c_i, of the ith pollutant equals the net changes due to five processes:

- advection by the mean wind components, u_j,
- turbulent diffusion characterized by gradient transport using eddy diffusivity, K_j,
- production and destruction of i through chemical reactions, R_i,
- addition of i by emission sources, S_i, and
- removal of i at the surface or by other physical processes, L_i.

Each pollutant is described with an ADE. The result is a set of coupled, nonlinear partial differential equations that satisfy conservation relationships in a turbulent flow. Coupling occurs between pollutant species in the reaction term and is an important source of the nonlinearity of the system. The equations require numerical, not analytic, solution.

For each time step, Δt, of a simulation, pollutant concentrations in grid cells change as they are gained (lost) through inflow (outflow) and chemical formation (destruction). Transport terms include wind-induced advection and turbulent diffusion. Emissions are an inflow at the ground level or, for large point sources, into a horizontal layer aloft. Typically, emissions from tall stacks occur above the surface layer, so they are assumed to inject into a horizontal layer that is above the surface. Refer to (12) or (13) for detailed reviews of model formulation.

TYPES OF PAQSM   The two types of PAQSM used today are distinguished by their frames of reference. Eulerian constructs overlay onto the modeling domain a three-dimensional (3-D) grid system of a particular resolution with a fixed frame of reference. Trajectory formulations start with a frame of reference that moves a control volume (which is often assumed to correspond to a particular air mass) over space and time using a prescribed meteorological variable, such as wind velocity.[5]

Eulerian models are the state of the science and require the least restrictive assumptions. In the United States, they are the models of choice for regulatory applications. However, they are computationally and data intensive. Oftentimes, there are insufficient data to support Eulerian model applications. Computational requirements may be a concern when considering the execution of a large number of simulations to fully explore model sensitivity or control strategy issues.

Trajectory models are less demanding computationally, require less input data, are a simpler representation of the physical system, and provide less information about the spatial character of pollutants. They use averages of observed wind speed and direction to transport a single air mass over space and time and, thus, have limited ability to represent complicated pollutant transport situations. The domain may be described as a single box, a zero-dimensional model (0-D), or as many boxes stacked vertically, a one-dimensional model (1-D), to allow for vertical mixing and pollutant concentrations that vary with altitude. The simplifications of trajectory models render them inappropriate for simulations extending beyond the period over which assumptions are valid. In particular, the integrity of the air column or boxes is violated over space and time in the presence of significant wind shear.

Many model uncertainty evaluations have been conducted using trajectory models because of their computational and input simplicity advantages, though recent efforts have used Eulerian models (14–20). It is easier to work with trajectory models, but their simplifying assumptions are violated more readily. Eulerian models

---

[5]Trajectory models are often referred to as Lagrangian formulations. The term is not used here because, strictly speaking, trajectory models are a simplification of Eulerian models that treat horizontal transport and turbulent diffusion as negligible.

are the dominant tools used for regional-scale air quality planning.[6] There is a trend toward simulating larger domains (i.e., regional and subcontinental-scales) and longer time periods (i.e., an entire ozone season lasting several months). Using larger domains reduces errors associated with boundary conditions and allows for the examination of pollutant transport over regional scales. Modeling a full ozone season addresses concerns about the representativeness of simulating only one or a few multi-day ozone episodes.

PAQSM INPUTS   PAQSM inputs may be categorized according to meteorology, emissions, topography, grid structure, and atmospheric concentrations specified at the outset of the simulation and at the boundary of the domain (12). The delineation of outputs and inputs is confounded by intermediate products; output from one model of a PAQSM can be input for another. Aerometric observations may be used to specify initial and boundary conditions, and to provide comparative data for model performance evaluation. The emissions and chemistry models rely on output from the meteorological model because chemical reactions and some emissions rates vary with actinic flux and air temperature.[7] Meteorological fields, emissions estimates, and chemical kinetics and rates (i.e., chemical mechanism) are inputs for the air quality model.

PAQSM OUTPUTS   Outputs are defined here as information produced by a PAQSM, notably estimated pollutant concentrations. Modelers use output, as well as intermediate products, to evaluate model performance. Policy makers are interested in predicted pollutant concentrations to determine "the emissions reductions needed to achieve the desired air-quality standards, such as the NAAQS for ozone" (2). The review by North American Research Strategy for Tropospheric Ozone (NARSTO) (4) identified four types of output:

1. Ozone concentrations estimated in space and time that result from estimated historical, current, or anticipated emissions.
2. Ozone precursors—concentrations of precursor (e.g., NO_x and hydrocarbons) or indicator species (e.g., CO) estimated in space and time. These chemical species are relevant and important, because they must be simulated accurately to conclude that the accuracy of ozone predictions is due to correct representation of relevant processes.
3. Ozone sensitivity—changes in ozone due to changes in precursor emissions or concentrations at the boundary.

---

[6]Point source dispersion models enjoy wide application for individual project permit applications. Because this review is concerned with regional-scale air quality planning, dispersion models are not reviewed.

[7]Although the dependency of emissions on meteorology is treated in PAQSM, feedback effects of chemical pollutant dynamics on meteorology are not. To the extent that emissions do not change dramatically, this assumption does not represent a significant source of error (12).

4. Transport—relative contributions from distant and local precursor emissions to peak ozone concentrations.

PAQSM Uncertainties

The uncertainties described in this section are found in the component models of a PAQSM, and they interact both within and across models. For organizational convenience, uncertainties pertaining to inputs, formulation, variability, and the use of results are discussed separately.

UNCERTAINTIES IN INPUTS   These uncertainies are described below in terms of emissions, observational data, meteorology, chemistry, and resolution.

Emissions   Estimates of emissions are among the most uncertain inputs of PAQSM (2, 4, 12). Emission accuracy determines estimation accuracy more than the choice of model or grid structure (12), although design features also matter [for example, see (21)].

Emissions from major industrial stacks are reasonably well known, with continuous monitors providing real-time emissions measurements for major facilities. This is not the case for emissions from residential, commercial, mobile, and biogenic sources. Industrial emissions from sources other than smokestacks (e.g., leaky pipes and valves) are not known accurately. Traditionally, motor vehicle and biogenic VOC emissions have been under- and overestimated, respectively [for examples, see (22) and (23)]. Russell (12) discussed how emissions estimates differ from actual values:

- Motor vehicle VOC exhaust emissions are underestimated by a factor of 2 to 4 (24–26).
- Biogenic VOC emissions are uncertain by a factor of 3 or more (27, 28).
- Other VOC sources, if studied in more detail, would be found to be very uncertain too.
- Mobile NO_x emissions are better understood than mobile VOC emissions (24, 26).
- Biogenic NO_x emissions estimates are still being developed and may be important in some areas [see (29)].

Adding to emissions' uncertainties is the need for their temporal and spatial specification. In one recent study, a fuel-based estimate of diesel truck emissions for the San Francisco Bay and San Joaquin Valley air basins found that emissions decrease 70%–80% on weekends (22). Emissions variation with meteorology is quite complicated, because changes in photolytic flux, temperature, and moisture can influence emissions (30, 31). Efforts to distinguish weekday and weekend emissions budgets are ongoing but hindered by limited knowledge of day-to-day changes in anthropogenic activity.

Emissions estimates typically have less spatial resolution than needed for a gridded modeling application (12, 26). All emissions, except some major point sources, are treated as area sources emitted at the surface because they are summed within grid cells and assumed to mix instantaneously in the cell. This may cause an important distortion in the chemistry in the case of large point sources (12). Assuming instantaneous pollutant mixing within grid cells has the effect of slowing down the chemistry at the source, where concentrations will be higher in reality, and speeding it up at distant parts of the grid, where concentrations would be lower in reality. Plume-in-grid modeling allows for simulation of subgrid, point source emissions, where the emissions plume is assigned to the appropriate horizontal layer based on consideration of plume rise and meteorology. Overlapping plumes are not treated explicitly in such plume-in-grid models.

Biogenic emissions estimates rely on knowledge of the surface area coverage of plant types, indices of leaf mass per plant type, and emissions rates per unit leaf mass per plant type. This is an active field of research because emissions rates are characterized incompletely for the myriad plant types and VOC species emitted.

Important assumptions used to estimate future emissions pertain to the rates used for population and economic growth and for land use conversion, forecasted changes in driving patterns, and the anticipated effectiveness and rates of implementation of emissions control technologies. Inevitably, these assumptions will lead to some error. None of these assumptions can account for unanticipated gradual changes, such as the rise in popularity of sport utility vehicles and light-duty trucks during the 1990s, or abrupt changes, such as a sudden increase in crude oil prices that leads power producers to switch from oil to natural gas fuel.

Observational data Observational data collected to initialize the modeling system, provide boundary conditions, and evaluate model performance have uncertainties due to limited characterization of their spatial and temporal variability. Observational data also have uncertainties caused by monitoring equipment, user error, and monitoring network design. Some pollutant species are easier to measure than others. For example, measurements of NO_x may actually capture NO_y, which includes NO_x plus products of NO_x oxidation.[8] Equipment may malfunction or may not be properly calibrated. Concentration estimated using canister samples may have errors due to a flawed analytical technique.

Monitor location can affect measurement bias. Routine monitoring stations are often located near sensitive receptors (e.g., population centers) or to emphasize some emissions sources over others. For example, stations may be sited near roadways to observe carbon monoxide hot spots. Measurements of ozone taken near roadways are underestimates of larger spatial scale concentrations due to local scavenging by vehicular nitrogen oxide emissions. Routine monitoring rarely

---

[8]NO_y may consist of HNO_3, HONO, N_2O_5, NO_3, peroxyacyl nitrates (PAN), organic nitrates, particulate nitrates, and any other reactive nitrogen compounds present (13).

characterizes ambient conditions aloft with sufficient spatial resolution, even though such observations are needed to initialize multilayer models.

Another concern is incommensurability between the spatial scales of estimated and observed pollutant concentrations. Measurements taken at one or several points within a grid cell typically represent volumes on the order of tens of cubic meters. Modeled concentrations are grid-cell averages for volumes ranging up to several hundred cubic kilometers (4). Surface layer grid cells range from 4 to 40 km in the horizontal and 50 to 200 m in height, which equals a volume range from less than 1 to 320 km^3.

Meteorology The meteorological model relies on observations typically lacking in the spatial and temporal detail needed to initialize meteorological fields. Interpolation using sparse observational data can lead to errors in calculated meteorological fields. The state of the science has progressed from objective interpolation to prognostic methods based on solution of fluid dynamics equations. Errors associated with initial and boundary conditions and with numerical solution methods can amplify temporally (32). The application of four-dimensional data assimilation dampens the temporal growth in errors by causing model results to conform to observations at regular intervals (33). Specifically, the three components of wind velocity calculated as a function of time are nudged toward measured values. Doing so, however, reduces the amount of observational data remaining for performance evaluation.

An important characteristic of meteorology is solar radiation, which influences temperature, photochemical reactions, and vertical mixing (12, 34, 35). Radiative transfer depends on incoming solar radiation, scattering and absorption by gases, aerosols and ground-level surfaces. Surface albedo influences actinic flux, which must be known to estimate chemical processing. The effects of aerosols on radiative transfer, both direct and indirect (i.e., due to clouds), are major sources of uncertainty. Actinic flux estimation requires description of aerosols spatially and temporally; only recently are observations available to do so accurately. There remain large uncertainties in aerosol concentrations, composition, and optical properties. Representations of key cloud chemistry and physics are also limited. With the exception of NO_2, atmospheric gases that affect radiative transfer are better characterized, and there are fewer uncertainties associated with their contributions.

Chemistry Atmospheric chemistry is known incompletely because it involves hundreds of pollutant species and thousands of reactions. Reaction rates and pathways are understood adequately for less than one quarter of the chemical species observed in the atmosphere (4). Even if known completely, atmospheric chemistry cannot be represented in its entirety because it would impose excessive computational demands. Fortunately, only a subset of essential reactions need be represented. Several approaches are used to simplify the chemistry, among these are the steady-state approximation for radical species and the use of structural and functional lumping for organic species (36, 37). Although they give similar results for ozone, they do not do so for other pollutant species (38). Uncertainties associated with atmospheric organic chemistry are more significant when ozone formation is limited by the availability of organic compounds; that is when the ratio of VOC to NO_x is small. Chemical kinetic parameters are determined experimentally, so the values are subject to experimental errors.

Resolution Representing the range of scales relevant to the physical system places great demands on a PAQSM (39). Models must span orders of magnitude in time and space, even though outputs are usually sought for time periods covering hours or days.[9] A compromise must be met between the inherent resolution of the processes of interest and scales imposed to manage the limitations of available information and computational intensity.

The spatial and temporal resolution of the inputs from the meteorological and emissions models are determined by modeling system specifications, such as grid structure (i.e., horizontal and vertical resolution). Emissions estimates and meteorological field inputs must be resolved to these scales. Furthermore, emissions descriptions must be compatible with the speciation requirements of the chemical mechanism.

Chemical and meteorological measurements are often not available at desired temporal or spatial resolution. No matter what grid size is selected for use, processes occurring at subgrid spatial scales are represented by average values used for grid cells. The significance of this limitation is still being explored (4).

There is a trade-off between grid structure resolution and computational intensity. Finer grids, both horizontally and vertically, reduce errors associated with numerical solution techniques, better represent point-oriented observations, and facilitate the approximation of physical processes, such as wind shear and vertical mixing. Data availability becomes limiting because finer resolution is not helpful when inputs, such as observations and estimates of emissions and meteorological variables, are not similarly resolved. New approaches, e.g., nested-grid refinements (40–42), might address this trade-off by providing finer spatial resolution for emissions hot spots.

UNCERTAINTIES IN MODEL FORMULATION Uncertainties associated with model formulation may be due to erroneous or incomplete representations, incommensurability, numerical solution techniques, and choice of modeling domain and grid structure. Simplified representations are necessary when knowledge is incomplete, or when more thorough or precise specification would increase computational intensity excessively. If more than one algorithm is available and appropriate, choosing one inevitably means accepting some uncertainties over others.

---

[9]The averaging times for ozone NAAQS concentration thresholds are one and eight hours.

Turbulence Uncertainties arise from the deterministic representation of turbulent diffusion transport using the gradient transport hypothesis in conjunction with the diffusivity coefficient, K_j. The approach limits the model applicability in the lower limits of the spatial and temporal scales (12). The validity of the ADE is predicated on two assumptions. Atmospheric turbulence is assumed stationary for the averaging time period of interest ($\sim$30 to 60 minutes for most applications). Also, the characteristic temporal and spatial scales in the gradients of the turbulent velocity correlations are assumed large compared with the time resolution and average distance that a fluid particle travels in that time period. These assumptions break down at small spatial and temporal scales.

Removal processes Uncertainties in estimating pollutant removal are associated with the treatment of pollutant transport near surfaces and the net flux of pollutants from various types of vegetation and soils. Deposition is the pathway by which pollutants are removed from the atmosphere via the physical transport to the surface and the physical/chemical interactions that occur there. The nature of these interactions for various species and surface types is a source of uncertainty. In wet conditions, deposition involves washout of pollutants with precipitation. Dry deposition involves no atmospheric hydrometeors (i.e., cloud and fog droplets, rain, or snow).

Available measurements of deposition are limited (43). Studies of the processes that control dry deposition require direct measurements of the air-to-surface exchange. Micrometeorological approaches used to characterize deposition, e.g., eddy correlation and gradients, are not well developed for nonuniform landscapes, such as hilly terrain, or for reactive pollutants, such as NO_2. The ability to parameterize the processes affecting dry deposition and reemission is limited by the complexity and variability of the chemical, physical, and biological characteristics of the surfaces and the diversity of pollutants and surface types.

Wet deposition and other aqueous phase physical and chemical interactions are among the most complex atmospheric processes to model. Indicative of the challenge are the range of scales (i.e., 10^{-6} m to 10^6 m) at which relevant processes occur, the multiple phases (i.e., gas, liquid, and aerosol), states of aqueous phases (e.g., cloud droplets, fog, rain, snow, and ice), and different processes occurring within and below clouds (13). For simulations involving short-term and urban-scale ozone episodes in areas of low humidity (e.g., western United States), wet deposition is not important because high ozone typically occurs on dry days. However, in humid areas (e.g., midwestern and eastern United States) and for regional-scale, seasonal-length modeling, precipitation scavenging and cloud dynamics become significant. These processes are treated using a washout parameter determined empirically or by calculating rates of pollutant diffusion into water droplets. Simulation is hindered by deficient or inaccurate knowledge of the size distributions of water droplets and ice crystals, as well as incomplete understanding of cloud dynamics. Consequently, wet deposition is one of the more uncertain outputs of meteorological models (44).

Another removal process is the entrainment of pollutants aloft (i.e., above the mixing layer). As modeled ozone episodes may last many days, overnight storage and subsequent reintroduction of aloft pollutants require description of the rate of vertical mixing. Doing so introduces uncertainty because knowledge of turbulent flow, vertical exchange, and pollutant concentrations at the top of the modeling domain is usually limited.

Aerosols Historically, models sometimes treated the transport of aerosols but never their physical and chemical processing. Gas and liquid phase chemistry requires specification, as does the chemistry involving pollutant reactions with aerosol and water droplet surfaces. This is especially so when simulating regional spatial scales and entire ozone seasons. Cloud droplets act as small reactors, influence pollutant mixing, compete with gas phase chemistry, and affect rates of wet deposition. Knowledge of heterogeneous (multiphase) reactions is severely deficient. Treating cloud processes is computationally intensive and requires input data that are rarely available. Complete treatment requires characterization of the size distributions of aerosols as well as their other chemical and physical properties. Consequently, there is considerable uncertainty associated with the treatment of cloud dynamics by deterministic meteorological models. Typifying how uncertainties are interdependent, those associated with cloud predictions exacerbate uncertainties in biogenic emission estimates that are sensitive to photolytic flux.

Numerical solution Solution techniques pertain to the numerical methods used to solve the set of coupled differential equations that cannot be solved analytically. Each of these conserves mass approximately (12). Solution-related errors tend to resemble artificial dispersion, thereby spreading would-be concentration peaks spatially. Nonetheless, solution techniques are believed to contribute a small amount of error to model predictions relative to errors associated with emissions estimates, representation of meteorology, and values used for boundary conditions (45).

VARIABILITY Variability refers to stochastic atmospheric and anthropo-genic processes. It contributes to uncertainties discussed previously, notably those associated with emissions estimates and representations of chemistry and meteorology. Here, its contribution to uncertainty is discussed in two respects: the implications of using means to represent values that vary and the inability to treat inherent variability.

The deterministic treatment of stochastic processes using nominal mean values is a source of uncertainty. For example, real motor vehicle driving activity and associated emissions vary over time, e.g., daily, hourly, monthly, annually. Attempts to estimate vehicular emissions introduces uncertainty associated with the choice of representation. Although it is desirable to generate separate estimates for weekdays and weekends, available information may not be adequate to do so.

Furthermore, when mean values are used, simulation of extreme realizations is prohibited (4).

Although it may be possible to represent stochastic processes using probabilistic methods, doing so does not eliminate the uncertainty inherent to variability. The estimate of vehicular emissions does not associate weather conditions and driving, so feedback effects are not represented. Extreme events are not represented either, such as changes in emissions from congestion caused by a traffic accident.

With few exceptions [for example, see (35)], neither the modeling systems nor the air quality planning efforts using modeling tools have incorporated representations of variability. At the modeling system level, emissions and meteorology are not characterized probabilistically. At the planning level, the few simulated ozone episodes may not represent the myriad conditions capable of causing violations of ozone air quality standards. With increases in computing capabilities and expanded observational databases, efforts are now under way to model full ozone seasons [see (46, 47)]; these presumably capture numerous ozone episodes to address concerns about meteorological and emissions variability. It may be necessary to model several ozone seasons to assess fully the range of variability and to evaluate air quality on days when ozone violates the 8-hour concentration threshold in addition to the 1-hour threshold. Doing so, however, may involve trade-offs. Although variability may be better represented, each modeled episode may be less accurate because it will receive less detailed attention and be based on routine rather than intensive observations.

UNCERTAINTIES IN USE OF MODELING RESULTS Although not strictly within the scope of this review, a fourth uncertainty relates to the use of PAQSM results. Decision makers must decide what to do with model output, which includes weighing it against other information. PAQSM output may be not compatible with the needs of decision makers. Consequently, there is uncertainty about how PAQSM output will be incorporated into decisions.

Another aspect of uncertainty arising from the use of model outputs is the characterization and incorporation of uncertainty. To date, formal model evaluation efforts have been inadequate (2, 4, 12, 39). Air quality planning oversight agencies provide limited guidance for treating uncertainty. Consequently, there is uncertainty about the nature of PAQSM output uncertainties, as well as how policy makers manage the limited knowledge they do have about uncertainties.

Finally, the possibility of uncertainties that are not yet known must be acknowledged. Unknown unknowns have frustrated past modeling and planning, and may continue to do so, as exemplified by the continual discovery of new sources of emissions.

Experiences with PAQSM Uncertainties

Now that models and their sources of uncertainty are described, experiences with them are discussed to indicate the potential benefits of rigorous uncertainty assessment. In one example, Hanna (20) queried experts to estimate the uncertainties of 128 key input variables of a modeling application. The experts were instructed to describe 95% confidence intervals. The modeling system in question was used by the Ozone Transport Assessment Group (OTAG) to evaluate emissions reductions needed to bring the northeastern United States into attainment with the ozone NAAQS. The effort was particularly concerned with long-range transport of emissions from midwestern states (48). Findings of Hanna (20) are listed in Table 1.

Although indicative of the range of input uncertainties, the study of OTAG modeling by Hanna (20) is not representative of modeling carried out elsewhere. [Hanna (20) used the estimates of input uncertainties to generate an estimate of output uncertainty. The results and limitations of that effort are discussed below.] Roth et al. (49) assess eleven urban-scale and four regional-scale modeling

TABLE 1 Experts' estimates of model input uncertainties (20, 86)

PAQSM input category	Input variable	Uncertainty range	Standard deviation (log-normal distribution unless noted)
Initial conditions	O_3 concentration	Factor of 3	0.549
	NO_x or VOC concentration	Factor of 5	0.805
Boundary conditions	O_3 concentration aloft or at side	Factor of 1.5	0.203
	NO_x or VOC concentration aloft or at side	Factor of 3	0.0549
Meteorology	Wind speed	Factor of 1.5	0.203
	Wind direction	+/− 40 degrees	20.0 (normal)
	Air temperature	+/− 3 K	1.5 (normal)
	Relative humidity	30%	15.0 (normal)
	Daytime vertical diffusivity below 1000 meters	Factor of 1.3	0.131
	Nighttime vertical diffusivity at all other times and heights	Factor of 3	0.549
	Rainfall amount	Factor of 2	0.347
	Cloud cover	30%	0.15 (normal)
	Cloud liquid water content	Factor of 2	0.347
Emissions	Major point source NO_x or VOC	Factor of 1.5	0.203
	All other emissions estimates[a]	Factor of 2	0.347
Photolysis rates	Six reactions	Factor of 2	0.347
Carbon bond IV reactions	Reactions 1 through 83	Factors ranging from 1.17 to 2.5	0.079–0.458

[a]Includes NO_x and VOC emissions estimated for biogenic, mobile, and area sources.

applications in the United States using 20 criteria describing the soundness of the model formulation, representativeness of the modeled episode(s), adequacy of the input database and emissions estimates, and the sufficiency of performance evaluation, peer review, and documentation. Modeling limitations were found to be extensive and ubiquitous. The average difference between observed and modeled 1-hour ozone concentrations ranged from 20%–35%. Although the regional studies tended to be more satisfactory than urban-scale studies, most were found to have some or major deficiencies and omissions. Furthermore, no study performed an adequate or satisfactory estimate of modeling uncertainties.

The work by Hanna, Roth, and colleagues indicates a commitment to acknowledge and evaluate uncertainties in PAQSM in the research realm. Although the findings of Roth et al. (49) indicate less interest in uncertainty for regulatory applications, such efforts certainly benefit from progress made by researchers. In addition to improvements noted above pertaining to meteorological and plume-in-grid modeling, the NARSTO Assessment (4) highlights several modeling advancements during the 1990s, which include:

- variable grid-size nesting to permit a range of spatial resolution within the modeling domain,
- improved treatment of biogenic emissions, including isoprene estimate accuracy and incorporation into chemistry representations, and
- progress toward multi-pollutant modeling, notably the development of algorithms to represent aerosol dynamics.

Furthermore, the NARSTO Assessment acknowledges improved approaches for conducting sensitivity analyses and for estimating error distributions of model outputs. These approaches are reviewed below after the suite of methods available to evaluate uncertainties in modeling is introduced.

III. FRAMEWORK FOR UNCERTAINTY ANALYSES

Uncertainty Analyses Defined

Uncertainty analysis is defined by Morgan & Henrion (9) as "the computation of the total uncertainty induced in the output by quantified uncertainty in the inputs and model, and the attributes of the relative importance of the input uncertainties in terms of their contributions." This approach involves sensitivity analyses that estimate output dependence on inputs, formulations, or design features (e.g., grid resolution). Sensitivity analyses are a component of the broader framework defined here as uncertainty analyses. When sensitivity studies are used to estimate total output uncertainty due to input uncertainties, it is sensitivity/uncertainty analysis.

The framework presented in this section provides the information per Morgan & Henrion (9), but it also examines performance in terms of intermediate products (e.g., meteorological fields) and includes the use of data and models exogenous to the PAQSM. Products of uncertainty evaluation may be qualitative or quantitative. A comprehensive model uncertainty evaluation will:

- quantify model sensitivities, notably the dependence of outputs on local changes in inputs, formulations, and design features, such as grid resolution;
- provide information to make probabilistic statements about the indications of model output, notably the likelihood that future air quality estimated by the model will be realized;
- increase confidence that the model is sufficiently valid for the decision-making need by identifying and correcting bias; and
- identify and assess the significance of compensating errors.

Before introducing the components of a comprehensive model uncertainty analysis, current regulatory requirements for performance evaluation are summarized to make a case for more extensive uncertainty assessment.

Operational Performance Evaluation

State and federal agencies establish formal processes for model validation, verification, and application. The EPA established guidelines on which PAQSM to use and how to apply and evaluate them (7, 50–54).[10] In California, CARB provided similar guidance (8). EPA and CARB requirements constitute an "operational analysis" that relies on comparison of estimated and observed peak ozone, expressed in terms of bias and error metrics.[11] Although necessary measures, these metrics are not sufficient indicators of reliable model performance. They do not address the concern that models may appear accurate for the wrong reasons. Errors that offset each other ("compensating errors") may indicate, incorrectly, adequate model performance. The risk of having such errors present is the development and adoption of ineffective or counterproductive emissions control strategies.

Biases or compensating errors are often hard to detect unless they are sought. The NARSTO Assessment offers two examples of compensating errors. In Kern County, California, two studies using the same model and input data produced conflicting conclusions about the relative effectiveness of pursuing NO_x or VOC control strategies, due to different assumptions about VOC concentrations aloft

---

[10]Additional guidance is provided for development and use of input data, notably emissions estimates [for examples, see (55–57)].

[11]Here, error and bias are defined strictly. Error is the mean of the absolute values of the differences between the computed (i.e., model estimated) and observed values; bias is simply the mean of the differences. Minimum performance criteria for PAQSM used in State Implementation Plans are that peak ozone predictions have paired bias and error normalized for peak ozone of less than 15% and 35%, respectively, and a bias unpaired in space and time of less than 20% (8).

and meteorological conditions in areas without observations (4). In another example, a modeling study in New York State yielded considerable differences in ozone estimates depending on the method used to generate wind fields and mixing heights (58).

Performance criteria measured in terms of error and bias metrics appear to be based largely on experiences with model performance (4). More relevant criteria would relate to what is meant to be learned by the modeling effort. For example, the needed accuracy in estimates of observed peak ozone concentrations might be determined by the amount of ozone reduction necessary to meet the standard.

Criteria based on past performance may lead to an approved model incapable of estimating future ozone with adequate reliability. Ozone control plans based on such models may be similarly unreliable. This concern is exacerbated by lower absolute values being modeled as peak observed ozone declines and by the lower concentration threshold of the new 8-hour ozone standard.

Statistical measures tell a partial story, one that is quite helpful when there is a big problem associated with performance, but less so (from the standpoint of uncertainty estimation) when there is not. Concerning limitations of operational evaluations to estimate uncertainty, one must consider that:

- Uncertainties associated with both observed and modeled concentrations should be taken into account.
- Some measurements do not compare exactly with the quantity modeled. Per the discussion of incommensurability above, observed and modeled concentrations represent different spatial averaging characteristics. In another example that also indicates uncertainties in measurements, what is often considered observed NO_2 will likely contain some peroxyactyl nitrate (PAN) and HNO_3 as well.
- The error and bias metrics used to summarize model performance indicate how well the model simulates the observed conditions, but they do not account for the possibility that the observed value may not be the true value of interest (e.g., peak ozone observed may not be the peak occurrence).
- Estimates of models may not be best estimates, and their expected bias should be considered. For example, ozone concentrations observed near roadways should be depressed relative to a model-estimated value due to reaction of ozone with NO. A less biased comparison would be made between observed and modeled "ozone + NO_2."

An unbiased, integrated estimate of uncertainty would take into account these additional factors. The NARSTO (4) and National Research Council (NRC) (2) assessments call for model uncertainty evaluations that extend beyond the criteria currently in force. Other researchers note that the practice of PAQSM performance analysis is wanting [for examples, see (12, 39, 49, 59)]. This review echoes those concerns.

Framework for Developing Uncertainty Information

Although CARB and EPA standardized the metrics for evaluating the adequacy of PAQSM performance, no comprehensive approach exists for estimating uncertainties in the results or outcomes of modeling (60, 61). Oftentimes uncertainties are not estimated. When they are, a necessarily limited approach is taken, such as the operational analyses just described. A typical uncertainty assessment will generally address one (or more) aspect(s) of uncertainty, but it will not provide a complete or encompassing estimate. The modeling community simply does not know how to do this (4).

Figure 2 introduces the several approaches now in use and shows how they might interact if applied in unison. Although not shown in the figure, a "code audit" or scientific evaluation of the process representations is another component of model evaluation (4).

Once the results of a given approach emerge, it is usually difficult to engage them with other sets of results. Methods of integration and synthesis are yet to be developed. The individual approaches represented in the diagram are:

- operational evaluation involving calculation of standard performance statistics,
- diagnostic analyses conducted typically to identify ways to improve operational performance and to assess the reasonableness of the representation of key atmospheric processes,
- sensitivity and sensitivity/uncertainty analyses,
- corroborative methods, and
- subjective judgment methods.

Assessing and estimating PAQSM uncertainties involves exercising the entire PAQSM or components of it. Modeling results may be corroborated through other means too. Diagnostic assessment focuses on individual models of the PAQSM. Corroborative methods include model-to-model comparisons, corroboration using different types of models (e.g., the EPA Mapper), data analyses, and executing the PAQSM with different scenarios of, for example, emissions estimates. Subjective judgment methods involve the solicitation and aggregation of expert opinions.

IV. SENSITIVITY ANALYSES

Overview

Model sensitivity analysis estimates model responses to changes in the model. When the effect of changing model inputs is sought, analyses are referred to as either parametric or functional sensitivity analysis; the respective distinction depends on whether the input in question is a constant or is distributed in space or time. When the effect of changing the representations of the chemical and physical

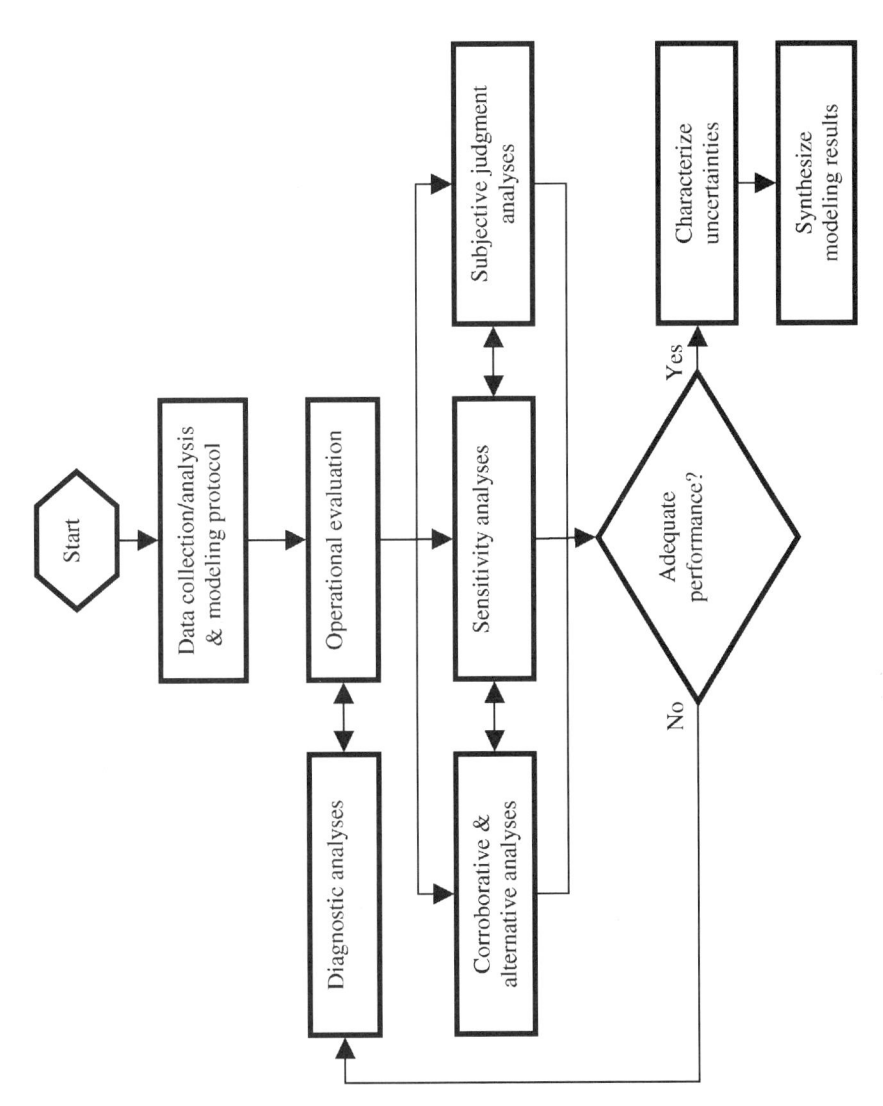

Figure 2 Comprehensive evaluation and analyses of PAQSM uncertainties.

processes is sought, analyses performed are structural sensitivity analyses. In this section, the use of sensitivity analysis for uncertainty estimation is discussed, and the constraints imposed by model formulation and by our knowledge of important input parameters are noted. So too are the various methods for computing sensitivities and uncertainties and pertinent examples of their application.

PARAMETRIC AND FUNCTIONAL SENSITIVITY ANALYSIS Parametric sensitivity analysis involves the calculation of system gradients, $\partial o_i/\partial z_u$, where o_i is the ith-dependent variable (i.e., output) and z_u is the uth input parameter. The system gradients describe the relationship between model responses and inputs. Referred to as sensitivity coefficients, the gradients reveal the importance of the various model parameters at a chosen point of operation. Sensitivity coefficients are quantitative measures of the significance of input parameters to outputs. Coefficient signs indicate directional response.

In air quality modeling, the dependent variables of particular interest are concentrations of pollutant species, such as ozone. Their sensitivities to input variables constitute the elementary sensitivity coefficients. Individual rate coefficients, emissions estimates, boundary conditions, and other input parameters are independent variables to be explored through sensitivity analyses. The aim is usually to identify the significance of the parameter. Often the product of an observable's sensitivity coefficient and a parameter uncertainty is taken as a measure of the parameter contribution to uncertainty in the observable. Additionally, the effect of neglected parameters (after assuming a nominal value) can also be determined by computing sensitivity coefficients for them.

When the parameters are distributed in space or time, functional derivatives, $\delta o_i/\delta z_u$, are the basic response functions associating incremental variations, δz_u, to corresponding changes in outputs, δo_i. An example of this is a chemical rate coefficient that varies with spatially and temporally varying temperature. Although functional sensitivity analysis has been used in other fields (62), this powerful technique has been applied to few air quality modeling studies.

One noteworthy example is Cho et al. (63), who used functional derivatives to explore the relationships among emissions sources, regional air quality, and acid deposition for the advection-diffusion equation. Functional derivatives are particularly useful for investigating source/receptor relationships in situations where the emission sources are distributed spatially and temporally within the modeling domain. The technique enabled Cho et al. to determine the region and magnitude of the influence of specific emission sources. The work by Cho et al. was undertaken in the late 1980s when the additional computational burden imposed by the calculation of sensitivity densities posed a more significant barrier than it would today with parallel computers. Consequently, the technique most certainly should be revisited.

Sensitivity analyses are often classified as local and global. Local sensitivity coefficients are the gradients about the nominal value of the input variables. They may be partial or functional derivatives and may include higher-order derivatives.

The key is that they are computed with respect to the nominal values of the parameters that define the problem. Oftentimes local methods are used to determine uncertainties in the dependent variable. Doing so requires variations in the input variable small enough to use a low-order Taylor series expansion or a first-order sensitivity coefficient of the dependent variable to describe the uncertainty. Too frequently modelers fail to verify that a first-order expansion is adequate.

For large variations, global methods must be used that take into account the range and statistical properties of the input variable to calculate average sensitivities, $\langle \partial o_i / \partial z_u \rangle$, over the range of the input parameter uncertainty. The simplest approach is repeatedly rerunning the model with variations of the parameter of interest. Parameter variations also may be generated systematically using factorial design and response surface approaches. Global analysis is difficult to achieve in practice because it presupposes reliable knowledge of the uncertainty in an input variable. Should one attempt a global analysis, an efficient way to conduct it would be to use local and global methods in concert. The local approach could be used to identify influential parameters to be subjects of a global analysis. Although not a formal global analysis, in the sense that average gradients associated with variations of specific parameters are not calculated, many applications of sensitivity/uncertainty analysis involve parameter variations that are larger than those associated with first- or second-order local analysis.

In addition to the various approaches to sensitivity analysis, there are myriad applications. Though several reviewers discuss applications (64, 65), Rabitz et al. (66) is particularly thoughtful in enumerating the uses for sensitivity analysis:

1. identifying influential or extraneous parameters and processes to deduce influence from the magnitude and sign of the sensitivity coefficient;
2. quantifying the extent and sources of error using a simple product of the sensitivity coefficient and an assumed error in a parameter to deduce the contribution the parameter makes to an observable's error;
3. identifying missing model components by allowing a parameter to be included in the model with zero value and computing its sensitivity coefficient, which, if large, suggests the parameter should be included in the model;
4. mapping parameter space for functional analysis whereby spatial and/or temporal regions of greatest influence are identified;
5. fitting a model to data to identify experimental conditions in which model components of interest are most sensitive to data; and
6. identifying steepest descent paths for optimization calculations to help search a multidimensional surface efficiently.

Applications 1 and 2 have been used extensively in air quality modeling. For example, sensitivity analysis is often used to determine how pollutants of interest respond to changes in emissions. The remaining four have been used in other fields (66). An application not mentioned in (66) is analyzing sensitivity coefficients to provide information about compensating errors. Good candidates are quantities that have sensitivity coefficients of nearly equal magnitudes and opposite sign.

Model sensitivity studies tend to be local parametric analyses that rely on the model being structurally correct. The range of applicability of sensitivity results is limited by the soundness and validity of the air quality modeling system and the supporting database employed to develop inputs. Although sensitivity analyses can be conducted using any model, the usefulness of such findings will be determined by how well the model actually represents key physical and chemical phenomena. Many sensitivity analyses have been conducted using models that do not provide a full representation of key atmospheric processes. Such studies using 0-D or 1-D models have limited scope and provide useful results within a restricted context, such as assessing the impact of uncertainties in chemical reaction rate constants on the calculated net ozone formation rate. The scaling of sensitivity results with model complexity is not understood. Neither are the limits of the usefulness of information derived from simple models for applications to more complex models. Considerable care must be exercised to determine the applicability of the findings in a regulatory regional air quality modeling context.

As mentioned previously, one application of sensitivity analysis relates the uncertainty in a quantity of interest, such as peak ozone concentration, to uncertainties in a suite of influential parameters. This type of analysis, referred to here as sensitivity/uncertainty analysis, most frequently estimates the uncertainty in model predictions resulting from uncertainties in inputs. Notable examples of the approach are reviewed herein. Before embarking on this discussion, however, attention is given to two important technical issues that have a significance for the validity and utility of sensitivity analysis results.

Air quality models are evaluated over a limited range of conditions, typically those associated with a set of historical meteorological events and their associated emissions conditions. Individual model components, such as the chemical mechanism, may be evaluated by independent means (e.g., smog chamber experiments) that cover a broader range of conditions. In designing sensitivity analyses and computer experiments that involve modification of model inputs, care must be exercised in (*a*) choosing the range over which parameters are evaluated and (*b*) evaluating the results in situations where the inputs are set to values that extend significantly beyond the range for which the model has been evaluated. Unfortunately, sensitivity studies are often conducted using models that have questionable or yet-to-be-determined capacity to replicate historical air quality events.

The second issue is correlation among the input variables. In selecting model input values, one must assure that all values are indeed plausible and consistent. Changes in correlated variables, such as emissions estimates and boundary conditions, may not be independent. Accurately representing such interdependencies among model inputs in the design of sensitivity experiments can (67–70) and should be achieved.

STRUCTURAL SENSITIVITY ANALYSIS   Structural sensitivity analysis is concerned with characterizing the response of the model outputs to a change in the basic representation of physical and chemical processes or in the structure of the model itself. Analyses explore the influences that representations have on estimated pollutant concentrations. For example, several investigators examined differences among various chemical mechanisms developed for use in air quality modeling [for examples, see (71) and (72)]. Similarly, alternative means are available for representing plume rise, turbulent diffusive transport, and for solving the governing equations themselves. Each of these choices has some impact on the resulting calculated pollutant levels. Comparing results generated using models of different dimensionality (i.e., 0-D, 1-D, 2-D, or 3-D) offers insights about the description of transport [for example, see (73)].

Although it is relatively easy to design mathematical and statistical methods to explore parametric sensitivity, the treatment of structural sensitivity and its ultimate relation to uncertainty is more challenging. Analyses of this type have principally relied on model-to-model comparisons and expert judgment, which are discussed below.[12] As improved representations of atmospheric processes are developed and incorporated into air quality models, structural sensitivity studies will provide a means for describing how the improvements may alter the outcome of previous regulatory modeling assessments. They may be used to support claims that the improved model performs as well as or better than other models that EPA or CARB have approved for use in regulatory applications. When structural sensitivity studies are performed using 0-D or 1-D models to reduce computational burden, the results may provide an initial indication of the sensitivities that may be found in more complex 3-D models. Such structural analyses provide an indication of the advantages and limitations of using less complex models for diagnostic purposes.

Like parametric and functional sensitivity analyses, the utility of results from structural sensitivity analysis is critically dependent on the ultimate soundness and validity of the modeling constructs and supporting databases. Of particular concern are situations where the results are being used to support regulatory decision making.

Methods

The starting point for any sensitivity analysis is an air quality model with a prescribed set of inputs that provide the best representation of all significant atmospheric phenomena. There are several approaches for calculating sensitivity coefficients, each with advantages and limitations.

Local parametric sensitivity analysis is the most prevalent type of sensitivity analysis applied to air quality modeling. Tilden et al. (64) presented a comprehensive

---

[12]In the interest of parsimony, literature pertaining to uncertainties associated with the representation of turbulent transport and meteorological modeling and parameterization is not reviewed in detail. See the reviews by Seaman (44) and Russell & Dennis (32).

early review of sensitivity techniques, which included some applications to atmospheric phenomena. Hamby (74) recently reviewed sensitivity analyses techniques applied to air quality modeling.

The simplest and most frequently used sensitivity analysis is the perturbative approach. Often referred to as the brute force method (BFM), a parameter value is perturbed, the model is rerun, and the change in observables is calculated to determine sensitivity coefficients. If the perturbation is small enough, as dictated by the numerics and the actual sensitivity of the parameter of interest, a first-order sensitivity coefficient is obtained. This approach can be used to check more refined methods and algorithms. Using large perturbations along with another more formal method allows one to deduce the limits of various orders of sensitivity coefficients. The BFM approach can also be used to conduct global sensitivity analysis.

The pertubative approach does not work well when there are a large number of observables or parameters of interest. When conducted using a 3-D model involving many input parameters, the computational requirements can quickly become overwhelming. To ameliorate this situation, simpler 0-D and 1-D models are often used to explore specific sensitivity issues. Given the large number of variables subject to study in a 3-D model, statistical design procedures are often used. Both fractional and second-order design procedures may be employed to reduce the number of model simulations to a more manageable level while providing reasonably accurate estimates of the sensitivity coefficients. When several model simulations are undertaken, considerable knowledge about model sensitivity characteristics is obtained. Thus, it may be possible to use existing findings of model sensitivity characteristics to update the experimental design to achieve desired goals more efficiently.

There are a number of approaches in which sensitivity differential equations are derived from the original parent equations and solved along with them. The equations can be derived analytically, as in the decoupled direct method (DDM) (75–77), or by using automatic differentiation, like Automatic Differentiation of Fortran (ADIFOR) (78, 79). A distinction needs to be made here: Most DDM applications focused on first-order sensitivity equations. A separate set of equations has to be derived for higher-order sensitivity coefficients. The number of second-order equations increases as the square of the number of first-order equations. Many DDM applications have been concerned with simpler models (0-D and 1-D). Recent research by Yang et al. and Dunker et al. [see (18) and (77)] developed the DDM approach for a 3-D model to explore the sensitivities of pollutant concentrations to initial conditions, boundary conditions, and emissions. To enhance computational efficiency without sacrificing accuracy Dunker et al. (77) developed an algorithm by deriving sensitivity equations from the formulas of the hybrid chemistry solver and the nonlinear advection algorithm. The effort produced highly accurate first-order sensitivity coefficients.

The advantage of DDM is that it computes systematically all sensitivity coefficients for parameters of a certain type for all dependent variables. The disadvantage is that it is computationally intensive and can be prone to numerical errors when approximations are made to enhance computational efficiency. Another disadvantage is that sensitivity coefficients calculated are almost always first order. When these coefficients are used in uncertainty calculations, parameter variations often exceed those for which the first-order approximation is valid.

The Green's function method (GFM) generates a Green's function (GF) or a propagator that can be used to compute all orders of sensitivity coefficients (80). For the ADE, the derived sensitivity equations are linear inhomogeneous equations with time-varying coefficients. The GF is the solution to the homogeneous equations derived from the sensitivity equations. If there are n observables, the GF dimension is $n \times n$ and most of the computational burden is involved with calculating it. If the number of parameters is large, the extra computational cost is only related to finding specific solutions for each parameter.

With efficiency comparable to DDM, the GFM offers several advantages. It provides sensitivities to initial conditions with no extra computational effort. It can be used to obtain higher-order sensitivities because sensitivity-governing equations of all orders have identical homogenous parts. Consequently, the only extra computational effort for computing higher-order sensitivities is in finding their particular solutions by quadrature. Furthermore, the GF is an actual sensitivity. The GFM can be used to explore how a dependent variable at a given location and time in the modeling domain is sensitive to the value of another dependent variable at another location and time. Second-order sensitivities are sensitivities of sensitivity coefficients. As such, they are useful for exploring parametric interdependencies, because they indicate how the sensitivity of one parameter changes with a perturbation in another parameter.

The adjoint approach is related to the GFM. As a transpose of the GF, the adjoint operator is useful for sensitivity and inverse analysis. It is especially attractive for air quality modeling when the number of input parameters is large relative to dependent variables of interest. Adjoint methods have been used for data assimilation to improve emissions estimates that bring modeled and measured results into closer agreement [see (81)].

Scale requirements (i.e., local or global) also have an impact on the sensitivity analysis approach. As the scale increases, there is a potential need to treat higher-order derivatives and interaction terms that might otherwise not be as important in a local analysis situation. This is especially important for the most influential variables that tend to have the largest sensitivity coefficients. For them, perturbations in excess of 15% often require second- and higher-order analyses.

The Fourier amplitude sensitivity test (FAST) method of (82) and (65) is a nonrandom, efficient sampling procedure defined by determining a search curve in the space of the input parameters so that the path length included in a given portion of parameter space is proportional to the joint probability distribution. Compared to random sampling, the main advantage of FAST is that it is relatively easy to determine the minimum number of sampling points required for obtaining reliable sensitivity coefficients. Like stochastic sensitivity analysis, FAST assumes that the uncertainty in each parameter can be described by a known probability distribution. It also assumes that all parametric variations are independent, which often is not the case.

Although sensitivity coefficients identify the most influential parameters and reveal how a system responds to changes, they do not indicate which parts of a model are most uncertain or assess the size of the uncertainty. Parameter uncertainties must be known or estimated prior to conducting uncertainty analysis with parametric sensitivity coefficients. Individual parameter uncertainties are best described by a probability distribution over the range of parameter uncertainty. Input values are sampled from the parameter probability distributions, and simulations are executed for each set of parameter values. In the majority of studies, the sampling is done in a random or quasi-random way, often using Monte Carlo techniques. The multiple simulations produce model output probability distributions that reflect the model uncertainty due to the parameter uncertainties. Frequently a constrained sampling scheme similar to Latin hypercube sampling, as developed by McKay et al. (83), is used to improve efficiency. Although sensitivity coefficients are not needed in these applications, statistical methods, such as multiple regression analysis, are often used to attribute the resulting uncertainty to the different input parameters. Doing so provides a measure of the sensitivity coefficients.

Tatang et al. (84) also developed an efficient approach for determining model uncertainty due to parameter uncertainty. They approximate a model response surface with orthogonal polynomials in the model parameters. The weighting functions of the polynomials are the probability density functions (PDFs) of the parameter uncertainty. The method is significantly faster than Monte Carlo approaches, but often the PDFs are not known.

An approach that appears quite attractive for sensitivity/uncertainty analysis is the use of Bayesian updating. This type of analysis incorporates actual observations, as best illustrated by example. Bergin & Milford (85) used Bayesian Monte Carlo analysis to refine the uncertainty estimates based on their previous work by using observations to update the uncertainty estimates. With a standard sampling technique, values are sampled according to the parameter a priori probability distributions, and each simulation is given an equal weight. When using Bayesian updating, observations are used to compute a likelihood function and a corresponding weight for each simulation. The weights are used to update a posteriori the uncertainty estimates for the model output and input parameters. Bayesian methods potentially allow for evaluations of the parameter uncertainty estimate by using additional information from pollutant concentration measurements. They may also be useful for comparing models that are structurally different, thus aiding in the difficult task of assessing structural uncertainty.

There are, however, important challenges associated with using Bayesian methods. Construction of the likelihood function requires a good understanding of the uncertainty in observations. Without this description, results may be unreliable. Furthermore, current techniques assume that variables used for updating have uncorrelated uncertainties. This is an important limitation when more than one observation variable is used (e.g., consecutive measurements of one concentration, concentrations of different species, or at different locations). At this point, the errors in observations may not be understood well enough to rely on Bayesian techniques for air quality modeling.

A closing note—sampling-based parametric sensitivity studies involve planning a set of simulations and conducting them in succession. The nth simulation in a set of p simulations is selected and designed based on what is known before any of these simulations is conducted. In contrast, Bayesian design involves planning the nth simulation using what is known at the beginning and what is learned through the $(n - 1)^{st}$ simulation. (In fact, this is what air quality modelers tend to do subjectively.) Thus, the choice of the nth simulation can be better informed and the set of simulations more efficient. In short, there is experience with less efficient parametric planning, but potentially more effective Bayesian methods are not well developed and are difficult to apply. Clearly, the development of practical and effective sequential planning techniques would be most welcome.

Applications

Selected sensitivity and sensitivity/uncertainty analyses are listed in Table 2.

Summary

Having reviewed research associated with conducting sensitivity and sensitivity/uncertainty analyses, several key observations emerge:

- The ultimate utility of sensitivity results is dependent on the soundness and validity of the model and supporting database. Care must be exercised to ensure that sensitivity results are used within their range of applicability.
- Few of the approaches demonstrated thus far have been used to contribute to model validation or diagnosis of sources of errors. There are promising new techniques for 3-D models.
- The usefulness and relationship of sensitivities calculated for 0-D and 1-D models to those associated with 3-D models is not well understood and warrants further investigation.
- With a few exceptions, second-order sensitivities estimation is generally lacking, but is especially useful for exploring interdependencies among inputs.
- Sampling requirements scale with input parameters; however, there is encouraging effort being directed toward the calculation of sampling needs and efficient, formal sampling techniques.
- Bayesian updating is a promising approach, yet remains limited by the need to understand a priori uncertainties and correlations associated with input parameters and observations used for updating. Nevertheless, in principle, sequential planning (i.e., Bayesian) techniques are inherently more efficient and, therefore, more attractive than simultaneous (i.e., parametric) planning techniques.

TABLE 2 Selected sensitivity studies using PAQSM

Method	Dimensionality	Types of analyses performed	References
Brute force method (BFM)	0-D[a] and 3-D[b]	Computed O_3 sensitivity to effects of motor vehicle emissions inventory updates and choice of chemical mechanism.	(25)
Direct decoupled method (DDM)	0-D, chemical mechanism of Regional Acid Deposition Model version 2 (RADM2)	Computed sensitivity of O_3, HCHO, HNO_3, peroxyacyl nitrates (PAN), and H_2O_2 to 157 reaction rate parameters and stochiometric coefficients of 34 reactions using a regional-scale gas-phase chemical mechanism. Sensitivity coefficients are combined with uncertainty estimates of the chemical mechanism input parameters to evaluate contributions to modeled pollutant concentration uncertainties.	(87)
Latin hypercube sampling (LHS) and multiple linear regression	0-D, chemical mechanism of RADM2	Uncertainties in estimated ozone reductions for three control strategies (reducing NO_x or VOC emissions by 25% or both by 25%) are computed under six different VOC-to-NO_x ratios with random sampling using a LHS/Monte Carlo technique. Multiple linear regression analysis is used to identify the most significant input parameter uncertainties.	(88)
LHS and multiple linear regression	1-D,[c] trajectory version of Carnegie/California Institute of Technology airshed model (CIT)	Computed the influence of uncertainties of input parameters (29 reaction rates, deposition affinities, emissions, wind direction, mixing height, and atmospheric stability) on uncertainty in estimated ozone concentrations. LHS is used to compute probability distributions for estimated concentrations of O_3, HCHO, HNO_3, PAN, and NO_y. Multiple linear regression analysis is used to attribute secondary pollutant concentration uncertainties to the input parameter uncertainties. Furthermore, peak ozone concentration uncertainties are estimated under two scenarios (25% motor vehicle NO_x or VOC emissions reductions).	(89)
DDM	0-D	Computed O_3 and PAN sensitivity to reaction rates and initial conditions.	(90)
DDM and LHS	0-D	Determined influence of reaction rate uncertainties on VOC reactivity.	(91)
DDM and LHS	0-D	Computed the influence of reaction rate uncertainties and alternative fuel exhaust variability on fuel reactivity adjustment factors, while considering product yields.	(92)
DDM	3-D CIT	Calculated ozone sensitivity to its initial concentration and deposition rate, selected reaction rates, precursor concentrations, and wind speeds.	(18)
Fourier amplitude sensitivity test (FAST)	0-D	Determined sensitivity and uncertainty due to reaction rates.	(93)
BFM	3-D	Investigated effects of NO_x and VOC controls on reducing O_3, PAN, and NO_3.	(14)

(*Continued*)

TABLE 2 (*Continued*)

Method	Dimensionality	Type of analyses performed	References
BFM	3-D	Explored using sum of total reactive nitrogen (NO$_y$) as a metric for determining ozone response to various reduction strategies.	(15)
BFM	3-D	Explored response of O$_3$ and its precursors to different emissions reduction strategies.	(94)
BFM	3-D	Estimated influence of reaction rate uncertainties on VOC reactivity due to uncertainty in 14 reaction rate parameters identified as the most influential by Yang et al. (91).	(17)
Monte Carlo (MC) with linear optimization	Uses optimization model	Used a cost-benefit framework to evaluate the use of VOC reactivity to identify reduction priorities to regulate urban O$_3$ given uncertainties in emissions and VOC reactivity parameters.	(95)
MC with subjective judgment analysis	3-D	Computed uncertainty in estimated O$_3$ concentrations due to uncertainties in over 100 input parameters that were estimated through elicitation of expert opinions.	(19, 20)
Green's function	0-D	Identified the most influential chemical reactions in photochemical smog production in terms of the sensitivities of pollutant concentrations with respect to rate constants and the sensitivities of one pollutant concentration at a specified time to concentrations of other pollutants at previous times. In addition, computed second-order sensitivity coefficients for exploring interdependencies between input parameters.	(80)
MC with Bayesian updating	1-D trajectory version of CIT	Used observations to modify uncertainties in input parameters, refined results of (89).	(85)
DDM	0-D	Compared alternative treatments of the organic chemistry kinetics using a formal gradient-based approach to compare three atmospheric chemical mechanisms. Computed sensitivities for O$_3$, H$_2$O$_2$, and HCHO.	(71)
Structural	0-D to 3-D	Summarized several modeling studies to compare urban ozone control. Examined uncertainty issues that arise when using VOC reactivity for ozone control.	(73)
DDM, BFM, and LHS	1-D and 3-D	Compared VOC reactivity changes determined in two models [3-D grid model and trajectory model used by Carter (96)] due to changes in VOC emission estimates. The emissions were changed by a fixed fraction, and the effect was determined using three metrics: peak O$_3$, population exposure, and spatial exposure.	(16)
Functional analysis	3-D	Functional sensitivities of an objective function were derived from sensitivity densities. Functional analysis was used to determine source-receptor relationships for acid deposition.	(63)

[a]0-D = single box, zero-dimensional model.
[b]3-D = gridded, three-dimensional model.
[c]1-D = column trajectory, one-dimensional model.

- Experience and methods are limited with respect to promising structural uncertainty assessment. Efforts to date have involved model-to-model comparisons and subjective analysis. Better theoretical understanding of structural sensitivity analysis in air quality modeling would greatly improve the reliability of models.

- Further work is needed to establish practical methods for using pertinent sensitivity/uncertainty analysis techniques to develop estimates of uncertainties associated with 3-D regional photochemical modeling results.

Although this summary highlights limitations associated with sensitivity analysis, such analyses are often the most expedient available. When conducted using a model that has undergone careful evaluation to identify and, where possible, to reduce or eliminate bias, sensitivity analysis may offer the best opportunity for understanding and estimating uncertainty.

V. DIAGNOSTIC ANALYSES

Overview

Diagnostic analyses are an important component of a comprehensive evaluation of air quality model performance (97, 98) and are carried out for two main purposes. When conducted in a prescriptive (or defined) manner, they provide insight into how well the modeling system represents particular physical or chemical reaction phenomena. Positive outcomes of such assessments help to bolster confidence in the modeling results. Equally important, indications that the modeling system is not simulating important phenomena adequately can help to direct subsequent efforts associated with the second type of diagnostic analyses aimed at rectifying model performance problems. In this case, the specific analyses undertaken depend on the nature of the modeling problem that has been encountered and the creativeness of the investigators in identifying the possible underlying causes based on the symptoms exhibited in the modeling results.

Diagnostic analyses evaluate modeled representations of particular phenomena that are known or thought to play key roles in influencing pollutant concentrations. Based on prevailing understanding and available measurements, specific analyses are designed and carried out to provide a quantitative determination of model performance in relation to the phenomena of concern. Analyses may involve the comparison of model variables, such as wind speeds and directions, temperatures, and ratios of selected pollutants with pertinent observations.

Diagnostic analyses should only be used to help point the way to modified treatments of atmospheric processes or model inputs based on sound scientific facts and representations. Particular care must be exercised in using such results to tune the model. In general, model tuning should be avoided. Scientific principals should determine how best to represent atmospheric processes and to develop model inputs.

Limitations of Available Measurement Data

Diagnostic analyses provide direct quantitative information concerning the representation of particular atmospheric phenomena in a PAQSM. The ability to assess the quality of representations is determined by the availability of pertinent measurements. The more suitable the available measurements, the more quantitative and substantive the assessment. If measurements are very limited or unavailable, then the assessments must of necessity be qualitative and based on the general knowledge of the investigator.

The data needed to support diagnostic analyses are generally only available through the conduct of special field measurement studies. Quantitative analyses will only be possible when such measurements are available. Routine measurement programs provide basic observations of surface pollutant concentrations and meteorological variables (such as wind velocity, temperature, and humidity) and are intended to fulfill regulatory requirements. They are not designed to provide information needed typically to support diagnostic analyses. Of particular concern is the general absence of air quality and meteorological data aloft. Detailed emissions data are rarely available with which to assess issues concerning the adequacy of the emissions inventory. Similarly, observations of dry deposition are rarely available.

When pertinent measurements are not available, analyses are formulated and assessed based on the general understanding of what may or may not be a reasonable representation of the phenomena of interest. For example, Jang et al. (21) applied process analysis techniques to obtain a better understanding of the high resolution version of the Regional Acid Deposition Model (HR-RADM) model results in the New York area. Although available pertinent measurements were limited, they were able to identify questionable behavior in the calculated pollutant concentrations.

Examples of Diagnostic Analyses

Four studies noted herein illustrate existing approaches for conducting diagnostic analyses. Jang et al. (21) applied process analysis techniques to investigate the effects of grid resolution on ozone formation chemistry. Chemical process analysis was used by Tonnesen & Wang (99) to examine a PAQSM applied to the Houston area. Roth et al. (100) and Vuilleumier et al. (101) provided examples of the types of diagnostic analyses that might be performed given the availability of extensive field measurements. And finally, a number of innovative analyses have been carried out in support of regulatory modeling in the northeastern United States (105–109).

PROCESS ANALYSIS TECHNIQUES   Jang et al. (21) studied the influence of grid resolution on calculated ozone levels in the New York area using the high-resolution version of a regional acid deposition model, HR-RADM. This model included provisions for producing detailed information on the contributions of key emissions, transport, and chemical reaction processes to calculated ozone levels. The technique is termed the integrated reaction rate/mass balance (IRR/MB) method, originally developed by Jeffries (102) to study chemical mechanisms. Details of the derivation are provided by Jeffries & Tonnesen (38). The technique was implemented in a trajectory model (103).

HR-RADM simulations for the northeastern United States were conducted for a multi-day ozone episode that occurred during the summer of 1988 using horizontal grid resolutions of 80, 40, and 20 km. The investigators noted peak ozone predictions near New York City that were 0.104 and 0.139 ppm using 80 km and 20 km grid resolutions, respectively. The IRR/MB method was used to investigate the ozone production processes at the two grid resolutions. The investigators were able to determine key differences between the 80 km and 20 km grid cases. They found that the interactions of chemistry and vertical transport, both competing for the emitted NO, was the cause of differences in results. This suggested that to improve model accuracy in calculating ozone formation, it was necessary to have adequate horizontal and vertical grid resolution and that the representation of the vertical transport process in the model needed a timescale corresponding to the relatively fast chemical reactions.

Tonnesen & Wang (99) discuss a more recent application of chemical process analysis to photochemical model simulations carried out in the Houston area. They conducted analyses to provide new insights into the chemical processes that affect ozone formation and to identify important sources for uncertainty. In particular, their analyses raised questions concerning the large fraction of NO_X emissions that were converted to inert HNO_3 during the nighttime N_2O_5 chemistry. There is a large uncertainty associated with the rate of this reaction, which in turn may have a significant influence on the responsiveness of the modeled ozone estimates to NO_X emissions changes. This could be quite important given the possible implementation of NO_X emission controls in the Houston area.

TECHNIQUES USING EXTENSIVE FIELD MEASUREMENTS   Extensive measurements were conducted in central California in the summer of 1990 as part of the SJVAQS/AUSPEX field measurement program to support a PAQSM application. DaMassa et al. (104) discussed the results of an operational evaluation of the modeling application. The SJVAQS/AUSPEX program provided a wealth of data with which to conduct diagnostic analyses of the meteorological, emissions, and air quality components of the modeling system.

Roth et al. (100) discussed the specification of process-related tests for a PAQSM. By constructing tests focusing on individual atmospheric processes, one can establish the accuracy of representation of these processes. If a particular model use is emphasized and requirements for accuracy of estimation are prescribed, "thresholds for acceptability of performance" of individual modules can be established through sensitivity analysis. Roth et al. (100) also introduced the concept of *thresholds triggering concern*, which connotes specified levels of bias in estimation which, if exceeded in performance, indicate the need for diagnosis of flaws and improvement in performance before the model can be tentatively accepted for use. A *stressfulness index* can be defined that describes the degree to which a model is forced to reveal flaws. The index provides a quantitative, albeit heuristic, measure of the degree of challenge offered a model through a suite of tests.

Roth et al. (100) developed a set of 24 questions for assessing the SJVAQS/AUSPEX Regional Mapping of Air Pollution (SARMAP) modeling system applied to the San Joaquin Valley, California. Two examples of these questions include:

- How well does the model simulate eddy circulation in the central and southern portions of the valley?
- Are ambient and emissions ratios of hydrocarbons to NO_x and CO to NO_x concentrations consistent?

Specific process-related tests were then derived to provide answers to each question. For each question, Roth et al. (100) provided commentary concerning the importance of the question, as well as a statement of the test, a specified threshold triggering concern, a brief discussion of the availability of data needed to support the proposed test, and an assessment of the feasibility of conducting a meaningful test.

Vuilleumier et al. (101) investigated sources of uncertainty in estimated photolysis reaction rates of NO_2 through comparisons with actual measured values from a chemical actinometer operated as part of the 1997 Southern California Ozone Study. The aerosol single scattering albedo was found to be a major source of uncertainty in the photolysis estimates, yielding biases between calculated and measured values ranging from 17%–36%.

A considerable body of analysis has been carried out to support regulatory modeling in the northeastern United States. For example, Hogrefe et al. (105–107) and Biswas et al. (108) demonstrate the application of spectral decomposition techniques to assess the ability of regional meteorological and air quality models to adequately represent observed intraday, diurnal, synoptic, and longer-term fluctuations in meteorological variables and primary and secondary pollutant concentrations. Using ambient pollutant measurements collected at the surface and by aircraft, Zhang et al. (109) examined the influence of high ozone trapped aloft at night on the temporal evolution as well as the peak ozone levels observed near the surface during the day.

Future Needs

To date, there is no formal guidance on how to conduct diagnostic analyses in a systematic manner. This may be reflective of the larger issue of the adequacy of aerometric databases available to support modeling. Until commitments to secure such databases are made, the possibilities for quantitative diagnostic analyses will be limited. Nevertheless, the application of process analysis to provide a general assessment of the representation of atmospheric processes in the modeling system is a viable alternative. Further effort is needed to develop guidelines for the implementation of such an approach and for the interpretation of the results.

Process-related tests employing available aerometric and emissions data provide another diagnostic assessment pathway. This approach is of particular value in cases for which a supplemental field measurement program has been implemented to provide a better characterization of key atmospheric processes. A design for such a testing program has been developed for model applications in central California. Actual implementation of the program is needed to assess the utility of the results and to provide guidance in how best to formulate extensions for application to other regions.

VI. CORROBORATIVE/ALTERNATIVE MODELING AND SUBJECTIVE JUDGMENT

Overview

Corroborative modeling analyses can play an important role in a comprehensive assessment of model performance by providing an independent means of assessing some aspect of the air quality model results, such as the likely influence of reducing emissions of VOCs or NO_X on ozone. Consistency of findings enhances confidence in the modeling results. An alternative modeling system might be applied that has been demonstrated to provide sound results in previous studies. The alternative base case approach provides a lower bound estimate of uncertainties in modeling results by using alternative sets of model inputs, each within its range of uncertainty. Finally, subjective judgment may be applied wherein the knowledge and experience of one or more individuals is employed to render an estimate of the uncertainty.

The utility of the information developed in the various corroborative approaches will depend on the methodology pursued and its applicability to the question of interest. Each approach to be considered must be evaluated a priori as to its merits. Yet, whatever the results, each will provide only partial information about the uncertainties of interest.

Subjective Judgment

Early efforts to query human judgments to support decision making and policy formulation resulted in the Delphi method (110, 111). Views of experts were solicited, summarized, and circulated in summary form among the same experts. The objective was to identify, resolve, and document differences—and iterate to a view that could be supported by all or most participants. In doing so, a fundamental constraint was to avoid creating an average or typical view.

Morgan & Henrion (9) recommended that expert elicitation be used to estimate uncertainties when needed, such as input parameter probability distributions for use in sensitivity/uncertainty simulations. Hanna et al. (20) pursued this course to evaluate uncertainties associated with modeling to identify emissions controls needed to attain the NAAQS for ozone in the eastern United States. As with most subjective methods, the following limitations pertain:

- Experts may differ substantially in their estimates, and those differences may be irresolvable due to insufficient available data.
- Experts have been and might be overconfident about the accuracy of their estimates of uncertainty.
- The estimates developed may be difficult to use.
- Because of questions surrounding their reliability, subjective uncertainty estimates may be disregarded in practice.

Nevertheless, expert judgment may be a welcome method for uncertainty estimation in the absence of feasible and reliable alternatives.

Corroborative Analyses

Corroborative analyses can provide an independent means of model evaluation (97, 98). Data analysis studies are an important source of information for corroborating model treatments of atmospheric processes and model results. Such studies can provide independent insights into the characteristics of key atmospheric phenomena. With such information, tests can be devised to assess the adequacy of model performance.

Another important avenue for corroborative analysis involves the application of observation-based methods. Such methods have been developed to determine if, for a region or subregion, VOC or NO_x controls are likely to be most effective in reducing ozone concentrations. For example, Blanchard et al. (112) use NO, NO_y, and O_3 data collected at the same location as input to a simple algebraic model described in Johnson & Azzi (113) to determine if VOC or NO_x control is preferable. Example applications of this procedure are provided in Blanchard et al. (114–116).

Developed by the Aeronomy Laboratory of the National Oceanic and Atmospheric Administration (117), a second approach relies on the use of a correlation between peak ozone and NO_y concentration. If an area is NO_x limited, NO_y and peak O_3 should correlate. If the area is VOC limited, they should not. Both procedures rely on the use of NO_y and O_3 data to make the necessary calculations, depend on data analysis alone, and bypass the need for modeling and compilation of an emissions estimate. However, accurate measurement of NO_y is quite difficult.

Cardelino & Chameides (118) use an observation-based model to describe O_3 production in terms of its precursors by employing the concept of relative incremental reactivity. Box model calculations are made to determine the amount of O_3 produced in daylight hours at specific sites, as well as the sensitivity of O_3 production to changes in precursor levels. An incremental reactivity is defined in terms of the O_3-forming potential difference for an assumed incremental change in the ratio of the precursor concentration and the integrated amount of precursor emitted or transported to each site. The method identifies four regimes of O_3 formation that range from NO_x limitation to VOC limitation and segregate the VOC into natural and anthropogenic contributions. Extensive discussions of the application of several contemporary observation-based analysis approaches are provided by Blanchard, Kleinman, and Trainer et al. (119–121).

Alternative modeling approaches may also be adopted in a corroborative manner. For example, an alternative prognostic meteorological model might be employed to develop meteorological inputs. Or, simulations might be conducted using a second air quality model that provides somewhat different treatments of one or more atmospheric processes. A good example of such an approach is being carried out to support SIP-related activities in the Houston area. Meteorological fields have been developed using three different meteorological models: Systems Applications International Mesoscale Meteorological Model (SAIMM), National Center for Atmospheric Research/Pennsylvania State University Meteorology Model (MM5), and Regional Atmospheric Modeling System (RAMS). In addition, air quality simulations have been conducted using two air quality models: Comprehensive Air Quality Model extended version (CAMx) and Community Multiscale Air Quality Model (CMAQ). Motivation for such efforts is related to the difficulties encountered in accurately simulating occurrences of high ozone concentrations. The ability to adequately simulate the complex meteorological phenomena that occur in the area continues to be a challenge. In addition, there is some evidence that highly reactive VOC emissions may be underestimated. Thus, efforts were undertaken to develop suitable adjustments to the estimate as an interim measure until more accurate emissions data are obtained. Documentation prepared by the Texas Commission on Environmental Quality discusses the various alternative modeling efforts (122).

A similar analysis for the northeastern United States using both MM5 and RAMS meteorological fields as inputs to the Variable Grid Urban Airshed Model (UAM-V) model is discussed by Biswas & Rao (123). While neither modeling system provided significantly better ozone performance, model-to-model and episode-to-episode differences were noted in individual grid cells with regard to the impacts of precursor emission reductions on calculated ozone levels.

Another corroborative approach is the concept of alternative base case (ABC) analysis (124, 125). The central premise of ABC analysis is that there are many combinations of model inputs that will produce model estimates—ozone concentrations as a function of location and time—that are similar and, in fact, are indistinguishable in accuracy within the error bounds accompanying the estimates. Possible combinations of alternative input settings are derived from an assessment of the uncertainties in each of the key input variables. Consideration is also given to the manner in which inputs were developed, particularly possible sources of compensating errors. The elements of ABC and sensitivity/uncertainty analysis (discussed in Section IV) have some common traits.

In a hypothetical and simple case of two sets of conditions [(*a*) VOC emissions, E_1, and VOC boundary conditions, B_1, and (*b*) VOC emissions, E_2, and VOC boundary conditions, B_2, and all other conditions the same as for case 1], estimated ozone concentrations as a function of time may be quite similar, with differences of the order of estimated measurement uncertainties. This situation can arise when the total loading of VOCs (initial conditions, boundary conditions, and emissions) is about the same magnitude, with similar spatial and temporal distributions for both cases. In practical applications, it may be possible to identify several sets of conditions that produce like outputs. Each may merit being accorded the status of base or reference case; selection becomes arbitrary. ABC analysis encourages identification of as many alternative base cases as possible. If five cases emerge from analysis, then each can be used as a reference case for examining emissions control strategies. Five results will be generated, and their spread in magnitude constitutes a lower bound on uncertainty in estimation of future ozone concentrations. If another ABC were to be identified, it can only increase (or maintain) the spread in outcomes. ABC analysis can be quite powerful, particularly in demonstrating the range of potential future outcomes for alternative model input conditions that are indistinguishable for a given data base.

To carry out such assessments, it is necessary to identify one or more suitable corroborative analysis approaches, such as those described above. Then a pertinent set of PAQSM results must be obtained that can be related to those produced by the selected analysis approach(es). After the appropriate analyses and model simulations are carried out, the consistency of the results must be determined. Further diagnostic and evaluation studies may be needed if the PAQSM results are not corroborated by the independent analyses.

Potential Uses Within Current Regulatory Context

Corroborative analysis approaches provide supplemental information that may confirm the findings of PAQSMs. In this context, they may contribute to weight of evidence arguments while helping to build confidence in findings. Equally important, the supplemental information may raise questions that motivate further diagnostic assessments before PAQSM findings are confirmed.

The utility of information derived from subjective judgment is dependent on the relevance of the experience of the participants. The information may be quite germane, or it may be incorrect and misleading.

Observation-based approaches can provide information within the range of circumstances represented by the available observation set. However, extrapolation beyond the range of existing conditions will involve considerable uncertainty. Consequently, observation-based methods have limited ability to estimate accurately the effects of emissions controls that significantly alter precursor emissions. They may be best suited for confirming PAQSM indications of the general directional effects of VOC and/or NO_x controls on ozone levels.

Application of sophisticated alternative modeling approaches can provide quantitative information about modeling uncertainties, especially when interpreted in the context of alternative base case analysis. However, if some aspect of the model is flawed, such as the meteorological or emissions inputs, then the resulting information will be of little value and possibly misleading.

Over the past several years, considerable effort has been devoted to developing and applying various corroborative analysis approaches. Although existing regulatory modeling guidance recognizes the potential value of such approaches, further effort is needed to clarify the range of applicability of each approach and to indicate how such information can be related to quantitative estimates of uncertainties associated with PAQSM results.

VII. LOOKING TO THE FUTURE

Several observations derive from review of the literature and knowledge of applications of photochemical models in air quality analysis.

1. Uncertainties pervade the use of models. Consequently, a range of model estimates may be anticipated for a given set of inputs and their associated uncertainties. Thus, estimates of uncertainties should be made and factored into processes involving model-based decision-making associated with air quality issues.

2. Methods available today that are truly useful either partially address the estimation need or focus on a defined, limited part of the problem. Unfortunately, no method is now available for estimating uncertainty in modeling that is comprehensive in scope.

3. A comprehensive method for analyzing uncertainty information would (*a*) propagate uncertainty from each component of the modeling system through the system into an estimate of uncertainty associated with model output, (*b*) elucidate bias, and (*c*) account for variability. The method would also synthesize and integrate results from the various methods employed to estimate uncertainty comprehensively. The products of a comprehensive uncertainty assessment would be distributions or probabilistic statements characterizing the uncertainty of model estimates.

4. Developing a comprehensive approach to uncertainty analysis would be very valuable. Its feasibility should be assessed. Such an approach may not be possible, because nothing in the literature suggests so.

5. In practical applications, visual inspection of plots of concentration versus time for pollutant species of interest provides adequate information to determine if model performance is sufficiently acceptable to merit proceeding with comprehensive uncertainty assessment. In many cases, model performance is wanting. Where performance is unacceptable, major flaws in the model should be corrected prior to obtaining uncertainty information.

6. Sensitivity/uncertainty analysis is by far the most frequently used method for estimating uncertainty. Its focus is on the response of dependent variables to changes in inputs. When the response is significant, uncertainty is likely to be important; when the response is small, the converse is expected.

Sensitivity analysis does not address bias as an element in uncertainty explicitly. Generally, it is not suited for this use, because the main assumption made is that the model is substantially correct in its representation of reality.

7. As the key element of a comprehensive assessment of uncertainty, the development and application of methods for identifying, estimating, and reducing biases (i.e., mitigating or eliminating flaws in model representations) should be made a priority. This includes determining when bias is present, how to identify it, and what to do when it corrupts modeling results. Through assessment of bias, model formulation may be improved to increase the probability that the model is performing acceptably well for the right reasons and that modeled sensitivities are reliable. Examining the issue of potential bias typically requires case-specific procedures.

8. In addition to the evaluation of bias, natural and human-induced variability should receive attention in the comprehensive estimation of uncertainty. Some deterministic modeling formulations may simulate well-characterized stochastic processes using statistical sampling techniques, whereas others, such as those used to derive meteorological inputs, are incapable of simulating stochastic processes. The appropriateness and feasibility of developing stochastic models merits attention because they are potentially attractive means for incorporating variability.

9. Designing a comprehensive approach to uncertainty assessment that can be implemented and that addresses bias and variability requires a major research effort. To date, no such effort has been formulated, let alone undertaken. Rather, the focus has been on portions of the problem, in the absence of a more encompassing plan that might foster a more integrated research program design.

ACKNOWLEDGMENT

This research was supported by the Assistant Secretary for Fossil Energy, Office of Natural Gas and Petroleum Technology, through the National Petroleum Technology Office under U.S. Department of Energy Contract No. DE-AC03-76SF00098.

The *Annual Review of Environment and Resources* is online at
http://environ.annualreviews.org

LITERATURE CITED

1. US Environ. Prot. Agency. 2002. *National Air Quality and Emissions Trends Report, 2000, Appendix A, Tables A-15, A-19*. Research Triangle Park, NC: US EPA, Off. Air Qual. Plan. Stand.
2. Natl. Res. Counc. 1991. *Rethinking the Ozone Problem in Urban and Regional Air Pollution*. Washington, DC: Natl. Acad.
3. Off. Technol. Assess. 1989. *Catching Our Breath: Next Steps for Reducing Urban Ozone*. Washington, DC: OTA

4. N. Am. Res. Strategy Tropospheric Ozone. 2000. Chapter 4: the air-quality modeling system. In *An Assessment of Tropospheric Ozone Pollution: A North American Perspective*. Palo Alto, CA: Electric Power Res. Inst./NARSTO
5. Am. Pet. Inst. 1989. *Detailed Analysis of Ozone State Implementation Plans in Seven Areas Selected for Retrospective Evaluation of Reasons for State Implementation Plan Failure.* Washington, DC: API, Health Environ. Sci. Dep.
6. Stokey E, Zeckhauser R. 1978. *A Primer for Policy Analysis.* New York: Norton
7. US Environ. Prot. Agency. 1996. *Guidance on the Use of Modeled Results to Demonstrate Attainment of the Ozone NAAQS.* Research Triangle Park, NC: US EPA, Off. Air Qual. Plan. Stand.
8. Calif. Air Resour. Board. 1992. *Technical Guidance Document: Photochemical Modeling.* Calif. EPA, Calif. Air Resour. Board., Sacramento, CA
9. Morgan MG, Henrion M. 1990. *Uncertainty: A Guide to Dealing with Uncertainty in Quantitative Risk and Policy Analysis.* New York: Cambridge Univ. Press
10. Deleted in proof
11. Cleary R. 1976. Mathematical Models. In *Boundaries of Analysis.* Cambridge, MA: Ballinger
12. Russell A. 1997. Regional photochemical air quality modeling: model formulations, history, and state of the science. *Annu. Rev. Energy Environ.* 22:537–88
13. Seinfeld J, Pandis S. 1998. *Atmospheric Chemistry and Physics: From Air Pollution to Climate Change.* New York: Wiley
14. Milford JB, Russell AG, McRae GJ. 1989. A new approach to photochemical pollution control: implications of spatial patterns in pollutant responses to reductions in nitrogen oxides and reactive organic gas emissions. *Environ. Sci. Technol.* 23:1290–301
15. Milford JB, Gao D, Sillman S, Blossey P, Russell AG. 1994. Total reactive nitrogen (NO_y) as an indicator of the sensitivity of ozone to reductions in hydrocarbon and NO_x emissions. *J. Geophys. Res.* 99:3533–42
16. Bergin MS, Russell AG, Milford JB. 1995. Quantification of individual VOC reactivity using a chemically detailed, three-dimensional photochemical model. *Environ. Sci. Technol.* 29:3029–37
17. Bergin MS, Russell AG, Milford JB. 1998. Effects of chemical mechanism uncertainties on the reactivity quantification of volatile organic compounds using a three-dimensional air quality model. *Environ. Sci. Technol.* 5:694–703
18. Yang YJ, Wilkinson JG, Russell AG. 1997. Fast, direct sensitivity analysis of multidimensional photochemical models. *Environ. Sci. Technol.* 31:2859–68
19. Hanna SR, Chang JC, Fernau ME. 1998. Monte Carlo estimates of uncertainties in predictions by a photochemical grid model (UAM-IV) due to uncertainties in input variables. *Atmos. Environ.* 32:3619–28
20. Hanna SR, Lu Z, Frey HC, Wheeler N, Vukuvich J, et al. 2001. Uncertainties in predicted ozone concentrations due to input uncertainties for the UAM-V photochemical grid model applied to the July 1995 OTAG domain. *Atmos. Environ.* 35(5):891–903
21. Jang J-CC, Jeffries HE, Tonnesen S. 1995. Sensitivity of ozone to model grid resolution—II. Detailed process analysis for ozone chemistry. *Atmos. Environ.* 29:3101–14
22. Marr L, Black D, Harley R. 2002. Formation of photochemical air pollution in Central California: 1. Development of a revised motor vehicle emission inventory. *J. Geophys. Res.* 107 (D6): 4047; doi:10.1029/2001JD000689
23. Marr L. 2002. Changes in ozone sensitivity to precursor emissions on diurnal, weekly and decadal time scales. In *Civil and Environmental Engineering*. Berkeley: Univ. Calif.

24. Pierson W, Gertler A, Bradow R. 1990. Comparison of the SCAQS tunnel study with other on-road vehicle emissions data. *J. Air Waste Manag.* 40:1495–504
25. Harley R, Sawyer R, Milford J. 1997. Updated photochemical modeling for California's south coast air basin: comparison of chemical mechanisms and motor vehicle emissions inventories. *Environ. Sci. Technol.* 31:135–54
26. Sawyer R, Harley R, Cadle S, Norbeck J, Slott R, et al. 2000. Mobile sources critical review: 1998 NARSTO Assessment. *Atmos. Environ.* 34:2161–81
27. Geron C, Guenther A, Pierce T. 1994. An improved model for estimating emissions of volatile organic compounds from forests in the eastern United States. *J. Geophys. Res.* 99:12773–91
28. Simpson D, Guenther A, Hewitt C, Steinbrecher R. 1995. Biogenic emissions in Europe. 1. Estimates and uncertainties. *J. Geophys. Res.* 100:22875–90
29. Matson P. 1997. NOx emission from soils and its consequences for the atmosphere and biosphere—critical gaps and research directions for the future. *Nutr. Cycl. Agroecosyst.* 48:1–6
30. Lamanna MS, Goldstein AH. 1999. In situ measurements of C2–C10 volatile organic compounds above a Sierra Nevada ponderosa pine plantation. *J. Geophys. Res.* 104:21,247–62
31. Schade G, Goldstein A, Lamana M. 1999. Are monoterpene emissions influenced by humidity? *Geophys. Res. Lett.* 26:2187–90
32. Russell A, Dennis R. 2000. NARSTO critical review of photochemical models and modeling. *Atmos. Environ.* 34:2283–324
33. Stauffer D, Seaman N. 1990. Use of four dimensional data assimilation in a limited area mesoscale, part I: experiments with synoptic data. *Mon. Weather Rev.* 118:1250–77
34. Vuilleumier L, Harley RA, Brown NJ, Slusser JR, Kolinski D, et al. 2001. Variability in ultraviolet total optical depth during the Southern California ozone study (SCOS97). *Atmos. Environ.* 35:1111–22
35. Vuilleumier L, Brown NJ, Harley RA, Reynolds SD. 2000. *Review and Improvement of Methods for Estimating Rates of Photolysis in Photochemical Models.* Vol. II: *User's Guide for TUVAQM Radiative Transfer and Photolysis Module.* Berkeley: Lawrence Berkeley Natl. Lab.
36. Lurmann F, Carter W, Coyner L. 1987. *A Surrogate Species Chemical Reaction Mechanism for Urban-Scale Air Quality Simulation Models*, Vols. I, II. Research Triangle Park, NC: US Environ. Prot. Agency
37. Gery MW, Whitten GZ, Killus JP, Dodge MC. 1989. A photochemical kinetics mechanism for urban and regional scale computer modeling. *J. Geophys. Res.* 94:12,925–56
38. Jeffries HE, Tonnesen S. 1994. A comparison of two photochemical reaction mechanisms using a mass balance and process analysis. *Atmos. Environ.* 28:2991–3003
39. Dennis R, Byun D, Novak J, Galluppi K, Coats C, et al. 1996. The next generation of integrated air quality modeling: EPA's Models-3. *Atmos. Environ.* 30:1925–38
40. Byun DW, Coats CJ, Hwang D, Fine S, Odman T, et al. 1995. Prototyping and implementation of multiscale air quality models for high performance computing. Presented at High Perform. Comput. Symp. 1995: Grand Chall. Comput. Simul. *Proc. 1995 Simul. Multiconf., Phoenix, AZ*, April 9–13, ed. AM Tentner, pp. 527–32. San Diego, CA: Soc. Comput. Simul.
41. Morris R, Myer T, Douglas S, Yocke M, Mirabella V. 1991. *Development of a nested-grid urban airshed model and application to Southern California.* Presented at 84th Natl. Air Waste Manag. Assoc. Meet., Vancouver, Can., June 16–21
42. Odman M, Russell A. 1991. Multiscale modeling of pollutant transport with chemistry. *J. Geophys. Res.* 96:7363–70

43. Wesely ML, Hicks BB. 2000. A review of the current status of knowledge on dry deposition. *Atmos. Environ.* 34:2261–82
44. Seaman NL. 2000. Meteorological modeling for air-quality assessments. *Atmos. Environ.* 34:2231–59
45. Dabdub D, Seinfeld JH. 1995. Extrapolation techniques used in the solution of stiff ODEs associated with chemical kinetics of air quality models. *Atmos. Environ.* 29:403–10
46. Winner DA, Cass GR. 1999. Modeling the long-term frequency distribution of regional ozone concentrations. *Atmos. Environ.* 33:431–51
47. Winner DA, Cass GR. 2001. Modeling the long-term frequency distribution of regional ozone concentrations using synthetic meteorology. *Environ. Sci. Technol.* 35:3718–26
48. Guinnup D, Collom B, cochairm . 1997. *Final Rep., Vol. I. Exec. Summ*: *OTAG Air Qual. Anal. Workgr.*, Ozone Transp. Assess. Group
49. Roth P, Tesche T, Reynolds S, Seinfeld J. 1997. *A Critical Review of Regulatory Air Quality Modeling for Tropospheric Ozone.* Washington, DC: Am. Pet. Inst. for NARSTO
50. US Environ. Prot. Agency. 1986. *Guideline on Air Quality Models (Revised).* Research Triangle Park, NC: US EPA. EPA-450/2-78-027R
50a. US Environ. Prot. Agency. 1987. *Guideline on Air Quality Models, Suppl. A.* Research Triangle Park, NC: US EPA. EPA-450/2-78-027R-A
51. US Environ. Prot. Agency. 1991. *Guideline for Regulatory Application of the Urban Airshed Model.* Research Triangle Park, NC: US EPA
52. US Environ. Prot. Agency. 1992. *Protocol for Determining the Best Performing Model.* Research Triangle Park, NC: US EPA, Off. Air Qual. Plan. Stand.
53. US Environ. Prot. Agency. 1993. *User's Guide for the Urban Airshed Model*, Vol. IV. Research Triangle Park, NC: US EPA, Off. Air Qual. Plan. Stand.
54. Deleted in proof
55. US Environ. Prot. Agency. 1993. *Guidance for Growth Factors, Projections and Control Strategies for the 15 Percent Rate-of-Progress Plans.* Research Triangle Park, NC: US EPA
56. US Environ. Prot. Agency. 1997. *Guidance for Emissions Inventory Development.* Research Triangle Park, NC: US EPA
57. US Environ. Prot. Agency. 1999. *Emissions Inventory Guidance for Implementation of Ozone and Particulate Matter National Ambient Air Quality Standards (NAAQS) and Regional Haze Regulations.* Research Triangle Park, NC: US EPA, Off. Air Qual. Plan. Stand.
58. Sistla G, Zhou N, Hao W, Ku J-Y, Rao ST, et al. 1996. Effects of uncertainties in meteorological inputs on urban airshed model predictions and ozone control strategies. *Atmos. Environ.* 30:2011–25
59. Roth P. 1999. A qualitative approach to evaluating the anticipated reliability of a photochemical air quality simulation model for a selected application. *J. Air Waste Mgmt. Assoc.* 49:1050–59
60. Woodward CS, Grant KE, Maxwell R. 2002. Applications of sensitivity analysis to uncertainty quantification for variably saturated flow. In *Computational Methods in Water Resources*, Vol. 1, ed. SM Hassanizadeh, RJ Schotting, WG Gray, GF Pinder, pp. 73–80. Amsterdam: Elsevier
61. Grant K, Woodward CS, Serban R, Brown PN, Maxwell R, et al. 2002. Sensitivity analysis based uncertainty estimation. Lawrence Livermore Natl. Lab. Tech. Rep. UCRL-PRES-150160, Dec.
62. Chang J, Brown NJ. 1996. Quantum functional sensitivity analysis of the $D + H_2$ reaction rate coefficient via the separable rotation approximation. *J. Chem. Phys.* 100:17740–55
63. Cho S-Y, Carmichael G, Rabitz H. 1988. Relationship between primary emissions

and regional air quality and acid deposition in Eulerian models determined by sensitivity analysis. *Water Air Soil Pollut.* 40:9–13
64. Tilden JW, Costanza V, McRae GJ, Seinfeld JH. 1981. Modeling of Chemical Reaction Systems, ed. KH Ebert, P Deuflhard, W Jager, pp. 69–91. Berlin: Springer-Verlag
65. Cukier RI, Levine HB, Shuler KE. 1978. Nonlinear sensitivity analysis of multi-parameter model systems. *Int. J. Chem. Kinet.* 11:1137–62
66. Rabitz H, Kramer M, Dacol D. 1983. Sensitivity analysis in chemical kinetics. *Annu. Rev. Phys. Chem.* 34:419–61
67. Iman RL, Conover WJ. 1982. A distribution-free approach to inducing rank correlation among input variables. *Commun. Stat.* B11:311–34
68. Iman RL, Conover WJ. 1982. Sensitivity analysis techniques: self-teaching curriculum. In *Nuclear Regul. Commission Rep., NUREG/CR-2350.* Albuquerque, NM: Sandia Natl. Lab.
69. Iman RL, Shortencarier MJ. 1984. A FORTRAN 77 program and user's guide for the generation of Latin hypercube and random samples for use with computer models. In *Nuclear Regul. Commission Rep., NUREG/CR-3624.* Albuquerque, NM: Sandia Natl. Lab.
70. Iman RL, Helton JC. 1985. *A Comparison of Sensitivity Analysis Techniques for Computer Models.* Livermore, CA: Sandia Natl. Lab.
71. Milford JB, Gao D, Russell AG, McRae GJ. 1992. Use of sensitivity analysis to compare chemical mechanisms for air-quality modeling. *Environ. Sci. Technol.* 26:1179–89
72. Kuhn M, Builtjes PJH, Poppe D, Simpson D, Stockwell WR, et al. 1998. Intercomparison of the gas-phase chemistry in several chemistry and transport models. *Atmos. Environ.* 32:693–709
73. Russell AG, Milford JB, Bergin MS, McBride SJ, McNair LA, et al. 1995. Urban ozone control and atmospheric reactivity of organic gases. *Science* 269:491–95
74. Hamby DM. 1994. A review of techniques for parameter sensitivity analysis of environmental models. *Environ. Monit. Assess.* 32:135–54
75. Dunker AM. 1981. Efficient calculation of sensitivity coefficients for complex atmospheric models. *Atmos. Environ.* 15:1155–61
76. Dunker AM. 1984. The decoupled direct method for calculating sensitivity coefficients in chemical kinetics. *J. Chem. Phys.* 81:2385–93
77. Dunker A, Yarwood G, Ortmann JP, Wilson GM. 2002. The decoupled direct method for sensitivity analysis in a three-dimensional air quality model—Implementation, accuracy and efficiency. *Environ. Sci. Technol.* 36:2965–76
78. Bischof C, Carle A, Corliss G, Griewank A, Hovland P. 1992. *ADIFOR Generating Derivative Codes from FORTRAN Programs.* Argonne, IL: Argonne Natl. Lab.
79. Bischof C, Carle A, Khademi P, Mauer A. 1994. *The ADIFOR2.0 System for the Automatic Differentiation of FORTRAN 77 Programs.* Argonne, IL: Argonne Natl. Lab.
80. Vuilleumier L, Harley R, Brown N. 1997. First- and second-order sensitivity analysis of a photochemically reactive system (a Green's Function approach). *Environ. Sci. Technol.* 31:1206–17
81. Elbern H, Schmidt H. 1999. A four-dimensional variational chemistry data assimilation scheme for Eulerian chemistry transport modeling. *J. Geophys. Res.* 104:18,583–98
82. Cukier RI, Fortuin CM, Shuler KE, Petschek AG, Schaibly JH. 1973. Study of the sensitivity of coupled reaction systems to uncertainties in rate coefficients. *J. Chem. Phys.* 59:3873–78
83. McKay MD, Beckman RJ, Conover WJ. 1979. A comparison of three methods for selecting values of input variables in the

analysis of output from a computer code. *Technometrics* 21:239–45
84. Tatang MA, Pan W, Prinn RG, McRae GJ. 1997. An efficient method for parametric uncertainty analysis of numerical geophysical models. *J. Geophys. Res.* 102:21,925–32
85. Bergin MS, Milford JB. 2000. Application of Bayesian Monte Carlo analysis to a Lagrangian photochemical air quality model. *Atmos. Environ.* 34:781–92
86. Hansen A. 2000. *Uncertainties in predicted ozone concentrations due to input uncertainties for the UAM-V photochemical grid model applied to the July 1995 OTAG domain.* Palo Alto, CA/St. Louis, MO: Electr. Power Res. Inst.
87. Gao D, Stockwell WR, Milford JB. 1995. First-order sensitivity and uncertainty analysis for a regional-scale gas-phase chemical mechanism. *J. Geophys. Res.* 100:23153–66
88. Gao D, Stockwell WR, Milford JB. 1996. Global uncertainty analysis of a region-scale gas-phase chemical mechanism. *J. Geophys. Res.* 101:9107–19
89. Bergin MS, Noblet GS, Petrini K, Dhieux JR, Milford JB, et al. 1999. Formal uncertainty analysis of a Lagrangian photochemical air pollution model. *Environ. Sci. Technol.* :1116–26
90. Stockwell WR, Milford JB, Gao D, Yang YJ. 1995. The effect of acetyl peroxy-peroxy radial reactions on peroxyacetyl nitrate and ozone concentrations. *Atmos. Environ.* 29:1591–99
91. Yang YJ, Stockwell WR, Milford JB. 1995. Uncertainties in incremental reactivities of volatile organic compounds. *Environ. Sci. Technol.* 29:1336–45
92. Yang YJ, Stockwell WR, Milford JB. 1996. Effect of chemical product yield uncertainties on reactivities of VOCs and emissions from reformulated gasolines and methanol fuels. *Environ. Sci. Technol.* 30:1392–97
93. Falls AH, McRae GJ, Seinfeld JH. 1979. Sensitivity and uncertainty analysis for a regional-scale gas-phase chemical mechanism. *Int. J. Chem. Kinet.* 11:1137–62
94. Milford JB, Gao D, Zafirakou A, Pierce T. 1994. Ozone precursor levels and responses to emissions reductions; analysis of regional oxidant model results. *Atmos. Environ.* 28:2093–104
95. McBride SJ, Oravetz MA, Russell AG. 1997. Cost-benefit and uncertainty issues in using organic reactivity to regulate urban ozone. *Environ. Sci. Technol.* 31:238A–44A
96. Carter WPL. 1994. Development of ozone reactivity scales for volatile organic compounds. *J. Air Waste Manag. Assoc.* 44:881–99
97. Reynolds SD, Roth PM, Tesche TW. 1992. *Guidance for evaluating photochemical model performance.* Presented at Air & Waste Manag. Assoc. 85th Annu. Meet. Exhib., Kansas City, MO, June 21–26
98. Reynolds SD, Roth PM, Tesche TW. 1994. *A Process for Stressful Evaluation of Photochemical Model Performance.* San Rafael, CA: Envair
99. Tonnesen G, Wang Z. 2001. *Interim rep.: evaluation of TNRCC SIP modeling using a chemical process analysis.* Univ. Calif. Irvine
100. Roth PM, Reynolds SD, Blanchard CL. 1998. *Protocol for Evaluating the Performance of the SARMAP Model.* San Anselmo: Envair
101. Vuilleumier L, Bamer JT, Harley RA, Brown NJ. 2001. Evaluation of nitrogen dioxide photolysis rates in an urban area using data from the 1997 Southern California ozone study. *Atmos. Environ.* 35:6525–37
102. Jeffries HE. 1984. *A Photochemical Reaction Mechanism Analysis Method Applied to Two Mechanisms.* Chapel Hill: Univ. North Carolina
103. Crouse RR. 1990. *Integrated reaction rate analysis of ozone prediction in a photochemical oxidant model.* Diss. Master,

Dep. Environ. Sci./Eng., Univ. N.C., Chapel Hill
104. DaMassa J, Tanrikulu S, Magliano K, Ranzieri A, Niccum L. 1996. *Performance Evaluation of SAQM in Central California and Attainment Demonstration for the August 3–6, 1990 Ozone Episode.* Sacramento: Calif. Air Resour. Board.
105. Hogrefe C, Rao ST, Kasibhatla P, Kallos G, Tremback CJ, et al. 2001. Evaluating the performance of regional-scale photochemical modeling systems: Part I, meteorological predictions. *Atmos. Environ.* 35:4159–74
106. Hogrefe C, Rao ST, Zurbenko IG, Porter PS. 2000. Interpreting the information in ozone observations and model predictions relevant to regulatory policies in the eastern United States. *Bull. Am. Meteorol. Soc.* 81:2083–106
107. Hogrefe C, Rao ST, Kasibhatla P, Hao W, Sistla G, et al. 2001. Evaluating the performance of regional-scale photochemical modeling systems: Part II, ozone predictions. *Atmos. Environ.* 35:4175–88
108. Biswas J, Hogrefe C, Rao ST, Hao W, Sistla G. 2001. Evaluating the performance of regional-scale photochemical modeling systems. Part III, precursor predictions. *Atmos. Environ.* 35:6129–49
109. Zhang J, Rao ST, Daggupaty SM. 1998. Meteorological processes and ozone exceedances in the northeastern United States during the 12–16 July 1995 episode. *J. Appl. Meteorol.* 37:776–89
110. Helmer O. 1963. *The Systematic Use of Expert Judgment in Operations Research.* Santa Monica: Rand Corp.
111. Dalkey N. 1968. *The Delphi Method: An Experimental Study of Group Opinion.* Santa Monica: Rand Corp.
112. Blanchard CL, Lurmann FW, Korc M, Roth PM. 1994. *The Use of Ambient Data to Corroborate Analyses of Ozone Control Strategies.* Research Triangle Park, NC: US EPA
113. Johnson GM, Azzi M. 1992. *Notes on the Derivation: The Integrated Empirical Rate Model (V2.2).* North Ryde, NSW, Aust.: CSIRO Div. Coal Energy Technol.
114. Blanchard CL, Roberts PT, Chinkin LR, Roth PM. 1995. *Application of smog production (SP) algorithms to the Coastal Oxidant Assessment for Southeast Texas (COAST) data.* Pap. 95-TP15.04 Presented at the Air Waste Manag. Assoc. 88th Annu. Meet. Exhib., San Antonio, TX, June 18–23
115. Blanchard CL, Roth PM, Tannenbaum SJ. 1997. *Development of a Method for Determining if the Control of VOC or NO_x Is Likely to Be More Effective for Reducing Ozone Concentrations.* Washington, DC: Am. Pet. Inst.
116. Blanchard CL, Lurmann FW, Roth PM, Jeffries HE, Korc M. 1999. The use of ambient data to corroborate analyses of ozone control strategies. *Atmos. Environ.* 33:369–81
117. Trainer M, Parrish D, Buhr M, Norton R, Fehsenfeld F, et al. 1993. Correlation of ozone with NO_y in photochemically aged air. *J. Geophys. Res.* 98:2917–26
118. Cardelino CA, Chameides WL. 1995. An observation-based method for analyzing ozone precursor relationships in the urban atmosphere. *J. Air Waste Manag.* 45:161–80
119. Blanchard CL. 2000. Ozone process insights from field experiments. Part III: extent of reaction and ozone formation. *Atmos. Environ.* 34:2035–43
120. Kleinman LI. 2000. Ozone process insights from field experiments. Part II: observation-based analysis for ozone production. *Atmos. Environ.* 34:2023–33
121. Trainer M, Parrish DD, Goldan PD, Roberts J, Fehsenfeld FC. 2000. Review of observation-based analysis of the regional factors influencing ozone concentrations. *Atmos. Environ.* 34:2045–61
122. Texas Comm. Environ. Qual. 2002. *Revisions to the State Implementation Plan (SIP) for the Control of Ozone Air Pollution: Post-1999 Rate-of-Progress and Attainment Demonstration Follow-up SIP*

for the Houston/Galveston Ozone Nonattainment Area. Austin: TCEQ

123. Biswas J, Rao ST. 2001. Uncertainties in episodic ozone modeling stemming from uncertainties in the meteorological fields. *J. Appl. Meteorol.* 40:117–36

124. Reynolds S, Michaels H, Roth P, Tesche TW, McNally D, et al. 1994. *The Importance of Using Alternative Base Cases in Photochemical Modeling.* Washington, DC: Am. Pet. Inst.

125. Reynolds S, Michaels H, Roth P, Tesche T, McNally D, et al. 1996. Alternative base cases in photochemical modeling: their construction, role, and value. *Atmos. Environ.* 30:1977–98

Transport of Energy, Information, and Material Through the Biosphere

William A. Reiners and Kenneth L. Driese
*Department of Botany and Wyoming Geographic Information Science Center
University of Wyoming, Laramie, Wyoming 82071; email: reiners@uwyo.edu,
kdriese@uwyo.edu*

■ **Abstract** A variety of transport processes operate within the biosphere at all temporal and spatial scales. Temporary events or chronic conditions, both scale-dependent, instigate the transport of entities having material, energetic, or informational properties via several different transport vectors. The fluxes and influences imparted by these transport phenomena shape the physical environment, underlie gene flow, facilitate animal communication, and constrain the nature of local systems. These transport phenomena have been highly altered in the last century as humankind has become an ever more potent force in the earth system. As a result, issues of environmental and earth system science are, to a considerable extent, aspects of transport phenomena. A general appreciation for transport phenomena, broadly defined, is vital to gaining an appropriate perspective on the fluid nature of the earth system and to defining system structure and function through present and past events.

CONTENTS

INTRODUCTION	108
CONCEPTUAL ORGANIZATION OF FLOWS AND MOVEMENTS	108
Flows and Movements as Propagations	108
KINDS OF PROPAGATIONS	113
Diffusion: Transport by Random Movements	113
Fluvial Transport: Propagation by Running Waters	114
Colluvial Transport: Mass Movement Through the Action of Gravity	115
Glacial Transport: Movement by Ice Masses	117
Sedimentation: Propagation by Particle Settling in Fluids	117
Lake and Ocean Currents	119
Wind Transport: Transport by Currents of the Atmosphere	121
Light: Propagation Through the Electromagnetic Spectrum	122
Sound: Propagation Through Acoustics	123
Animal Locomotion	123
ALTERATION OF TRANSPORT PHENOMENA BY HUMANS	124

INTRODUCTION

We live in a world of flows and movements that affect our everyday lives in many ways. This world of motion is sometimes exaggerated for us by romantic artists like Albert Bierstadt, who produced the agitated scene in Figure 1 (see color insert). The viewer is almost overwhelmed by the forces represented by towering clouds and smashing surf. Sunlight forces its way through clefts in the cloudscape; wind whips the tree foliage into pennants, the rain into sheets, and the surf into spume. Water cascades down mountain slopes in the background, rocks tumble off the eroded banks, and humans make their way through it all by boat and by foot. This dramatic scene highlights most of the ways that flows and movements shape our environment and participate in the functioning of the earth system.

As we seek to understand how Earth functions at the global scale, it is natural for us to think in terms of mixing and circulation in the atmosphere and oceans. These and other transport processes are central to our conceptualization of earth system functioning. The fact is, however, that these processes operate at all spatial and temporal scales throughout the biosphere. "Biosphere" is used here in the sense of that spherical volume at the surface of Earth in which life occurs. The movements of mass, energy, and information between portions of the biosphere are intrinsic to open systems. In a loosely defined sense, these transfers represent a complex system of connections between portions of the biosphere. Furthermore, these transfers have been highly altered in the last century as humankind has become an ever more potent force in the earth system. How we deal with those transfers is vital to our success in understanding and managing systems.

Transport processes comprise a broad range of physical and biological phenomena. These are complicated further by important differences in spatial and temporal scale, by the variety of underlying driving mechanisms, and by the logical difficulties in defining cause and effect. This subject is further exacerbated by difficulty in recognizing legacies of flows and movements of the past. The objective of this review is to address transport processes in the broadest context and to evaluate them as a kind of connectivity through the biosphere. This review is organized into three sections. We first present a system for conceptualizing the range of transport phenomena. We then review the major types of transport phenomena relevant to environmental science. Finally, we explore how transport phenomena are being increasingly altered by humans and how that may effect our research on the earth system.

CONCEPTUAL ORGANIZATION OF FLOWS AND MOVEMENTS

Flows and Movements as Propagations

Flows and movements can be described as propagation events (2, 3). "Propagation" is used in the sense of creating an effect at a distance, as by electromagnetic waves, compression waves, or mass movements that travel through space, which, on Earth,

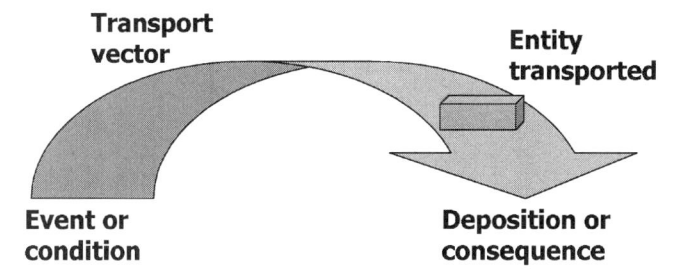

Figure 2 Generalized diagram of a propagation showing the initiating cause or condition, transmitting vector, entity propagated, and locus of effect or deposition.

is some form of physical medium (4). Propagations require four components: (a) initiating events or chronic conditions, (b) a conveyance mechanism or vector, (c) a conveyed entity, and (d) a locus of deposition or consequence (Figure 2). In some cases, propagations are the same as "communication" or "information transfer" (5) involving an information source, transmitter, signal, channel, and receptor. Propagations go beyond information transfer, however, because they include movements that cannot be interpreted as information. The transport of ash particles downwind from a forest fire may ultimately have biogeochemical influences, but it would not be useful or accurate to consider ash deposition a signal. Propagations are also related to "fluxes" in that with propagation, some quantity of an entity must move through some space or point at some rate. However, quantity and rate may not be the essence of many propagations so that "flux" is too narrow as a general descriptor. The following paragraphs elaborate on the four elements of propagation.

INITIATING EVENTS OR CONDITIONS   Events or conditions initiating propagation can range from spatially discrete and temporally brief phenomena, such as the excretion of an ant pheromone, to something as large and pervasive as a volcanic explosion injecting tons of materials into the upper troposphere and lower stratosphere. In fact, initiating causes can vary in at least seven distinct ways. The initiating cause

1. may be a discrete event or a chronic condition,
2. can be characterized by the kind of environment in which the event or condition occurs,
3. will have a spatial scale or extent,
4. may be of abiotic or biotic origin,
5. can emanate from a natural process or an anthropogenic action,
6. can vary in duration of the action, if it is a discrete event, and
7. may have a periodic character if it is a discrete phenomenon.

Determining whether or not an initiating cause is discrete in time will depend on the scalar context for time. The same is true for the spatial extent or duration of action or time frames for estimating periodicity. There is a relativism to these dimensions that has to be corrected with explicit definition of scalar context (6). Another kind of relativism exists for the definition of causation itself. The "butterfly effect" impacts each of these dimensions (7). We find, however, that moving too far from proximal to distal causation can frustrate understanding. It really is not useful to know that the stroke of a butterfly's wing ultimately caused a tornado in Kansas. It is more useful to seek causation at a more medial level (8), such as the meeting of air parcels over the Great Plains.

One should not confuse the extent of the initiating cause and the extent of environmental space that is impacted. The extent of a volcano may be a few square kilometers, but the extent of atmosphere affected by its effluvia may involve a sizeable fraction of Earth's atmosphere. Similarly with a chronic condition like a warm spring in the bottom of a lake, the spring source may occupy square centimeters, but the entire lake may be thermally and chemically affected.

ENTITIES   Propagations require that something be transported from the site of initiation to the locus of deposition (Figure 2). A neutral word for the item transported is "entity." Upon first consideration, characterization of entities seems straightforward. The sediment carried downstream by a creek consists of various sorts of detrital material, some inorganic, some organic. The entity is the mixture of clay, silt, sand, and variously fragmented units of organic matter. Similarly, sensible heat borne by desert winds across an irrigated golf course represents a form of thermal energy that contributes to evapotranspiration from well-watered greens. But what of bird calls, animal gestures, and exotic plant seeds borne in the mud coated under automobile wheel wells? How do we deal with these?

The simple approach is to divide entities into parcels of energy or matter or a combination of the two (Figure 3). Some parcels of energy may be pure energy such as electromagnetic energy or sound, but most are incorporated into matter, such as moving air, fluids, or solids. At the other extreme, some entities such as oxidized, inorganic matter may have no free energy associated with them at all (Figure 3). Of course, material entities often contain free energy in the form of reduced inorganic compounds such as sulfides, especially when they contain organic matter (Figure 3).

In fact, the most important character of an entity may be neither the energy nor the material content itself, but the information content that may impact the target destination. This is particularly true of biological targets (Figure 3). The transport of coded light signals emanating from certain insects and fish, of programmed sounds such as mating calls of birds, or of the genetic information bound in animal-, wind-, and water-borne spores, pollen, and seeds have importance from an informational point of view that far exceeds the incorporated energy and material content itself. This information content is vital to functioning of the biota. To the extent that the biota is the subject of interest, or has a broader function in earth system function

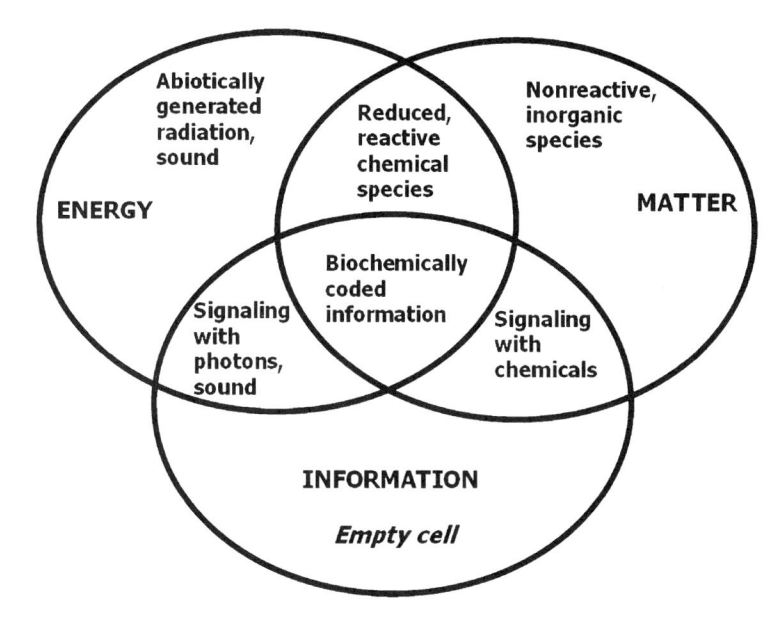

Figure 3 Classes of entities conveyed by propagations. Three simple classes, energy, matter, and information are represented by the ovals. The ovals overlap as described in the text.

such as metal reduction, then entities are characterized as parcels of information rather than as matter or energy.

More critical than the literal nature of entities is their relevance to their target destination; that relevance depends very much on the point of view of the observer. In the case of waves beating on the base of sea cliffs in Figure 1, they may be viewed as products of wind energy having been transformed to hydraulic energy that erodes the cliff base through mechanical action. Clearly, the individual waves are energetic entities. But the waves also consist of water, so that matter as well energy is being transported via the movement of water. As a parallel example, the wind blowing across the tree canopies in Figure 1 possesses kinetic energy and does work by transferring momentum to the tree canopies. If one is just interested in momentum transfer, then the wind is an energy entity. If one is interested in the chemical content of the air, then the wind is also a bearer of matter, specifically salt spray that can have a severe impact on leaf physiology. Then parcels of air borne by wind are defined as matter. But the wind may be bearing pathological spores as well, and the genetic information transport may be the entity of primary interest. Definition and characterization of entities depends on the phenomenon of interest to the observer.

VECTORS   Propagations require some mechanism to transport entities from place of origin to locus of deposition (Figure 2). Wiens (9) used "vector" as a term for phenomena playing this role. In this sense, vector means any agent providing

TABLE 1 Eleven general vectors at a medial level of causation that are responsible for propagation of ecological influences in the biosphere, and their ultimate underlying causation

Vector	Ultimate causation
Animal locomotion	Solar radiation
Colluvial transport	Radiogenic heating, gravity
Electromagnetic radiation	Solar radiation (directly and indirectly via animals)
Extra-tidal currents	Gravity, solar radiation
Fluvial transport	Solar radiation, gravity
Glacial transport	Solar radiation, gravity
Molecular diffusion	Solar radiation, radiogenic heating
Sedimentation	Solar radiation, gravity
Sound propagation	Miscellaneous, solar radiation via animals
Tidal currents	Gravity
Wind transport	Solar radiation, gravity

transmission of an entity across space. "Carrier" or "conveyor" have the same sense although with other nuances.

As was true for initiating causes, an operational level for determining vectors has to be selected. It is possible to broadly generalize and attribute a multitude of vectors under the category of gravity, e.g., surface and groundwater flows, tides, and mass wasting events. Obviously, assigning propagations at this level of causation is not useful. At the other extreme, we can describe vectors in extreme detail that extends to particular cases, such as the precise class of mass wasting process (10). We suggest a middle ground list of 11 vectors that serves well for general discussion (Table 1) [from (2)]. In the following we will review each of these vectors in terms of their properties with respect to mechanisms, entities typically involved, and their typical scales of occurrence.

CONSEQUENCES Propagation requires that the entity transported results in a consequence somewhere in environmental space (Figure 2). Whether the dissipation of heat, the triggering of a wildfire, or the subsidy of a limiting nutrient, the entity results in an effect. As should be clear from preceding discussion, how an observer records an effect depends on what the observer is observing. An observer can record the removal of material from a slope as the erosive consequence of a landslide or the accumulation of material at the bottom of the landslide as its depositional consequence. For classification and communication purposes, the observer defines the effect and in so doing defines the nature of the entity propagated. At the same time, the observer sets the scale of observation in space and in time, thereby defining other classificatory attributes of a propagation.

KINDS OF PROPAGATIONS

It is natural for people to define propagations in terms of the transmitting vector. Vectors seem to be the best organizing device for classification of propagation phenomena. Therefore, we review the vectors listed in Table 1 in the following sections to indicate the nature of these vectors and the ways in which they promote linkages through environmental space.

Diffusion: Transport by Random Movements

Diffusion is used in the narrow sense here as the transfer of mass by the movement of molecules, or very small particles, due to their kinetic energy (11, 12). The underlying mechanism of diffusion is random movements caused by collisions between small particles or molecules. These movements are a function of temperature and the material involved. If diffusion goes to completion, it results in an even distribution of the particles, but in nature that situation is rarely reached because of temporal variation in source and sink strength of the parts of the diffusing system. Fick's First Law suffices for a general conceptualization of diffusive transport; for a more formal mathematical treatment of diffusive transport see Campbell & Norman (13).

"Diffusion" is used to describe other flow processes that are complicated and difficult to treat more explicitly. For example, turbulent transfer in micrometeorology and hydrology, as well as the dispersion of plants or the movements of animals, can be successfully treated as diffusion if abstracted over a sufficient scale (14–18).

In addition to these uses, Hagerstrand (19) described further extensions of the term "diffusion" applying to sociocultural changes across space. He termed these "contagious," "stimulus," and "hierarchical" diffusion. These terms represent different mechanisms by which information is transferred in human societies, although they can be applied to other kinds of movements such as the dispersal of exotic species. Especially "hierarchical diffusion" (the case in which sensitive nodes are stimulated and they, in turn, stimulate a subordinate set of nodes in close proximity) is an appropriate application of this meaning of diffusion.

Diffusive transport can be considered both within homogeneous media and at interfaces between different media. Reiners & Driese (3) describe diffusive movement within gaseous, aqueous, and porous media. Within gaseous media, diffusive movement uncomplicated by mass flows includes the movement of gases around and within stomatal and intercellular spaces of plant leaves (20–22), the transport of pheromones between animals (23), and the dispersion of pollutants (14, 24, 25). Within aqueous media, pure diffusive transport includes cellular diffusion (26, 27), movement around plant roots (28, 29), and diffusion over short distances in lakes and streams (14, 30). Beyond distances of millimeters to centimeters, diffusive transport is usually supplanted by other mass transport vectors.

Diffusion rates in porous media are typically slower than in homogeneous gaseous or aqueous media because entities must take longer paths to avoid solid particles and because some of the transported entities are adsorbed (31). The most important porous media from an environmental point of view are sediments, soils (32–35), and snow (35–40).

As Reiners & Driese (3) point out, diffusion across media boundaries is arguably more important than within homogeneous media from an environmental point of view. These media interfaces include the soil-air (41–44), soil-snow (45), snow-air (40), ocean-air (46–49), and sediment-water column boundaries (50).

Diffusion is the most pervasive transport vector on Earth in terms of flux across surfaces. Although it is usually supplanted by other mass flow vectors at scales larger than centimeters, it is the dominant transport vector for fluid exchange between organisms and their environment, whether aqueous or atmospheric. In sum, diffusion is the primary propagation vector at the microscale. It propagates across short distances but within vast volumes and over immense surface areas. Viewing transport vectors collectively, diffusion is the base process from which many of the other vectors take over further transport.

Fluvial Transport: Propagation by Running Waters

Fluvial transport applies to the movement of water and incorporated materials on land and on and within glaciers. Running water is seen in Figure 1 in the mid background as a series of cataracts and falls cutting through the terrain. It moves huge quantities of materials rapidly via surface and groundwater flow at scales of centimeters to thousands of kilometers, all in response to gravity. Surface water flows to the sea are estimated to range from $33–47 \times 10^3$ km^3/yr, while groundwater flows, which are much more poorly constrained, may be in the order of 2×10^3 km^3/yr [(51) but also see Burnett et al. (52)]. Fluvially transported entities are essentially matter except that dissolved or suspended organic material has some biochemical free energy. Also, the hydraulic force and incorporated abrasive materials in the water have high erosive potential that must be recognized as energy if the consequence of flow is viewed as geomorphological (53). Sediment transported by rivers to the sea is estimated to be 13.7×10^9 tons/yr (51). Flux measurements for major ions and dissolved substances are also estimated by Reiners (51). Schlesinger (54) provides an excellent treatment on the general biogeochemical aspect of fluvial transport in his chapter on rivers and estuaries. Fluvial transport is a vital linkage of material flux from land to surface and groundwaters, and ultimately, to the sea.

Hydrology is the science underlying the principles of water movement (e.g., 31, 55–57) whereas fluvial geomorphology is the scientific discipline dealing with how water moves materials and reshapes the terrestrial landscape (10). The hydrology of surface flows involves inputs, infiltration, percolation, overland flow, and channel flow, all covered in the references cited above. In general, surface flow routing can be predicted from topography (58–60), but application of mathematical hydrologic principles is difficult due to geometric complexities. Also, surface channel routing can be modified by differential lithology (10), by historical events such as landscape exhumation at the million year scale (61), or by catastrophic floods such as the Missoula Lake floods in Washington state (62). These last two are historical legacies that must be accounted for in environmental analyses.

TRANSPORT PROCESSES IN THE BIOSPHERE   C-1

See legend on next page

Figure 1 "Puget Sound, on the Pacific Coast" by Albert Bierstadt, circa 1870. Almost all of the propagation vectors discussed in this review are dramatized in this large canvas, the original measuring 133.4 × 208.3 cm. Explicitly illustrated are transport by electromagnetic radiation (sunlight), wind (clouds and surf), water (streams on the mountain slopes), mass wasting (eroded lower slopes), sedimentation (rain and mist), and human locomotion. Implicit are the effects of Pleistocene glaciers on the lower slopes, the contribution of currents to the waves, diffusion—pervading everywhere, and the sounds of wind and surf. Printed with permission of Hudson Hills Press (1).

Groundwater hydrology requires a three-dimensional approach to transport and is further complicated by heterogeneities in flow path media. In general, water moves in response to pressure along flow paths of variable transmissivity due to porosity and the presence of joints, fractures, and other low-resistance features of the three-dimensional medium (57). Not surprisingly, there is an enormous range of groundwater flow rates. Groundwater flow rates can be as fast as found in open surface (m/s) where voids are large and continuous, as in carbonate or volcanic aquifers, or they can be extremely slow (mm/day) in sedimentary rocks with low transmissivities (56). Even less is known about groundwater inputs of nutrients into the sea [for local examples see (63, 64)].

Groundwater fluxes are immensely important in terms of the transport of materials as well as water itself. Pringle et al. (65) illustrated how groundwater geochemistry in a pristine volcanic terrain could influence surface water geochemistry and subsequently stream biology. An environmental arena of particular interest and importance is the hyporheic zone along and under stream channels, where groundwater mixes with, or becomes, surface water. The biogeochemical processes are varied and temporally varying in complicated ways in this zone (66–68). In human-dominated terrains, contaminants transported by groundwater may be derived from agriculture (particularly nitrogen); from mining (particularly iron, manganese, lead, chromium, and arsenic) and mining-associated acidity (usually derived from sulfides); and from industrial and domestic sources of organic compounds (69–71). Aquifers are more than passive conduits of these materials as chemical transformations can occur en route downstream (72). Communities dependent on groundwater must be vigilant against the upstream contamination and subsequent transport to wells (56). In these cases, laypersons become intensely concerned about propagation processes in the environment.

Fluvial transport pervades Earth's land surface, even in desert regions where the flows are infrequent but often violently energetic. Every point on Earth's surface not covered with glaciers is at least occasionally influenced by fluvial transport. Water is so mobile that where free water occurs, surfaces are intimately connected with channels and groundwater, and channels and groundwater are connected with one another and with the sea. Modeling of fluvial transport is well developed in the arenas of hydrologic, erosion, water quality, and groundwater modeling. These are reviewed by Reiners & Driese (3).

Colluvial Transport: Mass Movement Through the Action of Gravity

Fluvial and colluvial transport work together to lower the landscape, at first enhancing, then reducing, relief. Colluvial transport is synonymous with mass wasting or mass movement. An exacting definition of mass movement is "the downslope movement of slope material under the influence of the gravitational force of the material itself and without the assistance of moving water, air or ice" (10). Colluvial transport, often acting in concert with fluvial transport, shapes Earth's surface and results in a suite of secondary effects. As fluvial, glacial, or coastal erosion ensues, slopes steepen and material, if detached, moves downhill in response to gravity. Typically, that material is transported further along fluvial or glacial transport pathways. Mass wasting is seen in Figure 1 in terms of the undercut cliffs on the left and in the right background.

Colluvially transported material is mostly mineral matter but sometimes includes large loads of soil organic matter, organic detritus, and even living trees. Thus, the transported entity is matter of both abiotic and biotic origin. The energy of impact can also be a consideration. Wieczorek et al. (73) describe a series of rock falls in Yosemite Valley in 1996 for which the impact area was not particularly large, but the falls generated air blasts bearing dense clouds of abrasive sand that devastated larger areas downslope of the impact sites. Immediately downslope of the impacts, the air blast had velocities exceeding 110 m/s and toppled or snapped about 1000 trees. Even at distances of 0.5 km from impact, wind velocities snapped or toppled large trees, causing one fatality and several serious injuries.

Colluvial processes take many forms and mastery of all of the varieties composes a subfield of geomorphology. Summerfield (10) presents a table of 24 types under categories termed "creep," "flow," "slide," "heave," "fall" and "subsidence." All of these processes are described in detail in the geomorphological literature (10). Factors contributing to mass movement include slope steepening through undercutting, usually by river, glacier, or wave erosion; slope loading [e.g., (74)], usually with vegetation or water; lateral pressure generated by water-induced material swelling or freezing itself; transient stresses like earthquakes or movement of trees in the wind; and factors reducing shear strength of slope materials (10). Shear strength can be reduced by weathering, changes in pore-water pressure, changes in material structure, burrowing animals, and decaying tree roots (75). Subsidence is often related to subterranean solution erosion in karst terrain, removal of water from aquifers, or mining (76, 77).

Interaction between influences can trigger colluvial transport. In many cases, causal factors may themselves be a product of another propagation so that there is a concatenation of propagations and their consequences. Giani et al. (78) describe how a rock fall in the Italian Alps detached ice from a hanging glacier that, in turn, triggered a snow avalanche that partially destroyed a hotel and killed two skiers. As another example of concatenating events, a wildfire on Storm King Mountain in Colorado reduced the shear strength of slopes such that with the occurrence of a heavy rainstorm in 1994, debris flows were triggered in every drainage basin on the mountain (79). As with fluvial transport, the physics of colluvial transport is relatively well understood, and model development is mature. It is the parameterization of models to the complexities of the real world that is the primary problem. Reiners & Driese (3) review the types of models available for colluvial transport.

In summary, colluvial transport occurs wherever slopes occur. It is primarily a transport vector on land but is also important along submarine canyon walls, continental shelves, and trench walls in the sea. Although it can take place on relatively gentle terrain, its frequency of occurrence and the mass and energy transported increase with topographic relief. Climatic variables that control the type and rate of mineral weathering probably affect the styles of mass wasting in geographic regions.

Glacial Transport: Movement by Ice Masses

Glaciers are extremely effective transport vectors through the erosion, transport, and deposition of solid and liquid water along with incorporated mineral and organic matter. The plastic flow of ice confers similarities with fluvial transport, but the predominance of masses of mineral matter transported, often unsorted by size, also renders it similar to colluvial transport. Glacial transport is restricted to particular geographic conditions of climate and relief where ice can accumulate, only about 10% of today's continents. On the other hand, the historical imprint of glacial transport is enormous. It is thought that most of Earth was covered with ice for part of the Proterozoic Eon, and about 30% of continents were covered during glacial maxima of the Pleistocene Epoch (1.6 million to ca 12,000 ybp) (10). Where ice covered the land and some marine bays during the Pleistocene, its presence usually dominates topography and surficial geology through either its erosional or depositional effects. This, in turn, influences soil parent material and, to varying degrees, drainage patterns. The extensive glacial legacies of the Pleistocene in Europe and North America are general reductions in relief and the removal or deposition of soil parent material. South of the glacial boundary in Illinois, for example, the topography is much more like the hill country of Kentucky than the partially dissected till plains of the rest of the state.

Glacial erosion is powerful and rapid, particularly in mountainous terrain. It can move mass faster in a prolonged way than any other erosive force. Some have suggested that glacial erosion is the primary determinant of how high mountains are likely to be on Earth (80, 81) although the issue is complicated by the possibility that mountains can rise in response to material unloading (82). Where it occurs, glacial transport is rapid and involves large masses of material, but due to its present geographic restriction, it is now more important for its historical legacy. For further general reading on glacial transport see Eyles (83), Summerfield (10), and Evans (84). For examples of modeling applications see Koppes & Hallet (85), Konrad et al. (86), and Welch et al. (87).

Sedimentation: Propagation by Particle Settling in Fluids

In this treatment of sedimentation as a transport vector, we refer specifically to sedimentation as the downward flux of materials within fluids in response to gravity. The fluid media through which particles descend include the atmosphere, lakes, rivers, oceans, and magma chambers. This definition distinguishes the use of the term from lateral movement and subsequent deposition of sediment by water and wind (88–91). We consider those meanings to be the depositional parts of fluvial and wind transport. Sedimentation is driven by gravity; entities can be inorganic or organic materials, either living or dead (92), and can have material or information flow consequences. Sedimentation operates in Figure 1 as rainfall and fog droplets in the hazy atmosphere.

Sedimentation occurs in any fluid medium and can involve transport through kilometers of atmosphere or oceanic media. It is one process by which particles arrive on Earth from space (93). It contributes to the flux of particulate matter from the stratosphere to the troposphere (94), and from the troposphere to land and sea surfaces (14). Sedimentation is a principal pathway by which particulate matter, both mineral and organic, is transported from the epilimnions of lakes and oceans to the hypolimnions and subsequently to the benthic zones (95, 96).

As with diffusion, sedimentation is often involved with vectors of lateral transport. Turbulent flow in air or water overwhelms sedimentation depending on the velocity of the medium and the effective diameter and density of the particles. Stoke's Law describes the factors controlling the rate at which a particle will settle through the fluid column. The velocity of fall of a particle is directly proportional to the size of the particle and the difference between the density of the particle and the density of the fluid medium. It is inversely proportional to the viscosity of the medium (97). This means that a particle 1 μm in radius will fall through a 10°C oceanic water column at 0.00025 cm/sec while a particle 100 μm in radius will fall at a rate of 2.5 cm/sec (98). Because particulate sedimentation is so important to the carbon budget in the ocean (95), the size of particles produced in the photic zone is critical. The 1-μm particle described above will take 51 years to fall 4000 m through marine waters while the 100 μm particle will fall that distance in 2.7 days (98). Effective diameter is affected by shape. Some plankton have elaborated shapes that are hypothesized to be ecologically adaptive by slowing settling rates in the water column. Fluxes generated by sedimentation depend on the source strength as well as Stoke's Law relationships. More organic particles are produced in productive parts of the ocean (99, 100), while more mineral particles are introduced to the upper waters of the oceans near the mouths of rivers. On average, sediment accumulation on continental shelves is on the order of 1 m/1000 yr while in the deep ocean it is 0.1–10 mm/1000 yr (101).

It is difficult to measure dry deposition from the atmosphere to land or sea surfaces. It is even more difficult to differentiate sedimentation from other depositional processes like rainout, diffusion, and impaction, which are more closely related to motions of air (102). Nevertheless, sedimentation is clearly a major source of particulate deposition, especially of larger particles such as ash, soil dust, and fog droplets (103). Stoke's Law pertains to sedimentation in air as well as in water, but air speeds can be greater than water current speeds, so that impaction is likely to prevail over sedimentation during daytime conditions.

The sedimentation delivery of iron, phosphorus, and possibly nitrogen from the atmosphere to oligotrophic ocean waters (49, 104–106) appears to be of immense local importance. The same is true of phosphorous sedimentation to old, weathered soils (107, 108) and nitrogen to infertile soils (109). Not all atmospheric deposition is sedimentation (see above) but much of the mineral fraction, especially phosphorus and iron, can be. Considerable living material is transported in air and sedimented in a functional state. Besides biogeochemical implications, there are biological dispersal implications of atmospheric sedimentation for native and exotic species (92). In a specially interesting case, Shinn et al. (110) described a possible contamination of corals in the Caribbean by a fungus derived from dustfall originating in Africa.

Sedimentation is ubiquitous in occurrence throughout the atmosphere and ocean and lake water columns. The importance of the sedimentation vector depends, however, on location with respect to source strength on one hand and on sensitivity of ecosystems to the materials being deposited on the other. Some materials can have beneficial consequences for the system in which they are deposited, while some can be harmful in the cases of contaminants, toxins, or pest or disease species.

Lake and Ocean Currents

Currents are mass movements in large bodies of water, which are driven by wind, Coriolis force, or tidal forces that interact with the configurations of coastlines. Currents involve transport of enormous masses of water together with dissolved and particulate matter, both organic and inorganic, living and dead. We divide currents into those generated by tidal forces and those generated by wind and other forces. Currents are not obvious in Figure 1, but both tidal and nontidal currents probably contributed to wind generation of the waves breaking on the beach.

TIDAL CURRENTS   Tidal currents are generated by a combination of gravitational forces of the sun, other planets, the moon, and the centrifugal force from Earth's spin (101, 111). These gravitational interactions cause bulges and depressions that change water levels one or two times a day, thereby creating strong currents flowing from areas of high to low water. These flows interact with sea-bottom and coastline shapes to produce a wide range of tidal amplitudes from scarcely measurable to tens of meters (112). Tidal currents, along with nontidal currents, wind, and outflowing waters from land, make the coastal zone extraordinarily energy-rich both physically and biologically (113, 114).

Tides influence deep ocean mixing (115) but primarily dominate the physical environment of the coastal zone (114). On facing sea fronts like sea cliffs and beaches, tides alter sea level, including the location of waves and their mechanical effects on shoreline features. Both on sea fronts and within estuaries, periodic submergence and emergence of habitat create drastic contrasts in environmental resources and stresses, thus controlling the habitat zonation and the distributions of organisms (116). Powerful lateral currents effectively transport sediments (10, 112, 117–119), nutrients, and organic energy sources (120–122) as well as influence the dispersal of invertebrate larvae and other disseminules [e.g., (123, 124)].

Tidal currents are primarily effective in the coastal zone, but the zone is of enormous lateral extent on a global basis. The length of the coastal zone is a fractal problem but estimates range from 500,000 to 1,000,000 km in length. If continental shelves are included as part of the coastal zone, it comprises 8% of Earth's surface area (51). The coastal zone is a site of many resources and the location of the majority of human populations (51). Thus, tidal currents play crucial roles in natural and human-dominated ecosystems.

EXTRA-TIDAL CURRENTS   Planetary winds, Coriolis force, and gravity combine to move huge masses of water in lakes and oceans (101, 111). These movements have characteristic spatial patterns and temporal variability that create relatively stable (but see below) spatial-temporal patterns in transport of water mass and dissolved and particulate matter over distances of thousands of kilometers. These currents, together with atmospheric winds, comprise Earth's global scale transport systems that are so important in the distribution of thermal and latent heat energy, moisture, and biological disseminules in the atmosphere and (excepting latent energy) in the seas.

Currents occur in lakes as well as oceans. There are hundreds of thousands of lakes on Earth, and each is unique in critical ways, including the extent and pattern of currents. Some lakes have large-scale lateral currents, a fact perhaps most notable in the management of reservoir flow regimes. These lateral currents are controlled by basin morphometry and overall hydrology (125). Lakes also have a broad range of possible vertical movements and currents that are unique to each lake (96). These vertical movements result from the alternate development and destruction of thermal stratification, often referred to as lake turnover. Turnover is highly variable, ranging from nearly continuous vertical circulation to twice a year to once a year to rarely to never (96). Mixing (or not) is a fundamental property of lakes that affects virtually all of their other properties. This means that vertical transport sets much of the character of an individual lake.

Oceanic surface currents are caused by the planetary wind system and are directionally modified by the Coriolis effect and interactions with continental margins (112). Deep counter-currents match the hydraulic movements of surface currents. These abyssal currents are driven by gravitational effects on water of different densities, by the Coriolis effect, and by boundary constraints set by continents (95). Densities of ocean water differ through variations in temperature or salinity so the overall oceanic circulation system varies geographically with heating, evaporation, cooling, and freshwater inputs into regional waters (111). Surface and deep circulation patterns are connected by vertical sinking or upwelling movements, completing a complicated circulation system through the world's oceans that acts like a global conveyor system. This system is termed the "thermohaline circulation system."

Turnover times vary with different oceanic basins but range from 250 yr in the Indian Ocean to 510 yr in the Pacific Ocean (95), as well as represent a source and sink for trace gases (126), major atmospheric gases such as oxygen and CO_2 (127, 128) and forms of carbon composing the marine portion of the global carbon cycle. Concern has been expressed about how this system could be upset by anthropogenic actions (128–131). Few examples of transport systems are as central to our understanding and concern for the global system as this one.

Large-scale oceanic currents interact with continental and island masses such that the currents can set up more or less stable patterns of lateral and vertical flow. Upwellings, frequently occurring as western boundary currents, have large influences on the fertility of coastal seawater and the land climate (111, 112).

Transport in fluid environments, like the atmosphere, lakes, and oceans, accentuates two ways of looking at the environment that are not always appreciated by land-dwelling humans. The first is the dominance of movements over static structures. The second is the three-dimensional nature of the environment. Life on land is three-dimensional too, but we have a propensity to flatten it out into convenient two-dimensional conceptualizations and graphic representations. In lakes and seas, the ecological conditions of a point anywhere in their three-dimensional volumes is a function of the relationship of that point with respect to circulation systems bringing resources to [e.g., (132)], or exporting them from, that point [e.g., (133)].

Wind Transport: Transport by Currents of the Atmosphere

Wind is the motion of atmospheric air relative to objects. The action of wind is evident in Figure 1 in the shapes of the clouds and deciduous tree canopies and at the wave crests. Globally, wind is generated by unequal distribution of incoming radiation and the rotation of Earth (134). At the planetary level (ca >2 km altitude), winds transport sensible heat, latent heat, water vapor droplets, gases, and particles from original source areas over tens of thousands of kilometers. These particles include living organisms both active and dormant (92). Some of this air becomes mixed downward below the planetary boundary layer (1–2 km) where wind becomes turbulent due to interactions with topography and ground-level heating effects (135, 136). Some portion of this air comes into contact with the surface boundary layer (millimeters to meters) where it is altered into ever smaller eddies by friction and local heating effects, and where it exchanges energy and materials with surface features (12, 137).

Wind transport involves entrainment, movement, and deposition of entities. Entrainment of heat, gases, and particles (including organisms) involves the mixing of eddies near the surface source into larger eddies of wind at higher altitude. This entrainment depends on wind speed and the size and densities of particles in a manner similar to the Stoke's Law control of sedimentation (10, 92, 138–140). Movement requires sufficient upward mixing and wind velocity to carry materials some distance from the source. As air is mixing downward as well as upward, some of the airborne materials are returned to the surface where they can be deposited. Wind trajectories have characteristic geographic patterns and seasonal variability so that there is a statistical distribution of deposition downwind of source areas (141, 142). Deposition of materials from air takes place through several mechanisms: rainout, washout, sedimentation, impaction, and diffusion

(12, 136, 143). The mode of deposition depends on the nature of the transported material, moisture and precipitation conditions, and wind speed.

Wind transfers kinetic energy to water surfaces, generating waves, and to land surfaces, where it enhances turbulent mixing within the surface materials, such as vegetation. This mixing is necessary for both deposition and entrainment of materials (144). Sometimes the transfer of momentum exceeds the strength of forest vegetation leading to uprooting and bole breakage (145). This is one of the ways that propagations can leave a legacy on the landscape exceeding the life cycles of trees themselves (146).

Wind is also a vector for sensible and latent energy, both of which are important components of energy and water budgets (13, 147, 148). Wind entrains, translocates, and deposits trace gases (149), fog droplets (150, 151), snow (152), erodible soil particles (138), sand grains in dune fields (10, 153), and salt spray droplets from waves (51). Wind transport provides critically limiting nutrients in dust to oligotrophic portions of the open ocean (105, 154) and infertile land areas (107, 155). Wind transport can also have detrimental effects. It is responsible for global distribution of anthropogenically produced nitrogen leading to many potential changes in regional ecosystem function (109) as well as to deposition of acidity or acid forming substances (156, 157).

Wind as a transport vector is globally ubiquitous at the sea-, ice- and land-atmosphere interfaces. It transmits a wide variety of entities and operates over scales ranging from millimeters to global. Geographically, the relative importance of wind transport varies locally depending on source strengths, wind trajectories and velocities, and surface properties. Calculation of the importance of wind transport may often be quantitatively crude but can be constrained by chemical or isotope tracers.

Light: Propagation Through the Electromagnetic Spectrum

Light and sound are unique among the propagation vectors in that they exclusively do not involve material transfer and by the fact that the vectors and entities are the same. As used here, "light" includes a broad region of electromagnetic radiation (EMR) that can be perceived by organisms and used as cues or signals. The sun is the single largest source of EMR in the natural world, supporting most life on Earth (excluding life dependent on the flow of abiotically generated reduced compounds) by heating the surface and providing the energy driving photosynthesis.

These effects are obvious. Less obvious to physical scientists is the role of EMR in enabling and regulating the biological components of the earth system. The sun, together with the moon, also provides light for vision. By far more secondary, but biologically important, is the energetically costly biological light generated by nocturnal terrestrial and benthic organisms. These include bacteria, fungi, glow worms, beetles, fireflies, cephalopods, jellyfish, and fish (158). Reflected EMR and biological light underlie the generation of sensations and visual images by photoreceptors of many organisms (158–160). In response, plants and animals can make themselves more or less conspicuous by increasing or decreasing the contrast between themselves and their background via color, pattern, and movement (161). Much of the basis of crypsis and mimicry involves these adaptations (162).

The combined ability for light reception and production raises communication to high levels among animals [e.g., (163, 164)], and plant growth and differentiation are cued by EMR signals (165). It is difficult to exaggerate the adaptive significance of light reception and production through the broad diversity of the world's biota (158). The distributions of direct and reflected light in terrestrial environments and how they change through the diurnal cycle and alterations of the environment are subjects too complex for further review here (161, 166, 167).

Sound: Propagation Through Acoustics

Like electromagnetic radiation, sound is a wave-form of propagation for which the propagation is the entity. Unlike EMR, sound is mechanical energy transmitted through material media (air, water, soil, rocks, and structures) in longitudinal or transverse pressure waves. Sound is produced by a local concentration or rarefaction of molecules in a medium, producing variation in pressure. This pressure disturbance in local molecular concentration is propagated away from the source of the sound through collisions of successive layers of molecules and, in the absence of barriers, moves as a sphere of increasing radius. At each molecular collision, some of the energy in the disturbance is lost as heat until, at a sufficient distance from the source, all of the energy will be dissipated, and no sound will be detected (158). Reiners & Driese (3) elaborate further on the ecologically and environmentally relevant physics of sound.

Animal sounds vital to species fitness emanate from insects, fish, frogs, birds, and mammals. These signals involve attracting and bonding with mates, protecting territories, maintaining spacing between groups, communicating distress and hunger, and warning of danger from predators [e.g., (168–172)]. Some information propagation may be inadvertent, as when a territorial bird advertises its presence to a predator. Thus, there are two kinds of cost associated with biological sound propagation: revealing presence and the energy required to produce the sound (173, 174). The means, costs, and advantages of sound propagation and reception are subjects of long interest to animal behaviorists (158, 175–177).

Abiotically generated sound waves can have some influence on an abiotic environment, such as mechanical effects on slope stability. Thunder or a low-wave sound generated by earthquakes can travel enormous distances (178) and even generate mass movements. Abiotically generated sounds are ubiquitous and have some information value to a particularly attuned observer, but biologically produced sound is probably of greatest significance for this vector.

Animal Locomotion

Locomotory capacity can be found in some stage of all members of the biological kingdoms. However, biologically driven locomotion as a transport vector is restricted by us to animals and to organisms sometimes referred to as "protists," such as single-celled flagellates. These organisms are likely to disperse, forage, flee, and mate through some form of locomotion at some stage in their life cycle. By so doing, they act as vectors not only by transporting their own biomass but by translocating their effects on the environment. As a leaf miner works its way through the mesophyll of a birch leaf, it leaves behind a trail of excavated cells. As a bison herd makes its way across the plains, it leaves behind a trail of dung and partially consumed plants. Animals also act as vectors for other organisms by translocating plant spores and seeds (179) and animal spores and larvae. White-tailed deer act as vectors of Lyme disease by spreading ticks from one infested area to another during their perambulations (180). Humankind is undoubtedly the ultimate animal transport vector for worldwide transport of materials, energy, and exotic organisms.

The relative importance of animals as transport vectors depends on the locomotory capability of animal compared with the flows of other vectors (181). Many marine larval forms are only weakly motile compared with the currents in which they swim (123, 124) and thus scarcely qualify as transport vectors themselves. Other animals are strongly locomotory compared with abiotic vectors, such as some migratory birds and large mammals (182).

The role of animals as transport vectors is probably small in terms of mass but can be large in terms of impact, particularly when dispersal of other organisms is involved. It is impossible to generalize further about patterns of animal movement because the possibilities are as diverse as the global fauna itself. The subject is so important from other points of view that considerable research is directed at animal movement. See Dunning et al. (183) for deterministic movement modeling, Turchin (18) for more generalized diffusion models, and Scott et al. (184) for applications.

ALTERATION OF TRANSPORT PHENOMENA BY HUMANS

Environmental science, as a problem-centered, multidisciplinary field, arose in the mid-twentieth century with recognition that human impacts were widespread in extent and could lead to consequences at a distance. Three leading cases of the time were the production, dispersal, and impacts of radioactive fallout (185); biocides (186, 187); and acidity (188, 189). In all three cases, transport was an essential ingredient of these problems. Eventually, the concerns and approach of environmental science merged with those of earth, atmosphere, and ocean sciences, leading to an explicitly global perspective under the rubric of earth system science (ESS). According to Harte (190), ESS "seeks a predictive understanding of the complex system comprising organisms, atmosphere, fresh water, oceans, soil and human society." ESS involves many different issues, but the primary, interrelated foci are several aspects of atmospheric chemistry (191), land cover change (192), the global carbon and nitrogen cycles (109, 193–196), climate change (197), and changes in species composition through both extinctions and spread of exotic species to new ranges (198). ESS pursues understanding of how the earth system works through the widely varying conditions of earth history, but at the same time,

ESS scientists recognize that many earth processes are currently changing very rapidly due to human intervention. The various aspects of change are often referred to collectively as "global change."

Some elements of global change are based on local human impacts that are so widespread across the globe that they collectively amount to a global change. Examples of these are shifts in land cover and land use (199), the control and consumption of primary production and freshwater by humans (196), eutrophication of freshwater and coastal zone waters (113), and the planetary epidemic of species extinctions (198).

But other aspects of global change result from alterations in fluxes over distances of thousands of kilometers. Human activities appear to influence the trajectory, strength, and frequency of vectors, along with the quantity and quality of entities borne by these vectors. These long-distance propagations include transport of sensible and latent energy as they affect climate (200–202), chlorofluorocarbons to the stratosphere as they alter ozone concentrations (203), continental dust as it enhances marine productivity (204), nitrates as they increase terrestrial and marine primary production (109, 205), methane and nitrous oxide as they change net radiation transfer in the atmosphere (149, 206), heat and salt in ocean currents as they affect CO_2 transfer to deep oceanic waters and climate (207, 208), exotic species as they affect ecosystem function (209), and many others.

Recognizing the impact of an event or condition remote from its source is an especially exciting aspect of earth system science. However, the fact that human interventions lead to changes in transport processes at small spatial extents should not be overlooked. There is a reciprocity between small extent and large extent transport processes. While long distance transport such as dust deposition to oligotrophic ecosystems can lead to local changes, many, if not most, long distance propagations originate from changes effected over small extents. Dust from northern China originates, in part, from collective land use practices at the plot level in the loess covered regions of the country. Similarly, application of imported nitrogenous fertilizers enhances the microscale production and diffusion of nitrous and nitric oxide gases out of soils into the atmosphere, thereby contributing to local to regional ozone generation and the alteration in the balance of radiatively active gases at the global scale (210). These same small-scale processes lead to nitrate transport via fluvial pathways to local drainages and, ultimately, to the sea (109). The introduction of a single seed of an exotic plant to a garden can lead to disastrous infestations over many thousands of square kilometers (211). Transport processes are integrated across the full range of scales (Figure 4). A small environmental volume of a few cubic meters is interconnected with the larger biosphere through transport linkages operating at very small extents of soil aggregates to the global extents effected by atmospheric or oceanic circulation systems.

Understanding how Earth functions requires an appreciation of transport processes at all scales. This means that a broad understanding of how energy, information, and matter are propagated through multiple vectors must be an intrinsic part of education and research in environmental and earth system science. Understanding the flows and movements that interweave through the biosphere is as important

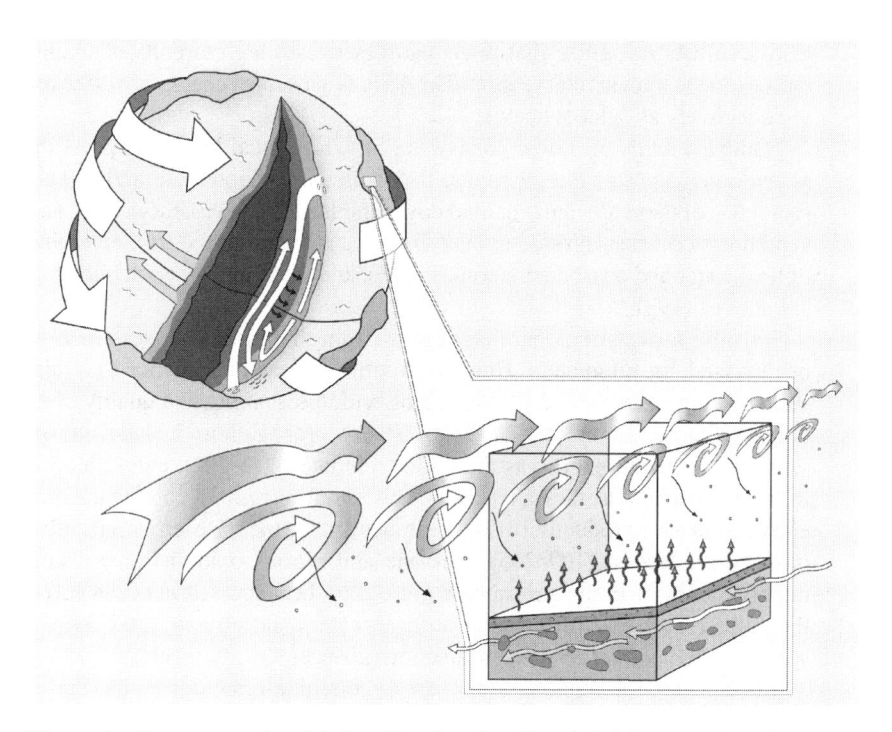

Figure 4 Transport at the global and local scales. The global figure on the left portrays atmospheric and oceanic circulation patterns as described in the text [redrawn from (111)]. The figure on the right represents a small volume of the biosphere indicating how it is imbedded in large scale wind fluxes through eddy transfer, how particles in the atmosphere are deposited from the wind column passing above, and how gases are diffusing from the soil at the base of the environmental volume. That same volume is connected to groundwater fluxes originating from adjacent environmental volumes up the groundwater gradient. Any volume of the global environment is connected to the greater biosphere through several propagation vectors by transfer mechanisms like these.

to earth system science as is the understanding of forces that drive physical and biological processes in situ.

ACKNOWLEDGMENTS

Preparation of this review was made possible by a grant from the Andrew W. Mellon Foundation and support from the National Center for Ecological Analysis and Synthesis at the University of California, Santa Barbara. Sarah Konrad helped to update the vast literature underlying this review, only a tiny portion of which is presented here. The authors extend their thanks to Ellen Axtmann for formatting and reviewing the citations and to Norma Reiners for critical editorial reading.

The *Annual Review of Environment and Resources* is online at
http://environ.annualreviews.org

LITERATURE CITED

1. Anderson NK, Ferber LS. 1990. *Albert Bierstadt: Art & Enterprise*. New York: Brooklyn Mus./Hudson Hills. 327 pp.
2. Reiners WA, Driese KL. 2001. The propagation of ecological influences across heterogeneous environmental space. *BioScience* 51:939–50
3. Reiners WA, Driese KL. 2003. *Propagation of Ecological Influences through Environmental Space*. Cambridge, UK: Cambridge Univ. Press: In press
4. Webster's. 1994. *New Universal Unabridged Dictionary*. Avenel, NJ: Barnes & Noble. 1854 pp.
5. Raisbeck G. 1963. *Information Theory*. Cambridge, MA: Mass. Inst. Technol. Press. 105 pp.
6. Peterson DL, Parker VT, eds. 1998. *Ecological Scale. Theory and Application*. New York: Columbia Univ. Press
7. Gleick J. 1987. *Chaos. Making a New Science*. New York: Viking. 352 pp.
8. Robertson GP. 1989. Nitrification and denitrification in humid tropical ecosystems: Potential controls on nitrogen retention. In *Mineral Nutrients in Tropical Forest and Savanna Ecosystems*, ed. J Proctor, pp. 55–69. Oxford: Blackwell Sci. Pub.
9. Wiens JA. 1992. Ecological flows across landscape boundaries: a conceptual overview. In *Landscape Boundaries. Consequences for Biotic Diversity and Ecological Flows*, ed. AJ Hansen, F diCastri, pp. 217–35. New York: Springer-Verlag
10. Summerfield MA. 1991. *Global Geomorphology*. Somerset: Wiley
11. Harris CJ. 1979. *Mathematical modelling of turbulent diffusion in the environment. Inst. Math. Appl. Conf. Ser.* London: Academic
12. Monteith JL, Unsworth M. 1995. *Principles of Environmental Physics*. London, UK: Arnold. 291 pp. 2nd ed.
13. Campbell GS, Norman N. 1998. *An Introduction to Environmental Biophysics*. New York: Springer-Verlag. 2nd ed.
14. Hemond H, Fechner-Levy EJ. 2000. *Chemical Fate and Transport in the Environment*. San Diego, CA: Academic. 433 pp. 2nd ed.
15. Choy B, Reible DD. 2000. *Diffusion Models of Environmental Transport*. Boca Raton: Lewis
16. Okubo A, Levin SA. 2001. *Diffusion and Ecological Problems: Modern Perspectives*. New York: Springer-Verlag. 467 pp. 2nd ed.
17. Pastor J, Dewey B, Moen R, Mladenoff DJ, White M, Cohen Y. 1998. Spatial patterns in the moose-forest-soil ecosystem on Isle Royale, Michigan, USA. *Ecological Applications* 8:411–24
18. Turchin P. 1998. *Quantitative Analysis of Movement. Measuring and Modeling Population Redistribution in Animals and Plants*. Sunderland, MA: Sinauer
19. Hagerstrand T. 1967. *Innovation Diffusion as a Spatial Process*. Chicago, IL: Univ. Chicago Press
20. Jarvis PG, McNaughton KG. 1986. Stomatal control of transpiration: scaling up from leaf to region. *Adv. Ecol. Res.* 15:1–49
21. Dickinson RE, Henderson-Sellers A, Kennedy PJ. 1993. *Biosphere-Atmosphere Transfer Scheme Version 1e as Coupled to the NCAR Community Climate Model. NCAR Technical Note NCAR/TN-387+STR*, Natl. Cent. Atmos. Res., Boulder, CO
22. Bugbee BG. 1985. Calculating CO_2 fluxes into leaves. In *Plant Physiology*, ed. FB Salisbury, CW Ross,

pp. 64–65. Belmont, CA: Wadsworth. 3rd ed.
23. Futrelle RP. 1984. How molecules get to their detectors. The physics of diffusion of insect pheromones. *Trends Neurosci.* 7:116–20
24. DeWispelaere C, eds. 1980. Air Pollution Modeling and Its Application I. *Proc. Intl. Tech. Meet. Air Pollution Model. Its Appl. Amsterdam, Neth.* New York: Plenum
25. Turner BD. 1994. *Workbook of Atmospheric Dispersion Modeling: An Introduction to Dispersion Modeling.* Boca Raton, FL: CRC
26. Brown GC, Cooper CE. 1995. *Bioenergetics: A Practical Approach.* New York: Oxford Univ. Press
27. Campbell NA, Reece JB, Mitchell LG. 1999. *Biology.* Menlo Park, CA: Benjamin/Cummings. 5th ed.
28. Nye PH, Tinker PB. 1977. *Solute Movement in the Soil-Root System.* Berkeley, CA: Univ. Calif. Press. 342 pp.
29. Chapin FSI. 1980. The mineral nutrition of wild plants. *Annu. Rev. Ecol. Syst.* 11: 233–60
30. Schnoor JL. 1996. *Environmental Modeling. Fate and Transport of Pollutants in Water, Air, and Soil.* New York: Wiley. 682 pp.
31. Freeze RA, Cherry JA, eds. 1979. *Groundwater.* Englewood Cliffs, NJ: Prentice-Hall
32. Campbell GS. 1985. *Soil Physics With Basic: Transport Models for Soil-Plant Systems.* Amsterdam, Neth.: Elsevier Sci.
33. Webb SW, Ho CK. 1998. Review of enhanced vapor diffusion in porous media. *Proc. TOUGH Workshop,* May 4–6, 1998, pp. 257–262. Berkeley, CA: Lawrence Berkeley Natl. Lab.
34. Livingston GP, Hutchinson GL. 1995. Enclosure-based measurement of trace gas exchange: applications and sources of error. In *Biogenic Trace Gases: Measuring Emissions from Soil and Water,* ed. PA Matson, RC Harriss, pp. 14–51. Cambridge, UK: Blackwell Sci.
35. van Bochove E, Bertrand N, Caron J. 1998. In situ estimation of the gaseous nitrous oxide diffusion coefficient in a sand loam soil. *Soil Sci. Soc. Am. J.* 62:1178–84
36. Massman W, Sommerfeld RA, Mosier AR, Zeller KF, Hehn TJ, Rochelle SG. 1997. A model investigation of turbulence-driven pressure pumping effects on the rate of diffusion of CO_2, N_2O and CH_4 through layered snow packs. *J. Geophys. Res.* 102:18,851–63
37. Brooks PD, Williams MW, Walker DA, Schmidt SK. 1995. The Niwot Ridge snow fence experiment: biogeochemical responses to changes in the seasonal snow pack. In *Biogeochemistry of Seasonally Snow-Covered Catchments (Proc. Boulder Symp., July),* pp. 293–302. Int. Assoc. Hydrol. Sci. Publ. No. 228
38. Oechel WC, Vourlitis G, Hastings SJ. 1997. Cold season CO2 emissions from arctic soils. *Glob. Biogeochem. Cycles* 11:163–72
39. Mast A, Kimberly KP, Wickland P, Striegl RT, Clow DW. 1998. Winter fluxes of CO2 and CH4 from subalpine soils in Rocky Mountain National Park, Colorado. *Glob. Biogeochem. Cycles* 12:607–20
40. van Bochove E, Jones HG, Bertrand N, Prévost D. 2000. Winter fluxes of greenhouse gases from snow covered agricultural soil: intra- and interannual variations. *Glob. Biogeochem. Cycles* 14: 113–25
41. Hillel D. 1998. *Environmental Soil Physics.* San Diego, CA: Academic
42. Liu S, Reiners WA, Keller M, Schimel DS. 1999. Model simulation of changes in N2O and NO emissions with conversion of tropical rain forests to pastures in the Costa Rican Atlantic Zone. *Glob. Biogeochem. Cycles* 13:663–77
43. Groffman PM, Brumme R, Butterbach-Bahl K, Dobbie KE, Mosier AR, et al. 2000. Evaluating annual nitrous oxide fluxes at the ecosystem scale. *Glob. Biogeochem. Cycles* 14:1061–70

44. Davidson EA, Keller M, Erickson HE, Verchot LV, Veldkamp E. 2000. Testing a conceptual model of soil emissions of nitrous and nitric oxides. *BioScience* 50:667–80
45. Sommerfeld RA, Mosier AR, Musselman RC. 1993. CO_2, CH_4 and N_2O flux through a Wyoming snowpack and implications for global budgets. *Nature* 361:140–42
46. Tarrason L, Turner S, Floisand I. 1995. Estimation of seasonal dimethyl sulphide fluxes over the North Atlantic Ocean and their contribution to European pollution levels. *J. Geophys. Res.* 100:11623–39
47. Sarmiento JL, LeQuere C. 1996. Oceanic carbon dioxide uptake in a model of century-scale global warming. *Science* 274:1346–50
48. Lai S, Patra PK. 1998. Variabilities in the fluxes and annual emissions of nitrous oxide from the Arabian Sea. *Glob. Biogeochem. Cycles* 12:321–27
49. Archer DE. 2000. A model of the iron cycle in the ocean. *Glob. Biogeochem. Cycles* 14:269–79
50. Boudreau BP, Huettel M, Forster S, Jahnke RA, MaLachan A, et al. 2001. Permeable marine sediments: overturning an old paradigm. *Eos, Trans. Am. Geophys. Union* 82:133, 135, 136
51. Reiners WA. 1995. Land-ocean interactions in the coastal zone. In *Encyclopedia of Environmental Biology*, ed. WA Nierenberg, pp. 403–15. San Diego: Academic
52. Burnett WC, Chanton J, Christoff J, Kontar E, Krupa S, et al. 2002. Assessing methodologies for measuring groundwater discharge to the ocean. *Eos, Trans. Am. Geophys. Union* 83:117–123
53. Harmon RS, Doe WW III, eds. 2001. *Landscape Erosion and Evolution Modeling*. New York: Kluwer Acad. 539 pp.
54. Schlesinger WH. 1997. *Biogeochemistry. An Analysis of Global Change*. San Diego, CA: Academic. 588 pp. 2nd ed.
55. Ward AD, Elliot WJ. 1995. *Environmental Hydrology*. Boca Raton, FL: CRC
56. Thompson SA. 1999. *Hydrology for Water Management*. Rotterdam, Neth.: Balkema. 362 pp.
57. Viessman W Jr, Knapp JW, Lewis GL, Harbaugh TE. 1977. *Introduction to Hydrology*. New York: Harper & Row. 704 pp. 2nd ed.
58. Bevan F, Moore ID. 1993. *Terrain Analysis and Distributed Modelling in Hydrology*. Chichester, UK: Wiley
59. Costa-Cabral MC, Burges SJ. 1994. Digital elevation model networks (DEMON): a model of flow over hillslopes for computation of contributing and dispersal areas. *Water Resourc. Res.* 30:1681–92
60. DeBarry PA, Quimpo RG, Garbrecht J, Evans TA, Garcia L, et al. 1999. *GIS modules and distributed models of the watershed*. ASCE Task Comm. GIS Modul. Distrib. Models of the Watershed, Spec. Rep., 120 pp. Am. Soc. Civ. Eng., Reston, Va
61. Hunt CB. 1967. *Physiography of the United States*. San Francisco: Freeman
62. Bretz JH. 1923. Glacial drainage on the Columbia Plateau. *Geol. Soc. Am. Bull.* 34:573–608
63. Giblin AE, Gaines AG. 1990. Nitrogen inputs to a marine embayment: the importance of groundwater. *Biogeochemistry* 10:309–28
64. Valiela I, Costa J, Foreman K, Teal JM, Howes B, Aubrey D. 1990. Transport of groundwater-borne nutrients from watersheds and their effects on coastal waters. *Biogeochemistry* 10:177–97
65. Pringle CM, Rowe GL, Triska GJ, Fernandez JF, West J. 1993. Landscape linkages between geothermal activity and solute composition and ecological response in surface waters draining the Atlantic Slope of Costa Rica. *Limnol. Oceanogr.* 38:753–74
66. Hedin LO, von Fischer JC, Ostrom NE, Kennedy BP, Brown MG, Robertson GP. 1998. Thermodynamic constraints on nitrogen transformations and other

biogeochemical processes at soil-stream interfaces. *Ecology* 79:684–703
67. Hill AR, Labadia CF, Sanmugadas K. 1998. Hyporheic zone hydrology and nitrogen dynamics in relation to the streambed topography of a N-rich stream. *Biogeochemistry* 42:285–310
68. Hill AR, DeVito KJ, Campagnolo S, Sanmugadas K. 2000. Subsurface denitrification in a forest riparian zone: interactions between hydrology and supplies of nitrate and organic carbon. *Biogeochemistry* 51:193–223
69. Deutsch WJ. 1997. *Groundwater Geochemistry. Fundamentals and Applications to Contamination*. Boca Raton, FL: Lewis. 221 pp.
70. Wierenga PA, Brusseau ML. 1995. Water and contaminant transport in the vadose zone. In *Environmental Hydrology*, ed. VP Singh, pp. 165–91. Dordrecht, Neth.: Kluwer Acad.
71. Bobba AG, Singh VP. 1995. Groundwater contamination modeling. See Ref. 70, pp. 225–319
72. Dagan G. 2002. An overview of stochastic modeling of groundwater flow and transport. From theory to applications. *Eos, Trans. Am. Geophys. Union* 83(53):621–25
73. Wieczorek GF, Snyder JB, Waitt RB, Morrissey MM, Uhrhammer RA, et al. 2000. Unusual July 10, 1996, rock fall at Happy Isles, Yosemite National Park, California. *Geol. Soc. Am. Bull.* 112:75–85
74. Dykes AP. 2002. Weathering-limited rainfall-triggered shallow mass movements in undisturbed steepland tropical rainforest. *Geomorphology* 46:73–93
75. Johnson AC, Wilcock P. 2002. Association between cedar decline and hillslope stability in mountainous regions of southeast Alaska. *Geomorphology* 46:129–42
76. Bell FG, Stacey TR, Genske DD. 2000. Mining subsidence and its effect on the environment; some differing examples. *Environ. Geol.* 40:135–52
77. Sidle RC, Kamil I, Sharma A, Yamashita S. 2000. Stream response to subsidence from underground coal mining in central Utah. *Environ. Geol.* 39:279–91
78. Giani GP, Silvano S, Zanon G. 2001. Avalanche of 18 January 1997 on Brenva glacier, Mont Blanc group, Western Italian Alps: an unusual process of formation. *Ann. Glaciol.* 32:333–38
79. Cannon SH, Kirkham RM. 2001. Wildfire-related debris-flow initiation processes, Storm King Mountain, Colorado. *Geomorphology* 39:171–88
80. Broecker WS. 1986. *How to Build a Habitable Planet*. Palisades, NY: Eldigio. 291 pp.
81. Brozovic N, Burbank DW, Meigs AJ. 1997. Climatic limits on landscape development in the Northwestern Himalaya. *Science* 276:571–74
82. Brocklehurst SH, Whipple KX. 2002. Glacial erosion and relief production in the eastern Sierra Nevada, California. *Geomorphology* 42:1–24
83. Eyles N, eds. 1983. *Glacial Geology. An Introduction for Engineers and Earth Scientists*. Oxford, UK: Pergamon. 409 pp.
84. Evans DJA. 2001. Glaciers. *Prog. Phys. Geogr.* 25:428–39
85. Koppes MN, Hallet B. 2002. Influence of rapid glacial retreat on the rate of erosion by tidewater glaciers. *Geology* 30:47–50
86. Konrad SK, Humphrey NF, Steig EJ, Clark DH, Potter N Jr, Pfeffer WT. 1999. Rock glacier dynamics and paleoclimatic implications. *Geology* 27:1131–34
87. Welch BC, Pfeffer WT, Harper JT, Humphrey NF. 1998. Mapping subglacial surfaces below temperate valley glaciers using 3-dimensional radio-echo sounding techniques. *J. Glaciol.* 44:164–70
88. Kent M, Giles TM, Owen NW, Dale P, Newnham RM. 2001. Studies of vegetation burial: a focus for biogeography and biogeomorphology. *Prog. Phys. Geogr.* 25:455–82
89. Smith GT, Ives LD, Nagelkerken IA, Ritchie KB. 1996. Caribbean sea fan mortalities. *Nature* 383:487

90. Soulsby C, Malcolm IA, Youngson AF, Moir HJ. 2001. Fine sediment influence on salmonid spawning habitat in a lowland agricultural stream: a preliminary assessment. *Sci. Total Environ.* 265:295–307
91. Bielders CL, Rajot JL, Amadou M. 2002. Transport of soil and nutrients by wind in bush fallow land and traditionally managed cultivated fields in the Sahel. *Geoderma* 109:19–39
92. Isard SA, Gage SH. 2001. *Flow of Life in the Atmosphere. An Airscape Approach to Understanding Invasive Organisms*. East Lansing, MI: Mich. State Univ. Press
93. Johnson KS. 2001. Iron supply and demand in the upper ocean: Is extraterrestrial dust a significant source of bioavailable iron? *Glob. Biogeochem. Cycles* 15:61–63
94. Tabazadeh A, Jensen EJ, Toon OB, Drdla K, Schoeberl MR. 2001. Role of the stratospheric polar freezing belt in denitrification. *Science* 291:2591–94
95. Murray JW. 1992. The oceans. In *Global Biogeochemical Cycles*, ed. SS Butcher, RJ Charleson, GH Orians, GV Wolfe, pp. 175–211. San Diego, CA: Academic
96. Wetzel RG. 1983. *Limnology*. New York: CBS Coll. Publ. 767 pp. 2nd ed.
97. Emiliani C. 1987. *Dictionary of the Physical Sciences. Terms, Formulas, Data*. New York: Oxford Univ. Press. 365 pp.
98. Turekian KK. 1968. *Oceans*. Englewood Cliffs, NJ: Prentice-Hall. 120 pp.
99. Redfield AC. 1958. The biological control of chemical factors in the environment. *Am. Sci.* 46:205–21
100. Lenton TM, Watson AJ. 2000. Redfield revisited. 1. Regulation of nitrate, phosphate, and oxygen in the ocean. *Glob. Biogeochem. Cycles* 14:225–48
101. Wells N. 1986. *The Atmosphere and Ocean: A Physical Introduction*. London: Taylor & Francis. 347 pp.
102. Hicks BB, McMillen RT. 1988. On the measurement of dry deposition using imperfect sensors and in non-ideal terrain. *Bound.-Layer Meteorol.* 42:79–94
103. Hicks BB, Matt DR. 1987. Combining biology, chemistry, and meteorology in modeling and measuring dry deposition. *J. Atmos. Chem.* 6:117–31
104. Bory AJM, Newton PP. 2000. Transport of airborne lithogenic material down through the water column in two contrasting regions of the eastern subtropical North Atlantic Ocean. *Glob. Biogeochem. Cycles* 14:297–315
105. Fung IY, Meyn SK, Tegen I, Doney SC, John JG, Bishop JKB. 2000. Iron supply and demand in the upper ocean. *Glob. Biogeochem. Cycles* 14:281–95
106. Jordan CE, Talbot RW. 2000. Direct atmospheric deposition of water-soluble nitrogen to the Gulf of Maine. *Glob. Biogeochem. Cycles* 14:1315–29
107. Chadwick OA, Derry LA, Vitousek PM, Huebert BJ, Hedin LO. 1999. Changing sources of nutrients during four million years of ecosystem development. *Nature* 397:491–97
108. Stoorvogel JJ, van Breemen N, Janssen BH. 1997. The nutrient input by Harmattan dust to a forest ecosystem in Cote d'Ivoire, Africa. *Biogeochemistry* 37:145–57
109. Matson PA, McDowell WH, Towsend AR, Vitousek PM. 1999. The globalization of N deposition: ecosystem consequences in tropical environments. *Biogeochemistry* 46:67–83
110. Shinn EA, Smith GW, Prospero JM, Betzer P, Hayes ML, et al. 2000. African dust and the demise of Caribbean coral reefs. *Geophys. Res. Lett.* 27:3029–32
111. Neshyba S. 1987. *Oceanography. Perspectives on a Fluid Earth*. New York: Wiley. 506 pp.
112. Levinton JS. 1995. *Marine Biology: Function, Diversity, Ecology*. New York: Oxford Univ. Press. 420 pp.
113. Holligan PM, Reiners WA. 1992. Predicting the responses of the coastal zone to climatic change. In *Global Climate Change. The Ecological Consequences*,

ed. FI Woodward, pp. 212–55. San Diego, CA: Academic
114. Williamson P. 1993. Global science at the coastal interface: fluxes, forcing factors and feedbacks. *Ambio* 22:59
115. Pinkel R, Munk W, Worcester P, Comuelle BD, Rudruck D, et al. 2000. Ocean mixing studied near Hawaiian Ridge. *Eos, Trans. Am. Geophys. Union* 81:545, 553
116. Carter RWG. 1988. *Coastal Environments. An Introduction to the Physical, Ecological and Cultural Systems of Coastlines.* San Diego: Academic
117. Davis RA Jr, ed. 1985. *Coastal Sedimentary Environments.* New York: Springer-Verlag. 420 pp. 2nd ed.
118. Dyer KR. 1986. *Coastal and Estuarine Sediment Dynamics.* Chichester: Wiley. 342 pp.
119. Seymour RJ. 1989. *Nearshore Sediment Transport.* New York: Plenum
120. Smith SV, Wiebe WJ, Hollibaugh JT, Dollar SJ, Hager SW, et al. 1987. Stoichiometry of C, N, P, and Si fluxes in a temperate-climate embayment. *J. Marine Res.* 45:427–60
121. Madden CJ, Day JW Jr, Randall JM. 1988. Freshwater and marine coupling in estuaries of the Mississippi deltaic plain. *Limnol. Oceanogr.* 33:982–1004
122. Smith SV, Hollibaugh JT. 1993. Coastal metabolism and the oceanic organic carbon balance. *Rev. Geophys.* 31:75–89
123. Chant RJ, Curran MC, Able KW, Glenn SM. 2000. Delivery of winter flounder (*Pseudopleuronectes americanus*) larvae to settlement habitats in coves near tidal inlets. *Estuarine Coast. Shelf Sci.* 51(5):529–41 (Abstr.)
124. Garland ED, Zimmer CA, Lentz SJ. 2002. Larval distributions in inner-shelf waters: the roles of wind-driven cross-shelf currents and diel vertical migrations. *Limnol. Oceanogr.* 47:803–17
125. Hutchinson GE. 1957. *A Treatise on Limnology.* Vol. 1. *Geography, Physics, and Chemistry.* New York: Wiley. 1015 pp.
126. Suntharalingam P, Sarmiento JL, Toggweiler JR. 2000. Global significance of nitrous-oxide production and transport from oceanic low-oxygen zones: a modeling study. *Glob. Biogeochem. Cycles* 14:1353–70
127. Archer DE, Eshel G, Winguth A, Broecker W, Pierrehumbert R, et al. 2000. Atmospheric pCO2 sensitivity to the biological pump in the oceans. *Glob. Biogeochem. Cycles* 14:1219–30
128. Sarmiento JL, Monfray P, Maier-Reimer E, Aumont O, Murnane RJ, Orr JC. 2000. Sea-air CO2 fluxes and carbon transport: a comparison of three ocean general circulation models. *Glob. Biogeochem. Cycles* 14:1267–81
129. Broecker WS. 1987. Unpleasant surprises in the greenhouse? *Nature* 328:123–26
130. Broecker WS. 1997. Thermohaline circulation, the Achilles heel of our climate system: Will man-made CO2 upset the current balance? *Science* 278:1582–88
131. Driscoll NW, Haug GH. 1998. A short circuit in thermohaline circulation: a cause for northern hemisphere glaciation? *Science* 282:436–38
132. Williams RG, McLaren AJ. 2000. Estimating the convective supply of nitrate and implied variability in export production over the North Atlantic. *Glob. Biogeochem. Cycles* 14:1299–1313
133. Laws EA, Falkowski PG, Smith WOJ, Ducklow D, McCarthy JJ. 2000. Temperature effects on export production in the open ocean. *Glob. Biogeochem. Cycles* 14:1231–46
134. Green J. 1999. *Atmospheric Dynamics.* Cambridge, UK: Cambridge Univ. Press. 213 pp.
135. Stull RB. 1988. *An Introduction to Boundary Layer Meteorology.* Dordrecht, Neth.: Kluwer Acad. 666 pp.
136. Garratt JR. 1992. *The Atmospheric Boundary Layer.* Cambridge, UK: Cambridge Univ. Press.
137. Raupach MR. 1995. Vegetation-atmosphere interaction and surface

conductance at leaf, canopy and regional scales. *Agric. Forest Meteorol.* 73:151–79
138. Foster GR. 1991. Advances in wind and water erosion prediction. *J. Soil Water Conserv.* 46:27–29
139. Taylor PA, Sykes RJ, Mason PJ. 1989. On the parameterization of drag over small-scale topography in neutrally-stratified boundary-layer flow. *Bound.-Layer Meteorol.* 48:409–22
140. Trimble SW, Crosson P. 2000. U.S. soil erosion rates—myth and reality. *Science* 289:248–50
141. Burrows FM. 1975. Calculation of the primary trajectories of dust seeds, spores and pollen in unsteady winds. *New Phytol.* 75:389–403
142. Sterk G, Stein A. 1997. Mapping windblown mass transport by modeling variability in space and time. *Soil Sci. Soc. Am. J.* 61:232–39
143. Kaimal JC, Finnigan JJ. 1994. *Atmospheric Boundary Layer Flows.* Oxford, UK: Oxford Univ. Press
144. Thom AS. 1975. Momentum, mass and heat exchange of plant communities. In *Vegetation and the Atmosphere*, ed. JL Monteith, pp. 57–93. New York: Academic
145. Foster DR. 1995. Land-use history and four hundred years of vegetation in New England. In *Principles, Patterns and Processes of Land Use Change: Some Legacies of the Columbian Encounter*, ed. BL Turner, pp. 253–319. New York: SCOPE/Wiley
146. Foster DR, Knight DH, Franklin JF. 1998. Landscape patterns and legacies resulting from large, infrequent forest disturbances. *Ecosystems* 1:497–510
147. Massman WJ. 1992. A surface energy balance method for partitioning evapotranspiration data into plant and soil components for a surface with partial canopy cover. *Water Resourc. Res.* 28:1723–32
148. Shuttleworth WJ. 1994. Large-scale experimental and modelling studies of hydrological processes. *Ambio* 23:82–86

149. Andreae MO, Shimel DS. 1989. *Exchange of Trace Gases between Terrestrial Ecosystems and the Atmosphere.* Chichester: Wiley. 363 pp.
150. Lovett GM, Reiners WA, Olson RK. 1982. Cloud droplet deposition in subalpine balsam fir forests. *Science* 218:1303–4
151. Lovett GM, Reiners WA. 1986. Canopy structure and cloud water deposition in subalpine coniferous forests. *Tellus* 38(B):319–27
152. Hiemstra CA, Liston GE, Reiners WA. 2002. Snow redistribution by wind and interactions with vegetation at upper treeline in the Medicine Bow Mountains, Wyoming. *Arct., Antarct. Alp. Res.* 34:262–73
153. Brandorf-Neilsen OE. 1990. *Sand, Dust and Soil in their Relation to Aeolian and Littoral Processes.* Sandbjerg, Den.: Math. Inst., Aarhus Univ.
154. Jickells TD, Dorling S, Deuser WG, Church TM, Arimoto R, Prospero JM. 1998. Air-borne dust fluxes to a deep water sediment trap in the Sargasso Sea. *Glob. Biogeochem. Cycles* 12:311–20
155. McDowell WH, Gines Sanchez C, Asbury CE, Ramos Perez CR. 1990. Influence of aerosols and long-range transport on precipitation chemistry at El Verde, Puerto Rico. *Atmos. Environ.* 24:2813–21
156. Gorham E. 1992. Atmospheric deposition to lakes and its ecological effects: a retrospective and prospective view of research. *Jpn. J. Limnol.* 53:231–48
157. Hicks BB, Hosker RP Jr, Womack JD. 1987. Comparison of wet and dry deposition: the first year of trial dry deposition monitoring. In *The Chemistry of Acid Rain*, ed. RW Johnson, GE Gordon, W Calkins, AZ Elzerman. Washington, DC: Am. Chem. Soc.
158. Bradbury JW, Vehrencamp SL. 1998. *Principles of Animal Communication.* Sunderland, MA: Sinauer. 882 pp.
159. Ali MA, Klyne MA. 1985. *Vision in Vertebrates.* New York: Plenum. 272 pp.
160. Goldsmith TH, Bernard GD. 1974.

The visual system of insects. In *The Physiology of Insecta*, ed. M Rockstein, pp. 165–272. New York: Academic. 2nd ed.

161. Endler JA, Thery M. 1996. Interacting effects of lek placement, display behavior, ambient light, and color patterns in three neotropical forest-dwelling birds. *Am. Nat.* 148:421–52

162. Owen DF. 1982. *Camouflage and Mimicry*. Chicago, IL: Univ. Chicago Press. 158 pp.

163. Warrant E. 2000. The eyes of deep-sea fishes and the changing nature of visual scenes with depth. *Philos. Trans. R. Soc. London B* 355:1155–59

164. Herring PJ. 2000. Species abundance, sexual encounter and bioluminescent signaling in the deep sea. *Philos. Trans. R. Soc. London B* 355:1273–76

165. Attridge TH. 1990. *Light and Plant Responses: A Study of Plant Photophysiology and the Natural Environment*. London: Edward Arnold. 148 pp.

166. Federer CA, Tanner CB. 1966. Spectral distribution of light in the forest. *Ecology* 47:555–60

167. Messier C, Bellefleur P. 1988. Light quantity and quality on the forest floor of pioneer and climax stages in a birch beech sugar maple stand. *Can. J. For. Res.* 18:615–22

168. MacKinnon JR. 1974. The ecology and behaviour of wild orangutans (*Pongo pygmaeus*). *Anim. Behav.* 22:3–74

169. Wasser P. 1977. Individual recognition, intragroup cohesion, and intergroup spacing: evidence from sound playback to forest monkeys. *Behaviour* 60:28–74

170. Duellman WE, Trueb L. 1986. *Biology of Amphibians*. New York: McGraw-Hill

171. Strahan R, eds. 1996. *Mammals of Australia*. Washington, DC: Smithsonian Inst. 2nd ed.

172. Poole JH. 1999. Signals and assessment in African elephants: evidence from playback experiments. *Anim. Behav.* 58:185–93

173. Brenowitz EA. 1986. Environmental influences on acoustic and electric animal communication. *Brain, Behav. Evol.* 28:32–42

174. Prestwich KN. 1994. The energetics of acoustic signaling in anurans and insects. *Am. Zool.* 34:625–43

175. Forrest TG. 1994. From sender to receiver: propagation and environmental effects on acoustic signals. *Am. Zool.* 34:644–54

176. Larom D, Garstang M, Payne K, Raspet R, Lindeque M. 1997. The influence of surface atmospheric conditions on the range and area reached by animal vocalizations. *J. Exp. Biol.* 200:421–31

177. Larom D, Garstang M, Lindeque M, Raspet R, Zunckel M, et al. 1997. Meteorology and elephant infrasound at Etosha National Park, Namibia. *J. Acoust. Soc. Am.* 101:1710–17

178. Bedard AJ Jr, Georges TM. 2000. Atmospheric infrasound. *Phys. Today* 53:32–37

179. Milton SJ, Dean WRJ. 2001. Seeds dispersed in dung of insectivores and herbivores in semi-arid southern Africa. *J. Arid Environ.* 47:465–83

180. Jones CG, Ostfeld RS, Richard MP, Schauber EM, Wolff JO. 1998. Chain reactions linking acorns to gypsy moth outbreaks and Lyme disease risk. *Science* 279:1023–26

181. Cowen RK, Lwiza KMM, Sonaugle S, Paris CB, Olson DB. 2000. Connectivity of marine populations: open or closed? *Science* 287:857–59

182. McLaren BE, Peterson RO. 1994. Wolves, moose, and tree rings on Isle Royale. *Science* 266:1555–58

183. Dunning JB Jr, Stewart DJ, Danielson BJ, Noon BR, Root TL, et al. 1995. Spatially explicit population models: current forms and future uses. *Ecol. Appl.* 5:3–11

184. Scott JM, Heglund PJ, Morrison M, Raphael M, Haufler J, Hall B, eds. 2002. *Predicting Species Occurrences: Issues of Scale and Accuracy*. Covello, CA: Island

185. Woodwell GM. 1969. Radioactivity and

fallout: the model pollution. *BioScience* 19:884–87
186. Carson R. 1962. *Silent Spring.* Cambridge, MA: Houghton Mifflin. 368 pp.
187. Woodwell GM, Craig PP, Johnson HA. 1971. DDT in the biosphere: Where does it go? *Science* 174:1101–7
188. Gorham E. 1955. On the acidity and salinity of rain. *Geochim. Cosmochim. Acta* 7:231–39
189. Likens GE, Bormann FH. 1974. Acid rain: a serious regional environmental problem. *Science* 184:1176–79
190. Harte J. 2002. Toward a synthesis of the Newtonian and Darwinian worldviews. *Phys. Today* 55:29–34
191. Graedel TE, Crutzen PJ. 1993. *Atmospheric Change: An Earth System Perspective.* New York: Freeman. 446 pp.
192. Houghton RA, Hobbie JE, Melillo JM, Moore B, Peterson BJ, et al. 1983. Changes in the carbon content of terrestrial biota and soils between 1860 and 1980: a net release of CO2 to the atmosphere. *Ecol. Monogr.* 53:235–62
193. Woodwell GM, Pecan EV, eds. 1973. *Carbon and the Biosphere.* Springfield, VA: Off. Inf. Serv., US Atomic Energy Comm. 392 pp.
194. McGuire AD, Sitch S, Clein JS, Dargaville R, Esser G, et al. 2001. Carbon balance of the terrestrial biosphere in the twentieth century: analyses of CO2, climate and land use effects with four process-based ecosystem models. *Glob. Biogeochem. Cycles* 15:183–206
195. Delwiche CC. 1970. The nitrogen cycle. *Sci. Am.* 223:136–46
196. Vitousek PM, Aber JD, Howarth RW, Likens GE, Matson PA, et al. 1997. Human alteration of the global nitrogen cycle: sources and consequences. *Ecol. Appl.* 7:737–50
197. Houghton JT, Ding Y, Griggs DJ, Noguer M, van der Linden PJ, et al., eds. 2001. *Climate Change 2001: The Scientific Basis.* Cambridge, UK: Cambridge Univ. Press. 882 pp.
198. Gaston KJ, eds. 1996. *Biodiversity: A Biology of Numbers and Difference.* Oxford, UK: Blackwell Sci. 396 pp.
199. Houghton RA. 1994. The worldwide extent of land-use change. *BioScience* 44:305–13
200. Kley D. 1997. Tropospheric chemistry and transport. *Science* 276:1043–45
201. Mahlman JD. 1997. Dynamics of transport processes in the upper troposphere. *Science* 276:1079–83
202. Volk CM, Elkins JW, Fahey DW, Salawitch RJ, Dutton GS, et al. 1996. Quantifying transport between the tropical and mid-latitude lower stratosphere. *Science* 272:1763–68
203. Cohn JP. 1987. Chlorofluorocarbons and the ozone layer. *BioScience* 37:647–50
204. Goudie AS, Middleton NJ. 2001. Saharan dust storms: nature and consequences. *Earth Sci. Rev.* 56:179–204
205. Galloway JN, Cowling EB. 2002. Reactive nitrogen and the world: 200 years of change. *Ambio* 21:64–71
206. Fung I, John J, Lerner J, Matthews E, Prather M, et al. 1991. Three-dimensional model synthesis of global methane cycle. *J. Geophys. Res.* 96:13033–65
207. Broecker WS. 1991. The great ocean conveyor. *Oceanography* 4:79–80
208. Bard E. 2002. Climate shock: Abrupt changes over millennial time scales. *Phys. Today* 55:32–38
209. Vitousek PM, D'Antonio CM, Loope LL, Westbrooks R. 1996. Biological invasions as global environmental change. *Am. Sci.* 84:468–78
210. Vitousek PM, Matson PA. 1993. Agriculture, the global nitrogen cycle, and trace gas flux. In *The Biogeochemistry of Global Change: Radiative Trace Gases,* ed. RS Oremland, pp. 193–208. New York: Chapman & Hall
211. Hengveld R. 1989. *The Dynamics of Biological Invasions.* New York: Chapman & Hall. 176 pp.

GLOBAL STATE OF BIODIVERSITY AND LOSS

Rodolfo Dirzo[1] and Peter H. Raven[2]

[1]*Instituto de Ecología, Departamento Ecología Evolutiva, Universidad Nacional Autónoma de México, Mexico DF 04510; email: urania@ecologia.unam.mx*
[2]*Missouri Botanical Garden, St. Louis, Missouri 63166-0299; email: praven@nas.edu*

Key Words biodiversity hotspots, endemism, extinction, species diversity, species threatening

■ **Abstract** Biodiversity, a central component of Earth's life support systems, is directly relevant to human societies. We examine the dimensions and nature of the Earth's terrestrial biodiversity and review the scientific facts concerning the rate of loss of biodiversity and the drivers of this loss. The estimate for the total number of species of eukaryotic organisms possible lies in the 5–15 million range, with a best guess of ∼7 million. Species diversity is unevenly distributed; the highest concentrations are in tropical ecosystems. Endemisms are concentrated in a few hotspots, which are in turn seriously threatened by habitat destruction—the most prominent driver of biodiversity loss. For the past 300 years, recorded extinctions for a few groups of organisms reveal rates of extinction at least several hundred times the rate expected on the basis of the geological record. The loss of biodiversity is the only truly irreversible global environmental change the Earth faces today.

CONTENTS

INTRODUCTION 138
THE FACETS OF BIODIVERSITY 138
BIODIVERSITY THROUGH TIME 140
GLOBAL MAGNITUDE OF BIODIVERSITY 141
    Species Diversity 141
    Intraspecific (Genetic) Diversity 142
    Endemism 144
    Domesticated Biodiversity 146
    Biodiversity Novelties 147
ECO-GEOGRAPHIC DISTRIBUTION 148
    The Distribution of Species, Families, and Orders 148
    Population and Genetic Diversity Distribution 150
    Distribution of Endemism 151
LOSS OF BIODIVERSITY 152
    Prehistoric and Recent Extinctions 152
    Threatened Species: How Many, Where, and Why 156
    Current and Future Rates of Extinction 161

1543-5938/03/1121-0137$14.00

Threats to Populations 162
EPILOGUE 163

INTRODUCTION

Biodiversity—the sum total of all of the plants, animals, fungi, and microorganisms on Earth; their genetic and phenotypic variation; and the communities and ecosystems of which they are a part—is more rich and varied now than ever before (1), but it is threatened with a major pulse of extinction to which some authors have referred as the sixth major extinction of the Phanerozoic Era (2). Even though there is no consensus as to the magnitude of biodiversity on Earth, it has clearly reached unprecedented diversity as a result of more than 3.5 billion years of organic evolution. At the same time, human domination of the planet is so extensive (3) that Crutzen (4) has gone so far as to refer to the present as "the Anthropocene Era" (4). It is obvious to most scientists that extinction is rampant at present, but a few skeptics have demurred, claiming that this is "a doomsday myth" (5) or that the estimates of extinction are "strident, inconsistent and data-free" (6).

In this paper we shall examine the dimensions and nature of the Earth's terrestrial biodiversity and review the scientific facts concerning the rate of loss of this biodiversity and the factors that are causing this loss. This review is important because (a) biodiversity is a central component of Earth's life support systems and directly relevant to human societies; (b) any attempt to defend a social cause, such as biodiversity, should rest on the best facts available; and (c) the loss of biodiversity is the only truly irreversible global environmental change the Earth faces today. We shall concern ourselves solely with eukaryotic organisms, because the facts are not yet available to support a comparable discussion of prokaryotic diversity.

THE FACETS OF BIODIVERSITY

The standard definition of biodiversity implies a logical link between the three levels it comprises: The organisms that make up a population of a given species behave and respond to their environment as they do as a result of the features determined by their genetic constitution. Species are constituents of communities that, with their physical environment, form the ecosystems, landscapes, and ultimately biomes.

Other facets of biodiversity are important from a functional and evolutionary point of view. These include the diversity of functional groups (or, in the case of plants, life forms); the proportion of endemic taxa; and the diversity of cultivated and domesticated species and their wild relatives. Life forms reflect the adaptive ways in which organisms respond to the selective pressures of the environment; in turn, the relative composition of life forms is reflected in the "spectra" characterizing a given kind of ecosystem (7). Such a classification helps also to define the structure and diversity of communities; an additional aspect of this approach is that it can facilitate comparisons between whole communities and their environments. For example, plant life form diversity in a tropical rain forest would include several species of herbs, epiphytic herbs, shrubs, hemiepiphytic trees, light-demanding and shade-tolerant trees, vines, lianas, palms, and parasitic plants; different types of forest will have contrasting relative abundances of each life form (8).

The proportion of taxa in a specified geographical area that is found nowhere else constitutes an important qualitative aspect of biodiversity—endemism. Initially, scientific interest in endemism was related to biogeographical and evolutionary studies, but currently an appreciation of endemism facilitates the formulation of conservation strategies worldwide. Endemism can be expressed at different levels; thus species, genera, families, orders or even phyla can be endemic to a given region. In a different sense, regions may have endemic life forms, as is the case of seasonally dry tropical forests of Madagascar, the Namib Desert, or Mexico, in which succulent and other unusual plants of bizarre form abound.

Domestication, the process by which plants and animals are selected from wild populations and adapted to special environments created by humans, is another important facet of biodiversity. Even though cultivated and domesticated plants and animals represent a very small fraction of the total species (see below), they constitute almost all of the food we consume and are thus of great importance (9).

Finally, another salient aspect of biodiversity is the occurrence, in some regions, of distinct biotic elements of different biogeographic origins in the same area. This includes the mingling of boreal temperate and Neotropical or Madrean elements, for example the co-occurrence of taxa of Nearctic and Neotropical origin in Mexico/Central America, or the confluence of animals and plants from the Indo-malaysian and Australasian regions in the islands between Java and New Guinea. Such meeting grounds of biogeographic provinces are reflected in unique assemblages of organisms including, for example, communities of boreal trees such as oaks, *Liquidambar*, and walnuts with austral *Cecropia*, *Nectandra*, and tree ferns in a small area in southeast Mexico and monkeys, marsupials, and cockatoos with other Asian and Australasian birds on a single tree in Indonesia (10).

Most analyses of biodiversity have been carried out at the level of species, even though the relationships both at higher taxonomic levels and genetic variation within species are also of great interest. Frequently in this paper, as in the literature generally, we shall use "biodiversity" to refer to species-level patterns of distribution.

In dealing with species diversity, the number of species per unit area or locality, one measure of the biological richness of a region, is termed alpha diversity. In contrast, beta diversity is a measure of the changes in species composition from one area to an adjacent one. If we speak comparatively of all the species in a given region, such as tropical America, or biome, such as the short-grass prairies of North America, we use the term gamma diversity. Thus a latitudinal gradient of higher tropical than temperate diversity of birds or plants is due to higher levels of alpha, beta, and gamma diversity.

BIODIVERSITY THROUGH TIME

Figure 1 (see color insert) shows the time-course of biological diversity throughout the Phanerozoic Period, the last 600 million years of life on Earth. The figure also shows the five major extinctions (arrows) that took place during this period.

Available fossil evidence suggests that diversity of families of multicellular marine organisms (Figure 1a) rose steadily through the Cambrian Period, attaining a plateau near the end of the Ordovician Period (about 440 million years ago) and then punctuated by a great wave of extinction in the Permian (290–245 million years ago), and subsequently increased steadily to the present. The trend in species number (not shown in Figure 1) is even more extreme: relatively low from the early Cambrian Period (some 540 million years ago) until the mid-Cretaceous Period, and then increasing tenfold over the past 100 million years (12). Terrestrial organisms first appeared about 440 million years ago, near the start of the Silurian Period, with the invasion of the land by the ancestors of plants, fungi, vertebrate animals, and arthropods—each group increasing rapidly in diversity from that time onward.

At the species level, vascular plants, an essentially terrestrial group, began to diversify markedly around 400 million years ago and declined during the worldwide Permian extinction event that also affected marine organisms profoundly (Figure 1b), and then began, like marine organisms, to diversify around the middle of the Cretaceous Period, some 100 million years ago, with the flowering plants (angiosperms) the dominant group thereafter.

The fossil records of both marine and terrestrial multicellular eukaryotes indicate maximum diversity at the present time (Figure 1). The present level of marine diversity is estimated to be about twice the average over the past 600 million years (12), and that of terrestrial diversity perhaps also about twice its historical average since organisms first invaded the land about 440 million years ago. The trend has been continually upward despite the five major extinction events that have occurred over the past 570 million years, which essentially covers the history of multicellular organisms (Figure 1). Nevertheless, this widely cited pattern of temporal increase in biodiversity through the Phanerozoic Era must be taken with caution. On the one hand, there is the "pull-of-the-recent effect" (13), whereby young rocks are more likely than old rocks to be well preserved, and thus the most recent occurrences of species are more likely to be found than the older occurrences. Moreover, a considerable fraction of the recent marine faunas are known from single rocks, from restricted localities. For example, Pliocene collections of macrofossils from the Isthmus of Panama constitute about 18% of the total Pliocene diversity, despite the fact that this area of Pliocene deposition is less than 0.1% of the 7 million km^2 of Pliocene deposition worldwide (14). It has been claimed that in order to accurately assess the trajectory of the increase in marine biodiversity during the Phanerozoic Period a comprehensive, global program directed to obtain new data is urgently needed (14).

The fossil record and the application of several analytical treatments to the data [largely the survivorship patterns of thousands of cohorts of fossil genera (15)] suggest that the average species has a life span of ~5–10 million years, including a range from about 1 to 13 million years for mammals and planktonic foraminifera, respectively (2). If throughout their geological history species last 10^6–10^7 years, it follows that their rate of extinction is 1-0.1 species per million species-years [see (16)]. However, because species longevities are based on the geological divisions in which they lived, species lifetimes may be overestimated while, conversely, records from single exposures of rock will lead to underestimates of species' true lifetimes. An important, independent source of information supports the million-year life span of species as a conservative estimate: molecular phylogenies that permit estimates of speciation rates (16). Since natural extinction rates cannot greatly exceed speciation rates, models in which lineages have the same probability of giving birth to a new lineage or going extinct allow the estimation of the rate parameters. The relevance of these estimates will become evident in our subsequent discussion of biodiversity loss.

GLOBAL MAGNITUDE OF BIODIVERSITY

Species Diversity

There are some 100 phyla of living organisms (17), but the total number of species they include is very poorly known. Complete catalogues of the described, valid species exist for only a few groups of organisms, and so the total can only be estimated; May (18) calculates it at 1.5 million species, lowering an earlier estimate by Hammond (9) at 1.75 million species. Much more difficult to estimate is the actual number of living eukaryotic species; moreover, methods of estimating the number and definition of prokaryotic species and viruses are still very limited, and we are omitting them from further consideration here. Relatively reliable estimates are available for some groups of vertebrate animals and some groups of plants and insects (e.g., butterflies and mosquitoes), but for others, especially nematodes, fungi, and mites, the estimates are much less certain–but the groups are certainly very large. Estimates of the total number of species of organisms are based on expert opinions by those who understand the level of diversity in a particular group of organisms well, extrapolations from an initial estimated number, or combinations of these methods. Thus sampling with an analysis of results has yielded estimates like Erwin's (19) of 30 million species of tropical arthropods based on the sampling of beetles in tropical tree canopies. The results of several of the expert opinions and extrapolations available are summarized by Pimm et al. (16). Such estimates deal essentially with possible orders of magnitude rather than actual numbers, leading to a fair degree of uncertainty [see (20)]. The number of described species typically falls 1–2 orders of magnitude below the extrapolated number, while expert opinions fall towards the middle of the range, and the extrapolated values move towards 10^6–10^8. The most recent, comprehensive, and careful effort to estimate the number of species overall is that of May (18), who reworked earlier estimates carefully from a statistical and factual point of view and effectively replaces Hammond's (9) earlier efforts in this area. May concludes that the best estimate for the total number of species of eukaryotic organisms possibly lies in the 5–15 million range, with a best guess of around 7 million species. Papers presented at a recent symposium (21) rework what can most logically be deduced about the number of species in individual groups and update the efforts of Hammond (9) in this regard.

Looking at the current rates of publication of new species [e.g., 13,000 animal species per year; see (9)], it is evident that the task of describing the total number of species on Earth will not be completed for many decades, even assuming they can all be collected and put into the hands of the appropriate experts. For flowering plants, Prance et al. (22), taking as their base the traditional estimate of 250,000 valid, described species, noting that an average of 2350 species had been described each year in the preceding nine-year period, and considering the rate of discovery of novelties throughout the world, estimated that perhaps 50,000 to 70,000 additional valid species remain to be described. Remarkably, recent estimates have strongly suggested that the assumption of 250,000 valid, described species may not be even approximately accurate! Thus, Bramwell (23), using the number of species of the largest country in a given region of the world as a "baseline flora" to which he added the number of local endemics from the other countries of that region, arrived at an estimated number of 421,968 species. This number is very similar to that suggested by Govaerts (24), 422,000, based on the enumerations presented in the first volumes of his *World Checklist of Seed Plants*. If these estimates are verified, then the total number of species of flowering plants could be as high as 500,000 or even more. A verified world checklist is urgently needed to provide an adequate baseline for knowledge about this extraordinarily important group of organisms.

Recent collections of papers and encyclopedias (21, 25, 26) present estimates of the total number of species either described or predicted for individual groups of organisms, and such efforts will and should continue as the base is made more secure. Despite all of the uncertainties, we can conclude with May (18) that the eukaryotic organisms can best be estimated as between 5 and 15 million but that it is still conceivable that the figure could be greatly increased, even by as much as an order of magnitude, by new discoveries (1, 16).

Intraspecific (Genetic) Diversity

In its broadest sense, genetic diversity embraces the diversity at all levels of an ecological or taxonomic hierarchy. Within species, this diversity exists at three levels: inside individuals, between individuals of a population, and between populations. Here we will stress variation within and between populations, the latter expressed as the relative proportion of the variation between and within populations, or population divergence. An enormous and only partly explored degree of genetic variation exists within populations.

A single, well-explored example will illustrate the richness and complexity of this variation. The following observations relate to plants of white clover (*Trifolium repens*), a stoloniferous perennial species, from a population growing in a 1-ha field in North Wales and analyzed for variation in those genes associated with different characters of known selective importance. Among 50 clones selected from the field, all but a few differed in the combinations of genes affecting their fitness in nature (27). For example, in a reciprocal transplant experiment, four different types of clover plants expressed differential competitive abilities depending on the neighboring grass species, each usually expressing its best performance when transplanted into conditions like those from which it originated (28). Another adaptive feature was marked by the occurrence of both cyanogenic and acyanogenic individuals, the former releasing cyanide when physically damaged by herbivores. Such individuals occurred in different parts of the field depending on the relative density of herbivores and thus the probability of being attacked (29). Furthermore, at least nine different morphs of leaf marks were found in different individuals (30); the character might be relevant in interactions with herbivores. Finally, several clover forms are known with different susceptibilities to being infected by nitrogen-fixing *Rhizobium* bacteria. These traits are mainly genetically determined, and even for the relatively few that we have mentioned here, the potential combinations of genetically distinct variants within this 1-ha field are very numerous. Comparable results have often been found for other species that have been investigated, and it is clear that the level of genetic diversity in out-crossing species generally is extremely large, as geneticists have demonstrated with increasing precision for populations of both plants and animals over the course of many decades.

Many species are composed of populations that are genetically more or less distinct from one another. A well-known example is the case of ecotypic differentiation, which has been demonstrated within many plant species over nearly a century [e.g., (31)]. Such differentiation occurs in relation to gradients in physical habitats, and it is widespread both in plants and in animals, sometimes even over short distances and relatively brief periods of time. A classic example here is the differentiation of plants that have invaded tailings from abandoned mines (32). In general, the more extensively such studies are conducted, the more variation is encountered.

What is the magnitude of population diversity at a global scale? The answer to this seemingly unmanageable question was attempted by Hughes et al. (33) by analyzing information on Mendelian populations of eukaryotic species. They first estimated the average number of populations per unit area from the literature on population differentiation [a total of 81 publications, including vertebrates (35), plants (23), arthropods (19), and one flatworm]. This estimate yielded a value of one population per 10,000 km^2 for an average species. To estimate the approximate average number of populations per species, they calculated the average range size per species from published range maps. The estimated value was 2.6 million km^2 (but they used the average for butterflies, 2.2 million km^2, as it was considered more conservative). The number of populations per unit area and the average range size were combined to estimate the number of populations per species, and this yielded a value of 220 (i.e., $2.2 \times 10^6/1 \times 10^4$). This value, multiplied by the presumed number of species on Earth, should give a global estimate. For the global species number, they used three values: 5, 14, and 30 million, and the corresponding populations were 1.1, 3.1, and 6.1 billion globally. Although very tentative, these estimates certainly illustrate the point that population diversity at the global scale is enormous. They also form a rough reference estimate for our subsequent discussion of the potential magnitude of biodiversity loss at the population level.

Endemism

Endemism refers to the restriction of kinds of organisms to particular geographical areas, with many different factors responsible for its nature and extent. In an interesting general analysis, Bykov [1979, 1983, cited in (34)] described the relationship between plant species endemism and area across a range of spatial scales, up to the size of the global, total land area. The magnitude of endemism of an area increases with size of that area. Given that the totality of all vascular plants is endemic to the total land area of earth, at this area the level of plant endemism is 100%, and should be lower for any smaller area. Bykov suggests that the lowest endemism for a "concrete" flora (i.e., one not truncated in number by the sample area being too small) should be 1%, which, he suggests, occurs at an area of 625 km², a size consistent with other minimum data points discussed by Major (34). This data point and that for the land area of the Earth (and its total flora) define a straight line on a log-log plot of percent endemism and area (Figure 2a). The precise size of the area at 1% endemism is arbitrary, but Bykov notes that the slope of the relationship is little influenced by changes in endemism values in the range 300 km² to a few thousand km².

Bykov's plot gives us a qualitative and quantitative means of assessing the relative degree of endemism for a given locality. Qualitatively, localities lying above the line will have less than normal endemicity; those below will have more, a useful point of reference. One can observe that the degree of endemism for the United States or Austria lie approximately on the line, whereas some small

Figure 2 Bykov's plant endemism plot [cited in (34)] showing (a) the relationship between percentage of endemic plant species in different floras and their corresponding area. The diagonal runs across a minimum of 1% endemic plant species and its corresponding area to the total number of plant species endemic to the Earth in the total surface land area; and (b) the location of Myers' et al. (35) hotspots of global biodiversity on Bykov's plant endemism plot. The 25 hotspots were plotted on the basis of data on percent endemism and their original area obtained from Myers et al. For identification of the 25 hotspots see (35). The shaded areas in both plots show the domain of endemism-rich regions. Figure modified from the original plot by Bykov, with permission.

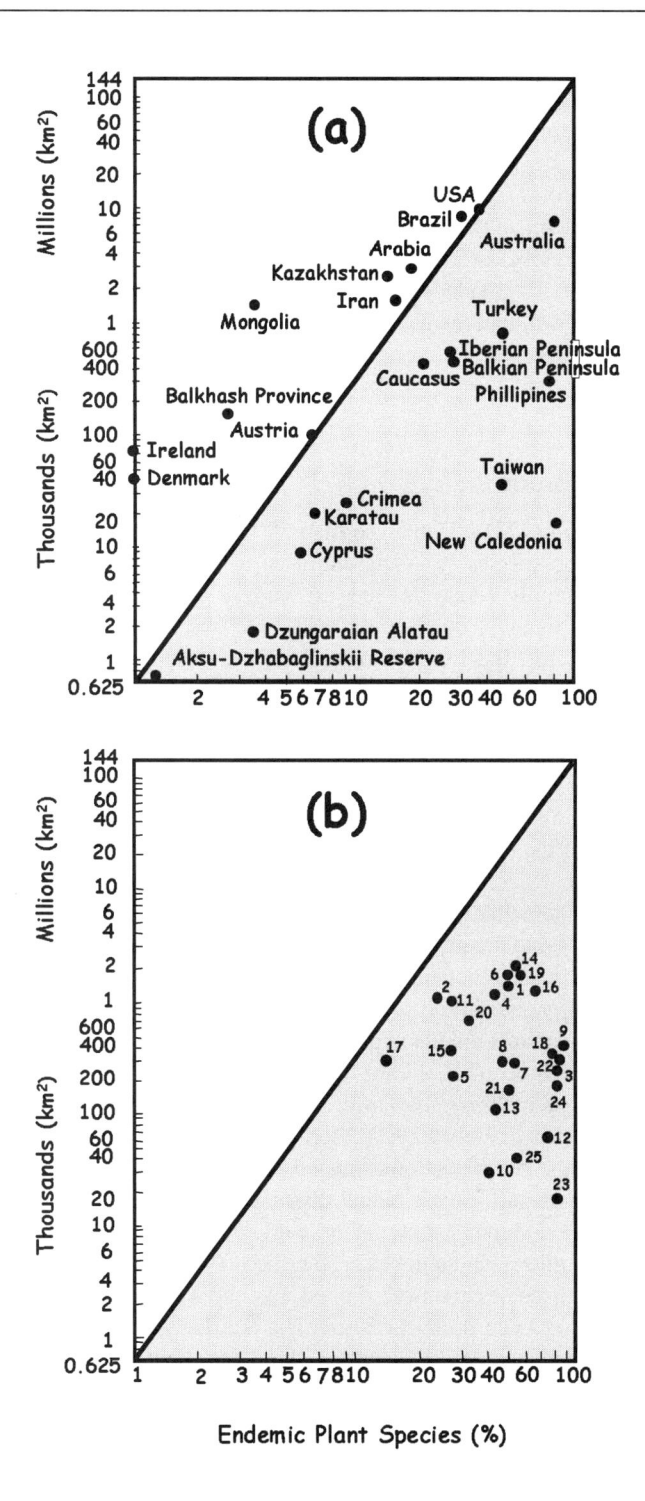

GLOBAL BIODIVERSITY AND LOSS 145

Endemic Plant Species (%)

countries such as Denmark or Ireland, depauperate in endemics, lie on the Y-axis, at a height of around the 50×10^3 km² tick. Areas that lie below the line, and particularly those located in the smallest possible quadrats in the lowest-right area of the plot, are the most endemic-rich. For example, New Caledonia has 68% endemic species in an area of 18.3×10^3 km². Quantitatively, Bykov defined an index of endemism l_e, on the basis of the degree of departure of our site of interest, E_f, from the global expected, normal value read off the line, E_n, as $l_e = E_f/E_n$. One then has to look for values greater or lower than 1.0 for sites with endemism levels greater or lower than the global normal, respectively. Biodiversity "hotspots" [see (35)], in terms of their degree of endemism, would be placed largely toward the plot's lower right sector. We shall discuss them further below.

Domesticated Biodiversity

About a third (173) of the more than 500 families of flowering plants have one or more crop species (9)—amounting to a total of about 2500 species overall. The grass family (Poaceae) has the largest number (379) and is closely followed by legumes, Fabaceae, with 337; the two families together include about 30% of all crop species. Ten more families (Apiaceae, Arecaceae, Asteraceae, Brassicaceae, Chenopodiaceae, Menthaceae, Rosaceae, Rutaceae, Solanaceae, and Zingiberaceae) have from a few to many dozens of crop species each, with the numerous other families including only one or a few species. Among the roughly 2500 crop species, just 103 supply over 90% of the calories humans consume, directly or indirectly (36), with just three grasses (cereals), rice, wheat, and maize, supplying over 60% of the total. More than 15 plants are cultivated as sources of fiber, and thousands more as ornamentals or sources of medicines. (Perhaps a tenth of the total species, more than 25,000 plant species overall, are or have been used as sources of medicines, but the great majority of these are collected directly from nature.)

Most crops are genetically diverse, as evidenced by the many land races that exist in the major cereals and such crops as bananas, cassava, potatoes, and tomatoes. Distinctive variants are also characteristic of many crops; for example, cabbage, cauliflowers, broccoli, kohlrabi, Brussels sprouts, calabrese, and kale are all selected variants of *Brassica oleracea*.

Of the approximately 50,000 described vertebrate species 30–40 species of birds and mammals have been domesticated. Apart from dogs and cats, four species of domestic mammals have a global distribution (except for the Antarctic) and are impressively dominant numerically: cattle (1300 million), sheep (1200 million), pigs (850 million), and chickens (10 billion) (9). Most of the remaining domesticated animal species are more limited, like those of the Andean camelids (llamas and vicuñas). As in domesticated crops, the degree of infraspecific variation in animals is astonishing: for example, there are about 800 distinct breeds each of cattle and sheep. Although the vast majority of the domesticated animals are used as food, they also provide wool, tallow, bone, manure for fuel and fertilizer, and leather, and they are used very widely as draft animals.

Biodiversity Novelties

With perhaps one in ten species of the Earth's eukaryotic organisms having been discovered, it should not be surprising that strikingly novel and wholly unexpected new taxa should continue to be discovered among the 15,000 to 20,000 new species that are annually described. Even for relatively well-known areas like the United States, the rate of discovery suggests that no more than a third to a half of the estimated total 500,000 to 750,000 species of organisms have yet been discovered. For flowering plants, perhaps 1000 new species await discovery in addition to the 18,000 already known to this country (37).

The number of new species has been rising over the past decade to levels comparable to those of the mid-eighteenth to late nineteenth century (38). Much of this discovery, as for mammals, seems to be directly correlated with serious exploration of new areas. Thus, fieldwork over the last decade in the Annamite mountains on the border of central Vietnam and Laos has brought to light a new bovid and at least three new species of muntjac deer, together with what seems to be a new genus of rabbit (39). Similar trends have been demonstrated for other groups of vertebrates (38).

Some of the new discoveries are of evident economic importance, such as a species of maize, *Zea diploperennis*, from the state of Jalisco in western Mexico, which is interfertile with cultivated maize but unique in its perennial habit; it is restricted to a disturbed area about the size of a football field and was discovered only 25 years ago (40).

Even a few new phyla and classes of eukaryotic organisms are being found each decade, mostly from marine habitats. The continued exploration of southern Mexico and Central America has led to the discovery of two new families of plants during the past two decades, one of them (Ticondendraceae) a locally fairly abundant tree species (41) and the other (Lacandoniaceae) comprising a slender, parasitic, achlorophyllous root-parasite, with a unique floral structure in which the pistillate organs surround the staminate ones (42). Occurring at a single locality in Chiapas, the latter plant is in danger of extinction. Other remarkable botanical examples, all newly discovered palms from Madagascar [narrated by Prance et al. in (22)], include the smallest palm (less than 27 cm in height), *Dypsis tenuissima*; an aquatic palm, *Ravenea musicalis*, with fruit and seeds with adaptations for flotation and aquatic dispersal and known only from a single population of about 450 plants along a river; and *Satranala* sp. nov. with a peculiar, hard endocarp that features flanges unlike those of any other palm endocarp, which may have facilitated the dispersal of its seeds by the recently extinct giant elephant bird.

Additional bizarre discoveries include many organisms, catalogued by Donoghue and Alverson (38), with unique life styles: an agaric fungus that fruits under the ice of lakes in far southern South America; an Australian frog that raises its tadpoles in its stomach; and a Brazilian caecilian that is three times the length (up to 0.8 m) of the largest lungless amphibian previously known. Most striking among the terrestrial invertebrates is the recent report of a new order of the class insecta from the Afrotropics (43)! This new order, the Mantophasmatodea, is represented by insects that look like a cross between a cricket and a stick insect, and it is the first of this taxonomic hierarchy to be discovered for more than 80 years. Once it was discovered in the field in Namibia, museum specimens collected over a period of more than a century were recognized from other parts of southern Africa. And the list goes on and on! Clearly we live in an age of discovery; one in which the geographic exploration of rapidly dwindling natural areas, coupled with increasingly deep phylogenetic analyses, is revealing much that has been unsuspected about the nature of life on Earth.

ECO-GEOGRAPHIC DISTRIBUTION

Many trends in the distributional patterns of biodiversity are well established. The most evident of these is that of species diversity, which increases from high to low latitudes in most groups that have been well analyzed. We show here that the distribution of higher taxonomic categories as well as other aspects of biodiversity tend to follow the same geographic gradient and review other additional eco-geographic trends as well. A comprehensive discussion of the causal factors underlying such gradients is, however, out of the scope of this paper.

The Distribution of Species, Families, and Orders

We begin with the interesting exercise carried out by Williams et al. (44). These authors combined the available data about the distribution of families for plants, amphibians, reptiles, and mammals using three combinatory approaches: summing the absolute family richness, the proportional family richness, and the proportional family richness weighted for the presumed total species richness of each family. The diversity of the groups for these parameters was mapped onto a cylindrical equal-area projection of the world, using equal-area grid cells of 10^0. The three approaches yielded similar results, which showed a consistent gradient of richness from high to low latitudes. In addition, the Americas were consistently richer than the Old World. The area of maximum family diversity was northern South America for two of the three analyses, with that for weighted family diversity being Central America. Kaufman (45) demonstrated a similar gradient for mammalian orders in the New World.

Latitudinal variation in species richness has been estimated in many different ways, including various arbitrary units of area, and these have yielded comparable gradients for the groups considered, with low latitudes in general richer in species than higher ones [see reviews in (1, 25, 26, 46)]. It also seems to apply to the fossil record, at least for the past 70 million years or so [see Figure 2.23 in (1) for fossil Foraminifera].

There are so many examples of studies of this kind that we selected only a few to review here—ones that illustrate the general principles. Global maps often show species richness of different taxa plotted as a world density surface. In the case of plants, for example, a map has been constructed based on ca. 1400 literature records from different geographic units with mapped richness values calculated on a standard area of 10,000 km² using a single species/area curve (47). The map in Figure 3 (see color insert) shows the Americas. Superimposed on this map we present plant species density data for specific localities sampled by A. Gentry (48). This remarkable data set corresponds to a large number of sites for which local species diversity of trees with a minimum diameter at breast height of 2.5 cm was enumerated at the scale of 0.1 ha with a highly standardized protocol and extremely high-quality species identification. In addition, we applied regression analysis of latitude with species diversity for the Gentry data. The three analyses show a very consistent latitudinal gradient of plant diversity. In broad geographic terms, species densities range from over 5000 species/10,000 km² in tropical regions to less than 100 in the highest latitudes. In terms of local species diversity values range from an average of 270 species per 0.1 ha in Colombia to ca. 15 near the U.S.-Canadian border. In addition, the relationship between latitude and local species diversity from the Gentry data was highly significant ($F = 33.1$; $P < 0.0001$; $R^2 = 0.56$). Furthermore, Figure 3 makes evident the occurrence of high-diversity centers, including western Amazonia, Brazil's Atlantic Coast, and Mesoamerica.

Similar analyses have been performed for other continents, and the overall results are consistent with those of Figure 3. Species density maps are also available for other groups [see (11) and http://stort.unep-wcmc.org]. For the botanical example just presented, data were not available to explore to what extent the latitudinal gradient is explained by species turnover. However, a recent study (49), comparing species composition among 20 tropical dry forest sites in Mexico, showed that 72% of a total of 917 sampled species were present only in a single site and that the average similarity (Sorensen's index) among sites was only 9%. Such a high species turnover in tropical sites has been found in other studies of plants and for vertebrates as well, as we discuss below.

Our final example concerns the distribution patterns of mammals (45). The species richness of mammals (excluding bats) for natural communities in the New World shows the same overall latitudinal gradient that we have mentioned for plants. In addition, an analysis of species turnover among localities showed that beta diversity was also higher at lower latitudes. These analyses indicate that the regional increase of species richness towards the equator (i.e., gamma diversity), appears to be a consequence of great increases both in local species richness (alpha diversity) and in species differentiation among communities (beta diversity).

Species number analyses of plants suggest that about 90,000 species, approximately twice as many as in Africa south of the Sahara, occur in the Neotropics and that the comparable area of Asia is roughly intermediate in this respect. This, then, is the same relationship as shown in the family analysis for plants and vertebrates presented above. Fogging sampling techniques using standardized protocols yield comparable data for canopy beetles (species/m³) and the results have the same tendency (although the values are even more contrasting than in the case of plants): 1.17 in Panama and 1.15 in Peru >0.29 in New Guinea >0.02 in Australia and Sulawesi. Similar tendencies have been observed in numerous other groups, including butterflies (Neotropics > Southeast Asia > Africa), frogs (Neotropics > Africa/Asia > Papua/Australia), and birds (Neotropics > Africa > Asia/Pacific > Australopapuan). In mammals, the number depends on the particular group (bats: Neotropical > Old World; primates: Old World > New World). It should be stressed, however, that many groups of eukaryotic organisms (e.g., nematodes, fungi, and mites) are so poorly known that we cannot at present state with confidence that they will, when better known, exhibit similar latitudinal or longitudinal patterns of species richness.

Our acceptance of the generality of the latitudinal gradient discussed above deserves two cautionary comments. On the one hand, there are a number of notable exceptions to the peak near the equator pattern, including ichneumonid wasps, shorebirds, penguins, and salamanders [see (26) for a discussion of these and additional examples], all of which have their diversity peaks at higher latitudes. Furthermore, as we noted earlier, we do not actually know enough about many groups to be sure whether their species would display a latitudinal gradient or, if they did, in which direction it may run. On the other hand, a very important determinant of the observed geographic patterns of species distribution, including the latitudinal gradient, is the "mid-domain effect" (50)—referring to the geometry of species ranges in relation to geographical boundaries. The principle of this effect is that species with wide ranges, when randomly placed within a bounded geographical domain, will tend to pile up in the middle (e.g., near the equator), while species with small ranges can, by chance alone, be anywhere. Such geometric models explain a significant proportion of the empirical variation in latitudinal richness for some wide-ranging taxa. The geographic patterns of narrow-ranging taxa, less constrained by geometry, are more likely to reflect local environmental and historical factors, and in the absence of a compelling theory of endemism, we will continue to be unable to understand why some groups of organisms sometimes match expected patterns of geographic distribution and sometimes do not.

Population and Genetic Diversity Distribution

The data concerning global variation in genetic diversity are extremely limited, but the few available studies suggest that, again, there is a significant latitudinal trend. On the one hand, evidence on genetic variation measured by allozyme diversity across phylogeny shows that genetic diversity varies nonrandomly among populations, species, and higher taxa and also among ecological parameters, including habitat type and climatic region. With regard to eco-geographic variation, a global study of 1111 species, analyzed for allozymic variation (an average of 23 loci per species) and 21 independent variables associated to them (51), found that ecological factors account for the highest proportion of the explained genetic variance among species, as compared with demographic and life history factors. The study shows that mean heterozygosity decreased in the direction tropical > temperate > arctic life zones. Higher genetic diversity, as far as our limited results to date allow us to extrapolate to the general pattern, characterizes species typical of tropical regions.

On the other hand, domesticated biodiversity provides insights related to genetic diversity and its geographic distribution. Simply, the location where the origination of crops and of agricultural development occurred provides a view of the distribution of this facet of biodiversity. The major crops have their centers of genetic diversity in geo-economically defined developing countries/regions, largely in the Neotropics, Middle East, the Mediterranean and Northern Africa region, East Africa, South and Southeast Asia, and China. Many of the countries with higher concentrations of species diversity are located in tropical regions, which also coincide with the location of many of the centers of origin and development of major crops, see (10).

Distribution of Endemism

Endemic taxa are very unevenly distributed across the Earth. The available literature makes evident the existence of significant centers of endemism both at regional and global scales and for a variety of taxa (52). Considering the absolute number of endemic species, we find a negative correlation with latitude for species richness in general (52), but the percentage of endemism may be lower at low latitudes. In addition, there are many exceptions to these general trends; for example, the percentages of endemics and often the absolute number are higher on islands and in areas of Mediterranean climate than they are elsewhere.

Centers of endemism (53) tend to be concentrated at lower latitudes in the Southern Hemisphere (where the continental masses are much more widely separated than in the North) and on islands. Myers et al. (35), elaborating on their earlier studies, presented centers of endemism as "hotspots" and defined them on the basis of their concentration of endemic plant (and to some extent vertebrate) species and the degree of threat to the long-term survival of natural habitats in the areas they selected. For an area to qualify as a hotspot, it must include a minimum of 1500 endemic plant species (equivalent to 0.6% of the 250,000 described species estimated to have been named at that time), and no more than 30% of its original vegetation remains. The 25 selected areas show a considerable congruence between the degree of endemism of plants and vertebrates. We carried out Spearman rank correlation analyses between percent plant endemism and plant and vertebrate species diversity, as well as percent endemic vertebrates, and in all cases the relationship was highly significant (plants: $r_s = 0.79, P < 0.0001$; vertebrates: $r_s = 0.49, P = 0.012$; percent endemic vertebrates $r_s = 0.63; P = 0.0007$). These remarkable areas contain an estimated 133,149 endemic plant species (44% of all plant species) and 9645 endemic vertebrate species (35% of the total) in an area of just 1.4% of the Earth's total. Not surprisingly, when we plot the position of the hotspots in Bykov's graph (Figure 2b), all 25 of them fall below the line of normal, globally expected levels of plant endemism. Only two of them fall relatively close but below the line because they have levels of endemism below 25%. While the 25 hotspots feature a variety of ecosystem types, the predominant ones are tropical moist forests, 15, and Mediterranean ecosystems, 5; 9 consist partly or completely of islands, and 16 are in the tropics at large.

In a recent analysis (54), the evolutionary history of two groups of mammals (primates and carnivores) residing in the hotspots was estimated by considering two measures: clade evolutionary history (the branch length within a clade in a phylogeny of the two groups) and species evolutionary history (the branch length from the present to the time of divergence for the species). The analysis indicated that, collectively, about 70% of the total evolutionary history of these two groups is found within the 25 hotspots. Thus not only 55% of the world's primates and 22% of the world's carnivores are endemic to the hotspots, but a large proportion of the evolutionary history of the two groups resides there.

The latitudinal gradient, the megadiversity countries, the centers of endemism, and the hotspots are all manifestations of the fact that global biodiversity is highly concentrated in a few patches of the Earth. Certainly the tropics, and particularly tropical moist forests, stand out as highly significant reservoirs of global biodiversity. Not surprisingly, the world's records for local biodiversity come from the tropics, particularly the moist tropics: 1200 species of beetle from a single tree species (19), 365 tree species in a 1-ha plot (55) or 365 plant species in a 0.1-ha plot, considering the contribution of non-tree plants (56) and, overall, an estimated half of the global species richness in just 6% to 7% of the land.

LOSS OF BIODIVERSITY

Prehistoric and Recent Extinctions

As we have seen, nature is patchy, plentiful, and beautiful. However such biological wealth is seriously threatened by human activities, and the threat is even more serious than it might appear at first. Next we review this extraordinarily important problem.

Extinction is the ultimate fate of all species. As we discussed earlier, given the known species life span, we can infer that the species currently living amount to only 2% to 3% of those that have ever lived (2). We also know that five significant extinction events occurred during the Phanerozoic Era (Figure 1), but because a lower number of species were present at all times in the past, these events collectively seem to have ended no more than 5% to 10% of the species that ever lived. The species at risk now represent an unusually high proportion of all those that ever lived.

Historically, it appears that a recent pulse of extinction started during the late Quaternary Period (57), intensified about 40,000 years ago, and apparently has not ended. An excellent summary of this is in Lovei (58), from which we sketch the salient points.

During the Wisconsin glaciation (ending ca. 10,000 years ago), about 71% of mammalian genera from mid-latitude North America were lost. Many of these lived through cycles of glacial-interglacial periods, with general conditions at their worst during the period prior to the extinctions. Indeed, conditions had improved at the time when most extinctions took place. The postglacial extinctions appear to be connected to the appearance of human beings in the affected areas. In addition to the mammals, 19 genera of large birds, mostly raptors, disappeared at this time. It is possible that the loss of mammals cascaded up to raptors, as happens in Africa when ungulate populations are reduced. In Australia, many species went extinct during the late Pleistocene, including all 19 marsupials heavier than 100 kg, most of the species of 10–100 kg body weight, three reptiles, an ostrich-sized bird, and an additional bestiary including tens of other large species. Recent evidence using refined radiocarbon dating (58) suggests that human predation is the probable cause of these Australian extinctions. The evidence for human-induced defaunation in Africa is limited and clearly needs additional study. Nevertheless, the coincidence of human presence (and the evidence of human proficiency at hunting) in North America and Australia with the selective loss of large animals, in what is geologically and evolutionarily a very short period, strongly suggests the causal role of humans in this wave of extinctions. Of the three hypotheses proposed to explain the megafaunal extinctions of this period, kill (overhunting), chill (low temperatures), and ill (pathogenic disease), overhunting seems to be the most consistent one (57–58a).

In addition, the extinction of many species on islands during the last 10,000 years is clearly correlated with the arrival of humans there (the so-called "first contact extinctions"). The examples are numerous. In Madagascar, massive extinctions started to take place soon after the arrival of human beings. Seven of the 17 primate genera have gone, while two more have lost their larger species, most of which were probably diurnal. Among the birds, extinction was significant for large-bodied, flightless species—the elephant birds. To this list we can add the pigmy hippo, the endemic aardvark, and two giant land tortoises, among others.

Before the arrival of humans in New Zealand, apart from two species of bats, there were no terrestrial mammals. In the absence of predators, birds, many of them flightless, prospered. There were two kinds of ratite birds, moas and kiwis. The dozen species of moas, with body sizes ranging from some 25 kg to 250 kg, were all exterminated as a consequence of intensive hunting by the Maori people as well, probably, as land clearing. In addition, the activities of the Maori were apparently responsible for the loss of a number of species of flightless, ground nesting, diurnal bird species, and a predator of the moas, the giant eagle (*Harpagornis moorei*), was lost along with its prey.

The colonization by humans of the Pacific Islands eastward and northeastward from southern Asia resulted in the elimination of some 1000 species of birds over a period of about 1000 years in this area alone—about a tenth of the world total that existed before the Polynesian colonizing voyages took place. Studies of these islands suggest that about half the species present when humans arrived have been preserved as fossils and that they and about an equal number of unknown species were lost as a result of human activities (59). For those bird species that have survived on Pacific islands, the future does not appear bright. Thus, of the estimated 125–145 nonmarine bird species that once lived in Hawaii, 27 have survived, but only 11 are abundant enough that their survival does not appear questionable.

The evidence that we have just reviewed indicates that a massive extinction event, driven by human beings, has been underway for some 40,000 years. In recent times, when we have more exact estimates of extinction, the situation has become far more drastic, as reviewed recently by the World Conservation Union (IUCN) (60), which we use as the basis of our review from the year 1500 A.D. onward. The total recorded extinctions for this 500-year period are 811 species, including 331 vertebrates, 388 invertebrates, and 92 plants. Figure 4 shows the proportional distribution among major groups for vertebrates, invertebrates, and plants. Among the vertebrates, the highest proportion is that of birds, followed by fish and mammals. Among the invertebrates, the largest contribution is due to terrestrial and freshwater mollusks, with 308 extinct species, the greatest total for any group for this period. In addition, 4 marine mollusks are known to have become extinct during this period. The figures for plants are too manifestly incomplete to form a useful basis for analysis.

In addition to these numbers, the 2002 IUCN list permits exploration of the changes in recorded extinctions between 1996 and 2002. During this seven-year period, the number of recorded vertebrate extinctions increased by 16 species and mollusks by 69 species, mostly because of increased exploration and taxonomic clarification within the United States.

A geographical analysis of the 811 recorded extinctions since 1500 shows that the occurrence is not random. Most have taken place on islands, although some studies suggest that the percentage of threat in continental areas may be underestimated (61); these calculations should be taken seriously in planning conservation strategies for the future. The statistics themselves must be viewed in the perspective of the very strict criteria employed by the IUCN for accepting that a species is extinct; for example, several hundred species of plants are considered extinct in current floras, but for one reason or another have not been listed by the IUCN. Examples include Goldblatt and Manning (62), who consider 36 plant species extinct in the Cape Floristic Province of South Africa, and the common understanding that well over 50 plant species have become extinct in Hawaii during the past two centuries (P.H. Raven, unpublished data). Whatever the true number, it would, since only a very few groups of organisms are well enough known to be assessed for extinction, clearly be only a very small fraction of the total species that have become extinct during that period of time. For tropical moist forests, some 19 of each 20 species would be unknown to science at present so the effects of burning forests of this kind result in a catastrophe beyond imagination.

What is clear is that extinction rates for the past several hundred years have been at least several hundred times historical values (63). The fact that we have documented so few extinctions does not mean that they are not happening. A compelling analysis (64) shows that sampling biases lead to artificially low estimates of extinction and threat in poorly studied taxa. In this analysis a positive and

Recorded Extinctions
(811)

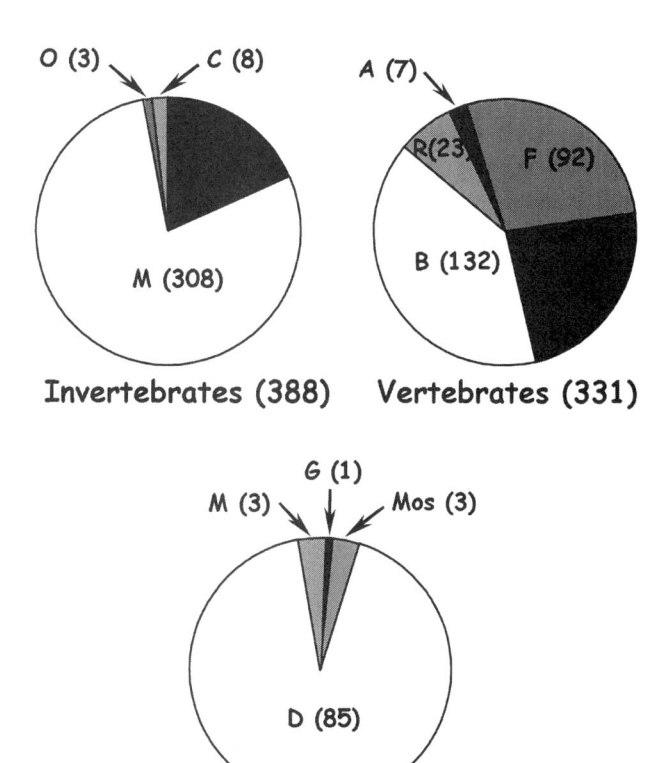

Invertebrates (388) O (3), C (8), M (308)

Vertebrates (331) A (7), R (23), F (92), B (132)

Plants (92) M (3), G (1), Mos (3), D (85)

Figure 4 Percentages (actual numbers are in parentheses) of recorded extinct species of vertebrates, invertebrates, and plants since 1500. The symbols used in the figure for vertebrates are: M, mammals; B, birds; R, reptiles; A, amphibians; F, fish. The symbols used for invertebrates are: I, insects; M, mollusks; C, crustaceans; O, onychophorans. Plant symbols are: M, mosses; G, gymnosperms; D, dicotyledons; Mo, monocotyledons. Derived from data in (60).

significant relationship was found between the magnitude of knowledge (defined by the percentage of recorded species) of several groups and the percentage of threatened and extinct species in such groups: The more under studied a group is, the more likely we are to miss extinctions of all but the most abundant and visible species. The groups that we know well enough to produce such estimates are diverse both in their life histories and in their geographical distributions. They are clearly typical of the many groups of organisms about which we know too little to make estimates of extinction. With widespread habitat destruction, increasingly adverse impact of alien invasive species, and overexploitation, there is no doubt that the rate of extinction will climb rapidly during the century we have just entered. We can gauge this by looking at the magnitude of threat and its geographic distribution.

Threatened Species: How Many, Where, and Why

The most comprehensive list of globally threatened species is the IUCN 2002 edition of threatened species (60). This list includes 11,167 threatened species (Figure 5) facing a high risk of extinction in at least the near future resulting both directly and indirectly from human activities. Although this is a small number relative to the total number of species (i.e., less than 1%), it includes 24% and 12% of all mammals and birds, respectively. The corresponding values for the other vertebrates are lower but still high if one considers the numbers as a proportion of

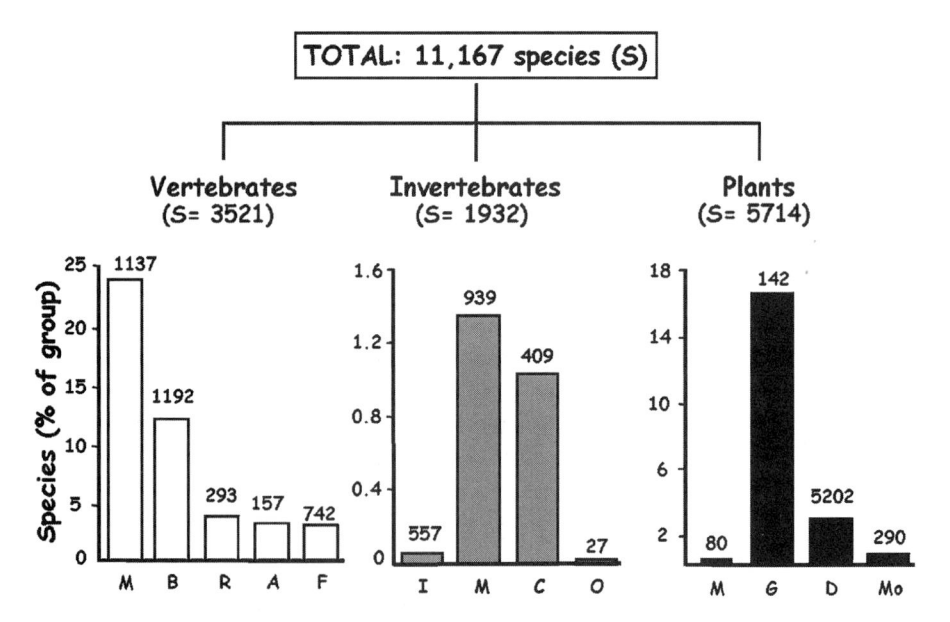

Figure 5 Percentages (and number) of threatened species of vertebrates, invertebrates, and plants in year 2002. The symbols used in the figure for vertebrates are: M, mammals; B, birds; R, reptiles; A, amphibians; F, fish. The symbols used for invertebrates are: I, insects; M, mollusks; C, crustaceans; O, others. Plant symbols are: M, mosses; G, gymnosperms; D, dicotyledons; Mo, monocotyledons. Derived with permission from data in (60).

the number of species actually evaluated, in which case about 25% of the reptiles, 21% of the amphibians, and 30% of the freshwater fish are threatened. Using very strict criteria, this would lead to a conclusion that approximately 20% of all vertebrates may actually be threatened at the present time. The real figure may very well be much higher. For invertebrates, only a few species have been evaluated and the statistics are too few to allow reasonable extrapolation.

For plants, the IUCN number represents only 2% to 3% of the known species, but that is clearly a serious underestimate. For gymnosperms, which are the only comprehensively assessed group, the value is 16%. Looking at individual countries, Master et al. (65) estimated that ca. 33% of the plant species native to the United States are threatened with extinction, including 24% of the conifers. Because the U.S. assessment also suggests that 14% of the birds and 16% of the mammals are threatened, figures relatively close to the IUCN world totals, they indicate that threatened plants are seriously underrepresented in the global figures. Freshwater species are the most seriously threatened in the United States with 37% of the fish, 69% of the freshwater mussels, and 51% of the crayfish considered to be in this status.

The 2002 IUCN report presents the data for animal species threatened in 1996 as well, and thus estimates can be made of the changes in the categories of threat among them. We calculated the proportional changes in the number of species in three categories of threat between 1996 and 2002 (Table 1). The salient aspects of this analysis are that proportional increases are considerable in the critically endangered and endangered categories. In the former, increases are particularly high in amphibians (a 66.7% increase, from 18 species in 1996 to 30 species in 2002) and reptiles, and in the latter the same occurs with birds, reptiles, and amphibians. There are two interesting decreases, mollusks in the critically endangered category and birds in the vulnerable category. In the former case, the explanation is that

TABLE 1 Percentage changes in the numbers of species of seven groups of animals in three categories of threat. The values were calculated as the proportional difference of the numbers recorded in each category in 1996 and 2002. Derived with permission from (60)

Group	Critically endangered	Endangered	Vulnerable
Mammals	7.1	7.6	0.8
Birds	8.3	38.7	−2.8
Reptiles	34.1	33.9	3.9
Amphibians	66.7	19.4	20.0
Fish	0	6.7	−0.2
Insects	4.5	1.7	4.2
Mollusks	−13.6	11.3	6.7

several of the mollusks in this category have been shown to become extinct, and in the birds of the 24 species that decreased, some were removed from it, but others moved to higher categories of threat. In sum, some of the changes resulted from new additions, but many were changes in status as a result of increasing threats; in particular, the situation of birds appears to be deteriorating.

The threats to biodiversity are not homogeneously distributed; the 2000 IUCN report (60a) allows for distinguishable patterns to be discerned with regard to geography and ecological (e.g., biome) affinity, among other things. Thus a large majority of the threatened mammal species occurs in tropical countries. The top of the list is Indonesia, with 135 species, followed by India, Brazil, China, and Mexico. As a percentage of the total number of mammal species in each country, the ranking of the top countries changes, but the majority of the countries, 8 out of the top 10, are still tropical. The significant outliers of a regression, between the total number of species versus threatened species, in all assessed countries constitute a group of nations that have more threatened species than expected. Of the 25 outliers, 19 are island states, but the group includes mainland countries such as India, Brazil, China, Bhutan, and Vietnam. This highlights the patchy nature of threats to biodiversity and a significant concentration in some tropical and island states. For birds, again, in absolute numbers, most of the countries with a high number of threatened species are tropical, Indonesia leading again with 115 species, closely followed by Brazil with 113. Here, the ranking changes notably when percentages of threatened species in faunas of particular countries are used. In this case, New Zealand is at the top of the list with 42% of its birds threatened, followed by the Philippines with 35%. The outliers of the regression analysis of species and endemism per country, again, include 15 island states and 10 continental nations in the tropics (Brazil, India, Colombia, Peru, and Ecuador; the most significant outliers) and outside the tropics (China and the Russian Federation). The United States is another outlier, but this is largely due to the situation in Hawaii and other islands that are included.

In the case of plants, the 1997 IUCN red list reports an overall figure of 13% species threatened. The numbers in the 2002 IUCN report have serious limitations as indicated above but, again, the tropical-insular predominance is evident: Malaysia has an extremely large number, 681 species, followed by Indonesia, 384; Brazil, 338; and Sri Lanka, 280; but it is clear that many factors have caused these assessments to be uneven. Some countries such as South Africa (60) and the United States (63) are clearly underrepresented, as are many poorly known tropical areas.

Recently, a new approach has been proposed to estimate global degree of endangerment for plants (66). This approach attempts to overcome the lack of information for tropical plants by considering that the number of plant species endemic to a country is a good proxy for the number that are threatened. For one well-studied tropical country, Ecuador, the authors estimate that approximately 83% of the endemic plant species qualify as threatened by the IUCN criteria. Because data on tropical endemism are better than for degree of threat, the use of such information and land area for 189 countries/regions led to five different estimates of global threat. The range of estimates (intended to take into consideration the effect of several potentially misleading factors, such as the fact that species endemic to small countries are more likely to be threatened than species endemic to large countries) varied from 22% to 47%. The latter figure results if the number of known species of flowering plants is estimated at 250,000, and the former if recent estimates of approximately 420,000 (reviewed above) are correct. Perhaps, then, a reasonable interim estimate would be that a third of the plant species of the world are threatened. This estimate, suggested against a background of inadequate knowledge, is extremely worrying considering our absolute dependency on plants and the many ways in which we expect to use them for our benefit in the future.

Considering that species with small ranges (i.e., endemic) are more apt to be threatened than those more widely distributed (16, 67), in the context of our lack of knowledge of many groups of organisms, 33% might be a reasonable estimate of the proportion of the world's biota that are threatened with extinction as we enter the twenty-first century. Such figures are likely to be higher for islands generally and also for Latin America, South Africa, and South and Southeast Asia, for reasons that we discussed earlier. Tropical forests of all kinds, with their very high concentrations of species, rapidly increasing human populations, rising expectations for living standards, and the globalization of the economy, are under particular threat.

We turn now to the question of drivers of extinction, which can be divided into two categories: proximal and ultimate. A revision of the ultimate drivers is outside the scope of this paper, but we refer to a synthetic statement of Ehrlich & Kremen (68). They refer to the $I = PAT$ equation: impact of the human enterprise on nature is the product of population, affluence (per capita consumption), and technology. The three variables causing the impact have to do with population growth, i.e., overconsumption, poorly designed environmental technologies, and faulty economic arrangements (for example, the fact that market prices of several resources do not reflect the real social costs). Biological extinction is ultimately rooted in these social, economic, and political drivers that, accordingly, require ultimate solutions from the social domains. To organize appropriate action, however, we also need relevant information on the nature, extent, and distribution of the proximal drivers, which we briefly review next.

The 2000 IUCN (60a) report analyzes the causes of threat to a sample of 720 mammalian threatened species, 1173 threatened birds, and 2274 plants. This survey shows that habitat loss/degradation is the most important threat to the three groups, affecting, respectively, 89%, 83%, and 91% of the sampled threatened mammals, birds, and plants. Specifically the primary causes of habitat loss are agricultural activities (including crop and livestock farming and plantations), extraction activities (mining, fishing, logging, and harvesting), and the development of infrastructure (such as human settlements, industry, roads, dams, and power lines). Of these specific drivers, agricultural activities affect 827 (70%) of the threatened species of birds, 1121 (49%) of the plant species, and apparently only 92 (13%) of the threatened species of mammals. Extraction has its greatest impact on plants, affecting 1365 (34%) species, but 622 bird species (53%) were also affected. Developmental activities affect 769 threatened plant species and 373 bird species, but only 59 (8%) of the threatened mammals. The low number of mammal species apparently affected by these drivers may reflect lack of information, and 495 mammal species (69%) were placed in this category. Studies at more local levels, for example in tropical forests of southeast Mexico (69), show that forest fragmentation is the leading cause for the local extinction of several mammal species with medium or large body size. Given the high concentration of threatened species in tropical ecosystems, and given the fact that tropical forests are clearly an endangered ecosystem because of deforestation, increasing utilization for various human activities, and fragmentation [see (70)], we can expect a tremendously high risk of extinction due to tropical deforestation.

The driver second in importance in the IUCN assessment is direct exploitation. The threats to 37%, 34%, and 8% of the sampled bird, mammal, and plant species arise from hunting, trading, and collecting. At a regional scale, hunting is particularly critical for mammals, especially in the tropics. It was estimated that subsistence hunting alone may be responsible for the killing of ca. 14 million animals per year in the Brazilian Amazon (71), and the problem is a very well known driver of extinction in Africa and Asia also.

Third in importance in the IUCN study is the introduction of alien invasive species of plants and animals, which affects 350 species (30%) of all threatened birds and 361 (15%) of the plants, but only 69 (10%) of the mammals. It is clear that this driver is especially serious for birds. In fact, a majority of the contemporary, since 1800, extinctions of birds, particularly on islands, can logically be attributed to the activities of introduced animals. Currently, it is estimated that virtually all (100%) of the threatened species on Hawaii are in danger of extinction because of the activities of introduced plants and animals. For the mainland United States, between 25% and 40% of the threats to extinction for native plants stem from the activities of introduced alien invasive plants and animals. In fact, it is likely that on a world scale, the introduction of alien invasive species is second only to habitat destruction as a source of extinction for plants and animals—a clear indication that conservation organizations and other bodies concerned with ameliorating threats to extinction need to deal with this problem much more seriously than has been traditional.

We now return to our discussion of the hotspots. As we have seen, in the scheme of Myers et al. (35), a hotspot has to have at least 1500 endemic plant species and only 30% of remaining natural habitat. Twenty-five such hotspots were identified (see Figure 2). Although collectively they covered 12% of the global land area, an average of seven eighths of their natural vegetation has been destroyed, so that the relatively natural areas in them now comprise only about 1.4% of the world's total land. Because taken together they contain nearly half of the world's plants and a third of all terrestrial vertebrates, they represent areas of enormous threat to a major proportion of the world's remaining biodiversity and, at the same time, afford hugely significant opportunities for conservation. Habitat loss within

the original hotspots has doubtless already driven many thousands of species, most of them unknown, to extinction with many more at threat now (72). They, along with oceanic islands, bodies of fresh water, and the tropics in general are especially critical to the survival of a major proportion of the existing biodiversity on Earth. In all of these areas, the huge and growing threats posed by introduced invasive alien species already present and potentially arriving in the future deserve much closer attention than they have received in the past as a major element in the depauperization of the world's endowment of biodiversity—our common heritage.

Current and Future Rates of Extinction

The background rate of species extinction over the past 65 million years has, as we have seen, amounted to 0.1–1 species per million species per year or less [see (16, 63)]. These estimates, based on information reviewed above, provide a yardstick for measuring current and projected future rates of extinction.

Over the last few thousand years humans have eliminated an estimated 10% of the world's species of birds. In some local instances, extinctions have reached more than 90%. This is documented information, not predictions. A thorough review of recorded extinction rates for vertebrates, plants, and some other groups of organisms for the past 300 years has revealed rates of extinction at least several hundred times the rate expected on the basis of the geological record (63). Such rates are particularly high for species with limited ranges, low local abundances, and geographic concentration in areas that are being changed rapidly.

The loss of habitat is the predominant driver of threat and extinction, so that principles that relate area loss and extinction/threat can operate as a useful tool to investigate current risk. These can be calibrated with known numbers of threatened/extinct species available for some places. This raises the question of how much area is necessary to conserve how many species.

Because habitat loss is the principal driver of extinction throughout the world, the survival times of species in small remaining areas of habitat should be considered in relation to their likely time of survival: How long does it take to lose species under such circumstances? The species (S)-area (A) relationship that has been shown to be valid for areas of similar habitat throughout the world is described by the power function $S = cA^z$, where c is a constant and z is the slope of the relationship. The slope, z, has typical values of about 0.15 for increasingly larger areas within a continuous habitat and higher ones, more like 0.25, for comparisons between actual islands in an archipelago. Because of this relationship, observations of habitat loss permit the prediction of the number of species that are likely to survive. For areas that have long been partly deforested, such as North America (73) where no more than a third of the total area of the eastern temperate forests survived at any one time in the past, the model predicts the loss of 4 species of birds, which is the actual number of bird species extinct or on the brink of extinction in the region. In contrast, in areas of recent deforestation, insular

Southeast Asia (74) and Brazil's Atlantic forest (75), the model adequately predicts the number of bird species threatened with extinction in the medium term.

For these cases we need to estimate how long it takes to lose species in fragmented habitats. The use of the species-area relationship permits estimates of the number of species in the pre-fragmentation stage and the number that will become extinct after fragmentation. These, together with a survey of the current species surviving in the fragmented habitat, permit in turn estimates of a "relaxation index," the ratio of the proportion of extinctions yet to occur after time t (e.g., years), to the proportion that will eventually occur. Such an index will equal 1.0 immediately after fragmentation and will eventually decline to zero. Assuming that the decline in species is exponential, we can characterize it by a fixed time to lose half its species, the "species half-life." An empirical study of these predictions in fragments of the Kakamega forests of western Kenya (76) calculated life times of birds to range between 25 and 75 years, 50 years on the average. This means that of the contingent of species the fragments are going to lose, they will lose half in about 50 years, and about three quarters of them in a century.

We can now put the findings of these studies and our knowledge of threats together to get a global picture of extinction. In the case of birds, the current number of threatened species is 1192, largely due to habitat loss and fragmentation. To use conservative and round numbers, we can predict that at least 500 (but probably closer to 600) of them will go extinct in the next 50 years, yielding an extinction rate of over 1000 extinctions per million species per year—some 1000 times higher than the background rate of 1.0. Using the same half-life of 50 years, we can predict that some 565 of the 1137 threatened species of mammals will go extinct within the next 50 years due to habitat loss and fragmentation. The corresponding prediction of the relative rate using again a conservative value of 500 (instead of 565) produces an extinction rate of over 1000 species per million species per year. Similar exercises using the values of Figure 5 yield a panorama of widespread extinctions in fragmented habitats within a period of some five decades, again, with extinction rates 2+ orders of magnitude higher than background rates.

Threats to Populations

Undoubtedly, a major pulse of extinction has already occurred, is currently taking place, and will continue to occur at the population level. Estimates of species extinction/threat will underestimate such intraspecific extinctions. No data are available to document these massive biological extinctions. Hughes et al. (33) proposed that we may assume a populations-area relationship in a one-to-one (linear) pattern, as opposed to a typical species-area relationship under the $S = cA^z$ model. This is due to a question of size: a population occupies a small area, relative to a species. In this way, when a large amount of area is destroyed, several populations may go extinct while few species are likely to be lost, because other populations of the species exist elsewhere, and the rate of population extinction will be faster than that of species extinction. For example, with a slope (the z value) of

GLOBAL BIODIVERSITY AND LOSS   C-1

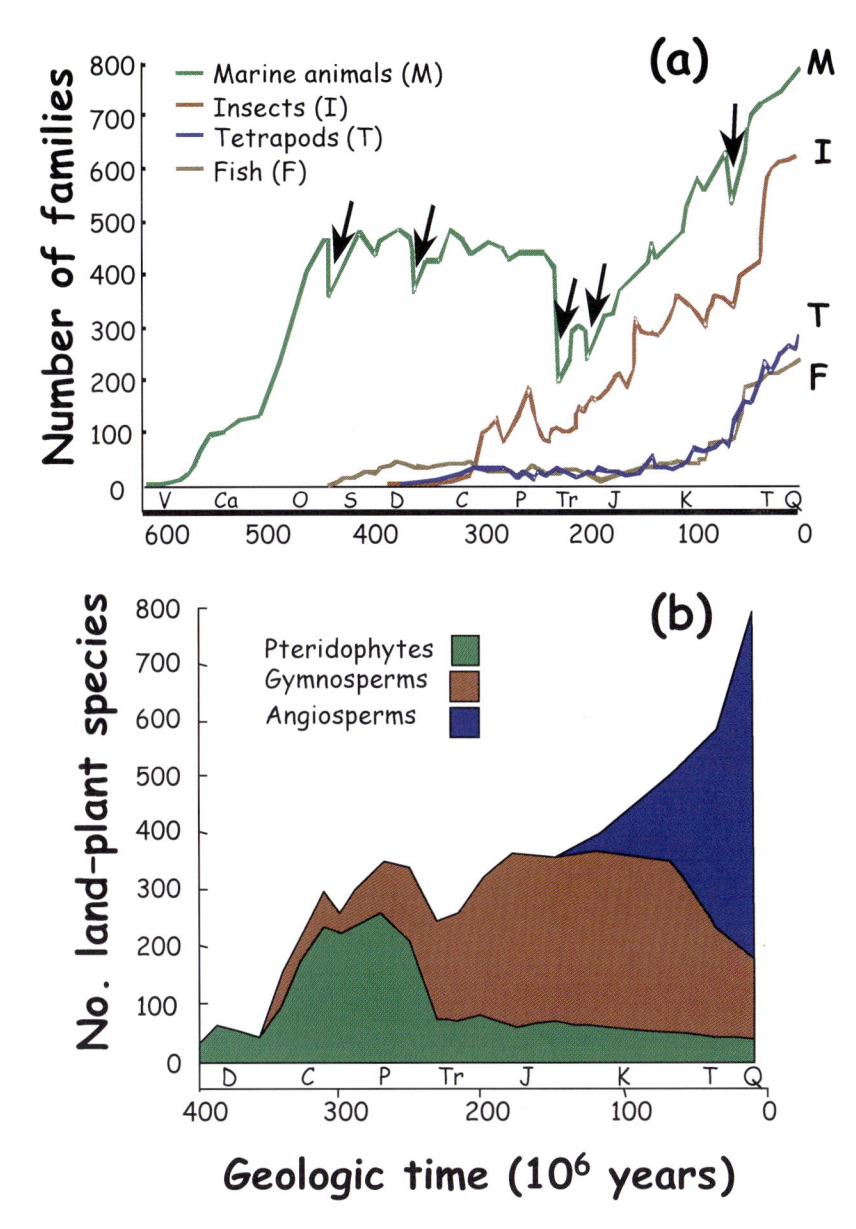

Figure 1 (*a*) The number of families of marine animals, insects, tetrapods, and fish through the last 600 million years, and (*b*) the number of land-plant fossil species, including three major groups, Angiosperms, Gymnosperms, and Pteridophytes, through the last 400 million years. The symbols used are: V, Vendian; Ca, Cambrian; O, Ordovician; S, Silurian; D, Devonian; C, Carboniferous; P, Permian; Tr, Triassic; J, Jurassic; K, Cretaceous; T, Tertiary; and Q, Quaternary. Modified from (11), with permission.

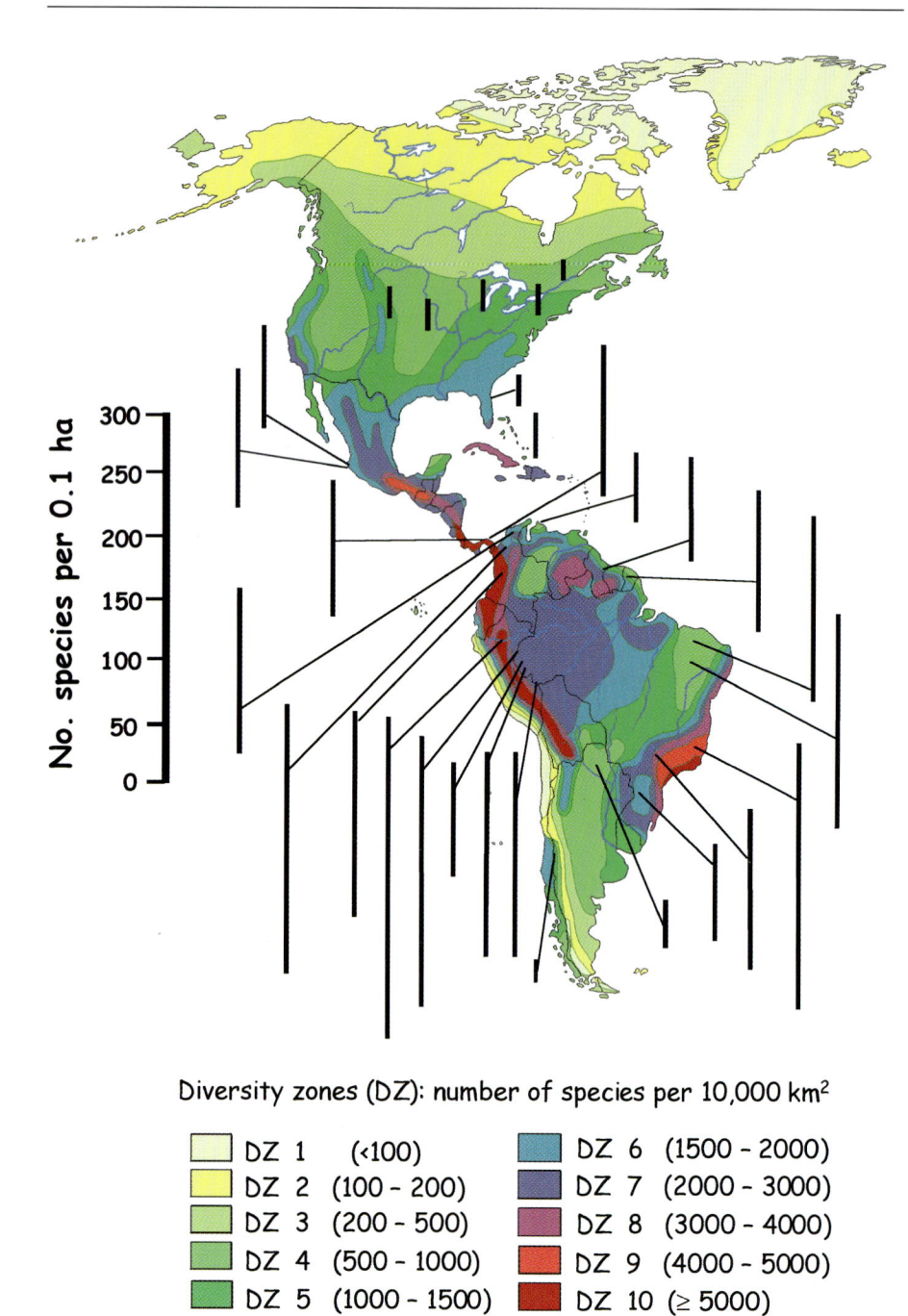

Diversity zones (DZ): number of species per 10,000 km²

- DZ 1 (<100)
- DZ 2 (100 – 200)
- DZ 3 (200 – 500)
- DZ 4 (500 – 1000)
- DZ 5 (1000 – 1500)
- DZ 6 (1500 – 2000)
- DZ 7 (2000 – 3000)
- DZ 8 (3000 – 4000)
- DZ 9 (4000 – 5000)
- DZ 10 (≥ 5000)

See legend on next page

Figure 3 Map of plant species diversity by density surfaces (number of species per 10,000 km^2) in the Americas and the number of plant species per 0.1 ha in different localities throughout the region. Each bar represents the average value for lowland sites (up to 1000 m above sea level) located in close proximity within a latitudinal band. (The number of sites for each average value varies. Files with details on site identity and number of species can be obtained from R. Dirzo upon request.) The number of species per 0.1 ha was obtained from data of Alwyn Gentry, reported in (48). The map was modified from (47) in the *Acta Botanica Fennica*, Volume 162, and published with permission of the Finnish Zoological and Botanical Publishing Board and the authors.

0.30, a habitat loss of 90% will commit 50% of the species to extinction, while 90% of the populations in the original habitat will be lost. Hughes et al. (33) did a thought experiment assuming an annual tropical deforestation of 0.8%, a global population diversity of 3 billion (two thirds of which exist in tropical regions), and calculated an extinction rate of 16 million populations per year. These calculations may be debatable, yet their message is obvious: a major pulse of biological extinction is and will be taking place at the population level. For example, a study of 173 mammalian species on six continents shows that, collectively, these species have lost over 50% of the areas of their historic ranges, especially in regions where human activities are intense (77).

EPILOGUE

The described current patterns of biodiversity distribution and extinction and its drivers underscore the urgent need to protect habitats, particularly habitats rich in species and particularly those rich in endemic species. The 1994 IUCN assessment of protected areas (78) shows a rather gloomy perspective. The assessment indicates that 8641 protected areas in categories I–V (those with low/no human intervention) existed, covering an area of 7.9 million km^2, equivalent to 5.3% of the Earth's surface. However, only 3.7% were in categories I–III, those with the best conservation potential. In addition, the frequency distribution of park sizes is strongly right-skewed, with most of them of small area and only a few large ones. Although a 5.3% area of habitat may imply a rough potential for conservation of 50% of the global species diversity (on the basis of the species-area relationship), a closer look at the regional distribution of protected areas shows that the percentage ranges from 0.3 to 10.9 with the highest values in North America (10.9%), Europe (9.1%), and Australia (10.6%), while many of the critical biodiversity areas have lower values. In addition, many parks in general only exist as "paper parks" without an effective and comprehensive protective scheme in place.

The regions used in the 1994 IUCN assessment are artificial. From an ecological standpoint, it is of great importance that the rate of creation of protected areas in tropical forests peaked in the 1980s, and has tended to fall since. It is therefore doubtful that more than 10% of the tropical forests will be protected, and probably more realistic to think of 5% surviving the next 50 years. Such a reduction in the area of these forests would lead, ultimately, to the extinction of perhaps three quarters of the species living in the forests originally with no more than 1 in 10 of the species ever having been discovered or described scientifically. The restoration of deforested or damaged areas will have a very beneficial effect on the survival of many of the species that may be hanging on in fragments of forest now. At any event, more than a third of the existing species on Earth could disappear with the destruction of the tropical forests.

Considering the wider threats to species in other tropical areas, on islands, and in nontropical hotspots because of alien invasive plants and animals that are spreading rapidly over the face of the globe and the selective hunting or gathering of wild species, it is reasonable, although pessimistic, to envision the loss of two thirds of the species on Earth by the end of the twenty-first century—an incalculable loss for the Earth and for humanity and the prosperous, sustainable future of mankind. We must do what we can to prevent such a loss, to limit it, by the most careful planning of which we are capable and the appropriate allocation of resources worldwide. The dimensions of the sixth great extinction are still matters of human choice, and millions of species that otherwise could be lost during the course of this century can be saved by decisive and appropriate actions, well considered and taken as soon as possible.

ACKNOWLEDGMENTS

We are grateful to Stuart L. Pimm for his enthusiastic and valuable help in all stages of the preparation of this review, including constructive comments on previous drafts. We thank Guillermina Gómez, Arturo Dirzo, Laura Zenteno, and Raúl I. Martínez for their help in the preparation of figures and literature search.

The *Annual Review of Environment and Resources* is online at
http://environ.annualreviews.org

LITERATURE CITED

1. Rozensweig ML. 1995. *Species Diversity in Space and Time*. Cambridge, GB: Cambridge Univ. Press
2. May RM, Lawton JH, Stork NE. 1995. Assessing extinction rates. In *Extinction Rates*, ed. JH Lawton, RM May, pp. 1–24. Oxford: Oxford Univ. Press
3. Vitousek P, Mooney HA, Lubchenco J, Melillo JL. 1997. Human domination of Earth's ecosystems. *Science* 277:494–99
4. Crutzen PJ. 2002. Geology of mankind. *Nature* 415:23
5. Budiansky S. 1993. The doomsday myths. *US News World Rep.* Dec. 13:81–83
6. Mann CC, Plummer ML. 1995. *Noah's Choice*. New York: Knopf
7. Raunkiaer C. 1934. *The Life Forms of Plants*. Oxford: Oxford Univ. Press
8. Dirzo R. 2001. Tropical forests. In *Global Biodiversity in a Changing Environment. Scenarios for the 21st Century*, ed. FS Chapin, OE Sala, E Huber-Sannwald, pp. 251–276. New York: Springer
9. Hammond PM. 1995. Magnitude and distribution of biodiversity. In *Global Biodiversity Assessment*, ed. VH Heywood. Cambridge, GB: Cambridge Univ. Press
10. Sarukhán J, Dirzo R. 2001. Biodiversity-rich countries. See Ref. 26, 1:419–36
11. Groombridge B, Jenkins MD. 2002. *Global Biodiversity: Earth's Living Resources in the 21st Century*. Cambridge, GB: World Conserv. See also http://stort.unep-wcmc.org
12. Sepkoski JJ Jr. 1992. Phylogenetic and ecologic patterns in the Phanerozoic history of marine biodiversity. In *Systematics, Ecology, and the Biodiversity Crisis*, ed. N Eldridge, pp. 77–100. New York: Columbia Univ. Press
13. Raup DM. 1972. Taxonomic diversity during the Phanerozoic. *Science* 177:1065–71
14. Jackson JBC, Johnson KG. 2001. Measuring past biodiversity. *Science* 293:2401–04

15. Raup DM. 1978. Cohort analysis of generic survivorship. *Paleobiology* 4:1–15
16. Pimm SL, Russell GJ, Gittleman JL, Brooks TM. 1995. The future of biodiversity. *Science* 269:347–50
17. Margulis L, Schwartz KV. 1998. *Five Kingdoms, An Illustrated Guide to the Phyla of Life on Earth.* New York: Freeman
18. May RM. 2000. The dimensions of life on Earth. In *Nature and Human Society: The Quest for a Sustainable World*, ed. PH Raven, T Williams, pp. 30–45. Washington, DC: Natl. Acad.
19. Erwin TL. 1982. Tropical forests: their richness in Coleopteran and other arthropod species. *Coleopt. Bull.* 36:74–75
20. Gaston KJ. 1991. The magnitude of global insect species richness. *Conserv. Biol.* 5:283–96
21. Raven PH, Williams T, eds. 2000. *Nature and Human Society: The Quest for a Sustainable World.* Washington, DC: Natl. Acad.
22. Prance GT, Beetle H, Grandfield J, Johns R. 2000. The tropical flora remains undercollected. *Ann. Missouri Bot. Gard.* 87:67–71
23. Bramwell D. 2002. How many plant species are there? *Plant Talk* 28:32–34
24. Govaerts R. 2001. How many species of seed plants are there? *Taxon* 50:1085–90
25. Heywood VH, ed. 1995. *Global Biodiversity Assessment.* Cambridge, GB: Cambridge Univ. Press
26. Levin SA, ed. 2001. *Encyclopedia of Biodiversity.* San Diego: Academic. 5 Vols.
27. Burdon JJ. 1980. Intraspecific diversity in a natural population of *Trifolium repens*. *J. Ecol.* 68:717–35
28. Turkington R, Harper JL. 1979. The growth, distribution and neighbour relationships of *Trifolium repens* in a permanent pasture. IV. Fine scale biotic differentiation. *J. Ecol.* 67:245–54
29. Dirzo R, Harper JL. 1982. Experimental studies on slug-plant interactions. IV. The performance of cyanogenic and acyanogenic morphs of *Trifolium repens* in the field. *J. Ecol.* 70:119–38
30. Cahn M, Harper JL. 1976. The biology of the leaf mark polymorphism in *Trifolium repens* L. I. Distribution of phenotypes at a local scale. *Heredity* 37:309–25
31. Turesson G. 1922. The genotypical response of the plant species to the habitat. *Hereditas* 6:147–236
32. Antonovics J, Bradshaw AD. 1970. Evolution in closely adjacent populations. VIII. Clinal patterns at a mine boundary. *Heredity* 25:349–62
33. Hughes JB, Daily GC, Ehrlich PR. 1997. Population diversity: its extent and extinction. *Science* 278:689–91
34. Major J. 1988. Endemism. A botanical perspective. In *Analytical Biogeography. An Integrated Approach to the Study of Plant and Animal Distributions*, ed. AA Myers, PS Giller, pp. 117–46. New York: Chapman & Hall
35. Myers N, Mittermeier RA, Mittermeier C, da Fonseca GAB, Kent J. 2000. Biodiversity hotspots for conservation priorities. *Nature* 403:853–58
36. Prescott-Allen R, Prescott-Allen C. 1990. How many plants feed the world? *Conserv. Biol.* 4:365–74
37. Ertter B. 2000. Floristic surprises in North America North of Mexico. *Ann. Missouri Bot. Gard.* 87:81–109
38. Donoghue MJ, Alverson WS. 2000. A new age of discovery. *Ann. Missouri Bot. Gard.* 87:110–26
39. Ginsberg JR. 2001. Biodiversity of mammals. See Ref. 26, 3:777–810
40. Iltis HH, Doebley JF, Guzmán R, Pazy B. 1979. *Zea diploperennis* (Graminae): a new teosinte from México. *Science* 203:186–88
41. Gómez-Laurito J, Gómez LD. 1989. *Ticodendron*: a new tree from Central America. *Ann. Missouri Bot. Gard.* 76:1148–51
42. Martínez E. 1989. Lacandoniaceae (Triuridales): una nueva familia de México. *Ann. Missouri Bot. Gard.* 76:128–35
43. Klass KD, Zompro O, Kristensen NP, Adis

J. 2002. Mantophasmatodea: a new insect order with extant members from the Afrotropics. *Science* 296:1456–59

44. Williams PH, Gaston KJ, Humphries CJ. 1997. Mapping biodiversity value worldwide: combining higher-taxon richness from different groups. *Proc. R. Soc. Lond. B.* 264:141–48

45. Kaufman DM. 1995. Diversity of New World mammals: universality of the latitudinal gradients and bauplans. *J. Mammal.* 76:322–34

46. Willig MR. 2001. Latitude, common trends within. See Ref. 26, 3:701–14

47. Barthlott W, Biedinger N, Braun G, Feig F, Kier G, Mutke J. 1999. Terminological and methodological aspects of the mapping and analysis of global biodiversity. *Acta Bot. Fennica* 162:103–10. See also http://www.botanik.uni-bonn.de/system/biomaps.htm#worldmap

48. Phillips O, Miller JS. 2002. *Global Patterns of Plant Diversity: Alwyn H. Gentry's Forest Transect Data Set.* St. Louis, MO: Missouri Bot. Gard.

49. Trejo R, Dirzo R. 2002. Floristic diversity of Mexican seasonally dry tropical forests. *Biodivers. Conserv.* 11:2063–48

50. Colwell RK, Lees DC. 2000. The mid-domain effect: geometric constraints on the geography of species richness. *TREE* 15:70–76

51. Nevo E. 2001. Genetic diversity. See Ref. 26, 3:195–213

52. Cowling R. 2001. Endemism. See Ref. 26, 2:497–507

53. Bibby CJ, Crosby MJ, Johnson TH, Long AJ, Sathersfield AJ, Thirgood SJ. 1992. *Putting Biodiversity on the Map: Global Priorities for Conservation.* Cambridge, GB: Int. Counc. Bird Preserv.

54. Sechrest W, Brooks TM, Fonseca GAB, Konstant WR, Mittermeier RA, et al. 2002. Hotspots and the conservation of evolutionary history. *Proc. Natl. Acad. Sci. USA* 99(4):2067–71

55. Valencia R, Valslev H, Paz y Miño GC. 1994. High tree alpha-diversity in Amazonian Ecuador. *Biodivers. Conserv.* 3:21–28

56. Gentry AH, Dodson CH. 1987. Contribution of nontrees to species richness of a tropical rain forest. *Biotropica* 19:149–56

57. Martin PS, Klein RG, eds. 1984. *Quaternary Extinctions: A Prehistoric Revolution.* Tucson: Univ. Ariz. Press

58. Lövei GL. 2001. Modern examples of extinctions. See Ref. 26, 2:731–43

58a. Alroy J. 2001. A multi-species overkill simulation of the end-Pleistocene megafaunal extinction. *Science* 292:1893–96

59. Pimm SL, Moulton MP, Justice LJ. 1994. Bird extinctions in the Central Pacific. *Phil. Trans. R. Soc. London Ser. B* 344:27–33

60. Hilton-Taylor C. 2002. *IUCN Red List of Threatened Species.* http://www.redlist.org

60a. Hilton-Taylor C. 2000. *IUCN Red List of Threatened Species.* World Conserv. Union, Gland Switzerland

61. Manne LL, Brooks TM, Pimm SL. 1999. Relative risk of extinction of passerine birds on continents and islands. *Nature* 399:258–61

62. Goldblat P, Manning JC. 2002. Plant diversity in the Cape Region of southern Africa. *Ann. Missouri Bot. Gard.* 89:281–302

63. Pimm SL, Brooks TM. 2000. The sixth extinction: how large, where and when? In *Nature and Human Society: The Quest for a Sustainable World,* ed. PH Raven, T Williams, pp. 46–62. Washington, DC: Natl. Acad.

64. McKinney ML. 1999. High rates of extinction and threat in poorly studied taxa. *Conserv. Biol.* 13:1273–81

65. Master LL, Stein BA, Kutner LS, Hammerson GA. 2000. Vanishing assets. Conservation status of the US species. In *Precious Heritage, The Status of Biodiversity in the United States,* ed. BA Stein, LS Kutner, JS Adams, pp. 93–118. New York: Oxford Univ. Press

66. Pitman NCA, Jørgensen PM. 2002. Estimating the size of the world's threatened flora. *Science* 298:989
67. Pimm SL, Raven P. 2000. Extinction by numbers. *Nature* 403:843–45
68. Ehrlich P, Kremen C. 2001. Human effects on ecosystems, overview. See Ref. 26, 3:383–93
69. Dirzo R, Miranda A. 1991. Altered patterns of herbivory and diversity: a case study of the possible consequences of contemporary defaunation. In *Plant-Animal Interactions: Evolutionary Ecology in Tropical and Temperate Regions*, ed. PW Price, TM Lewinsohn, GW Fernandes, WW Benson. New York: Wiley
70. Laurance WF, Bierregaard RO Jr, eds. 1997. *Tropical Forest Remnants: Ecology, Management, and Conservation of Fragmented Communities*. Chicago: Chicago Univ. Press
71. Redford KH. 1992. The empty forest. *BioScience* 42:412–26
72. Brooks TM, Mittermeier RA, Mittermeier CG, Fonseca GAB, DA Rylands AB, et al. 2002. Habitat loss and extinction in the hotspots of biodiversity. *Conserv. Biol.* 16:909–23
73. Pimm SL, Askins RA. 1995. Forest losses predict bird extinctions in eastern North America. *Proc. Natl. Acad. Sci. USA* 92:9343–47
74. Brooks TM, Pimm SL, Collar NJ. 1997. Deforestation predicts the number of threatened birds in insular Southeast Asia. *Conserv. Biol.* 11:382–94
75. Brooks TM, Balmford A. 1996. Atlantic forest extinctions. *Nature* 380:115
76. Brooks TM, Pimm SL, Oyugi JO. 1999. Time lag between deforestation and bird extinction in tropical forest fragments. *Conserv. Biol.* 15:1140–50
77. Ceballos G, Ehrlich PR. 2002. Mammal population losses and the extinction crisis. *Science* 296:904–7
78. McNeely JA, Harrison J, Dingwall P. 1994. *Protecting Nature: Regional Reviews of Protected Areas*. Cambridge, UK: IUCN Publ. Serv. Unit

PATTERNS AND MECHANISMS OF THE FOREST CARBON CYCLE[1]

Stith T. Gower
Department of Forest Ecology and Management, University of Wisconsin, Madison, Wisconsin 53706; email: stgower@wisc.edu

Key Words global change, disturbance, net primary production, net ecosystem production, carbon sequestration, forest products

■ **Abstract** Forests are an important source for fiber and fuel for humans and contain the majority of the total terrestrial carbon (C). The amount of C stored in the vegetation and soil are strongly influenced by environmental constraints on annual C uptake and decomposition and time since disturbance. Increasing concentrations of atmospheric carbon dioxide (CO_2), nitrogen deposition, and climate warming induced by greater greenhouse gas (GHG) concentrations in the atmosphere influence C accumulation rates of forests, but their effects will likely differ in direction and magnitude among forest ecosystems. The net interactive effect of global change on the forest C cycle is poorly understood. The growing demand for wood fiber and fuel by humans and the ongoing anthropogenic perturbations of the climate have changed the natural disturbance regimes (i.e., frequency and intensity); these changes influence the net exchange of CO_2 between forests and the atmosphere. To date, the role of forest products in the global C cycle have largely been ignored, and important emissions associated with the production, transport, and utilization of the forest products have been excluded, leading to erroneous conclusions about net C storage in forest products.

CONTENTS

THE FOREST C CYCLE AND GLOBAL CHANGE	170
THE FOREST RESOURCE	173
THE FOREST ECOSYSTEM C CYCLE	174
Net Primary Production	176
Soil Surface CO_2 Flux	179
Net Ecosystem Production	180

---

[1]Abbreviations used include: P_{vi}, biomass production of the ith tissue and vth vegetation strata; C, carbon; CO_2, carbon dioxide; D, detritus; FACE, free-air CO_2 exchange; GHG, greenhouse gas; GPP, gross primary production; H, herbivory; IGBP, International Geosphere-Biosphere Program; LAI, leaf area index; NBP, net biome production; NEP, net ecosystem production; NPP, net primary production; NPP_A, net primary production aboveground; PAR, photosynthetic active radiation; R_A, autotrophic respiration; R_H, heterotrophic respiration; S, soil surface CO_2 flux.

1543-5938/03/1121-0169$14.00

DISTURBANCES AND FOREST BIOLOGICAL C CYCLE 183
   Initial Disturbance Effects on C Pools 183
   Changes in the C Cycle During Succession 184
ATMOSPHERIC POLLUTANTS AND THE
   FOREST BIOLOGICAL C CYCLE 187
   Atmospheric N Deposition 187
   Climate Warming 188
   Elevated Atmospheric CO_2 Concentration 189
GREENHOUSE GAS MANAGEMENT AND
   THE ROLE OF FORESTS 192
   Carbon Sequestration Potential in Vegetation and Soil 192
   Carbon Sequestration in Forest Products 193
   Offset Fossil Fuel Emissions by Substituting
      Wood/Paper Material 194
IMPORTANT ISSUES FOR FUTURE RESEARCH 195

THE FOREST C CYCLE AND GLOBAL CHANGE

The forest carbon (C) cycle is characterized by a biological (forest ecosystem) and industrial (forest products) cycle (Figure 1). The vast majority of forest C cycle research has focused on the biological C cycle, for good reason. Forests cover 65% of the total land surface, they contain 90% of the total vegetation C in terrestrial ecosystems, they contain 80% of the total soil C in terrestrial ecosystems, and they assimilate 67% of the total CO_2 removed from the atmosphere by all terrestrial ecosystems (1). However, it is increasingly important to consider the industrial C cycle because humans harvest the forests and transport the wood fiber to production facilities where the C is stored in wood and paper products; eventually these products are incinerated, recycled, or landfilled as waste (2).

The most dramatic changes to the forest C cycle are society's increased reliance on forests for fiber and fuel and its conversion of forests to cropland and pasture (3, 4). Deforestation to develop cropland and pasture was the dominant land use change in temperate regions in the past and is now the dominant land use change in tropical regions (5). Other disturbances, such as wildfire and insect outbreaks, are natural processes in forest ecosystems, but there is growing evidence that the frequency and severity of these disturbances are increasing as an indirect result of human activities (6, 7).

Land use and human-modified rates of natural disturbance have directly and indirectly altered the exchange of carbon dioxide (CO_2) between forests and the atmosphere. The atmospheric concentration of CO_2, a greenhouse gas (GHG), has increased by 30% since the preindustrial era. Most scientists agree that increased concentrations of CO_2 and other GHG are responsible for climate warming (8). Multi-model simulation ensembles suggest that the average change in global surface air temperature from the 1961–1990 period to the 2071–2100 period will be +3°C (with a range of 1.3 to 4.5°C) with the greater warming in high versus low

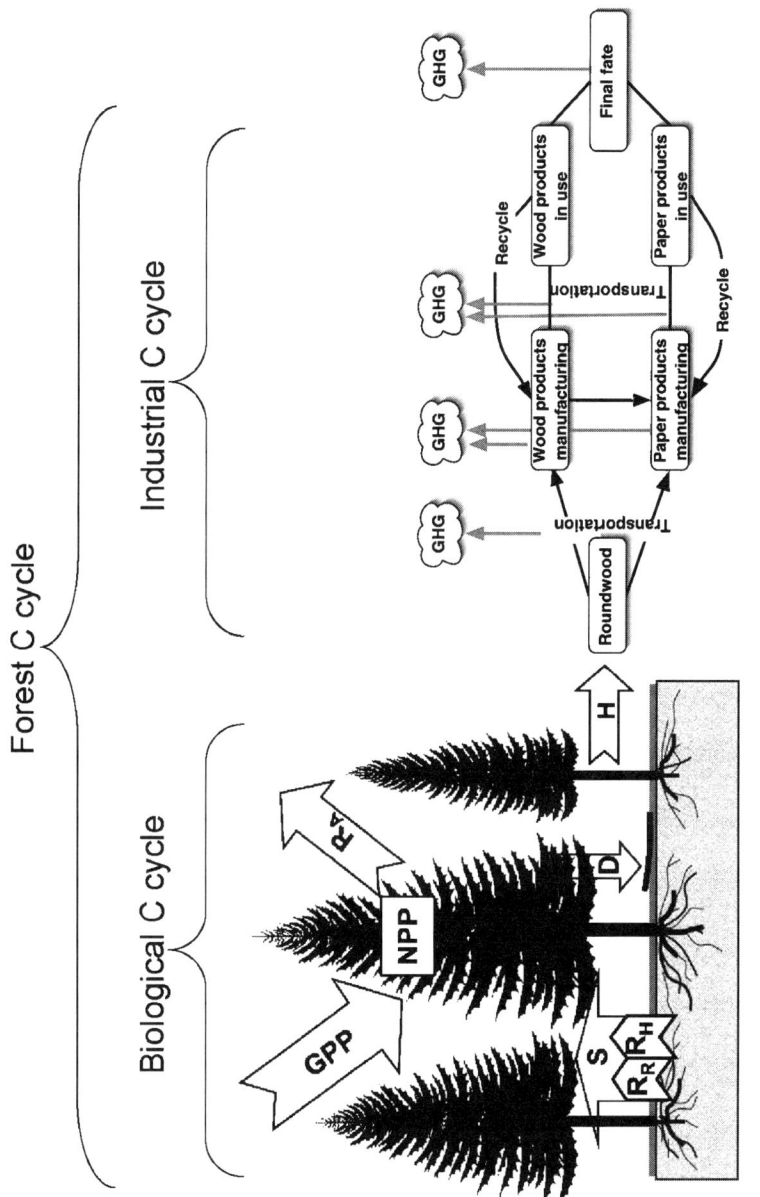

Figure 1 Conceptual diagram of the forest C cycle. The forest C cycle is comprised of a biological cycle (i.e., forest ecosystem) and an industrial cycle (i.e., forest products).

latitude zones (8). The effect of warming on the C budget of boreal forests is of particular interest because it is the second largest forest biome (9), and the soil C density is greater for boreal forest and peatland soils than for soils of other forest biomes.

The concentrations of other pollutants are also changing regionally, and forests will experience different exposures to these other pollutants, relative to the uniform increase in CO_2, depending upon their location to regional sources of ozone, nitrogen (N) deposition, and other pollutants. Chronic N deposition is a growing concern in highly industrialized regions of the world, and its effect on forest C cycle will change as total deposition increases (10). Ozone, a strong oxidant that adversely affects forest productivity (11, 12), now frequently exceeds critical threshold values in many forests near large industrial areas (13, 14).

In stark contrast to the myriad of studies that have quantified one or more of the major C fluxes of forest ecosystems, few studies have quantified the C content and emissions of the wood and paper products chains (2, 15). Yet, C storage in wood and paper products and their waste is increasing, and the production of some forest products requires large quantities of energy. For example, total world annual consumption of paper is approximately 270 million metric tons (16), and the pulp and paper industry is the fifth largest consumer of energy in the world (17).

The objective of this review is to summarize the major components of the forest C cycle and examine how global changes may affect the exchange of C between forests and the atmosphere. The first section of the paper briefly reviews the forest resource and the biological, or forest ecosystem, C cycle and its major components. The second section examines the environmental controls on (a) net primary production (NPP), (b) soil surface CO_2 flux (S), and (c) net ecosystem production (NEP). Comparisons of NPP, S, and NEP are provided to illustrate the general magnitudes of difference among forest ecosystems. The third section summarizes the effects of disturbance on forest ecosystem C cycle. The review includes initial changes in C pools directly caused by the disturbances and changes to the components of the forest C cycle during forest succession. The fourth major section reviews the effects of (a) climate warming, (b) elevated atmospheric CO_2 concentration, and (c) nitrogen deposition on forest ecosystem C cycle. The effects of multiple pollutants are briefly discussed. The fifth and last major section of the paper examines the role of forests in the GHG management schemes such as the Kyoto Protocol. The section begins by reviewing potential roles of forest ecosystems in meeting the Kyoto Protocol, which defines the first steps toward reducing the net emissions of GHG from terrestrial ecosystems. To date, most research on forest C cycle has focused on forest ecosystems but ignored the industrial C cycle. Important goals of this paper are to increase the readers' awareness of the important role forest products play in the forest C cycle and to demonstrate the great need for more rigorous analyses of this component of the forest C cycle. The paper concludes with a summary of critical issues that need to be resolved to reduce uncertainties of the forest C budget.

Tropical region   **Nontropical region**

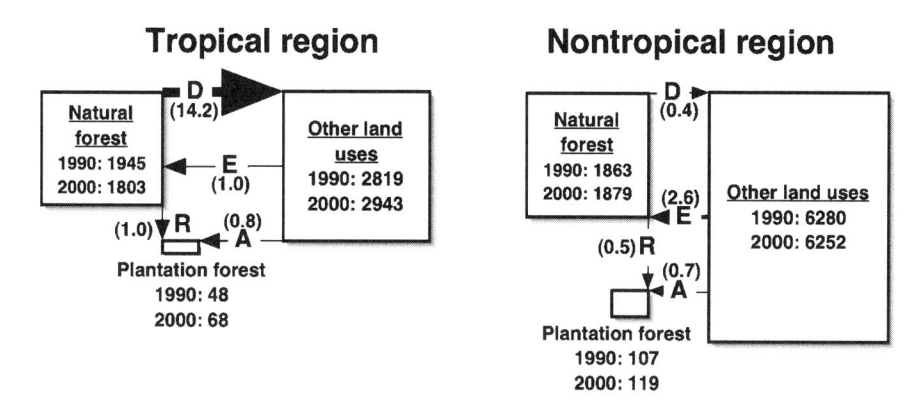

```
Natural     D (14.2)              Natural      D (0.4)
forest   ────────▶  Other land    forest    ────────▶  
1990: 1945           uses         1990: 1863            Other land uses
2000: 1803   E       1990: 2819   2000: 1879   (2.6)    1990: 6280
         ◀──(1.0)    2000: 2943            ◀── E        2000: 6252
   (1.0) ▼ R (0.8)                 (0.5) R
         ◀── A                           ◀── (0.7) A
Plantation forest                  Plantation forest
1990: 48                           1990: 107
2000: 68                           2000: 119
```

Figure 3 Forest land use change dynamics for tropical and nontropical regions. All data are averages for 1990–2000, and the units are million (10^6) hectares. Pools (*squares*) and fluxes (*arrows*) are drawn approximately to scale. Abbreviations for fluxes are D, deforestation; E, expansion of natural forests; R, reforestation; and A, afforestation. Redrawn from (3).

THE FOREST RESOURCE

Figure 2 (see color insert) illustrates the distribution of the major forest biomes of the world based on the International Geosphere Biosphere Program (IGBP) land cover classification scheme and 2000–2001 remotely sensed imagery from the moderate infrared spectrophotometer (MODIS). Scientists use different classification schemes to characterize global forest attributes such as land cover, soil and vegetation C content, and S because a universally applicable classification scheme does not exist. As a result, several vegetation classification schemes were used in this review. The lack of a universal scheme is partly historic and should be resolved with the widespread acceptance of the IGBP land cover classification scheme.

There are basic differences in the land use change dynamics between tropical and nontropical (temperate and boreal) regions (Figure 3). In 2000, natural forests comprised 38% and 23%, respectively, of the total land area in tropical and nontropical regions. During the 1990s deforestation was the dominant land use change process in tropical regions and occurred at a rate 14 times greater than each of the other land use changes (i.e., reforestation, afforestation, and natural forest expansion). The net loss of 7% of natural tropical forests annually during the 1990s differs greatly from the 1% increase in area of nontropical natural forests during the same time period. Natural expansion of forests was the dominant land use change process for nontropical forests during the 1990s and occurred at a rate 6.5 times greater than deforestation.

Natural forests cover approximately 4165×10^6 hectares, or approximately 65% of the Earth's land surface. Forest plantations cover an additional 112 to 187×10^6 hectares of the Earth's land surface (5, 18, 19). Low latitude tropical forests, including both evergreen and deciduous forests, cover 1755×10^6 hectares, or approximately 42% of all forested area (Figure 4a). Over half of the low latitude tropical forests occur in Central and South America. Area estimates for boreal forests range from 900 to 2110 × 10⁶ hectares (9). Dixon et al. reported high latitude forests cover 1560 × 10⁶ hectares, making these forests the second largest biome. Midlatitude or temperate forests comprise 25% of the total global forest area (18).

Early estimates of forest C content were based on values from isolated studies reported in the literature that were never intended to be representative of the different types and age classes of forest ecosystems. The use of national forest inventory data and remotely sensed estimates of land use change have improved the accuracy of estimates of C content of world forests. Dixon et al. (18) estimated that the forest vegetation and soil contain 359 and 787 Pg C, respectively (Figure 4b). The boreal forest contains a greater amount of C than low latitude forests, although the latter is larger in area (Figure 4a). The C density, defined as the C content per unit area, of vegetation averages 127, 63, and 50 MgC ha^{-1}, respectively, for tropical, temperate, and boreal forests, but there is substantial variation among geographic regions within the same zone (Figure 4c). Despite the twofold greater C density of vegetation in tropical than boreal forests, the total (vegetation + soil) C density is almost 50% greater for the boreal than tropical forests.

Although tropical and temperate forest have four to five and two to three times more fine littterfall than boreal forests, the cold climate and poorly drained soils of the boreal forests severely restrict decomposition of detritus (D), resulting in large accumulations of C in the soil, much of it frozen in the permafrost (20, 21). The fraction of total C content (density × area) contained in the soil generally decreases from high to low latitude forests, with boreal forest soils containing almost 60% of the total C content of boreal forests. The midlatitude forests account for the smallest percentage of the total forest C pool because temperate forests comprise a smaller percentage of the global forests and because the C density is lower for temperate forests than boreal and tropical forests (18). However, the midlatitude forests are young and increasing in area (Figure 3) and will accumulate C (see disturbance section below).

THE FOREST ECOSYSTEM C CYCLE

The net exchange of C between the forest and atmosphere is described by Equation 1.

$$CO_2 + H_2O \leftrightarrow CH_2O + O_2. \qquad 1.$$

Photosynthesis is the assimilation of CO_2 from the atmosphere by plants and the conversion to carbohydrates (CH_2O) that plants use to build organic matter. Respiration is the oxidation of carbohydrates and release of CO_2 to the atmosphere. The net difference between the two processes over time determines the net accumulation of C, assuming the C is not removed by disturbance (see below).

Gross primary production (GPP) is the total amount of CO_2 assimilated by all vegetation strata (i.e., overstory, shrub, herbs, and bryophytes) (Figure 1). Approximately 50% of the CO_2 assimilated by vegetation is used to construct

THE FOREST CARBON CYCLE   175

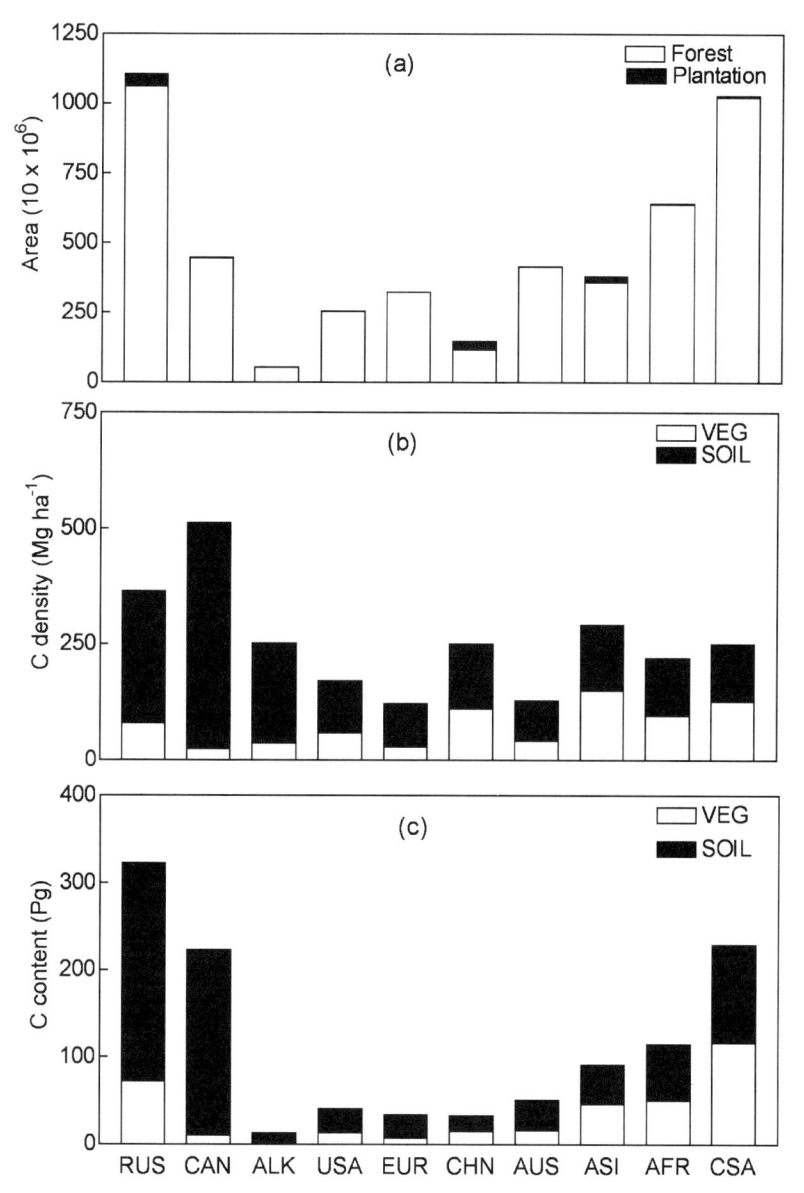

Figure 4 World forest summary estimates for (a) area in hectares, (b) carbon content, and (c) average carbon density. World forests were classified into low (0° to 25°), mid (25° to 50°), and high (50° to 75°) latitudinal zones that roughly correspond to tropical, temperate, and boreal forests, respectively. Abbreviations used are: RUS, Russia; CAN, Canada; ALK, Alaska; USA, United States; EUR, Europe; CHN, China; AUS, Australia; ASI, Asia; AFR, Africa; and CSA, Central and South America. Adapted from (18).

new tissue (growth respiration) and repair and maintain existing tissues (maintenance respiration). The sum of maintenance and growth respiration is referred to as autotrophic respiration (R_A) and results in a loss of CO_2 from the vegetation to the atmosphere (Figure 1).

NPP (Figure 1) is the balance between GPP and R_A (Equation 2).

$$NPP = GPP - R_A. \qquad 2.$$

NPP is expressed on a dry organic matter or C basis, per unit area per year. Dry mass values can be converted to a C basis by assuming C: organic matter ratios of 0.45 for foliage, herbaceous vegetation, and fine roots and 0.50 for woody tissues such as stem wood, bark, branches, and coarse roots (22). GPP is difficult to measure directly; instead it is commonly simulated using an ecosystem process model or indirectly estimated from net ecosystem CO_2 flux data. NPP is calculated as the sum of the annual production (P) of all tissues (i) for all vegetation strata (j) (Equation 3).

$$NPP = \sum (P_{ij}) + H. \qquad 3.$$

All tissues (e.g., stem, branch, foliage, coarse roots, fine roots, and mycorrhizae, reproduction) for all vegetation strata (overstory, understory, and ground cover) should be included. Fine root and mycorrhizae are the tissues that are most often excluded (22). Vogt et al. estimated mycorrhizae NPP comprised 15% of NPP in a cold temperate conifer forest, but it is not known if mycorrhizae comprise a similar fraction of total NPP in other forest ecosystems (23). A second bias is the exclusion of herbivory (H). The few studies that have quantified this loss of NPP have concluded that less than 10% of NPP of forests is consumed, except during insect outbreaks in some tropical forests (1, 24).

NEP is the annual net exchange of C, in the form of CO_2 between the atmosphere and terrestrial ecosystems, including the vegetation and soil (Figure 1). NEP is the difference between NPP and heterotrophic respiration (R_H). The sign convention for NEP used throughout this paper is NEP > 0, which implies a net transfer of C from the atmosphere to the forest ecosystem (C sink), and NEP < 0 implies a net transfer of C from the forest ecosystem to the atmosphere (C source). The efflux of CO_2 from the soil surface (S) results from the oxidation of soil organic matter by heterotrophic organisms (R_H) and root respiration (R_R) (Figure 1). The net exchange of C from the soil (S) is the difference between detritus (D) inputs (i.e., foliage, fine and coarse woody D production, and fine root turnover) and R_H. The loss of C via erosion and leached dissolved organic C should also be included (25). Net biome production (NBP) is the sum of NEP for all terrestrial ecosystems comprising a landscape, and accounts for C losses from disturbances.

Net Primary Production

Most plants are photoautotrophs, which acquire energy from solar radiation. Photosynthesis by leaves is proportional to absorbed visible quanta—or photosynthetic active radiation (PAR) (26). Although the light-photosynthesis relationship is

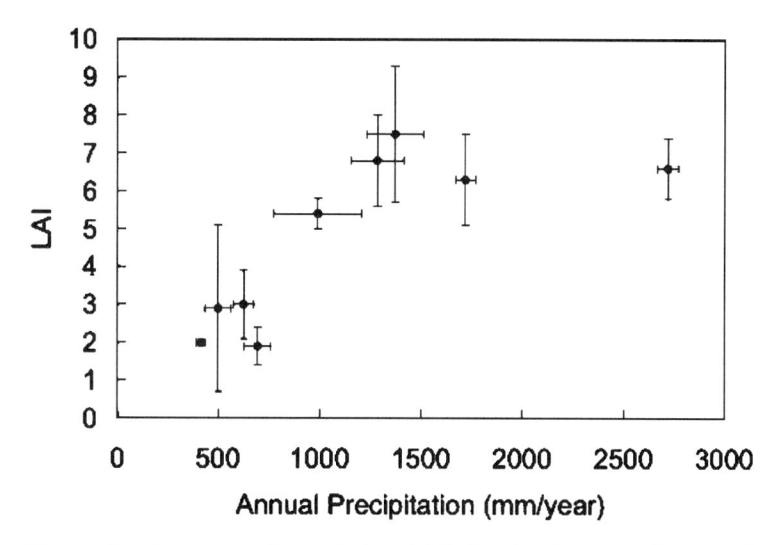

Figure 5 Average leaf area index (LAI) for the dominant forest and woodland biomes and its relationship to annual precipitation. Adapted from (32).

nonlinear for individual leaves, it is linear for most canopies (27–30), reducing the stand-level canopy photosynthesis to three primary factors: incident PAR, leaf area index (LAI), and environmental constraints on stomatal conductance. Incident PAR is strongly influenced by latitude, aspect, and cloud cover (31). The fraction of absorbed PAR that is usable by plants is strongly influenced by environmental constraints on stomatal conductance. Extreme cold temperatures, high vapor pressure deficits, inadequate soil moisture, and nutrient deficiencies restrict canopy conductance (28).

Average LAI varies fourfold among woodland and forest biomes, ranging from 1.9 for woodlands to 7.5 for tropical deciduous broadleaf forests (Figure 5). These biome-wide averages are based on literature reviews that may not be representative for all biomes. At the biome scale LAI is positively correlated to annual precipitation (Figure 5). Grier & Running first demonstrated the strong positive relationship between site water balance and LAI for terrestrial biomes (e.g., coniferous forests, woodland, and shrubland) occurring across a broad precipitation gradient in Oregon (33). This relationship is much weaker at the smaller forest ecosystem scale; instead LAI is positively correlated to soil water holding capacity (34).

The strong positive relationship between LAI and water availability results from the optimization of NPP. The simultaneous processes of photosynthesis and transpiration couple the C and water budgets of forests. Plants do not support a large LAI in drier environments because the soil moisture deficit and vapor pressure deficit severely restrict stomatal conductance and preclude CO_2 uptake, while constant foliage respiration costs reduce the net C uptake. The allocation of C to LAI appears to be in quasi-equilibrium with the environment in which they occur (35).

The availability of nutrients also influences the allocation of NPP to biomass components (1). Foliage has the highest nutrient concentrations of any major plant tissues (stem, branch, and roots), and large amounts of nutrients are required to construct a canopy. Evergreen forests have partially reduced the nutritional constraint on annual leaf production by retaining needles for several years, but the trade-off is that an evergreen canopy has a lower average photosynthetic rate than deciduous canopy (36). There is increasing evidence that plants optimize C allocation to equalize multiple resource limitations, thereby maximizing C gain. To optimize C uptake, trees allocate less biomass to foliage production and more to fine roots and mycorrhizae production to increase nutrient acquisition on infertile soils and visa versa on fertile soils (37, 38).

The ratio of NPP per unit of absorbed PAR is referred to as light use efficiency (LUE) or epsilon (ε). The lack of a universal acceptance of units for NPP (i.e., dry mass or C) and solar quanta [i.e., intercepted PAR, absorbed PAR, intercepted solar radiation (SR), and absorbed (SR)] has caused unnecessary variation in LUE values reported in the literature. Gower et al. standardized LUE coefficients reported in the literature to common units for the major terrestrial biomes and found the values were similar among forest biomes, although LUE was consistently greater for deciduous than evergreen forests for a given biome (22). If there really are no large differences in LUE among forest biomes, then the observed differences in NPP are largely the result of environmental controls on LAI. LUE coefficients based on GPP may vary greatly among biomes because many of the environmental constraints lie in controls on R_A resulting from varying C allocation patterns.

Average NPP values for the major forest biomes range from a low of 330 gC m^{-2} yr^{-1} for boreal forests to highs of 820 and 1000 gC m^{-2} yr^{-1}, respectively, for tropical broadleaf evergreen and temperate broadleaf evergreen forests (Figure 6).

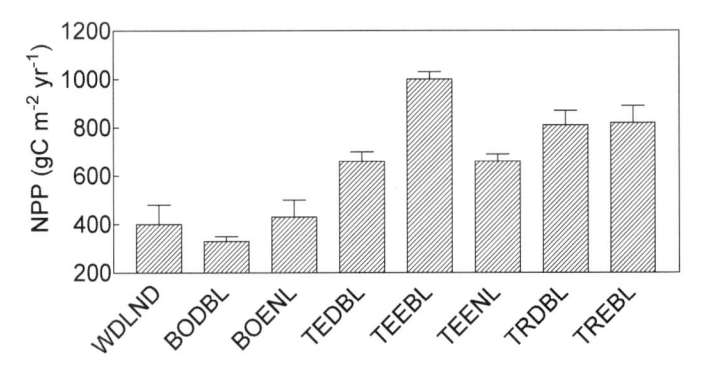

Figure 6 Average total net primary production (NPP) for the major forest biomes and woodlands of the world. Forest biome nomenclature used throughout this paper is as follows: WDLND, woodlands; BODBL, boreal deciduous broadleaf; BOENL, boreal evergreen needleleaf; TEDBL, temperate deciduous broadleaf; TEEBL, temperate evergreen broadleaf; TEENL, temperate evergreen needleleaf; TRDBL, tropical deciduous broadleaf; and TREBL, tropical evergreen broadleaf. Modified from (22).

The short growing season, caused by frozen soils in the spring and cold nighttime air temperatures in the fall, and infertile soils are the primary constraints on NPP of boreal forests. Interannual coefficients of variation for aboveground NPP (NPP$_A$) are several fold greater for nonforests than forests (39). Because the distribution, structure, and NPP of forest biomes are controlled by different environmental constraints, it is unlikely that the effect of climate change on NPP will be of similar magnitude or direction (40, 41). The physiologically-based interrelationships among water availability, LAI, and NPP suggest that changes in water balance, caused by changes in precipitation, temperature, or evaporative demand, will influence the structure and NPP of forest ecosystems differently depending upon the relative limitation of water versus nutrient(s), temperature, and light on NPP (42). Climate-induced changes in disturbance regimes could have greater effects than physiological responses (see the Disturbance section below).

Soil Surface CO$_2$ Flux

Forest soil scientists have long recognized the importance of soil organic matter because of its beneficial physical, chemical, and hydrological attributes to tree growth. Soil C is included in the organic layers composed of fine and coarse woody D and the mineral soil, with most of the C contained in the mineral soil. The notable exception is poorly drained boreal forest soils that contain as much as 90% of the C in peat. Forest soils are an important component of the global C cycle because of the large amount of C contained in the soil (Figure 4b,c).

Soil surface CO$_2$ flux, the sum of R$_H$ and root respiration, is positively correlated to near-surface soil temperature and is most commonly modeled using a simple Q$_{10}$ or Arrhenius function (43). These simple empirical models commonly explain 70%–90% of the variation in instantaneous chamber-based flux measurements during the year(s); however these same model forms explain only 34% to 50% of the variation among major terrestrial biomes of the world (44). Methodological differences may be responsible for some of the variation (45). Other important factors that influence S are (a) moisture (46, 47), (b) substrate quality (48), (c) fine root dynamics (49, 50), and (d) population and community dynamics of soil microbes (51, 52).

Average annual S ranges from 360 gC m^{-2} yr^{-1} for boreal evergreen needle-leaf forests to 1540 for tropical evergreen broadleaf forests (Figure 7). The almost twofold difference in S between boreal deciduous and evergreen is based on four studies; two values range from 430 to 450 and two values range from 860 to 870 gC m^{-2} yr^{-1}. Interannual variation in S varied by 34%–55% and exceeded the interannual variation of NEP for an eastern deciduous forest (55). The importance of temperature and moisture control on S varies seasonally and with soil drainage; this suggests that climate change will not have a uniform effect on S for all forests.

Raich et al. used a simple temperature model to estimate S from satellite-derived estimates of temperature (56). The annual average for a fifteen year period was 80.4 PgC, of which forests and woodlands comprise 57% of the total. The

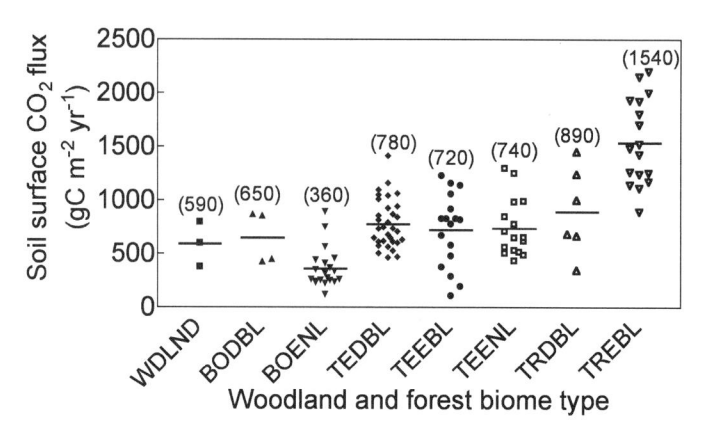

Figure 7 Average annual soil surface CO_2 (S) for major forest biomes and woodlands. Values were excluded if they were not for a full year or were for a treated (i.e., fertilized, drained, recently burned, or harvested) forest. See Figure 6 for forest biome nomenclature. Data sources were (44, 53, 54).

authors did not separate forest biomes by climate zone, but evergreen broadleaf forests contributed a greater fraction (0.30) of total biosphere S to the atmosphere than any other vegetation type. The modeled interannual variation in S suggested that precipitation explained the greatest amount of observed variation in S for seasonally dry biomes, but at the global scale interannual S variation was positively correlated ($r^2 = 0.78$) to mean annual temperature, as would be expected with the use of temperature relationships.

Partitioning S into heterotrophic (R_H) and autotrophic root respiration (R_R) is useful because the responses of the two fluxes to temperature differs (49). Also, R_H can be subtracted from NPP to estimate NEP, which provides a second independent approach that can be compared to the eddy covariance approach (57). R_H is commonly estimated using (a) independent estimates of litter, soil, and roots plus mycorrhizae, (b) flux measurements from soil plots with and without roots, or (c) natural abundance of stable isotopes (58). The contribution of root respiration to total S averages 0.54, 0.41, 0.56, 0.22, and 0.50 for boreal evergreen needleleaf, temperate deciduous broadleaf, temperate evergreen needleleaf, temperate evergreen broadleaf, and tropical evergreen broadleaf forests, respectively (Figure 8). The ratio of R_R:S varies seasonally (50) and during stand development (53) as root biomass changes.

Net Ecosystem Production

NEP is commonly measured using a micrometeorological technique known as eddy covariance (57). During the last decade the number of eddy flux towers has increased dramatically, allowing comparison of NEP among major biomes, seasonal patterns of net CO_2 exchange for ecosystem, and even interannual variation

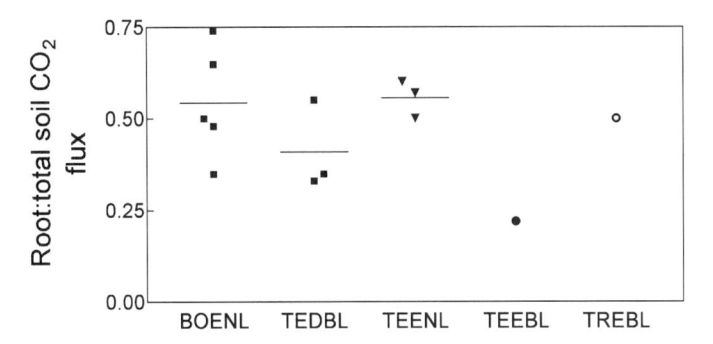

Figure 8 The contribution of root respiration to total soil surface CO_2 flux for forest biomes of the world. See Figure 6 for forest biome nomenclature. Data sources were (1, 53, 59).

of NEP. NEP and GPP generally increase from boreal to tropical forests, but there is sizable variation within a biome (Figure 9). Valentini et al. summarized the eddy covariance sites in Europe (EUROFLUX) and reported a significant inverse relationship between NEP and latitude (60); although this relationship did not hold when North American forest NEP data from the AMERIFLUX network were added. The lack of a simple relationship between NEP and latitude is not surprising

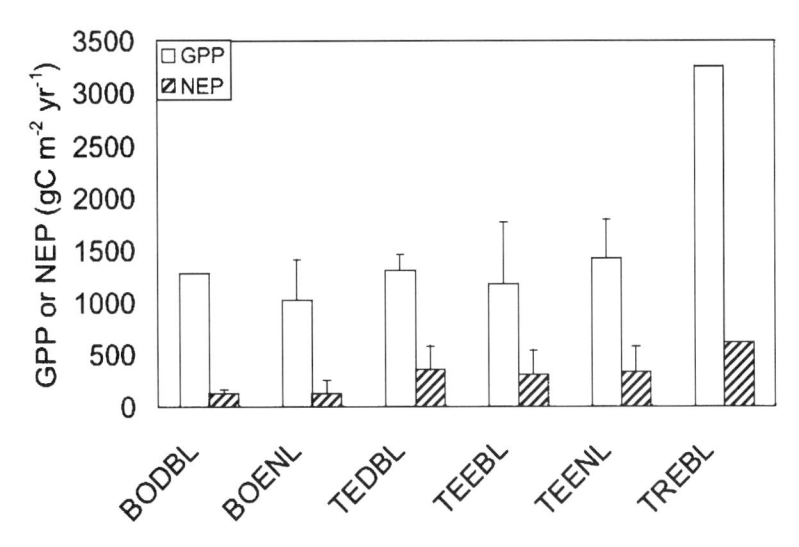

Figure 9 Summary of gross primary production (GPP, gC m^{-2} yr^{-1}) and net ecosystem production (NEP, gC m^{-2} yr^{-1}) for forest biomes of the world. Data sources (60–64). In some cases data originally published in Valentini et al. (60) were revised, as gap-filling approaches became more sophisticated, and republished by Falge et al. (61).

given the myriad of factors that influence NEP. Most, if not all, of the forests in Europe have a more maritime climate than the AMERIFLUX forests, which have a more continental climate. Differences in annual N deposition rates, stand age, soil edaphic, and management activity may also contribute to the large intrabiome variation in NEP. The metabolic activity of the plants (NPP) and microbes (R_H), which together determine NEP, are affected by both the phenology and quantity of a suite of environmental variables, and each will respond differently to interannual climate variation (65, 66).

Few sites have sufficient continuous eddy covariance measurements to examine interannual NEP variation, but those that do suggest that interannual variation of NEP can exceed observed variation in NEP among boreal and temperate forest biomes (Figure 10). For example, Arain et al. (62) reported NEP varied 3.5-fold (80 to 290 gC m^{-2} yr^{-1}) over a five year period for a boreal trembling aspen (*Populus tremuloides*) forest in central Saskatchewan, Canada, and Barford et al. (66) reported NEP varied two-fold (+120 to +250 gC m^{-2} yr^{-1}) over a nine year period for a mixed eastern deciduous forest in Massachusetts. Few of the scientists provided quantitative analysis of the source of the interannual NEP variation, but most suggested potential causes. Warm early springs appear to increase NEP of boreal forests (62, 67, 71). Other sources of interannual NEP variation were drought

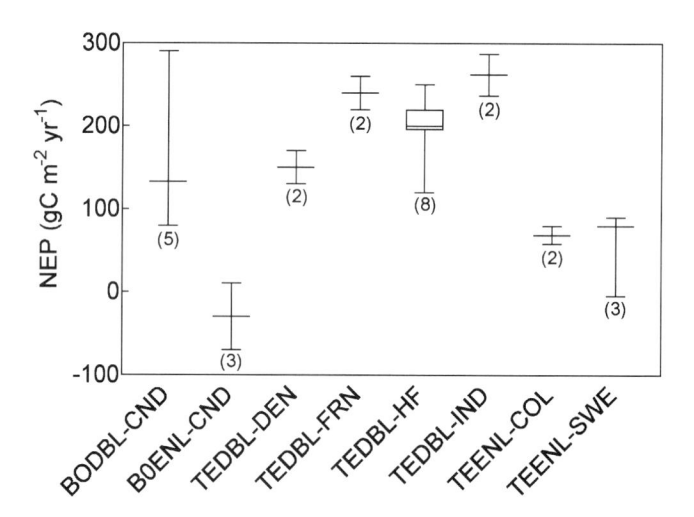

Figure 10 Interannual NEP variation for select forest biomes shown in box-and-whisker plots. The values in parentheses denote the number of years of measurements. The prefix for each observation describes the biome (see Figure 6 for forest biome nomenclature) and the last three letters depict the site location: BODBL-CND, Saskatchewan, Canada (62); BOENL-CND, Manitoba, Canada (67); TEDBL-DEN, Denmark [cited in (60)]; TEDBL-FRN, France (69); TEDBL-HF, Harvard Forest, Massachusetts (66, 72); TEDBL-IND, Indiana (68); TEENL-COL, Colorado (63); and TEENL-SWE, Sweden (70).

(63, 66, 67, 71), incident PAR and air humidity (68), winter snow cover (66), and fraction of incident diffuse:total PAR (63). Lagged ecosystem effects also influence interannual variation in NEP, so some year-to-year variation reflects environmental conditions of previous years (65). The magnitude and direction of the lagged effects differs among biomes depending upon whether the interannual variation in climate increased or decreased the environmental constraint(s) on C assimilation.

The importance of diffuse radiation C assimilation and net exchange of CO_2 between terrestrial ecosystems and the atmosphere is particularly relevant to global change because the increased fire frequency and cloud cover, products of global change, will increase the fraction of diffuse radiation. Diffuse radiation provides more uniform distribution of PAR over all foliage elements in the canopy than direct beam radiation that saturates the outer leaves but poorly illuminates shade foliage (22).

DISTURBANCES AND FOREST BIOLOGICAL C CYCLE

Disturbance is an important component of global change that influences forest ecosystem C budgets. Harvesting, fire, insects, pathogens, and wind are important disturbances, and the intensity of each varies greatly over time and space. For example, harvesting can range from single-tree removal to conventional harvesting that removes the stem wood up to a minimum top diameter, to whole-tree harvesting that removes the entire stem, branches, and sometimes foliage. While these disturbances are dramatic, they generally do not permanently change the vegetation composition and structure. For simplicity, it is convenient to categorize the effects of disturbance on the C cycle into two phases: initial disturbance effects on C pools and changes in C cycle processes during ecosystem recovery or succession. The phases are arbitrary, but they provide a useful framework to discuss the effects of disturbance on forest C cycles.

Initial Disturbance Effects on C Pools

The effects of land use change and forest management practices, especially harvesting, on soil C content is an important topic in global C cycles as more forests are harvested for the first time or are subject to more intense practices to meet the growing demand for fiber. Johnson & Curtis concluded that harvesting, on average, had little or no effect on the C content of the A horizon (73). They did note that whole-tree harvesting decreased C content of the A horizon by 6% while stem-only or conventional harvesting increased C content of the A horizon by 18%. Fertilization and planting N-fixing plants, two forest management practices to increase N availability, increased C content in the A horizon and in the total soil. The lack of standard sampling protocols and omission of certain components (i.e., fine and coarse woody D and deep soils) is a serious problem that prohibits a rigorous analysis of the effects of harvesting on total soil C content. In the future scientists need to quantify all soil and D pools; otherwise, it is impossible to determine if a disturbance causes a net C loss or merely a redistribution of C into one or more unmeasured pools.

Fire consumes organic matter in the vegetation and D, and it is an important source of C emissions to the atmosphere (74, 75). Fire generally does not effect the C content of the upper mineral soil (73). Amiro et al. estimated that wildfires in Canadian boreal forests consumed 1.3 kgC m^{-2} (75) or roughly 15% of the forest floor. The effects of fires on soil C content differ from harvesting in several important ways. First, most fires consume a small fraction of the C contained in the woody biomass although harvesting removes 50%–80% of total aboveground woody biomass (76–78). Decomposition of standing dead stem is slow until the stem falls and makes contact with the soil, which facilitates colonization of the wood by heterotrophs and increases moisture in the woody tissue (79–81). Bond-Lamberty et al. reported a 50 t C input of coarse woody debris around year 12 after a stand-killing wildfire in a boreal black spruce forest (81). Processes that increase C accumulation in the soil are (a) incorporation of charcoal recolonization of early seres by nitrogen-fixing plants and (b) downward transport and deposition of hydrophobic organic compounds into the soil (82).

The effects of disturbance on soil C pools are highly variable for several reasons: (a) varying disturbance and management intensities and their effects on soil and detritus C pools (73, 83), (b) inconsistent treatment or exclusion of some detritus C pools, the most notorious being coarse woody debris (79), and (c) past land use and historic disturbance legacies (84). All of these factors make it extremely difficult, if not impossible, to detect small changes in the C content of the large and heterogeneous soil C pool (85).

Changes in the C Cycle During Succession

The rate of ecosystem recovery following a stand-killing disturbance depends on climate, edaphic soil conditions, and disturbance intensity, but the general ecosystem functional characteristics are thought to follow predictable patterns (86). Odum hypothesized that during forest succession (a) NPP and GPP would reach a maximum and decrease, (b) R_A would steadily increase, and (c) NEP would reach a maximum in synchrony with NPP and decline to a steady state near zero. Sufficient data have been compiled during the past several decades to begin to examine Odum's predictions.

Forest chronosequence studies reveal that NPP_A reaches a maximum during the early life of the stand, often corresponding to maximum LAI, and then declines (87, 88). Age-related NPP_A decline averages 37% across all forest biomes, but it is more pronounced (54%) in boreal forests (Figure 11). The age-related NPP decline often corresponds to a decrease in LAI (88). The physiological causes for this age-related NPP decline are not well understood, but it has been observed in almost every forest biome of the world (87). Kira & Shidei first hypothesized that the decline in NPP with stand age was due to an altered balance between respiring and photosynthetic tissue (92). This hypothesis persisted in the ecological literature for several decades before being tested and found not to be the primary cause

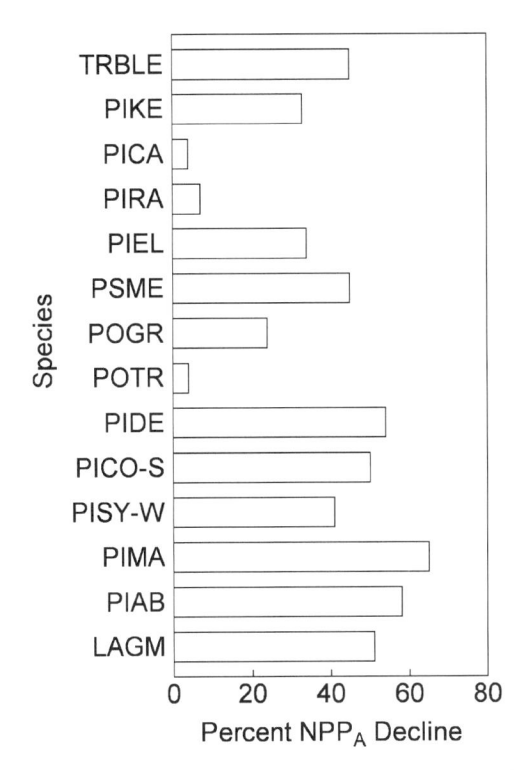

Figure 11 Summary of age-related aboveground net primary production decline for forest ecosystems in contrasting climates. Age-related NPP$_A$ decline was calculated as (maximum NPP$_A$ − minimum NPP$_A$, after maximum NPP$_A$ occurred)/maximum NPP$_A$. The primary data source was (87), and additional data sources were (89–91). Species codes for boreal forests are; and TRBLE, tropical broadleaf evergreen mixed forest; PIKE, *Pinus keysia*; PICA, *Pinus caribaea*; and PIRA, *Pinus radiata* for subtropical and tropical forests; PIEL, *Pinus elliottii*; PSME, *Pseudotsuga menziesii*; POGR, *Populus grandidentata*; POTR, *Populus tremuloides*; PIDE, *Pinus densiflora*; PICO-S, *Pinus contorta*; PISY-W, *Pinus sylvestris* for temperate forests; and PIMA, *Picea mariana*; PIAB, *Picea abies*; and LAGM, *Larix gmelinii* for boreal forests.

(87, 93, 94). The two most plausible explanations for the age-related decline in NPP are increased nutrient limitation and hydraulic constraint (87, 88), but other causes have been hypothesized (88).

More research is needed to elucidate the mechanism(s) responsible for the age-related NPP decline because NPP is a major component of NEP. Ongoing efforts to simulate global forest NPP must account for changes in NPP during succession. Ecosystem biogeochemical models need to incorporate the correct mechanism(s) that constrain NPP and C allocation because climate change, increased nitrogen deposition, and elevated CO$_2$ directly or indirectly affect water and nutrient availability, two of the major factors thought to affect the magnitude and timing of the age-related NPP decline.

NEP, the net exchange of CO_2 between terrestrial ecosystems and the atmosphere, is the difference between two large fluxes of opposite effect on atmospheric CO_2 concentration. Results from a boreal forest wildfire chronosequence near Thompson, Manitoba, Canada provides the first comprehensive assessment of how NEP, and its major components, change during forest succession (Figure 12). NPP increased as the leaf area increased (96) and peaked 35 to 70 years after

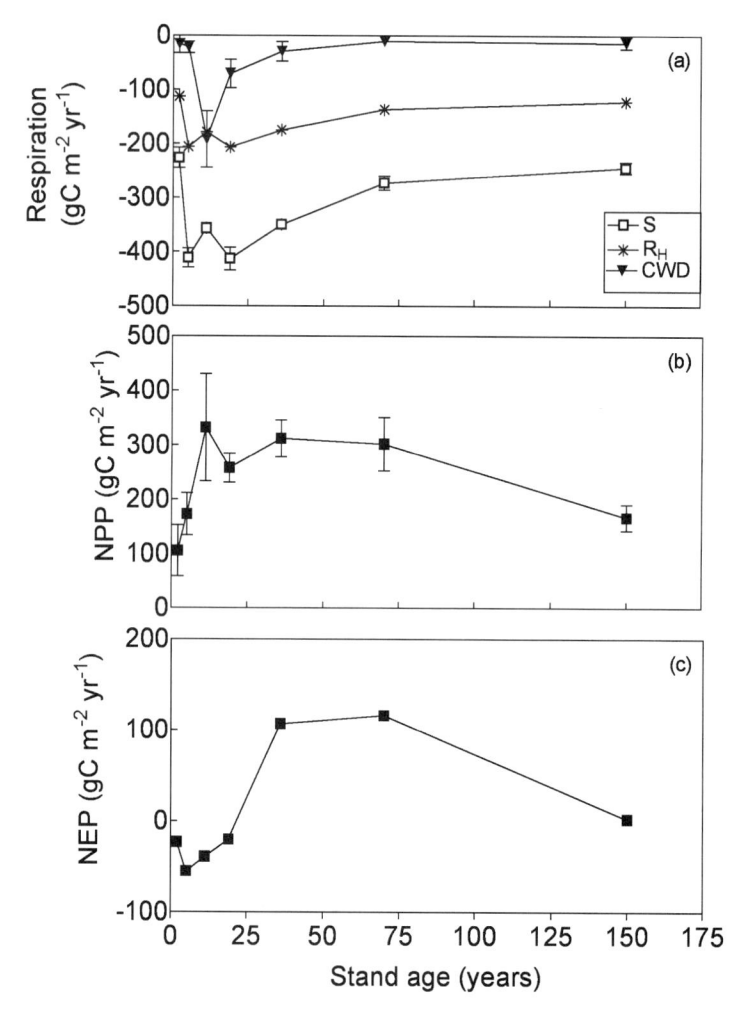

Figure 12 Comparison of (*a*) soil surface + coarse woody debris (CWD) CO_2 flux (*b*) NPP, (*c*) and NEP for a well-drained boreal black spruce chronosequence. Data sources were (53, 54, 89).

the stand-killing wildfire, and then it declined by 50%–60% depending upon soil drainage (89). During early succession, R_H from the soil and coarse woody debris were greater than NPP, causing NEP to be negative for several decades. Maximum NEP occurred at a similar stage in succession, and NPP and NEP both slowly declined with NEP approaching zero for the 150-year-old black spruce stand. The NBP was 48 gC m^{-2} yr^{-1} for the boreal forest landscape near Thompson, Manitoba, Canada (89). The observed patterns are very similar to the hypothesized patterns proposed over 40 years ago (86).

ATMOSPHERIC POLLUTANTS AND THE FOREST BIOLOGICAL C CYCLE

Humans have greatly altered atmospheric CO_2 concentrations, nitrogen deposition from the atmosphere, and tropospheric ozone concentrations (3). Much has been learned about the rates of increase of the various pollutants and their effects on forest ecosystems during the past several decades. A CO_2 enriched atmosphere and modest deposition of nitrogen may stimulate C uptake by forests temporarily, but the long-term effects may be negligible or possibly detrimental. Climate change is now well accepted by international scientists and policy makers (8, 40). Warming is the most publicized aspect of climate change, and there is now substantial evidence that increases in GHG in the atmosphere are responsible for the 0.3 to 0.6°C increase in air temperature over the last century (40, 97, 98). The effects of each of the pollutants and climate warming on the forest ecosystem C cycle are reviewed below.

Atmospheric N Deposition

Human activities have more than doubled the deposition of nitrogen (N) from the atmosphere to terrestrial ecosystems, with much of the annual deposition of 140 Tg yr^{-1} occurring in industrialized regions (99). Several excellent reviews on the effects of atmospheric N deposition and ecosystem responses have been published recently (100–103); therefore, the focus of this paper is on reported effects of atmospheric N deposition on forest C sequestration. The productivity of many temperate and boreal forest ecosystems are limited by nitrogen availability, and fertilization routinely increases annual C sequestration in the vegetation (1) and soils (73). Several experimental studies have shown that fertilization increased forest growth more than decomposition—implying N increased net C sequestration (104, 105). Estimates of the effects of N deposition on C sequestration by global forests ranges from 0.1 to 2.3 Pg C yr^{-1} (106–109).

However, not all evidence suggests that atmospheric N deposition enhances C sequestration. Results from modest ^{15}N additions in six European and three North American forests suggested that forest vegetation was a small sink (110). An even greater concern is that chronic N deposition will cause the terrestrial ecosystem to become nitrogen saturated and eventually lead to large nitrogen leaching losses and decreased forest productivity (10, 100). In addition, because of the catalytic role of reactive nitrogen, atmospheric N deposition is often correlated to the deposition of other pollutants such as ozone (109). Long-term (1969–1990) fertilization studies of two Swedish forests added 1740 and 2160 kgN ha^{-1} over a +20-year period and reported continued greater C accumulation in the vegetation and soil of the fertilized than control plots if nutrient imbalances were avoided by adding all plant-required elements (101). This study provides evidence that the N saturation threshold can be extremely high. The wide range of observed forest growth responses to atmospheric N deposition may be influenced by variations in such factors as the successional stage of development, forest type (evergreen versus deciduous), stand history, soil nitrogen accumulation, topography, and climate. All of these factors influence forest growth and most likely will help determine forest growth response to chronic atmospheric N deposition (100, 103). Understanding these determinants will be necessary in order to predict the effects of atmospheric N deposition on C sequestration in different forest types in the future.

Climate Warming

The sensitivity of terrestrial C cycles to climate warming is one of the most pressing scientific environmental problems. Views on the effect of climate change on the C cycling processes, especially respiration, have changed in recent years. The dominant paradigm once was that R_A and R_H were more positively temperature-dependent than GPP, which means that the R_A:GPP ratio would increase in a warmer climate (111, 112). However, comparative whole stand C budget studies have shown that the ratio of R_A:GPP for forests in contrasting climates is relatively stable, averaging around 0.50 (1). Adjustments in C allocation to various biomass components and physiological acclimation of respiration to temperature appear to be the most important mechanisms that maintain a stable proportion of GPP allocated to R_A (113). Dewar et al. (114), using a model, demonstrated that the short-term increase in respiration and long-term temperature acclimation of plants in response to warming could be explained by transient dynamics of nonstructural carbohydrate and protein pools. Results from experimental warming studies in greenhouses and growth chambers have further demonstrated that the acclimated R_A:GPP ratio is relatively insensitive to temperature (115–117).

The effect of climate warming on S is one of the most important and controversial topics related to global change and the C cycle. The issue is of great importance because soil contains twice as much C as the atmosphere (118), and small changes in S would have a pronounced effect on CO_2 concentrations in the atmosphere (119–121).

Numerous empirical studies have demonstrated a positive exponential relationship between S and soil temperature (see Soil Surface CO_2 Flux, above). Scientists have used these empirical models to predict S for a warmer climate and reported moderate to large losses of C to the atmosphere (119–121). Data from long-term eddy flux measurements have lead scientists to conclude that warming causes terrestrial ecosystems to become a weaker C sink or even a C source (67, 122).

However, experimental data on the effects of climate warming on C sink strength of terrestrial ecosystems do not fully support modeling results. Peterjohn et al. reported little or no increase in S from an eastern deciduous forest soil that was heated 5°C above an adjacent unheated forest soil (123). Stromgren et al. (124) measured S in replicate irrigated-fertilized unheated and irrigated-fertilized heated Norway spruce stands in northern Sweden and reported a 17% greater S for the heated (760 gC m^{-2} yr^{-1}) than the control (680 gC m^{-2} yr^{-1}). Much of the greater C loss from the heated plots was attributed to the 12% increase in the length of the soil frost-free period. However, the modest increase in S in the heated stands was offset by a 280 gC m^{-2} yr^{-1} increase in NPP$_A$ in the heated compared to the control (105). The results from the boreal warming experiment in northern Sweden are consistent with the meta-analysis results for warming experiments conducted in a variety of ecosystems using different artificial warming approaches. Rustad et al. (125) reported a similar, modest average increase in S (20%) and NPP$_A$ (19%), providing little or no support for the hypothesis that warming will increase net C exchange to the atmosphere.

The discrepancy between the results from experimental studies and modeling is likely explained by the fact that most models use empirical zero-order temperature functions derived from quasi steady-state control ecosystems to predict S for ecosystems that are no longer at steady-state because of climate change and increased soil N mineralization (125–127). Over time periods greater than one year, S should be strongly correlated to D production, which is directly proportional to NPP. Annual S can be less than NPP over long time periods (i.e., decades to centuries), in which case the ecosystem accumulates C (128).

More problematic uncertainties of future global forest C budgets are the potential redistribution of ecosystem boundaries and its effect on C storage (129). Rapid changes in climate may cause large transient losses of C (130). In addition, large scale changes in the distribution of biomes may alter the structural characteristics (e.g., albedo and LAI) that produce climate feedback mechanisms, which can have positive or negative effects on climate change relative to the positive effect of radiative forcing (131). The magnitude and direction of the feedback are dependent the effects of elevated CO$_2$ and warming on vegetation growth and on the extent of vegetation-atmosphere coupling.

Elevated Atmospheric CO$_2$ Concentration

A central question related to global change and the C cycle is the response of terrestrial ecosystems to elevated atmospheric CO$_2$ concentration. Specifically, will elevated CO$_2$ stimulate NPP and result in greater C storage in long-lived tissues (i.e., wood) and humus, or alternatively, will stimulated NPP largely occur in short-lived tissues (i.e., foliage and fine roots) that decompose rapidly in the soil and contribute little to net C sequestration? This whole-ecosystem question is being addressed with free-air CO₂ enrichment (FACE) experiments. The advantage of FACE studies is they have minimal effect on the microclimate, and they allow for feedbacks between vegetation and the soil (132).

CO_2 fertilization increased NPP by 21% and 25% during the first two years of enrichment at a warm temperate needleleaf evergreen (*Pinus taeda*) and broadleaf deciduous (*Liquidambar styraciflua*) forests (Figure 13). These short-term responses suggest only modest C accumulation in woody tissue and limited increase in C storage in the soil and litter (133, 134). However, the results from the two forest FACE experiments should be considered preliminary because it is unclear if the observed responses represent a new equilibrium or a transient response (135, 136). The measured growth response of the young stands to CO_2 enrichment may be the upper limit for forest C sequestration because the demand for nutrients may exceed nutrient mineralization rates in the soil. A decline in growth response to

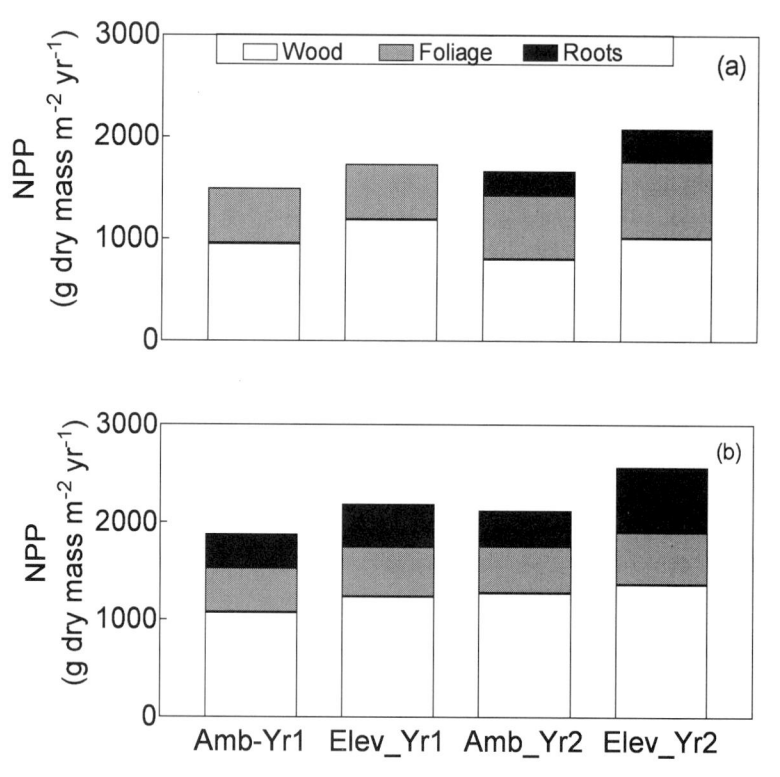

Figure 13 Comparison of NPP for (*a*) loblolly pine and (*b*) sweetgum grown in control and enriched atmospheric CO_2. The abbreviations are: Amb, ambient atmospheric CO_2 concentration; Elev, elevated atmospheric CO_2 concentration; Yr1, year 1 of treatment; and Yr2, year 2 of treatment. Data sources were (126, 127).

long-term CO_2 enrichment has been observed for individual trees grown in elevated CO_2 concentrations (137), *Quercus ilex* trees at a natural CO_2 spring (138), and *P. taeda* growth at the original, unreplicated FACE stand in North Carolina (139).

A pressing research need is the multiplicative effects of multiple atmospheric pollutants on the forest C cycle. Tropospheric ozone (O_3), a strong oxidant that is phytotoxic to many plants (11, 12), exceeds the deleterious threshold of 60 ppb in over 29% of all temperate and subboreal forests. Ozone concentrations are predicted to triple during the next 30 to 40 years and adversely affect over 50% of all temperate and subboreal forests by 2100 (13, 14, 140, 141). The increased concentrations of CO_2 and ozone have opposite effects on plant growth, but their interactive effect is poorly understood (140). In an ongoing study, NPP_A for aspen and mixed aspen + birch was greater (36%–62%) in elevated CO_2 than control FACE rings, less (2%–23%) in elevated O_3 than control FACE rings, and similar for $CO_2 + O_3$ and control FACE rings after three years of treatment (Figure 14).

Predicting the effect of atmospheric pollutants on forest ecosystem C budgets is complicated by the fact that stressed plants are more susceptible to insects and pathogens. Insect outbreaks, such as those by forest tent caterpillar, predispose the trees to disease and other environmental stresses that may result in large-scale dieback and increased fire susceptibility. Aspen trees exposed to ozone had lower concentration of phenolic glycoside, an antiherbivore defense compound, and greater growth of tent caterpillar pupae than aspen grown in ambient FACE rings (141). However, the adverse effects of ozone were ameliorated when aspen was grown in elevated $CO_2 + O_3$. The interactive effects of multiple atmospheric pollutants on forest C storage and cycling warrant greater attention, especially because it relates to increased susceptibility to stand-killing perturbations.

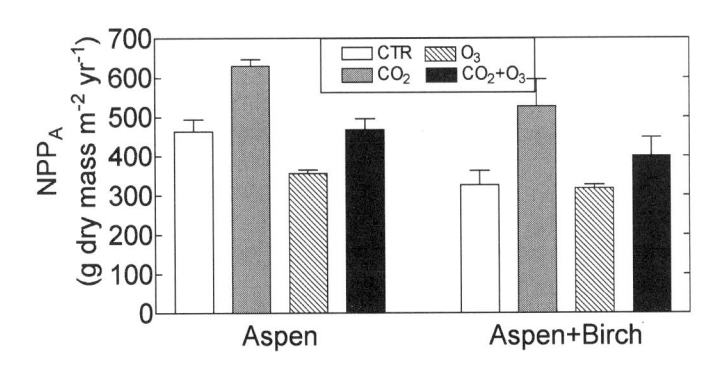

Figure 14 Comparison of NPP_A for mixed trembling aspen and birch trees grown in ambient or control atmospheric CO_2 concentration (CTR), enriched CO_2, elevated ozone, and ozone + enriched CO_2 FACE rings. (Data were generously provided by E. Kruger, University of Wisconsin.)

GREENHOUSE GAS MANAGEMENT AND THE ROLE OF FORESTS

The Kyoto Protocol, an international treaty to decrease GHG concentrations in the atmosphere by reducing fossil fuel emissions, now awaits final ratification by individual nations (142). During the negotiation process, the focus shifted from reducing fossil fuel emissions toward implementation of biological sinks (8, 143). The final version of the Kyoto Protocol included afforestation, reforestation, and changes in the management of agriculture and forestry as allowable biological C sequestration activities. As the Kyoto Protocol is now written, the sum of the sequestered C resulting from the three practices cannot comprise more than 80% of the required 5% reduction in fossil fuel emissions below the base year (1990).

Forest landowners and associated forest product industries have three broad potential management options to offset rising CO_2 concentrations in the atmosphere: (a) C sequestration in forest vegetation and soil, (b) C sequestration in wood and paper products, and (c) offset fossil fuel emissions by substituting wood/paper material. The biological feasibility of each of these management opportunities is examined in the following sections. The socioeconomic and cultural constraints for the three management opportunities are not discussed in this review but are an integral part of a successful forest C sequestration management program (144, 145).

Carbon Sequestration Potential in Vegetation and Soil

Figure 6 summarizes average NPP rates for the dominant forest biomes of the world. Forest management activities can increase NPP, but few studies have quantified maximum C sequestration rates for different forest regions. Removing nutrient and water limitations are two obvious approaches, and there are several studies that have added sufficient water and nutrients to remove these constraints on NPP (146–148). The relative importance of water and nutrient limitations varied among forests. Irrigation and fertilization together (IF) increased NPP_A of radiata pine (*Pinus radiata*) in New South Wales, Australia; Scots pine (*Pinus sylvestris*) in southern Sweden; and loblolly pine (*Pines taeda*) in North Carolina, by 70%, 78%, and 154%, respectively. The effect of IF was additive for loblolly pine, but it was multiplicative for *P. radiata*.

Nutrient and water amendments clearly increased the gross C sequestration rates of the forests, and the rates appear promising from the point of view of C sequestration. However, gross C sequestration rates are misleading because they exclude GHG emissions required to manage the forest [GHG emitted from the production of fertilizers added to the forest (149)] and emissions produced via energy consumption during the production and transportation of the final products. For example, 0.58 mol of C is released as CO_2 per mol of N produced in fertilizer, and this factor increases to 1.4 if production, transport, and application of the fertilizer are included (150, 151). Future forest C sequestration management plans should be based on a complete accounting of all GHG emissions associated with the management practices proposed to increased tree growth. The relationship between forest management intensity and net forest C sequestration is unknown and warrants investigation.

Land use changes such as afforestation, deforestation, and conversion of natural forests to plantation change the land cover compared to natural disturbances that often only reset the successional stage of the terrestrial ecosystem. The effects of land use change on soil C pools are of great importance to scientists and policy makers trying to reduce GHG emissions or enhance C sequestration, as mandated by the Framework Convention on Climate Change. Guo & Gifford (152) performed a meta-analysis on the effects of land use change on soil C stocks, and they found that conversion of forest to crops decreased soil C content by 42%, but afforestation of cropland increased soil C content by 53%. Conversion of natural forests to plantations decreased soil C content by 13%.

There are very few replicated afforestation studies that have quantified C accumulation rates and distribution for all major components (i.e., mineral soil, D, and vegetation) of a forest. The accumulation of C in D and mineral soil has a greater permanence than in vegetation, and it is therefore more desirable from a GHG management perspective. The pattern that emerges from a few studies is that 80%–90% of the total ecosystem carbon accumulation occurs in the forest vegetation, followed by forest floor and mineral soil (153, 154). C accumulation in mineral soil was extremely low after 40 years for both afforestation studies—a finding that corroborates earlier soil-only studies that concluded average C accumulation rates for a variety of forest ecosystems were near zero for most reforestation and modest for temperate and boreal afforestation activities (1). The general conclusion is that storing large amounts of C in the soil is not feasible, at least on a timescale of the life of a stand, and the focus should be of fate of the C contained in the trees.

Carbon Sequestration in Forest Products

Recently scientists have quantified the gross amount of C contained in paper and wood products in the United States (2, 155), Finland (156, 157), and in the major countries of the world (15). Since 1910, 2.7 Pg C, an amount that is equivalent to 20% of the total C contained in forest trees in the United States, has accumulated in wood and paper products that are currently in use or buried in landfills, and the annual C accumulation rate is projected to increase from present-day 61 Tg C yr^{-1} to 74 Tg C yr^{-1} by 2040 (2). The growing demand for wood and paper products and changed disposal practices are the primary factors responsible for the increased rate of gross C accumulation in forest products. Before 1986 wood and paper waste was disposed in dumps, where it was often burned; however, waste is now placed in landfills or recycled. The anaerobic conditions of landfills and high lignin concentration of wood and paper products make forest products extremely resistant to decay. On average, only 3%, 16%, 18%, and 38% of the total C contained in solid wood products, newsprint, coated paper (i.e., magazines), and office paper, respectively, are ever released back to the atmosphere when placed in landfills (2).

Côté et al. completed a C mass balance analysis for an integrated pulp mill in Texarkana, Texas, that produces bleached board and cupstock grades of paper (158). The rolls of product are transported to other locations where the paper is converted into milk and juice cartons. They concluded that the integrated mill and fiber basket (the forest that provides the fiber for the mill) were a net C sink. In other words, the C sequestered by their forests for that year exceeded the C released to produce the paper products by a factor of 1.4 to 2.8.

It is extremely important to note that almost all the forest product sequestration estimates are based on gross C accumulation. That is to say, GHG emissions from harvest, transportation of the roundwood or chips to processing plants (i.e., pulp and paper mills, saw mills), mill emissions, and transportation of the forest products to regional distributors and consumers are ignored (see Figure 1).

Industrial ecology is a rapidly emerging discipline that studies "technological ecosystems," their consumption and recycling of resources, their potential impacts on the environment, and the ways in which the biological and technological ecosystems can be restructured to enable global sustainability (159). Life cycle analysis (LCA) is an important tool used in industrial ecology and can be used to quantify total GHG emissions for a forest product from cradle (i.e., forest establishment) to grave (i.e., final fate). The chain should include the entire life cycle of the product, process, or activity and encompass the extraction and processing of raw materials, manufacturing, transportation, distribution, use, reuse, maintenance, recycling, and final disposal, which includes the release of CO_2 and CH_4 from the landfills (160). LCA studies can be used to identify and quantify GHG emissions for all processes in the product chain. Such studies are greatly needed to identify potential management opportunities to reduce GHG emissions, increase biological C sequestration, and assess optimal disposal practices of end products. Scientists have yet to demonstrate that there is a net C storage in forest products if a complete LCA, from cradle to grave, is completed.

Offset Fossil Fuel Emissions by Substituting Wood/Paper Material

Many wood product and paper production mills generate some of their energy from wood waste (i.e., chips, bark, and sawdust) and paper waste recovered from the harvesting and manufacturing processes. The CO_2 emitted when wood and paper waste is burned is equivalent to the atmospheric CO_2 that was sequestered by the tree during growth and transformed into organic carbon compounds; hence there is no net contribution to the atmospheric CO_2 concentration, and the material is considered to be C neutral (161). The use of wood and paper waste as a biofuel is desirable because it is a C neutral energy source, and it decreases human dependency on non-C neutral fossil fuels. Row & Phelps (155) estimated that the use of wood and paper waste products as fuel in the United States prevented the release of 50×10^6 metric tons C from the combustion of fossil fuel annually.

THE FOREST CARBON CYCLE C-1

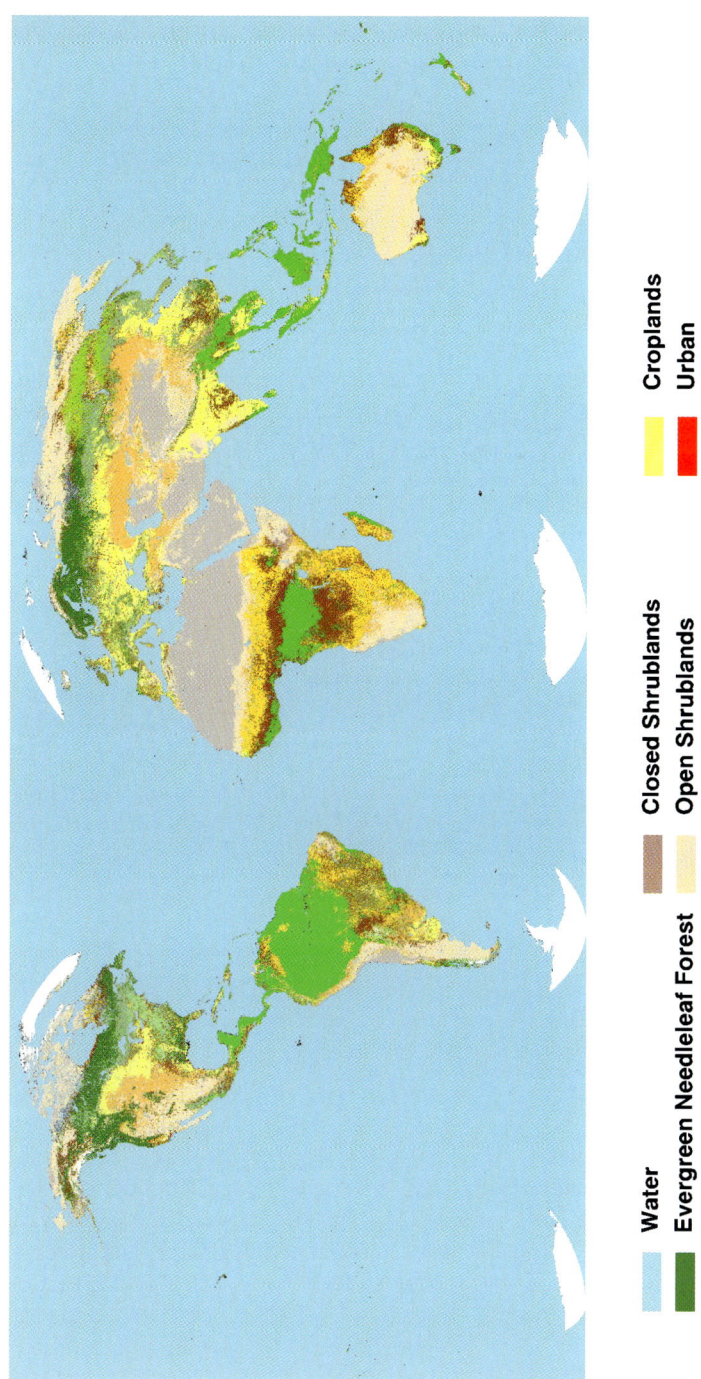

See legend on next page

Figure 2 Map of the major terrestrial ecosystems of the world based on MODIS 2000–2001 imagery and the IGBP land cover classification system. Source is Boston University http://geography.bu.edu/landcover/userguidelc/intro.html

Approximately 270×10^6 tons of paper are consumed annually worldwide (16), and the consumption of energy by the pulp and paper industry makes it the fifth largest consumer of energy in the world (17). The fiber used to produce paper is supplied by virgin fiber (e.g., wood) and recycled paper products. Different processes, which differ in energy requirements, material efficiencies, and paper characteristics (i.e., brightness, strength, and opacity), are used to manufacture wood into pulp—the primary material used to make paper. The kraft, or chemical, pulping process requires very little purchased power because almost all (>94%) of the required energy is derived from wood waste at the mill and black liquor (a by-product of the bleached kraft pulping of virgin fiber) that is produced in the kraft process. The carbon neutral wood waste and black liquors are burned to produce steam and electricity, which thus decreases the need for purchased energy that is commonly derived from fossil fuels. Mechanical pulping processes, the most prominent being stone-ground wood and thermomechanical, require large quantities of energy because mechanical pulping does not generate chemical by-products that can be burned to produce steam and electricity. However, the pulping yield coefficient (paper produced per ton of wood fiber consumed) is lower for kraft pulping (40% to 65%) than mechanical pulping (>80%) processes (16) because the kraft processes extract the lignin and other components. Many paper products are produced from a mixture of kraft and mechanical pulp to achieve (a) required paper characteristics (e.g., kraft pulp has greater strength and durability needed for printing, writing paper, packaging, and construction board products) and (b) desired characteristics by consumers. Policy decision makers, pulp and paper industry executives, and society are confronted with multiple goals of preserving forest biodiversity, fiber conservation, energy conservation, and the use of biomass for fossil fuel substitution. The trade-offs between the pulping processes (kraft versus mechanical) and virgin fiber versus recycled paper have numerous, complex implications on net energy consumption and warrant immediate study.

IMPORTANT ISSUES FOR FUTURE RESEARCH

Our knowledge of the factors controlling the carbon budgets of forests has increased dramatically during the past several decades and has helped focus new questions. Disturbance has a greater effect on NPP, R_H, and NEP than other aspects of global change such as warming or elevated CO_2 concentration. More process-based chronosequence studies for different types of disturbance regimes are warranted to elucidate physiological principles that need be incorporated into physiologically-based models. Rates of climate warming are predicted to differ among forest biomes, and the effects of warming on the structure and function of terrestrial ecosystems are likely to be complex and differ among ecosystems (162).

Important global change questions that remained unanswered include:

1. How will warming influence soil carbon dynamics and the net exchange of carbon between forests and the atmosphere?

2. What effect does past land use history have on current carbon budgets of forests?

3. How are disturbance regimes (i.e., frequency and intensity) for wildfire, harvesting, and insect outbreak changing? What effect will they have on carbon exchange between forests and the atmosphere?

4. What is the net effect of the multiple changes in atmospheric chemistry on forest carbon budgets?

5. What are the CO_2 and other GHG shadows for the major forest products? What are the near- and long-term opportunities to reduce GHG emissions for each chain? What intensity level of forest management maximizes net C sequestration?

The science questions outlined above will require the use of numerous research tools and approaches that can only be provided by interdisciplinary science teams. All the questions have direct implications to private, state, and federal forest managers, as well as policy makers. The forest C cycle is inextricably linked to the forest product industries that are very dependent upon fossil fuels for power to manufacture wood and paper products and that transport final wood fiber to the mills and final products to consumers. The interrelationships among the various industries provide many opportunities to reduce fossil fuel emissions. Forest product, energy, transportation, and waste management industries have the greatest understanding and insight into their respective components of forest product chains, and scientists must actively include these parties in future analyses and policy discussions.

ACKNOWLEDGMENTS

The author was supported by a NASA (NAG5-8069) and NSF (DEB-0077881) grants during the preparation of this paper. Ben Bond-Lamberty, Pamela Matson, and David Schimel provided numerous suggestions that greatly improved the manuscript. Doug Ahl generously prepared Figure 2.

The *Annual Review of Environment and Resources* is online at
http://environ.annualreviews.org

LITERATURE CITED

1. Landsberg JJ, Gower ST. 1997. *Applications of Physiological Ecology to Forest Management*. San Diego, CA: Academic. 354 pp.
2. Skog KE, Nicholson GA. 2000. *Carbon sequestration in wood and paper products*. USDA For. Serv. Gen. Tech. Rep. *RMRS-GTR-59*, pp. 79–88, Washington, DC
3. Food Agric. Organ. U.N. 2001. *Global Forest Resources Assessment 2000. FAO-For. Pap. 140*. Rome. 479 pp.
4. Vitousek PM, Mooney HA, Lubchenco J, Melillo JM. 1997. Human domination of Earth's ecosystems. *Science* 277:494–99
5. Watson RT, Noble IR, Bolin B, Ravindranath NH, Verardo DJ, Dokken DJ, eds. 2000. *Land use, land use change, and*

forestry. Spec. Rep. Intergov. Panel Clim. Chang. Cambridge Univ. Press, Cambridge, UK.
6. Flannigan MD, Bergeron Y, Engelmark O, Wotton BM. 1998. Future wildfire in circumboreal forests in relation to global warming. *J. Veg. Sci.* 9:469–76
7. Kurz WA, Apps MJ. 1999. The carbon budget of Canadian forests: sensitivity analysis of changes in disturbance regimes, growth rates, and decomposition rates. *Environ. Pollut.* 83:55–61
8. Intergov. Panel Clim. Chang. 2001. *Third assessment report (TAR), climate change 2001: The scientific basis. Work. Group 1 Rep. Tech. Summ.* IPCC Natl. Greenh. Gas Inventory Program, New York City
9. Gower ST, Krankina O, Olson RJ, Apps M, Linder S, Wang C. 2001. Net primary production and carbon allocation patterns of boreal forest ecosystems. *Ecol. Appl.* 11:1395–411
10. Aber J, McDowell W, Nadelhoffer K, Magill A, Berntson G, et al. 1998. Nitrogen saturation in temperate forest ecosystems. *BioScience* 48:921–34
11. Reich PB. 1987. Quantifying plant response to ozone: a unifying theory. *Tree Physiol.* 3:63–91
12. Pye JM. 1988. Impact of ozone on the growth and yield of trees: a review. *J Environ. Qual.* 17:347–60
13. Chameides WL, Kasibhatla PS, Yienger J, Levy H II. 1994. Growth of continental-scale metro-agro-plexes, regional ozone pollution, and world food production. *Science* 264:74–77
14. Fowler D, Cape JN, Coyle M, Flechard C, Kuylenstierna J, et al. 1999. The global exposure of forests to air pollutants. *Water Air Soil Pollut.* 116:5–32
15. Winjum JK, Brown S, Schlamadinger B. 1998. Forest harvests and wood products: sources and sinks of atmospheric carbon dioxide. *For. Sci.* 44:272–84
16. Ruth M, Harrington T Jr. 1998. Dynamics of material and energy use in U.S. pulp and paper manufacturing. *J. Ind. Ecol.* 1:147–68
17. Pulp Pap. Int. 1996. International fact and price book. Brussels: Miller Freeman
18. Dixon RK, Brown S, Houghton RA, Solomon AM, Trexler MC, et al. 1994. Carbon pools ands fluxes of global forest ecosystems. *Science* 263:185–90
19. Winjum JK, Schroeder PE. 1997. Forest plantations of the world: their extent, ecological attributes and carbon storage. *Agric. For. Meteorol.* 84:153–67
20. Gorham E. 1991. Northern peatlands: role in the carbon cycle and probable responses to climatic warming. *Ecol. Appl.* 1:182–95
21. Gower ST, Vogel JV, Norman JM, Kucharik CJ, Steele SJ, Stow TK. 1997. Carbon distribution and net primary production of aspen, jack pine and black spruce BOREAS forests. *J. Geophy. Res.* 102(D24):29029–41
22. Gower ST, Kucharik CJ, Norman JM. 1999. Direct and indirect estimation of leaf area index, f_{APAR}, and net primary production of terrestrial ecosystems. *Remote Sens. Environ.* 70:29–51
23. Vogt KA, Grier CC, Meier CE, Edmonds RL. 1982. Mycorrhizal role in net primary production and nutrient cycling in Abies amabilis ecosystems in western Washington. *Ecology* 63:370–80
24. Schowalter TD, Hargrove WW, Crossley DA. 1986. Herbivory in forested ecosystems. *Annu. Rev. Entomol.* 31:177–96
25. Randerson JT, Chapin FS, Harden JW, Neff JW, Harmon ME. 2002. Net ecosystem production: a comprehensive measure of net carbon accumulation by ecosystems. *Ecol. Appl.* 12:937–47
26. McCree KJ. 1972. The action spectrum, absorptance, and quantum yield of photosynthesis in crop plants. *Agric. Meteorol.* 9:191–216
27. Monteith JL. 1972. Solar radiation and production in tropical ecosystems. *J. Appl. Ecol.* 9:747–66
28. McMurtrie RE, Gholz HL, Linder S,

Gower ST. 1994. Climatic factors controlling the productivity of pine stands: a model-based analysis. *Ecol. Bull.* 43:173–88

29. Landsberg JJ, Prince SD, Jarvis PJ, McMurtrie RE, Luxmoore R, Medlyn BE. 1997. Energy conversion and use in forests: the analysis of forest production in terms of radiation utilization efficiency. In *The Use of Remote Sensing in the Modeling of Forest Productivity at Scales from Stands to Globe*, ed. HL Gholz, K Nakane, H Shirada, pp. 273–98. Dordrecht, Neth.: Kluwer Acad.

30. Medlyn B. 1998. Physiological basis of the light use efficiency model. *Tree Physiol.* 18:167–76

31. Waring RH, Running SW. 1998. *Forest Ecosystems: Analysis at Multiple Scales.* San Diego: Academic

32. Gower ST. 2001. Production of terrestrial ecosystems. In *Encyclopedia of Global Change*, ed. HA Mooney, P Canadell. pp. 516–21. Chichester, UK: Blackwell Sci.

33. Grier CC, Running SW. 1977. Leaf area of mature northwestern coniferous forests: relation to site water balance. *Ecology* 58:893–99

34. Fassnacht KS, Gower ST. 1997. Interrelationships among edaphic and stand characteristics, leaf area index, and aboveground net primary productivity for upland forest ecosystems in north central Wisconsin. *Can. J. For. Res.* 27:1058–67

35. Nemani RR, Running SW. 1989. Testing a theoretical climate-soil-leaf area hydrologic equilibrium of forests using satellite data and ecosystem simulation. *Agric. For. Meteorol.* 44:245–60

36. Gower ST, Richards JH. 1990. Larches: deciduous conifers in an evergreen world. *BioScience* 40:818–26

37. Gower ST, Vogt KA, Grier CC. 1992. Carbon dynamics of Rocky Mountain Douglas-fir: influence of water and nutrient availability. *Ecol. Monogr.* 62:43–65

38. Gower ST, Isebrands JG, Sheriff D. 1995. Factors influencing carbon assimilation and allocation in conifer forests. In *Resource Physiology of Conifers*, ed. WK Smith, TM Hinckley, pp. 217–54. San Diego: Academic

39. Knapp AK, Smith MD. 2001. Variation among biomes in temporal dynamics of aboveground primary production. *Science* 291:481–84

40. Intergov. Panel Clim. Chang. 1996. *Climate Change 1995: The Science of Climate Change.* Cambridge, UK: Cambridge Univ. Press. 572 pp.

41. Schimel D, Melillo J, Tian H, McGuire AD, Kicklighter D, et al. 2000. Contribution of increasing CO_2 and climate to carbon storage by ecosystems in the United States. *Science* 287:2004–6

42. Running SW, Nemani R. 1991. Regional hydrologic and carbon balance responses of forests resulting from global climate change. *Clim. Change* 19:349–68

43. Lloyd J, Taylor JA. 1994. On the temperature dependence on soil respiration. *Func. Ecol.* 8:315–23

44. Raich JW, Schlesinger WH. 1992. The global carbon dioxide flux in soil respiration and its relationship to vegetation and climate. *Tellus B* 44:81–99

45. Norman JM, Kucharik CJ, Gower ST, Baldocchi DD, Crill PM, et al. 1997. A comparison of six methods for measuring soil-surface carbon dioxide fluxes. *J. Geophys. Res.* 102:28771–77

46. Howard DM, Howard PJA. 1993. Relationships between CO_2 evolution, moisture content, and temperature for a range of soil types. *Soil Biol. Biochem.* 25:1537–46

47. Davidson EA, Belk E, Boone RD. 1998. Soil water content and temperature as independent or confounded factors controlling soil respiration in a temperate mixed hardwood forest. *Glob. Chang. Biol.* 4:217–28

48. Vance ED, Chapin FS III. 2001. Substrate limitations to microbial activity in taiga forest floors. *Soil Biol. Biochem.* 33:173–88

49. Boone RD, Nadelhoffer KJ, Canary JD, Kaye JP. 1998. Roots exert a strong influence on the temperature sensitivity of soil respiration. *Nature* 396:570–72
50. Bisbee K, Gower ST, Norman JM. 2003. Carbon budgets of contrasting boreal black spruce forests. *Ecosystems*: 6:248–60
51. Zogg GP, Zak DR, Ringelberg DB, MacDonald NW, Pregitzer KS, et al. 1997. *Soil Sci. Soc. Am. J.* 61:475–81
52. Panikov NS. 1999. Understanding and prediction of soil microbial community dynamics under global change. *Appl. Soil Ecol.* 11:161–76
53. Wang C, Bond-Lamberty B, Gower ST. 2003. Soil surface CO_2 flux in a boreal black spruce fire chronosequence. *J. Geophys. Res.* 108(D3) art. no. 8224
54. Davidson EA, Savage K, Bolstad P, Clark DA, Curtis PS, et al. 2002. Belowground carbon allocation in forests estimated from litterfall and IRGA-based soil respiration measurements. *Agric. For. Meteorol.* 13:39–51
55. Savage KE, Davidson EA. 2001. Interannual variation of soil respiration in two New England forests. *Glob. Biogeochem. Cycles* 15:337–50
56. Raich JW, Potter CS, Bhagawati D. 2002. Interannual variability in global soil respiration, 1980–1994. *Glob. Chang. Biol.* 8:800–12
57. Baldocchi D, Falge E, Gu L, Olson R, Hollinger D, et al. 2001. FLUXNET: a new tool to study the temporal and spatial variability of ecosystem scale carbon dioxide, water vapor, and energy flux densities. *Bull. Am. Meteorol. Soc.* 82:2415–34
58. Hanson PJ, Edwards NT, Garten CT, Andrews JA. 2000. Separating root and soil microbial contributions to soil respiration: a review of methods and observations. *Biogeochemistry* 48:115–46
59. Ekblad A, Högberg P. 2001. Natural abundance of ^{13}C in CO_2 respired from forest soils reveals speed of link between tree photosynthesis and root respiration. *Oecologia* 127:305–8
60. Valentini R, Matteucci G, Dolman AJ, Schulze E-D, Rebmann C, et al. 2000. Respiration as the main determinant of carbon balance in European forests. *Nature* 404:861–65
61. Falge E, Baldocchi D, Tenhunen J, Aubinet M, Bakwin P, et al. 2002. Seasonality of ecosystem respiration and gross primary production as derived from FLUXNET measurements. *Agric. For. Meteorol.* 113:53–74
62. Arain MA, Black TA, Barr AG, Jarvis PG, Massheder JM, et al. 2002. Effects of seasonal and interannual climate variability on net ecosystem production of boreal deciduous and conifer forests. *Can. J. For. Res.* 32:878–91
63. Monson RK, Turnipseed AA, Sparks JP, Harley PC, Scott-Denton LE, et al. 2002. Carbon sequestration in a high-elevation subalpine forest. *Glob. Chang. Biol.* 8:459–70
64. Curtis PS, Hanson PJ, Bolstad P, Barford C, Randolph JC, et al. 2002. Biometric and eddy-covariance based estimates of annual carbon storage in five eastern North American deciduous forests. *Agric. For. Meteorol.* 113:3–19
65. Braswell BH, Schimel DS, Linder E, Moore B III. 1997. The response of global terrestrial ecosystems to interannual temperature variability. *Science* 278:870–72
66. Barford CC, Wofsy SC, Goulden ML, Munger JW, Pyle EH, et al. 1999. Factors controlling long- and short-term sequestration of atmospheric CO_2 in a mid-latitude forest. *Science* 294:1688–91
67. Goulden ML, Wofsy SC, Harden JW, Trumbore SE, Crill PM, et al. 1998. Sensitivity of boreal forest carbon balance to soil thaw. *Science* 279:214–17
68. Ehman JL, Schmid HP, Grimmond CSB, Randolph JC, Hanson PJ, et al. 2002. An initial intercomparison of micrometeorological and ecological inventory estimates of carbon exchange in a mid-latitude

deciduous forest. *Glob. Chang. Biol.* 8:575–89
69. Aubinet M, Heinesch B, Longdoz B. 2002. Estimation of the carbon sequestration by a heterogeneous forest: night flux corrections, heterogeneity of the site and inter-annual variability. *Glob. Chang. Biol.* 8:1053–71
70. Lindroth A, Grelle A, Moren A-S. 1998. Long-term measurements of boreal forest carbon balance reveal large temperature sensitivity. *Glob. Chang. Biol.* 4:443–50
71. Chen WJ, Black TA, Yang PC, Barr AG, Neumann HH, et al. 1999. Effects of climatic variability on the annual carbon sequestration by a boreal aspen forest. *Glob. Chang. Biol.* 5:41–53
72. Goulden ML, Munger JW, Fan S-M, Daube BC, Wofsy SC. Exchange of carbon dioxide by a deciduous forest: response to climate variability. *Science* 271:1576–78
73. Johnson DW, Curtis PS. 2001. Effects of forest management on soil C and N storage: meta analysis. *For. Ecol. Manag.* 140:227–38
74. Wang C, Gower ST, Wang Y, Zhao H, Yan P, Bond-Lamberty B. 2001. Influence of fire on carbon distribution and net primary production of boreal *Larix gmelinii* forests in northeastern China. *Glob. Chang. Biol.* 7:719–30
75. Amiro BD, Todd JB, Wotton BM, Logan KA, Flannigan MD, et al. 2001. Direct carbon emissions from Canadian forest fires, 1959–1999. *Can. J. For. Res.* 31:512–25
76. Brown S. 1997. *Estimating biomass and biomass change of tropical forests: a primer. FAO For. Pap. 134*, Food Agric. Organ. U.N., Rome
77. Brown S, Lugo AE. 1992. Aboveground biomass estimates for tropical moist forests of the Brazilian Amazon. *Interciencia* 17:1–18
78. Schroeder PE, Brown S, Mo J, Birdsey R, Cieszewaski C. 1997. Biomass estimation for temperate broad-leaf forests of the U.S. using inventory data. *For. Sci.* 43:424–34
79. Harmon ME, Franklin JF, Swanson FJ, Sollins P, Gregory SV, et al. 1986. Ecology of coarse woody debris in temperate ecosystems. *Adv. Ecol. Res.* 15:133–302
80. Wang C, Bond-Lamberty B, Gower ST. 2002. Environmental controls on carbon dioxide flux from black spruce coarse woody debris. *Oecologia* 132:374–81
81. Bond-Lamberty B, Wang C, Gower ST. 2003. Annual carbon flux from woody debris for a boreal black spruce fire chronosequence. *J. Geophys. Res.* 108(D3): art. no. 8220
82. Harden JW, Trumbore SE, Stocks BJ, Hirsch A, Gower ST, et al. 2000. The role of fire in the boreal carbon budget. *Glob. Chang. Biol.* 6:174–84
83. Wirth C, Schulze E-D, Lühker B, Grigoriev S, Siry M, et al. 2002. Fire and site type effects on the long-term carbon and nitrogen balance in pristine Siberian Scots pine forests. *Plant Soil* 242:41–63
84. Currie WS, Nadelhoffer KJ. 2002. The imprint of land-use history: patterns of carbon and nitrogen in downed woody debris at the Harvard Forest. *Ecosystems* 5:446–60
85. Homann PS, Bormann BT, Boyle JR. 2001. Detecting treatment differences in soil carbon and nitrogen resulting from forest manipulations. *Soil Sci. Soc. Am. J.* 65:463–69
86. Odum E. 1969. The strategy of ecosystem development. *Science* 164:262–70
87. Gower ST, McMurtrie RE, Murty D. 1996. Aboveground net primary production decline with stand age: potential causes. *Trends Ecol. Evol.* 11:378–82
88. Ryan MG, Binkley D, Fownes J. 1996. Age related decline in forest productivity: pattern and process. *Adv. Ecol. Res.* 214–52
89. Bond-Lamberty B, Wang C, Gower ST. 2003. Net primary production of a boreal black spruce wildfire chronosequence. *Ecol. Monogr.* In press

90. Wirth C, Schilze E-D, Kusznetova V, Milyukova I, Hardes G, et al. 2002. Comparing the influence of site quality, stand age, fire and climate on aboveground tree production in Siberian Scots pine forests. *Tree Physiol.* 22: 537–52
91. Smith FW, Resh SG. 1999. Age-related changes in production and belowground carbon allocation in Pinus contorta forests. *For. Sci.* 45:333–41
92. Kira T, Shedei T. 1967. Primary production and turnover of organic matter in different forest ecosystems of the western Pacific. *Jpn. J. Ecol.* 13:273–83
93. Ryan MG, Waring RH. 1992. Maintenance respiration and stand development in a subalpine lodgepole pine forest. *Ecology* 73:2100–8
94. Murty D, McMurtrie RE, Ryan MG. Declining forest productivity in aging forest stands—a modeling analysis of alternative hypotheses. *Tree Physiol.* 16:187–200
95. Deleted in proof
96. Bond-Lamberty B, Wang C, Gower ST, Norman JM. 2002. Leaf area dynamics of a boreal black spruce fire chronosequence. *Tree Physiol.* 22:993–1001
97. Rind D. 1999. Complexity and climate. *Science* 284:105–7
98. Karl TR, Knight RW, Baker B. 2000. The record breaking global temperature of 1997 and 1998: evidence for an increase in the rate of global warming? *Geophys. Res. Lett.* 27:719
99. Vitousek PM, Aber JD, Howarth RW, Likens GE, Matson PA, et al. 1997. Human alteration of the global nitrogen cycle: sources and consequences. *Ecol. Appl.* 7:737–50
100. Fenn ME, Poth MA, Aber JD, Baron JS, Bormann BT, et al. 1998. Nitrogen excess in North American ecosystems: predisposing factors, ecosystem responses, and management strategies. *Ecol. Appl.* 8:706–33
101. Matson PA, McDowell WH, Townsend AR, Vitousek PM. 1999. The globalization of N deposition: ecosystem consequences in tropical environments. *Biogeochemistry* 46:67–83
102. Tamm CO, Aronsson A, Popovic B, Flower-Ellis J. 1999. Optimum nutrition and nitrogen saturation in Scots pine stands. *Stud. For. Suec. No. 206.* Swed. Univ. Agric. Sci., Uppsala, Swed. 126 pp.
103. Matson P, Cohse KA, Hall SJ. 2002. The globalization of nitrogen deposition: consequences for terrestrial ecosystems. *Ambio* 31:113–19
104. Aber JD, Magill A, McNulty SG, Boone RD, Nadelhoffer KJ, et al. 1995. Forest biogeochemistry and primary production altered by nitrogen saturation. *Water Air Soil Pollut.* 85:1665–70
105. Stromgren M. 2001. *Soil surface CO_2 flux and growth in a boreal Norway spruce stand: effects of soil warming and nutrition.* PhD. dissertation. Silvestria 220 Swed. Univ. Agric. Sci., Uppsala, Swed.
106. Peterson BJ, Melillo JM. 1985. The potential storage of carbon caused by eutrophication of the biosphere. *Tellus B* 37:117–27
107. Schindler DW, Bayley SE. 1993. The biosphere as an increasing sink for atmospheric carbon: estimates from increasing nitrogen deposition. *Glob. Biogeochem. Cycles* 7:717–34
108. Townsend AR, Braswell BH, Holland EA, Penner JE. 1996. Spatial and temporal patterns in terrestrial carbon storage due to deposition of fossil fuel nitrogen. *Ecol. Appl.* 6:806–14
109. Holland EA. 1997. Variations in the predicted spatial distribution of atmospheric nitrogen deposition and their impact on carbon uptake by terrestrial ecosystems. *J. Geophys. Res.* 102:15849–66
110. Nadelhoffer KJ, Emmett BA, Gundersen P, Kjonaas OJ, Koopmans CJ, et al. 1999. Nitrogen deposition makes a minor contribution to carbon sequestration in temperate forests. *Nature* 398:145–48
111. Woodwell GM. 1983. *Biotic Effects on the Concentration of Atmospheric Carbon*

Dioxide: A Review and Projection. pp. 216–41. Washington, DC: Natl. Acad.
112. Woodwell GM. 1990. The effects of global warming. In *Global Warming: The Greenpeace Report*, ed. J Leggett, pp. 116–32. Oxford, UK: Oxford Univ. Press
113. Ryan MG, Linder S, Vose JM, Hubbard RM. 1994. Respiration of pine forests. *Ecol. Bull.* 43:50–63
114. Dewar RC, Medyln BE, McMurtrie RE. 1999. Acclimation of the respiration/photosynthesis ratio to temperature: insights from a model. *Glob. Chang. Biol.* 5:615–22
115. Gifford RM. 1994. The global carbon cycle: a viewpoint on the missing sink. *Aust. J. Plant Physiol.* 21:1–5
116. Gifford RM. 1995. Whole plant respiration and photosynthesis of wheat under increased CO_2 concentration and temperature: long-term vs short-term distinctions for modeling. *Glob. Chang. Biol.* 1:385–96
117. Tjoelker MG, Oleksyn J, Reich PR. 1999. Acclimation of respiration to temperature and CO_2 in seedlings of boreal tree species in relation to plant size and relative growth rate. *Glob. Chang. Biol.* 49:679–91
118. Batjes NH. 1996. Total carbon and nitrogen in soils of the world. *Eurasian J. Soil Sci.* 47:151–63
119. Jenkinson DS, Adams DE, Wild A. 1991. Model estimates of CO_2 emissions from soil in response to global warming. *Nature* 351:304–6
120. Kirschbaum MUF. 2000. Will changes in soil organic carbon act as a positive or negative feedback on global warming? *Biogeochemistry* 48:21–51
121. McGuire AD, Sitch S, Clein JS, Dargaville R, Esser G, et al. 2001. Carbon balance of terrestrial ecosystems in the twentieth century: analyses of CO_2, climate and land use effects with four process-based ecosystem models. *Glob. Biogeochem. Cycles* 15:183–206
122. Oechel WC, Vourlitis GL, Hastings SJ, Bochkarev SA. 1995. Changes in arctic CO_2 flux over two decades: effects of climate change at Barrow, Alaska. *Ecol. Appl.* 5:846–55
123. Peterjohn WT, Melillo JM, Steudler PA, Newkirk KM, Bowles FP, et al. 1994. Responses of trace gas fluxes and N availability to experimentally elevated soil temperatures. *Ecol. Appl.* 4:617–25
124. Strömgren M, Gower ST, Linder S. 2003. Effects of soil warming on soil carbon dynamics of a boreal Picea abies forest. *Glob. Chang. Biol.* In press
125. Rustad LE, Campbell JL, Marion GM, Norby RJ, Mitchell MJ, et al. 2001. A meta-analysis of the response of soil respiration, net nitrogen mineralization, aboveground plant growth to experimental ecosystem warming. *Oecologia* 126:543–62
126. Schimel DS. 1995. Terrestrial ecosystems and the carbon cycle. *Glob. Chang. Biol.* 1:77–91
127. Schimel DS, Braswell BH, Holland EA, McKeown R, Oijima DS, et al. 1994. Climatic, edaphic, and biotic controls over storage and turnover of carbon in soils. *Glob. Biogeochem. Cycles* 8:279–93
128. Harden JW, Sundquist ET, Stallard RF, Mark RK. 1992. Dynamics of soil carbon during deglaciation of the Laurentide Ice Sheet. *Science* 258:1921–24
129. Reilly J, Prinn R, Harnisch J, Fitzmaurice J, Jacoby H, et al. 1999. Multi-gas assessment of the Kyoto Protocol. *Nature* 401:549–55
130. Woodwell GM, MacKenzie FT, Houghton RA, Apps MJ, Gorham E, Davidson EA. 1995. *Biotic Feedbacks in the Global Climatic System*, ed. GM Woodwell, FT Mackenzie, pp. 395–411. New York, NY: Oxford Univ. Press
131. Betts RA, Cox PM, Lee SE, Woodward FI. 1997. Contrasting physiological and structural vegetation feedbacks in climate change simulations. *Nature* 387:796–99
132. Hendry GR, Ellsworth DS, Lewin KF, Nagy J. 1999. A free-air enrichment system for exposing tall forest vegetation to

elevated atmospheric CO_2. *Glob. Chang. Biol.* 5:293–309
133. DeLucia EH, Hamilton JG, Naidu SL, Thomas RB, Andrews JA, et al. 1999. Net primary production of a forest ecosystem with experimental CO_2 enrichment. *Science* 284:1177–79
134. Norby RJ, Hanson PJ, O'Neill EG, Tschaplinski TJ, Weltzin JF, et al. 2002. Net primary productivity of a CO_2-enriched deciduous forest and the implications for carbon storage. *Ecol. Appl.* 12:1261–66
135. Schlesinger WH, Lichter J. 2001. Limited carbon storage in soil and litter of experimental plots under elevated atmospheric CO_2. *Nature* 411:466–69
136. Luo Y. 2001. Transient ecosystem responses to free-air CO_2 enrichment (FACE): experiments to predict carbon sequestration in natural ecosystems. *New Phytol.* 152:3–8
137. Idso SB. 1999. The long-term response of trees to atmospheric CO_2 enrichment. *Glob. Chang. Biol.* 5:493–95
138. Hättenschwiler S, Miglietta F, Raschi A, Körner Ch. 1997. Thirty years of in situ tree growth under elevated CO_2; a model for future forest responses? *Glob. Chang. Biol.* 3:463–71
139. Oren R, Ellsworth DS, Johnson KH, Phillips N, Ewers BE, et al. 2001. Soil fertility limits carbon sequestration by forest ecosystems in a CO_2-enriched atmosphere. *Nature* 411:466–69
140. McLaughlin SB, Percy KE. 1999. Forest health in North America: some perspectives on actual and potential roles of climate and air pollution. *Water Air Soil Pollut.* 116:151–97
141. Percy KE, Awmack CS, Lindroth RL, Kubiske ME, Kopper BJ, et al. 2002. Altered performance of forest pests under atmospheres enriched by CO_2 and O_3. *Nature* 420:403–7
142. UN Framew. Conv. Clim. Change Kyoto Protocol to the United Nations Framework Convention on Climate Change.
1997. http://www.unfccc.int/resource/docs/convkp/kpeng.pdf
143. Schulze E-D, Valentini R, Sanz M-J. 2002. The long way from Kyoto to Marakesh: implications of the Kyoto Protocol negotiations for global ecology. *Glob. Chang. Biol.* 8:505–18
144. Missfeldt F, Haites E. 2001. The potential contribution of sinks to meeting the Kyoto protocol commitments. *Environ. Sci. Policy* 4:269–92
145. Martin PH, Nabuurs G-J, Aubinet M, Karajalainen T, Vine EL, et al. 2001. Carbon sinks in temperate forests. *Annu. Rev. Energy Environ.* 26:435–65
146. Linder S, Axelsson B. 1982. Changes in carbon uptake and allocation patterns as a result of irrigation and fertilization in a young Pinus sylvestris stand. In *Carbon Uptake and Allocation: Key to Management of Subalpine Forest Ecosystems*, ed. RH Waring, pp. 38–44. IUFRO Workshop. For. Res. Lab., Corvallis, Or.
147. Snowdon P, Benson ML. 1992. Effects of combinations of irrigation and fertilization on the growth and above-ground biomass production of Pinus radiata. *For. Ecol. Manag.* 52:87–116
148. Albaugh TJ, Allen HL, Dougherty PM, Kress LW, King JS. 1997. Leaf area and above- and belowground growth responses of loblolly pine to nutrient and water additions. *For. Sci.* 44:317–27
149. Matson PA, Volkman C, Gower ST, Grier CC. 1992. Soil nitrogen cycling and nitrous oxide flux from fertilized high-elevation Douglas-fir forests in New Mexico. *Biogeochemistry* 18:101–17
150. Cole CV, Flach K, Lee J, Sauerbeck D, Stewart B. 1993. Agricultural sources and sinks of carbon. *Water Air Soil Pollut.* 70:111–22
151. Izaurralde RC, McGill WB, Bryden A, Graham S, Ward M, Dickey P. 1998. Scientific challenges in developing a plan to predict and verify carbon storage in Canadian prairies soils. In *Management of Carbon Sequestration in Soil*, ed. R Lal, JM

Kimble, RF Follett, BA Stewart, pp. 433–46. Boca Raton, FL: CRC
152. Guo LB, Gifford RM. 2002. Soil carbon stocks and land use change: a meta analysis. *Glob. Chang. Biol.* 8:345–60
153. Richter DD, Markewitz D, Trumbore SE, Wells CG. 1999. Rapid accumulation of soil carbon in re-establishing forest. *Nature* 400:56–58
154. Gower ST, Barger D. 2003. Biological and economic feasibility of afforestation to sequester carbon: a case study. *J. Environ. Qual.* In press
155. Row C, Phelps RB. 1996. Wood carbon flows and storage after timber harvest. In *Forests and Global Change. Vol. 2. Forest Management Opportunities for Mitigating Carbon Emissions*, ed. RN Sampson, D Hair, pp. 27–58. Washington, DC: Am. Forests
156. Karjalainen T. 1996. Dynamics and potentials of carbon sequestration in managed stands and wood products in Finland under changing climatic conditions. *Forest Ecol. Manag.* 80:113–32
157. Karjalainen TS, Kellomaki S, Pussinen A. 1994. Role of wood-based products in absorbing atmospheric carbon. *Silva Fenn.* 28:67–80
158. Côté WA, Young RJ, Riese KB, Costanza AF, Tonelli JP, Lenocker C. 2002. A carbon balance method for paper and wood products. *Environ. Pollut.* 116:S1–6
159. Graedel TE, Allenby BR. 1995. *Industrial Ecology*. Upper Saddle River, NJ: Prentice Hall. 412 pp.
160. Consoli F, Allen D, Boustead I, Fava James, Franklin W, et al. eds. 1993. *Guidelines for Life-Cycle Assessment: A Code of Practice*. Brussels: Soc. Environ. Toxicol. Chem. 13 pp.
161. World Resourc. Inst., World Bus. Counc. Sustain. Dev. 2001. *The Greenhouse Gas Protocol: a Corporate Accounting and Reporting Standard*. Washington, DC: WRI. http://www.ghgprotocol.org/standard/ghg.pdf
162. Shaver GR, Canadell J, Chapin FS III, Gurevitch J, Harte J, et al. 2000. Global warming and terrestrial ecosystems: a conceptual framework for analysis. *BioScience* 50:871–82

DYNAMICS OF LAND-USE AND LAND-COVER CHANGE IN TROPICAL REGIONS

Eric F. Lambin,[1] Helmut J. Geist,[2] and Erika Lepers[2]

[1]*Department of Geography, University of Louvain, Place Louis Pasteur 3, B-1348 Louvain-la-Neuve, Belgium; email: lambin@geog.ucl.ac.be*
[2]*LUCC International Project Office, Department of Geography, University of Louvain, Place Louis Pasteur 3, B-1348 Louvain-la-Neuve, Belgium; email: geist@geog.ucl.ac.be, lepers@geog.ucl.ac.be*

Key Words deforestation, agriculture, urbanization, land degradation, landscape

■ **Abstract** We highlight the complexity of land-use/cover change and propose a framework for a more general understanding of the issue, with emphasis on tropical regions. The review summarizes recent estimates on changes in cropland, agricultural intensification, tropical deforestation, pasture expansion, and urbanization and identifies the still unmeasured land-cover changes. Climate-driven land-cover modifications interact with land-use changes. Land-use change is driven by synergetic factor combinations of resource scarcity leading to an increase in the pressure of production on resources, changing opportunities created by markets, outside policy intervention, loss of adaptive capacity, and changes in social organization and attitudes. The changes in ecosystem goods and services that result from land-use change feed back on the drivers of land-use change. A restricted set of dominant pathways of land-use change is identified. Land-use change can be understood using the concepts of complex adaptive systems and transitions. Integrated, place-based research on land-use/land-cover change requires a combination of the agent-based systems and narrative perspectives of understanding. We argue in this paper that a systematic analysis of local-scale land-use change studies, conducted over a range of timescales, helps to uncover general principles that provide an explanation and prediction of new land-use changes.

CONTENTS

INTRODUCTION 206
RECENT ESTIMATES OF GLOBAL LAND-USE/COVER CHANGE 208
   Historical Changes 208
   Most Rapid Land-Cover Changes of the Last Decades 209
   The Still Unmeasured Land-Cover Changes 213
THE COMPLEX NATURE OF LAND-COVER CHANGES 213
   Conversion Versus Modification in Land Cover 213
   Progressive Versus Episodic Land-Cover Changes 215
EMPIRICAL EVIDENCE ON THE CAUSES OF LAND-USE CHANGE 216

Proximate Versus Underlying Causes 216
General Insights on Sectoral Causes of Land-Use Change 217
A Finite Set of Pathways of Land-Use Change 221
A SYNTHESIS OF THE CAUSES OF LAND-USE CHANGE AND
  THEIR INTERACTIONS 223
  The Five Fundamental High-Level Causes of Land-Use Change 223
  Mode of Interactions Between Causes of Change 225
  Feedback and Endogeneity 226
  Land-Use Change as an Emergent Property of Complex Adaptive
    Systems 227
  Land-Use Transitions 228
INTEGRATIVE FRAMEWORKS TO UNDERSTAND
  LAND-USE/COVER CHANGES 228
  Agent-Based Perspective 229
  Systems Perspective 230
  Narrative Perspective 230
CONCLUSION AND FUTURE RESEARCH 231

INTRODUCTION

Concerns about land-use/cover change emerged in the research agenda on global environmental change several decades ago with the realization that land surface processes influence climate. In the mid-1970s, it was recognized that land-cover change modifies surface albedo and thus surface-atmosphere energy exchanges, which have an impact on regional climate (1–3). In the early 1980s, terrestrial ecosystems as sources and sinks of carbon were highlighted; this underscored the impact of land-use/cover change on the global climate via the carbon cycle (4, 5). Decreasing the uncertainty of these terrestrial sources and sinks of carbon remains a serious challenge today. Later, the important contribution of local evapotranspiration to the water cycle—that is precipitation recycling—as a function of land cover highlighted yet another considerable impact of land-use/cover change on climate, at a local to regional scale in this case (6).

A much broader range of impacts of land-use/cover change on ecosystem goods and services were further identified. Of primary concern are impacts on biotic diversity worldwide (7), soil degradation (8), and the ability of biological systems to support human needs (9). Land-use/cover changes also determine, in part, the vulnerability of places and people to climatic, economic, or sociopolitical perturbations (10). When aggregated globally, land-use/cover changes significantly affect central aspects of earth system functioning. All impacts are not negative though, as many forms of land-use/cover changes are associated with continuing increases in food and fiber production, in resource use efficiency, and in wealth and well-being.

Understanding and predicting the impact of surface processes on climate required long-term historical reconstructions and projections into the future of land-cover changes at regional to global scales (11, 12). Quantifying the contribution of terrestrial ecosystems to global carbon pools and flux required accurate mapping of land cover and measurements of land-cover conversions worldwide (13–15). Fine resolution, spatially explicit data on landscape fragmentation were required to understand the impact of land-use/cover changes on biodiversity (16, 17). Predicting how land-use changes affect land degradation, the feedback on livelihood strategies from land degradation, and the vulnerability of places and people in the face of land-use/cover changes requires a good understanding of the dynamic human-environment interactions associated with land-use change (10).

Over the last few decades, numerous researchers have improved measurements of land-cover change, the understanding of the causes of land-use change, and predictive models of land-use/cover change, in part under the auspices of the Land-Use and Land-Cover Change (LUCC) project of the International Geosphere-Biosphere Programme (IGBP) and International Human Dimensions Programme on Global Environmental Change (IHDP) (18, 19). Many scientists, especially in the natural sciences, previously assumed that generating local- to global-scale projections of land change several centuries into the past and about 100 years into the future would be easy. Actually, many thought land changes consisted mostly in the conversion of pristine forests to agricultural uses (deforestation) or the destruction of natural vegetation by overgrazing, which leads to desert conditions (desertification). These conversions were assumed to be irreversible and spatially homogeneous and to progress linearly. Only the growth of the local population and, to a lesser extent, its increase in consumption were thought to drive the changes in land conditions.

Recent research has largely dispelled these simplifications and replaced them by a representation of much more complex, and sometimes intricate, processes of land-use/cover change. A consensus is progressively being reached on the rate and location of some of the main land changes, but other forms of change, such as desertification, are still unmeasured and controversial. Understanding of the causes of land-use change has moved from simplistic representations of two or three driving forces to a much more profound understanding that involves situation-specific interactions among a large number of factors at different spatial and temporal scales. The richness of explanations has greatly increased, often at the expense of generality of the explanations. Today, only a very few models of land-use change can generate long-term, realistic projections of future land-use/cover changes at regional to global scales. The last decade, however, has witnessed innovative methodological developments in the modeling of land-use change at local to regional scales (20–22). Nevertheless, the recent progress in our understanding of the causes of land-use change still has to be fully integrated in models of the process.

This review describes how our understanding of land-use/cover change has moved from simplicity to greater realism and complexity over the last decades. The main emphasis of the review is on tropical regions. Our goal is to extract from this complexity a general framework for a more general understanding of land-use/cover change. First, the most recent estimates of the magnitude of land-use/cover change are summarized. Second, the complex nature of land-cover change is discussed to emphasize the need to integrate all scales and processes of change. Third, a synthesis of recent case study evidence on the causes of land-use change is presented, with emphasis on the mode of interaction between diverse causes and dominant pathways of change. Fourth, the complexity of land-use change is described using the notions of complex adaptive systems and transition. Integrative perspectives to analyze land-use/cover changes are then discussed. The review highlights the dynamic nature of coupled human-environment systems in relation to land-use/cover change.

RECENT ESTIMATES OF GLOBAL LAND-USE/COVER CHANGE

Historical Changes

Since humans have controlled fire and domesticated plants and animals, they have cleared forests to wring higher value from the land. About half of the ice-free land surface has been converted or substantially modified by human activities over the last 10,000 years. A recent study estimated that undisturbed (or wilderness) areas represent 46% of the earth's land surface (23). Forests covered about 50% of the earth's land area 8000 years ago, as opposed to 30% today (24). Agriculture has expanded into forests, savannas, and steppes in all parts of the world to meet the demand for food and fiber. Agricultural expansion has shifted between regions over time; this followed the general development of civilizations, economies, and increasing populations (25).

Two recent studies estimated historical changes in permanent cropland at a global scale during the last 300 years by spatializing historical cropland inventory data based on a global land-cover classification derived by remote sensing, which used a hindcasting approach (11), or based on historical population density data (26). The area of cropland has increased globally from an estimated 300–400 million ha in 1700 to 1500–1800 million ha in 1990, a 4.5- to fivefold increase in three centuries and a 50% net increase just in the twentieth century. The area under pasture—for which more uncertainties remain—increased from around 500 million ha in 1700 to around 3100 million ha in 1990 (27). These increases led to the clearing of forests and the transformation of natural grasslands, steppes, and savannas. Forest area decreased from 5000–6200 million ha in 1700 to 4300–5300 million ha in 1990. Steppes, savannas, and grasslands also experienced a rapid decline, from around 3200 million ha in 1700 to 1800–2700 million ha in 1990 (11, 26) (Table 1).

Europe, the Indo-Gangetic Plain, and eastern China experienced first the most rapid cropland expansion during the eighteenth century. Starting in the nineteenth century, the newly developed regions of North America and the former Soviet Union followed suit. China experienced a steady rate of expansion throughout the last three centuries (28). A very gradual cropland expansion occurred in Africa, south and Southeast Asia, Latin America, and Australia until 1850, but since then,

TABLE 1 Historical changes in land use/cover at a global scale over the last 300 years (11, 26, 27)

	Forest/woodland (10^6 ha)	Steppe/savanna/grassland (10^6 ha)	Cropland (10^6 ha)	Pasture (10^6 ha)
1700	5000 to 6200	3200	300 to 400	400 to 500
1990	4300 to 5300	1800 to 2700	1500 to 1800	3100 to 3300

these regions have experienced dramatic increases in cropland, especially during the second half of the twentieth century. The greatest cropland expansion in the twentieth century occurred in south and Southeast Asia (28). The Corn Belt in the United States, the prairie provinces in Canada, the pampas grassland region in Argentina, and, a few decades later, southeast Brazil have also seen rapid expansion of permanent cropland early in the twentieth century (28).

Most Rapid Land-Cover Changes of the Last Decades

RECENT FOREST-COVER CHANGES Deforestation occurs when forest is converted to another land cover or when the tree canopy cover falls below a minimum percentage threshold—10% for the United Nations (U.N.) Food and Agriculture Organization (F.A.O.) (29). On the basis of national statistics, inventory reports, estimates by experts, and a pantropical remote sensing survey for tropical forests only, the Global Forest Resources Assessment 2000 (29) estimated that the world's natural forests decreased by 16.1 million hectares per year on average during the 1990s; that is a loss of 4.2% of the natural forest that existed in 1990. However, some natural forests were converted to forest plantations. Gains in forest cover arose from afforestation on land previously under nonforest land use (1.6 million hectares per year globally) and the expansion of natural forests in areas previously under agriculture, mostly in western Europe and eastern North America (3.6 million hectares per year globally). The net global decrease in forest area was therefore 9.4 million hectares per year from 1990 to 2000 (29). The total net forest change for the temperate regions was positive, but it was negative for the tropical regions.

FAO estimated that tropical regions lost 15.2 million hectares of forests per year during the 1990s. Recent estimates for only the world's humid tropical forests (30), based on a sampling strategy of remote sensing data, revised downward by 23% FAO's net rate of change in forest cover for the humid tropics, which exclude tropical dry forests. According to Achard et al. (30), between 1990 and 1997, 5.8 ± 1.4 million hectares of humid tropical forest were lost each year (Table 2). Forest regrowth accounted for 1.0 ± 0.32 million hectares. The annual rate of net cover change in humid tropical forest was 0.43% during that period. A further 2.3 ± 0.7 million hectares of forest were visibly degraded. This figure does not include forests affected by selective logging. Southeast Asia has experienced the highest

TABLE 2 Mean annual change estimates of humid tropical forest cover during the 1990–1997 period[a]

	Forest cover in 1990 (10⁶ ha)	Annual net cover change 10⁶ ha	%	Annual deforestation 10⁶ ha	%	Annual forest regrowth 10⁶ ha	%	Annual forest degradation 10⁶ ha	%
Latin America	669 ± 57	−2.2 ± 1.2	0.33	2.5 ± 1.4	0.38	0.28 ± 0.22	0.04	0.83 ± 0.67	0.13
Africa	198 ± 13	−0.71 ± 0.31	0.36	0.85 ± 0.30	0.43	0.14 ± 0.11	0.07	0.39 ± 0.19	0.21
Southeast Asia	283 ± 31	−2.0 ± 0.8	0.71	2.5 ± 0.8	0.91	0.53 ± 0.25	0.19	1.1 ± 0.44	0.42
Global	1150 ± 54	−4.9 ± 1.3	0.43	5.8 ± 1.4	0.52	1.0 ± 0.32	0.08	2.3 ± 0.71	0.2

[a]Abstracted with permission from Achard F, Eva HD, Stibig HJ, Mayaux P, Gallego J, et al. 2002. Determination of deforestation rates of the world's humid tropical forests. *Science* 297:999–1002. Copyright 2002 American Association for the Advancement of Science, http://www.sciencemag.org.

rate of net cover change (0.71% per year), whereas Africa and Latin America present lower rates (respectively 0.36% and 0.33%). Latin America, however, lost about the same area of forest as Southeast Asia during the 1990–1997 time period (30). Forest degradation was most extensive in Southeast Asia (0.42% per year), lowest in Latin America (0.13% per year), and intermediate in Africa (0.21% per year). Forest regrowth was more extensive, both in absolute and relative terms, in Southeast Asia than in the other humid tropical regions (0.19% for Southeast Asia, 0.04% for Latin America, and 0.07% for Africa) (30).

These recent assessments of deforestation, as well as another remote sensing survey at a coarser spatial resolution but covering the entire tropical belt (31), concur to estimate less deforestation in the 1990s than was observed in the 1980s. Still, it is unlikely that deforestation has significantly slowed down, because differences in methods of assessment and definitions used may account for at least part of the difference (32). Moreover, deforestation in the dry tropical forests may often be underestimated.

In Latin America, large-scale forest conversion and colonization for livestock-based agriculture is prevalent, whereas cropland expansion by smallholders dominates in Africa. In Asia, intensified shifting agriculture, including migration into new areas, gradual change of existing areas toward more permanent agriculture, and logging explain most of the deforestation (29, 30, 33). Within these regions, deforestation is largely confined to a few areas undergoing rapid change, with annual rates of deforestation from 2% to 5% (Figure 1) (see color insert). The largest deforestation front is the *arc of deforestation* of the Brazilian Amazon, which extends more recently outside Brazil, east of the Andes, and along the road from Manaus to Venezuela. More scattered areas of forest loss are detected in the Chaco and Atlantic forest areas in South America. Central America has significant deforestation fronts in the Yucatán and at the Nicaraguan border with Honduras and Costa Rica. In Africa, forest-cover change is very rapid in Madagascar, Côte d'Ivoire, and the Congo basin, in small scattered hot spots. In Southeast Asia several deforestation fronts are found around Sumatra, Borneo, Vietnam, Cambodia, and Myanmar.

RECENT CHANGES IN AGRICULTURAL AREAS   Historically, humans have increased agricultural output mainly by bringing more land into production. The greatest concentration of farmland is found in Eastern Europe, with more than half of its land area in crop cover (28). In the United Kingdom, about 70% of its area is classified as agricultural land (cropland, grassland/rough grazing), with agriculture and areas set aside for conservation or recreation intimately intertwined (37). Despite claims to the contrary, the amount of suitable land remaining for crops is very limited in most developing countries (38, 39), where most of the growing food demand originates. Where there is a large surplus of cultivable land, land is often under rain forest or in marginal areas (38, 39).

The period after 1960 has witnessed a decoupling between food production increase and cropland expansion (Table 3). The 1.97-fold increase in world food production from 1961 to 1996 was associated with only a 10% increase of land under cultivation but also with a 1.68-fold increase in the amount of irrigated cropland and a 6.87- and 3.48-fold increase in the global annual rate of nitrogen and phosphorus fertilization (40). In 2000, 271 million ha were irrigated (25). Globally, the cropland area per capita decreased by more than half in the twentieth century, from around 0.75 ha per person in 1900 to only 0.35 hectare per person in 1990 (28). Note, however, that national statistics in developing countries often substantially underreport agricultural land area (28, 38), e.g., by as much as 50% in parts of China (41).

The mix of cropland expansion and agricultural intensification has varied geographically (25). Tropical Asia increased its food production mainly by increasing

TABLE 3 Increase in world food production and agricultural inputs from 1961 to 1996, based on FAO data (40)

	Number-fold increase in 35 years (1961–1996)
World food production	1.97
Land under cultivation	1.098
Proportion of irrigated land	1.68
Nitrogen fertilization	6.87
Phosphorus fertilization	3.48

fertilizer use and irrigation. Most of Africa and Latin America increased their food production through both agricultural intensification and extensification. Western Africa is the only part of the world where, overall, cropland expansion was accompanied by a decrease in fertilizer use (−1.83% per year) and just a slight increase in irrigation (0.31% per year compared to a world average of 1.22% per year). In 1995, the global irrigated areas were distributed as 68% in Asia, 16% in the Americas, 10% in Europe, 5% in Africa, and 1% in Australia (42). In western Europe and the northeastern United States, cropland decreased during the last decades, after abandonment of agriculture or, in a few cases, following land degradation mostly on marginal land. Globally, this change has freed 222 million ha from agricultural use since 1900 (28).

RECENT CHANGES IN PASTORAL AREAS   Natural vegetation covers have given way not only to cropland but also to *pasture*—defined as land used permanently for herbaceous forage crops, either cultivated or growing wild (25). The distinction between pasture and natural savannas or steppes is not always clear. Most pastures are located in Asia (33%) and Africa (28%), with only a small portion being located in Europe and North America (7%) (25). During the last decade, pastures increased considerably in nontropical Asia (at an annual rate of 4.78%), whereas data suggest that pasture land has apparently decreased in eastern Africa. As eastern Africa recorded a large increase in head of cattle over this period [872,000 additional head of cattle per year between 1992 and 1999, according to FAO (25)], it is likely that many areas in pastoral use in Africa are classified as natural vegetation.

RECENT CHANGES IN URBANIZATION   In 2000, towns and cities sheltered more than 2.9 billion people, nearly half of the world population (43). Urban population has been growing more rapidly than rural population worldwide, particularly in developing countries. According to the U.N. Population Division (43), the number of megacities, defined here as cities with more than 10 million inhabitants, has changed from one in 1950 (New York) to 17 in 2000, the majority of which are in developing countries. Urban form and function have also changed rapidly. Built-up or paved-over areas are roughly estimated to occupy from 2% to 3% of the earth's land surface (38, 44). For example, in 1997, the 7 million inhabitants of Hong Kong were supported on as little as 120 km^2 of built-up land (45). However, urbanization affects land in rural areas through the *ecological footprint* of cities. This footprint includes, but is not restricted to, the consumption of prime agricultural land in peri-urban areas for residential, infrastructure, and amenity uses, which blurs the distinction between cities and countryside, especially in western developed countries. Urban inhabitants within the Baltic Sea drainage, for example, depend on forest, agriculture, wetland, lake, and marine systems that constitute an area about 1000 times larger than that of the urban area proper (46). In 1997, total nonfood material resources consumed in Hong Kong (i.e., its urban material metabolism) were nearly 25 times larger than the total material turnover of the natural ecosystem. Fossil fuel energy consumed in this city (i.e., its urban energy metabolism) exceeded photosynthetically fixed solar energy by 17 times (45). Time series of global maps of nighttime lights detected by satellite (47) illustrate the rapid changes in both urban extent and electrification of the cities and their surroundings. A question still being debated is whether urban land use is more efficient than rural land use and, therefore, whether urbanization saves land for nature.

The most populated clusters of cities are mainly located along the coastal zones and major waterways—in India, East Asia, on the eastern U.S. coast, and in western Europe (Figure 2) (see color insert). The cities experiencing the most rapid change in urban population between 1990 and 2000 are mostly located in developing countries (48) (Figure 2). It is estimated that 1 to 2 million ha of cropland are being taken out of production every year in developing countries to meet the land demand for housing, industry, infrastructure, and recreation (39). This is likely to take place mostly on prime agricultural land located in coastal plains and in river valleys. Note that rural households may consume more land per capita for residential purposes than their urban counterparts (39).

The Still Unmeasured Land-Cover Changes

Other forms of rapid land-cover change that are thought to be widespread are still poorly documented at the global scale. Local- to national-scale studies, however, demonstrate their importance and ecological significance. Prominent among these are changes in the (sub)tropical dry forests (e.g., Miombo forests in southern Africa and Chaco forests in South America); forest-cover changes caused by selective logging, fires, and insect damage; drainage or other forms of alteration of wetlands; soil degradation in croplands; changes in the extent and productive capacity of pastoral lands; and dryland degradation, also referred to as desertification, which remains a controversial issue.

THE COMPLEX NATURE OF LAND-COVER CHANGES

Conversion Versus Modification in Land Cover

The land cover is defined by the attributes of the earth's land surface and immediate subsurface, including biota, soil, topography, surface and groundwater, and human structures. Data sets used in land-use/cover change research represent the land surface by a set of spatial units, each associated with attributes. These attributes are either a single land-cover category (i.e., leading to a discrete representation of land cover) (49) or a set of values for continuous biophysical variables (i.e., leading to a continuous representation of land cover) (50). The discrete representation of land cover has the advantages of concision and clarity, but it has led to an overemphasis of land-cover conversions and a neglect of land-cover modifications. *Land-cover conversions* (i.e., the complete replacement of one cover type by another) are measured by a shift from one land-cover category to another, as is the case in agricultural expansion, deforestation, or change in urban extent. *Land-cover modifications* are more subtle changes that affect the character of the land cover without changing its overall classification.

Recently, there has been increased recognition of the importance of the processes of modification of land attributes. For example, mostly *agricultural intensification*—defined as higher levels of inputs and increased output of cultivated or reared products per unit area and time—permitted an increase in the world's food production over the last decades (40). Thanks to the use of high-yielding crop varieties, fertilization, irrigation, and pesticides on land already under agriculture, crop yield increases have outpaced global human population growth (51). In the Brazilian Amazon, every year forest impoverishment caused by selective logging and fires affects an area at least as large as the area affected by forest-cover conversion (52). The expansion of woody shrubs in the western United States grasslands, following fire suppression and overgrazing, contributed to a large carbon sink (14, 53). The severity of soil erosion and its impact on associated resources in the United States has been debated because of discrepancies between estimates based on models and observed sediment budgets (8). Declines in tree density and species richness in the last half of the twentieth century were measured in a region of Senegal, in the West African Sahel, and provided evidence of desertification in that region (54). Another study in western Sudan, a region that was allegedly affected by desertification, did not find any decline in the abundance of trees despite several decades of droughts (55).

The monitoring of land-cover conversion can be performed by a simple comparison of successive land-cover maps. By contrast, the detection of subtle changes within land-cover classes—that is modifications—requires a representation of land cover where the surface attributes vary continuously in space and time, at the seasonal and interannual scales (50, 56). This representation allows detection of, for example, changes in tree density, in net primary productivity, or in the length of the growing season. Earth observation from satellite sensors provides repetitive and spatially explicit measurements of biophysical surface attributes, such as vegetation cover, biomass, vegetation community structure, surface moisture, superficial soil organic matter content, and landscape heterogeneity.

Analyses of multiyear time series of these attributes, their fine-scale spatial pattern, and their seasonal evolution have led to a broader view of land-cover change. Remote sensing data highlight high temporal frequency land-cover modifications of great importance for earth system processes. In particular, data from wide-field-of-view satellite sensors reveal patterns of seasonal and interannual variations in land surface attributes that are driven not by land-use change but rather by climatic variability. These variations include the impact on vegetation and surface moisture of the El Niño Southern Oscillation (ENSO) phenomena (57–59), natural disasters such as floods and droughts (60, 61), changes in the length of the growing season in boreal regions (62), and changes in vegetation productivity due to erratic rainfall fluctuations in the African Sahel, which lead to an expansion and contraction of the Sahara (63).

A study linking coarse resolution remote sensing data with rainfall data tested whether there was a decadal trend in the rain-use efficiency of the African Sahel region. It revealed the absence of widespread subcontinental-scale dryland degradation, although some areas did show signs of degradation (64). These results suggested that the resilience of the Sahel in primary production per unit rainfall has not changed despite serious droughts in the 1970s and 1980s. The impact of fires on land cover has also been well documented with remote sensing data (65), both for the mostly anthropogenic fires in tropical regions (66) and the mostly natural fires in boreal regions (67). Fires result from a combination of climatic factors, which determine fuel availability, fuel flammability, and ignition by lightning, and factors related to land-use/cover change that control fire propagation in the landscape and human ignition.

A combination of coarse and fine spatial resolution satellite sensors allowed measuring at the global scale land-cover changes caused by land-use change, such as deforestation in the humid tropics (30, 31) and change in nighttime city lights, which is a proxy for changes in urban extent and electrification (47). Although numerous local scale studies have mapped and quantified land-cover change with fine resolution remote sensing data, and there are a few subnational- to national-scale studies (35), there are remarkably few such studies at the regional to global scales. National-scale forest inventory and agricultural census data have also been analyzed, in some cases with remote sensing data, to refine estimates of rates and geographic patterns of change in forest cover and cropland (11, 14). Overall, the quantification of areas of rapid land-cover change still suffers from large uncertainties (36).

Progressive Versus Episodic Land-Cover Changes

Time series of remote sensing data reveal that land-cover changes do not always occur in a progressive and gradual way, but they may show periods of rapid and abrupt change followed either by a quick recovery of ecosystems or by a nonequilibrium trajectory. Such short-term changes, often caused by the interaction of climatic and land-use factors, have an important impact on ecosystem processes. For example, droughts in the African Sahel and their effects on vegetation are reinforced at the decadal timescale through a feedback mechanism that involves land surface changes caused by the initial decrease in rainfall (68). Grazing and conversion of semiarid grasslands to row-crop agriculture are the source of another positive desertification feedback by increasing heterogeneity of soil resources in space and time (69). The role of the Amazonian forest as a carbon sink (in natural forests) and source (from land-use changes and fires) varies from year to year as a result of interactive effects between deforestation, abandonment of agricultural land reverting to forests, fires, and interannual climatic variability (70, 71). In Indonesia, periodic El Niño-driven droughts lead to an increase in the forest's susceptibility to fires. Accidental fires are more likely under these conditions and lead to the devastation of large tracts of forests (72) and to the release of huge amounts of carbon from peatland fires (73). Large landholders also seize the opportunity of drought conditions to burn large tracts of forest to convert them to plantations. Forests that have been affected by forest fragmentation, selective logging, or a first fire subsequently become even more vulnerable to fires as these factors interact synergistically with drought (72, 74).

In summary, both land-cover modifications and rapid land-cover changes need to be better taken into account in land-cover change studies. Climate-driven land-cover modifications do interact with land-use changes. Slow and localized land-cover conversion takes place against a background of high temporal frequency regional-scale fluctuations in land-cover conditions caused by climatic variability, and it is often linked through positive feedback with land-cover modifications. These multiple spatial and temporal scales of change, with interactions between climate-driven and anthropogenic changes, are a significant source of complexity in the assessment of land-cover changes. It is not surprising that the land-cover changes for which the best data exist—deforestation, changes in the extent of cultivated lands, and urbanization—are processes of conversion that are not strongly affected by interannual climatic variability. By contrast, few quantitative data exist at the global scale for processes of land-cover modification that are heavily influenced by interannual climatic fluctuations, e.g., desertification, forest degradation and rangeland modifications.

EMPIRICAL EVIDENCE ON THE CAUSES OF LAND-USE CHANGE

Proximate Versus Underlying Causes

Land use is defined by the purposes for which humans exploit the land cover. There is high variability in time and space in biophysical environments, socioeconomic activities, and cultural contexts that are associated with land-use change. Identifying the causes of land-use change requires an understanding of how people make land-use decisions and how various factors interact in specific contexts to influence decision making on land use. Decision making is influenced by factors at the local, regional, or global scale. Proximate (or direct) causes of land-use change constitute human activities or immediate actions that originate from intended land use and directly affect land cover (75). They involve a physical action on land cover. Underlying (or indirect or root) causes are fundamental forces that underpin the more proximate causes of land-cover change. They operate more diffusely (i.e., from a distance), often by altering one or more proximate causes (76). Underlying causes are formed by a complex of social, political, economic, demographic, technological, cultural, and biophysical variables that constitute initial conditions in the human-environment relations and are structural (or systemic) in nature (33, 77, 78).

Proximate causes generally operate at the local level (individual farms, households, or communities). By contrast, underlying causes may originate from the regional (districts, provinces, or country) or even global levels, with complex interplays between levels of organization. Underlying causes are often exogenous to the local communities managing land and are thus uncontrollable by these communities. Only some local-scale factors are endogenous to decision makers. An important system property associated with changes in land use is feedback that can either accentuate or amplify the speed, intensity, or mode of land change, or constitute human mitigating forces, for example via institutional actions that dampen, impede, or counteract factors or their impacts. Examples are the direct regulation of access to land resources, market adjustments, or informal social regulations (e.g., shared norms and values that give rise to shared land management practices).

Place-based research followed by systematic comparative analyses of case studies of land-use dynamics have helped to improve understanding of the causes of land-use change (10, 33, 79–83). These syntheses produced general insights on sectoral causes of land-use change and on the mode of interaction between various causes. They identified dominant pathways—also referred to as spirals, trajectories, or syndromes—leading to specific types of change. What has been lacking so far is the development of an integrative framework that would provide a unifying theory for these insights and pathways of land-use change and a more process-oriented understanding of how multiple macrostructural variables interact to affect micro agency with respect to land.

General Insights on Sectoral Causes of Land-Use Change

MULTIPLE CAUSES Land-use change is always caused by multiple interacting factors originating from different levels of organization of the coupled human-environment systems. The mix of driving forces of land-use change varies in time and space, according to specific human-environment conditions. Driving forces can be slow variables, with long turnover times, which determine the boundaries of sustainability and collectively govern the land use trajectory (such as the spread of salinity in irrigation schemes or declining infant mortality), or fast variables, with short turnover times (such as food aid or climatic variability associated with El Niño oscillation). Biophysical drivers may be as important as human drivers. The former define the natural capacity or predisposing conditions for land-use changes. The set of abiotic and biotic factors that determine this natural capacity varies among localities and regions. Trigger events, whether these are biophysical (a drought or hurricane) or socioeconomic (a war or economic crisis), also drive land-use changes. Changes are generally driven by a combination of factors that work gradually and factors that happen intermittently (82).

NATURAL VARIABILITY Natural environmental change and variability interact with human causes of land-use change. Highly variable ecosystem conditions driven by climatic variations amplify the pressures arising from high demands on land resources, especially under dry to sub-humid climatic conditions. Natural and socioeconomic changes may operate as synchronous but independent events. In the Iberian Peninsula during the sixteenth and seventeenth centuries, the peak of the Little Ice Age occurred almost simultaneously with large-scale clearing for cultivated land following the consolidation of Christian rule over the region. This cultivation triggered changes in surface hydrology and significant soil erosion (84). Natural variability may also lead to socioeconomic unsustainability, for example when unusually wet conditions alter the perception of drought risks and generate overstocking on rangelands. When drier conditions return, the livestock management practices are ill adapted and cause land degradation. This overstocking happened several times in Australia and, in the 1970s, in the African Sahel (84). Land-use change, such as cropland expansion in drylands, may also increase the vulnerability of human-environment systems to climatic fluctuations and thereby trigger land degradation.

ECONOMIC AND TECHNOLOGICAL FACTORS   Available case studies highlight that, at the timescale of a couple of decades or less, land-use changes mostly result from individual and social responses to changing economic conditions, which are mediated by institutional factors. Opportunities and constraints for new land uses are created by markets and policies and are increasingly influenced by global factors (82, 85). Economic factors and policies define a range of variables that have a direct impact on the decision making by land managers, e.g., input and output prices, taxes, subsidies, production and transportation costs, capital flows and investments, credit access, trade, and technology (86). Internal consumption affects land less than external demand, so subsistence croplands consequently decrease while land under crops for markets increases with a parallel increase in agricultural intensity (87). Market access is largely conditioned by state investments in transportation infrastructure. The unequal distribution of wealth between households, countries, and regions determines geographic differences in economic opportunities and constraints. It affects, for example, who is able to develop, use, and profit from new technologies that increase efficiency in land management.

Improving agricultural technology—as much as providing secure land tenure and giving farmers better access to credit and markets—can potentially encourage more deforestation rather than relieving pressure on the forests (88). The differing impact of agricultural development on forest conversion depends on how the new technologies affect the labor market and migration, whether the crops are sold locally or globally, how profitable farming is at the forest frontier, as well as on the capital and labor intensity of the new technologies (88).

DEMOGRAPHIC FACTORS   At longer timescales, both increases and decreases of a given population also have a large impact on land use. Demographic change does not only imply the shift from high to low rates of fertility and mortality (as suggested by the demographic transition), but it is also associated with the development of households and features of their life cycle. The family or life-cycle features relate mainly to labor availability at the level of households, which is linked to migration, urbanization, and the breakdown of extended families into several nuclear families. As an example of the latter phenomenon, the splintering of family herds in the West African Sudan-Sahel zone over the past 25 years—due to increases in nuclear households and the transfer of livestock wealth from herding families to merchants, agriculturalists, and government officials—led to increased investment in crop production, reduced labor availability among pastoral households, lower energy and skills applied to livestock husbandry, and reduced livestock mobility, which increased the risk of land degradation (89). Fuelwood demand by households in Africa differs between nuclear family units and larger consuming units; the latter are generally more energy efficient. Small consuming units thus cause more forest degradation, especially in peri-urban environments (90).

The internal dynamics of traditional and colonist families in humid forest frontiers in South America, which are mainly related to households' capital and labor constraints, explain the microlevel dynamics of land-cover modification by forest types (91), land quality (92), and gender division, as well as the changing social context of deforestation in the Amazon Basin (93–95). Forest clearing is caused by a variety of actors, with differing effects: recent in-migrants practice slash-and-burn agriculture; their children's families shift to fallow agriculture; long-settled families have diversified production; small families have crop/livestock combinations (associated with high rates of forest losses); large families have perennial production modes (associated with low rates of forest losses); and small ranchers are displaced by large ranchers, and upland croppers are displaced by lowland ranchers (96–99).

Life-cycle features arise from and affect rural as well as urban environments. They result from households' strategic responses to both economic opportunities (for example, market signals indicating higher crop profitability) and constraints (due to economic crisis conditions, for example). They shape the trajectory of land-use change, which itself affects the household's economic status (100, 101). Therefore, a population analysis of great nuances is required.

Migration in its various forms is the most important demographic factor causing land-use change at timescales of a couple of decades (33, 102). Migration operates as a significant driver with other nondemographic factors, such as government policies, changes in consumption patterns, economic integration, and globalization (87). Some policies resulting in land-use change either provoke (87) or are intricately linked with (103) increased migration.

The growth of urban aspirations, the urban-rural population distribution, and the impact of rapidly growing cities on ecosystem goods and services are likely to become dominant factors in land-use change in the decades to come, be it in major urban or peri-urban areas (87) or in remote hinterland or watershed areas (96, 104–106). Many new urban dwellers in developing countries still own rural landholdings (107). Although the growth of urban areas creates new local and regional markets for livestock, timber, and agricultural products, it also increases urban remittances to the countryside (82).

INSTITUTIONAL FACTORS   To explain land-use changes, it is also important to understand institutions (political, legal, economic, and traditional) and their interactions with individual decision making (85, 108). Access to land, labor, capital, technology, and information is structured (and is frequently constrained) by local and national policies and institutions (109). Land managers have varying capabilities to participate in and to define these institutions. Relevant nonmarket institutions include: property-rights regimes; environmental policies; decision making systems on resource management (e.g., decentralization, democratization, and the role of the public, of civil society, and of local communities in decision making); information systems related to environmental indicators as they determine perception of changes in ecosystems; social networks representing specific interests related to resource management; conflict resolution systems concerning access to resources; and institutions that govern the distribution of resources and thus control economic differentiation.

There is often a mismatch between environmental signals reaching local populations and the macrolevel institutions (87, 110). Therefore, the rules used for making policies are important to ensure that local users are able to influence resource-management institutions (111). Institutions need to be considered at various scales, to identify the local mediating factors and adaptive strategies and to understand their interactions with national- and international-level institutions.

Many land-use changes are due to ill-defined policies and weak institutional enforcement, as exemplified by the widespread illegal logging in Indonesia linked to corruption and to the devolving of forest management responsibilities to the district level (112). On the other hand, recovery or restoration of land is also possible with appropriate land-use policies. Consolidation of landholdings and the shift from communal, traditional systems to formal, state-sanctioned regimes is a trend observed throughout the developing world (83). Examples of policies that influence land-use change are state policies to attain self-sufficiency in food (113); taxation, fiscal incentives, subsidies, and credits (93, 97, 114–116); price controls on agricultural inputs and outputs (87, 116); decentralization (113, 117); infrastructure support (87); (low) investments in monitoring and formally guarding natural resources (85); resource commodification (87, 116, 118, 119); land consolidation (120, 121), nationalization, and collectivization (87, 113); structural adjustment measures (101, 106, 122); and international environmental agreements.

With increasingly interconnected market forces and the rise of international environmental conventions, the impact of institutional drivers moves from the local to the global level. Land degradation is more prominent when macropolicies, either capitalist or socialist, undermine local adaptation strategies. In particular, perverse subsidies for road construction, agricultural production, forestry, and so forth are thought to be one of the biggest impediments to environmental sustainability (123).

CULTURAL FACTORS   Numerous cultural factors also influence decision making on land use. Land managers have various motivations, collective memories, and personal histories. Their attitudes, values, beliefs, and individual perceptions influence land-use decisions—for instance through their perception of and attitude toward risk. Land-use decisions have intended and unintended consequences on ecosystems; these depend on the knowledge, information, and management skills available to land managers. Culture is often linked with political and economic inequalities, e.g., the status of women or ethnic minorities (76, 87), that affect resource access and land use. Understanding the controlling models of various actors may thus explain the management of resources, adaptive strategies, compliance or resistance to policies, or social learning and therefore social resilience in the face of land-use change.

GLOBALIZATION   Researchers have recently argued that cross-cutting the local and national pathways of land-use/cover change are the many processes of globalization that amplify or attenuate the driving forces by removing regional barriers, weakening national connections, and increasing the interdependency among people and between nations. Globalization as such is not a driver of land-use change but is a process that underlies the other driving forces discussed above. Globalization accelerates or buffers the impact of these drivers on land use. For example, Barbier (124) identified land-use change as the immediate and principal environmental impact of economic liberalization and globalization—mostly trade liberalization and reforms to open up the agro-industrial sector—in Ghana and Mexico. Directly, increased agricultural productivity triggered forest conversion and increased land degradation from unsustainable production methods. Indirectly, agro-industrial development displaced the landless and rural poor, who were then pushed to marginal agricultural lands or to the forest frontier. Although the environmental effects of macroeconomic policies and trade liberalization are particularly important in countries with fragile ecosystems (e.g., semiarid lands and mangrove forests), international trade and other forms of globalization can also improve environmental conditions through green certification and eco labeling, wider and more rapid spread of technologies, better media coverage allowing international pressure on states that degrade their resources, and free circulation of people, which provides better educational and employment opportunities. Naylor et al. (125) showed, for example, that in a small island of Micronesia, international migration, foreign aid, and monetary remittances from family members living overseas have relieved the pressures of economic crowding on mangrove forests, despite an increase in population and a decline in local government jobs.

International institutions (including organizations within the U. N. system and nongovernmental organizations) can be instrumental in promoting and funding policies aimed at combating environmental degradation, setting political agendas, building consensus, and creating constraints and incentives for sustainable land management (126).

A Finite Set of Pathways of Land-Use Change

The various sectoral drivers of land-use change discussed above are strongly linked within and between levels of organization of human-environment systems. They interact directly, are linked via feedback, and thus often have synergetic effects. Any land manager also constantly makes trade-offs between different land-use opportunities and constraints associated with a variety of external factors. Moreover, various human-environment conditions react to and reshape the impacts of drivers differently, which leads to specific pathways of land-use change (82). The complexity in the combinations of causes giving rise to land-use change can be greatly reduced by recognizing that there are a limited number of ways in which these causes interact. In other words, a limited suite of processes and variables at any scale makes the problem tractable (127). The critical challenge is thus to identify dominant pathways and associated causes of land-use change. The risk factors associated with each pathway can then be identified.

Certain conditions appear repeatedly in case studies. They include but are not restricted to: loss of land productivity on sensitive areas following inappropriate use or the failure to maintain protective works (128, 129); development of the forest frontiers by weak state economies, for geopolitical reasons or to promote interest groups (94, 104); institutions in transition from communal to private land ownership in developing regions (93, 130); loss of entitlements to environmental resources (e.g., expropriation for large-scale agriculture, large dams, forestry projects, tourism, and wildlife conservation), that lead to an ecological marginalization of the poor (80, 131, 132); decrease in land availability due to encroachment by other land uses, such as land zoning for forest reserves, wilderness areas or agro-industrial plantations, which leads to the so-called tragedy of enclosure (96, 133); induced innovation and intensification (87, 134, 135), especially in peri-urban and market-accessible areas of developing regions (136); urbanization followed by changes in consumption patterns and in income distribution with differential rural impacts (87, 96, 120); new economic opportunities linked to new market outlets, changes in economic policies, or capital investments (114, 130, 137–139); breakdown of extended families with impacts on resource use efficiency (89, 90); inappropriate policy intervention giving rise to rapid modifications of landscapes and ecosystems (103, 140, 141); macroeconomic shocks and structural adjustment policies with undesirable consequences on natural resources (101, 106, 122, 142); lack of community's ability to cope with a deteriorating environmental situation, combined with absence of political will to mitigate damage and to alter the trajectory of change, which leads to delayed and ineffective social responses (10).

Case studies show that not all causes of land-use change and all levels of organization are equally important. For any given human-environment system, a limited number of causes are essential to predict the general trend in land use (127). This is the basis, for example, for the syndrome approach, which describes archetypical, dynamic, coevolutionary patterns of human-environment interactions (81). A taxonomy of syndromes links processes of degradation to both changes over time and status of state variables. The approach is applied at the intermediate functional scales that reflect processes taking place from the household level up to the international level. For example, the *overexploitation syndrome* represents the natural and social processes governing the extraction of biological resources through unsustainable industrial logging activities or other forms of resource use. Policy failure is one of the essential underlying driving forces of this syndrome (e.g., corruption, lobbyism, and weak or no law enforcement) (81). The typology of syndromes reflects expert opinion based on local case examples. The syndrome approach aims at a high level of generality in the description of mechanisms of environmental degradation.

Another approach, which has provided a classification of the situations in which environmental degradation occurs, is the study of regions at risk and environmental criticality by Kasperson et al. (10). Several case studies of regions under environmental degradation were described qualitatively by their histories. These qualitative trajectories were represented in terms of development of the wealth of the inhabitants and the state of the environment. A *critical environment* was defined as one in which the extent or the rate of environmental degradation precludes the maintenance of current resource-use systems or levels of human well-being, given feasible adaptations and the community's ability to mount a response (10). Different typical time courses of these variables were identified and interpreted with respect to more or less problematic future development of the regions. The Aral Sea, for example, was unquestionably a critical region after a few decades of Soviet-sponsored, ill-conceived large-scale irrigation schemes. Subsuming a particular case (e.g., the present situation and the history in a specified region) under one of these classes should allow for a restricted prognosis of its possible future development, which is a prerequisite for mitigation or adaptation.

Generic principles leading to environmental degradation can also emerge from careful comparison of diverse case studies. Kates & Haarmann (80) found a set of common interactive processes linking poverty and environmental degradation. Case studies told common tales of poor people's displacement from their lands, the division of their resources, and the degradation of their environments, which culminated in three major spirals of household impoverishment and environmental degradation driven by combinations of development and commercialization, population growth, poverty, and natural hazards. Lambin et al. (82) similarly identified typical pathways leading to tropical deforestation, agricultural intensification, rangeland modifications, and urbanization.

In summary, despite the large diversity of causes and situations leading to land-use change, there are some generalizable patterns of change that result from recurrent interactions between driving forces, following specific sequences of events. Even though, at the detailed level, these sequences may play out differently in specific situations, their identification may confer some predictive power by analogy with similar pathways in comparable regional and historical contexts.

A SYNTHESIS OF THE CAUSES OF LAND-USE CHANGE AND THEIR INTERACTIONS

The Five Fundamental High-Level Causes of Land-Use Change

Summarizing a large number of case studies, we find that land-use change is driven by a combination of the following fundamental high-level causes (Table 4):

TABLE 4 Typology of the causes of land-use change

	Resource scarcity causing pressure of production on resources	Changing opportunities created by markets	Outside policy intervention	Loss of adaptive capacity and increased vulnerability	Changes in social organization, in resource access, and in attitudes
Slow	Natural population growth and division of land parcels Domestic life cycles that lead to changes in labor availability Loss of land productivity on sensitive areas following excessive or inappropriate use Failure to restore or to maintain protective works of environmental resources Heavy surplus extraction away from the land manager	Increase in commercialization and agro-industrialization Improvement in accessibility through road construction Changes in market prices for inputs or outputs (e.g., erosion of prices of primary production, unfavorable global or urban-rural terms of trade) Off-farm wages and employment opportunities	Economic development programs Perverse subsidies, policy-induced price distortions and fiscal incentives Frontier development (e.g., for geopolitical reasons or to promote interest groups) Poor governance and corruption Insecurity in land tenure	Impoverishment (e.g., creeping household debts, no access to credit, lack of alternative income sources, and weak buffering capacity) Breakdown of informal social security networks Dependence on external resources or on assistance Social discrimination (ethnic minorities, women, members of lower classes or castes)	Changes in institutions governing access to resources by different land managers (e.g., shift from communal to private rights, tenure, holdings, and titles) Growth of urban aspirations Breakdown of extended family Growth of individualism and materialism Lack of public education and poor information flow on the environment
Fast	Spontaneous migration, forced population displacement, refugees Decrease in land availability due to encroachment by other land uses (e.g., natural reserves)	Capital investments Changes in national or global macro-economic and trade conditions that lead to changes in prices (e.g., surge in energy prices or global financial crisis) New technologies for intensification of resource use	Rapid policy changes (e.g., devaluation) Government instability War	Internal conflicts Illness (e.g., HIV) Risks associated with natural hazards (e.g., leading to a crop failure, loss of resource, or loss of productive capacity)	Loss of entitlements to environmental resources (e.g., expropriation for large-scale agriculture, large dams, forestry projects, tourism and wildlife conservation), which leads to an ecological marginalization of the poor

1. resource scarcity leading to an increase in the pressure of production on resources,
2. changing opportunities created by markets,
3. outside policy intervention,
4. loss of adaptive capacity and increased vulnerability, and
5. changes in social organization, in resource access, and in attitudes.

Some of these fundamental causes are experienced as constraints. They force local land managers into degradation, innovation, or displacement pathways. The other causes are associated with the seizure of new opportunities by land managers who seek to realize their diverse aspirations.

Each of these high-level causes can apply as slow evolutionary processes that change incrementally at the timescale of decades or more, or as fast changes that are abrupt and occur as perturbations that affect human-environment systems suddenly (Table 4). Only a combination of several causes, with synergetic interactions, is likely to drive a region into a critical trajectory (84).

Some of the fundamental causes leading to land-use change are mostly endogenous, such as resource scarcity, increased vulnerability and changes in social organization, even though they may be influenced by exogenous factors as well. The other high-level causes, such as changing market opportunities and policy intervention, are mostly exogenous, even though the response of land managers to these external forces is strongly mediated by local factors.

Mode of Interactions Between Causes of Change

The representation of interactions between these various causes of land-use change may be based on different patterns: one cause may completely dominate the other causes, assuming that land use in a given locality is influenced by whatever factor exerts the greatest constraint; factors driving land-use change can be connected as causal chains, i.e., interconnected in such a way that one or several variables (underlying causes, mainly) drive one or several other variables (proximate causes, mainly); different factors can intervene in concomitant occurrence, i.e., independent but synchronous operation of individual factors leading to land change; they may also intervene in synergetic factor combinations, i.e., several mutually interacting variables driving land-use change and producing an enhanced or increased effect due to reciprocal action and feedbacks between causes.

In meta-analyses of case studies of tropical deforestation (33) and dryland degradation or desertification by the same authors, the proportion of cases in which dominant, single, or key factors operate at either the proximate or underlying level was low (ca. 10% of the cases), as was the case with pure causal chains (ca. 5% to 8%). Concomitant occurrence of causes was more widespread (ca. 25%). The most common type of interaction was synergetic factor combinations (in 70% to 90% of the case studies reviewed).

In short,

Land use = f(pressures, opportunities, policies, vulnerability, and social organization);

with

pressures = f(population of resource users, labor availability, quantity of resources, and sensitivity of resources);
opportunities = f(market prices, production costs, transportation costs, and technology);
policies = f(subsidies, taxes, property rights, infrastructure, and governance);
vulnerability = f(exposure to external perturbations, sensitivity, and coping capacity); and
social organization = f(resource access, income distribution, household features, and urban-rural interactions)

with the functions f having forms that account for strong interactions between causes of land-use change.

Feedback and Endogeneity

In most cases, the patterns of causation discussed above are simplifications that are useful for communicating about particular environmental issues or for modeling. In reality, there are functional interdependencies between all the causes of land-use change, both at each organizational level, "horizontal interplay," and between levels of organization, "vertical interplay" (143).

Even at short timescales, the direction of causality may be difficult to establish, as illustrated by the case of roads and deforestation. For example, 81% of the deforestation in the Brazilian Amazon between 1991 and 1994 occurred within 50 kilometers of four major road networks (144). Is it the national demand for land and the high agricultural suitability of some forest areas that lead to policy decisions to expand the road network in these areas, which then gives access to the forest for migrants who clear land? Or is it the expansion of local logging or agricultural activities in some forest areas that then justifies the construction of new roads to link these active production areas to existing markets? Or does the construction of a road for reasons unrelated to land use in the forest (e.g., to connect major cities) induce new deforestation by its mere presence, through a spatial redistribution of population and activities? Or, in the latter case, does the road simply attract to a given location a preexisting demand for land that would have led to deforestation elsewhere if the road had not been built? In other words, is a road an endogenous or exogenous factor in deforestation and does it affect just the location or also the quantity of deforestation in a given country? The likely answer to these questions is that, in most cases, national demand for land, policies to develop the forest frontier, capital investments in logging and agricultural

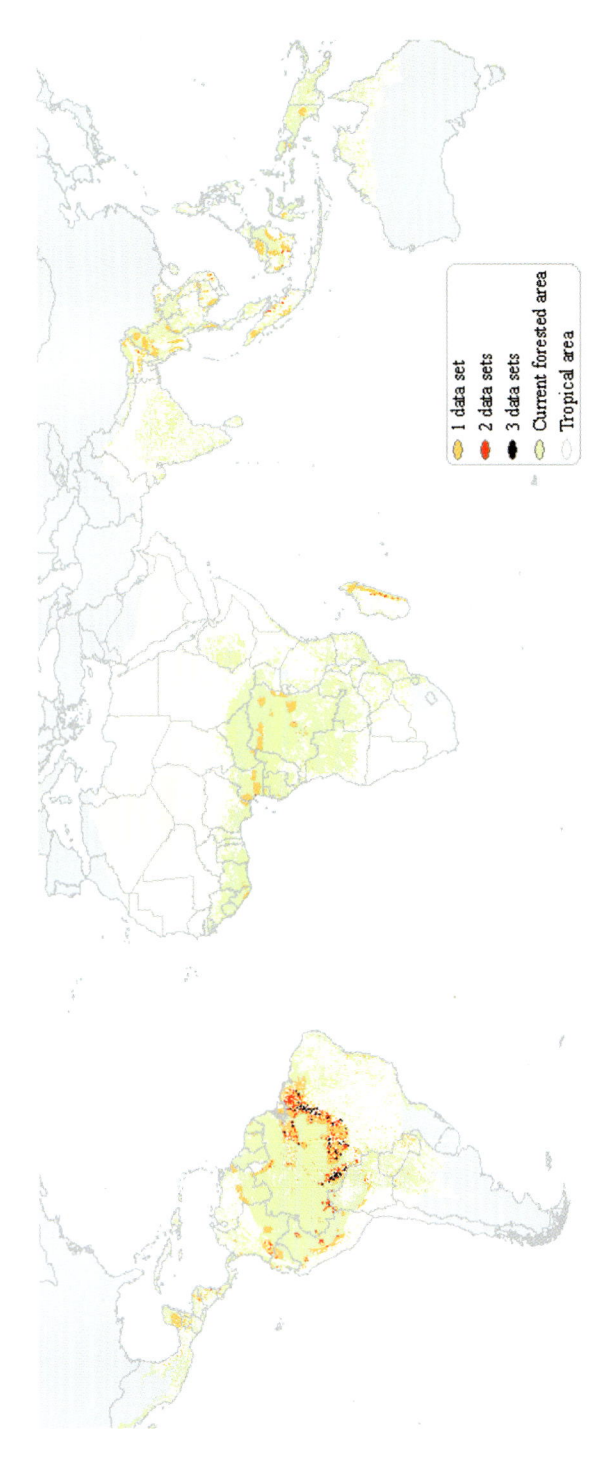

Figure 1 Main tropical deforestation fronts in the 1980s and 1990s. The map is based on three data sets: (a) the deforestation hotspots in the humid tropics of the Tropical Ecosystem Environment Observation by Satellite (TREES) project (34), (b) a time series analysis of tree cover based on 8-km resolution data from the National Oceanic and Atmospheric Administration's advanced very high resolution radiometer (AVHRR) (31), and (c) the Amazon Basin deforestation maps derived from time series of Landsat Thematic Mapper (Landsat TM) data (35). These maps were overlaid and combined to identify areas where high rates of deforestation were measured by several of the datasets. *Green* areas are intact forests. The map indicates the number of times each 0.1° grid was identified as being affected by rapid deforestation by the different datasets (*orange*, pixels detected as hotspot by one dataset, *red*, pixels detected as hotspot by two datasets, *black*, pixels detected as hotspot by three datasets) (36).

Legend:

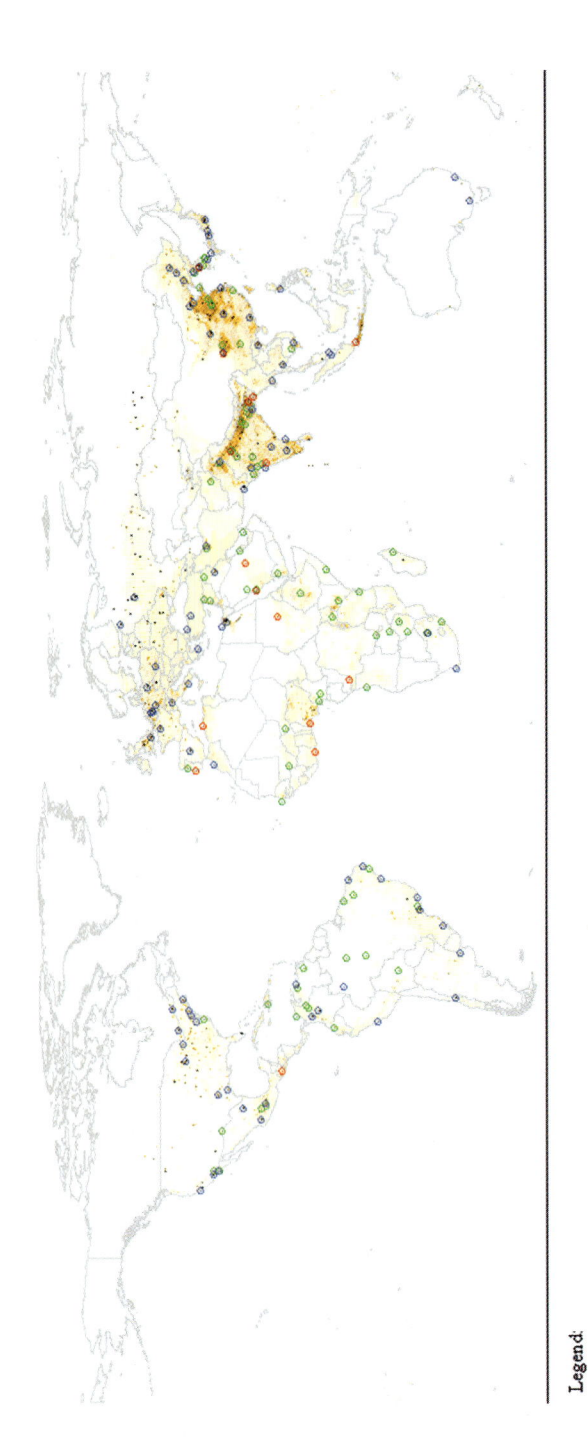

Population density (inhabitants/km²) in 1995

- < 5
- 6 - 10
- 11 - 25
- 26 - 50
- 51 - 100
- 101 - 150
- 151 - 200
- 201 - 250
- 251 - 300
- 301 - 350
- 351 - 400
- 401 - 450
- 451 - 500
- 501 - 600
- 601 - 700
- 701 - 800
- 801 - 900
- 901 - 1000
- 1001 - 1250
- 1251 - 1500
- 1500 - 1750
- > 1750

"Gridded population of the world" dataset [43]

- ◇ Most changing cities between 1990 and 2000
- ◇ Most populated cities in 2000
- ◇ Most populated and changing cities

"World Urbanisation Prospects", population estimates for cities of more than 750,000 inhabitants [48]

See legend on next page

Figure 2 Population density in 1995 and most populated and changing cities from 1990 to 2000. The map is based on the 2001 revision of the "World Urbanization Prospects" (43), which provides population estimates in cities of more than 750,000 inhabitants for the years 1990 and 2000, and the "gridded population of the world" (48), which provides population estimates in 1995. The first dataset focuses on megacities whereas the second includes less populated areas. *Green circles* represent the most changing cities between 1990 and 2000, *blue circles* the most populated cities in 2000, and *red circles* the most changing and populated cities. The background color scale represents the population densities in 1995 (from less than five inhabitants in *gray* to more than 1750 inhabitants/km² in *dark orange*) (36).

activities, population movements, commodification of the economy, the development of urban markets, and infrastructure expansion are highly interdependent and coevolve in close interaction as part of a general transformation of society and of its interaction with its natural environment.

As the timescale of analysis expands, all causes of land-use change—from demographic changes to technological innovations, which include new environmental policies—become endogenous to the human-environment system and are affected in some degree by land-use change. Actually, the changes in ecosystem goods and services that result from land-use change lead to important feedback on the drivers of land-use change. Changes in ecosystems affect the availability and quality of some of the natural resources that are essential to sustain livelihood, create opportunities and constraints for new land uses, induce institutional changes at the local to global levels in response to perceived and anticipated resource degradation, modify the adaptive capacity of land managers (by affecting their health, for example), and give rise to social changes in the form of income differentiation (when there are winners and losers in environmental change) or increased social complexity (e.g., by increasing interactions between urban and rural systems).

Land-Use Change as an Emergent Property of Complex Adaptive Systems

Land use is never static, but it is constantly changing in response to dynamic interaction between drivers and feedback from land-use change to these drivers. In other words, human-environmental systems are complex adaptive systems in which properties, such as land use, emerge from the interactions among the various components of the entire system, which themselves feed back to influence the subsequent development of those interactions (127). Land-use change is a spatial property observed at the scale of a landscape. It is the sum of many small, local-scale changes in land allocation that reinforce or cancel each other. These changes are the product of multiple decisions resulting from interactions between diverse agents, who act under certain conditions, anticipate future outcomes of their decisions, and adapt their behaviors to changes in external (e.g., the market) and internal (e.g., their aspirations) conditions. In most cases, these decisions are made without central direction, unless there are central planning systems. Land-use change is thus a complex large-scale spatial behavior that emerges from the aggregate interactions of less complex agents. Human-environment systems associated with land use have similar attributes and are governed by mechanisms and processes similar to those of other complex adaptive social or biological systems (145–147).

The exact future of the behavior of coupled human-environment systems is often unpredictable because it is emergent rather than predetermined. Hence, there is an interest in place-based research as a method to reveal a large repertoire of pathways of land-use change, in a range of human-environment conditions.

Land-Use Transitions

Land-use change is associated with other societal and biophysical changes through a series of transitions (148). A transition can be defined as a process of societal change in which the structural character of society (or a complex subsystem of society) transforms (149). It results from a set of connected changes, which reinforce each other but take place in several different components of the system. Multiple causality and coevolution of different sectors of society caused by interacting developments are central to the concept of transition. Transitions in land use must be viewed as multiple and reversible dynamics. A transition is not a fixed pattern, nor is it deterministic. It is not set in advance, and there is large variability in specific trajectories. There is thus a strong notion of instability and indeterminacy in land-use transitions. Transitions should be viewed as "possible development paths where the direction, size, and speed can be influenced through policy and specific circumstances" (149).

The concept of transition has been applied in land-use change studies at different spatial and temporal scales. A forest transition has been described at a national scale to represent the change from decreasing to expanding national forest areas that has taken place over a century or more in several European countries and in North America, by afforestation and natural regeneration mostly on abandoned marginal agricultural land once societies began to industrialize and urbanize (150, 151). Forests in the Mediterranean basin did not make this transition. Some regions in the tropics currently show signs of significant reforestation. A predominantly national focus in forest transition studies (150–152) has been increasingly complemented by analyses at the subnational scale (153, 154). Case studies have also identified transition-like trajectories that suggest, over a decade or so, households undertake management of already cleared areas following a period of rapid deforestation, stop deforesting, and even undertake afforestation within their individual parcels (155–157).

INTEGRATIVE FRAMEWORKS TO UNDERSTAND LAND-USE/COVER CHANGES

How to overcome the somewhat futile observation that everything is interrelated? The level of integration in research on land-use/land-cover change requires a combination of perspectives of understanding: the agent-based, the systems, and the narrative approaches (19). Each perspective approaches the impact on land of the interactions between macrostructure and microagency from a different vantage point. These perspectives can be and are combined in various ways in integrated, place-based research on causes and impacts of land-use change; examples include the Yucatán (158), the Serengeti-Mara ecosystem (132), the Nang Rong District in northeastern Thailand (159, 160), the Ecuadorian Amazon (161), the Belgian Ardennes (162), the Yaqui valley in Mexico (163), the African Sahel

(164, 165), and other integrated land change studies over a particular geographical region. These perspectives still have to be integrated in the modeling of land-use change.

Agent-Based Perspective

The agent-based perspective is centered on the general nature and rules of land-use decision making by individuals. It represents the motivations behind decisions and the external factors that influence decisions about land use. It applies approaches that range from the rational decision making of neoclassical economics to household, gender, class, and other dimensions common to the social and behavioral sciences. Local ecosystem managers have many motives, some intentional and others unconscious, related to economic, traditional, emotional or biophysical factors (76). Economic models of land-use change, for example, assume that land managers attempt to fulfill their needs and meet their expectations by accommodating economic, social, and environmental constraints (utility optimization). Land managers evaluate expected outcomes of their land-use decisions. If undesired environmental impacts are foreseen, they modify factor allocation (22).

As an example of the agent-based perspective, authors have analyzed the diversity of responses by land managers to population growth. Whereas the emphasis of Boserup's work (166) is on technological responses, Bilsborrow (167) analyzed several demographic responses in the face of land shortage and declining yields. They are of two sorts: outmigration and fertility reduction through postponement of marriage or reduction in marital fertility. Bilsborrow & Ogendo (168) further describe local changes in tenure arrangements, which can be the first adaptations of land-use practices to population growth. They usually follow the sequence of distribution of idle land for agricultural use, reduction of landholding size in the community, creation of new categories of access rights, and reclassification of old ones to exclude nonpermanent members. Moreover, these tenurial, technological, and demographic responses can be multiphasic, i.e., occurring simultaneously—as conceptualized by Davis (169), rather than sequential. Their effects are thus difficult to separate.

Microeconomic approaches to land-use changes explain spatial configurations of changes. Any parcel of land, given its attributes and location, is assumed to be allocated to the use that earns the highest rent (170). This rent is a function of the returns and costs of land conversion, given supply and demand functions of the land market, which is assumed to be competitive (171). Deforestation, for example, is driven by choices by land managers among alternative rents (172, 173). Microeconomic approaches usually assume that the agents have the ability to make informed predictions and plans and that they are risk minimizers. After exploring all options available to them, individuals make rational decisions based on available information, obligations, and expectations (social as well as economic) to balance anticipated returns and risks.

Systems Perspective

The systems/structures perspective explains land-use change through the organization and institutions of society (174). Institutions, such as governments, communities, or markets, operate interactively at different spatial and temporal scales; the institutions link local conditions to global processes and vice versa. Although some institutions are direct drivers of change, others, such as markets, are intricately linked to individual decisions. The systems perspective represents the dynamics of economy-environment linkages operating at regional to global scales. It has to cope with issues that include technological innovations, policy and institutional changes, collective ownership of land resources, rural-urban dynamics, and macroeconomic transformations.

The systems perspective highlights, for example, how communities are trapped in a degradational pathway given complex mechanisms that may have their roots outside the area subjected to degradation. For instance, Blaikie & Brookfield (175), Leonard (131) and Kates & Haarman (80) discuss the process of marginalization of poor people in remote and ecologically fragile rural areas. This ecological marginalization usually follows population growth, agricultural modernization—associated with mechanization and land consolidation—inequalities in land tenure in the most fertile and accessible agricultural regions, or other pressures of social or political origin. It leads to migration of poor farmers into areas with a high ecological sensitivity for which existing management practices may be inadequate.

Narrative Perspective

The narrative perspective seeks depth of understanding through historical detail and interpretation (176, 177). It tells a land-use/cover change story for a specific locality (178–180). Historical analyses of landscape grasp all the complexity of events, in particular stochastic or nonrandom but unpredictable events that significantly affect land-use/land-cover changes. It includes changing political economies, environmental feedback on land use, and external shocks (181). The narrative perspective recognizes the path dependence of recent evolutions. It avoids the simplifications and erroneous interpretations that could result from studies focused only on the present and immediate past, outside the context of longer histories of human-environment interactions (109). For example, Fairhead & Leach's (182) historical study of contemporary forest islands in Guinea showed that these were human creations in a savanna landscape, where farmers have turned fallow vegetation more woody around their villages. These patches of dense forests in the savanna had long been regarded as the last relics of a once more extensive forest cover, degraded due to its inhabitants' land use. The narrative approach also allows distilling from changing human-environment conditions those dynamics crosscutting different eras or episodes of use and occupation and those unique to individual episodes (181).

Scenarios generated to project future land-use changes or to identify land-use patterns with certain optimality characteristics are based on narrative story lines to describe consistently the relationships between driving forces of environmental changes and their evolution (183). The scenarios are hypothetical sequences of events that provide alternative images of how the future might unfold. Scenarios consist of states, driving forces, events, consequences, and actions that are internally consistent and plausible (183). They provide insights into the present by drawing analogies between historical and current situations.

CONCLUSION AND FUTURE RESEARCH

Significant progress in the quantification and understanding of land-use/cover changes has been achieved over the last decade. Much remains to be learned, however, before we can fully assess and project the future role of land-use/cover change in the functioning of the earth system and identify conditions for sustainable land use. New estimates of areas and rates of major land-use/cover conversions have greatly narrowed down uncertainties. Sometimes initial estimates of the spatial importance of these changes have been revised downward. But often, the significance of land-use/cover change for earth system processes has been revised upward. A number of more subtle land changes still need to be better quantified at a global scale. This is particularly the case for anthropogenic changes that strongly interact with natural environmental variability and therefore require longitudinal data over a long time period for a reliable assessment.

Analyses of the causes of land-use change have moved from simplistic single-cause explanations to an understanding that integrates multiple causes and their complex interactions. A few general pathways leading to land-use change have been identified from a wealth of local case studies. This inductive process of generalization paves the way for the development of more realistic models of land-use change. Nevertheless, different perspectives of understanding still tend to follow different lines of explanation of the causes of land-use change because each focuses on specific organizational levels and temporal scales of the human-environment systems. Whereas a systems perspective tends to focus on gradual and progressive processes of change at the scale of large entities, the agent-based perspective deals with people's own foreseeable futures at the individual level, and the narrative perspective adopts a much longer time horizon and focuses on critical events and abrupt transitions. Different assumptions about temporality lead to varying explanations and interpretations of the causes and significance of environmental changes. These assumptions should be made explicit to facilitate the development of an integrative theory of human-environment relationships. We also argued in this paper that a systematic analysis of local scale land-use change studies, conducted over a range of timescales, helps to uncover general principles to provide an explanation and prediction of new land-use changes.

Improved understanding of the complex dynamic processes underlying land-use change will allow more reliable projections and more realistic scenarios of future changes. Crucial to projections is understanding factors that control positive and negative feedback in land-use change. Positive feedback loops amplify change and lead, in some cases, to a rapid degradation of ecosystems and the impoverishment of the societies using these ecosystems. By contrast, institutional and technological innovations may lead to negative feedback loops that decrease the rate of change or even reverse land-use/cover change trends. The relative strength of amplifying and attenuating feedback can be influenced by policies that control switches between land-use/cover change regimes dominated by positive or negative feedback. The analysis of interaction, coherence, or conflict between social and biophysical responses to changes in both ecosystem services and earth system processes caused by land changes is still a largely unresearched area. It will be a central focus of the new Land project of the IGBP and IHDP.

Improved understanding of processes of land-use change has led to a shift from a view condemning human impact on the environment as leading mostly to a deterioration of earth system processes to emphasis on the potential for ecological restoration through land management (184). This change reflects an evolution of the research questions, methods, and scientific paradigm.

First, initial concerns about global land-use/cover change arose from the realization that land transformation influences climate change and reduces biotic diversity, hence the interest in deforestation, desertification, and other changes in natural vegetation. The more recent focus on issues related to ecosystem goods and services, sustainability, and vulnerability has led to a greater emphasis on the dynamic coupling between human societies and their ecosystems at a local scale.

Second, research methods applied in land-use/cover change research were initially largely influenced by advances in remote sensing. This technology has led to an emphasis on short timescales, because earth observation data have been available only for a few decades. Recently, a wide range of other methods have been used to reconstruct long-term changes in landscapes. This change in temporal frame has led to a greater consideration of the long-term processes of ecological restoration and land-use transition.

Finally, whereas the notion of equilibrium used to dominate thinking about environmental change, a nonequilibrium paradigm, as well as concepts related to complex system dynamics, is now influencing land-use/cover change research. Rather than interpreting deviations from a predisturbance state as problematic, land-use changes are now increasingly analyzed as part of the system interactions leading to coevolution of natural and social systems. Throughout their history, human societies have coevolved with their environment through change, instability, and mutual adaptation. The coupled human-environment systems should therefore be considered as a whole when we assess sustainability and vulnerability.

ACKNOWLEDGMENTS

This review was prepared while Eric Lambin was a Fellow at the Center for Advanced Study in the Behavioral Sciences at Stanford, California. Eric Lambin is grateful for the financial support provided by The William and Flora Hewlett

Foundation (Grant #2000-5633). The authors are also grateful for the support from the Services of the Prime Minister of Belgium, Office for Scientific, Technical, and Cultural Affairs. This paper has greatly benefited from ideas developed within the LUCC project of the IGBP and IHDP. The contribution of the past and present members of the LUCC Scientific Steering Committee is particularly acknowledged. We thank Jane Guyer and Karen Seto for comments on an earlier version of the paper and thank Kathleen Mulch for editorial assistance.

The *Annual Review of Environment and Resources* is online at
http://environ.annualreviews.org

LITERATURE CITED

1. Otterman J. 1974. Baring high-albedo soils by overgrazing: a hypothesised desertification mechanism. *Science* 86:531–33
2. Charney J, Stone PH. 1975. Drought in the Sahara: a biogeophysical feedback mechanism. *Science* 187:434–35
3. Sagan C, Toon OB, Pollack JB. 1979. Anthropogenic albedo changes and the earth's climate. *Science* 206:1363–68
4. Woodwell GM, Hobbie JE, Houghton RA, Melillo JM, Moore B, et al. 1983. Global deforestation: contribution to atmospheric carbon dioxide. *Science* 222:1081–86
5. Houghton RA, Boone RD, Melillo JM, Palm CA, Myers N, et al. 1985. Net flux of carbon dioxide from tropical forest in 1980. *Nature* 316:617–20
6. Eltahir EAB, Bras RL. 1996. Precipitation recycling. *Rev. Geophys.* 34:367–78
7. Sala OE, Chapin FS, Armesto JJ, Berlow E, Bloomfield J, et al. 2000. Biodiversity—global biodiversity scenarios for the year 2100. *Science* 287:1770–74
8. Trimble SW, Crosson P. 2000. Land use—US soil erosion rates: myth and reality. *Science* 289:248–50
9. Vitousek PM, Mooney HA, Lubchenco J, Melillo JM. 1997. Human domination of earth's ecosystems. *Science* 277:494–99
10. Kasperson JX, Kasperson RE, Turner BL, eds. 1995. *Regions at Risk: Comparisons of Threatened Environments.* Tokyo: UN Univ. Press. 588 pp.
11. Ramankutty N, Foley JA. 1999. Estimating historical changes in global land cover: croplands from 1700 to 1992. *Glob. Biogeochem. Cycles* 13(4):997–1027
12. Taylor C, Lambin EF, Stephenne N, Harding R, Essery R. 2002. The influence of land-use change on climate in the Sahel. *J. Clim.* 15(24):3615–29
13. Dixon RK, Brown S, Houghton RA, Solomon AM, Trexler MC, Wisniewski J. 1994. Carbon pools and flux of global forest ecosystems. *Science* 263:185–90
14. Houghton RA, Hackler JL, Lawrence KT. 1999. The US carbon budget: contribution from land-use change. *Science* 285:574–78
15. McGuire AD, Sitch S, Clein JS, Dargaville R, Esser G, et al. 2001. Carbon balance of the terrestrial biosphere in the twentieth century: analyses of CO_2, climate and land-use effects with four process-based ecosystem models. *Glob. Biogeochem. Cycles* 15(1):183–206
16. Margules CR, Pressey RL. 2000. Systematic conservation planning. *Nature* 405:243–53
17. Liu JG, Linderman M, Ouyang Z, An L, Yang J, Zhang H. 2001. Ecological degradation in protected areas: the case of Wolong Nature Reserve for Giant Pandas. *Science* 292:98–101
18. Turner BL, Skole D, Sanderson S, Fischer

G, Fresco L, Leemans R. 1995. Land-use and land-cover change science/research plan. *IGBP Glob. Change Rep. 35/HDP Rep. 7*, Int. Geosph.-Biosph. Program., Hum. Dimens. Glob. Environ. Change Program., Stockholm/Geneva

19. Lambin EF, Baulies X, Bockstael N, Fischer G, Krug T, et al. 1999. Land-use and land-cover change (LUCC): implementation strategy. *IGBP Rep. 48, IHDP Rep. 10*, Int. Geosph.-Biosph. Program., Int. Hum. Dimens. Glob. Environ. Change Program., Stockholm/Bonn

20. Liu JG. 2001. Integrating ecology with human demography, behavior, and socioeconomics: needs and approaches. *Ecol. Model.* 140(1–2):1–8

21. Veldkamp A, Lambin EF. 2001. Predicting land-use change: editorial. *Agric. Ecosyst. Environ.* 85(1–3):1–6

22. Parker DC, Manson SM, Janssen MA, Hoffmann MJ, Deadman P. 2003. Multi-agent system models for the simulation of land-use and land-cover change: a review. *Ann. Assoc. Am. Geogr.* 93(2):314–37

23. Mittermeier R, Mittermeier CG, Gil PR, Pilgrim J, Fonseca G, et al. 2003. *Wilderness: Earth's Last Wild Places*. Chicago: Univ. Chicago Press. 576 pp.

24. Ball JB. 2001. Global forest resources: history and dynamics. In *The Forests Handbook*. Vol. 1, ed. J Evans, pp. 3–22. Oxford: Blackwell Sci. 418 pp.

25. UN Food Agric. Organ. 2001. *FAO Statistical Databases*. http://apps.fao.org

26. Goldewijk KK. 2001. Estimating global land use change over the past 300 years: the HYDE database. *Glob. Biogeochem. Cycles* 15(2):417–34

27. Goldewijk KK, Ramankutty N. 2003. Land cover change over the last three centuries due to human activities: assessing the differences between two new global data sets. *GeoJournal* : In press

28. Ramankutty N, Foley JA, Olejniczak NJ. 2002. People on the land: changes in global population and croplands during the 20th century. *Ambio* 31(3):251–57

29. UN Food. Agric. Organ. 2001. Global forest resources assessment 2000 (FRA 2000): main report, *FAO For. Pap. 140*, FAO, Rome

30. Achard F, Eva HD, Stibig HJ, Mayaux P, Gallego J, et al. 2002. Determination of deforestation rates of the world's humid tropical forests. *Science* 297:999–1002

31. DeFries R, Houghton RA, Hansen MC, Field CB, Skole D, Townshend J. 2002. Carbon emissions from tropical deforestation and regrowth based on satellite observations for the 1980s and 1990s. *Proc. Natl. Acad. Sci. USA* 99(22):14256–61

32. Matthews E. 2001. *Understanding the FRA 2000. Forest briefing 1*, World Resourc. Inst., Washington, DC

33. Geist HJ, Lambin EF. 2002. Proximate causes and underlying driving forces of tropical deforestation. *BioScience* 52(2):143–50

34. Achard F, Eva HD, Glinni A, Mayaux P, Richards T, Stibig HJ. 1998. *Identification of deforestation hot spot areas in the humid tropics, TREES Publ. Ser. B: Res. Rep. 4*, Eur. Comm., Luxembourg

35. Skole D, Tucker C. 1993. Tropical deforestation and habitat fragmentation in the Amazon: satellite data from 1978 to 1988. *Science* 260:1905–10

36. Lepers E, Lambin EF, Janetos T, DeFries R, Geist H, et al. 2003. *Areas of rapid land-cover change of the world. MEA Rep.*, Millenium Ecosyst. Assess., Penang, Malaysia

37. Hails RS. 2002. Assessing the risks associated with new agricultural practices. *Nature* 418:685–88

38. Young A. 1999. Is there really spare land? A critique of estimates of available cultivable land in developing countries. *Environ. Dev. Sustain.* 1:3–18

39. Döös BR. 2002. Population growth and loss of arable land. *Glob. Environ. Change: Hum. Policy Dimens.* 12(4):303–11

40. Tilman D. 1999. Global environmental impacts of agricultural expansion: the

need for sustainable and efficient practices. *Proc. Natl. Acad. Sci. USA* 96(11): 5995–6000

41. Seto KC, Kaufmann RK, Woodcock CE. 2000. Landsat reveals China's farmland reserves, but they're vanishing fast. *Nature* 406:121

42. Döll P, Siebert S. 2000. A digital global map of irrigated areas. *Int. Comm. Irrig. Drain. J.* 49(2):55–66

43. Popul. Div., Dep. Econ. Soc. Aff., UN Secr. 2002. *World Urbanization Prospects: The 2001 Revision* (ESA/P/WP.173) New York: UN Publ. 328 pp. http://www.un.org/esa/population/publications/wup2001/wup2001dh.pdf

44. Grübler A. 1994. Technology. In *Changes in Land Use and Land Cover: A Global Perspective*, ed. WB Meyer, BL Turner, 287–328. Cambridge, UK: Cambridge Univ. Press

45. Warren-Rhodes K, Koenig A. 2001. Escalating trends in the urban metabolism of Hong Kong: 1971–1997. *Ambio* 30(7): 429–38

46. Folke C, Jansson Å, Larsson J, Costanza R. 1997. Ecosystem appropriation by cities. *Ambio* 26(3):167–72

47. Elvidge CD, Imhoff ML, Baugh KE, Hobson VR, Nelson I, et al. 2001. Night-time lights of the world: 1994–1995. *Int. Soc. Photogramm. Remote Sens. J.* 56(2):81–99

48. Deichmann U, Balk D, Yetman G. 2001. Transforming population data for interdisciplinary usages: from census to grid. Work. Pap., Cent. Int. Earth Sci. Inf. Netw., Columbia Univ.

49. Loveland TR, Zhu Z, Ohlen DO, Brown JF, Reed BC, Yang LM. 1999. An analysis of the IGBP global land-cover characterization process. *Photogramm. Eng. Remote Sens.* 65(9):1021–32

50. DeFries RS, Field CB, Fung I, Justice CO, Los S, et al. 1995. Mapping the land surface for global atmosphere-biosphere models: toward continuous distributions of vegetation's functional properties. *J. Geophys. Res. Atmos.* 100(D10):20867–82

51. Matson PA, Parton WJ, Power AG, Swift MJ. 1997. Agricultural intensification and ecosystem properties. *Science* 277:504–9

52. Nepstad DA, Veríssimo A, Alencar A, Nobre C, Lima E, et al. 1999. Large-scale impoverishment of Amazonian forests by logging and fire. *Nature* 398:505–8

53. Pacala SW, Hurtt GC, Baker D, Peylin P, Houghton RA, et al. 2001. Consistent land- and atmosphere-based US carbon sink estimates. *Science* 292:2316–20

54. Gonzalez P. 2001. Desertification and a shift of forest species in the West African Sahel. *Clim. Res.* 17(2):217–28

55. Schlesinger WH, Gramenopoulos N. 1996. Archival photographs show no climate-induced changes in woody vegetation in the Sudan, 1943–1994. *Glob. Change Biol.* 2(2):137–41

56. Lambin EF. 1999. Monitoring forest degradation in tropical regions by remote sensing: some methodological issues. *Glob. Ecol. Biogeogr.* 8(3–4):191–98

57. Eastman JR, Fulk M. 1993. Long sequence time series evaluation using standardized principal components. *Photogramm. Eng. Remote Sens.* 59(8):991–96

58. Plisnier PD, Serneels S, Lambin EF. 2000. Impact of ENSO on East African ecosystems: a multivariate analysis based on climate and remote sensing data. *Glob. Ecol. Biogeogr.* 9(6):481–97

59. Behrenfeld MJ, Randerson JT, McClain CR, Feldman GC, Los SO, et al. 2001. Biospheric primary production during an ENSO transition. *Science* 291:2594–97

60. Lambin EF, Ehrlich D. 1997. Land-cover changes in sub-Saharan Africa, 1982–1991: application of a change index based on remotely sensed surface temperature and vegetation indices at a continental scale. *Remote Sens. Environ.* 61(2):181–200

61. Lupo F, Reginster I, Lambin EF. 2001. Monitoring land-cover changes in West

Africa with SPOT vegetation: impact of natural disasters in 1998–1999. *Int. J. Remote Sens.* 22(13):2633–39
62. Myneni RB, Keeling CD, Tucker CJ, Asrar G, Nemani RR. 1997. Increased plant growth in the northern high latitudes from 1981 to 1991. *Nature* 386:698–702
63. Tucker CJ, Dregne HE, Newcomb WW. 1991. Expansion and contraction of the Sahara desert from 1980 to 1990. *Science* 253:299–301
64. Prince SD, De Colstoun EB, Kravitz LL. 1998. Evidence from rain-use efficiencies does not indicate extensive Sahelian desertification. *Glob. Change Biol.* 4(4):359–74
65. Dwyer E, Pereira JMC, Grégoire JM, DeCamara CC. 2000. Characterization of the spatio-temporal patterns of fire activity using satellite imagery for the period April 1992 to March 1993. *J. Biogeogr.* 27(1):57–69
66. Pereira JMC, Pereira BS, Barbosa P, Stroppiana D, Vasconcelos MJP, Gregoire JM. 1999. Satellite monitoring of fire in the EXPRESSO study area during the 1996 dry season experiment: active fires, burnt area, and atmospheric emissions. *J. Geophys. Res. Atmos.* 104(D23):30701–12
67. Kasischke ES, Williams D, Barry D. 2002. Analysis of the patterns of large fires in the boreal forest region of Alaska. *Int. J. Wildland Fire* 11(2):131–44
68. Zeng N, Neelin JD, Lau KM, Tucker CJ. 1999. Enhancement of interdecadal climate variability in the Sahel by vegetation interaction. *Science* 286:1537–40
69. Schlesinger WH, Reynolds JF, Cunningham GL, Huenneke LF, Jarrell WM, et al. 1990. Biological feedbacks in global desertification. *Science* 247:1043–48
70. Tian HQ, Melillo JM, Kicklighter DW, McGuire AD, Helfrich JVK, et al. 1998. Effect of interannual climate variability on carbon storage in Amazonian ecosystems. *Nature* 396:664–67
71. Houghton RA, Skole DL, Nobre CA, Hackler JL, Lawrence KT, Chomentowski WH. 2000. Annual fluxes of carbon from deforestation and regrowth in the Brazilian Amazon. *Nature* 403:301–4
72. Siegert F, Ruecker G, Hinrichs A, Hoffmann AA. 2001. Increased damage from fires in logged forests during droughts caused by El Niño. *Nature* 414:437–40
73. Page SE, Siegert F, Rieley JO, Boehm HDV, Jayal A, Limin S. 2002. The amount of carbon released from peat and forest fires in Indonesia during 1997. *Nature* 420:61–65
74. Cochrane MA. 2001. Synergistic interactions between habitat fragmentation and fire in evergreen tropical forests. *Conserv. Biol.* 15(6):1515–21
75. Ojima DS, Galvin KA, Turner BL II. 1994. The global impact of land-use change. *BioScience* 44(5):300–4
76. Leemans R, Lambin EF, McCalla A, Nelson J, Pingali P, Watson B. 2003. Drivers of change in ecosystems and their services. In *Ecosystems and Human Well-Being: A Framework for Assessment*, ed. H Mooney, A Cropper, W Reid. Washington, DC: Island. In press
77. Ledec G. 1985. The political economy of tropical deforestation. In *Diverting Nature's Capital: The Political Economy of Environmental Abuse in the Third World*, ed. HJ Leonard, 179–226. New York/London: Holmes & Meier
78. Contreras-Hermosilla A. 2000. The underlying causes of forest decline. *CIFOR Occas. Pap. 30*, Center Int. Forestry Res., Bogor, Indones.
79. Wiggins S. 1995. Change in African farming systems between the mid 1970s and the mid 1980s. *J. Int. Dev.* 7(6):807–48
80. Kates RW, Haarmann V. 1992. Where the poors live: Are the assumptions correct? *Environment* 34(4):4–28
81. Petschel-Held G, Lüdeke MKB, Reusswig F. 1999. Actors, structures and environments: a comparative and transdisciplinary view on regional case studies of global environmental change. In *Coping*

with Changing Environments: Social Dimensions of Endangered Ecosystems in the Developing World, ed. B Lohnert, H Geist, pp. 255–92. Singapore/Sydney: Ashgate
82. Lambin EF, Turner BL, Geist H, Agbola S, Angelsen A, et al. 2001. The causes of land-use and land-cover change: moving beyond the myths. *Glob. Environ. Change* 11(4):261–69
83. McConnell W, Keys E. 2003. Meta-analysis of agricultural change. In *Seeing the Forest and the Trees: Human-Environment Interactions in Forest Ecosystems*, ed. E Moran, Bloomington, IN: Cent. Study Instit., Popul., Environ. Change. In press
84. Puigdefábregas J. 1998. Ecological impacts of global change on drylands and their implications for desertification. *Land Degrad. Dev.* 9(5):393–406
85. Agrawal A, Yadama GN. 1997. How do local institutions mediate market and population pressures on resources? Forest *Panchayats* in Kumaon, India. *Dev. Change* 28:435–65
86. Barbier EB. 1997. The economic determinants of land degradation in developing countries. *Philos. Trans. R. Soc. London Ser. B* 352:891–99
87. Indian Natl. Sci. Acad., Chin. Acad. Sci., US Natl. Acad. Sci. 2001. *Growing Populations, Changing Landscapes: Studies from India, China, and the United States*. Washington, DC: Natl. Acad. 324 pp.
88. Angelsen A, Kaimowitz D. 2001. *Agricultural Technologies and Tropical Deforestation*. Wallingford, UK: CABI Publ. 440 pp.
89. Turner MD. 1999. Labor process and the environment: the effects of labor availability and compensation on the quality of herding in the Sahel. *Hum. Ecol.* 27(2):267–96
90. Cline-Cole RA, Main HAC, Nichol JE. 1990. On fuelwood consumption, population dynamics and deforestation in Africa. *World Dev.* 18:513–27

91. Coomes OT, Grimard F, Burt GJ. 2000. Tropical forests and shifting cultivation: secondary forest fallow dynamics among traditional farmers of the Peruvian Amazon. *Ecol. Econ.* 32(1):109–24
92. Marquette CM. 1998. Land use patterns among small farmer settlers in the northeastern Ecuadorian Amazon. *Hum. Ecol.* 26(4):573–98
93. Pichón FJ. 1997. Settler households and land-use patterns in the Amazon frontier: farm-level evidence from Ecuador. *World Dev.* 25(1):67–91
94. Sierra R, Stallings J. 1998. The dynamics and social organization of tropical deforestation in Northwest Ecuador, 1983–1995. *Hum. Ecol.* 26(1):135–61
95. Perz SG. 2002. The changing social contexts of deforestation in the Brazilian Amazon. *Soc. Sci. Q.* 83(1):35–52
96. Humphries S. 1998. Milk cows, migrants, and land markets: unravelling the complexities of forest to pasture conversion in Northern Honduras. *Econ. Dev. Cult. Change* 47(1):95–124
97. McCracken SD, Brondizio ES, Nelson D, Moran EF, Siqueira AD, Rodriguez-Pedraza C. 1999. Remote sensing and GIS at farm property level: demography and deforestation in the Brazilian Amazon. *Photogr. Eng. Remote Sens.* 65(11):1311–20
98. Walker R, Moran E, Anselin L. 2000. Deforestation and cattle ranching in the Brazilian Amazon: external capital and household processes. *World Dev.* 28(4):683–99
99. Walker R, Perz S, Caldas M, Silva LGT. 2002. Land use and land cover change in forest frontiers: the role of household life cycles. *Int. Reg. Sci. Rev.* 25(2):169–99
100. Walker RT, Homma A. 1996. Land use and land cover dynamics in the Brazilian Amazon: an overview. *Ecol. Econ.* 18(1):67–80
101. Sunderlin WD, Angelsen A, Resosudarmo DP, Dermawan A, Rianto E. 2001. Economic crisis, small farmer well-being,

and forest cover change in Indonesia. *World Dev.* 29(5):767–82
102. Angelsen A, Kaimowitz D. 1999. Rethinking the causes of deforestation: lessons from economic models. *World Bank Res. Obs.* 14(1):73–98
103. Fearnside PM. 1997. Transmigration in Indonesia: lessons from its environmental and social impacts. *Environ. Manag.* 21(4):553–70
104. Fox J, Krummel J, Yarnasarn S, Ekasingh M, Podger N. 1995. Land use and landscape dynamics in northern Thailand: assessing change in three upland watersheds. *Ambio* 24(6):328–34
105. Indrabudi H, de Gier A, Fresco LO. 1998. Deforestation and its driving forces: a case study of Riam Kanan watershed, Indonesia. *Land Degrad. Dev.* 9(4):311–22
106. Mertens B, Sunderlin WW, Ndoye O, Lambin EF. 2000. Impact of macro economic change on deforestation in South Cameroon: integration of household survey and remotely-sensed data. *World Dev.* 28(6):983–99
107. Browder JO, Godfrey BJ. 1997. *Rainforest Cities, Urbanization, Development, and Globalization of the Brazilian Amazon*. New York: Columbia Univ. Press. 424 pp.
108. Ostrom E, Burger J, Field CB, Noorgaard RB, Policansky D. 1999. Sustainability—revisiting the commons: local lessons, global challenges. *Science* 284:278–82
109. Batterbury SPJ, Bebbington AJ. 1999. Environmental histories, access to resources and landscape change: an introduction. *Land Degrad. Dev.* 10(4):279–89
110. Redman CL. 1999. *Human Impact on Ancient Environments*. Tucson: Arizona Univ. Press. 288 pp.
111. Poteete A, Ostrom E. 2004. An institutional approach to the study of forest resources. In *Human Impacts on Tropical Forest Biodiversity and Genetic Resources*, ed. J Poulsen, New York: CABI Publ. In press
112. Jepson P, Jarvie JK, MacKinnon K, Monk KA. 2001. The end for Indonesia's lowland forests? *Science* 292:859–61
113. Xu J, Fox J, Lu X, Podger N, Leisz S, Ai XH. 1999. Effects of swidden cultivation, state policies, and customary institutions on land cover in a Hani village, Yunnan, China. *Mt. Res. Dev.* 19(2):123–32
114. Hecht SB. 1985. Environment, development and politics: capital accumulation and the livestock sector in eastern Amazonia. *World Dev.* 13(6):663–84
115. Barbier EB. 1993. Economic aspects of tropical deforestation in Southeast Asia. *Glob. Ecol. Biogeogr.* 3(4–6):215–34
116. Deininger KW, Minten B. 1999. Poverty, policies, and deforestation: the case of Mexico. *Econ. Dev. Cult. Change* 47(2):313–44
117. Becker CD. 1999. Protecting a Garua forest in Ecuador: the role of institutions and ecosystem valuation. *Ambio* 28(2):156–61
118. Remigio AA. 1993. Philippine forest resource policy in the Marcos and Aquino governments: a comparative assessment. *Glob. Ecol. Biogeogr.* 3(4–6):192–212
119. Sohn YS, Moran E, Gurri F. 1999. Deforestation in north-central Yucatán (1985–1995): mapping secondary succession of forest and agricultural land use in Sotuta using the cosine of the angle concept. *Photogramm. Eng. Remote Sens.* 65(8):947–58
120. Imbernon J. 1999. A comparison of the driving forces behind deforestation in the Peruvian and the Brazilian Amazon. *Ambio* 28(6):509–13
121. Pfaff ASP. 1999. What drives deforestation in the Brazilian Amazon? Evidence from satellite and socioeconomic data. *J. Environ. Econ. Manag.* 37(1):26–43
122. Kaimowitz D, Thiele G, Pacheco P. 1999. The effects of structural adjustment on deforestation and forest degradation in lowland Bolivia. *World Dev.* 27(3):505–20

123. Myers N, Kent J. 2001. *Perverse Subsidies: How Tax Dollars Can Undercut the Environment and the Economy.* Washington, DC: Island. 277 pp.
124. Barbier EB. 2000. Links between economic liberalization and rural resource degradation in the developing regions. *Agric. Econ.* 23(3):299–310
125. Naylor RL, Bonine KM, Ewel KC, Waguk E. 2002. Migration, markets, and mangrove resource use on Kosrae, Federated State of Micronesia. *Ambio* 31:340–50
126. Lambin EF, Chasek PS, Downing TE, Kerven C, Kleidon A, et al. 2002. The interplay between international and local processes affecting desertification. In *Global Desertification: Do Humans Cause Deserts?*, ed. JF Reynolds, DM Stafford Smith, 387–401. Berlin: Dahlem Univ. Press
127. Stafford Smith DM, Reynolds JF. 2002. Desertification: a new paradigm for an old problem. See Ref. 126, pp. 403–24
128. Saiko TA, Zonn IS. 2000. Irrigation expansion and dynamics of desertification in the Circum-Aral region of Central Asia. *Appl. Geogr.* 20(4):349–67
129. Nielsen TL, Zöbisch MA. 2001. Multifactorial causes of land-use change: land-use dynamics in the agropastoral village of Im Mial, northwestern Syria. *Land Degrad. Dev.* 12(2):143–61
130. Imbernon J. 1999. Pattern and development of land-use changes in the Kenyan highlands since the 1950s. *Agric. Ecosyst. Environ.* 76(1):67–73
131. Leonard HJ. 1989. Environment and the poor: development strategies for a common agenda. *US-Third World Policy Perspect.* 11:3–45
132. Homewood K, Lambin EF, Coast E, Kariuki A, Kikula I, et al. 2001. Long term changes in Serengeti-Mara wildebeest and land cover: pastoralism, population or policies? *Proc. Natl. Acad. Sci. USA* 98(22):12544–49
133. Sussman RW, Green GM, Sussman LK. 1994. Satellite imagery, human ecology, anthropology, and deforestation in Madagascar. *Hum. Ecol.* 22(3):333–54
134. Netting RM. 1993. *Smallholders, Householders, Farm Families and the Ecology of Intensive, Sustainable Agriculture.* Stanford: Stanford Univ. Press. 389 pp.
135. Turner BL, Ali AMS. 1996. Induced intensification: agricultural change in Bangladesh with implications for Malthus and Boserup. *Proc. Natl. Acad. Sci. USA* 93(25):14984–91
136. Guyer JI, Lambin EF. 1993. Land use in an urban hinterland: ethnography and remote sensing in the study of African intensification. *Am. Anthropol.* 95:839–59
137. Stonich SC. 1989. The dynamics of social processes and environmental destruction: a Central American case study. *Popul. Dev. Rev.* 15(2):269–96
138. Angelsen A. 1995. Shifting cultivation and "deforestation": a study from Indonesia. *World Dev.* 23(10):1713–29
139. Abbot JIO, Homewood K. 1999. A history of change: causes of *miombo* woodland decline in a protected area in Malawi. *J. Appl. Ecol.* 36 (3):422–33
140. Colchester M. 1993. Pirates, squatters and poachers: the political ecology of dispossession of the native peoples of Sarawak. *Glob. Ecol. Biogeogr.* 3(4–6):158–79
141. Genxu W, Guodong C. 1999. Water resource development and its influence on the environment in arid areas of China: the case of the Hei River basin. *J. Arid Environ.* 43(2):121–31
142. Wunder S. 2000. *The Economics of Deforestation: The Example of Ecuador.* Houndmills: Macmillan. 256 pp.
143. Young OR. 2002. *The Institutional Dimensions of Environmental Change.* Cambridge, MA: MIT Press. 232 pp.
144. Lele U, Viana V, Veríssimo A, Vosti S, Perkins K, Husain SA. 2000. *Brazil, forests in the balance: challenges of conservation with development. Eval. Ctry. Case Study Ser.*, Oper. Eval. Dep. World Bank, Washington, DC
145. Holland JH, Mimmaugh H. 1995. *Hidden*

Order: How Adaptation Builds Complexity. Reading, MA: Addison-Wesley. 208 pp.
146. Levin SA. 1998. Ecosystems and the biosphere as complex adaptive systems. *Ecosystems* 1(5):431–36
147. Ostrom E. 1999. Coping with tragedies of the commons. *Annu. Rev. Polit. Sci.* 2:493–535
148. Raskin P, Banuri T, Gallopín G, Gutman P, Hammond A, et al. 2002. Great transition: the promise and lure of the times ahead. *Glob. Scenar. Group, SEI Pole Star Ser. Rep. 10*, Stockholm Environ. Inst., Boston
149. Martens P, Rotmans J, eds. 2002. *Transitions in a Globalising World.* Lisse, Neth: Swets & Zeitlinger. 135 pp.
150. Mather AS, Needle CL. 1998. The forest transition: a theoretical basis. *Area* 30(2):117–24
151. Mather AS, Fairbairn J, Needle CL. 1999. The course and drivers of the forest transition: the case of France. *J. Rural Stud.* 15(1):65–90
152. Rudel TK, Perez-Lugo M, Zichal H. 2000. When fields revert to forest: development and spontaneous reforestation in postwar Puerto Rico. *Prof. Geogr.* 52(3):386–97
153. Weinhold D. 1999. Estimating the loss of agricultural productivity in the Amazon. *Ecol. Econ.* 31(1):63–76
154. Rudel TK, Bates D, Machinguiashi R. 2002. A tropical forest transition? Agricultural change, out-migration, and secondary forests in the Ecuadorian Amazon. *Ann. Assoc. Am. Geogr.* 92(1):87–102
155. Moran EF, Brondizio E. 1998. Land-use change after deforestation in Amazonia. See Ref. 185, pp. 94–120
156. Moran EF, Brondizio ES, McCracken SD. 2002: Trajectories of land use: soils, succession, and crop choice. In *Deforestation and Land Use in the Amazon*, ed. CH Wood, R Porro, pp. 193–217. Gainesville: Univ. Florida Press
157. McCracken SD, Boucek B, Moran EF. 2002. Deforestation trajectories in a frontier region of the Brazilian Amazon. See Ref. 186, pp. 215–34
158. Turner BL, Villar SC, Foster D, Geoghegan J, Keys E, et al. 2001. Deforestation in the southern Yucatán peninsular region: an integrative approach. *For. Ecol. Manag.* 154(3):353–70
159. Entwisle B, Walsh SJ, Rindfuss RR, Chamratrithirong A. 1998. Land-use/land-cover and population dynamics. See Ref. 185, pp. 121–44
160. Walsh SJ, Evans TP, Welsh WF, Entwisle B, Rindfuss RR. 1999. Scale-dependent relationships between population and environment in northeastern Thailand. *Photogr. Eng. Remote Sens.* 65(1):97–105
161. Walsh SJ, Messina JP, Crews-Meyer KA, Bilsborrow RE, Pan WK. 2002. Characterizing and modeling patterns of deforestation and agricultural extensification in the Ecuadorian Amazon. See Ref. 186, pp. 187–214
162. Petit CC, Lambin EF. 2002. Long-term land-cover changes in the Belgian Ardennes (1775–1929): model-based reconstruction versus historical maps. *Glob. Change Biol.* 8(7):616–31
163. Riley WJ, Ortiz-Monasterio I, Matson PA. 2001. Nitrogen leaching and soil nitrate, nitrite, and ammonium levels under irrigated wheat in northern Mexico. *Nutr. Cycl. Agroecosyst.* 61(3):223–36
164. Raynaut C. 1997. *Societies and Nature in the Sahel: Rethinking Environmental Degradation.* London: Routledge. 376 pp.
165. Mortimore M, Adams WM. 1999. *Working the Sahel: Environment and Society in Northern Nigeria.* London: Routledge. 226 pp.
166. Boserup E. 1965. *The Conditions of Agricultural Growth: The Economics of Agrarian Change under Population Pressure.* Chicago: Aldine. 124 pp.
167. Bilsborrow RE. 1987. Population pressures and agricultural development in developing countries: a conceptual framework and recent evidence. *World Dev.* 15(2):183–203

168. Bilsborrow RE, Ogendo HWOO. 1992. Population-driven changes in land use in developing countries. *Ambio* 21(1):37–45
169. Davis K. 1963. The theory of change and response in modern demographic history. *Popul. Index* 29(4):345–66
170. Chomitz KM, Gray DA. 1996. Roads, land use, and deforestation: a spatial model applied to Belize. *World Bank Econ. Rev.* 10(3):487–512
171. Panayotou T, Sungsuwan S. 1989. *An econometric study of the causes of tropical deforestation: the case of Northeast Thailand*. Dev. Disc. Pap. 284, Harvard Inst. Int. Dev., Cambridge, MA
172. Mertens B, Lambin EF. 2000. Land-cover change trajectories in South Cameroon. *Ann. Assoc. Am. Geogr.* 90(3):467–94
173. Cervigni R. 2001. *Biodiversity in the Balance: Land Use, National Development and Global Welfare*. Cheltenham: Edward Elgar. 271 pp.
174. Ostrom E. 1990. *Governing the Commons: The Evolution of Institutions for Collective Action*. Cambridge, UK: Cambridge Univ. Press. 280 pp.
175. Blaikie P, Brookfield H. 1987. *Land Degradation and Society*. London: Methuen. 296 pp.
176. Richards P. 1990. Land transformation. In *The Earth as Transformed by Human Action: Global and Regional Changes in the Biosphere over the Past 300 Years*, ed. BL Turner, WC Clark, RW Kates, JF Richards, J Mathews, WB Meyer, 163–78. Cambridge, UK: Cambridge Univ. Press
177. Crumley CL, eds. 1994. *Historical Ecology: Cultural Knowledge and Changing Landscapes*. Santa Fe: Sch. Am. Res. 304 pp.
178. Netting RM. 1981. *Balancing on an Alp: Ecological Change and Continuity in a Swiss Mountain Community*. Cambridge, UK: Cambridge Univ. Press. 436 pp.
179. Conte CA. 1999. The forest becomes a desert: forest use and environmental change in Tanzania's west Usambara Mountains. *Land Degrad. Dev.* 10(4):291–309
180. Abrol YP, Sangwan S, Tiwari MK, eds. 2002. *Land Use: Historical Perspectives, Focus on Indo-Gangetic Plains*. New Delhi: Allied. 667 pp.
181. Klepeis P, Turner BL. 2001. Integrated land history and global change science: the example of the Southern Yucatán Peninsular Region Project. *Land Use Policy* 18(1):27–39
182. Fairhead J, Leach M. 1996. *Misreading the African Landscape: Society and Ecology in a Forest-Savanna Mosaic*. Cambridge, UK: Cambridge Univ. Press. 374 pp.
183. Rotmans J, van Asselt M, Anastasi C, Greeuw S, Mellors J, et al. 2000. Visions for a sustainable Europe. *Futures* 32(9–10):809–31
184. Victor DG, Ausubel JH. 2000. Restoring the forests. *Foreign Aff.* 79(6):127–44
185. Liverman D, Moran EF, Rindfuss RR, Stern PC, eds. 1998. *People and Pixels: Linking Remote Sensing and Social Science*. Washington, DC: Natl. Acad.
186. Walsh-Meyer S, Crews K, eds. 2002. *Linking People, Place, and Policy: A GIScience Approach*. Dordrecht: Kluwer

URBAN CENTERS: An Assessment of Sustainability

Gordon McGranahan and David Satterthwaite

International Institute for Environment and Development, London WC1H ODD, United Kingdom; email: Gordon.Mcgranahan@iied.org, David.Satterthwaite@iied.org

Key Words urbanization, sustainable development, cities, ecological footprint

■ **Abstract** As increasing proportions of the world's population, production, and consumption become concentrated in urban areas, the need for urban development patterns that are more ecologically sustainable becomes obvious. A large proportion of the world's urban population also has needs that are unmet. We review the scale and nature of urban change worldwide, the environmental impacts of these changes, and the potentials and the difficulties in better meeting sustainable development goals in urban centers. The discussion of the interaction between city-based production and consumption and the resources and sinks on which these rely that are outside city boundaries is a reminder that the goal is not sustainable cities but cities that contribute to sustainable development within their boundaries, in the region around them, and globally.

CONTENTS

INTRODUCTION	244
AN URBANIZING WORLD	245
THE CONTROVERSIES OVER SUSTAINABLE DEVELOPMENT AND CITIES	249
WHAT CRITERIA SHOULD BE USED TO JUDGE SUSTAINABLE DEVELOPMENT IN URBAN AREAS?	251
ECOLOGICAL FOOTPRINTS OF CITIES	256
NONRENEWABLE RESOURCES AND SINKS	257
URBAN CENTERS AND GLOBAL SYSTEMS	259
WHAT SUSTAINABLE DEVELOPMENT IMPLIES FOR URBAN AUTHORITIES	260
BUILDING SYNERGIES, AVOIDING CONFLICTS	263
ENABLING LOCAL ACTION WHILE MEETING NATIONAL AND GLOBAL GOALS	265
IMPLEMENTING SUSTAINABLE DEVELOPMENT IN CITIES	267
THE GLOBAL CONTEXT FOR SUSTAINABILITY AND DEVELOPMENT	269

INTRODUCTION

At its core, the concept of sustainable development is about reconciling "development" and "environment." Development, i.e., the meeting of people's needs, requires use of resources and implies generation of wastes. The environment has finite limits to the use of many resources and on the capacity of ecosystems to absorb or breakdown wastes or render them harmless at local, regional, and global scales. If development implies extending to all current and future populations the levels of resource use and waste generation that are the norm among middle-income groups in high-income nations, it is likely to conflict with local or global systems with finite resources and capacities to assimilate wastes. There is good evidence that such conflicts are occurring in more and more localities and also that the richest localities have overcome local constraints by drawing on the resources and sinks of other localities to the point where some resources and ecological processes are threatened both in these localities and globally (1). This implies that sustainable development requires a commitment to ensuring everyone's needs are met with modes of development that are less rooted in high-consumption, high-waste lifestyles.

Urban centers have particular relevance to any discussion of sustainable development for three reasons. The first is an increasingly urbanized world; today close to half the world's population live in urban centers, and the proportion is likely to continue growing as an increasing amount of the world's economic activities concentrate in urban centers (2). As described below, a significant proportion of the world's population with unmet needs lives in urban areas. The second reason is that urban centers concentrate most of the world's economic activities, including most industrial production, and thus are the sites that concentrate most demands for the natural resources used in such production and the sites that generate most industrial wastes. The third is that much of the world's middle- and upper-income groups live and work in urban centers, and it is their demands for goods and services that underpin most of the (rural and urban) resource demands and waste outputs from production worldwide. As a result of urban centers' concentration of middle- and upper-income groups and of the world's nonagricultural production, inevitably they are also the sites for the generation of a high proportion of greenhouse gases. In addition, many of the greenhouse gases generated outside urban centers are linked to urban-based demands—as in the greenhouse gases generated by fossil-fuel power stations, oil wells, and farms that are outside urban boundaries but where the electricity, oil, and farm products are destined for urban producers or consumers. Thus, the quality of environmental management within urban centers, which include measures to increase resource use efficiency and reduce waste generation, heavily influences not only the quality of life for the urban population but also populations that may be far outside of urban areas. As a result, the scale of resource use and waste generation arising from production and consumption located in urban centers has major implications for broad ecological sustainability. Thus, the key ecological issue for urban centers is not sustainable cities but cities and smaller urban centers that have production systems and inhabitants with patterns of consumption that are compatible with sustainable development within their region (encompassing both rural and urban areas) and globally.

AN URBANIZING WORLD

By 2003, the world's urban population reached 3 billion people, around the same size as the world's total population in 1960 (3). Close to half of the world's population now lives in urban centers, compared to less than 15% in 1900 (4). During the twentieth century, the world's urban population increased more than tenfold, and many aspects of urban change over the last fifty years are unprecedented. These include not only the world's level of urbanization and the size of its urban population but also the number of countries becoming more urbanized and the size and number of very large cities. Many cities have had populations that grew ten to twentyfold in the last 30 years (2). Most of the world's largest cities are now in Asia, not in Europe or North America.

Table 1, with statistics on the scale of urban change in each region between 1950 and 2000, shows that most of the world's urban population is now outside Europe and North America. Asia alone contains almost half the world's urban population, even if more than three fifths of its people still live in rural areas. Africa, which is generally perceived as overwhelmingly rural, now has close to two fifths of its population in urban areas and a larger total urban population than North America. The urban population of Africa, Asia, Latin America, and the Caribbean is now nearly three times the size of the urban population of the rest of the world. United Nations' (U.N.) projections suggest that urban populations are growing so much faster than rural populations that 85% of the growth in the world's population between 2000 and 2010 will be in urban areas, and virtually all of this growth will be in Africa, Asia, and Latin America (3).

Some care is needed in interpreting the urban statistics in Table 1. Aggregate statistics for regions obscure the great diversity in urban trends among nations. Most nations may be urbanizing, but a large proportion of the world's urban centers are not growing rapidly. Many even have more people moving out than in, so they either have declining populations or populations growing below their rate of natural increase. These include many of the world's largest cities (Mexico City, Sao Paulo, Buenos Aires, Kolkata—formerly Calcutta—and Seoul) (2). The increasing number of cities with 10 million or more inhabitants may seem to be a cause for concern, but there are relatively few of them—16 by 2000—and in this year, they concentrated less than 4% of the world's population (2, 3).

The statistics in Table 1 also tell us nothing about the complex and often rapidly changing movements of people in and out of most urban centers. There are no agreed international criteria for how city boundaries should be defined. Many large cities have their population undercounted as suburban settlements have long spilled over the city boundaries. However, for other cities, their population is

TABLE 1 The distribution of the world's urban population by region, 1950–2010

Region	1950	1970	1990	2000[a]	Projection for 2010
Urban population (millions of inhabitants)					
World	751	1357	2286	2862	3514
Africa	32	82	197	295	426
Asia	244	501	1023	1376	1784
Europe	287	424	521	534	536
Latin America and the Caribbean	70	164	313	391	470
Northern America	110	171	213	243	273
Oceania	8	14	19	23	26
Percentage of population living in urban areas					
World	29.8	36.8	43.5	47.2	51.5
Africa	14.7	23.1	31.8	37.2	42.7
Asia	17.4	23.4	32.2	37.5	43.0
Europe	52.4	64.6	72.1	73.4	75.1
Latin America and the Caribbean	41.9	57.6	71.1	75.4	79.0
Northern America	63.9	73.8	75.4	77.4	79.8
Oceania	61.6	71.2	70.8	74.1	75.7
Percentage of the world's urban population living in					
World	100	100	100	100	100
Africa	4.3	6.1	8.6	10.3	12.1
Asia	32.5	37.0	44.8	48.1	50.8
Europe	38.3	31.3	22.8	18.7	15.3
Latin America and the Caribbean	9.3	12.1	13.7	13.7	13.4
Northern America	14.6	12.6	9.3	8.5	7.8
Oceania	1.0	1.0	0.8	0.8	0.8

[a]The statistics for 2000 in this table are an aggregation of national statistics; many of which draw on national censuses held in 1999, 2000, or 2001. But some are based on estimates or projections from statistics drawn from censuses held around 1990. There is also a group of countries (mostly in Africa) for which there are no census data since the 1970s or early 1980s, so all figures for their urban (and rural) populations are based on estimates and projections. The statistics are drawn or derived from (3).

overstated because city boundaries have been redefined to encompass several thousand square kilometers and include large rural populations and populations of separate urban centers. Population statistics also tell us nothing of the very large economic, social, political, and demographic changes that have underpinned the trend toward increasingly urbanized societies. The most important underpinning of urban change during the twentieth century was the large increase in the size of the global economy. In general, the nations with the largest cities and with the most rapid increase in their levels of urbanization are the nations with the largest increases in their economies (2, 5). There is an economic logic underlying the distribution of the world's urban population, which includes its largest cities, as can be seen in the concentration of the world's "million cities" (cities with one million or more inhabitants) and megacities in its largest economies. In 2000, the world's 5 largest economies (those in the United States, China, Japan, India, and Germany) had 9 of the world's 16 megacities and 46% of its million cities. By 2000, all but 2 of the world's 16 megacities and more than two thirds of its million cities were in the 20 largest economies. Similarly, within each of the world's regions, most of the largest cities are concentrated in the largest economies—for instance, Brazil and Mexico in Latin America and China, India, Indonesia, and the Republic of Korea in Asia (2). However, there are also other important underpinnings of urbanization in many nations. For example, in most African nations, rapid urbanization just before and after achieving independence reflects both the removal of colonial controls on the right of their population to live in urban centers and the building of the institutional base for independent nations.

Taking a long-term view of urban change, it is not surprising that Asia has most of the world's largest cities, because throughout most of history this has been the case. The growing number of large Asian cities reflects the region's growing importance within the world economy. In addition, although rapid urban growth is often seen as a problem, it is generally the nations that have urbanized most in the last 50 years that have the highest average life expectancies or the largest increase in their life expectancies. In addition, the megacities may appear chaotic and out of control, but most have life expectancies and provision for piped water, sanitation, schools, and health care that are well above their national average or the average for smaller urban centers—even if the aggregate statistics for some of the better served megacities hide significant proportions of their population who live in very poor conditions (5–7).

Recent censuses also show that the world today is less dominated by large cities than had been anticipated. For instance, Mexico City had 18 million people in 2000 (8)—not the 31 million people predicted 25 years ago (9). Kolkata (formerly Calcutta) had around 13 million by 2000, not the 40–50 million that had been predicted during the 1970s (10). Sao Paulo, Rio de Janeiro, Seoul, Chennai (formerly Madras), and Cairo are among the many other large cities that, by 2000, had several million inhabitants fewer than had been predicted. In addition, the actual number of megacities with more than 10 million inhabitants in 2000 is fewer than had been expected (2). This is often because smaller cities have successfully attracted new investments away from the very large cities. For instance in southeast Brazil, over the last 20 years, Sao Paulo has lost new investments to a network of smaller cities, which include Porto Alegre and Curitiba, and in Mexico, much new investment has been in cities on or close to the border with the United States and not in Mexico City. In addition, as in Europe and North America, well-managed smaller cities often attract businesses and middle- and upper-income groups away from large cities because of a better quality of life, including a capacity to offer better quality, affordable housing.

The world also proved to have a smaller urban population and to be less urbanized than expected in 2000. By this date, the world's urban population had 270 million people fewer than had been predicted 20 years previously (2). The main reason for this is the slow economic growth (or economic decline) that many low- and middle-income nations have experienced since 1980. This helps explain slower population growth rates for many cities in Africa and Latin America. Part of this is also related to structural adjustment policies that brought declines in employment, falling real incomes and declining urban welfare, and proved to be less successful than hoped in stimulating economic growth (11). For most nations, urban population growth rates also dropped due to falling fertility rates. For some, it was also because of rising mortality rates. By the late 1990s, this included large and growing levels of mortality from HIV/AIDS. This is particularly apparent in certain sub-Saharan African nations with high levels of infection and the absence of affordable drugs. The illness is reshaping urban trends in many nations (11).

There is an obvious association between the world's largest cities and globalization. Growing cross-border flows of raw materials, goods, information, income, and capital, much of it managed by transnational corporations, underpin a network of what can be termed "global cities" that are the sites for the management and servicing of the global economy (12). Most international investment is concentrated in a relatively small proportion of the world's cities. Many of the world's fastest growing cities are also the cities that have had most success in attracting international investment. The remittance flows created by large-scale international migration associated with globalization have also had a profound impact in cities and smaller urban centers where many migrants come from. The income flows to households in low- or middle-income countries from those working abroad and often supports not only higher consumption levels but also more investment in housing. For many low- and middle-income nations, the total value of remittance flows from migrants working abroad is larger than total aid flows (13).

However, the association between globalization and large cities is moderated by two factors. The first is that advanced telecommunications systems allow a separation of the production process from those who manage and finance it. For example, the economies of London and New York may depend heavily on growing markets for industrial goods, but they have very little such industrial production themselves. The second, linked to this, is the more decentralized pattern of urban development that is possible within regions with well-developed transport and communications infrastructure. Many of the most successful regions have urban forms that are not dominated by a large central city and have new enterprises developing in a network of smaller cities and greenfield sites. In all high-income nations and many middle- and low-income nations, there has been a growing capacity of cities outside the very large metropolitan areas to attract a significant proportion of new investment. In the nations that have had effective decentralizations, such as Brazil and, in part, India, urban authorities in smaller cities have more resources and capacity to compete for new investment. Trade liberalization and a greater emphasis on exports have also increased the comparative advantage of many smaller cities, while advances in interregional transport and communications have lessened the advantages for businesses in locating in the largest cities.

However, there are also large cities whose population growth rates remained high during the 1980s and 1990s—for instance Dhaka (Bangladesh) and many cities in India and China—and strong economic performance by such cities is the most important factor in explaining this. China has many examples of cities with very rapid population growth rates, which is hardly surprising given the very rapid economic growth that it has sustained over the last two decades. Thus, although some existing large cities may continue to grow rapidly in the low- and middle-income nations with strong economic performance, in general, the urban future is likely to be less dominated by megacities and more by highly connected urban systems. In general, most urbanization in the future will come in low- and middle-income nations with the best economic performance. As such nations invest in improved transport and communications to support this, urban systems will generally become more decentralized. This process will be reinforced if decentralization really increases the capacity and competence of local (municipal, city, and metropolitan) governments.

THE CONTROVERSIES OVER SUSTAINABLE DEVELOPMENT AND CITIES

Although there is a large and diverse literature about sustainable development that goes back 30 years, much of it ignores urban centers or sees urban centers as the problem, with little or no discussion of the role of urban policies and urban management in meeting sustainable development goals. Many national strategies for sustainable development include little or no discussion about urban policy (6). Most of the global reports about sustainability or sustainable development produced by international nongovernmental organizations or U.N. agencies give little detailed consideration to the role of urban policies, the urban governance structures needed to implement sustainable development goals, and often give little attention to the scale of unmet needs in urban areas. The report of the Brundtland Commission, *Our Common Future*, published in 1987, which had considerable importance in getting sustainable development issues more widely discussed by governments and international agencies, was unusual in that it had a chapter on urban issues (14), but this chapter was nearly dropped because of the opposition to a chapter on such issues by some Commission members. The early drafts of Agenda 21, the blueprint for sustainable development, that came out of the Earth Summit, the UN Conference on Environment and Development, hardly mentioned urban centers, and it was only through intensive lobbying by particular U.N. agencies, who felt that urban issues were important, that this omission was addressed in the final version.

When consideration is given to urban centers in discussions of sustainable development, it is usually to their role as centers of pollution and waste. But it can be misleading to attribute to urban centers the resource use, waste, pollution, and greenhouse gas emissions that occur within their boundaries. These arise as a result of particular industries and commercial and industrial enterprises (or corporations) and middle- and upper-income groups with high consumption lifestyles. They may be concentrated in (particular) urban centers, but it is not only their concentration in these urban centers that is environmentally destructive but also their level of resource use and waste generation. If these production units were dispersed in rural areas, they could reduce their local ecological impact (very large cities generally exceed the capacity of local ecosystems for freshwater, and wastes generated within the city often damage local and sometimes regional water bodies), but their total draw on resources and generation of wastes would not change. A coal fired power station or cement factory does not reduce its fuel use or its generation of greenhouse gases by being located outside a city. By some criteria, the ecological impact of industries and wealthy households would increase if they were dispersed in rural areas, because their spatial dispersion would imply a greater need for motorized transport. Concentrating people and production in cities gives more possibilities of waste reduction, reuse, and recycling and also makes good environmental management cheaper since it is difficult for any environmental agency to check on the emissions and waste disposal practices of industries dispersed through rural regions (6). In addition, concentrating people in cities reduces their per capita resource use. In high-income countries and in the wealthier cities or regions in middle-income countries, it is the middle- or upper-income households with two or more automobiles living in rural areas, small towns, or low density outer suburbs of cities that generally have the highest consumption of resources, generally much more so than those with similar incomes living in cities (15). Thus, in any discussion of how different urban centers perform in regard to sustainable development, it is important to scrutinize the activities taking place and the people living within these urban centers. One particularly wealthy, high-consumption individual or household with several large automobiles, a large inefficiently heated or cooled home, and with frequent use of air travel (for pleasure and work) can have a more damaging global ecological impact than thousands of urban dwellers in informal settlements in low-income nations (6).

There are few valid generalizations for urban centers because of their diversity in terms of size, quality of life, and total or average per capita resource use. Urban centers vary in size from city/regions with tens of millions of people to settlements with a few hundred inhabitants. There is considerable variation in the way that different governments define urban centers; most use population thresholds of between 1000 and 5000 inhabitants to distinguish rural from urban settlements, and some also add criteria regarding density and nonagricultural employment (2, 3). In terms of development, they vary from urban centers in many low-income nations where average life expectancies are very short (below 40 years) and one child in three dies before the age of 5 (virtually all from easily prevented causes) to urban centers where average life expectancies are 80 years and only one child in 200 dies before the age of five. In the urban centers with the very short life expectancies, environmental hazards contribute much to premature death, most of it from infectious diseases and physical accidents; in the urban centers with high life expectancies, their contribution is much less significant (6, 16). In terms of ecological sustainability, urban centers vary from those with very low levels of resource use and waste generation (and almost insignificant contributions to regional or global ecological problems) to those with very high levels of resource use, waste generation, and regional and global impacts. Unfortunately, the urban centers that perform best by development criteria such as high life expectancy and low infant mortality generally perform worst by ecological sustainability criteria, such as fresh water use, waste volumes, and greenhouse gas emissions per person. As discussed below, however, this is not always the case and need not be so.

Thus, it is difficult to generalize about urban centers' performance in regard to meeting needs and in regard to the use of natural capital. In addition, generalizations about the nature of their problems may be misleading. For instance, much of the literature on current or likely future freshwater shortages suggests the inadequacies in provision for water are linked to water stress. However, an analysis of nations' level of water stress and of the extent of urban provision for water found no association; indeed, those low- and middle-income nations that faced water stress had, on average, better urban provision for water and sanitation than nations with similar per capita incomes that did not (7).

WHAT CRITERIA SHOULD BE USED TO JUDGE SUSTAINABLE DEVELOPMENT IN URBAN AREAS?

Figure 1 summarizes the multiple goals that are within any commitment to sustainable development. According to its original meaning and the one taken up by the World Commission on Environment and Development, or the Brundtland Commission in 1987 (14), the goals are to meet the needs of the present generation without compromising the ability of future generations to meet their own needs. The development component for urban centers is the extent to which their inhabitants' needs are met. These include the need for adequate livelihoods, for adequate shelter [secure, good quality housing with basic infrastructure (for water piped into homes and provision for sanitation, drainage, and solid waste removal)] and for services (including schools, health care and emergency services). During the 1990s, the discussions about urban development in low- and middle-income nations came to recognize that reducing poverty meant not only more secure livelihoods and better housing but also ensuring all urban citizens had the right to exercise their civil and political rights and that they were protected by the rule of law against violence, other crimes, and unsafe working conditions (6, 17). This has an important environmental component because (a) the quality of the home, work, neighborhood, and city environment and (b) the extent to which the inhabitants are protected from biological pathogens and chemical pollutants (in the water, air, soil, or food) or other environmental hazards have a major influence on the health and well-being of the population (6, 18).

Meeting the needs of the present, the development component of sustainable development, requires consideration of whose needs are to be met, what needs, who defines needs, and who obtains more power and resources to ensure they are met. These include economic, social, cultural, health, and political needs as outlined in Figure 1. Major changes are required to meet needs, given that more

MEETING THE NEEDS OF THE PRESENT...

Economic needs---include access to an adequate income/livelihood or productive assets; also economic security when unemployed, ill, disabled, or otherwise unable to work.

Environmental needs---include accommodation that is healthy and safe with adequate provision for piped water, sanitation, and drainage. Also a home, workplace, and living environment protected from environmental hazards, which include air and water pollution. Provision for recreation and for children's play. Shelters and services must meet the specific needs of children and of adults responsible for most child rearing (usually women).

Social, cultural, and health needs---include health care, education, and transportation. Needs related to people's choice and control---including homes and neighborhoods that they value and where their social and cultural priorities are met.

Political needs---include freedom to participate in national and local politics and in decisions regarding management and development of one's home and neighborhood within a broader framework that ensures respect for civil and political rights and the implementation of environmental legislation.

SUSTAINABLE DEVELOPMENT AND CITIES

Figure 1 The multiple goals of sustainable development as applied to cities (6).

... WITHOUT COMPROMISING THE ABILITY OF FUTURE GENERATIONS TO MEET THEIR OWN NEEDS

Minimizing use or waste of nonrenewable resources---includes minimizing the consumption of fossil fuels in housing, commerce, industry, and transport plus substituting renewable sources where feasible. Also, minimizing waste of scarce mineral resources (reduce use, reuse, recycle, and reclaim). There are also cultural, historical, and natural assets within cities that are irreplaceable and thus nonrenewable---for instance, historic districts, and parks and natural landscapes that provide space for play, recreation, and access to nature.

Sustainable use of finite renewable resources---cities drawing on freshwater resources at levels that can be sustained (with efficient use, recycling, and reuse promoted). Keeping to a sustainable ecological footprint in terms of land area on which city-based producers and consumers draw for agricultural, forest products, and biomass fuels.

Biodegradable wastes not overtaxing capacities of renewable sinks (e.g., capacity of a river to break down biodegradable wastes without ecological degradation).

Nonbiodegradable wastes/emissions not overtaxing (finite) capacity of local and global sinks to absorb or dilute them without adverse effects (e.g., especially persistent organic pollutants, greenhouse gases, and stratospheric ozone-depleting chemicals).

Social/human capital that future generations need includes institutional structures to support human rights and good governance and more generally to receive each nation's or social group's rich cultural heritage, knowledge, and experience.

Figure 1 (*Continued*)

than 600 million urban dwellers live in tenements or informal settlements where their lives are constantly at risk (and thus have much reduced life expectancies) because of overcrowded poor quality housing and lack of basic services (6, 16). Much of the urban population in low- and middle-income nations lack safe, regular, and easily accessed piped water supplies and good quality provision for sanitation and drainage (7). A U.N. report published in 2003 shows that the deficiencies in provision for water and sanitation in urban areas of Africa, Asia, and Latin America are much worse than had previously been suggested by official statistics; for instance, it suggests that at least 35 percent of the urban population in Africa and Asia have inadequate provision water and at least half have inadequate provision for sanitation (7). As many as 100 million urban dwellers in low- and middle-income nations have to resort to open defecation, because of the lack of toilet facilities in their homes or nearby (7). Within these nations, it is also common for 30–60 percent of a city's population to live in poor quality one or two-room shacks in squatter settlements or illegal subdivisions; most have very inadequate provision for infrastructure and services, and a high proportion are at constant risk of eviction (5, 6, 19). Many of these informal or illegal settlements are located on land sites in flood plains, along river banks, or on steep slopes (that are at risk from landslides) because these were the only sites in or close to cities on which their inhabitants were able to settle; landowners and governments would not have permitted them to settle on better quality sites (6).

The ecological sustainability component of sustainable development is largely concerned with minimizing the depletion or degradation of the four types of natural capital listed in the lower box of Figure 1. All urban centers depend on renewable resources such as fresh water and the soils and forests from which food, other agricultural crops, and forest products are produced. The economy of a high proportion of all urban centers in low- and middle-income nations is also intimately linked to rural areas because they serve as markets and service centers for the products of agriculture and forests and for those working in rural areas. Many major cities first grew as markets, service centers, and agricultural processing locations for the crops produced in their regions, such as coffee towns, tea towns, fruit and wine towns, sugar towns, or silk-mulberry towns (20).

All urban centers (or rather the population and production systems concentrated there) rely on the renewable sink capacity of the ecosystems within which they are located or adjacent ecosystems to break down the biodegradable wastes they generate. Most wastes arising from production and consumption are biodegradable, but large waste volumes can overwhelm local capacities. Each water body has a finite capacity to break down biodegradable wastes without becoming degraded (and ultimately dead). There are also conflicts between protecting some renewable resources and using sinks, especially as the disposal of wastes into freshwater resources (for instance industries dumping their wastes into rivers or down wells) reduces their quality and/or availability for human use. Most major cities and many smaller urban centers in Africa, Asia, and Latin America have rivers running through them that are heavily polluted, often destroy or damage fisheries, and pose serious hazards for communities downriver who use the water (6).

Any examination of the use made by urban consumers and businesses of renewable resources and sinks and of their linkages with rural producers and ecosystems within their own region and beyond highlights how sustainable urban development and sustainable rural development cannot be separated. The rural-urban linkages can be positive in both developmental and environmental terms. Demand for rural produce from urban-based enterprises and households can support prosperous farms and rural settlements, where natural capital is not being depleted. Few governments appreciate the extent to which productive intensive agriculture can support development goals in both rural and urban areas, in part because no professional group or government institution has the responsibility to understand and support this (21, 22). Increasing agricultural production can also support urban development within or close to the main farming areas—the two supporting each other. Although for this to happen, generally a relatively equitable land owning structure and a concentration of relatively small farms (each producing good livings for those farming them based on relatively high-value crops) are required (20, 21). There are also many examples of less ecologically damaging interactions between urban wastes and surrounding areas. For instance, organic solid and liquid wastes that originate from urban-based consumers or industries are returned to soils, which demonstrates alternatives to the heavy use of artificial fertilizers and to the disregard of nutrients within city wastes (23). Urban agriculture also has particular importance in much of Africa, Asia, and Latin America, both as a livelihood or part of a livelihood for many households and as a system of production that is relatively efficient in energy input terms and helps keep food costs down (24). However, there are also the negative aspects that rural-urban links can have. For instance, when agricultural land is lost as cities' built-up areas expand without control, land speculation on urban fringes drives out cultivators. Enterprises on city fringes can also damage agricultural production; examples include quarries, brick-making plants, and sites from which landfill is drawn that expand over farmland (6).

Thus, if urban citizens and their governments are committed to sustainable development, they should be concerned about the impact of their resource use and waste generation on the region around the city, even though much of this is generally outside the official urban boundaries and outside the city government's jurisdiction. For instance, consider the importance of protecting trees, woods, and forests in the region around cities. Forests have key local ecological roles in protecting watersheds (and preventing soil erosion), regulating water flows (and preventing floods), maintaining local biodiversity, and moderating climatic extremes (25). A great range of forest products are important for city consumers and producers—especially in regions where fuelwood or charcoal are still widely used as fuels by urban households. Other important forest derivatives include timber and "a variety of foods including bushmeat . . . framing, panelling and thatching materials, and a range of other goods including berries, nuts, fruit, wild animals, honey, resins, oils, rattan and medical products" (26). Forests are also a key part of natural landscapes to which city dwellers want access for recreation. In addition, forests have key global roles within the carbon cycle and with maintaining global biodiversity.

Deforestation or forest depletion is likely to have a number of effects on urban centers. Perhaps the most serious economic impacts are the loss of employment, income, and consumption goods for urban centers in areas where forest exploitation is a significant part of the local economy. There is also the increasing difficulty experienced by those living in such settlements in obtaining fuel. The ecological effects of deforestation, which include changes in runoff and subsequent erosion, may add to the risk of small floods, reduce the capacity of hydroelectric stations (whose electricity is usually destined for urban consumers or enterprises), and reduce the productivity of agriculture. Deforestation of river catchments and associated soil erosion may be a contributory factor in floods that devastate large areas downstream, in cities or city districts built alongside rivers (27). All this highlights the need for good forest protection and management in and around cities, within governance structures that ensure that such management is not oriented only to the needs of powerful groups. But this usually does not happen, because the areas in most need of good management typically fall outside the boundaries of city authorities or because of the incapacity or unwillingness of government agencies to control private developments that cause deforestation. However, no assumption should be made that city development in low-income nations is associated with widening circles of deforestation because of demand for fuelwood or charcoal; in many instances, it is not. Demand can stimulate reforestation or cause much of the city population to shift to the use of other fuels (28).

The need for much improved management of coastal areas provides another example of the institutional difficulties. A large proportion of the world's urban population (and many of its largest cities) is in coastal areas. Tens of millions of people depend, directly or indirectly, on coastal and marine ecosystems for their livelihoods from fishing and also from tourism. A great range of resources is drawn from such ecosystems, in part, because of the high productivity of near-shore waters and mangroves. Coastal areas are also widely used as sources of building materials and as dumping grounds for sewage, storm and surface runoff, industrial effluents (often including toxic wastes), and garbage. In most coastal areas in low- and middle-income nations, there is little provision to protect key resources such as mangroves and coral reefs with their multiple productive and protective functions. The result is that they are generally being used and degraded or polluted by powerful economic interests to the detriment not only of the environment but also of the livelihoods of large numbers of low-income groups.

ECOLOGICAL FOOTPRINTS OF CITIES

Consideration of the use of resources and sinks by producers and consumers located in any urban center must also take into account the ecological impacts of this use in distant regions. In general, the larger and wealthier the urban center, the larger the area from which resources are drawn. Many cities now draw on the freshwater resources of distant ecosystems, as their demand for freshwater has long exceeded local capacities and often destroyed local capacities by overexploiting groundwater and polluting surface water (7). Dakar, the capital of Senegal, now needs to draw water from a lake 200 km away (29); Mexico City has to supplement local supplies with water drawn from neighboring basins that has to be pumped over 1000 meters in height and drawn from up to 150 km away (30). Prosperous cities also draw heavily on the resources and waste-assimilation capacities of "distant elsewheres"—as highlighted by the concept developed by William Rees of cities' ecological footprints (31, 32). A city may perform extremely well in environmental terms in regard to having a safe, stimulating environment for its inhabitants and a very well-managed region around it (with good watershed management, many forests, and careful protection of sites of particular scientific interest), yet it can have a very high environmental impact on distant regional systems and on global systems because of the high demand from its population and businesses for goods whose fabrication and transport to that city required high resource inputs and generated high levels of pollution and greenhouse gas emissions. This is part of a more general tendency for cities to pass on environmental burdens to other people, other ecosystems, or to global systems as they become more prosperous and larger (33). The lower Fraser Valley, in which the city of Vancouver is located, has an ecological footprint that is about 20 times its actual area, to produce the food and forestry products its inhabitants and businesses use and to grow vegetation to absorb the carbon dioxide that they create (31). London's ecological footprint is estimated to be 125 times its actual size, based on similar criteria (34). Small relatively poor urban centers generally have ecological footprints that are relatively small and very local. Most of the largest more wealthy cities draw resources from huge areas; many extend beyond their nations' borders and have high levels of greenhouse gas emissions as discussed in detail below. It can be misleading to compare the ecological footprints of cities in that there are large disparities within any city population in regard to a household's ecological footprint. For instance, the poorest 20 percent of Canada's population have average ecological footprints that are less than a quarter of those of the wealthiest 20 percent of the population (32). The disparities between the ecological footprints of high-income and low-income households in cities in low- and middle-income nations is likely to be much larger than this.

NONRENEWABLE RESOURCES AND SINKS

There are also dramatic contrasts between high-income nations and low-income nations in regard to the use of nonrenewable resources and sinks. Most high-income nations have levels of commercial energy consumption per person that are 20 to 30 times that in many low-income nations (35). Comparable contrasts exist between per capita consumption in rich and poor nations for most nonrenewable resources. There are fewer figures comparing city populations' nonrenewable resource consumption, but those that do exist also show very large differences. Gasoline use per capita in cities, such as Houston, Detroit, and Los Angeles, with among the world's highest consumption levels, are 100 times or more those of most cities in low-income nations (36). Average waste generation per inhabitant in urban centers can vary more than 20-fold when comparing urban citizens in high-income nations (who may generate 1000 kg or more of waste per person per year) to those in some of the lowest-income nations (who may generate less than 50 kg per person per year) (5, 6). The disparities in terms of the amount of nonrenewable resources thrown away in the garbage (especially metals) are much higher because of the higher proportion of metals discarded in the household wastes in cities in high-income nations. Indeed, many low-income urban dwellers in Africa and Asia hardly throw away any nonrenewable resources because they cannot afford goods made from such resources; many do the opposite (in effect they create nonrenewable resources) because their livelihoods are based on finding and reclaiming items from waste streams for reuse or recycling (5).

This comparison of nonrenewable resource consumption between nations or between cities can be misleading in that it is the middle- and upper-income groups that account for most resource use and most generation of household wastes. This becomes a high-income:low-income country issue (or a North:South issue) because most of the world's middle- and upper-income people with high consumption lifestyles live in Europe, North America, and Japan, and because international politics reflect this imbalance. High-income households in cities such as Lagos, Sao Paulo, and Bangkok may have levels of nonrenewable resource use comparable to high-income households in Los Angeles or Houston; it is primarily the fact that there are fewer of them within the city population that keeps city averages much lower.

It can also be misleading to measure each person's contribution to unsustainable levels of resource use and waste generation by the total waste volumes they generate in that it is their use of particular resources and generation of particular wastes that threaten ecological sustainability. If we focus on those consumer goods whose fabrication involved high levels of pollution (including for instance persistent organic pollutants) and on wastes that have worrying ecological implications (such as used batteries), the differentials between low- and high-income groups is likely to be even larger than just for waste volumes. The dates at which the price of nonrenewable resources will begin to rise rapidly, reflecting depletion of their stocks, may have been overstated in the various reports produced during the 1970s, but the finite nature of nonrenewable resource stocks is not in doubt. There may be sufficient nonrenewable resources to ensure that 9–10 billion people on earth, late in this century, have their needs met. But it is unlikely that the world's resource base could sustain a world population of 9 or 10 billion with a per capita consumption of nonrenewable resources similar to those enjoyed by the richest households today. However, one of the important shifts in our understanding of the ecological limits to growth since the 1970s has been that these center much more on the likely costs that will arise if greenhouse gas emissions are not controlled and on the depletion or degradation of resources that should be renewable (soils, forests, and freshwater) than from the depletion of the nonrenewable resource base.

URBAN CENTERS AND GLOBAL SYSTEMS

The disparities in greenhouse gas emissions per person between countries or cities in high-income and low-income countries are as striking as those outlined above in terms of nonrenewable resource use (to which many are obviously related). Per capita carbon dioxide emissions in 1996 in the United States were 200 to 500 times those in many low-income nations (37). Cities such as Canberra, Chicago, and Los Angeles have between 6 and 9 times the carbon dioxide emissions per person of the world's average and 25 or more times that of cities such as Dhaka (38). There is also the issue not only of who is currently contributing most to global warming but who historically contributed most. One estimate suggests that Western Europe and North America together have been responsible for 61 percent of all emissions since 1800, although they only contain 10 percent of the world's population (39). Before the international measures taken to control their use, the per capita disparities for the use of chlorofluorocarbons and halons (the main causes of stratospheric ozone depletion) were just as striking; figures for 1986 show that most high-income countries had around 100 times the use of many low-income nations (40). This discussion of the interaction between city-based production and consumption and resources and sinks from beyond the city boundaries is a reminder that the goal is not sustainable cities but cities that contribute to sustainable development goals—within their boundaries, in the region around them, and globally. A concentration on sustainable cities focuses too much on achieving ecological sustainability within increasingly isolated ecoregions or bioregions. Seeking sustainable cities implies that each city has to meet the resource needs of the population and enterprises located there from its immediate surrounds. But the goals of sustainable development are the meeting of human needs within all cities (and rural areas) with a level of resource use and waste generation within each region, the nation, and the planet that is compatible with ecological sustainability. It is unrealistic to demand that major cities should be supported by the resources produced in their immediate surrounds, but it is entirely appropriate to require that consumers and producers in high-consumption, high waste cities reduce their level of resource use and waste and reduce or halt the damaging ecological impacts of their demands for freshwater and other resources on their surrounds (41).

Although the discussions and recommendations about sustainable cities have much relevance to reducing the depletion of natural capital caused by production and consumption in cities in high-income nations, they concentrate too much on individual city performance. What is more important for sustainable development is the local, national, and international frameworks needed to ensure the achievement of sustainable development goals worldwide, including the appropriate frameworks for cities and smaller urban centers.

WHAT SUSTAINABLE DEVELOPMENT IMPLIES FOR URBAN AUTHORITIES

A commitment to sustainable development by city or municipal authorities means adding new goals to those that are their traditional concerns. Meeting development goals has long been among their main responsibilities. These generally include attracting new investment, better social conditions (and fewer social problems), ensuring basic services and adequate housing, and (more recently) better environmental standards within their jurisdiction. This does not imply that city and municipal authorities need be major providers of housing and basic services, but they can act as supervisors and/or supporters of private or community provision.

A concern for sustainable development retains these conventional concerns and adds two more. The first is a concern for the environmental impact of urban-based production and consumption on the needs of all people, not just those within their jurisdiction. The second is an understanding of the finite nature of many natural resources (or the ecosystems from which they are drawn) and of the capacities of natural systems in the wider regional, national, and international context to absorb or break down wastes. Historically, these have not been considered within the purview of city authorities. Indeed, many cities in high-income nations have only made considerable progress in achieving sustainable development goals within their own boundaries (i.e., reducing poverty, ensuring high quality living environments, protecting local ecosystems, and developing more representative and accountable government) by drawing heavily on the environmental capital of other regions or nations and on the waste absorption capacity of "the global commons" (31, 33). But in the long term, all cities will suffer if the aggregate impact of all cities' production and their inhabitants' consumption draws on global resources at unsustainable rates and deposits wastes in global sinks at levels that disrupt the functioning of ecosystems and global cycles. A large proportion of the world's urban population are particularly at risk from the growth in the number and intensity of extreme weather events that are likely to occur if greenhouse gas emissions are not controlled (42).

Adding a concern for ecological sustainability onto existing development concerns means setting limits on the rights of city enterprises or consumers to use scarce resources (wherever they come from) and to generate nonbiodegradable wastes. Such limits can be implemented through local authorities' guidelines and regulations in planning and regulating the built environment, e.g., building material production, construction, building design and performance, site and settlement planning, and efficiency standards for appliances and fixtures. Goals relating to local or global ecological sustainability can be incorporated into the norms, codes, and regulations that influence the built environment and its heating or cooling. But city authorities need national guidelines and often national encouragement. In most political systems, national governments have the primary role in developing guidelines and supporting innovation allied to regional or global conventions or guidelines where international agreement is reached on setting such limits.

But care is needed not to stifle local innovation with national standards. Urban authorities need a national policy with a supporting legislative, fiscal, and regulatory framework to help them add a concern for ecological sustainability into their policies, regulations, and investment patterns. It also remains the task of national government to consider the social and environmental impacts of macroeconomic and sectoral policies, which may contribute to the very problems their sustainable development policies are seeking to avoid. But urban authorities have the most critical role in actually implementing sustainability measures. Even in the absence of national policies, many city authorities have demonstrated their commitment to sustainable development, as in the many local authorities in the United States who have committed themselves to reducing greenhouse gas emissions within their boundaries, despite the U.S. government's opposition to a global convention that would require such reductions. Indeed, one of the most important roles for urban authorities in high-income nations and in the more prosperous cities in middle-income nations is promoting the necessary delinking of high standards of living/quality of life from high levels of resource use and waste generation. The different environmental emphases that can be given within any sustainable development policy is made clear by Haughton's unpacking of the different aspects of environmental equity. He suggests that we think of sustainable development as seeking to reconcile five different dimensions of environmental equity:

- Intragenerational equity (as measured by equity in access to basic services, such as water supply, sanitation, and primary health care, and in protection from environmental hazards, especially flooding, landslides, and high levels of air pollution);
- intergenerational equity (as measured by the extent to which there are effective policies to help conserve soils and forests, make efficient use of freshwater resources, reduce nonbiodegradable wastes, and keep down greenhouse gas emissions);
- geographical or trans-boundary equity (as measured by the extent to which environmental cost transfers from city-based production or consumption are avoided, such as in damage to local water bodies from liquid and solid wastes and control of air pollution that causes acid rain);
- procedural equity grounded in legal and political systems that treat all sections of the population equally (as measured by the extent to which different stakeholders benefit from public investments and policies and the extent to which they are involved in developing and implementing local environmental plans); and
- interspecies equity, as measured by the extent to which preserving ecosystem integrity and areas of particular importance for biodiversity are integrated into environmental plans (43).

Many proponents of sustainable development concentrate on only one or two of these aspects and may indeed promote actions that go against the other dimensions, as in forcing local populations off land they have long utilized (and may even own) to create wildlife reserves or green belts. However, while Figure 1 and the above checklist are useful for governments in developing policies to contribute toward sustainable development goals, experience to date suggests that the actual policies and the priorities must be developed locally, so they respond to local circumstances, including local opportunities and constraints. Given the diversity of cities and smaller urban centers in terms of their size and population growth rates and of their economic, social, political, cultural, and ecological underpinnings, it is difficult to consider urban policy and management for sustainable development in general terms. Priorities in a move toward sustainable development are going to differ greatly from city to city. For cities (or urban systems) with high levels of nonrenewable resource use, the main need is to reduce fossil fuel use and waste generation (through reducing waste levels and through more recycling) while maintaining a productive, stable, and innovative economy and a better record in ensuring benefits for lower-income or otherwise disadvantaged groups. Some clues as to how this can be achieved might be found in the cities that currently have among the world's best living standards but a relatively small draw on environmental capital, and this is not simply the result of a less energy intensive economic base. For instance, cities, such as Copenhagen and Amsterdam, have one third of the carbon dioxide emissions per person from transport of Detroit and Houston, yet many would consider Copenhagen and Amsterdam to have a superior quality of life (36). There is also the growing body of evidence that increasing prosperity need not imply increased resource use and waste; indeed, prosperity can increase while resource use and waste generation are cut (44).

For cities or smaller urban centers with low levels of nonrenewable resource use and waste generation (which usually implies a relatively low-income city), the priority is meeting development needs, but there are precedents to show that this is not incompatible with policies and practices that ensure the efficient use of natural capital. For example, some urban governments' responses to the action plan of the U.N. Conference on Environment and Development in 1992 (Agenda 21) were remarkable, especially in light of the relatively modest sums national governments and international development agencies devoted to these Local Agenda 21s. Some of the most successful Local Agenda 21s have been in Latin America, and in particular in those urban centers where a combination of democratization, decentralization, and growing environmental awareness was already spurring socially-concerned environmental movements (6, 45–47). By combining environmental awareness with good local governance, it is clearly possible to reconcile development and environmental imperatives.

If low- and middle-income nations are able to develop more stable and prosperous economies, they make increased use of nonrenewable resources, and their greenhouse gas emissions per capita are also likely to increase. The extent of this growth in the use of natural capital depends not only on the level of wealth created and its distribution but also on the extent to which provisions are made, now and in the immediate future, to promote efficient resource use and waste minimization.

For example, in rapidly growing cities, measures to encourage fuel-efficient buildings and land use patterns that respond to citizens' priorities for easy access to employment and services within fuel-efficient transport systems can, over time, bring increasingly large savings in the use of fossil fuels (and thus also in the emissions of greenhouse gases) relative to wealth. Curitiba in Brazil is now applauded for its innovative and widely used public transport systems, but the innovations that led to this were put in place nearly 40 years ago (48). Major cities in the western United States, including Los Angeles, have continued to grow over the past several decades, but their total water use has leveled off or even declined as overall water-use efficiency and productivity has improved (49).

BUILDING SYNERGIES, AVOIDING CONFLICTS

When city governments consider how to apply a sustainable development framework to their operations and their urban policies and projects (or national governments and international agencies seek to support them in doing so), there are obvious tensions between different goals within the two boxes in Figure 1 and also between the five different equity goals noted above. Most center on the extent to which projects or investments justified for their contribution to expanding production (which in turn is meant to increase incomes and help meet human needs) contribute to the depletion of one or more aspects of natural capital; for instance, fossil-fueled power stations or much expanded highway systems that will increase motor-vehicle use and therefore increase greenhouse gas emissions. Within environmental policies, there are obvious conflicts between what is often termed "the brown agenda," which concentrates on environmental health, and "the green agenda," which concentrates on the contribution of urban-based production, consumption, and waste generation to ecosystem disruption, resource depletion, and global climate change (50). There are also rural versus urban conflicts as in, for instance, large hydroelectric dams whose construction involves flooding large areas of agricultural land and forest with most of the electricity destined for urban enterprises or consumers. Expanding urban areas inevitably draw more on the resources of their wider regions; increasingly prosperous urban areas almost inevitably draw more heavily on nonrenewable resources and create more wastes.

In part, it is only when the different goals are pursued independently that there are serious conflicts. If pursued in tandem, important complementaries can be found between safer, healthier city environments and reduced depletion of natural capital. Such complementarities include:

1. Systems for the management of liquid and solid wastes that reduce environmental hazards for city dwellers and also reduce nonrenewable resource use (through promoting waste minimization, reuse, and recycling) and reduce the ecological damage that previously arose from polluted surface runoff.

2. Improvements to public transport that better meet the transport needs of most citizens (especially lower-income groups), reduce physical hazards

(road accidents are often among the main causes of premature death and serious injury for adults), and keep down air pollution and greenhouse gas emissions.

There are often more complementarities between contrasting agendas than might initially appear evident. For instance, the priority of those espousing the brown agenda to expand the number of households connected to piped water systems (which implies increased household consumption for those who previously relied on public standpipes or vendors) seems to conflict with those espousing a green agenda who want to keep down the use of freshwater (to avoid depleting groundwater reserves or drawing water from more distant watersheds) and who recommend increasing water prices to encourage conservation. But both agendas can be served by better water management. Support for improving water-use efficiency and better maintenance of piped water systems can often free up sufficient new water supplies for ecosystem restoration or new users, and extending the piped water systems can help ensure that this new water can be accessed by those who need it most. In addition, the cost of extending water supplies can in part be met by charging the enterprises and households who are connected to the system more realistic prices, with tariff structures that discourage high consumption levels while ensuring that poorer populations can afford water for basic needs (7, 51). Although there will still be trade-offs—for instance, the cheapest or most robust buses may not be the best performers in terms of polluting emissions and fuel use, decisions made within an awareness of such trade-offs and with procedural equity should considerably reduce the conflicts between ecological sustainability and development.

One of the more controversial aspects is in regard to the choice of systems to improve sanitation, but health and ecological concerns can be combined. For those whose primary concern is public health, water-borne sewers are often seen as the best sanitation system for large and dense cities. When well managed, they provide a very safe and convenient way by which households can dispose of their human wastes. From an environmental health perspective, they are very effective because the diseases caused by human excreta and inadequate waste-water management are among the world's main causes of infant and child death and illness (18). Although water-borne sewers are considered to be expensive solutions for the poor, there are also examples, such as the Orangi Project in Pakistan, where costs were kept down to the point where little or no subsidy was needed in providing low-income households with sewers (52). But from an ecological perspective, city sewer systems generally require high levels of freshwater use and by collecting all the wastes within a single system, they can present serious problems in regard to what can be done with the large volume of sewage. Sewage can be treated, but for low- and middle-income nations, going beyond primary treatment is expensive if centralized mechanical systems are used. Disposing of sewage sludge is also a problem, especially for large sewer systems. However, potential conflicts can be minimized if decisions about which sanitation system best addresses the needs and resources of the inhabitants of a city or settlement are made within an awareness of both the human and ecological consequences. There are many sewer systems and water-flushed toilets in operation that minimize the volume of water needed. There are also systems in which treatment is decentralized, and the ecological impacts of the whole sewer and drainage system are much reduced. There are examples of "sewage farming" and sewage-fed aquaculture, which make use of the nutrients in sewage and act as treatment, although care must be taken to minimize health risks for those working in these activities and to ensure no health risk to those who consume the products of sewage farming. It is important that the full range of potential solutions to sanitation problems in any city or city district are considered, but with the needs and priorities of those whose sanitation is most in need of improvement should also have a central role. In pursuing sanitation systems with less ecological impact, there is a danger of promoting systems that bring inconvenience, higher maintenance costs, and greater environmental risks to the users—or of simply producing latrines that the population does not use (7).

ENABLING LOCAL ACTION WHILE MEETING NATIONAL AND GLOBAL GOALS

As noted earlier, the literature on sustainable development often concentrates too much on national policies and national strategies but gives too little attention to the changes needed in each locality and in the role of local governments. Is it possible to reconcile a concern for global sustainability with the need for development determined within democratic local structures? There is an obvious need for international agreements to set limits for each national society's consumption of resources and use of the global sink for their wastes. But many of the actions to achieve this depend on actions taken locally—by households, businesses, and local governments. The interaction of each city with local and regional ecosystems is unique, which implies the need for optimal use of local resources, knowledge, and skills. This demands a considerable degree of local self-determination, because centralized decision-making structures have great difficulty in developing policies that respond appropriately to such diversity.

Much of what has been discussed above stresses the concept of central government as an enabler, developing the laws, institutions, and policies that support and encourage individuals, households, communities, enterprises, and local governments to undertake economic, social, and environmental activities, which contribute to sustainable development. The discussion of government as an enabler has a long history. Within the evolution of development theory, it is perhaps through discussions of appropriate housing policies that the importance of an enabling policy has been stressed, and its form made most explicit. The origins of the idea that government actions in regard to housing should concentrate on enabling and supporting the efforts of citizens and their community organizations to develop their own housing goes back at least to the 1950s and perhaps earlier (53, 54). The concept of enablement has also spread to many other sectors; for instance, in the organization of agricultural extension services (with the shift to participatory learning and action) and in the construction, organization, and management of many forms of infrastructure and services at the community or neighborhood level (e.g., for health care services, water supplies, and provision for sanitation). However, it is also often appropriate to set national standards. In the United States, a national standard for water use by toilets was set at 1.6 gallons per flush, and this took the decision about water use in toilets out of the hands of individual manufacturers and local and state governments.

The concept of enablement is based on the understanding that most human investments, activities and choices that influence the achievement of development goals and sustainability goals take place outside government. Most are beyond the control of governments (or at least of democratic governments) even where governments seek some control. In cities in Africa and much of Asia and Latin America, the point is particularly valid because most homes, neighborhoods, jobs, and incomes are created outside of government and often in contravention of official rules and regulations (6, 19). There is the long-established understanding that inappropriate government controls and regulations discourage and distort the scale and vitality of individual, family, and community investments and activities. But there is also recognition that without scrupulously enforced controls and regulations, individuals, communities, and enterprises can impose their externalities on others. The wave of environmental health centered reforms of city and municipal governments in Europe and North America in the late nineteenth and early twentieth centuries developed systems of urban governance to ensure better provision in the supply of water and the disposal of liquid and solid wastes. Similar reforms were also evident in many Latin American countries. Environmental legislation in the second half of the twentieth century has centered on government control of air, water pollution, and solid waste generation and disposal that imposed costs on urban citizens and on the citizens and ecosystems beyond the city boundaries. In each instance, central government had to provide the framework for action, and it was generally city and municipal governments that had to act; successful government enablement is always a careful balance between encouragement and control.

The need for governments to seek a balance between encouragement and control has received considerable support from the growing recognition that democratic and participatory government structures are not only important goals of development but also important means for achieving development goals. Participation and enablement are inseparable since popular priorities and demands should be a major influence on the development of enabling policies, while these policies in turn should provide plenty of scope for locally-determined solutions. The concept of government policies and institutions as rooted in enablement has a much wider relevance because it is important to the promotion of greater ecological sustainability as well as development. It would be politically unacceptable in most societies for governments to substantially restrict individual consumption levels, but sustainable development worldwide is impossible without national frameworks that promote substantially lower levels of demand by wealthy households on the world's natural capital.

IMPLEMENTING SUSTAINABLE DEVELOPMENT IN CITIES

The regulations and incentives needed to support the achievement of development goals, within a framework that promotes local and global ecological sustainability, is relatively easy to conceive as an abstract exercise. The poverty suffered by the minority of urban dwellers in richer nations and the majority in poorer nations can be drastically reduced without a large expansion in resource use (and waste generation). The economic and ecological costs of providing safe and sufficient water supplies, provision for sanitation, garbage removal, and health care and ensuring safe, secure shelters are often overstated. The quality of life of wealthy (generally high-consumption) individuals and households need not diminish and in certain aspects may indeed improve within a long-term program to cut their draw on the world's natural capital (44).

But translating this into reality within nations and globally is another issue. Powerful vested interests oppose most of the needed policies and priorities. For instance, reducing the resource use and greenhouse gas emissions of middle- and upper-income groups implies less profits for many companies and their politically influential coalitions, and the fact that it may also mean more profits for as yet unformed coalitions is largely irrelevant politically. Economic vested interests are particularly strong in the richest nations, but it is in these nations where changes are also most needed, for at least three reasons:

1. These are the nations with the highest current and historic contributions to greenhouse gases.
2. These nations have no moral basis for demanding more resource conserving (less greenhouse gas emitting) patterns of development among lower income nations unless they (and their wealthiest citizens) set an example of how to combine high quality lives with much lower resource use and waste generation.
3. Low-income nations that need to develop a stronger and more prosperous economic base will generally need to increase their greenhouse gas emissions, and only by reducing emissions per person in the richer nations can this be possible, within a commitment to restrict global greenhouse gas emissions.

Large cuts in greenhouse gas emissions within the richest countries will bring higher costs, especially to those who currently consume most. Technological change can help limit the rise in costs. Examples include moderating the impact of rising gasoline prices through the relatively rapid introduction of increasingly fuel-efficient automobiles and moderating the impact of higher electricity prices (especially where these are generated by fossil-fueled power stations) through more efficient electrical appliances and better designed and managed buildings that restrict the need for space heating or cooling. Many industries can also limit the impact of higher fossil fuel prices or water scarcity by increasing the efficiency with which fuel or water is used. In addition, a steady increase in the price of resources increases the economic incentives to replace them with renewable sources or improvements in efficiency (and technological change helps reduce the cost of tapping alternative resources). The scope for using renewable energy resources for space heating and cooling is also much increased in energy-efficient buildings. But if combating atmospheric warming does demand a rapid reduction in greenhouse gas emissions in high-income nations, this may require limitations in middle- and upper-income groups' right to use inefficient private automobiles, have unlimited air travel, and use inefficient space heating or cooling, which cannot be met by new technologies and alternative (renewable) fuels—at least at costs which will prove politically possible. In addition, so many existing commercial, industrial, and residential buildings and urban forms (for instance low density suburban developments and out-of-town shopping malls) have high levels of energy use built into them, and these are not easily or rapidly changed.

At the same time, in Africa, Asia, and Latin America, the achievement of development goals that minimize the call on local and global natural capital demands a competence and capacity to act by city and municipal government that is currently rarely present. There is a widely shared recognition that too little attention has been paid by most governments in low-income nations and by most international agencies to developing the competence, capacity, and accountability of urban governments (5, 6). As noted by Stren, one of the most experienced specialists on issues of urban governance, in a review of African cities: "ultimately, solutions to problems of urban finance, housing, public transport, the siting and standards of urban infrastructure, public health and public cleansing services, water, electricity and numerous other urban amenities must be formulated locally, by local people, on the basis of local experience and information" (55). It is difficult to see much success in the achievement of both the development and the ecological sustainability components of sustainable development in urban areas in low- and middle-income nations without more competent, effective, accountable local governments. Local governments cannot take on these roles without a stronger financial base, the support of national government, and an appropriate legislative, regulatory, and incentive structure (5, 6). There is also the need for mechanisms to allow resource transfers between local governments otherwise only local governments in more prosperous areas will have the resources to address development and sustainability goals.

There is also a recognition that the capacity of local government to work in partnership with community organizations, nongovernment organizations, nonprofit foundations, and private sector enterprises is central to the achievement of development goals, and this is especially true when economic circumstances limit the investment capacity of local government. This stress on the importance of such partnerships is evident in Agenda 21 that came out of the U.N. Earth Summit in 1992 and also in the recommendations that came out of the 2002 U.N. Summit on Sustainable Development. A stress on enablement at local level is to provide the support and advice that will encourage community initiatives and multiply many-fold the number that start and succeed. Such policy directions imply the need for new kinds of enabling institutions widely distributed within each nation to provide funding and technical advice (56).

THE GLOBAL CONTEXT FOR SUSTAINABILITY AND DEVELOPMENT

Citizen pressure has often helped persuade city and municipal governments to pursue more sustainable patterns of resource use and waste minimization, where the ecological impacts are local, regional, or (on occasion) national. This can be seen in the environmental movements and in the role taken by environmental issues in election campaigns. But most of these have been driven by citizen concern for their own health or quality of life. As Haughton points out, nearly everyone is an environmentalist in the sense of wanting a good environment for themselves. But so much environmental pressure is by groups with power wanting to protect or improve their environment at the expense of others (43). Examples include:

1. Parks and nature reserves that serve to prevent low-income groups from accessing land on which to develop their own homes,
2. Middle class pressure that ensures dirty industries or facilities are located in low-income areas, and
3. Cities that export their environmental problems.

There is less citizen pressure on city and municipal governments for changes in production and consumption patterns that have their most serious ecological impacts overseas or on global cycles. Yet the achievement of sustainable development depends on city residents, businesses, and governments reducing the ecological damage to which they contribute far beyond the city boundaries and reducing greenhouse gas emissions. There are some important signs of change. One example is termed "green consumerism" in which consumers choose goods whose fabrication or use has less damaging environmental consequences; this is supported by ecolabeling and has put pressure on many manufacturers to address the environmental implications of their products' fabrication, use, and disposal. In the European Ecolabel scheme set up by the European Union, which operates in 18 nations, enterprises can use the label on their products if they have below average environmental impacts on the basis of life cycle assessments, and in each nation, a national body is responsible for administering the program (57). The International Standards Organization (ISO) also seeks to promote better working practices, environmental management, and product standards through the various

ISO standards awarded to products. The "fair-trade" campaigns and the sale of fair-trade goods have helped to raise issues such as the wages and/or working conditions of those who make the goods and the prices they are paid. Many European nations have fair-trade labeling organizations, and by 2002, 350 fair-trade certified producer groups in 36 nations were selling to importers and retailers in 17 nations (58). In the United Kingdom, the retail value of fair-trade products reached more than US$65 million in 2001, some 16 times more than in 1994 (58). Human rights campaigns and environmental groups have put pressure on large producers and retailers to take what is usually termed "ethical sourcing" more seriously by avoiding the use of goods produced in countries, or by companies, with poor human rights, labor, and environmental records. Many companies' unethical investments, products, or poor environmental performance have been exposed by campaigns to promote consumer boycotts of their products (for instance, to boycott the products of Nestle because of their promotion of alternatives to breast milk in countries where this often increases health risks for babies) or by environmental or human rights campaigners who purchase some shares and bring pressure on the company at shareholder meetings. There are examples of companies (including multinational corporations) that have made explicit commitments to improve environmental performance or to provide better wages and working conditions for their workforce or for those working for major subcontractors. Gap Incorporated reports that it has developed a code for the companies from which it purchases goods that spells out its expectations regarding wages, child labor, health, and safety issues and respecting the rights of the workers, and it has a Global Compliance department to monitor suppliers' performance (59). There are even some companies that allow independent audits to check on their claims. Governments in most high-income nations have encouraged or supported ecolabeling and the control of certain imports for ethical or environmental reasons. All these have importance because they show ways of lessening the human and environmental costs of production in distant elsewheres.

But the extent to which this can become sufficiently effective on a global scale is in doubt. Labeling schemes implemented or checked by independent third parties can have beneficial impacts and can influence a proportion of the market, but they are unlikely to influence enough of it to make the needed difference. Up to a point, the demand for products with lower human and environmental costs can be met by reshuffling the existing product mix, which increases the average human and environmental cost of unlabeled products. The perception that this is happening (whether or not it actually is) can further undermine the demand for ecolabeled products.

Then there are the vast imbalances in power between multinational companies with their chains of production, distribution, sale, and promotion and the citizen groups that raise these issues. The people who are currently affected most by the international transfer of environmental costs, i.e., the workforce exposed to dangerous or oppressive working conditions and the inhabitants suffering from high air pollution levels and other environmental impacts, often have little political influence in the countries where they live and none at all on the governments of the nations to which the goods they helped produce are exported.

Individually, they are often free to choose between dangerous working conditions and even lower incomes (if they give up their jobs), but even collectively they have little influence over how and to what extent their employers can be held responsible for improving their working conditions. Individually, they are often free to choose between unhealthy living environments and an even higher cost of living (implying lower consumption), but they rarely have the opportunity to promote the sort of changes that might help them and their neighbors avoid such predicaments. They often face difficulties within their own nations because they risk losing their livelihood if they are part of any protest against low wages, working conditions, or environmental abuses. It is perhaps difficult for those of us living in high-income countries to appreciate this, but it is often politically dangerous to protest. Two of the Peruvians who helped launch the campaign against pollution in Chimbote (Peru) and helped develop the city's Local Agenda 21 were imprisoned for 13 months and falsely accused of being terrorists; it was only after a strong national and international campaign that they were released (60). Meanwhile, national and city governments desperate to attract new investment and to boost exports so often do not support citizens' environmental concerns. And if the key needs and priorities of so much of the present generation cannot be protected from international production and trading systems, how much less are the needs and priorities of future generations likely to be protected?

There is some international action to prevent the most obvious and blatant international transfers of environmental costs, such as in the controls on the export of hazardous wastes, and on the trade in endangered species or products derived from them. But the interests of many of the world's most powerful companies and corporations would be threatened if action extended to address all such transfers—for instance, if governments in Europe and North America only permitted imports from countries where good standards of occupational health and safety are maintained. Another control might permit the import of goods produced by multinational companies only if the company and its main subcontractors met agreed standards for good environmental practices in the use of resources and the generation and management of wastes in all its operations in different countries and allowed independent groups to monitor their performance. Moreover, even if such standards were agreed upon, there is the danger that those affected by the environmental transfers would not be effectively represented in their negotiation, and the resulting agreements might do them more harm than good by undermining rather than enhancing their local negotiating positions.

In conclusion, two international issues can be highlighted as central to the achievement of sustainable development goals. The first is whether it is politically possible to combine the pursuit of increased wealth and development by national societies (most of whose members have strong preferences for minimal constraints on their consumption levels) with a respect for the ecological and material limits of the biosphere. To realize this possibility, international and national policies and agreements are needed to ensure that the needs of future generations, as well those of the present, are considered. The second is whether the international development system can become far more effective at ensuring people's needs are met (and building local capacities to ensure they are met), especially in low-income nations. Both require more competent, effective city and municipal governments. It is time the debates about sustainable development (and sustainable cities) gave more attention to this.

The *Annual Review of Environment and Resources* is online at
http://environ.annualreviews.org

LITERATURE CITED

1. Rees WE. 1995. Achieving sustainability: reform or transformation? *J. Plan. Lit.* 9(4):343–61
2. Satterthwaite D. 2002. *Coping With Rapid Urban Growth*. London: R. Inst. Chart. Surv. 35 pp.
3. UN Popul. Div. 2002. *World Urbanization Prospects: The 2001 Revision*. New York: UN Dep. Econ. Soc. Aff., ST/ESA/SER.A/216. 321 pp.
4. Graumann JV. 1977. Orders of magnitude of the world's urban and rural population in history. *UN Popul. Bull.* 8:16–33
5. UN Cent. Hum. Settl. (Habitat). 1996. *An Urbanizing World: Global Report on Human Settlements, 1996*. Oxford: Oxford Univ. Press. 559 pp.
6. Hardoy JE, Mitlin D, Satterthwaite D. 2001. *Environmental Problems in an Urbanizing World: Finding Solutions for Cities in Africa, Asia and Latin America*. London: Earthscan. 470 pp.
7. UN Habitat. 2003. *Water and Sanitation in the World's Cities*. London: Earthscan. 274 pp.
8. Garza G. 2002. *Urbanisation of Mexico during the twentieth century*. Urban Change Work. Pap. 7, Int. Inst. Environ. Dev., London
9. UN Popul. Div. 1975. *Trends and Prospects in the Population of Urban Agglomerations as assessed in 1973–75*. ESA/P/WP.58 New York: UN Dep. Int. Econ. Soc. Aff.
10. Brown L. 1974. *In the Human Interest*. New York: Norton
11. Potts D. 2001 . *Urban growth and urban economies in eastern and southern Africa: an overview*. Presented at Workshop Afr. Urban Econ.: Viability Vitality Vitiation Major Cities East South. Afr., Nov. Neth.
12. Sassen S. 2002. Locating cities on global circuits. *Environ. Urban.* 14(1):13–30
13. World Bank. 2003. *Global Development Finance 2003*. Table A 19, Stat. Annex, p. 198. Washington, DC: World Bank
14. World Comm. Environ. Dev. 1987. *Our Common Future*. Oxford: Oxford Univ. Press. 383 pp.
15. Newman P. 1996. Reducing automobile dependence *Environ. Urban.* 8(1):67–92
16. World Health Organ. 1999. Creating healthy cities in the 21st century. Chapter 6. In *The Earthscan Reader on Sustainable Cities*, ed. D Satterthwaite, pp. 137–72. London: Earthscan
17. Wratten E. 1995. Conceptualizing urban poverty. *Environ. Urban.* 7(1):11–36
18. World Health Organ. 1992. *Our planet our health*. Rep. Comm. Health Environ. Geneva 282 pp.
19. Hardoy JE, Satterthwaite D. 1989. *Squatter Citizen: Life in the Urban Third World*. London: Earthscan. 388 pp.
20. Satterthwaite D, Taneja B. 2003. *Agriculture and urban development*. Presented at World Bank, Washington, DC, 28 pp.

http://www.worldbank.org/urban/urbanruralseminar/

21. Hardoy JE, Satterthwaite D. 1988. Small and intermediate urban centres in the Third World; what role for government? *Third World Plan. Rev.* 10(1):5–26

22. Tacoli T. 1998. Bridging the divide: rural-urban interactions and livelihood strategies. Gatekeeper Ser. 77. Int. Inst. Environ. Dev., Sustain. Agric. Rural Livelihoods Programme, London. 17 pp.

23. Eaton D, Hilhorst T. 2003. Opportunities for managing solid waste flows in the peri-urban interface of Bamako and Ouagadougou. *Environ. Urban.* 15(1):53–64

24. Smit J, Ratta A, Nasr J. 1996. *Urban Agriculture: Food Jobs and Sustainable Cities.* Publ. Ser. Habitat II, Vol. 1. New York: UN Dev. Programme. 302 pp.

25. Mayers J, Bass S. 1999. *Policy That Works for Forests and People.* London: Int. Inst. Environ. Dev. 324 pp.

26. Rietbergen S. 1989. Africa. In *No Timber Without Trees*, ed. D Poore, pp. 40–73. London: Earthscan

27. Bhatt CP. 1990. The Chipko Andolan: forest conservation based on people's power. *Environ. Urban.* 2(1):7–18

28. Leach G, Mearns R. 1989. *Beyond the Woodfuel Crisis: People, Land and Trees in Africa.* London: Earthscan. 309 pp.

29. White R. 1992. The international transfer of urban technology: Does the North have anything to offer for the global environmental crisis? *Environ. Urban.* 4(2):109–20

30. Connolly P. 1999. Mexico City: our common future? *Environ. Urban.* 11(1):53–78

31. Rees WE. 1992. Ecological footprints and appropriated carrying capacity: what urban economics leaves out. *Environ. Urban.* 4(2):121–30

32. Wackernagel M, Rees WE. 1995. *Our Ecological Footprint: Reducing Human Impact on the Earth.* Gabriola Isl., Can.: New Society. 176 pp.

33. McGranahan G, Jacobi P, Songsore J, Surjadi C, Kjellén M. 2001. *Citizens at Risk: From Urban Sanitation to Sustainable Cities.* London: Earthscan

34. Jopling J, Girardet H. 1996. *Creating a Sustainable London.* London: Sustain. London Trust. 45 pp.

35. World Bank. 1999. *Entering the 21st Century: World Development Report 1999/2000.* Oxford/New York: Oxford Univ. Press. 300 pp.

36. Newman P, Kenworthy J. 1999. *Sustainability and Cities: Overcoming Automobile Dependence.* Washington, DC: Island. 442 pp.

37. World Resourc. Inst. 2000. *World Resources 2000–2001: People and Ecosystems: the Fraying Web of Life.* Table AC.1. Washington, DC: World Resourc. Inst.

38. Nishioka S, Noriguchi Y, Yamamura S. 1990. Megalopolis and climate change: the case of Tokyo. In *Cities and Global Climate Change*, ed. J McCulloch, pp. 108–33. Washington, DC: Clim. Inst.

39. Agarwal A, Narain S, Sen S, eds. 1999. *State of India's Environment: The Citizens' Fifth Report.* New Delhi: Cent. Sci. Environ. 300 pp.

40. UN Environ. Programme. 1991. *Environmental Data Report, 1991–2*, GEMS Monit. Assess. Res. Cent. Oxford: Blackwell. 408 pp.

41. Satterthwaite D. 1997. Sustainable cities or cities that contribute to sustainable development. *Urban Stud.* 34(10):1667–91

42. Scott M, Gupta S, Jáuregui E, Nwafor J, Satterthwaite D, et al. 2001. Human settlements, energy and industry. In *Climate Change 2001; Impacts, Adaptation, and Vulnerability*, ed. JJ McCarthy, OF Canziani, NA Leary, DJ Dokken, KS White, pp. 381–416. Cambridge: Cambridge Univ. Press

43. Haughton G. 1998. Environmental justice and the sustainable city. *J. Plan. Edu. Res.* 18(3):233–43

44. Von Weizsäcker E, Lovins AB, Lovins LH. 1997. *Factor Four: Doubling Wealth,*

Halving Resource Use. London: Earthscan. 322 pp.
45. Velasquez LS. 1998. Agenda 21; a form of joint environmental management in Manizales, Colombia. *Environ. Urban.* 10(2):9–36
46. Miranda L, Hordijk M. 1998. Let us build cities for life: the national campaign of local Agenda 21s in Peru. *Environ. Urban.* 10(2):69–102
47. Menegat R. 2002. Participatory democracy and sustainable development: integrated urban environmental management in Porto Alegre, Brazil. *Environ. Urban.* 14(2):181–206
48. Rabinovitch J. 1992. Curitiba: towards sustainable urban development. *Environ. Urban.* 4(2):62–77
49. Gleick PH. 2003. Water use. *Annu. Rev. Environ. Resour.* 28:275–314
50. McGranahan G, Satterthwaite D. 2000. Environmental health or ecological sustainability? Reconciling the brown and green agendas in urban development. In *Sustainable Cities in Developing Countries*, ed. Cedric Pugh, pp. 73–90. London: Earthscan
51. McGranahan G. 2002. *Demand-Side Water Strategies and the Urban Poor.* PIE Ser. 4 London: Int. Inst. Environ. Dev. 67 pp.
52. Hasan A. 1997. *Working with Government: The Story of the Orangi Pilot Project's Collaboration with State Agencies for Replicating its Low Cost Sanitation Programme.* Karachi: City Press. 269 pp.
53. Mangin W. 1967. Latin American squatter settlements; a problem and a solution. *Latin Am. Res. Rev.* 2(3):65–98
54. Turner JFC. 1969. Uncontrolled urban settlements: problems and policies. In *The City in Newly Developed Countries*, ed. G Breese, pp. 507–34. New Jersey: Prentice Hall
55. Stren RE. 1989. Administration of urban services. In *African Cities in Crisis*, ed. RE Stren, RR White, pp. 37–67. Boulder: Westview
56. Satterthwaite D. 2001. Reducing urban poverty: constraints on the effectiveness of aid agencies and development banks and some suggestions for change. *Environ. Urban.* 13(1):137–57
57. Dep. Environ. Food Rural Aff. 2003. *Consumer Products: The European Ecolabel.* http://www.defra.gov.uk/environment/consumerprod/ecolabel/
58. Fairtrade Found. 2003. *Why Fairtrade?* http://www.fairtrade.org.uk
59. Gap Inc. 2003. *Beyond the Label: Gap Inc.'s Commitment to Ethical Sourcing.* http://www.gapinc.com/social_resp/sourcing_body.shtm
60. Foronda ME. 1998. Chimbote's Local Agenda 21: initiatives to support its development and implementation. *Environ. Urban.* 10(2):129–47

WATER USE

Peter H. Gleick
Pacific Institute, 654 13th Street, Oakland, California 94612;
email: pgleick@pipeline.com

Key Words water consumption, withdrawal, scenarios, freshwater, conservation, water-use efficiency, water productivity

■ **Abstract** Water managers and planners are slowly beginning to change their perspective and perceptions about how best to meet human needs for water; they are shifting from a focus on building supply infrastructure to improving their understanding of how water is used and how those uses can best be met. This review discusses definitions of water use, explores the history of water use around the world and in characteristic regions, identifies problems with collecting and analyzing water data, and addresses the question of improving water-use efficiency and productivity in different regions and economic sectors. There is growing interest on the part of water managers around the world to implement these approaches to lessen pressures on increasingly scarce water resources, reduce the adverse ecological effects of human withdrawals of water, and improve long-term sustainable water use.

CONTENTS

INTRODUCTION	276
Needs Versus Wants for Water	277
Definitions of Water Use, Conservation, and Efficiency	278
HOW IS WATER USED?	280
Data Problems	281
ESTIMATES OF CURRENT WATER USE	282
Global Water Use	282
Regional Water Use: National Water-Use Estimates	284
Experience from the United States	290
FORECASTING WATER USE	292
THE CONNECTION BETWEEN WATER USE AND HUMAN WELL-BEING	296
CHANGING WATER-USE PATTERNS: THE POTENTIAL FOR IMPROVING WATER-USE EFFICIENCY	298
Cost-Effectiveness of Efficiency Improvements	303
Urban Improvements: The Example of California	309
CONCLUSIONS	310

INTRODUCTION

The history of human civilization is entangled with the history of the ways humans have learned to manipulate and use fresh water. The earliest agricultural communities depended on the vagaries of natural rainfall and runoff. Engineering advances came with simple dams and irrigation canals that permitted greater crop production and longer growing seasons. The expansion of urban areas eventually required the development of sophisticated piping and aqueducts, to bring water to users, and of innovative systems to remove wastes, some of which were put in place thousands of years ago (1, 2).

During the industrial revolution and population explosion of the nineteenth and twentieth centuries, the demand for water rose dramatically. Unprecedented construction of tens of thousands of monumental engineering projects designed to control floods, protect clean water supplies, and provide water for irrigation or hydropower brought great benefits to hundreds of millions of people. Thanks to improved sewer systems, water-related diseases such as cholera and typhoid, once endemic throughout the world, have largely been conquered in the more industrialized nations. Huge cities survive on water brought from hundreds and even thousands of kilometers away. Food production to meet the needs of more than six billion people is now largely dependent on artificial irrigation systems. Nearly one fifth of all of the electricity generated worldwide is produced by hydroelectric turbines. Even today, $30 to $40 billion are spent annually on new dams (3).

A wide variety of forces, however, are driving a shift away from the construction of new water infrastructure. Most important is the improved understanding of the true economic, social, and environmental costs of that infrastructure. As a result, water planners and managers are on the verge of a fundamental change in thinking about water—a change from a focus on new construction to a focus on evaluating how best to meet human needs and desires. New water facilities are still needed in many parts of the world, and the existing infrastructure must be maintained in order to keep the flow of benefits coming. But those responsible for water are now beginning to pay far more attention to the other side of the equation—how society uses water.

Most water planners throughout the world are not trained to think about water use in a systematic way. Definitions are used inconsistently and incorrectly. Forecasts of water use are made with inappropriate and irregular assumptions. And both water experts and policy makers often misunderstand the role of water use in water policy. New approaches to water planning and management are beginning to address issues of use directly, which lead to changes in management and to improvements in long-term sustainable water use. This review discusses definitions of water use, explores the history of water use around the world and in characteristic regions, identifies problems with collecting and analyzing water data, and addresses the question of improving the efficiency and productivity of water use in different regions and economic sectors.

Needs Versus Wants for Water

A shift in emphasis is underway away from evaluating broad demands for water to a better understanding of water needs and uses. Discussion of the differences between needs and wants has recently appeared in the resource literature (4). People need only basic amounts of water for drinking, cooking, cleaning, and hygiene to maintain human well-being (5). Rather, people seek water for goods and services, such as the production of food and industrial items, transportation, communications, and the elimination of wastes. In addition, people want goods and services beyond their basic needs; some of the wanted items are recreation, leisure, and luxury goods. Providing these needs and wants can be accomplished in many ways, which depend on technology, prices, cultural traditions, and other factors, often with radically different implications for water.

Traditional approaches to meeting water needs have focused on how to design, fund, and build water-supply systems; these range from dams and aqueducts to water treatment and distribution facilities. Water-supply systems have brought great benefits to water users by improving the reliability of supply, reducing water-related diseases associated with poor water quality, and buffering the impacts of extreme hydrologic events such as floods and droughts. They have also brought great costs, which include ecological and environmental degradation, social disruption associated with infrastructure construction, and economic problems.

An alternative approach, dubbed the "soft" path, also relies on centralized infrastructure but complements it with investment in decentralized facilities, efficient technologies, and human capital (6–8). It strives to improve the overall productivity of water use rather than seek endless sources of new supply. It delivers diverse water services matched to the users' needs and works with water users at local and community scales.

A good example of the difference between needs and wants can be seen in approaches for disposing of human wastes. Waste disposal does not require any water, although using some amount of water for this purpose may be appropriate or culturally preferred. In many parts of the world, human wastes are disposed of safely without any water at all (except for modest amounts for hygiene and washing). In industrial nations, however, we have grown accustomed to flush toilets. Indeed, toilet flushing is usually the largest indoor residential use of water in richer nations. Yet even here, substantial improvements in technology in the past two decades have led to a 75% decrease in water used by toilets in the United States, and even greater improvements are achieved in toilets used widely in Australia, Japan, and Europe. All toilets manufactured in Australia are now dual-flush systems using either six liters or three liters per flush (9).

Many traditional approaches can also be used to manage human wastes without any water, and new technology can do this even in wealthier countries accustomed to traditional flush systems. At the high end, electrically mixed, heated, and ventilated composting toilets, which have no odors or insect problems, are available (10). These devices safely and effectively biodegrade human wastes into water, carbon dioxide, and a soil-like residue that can be used as compost. Although they can use substantial amounts of electricity, they can displace an equal or greater amount of electricity currently used to deliver water and treat wastewater.

Similarly, farmers do not want to use water, per se; they want to grow crops profitably and sustainably. Manufacturers are not interested in using water but in producing goods. Soft-path water planners would therefore argue that farmers and manufacturers are likely to implement any water-conserving technologies that make practical, economic, and social sense while permitting them to meet their needs. Comparable examples of technologies and practices that permit us to meet our needs and wants with less and less water can be found in every sector of society (11).

Definitions of Water Use, Conservation, and Efficiency

There is considerable confusion in the water literature about the terms use, need, withdrawal, demand, consumption, and consumptive use. Great care should be used when interpreting or comparing different studies or assumptions about water use. The term *water use*, while common, can mean many different things, referring at times to consumptive use and at times to withdrawals of water.

Withdrawal usually refers to water removed from a source and used for human needs. Some of this water may be returned to the original source with changes in the quantity and quality of the water, but some may be used consumptively. The term *consumptive use* or *consumption* typically refers to water withdrawn from a source and made unavailable for reuse in the same basin, such as through conversion to steam, losses to evaporation, seepage to a saline sink, or contamination. Consumptive use is sometimes referred to as irretrievable or irrecoverable loss (12). Thus a power plant may withdraw substantial amounts of water for cooling from a river but use that water in a way that permits it to be returned directly to the river, perhaps a bit warmer, for use by the next downstream user. A farmer may withdraw the same amount of water for irrigation, but the vast majority of it may be used consumptively by plants and become unavailable for any other activity.

Need for water is also a subjective term, but typically it refers to the minimum amount of water required to satisfy a particular purpose or requirement. It also sometimes refers to the desire for water on the part of a water user. *Demand* for water is an economic concept often used to describe the amount of water requested or required by a user (13). The level of demand for water may have no relationship to the minimum amount of water required to satisfy a particular requirement. Water demand to flush a toilet can range from six gallons in an old, inefficient U.S. toilet, to 1.6 gallons in a model that meets current U.S. standards, to zero gallons in an efficient composting toilet. What is actually being demanded is not a specific amount of water but the service of reliably and safely removing wastes.

A considerable number of other confusing terms have appeared in the water literature in the past few years. Among them are terms used to describe the kinds of water that might be saved by changes in technology and water policies, including real water, paper water, and new water. Some of these distinctions have been valuable in identifying where and when conservation is most beneficial and have allowed planners to focus on the improvements in water-use efficiency that are the most appropriate and valuable (14–17). Some of these distinctions, however, have been misleading or have misrepresented the value of efficiency improvements.

As noted above, consumptive uses of water prevent water from being reused in a watershed or system. Efforts to reduce consumptive uses clearly save real, physical water that can be made available to other users. But some planners are confused about the value of nonconsumptive uses of water: uses that permit later reuse.

The California Department of Water Resources (CDWR), for example, miscalculated the value of water-use efficiency efforts to reduce nonconsumptive uses in water plans prepared in the 1990s. The CDWR argued that upstream reductions in nonconsumptive use are *paper* water, i.e., they do not produce *new* water (by which they mean additions to supply), and hence do not help satisfy water demands (18, 19). Under this line of thought, Sacramento, an inland city, would not benefit from efforts to install residential water meters or retrofit houses with low-flow showerheads or efficient toilets because water used inefficiently (but nonconsumptively) in Sacramento is already being used by downstream users.

While no new water would be produced in this case, the water savings from efficiency improvements in Sacramento would nevertheless be a real reduction in demand that displaces the need for new supplies, because they would permit new customers and new demands in Sacramento to be satisfied without expanding capacity or infrastructure. Moreover, such reductions in demand would reduce the need to take water out of local rivers and aquifers, improve water quality and environmental values downstream of Sacramento, and provide enhanced recreation, fishing, tourism, and other benefits. This misunderstanding led state water planners to ignore or underemphasize improvements in urban water-use efficiency in inland regions. That, in turn, led to a potential overestimate of future increases in urban demand in California in 2020 by more than a billion cubic meters, which could in turn lead policy makers to commit major financial resources to unnecessary new supply projects (19). As will be described later, water forecasts leading to overestimates of future water needs are common.

Similarly, water accounts for the Nile River indicate that only 20%–30% of irrigation water diverted from the Nile is evaporated or transpired by crops (15). The remainder is return water typically reused downstream. Some have claimed that upstream reductions in nonconsumptive use are relatively unimportant because water loss is not the same as water waste (20). Of course this is strictly correct: Irrigation return flows are not wasted if they are used downstream. But upstream conservation efforts have other benefits: They would allow a larger upstream area to be irrigated, improve the navigability of the Nile, or as in the California example, improve water quality for downstream natural systems or users.

Related to problems of defining water use is the challenge of defining how to improve that use. The terms conservation, efficiency, and productivity are often used interchangeably to get across the idea of doing more with less. Used most generally, the term *water conservation* simply refers to reducing water use by any amount or any means, which may include applying new technology, improving old technology, and instituting behavioral changes.

Baumann et al. more explicitly defined *water conservation* as any socially beneficial reduction in water use or water loss. This definition suggests that efficiency measures should, in addition to reducing water use per unit of activity, make sense economically and socially (21). This leads to economically efficient outcomes, taking into account all costs, by pushing forward with conservation up to the point where the incremental cost of demand reduction is the same as the incremental cost of supply augmentation. The advantage of this definition is that it focuses on comprehensive demand and supply management with the goal of increasing overall well-being per unit of water used.

Water-use efficiency is a more precise measure of water conservation: how much water is actually used for a specific purpose compared to the minimum amount necessary to satisfy that purpose. Under this definition, the theoretical maximum water-use efficiency occurs when society actually uses the minimum amount of water necessary to do something. In reality, however, this theoretical maximum efficiency is rarely, if ever, achieved because the technology is not available or commercialized, because the economic cost is too high, or because societal or cultural preferences rule out particular approaches.

Finally, the concept of water productivity is useful in discussions about water use. *Water productivity* usually refers to the amount of measurable output per unit of water that is used. The units of output can be physical (e.g., tons of wheat) or economic (e.g., the dollar value of the good or service produced). Hence, the term water productivity is a comprehensive way to combine the ideas of doing more with less water.

HOW IS WATER USED?

Water is used for many different purposes throughout our economies and natural ecosystems. Agriculture is the largest consumer of water used by humans worldwide. Most observers put total consumptive use of water worldwide for irrigated agriculture at nearly 85% of total human consumptive use. This water is vital for the production of food. In 2000, around 270 million hectares of land were irrigated worldwide, which is 18% of total cropland (22). Around 40% of all agricultural production comes from these irrigated areas. As a result, evaluations of water use must pay particular attention to this sector.

Water is used by agriculture for a number of critical services. Water is necessary for growing biota, for maintaining temperature balances within plants, for leaching salts and other minerals away from the root zone, and more. Water diverted for agriculture is depleted by transpiration of the plants, by evaporation from soil and free water surfaces, and by deep percolation to groundwater. Some of this water can be considered to be used beneficially while a portion is lost to nonbeneficial uses.

In urban or residential settings, water is used for a wide range of daily activities, which include cooking, cleaning and bathing, small-scale irrigation for gardens or municipal landscapes, waste disposal, and commercial and industrial activities. Almost all forms of production of goods and services require water. Sometimes water is actually embodied in the production of a good, such as water used to can fruits and vegetables or to make beverages. Other times, water is simply used to clean, cool, or operate machinery. A substantial fraction of total water withdrawals in some industrialized nations is used for the production of energy, either directly in hydroelectric plants or indirectly for power plant cooling. Most of this water is not used consumptively. In the United States, 47% of total water withdrawals went to power plant cooling. In Europe, 32% went for these purposes (23–25).

Finally, there is a whole series of water uses by natural ecosystems that are almost always ignored in surveys or assessments of water use. Many of these environmental uses of water are not directly human uses, although they nonetheless contribute to maintaining the ability of natural ecosystems to provide certain kinds of goods and services critical for human well-being. While there are no satisfactory standards for how to account for this kind of water use, it is receiving growing attention in the water-use field. Indeed, the government of South Africa has formally acknowledged, the need to maintain basic water flows for the environment in its post-apartheid water laws (26).

Data Problems

Compounding problems with definitions of water use are serious problems with data. Data on water use are collected around the world to support scientific research, facilitate the operation of water-supply systems, and improve water-policy decisions. The types of data collected, the frequency and accuracy of collection, and the availability vary widely from place to place. Compared with data on the hydrologic cycle, such as rainfall, runoff, and temperature, data on water use are inadequate and incomplete, and pressures are growing to cut back collection for financial reasons (27, 28). Several serious problems hinder water-use analyses:

SYSTEMATIC COLLECTION OF WATER-USE DATA IS RARE Far fewer data are collected on water use than on water supply and availability. Domestic water use is often not measured directly, and details on how that water is used are rarely collected. Data on surface water are collected more frequently than data on the use or condition of groundwater. Data on urban water uses are more readily available than data on rural and agricultural uses, but even details of industrial and commercial water uses are inventoried infrequently or not at all. Even when water-use data are collected, information on changing water-use patterns over time is often not available; this makes analysis of trends difficult.

SOME WATER USES OR NEEDS ARE UNQUANTIFIED OR UNQUANTIFIABLE Some water uses and needs have never been adequately catalogued; others are unlikely ever to be accurately determined. For example, ecological needs, recreational uses, water for hydropower production or navigation, and reservoir losses to seepage or evaporation are often difficult to calculate with any accuracy. Information on total withdrawals is reported more frequently than information on consumptive uses. But water may be withdrawn once and then used several times in a process; so data on withdrawals may be an inadequate measure of overall use or need. These kinds of water-use distinctions and activities must be measured if effective water management is to be done.

THERE ARE SERIOUS GLOBAL AND REGIONAL DISPARITIES IN COLLECTION   Although water-use data are usually more reliably and consistently collected in the industrialized nations, some regions have few or no programs in place to survey water uses. There are also regional disparities in the scope and quality of water-use data collection within countries, and even in wealthier countries, programs to evaluate water use are often the first victims of budget cuts during fiscal crises.

MANY DATA ARE INACCURATE   Even when data are collected, inaccurate measurement and reporting are common. As mentioned above, confusion over definitions of withdrawals, consumption, and reuse make some comparisons difficult. It is difficult to determine water use when no meters or measuring devices are in place. And determining specific uses often requires estimates based on indirect factors, such as climate, typical crop characteristics, or assumptions about the performance of water-use technology. For example, showerheads that are designed to flow at a rate of 2.5 gallons per minute (the current U.S. standard) may actually flow at rates above or below this standard because of local differences in pipe pressure. Crops estimated to evapotranspire a certain amount of water may use more or less than that because of differing soil conditions, temperatures, or even local wind regimes.

ESTIMATES OF CURRENT WATER USE

As described above, collecting and reporting water-use data entail enormous challenges due to problems with the quality of data and differing definitions and standards for measurement. Because of these difficulties, estimates of current water use at the national or global level must only be considered approximations, even in the best of circumstances. Nevertheless, a number of comprehensive assessments have been done in an effort to get a broader picture of critical water concerns. Most global studies typically consist of separate regional or sectoral evaluations conflated to provide a global view. In this section, several global and regional water-use estimates are reviewed, and an overview of water use by major sectors is presented.

Global Water Use

Many factors determine water-use levels around the world: the extent and form of socioeconomic development, population size, climatic conditions, and the physical nature of a region. Various assessments have been made of global water use, typically by combining regional analyses that take these different factors into account. Shiklomanov and a group of researchers at the State Hydrologic Institute (SHI) of St. Petersburg have produced one of the most comprehensive and recent assessments. In this analysis, total water withdrawals and consumption were estimated for urban needs (domestic water consumption), industrial use (including power generation), irrigated agriculture, and evaporation losses from reservoir surfaces. Estimates were made for various periods, including 1900, 1940, 1950, 1960, 1970, 1980, 1990, and 1995 (12, 29).

The SHI estimated water use for approximately 150 countries, and the data were then generalized for larger economic regions and summed by continents. Preference was given to using actual reported data from individual countries or groups of countries, but when actual data were not available, estimates were derived by using information on reported economic activity using assumptions about the water implications of different activities or by drawing analogies with countries with similar physiographic and economic conditions.

Table 1 shows Shiklomanov's (29) estimates of both water withdrawals and consumption (reported as irrecoverable losses) by continental regions for decades from 1900 to the mid-1990s. As might be expected, water uses around the world are very uneven, both spatially and temporally. The data also indicate the quite strong and dramatic increases in total fresh water withdrawals and consumption in the twentieth century, which led to the widespread construction of large water systems. According to these estimates, water withdrawals in 1995 totaled 3765 cubic

TABLE 1 Water withdrawal and consumption estimates and projections in cubic kilometers (29)

Continent	Historical estimates of use									Forecasted use		
	1900	1940	1950	1960	1970	1980	1990	1995	2000	2010	2025
Europe	37.5[a]	71	93.8	185	294	445	491	511	534	578	619
	17.6[b]	29.8	38.4	53.9	81.8	158	183	187	191	202	217
North America	70	221	286	410	555	677	652	685	705	744	786
	29.2	83.8	104	138	181	221	221	238	243	255	269
Africa	41.0	49.0	56.0	86.0	116	168	199	215	230	270	331
	34.0	39.0	44.0	66.0	88.0	129	151	160	169	190	216
Asia	414	689	860	1222	1499	1784	2067	2157	2245	2483	3104
	322	528	654	932	1116	1324	1529	1565	1603	1721	1971
South America	15.2	27.7	59.4	68.5	85.2	111	152	166	180	213	257
	11.3	20.6	41.7	44.4	57.8	71.0	91.4	97.7	104	112	122
Australia & Oceania	1.6	6.8	10.3	17.4	23.3	29.4	28.5	30.5	32.6	35.6	39.6
	0.6	3.4	5.1	9.0	11.9	14.6	16.4	17.6	18.9	21	23.1
Total (rounded)[c]	579	1065	1366	1989	2573	3214	3590	3765	3927	4324	5137
	415	704	887	1243	1536	1918	2192	2265	2329	2501	2818

[a]Underlined numbers show water withdrawal.
[b]Italic numbers show water consumption.
[c]Includes about 270 cubic kilometers in water losses from reservoirs for 2025.

kilometers annually, compared with 579 cubic kilometers in 1900. Consumptive uses in 1995 were estimated at 2265 cubic kilometers, up from 415 km^3 in 1900. Use in North America and Europe accounted for 19% of total estimated withdrawals at the beginning of the twentieth century. By 1995, withdrawals in North America and Europe had increased to 30% of the total, which reflects increased industrialization.

From a practical point of view, however, absolute measures of water use are sometimes less valuable than comparing water use with water availability, which can give a better sense of how close a region may be to stress or scarcity. For example, total water withdrawals at the end of the twentieth century comprised as much as 15% to 17% of total renewable water availability in Europe and Asia, but only 1% to 2% of availability in South America and Oceania. On an even finer regional scale, current water withdrawals are already as much as 24% to 30% of total supply in parts of southern and central Europe; at the same time in the northern part of the continent, there are regions where these values never exceed 3%. In Canada, water withdrawals are only about 1% of total water resources. Just to the south, the United States uses as much as 28% of total availability, and there are watersheds in the United States where water use approaches or even occasionally exceeds total regional water availability (due to unsustainable overdraft of local groundwater resources to supplement renewable supplies).

A slightly different approach to estimating water use at the global scale was taken by Postel et al. (30). In their analysis, they estimate the portion of the Earth's renewable water resources accessible to humans and the portion of this supply now being used. They use the estimates of Shiklomanov to calculate municipal uses and add water required for agricultural production and instream flows for human needs such as waste dilution, navigation, recreation, and environmental uses. Overall, Postel et al. (30) estimate that withdrawals from rivers, streams, and aquifers combined with instream flow requirements already total 6780 cubic kilometers per year and that these uses account for 54% of total accessible runoff.

Regional Water Use: National Water-Use Estimates

Data on water use by countries and by different economic sectors are among the most sought-after and unreliable in the water resources area. In recent years, more concerted and consistent efforts to collect and report national water-use estimates have been made by national water agencies and by the United Nations Food and Agriculture Organization (FAO) (31–34). The recent FAO reports cover most countries of Africa, the Near East, the former Soviet Union, Asia, Latin America, and the Caribbean. New, consistent estimates on use have yet to be done for Europe and North America, though national estimates from these regions are done on a more regular basis by those countries themselves. Within each of the continental reports, some of the national water-use data are still incomplete or grossly outdated. For Africa, for example, some of the data are more than 30 years old.

The most up-to-date national data on water use are reviewed and summarized every two years in the biennial book *The World's Water*. These data are reproduced here from the most recent volume (see Table 2) (35). This table shows total

TABLE 2 Freshwater withdrawal, by country and sector[a]

Region and country	Year	Total freshwater withdrawal (km³/yr)	Per capita withdrawal (m³/p/yr)[b]	Domestic use (%)	Industrial use (%)	Agricultural use (%)
Africa						
Algeria	1990	4.50	142	25	15	60
Angola	1987	0.48	38	14	10	76
Benin	1994	0.15	23	23	10	67
Botswana	1992	0.11	70	32	20	48
Burkina Faso	1992	0.38	31	19	0	81
Burundi	1987	0.10	14	36	0	64
Cameroon	1987	0.40	26	46	19	35
Cape Verde	1990	0.03	59	10	19	88
Central African Republic	1987	0.07	19	21	5	74
Chad	1987	0.18	25	16	2	82
Comoros	1987	0.01	14	48	5	47
Congo	1987	0.04	13	62	27	11
Congo, Democratic Republic of (formerly Zaire)	1990	0.36	7	61	16	23
Cote D'Ivoire	1987	0.71	47	22	11	67
Djibouti	1985	0.01	11	13	0	87
Egypt	1993	55.10	809	6	8	86
Equatorial Guinea	1987	0.01	22	81	13	6
Ethiopia (and Eritrea)	1987	2.20	31	11	3	86
Gabon	1987	0.06	49	72	22	6
Gambia	1982	0.02	16	7	2	91
Ghana	1970	0.30	15	35	13	52
Guinea	1987	0.74	94	10	3	87
Guinea-Bissau	1991	0.02	14	60	4	36
Kenya	1990	2.05	68	20	4	76
Lesotho	1987	0.05	22	22	22	56
Liberia	1987	0.13	40	27	13	60
Libya	1994	4.60	720	11	2	87
Madagascar	1984	16.30	937	1	0	99
Malawi	1994	0.94	85	10	3	86
Mali	1987	1.36	108	2	1	97
Mauritania	1985	1.63	632	6	2	92
Mauritius	1995	0.62	522	18	8	75
Morocco	1991	11.05	381	5	3	92
Mozambique	1992	0.61	31	9	2	89
Namibia	1991	0.249	144	29	3	68
Niger	1988	0.50	46	16	2	82

(*Continued*)

TABLE 2 (*Continued*)

Region and country	Year	Total freshwater withdrawal (km³/yr)	Per capita withdrawal (m³/p/yr)[b]	Domestic use (%)	Industrial use (%)	Agricultural use (%)
Nigeria	1987	3.63	28	31	15	54
Rwanda	1993	0.77	100	5	2	94
Senegal	1987	1.36	143	5	3	92
Sierra Leone	1987	0.37	76	7	4	89
Somalia	1987	0.81	70	3	0	97
South Africa	1990	13.31	288	17	11	72
Sudan	1995	17.80	597	4	1	94
Swaziland	1980	0.66	667	2	2	96
Tanzania	1994	1.17	35	9	2	89
Togo	1987	0.09	19	62	13	26
Tunisia	1990	3.08	313	9	3	89
Uganda	1970	0.20	9	32	8	60
Zambia	1994	1.71	187	16	7	77
Zimbabwe	1987	1.22	98	14	7	79
North and Central America						
Antigua and Barbuda	1990	0.005	75	60	20	20
Barbados	1996	0.08	312	77	0	23
Belize	1993	0.095	396	12	88	0
Canada	1990	43.89	1431	11	80	8
Costa Rica	1997	5.77	1520	13	7	80
Cuba	1995	5.21	465	49	0	51
Dominica	1996	0.02	239	0	0	100
Dominican Republic	1994	8.34	982	11	0	89
El Salvador	1992	0.73	115	34	20	46
Guatemala	1992	1.16	95	9	17	74
Haiti	1991	0.98	125	5	1	94
Honduras	1992	1.52	234	4	5	91
Jamaica	1993	0.90	348	15	7	77
Mexico	1998	77.81	787	17	5	78
Nicaragua	1998	1.29	274	14	2	84
Panama	1990	1.64	575	28	2	70
St. Lucia	1997	0.01	89	100	0	0
St. Vincent and the Grenadines	1995	0.01	88	100	0	0
Trinidad and Tobago	1997	0.30	221	68	26	6
United States of America	1995	469.00	1688	12	46	42

(*Continued*)

TABLE 2 (*Continued*)

Region and country	Year	Total freshwater withdrawal (km³/yr)	Per capita withdrawal (m³/p/yr)[b]	Domestic use (%)	Industrial use (%)	Agricultural use (%)
South America						
Argentina	1995	28.58	772	16	9	75
Bolivia	1987	1.21	145	10	3	87
Brazil	1992	54.87	324	21	18	61
Chile	1987	20.29	1334	5	11	84
Colombia	1996	8.94	230	59	4	37
Ecuador	1997	16.99	1343	12	6	82
Guyana	1992	1.46	1670	1	0	99
Paraguay	1987	0.43	78	15	7	78
Peru	1992	18.97	739	7	7	86
Suriname	1987	0.46	1018	6	5	89
Uruguay	1965	0.65	199	6	3	91
Venezuela	1970	4.10	170	44	10	46
Asia						
Afghanistan	1991	26.11	1020	1	0	99
Bahrain	1991	0.24	387	39	4	56
Bangladesh	1990	14.64	114	12	2	86
Bhutan	1987	0.02	10	36	10	54
Brunei	1994	0.92	2788	—	—	—
Cambodia	1987	0.52	46	5	1	94
China	2000	549.76	431	11	21	69
Cyprus	1993	0.21	267	7	2	91
India	1990	500.00	497	5	3	92
Indonesia	1990	74.35	350	6	1	93
Iran	1993	70.03	916	6	2	92
Iraq	1990	42.80	1852	3	5	92
Israel	1990	1.70	280	16	5	79
Japan	1992	91.40	723	19	17	64
Jordan	1993	0.98	155	22	3	75
Korea, Democratic People's Republic	1987	14.16	592	11	16	73
Korea Republic	1994	23.67	505	26	11	63
Kuwait	1994	0.54	274	37	2	60
Laos	1987	0.99	174	8	10	82
Lebanon	1994	1.29	393	28	4	68
Malaysia	1995	12.73	571	10	13	77
Maldives	1987	0.003	10	98	2	0
Mongolia	1993	0.43	157	20	27	53
Myanmar	1987	3.96	80	7	3	90
Nepal	1994	28.95	1189	1	0	99
Oman	1991	1.22	450	5	2	94

(*Continued*)

TABLE 2 (*Continued*)

Region and country	Year	Total freshwater withdrawal (km³/yr)	Per capita withdrawal (m³/p/yr)[b]	Domestic use (%)	Industrial use (%)	Agricultural use (%)
Pakistan	1991	155.60	997	2	2	97
Philippines	1995	55.42	739	8	4	88
Qatar	1994	0.28	476	23	3	74
Saudi Arabia	1992	17.02	786	9	1	90
Singapore	1975	0.19	53	45	51	4
Sri Lanka	1990	9.77	519	2	2	96
Syria	1993	14.41	894	4	2	94
Thailand	1990	33.13	548	5	4	91
Turkey	1992	31.60	481	16	11	72
United Arab Emirates	1995	2.11	863	24	9	67
Vietnam	1990	54.33	674	4	10	86
Yemen	1990	2.93	162	7	1	92
Europe						
Albania	1970	0.20	57	6	18	76
Austria	1991	2.52	304	19	73	8
Belgium	1990	9.00	877	11	85	4
Bulgaria	1988	13.90	1673	3	75	22
Czech Republic	1991	2.74	269	23	68	9
Denmark	1995	1.00	190	30	27	43
Finland	1994	2.43	469	12	85	3
France	1994	34.88	591	16	69	15
Germany	1990	58.85	712	14	68	18
Greece	1990	6.00	566	8	29	63
Hungary	1991	6.81	694	9	55	36
Iceland	1994	0.16	567	31	63	6
Ireland	1990	1.20	336	16	74	10
Italy	1990	56.20	983	14	27	59
Luxembourg	1994	0.06	133	42	45	13
Malta	1995	0.06	147	87	1	12
Netherlands	1991	7.80	491	5	61	34
Norway	1985	2.03	461	20	72	8
Poland	1991	12.28	317	16	60	24
Portugal	1990	7.29	745	15	37	48
Romania	1994	26.00	1155	8	33	59
Slovak Republic	1991	1.78	331	—	—	—
Spain	1994	33.30	837	12	26	62
Sweden	1994	2.96	333	36	55	9
Switzerland	1994	2.60	351	23	73	4
United Kingdom	1994	11.75	201	20	77	3
Yugoslavia[c]	1980	8.77	368	16	72	12

(*Continued*)

TABLE 2 (*Continued*)

Region and country	Year	Total freshwater withdrawal (km³/yr)	Per capita withdrawal (m³/p/yr)[b]	Domestic use (%)	Industrial use (%)	Agricultural use (%)
Former Soviet Union						
Armenia	1994	2.93	800	30	4	66
Azerbaijan	1995	16.53	2112	5	25	70
Belarus	1990	2.73	265	22	43	35
Estonia	1995	0.16	113	56	39	5
Georgia	1990	3.47	640	21	20	59
Kazakhstan	1993	33.67	1989	2	17	81
Kyrgyz Republic	1994	10.09	2221	3	3	94
Latvia	1994	0.29	121	55	32	13
Lithuania	1995	0.25	68	81	16	3
Moldova	1992	2.96	664	9	65	26
Russian Federation	1994	77.10	527	19	62	20
Tajikistan	1994	11.87	1855	3	4	92
Turkmenistan	1994	23.78	5309	1	1	98
Ukraine	1992	25.99	512	18	52	30
Uzbekistan	1994	58.05	2320	4	2	94
Oceania						
Australia	1995	17.80	945	15	10	75
Fiji	1987	0.03	35	20	20	60
New Zealand	1991	2.00	532	46	10	44
Papua New Guinea	1987	0.10	21	29	22	49
Solomon Islands	1987	—	—	40	20	40

[a]See (35) for details on original data. Figures may not add to totals due to independent rounding.
[b]Per capita figures calculated using 2000 population numbers: medium UN variant.
[c]Includes Bosnia and Herzegovina, Macedonia, Croatia.

freshwater withdrawals by country in cubic kilometers per year and cubic meters per person per year, using estimated water withdrawals for the year noted and the United Nations population estimates (medium variant) by country for the year 2000. The table also gives the reported breakdown of that water use for the domestic, agricultural, and industrial sectors, in percent of total water use. The independent data sources are identified in the original table [see (35)]. The domestic sector typically includes household and municipal uses as well as commercial and governmental water use. The industrial sector typically includes water used for power plant cooling and industrial production. The agricultural sector includes water for irrigation and livestock.

Extreme care should be used when applying these data; as noted earlier, they are often the least reliable and most inconsistent of all water-resources information. Despite the efforts of FAO to standardize reporting, the data still come from a wide variety of sources and are collected using different approaches, with few formal standards. As a result, this table includes data that are measured, estimated, and modeled using different assumptions or derived from other data. The data also come from different years, which makes direct comparisons difficult. As examples of some of the inconsistencies and gaps, separate data are not available for the former states of Yugoslavia; industrial withdrawals for Panama, St. Lucia, St. Vincent, and the Grenadines are included in the domestic category; and none of the national data include the use of rainfall in agriculture. Many countries use a significant fraction of the rain falling on their territory for agricultural production, but this category of water use is neither accurately measured nor reported.

Despite these data constraints, Table 2 offers dramatic insights into differences in water use around the world, especially when normalized for population. In Africa, for example, reported water uses range from approximately 600 to 800 cubic meters per person per year (m^3/p/yr) in Egypt, Libya, the Sudan and a handful of other countries to under 20 cubic meters per person per year in the poorest countries of the continent. For many countries of Africa, as much as 90% or more of reported withdrawals go to agricultural uses.

In contrast, almost no country in Europe reports per capita withdrawals of less than several hundred m^3/p/yr (estimates of 50 m^3/p/yr from Albania are more than 30 years old and highly suspect), and several exceed 800 m^3/p/yr, even with almost no irrigated agriculture. Another major difference between the two continents is the far higher proportion of total water use reported in the industrial sector in Europe, where industry commonly accounts for 60% or more of total withdrawals.

Experience from the United States

Few regions or countries have better long-term information on water use than the United States. Beginning in 1951, the U.S. Geological Survey published a series of comprehensive reports on water use in the United States at approximately five-year intervals (36–39). These water-use studies include compilations and estimates of surface and groundwater water use for all states and for various use categories by state and by major hydrologic region. The initial study estimated water use for all withdrawals, which included municipal, rural domestic and livestock, irrigation, industrial use, and hydroelectric power. Water for instream flows such as navigation, recreation, and fish and wildlife were also addressed, though only qualitatively. Consumptive use of water began to be estimated in the 1960 report, and estimates were also made of water use in the early decades of the century, beginning in 1900 (37, 40, 41).

Differences among the states in types of water use, methods of data collection, reliability of reporting, and funding priorities have resulted in unevenness in the breadth and depth of available information (42). As a result, the U.S. National Research Council (43) has recommended a series of improvements in the U.S. National Water-Use Information Program to help provide more comprehensive and

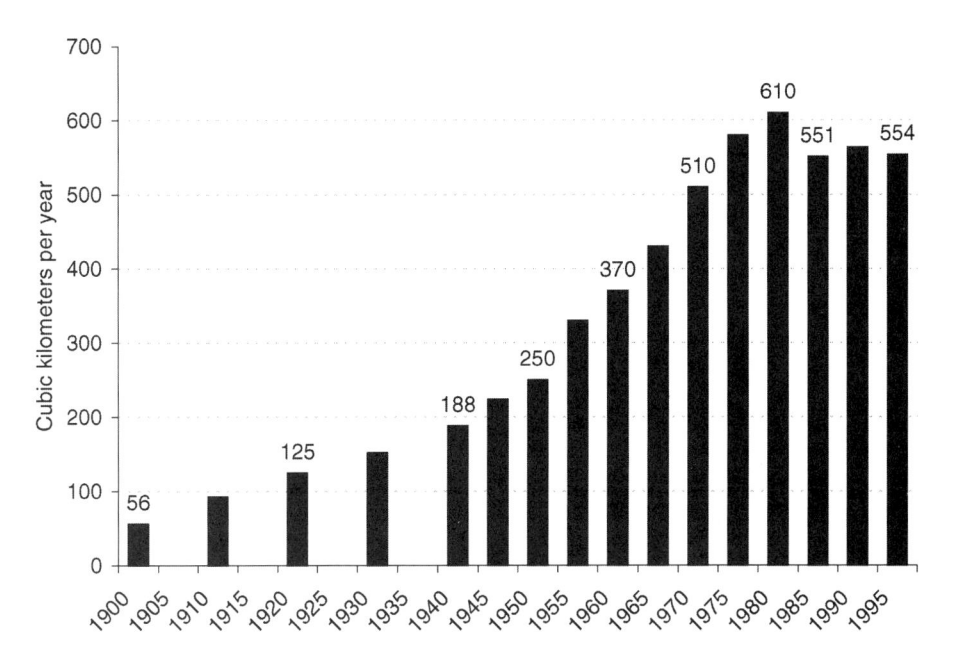

Figure 1 Total U.S. water withdrawals 1900 to 1995. The peak of withdrawals occurred in the 1980s and was followed by a decline as the efficiency of water use nationwide improved and as the economy shifted to less water-intensive uses.

accurate water-use data. Despite these problems, this series of water-use studies has proven to be extremely valuable for researchers and policy makers.

One of the most important findings from the long-term data provided by these reports has been an unexpected change in the trend of water use in the country. Figure 1 graphs total U.S. water withdrawals from 1900 to 1995 and shows rapid growth up until the mid- to late-1980s. Water withdrawals then began to level off and even decline, a change not noted or recognized by water managers or policy makers until the 1990s. This decline, however, has persisted; indeed, it is even more apparent when per capita use is measured. Figure 2 shows per capita water withdrawals (fresh and saline) from 1900 to 1995 together with U.S. population. Since 1980, per capita withdrawals have decreased 20% and now are at levels comparable to those of the mid-1960s. Yet U.S. population has grown from approximately 175 million in 1960 to over 270 million in 1995.

The implications of these trends for water planning and policy, and hence the value of consistency in collecting and reporting water-use data, are dramatic. In particular, they challenge the assumption of planners that economic and population growth lead inevitably to growth in water withdrawals and necessary expansion of supply. And they support the idea that improvements in water-use efficiency and shifts in economic structure can reduce resource use, even in an expanding economy (44).

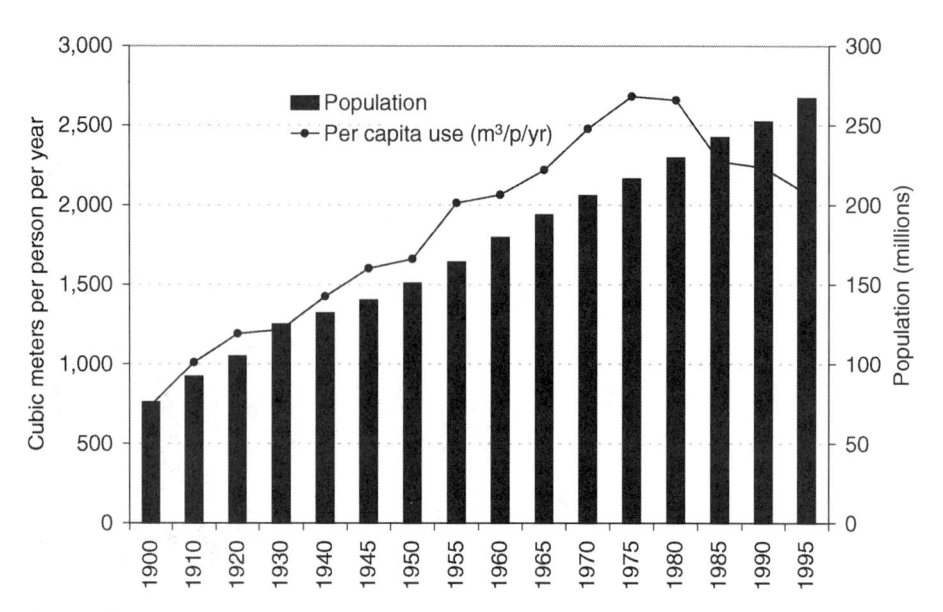

Figure 2 U.S. population and per capita water withdrawals (fresh and saline) from 1900 to 1995 (36–40, 93).

Despite the value and importance of regular reports on water use, financial and institutional pressures are forcing many water agencies to cut back, rather than expand, data collection. In the United States, fiscal policies are leading to reductions in data collection, analysis, and presentation on water use. The 2000 U.S. Geological Survey national water-use report (scheduled to be released in 2003), for example, will cut back on collection and presentation of data for several categories; these include mining, livestock, and aquaculture. Data will only be compiled for states where water uses in these categories are large. Withdrawals from major groundwater aquifers are only being reported for public supply, irrigation, and industry. Data on commercial water use, wastewater treatment, reservoir evaporation, and hydroelectric power are no longer being collected nor is information on consumptive use, reclaimed wastewater, return flows, or deliveries from public suppliers (41). These cutbacks in data collection will seriously imperil the long-term value of the U.S. time series on water use.

FORECASTING WATER USE

Humans have always thought about possible futures, explored plausible paths, and tried to identify risks and benefits associated with different choices. In recent years, this has led to a growing interest in scenarios, forecasting, and "future" studies [see, for example, Schwartz (45)]. Scenario planning has more than academic implications. Water planners are among the few natural resource managers to think more than a few years into the future. Designing and building major water infrastructure can take years, and dams, reservoirs, aqueducts, and pipelines may last for decades or even centuries, which requires planners to take a relatively long view.

In the water sector, expectations about future water use drive huge financial expenditures for water-supply projects. These projects, in turn, have significant human and ecological impacts. At the same time, not making necessary investments can lead to the failure to meet fundamental human water needs. The challenge facing water planners is to balance the risks and benefits of these kinds of efforts.

What will future water uses be? How can they be predicted, given all the uncertainties involved in looking into the future? At the global level, various projections and estimates of future freshwater demands have been made over the past half century; some extended out as much as 60 or 70 years. Reviewing the major studies that have been done reveals two noteworthy trends: Overestimating future water demand, often substantially, is the norm, not the exception; and as tools and methods for making forecasts improve, forecasts of future water needs drop.

Figure 3 and Table 3 show more than 25 different water projections made before 2000 for various points during the twenty-first century, along with an estimates

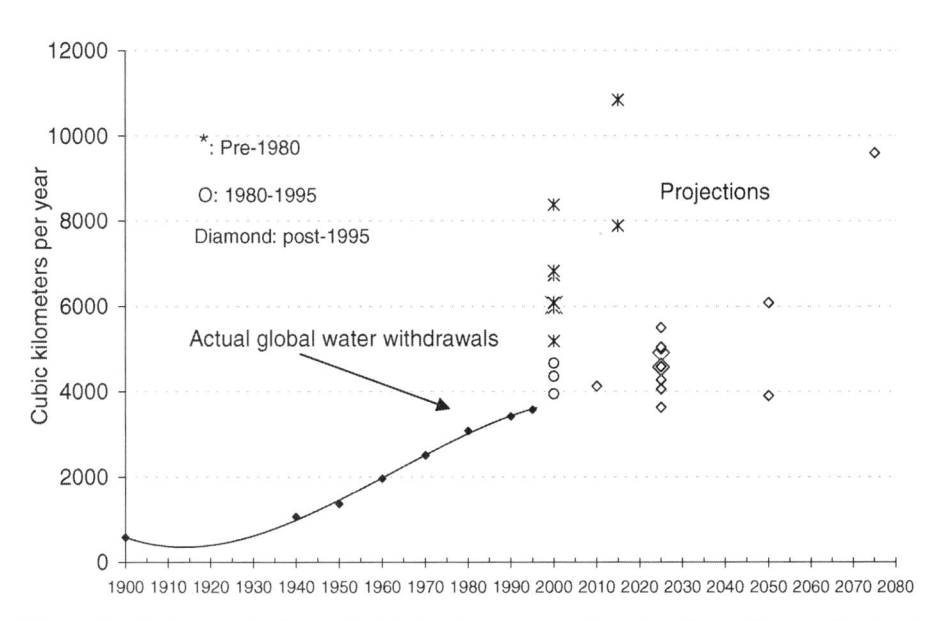

Figure 3 Various projections of global water use over time, together with an estimate of actual water withdrawals (29). Projections made in the 1960s and 1970s greatly overestimated water use in 2000. Even more recent projections tend to overestimate future use because of simplistic assumptions of the relation between population, economic growth, and water.

TABLE 3 Summary of various global water forecasts

Author	Scenario	Publication year	Forecast year	Estimated withdrawal (km^3/yr)
Nikitopoulos		1967	2000	6,730
L'vovich	Rational use	1974	2000	6,325[a]
L'vovich	Conventional	1974	2000	12,270[a]
Kalinin & Shiklomanov		1974	2000	5,970
Falkenmark & Lindh		1974	2000	6,030
Falkenmark & Lindh		1974	2000	8,380
Falkenmark & Lindh		1974	2015	10,840
Falkenmark & Lindh		1974	2015	7,885
De Mare		1976	2000	5,605[a]
Belyaev		1990	2000	4,350
World Resources Institute		1990	2000	4,660
Shiklomanov & Markova		1987	2000	4,976[a]
Shiklomanov		1998	2000	3,717[a,b]
Shiklomanov		1998	2010	4,089[a]
Shiklomanov		1998	2025	4,867[a]
Raskin et al.	Low	1997	2025	4,500
Raskin et al.	Mid	1997	2025	5,000
Raskin et al.	High	1997	2025	5,500
Gleick	Sustainable vision	1997	2025	4,270[a]
Alcamo et al.	Medium 2025	1997	2025	4,580
Alcamo et al.	Medium 2075	1997	2075	9,496
Raskin et al.	Reference 2025	1998	2025	5,044
Raskin et al.	Reference 2050	1998	2050	6,081
Raskin et al.	Policy reform 2025	1998	2025	4,054
Raskin et al.	Policy reform 2050	1998	2050	3,899
Seckler et al.	Business as usual	1998	2025	4,569
Seckler et al.	High irrigation efficiency	1998	2025	3,625

[a]These studies included estimates for water lost from reservoir evaporation. In order to make more consistent comparisons here with those studies that failed to estimate reservoir evaporative losses, those estimates are subtracted from total withdrawals. The numbers here thus represent withdrawals without reservoir evaporation. See Gleick (94) for specific assumptions underlying each projection and for full citations.

[b]Actual 1995 water withdrawals were estimated to be 3,765 km^3 by Shiklomanov (29).

of actual water use up to 2000. As the figure shows, every one of the projections made before 1995 greatly overestimated future water demands by assuming that use would continue to grow at, or even above, historical growth rates. Actual global water withdrawals in the late 1990s were only around half of what they were expected to be by most forecasts 30 years earlier. The inaccuracy of these past projections highlights the importance of developing better methods for making projections of future needs.

The earliest projections routinely, and significantly, overestimated future water demands because of their dependence on relatively simplistic extrapolation of existing trends. Most of the earliest projections used variants on the same methodology: Future water use was based on population projections; simple assumptions of industrial, commercial, and residential water-use intensity (e.g., water per unit population or income); and basic estimates of future crop production as a function of irrigated area and crop yield. Early scenarios were typically single, business-as-usual projections with no variants. Most scenarios ignored water requirements for instream ecological needs, navigation, hydropower production, and recreation. And almost all of these forecasts showed dramatic increases in demand over time, sometimes to implausible levels that led many observers to worry about water shortfalls and shortages. In some areas of the world, such shortages and shortfalls are already manifest, and new problem areas are likely to emerge in coming years. But it is also important to note that every one of the early global water projections estimated far greater demands for water, many of them by a substantial margin, than have actually materialized. This suggests that the traditional methods used by water-scenario developers are missing some critically important real-world dynamics.

One of the earliest and most comprehensive assessments was prepared in 1974 by L'vovich (46). Detailed assumptions were made for a variety of human uses to the year 2000; these included domestic and industrial water use, irrigated and nonirrigated agricultural water demands, and hydropower, navigation, and fishery water requirements. In his business-as-usual scenario, L'vovich assumed that domestic per capita withdrawals would continue to increase, that water consumption for energy production would grow by a factor of 20, while water consumption per unit energy would be cut in half, gross industrial water use would increase by a factor of 15, and agricultural water-use efficiency would increase slightly while total demands doubled with population. All together, he projected water demands in 2000 of more than 12,000 cubic kilometers, a fourfold increase over 1974. The work of L'vovich served as the basis for many later projections, which may have used different assumptions, baseline data, and details, but all approached the idea of water-use projections in the same way (47–49).

The methods and tools used for forecasting and scenario analysis have been getting more and more sophisticated and permit a better understanding of the driving factors behind changes in demands for water. New projections are taking advantage of advances in computer capabilities, the availability of better water data, and new concepts of scenario development. These estimates have begun to include reassessments of actual water needs and water-use efficiencies, dietary requirements, cropping patterns and types, and ecosystem functions (50, 51). Large-scale water-use projections have also become increasingly sophisticated due to the growing capability of easily accessible computers to handle significant numbers of calculations and the growing availability of water-use data. Assessments that were conducted for continental areas or on a national basis are now being done for watersheds on smaller and smaller temporal and spatial scales (52, 53).

THE CONNECTION BETWEEN WATER USE AND HUMAN WELL-BEING

The common assumption that growing populations and economic development will inevitably lead to greater human uses of water drove most of the projections described previously. This assumption, however, deserves closer scrutiny, especially if the idea of a soft path requires us to reconsider the distinction between water use and water needs (6–8). And when a closer look is taken, there are important examples for which, and reasons why, the assumption that increases in human well-being require ever larger uses of water breaks down.

Figure 4 shows the relationship between per capita GDP (a well-understood, albeit imperfect, measure of well-being) and per capita water use for a wide range of countries. As this graph suggests, there is no clear connection between these two variables. Several high water–using nations have very low per capita GDP, and several of the wealthiest nations have very low per capita water use.

A far more important determinant of water use is the extent to which countries commit their water resources to the production of food, especially irrigated agriculture. Large grain-producing countries, such as Canada, the United States, Argentina, and Australia, all have significantly higher per capita water use than average. Figure 5 shows per capita grain production and per capita water withdrawals for the world's major grain producers. The countries in the top right of the graph are those that produce large amounts of grain and serve as the world's leading grain exporters. As this graph suggests, a commitment to this level of agricultural production requires a commitment of a substantial amount of water.

This evidence also suggests that countries can have quite high standards of living (as measured by GDP) at modest per capita levels of water withdrawals, as long as someone is producing and exporting sufficient food to satisfy all needs. Indeed, the trade in grain has recently been acknowledged to be a trade in water as well—the water embodied in trade goods has been dubbed "virtual" water (54).

Many water planners still believe that using less water somehow means a loss of prosperity. The traditional assumption, repeated over and over in water plans and discussions about the risk of future water shortages, is that continued increases in population and improvements in well-being require continued increases in water use. This might be true in the absence of improvements in technology or water

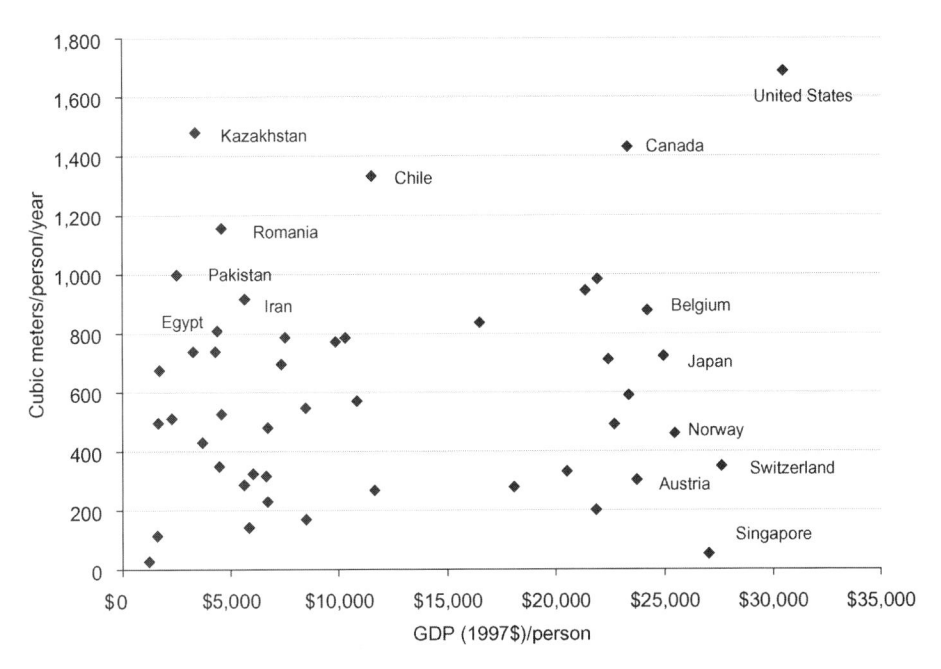

Figure 4 Per capita gross domestic product (GDP) plotted against per capita water withdrawals for a wide range of countries. No clear relationship can be seen from this graph, which suggests that the relationship between GDP and water use is not a simple one.

management, but with such improvements, there is enormous room for economic growth without growth in water use. For example, producing a ton of steel before World War II required 100 to 200 tons of water (55, 56). Today, each ton of steel can be produced with less than four tons of water: a vast improvement in water productivity (57). Furthermore, because a ton of aluminum can be produced using only one and a half tons of water, replacing the use of steel with aluminum, as has been happening for many years in the automobile industry, can further lower water use without reducing economic activity (6).

The links between water use, population, and economic well-being are not immutable. They can be modified and even broken, as has already happened in the United States, China, and elsewhere. For example, Japan used nearly 50 million liters of water to produce a million dollars of commercial output in 1965; by 1989 this had dropped to 14 million liters per million constant (inflation-adjusted) dollars of commercial output, which quadrupled water productivity (58).

The evidence for the changing connections between economic well-being and total water use can be seen by graphically comparing long-term data on water use, population, and gross domestic product for different regions. Serious data constraints limit the comparisons that can be made, especially constraints on the availability of reliable long-term water-use data. Nevertheless, data from a variety

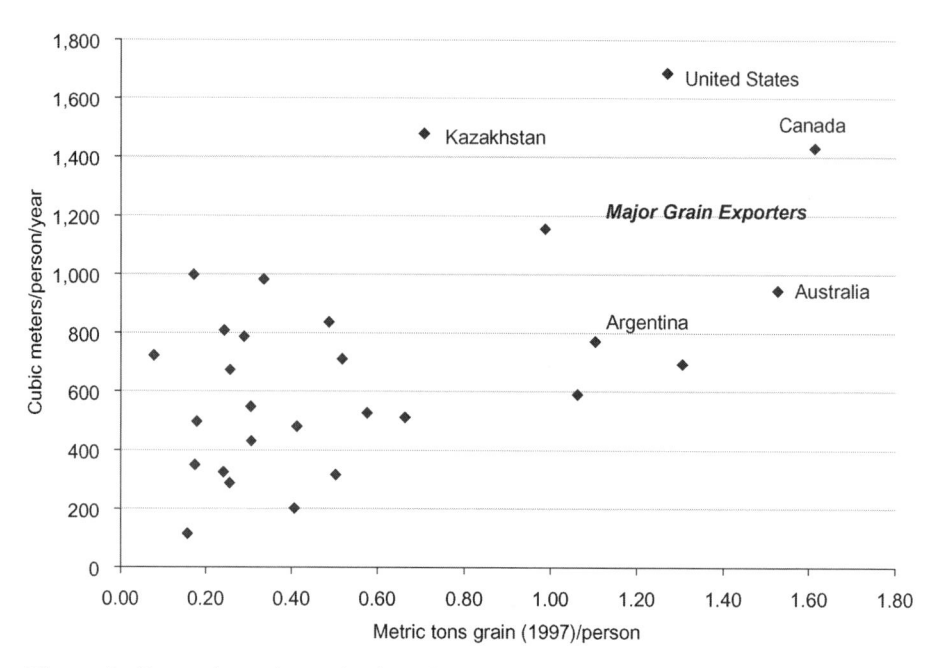

Figure 5 Per capita grain production plotted against per capita water withdrawals for a wide range of countries. Countries with major grain production also have major water use because of the need to supply substantial irrigation water.

of regions show the traditional increases in water use associated with increases in population and GDP, up to a point, followed by a divergence between these factors as countries begin to shift from a focus on supply and water development to one focused on water use and efficiency.

Figures 6, 7, 8, 9, 10, and 11 show estimates of total water use over time for a number of countries or regions plotted against GDP or population. The challenge for water managers in coming years is how to make the transition from the false assumption that growing populations and growing economies require ever increasing amounts of water.

CHANGING WATER-USE PATTERNS: THE POTENTIAL FOR IMPROVING WATER-USE EFFICIENCY

The relationship between water use and well-being is changing for two major reasons. First, improvements in technology and management approaches are permitting needs to be met with less water, and second, the nature of economies is shifting away from water-intensive goods and services toward lower water-using, higher-valued production. These changes permit nonstructural solutions to be considered as useful and practical tools for meeting future expectations about water demand.

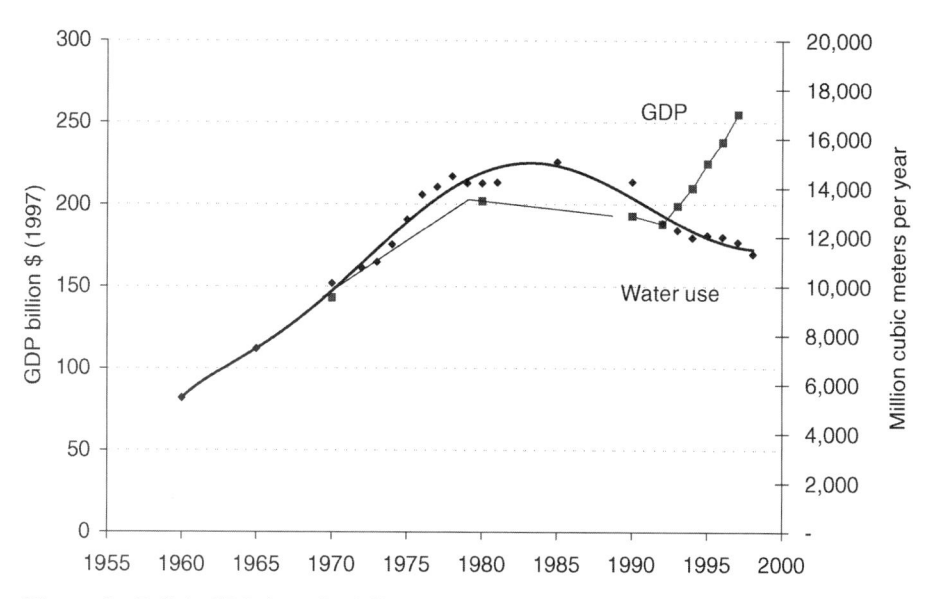

Figure 6 Polish GDP in U.S. dollars (*squares*) and total water withdrawals in Poland (*diamonds*). After democratization in Poland, economic productivity soared, and water use (represented as the trend line) decreased as industries rapidly improved overall efficiency.

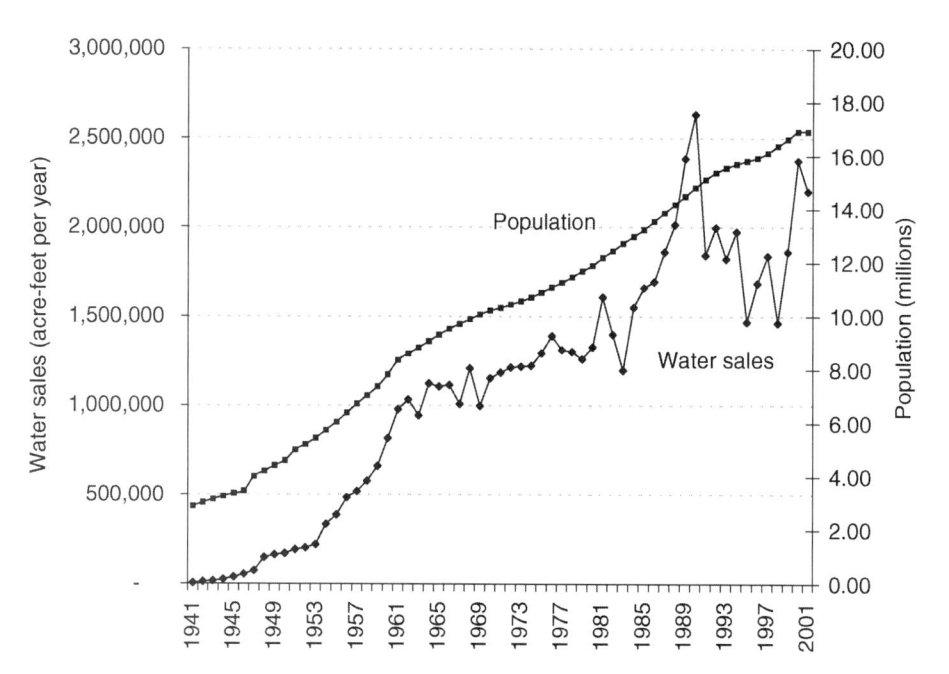

Figure 7 Water sales and population for the Metropolitan Water District of Southern California, which serves 17 million people. Water conservation and efficiency programs have led to a leveling off of demand, despite growing populations.

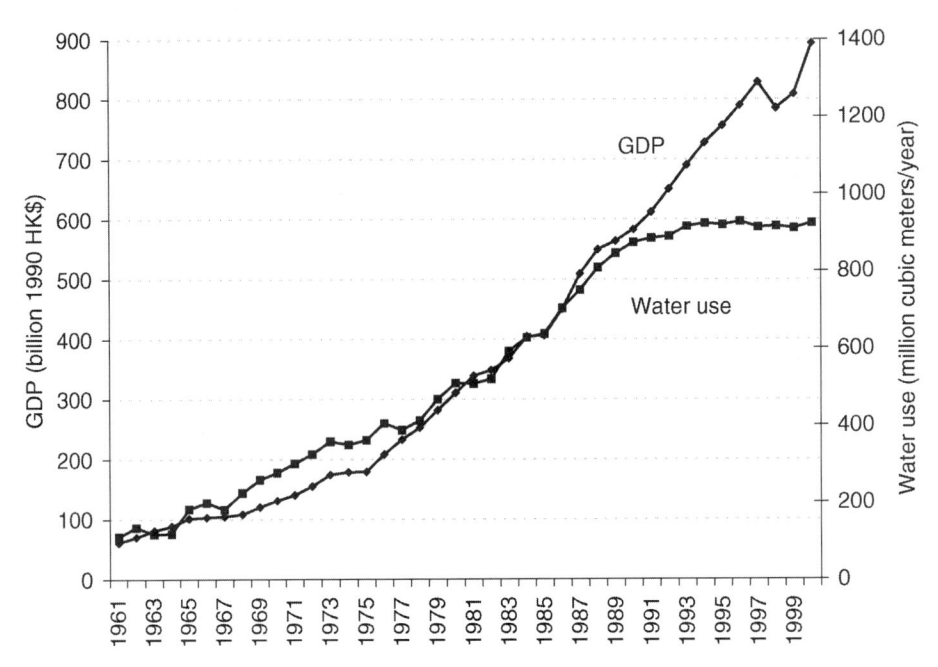

Figure 8 Hong Kong GDP and total water withdrawals. The curves appear to follow the water use in most classic industrialized countries, with a break between rising GDP in constant 1990 Hong Kong dollars and water use, which in this case occurred around 1990 (D. Chen, Chinese University of Hong Kong, personal communication).

The concept of integrating nonstructural water-management approaches into water planning goes back many decades. In 1950, the Water Resources Policy Commission of the United States published *A Water Policy for the American People*, which noted that

> We can no longer be wasteful and careless in our attitude towards our water resources. Not only in the West, where the crucial value of water has long been recognized, but in every part of the country, we must manage and conserve water if we are to make the best use of it for future development (59).

In the early 1960s, White called for broadening the range of alternatives examined by water managers who had previously only focused on structural solutions to water problems (60). Under White's approach, managers should consider both structural and nonstructural alternatives, including zoning, land-use planning, and changing water-use patterns. Unfortunately, traditional water management has, in general, continued to concentrate heavily on the construction of physical infrastructure.

Wherever fresh water was abundant historically, end-use technologies were simple. Washbasins, with or without running water, or pipes located at the proper height over well-drained surfaces were adequate for drinking, cooking, bathing,

WATER USE **301**

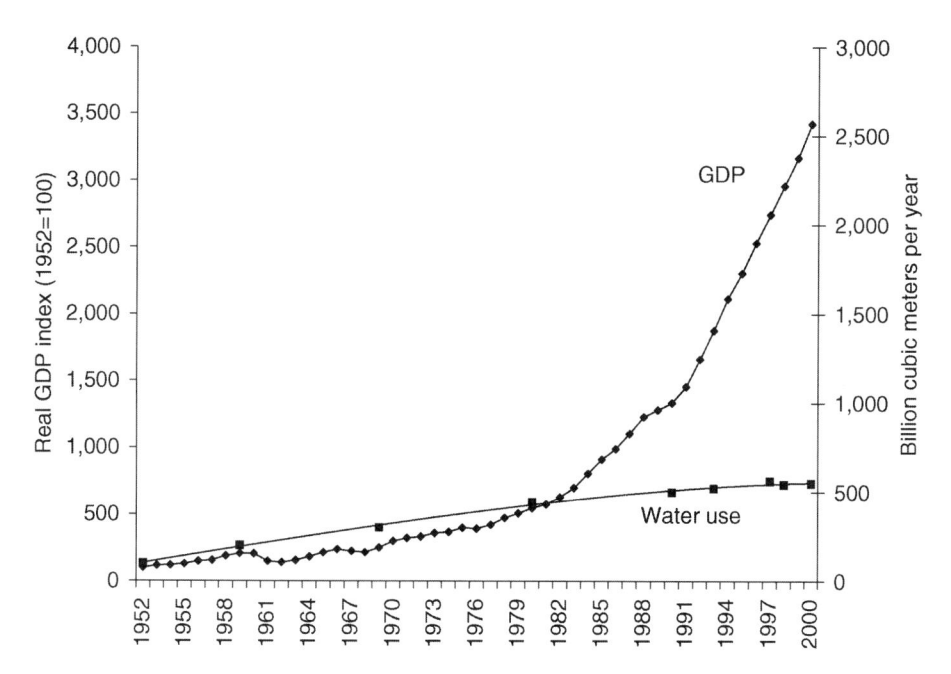

Figure 9 China's GDP index (1952 = 100) and total water withdrawals.

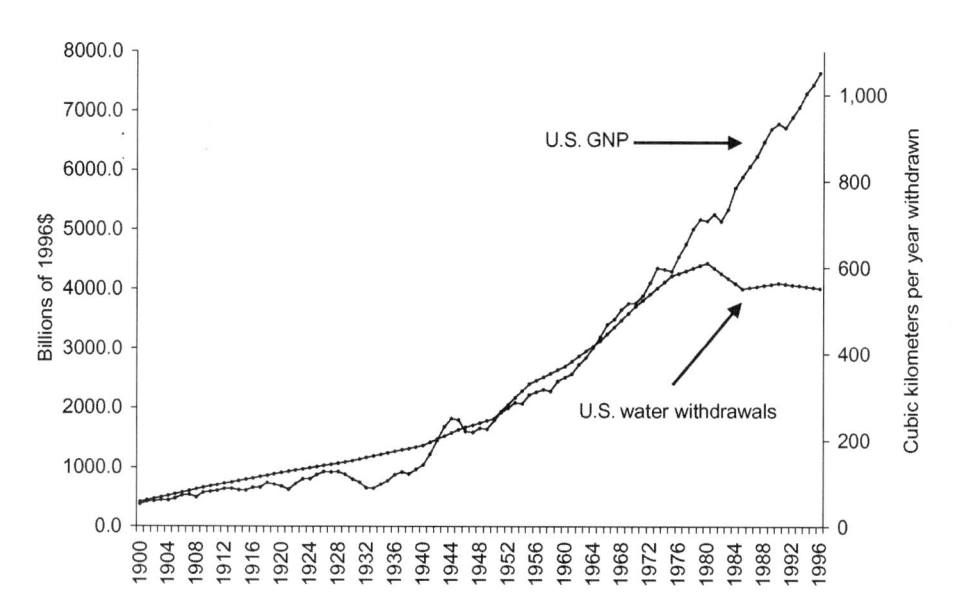

Figure 10 U.S. GNP (1996 dollars) and total water withdrawals in the United States. U.S. water use rose consistently with GDP up until the 1980s when the two curves split apart. Total water use in the United States is now actually well below its peak level, because the economic productivity of water use in the United States has improved.

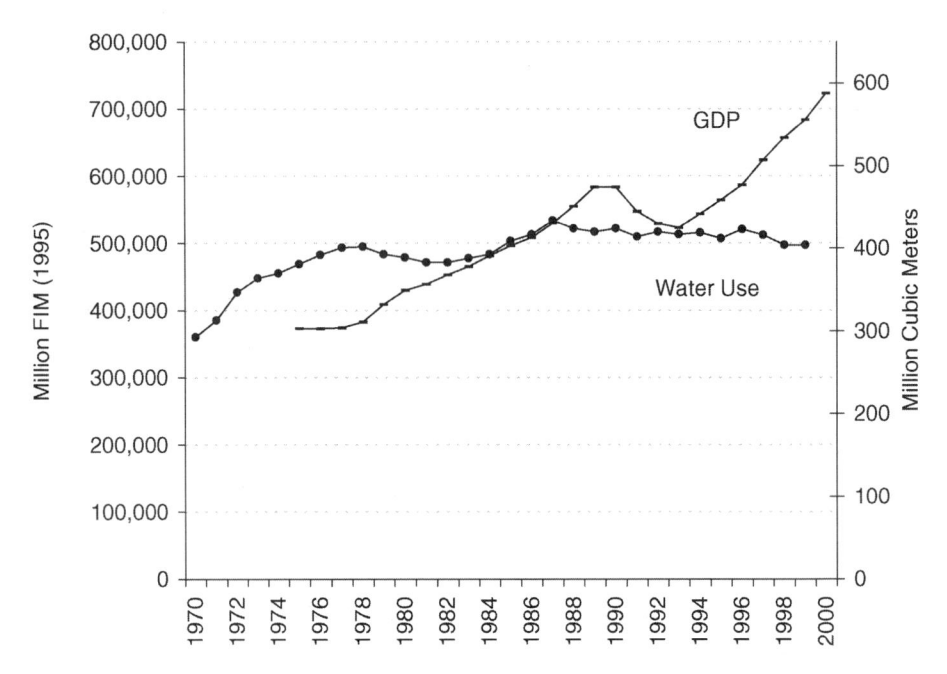

Figure 11 Total Finish GDP (1995 FIM) and water withdrawals in Finland.

and clothes washing. Machinery that used water, such as electrically powered clothes washers, were designed much later to replace human labor, not to use water more efficiently. Sophisticated and technically efficient water measurement and use devices, a key component of soft path water systems, were not necessary and did not develop as rapidly as did water collection and distribution technologies.

Where water was scarce, more efficient technologies and patterns of use were developed. The choice of crops is a good example: People need nutritional food but can choose among a variety of crops to meet that need. Olives are an important part of Middle Eastern and Mediterranean cultures because they are well adapted to semiarid regions. Rice was grown in wetter regions of the world and did not appear in arid regions prior to the availability of inexpensive energy and irrigation water. Such crop choices are examples of appropriate decisions when water is scarce.

Most water managers have a background in engineering with a focus on building structures to capture and deliver water and water services (61). Thus the idea that rice can be grown in water-scarce regions seems like a simple problem of figuring out how to move water from elsewhere. Efficiency improvements, however, depend on the behavior of water users, rather than water agency or company personnel, and on the application of technologies at the end-use level. Capturing these improvements requires different professional skills and training than are traditionally taught in water management schools. As the water-use efficiency and management field matures, however, water utilities will increasingly demand training in people management, the application of small-scale technology, and water-use assessment. Indeed, growing numbers of water agencies now have water conservation departments, and professional societies, such as the American Water Works Association and the International Water Resources Association, are promoting efficiency discussions and adding water-use experts and groups (62, 62a).

To compound the problem of training and the need for new professional skills, the economics of efficiency improvements have been poorly understood and inaccurately estimated by traditional methods. As a result, estimates of the potential for improving water-use efficiency are almost always lower than the true potential, as the inaccurate projections described earlier suggest. In places where an effort has been made to identify and capture improvements in water-use efficiency, water demands have been cut by 20%, 30%, 40% or more (11, 58, 63).

Cost-Effectiveness of Efficiency Improvements

Centralized water facilities were historically lower in cost, within a narrow accounting methodology, than decentralized investments in efficiency. This may still be the case in some circumstances. But the belief that efficiency improvements are more expensive than new or expanded centralized water supply is incorrect in most circumstances (64, 65). In addition, it is increasingly apparent that most cost projections of new large, centralized systems are routinely and often substantially underestimated, even without accounting for hard-to-measure environmental and social costs. Although this is a problem common to many large capital projects, it has received considerable attention around the construction of dams and reservoirs, which often end up costing much more than originally projected (66). World Bank statistics on dam construction projects suggest that construction cost overruns averaged 30% on the 70 hydropower projects funded by the Bank since the 1960s (67). Other World Bank studies found that three quarters of the 80 hydro projects completed in the 1970s and 1980s had costs in excess of their budgets, and almost one third of the projects studied had actual costs that exceeded estimates by 50% or more (68).

There are many reasons for cost overruns; these include delays, design errors, poor quality construction, or corruption of project advocates and managers. For example, the Chixoy Dam in Guatemala was delayed for nine years by the collapse of poorly designed tunnels, social opposition, and corruption. Its final cost of $1.2 billion was more than five times its initial cost estimate, and some studies suggest the final cost may have been as high as $2.5 billion (69). The Yacyreta Dam on the Parana River between Argentina and Paraguay became known as a "monument to corruption" as the cost of the project increased to $8 billion from an original estimate of $1.6 billion (67). Cost overruns are not restricted to projects in less developed countries. In 2000, an economist at the U.S. Army Corps of Engineers blew the whistle on biased cost-benefit studies for projects along the Missouri and Mississippi rivers, which led to calls for reform of the cost estimating and evaluation (70).

In contrast, the cost of efficiency improvements seems to be decreasing over time as technologies and conservation programs mature and as rate designs begin to account for the true costs of water supply (71, 72). In the United States, the best low-flow toilets cost no more on average than inadequate low-flow models or older wasteful models, especially over the lifetime of the product (11). As water suppliers have learned which models reliably save water, and provided this information to their customers, the cost of conserving water via low-flow toilet installation has fallen. This trend will continue as the technology for pressure-flush toilets (around 0.6 gallons per flush) and waterless toilets and urinals improves.

Another reason for the belief that efficiency improvements are too expensive is that traditional water planners usually estimate the cost of efficiency improvements without accounting for secondary benefits. Such secondary benefits, such as energy savings, can be substantial. In the residential sector in California, without accounting for the avoided energy expense for water heating, for example, only efficient toilets and showerheads are cost-effective compared with new water supply projects at any water price exceeding $0.05 per cubic meter. After accounting for energy benefits, efficient clothes- and dishwashers would be highly cost-effective, even if new water supply could be obtained for free (7, 73)

There are other secondary benefits to be gained as well that are rarely calculated. Among these are

- Reductions in peak water system loads. Peak loads determine the size of capital facilities required, hence capital costs. Lower peak loads mean that existing capital facilities can serve more customers and avoid or reduce the expense of these facilities.

- Reductions in peak energy demands. Energy and water supply networks are similar in many ways. Reduction of peak energy demands that result from efficiency improvements and a decrease in water pumping, treatment, or heating needs will similarly allow energy utilities to serve more customers with existing capital facilities and avoid or reduce capital expenses that are ultimately paid by energy purchasers.

- Reductions in wastewater treatment expenses, both operational expenses and costs for expanding sewers or treatment facilities.

- Reductions in environmental damage from water withdrawals or wastewater discharges in environmentally sensitive locations.

- Increases in employment, for example, by increasing the rate at which appliances or irrigation systems are monitored, serviced, or replaced. Investments in large, centralized capital facilities increase employment during construction but use relatively little labor once construction is complete (73, 74).

The belief that efficiency improvements are not economically competitive with expansion of centralized supplies is slowly being overcome. Water planners are beginning to realize that the cost escalation, construction delays, and interest charges that so often plague large capital-intensive water projects rarely occur in conservation programs. This has been seen over and over again. For example, in Santa Barbara, California, a severe drought in the late 1970s stimulated local residents to support the construction of a large desalination plant, as well as a pipeline to connect to the centralized state water project. When the very high economic costs of those facilities were passed on to consumers, conservation and efficiency improvements reduced demand so fast that the need for the new facilities disappeared (75). The desalination plant was never put into routine operation and is mothballed (partially decommissioned). If effective pricing programs, education, and community planning had been done first, the expense of these facilities could have been long delayed and perhaps completely avoided.

A number of municipal water suppliers around the world have implemented aggressive water conservation programs. Municipal conservation programs that are fully integrated have shown impressive successes. Postel (63) includes an excellent summary of successful municipal programs in Jerusalem, Israel; Mexico City, Mexico; Los Angeles, California; Beijing, China; Singapore; Boston, Massachusetts; Waterloo, Canada; Bogor, Indonesia; and Melbourne, Australia. Reductions in water demand varied from 10%–30%. Vickers (11, 76) updates the results from the Massachusetts Water Resources Authority, which serves the Boston area, and presents data for the City of Albuquerque, New Mexico, and many other communities. Several municipalities have reported reductions of 25% or more. Owens-Viani (77) presents results from the Marin Municipal Water District in Northern California, where a conservation management plan led to a reduction in demand of about 15% in the first 10 years of implementation, despite a 7.5% increase in the district's population. This is only about half of their 20-year target of up to a 32% reduction in absolute demand despite increases in population. After adjusting for population growth, this 20-year target, already half achieved, amounts to a reduction in water use of approximately 45% per capita.

There are many opportunities for improving the efficiency of commercial, industrial, and institutional water uses. Pike (78) evaluated opportunities for various commercial and institutional water users in the United States and found that average potential savings vary from 9% to 31% within 18 categories of users (e.g., eating and drinking places, vehicle dealers, and services). Gleick et al. (73) found that overall savings potential in California's commercial and industrial sector was nearly 40% with existing technology. Similar statistics are provided by Vickers (11), who includes examples from outside the United States where potential reductions in industrial water use are often larger when combined with aggressive leak detection and repair. In many developing countries, 20% to 40%, or even more, of the water put into a system never reaches consumers because of leaks. Table 4 from Gleick (17) summarizes information on "unaccounted for water" from cities and countries around the world.

Most of these opportunities are cost effective and widely applicable. For industrial savings, one analysis found typical reductions of 30%–40% with estimated payback periods of less than one year (79). The report concluded: "The cost

TABLE 4 Unaccounted for water (17). See original for details on sources

Location	Period/year	Percent
Africa (large city average)	1990s	39
Algiers, Algeria	1990s	51
Amman, Jordan	1990s	52
Asia (large city average)	1990s	35 to 42
Bahrain	1993	36
Bahrain	2000	24
Barbados	1996	43
Buenos Aires, Argentina	1993	43
Buenos Aires, Argentina	1996	31
Canada (average)	1990s	15
Casablanca, Morocco	1990s	34
Damascus, Syria	1995	64
Dubai, United Arab Emirates	1990s	15
Gaza	1995	47
Gaza	1999	31
Haiphong, Vietnam	1998	70
Hanoi, Vietnam	1995	63
Hebron	1990s	48
Johor Bahru, Malaysia	1995	21
Kansas, United States (average)	1997	15
Kansas, United States (range)	1997	3 to 65
Lae, Papua New Guinea	1995	61
Latin America/Caribbean (large city average)	1990s	42
Lebanon	1990s	40
Male, Maldives	1995	10
Mandalay, Myanmar	1995	60
Mexico City, Mexico	1997	37
Mexico City, Mexico	1999	32
Nairobi, Kenya	2000	50
Nicosia, Cyprus	1990s	16
North America (large city average)	1990s	15
Oran, Algeria	1990s	42
Penang, Malaysia	1995	20
Phnom Penh, Vietnam	1995	61

(*Continued*)

TABLE 4 (*Continued*)

Location	Period/year	Percent
Poland (medium utility range)	1990s	19 to 51
Rabat, Morocco	1990s	18
Ramallah	1990s	25
Rarotonga, Cook Islands	1995	70
Sana'a, Yemen	1990s	50
Seoul, South Korea	1996	35
Singapore	1990s	11
Singapore	1995	6
Sydney, Australia	1990s	13.4
Tamir, Yemen	1990s	28
Teheran, Iran	1990s	35
Tunisia (large utility range)	1990s	8 to 21
United Kingdom (small utility range)	1990s	14 to 30
United States (average)	1990s	12
Vietnam (average)	1998	50
Washington, DC area suppliers	1999	10 to 28

effective water conservation measures successfully used at the case study facilities can readily be adopted by other facilities and other industries."

Major efficiency improvements are possible in the agricultural sector as well, and because this sector consumes such a large fraction of total human water use, it is deserving of special attention (80–82). Traditional irrigation methods are very inefficient. Furrow or flood irrigation is the simplest form of irrigation, with water delivered to rows of crops from a ditch or pipeline. As water moves into each row, it infiltrates the soil. For ideal irrigation, the amount of water infiltrated is just adequate to replace depleted soil water. In actuality, however, soils at the top end of rows receive more water than necessary to ensure that water reaches the end of each furrow, even if land is leveled to permit full coverage. These systems are among the most inefficient available, though experienced irrigators and careful tuning can somewhat reduce losses.

More efficient sprinkler systems that can apply water more accurately and carefully than flood systems are available. Sprinklers can be fixed or moving and require pumps to provide pressure necessary to distribute water through pipes. Fixed sprinklers require sufficient pipes and sprinkler heads to cover an entire field. To irrigate the field, sprinklers need only to be turned on and off. Moving sprinkler systems permit a small system to cover larger areas and can include periodically moved systems or constantly moved systems. Center-pivot and lateral-move systems are the most common, with a lateral pipeline that moves continuously in a direction perpendicular to the lateral or is fixed at one end to irrigate a large circular area. A modification of these moving systems is the low-energy, precision application (LEPA) system that discharges water just above the soil surface and reduces unproductive evaporative losses (83, 84).

Water productivity improvements can also be gained from techniques such as furrow diking, land leveling, direct seeding, drip irrigation, micro sprinklers, careful scheduling of irrigation, water recycling, and careful water accounting (85). For example, micro-irrigation systems (primarily drip and micro sprinklers) often achieve efficiencies in excess of 95% as compared with flood irrigation efficiencies of 60% or less (11, 86). As of 2000, however, the area under micro irrigation is around 2.8 million ha, only about 1% of all irrigated land (87). In China, vast quantities of the water used in agriculture are used inefficiently. In 2000, 97% of all Chinese irrigation used furrow/flood irrigation; 3% of the irrigated area was watered with sprinkers and drip systems (88). Even in California, a small fraction of all cropland was irrigated with drip systems in the mid-1990s (6).

Another example is laser leveling of fields, which permits water to be distributed more uniformly. This reduces the water required to ensure that all parts of the field are irrigated adequately. Recent experience growing wheat, alfalfa, and cotton in the Welton-Mohawk Valley of Arizona found that water use declined between 20%–32% as a result of laser leveling, and yields increased from 12%–22% (11). This practice requires that land be leveled every two to five years, at a relatively modest cost, ~$100 per hectare.

Precision irrigation remains expensive, which makes it suitable only for higher-value crops. Extending more efficient irrigation systems to the vast numbers of small farmers is critical if significant new improvements in agricultural water use are to be captured. Most of the world's 1.1 billion farmers live in developing countries and cultivate plots smaller than two hectares (89). These farmers cannot afford sophisticated and costly precision irrigation systems, yet they would benefit from access to better equipment. In recent years, new low-cost drip techniques have begun to emerge and open up vast potential for the poor small farmers of developing countries. International Development Enterprises has helped push the development of simple but functional low-cost solutions using cloth filtration, a bucket as a container, and inexpensive drip lines. These systems can reduce the capital costs from $2500 to $250 per hectare, reduce water use by 50%, and increase yields (90–92). Widespread expansion of such low-cost drip systems has the potential to boost farmer incomes, raise yields and crop productivity, and ameliorate persistent hunger, while reducing overall water use in agriculture. It remains to be seen if the barriers to widespread application of inexpensive efficiency systems, such as higher production and maintenance expenses, the need for local production of equipment, and farmer reluctance to adopt unfamiliar technology, can be overcome.

Urban Improvements: The Example of California

California has begun to explore the potential for improving the efficiency of water use in every sector because of growing constraints on new supply. New studies suggest that the future potential for improving urban water-use efficiency is large even in regions and sectors that have already conserved a considerable amount of water (73). Figure 12 shows indoor residential water use in California under a business as usual scenario through 2020 and an estimate of total indoor residential use if currently cost-effective technologies and policies are implemented. The upper line in this figure indicates the level of water use statewide without implementing efficiency measures and would require the state to develop new water supplies to meet this projected need. The lower line in the figure is the maximum practical savings from implementing the current best practical technologies.

The two curves show that a traditional water policy would require about a 45% increase (over 1.1 billion cubic meters per year from current levels) in water supply for indoor residential purposes by the year 2020, but an efficient path actually reduces total indoor residential demand by about 25% (over 600 million

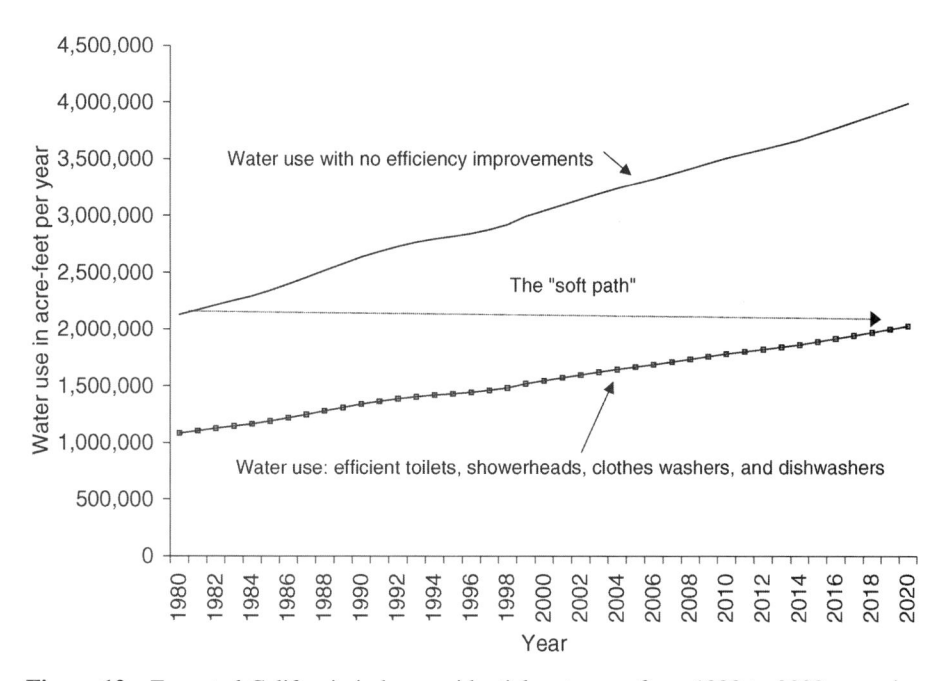

Figure 12 Expected California indoor residential water use from 1998 to 2020 assuming no improvements in efficiency (*top curve*) and assuming that all cost-effective improvements using existing technology are implemented (*bottom curve*). If all efficiency improvements are implemented, total indoor residential water use in 2020 could be below the level of actual water use in 1980, despite a 50% increase in population.

cubic meters) despite population growth. This means that the soft path for indoor residential use can cost-effectively conserve about 1.7 billion cubic meters of water by the year 2020 (73). This simple example, for a single sector of California water use, shows the dramatic gains possible by putting more effort into demand-management of water.

CONCLUSIONS

The focus of water planning and management is slowly shifting from the development of water-supply systems to more integrated analysis of how and why humans use water. By better understanding water needs, improvements in the overall productivity of human activities can be identified and achieved, which will reduce water use and the adverse implications of that use.

Water use is still poorly understood and inadequately measured and reported. Problems with definitions and data collection hinder efforts to improve water-use efficiency. Inappropriate water planning still results from simplistic assumptions about how water uses will change in the future. Nevertheless, a substantial shift in thinking has occurred in recent years as the social, political, economic, and environmental costs of traditional water developments have become apparent. There is growing evidence and experience that shows how improvements in water-use efficiency can offer the fastest and cleanest sources of new supply by reducing overall demands for water in every sector. In some countries, water use is even beginning to level off or decline despite growing populations and economies and offers the hope that smart management will be an effective tool in sustainable water systems.

The *Annual Review of Environment and Resources* is online at
http://environ.annualreviews.org

LITERATURE CITED

1. Crouch DP. 1993. *Water Management in Ancient Greek Cities*. New York: Oxford Univ. Press
2. Landels JG. 2000. *Engineering in the Ancient World*. Berkeley, CA: Univ. Calif. Press
3. World Comm. Dams. 2000. *Dams and Development: A New Framework for Decision-Making*. London: Earthscan
4. Douglas M, Gasper D, Ney S, Thompson M. 1998. Human needs and wants. In *Human Choices and Climate Change*, Vol. 1, ed. S Rayner, E Malone, pp. 195–263. Columbus, OH: Battelle
5. Gleick PH. 1996. Basic water requirements for human activities: meeting basic needs. *Water Int.* 21:83–92
6. Gleick PH. 2002. Soft water paths. *Nature* 418:373
7. Wolff G, Gleick PH. 2002. The soft path for water. In *The World's Water 2002–2003*, ed. PH Gleick, WCG Burns, EL Chalecki, M Cohen, KK Cushing, et al., pp. 1–32. Washington, DC: Island
8. Brooks D. 2003. *Another path not taken: a methodological exploration of water soft paths for Canada and elsewhere*. Friends of the Earth Can. Rep. (March) pp. 67
9. White S. 1999. Integrated resource

planning in the Australian water industry. *Proc. CONSERV99, Am. Water Works Assoc., Monterey, CA*, Feb.
10. Del Porto D, Steinfeld C. 1999. *The Composting System Toilet Book*. Concord, MA: Cent. Ecol. Pollut. Prev.
11. Vickers AL. 2001. *Handbook of Water Use and Conservation*. Amherst, MA: WaterPlow. 439 pp.
12. Shiklomanov IA. 1993. World fresh water resources. In *Water in Crisis: A Guide to the World's Fresh Water Resources*, ed. PH Gleick, pp. 13–24. New York: Oxford Univ. Press
13. Boland JJ, Dziegielewski B, Bauman DD, Opitz EM. 1984. *Influence of Price and Rate Structures on Minimum and Maximum Water Use*. Carbondale, IL: Plan. Manag. Consult.
14. Keller A, Keller J. 1995. *Effective efficiency: A water use efficiency concept for allocating freshwater resources*. Water Resour. Irrig. Div. Discuss. Pap. 22. Cent. Econ. Policy Stud. Arlington, VA
15. Molden D. 1997. *Accounting for water use and productivity. System-wide initiative on water management (SWIM). Rep. 1*. Int. Irrig. Manag. Inst., Colombo, Sri Lanka
16. Seckler D. 1996. *The new era of water resources management: from dry to wet water savings. Res. Rep. 1*. Int. Irrig. Manag. Inst., Colombo, Sri Lanka
17. Gleick PH. 2002. *The World's Water 2002–2003*. Washington, DC: Island
18. Calif. Dep. Water Resour. 1998. *The California Water Plan Update*. Bull. 160–98, Sacramento, CA
19. Gleick PH, Haasz D. 1998. *Review of the CalFed water-use efficiency component technical appendix. Rep*. Pac. Inst. Stud. Dev., Environ., Secur. Oakland, CA
20. Palacios-Velez E. 1994. Water use efficiency in irrigation districts. In *Efficient Water Use*, ed. H Garduno, F Arreguin-Cortes. Montevideo: UN Educ. Sci. Cult. Organ./Reg. Off. Sci. Technol. Lat. Am. Caribb.
21. Baumann DD, Boland JJ, Sims JH. 1980. *The problem of defining water conservation*. Cornett Pap., Univ. Victoria, Vic., BC, Can. pp. 125–34
22. UN Food Agric. Organ. 2002. FAOSTAT AQUASTAT database. www.fao.org
23. Solley WB, Pierce RR, Perlman HA. 1998. *Estimated Use of Water in the United States*. US Geol. Surv. Circ. 1200. Denver, CO
24. Eurostat Year B. 1997. *Statistics of the European Union*. EC/C/61 Ser.26GT. Luxembourg
25. Eur. Environ. Agency. 1999. *Sustainable Water Use in Europe*. Copenhagen, Den.: EEA
26. Gov. S. Afr. 1998. *National Water Act 36 of 1998*. Pretoria: Gov. S. Afr.
27. Schultz GA. 2000. Potential of modern data types for future water resources management. *Water Int*. 25(1):89–109
28. Simonovic SP. 2000. Tools for water management: one view of the future. *Water Int*. 25(1):76–88
29. Shiklomanov IA. 1998. *Assessment of water resources and water availability in the world. UN Rep. Compr. Assess. Freshw. Resour. World*, Data arch. CD-ROM State Hydrol. Inst., St. Petersburg, Russia
30. Postel SL, Daily GC, Ehrlich PR. 1996. Human appropriation of renewable fresh water. *Science* 271:785–88
31. UN Food Agric. Organ. 1995. *Irrigation in Africa in figures*. Water Rep. 7. Rome, Italy
32. UN Food Agric. Organ. 1997. *Irrigation in the Near East region in figures*. Water Rep. 9. Rome, Italy
33. UN Food Agric. Organ. 1997. *Irrigation in the former Soviet Union in figures*. Water Report No. 15. Rome, Italy
34. UN Food Agric. Organ. 2000. *Irrigation in Latin America in figures*. Water Rep. 20. Rome, Italy
35. Gleick PH, Burns WCG, Chalecki EL, Cohen M, Cushing KK, et al. *The World's Water 2002–2003, Table 2*, pp. 243–51. Washington, DC: Island

36. MacKichan KA. 1951. *Estimated Water Use in the United States, 1950*: US Geol. Surv. Circ. 115. Reston, VA. 13 pp.
37. MacKichan KA. 1957. *Estimated Water Use in the United States, 1955*: U.S. Geol. Surv. Circ. 398. Reston, VA. 18 pp.
38. MacKichan KA, Kammerer JC. 1961. *Estimated Use of Water in the United States, 1960*: U.S. Geol. Surv. Circ. 456. Reston, VA. 26 pp.
39. Solley WB, Pierce RR, Perlman HA. 1998. *Estimated Use of Water in the United States*. U.S. Geol. Surv. Circ. 1200. Denver, CO
40. Natl. Res. Counc. 2002. *Estimating Water Use in the United States: A New Paradigm for the National Water-Use Information Program*. Washington, DC: Natl. Acad.
41. Counc. Environ. Qual. 1991. *Environmental Quality: 21st Annu. Rep.*, Washington, DC
42. US Dep. Inter. 2002. *Rep. Cong. Concepts for National Assessment of Water Availability and Use*. Circ. 1223, US Geol. Surv. Reston, VA
43. Natl. Res. Counc. 2002. *Estimating Water Use in the United States: A New Paradigm for the National Water-Use Information Program*. Washington, DC: Natl. Acad.
44. Cole MA. 2003. Economic growth and water use. *Appl. Econ. Lett.* 10: In press
45. Schwartz P. 1991. *The Art of the Long View*. New York: Currency/Doubleday
46. L'vovich MI. 1974. *World Water Resources and Their Future*. Transl. R Nace, 1979, Washington, DC: Am. Geophys. Union 415 pp.
47. De Mare L. 1976. *Resources—Needs—Problems: An assessment of the World Water Situation by 2000*. Lund, Swed.: Inst. Technol./Univ. Lund
48. Falkenmark M, Lindh G. 1974. How can we cope with the water resources situation by the year 2050? *Ambio* 3(3–4):114–22
49. Kalinin GP, Shiklomanov IA. 1974. *USSR: World Water Balance and Water Resources of the Earth*. USSR Natl. Comm. IHD, Leningrad (In Russian)
50. Raskin P, Gleick PH, Kirshen P, Pontius G, Strzepek K. 1997. *Water Futures: Assessment of Long-range Patterns and Problems*. Backgr. Doc. Chapter 3 Compr. Assess. Freshw. Resour. World. Stock. Environ. Inst. Boston, MA. 77 pp.
51. Seckler D, Amarasinghe U, Molden D, de Silva R, Barker R. 1998. *World water demand and supply, 1990 to 2025: scenarios and issues*. Res. Rep. 19, Int. Water Manag. Inst., Colombo, Sri Lanka
52. Gleick PH. 1997. *Water 2050: Moving Toward A Sustainable Vision for the Earth's Fresh Water*. Rep. Pac. Inst. Stud. Dev., Environ., Secur., Oakland, CA
53. Alcamo J, Döll P, Kaspar F, Siebert S. 1997. *Global change and global scenarios of water use and availability: An application of Water GAP 1.0*. Rep. Wiss. Zent. Für Umweltsystemforschung, Univ. Gesamthochsch. Kassel, Ger.
54. Allan T. 1997. *'Virtual water': a long term solution for water short Middle Eastern economies?* Presented at Br. Assoc. Festiv. Sci.,Univ. Leeds,UK. Sept. 9. http://www2.soas.ac.uk/Geography/WaterIssues/OccasionalPapers/AcrobatFiles/OCC03.PDF
55. Natl. Assoc. Manufact. 1950. *Water in industry*. Rep. Econ. Policy Div. Ser. 36, Append. C. Washington, DC
56. Kollar KL, MacAuley P. 1980. Water requirements for industrial development. *J. Am. Water Works Assoc.* 72 (1):2–9
57. Posco Steel. 2002. *Environmental Progress Report: Environmentally Sound and Sustainable Development*. Pohang, Korea. http://www.posco.co.kr/en/sustain/environment04_01.html
58. Gleick PH. 2001. Making Every Drop Count. *Sci. Am.* Feb.:28–33
59. Water Resour. Policy Comm. 1950. *A Water Policy for the American People, The Report of the President's Water Resources Policy Commission, Vol. 1*. Washington, DC: US GPO. 445 pp.

60. White GF. 1961. The choices of use in resource management. *Nat. Resour. J.* 1:23–40
61. Schultz GA. 1998. A change of paradigm in water sciences at the turn of the century? *Water Int.* 23(1):37–44
62. Am. Water Works Assoc. *Water Conservation Around the Home.* http://www.awwa.org/Advocacy/learn/conserve/
62a. Metrop. Water Dist. South. Calif. *Conservation and the Environment.* http://www.mwd.dst.ca.us/mwdh2o/pages/conserv/conserv01.html
63. Postel S. 1997. *Last Oasis: Facing Water Scarcity.* New York: Norton. 239 pp.
64. Macy P, Maddaus W. 1989. Cost-benefit analysis of conservation programs. *J. Am. Water Works Assoc.* 81:3–43
65. Maddaus WO. 1999. Realizing the benefits from water conservation. *Water Resour. Update* 114:8–17
66. World Comm. Dams. 2000. *Overview summary. Dams and development: a new framework for decision-making. Rep.* http://www.dams.org/report/wcd_overview.htm
67. McCully P. 1996. *Silenced Rivers: The Ecology and Politics of Large Dams.* London: Zed Books. 350 pp.
68. Morrow EW, Shangraw RF Jr. 1990. *Understanding the costs and schedules of World Bank supported hydroelectric projects. Rep.*, World Bank Ind. Energy Dep. July. Washington, DC
69. Chen C. 2000. *The Chixoy Dam Case Study.* World Comm. Dams. Submiss. soc073. http://www.dams.org/kbase/submissions/sublist.php
70. US Off. Spec. Counc. 2000. *Letter to the President, Dec. 6. USOSC File No. DI-00-0792.* Washington, DC
71. Goldstone J. 1986. Full-cost water pricing. *Am. Water Works Assoc. J.* 78(2):52–61
72. Chesnutt TW, Beecher JA, Mann PC, Clark DM, Hanemann WM, Raftelis GA. 1997. *Designing, Evaluating and Implementing Conservation Rate Structures: A Handbook.* Sacramento, CA: Calif. Urban Water Conserv. Counc.
73. Gleick PH, Haasz D, Henges-Jeck C, Srinivasan V, Wolff GH, Mann A. 2003. *Waste not, want not: the potential for urban water conservation and efficiency in California. Rep.* Pac. Inst. Stud. Dev., Environ., Secur. Oakland, CA. In press
74. Dziegielewski B. 1999. Management of water demand: unresolved issues. *Water Resour. Update* 114:1–7
75. Calif. Resour. Agency. 1997. *California's Ocean Resources: An Agenda for the Future.* Sacramento, CA http://resources.ca.gov/ocean/97Agenda/97Agenda.html
76. Vickers AL. 1999. The future of water conservation: challenges ahead. *Water Resour. Update* 114:49–51
77. Owens-Viani L. 1999. Marin Municipal Water District's innovative integrated resource management program. In *Sustainable Use of Water: California Success Stories*, ed. L Owens-Viani, AK Wong, PH Gleick, pp. 11–26. Oakland, CA: Pac. Inst. Stud. Dev., Environ., Secur.
78. Pike C. 1997. *Some implications of the 1997 California food processor survey.* Presented at 214th Am. Chem. Soc. Natl. Meet., Sept. 9. Las Vegas, NV
79. Brown & Caldwell, Inc. 1990. *Case studies of industrial water conservation in the San Jose area.* Brown & Caldwell, Pleasant Hill, CA
80. Molden D, Sakthivadivel R, Perry CJ, de Fraiture C, Kloezen WH. 1998. *Indicators for comparing performance of irrigated agricultural systems. Int. Water Manag. Inst. Res. Rep. 20.* Colombo, Sri Lanka
81. Natl. Res. Counc. 1996. *A New Era for Irrigation.* Washington, DC: Natl. Acad.
82. Counc. Agric. Sci. Technol. 1988. *Effective use of water in irrigated agriculture.* Task Force Rep. 113. Ames, IA
83. Schneider AD, Howell TA, Evett SR. 2001. *Comparison of SDI, LEPA, and spray irrigation efficiency.* Agric. Res. Serv. Pap. 012019 2001. Presented at ASAE Annu. Int. Meet., Sacramento, CA.

84. Fipps G, New LL. 1994. Improving the efficiency of center pivot irrigation with LEPA. In *Efficient Water Use*, ed. H Garduño, F Arreguín-Cortés. Montevideo, Urug: UN Educ. Sci. Cult. Organ./Reg. Off. Sci. Technol. Lat. Am. Caribb. 379 pp.
85. Guerra LC, Bhuiyan SI, Tuong TP, Barker R. 1998. *Producing more rice with less water from irrigated systems*. Int. Water Manag. Inst. SWIM Pap. 5. Colombo, Sri Lanka
86. Keller J, Bliesner RD. 1990. *Sprinkle and Trickle Irrigation Design*. New York: Van Nostrand Reinhold
87. Postel S. 1999. *Pillar of Sand: Can the Irrigation Miracle Last?* New York: Norton. 313 pp.
88. Jin L, Young W. 2001. Water use in agriculture in China: importance, challenges, and implications for policy. *Water Policy* 3(3):215–28
89. Van Hofwegen P, Svendsen M. 2000. *A vision of water for food and rural development*. Presented at 2nd World Water Forum. The Hague, Neth.
90. Polak P, Nanes Adhikari D. 1997. A low-cost drip irrigation system for small farmers in developing countries. *J. Am. Water Resour. Assoc.* 33(1):119–24
91. Postel S, Polak P, Gonzales F, Keller J. 2001. Drip irrigation for small farmers: A new initiative to alleviate hunger and poverty. *Water Int.* 26(1):3–13
92. Int. Dev. Enterprises. 2002. *Low Cost Drip Irrigation Fact Sheet*. http://www.ideorg.org/html/gallery/drip.html
93. Gleick PH. 1998. The changing water paradigm. In *The World's Water 1998-1999*, ed. PH Gleick, pp. 5–37. Washington, DC: Island
94. Gleick PH. 2000. Pictures of the future: a review of global water resources projections. In *The World's Water 2000–2001*, ed. PH Gleick, pp. 39–61. Washington, DC: Island

… Annu. Rev. Environ. Resour. 2003. 28:315–58 …

MEETING CEREAL DEMAND WHILE PROTECTING NATURAL RESOURCES AND IMPROVING ENVIRONMENTAL QUALITY

Kenneth G. Cassman, Achim Dobermann, Daniel T. Walters, and Haishun Yang

Department of Agronomy and Horticulture, University of Nebraska, Lincoln, Nebraska 68583; email: kcassman1@unl.edu, adobermann2@unl.edu, dwalters1@unl.edu, hyang2@unl.edu

Key Words carbon sequestration, food security, nitrogen use efficiency, yield potential

■ **Abstract** Agriculture is a resource-intensive enterprise. The manner in which food production systems utilize resources has a large influence on environmental quality. To evaluate prospects for conserving natural resources while meeting increased demand for cereals, we interpret recent trends and future trajectories in crop yields, land and nitrogen fertilizer use, carbon sequestration, and greenhouse gas emissions to identify key issues and challenges. Based on this assessment, we conclude that avoiding expansion of cultivation into natural ecosystems, increased nitrogen use efficiency, and improved soil quality are pivotal components of a sustainable agriculture that meets human needs and protects natural resources. To achieve this outcome will depend on raising the yield potential and closing existing yield gaps of the major cereal crops to avoid yield stagnation in some of the world's most productive systems. Recent trends suggest, however, that increasing crop yield potential is a formidable scientific challenge that has proven to be an elusive goal.

CONTENTS

INTRODUCTION 316
ARABLE LAND RESOURCES 318
   Estimating Land Reserves 318
   Case Studies: Sub-Saharan Africa and China 319
   Preserving Natural Ecosystems 320
YIELD POTENTIAL AND EXPLOITABLE YIELD GAPS 321
   Definitions 321
   Importance of Maintaining an Exploitable Yield Gap 321
   Estimating Trends in Rice Yield Potential 324
   Estimating Trends in Yield Potential of Maize and Wheat ... 327
   Are Existing Yield Gaps Large Enough? 328

1543-5938/03/1121-0315$14.00

NITROGEN EFFICIENCY AND TRENDS IN
NITROGEN FERTILIZER USE 330
   Inorganic Versus Organic Nitrogen Sources 330
   Nitrogen Efficiency at the Field Level 331
   Global Trends in Cereal Production and Nitrogen Fertilizer Use 334
   Disaggregating Trends in Cereal Yields and Nitrogen Fertilizer Use 336
   Projection of Future Nitrogen Fertilizer Requirements 340
   Improving Nitrogen Use Efficiency 342
CARBON SEQUESTRATION, GREENHOUSE FORCING, AND
SOIL QUALITY 343
   Carbon Sequestration and Greenhouse Gas Emissions 343
   Soil Quality, Nitrogen Requirements, and
   Greenhouse Gas Emissions 346
CONCLUSIONS 349

INTRODUCTION

Agriculture currently appropriates a substantial portion of the Earth's natural resources. Crop production, pasture, and livestock grazing systems occupy 38% of total land area (1). Water used for irrigation accounts for 80% of all freshwater consumption (2). Nitrogen (N) fertilizer applied to agricultural land comprises more than 50% of the global reactive[1] N load attributable to human activities (3). The use of these resources has a number of negative environmental consequences (4–6). Land conversion from natural forests, wetlands, and grasslands to highly productive but simplified agroecosystems results in a substantial reduction in biodiversity on the converted land and a decrease in habitat for displaced wildlife and plant communities. Irrigation withdrawals from river systems and water bodies alter riparian habitat and reduce water quality necessary to support wildlife and native plant populations. Nitrogen losses associated with use of N fertilizer can result in nitrate contamination of water resources and increased emissions of nitrous oxide (N_2O), a potent greenhouse gas with a forcing potential about 300-fold greater than CO_2. Reduced water quality from irrigation withdrawals and nutrient losses from agricultural runoff have a negative impact on aquatic recreational activities that depend on pristine rivers, lakes, and coastlines.

Although production trends of the past 40 years have kept pace with food demand (Figure 1), at issue is whether the projected increases in food requirements can be met while protecting natural resources for future generations. Grain demand is expected to increase at a faster rate than population growth because economic development and urbanization will result in greater per capita consumption of livestock products in developing countries, where more than 95% of the population

---

[1]Reactive N refers to all N compounds in the atmosphere and biosphere that are biologically, photochemically, or radiatively active. The reactive N pool includes inorganic reduced (e.g., NH_3, NH_4^+) and oxidized (e.g., NO_x, HNO_3, N_2O, NO_3^-) compounds and organic compounds (e.g., urea, amines, proteins, amides).

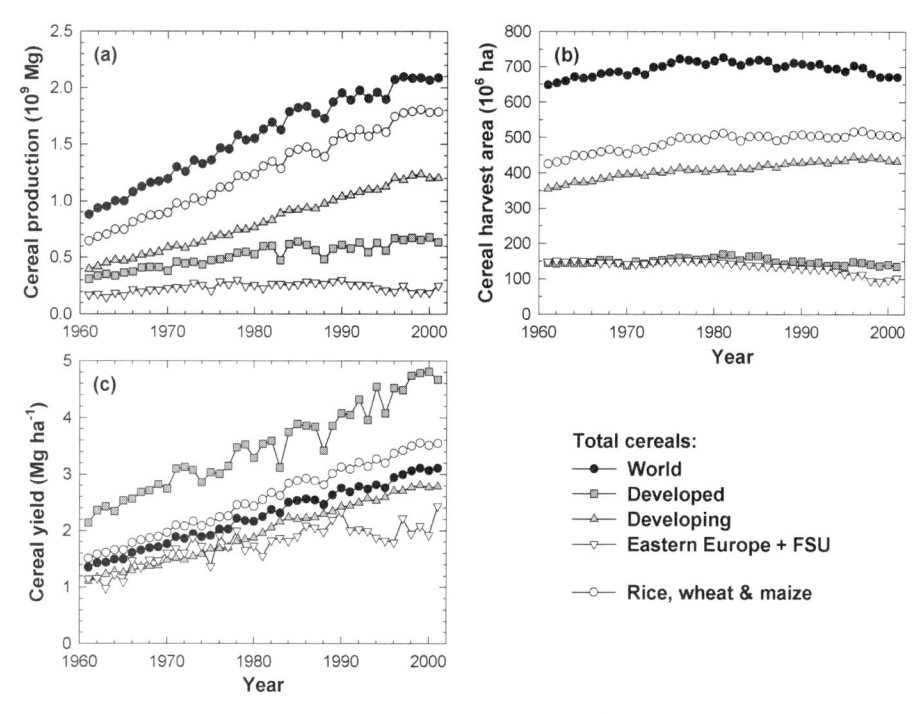

Figure 1 Trends in global cereal production, harvested area, and yield from 1960 to 2001. Developed countries include those in Western Europe and North America, Australia, New Zealand, South Africa, Israel, and Japan. Developing countries include those in Latin America, Africa, Near East, Asia, and Oceania (except those included in developed countries). Eastern Europe + FSU include the 14 countries of central and eastern Europe and all 15 countries of the Former Soviet Union (FSU) (9).

growth will occur (7). Feed grains are projected to account for 35% of the increase in global cereal production to 2020 because the majority of increase in meat production will most likely come from grain-fed poultry and swine produced in confined feeding operations, which require about 3 kg grain to produce 1 kg of meat (8). Therefore, world cereal demand is projected to increase by about 1.3% annually to 2025 (Table 1).

To evaluate prospects for conserving natural resources and improving environmental quality while meeting increased food demand, we interpret recent trends and future trajectories in land use, crop yields, nitrogen fertilizer use, carbon sequestration, and greenhouse gas emissions to identify key issues and challenges. Our discussion will emphasize cropping systems that produce maize, rice, and wheat because these three cereals provide about 60% of all human calories, either directly as human food or indirectly as feed grains for livestock, and will likely remain the foundation of the human food supply because of their high yield potential

TABLE 1 Projected changes in population, cereal demand, yields, area, and prices from 1995 to 2025. Values shown refer to the business-as-usual scenario of food and water demand and supply based on the International Model for Policy Analysis of Agricultural Commodities and Trade (IMPACT) model (2). Population projections are based on the medium scenario of the United Nations' 1998 projection (70)

Indices	1995	2025	Annual rate of change (%)
Global population (billion)	5.66	7.90	1.12
Global demand for rice, wheat, and maize (10^6 Mg)[a]	1657	2436	1.29
Total rice, wheat, and maize area (10^6 ha)	506	556	0.31
Mean rice, wheat, maize yield (Mg ha^{-1})[a]	3.27	4.38	0.98
World rice price (U.S. dollars Mg^{-1}, milled rice)	285	221	−0.84
World wheat price (U.S. dollars Mg^{-1})	133	119	−0.37
World maize price (U.S. dollars Mg^{-1})	103	104	0.03

[a]Numbers for cereal demand and yields are higher than those published in Rosegrant et al. (2) because rice is included as rough rice (paddy).

and ease of storage and transport. We will not cover the availability of water for irrigation, which is another critical resource for cereal production, because several recent reviews provide a thorough examination of the issues related to freshwater supplies for irrigated agriculture (2, 10–12).

ARABLE LAND RESOURCES

Estimating Land Reserves

Assessment of land resources available for agricultural expansion is estimated by the difference between land area currently used for crop production and land area that has the potential to produce crops. Most recent assessments rely on the land and crop database of the United Nations Food and Agriculture Organization (FAO) (9). Based on this approach, arable land reserves are estimated to be at least equal in size to the present area of cultivated land. For example, total land area suitable for production of at least one food crop was estimated at 3325 million ha (Mha), while existing irrigated and rain-fed cropland was estimated at 1505 Mha in 1994–1996, with another 156 Mha in settlements, roads, and infrastructure (13). By difference, the land reserve available for crop production was estimated at 1664 Mha, which is larger than the amount of cropland in current production.

Given this seemly large land reserve, econometric models developed to predict future food demand-supply scenarios are typically based on the assumption that availability of arable land is not a constraint to expansion of cropped area (14). Instead, cereal prices have the greatest influence on cropped area expansion. One such model is the International Model for Policy Analysis of Agricultural Commodities and Trade (IMPACT) model developed by the International Food Policy Research Institute, which projects a 10% increase (50 Mha) in harvested cereal area from 1995 and 2025 (Table 1), an increase that is about double the current U.S. maize area. Expansion of cereal production area in sub-Saharan Africa and South America is expected to account for most of this increase. Because this expansion is associated with constant or declining cereal prices, the increase in cropped area would be much greater if cereal prices were to rise.

In contrast to this reassuring scenario of surplus arable land, Young (15) argues that the difference method is grossly misleading because it overestimates the amount of uncultivated land that can be farmed in a sustainable fashion, underestimates the amount of land currently in crop production, and neglects the increasing demand for land used for nonagricultural purposes. For example, annual cereal cropping currently practiced on steeply sloping cropland in South and Central America, the Great Lakes region of Central Africa, and in southern China is not likely to be sustainable over the longer term because of severe erosion risk. Perennial crops and agroforestry systems are better suited to these environments. Likewise, sustained cereal production is questionable in the semiarid zones of sub-Saharan Africa where population pressure has forced increased cropping intensity on soils of low fertility.

Case Studies: Sub-Saharan Africa and China

A critical issue for sub-Saharan Africa is whether food demand can be met by intensification of crop production on existing cropland without further expansion of agriculture into more marginal production areas where the risk of crop failure, soil degradation, and environmental damage is high. Unfortunately, FAO statistics provide little insight into this issue because only harvested area is reported. For example, the increase in harvested crop area accounted for nearly all of the increase in food production in sub-Saharan Africa between 1989–1999, when there was little increase in yield of the major food crops (Table 2). It is impossible, however, to determine the relative contributions of intensification from growing two or more crops per year on the same piece of land in subhumid and humid areas, versus a reduction in length of the fallow period in semiarid zones, or actual expansion of cropped area into previously uncultivated areas. Lack of such data makes it difficult to estimate available land reserves to support sustainable crop production in sub-Saharan Africa.

Cultivated land area also is underestimated in some highly productive regions. Recent estimates of cropland in China, confirmed by remote sensing, are 35%–40% greater than the cultivated area reported in official government land-use statistics (16). But even with this larger estimate of cropped area, the land difference method suggests an additional land reserve of 30 Mha suitable for grain production. Such estimates do not account for the areas currently in cereal production systems that are not sustainable and the increasing amount of land needed for purposes other

TABLE 2 Annual percentage rates of change in area, yield, and production of the major food crops in sub-Saharan Africa, 1989–1999[a]

Crop	Area	Yield	Production
Cassava	2.6	0.7	3.3
Maize	0.8	0.2	1.0
Yam	7.2	0.4	7.6
Cowpea	7.6	−1.1	6.5
Plantain	1.9	0.1	2.0

[a]Annual growth rates in area, yield, and production were estimated from three-year means in 1988–1990 and 1998–2000 (9).

than agriculture. More than 2 Mha of agricultural land in China were converted to other uses from 1985 to 1995 (14). If China continues to follow trends in developed countries, the demand for national parks, recreation areas, and scenery will increase rapidly as economic development proceeds. Moreover, the process of industrialization and urbanization will continue to encroach on existing highly productive agricultural land while expansion of cropping will occur on more marginal land. Similar development processes will reduce arable land reserves for agriculture in other densely populated regions of South and Southeast Asia, which are currently major centers of cereal production. Assuming a requirement for housing and infrastructure of 40 ha per 1000 people, FAO estimates a need for an additional 100 Mha of urban land in developing countries by 2030 (14).

Preserving Natural Ecosystems

Native forests, savannas, and wetlands account for a large portion of the remaining land reserves worldwide. Forests currently occupy about 27% of the uncultivated land in South and Central America and Africa (13). Preserving a large portion of these forest ecosystems is crucial for protecting the biodiversity and environmental services they provide. In addition, much of the remaining uncultivated land has severe constraints to crop production from soils that have physical or chemical properties that would limit plant growth without ameliorative amendments. Recent estimates suggest that only 7% and 12% of the potentially arable land in Africa and Latin America, respectively, are free of soil constraints (1). Sustaining productivity on such land requires proper soil management technologies and improved use of nutrients and other amendments to maintain soil quality. It should also be noted that the current status of land degradation is not precisely known because the most comprehensive survey to date, the Global Assessment of Land Degradation (GLASOD), was conducted more than 12 years ago (14). The GLASOD assessment estimated the total area of degraded land to be 1964 Mha, with nearly half of this area degraded to at least a moderate degree. Most of this degradation was the result of inappropriate agricultural practices.

Recent trends indicate that total harvested cereal area has been decreasing since 1980 (Figure 1b). Although most of the decrease has occurred in developed countries, especially in Eastern Europe and the Former Soviet Union (FSU), harvested area has also decreased slightly in some developing countries since 1995. This trend raises the issue of whether the cost-benefit ratio of expanding cereal area in developing countries will be favorable if cereal prices continue a slow decline as predicted by the IMPACT model (Table 1). Given the uncertainty in the estimates of land reserves for sustainable crop production, the steady conversion of agricultural land to other uses, and the need to protect large tracts of natural ecosystems, it seems prudent to establish policies at national and regional levels that minimize expansion of agriculture into uncultivated areas by meeting increased food demand with greater yields on existing cropland (17). Increased yields, however, depend on maintaining an exploitable yield gap and the use of management practices that maintain soil quality and reduce the negative effects of crop cultivation on environmental quality.

YIELD POTENTIAL AND EXPLOITABLE YIELD GAPS

Definitions

Yield potential is defined as the yield of a crop cultivar when grown in environments to which it is adapted, with nutrients and water nonlimiting and pests and diseases effectively controlled (18). Hence, for a given crop variety or hybrid in a specific field environment, yield potential is determined by the amount of incident solar radiation, temperature, and plant density—the latter governs the rate at which the leaf canopy develops. The difference between yield potential and the actual yield achieved by farmers represents the exploitable yield gap (Figure 2). Yield potential can be reduced by insufficient water supply, either from inadequate rainfall in rain-fed cropping systems or from suboptimal irrigation in irrigated systems. Hence, genotype, solar radiation, temperature, plant population, and degree of water deficit determine water-limited yield potential. In addition to yield reduction from limited water supply, actual farm yields are determined by the magnitude of yield loss from factors such as nutrient deficiencies or imbalanced nutrition, diseases, insect pests, and weed competition.

As average farm yields approach the yield potential threshold, it becomes more difficult for farmers to sustain yield increases because further gains require the elimination of small imperfections in the integrated management of soil, crops, water, nutrients, and pests. In general, such rigorous fine-tuning is not economically viable on a production scale such that yield stagnation typically occurs when average farm yields reach about 80% of the yield potential ceiling (20).

Importance of Maintaining an Exploitable Yield Gap

Lack of an increase in rice yield potential is a mounting concern because yield stagnation is occurring in some of the world's most productive rice-producing

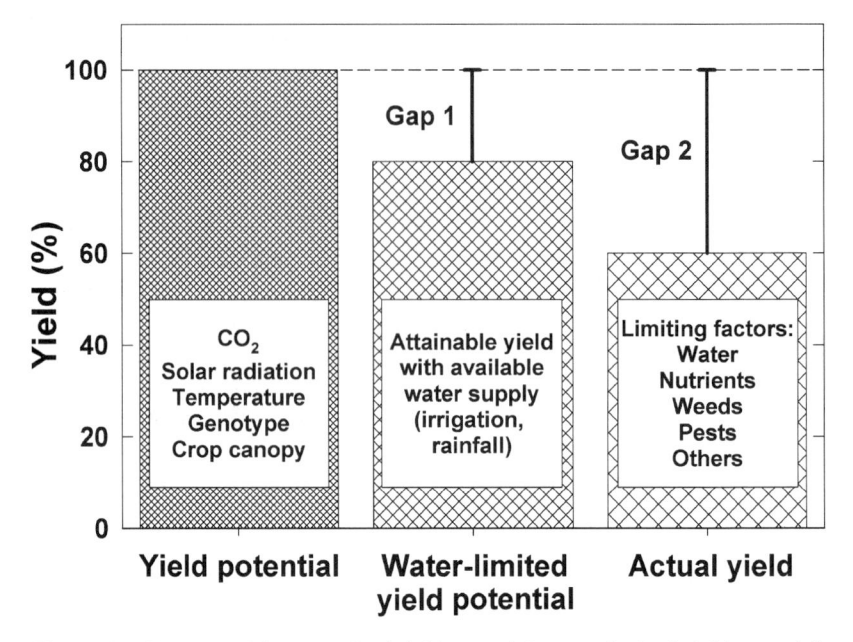

Figure 2 Conceptual framework of yield potential, water-limited yield potential, and actual farm yields as constrained by a number of production factors. Modified from van Ittersum & Rabbinge (19).

regions as a result of a diminishing exploitable yield gap. Although aggregate rice yields in China appear to continue at a linear rate of increase established during the past 35 years (Figure 3a), yields are now approaching the 80% yield potential threshold in several major rice-producing provinces. For example, clear trends of yield stagnation are evident in three of China's major rice-producing provinces, which account for more than 35% of Chinese rice production (Figure 3b). Likewise, yields are increasing very slowly in Japan (Figure 3a) and Korea (data not shown), where average farm yields are currently about 80% of yield potential estimated by crop simulation models (21).

Yields are also stagnating in major rice-producing provinces of India (Punjab), the Philippines (Central Luzon), and Indonesia (Central Java), although these yield plateaus appear to be well below the 80% yield potential level (Figure 3c). Substantial reductions in yield growth at levels below the 80% yield potential threshold are typical of trends observed in a number of other regions and countries where modern rice production technologies have been practiced for several decades. Specific reasons for the yield stagnation in these regions have not yet been identified due to a lack of long-term monitoring data on biophysical and socioeconomic determinants of yield and productivity (22). Because yield stagnation in these areas is not associated with a diminishing exploitable yield gap, available evidence suggests productivity constraints from factors such as deterioration of soil and water

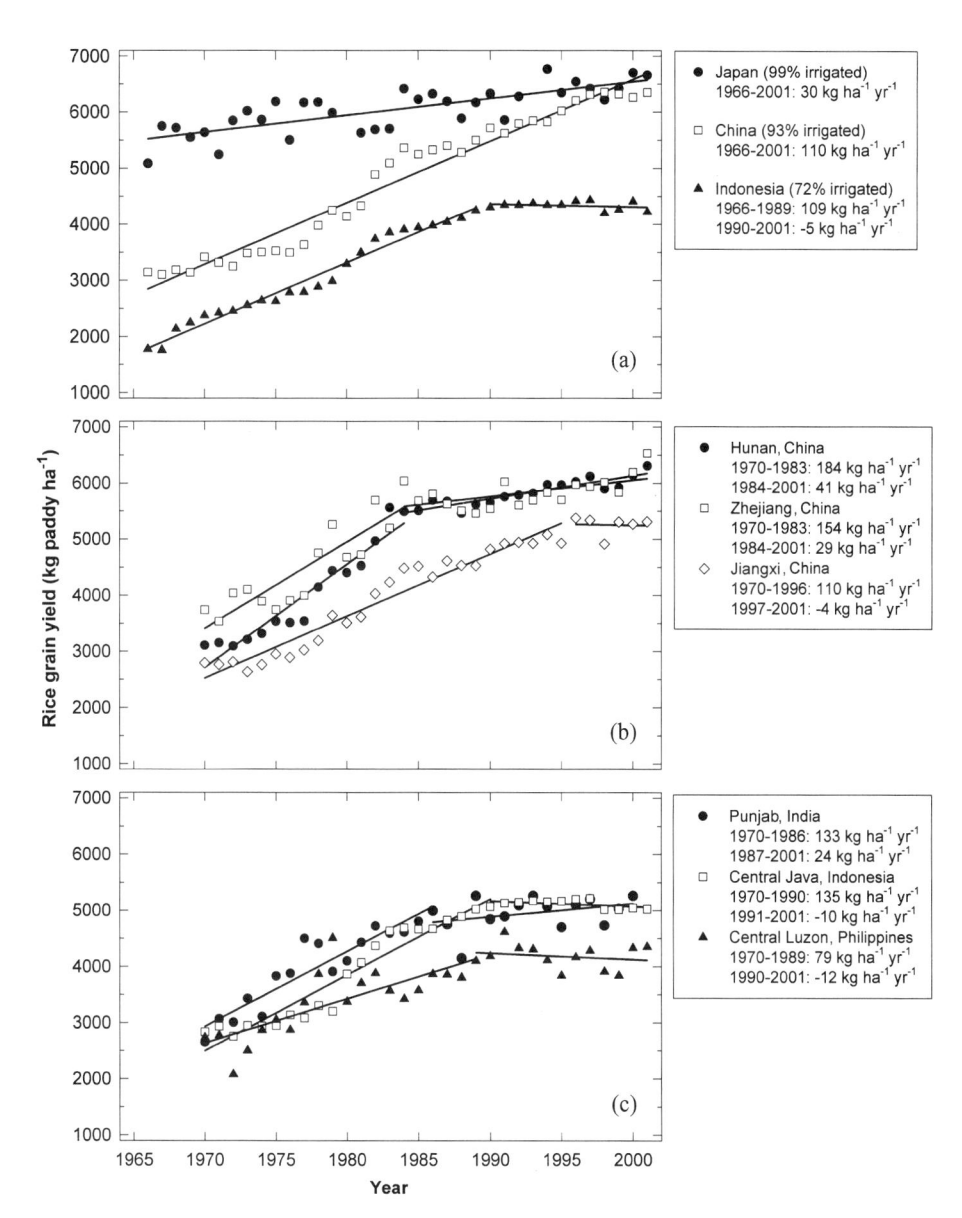

Figure 3 Yield trends in major rice-producing countries and provinces where there is evidence of stagnation in the rate of gain in average rice yields. Country data obtained from (9). Province data were based on national agricultural statistics provided by D. Dawe, Social Sciences Division, International Rice Research Institute (IRRI). Note that yield data for China refer to official statistics. Actual yields are likely to be lower because of the apparent underestimation of crop harvest area in China (20).

quality, reduced access to irrigation water, and imbalanced nutrient use. It is also noteworthy that researchers have found it difficult to maintain yields at 80% of yield potential in all but a few of the long-term experiments on intensive irrigated rice systems in the developing countries of Asia (23).

Estimating Trends in Rice Yield Potential

Maintaining an exploitable yield gap as average farm yields approach 80% of yield potential depends on achieving increases in yield potential through genetic improvement. Estimating trends in crop yield potential over time, however, is not a straightforward proposition. The most common method compares a time series of historical cultivars in a replicated field study. Cultivars chosen for such evaluations are typically the most widely used commercial varieties or hybrids of their time. The change in yield potential is estimated by plotting the yield of each cultivar against its year of release. A significant positive slope between yield and year of release is assumed to estimate the gain in yield potential—assuming the experiment is grown under nonlimiting conditions. This method places older cultivars at a disadvantage, however, because they were selected to withstand pathogens, insects, and soil and atmospheric conditions that existed during the period in which they were selected. But pathogen and insect pest populations evolve to overcome a cultivar's resistance to infection or infestation, soil properties change with intensive cropping, and atmospheric temperature and [CO_2] have risen steadily during the past 50 years. Whereas newly released cultivars are selected against contemporary conditions and are adapted to withstand them, older cultivars were not. Therefore, even with the best possible management practices to minimize the confounding effects of selection under different environmental conditions, it is not always possible to fully protect and optimize growth conditions for older cultivars.

Such a scenario is representative of modern rice-breeding efforts for intensive rice systems in tropical Asia. When historical inbred *indica* rice cultivars were grown in a replicated field study at two sites in 1996, there was a positive linear relationship between yield and year of release since 1966, with a slope of 75 kg ha^{-1} yr^{-1} (Figure 4). The oldest cultivar in this time series is IR8, which was released in 1966 and was the first widely grown modern inbred *indica* rice variety in tropical Asia. Although IR8 had the smallest yield when grown in 1996, it often attained yields of 9–10 Mg ha^{-1} when grown in the first years after it was released, and this yield level is comparable to the yield potential of the most recently released cultivars. The yield potential for this environment estimated by simulation is also 9–10 Mg ha^{-1} in years with typical weather patterns (21, 24). Hence, there has been no detectable increase in the yield potential of inbred rice varieties in 37 years since the release of IR8 (25, 26). Despite lack of progress towards greater yield potential, maintenance breeding efforts were highly successful in improving grain quality and maintaining yields in the face of substantial increases in disease and insect pressure—accomplishments of tremendous importance to sustaining rice production increases in Asia without expanding crop area.

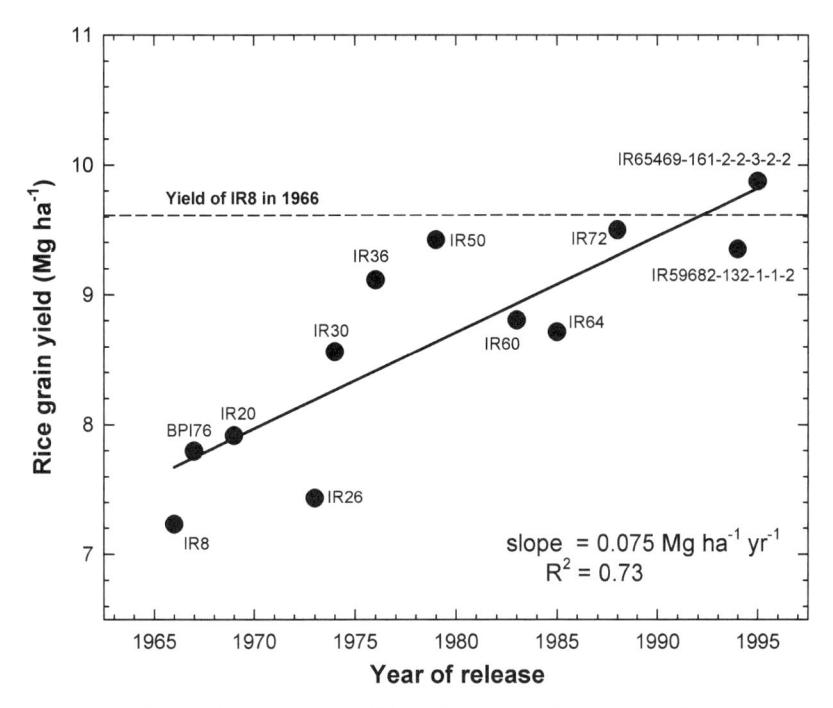

Figure 4 Yield trend of cultivars and lines developed since 1966 at the International Rice Research Institute (IRRI) in the Philippines and by the Bureau of Plant Industry, Department of Agriculture, Philippines. The twelve cultivars and two lines were grown at the IRRI Research Farm and the Philippines Rice Research Institute Research Farm in the 1996 dry season with optimum crop management. Each data point is a mean of the two locations. The dashed line represents the maximum yield obtained with IR8 when grown at the IRRI Research Farm 30 years earlier, in the dry season of 1966 (28). The figure is modified from Peng et al. (27).

When older cultivars are at a disadvantage in a historical time series comparison, a positive slope in the relationship between cultivar yield and year of release provides an estimate of resistance to contemporary stresses rather than an estimate of yield potential as shown conceptually in Figure 5. Under this scenario, new cultivars of a given crop are released at regular intervals, and the yield of each cultivar declines as they become less adapted to evolving conditions in the agro-ecosystem. While maintenance breeding continuously identifies new cultivars with yield potential equivalent to older cultivars, there is no increase in yield potential per se.

Although there has been little, if any, improvement in yield potential of inbred *indica* rice varieties, there is convincing evidence of gains in yield potential from hybrid rice. Direct field comparisons of recently released *indica* rice hybrids with recently released inbred *indica* varieties have clearly documented that rice hybrids

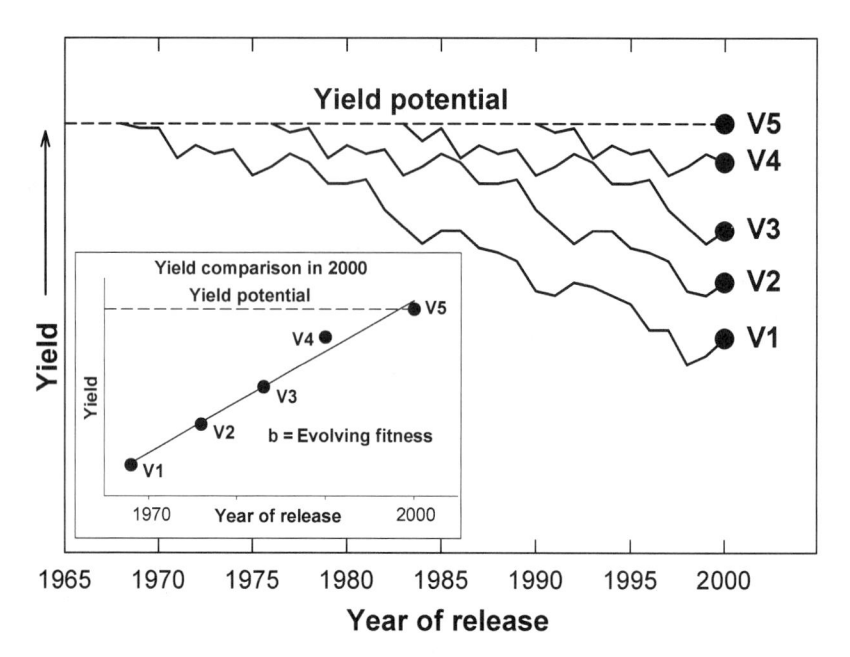

Figure 5 Conceptual framework for breeding to maintain yields against evolving sensitivity to pathogens, insect pests, and abiotic environmental conditions without an increase in yield potential.

have a 9% advantage in yield potential when grown in tropical lowland environments (25). Hybrid rice presently accounts for about 50% of the rice area in China. Adoption of hybrids is beginning to occur in Vietnam, India, the Philippines, and Bangladesh, although they currently account for only 1.2% of global rice area outside China. Recent trends indicate that hybrid rice area in China has remained stagnant, and there are major impediments to commercialization in other countries. These impediments include the low yield of hybrid seed production, high seed cost, and poor grain quality of hybrid rice varieties. Moreover, the 9% yield potential advantage of hybrid rice represents a onetime gain from hybrid vigor rather than a sustained increase in yield potential over time.

In addition to hybrid rice, efforts are currently in progress to create new plant types with higher yield potential by crossing germplasm from tropical *japonica* germplasm with inbred *indica* varieties (26). These efforts follow upon a 10-year breeding program, beginning in 1990, which developed the tropical *japonica* germplasm into lines that were adapted to lowland tropical environments. With continued investment in this program, it may be possible to increase rice yield potential by 5%–10%. While an increase of this magnitude is far less than the 25%–50% increases that the International Rice Research Institute (IRRI) had initially hoped for, even a small boost should be considered a major accomplishment given the lack of increase in *indica* inbred rice yield potential since 1966.

Estimating Trends in Yield Potential of Maize and Wheat

Estimating trends in maize yield potential is also difficult. Although maize breeders have been successful in developing hybrids with greater stress resistance, there is little evidence of an increase in yield potential (29). In part, the lack of evidence reflects the scarcity of research investment in maize yield potential in both the private and public sectors. It may also reflect the brute force empirical selection approach used by maize breeders, which relies on testing tremendous numbers of hybrid lines in thousands of on-farm strip trials with primary emphasis on yield and yield stability. Such on-farm trials rarely provide management practices that support yields that approach yield potential levels. The result has been substantial improvements in resistance to the wide range of abiotic and biotic stresses that occur under on-farm conditions and greater adaptation to intensified crop management practices adopted by farmers during the past 40 years.

Without explicit research efforts on maize yield potential, the highest reported maize yields come from nationally sanctioned yield contests that include hundreds of farmers who adhere to contest guidelines with regard to minimum field size, harvest area, and independent verification (30). Yield trends of contest winners for irrigated systems in the state of Nebraska indicate no increase in yield potential in the past 20 years, with a mean winning yield of 18.8 Mg ha^{-1} (Figure 6). In contrast, contest-winning yields in rain-fed systems have increased markedly and are approaching the yield potential ceiling indicated by the irrigated contest-winning yields.[2] And while the current average irrigated maize yield is only 50% of yield potential, average yields are steadily increasing and will eventually approach the 80% yield potential threshold where stagnation occurs. In fact, a number of progressive maize farmers currently achieve yields that exceed 80% of yield potential in irrigated systems.

Investment in research to improve yield potential of wheat has been much greater than that for rice or maize. A number of field studies have compared yield trends of an historical time-series of wheat varieties (31–33). Although these studies suffer from the same confounding factors as comparable studies with rice, the wheat evaluations were more rigorous because yield gains were quantified with and without fungicide protection against diseases and at different levels of N fertilization. Results consistently document a linear increase in wheat cultivar yields versus year of release. The greater number of investigations and wider range of environments in which these tests were conducted give greater weight to evidence of genetic gain in wheat yield potential. Despite this apparent success, the rate of

---

[2]Although there are reports of considerably higher contest-winning yields at one site in Iowa, these yield levels are up to 50% greater than the yield potential simulated by existing maize models using actual data on climate, soil properties, planting date, and maturity of the hybrid used at the site (H. Yang, unpublished data). In contrast, the contest-winning yields in Nebraska fall comfortably within the range of simulated yield potential for these sites. Hence, we believe the contest-winning yields in Nebraska provide the most reliable estimate of maize yield potential in the north-central United States.

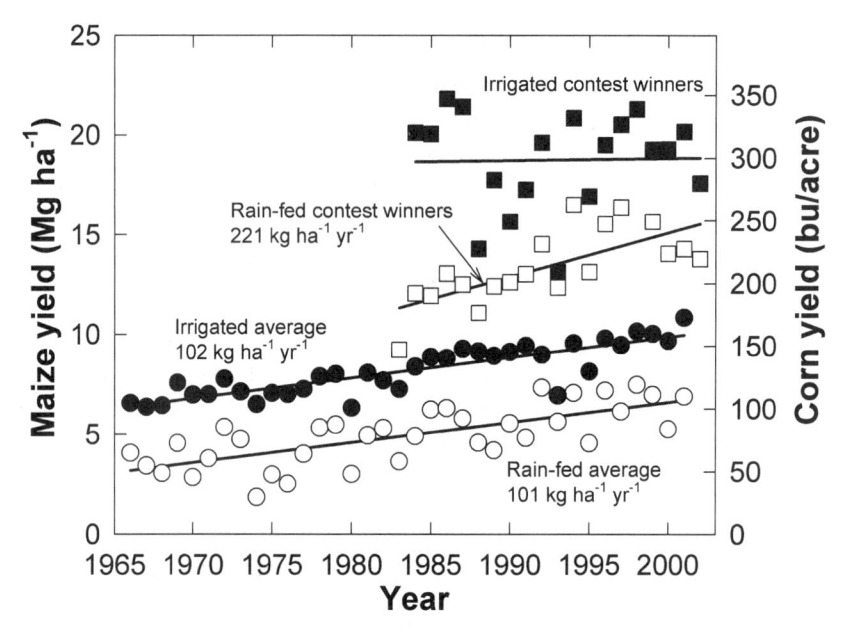

Figure 6 Yield trends in yield contests sanctioned by the National Corn Growers Association for irrigated and rain-fed maize systems in Nebraska and average farm yields in Nebraska for irrigated and rain-fed maize production.

gain in these studies was estimated at 38 to 60 kg ha^{-1} yr^{-1}, which is considerably less than 1% of the yield of the best-yielding cultivar. Because the rate of yield improvement was strongly linear in these studies, the proportional rate of gain will steadily decrease as yield potential increases. With annual wheat demand projected to rise by a compound annual rate of 1.1% to 2025, the exploitable gap between yield potential and average farm yields will also diminish in high-yielding wheat systems. Evidence of yield stagnation is apparent in the Yaqui Valley of Mexico, where the International Maize and Wheat Improvement Center (CIMMYT) conducts much of its wheat-breeding effort, and the linear yield trajectory in the Indian states of Punjab and Haryana will soon reach yield levels at which stagnation begins to occur in the Yaqui Valley (Figure 7). Together, the Punjab and Haryana states account for 34% of Indian wheat production. These trends emphasize the importance of continued efforts to increase wheat yield potential for sustaining yield gains at the farm level in major wheat-producing regions.

Are Existing Yield Gaps Large Enough?

To answer this question requires estimation of mean crop yield potential in the most important cereal-producing areas worldwide and data on current yields in these areas. To estimate current crop yield potential requires a robust crop simulation model that has been validated against direct measurements of maximum attainable

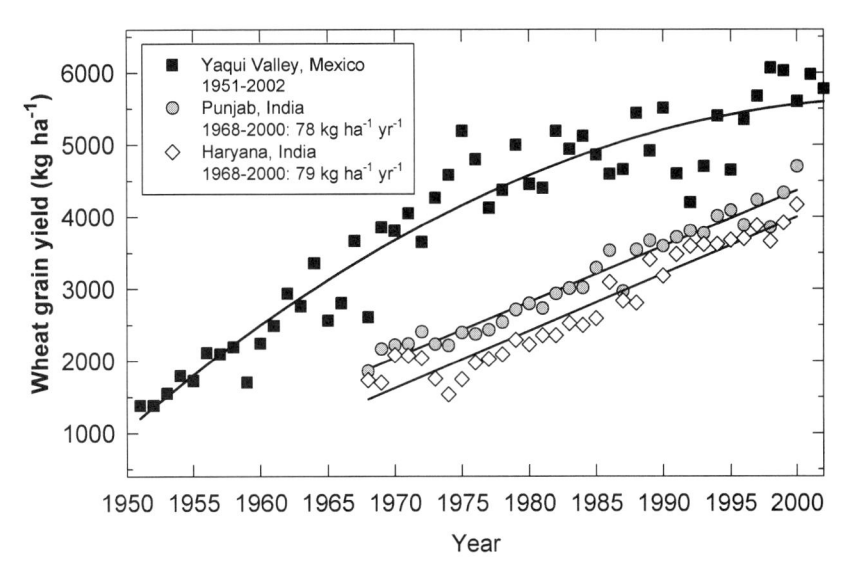

Figure 7 Yield trends of wheat in the Yaqui Valley of Mexico and major wheat-producing provinces in India. Data for the Yaqui Valley were provided by K. Sayre, CIMMYT, and data for the Indian provinces were provided by D. Byerlee, World Bank.

crop yields from a number of environments and a long-term climate database for each of the major cereal-producing domains. Such geospatial modeling of yield potential and possible effects of different scenarios for global climate change have been evaluated for rice in Asia (21, 34). Based on this analysis, it is clear that yield potential must be increased to meet future demand projections without a large increase in rice production area because current irrigated rice yields have already approached or will soon approach 80% of current yield potential. As a result, yield stagnation is already occurring in many of the world's most productive rice domains (Figure 3a,b).

There has been no comparable effort to estimate maize and wheat yield potential in the most productive areas for these crops. Lack of such an analysis makes it difficult to estimate whether closure of existing yield gaps will meet projected demand for these cereals without expanding crop-production area. While the contest-winning U.S. maize yield typically ranges from about 15.7 to 20.0 Mg ha^{-1} depending on year (30),[2] the average yield potential is much smaller because the contest-winning yield represents the highest possible yield achieved under the most favorable combination of soil, climate, and crop management. Current average U.S. maize yields are 8.6 Mg ha^{-1} (1999–2001), which is perhaps 55% to 65% of the mean U.S. yield potential. Current average maize yields in developing countries, including China, are much smaller (2.96 Mg ha^{-1} in 1999–2001) because of greater constraints from poor soils, water deficits, nutrient deficiencies, and pests in many production areas. Despite these constraints, numerous studies have shown considerable potential to increase yields with improved crop and soil management that includes nutrient input, weed control, and integrated pest management. Achieving adoption of such improved practices, however, will require substantial investment in applied research, extension, and market infrastructure—investments that are lacking in many developing countries.

Although it is clear that meeting projected rice demand will require both closure of the current exploitable yield gap and an increase in rice yield potential, the prognosis for maize and wheat is less certain. Our best guess is that closing the current yield gaps for maize and wheat is sufficient to satisfy demand for the next 20 to 25 years, but it will not be sufficient to meet the needs of a human population expected to reach 9 billion within 40 to 50 years. Hence, increasing yield potential of these cereals will also be a pivotal component of global food security.

NITROGEN EFFICIENCY AND TRENDS IN NITROGEN FERTILIZER USE

Adequate N supply is required for achieving high cereal yields (35), but negative effects from improper N fertilizer use threaten environmental quality and human health at both local and global scales as a result of water pollution from nitrate leaching or runoff, air pollution, and greenhouse gas emissions. Estimates for the United Kingdom (36) and Germany (37) suggest that the environmental costs of N fertilizer use are equal to one third the total value of all farm goods produced. Because the relationship between crop yield and N uptake is tightly conserved (38), achieving further increases in grain production will require greater N uptake by these crops. Hence, the key challenge going forward is to meet the greater N requirements of higher-yielding crops while concurrently increasing N use efficiency and reducing the reactive N load attributable to agriculture. To address this challenge requires detailed understanding of crop response to N and reliable projections of cereal production increases at local, regional, and global scales.

Inorganic Versus Organic Nitrogen Sources

Concern about the reactive N load from agriculture has led to calls for greater utilization of organic N sources and regulations reducing N fertilizer use. Organic production systems rely entirely on organic N sources. Even though only 1% of the world's cropland (about 16 Mha) is currently under certified organic production, demand for organic food is expected to grow, especially in developed countries, and organic agriculture may become a more widespread alternative to traditional agriculture in the next 30 years (14).

Although it is generally believed that organic agriculture offers environmental benefits associated with a reduction in pesticide use (14), the benefits from reliance on organic N sources have not been established, and the scientific basis for such a perception has not been documented. Controlling the fate of N from organic sources is just as difficult as managing the fate of mineral N fertilizer (39).

For example, nitrate leaching or runoff occurs whenever nitrate accumulation in soil coincides with a period of high rainfall or irrigation. Incorporating grass and legume cover crops, long fallow periods, mineral or organic N applications at the wrong time of the year, or small plant N demand (poor crop growth) can result in large nitrate leaching losses (40, 41). Case studies have shown comparable or increased potential losses (42), or decreased potential losses (43, 44) due to nitrate leaching and runoff from organic N sources as compared to fertilizer N. Many of these comparisons are flawed, however, because they compare different cropping systems, different amounts of applied N, and different yield levels. Under similar cropping systems with equivalent N input levels, nitrate losses from organic systems in the United Kingdom were similar to or slightly smaller than those from conventional farms following best management practices (45). Overall, the available literature provides no clear evidence that nitrate losses are reduced by the introduction of organic farming practices if the goal is to maintain the same crop yield levels as conventional farming systems (46).

Similar principles apply to other potentially harmful N loss mechanisms, such as gaseous N losses. In a study on a cultivated organic soil in southern Germany, total annual N_2O-N losses were 4, 16, 20, and 56 kg ha^{-1}, respectively, for a fertilized meadow, a fertilized arable field, an unfertilized meadow, and an unfertilized arable field (47). Although conversion from conventional to organic farming can sometimes reduce N_2O emissions on an area basis, both systems emit similar amounts of N_2O per unit of harvested yield (48, 49). In irrigated rice systems where rice is typically grown in flooded soil, methane emissions increase with the addition of manure and straw compared to systems that only receive mineral fertilizer N (50, 51). Reduction of N losses is therefore not a question of organic or conventional farming, but rather of using appropriate N management practices tailored to the needs of the particular cropping system.

Yield reductions are often associated with agricultural systems that follow organic practices (52, 53), and these systems appear to require both premium prices and government subsidies to remain economically viable. They also require copious amounts of organic N sources or increased land requirements to accommodate rotations with leguminous green manures to provide an adequate N supply. While this is feasible in industrialized countries, organic or low-input agriculture cannot secure the future food supply in the developing world, where maintaining low food prices contributes most to reducing poverty and increasing economic wealth (54, 55). Whereas organic N sources are critical components of the agricultural N cycle and should be utilized when they are available and cost-effective, cereal production at a global scale will largely depend on mineral N fertilizer to meet current and future food demand.

Nitrogen Efficiency at the Field Level

The relationship between crop yield and N supply follows a diminishing return function that makes it difficult to achieve high yields and high N efficiency without increasing nitrate leakage or N_2O emissions (38). At the scale of an individual field or experimental plot, grain yield (Y) and N uptake (U) increase with increasing N rate (F) and gradually approach a ceiling, which is determined by the site yield potential (Figure 8a,c). At low levels of N supply, rates of increase in yield and N uptake are large because N is the primary factor limiting crop growth and final yield. As the N supply increases, incremental yield gains are smaller because yield determinants other than N become more limiting. The broadest measure of N use efficiency is the ratio of yield to the amount of applied N (NUE = Y/F, also called the partial factor productivity of applied N), which declines from large values at small N rates to much smaller values at high N application rates.

Crop yield response functions to N vary widely among different environments, and they can be shifted due to technological, environmental, or economic factors (56). For example, the introduction of improved varieties with better adaptation to stress or innovations in N fertilizer management that improve the timing of N applications will shift the fertilizer response function up, which results in greater yield at the same level of N input (increase in NUE). Factors such as insufficient water supply, a decline in the indigenous N-supplying capacity of soil, a decrease in the uptake capacity of the root system due to soil toxicities or pathogens, yield limitations from deficiencies of nutrients other than N, and yield losses from insects, disease, and weeds can shift the response function down (decrease in NUE).

Nitrogen use efficiency is an aggregate efficiency index that incorporates the contributions from indigenous soil N, fertilizer uptake efficiency, and the efficiency with which N acquired by the plant is converted into grain yield. Evaluation of NUE requires separation of this aggregate efficiency index into component indices to understand the factors governing N uptake and fertilizer efficiency, to compare NUE in different environments, and to assess the effects of different N management options. To evaluate these components, agronomists typically estimate agronomic (AE), recovery (RE), and physiological (PE) efficiencies from applied N based on differences in yield and N uptake between fertilized plots and an unfertilized control (57, 58). Alternatively, the continuous response functions between yield, plant N uptake, and fertilizer N input illustrate the curvilinear nature of crop response to N application (Figure 8a,b,c). The incremental yield increase that results from N application can be defined as the incremental agronomic efficiency from applied N ($AE_i = dY/dF$ in Figure 8a). The AE_i is the product of the efficiency of N recovery from applied N sources (incremental recovery efficiency, $RE_i = dU/dF$ in Figure 8c) and the efficiency with which the plant uses each unit of N acquired from applied N to produce grain (incremental physiological efficiency,

Figure 8 Relationships among grain yield, plant N accumulation, and the amount of applied N in irrigated maize and their effects on different components of N use efficiency. Measured values (*symbols*) and fitted curves are based on a field experiment conducted in eastern Nebraska, which represents a favorable environment with fertile soils, use of a well adapted hybrid, and good pest control.

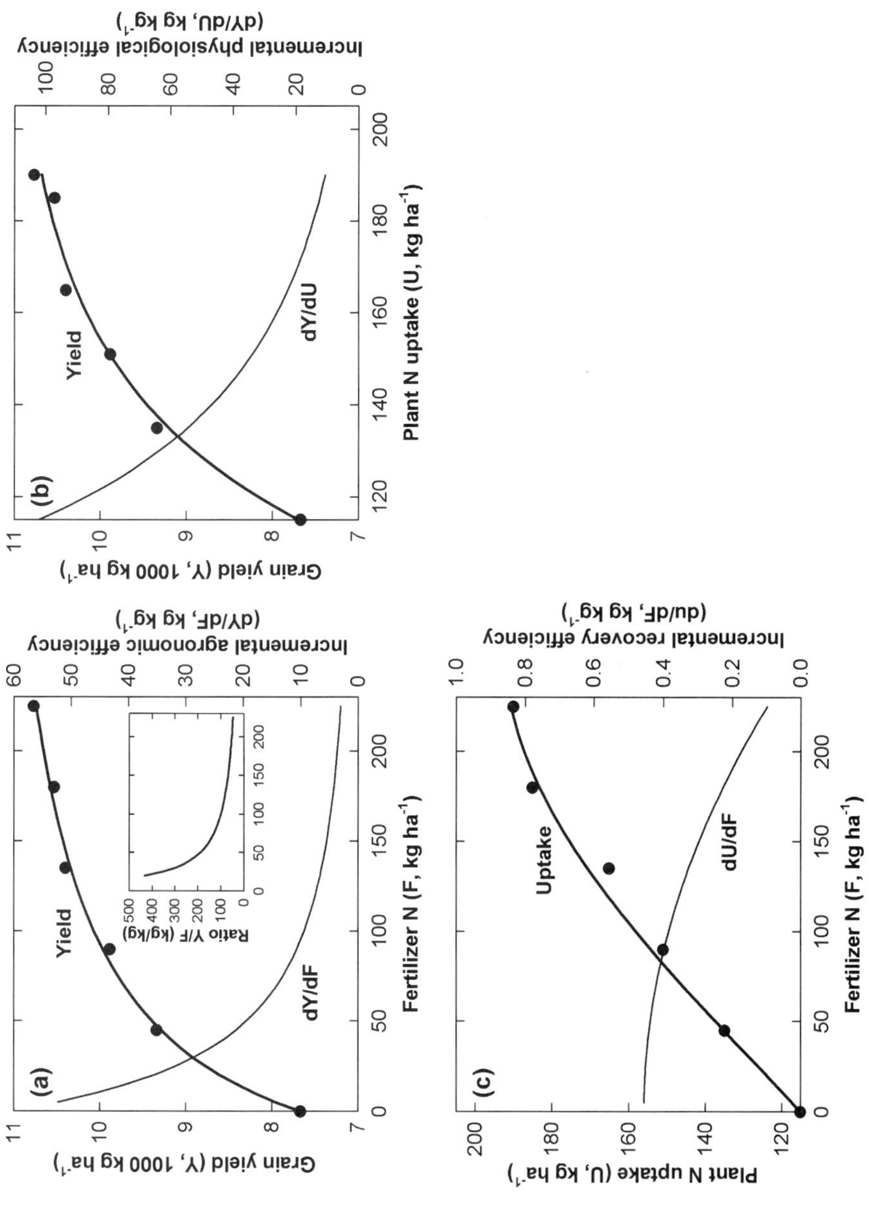
(a)
Yield
dY/dF
Grain yield (Y, 1000 kg ha-1)
Incremental agronomic efficiency (dY/dF, kg kg-1)
Fertilizer N (F, kg ha-1)
Ratio Y/F (kg/kg)
(b)
Yield
dY/dU
Grain yield (Y, 1000 kg ha-1)
Incremental physiological efficiency (dY/dU, kg kg-1)
Plant N uptake (U, kg ha-1)
(c)
Uptake
dU/dF
Plant N uptake (U, kg ha-1)
Incremental recovery efficiency (du/dF, kg kg-1)
Fertilizer N (F, kg ha-1)

$PE_i = dY/dU$ in Figure 8b). The RE_i largely depends on the degree of congruence between plant N demand and the available supply of N from applied fertilizer or organic N sources. Consequently, optimizing the timing, quantity, and availability of applied N is the key to achieving high RE_i.

In addition to N uptake by the crop and N losses, a portion of the N from applied fertilizer and organic sources is retained in soil as residual inorganic N (either ammonium or nitrate) or incorporated into various organic N pools; these include microbial biomass and soil organic matter. Such retention should be considered a positive contribution to N input efficiency only when there is a net increase in total soil N content. Because more than 95% of total soil N is typically found in organic N pools, an increase in soil organic matter (i.e., carbon sequestration) is required to achieve increases in total soil N. Sustained increases in organic matter in cropping systems practiced on aerated soils (e.g., maize- and wheat-based systems without irrigated rice) result in greater indigenous N supply from decomposition of the organic N pools, which can reduce N fertilizer requirements to maintain yields and thereby increase NUE (59, 60). In contrast, greater soil organic matter in continuous irrigated rice systems does not necessarily result in an increase in N mineralization because there is little relationship between soil organic matter content and indigenous soil N supply in anaerobic soils (61, 62). For cropping systems in which soil organic matter is declining over time, there is an additional loss of N above that from applied N fertilizer and organic N sources. This additional loss of N reduces NUE, and greater amounts of applied N are required to maintain yields.

Global Trends in Cereal Production and Nitrogen Fertilizer Use

Aggregate data on global crop production and fertilizer N consumption have often been used to estimate agriculture's contribution to the reactive N load in the global N cycle (3, 17, 63). At a global scale, cereal yields (Figure 1c, slope = 45 kg ha^{-1} yr^{-1}), cereal production (Figure 1a, slope = 31 × 10^6 Mg yr^{-1}) and fertilizer N consumption (Figure 9a, slope = 2 Mt yr^{-1}) have increased in a near-linear fashion during the past 40 years and are highly correlated with one another. Recent estimates indicate that the three major cereals receive 56% of global N fertilizer use while other cereals account for an additional 8% (64).

In developing countries, cereal yields and production from 1960 to 2001 follow a linear trend (Figure 1a,c). At the beginning of this time series, N fertilizer use was very small and increased exponentially during the course of the Green Revolution, resulting in a steep, nonlinear decline in the ratio of yield:N fertilizer use over time (Figure 9b). The rapid increase in N fertilizer use followed the rapid adoption of modern high-yielding varieties that could respond to the increased N supply and cropping intensity (66). The decrease in NUE occurs as farmers move yields higher along a fixed response function unless offsetting factors, such as improved management or yield limitations, shift the response function up or down (56).

In developed countries excluding those in Eastern Europe and the FSU, cereal yields continue to increase linearly (Figure 1c) while harvested area has declined

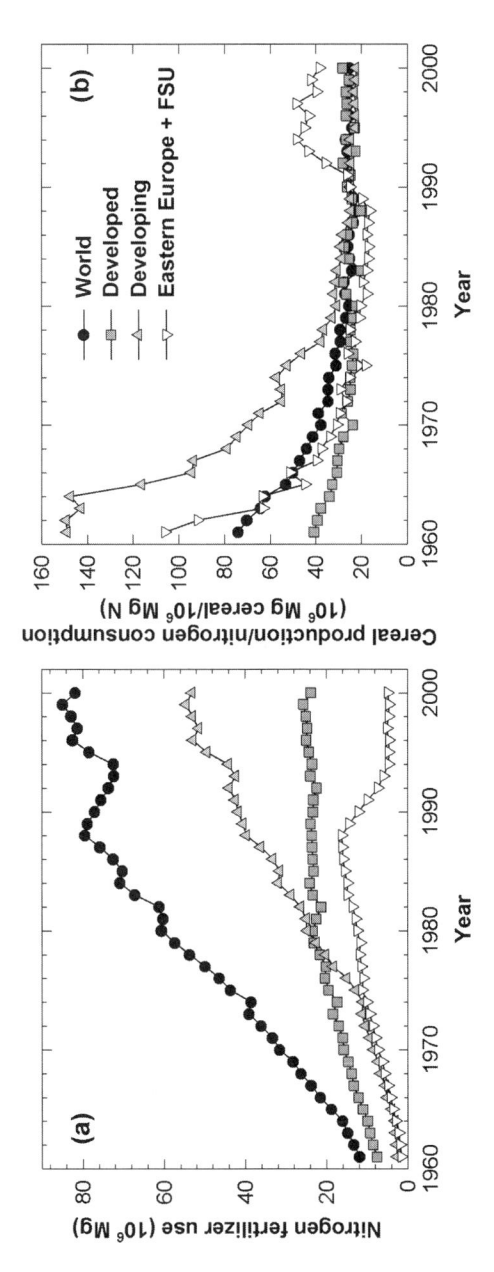

Figure 9 Trends in global consumption of N fertilizer and the ratio of cereal production to N fertilizer consumption. *Developed countries* include those in Western Europe, North America, Australia, New Zealand, South Africa, Israel, and Japan. *Developing countries* include those in Latin America, Africa, Near East, Asia, and Oceania (except those included in developed countries). *Eastern Europe + the former Soviet Union (FSU)* include the 14 countries of central and eastern Europe and all 15 countries of the FSU. Sources: Production data obtained from FAOSTAT (9). Fertilizer consumption data obtained from the IFADATA database (65).

since the 1980s (Figure 1*b*), and total production (Figure 1*a*) and N fertilizer use (Figure 9*a*) have remained relatively constant. In Eastern Europe and countries of the FSU, N consumption dropped in the late 1980s as a result of political and economic turmoil. In these countries, the ratio of cereal yield:N fertilizer use doubled from 1988 to 2000 without improvements in yield potential or major changes in N management, and the ratio is now greater than in developing countries (Figure 9*a,b*).

The fact that trajectories of cereal production and N fertilizer use in developing and developed countries deviate from linearity is hidden in trends estimated from aggregate global data. Hence, the regression of global cereal production on global N use (Figure 9*b*) represents a crude index of global N use efficiency because this relationship is affected by changes in land area and yield, by stage of economic development, and by shifts in the yield response to N caused by adoption of improved germplasm and crop management technologies. Projections of future N fertilizer needs based on aggregated data can therefore be misleading unless these dissimilarities are considered.

Disaggregating Trends in Cereal Yields and Nitrogen Fertilizer Use

The ratio of global cereal production to global fertilizer N consumption has been used to illustrate trends in NUE over time and shows a curvilinear decline in the past 40 years (Figure 9*b*). This decrease has raised concerns that future increases in N fertilizer use are unlikely to be as effective in raising yields as in the past (17). Aggregate global data, however, do not provide a sound basis for estimating future trends because these trends differ widely between developing and developed countries, as discussed above, between different countries, and among the different cereal crops.

The relationship between the mean national yield of maize, rice, and wheat and the mean rate of N fertilizer applied to each of these cereal crops on a country-by-country basis is linear (Figure 10). The slope (AE) of the combined regression suggests that cereal yields will increase by 37 kg ha^{-1} for each kg of additional N fertilizer. The slopes and intercepts (Y at zero N applied), however, differ significantly among the three crops.

While the regressions in Figure 10 can identify major differences in N efficiency among crops or countries, they are of limited value for projecting future N fertilizer requirements because the combined regression includes countries with substantial differences in soil fertility and in the technological sophistication of crop management. Relationships between yield and N use within a country differ significantly from this global regression. For example, regression of average maize yield and N fertilizer rate for each of the major U.S. maize-producing states explains 26% of the variation in U.S. maize yield and has a slope (AE) of only 13 kg kg^{-1} (Figure 11), which is nearly 70% less than the global AE for maize (Figure 10). In contrast, the U.S. regression has a large intercept of 6.1 Mg ha^{-1}, which is more than sevenfold greater than the global intercept because maize is generally grown on fertile soils

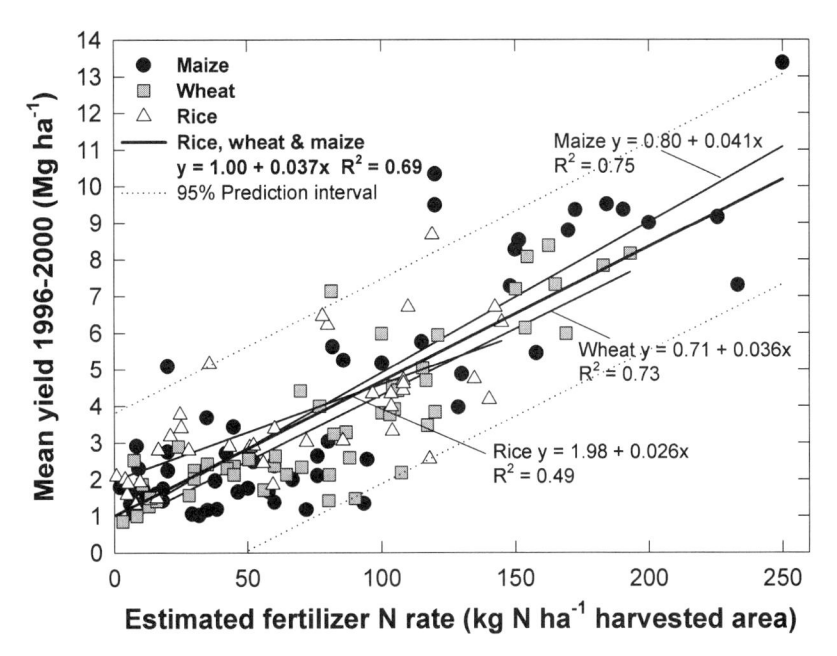

Figure 10 Relationships between yield of maize, rice, and wheat and average N rates applied in each country. Each data point represents one country (rice, 37 countries; wheat, 53 countries; maize, 56 countries). Sources: yield data were obtained from FAOSTAT (9); fertilizer N rates represent country-specific estimates for each crop based on surveys and industry sources, as summarized in the 5th edition (2002) of the IFA/IFDC/IPI/PPI/FAO database on fertilizer use by crops (64). Values for each country refer to the average amount of N applied to the entire harvested area for each cereal crop.

in the U.S. Corn Belt. Increasing the N rate in the United States has relatively little effect on average yields because yield levels are already high and are approaching the nonlinear range of the N response curve (Figure 8a). Differences in the ratio of yield:N fertilizer rate among states are associated with substantial differences in soil quality and crop management. For example, the small yield:fertilizer N ratio in North Carolina is associated with the prevalence of highly weathered soils of relatively poor quality and small indigenous N supply in that state. In contrast, the larger yield:fertilizer N ratios in Wisconsin and Minnesota are associated with the higher quality of loess soils in those states, which have a greater indigenous N supply that shifts the N response curve upwards.

Relationships between yield and fertilizer N rate become even more scattered if farm-scale data are evaluated as seen in relationships among yield, plant N uptake, and fertilizer N rate from 179 fields under intensive rice cropping in Asia (Figure 12). These data are representative of much of the irrigated rice area in Asia. Average farm yields varied widely, but the mean yield of 5.1 Mg ha^{-1} was

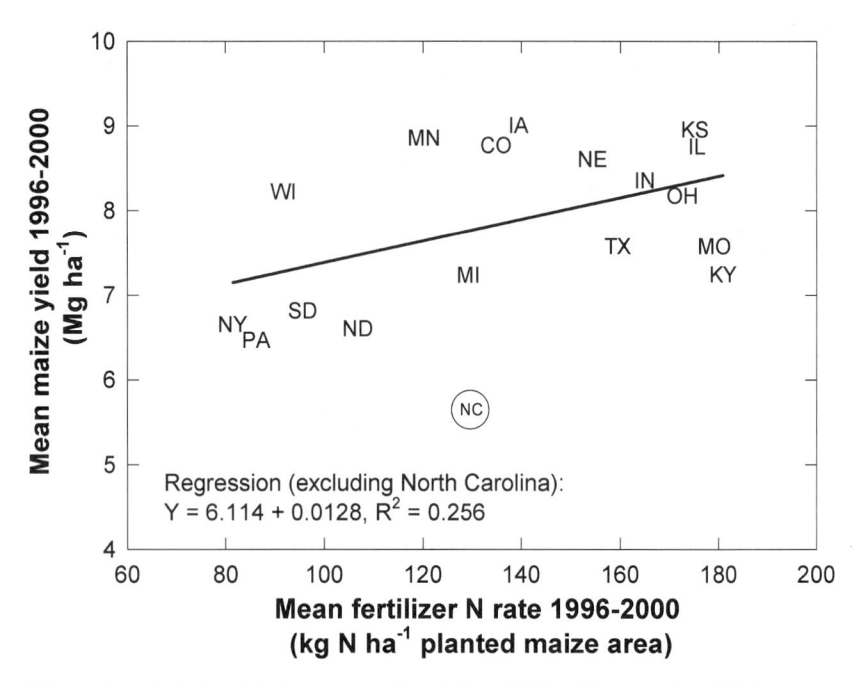

Figure 11 Relationship between maize yield and N fertilizer rate in 18 U.S. states. Values shown are mean maize yields and the average fertilizer N use in each state during the period 1996 to 2000 (67).

close to the global average yield for irrigated rice of about 5.2 Mg ha^{-1} (69). Average N rates applied by these farmers varied from 56 to 198 kg N ha^{-1}, but across farms there was no relationship between rice yield and N fertilizer rate, or between plant N uptake and N rate (Figure 12a,c). Yield was closely correlated with plant N uptake and formed an upper boundary line representing the most efficient N use for a given N rate at sites where N was the dominant yield-limiting factor (Figure 12b). This boundary line becomes nonlinear as yields approach high levels; which confirms the curvilinear nature of the relationship between yield and N uptake at the field level (Figure 8b). Numerous farms fell below this upper boundary, indicating that factors in addition to N limited yield, which explains the lack of a relationship between yield and N rate (Figure 8a). Among the factors that limit on-farm yields in addition to rate of N application are climate, the supply of other essential nutrients, disease, insect pest, weed pressure, stand establishment, and N management technology (e.g., timing, forms, and placement). As a result, the wide variation in NUE (46 to 88 kg grain kg^{-1} per kg of applied N) was largely determined by the large variation in RE (0.05 to 0.64 kg plant N per kg of N uptake from fertilizer).

As a result of the large differences in NUE among countries, regions, farms, fields within a farm, and crop species, policies that promote an increase or decrease

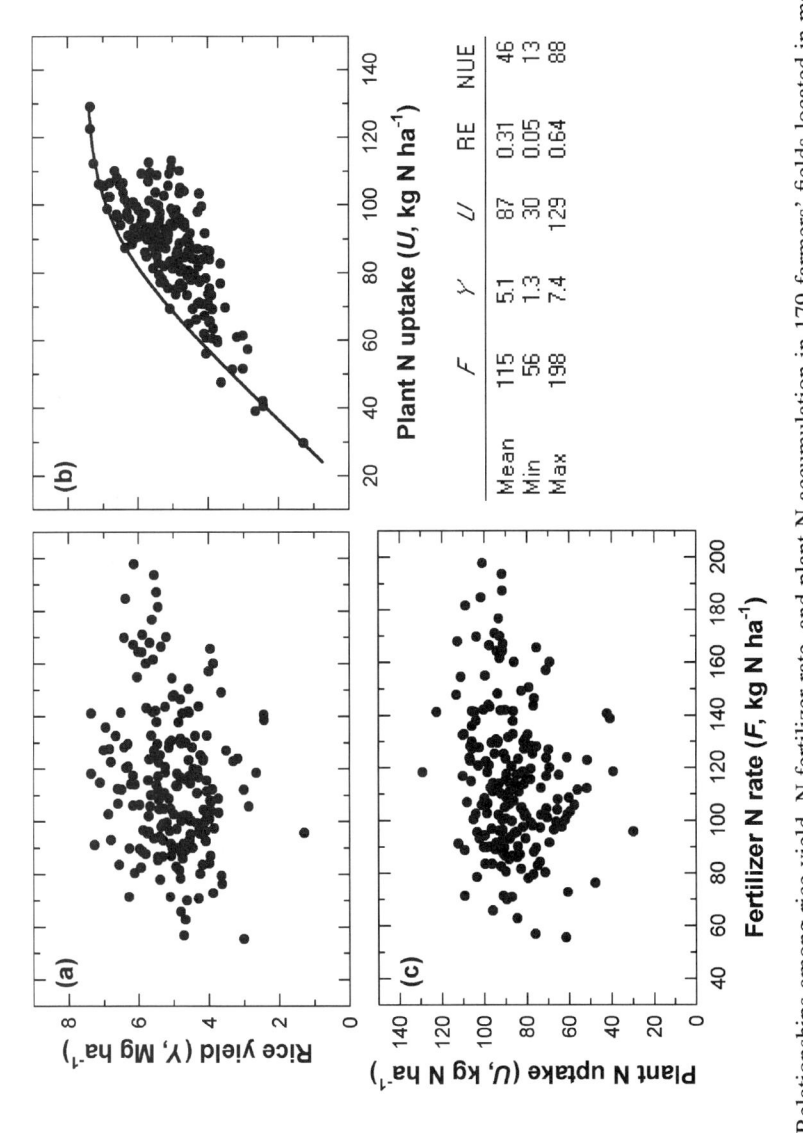

Figure 12 Relationships among rice yield, N fertilizer rate, and plant N accumulation in 179 farmers' fields located in major irrigated rice areas of China, India, Indonesia, the Philippines, Thailand, and Vietnam. Data points represent means of individual rice farms (15 to 26 farms per country) for four consecutive rice crops grown from 1997 to 1999 based on data reported by Dobermann et al. (68).

in N fertilizer use at a state or national level would have a widely varying impact on yields, farm profitability, and environmental quality. Instead, achieving greater NUE at state or national levels will require policies that favor increases in NUE at the field scale with emphasis on technologies that can achieve greater congruence between crop N demand and N supply from all sources, which include fertilizer, organic inputs, and indigenous soil N (38).

Projection of Future Nitrogen Fertilizer Requirements

Estimates of future growth in global fertilizer consumption differ because of different forecasting methods and underpinning assumptions about food demand, land area, yields, and trends in NUE. Because rice, wheat, and maize account for 56% of the global fertilizer N consumption, we evaluated nine scenarios of global fertilizer N consumption by the three major cereals to 2025 (Table 3). The different scenarios illustrate the sensitivity of N fertilizer requirements to trends in cereal yields, harvested area, and NUE.

At one extreme, scenario Ca, the harvested area declines by 7.4% due to decreasing availability of agricultural land at a rate similar to land use trends since 1980 (Figure 1b) and NUE decreases by 15%. Global N fertilizer consumption for rice, wheat, and maize in 2025 would be 61% larger in 2025 than in 2000 (1.9% yr^{-1}) under this scenario. The annual rate of yield increase (1.6%) must be large enough to meet increased food demand (1.3%) and offset the decrease in harvested area (-0.3% yr^{-1}). The average N rate to achieve the required yield level in 2025 is 151 kg N ha^{-1}, which is 74% above the current mean N rate. This large increase in N rate would increase environmental risks from N losses due to nitrate leaching, runoff, and N$_2$O emissions because it is more difficult to match crop demand with N supply at higher rates of applied N.

Scenario Ab assumes that harvested cereal area increases at a rate of 0.3% yr^{-1} from both area expansion and increasing cropping intensity. While this scenario is not consistent with global land-use trends of the past 20 years (Figure 1b), it is similar to the rate of increase in cultivated area predicted by the IMPACT model (2, 14). It is also assumed that NUE remains unchanged, although this will require continuing progress in crop genetics (increase in stress resistance and small increases in yield potential) and improved crop management technologies (reduction of yield gaps). Consequently, average N rates would rise by only 28% (1.0% yr^{-1}) and global N consumption would increase at the same rate as cereal production (1.3% yr^{-1}). The other scenarios with constant NUE (Bb, Cb) give equivalent projections for N fertilizer consumption because grain yield increases are proportional to increases in total N use. The assumption of constant NUE was also used to predict future N fertilizer consumption by the FAO baseline scenario (71), by the econometric model of Bumb & Banaante (72), and by Frink et al. (73) who based their projection on a model that considered population growth, gross domestic product, and crop production potential. Each of these models predicts an annual increase in N fertilizer consumption of 1.0% to 1.2% depending on the amount of expansion in cropped area in the different models.

TABLE 3 Projected changes in N fertilizer requirements of the major cereals (rice, wheat, and maize) from 2000 to 2025 as affected by changes in harvested land area and N use efficiency (NUE in kg grain per kg of applied N fertilizer). All values refer to the sum or averages of global rice, wheat, and maize production[a]

	Change in harvested area[b]			
	A. Increase	B. Constant	C. Decrease	All
	Average N amount applied			Total N consumption
Change in N efficiency[b]	kg N ha^{-1}			10^6 Mg
a. Decrease	130.2	139.9	151.1	71.6
b. Constant	110.7	118.9	128.4	60.9
c. Increase	96.3	103.4	111.7	53.0
	Cumulative change (%)			
a. Decrease	50.2	61.4	74.3	61.3
b. Constant	27.7	37.1	48.1	37.2
c. Increase	11.1	19.3	28.8	19.3
	Annual rate of change (%)			
a. Decrease	1.6	1.9	2.2	1.9
b. Constant	1.0	1.3	1.6	1.3
c. Increase	0.4	0.7	1.0	0.7

[a] All scenarios assume that global population increases to 7.9 billion people (70) and that cereal demand increases by 37% (1.3% per year) to 2436 Mt in 2025 (2). Baseline global data for the year 2000 were a harvested area of 512 Mha, mean cereal yield of 3.47 Mg ha^{-1}, total production of 1777 Mt (averages for 1996 to 2000), and total fertilizer N consumption of 44.4 Mt (64). The global mean N fertilizer rate applied to rice, wheat, and maize was about 87 kg N ha^{-1} in 2000 with a mean NUE of about 40 kg grain per kg N applied.

[b] *Area scenarios*: (A) Increase: Harvested area increases to 550 Mha in 2025 (+7.4%, +0.3% per year), mainly in sub-Saharan Africa and Latin America. Grain yield must increase to 4.43 Mg ha^{-1} in 2025 (+28%, +1.0%/yr). This scenario is similar to the business-as-usual scenario in Rosegrant et al. (2). (B) Constant: Harvested area remains unchanged at 512 Mha. Grain yield must increase to 4.76 Mg ha^{-1} in 2025 (+37%, +1.3%/yr). (C) Decrease: Harvested area decreases to 474 Mha in 2025 (−7.4%, −0.3% per year). Grain yield must increase to 5.14 Mg ha^{-1} in 2025 (+48%, +1.6%/yr).

[c] *Nitrogen efficiency scenarios*: (a) Decrease: Insufficient investment in research that emphasizes improving crop management and increasing crop yield potential in favorable production areas such that NUE decreases to 34 kg grain kg^{-1} applied N in 2025 (−15%, −0.6% per year). (b) Constant: NUE remains unchanged at 40 kg grain kg^{-1} applied N. (c) Increase: Adequate investment in research that emphasizes improving crop management and increasing crop yield potential in favorable production areas such that NUE increases to 46 kg grain kg^{-1} applied N in 2025 (+15%, +0.6% per year).

Scenario Ac is the most optimistic with regard to total N fertilizer requirements and minimizing negative environmental risks from the applied N because it assumes an increase in both area (+7.4%, or 0.3% yr^{-1}) and NUE (+15%, or 0.6% yr^{-1}). An increase in NUE could result from greater investment in research on genetic improvement and on research and extension to develop and implement improved crop and N management practices. This scenario gives a yield increase of 28% by 2025 (1.1% yr^{-1}) with an average N rate of only 96 kg N ha^{-1} (+11%, or 0.4% yr^{-1}) as compared to present levels. The additional environmental risk from greater N fertilizer use would be minimized because of smaller N rates and a total increase in N fertilizer use of only 19% (0.7% yr^{-1}). Although this scenario minimizes environmental risk from N fertilizer, it increases the negative effects on natural resource conservation from expansion of cultivated area, especially if such expansion occurs at the expense of natural ecosystems or onto marginal land that cannot sustain intensive cereal production. Hence, Bc is perhaps the best overall scenario because it would increase NUE with no net change in harvested crop area and thereby achieve the required 37% increase in cereal production with a 19% increase in both N fertilizer use and N rate.

All of the scenarios of total N fertilizer use in Table 3 are much smaller than those from other studies that did not account for the interactive effects of changes in land area, yields, and NUE (66, 67, 77). Because N fertilizer requirements are sensitive to these factors and given the most likely trends in harvested area and NUE (Table 3), we believe our projections of global N fertilizer use on rice, wheat, and maize in 2025 (53 to 72 Mt N) represent a plausible range. Further improvements in predicting global N fertilizer use will require specifying the locations and cropping systems that will provide the increase in cereal production and the primary determinants of NUE in those environments.

Improving Nitrogen Use Efficiency

The key question is whether the increase in NUE proposed in scenarios Ac, Bc, or Cc is realistic? We assumed a modest increase of 15% over a 25-yr period (0.6% yr^{-1}), which results in an average of NUE of 46 kg grain kg^{-1} N applied as compared to 40 kg grain kg^{-1} N at present. Far larger increases in NUE have been achieved in recent years in various developed countries. In U.S. maize systems, NUE increased from 42 kg kg^{-1} in 1980 to 57 kg kg^{-1} in 2000 (38), which represents a 36% increase (1.6% yr^{-1}). Three factors contributed to this improvement: (a) increased yields and more vigorous crop growth associated with greater stress tolerance of modern hybrids (29), (b) improved management of production factors other than N (conservation tillage, seed quality, and higher plant densities), and (c) improved N fertilizer management (74). In Japan, NUE of rice remained virtually constant at about 57 kg kg^{-1} from 1961 to 1985 but has increased to more than 75 kg kg^{-1} (32%, 1.8% yr^{-1}) in recent years (75, 76). Key factors contributing to this increase were a shift to rice varieties with better grain quality, which also had lower yield potential and nitrogen concentrations, and the adoption of more knowledge-intensive N management technologies (75); this resulted in a 17% decrease in the average N rate without a reduction in yield.

Increasing NUE in the developing world presents a greater challenge. Nitrogen use efficiency is particularly low in intensive irrigated rice systems of subtropical and tropical Asia, and the available evidence suggests that NUE has remained virtually unchanged during the past 20 to 30 years, despite increases in yield over time (74). Carefully conducted research has demonstrated, however, that rice is capable of taking up fertilizer N very efficiently (77) provided the timing of N applications is congruent with the dynamics of soil N supply and crop N demand (78). These principles have recently become embedded in a new approach for nutrient management (79, 80). In field testing conducted in 179 rice farms throughout Asia, average grain yield increased by 0.5 Mg ha^{-1} (11%) and N fertilizer rate decreased by 5 kg N ha^{-1} with field-specific management compared to the baseline farmers' fertilizer practice (68). Mean RE of applied N increased from 30% with farmers' practices to 40% with field-specific management that takes into account the large field-to-field variation in the indigenous soil N-supplying capacity. Studies in China documented even larger gains (81). Improving the congruence between crop N demand and N supply also were found to substantially increase N fertilizer efficiency of irrigated wheat in Mexico (82, 83).

These results highlight the potential for field-specific management in small-scale farming systems in developing countries, provided the technologies chosen match the biophysical and socioeconomic characteristics of the agroecosystem. Such improvements will require significant long-term investments in research and extension education. Several years of on-farm experimentation are required to develop an optimal N management scheme for a particular location that is characterized by a set of common environmental, socioeconomic, and cropping characteristics. Seasonal variation is large and fine-tuning of N management must be accomplished in accordance with other management factors that influence NUE, such as balanced supplies of macro- and micronutrients, water management, optimal plant density, and pest control. In addition, substantial investments in research to raise rice yield potential also will be required because many intensive rice-producing regions are currently approaching the yield potential ceiling (Figure 3), and the yield response to applied N becomes strongly curvilinear in this region of the response function. At present, we suspect that current investment in such research and extension efforts is grossly inadequate.

CARBON SEQUESTRATION, GREENHOUSE FORCING, AND SOIL QUALITY

Carbon Sequestration and Greenhouse Gas Emissions

The degree to which crop production systems contribute to increases or decreases in greenhouse gas concentrations is another issue of concern given modern trends in atmospheric composition and putative changes in global climate (84, 85). Over the past 52 years, atmospheric CO_2 concentrations have risen by 18%, which may contribute to global warming (86). Soil represents one of the largest pools of carbon (C) in the terrestrial biosphere and contains about 1500 Pg C in organic forms, which is roughly three times the size of the biotic pool of C in terrestrial ecosystems (87). Hence, small changes in size of the soil organic C (SOC) pool have a dramatic effect on the atmospheric C balance. Although most of the increase in atmospheric CO_2 has been driven by accelerated fossil-fuel use, agricultural activity through deforestation and soil cultivation has contributed an estimated 55 Pg C loss from decomposition of SOC and release of CO_2 to the atmosphere during the past 150 years (86). Current estimated annual net SOC loss from land use change is in the range of 1 to 2 Pg C yr^{-1}, which occurs primarily in the tropics (88). Agriculture also contributes to greenhouse forcing through the emission of N_2O associated with the application of N fertilizer and through the consumption of fossil-fuel energy in the manufacture, distribution, and use of agricultural inputs and machinery. For example, application of N fertilizer accounts for about 60% of the fossil-fuel energy consumed in the production of U.S. maize (89).

The net effect of a cropping system on greenhouse forcing potential can be estimated by accounting for all greenhouse gases emitted to the atmosphere or sequestered in soil or plant biomass. Such an analysis must consider the greenhouse gas emissions associated with all inputs and outputs used in the production system. Rates of CO_2 oxidation from SOC in a given cultivated field vary in relation to soil moisture and temperature regime, soil physical and chemical properties, the amount of carbon (C) input from crop residues, the chemical composition of organic C in these residues, and the degree of physical soil disruption (e.g., tillage). Consequently there is considerable potential to minimize the oxidation of existing SOC and to increase the inputs of crop residue-C through changes in crop and soil management. The potential for C sequestration in stable soil organic matter has been estimated in several studies (90–94). Estimates of C sequestration potential in U.S. crop agriculture range from 0.075 to 0.208 Pg C yr^{-1}, which is equivalent to 5 to 12% of CO_2 emissions from total U.S. fossil-fuel consumption (Figure 13).

Global estimates of the mitigation potential of C sequestration in agricultural soils are in the 0.4 to 0.6 Pg C yr^{-1} range, or less than 10% of the current annual C emissions from fossil fuels (93). In general, comparison of C sequestration rates in forest and agroecosystems suggest that sequestration potential is greater in timber production systems. However, recent results indicate that rapid turnover of organic C in the litter layer and N limitations to primary productivity of forest ecosystems, which are typically located on relatively poor soils, may limit the potential size of forest C sinks (95).

The estimates of C sequestration in cropping systems are derived from direct measurements in long-term experiments and monitoring sites coupled with simulation and extrapolation of these point estimates to regional, national, and global scales. Decreased tillage intensity, reduced bare fallow, improved fertilizer management, crop rotation, and cover crops are factors identified as having the greatest potential to increase C sequestration (92, 96). From our view, however, these estimates of agricultural C-sequestration potential are constrained by two factors. First, they are based on cropping systems that give average yields with average crop management despite the fact that average yields and biomass accumulation of the major cereal crops have increased steadily due to genetic improvements in crop cultivars and improved management of soil and inputs (18, 97, 98). For

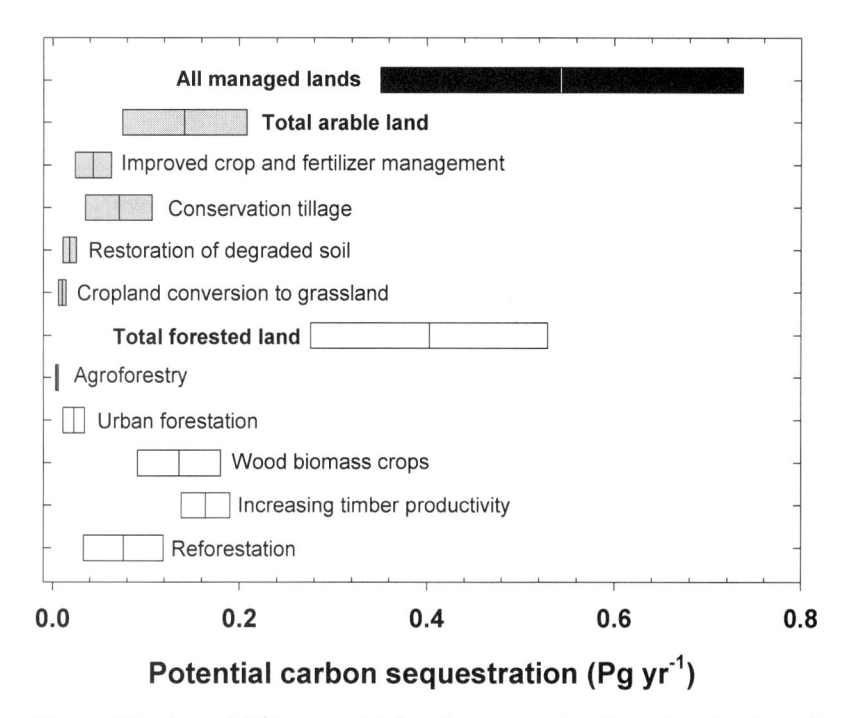

Figure 13 Annual U.S. potential for C sequestration from the adoption of alternative land use options in managed forests and arable lands. Bars indicate current high and low estimates of potential C sequestration. Adapted from (85).

example, average U.S. maize yields have increased linearly for the past 35 years at a rate of about 109 kg ha^{-1} per year. Moreover, many progressive U.S. farmers currently produce maize yields that are 55% to 75% greater than today's average farm yield. Similarly, comparisons of cropping systems are questionable when crop management is not clearly defined with regard to the yield potential of the each system. For example, West & Post (99) compared C sequestration as affected by changing from conventional tillage to no-till in 67 long-term experiments from across the United States. They reported a mean C-sequestration rate of 900 kg C ha^{-1} yr^{-1} for maize–soybean rotations (n = 14) but only 440 kg C ha^{-1} yr^{-1} for continuous maize (n = 11). Yet analysis of the same data set with respect to the overall rate of C sequestration in response to a change from continuous maize to maize-soybean gave a mean annual C-sequestration rate of -190 kg C ha^{-1} yr^{-1}. Such discrepancies are likely to result from variation in the optimization of crop management and differences in sampling and measurement methods among these long-term experiments. Therefore, we believe that the most useful estimates of C-sequestration potential are derived from cropping systems managed to achieve yields that approach 80% of yield potential, which are attainable with progressive intensification strategies that increase both yields and input use efficiency. Such estimates would provide a more realistic prognosis for C-sequestration potential than estimates based on today's average yield with average management.

Second, the validity of C-sequestration assessments depends on the accuracy of estimated or simulated net primary productivity, the proportion of plant biomass that is returned to soil, and the rate of C transformations and turnover in soil. Several recent studies have attempted to assess current and future soil C-sequestration potential at a continental scale for Europe and North America based on ecosystem simulation models (89, 94, 100–105). Because these models are typically validated against data from long-term experiments in which net primary productivity and management follow current average practices, or even antiquated practices, their ability to simulate future scenarios outside the range of validation is questionable. For instance, three of the most widely used maize simulation models, CERES-Maize (106), Muchow-Sinclair-Bennett (107), INTERCOM (108), and the ecosystem C balance model CENTURY (109, 110), underestimated recycled aboveground crop residues by 13% to 47% when compared with field measurements in a high-yield long-term experiment at Lincoln, Nebraska (Figure 14). In addition to underestimation of crop residue yields, the CENTURY model overestimates root biomass. In one field study at Mead, Nebraska, measured maize root biomass was 1.9 Mg ha^{-1} at anthesis, which is the point of maximum root biomass, but the CENTURY model predicted a root biomass more than threefold greater (D.T. Walters et al., unpublished data). Although current ecosystem C balance models are useful to explore future trends under different scenarios, more accurate and robust models are needed to provide reliable estimates of the actual magnitude of C sequestration in response to changes in crop management and climate—especially at crop yield levels that are substantially higher than current average yields of maize, rice, and wheat systems.

Soil Quality, Nitrogen Requirements, and Greenhouse Gas Emissions

In addition to mitigation of greenhouse gas emissions, C sequestration benefits soil quality by increasing organic matter content (111, 112). Soil organic matter contributes to soil quality and ecosystem function through its influence on soil physical stability, soil microbial activity, nutrient storage and release, and environmental quality (113). The essential plant nutrients N, phosphorus (P), and sulfur (S) are components of the chemical building blocks that form soil humus. These nutrients are mineralized into plant-available forms by microbial activity that decomposes the humus. Humus is especially rich in N, which comprises 4%–6% of soil organic matter mass. Hence, C sequestration in soil humus requires input of both N and C that exceeds the output of these elements from an ecosystem. Thus, in many cropping systems, the application of N fertilizer increases soil C sequestration through augmented plant productivity and increased return of crop residues (114, 115).

When the net C and N balance results in C sequestration, the larger size of the SOC pool results in greater rates of SOC decomposition in aerobic soils. Because

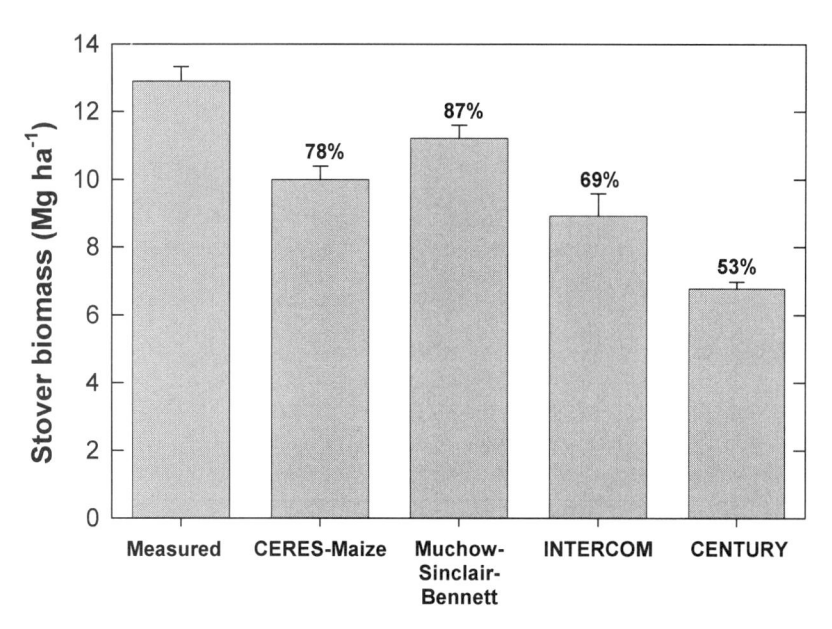

Figure 14 Aboveground maize vegetative biomass (stover) at maturity as measured in a high-yield field experiment at Lincoln, Nebraska, and corresponding estimates of biomass yield by four widely used simulation models. Values shown are means and standard errors for three years (1999 to 2001) and three plant population treatments in each year (n = 9). Numerical values above simulation bars represent the percentage of the measured biomass yield. In this field study, the maize crop was managed to achieve the minimal possible stress from biotic and abiotic factors.

the C:N ratio of SOC is relatively stable, an increase in SOC decomposition will result in a greater indigenous supply of plant-available N and a reduction in N fertilizer requirements (scenario B, Figure 15). Additional improvement in NUE can occur when the benefits of C sequestration are coupled with increases in crop yields from adoption of cultural practices that reduce yield losses from abiotic and biotic stresses and improve N fertilizer efficiency (scenario C). Therefore, management practices and policies that encourage enhancement of soil quality through C sequestration will also lead to a reduction in N fertilizer requirements per unit of yield in cropping systems on upland (i.e., aerated) soils. The effect of enhanced soil quality from C sequestration also can improve crop yields from postive effects on other soil physical and chemical properties that influence root development, water-holding capacity, water infiltration rate, and the availability of P and S.

Nitrous oxide losses via nitrification and denitrification are estimated to average $1.25 \pm 1.0\%$ of applied N fertilizer (116, 117). Although this reference value is widely used to estimate N_2O emissions from agriculture, the proportional loss

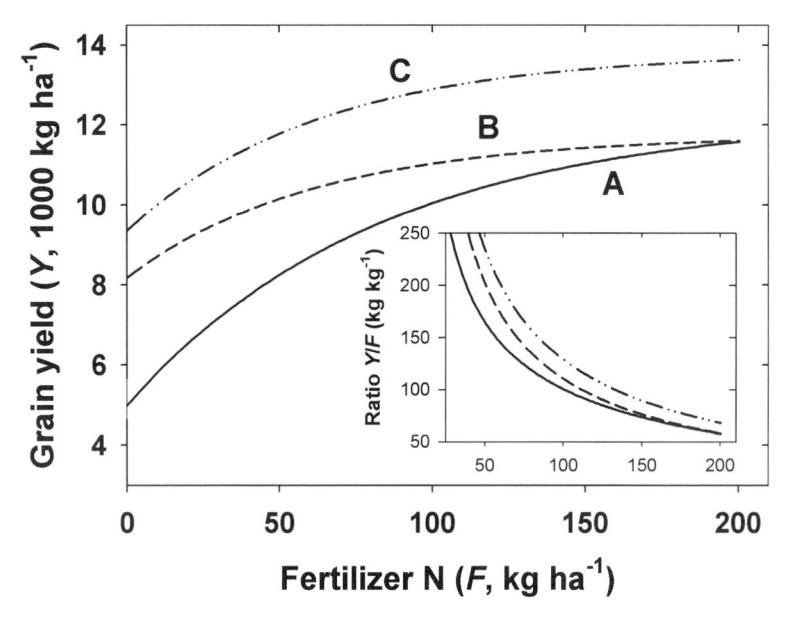

Figure 15 Hypothetical relationship between maize yield (Y) and the N application rate (F) for average soil quality and average yield (*curve A*), average yield and increased soil organic matter content and associated indigenous N supply (*curve B*), and increased soil organic matter content and indigenous N supply with improved crop management to achieve greater N fertilizer efficiency at all rates of applied N (*curve C*). Scenarios B and C assume an increase of 50 kg N ha^{-1} in indigenous N supply from the increase in soil organic matter. Insert shows the overall N use efficiency (Y/F) for each scenario.

may vary considerably as influenced by management practices, crop vigor, climate, and soil properties (118–120). Losses also differ among N fertilizer formulations with the greatest losses occurring from anhydrous ammonia (121). Despite this variation, denitrification losses are typically proportional to the amount of applied N fertilizer because the nitrification of NH_4^+ is associated with constituitive formation of small amounts of N_2O, and because nitrate is denitrified to N_2O by anerobic reduction mediated by facultative microbes under wet soil conditions.

Recent field (122) and simulation studies (103) have demonstrated that trace gas fluxes and whole-system energy balance must be considered in quantifying the greenhouse forcing potential of different land management options. For example, maize-based cropping systems that dominate agricultural land use in the north-central United States are considered to have significant under-utilized C-sequestration potential (123), but they also contribute significantly to global greenhouse gas emissions. Hence, the positive effects of sequestering C can be offset by emissions of greenhouse gases such as nitrous oxide (N_2O) or inefficient use of fossil-fuel energy embodied in other crop and soil management operations (122). Previous research has illustrated effects of crop rotation, tillage, irrigation, crop residues, soil conditions (temperature, water status, pH, salt content, and available C), manure, and fertilizer use on emissions of N_2O and other greenhouse gases from maize-based systems in the north-central United States (119, 121, 124–129). However, most of these estimates were obtained from small experimental field plots, which may not be representative of production-scale fields. Therefore, most currently used simulation models fail to account for large pulses of N_2O emissions caused by spring thawing (130), rapid soil warming (131), tillage and irrigation events (132), and N application (120), which may greatly affect annual emission rates and the net global warming potential of an agroecosystem (133). And although C sequestration is often increased in systems that receive N fertilizer, the energy costs of N fertilizer and associated CO_2 emissions must also be included in the net greenhouse forcing budget (134).

In summary, a number of uncertainties exist about the design of optimal management practices to sustain increases in food production while optimizing N use efficiency and C sequestration and minimizing greenhouse gas emissions. Resolving these uncertainties will require carefully designed, interdisciplinary field studies to improve fundamental understanding of crop growth and C and N cycling in response to management and environment. This knowledge can then be used to develop robust ecosystem models that accurately simulate C and N balance across a wide range of environmental conditions. Greater emphasis on conducting such studies in production-scale fields with progressive management practices are also needed to obtain realistic estimates of future C-sequestration potential and effects on greenhouse forcing.

CONCLUSIONS

A declining birth rate and projections for stable or decreasing human population within the next 40–50 years present an historical opportunity to protect natural resources for future generations. The degree to which agriculture contributes to resource conservation while meeting increased food demand is a critical component of this scenario. Increasing yields on existing cropland, limiting expansion of cultivated area, achieving a substantial increase in N fertilizer efficiency, and improving soil quality through C sequestration will be required to avoid severe natural resource degradation and to reduce emissions of greenhouse gases.

Although harvested cereal production area has remained relatively constant during the past 20 years, evidence of yield stagnation in several major cropping systems will make it increasingly difficult to sustain increases in food production without an expansion in cultivated area. Intensification of cereal production on existing cropland is required because loss of land to urbanization and industrialization largely occurs on prime agricultural land, and cropland replacement occurs at the expense of remnant forests and grasslands that typically have poorer soils and climate for intensive crop production. Lack of progress in raising yield potential is another threat to maintaining yield advances on existing agricultural land, and the scientific challenge of increasing crop yield potential appears to have been underestimated.

Intensification presents a challenge to reducing the negative effects of N fertilizer because crop yield response to applied N follows a diminishing return function at the field level. Organic farming is not a panacea because it is equally difficult to control the fate of N from organic N sources as it is from fertilizer, especially in systems that produce at equivalent yield levels. Technologies that improve the congruence between crop N demand and the N supply from soil and fertilizer have the greatest potential to improve N efficiency. Precise N management in time and space is required, which depends on accurate prediction of soil N supply and real-time crop N demand on a field-specific basis for small farms and a site-specific basis in large production fields. Significant strides have been made towards developing this capability, but continued investment in research and extension will be needed to assure practical management options and farmer adoption. Trends in NUE and cultivated area will ultimately determine global N fertilizer requirements and the risk of N losses to the environment.

The degree to which agriculture contributes to solving or aggravating atmospheric greenhouse gas composition depends on trends in soil C sequestration and NUE. Intensive cereal production systems appear to have considerable scope for sequestering C, which can reduce net greenhouse forcing potential when NUE is high and N_2O emissions are low. Perhaps the greatest potential for short-term gain in C sequestration exists in the reversion of marginal lands currently under cultivation and unsuitable for sustainable production to native vegetation. Avoiding further expansion of agriculture into natural ecosystems is another key factor in limiting greenhouse gas emissions. Enacting policies to support the reversion of marginal lands and protection of natural ecosystems from agricultural expansion will place an additional burden on existing highly productive cultivated areas to meet future food demand. These same productive soils also have the greatest potential for C sequestration and increased NUE.

A number of influential crop scientists and economists see few technological or biophysical constraints to meeting global food requirements of an expanding human population (97, 135–137). These optimistic scenarios are based on two pivotal assumptions: (a) there is adequate arable land of sufficient quality to support increased grain production, and (b) an exploitable gap can be maintained between average farm yields and the genetic yield potential of the major cereal crops to allow sustained increases in crop yields. Our analysis suggests considerable uncertainty in both assumptions.

We conclude that an environmentally proactive agriculture will be required to meet food demand and protect natural resources and environmental quality. It will require policies and markets that direct intensification to existing prime agricultural land while avoiding expansion of cultivated area into natural ecosystems. It also will require substantial investments in research and extension to support scientific advances and timely development and adoption of innovative new technologies that help to close the exploitable yield gap, increase crop yield potential and N fertilizer efficiency, and improve soil quality.

ACKNOWLEDGMENTS

We thank Patrick Heffer and Olivier Rousseau, International Fertilizer Industry Association, Paris, for providing the most recent statistics on global fertilizer consumption and fertilizer use by crops; Derek Byerlee, The World Bank, and David Dawe, IRRI, for providing data on wheat and rice yield trends; and Ken Sayre, CIMMYT, for providing data on wheat yield trends in the Yaqui Valley. We are grateful to Shaobing Peng and John Sheehy, IRRI, for information about progress in research on increasing rice yield potential, and to Rosalind Naylor and Pamela Matson, Stanford University, for constructive comments on an earlier draft of this manuscript. This research was supported by (a) the U.S. Department of Energy EPSCoR program, Grant No. DE-FG-02-00ER45827, (b) the U.S. Department of Energy, Office of Science, Biological and Environmental Research Program, Grant No. DE-FG03-00ER62996, (c) the Cooperative State Research, Education, and Extension Service, U.S. Department of Agriculture, under Agreement No. 2001-38700-11092. This paper has been assigned Journal Series No. 14004, Agricultural Research Division, University of Nebraska.

The *Annual Review of Environment and Resources* is online at
http://environ.annualreviews.org

LITERATURE CITED

1. Wood S, Sebastian K, Scherr SJ. 2000. *Pilot Analysis of Global Ecosystems: Agroecosystems.* Washington, DC: Int. Food Policy Res. Inst., World Resourc. Inst.
2. Rosegrant MW, Cai X, Cline SA. 2002. *World water and food to 2025: dealing with scarcity.* Washington, DC: Int. Food Policy Res. Inst. 338 pp.
3. Smil V. 1999. Nitrogen in crop production: An account of global flows. *Glob. Biochem. Cycles* 13:647–62
4. Dobson P, Bradshaw AD, Baker JM. 1997. Hopes for the future: restoration ecology and conservation biology. *Science* 277:515–22
5. Matson PA, Parton WJ, Power AG, Swift MJ. 1997. Agricultural intensification and ecosystem properties. *Science* 277:504–9
6. Vitousek PM, Mooney HA, Lubchenco J, Melillo JM. 1997. Human domination of Earth's ecosystems. *Science* 277:493–99
7. Rosegrant MW, Paisner MS, Meijer S, Witcover J. 2001. *Global Food Projections to 2020: Emerging Trends and Alternative Futures.* Washington, DC: Int. Food Policy Res. Inst.
8. Bradford E, Baldwin RL, Blackburn H, Cassman KG, Crosson PR, et al. 1999. *Animal agriculture and global food supply. Task Force Rep. 135* Counc. Agric. Sci. Technol. Ames, IA
9. Food Agric. Organ. UN. 2003. *FAOSTAT Database–Agricultural Production.* http://apps.fao.org
10. Pimentel D, Houser J, Preiss E, White O, Fang H, et al. 1997. Water resources: agriculture, the environment, and society. *BioScience* 47:97–109

11. Postel SL. 1998. Water for food production: Will there be enough in 2025? *BioScience* 48:629–37
12. Naylor RL. 1996. Energy and resource constraints on intensive agricultural production. *Annu. Rev. Energy Environ.* 21:99–123
13. Fischer G, Shah M, van Velthuizen H, Nachtergaele FO. 2000. *Global Agro-Ecological Assessment for Agriculture in the 21st Century.* Vienna: Int. Inst. Appl. Syst. Anal.
14. Food Agric. Organ. UN. 2002. *World Agriculture: Towards 2015/2030.* Rome: FAO UN. 97 pp.
15. Young A. 1999. Is there really spare land? A critique of estimates of available cultivable land in developing countries. *Environ. Dev. Sustain.* 1:3–18
16. Heilig GK. 1999. *China food: Can China feed itself?* CD-ROM Vers. 1.1 Laxenburg, Austria: Int. Inst. Appl. Syst. Anal.
17. Tilman D, Cassman KG, Matson PA, Naylor RL, Polasky S. 2002. Agricultural sustainability and intensive production practices. *Nature* 418:671–77
18. Evans LT. 1993. *Crop Evolution, Adaptation, and Yield.* Cambridge, UK: Cambridge Univ. Press. 500 pp.
19. van Ittersum MK, Rabbinge R. 1997. Concepts in production ecology for analysis and quantification of agricultural input-output combinations. *Field Crops Res.* 52:197–208
20. Cassman KG. 1999. Ecological intensification of cereal production systems: yield potential, soil quality, and precision agriculture. *Proc. Natl. Acad. Sci. USA* 96:5952–59
21. Matthews RB, Kropff MJ, Horie T, Bachelet D. 1997. Simulating the impact of climate change on rice production in Asia and evaluating options for adoption. *Agric. Syst.* 54:399–425
22. Dawe D, Dobermann A. 2001. Yield and productivity trends in intensive rice-based cropping systems of Asia. In *Yield Gap and Productivity Decline in Rice Production*, pp. 97–115. Rome: FAO UN
23. Dawe D, Dobermann A, Moya P, Abdulrachman S, Bijay S. et al. 2000. How widespread are yield declines in long-term rice experiments in Asia? *Field Crops Res.* 66:175–93
24. Kropff MJ, Cassman KG, Peng S, Mathews RB, Setter TL. 1994. Quantitative understanding of yield potential. In *Breaking the Yield Barrier*, ed. KG Cassman, pp. 21–38. Los Baños, Philipp.: Int. Rice Res. Inst.
25. Peng S, Cassman KG, Virmani SS, Sheehy JE, Khush GS. 1999. Yield potential trends of tropical rice since the release of IR8 and the challenge of increasing rice yield potential. *Crop Sci.* 39:1552–59
26. Peng S, Khush GS. 2003. Four decades of breeding for increased yield potential of irrigated rice in the International Rice Research Institute. *Plant Prod. Sci. (Jpn.)* 6(3):157–64
27. Peng S, Laza RC, Visperas RM, Sanico AL, Cassman KG, Khush GS. 2000. Grain yield of rice cultivars and lines developed in the Philippines since 1966. *Crop Sci.* 40:307–14
28. De Datta SK, Tauro AC, Baloing SN. 1968. Effect of plant type and nitrogen level on growth characteristics and grain yield of indica rice in the tropics. *Agron. J.* 60:643–47
29. Duvick DN, Cassman KG. 1999. Post-green revolution trends in yield potential of temperate maize in the North-Central United States. *Crop Sci.* 39:1622–30
30. Natl. Corn Grow. Assoc. 2003. *National Corn Growers Association—Corn Yield Contest.* http://www.ncga.com//02profits/CYC/main/index.html
31. Austin RB, Ford MA. 1989. Effects of nitrogen fertilizer on the performance of old and new varieties of winter wheat. *Vortr. Pflanzenzucht* 16:307–15
32. Sayre KD, Singh RP, Huerta-Espino J, Rajaram S. 1998. Genetic progress in

reducing yield losses to leaf rust in CIMMYT-derived Mexican spring wheat cultivars. *Crop Sci.* 38:654–59
33. Brancourt-Hulmel M, Doussinault G, Lecomte C, Berard P, Le Buanec B, Trotter M. 2003. Genetic improvement of agronomic traits of winter wheat cultivars released in France from 1946 to 1992. *Crop Sci.* 43:37–45
34. Matthews RB, Kropff MJ, Bachelet D, van Laar HH. 1995. *Modeling the impact of climate change on rice production in Asia.* Wallingford, UK: CAB Int., Int. Rice Res. Inst.
35. Sinclair TR, Horie T. 1989. Leaf nitrogen, photosynthesis, and crop radiation use efficiency: a review. *Crop Sci.* 29:90–98
36. Pretty J, Brett C, Gee D, Hine RE, Mason CF, et al. 2000. An assessment of the total external costs of UK agriculture. *Agric. Syst.* 65:113–36
37. Schweigert P, van der Ploeg RR. 2000. Nitrogen use efficiency in German agriculture since 1950: facts and evaluation. *Ber. Landwirtsch.* 80:185–212
38. Cassman KG, Dobermann A, Walters DT. 2002. Agroecosystems, nitrogen-use efficiency, and nitrogen management. *Ambio* 31:132–40
39. Poudel DD, Horwath WR, Lanini WT, Temple SR, van Bruggen AHC. 2002. Comparison of soil N availability and leaching potential, crop yields and weeds in organic, low-input and conventional farming systems in northern California. *Agric. Ecosyst. Environ.* 90:125–37
40. Di HJ, Cameron KC. 2002. Nitrate leaching in temperate agroecosystems: sources, factors and mitigating strategies. *Nutr. Cycl. Agroecosyst.* 64:237–56
41. Hansen B, Alroe HF, Kristensen ES. 2001. Approaches to assess the environmental impact of organic farming with particular regard to Denmark. *Agric. Ecosyst. Environ.* 83:11–26
42. Stivers LJ, Shennan C. 1991. Meeting the nitrogen needs of processing tomatoes through winter cover cropping. *J. Prod. Agric.* 4:330–35
43. Schluter W, Hennig A, Brummer G. 1997. Nitrate transport in soils of a river flood plain under organic and conventional farming - analytical results, modeling and balances. *Z. Pflanzenernaehr. Bodenk.* 160:57–65
44. Eltun R. 1995. Comparisons of nitrogen leaching in ecological and conventional cropping systems. *Biol. Agric. Hortic.* 11:103–14
45. Stopes C, Lord EI, Philipps L, Woodward L. 2002. Nitrate leaching from organic farms and conventional farms following best practice. *Soil Use Manag.* 18:256–63
46. Kirchmann H, Bergstroem L. 2001. Do organic farming practices reduce nitrate leaching? *Commun. Soil Sci. Plant Anal.* 32:997–1028
47. Flessa H, Wild U, Klemisch M, Pfadenhauer J. 1998. Nitrous oxide and methane fluxes from organic soils under agriculture. *Eur. J. Soil Sci.* 49:327–35
48. Flessa H, Ruser R, Dorsch P, Kamp T, Jimenez MA, et al. 2002. Integrated evaluation of greenhouse gas emissions (CO_2, CH_4, N_2O) from two farming systems in southern Germany. *Agric. Ecosyst. Environ.* 91:175–89
49. van der Werden TJ, Sherlock RR, Williams PH, Cameron K. 2000. Effect of three contrasting onion (*Allium cepa L.*) production systems on nitrous oxide emissions from soil. *Biol. Fertil. Soils* 31:334–42
50. Wang ZY, Xu YC, Li Z, Guo YX, Wassmann R, et al. 2000. A four-year record of methane emissions from irrigated rice fields in the Beijing region of China. *Nutr. Cycl. Agroecosyst.* 58:55–63
51. Wassmann R, Neue HU, Alberto MCR, Lantin RS, Bueno C, et al. 1996. Fluxes and pools of methane in wetland rice soils with varying organic inputs. *Environ. Monit. Assess.* 42:163–73
52. Mäder P, Fliessbach A, Dubois D, Gunst L, Fried P, Niggli U. 2002. Soil fertility

and biodiversity in organic farming. *Science* 296:1694–97
53. Eltun R, Korsaeth A, Nordheim O. 2002. A comparison of environmental, soil fertility, yield, and economical effects in six cropping systems based on an 8-year experiment in Norway. *Agric. Ecosyst. Environ.* 90:155–68
54. Dawe D. 2000. The contribution of rice research to poverty alleviation. In *Redesigning Rice Photosynthesis to Increase Yield*, ed. JE Sheehy, PL Mitchell, B Hardy, pp. 3–12. Makati City, Philipp./Amsterdam: Int. Rice Res. Inst., Elsevier Sci.
55. Senauer B, Sur M. 2001. Ending global hunger in the 21st century: projections of the number of food insecure people. *Rev. Agric. Econ.* 23:68–81
56. Dawe D, Dobermann A. 1999. *Defining productivity and yield. IRRI Discuss. Pap. Ser. 33*. Int. Rice Res. Inst. Makati City, Philipp.
57. Novoa R, Loomis RS. 1981. Nitrogen and plant production. *Plant Soil* 58:177–204
58. Cassman KG, Gines HC, Dizon M, Samson MI, Alcantara JM. 1996. Nitrogen-use efficiency in tropical lowland rice systems: contributions from indigenous and applied nitrogen. *Field Crops Res.* 47:1–12
59. Bell MA. 1993. Organic matter, soil properties, and wheat production in the high valley of Mexico. *Soil Sci.* 156:86–93
60. Kolberg RL, Westfall DG, Peterson GA. 1999. Influence of cropping intensity and nitrogen fertilizer rates on in situ nitrogen mineralization. *Soil Sci. Soc. Am. J.* 63:129–34
61. Cassman KG, Dobermann A, Santa Cruz PC, Gines HC, Samson MI, et al. 1996. Soil organic matter and the indigenous nitrogen supply of intensive irrigated rice systems in the tropics. *Plant Soil* 182:267–78
62. Dobermann A, Witt C, Abdulrachman S, Gines HC, Nagarajan R, et al. 2003. Estimating indigenous nutrient supplies for site-specific nutrient management in irrigated rice. *Agron. J.* 95:924–35
63. Tilman D, Fargione J, Wolff B, D'Antonio C, Dobson A, et al. 2001. Forecasting agriculturally driven global environmental change. *Science* 292:281–84
64. Int. Fertil. Ind. Assoc. 2002. *Fertilizer use by crop*. Rome: IFA, IFDC, IPI, PPI, FAO
65. Int. Fertil. Ind. Assoc. 2003. *IFADATA Statistics*. http://www.fertilizer.org/ifa/statistics.asp
66. Cassman KG, Pingali PL. 1995. Intensification of irrigated rice systems: learning from the past to meet future challenges. *GeoJ.* 35:299–305
67. US Dep. Agric., Natl. Agric. Stat. Serv. 2003. *Agricultural Statistics Database*. http://www.nass.usda.gov
68. Dobermann A, Witt C, Dawe D, Gines GC, Nagarajan R, et al. 2002. Site-specific nutrient management for intensive rice cropping systems in Asia. *Field Crops Res.* 74:37–66
69. Dobermann A. 2000. Future intensification of irrigated rice systems. In *Redesigning Rice Photosynthesis to Increase Yield*, ed. JE Sheehy, PL Mitchell, B Hardy, pp. 229–47. Makati City, Philipp./Amsterdam: Int. Rice Res. Inst., Elsevier Sci.
70. UN. 1998. *World Population Prospects*. New York: UN
71. Food Agric. Organ. UN. 2000. *Fertilizer Requirements in 2015 and 2030*. Rome: FAO UN
72. Bumb B, Baanante CA. 1996. *The role of fertilizer in sustaining food security and protecting the environment to 2020. Discuss. Pap. 17*. Washington, DC: Int. Food Policy Res. Inst.
73. Frink CR, Waggoner PE, Ausubel JH. 1999. Nitrogen fertilizer: retrospect and prospect. *Proc. Natl. Acad. Sci. USA* 96:1175–80
74. Dobermann A, Cassman KG. 2002. Plant nutrient management for enhanced productivity in intensive grain production systems of the United States and Asia. *Plant Soil* 247:153–75

75. Suzuki A. 1997. *Fertilization of Rice in Japan*. Tokyo, Jpn.: Jpn. FAO Assoc. 1–111 pp.
76. Mishima S. 2001. Recent trend of nitrogen flow associated with agricultural production in Japan. *Soil Sci. Plant Nutr.* 47:157–66
77. Peng S, Cassman KG. 1998. Upper thresholds of nitrogen uptake rates and associated N fertilizer efficiencies in irrigated rice. *Agron. J.* 90:178–85
78. Peng S, Garcia FV, Laza RC, Sanico AL, Visperas RM, Cassman KG. 1996. Increased N-use efficiency using a chlorophyll meter on high-yielding irrigated rice. *Field Crops Res.* 47:243–52
79. Dobermann A, White PF. 1999. Strategies for nutrient management in irrigated and rainfed lowland rice systems. *Nutr. Cycl. Agroecosyst.* 53:1–18
80. Witt C, Balasubramaniam V, Dobermann A, Buresh RJ. 2002. Nutrient management. In *Rice: A Practical Guide to Nutrient Management*, ed. TH Fairhurst, C Witt, pp. 1–45. Manila/Singapore: Int. Rice Res. Inst., Potash & Phosphate Inst./Potash & Phosphate Inst. Can.
81. Wang GH, Dobermann A, Witt C, Sun QZ, Fu RX. 2001. Performance of site-specific nutrient management for irrigated rice in southeast China. *Agron. J.* 93:869–78
82. Matson PA, Naylor RL, Ortiz-Monasterio I. 1998. Integration of environmental, agronomic, and economic aspects of fertilizer management. *Science* 280:112–15
83. Riley WJ, Ortiz-Monasterio I, Matson PA. 2003. Nitrogen leaching and soil nitrate, nitrite, and ammonium levels under irrigated wheat in Northern Mexico. *Nutr. Cycl. Agroecosyst.* 61:223–36
84. Melillo JM, Prentice IC, Farquhar GD, Schulze ED, Sala OE. 1996. Terrestrial biotic responses to environmental change and feedbacks to climate. In *Climate Change 1995. The Science of Climate Change*, ed. JT Houghton, LG Meira Filho, BA Callander, N Harris, A Kattenberg, K Maskell, pp. 445–481. Cambridge, UK: IPCC, Cambridge Univ. Press
85. Metting FB, Smith JL, Amthor JS. 1998. Science needs and new technologies for soil carbon sequestration. In Carbon sequestration in soils: science, monitoring, and beyond. *Proc. St. Michaels Workshop, Dec.*, ed. NJ Rosenberg, pp. 1–34. Columbus, OH: Battelle
86. Intergov. Panel Clim. Chang. 1996. *Climate change 1995. The science of climate change*. Work. Group 1. Cambridge: IPCC., Cambridge Univ. Press.
87. Schlesinger WH. 1984. Soil organic matter: a source of atmospheric CO_2. In *The Role of Terrestrial Vegetation in the Global Carbon Cycle: Measurement by Remote Sensing*, ed. GM Woodwell, pp. 111–27. New York: Wiley
88. Houghton RA. 1995. Changes in the storage of terrestrial carbon since 1850. In *Soils and Global Change*, ed. R Lal, JM Kimble, E Levine, BA Stewart, pp. 45–65. Boca Raton, FL: CRC
89. West TO, Marland G. 2002. A synthesis of carbon sequestration, carbon emissions, and net carbon flux in agriculture: comparing tillage practices in the United States. *Agric. Ecosyst. Environ.* 91:217–32
90. Hair D, Sampson RN, Hamilton TE. 1996. Summary: forest management opportunities for increasing carbon storage. In *Forests and Global Change*: Vol. 2: *Forest Management Opportunities for Mitigating Carbon Emissions*, ed. RN Sampson, D Hair, pp. 237–54. Washington, DC: Am. Forests
91. Lal R, Kimble JM, Follett RF, Cole CV. 1998. *The Potential of U.S. Cropland to Sequester Carbon and Mitigate the Greenhouse Effect*. Chelsea, MI: Ann Arbor. 128 pp.
92. Intergov. Panel Clim. Chang. 2000. *Land use, land–use change, and forestry. Spec. Rep.* IPCC, Cambridge, UK
93. Paustian K, Andren O, Janzen HH, Lal R, Smith P, et al. 1997. Agricultural soils as

sink to mitigate CO$_2$ emissions. *Soil Use Manag.* 13:230–44
94. Dumanski J, Desjardins RL, Tarnocai C, Monreal C, Gregorich EG, et al. 1998. Possibilities for future carbon sequestration in Canadian agriculture in relation to land use changes. *Clim. Chang.* 40:81–103
95. Schlesinger WH, Lichter A. 2001. Limited carbon storage in soil and litter of experimental forest plots under increased atmospheric CO$_2$. *Nature* 411:466–69
96. Lal R, Kimble JM, Follett RF. 1999. Agricultural practices and policies for carbon sequestration in soil. *Recomm. Conclus. Int. Symp.* 19–23 July, Columbus, OH, 12 pp.
97. Waggoner PE. 1994. *How much land can ten billion people spare for nature? Task Force Rep. 121.* Counc. Agric. Sci. Technol. Ames, IA
98. Cassman KG. 2001. *Crop science research to assure food security.* In Crop science: progress and prospects. Presented at 3rd Int. Crop Sci. Congr., Hamburg, Ger., 2000, ed. J Nösberger, HH Geiger, PC Struik, pp. 33–51. Wallingford, UK: CABI
99. West TO, Post WM. 2002. Soil organic carbon sequestration rates by tillage and crop rotation: a global data analysis. *Soil Sci. Soc. Am. J.* 66:1930–46
100. Dick WA, Blevins RL, Frye WW, Peters SE, Christenson DR, et al. 1998. Impacts of agricultural management practices on C sequestration in forest-derived soils of the eastern Corn Belt. *Soil Tillage Res.* 47:235–44
101. Natl. Assess. Synth. Team. 2000. *Climate Change Impacts on the United States: The Potential Consequences of Climate Variability and Change.* Washington, DC: US Glob. Chang. Res. Program
102. Vleeshouwers LM, Verhagen A. 2002. Carbon emission and sequestration by agricultural land use: a model study for Europe. *Glob. Chang. Biol.* 8:519–30
103. Smith P, Goulding KWT, Smith KA, Powlson DS, Smith JU, et al. 2001. Enhancing the carbon sink in European agricultural soils: including trace gas fluxes in estimates of carbon mitigation potential. *Nutr. Cycl. Agroecosyst.* 60:237–52
104. Eve MD, Sperow M, Howerton K, Paustian K, Follett RF. 2002. Predicted impact of management changes on soil carbon storage for each cropland region of the conterminous United States. *J. Soil Water Conserv.* 57:196–204
105. Smith P, Powlson DS, Smith JU, Falloon P, Coleman K. 2000. Meeting Europe's climate change commitments: quantitative estimates of the potential for carbon mitigation by agriculture. *Glob. Chang. Biol.* 6:525–39
106. Jones CA, Kiniry JR. 1986. *CERES-Maize: A Simulation Model of Maize Growth and Development.* College Station: Tex. A&M Univ. Press
107. Muchow RC, Sinclair TR, Bennett JM. 1990. Temperature and solar radiation effects on potential maize yields across locations. *Agron. J.* 82:338–42
108. Kropff MJ, van Laar HH. 1993. *Modelling Crop-Weed Interactions.* Wallingford, UK: CABI
109. Parton WJ, Schimel DS, Cole CV, Ojima DS. 1987. Analysis of factors controlling soil organic matter levels in Great Plains grasslands. *Soil Sci. Soc. Am. J.* 51:1173–79
110. Metherell AK, Harding LA, Cole CV, Parton WJ. 1993. *Century Soil Organic Matter Model Environment. Technical Documentation, Agroecosystem Version 4.0.* Fort Collins, CO: USDA, Agric. Res. Serv.
111. Greenland DJ. 1998. Carbon sequestration in soil: knowledge gaps indicated by the symposium presentations. See Ref. 138, pp. 591–94
112. Izaurralde RC, Rosenberg NJ, Lal R. 2001. Mitigation of climatic change by soil carbon sequestration: issues of science, monitoring, and degraded lands. *Adv. Agron.* 70:1–75

113. Herrick JE, Wander MM. 1997. Relationship between soil organic carbon and soil quality in cropped and rangeland soils: the importance of distribution, composition and soil biological activity. See Ref. 138, pp. 405–25
114. Paustian K, Collins HP, Paul EA. 1997. Management controls on soil carbon. In *Soil Organic Matter in Temperate Agroecosystems*, ed. EA Paul, K Paustian, ET Elliott, CV Cole, pp. 15–49. Boca Raton, FL: CRC
115. Halvorson AD, Reule CA, Follett RF. 1999. Nitrogen fertilization effects on soil carbon and nitrogen in a dryland cropping system. *Soil Sci. Soc. Am. J.* 63:912–17
116. Bouwman AF. 1990. Exchange of greenhouse gases between terrestrial ecosystems and the atmosphere. In *Soils and the Greenhouse Effect*, ed. AF Bouwman, pp. 61–127. Chichester, UK: Wiley
117. Intergov. Panel Clim. Chang. 1996. *The Revised 1996 Guidelines for National Greenhouse Gas Inventories*. Vol. 1–3. Geneva, Switz.: IPCC
118. Smith KA, Mctaggart IP, Tsuruta H. 1997. Emissions of N_2O and NO associated with nitrogen fertilization in intensive agriculture, and the potential for mitigation. *Soil Use Manag.* 13:296–304
119. Breitenbeck GA, Bremner JM. 1986. Effects of rate and depth of fertilizer application on emission of nitrous oxide from soil fertilized with anhydrous ammonia. *Biol. Fertil. Soils* 2:201–4
120. Simojoki A, Jaakkola A. 2000. Effect of nitrogen fertilization, cropping and irrigation on soil air composition and nitrous oxide emission in a loamy clay. *Eur. J. Soil Sci.* 51:413–24
121. Eichner MJ. 1990. Nitrous oxide emissions from fertilized soils: summary of available data. *J. Environ. Qual.* 19:272–80
122. Robertson GP, Paul EA, Harwood RR. 2000. Greenhouse gases in intensive agriculture: contributions of individual gases to the radiative forcing of the atmosphere. *Science* 289:1922–25
123. Collins HP, Blevins RL, Bundy LG, Christenson DR, Dick WA, et al. 1999. Soil carbon dynamics in corn-based agroecosystems: results from carbon-13 natural abundance. *Soil Sci. Soc. Am. J.* 63:584–91
124. Aulakh MS, Doran JW, Walters DT, Mosier AR, Francis DD. 1991. Crop residue type and placement effects of denitrification and mineralization. *Soil Sci. Soc. Am. J.* 55:1020–25
125. Weier KL, Doran JW, Power JF, Walters DT. 1993. Denitrification and the dinitrogen/nitrous oxide ratio as affected by soil water, available carbon, and nitrate. *Soil Sci. Soc. Am. J.* 57:66–72
126. Qian JH, Doran JW, Weier KL, Mosier AR, Peterson TA, Power JF. 1997. Soil denitrification and nitrous oxide losses under corn irrigated with high-nitrate groundwater. *J. Environ. Qual.* 26:348–60
127. Cates RL, Keeney DR. 1987. Nitrous oxide production throughout the year from fertilized and manured maize fields. *J. Environ. Qual.* 16:443–47
128. Cochran VL, Elliott LF, Papendick RI. 1981. Nitrous oxide emissions from a fallow field fertilized with anhydrous ammonia. *Soil Sci. Soc. Am. J.* 45:307–10
129. Bronson KF, Mosier AR, Bishnoi SR. 1992. Nitrous oxide emissions in irrigated corn as affected by nitrification-denitrification. *Soil Sci. Soc. Am. J.* 56:161–65
130. Papen H, Butterbach-Bahl K. 1999. A 3-year continuous record of nitrogen trace gas fluxes from untreated and limed soil of a N-saturated spruce and beech forest ecosystem in Germany. 1. N_2O emissions. *J. Geophys. Res.* 104:18487–503
131. Hutchinson GL, Guenzi WD, Livingston GP. 1993. Soil water controls on aerobic emissions of gaseous N oxides. *Soil Biol. Biochem.* 25:1–9
132. Kessavalou A, Doran JW, Mosier AR, Drijber RA. 1998. Greenhouse gas fluxes

following tillage and wetting in a wheat-fallow cropping system. *J. Environ. Qual.* 27:1105–16

133. Hutchinson GL, Vigil MF, Doran JW, Kessavalou A. 1997. Coarse-scale soil-atmosphere NO_x modeling: status and limitations. *Nutr. Cycl. Agroecosyst.* 48:25–35

134. Schlesinger WH. 2000. Carbon sequestration in soils: some cautions amidst optimism. *Agric. Ecosyst. Environ.* 82:121–27

135. Pinstrup-Andersen P, Pandya-Lorch R, Rosegrant MW. 1999. *World Food Prospects: Critical Issues for the Early Twenty-First Century.* Washington, DC: Int. Food Policy Res. Inst. 32 pp.

136. Evans LT. 1998. *Feeding the Ten Billion: Plants and Population Growth.* Cambridge, UK: Cambridge Univ. Press

137. Dyson T. 1996. *Population and Food: Global Perspectives.* London: Routledge

138. Lal R, Kimble JM, Stewart BA, eds. 1998. *Soil Processes and the Carbon Cycle.* Boca Raton, FL: CRC

STATE OF THE WORLD'S FISHERIES

Ray Hilborn, Trevor A. Branch, Billy Ernst, Arni Magnussson, Carolina V. Minte-Vera, Mark D. Scheuerell, and Juan L. Valero

School of Aquatic and Fishery Sciences, University of Washington, Box 355020, Seattle, Washington 98195; email: rayh@u.washington.edu, tbranch@u.washington.edu, biernst@u.washington.edu, arnima@u.washington.edu, cminte@u.washington.edu, mark.scheuerell@noaa.gov, juan@u.washington.edu

Key Words fishery, catch, exploitation, management, marine, ecosystem, humans

■ **Abstract** The total world catch from marine and freshwater wild stocks has peaked and may be slightly declining. There appear to be few significant resources to be developed, and the majority of the world's fish stocks are intensively exploited. Many marine ecosystems have been profoundly changed by fishing and other human activities. Although most of the world's major fisheries continue to produce substantial sustainable yield, a number have been severely overfished, and many more stocks appear to be heading toward depletion. The world's fisheries continue to be heavily subsidized, which encourages overfishing and provides society with a small fraction of the potential economic benefits. In most of the world's fisheries there is a "race for fish" in which boats compete to catch the fish before a quota is achieved or the fish are caught by someone else. The race for fish leads to economic inefficiency, poor quality product, and pressure to extract every fish for short-term gain. A number of countries have instituted alternative management practices that eliminate the race for fish and encourage economic efficiency, use lower exploitation rates that deliberately do not attempt to maximize biological yield, and encourage reduced fishing costs and increased value of products. In fisheries where this transition has taken place, we see the potential for future sustainability, but in those fisheries where the race for fish continues, we anticipate further declines in abundance, further loss of jobs and fishing communities, and potential structural change to marine ecosystems.

CONTENTS

INTRODUCTION 360
HISTORICAL PERSPECTIVE ON IMPACTS OF HUMANS ON FISH
  STOCKS 363
  Harvesting and Sequential Depletion 363
  Climate 364
  Pollution and Introduction of Exotic Species 367
  Inland Fisheries 367
  Summary 368

STATUS OF FISHERIES AND ECOSYSTEMS 368
    Stock Status 368
    Discarding and Waste 370
    Habitat Impacts of Fishing 372
    Extinction and Ecosystem Impacts 373
SOCIAL AND ECONOMIC STATUS OF FISHERIES 375
THE SCIENCE OF SUSTAINABLE HARVESTING 375
    Single-Species Sustainability 377
    Multispecies and Ecosystem Analysis 379
THE BEHAVIOR OF FISHING FLEETS 381
METHODS OF FISHERIES MANAGEMENT 382
    Institutional Structure and Governance 382
    Allocating Fish Among Users 384
    Illegal Fishing 386
    New Solutions: The Precautionary Approach and Marine Protected
      Areas 387
WHAT DETERMINES SUCCESS AND FAILURE? 387
THE FUTURE OF WORLD FISHERIES 390

INTRODUCTION

The collapse of the Newfoundland cod stock and closure of the fishery in 1992 illustrates the crisis facing the world's fisheries. Before Columbus came to America, Basque fishermen were sailing to the Grand Banks to fish for cod; indeed, the cod fishery was the reason for the settlement of Newfoundland. The fishery was sustainably harvested for 500 years, but in a few decades beginning in the 1960s, several million tonnes of fish stocks were reduced to a small remnant that shows no sign of rebuilding (Figure 1). The cod collapse caused enormous social upheaval: 20,000 people were put out of work, the economy of Newfoundland was severely damaged, Canadian taxpayers paid over Can$1 billion per year to support unemployed fishermen, and the whole culture of an island built on cod fishing was shaken (1).

The cause of the cod collapse was clearly overfishing because the fish were harvested too hard and too young (2, 3). Modern fishing vessels pursued the cod over their entire range onto their spawning grounds, instead of only fishing when the cod came inshore. The destruction began with large foreign fleets moving onto the Grand Banks, was temporarily stopped in 1977 when Canada declared a 200-mile limit that excluded most foreign fishing, and then continued with the building of Canada's own offshore fleet, a fleet that was much too large based on overly optimistic scientific assessments of long-term sustainable yield. Ultimately, it was the Canadian fleet, with Canadian scientists providing advice and Canadian managers in charge, that led to the demise of this fishery. In theory, this was a management system the world could admire, with modern research surveys, state-of-the-art computer models to assess stock status, and extensive peer review by experts. Yet it failed totally.

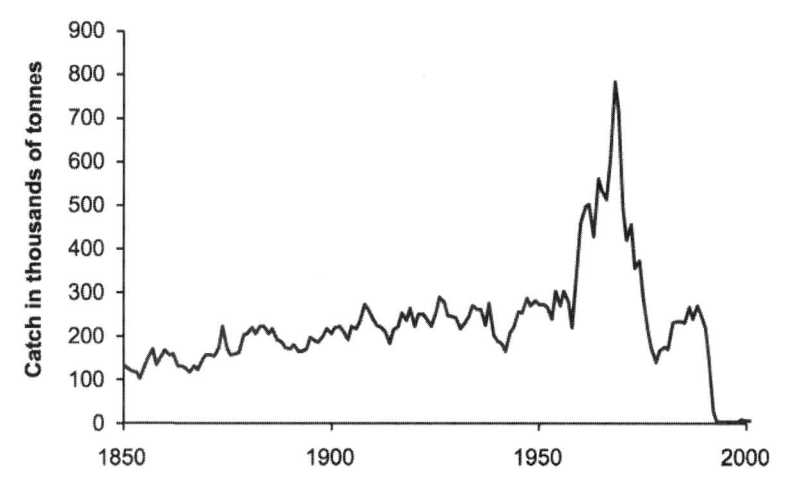

Figure 1 Catches of Newfoundland (northern) cod since 1850 in thousands of tonnes. Catches are for statistical areas 2J and 3KL. Data taken from (155).

The failure of the fishery was not simply a failure of the cod to reproduce. Although the value of groundfish (with cod being the most important) declined dramatically, an increase in shellfish (lobster, shrimp, and crab) more than made up—in economic value—for the loss of groundfish (Figure 2). By 1996, the value of Newfoundland fisheries landings was greater than it had been before the

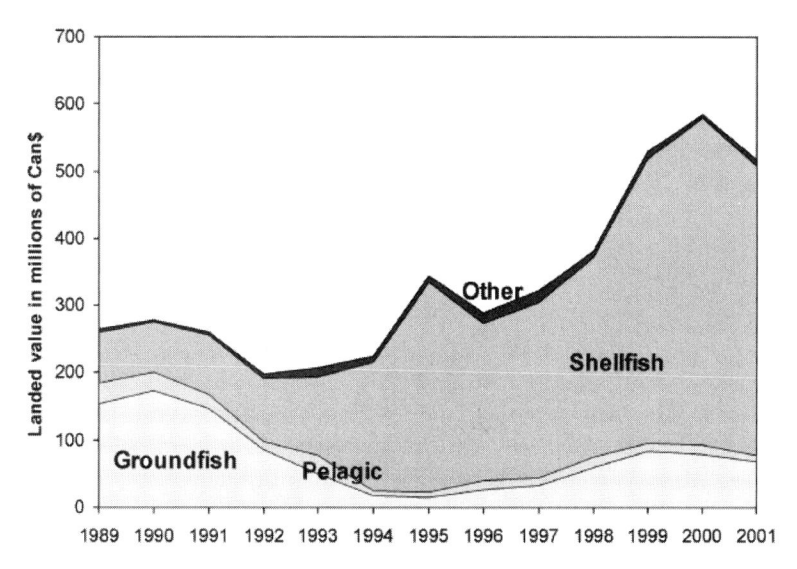

Figure 2 The economic value of landings for groundfish (mainly cod) and shellfish (lobster, shrimp, and crab) in Newfoundland from 1989 to 1996. Pelagic species and other species are minor and shown as smaller contributors. Source (5a).

cod collapse. The same is true for eastern Canada as a whole. Moreover, this is not a simple case of the fishing fleets moving from cod onto shrimp, lobster, and crab. Rather, a substantial increase in the abundance of shellfish coincided with the groundfish collapse. Considerable evidence suggests this was because of reduced groundfish predation (4, 5). The important point is that during the 1990s there was a reasonably continuous stream of income available to sustain fishing communities. In fact, communities were not sustained. The fishermen and plant workers who relied on cod remained unemployed and received part of the Can$1 billion annual payments (much greater than the economic value of the fishery), while fishermen who held shellfish licenses became wealthy. Prior to 1950, fishing communities had a mixed fishing pattern, with individuals fishing cod, lobster, crab, shrimp, and seals. If this structure had been in place in the 1990s, the economic impacts of the collapse of cod would have been largely ameliorated by the increased income to the fishermen from increased take of shellfish. However, during the 1960s and 1970s, Canada instituted programs to restrict entry into fisheries, forcing individuals to specialize. When the cod collapsed in 1991, cod fishermen were therefore not allowed to switch. The collapse of the cod stock was clearly due to overfishing. But the collapse of the Newfoundland fishery was due primarily to an institutional structure that forced specialization, which reduced the ability of fishermen to adapt to change.

The Newfoundland cod collapse illustrates the interaction between marine ecosystems and their products, humans who exploit the fish, the social and economic fabric of communities and markets, and the governmental institutions that regulate the fisheries. Is this the future, or indeed the present, for the world's fisheries? There is no shortage of evidence that fishing fleets are too large, science too imprecise, and management institutions too ineffective to prevent the Newfoundland cod story from being repeated again and again, as indeed it has been since humans first acquired the technology to exploit the resources of the sea. Nonetheless, there are signs of hope. Fisheries have been and can be managed sustainably. It has become clear that the greatest mistake in understanding fisheries systems is to think of fish as their centerpiece. In fact, society seeks to maintain sustainable fisheries, not just fish. People want sustainable ecosystems, sustainable communities, and sustainable economic activity. As we will show, most of the world's fisheries are intensively exploited, and many may indeed be going the way of the Newfoundland cod. If the fish were the only important component of the system, society could simply stop fishing. This, however, would often destroy the fishing communities that are the principal reason that most people care about the existence of fisheries. In this review, we explore the state of the world's fisheries, including the fish, the people who harvest them, and the institutions that regulate them. We use the term fisheries to refer to the natural and human system and fish stocks to refer to the species and the ecosystems in which they live. We use the terms fisherman and fishermen throughout the report because this is how practitioners of fishing (both male and female) tend to refer to themselves in the United States. We will seek examples of management solutions that ensure the sustainability of all of these components. We include in "the world's fisheries" the fisheries that harvest wild stocks of marine and freshwater fish, invertebrates, and mammals. We specifically exclude aquaculture and will treat freshwater and recreational fisheries only slightly.

HISTORICAL PERSPECTIVE ON IMPACTS OF HUMANS ON FISH STOCKS

Fisheries have played a significant role in human history. The search for cod led to much of the early exploration of North America (6); the trade in cod and whales was a major component of European economic activity in the sixteenth through nineteenth centuries, and fluctuations in herring stocks in Scandinavia shook local economies (7). In the twentieth century, the collapse of the Peruvian anchovetta stock rocked the Peruvian economy, and the economy of Iceland was dominated by fish products. Therefore the interaction between society and fish stocks has been and continues to be important to hundreds of millions of people and national governments. This explains, to a great extent, the worldwide publicity that many recent fishery crises have received and the widespread public interest in the status of fisheries and in particular how human activity has impacted fish stocks.

The impact of mankind on marine ecosystems has long been a subject of controversy. In the late nineteenth century it was still possible to argue "that the cod fishery, the herring fishery, the pilchard fishery, the mackerel fishery, and probably all the great sea-fisheries, are inexhaustible; that is to say that nothing we do seriously affects the number of fish" (8) quoted in (9).

Other scientists, however, have long expressed the view that fishing would inescapably degrade fish populations. "We have ... to face the established fact that the bottom fisheries are ... in rapid and continuous process of exhaustion; that the rate at which sea fishes multiply and grow, even in favorable seasons, is exceeded by the rate of capture" (10) quoted in (9).

Harvesting and Sequential Depletion

The exhaustible nature of fish stocks was firmly demonstrated by "The Great Fishing Experiment," also known as World War I, which halted fishing in the North Sea for five years. When fishermen returned after the war, they found that fish had increased dramatically in size and abundance (9). This was clear evidence that the abundance of the stocks had been reduced before the war by fishing. It is now widely accepted that fishing can and does seriously affect fish stock abundance, in the same way that whaling was responsible for the sequential depletion, and in some cases destruction, of cetacean populations worldwide. By the twentieth century, southern right whales were almost wiped out, and modern whaling fleets were embarking on huge harvests of large cetaceans in the Southern Hemisphere, focusing on less and less valuable species: humpback, blue, fin, sperm, and sei whale populations were sequentially depleted (Figure 3).

Southern Hemisphere whales are only the most recent of a long series of groups of aquatic organisms that have suffered substantial depletion. Formerly widespread salmon are now absent from most European rivers (11), and marine mammals like seals and sea lions were hunted to near extinction worldwide (12). Sea otters in the North Pacific were formerly abundant from California to the tips of the Aleutian Islands before unrestricted fur hunting reduced them to near extinction at the start of the twentieth century. The International Fur Seal Treaty then afforded them protection, and many areas managed to repopulate and recover to their former densities.

In most natural ecosystems, large consumer species like whales, manatees, turtles, and monk seals were rapidly wiped out by intensive hunting. Species in similar trophic levels then took over the roles of the missing top consumers until they in turn were overfished or depleted through disease or other natural causes (13). Sometimes, decades or even centuries after the original consumer species were eliminated, the entire ecosystem collapsed, as happened to western Atlantic coral reefs. These reefs suffered massive mortality in the 1980s when they were smothered by seaweeds (13). The too-obvious cause of the algal profusion was the loss of an abundant sea urchin species, but the ultimate reason was the fishery caused depletion of herbivorous fish at the start of the twentieth century, which left the sea urchin as the sole algal control agent protecting the coral reefs.

These changes, often taking centuries, alter human perception of what is natural or desirable. Fishery scientists of each generation accept the natural state of fisheries as being the stock levels when their careers started and neglect the fact that stocks may have declined before they started working. This has been termed the "shifting baseline syndrome" (14) and Pauly has argued that this leads fishery managers to progressively accept degraded systems as the target they would like to achieve, because they have no understanding of the real natural condition that may have existed decades or centuries before.

Climate

Not all changes in marine fish stocks are due to fishing pressure. In many fish stocks, climate change and long-term natural fluctuations also play an important role (7). Reconstructions of Bristol Bay salmon abundance over the past 2200 years show a pattern of high natural variability (Figure 4) (15, 16). At the decadal scale, changes appear to be related to climate changes and are asynchronously linked to changes in far-flung systems like sardine and anchovy populations in California. At the level of centuries, this synchrony breaks down, but there are long-term underlying patterns of low salmon abundance from 100 BC to 800 AD, and high salmon abundance from 1200 to 1900 AD. Long-term records show that other species also vary naturally over one or two orders of magnitude (17–19). Climate variability can simultaneously contribute to increases in some stocks at the same time it helps to bring about decreases in others. In the most recent century, global

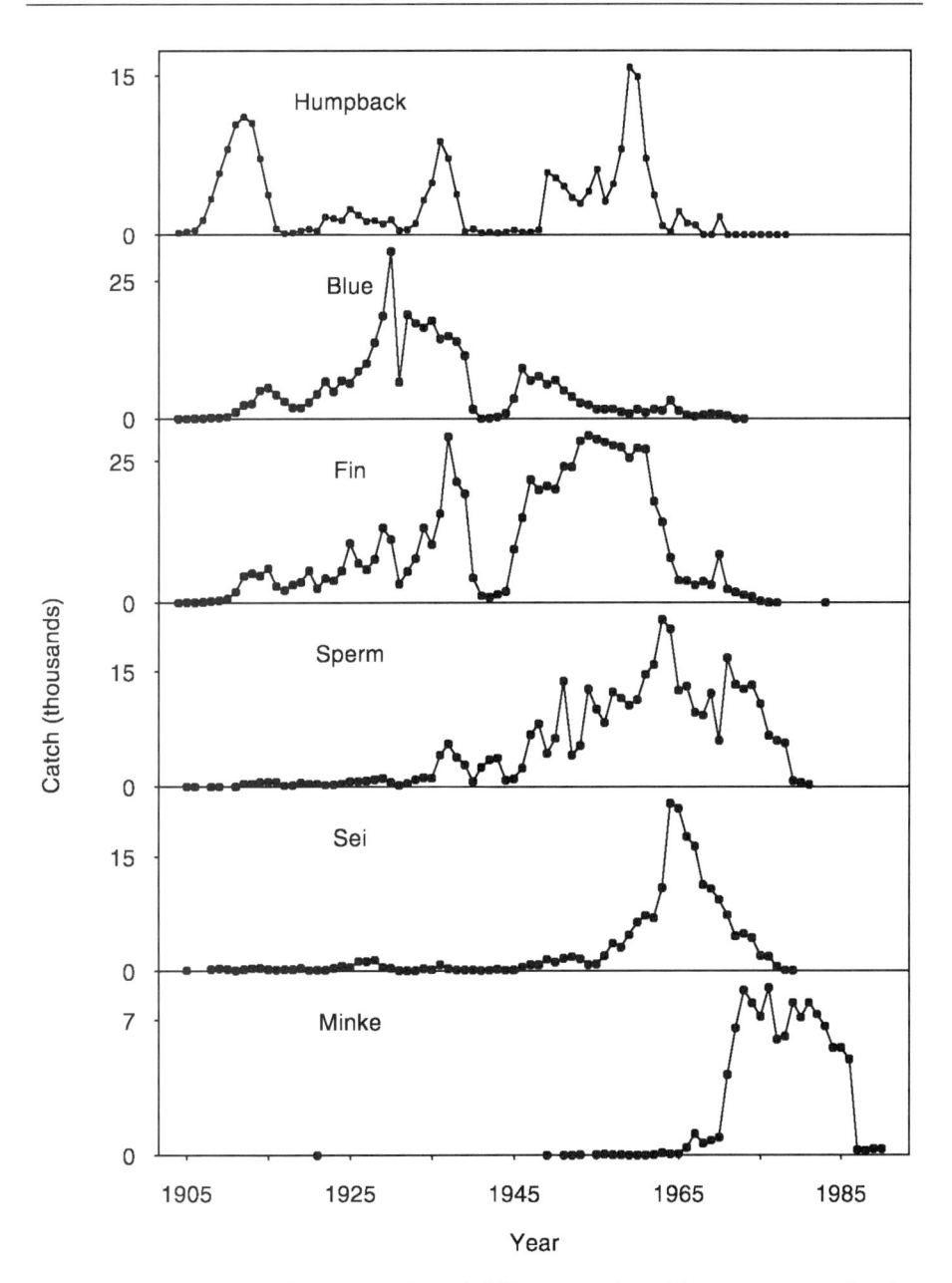

Figure 3 Southern Hemisphere catches of different species of large cetaceans showing the pattern of discovery, exploitation, and subsequent collapse of each species (C. Allison, International Whaling Commission, personal communication, December 2002). Southern right whales (not shown here) were already severely depleted by the mid-1800s. Catches dropped nearly to zero during World War II.

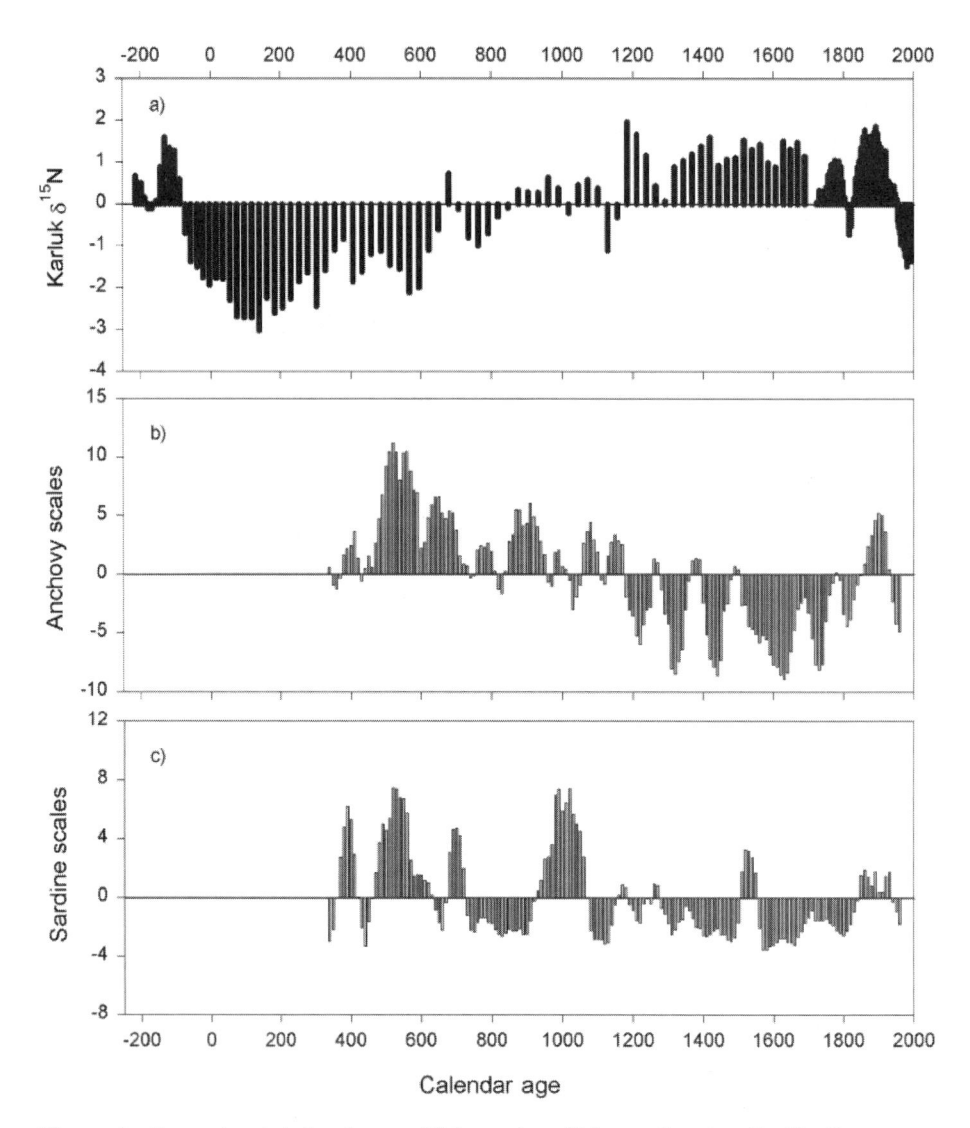

Figure 4 Reconstructed abundance of fish species off the northeastern Pacific Ocean over the past 2200 years, repeated with permission from (16). (*a*) Sockeye salmon abundances in Karluk Lake reconstructed from $\delta^{15}N$ (‰) sediment series (16). (*b,c*) Northern anchovy and sardine scales (per 1000 cm^2 per year) from sediments off Santa Barbara, California, smoothed by a 50-year running average (17).

catches demonstrate striking asynchronous periods of success and failure of sardine and anchovy species (20, 21). Climate clearly has strong impacts on fish abundance and caused "crashes" in fish stocks long before humans had any impact on them.

Pollution and Introduction of Exotic Species

Pollution from human industry and agriculture (22) is an additional impact on fish stocks. Persistent toxic chemicals such as DDT, PCBs, and heavy metals may disrupt the immune and reproductive systems of organisms, particularly those that feed high in the food web like marine mammals and humans (23). Concentrations of these chemicals are much higher in the Northern than in the Southern Hemisphere, because of greater human population densities and their associated impacts (24). Oil spills have been decreasing over the past 30 years, but they continue to be more devastating than oil exploration due to their intensity (23), and the ecological damage from the 1989 *Exxon Valdez* spill is widely considered the worst ever (25). Nutrients from agricultural and livestock production, sewage discharge, and the combustion of fossil fuels have essentially "fertilized" many coastal ecosystems throughout North America, Europe, and Asia (26–29). In some cases, excessive nitrogen and phosphorus have increased primary production and subsequent decomposition enough to deplete the oxygen levels in the water (30). These hypoxic areas can be extensive, covering over 20,000 km^2 in the Gulf of Mexico and the Black Sea and up to 70,000 km^2 in the Baltic Sea (30), with important economic and ecological implications (31). Historically, chemical and nutrient pollution has interacted with overfishing to impact coastal ecosystems and their associated fisheries (32, 33). These effects persist today and will likely continue into the future.

Introduction of exotics is another form of "pollution" affecting marine fish stocks, particularly in coastal ecosystems. Native species in many of the world's estuaries have been replaced by exotic introductions, and with increasing world trade, the frequency of introductions is almost certainly going to grow (34, 35).

Inland Fisheries

Fishing, climate, and pollution have had similar, if not stronger, impacts on inland fish stocks. Exploitation by recreational fisheries has led to collapses of freshwater stocks in Canada and is probably occurring elsewhere across the globe (36). As in marine ecosystems, climate change, eutrophication, pollution, dams and diversions, habitat destruction, and overexploitation all threaten the well-being of freshwater fisheries (37). One of the most important issues is that of introduced species, which in the United States have resulted in large-scale homogenization of fish faunas, particularly in the western continental states (38). Introduced species often cause extinctions among endemics (39) and can lead to either severe economic losses (40) or to the development of valuable fisheries based on the exotic species. For example, in Lake Victoria the exotic Nile perch and Nile tilapia have caused mass extinctions among the incredibly diverse native fish species (41), but they have also led to a fourfold increase in overall fishery yield (42). A similar increase in yield was obtained when the North American Great Lakes were stocked with exotic Pacific salmon in the 1970s and 1980s to control booming populations of introduced alewife and improve recreational fishing (40). These exotic salmonids now support a US$3–5 billion recreational fishing industry annually (43).

Summary

For centuries ecosystems and fish stocks have been affected by harvesting, pollution, climate, and introduction of exotics. Recent attention on fisheries has focused on harvesting, both because harvesting pressure grew enormously in the twentieth century and because it is the one human activity that is most easily regulated. Having seen how these multiple factors can affect fish stocks, we now look at the current status of fish stocks, fisheries, and marine ecosystems.

STATUS OF FISHERIES AND ECOSYSTEMS

In the last decade the general public has been bombarded with stories about the collapse of the world's fish stocks. United Nations (UN) Food and Agriculture Organization's (FAO) estimate that "75% of the world's fisheries are fully or overexploited" has been widely quoted (44). Considering that being fully exploited is the objective of most national fishery agencies (and therefore not necessarily alarming), of more concern is the estimate that 33% of the U.S. fish stocks are overfished or depleted (45). The historical catch trends in Figure 5 show very little if any decline in world catch and are therefore surprising.

The state of the world's fisheries is extremely difficult to assess. Shepherd, an English fisheries scientist, once said "Counting fish is just as easy as counting trees, except they are invisible and they move." Nevertheless, a number of methods have been tried including (*a*) trends in catch (46), (*b*) stock-by-stock classification based on assessment of current stock size in relation to historical stock size (45), (*c*) trends in the trophic level of catches (47), and (*d*) trends in catches for individual stocks (44). Each of these approaches has its limitations. Trends in total yield suggest stability (Figure 5*B*) and therefore sustainability at current levels, but these may mask a sequential depletion of individual stocks, so that the apparent stability may be a precursor to terminal decline as the last accessible fish stocks are depleted.

Stock Status

Stock-by-stock classifications are probably the best approach but are data intensive and available only in a few countries. Where they are possible, such classifications may be misleading. For instance, in the United States, 33% of the fish stocks that have been classified are "overfished or depleted" (45), but the vast majority of these resources are still producing considerable yield, and many stocks are classified as overfished even if rebuilding. Assuming that the sustainable yield from overfished

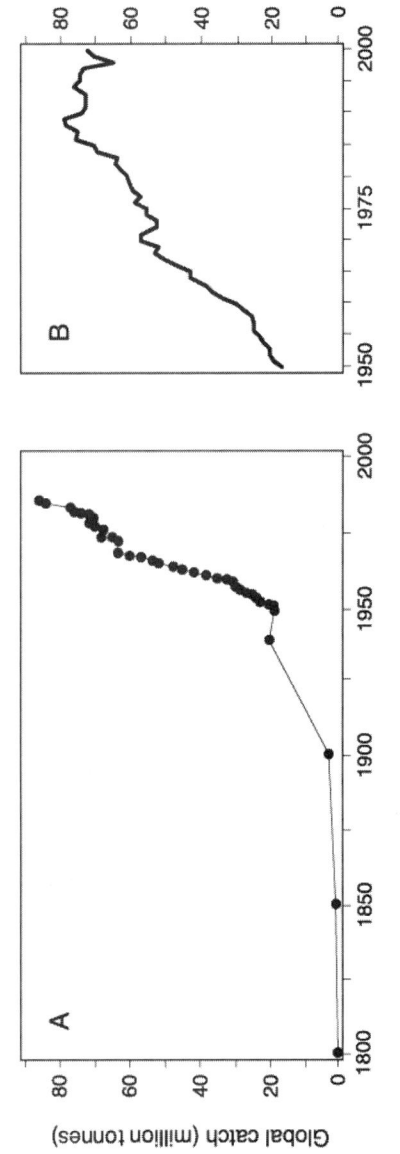

Figure 5 (*A*) Historical world fisheries catches redrawn from (115). (*B*) Recent catches based on FAO catch statistics, which exclude aquaculture production (48). Catches from China are excluded because of concerns about overreporting in recent years (45a).

stocks is only half of the potential yield if they were not overfished, the U.S. production would be at 84% of maximum, a picture far different from that implied by the often-used figure of 75% overfished or fully exploited. Indeed, many stocks in the United States may be legally classified as overfished even if they are at a stock size that will produce maximum possible yield—the distinction between legal and biological classifications can be considerable.

Analysis of trends in landings for individual stocks is widely applicable because landing data are easily available. As an example, of the six largest fisheries in Australia, four are stable (the two lobster fisheries, whiting, and Australian salmon), whereas the other two (southern bluefin tuna and orange roughy) have both shown considerable declines in catch (48) because early high landings during the fishing-down phase have reduced fish stocks, sometimes rapidly, to long-term sustainable levels. We can use these data to measure the stock status by dividing current landings by the maximum historical landings after using a five-year running average to smooth the data. For the two lobster fisheries, Australian salmon and whiting, the stock status estimates are 100%, 61%, 87%, and 53%, respectively; yet for orange roughy and southern bluefin tuna, they are 47% and 30%, respectively. The unweighted average stock status among Australian major fisheries is thus 63%. This does not imply that the current yields are 63% of maximum potential because the catches for orange roughy and southern bluefin tuna were far in excess of sustainable levels as the fisheries developed.

When the 495 largest fisheries (those with cumulative catches $\geq 100,000$ t from 1970 to 2000, excluding Chinese fisheries) in the FAO database (48) are analyzed in the same way, we see that many of the world's fisheries are near their peak production, with a wide range in production levels among the other fisheries (Figure 6). Considerable care is needed in interpreting these results; many fisheries that are at or near maximum historical production may be currently fished far above sustainable levels. In contrast, many of the fisheries with low current yield may reflect the reduction of yields from high nonsustainable levels to lower sustainable levels, or changes in access, particularly in association with the expansion of Exclusive Economic Zones (EEZ) to 200 miles.

If we extend this analysis to individual countries, we see that many developing countries have fisheries that are new and growing and hence still have landings near their short-term historical maxima, yet countries such as Japan and South Korea suffered the closure of many fisheries when they lost access to distant water fishing grounds (Figure 7). It would be most interesting to know, on a stock-by-stock basis, where the sustainable yield is in relation to the maximum sustainable yield, but this analysis has only been attempted in a few countries such as the United States (45).

Discarding and Waste

Discarded fish are a major issue in fisheries. The most recent survey available shows 26% of the world's catch is discarded annually (49). Discarding is usually caused by economic or regulatory constraints. Economic discards include catch

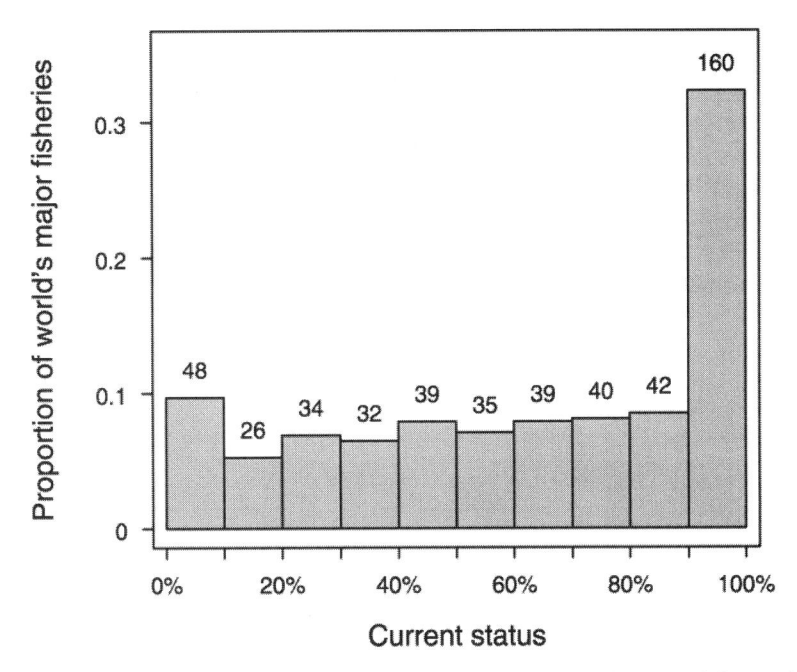

Figure 6 Current yield divided by maximum historical yield for 495 of the world's major fisheries. Each fishery is a unique species-area combination, as defined in the FAO database (48). Numbers at top of bars show number of stocks represented in each category. Catches from China are excluded because of concerns about overreporting in recent years (45a).

that is unwanted because the fish are too small, or the species is unmarketable. Regulatory-induced discarding involves catch of species, or size of fish, in excess of that which a particular fishery is allowed to retain (50). Bycatch (the unintended catch of nontarget species) can be an important management concern for many reasons. 1. It can be a substantial component of fishing mortality. 2. It may aggravate overfishing. 3. It may impact other highly regulated fisheries. 4. It may have undesirable impacts on a particular nontarget species or group of species. 5. It is a waste of important natural resources. 6. It may cause allocation conflicts between competing socioeconomic interests (50).

Discards are highest in shrimp and prawn trawl fisheries that discard an average of 5.2 kg (and a maximum of 136 kg) for every kg of landed catch (49). The greatest total discards are in the northwest Pacific, a region where shrimp fisheries discards account for 50% of the total discard by all fisheries. Most discards in shrimp fisheries are finfish and other crustaceans that do not attract public attention as much as large charismatic animals like dolphins. Public activism over high dolphin bycatch in tuna fisheries in the 1980s (133,000 dolphins were killed in 1986) translated into consumer avoidance of tuna products and made fishermen aware

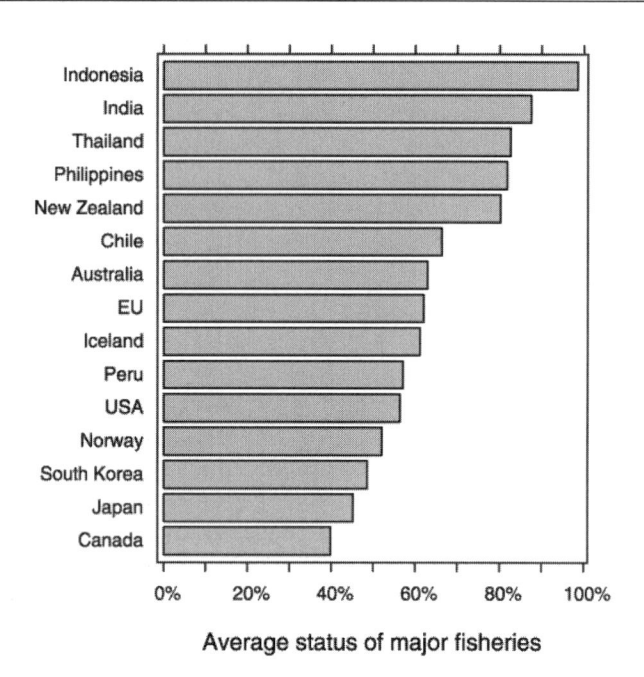

Figure 7 Current yield divided by maximum historical yield for some major fishing nations, averaged across their major stocks. The EU label pools the member countries of the European Union.

that their practices had to change if they wanted to remain in business. Solutions came from the fishermen themselves, highly motivated by the need to survive, who managed to reduce dolphin bycatch to just 1877 by 1998 (51) by reducing the bycatch per unit of effort (52). Another way to control the problem of bycatch is reducing the total effort, as happened in the case of long driftnets that were banned by a UN treaty as a result of increased public awareness caused by a coalition of governments and private conservation groups. As a result, more than 15,000 people lost their jobs in the participating countries (51). Bycatch problems have also been addressed in other ways. In Norway, fishermen are obligated by law to land all their bycatch (51, 53). Naturally, the success of a program like this will depend largely on enforcement, but there is at least a clear incentive toward research on bycatch reduction gear, behavioral changes, and the reduction of waste, with a possible downside—the development of markets for undersized fish (51).

Habitat Impacts of Fishing

The act of fishing can have wide-ranging, negative impacts on ecosystems (54, 55). Bottom trawling, dredging, and trapping often reduce hard substrate and simplify the bottom topography, which results in coral destruction and the leveling of seamount tops (56, 57). In other cases, heavy doors on bottom trawls can leave large furrows in the sea floor (58). In regions of the ocean with soft sediments, fishing practices disturb the sediments with mixed effects on benthic invertebrates (59). In Australia, trawling reduced the density and biomass of soft-bodied, immobile taxa by more than 80% (56), but less than 5% of the disturbed biomass was typically retained in the trawl gear (60); this makes it difficult to assess the impact of trawling from what is seen on the surface. In the Bering Sea, similar reductions were found in small benthos, but larger organisms such as crabs and sea stars had a mixed response (61). In the Grand Banks, large species such as crabs and urchins suffered severe declines, whereas smaller sediment-dwelling organisms were relatively unaffected (62). While targeting shellfish in estuaries along the Atlantic coast of the United States, fisherman also greatly reduced the extent of important seagrass beds (63). However, these various effects of physical disturbance may be relatively short lived. Several studies suggest that trawl fisheries mimic natural disturbances and that their negative effects persist for less than a year (59, 64, 65). Clearly any physical effects of a fishery will vary with geographical region, fishing intensity, and the gear used. The spatial extent of impact of trawl gear on the sea floor was reviewed for the United States (66), but the report did not address whether these impacts had a positive or negative effect on fish production. It seems quite likely that some important commercial species may benefit from these impacts, while other species may be harmed, but there is no substantial data available at present.

Extinction and Ecosystem Impacts

The extinction of marine fish, invertebrates, and plants may seem unlikely, given that most marine species produce such prolific quantities of eggs and are spread so widely over such diverse habitats. However, well-documented cases of extinction from natural causes include the eelgrass limpet, *Lottia alveus*, which was eliminated when disease wiped out suitable eelgrass habitat (67), and the Galapagos damselfish which disappeared after the 1982–1983 El Niño (68). Extinctions can also be caused directly by fishing pressure. The California white abalone, formerly present in densities of $1/m^2$ from Point Conception, California, to Baja California, was the target of a fishery in the early 1970s, which peaked at 65 tonnes in 1972. The population was rapidly reduced below densities that could produce sufficient sperm concentrations to ensure fertilization during broadcast spawning, although disease may have also contributed their decline. The last major recruitment event occurred in the late 1960s, and white abalone populations have declined ever since. Although for economic reasons, commercial fishing is unlikely to target a species once it reaches very low densities, many fish species are caught as bycatch in fisheries that are directed at other species. The target fishery can be maintained while nontarget species decline due to a lower intrinsic rate of increase or because they are more readily caught than the target species. Sharks in the northwest Atlantic have declined by 50%–90% in the past 15 years because of bycatch in the tuna and swordfish longline fisheries (69). At least two other widely distributed species have been brought to the brink of extinction in this manner: so-called common skates in the Irish Sea and barndoor skates, the largest skates in the northwest

Atlantic (70, 71). In the skate examples, near extinction occurred without fanfare, so it is likely that other fish species could disappear in the same way.

Fisheries' exploitation often leads to dramatic changes in the size structure and abundance of targeted species, as well as shifts in the overall fish assemblage (72). This fishing pressure may reduce the mean trophic level of the fish community (47, 73) due to greater declines in larger, slow-growing species relative to smaller, faster-growing species (74). In a review of 45 years of global fishery landings, Pauly et al. (47) found a dramatic decrease in the mean trophic level of harvested fish in both marine and inland ecosystems (Figure 8). They argue that their observed shift in landings from larger piscivorous fish toward smaller planktivorous fish and invertebrates reflects direct effects of the fishery on ecosystem structure. These results were challenged by Caddy et al. (75, 76) who raised several objections regarding the methods and interpretation of Pauly et al. (47) including taxonomic resolution, use of fishery landings data, development of aquaculture, bottom-up effects of eutrophication, technological improvements, market forces, and long-term environmental change. Nevertheless, other techniques have also demonstrated similar declines in the mean trophic level of fishery landings for specific regions such as the Gulf of Thailand (77), the Celtic Sea (78), and on both coasts of Canada (79). This shift toward exploitation of lower trophic-level fish combined with their already decreasing stock sizes may signal future fishery collapses and changes in ecosystem structure (23).

However, declining trends in average trophic levels are also the natural consequence of fisheries developing to a sustainable level and may not be a precursor of ecosystem change or collapse. In the Mediterranean Sea, an area that has been heavily exploited for a very long time and one where the mean trophic level is very low, there is little evidence of ecosystem collapse or declining trophic levels. In

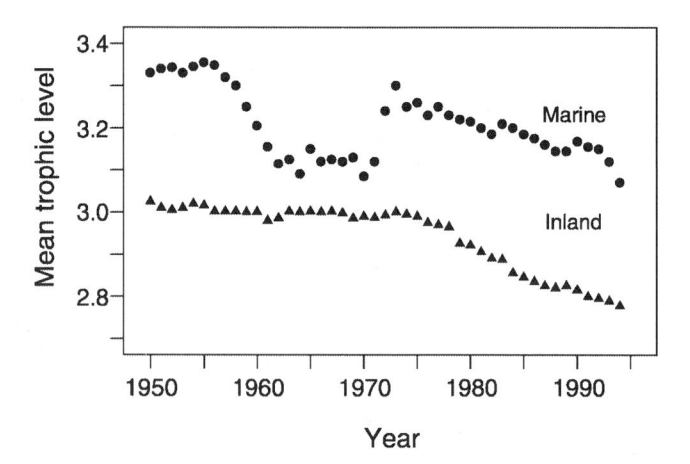

Figure 8 Change in the mean trophic level of global fisheries landings for marine and inland areas. Redrawn from (47).

fact, productivity has continued to increase, perhaps because of increased nutrient enrichment from human activities (80). The current trends in the Mediterranean may suggest that (*a*) intense fisheries low on the food chain may be sustained, (*b*) ecosystem collapse (13) is not a necessary consequence of intense fishing, and (*c*) declining mean trophic level (47) is not necessarily a precursor to disaster.

SOCIAL AND ECONOMIC STATUS OF FISHERIES

Fish stocks are only one component of fisheries, and we are equally interested in the social and economic health of fisheries. No national or international agencies attempt to define or summarize economic health; the only statistics available are on employment, income, exports, and subsidies. We saw earlier that the economic value of the Newfoundland fishery increased after the groundfish closures; this emphasizes the fact that economic statistics may not well reflect the health of the fishing communities.

Fisheries constitute a highly variable portion of national exports: less than 1% for countries such as Korea and the Netherlands; under 10% for most countries such as Australia, New Zealand, Thailand, Norway, and China; but represent 16% of Peru's exports and 64% of Iceland's. These statistics provide an indication of the importance but not a real index of the economic health of the fishery in each country.

Subsidies may constitute a better indication of economic health. Fisheries are often subsidized to maintain economically fragile industries. The total expenditure on fisheries subsidies worldwide is estimated to be US$14–21 billion per year (81). At least half of these subsidies come from Organisation for Economic Co-operation and Development (OECD) countries (Table 1) (81, 82). Other sectors which exploit natural resources are also heavily subsidized, such as forestry (US$35 billion) and mining (US$30 billion) (46). Perhaps nothing reflects the poor economic health of the world's fisheries than the fact that subsidies for OECD countries constitute 17% of the landed value. Estimates of profitability made by the FAO indicate that 97% of the 108 types of fishing vessels studied had a positive gross cash flow (83). However, if subsidies had not been in place, most vessel types would have reduced earnings, and some would lose money.

Subsidies encourage vessel construction, retention of economically inefficient harvesting, and overcapitalization of the harvesting industry. While subsidies do stimulate employment and thus contribute to one of the common goals of national fisheries policy, subsidies are widely regarded as having a negative impact on the sustainability of fisheries by encouraging overcapitalization (84).

THE SCIENCE OF SUSTAINABLE HARVESTING

For the last 100 years scientists have been studying the biology of fish and how to sustainably harvest them, and there is a well-developed body of knowledge under the general title of fisheries stock assessment (85, 86). For many populations

TABLE 1 Estimates of government fisheries subsidies from OECD countries in 1997. These countries account for at least half of the world total of US$14–20.5 billion a year (81). Partial subsidies = direct payments + cost-reducing transfers. Total subsidies also include general services (82)

	Subsidies (US$ millions)					Subsidies (% of landed value)	
	Direct payments	Cost-reducing transfers	General services	Total	Landed value	Partial	Total
Australia[a]	5	7	11	23	259	5	9
Belgium	0	3	2	5	99	3	5
Canada	252	18	135	405	1,621	17	25
Denmark	20	0	62	82	521	4	16
Finland	3	2	21	26	29	18	90
France	22	14	104	139	756	5	18
Germany	8	3	52	63	194	5	32
Greece	12	0	38	50	387	3	13
Iceland	0	18	18	36	877	2	4
Ireland	5	3	96	104	220	3	47
Italy	24	5	64	92	1,749	2	5
Japan	25	22	2,899	2,946	14,117	<0.5	21
Korea	30	59	253	342	4,929	2	7
Mexico	0	0	17	17	1,017	0	1
Netherlands	4	0	32	36	466	1	8
New Zealand	0	0	17	17	475	0	4
Norway[b]	3	62	98	163	1,343	5	12
Poland	0	0	8	8	215	0	4
Portugal	32	<0.5	34	66	319	10	21
Spain[c]	205	81	59	345	3,443	8	10
Sweden	9	0	45	54	129	7	42
Turkey	0	1	27	29	212	1	13
United Kingdom	23	4	101	128	1,012	3	13
United States	21	194	662	877	3,644	6	24
European Union[d]	366	358	710	1,434	9,324	8	15
OECD Total	702	740	4,856	6,298	38,032	4	17

[a]Commonwealth fisheries only.
[b]Landed value for Norway based on 1996 data.
[c]Landed value for Spain does not include national landings in foreign ports.
[d]European Union (EU) values are the sum of all EU Member State values. The exception to this is cost reducing transfers, i.e., payments for access for third country waters are not allocated among each Member State. Instead, the value is added to the EU total figure.

the factors affecting birth and death rates are understood, and harvest guidelines that lead to long-term sustainability are easily calculated. The key to sustainable harvesting is being able to measure the trend in population abundance and having the institutional capability to regulate harvest (87). If Canadian scientists had known the true trend in stock abundance in the 1980s, the Newfoundland cod collapse would probably not have happened. If the abundance trend is known then, in theory, catch can be reduced until the stock stops declining. This guarantees that the stock will not collapse, but it does not insure that the yield is maximized. However if maximum yields are desired, then the relationship between population size and sustainable harvest needs to be understood, not only to insure the stock does not collapse, but to identify and reach the population size that provides maximum harvest. This requires a much more detailed understanding of fish biology.

Single-Species Sustainability

A key lesson from the collapse of the Newfoundland cod fishery, and indeed many other stock declines and collapses, is that harvest rates were too high. In some years, over 50% of the fish large enough to be captured in the fishing gear were harvested. Overfishing is caused by taking too large a fraction of the population each year. The question is what fraction is too large? To understand the basic elements of single-species sustainability, we need to define some basic terms and concepts.

Figure 9 shows the idealized relationship between population size (X axis) and sustainable yield (Y axis). Another word for sustainable yield is "surplus production," which is how much the population would grow in the absence of harvesting. If the population remained unharvested for many years, it would increase to the point where competition for food, space, or some resource was limiting. There

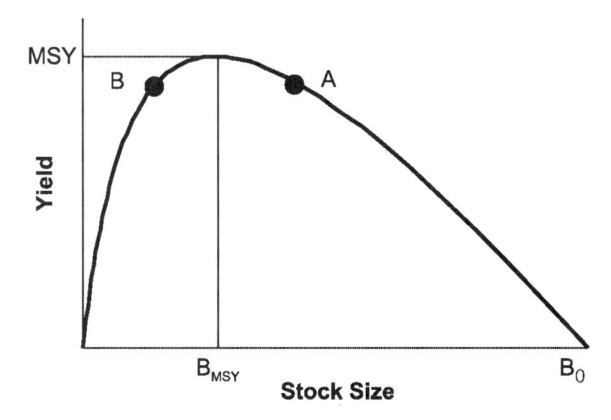

Figure 9 The relationship between spawning stock biomass and sustainable yield.

would be no surplus production, and the population would stop growing. This point is called virgin biomass, carrying capacity, or simply B_{zero}. When there are no fish in the population, the surplus production would also be zero. By definition at some point between zero biomass and B_{zero}, the surplus production, and therefore sustainable yield, will be maximized. The yield at this point is called maximum sustainable yield (MSY), and the stock size that produces it is referred to as B_{MSY}. The traditional fisheries policy from the 1950s until recent years was to manage populations for MSY. Although MSY is often regarded as an outmoded concept (88), it remains a central element of many national fisheries law including the Magnusson-Stevens Act. The ratio between MSY and B_{MSY} is the fraction of the population that would be harvested at MSY and is roughly the exploitation rate that fishery managers try to achieve.

In the last decade, general rules of thumb have evolved regarding which levels of exploitation are sustainable (89, 90). One key determinant of sustainable exploitation rate is the natural mortality rate of mature individuals. Long-lived animals have low natural mortality and can sustain low fishing mortality, and conversely, populations with higher natural mortality rates can generally sustain higher fishing mortality rates. A second key determinant is the intrinsic rate of increase of the population at low densities. Populations that are in good habitat, with consequent high survival in the early life history, must by definition be capable of sustaining a higher harvest rate than those populations that cannot increase rapidly.

Within the United States and Canada, a form of fisheries management has evolved in which target exploitation rates are tied to the estimated stock size in relation to virgin biomass. Such a rule is used by the Pacific Fisheries Management Council (PFMC) in the United States (91). When the stock is above 40% of virgin biomass, then a target exploitation rate is set that is related primarily to the natural mortality rate. As the stock drops below 40% of virgin biomass, the target exploitation rate is decreased until it is zero at 10% of virgin biomass. The PFMC has adopted a rule so that once a stock drops below 25% of virgin biomass the stock is officially listed as overfished, and new rules, called "rebuilding plans," must be put in place that provide for the stock to rebuild to 40% of virgin biomass in a specified time. The values of 25% as overfished, and 40% as rebuilt are known as reference points. The rebuilt value is chosen as a rule-of-thumb where MSY could be achieved, and the overfished level as a threshold below which there are serious risks of reduced recruitment and possible stock collapse.

The example of the PFMC's management rules are typical of those adopted in a wide range of management arenas and are characterized by target and limit reference points. Targets are stock sizes or exploitation rates that the agencies try to achieve, and limits are those they try to not exceed. For the PMFC, 40% of virgin biomass is the target, and 25% is the limit. Although many institutions chose targets and limits based on estimates of virgin biomass, this approach has been criticized because virgin biomass is very difficult to determine

(91), and setting reference points in relation to virgin biomass is not a universal practice.

While long-term sustainable yield is maximized in theory at B_{MSY}, the biology of most fish stocks produces yield curves similar to that seen in Figure 9 in which the sustainable yield is similar over a reasonably large range of stock sizes, which constitute roughly the area between points A and B. Managers and scientists have generally moved to higher stock sizes than B_{MSY} to achieve multiple objectives including (*a*) larger stock sizes provide a better buffer for environmental variation and insurance against dropping to low stock sizes, (*b*) at higher stocks sizes the catch rate and therefore economic performance in the fishery is better, and (*c*) at higher stock sizes there is less impact on other components of the ecosystem (84). Many of the current controversies in fisheries management occur when the stock size is low, as at point B, and managers want to move to point A. This is a rebuilding plan. Points A and B have similar yield on the Y axis, but they are reasonably far apart on the X axis and moving from B to A involves more than doubling the population size. To move from B to A requires significant reductions in catch, and yet promises reasonably little, if any, increase in long-term catch. It is little wonder, therefore, that commercial fishing groups tend to resist these rebuilding plans.

The theory of single-species management is well refined, and many of the success stories of fisheries management (87), such as West Australian Rock Lobster, Pacific Halibut, and Alaskan Salmon, are places where the theory has been effectively implemented. Increasingly, however, single-species management is running into major obstacles. There are two potential limitations in single-species management theory and practice. First, many fisheries catch a wide range of stocks, and it is often impossible to manage stocks separately. Managers cannot achieve the target exploitation rate or stock size on multiple species simultaneously. While it has long been known (92) that maximization of yield from these multispecies fisheries will lead some of the species to be overexploited and some underexploited, the trend in the United States, at least, is to avoid overharvesting any stock, which thus requires substantial loss in yield from the mix of stocks (93, 94). The second limitation of single-species theory is that it ignores ecosystem interactions. This is covered in the next section.

Multispecies and Ecosystem Analysis

It is now widely argued that single-species management is insufficient for long-term sustainability, and a broader recognition of ecosystem concerns needs to pervade fisheries decision making (13, 95). Some point to a number of significant ecosystem changes caused by fishing (66), such as when elimination of the sea otter through most of the northeast Pacific led to loss of the kelp forests and establishment of sea urchin dominated barrens. However, the examples of major ecosystem shifts caused by fishing are cases that good single-species management would have avoided. Sea otters were hunted below 1% of their original numbers, whereas single-species management for marine mammals would prescribe a level in excess of 50% (96, 97). Thus although the call for ecosystem management is predicated on the failure of single-species management, it is not clear that single-species management, if properly applied, would have failed. Nevertheless, there is growing effort to incorporate ecosystem concerns in the management process.

Ecosystem interactions are usually omitted in stock assessment models due to the demands such models place on data and biological understanding. However, there has been recognition that species interactions, particularly predator-prey interactions, have an important role in the dynamics of target species and exploited ecosystems. For example, in the North Sea this recognition resulted in the creation of the International Council for the Exploration of the Sea (ICES) multispecies assessment group and in the application of multispecies virtual population analysis (MSVPA) (98). An international effort was made to analyze species diet during the "year of the stomach" (99). MSVPA includes the dynamics of several species, linking them through predation mortality. Another modeling approach that includes trophic interactions is the mass balance model ECOPATH (100–103), which assumes that after perturbations the ecosystem will eventually return to its original state (104). There are over 150 published ECOPATH models (www.ecopath.org) that are gaining importance in understanding ecosystem structure. ECOPATH models have been used to calculate that 8% of oceanic primary production is required to sustain global fisheries and up to 25%–30% on continental shelves (105). Those two approaches are the most popular among many other models (106). Multispecies models provide an opportunity for including more biological realism, but it is not clear that this will generate better advice for management. Their roles seem to be in improving estimates of natural mortality, promoting better understanding of spawner-recruit relationship and variability in growth rates, providing alternative views on biological reference points, and creating a framework for evaluating ecosystem properties (106).

Conventional fisheries assessment and management approaches assume that fish comprise a single mobile stock, that their dynamics are spatially homogeneous, and that local fishing effects are diluted in the larger pool of fish. Fisheries dominated by spatial heterogeneity due to limited mobility of organisms and habitat differences do not fit the assumption of spatial homogeneity. Strong spatial effects on growth, reproduction, recruitment, and fishing may lead to sequential depletion of stocks on small spatial scales as fishing effort moves farther and farther from the initial discovery of the resource (107). Sedentary stocks such as benthic invertebrates are typically structured as metapopulations, in which subpopulations of relatively sedentary adults are interconnected through larval and/or juvenile dispersal (108). Spatial heterogeneity substantially increases the dimension of the problem in terms of data requirements, analysis, and traditional implementation of management measures, especially in already data-poor or management-troubled fisheries. Alternatives to single stock management such as spatially explicit strategies (rotation of areas or reserves) has proven successful, with the Chilean benthic fisheries as the best documented (109, 110).

THE BEHAVIOR OF FISHING FLEETS

A central lesson from 100 years of fisheries management is that fishermen respond to the economic opportunities of fishing and to regulation (84, 111, 112). If new markets develop or new stocks are discovered or become available to a new technology, fishermen will pursue the economic potential of these resources. If management agencies limit the number of boats, then fishermen will build larger boats. If the boat length is limited, the boats become wider, higher, and have larger engines. While individual motivation may vary, the behavior of fishing fleets can be understood by simple economic optimization; if money is to be made, some element of the fleet will figure out how to do it, and others will follow. The economic behavior of fishing fleets leads directly to one of the basic truths of fisheries: In unregulated fisheries, fishing effort increases until all profit is consumed (113). The natural dynamic of fish-fishermen interactions is to move to the point where an additional unit of effort would prove unprofitable, and this point, the so-called bionomic equilibrium, may leave the stock lightly exploited, overexploited, or commercially extinct (114). If costs of fishing are low and prices are high, then fishermen can take nearly the last animal as happened with North Pacific sea otters, many fur seals and sea lions, and almost happened with the great whales before bans on whaling (115). The natural dynamic of fisheries is to deplete a stock as far as the technology and markets will allow, and then move onto the next stock, which generates the all too familiar pattern of sequential depletion shown in Figure 3. The dominant focus of fisheries management has been to try to prevent this pattern and restrict exploitation so that individual stocks are not depleted.

Although the natural dynamic of a fisherman as a hunter is sequential depletion of the resources, markets want a stable supply of products. In unregulated fisheries, market considerations enter only in what price the fisherman will get for his product and whether it is still profitable to chase the prey. The fisherman maximizes his income by catching as many fish as fast as possible, with little attention paid to quality. When the race for fish is removed, fishermen improve their incomes by improving quality. Boom and bust fisheries, short fishing seasons, and highly fluctuating yields all detract from the potential to maximize revenue from the fish. Finally, in many fisheries there is a significant effect of supply and demand. Years of large catch often lead to lower price, and similarly reduced catches are often compensated to some extent by higher prices (116).

Recognizing that fishing is largely an economic activity, it is surprising how little attention is paid to the economics of fisheries sustainability. Almost all intellectual and political energy has gone into the biological aspects of sustainability. For half a century, economists have pointed out that the economic optimum yield from a fishery will almost always occur at larger stock sizes and lower fishing efforts than the biological optimum yield, yet invariably the dynamics of fish, fishermen, and fisheries managers has led to us pushing the limit of biological sustainability, far beyond any sensible level of fishing effort based on economics (84, 117). In fisheries where various forms of regulation have solved the race for fish, fishermen concentrate on economic maximization. For example in the cooperative fisheries for pollock and hake in the western United States, in the halibut and sablefish fisheries of the West Coast of the United States and Canada, and in the fisheries of New Zealand, most of the energy of the fishing industry is devoted to quality improvement and reductions in the costs of fishing (116). In a number of fisheries, including the Tasmanian abalone fishery and the New Zealand rock lobster fishery in Gisborne, fishermen have volunteered to accept catch reductions knowing it would lead to higher prices and lower costs of fishing (118, 119).

For economic, biological, ecosystem, and social reasons, society should manage fish stocks toward the higher end of abundance rather than the lower end. This is undisputed. Yet in the majority of the world's fisheries, stocks are at low levels of abundance (fully or over-exploited), and indeed fisheries targets of the last 50 years have been toward the biomass that produces MSY, below that which produces optimum economic yield. Further, stocks may be at low abundance for reasons of climate change or random environmental variation. Given that stocks are often below the biomass that will produce maximum economic yield, how do managers move the stocks to the more desirable state of high abundance and is it even worth the cost of making this transition? The only tool available to managers to move stocks from low abundance to high abundance is by reducing exploitation rates, with the commensurate cost of reduced yield. Whether such loss of yield is worth the cost is a much harder question. In the major fishery for snapper in New Zealand, a court case was fought over a proposed rebuilding plan that would have involved a 40% reduction in catch for 20 years to double the stock size. The scientists estimated this would have produced an 8% increase in biological yield (120). Few individuals would consider an 8% increase in income an adequate compensation for a 40% reduction in income for 20 years. Admittedly there would be additional benefits of larger stock size (such as lower fishing costs), but this does illustrate the high potential cost of making the transition from low stock size to high.

METHODS OF FISHERIES MANAGEMENT

Institutional Structure and Governance

Fisheries management acts directly by regulating fishing activity and involves two basic processes: allocating the fish among users and determining the allowable harvest. These decisions are imbedded in institutional systems, and there is growing recognition that the institutional structure, sometimes known as governance system, and the incentives it provides are the primary determinants of the success or failure of fisheries (117, 121).

The major issues in fisheries governance are (*a*) who makes decisions about allocation and harvest, (*b*) are such decisions made by executive fiat, majority voting, or consensus, (*c*) how allocation among users is related to determining allowable harvest, (*d*) the role of science in setting catch levels, and (*e*) how can decision making about harvest levels be made less political.

Responsibility for regulatory decision making takes many forms. Most commonly a governmental official, often a Minister of Fisheries, has ultimate responsibility but takes advice from government staff and stakeholders. In some countries, decision making is devolved to a commission or board, perhaps in an attempt to remove the heat of politics from elected officials. The U.S. fisheries management councils have such a system, and decisions are made by majority vote. International Commissions almost universally have ultimate decision making vested in the members of the commission, who are appointed by the national member governments. The major difference between commissions is whether decisions are made by consensus, majority, or super-majority and whether decisions are binding on the members.

Because fisheries management frequently involves trade-offs between assured short-term reductions in catch against uncertain long-term consequences in stock size and future catch, there are always strong arguments from fishermen to not reduce catches. Management systems that require consensus have much more difficulty in accepting catch reductions than systems by majority vote or executive fiat.

When allocation among competing users is not separated from process of setting allowable harvests, all harvest decisions have allocation implications and conservation often suffers (122). These two types of decisions need to be separated to achieve the social, economic, and biological objectives of most fisheries systems. Systems that regulate number of boats, fishing season, and gear efficiency do not provide formal allocation among users; other allocation systems discussed below, such as individual quotas and territorial fishing rights, do distinguish between allocation and harvest decisions.

Some jurisdictions recognize the clear distinction between scientific advice on the status of the stocks and consequences of alternative regulations and the decision-making process, which involves weighing trade-offs in the consequences. In these systems, scientists make no yield recommendations, and the decision makers directly confront the trade-off between biological risk and expected yield. In other systems, scientists are asked to both estimate stock status and recommend catch levels, usually on the basis of harvest strategies. The harvest strategies themselves are often developed by the scientists and then approved by the decision-making body, which means in the end that scientists made the decisions about the trade-off between short- and long-term yield and the trade-off between biological risk and economic return. There are frequent pleas for harvest decisions to be science based (indeed the best available science is enshrined in the Magnusson-Stevens Act), but such calls fail to recognize that science cannot provide advice on catch levels without unambiguous determination of management objectives from managers (123), and these objectives are rarely if ever stated explicitly. Because setting annual catches involves major economic consequences, it is not surprising that it has become highly political and frequently is the subject of court action.

To avoid the problems of determining annual catch quotas in a highly political environment, a number of jurisdictions are moving to a much more formal automated process known as "management procedures" that completely specify (a) what data will be collected, (b) how the data will be analyzed, and (c) how the catch regulations will change in relation to the analysis (124, 125). When a management procedure is in place, the annual cycle of decision making is automatic, the data collected automatically determine what the catch level will be, there are no scientific or political decisions to be made, and they are incorporated as part of the management procedure. Once the decision makers adopt a management procedure, it runs automatically. Formal management procedures have many advantages to managers, scientists, and fishermen. The advantages include the transparency of decision making to users, the ability to evaluate the consequences and risks for any hypothesized ecosystem behavior, the elimination of arbitrary decisions on how to determine stock status, which removes politics from the annual decision making cycle, and significant cost savings because the expense of annual meetings and scientific work on stock status are eliminated.

Many of the most successful fisheries, e.g., the West Australia rock lobster, Bristol Bay salmon, and Pacific halibut, all involve single-species management by single agencies. Single-species fisheries are much easier to manage than complex mixed stock fisheries, and it is no surprise that many successful fisheries target single species. A simple institutional structure may be another great advantage, and there are few examples of fisheries successes among the international fisheries agencies that involve multiple countries. Unfortunately, we have not been able to find any agreed metric of fisheries success in order to compare institutional complexity and successful management, but we believe this relationship is widely accepted among practicing fisheries professionals.

Allocating Fish Among Users

Throughout most of the twentieth century, distant water fleets from any country could fish in most areas, except for a narrow strip usually within 3–12 nautical miles from land. This era of open access ended abruptly in the 1970s with the worldwide expansion of EEZs to 200 nautical miles, which gave countries the legal authority to prevent overfishing in their territorial waters (117). Most countries therefore scrambled to build up domestic fishing capacity through massive direct and indirect subsidies; this reduced fishing costs and ultimately often increased total fishing capacity well above the levels that would be needed to harvest their fish stocks. It soon became obvious that an open-access policy in territorial waters would lead to the destruction of most fish stocks. Limits on fishing gear, seasonal closures, and restrictions on fishing effort were all imposed with varying degrees of success. Limited-entry programs followed to restrict not only fishing power, but the number of vessels in the fishery. However, unless individual catches are restricted, a limit to the total catch merely results in increased fishing power in whichever way they are allowed to increase. Fish stocks continued to be depleted and potential economic gains dissipated because there were no incentives for fishermen to conserve the resource or to increase their income, except by competing frantically with each other to catch a limited total number of fish (84, 117, 122).

Long before the advent of the 200 mile EEZ, economists and political scientists were addressing the problem of economic efficiency and regulatory structures in fishing fleets (113, 114). These authors recognized that the fisheries problem was too many boats fishing for declining fish populations, and economic efficiency could only be achieved by reducing the fishing pressure to the level stocks could sustain. Potential methods of control fall into two basic classes. First are those that limit the amount of fishing (called input controls) and include gear restrictions, limited fishing seasons, closed areas, and limiting the number of vessels. Most regulated fisheries followed this sequence in adopting increasing levels of restriction. Second are measures that specifically regulate the number of fish caught and include setting a total allowable catch for the fishery (usually called TAC) and assigning specific catch limits to individual fishermen or fishing vessels [commonly called individual quotas (IQs) or individual vessel quotas (IVQs)]. IQ rights are generally allocated based on historical catch records but can also be allocated by auction.

Economists have almost universally favored output controls (116, 126, 127), and throughout the 1980s and 1990s, many fisheries moved to IQs. Some countries, notably Australia, Iceland, and New Zealand, adopted IQ systems for most of their fisheries and often moved a step further by giving fishermen a share of the total catch in perpetuity and allowing them to buy, sell, and transfer their quota share. This system became known as individual transferable quotas (ITQs). Those allocated ITQs gained an asset of considerable value and in general became wealthy. The introduction of ITQs resulted in greater efficiency in fishing fleets, more involvement of fishermen in research spending and decision making, higher product prices, and greater safety (116).

For example, the Alaskan halibut fishery is worth about US$160 million per year (116). It was closed to foreign vessels in 1978 but remained open to all domestic vessels until 1995. Total catches were limited, and effort was regulated by season and gear restrictions. As thousands of vessels queued to catch their share of the lucrative fishery, the season length was continually reduced, falling from more than 100 days in the early 1970s to 2–3 days or shorter by the late 1980s. This excessive harvesting capacity resulted in a glut of fish being processed, lower returns to fishermen, fishing in dangerous conditions, loss of gear that continued to "ghost fish," overspending on equipment to maximize catching and processing power, and many other problems. To solve these problems, ITQs were approved in 1991 and implemented in 1995, with quota shares allocated to 5484 vessel owners. Fishermen are allowed to transfer their quota to other fishermen, but there are limits (generally 1% of the total quota) on how much quota any individual may own (128). Changes in the fishery have been dramatic. The season length is now 245 days; this improves the availability and quality of halibut product and allows the fishermen to maximize the value of the product. Fishing mortality from abandoned gear has decreased 75%, and discards of halibut bycatch reduced by 80% (128). The number of vessels in the fishery has decreased by 50%, and the number of Coast Guard rescue missions required for the fishery was a third of the pre-ITQ levels (128).

ITQ systems have been the subject of much controversy (18, 116, 127). The concerns raised include (*a*) equity of allocation of valuable rights to vessel owners, with consequent negative impacts on crew members and processors and no direct revenue benefit to the public; (*b*) the growth of shore-based ownership of the fishing rights and subsequent lack of ownership of these rights by active fishermen; and (*c*) incentives for ITQ owners to sort through their catch for the fish that are most valuable per unit of ITQ fishing right.

An alternative to allocating fishing rights to individuals is to auction fishing rights with the government receiving the auction fee (127). Such a system was proposed for almost all Canadian west coast fisheries in 1981 (90), but it received no support from the fishing industry and was never implemented. New Zealand's ITQ system initially included auctioning of new quota (129). The harvest rights in Falkland/Malvinas Island squid fishery are auctioned each year; the geoduck fishery in Washington state is run on a similar basis (130). ITQs are auctioned in some Chilean fisheries (131), and many Russian fisheries have moved to auctions. Auction systems have been strongly opposed by existing fishermen and have not been actively considered as management options within U.S. fishery management councils.

Two additional management systems have emerged that are variations on the traditional input and output controls. The first is fishermen's cooperatives; fishermen agree among themselves how to partition the TAC and form informal IQ systems. This has happened in the very large factory trawler fleet for pollock in the Bering Sea, the factory trawler fleet for hake on the West Coast of the United States and the salmon fishery in Chignik, Alaska. Cooperatives are able to achieve the economic efficiency of IQ systems without the legal difficulties of implementation. Territorial fishing rights are another management system that has been effectively implemented in Chilean artisanal fisheries (109, 110) and have been proposed as widely applicable to sedentary species (119).

Illegal Fishing

Illegal fishing is a growing problem in many parts of the world (132), particularly for high-value species such as lobster and abalone. In Australia, New Zealand, and South Africa, high-value lobster and abalone are almost impossible to find anywhere near major cities, and substantial undercover work suggests that extensive rings of illegal fishing operate broadly (133). The Chilean fishery for loco was almost totally dominated by illegal catch; this forced the complete closure of the fishery twice in the last 15 years (110). Few fisheries agencies can field the resources necessary to monitor and prevent illegal fishing. Local cooperation and control is the appropriate approach. Chile solved their illegal fishing problem by granting ownership of the fishing beds to local cooperatives that police and protect their fishing grounds (109). Territorial fishing rights have also been shown to provide significant protection from unauthorized fishing in traditional Pacific Islands (134).

The problems of illegal fishing and by-catch discards by licensed commercial fishermen at sea are even more difficult, but some fisheries, e.g., the British Columbia groundfish fishery, have implemented 100% coverage of all vessels by observers to address this problem (135).

New Solutions: The Precautionary Approach and Marine Protected Areas

Concern about the failure of traditional management systems has led to increasing calls for completely new methods to manage fisheries (95). Two ideas have emerged from this concern and discussion, the precautionary approach (136) and the use of marine protected areas (137). In this review, we briefly discuss the primary components of these two approaches and point readers to the extensive literature on each.

The precautionary approach is built around the concept that managers should not wait until they have unequivocal evidence that fishing effort needs to be reduced before acting, and it is intended to protect fisheries from overexploitation in the face of uncertainty. There are several ways the precautionary approach could be implemented: (*a*) No fishing is allowed if the harvest policy has not been demonstrated to be sustainable (136), (*b*) cautious harvest levels are adopted and guided by biological reference points, and (*c*) institutional arrangements are changed to ensure fisheries monitoring, feedback to regulations, and effective implementation of those regulations (138). In the United States, the precautionary approach is often identified with the biological reference points. Moving target reference points from B_{MSY} to biomasses higher than B_{MSY}, and similarly more conservative reference points have become the key elements of precaution with U.S. fisheries policy (138).

Marine protected areas (MPA) are the other recent concept being advocated as a solution to the concerns about overexploitation or marine fisheries. The concept is simply to set aside areas of marine habitat that are protected from fishing. Although some areas have been protected in the past, MPA advocates generally argue to protect approximately 20% of habitat from fishing (137, 139). It seems clear that the abundance of fish in protected areas is higher than outside protected areas (140), but whether MPAs will help improve fish harvests is subject to considerable controversy (141–143).

WHAT DETERMINES SUCCESS AND FAILURE?

Fisheries success can be defined in at least two ways: Biological success is the maintenance of healthy stock size near or above the levels that produce maximum harvestable surplus, and economic success could in theory be measured by profitability of the fishing industry. Other performance measures might include employment and amount of controversy over management actions (lawsuits for instance), but we do not attempt to address those issues.

We postulate the following hypothesis. Fisheries management success depends on three primary elements: (a) the simplicity of the decision making system, (b) the method used to allocate catch and regulate yield and its incentives, and (c) the biology of the species and its relation to the scale of management. This hypothesis suggests that complex management institutions have difficulty reducing catches, and the complexity leads to indecision and ultimately poor results (144). Simpler management systems with fewer powerful actors are more likely to have a common objective and make hard decisions. Management systems that exclude fishermen from the decision making process are more likely to encounter resistance and opposition to change than those that actively involve fishermen. Second, governance systems that provide incentives to avoid the race for fish are more likely to avoid excess fleet capacity, which leads both to poor profitability and political pressure from fishermen to extract the maximum possible catch (117). Third, species that have very low rates of increase, low fecundity, or whose abundance are particularly difficult to measure are more prone to overcapitalization because of low sustainable yields in relation to virgin biomass (86) or of the difficulty in determining trends in abundance. Species that are highly sedentary need management systems that have small-scale spatial management structure.

It would be desirable to compare a wide range of species on these three dimensions and to determine if they do indeed prove to explain much of the variability in fisheries success and failure. In the United States, data are available for the current status of most major stocks, but we found no reliable way of measuring economic success. Fisheries that closed or dramatically reduced catches to rebuild stock size are almost certainly economic failures, and as a surrogate we used the current catch in relation to maximum catch. A thorough study of this scale is beyond the scope of this review, and in lieu of this we present a list of some notable fisheries successes (Table 2) and failures (Table 3). For each fishery, the tables provide a measure of biological health (generally status in relation to B_{MSY}) and economic health (current catch in terms of long-term maximum).

Admittedly the lists in Tables 2 and 3 are short and not randomly selected, but they illustrate both the general elements of our hypothesis and some of the complexities. None of the successes is from a complex institution, but many of the failures are from simpler institutions. Only the Western Australian (WA) rock lobster fishery, among one of the successes, is one that has a race for fish. The WA rock lobster fishery has a very effective limit on the number of pots-per-boat that has consistently been reduced in order to prevent growth in fishing power.

Among the abalone, only the Tasmanian fishery stands out as a success. The race for fish was stopped by an early ITQ program while the stock was still abundant, but perhaps more importantly the island of Tasmania is far from potential markets for illegal harvesting, and the licensed ITQ fishermen are actively on the water and on the lookout for poachers. The Canadian abalone fishery is also an ITQ fishery, but since it closed, there is little active protection from poaching. Orange roughy

TABLE 2 List of fishery management successes of different stocks of the world. Landing indicator is computed as the ratio of the current to the maximum catch in the catch history available to us

Species	Biological status	Landings indicator	Major regulatory implement	Institutional complexity	Reference
Rock lobster (West Australia)	Near B_{MSY}	0.77	Limited effort	Single state agency	(145)
Abalone (Tasmania)	Near B_{MSY}	0.61	ITQ	Single state agency	(146)
Hoki (New Zealand)	Near B_{MSY}	0.86	ITQ	Single national agency	(147)
Rock lobster (New Zealand)	Near B_{MSY}	0.45	ITQ	Single national agency	(148)
Orange roughy (New Zealand area 3b)	Near B_{MSY}	0.28	ITQ	Single national agency	(149)
Pacific halibut (United States/ Canada)	Near B_{MSY}	0.97	ITQ	Two-country international agency	(150)
Pacific cod (Bering Sea, United States)	Above B_{MSY}	0.51	TAC	Management council	(151)
Salmon (Alaska)	Near B_{MSY}	0.55	TAC	Single state agency	(152)
Pollock (Bering Sea, United States)	Above B_{MSY}	1.00	TAC	Management council	(153)
Ilex squid (Falkland/ Malvinas Islands)	Abundant	1.00	Auction	Independent management agency	(154)

are a difficult species to manage because of their long life and the difficulty in measuring abundance. The major New Zealand orange roughy fishery (Area 3B) remains healthy because, in part, large amounts of money have been spent on measuring abundance. Whereas, the Challenger Plateau population is in poor state and has never had expensive trawl or hydroacoustic surveys conducted. Sharks have very low fecundity and are easily overexploited.

We have learned that some of the basic assumptions and approaches of the past have been the causes of fisheries failures. These sins of the past include 1. freedom of the seas in which unregulated fishing was allowed until sufficient evidence

TABLE 3 List of fishery management failures of different stocks of the world. Landing indicator is computed as the ratio of the current to the maximum catch in the historical data

Species	Biological status	Landings indicator	Major regulation	Institutional complexity	Reference
Northern cod (Canada)	Severely depleted	0.006	TAC	Federal provincial committee	(155)
North Sea cod (Europe)	Rebuilding	0.14	TAC	Multicountry EU	(156)
Gemfish (Eastern Australia)	Severely depleted	Closed	TAC	Single national agency	(157)
Southern school sharks (Australia)	Depleted	0.07	ITQ	Single national agency	(158)
Orange roughy (New Zealand area 7)	Depleted	0.11	TAC	Single national agency	(159)
Abalone (British Columbia)	Severely depleted	Closed	IQ	Single national agency	(160)
Abalone (California)	Severely depleted	Closed	Bag limits	Single state agency	(161)
Abalone (Alaska)	Severely depleted	Closed	Effort limitation	Single state agency	(162)

of harm accumulated; 2. large-scale management in which complex agencies attempted to collect data on, manage, and enforce regulations over large geographic areas and mixtures of stocks; 3. top-down control that does not provide incentives for fishermen to avoid the race for fish, prevent illegal fishing, and reduce pressure for overcapitalization and overexploitation; 4. maximization of yield in which managers attempted to squeeze every last bit of sustainable yield from stocks (because of overcapitalization) despite poor biological understanding; and 5. failure to separate allocation from conservation, which results in conservation goals being lost in allocation battles.

THE FUTURE OF WORLD FISHERIES

We see two very different paths fisheries may take in the future. One is that fishing pressure may remain high. Attempts to extract the maximum yield from fisheries will continue to lead to intense harvesting, and sequential depletion of major fisheries will result. Economics will cause fishing pressure to move lower down the food chain, so that fish species that are currently largely discarded will dominate the catch. Alternatively, we envision a future in which the race for fish is eliminated by appropriate institutional incentives, fishing pressure is reduced, stock abundance generally increases, and most depleted stocks recover. Commercial fisheries will strive for stability and profitability rather than maximization of yield.

These two possible futures are now taking place. In some locations (much of Africa and Asia, Argentina, New England, and Europe for example), the race for fish is in full swing, pressure to maximize yield continues to lead to intense fishing pressure, and the pessimistic future is developing. However, New Zealand, Chile, Australia, some Pacific Island countries, and some U.S. and Canadian fisheries have identified the problems and put in place appropriate incentives. In these places, the more optimistic future is unfolding. The race for fish has been halted, and economic and biological sustainability head the agenda. Ignorance is no longer an excuse; the question is whether regions, states, and communities can assemble the political will to choose the kind of fishery they want.

ACKNOWLEDGMENTS

T.A.B. was funded by NMFS grant NA07FE0473 and the South African National Research Foundation. C.V.M.V. was funded by CAPES/Brazil. The authors thank C. Allison for providing updated Southern Hemisphere whale catch data. All junior authors of this review were listed alphabetically.

The *Annual Review of Environment and Resources* is online at
http://environ.annualreviews.org

LITERATURE CITED

1. Harris M. 1998. *Lament for an Ocean. The Collapse of the Atlantic Cod Fishery: A True Crime Story*. Toronto: McClelland & Stewart. 342 pp.
2. Myers R, Hutchings A, Barrowman N. 1997. Why do fish stocks collapse? The example of cod in Atlantic Canada. *Ecol. Appl.* 7:91–106
3. Hutchings A, Myers R. 1994. What can be learned from the collapse of a renewable resource? Atlantic cod, *Gadus morhua*, of Newfoundland and Labrador. *Can. J. Fish. Aquat. Sci.* 51:2126–46
4. Bundy A. 2001. Fishing on ecosystems: the interplay of fishing and predation in Newfoundland-Labrador. *Can. J. Fish. Aquat. Sci.* 58:1153–67
5. Worm B, Myers RA. Top-down versus bottom-up control in oceanic food webs: a meta-analysis of cod-shrimp interactions in the North Atlantic. *Ecology* 84(1):162–73
5a. Can. Dep. Fish. Oceans. *Canada Landings Informantion*. http://www.dfo-mpo.gc.ca/communic/statistics/landings/land_e.htm
6. Kurlansky M. 1997. *Cod: A Biography of the Fish that Changed the World*. New York: Walker 294 pp.
7. Cushing DH. 1982. *Climate and*

Fisheries. London/New York: Academic. 373 pp.
8. Huxley TH. 1884. Inaugural address. *Fish. Exhib. Lit.* 4:1–22
9. Smith TD. 1994. *Scaling Fisheries: The Science of Measuring the Effects of Fishing, 1855–1955*. Cambridge, UK: Cambridge Univ. Press. 392 pp.
10. Garstang W. 1900. The impoverishment of the sea: a critical summary of the experimental and statistical evidence bearing upon the alleged depletion of the trawling grounds. *J. Marine Biol. Assoc.* 6:1–69
11. Parrish DL, Behnke RJ, Gephard SR, McCormick SD, Reeves GH. 1998. Why aren't there more Atlantic salmon (*Salmo salar*)? *Can. J. Fish. Aquat. Sci.* 55:281–87
12. Van Blaricom GR, Gerber LR, Brownell RL. 2001. Marine mammals, extinctions of. In *Encyclopedia of Biodiversity*. London/New York: Academic
13. Jackson JBC, Kirby MX, Berger WH, Bjorndal KA, Botsford LW, et al. 2001. Historical overfishing and the recent collapse of coastal ecosystems. *Science* 293:629–38
14. Pauly D. 1995. Anecdotes and the shifting baseline syndrome of fisheries. *Trends Ecol. Evol.* 10:430
15. Finney BP, Gregory-Eaves I, Sweetman J, Douglas MSV, Smol JP. 2000. Impacts of climatic change and fishing on Pacific salmon abundance over the past 300 years. *Science* 290:795–99
16. Finney BP, Gregory-Eaves I, Douglas MSV, Smol JP. 2002. Fisheries productivity in the northeastern Pacific Ocean over the past 2200 years. *Nature* 416:729–33
17. Baumgartner TR, Soutar A, Ferreira-Bartrina V. 1992. Reconstruction of the history of Pacific sardine and northern anchovy populations over the past two millennia from sediments of the Santa Barbara basin, California. *Calif. Coop. Ocean. Fish. Investig. Rep.* 33:24–40
18. De Vries TJ, Pearcy WG. 1982. Fish debris in sediments of the upwelling zone off central Peru: a late Quaternary record. *Deep-Sea Res.* 28:87–109
19. Shackleton LY. 1987. A comparative study of fossil fish scales from three upwelling regions. *S. Afr. J. Mar. Sci.* 5:1–8
20. Schwartzlose RA, Alheit J, Bakun A, Baumgartner TR, Cloete R, et al. 1999. Worldwide large-scale fluctuations of sardine and anchovy populations. *S. Afr. J. Mar. Sci.* 21:289–347
21. Chavez FP, Ryan J, Lluch-Cota SE, Ñiquen CM. 2003. From anchovies to sardines and back: multidecadal change in the Pacific Ocean. *Science* 299:217–21
22. Natl. Res. Counc. 1995. *Understanding Marine Biodiversity: A Research Agenda for the Nation*. Washington, DC: Natl. Acad. 114 pp.
23. Verity PG, Smetacek V, Smayda TJ. 2002. Status, trends and the future of the marine pelagic ecosystem. *Environ. Conserv.* 29:207–37
24. Moore MR, Vetter W, Gaus C, Shaw GR, Muller JF. 2002. Trace organic compounds in the marine environment. *Mar. Pollut. Bull.* 45:62–68
25. Peterson CH. 2001. The "Exxon Valdez" oil spill in Alaska: acute, indirect and chronic effects on the ecosystem. *Adv. Mar. Biol.* 39:1–103
26. Nixon SW. 1995. Coastal marine eutrophication: a definition, social causes, and future concerns. *Ophelia* 41:199–219
27. Howarth RW, Billen G, Swaney D, Townsend A, Jaworski N, et al. 1996. Regional nitrogen budgets and riverine N&P fluxes for the drainages to the North Atlantic Ocean: natural and human influences. *Biogeochemistry* 35:75–139
28. Cloern JE. 2001. Our evolving conceptual model of the coastal eutrophication problem. *Mar. Ecol.-Prog. Ser.* 210:223–53
29. Boesch DF. 2002. Challenges and opportunities for science in reducing nutrient over-enrichment of coastal ecosystems. *Estuaries* 25:886–900

30. Rabalais NN, Turner RE, Scavia D. 2002. Beyond science into policy: Gulf of Mexico hypoxia and the Mississippi River. *BioScience* 52:129–42
31. Leming TD, Stuntz WE. 1984. Zones of coastal hypoxia revealed by satellite scanning have implications for strategic fishing. *Nature* 310:136–38
32. Boesch D, Burreson E, Dennison W, Houde E, Kemp M, et al. 2001. Factors in the decline of coastal ecosystems. *Science* 293:1589–91
33. Peterson C, Jackson J, Kirby M, Lenihan H, Bourque B, et al. 2001. Factors in the decline of coastal ecosystems (response). *Science* 293:1589–91
34. Cohen AN, Carlton JT. 1998. Accelerating invasion rate in a highly invaded estuary. *Science* 279:555–58
35. Carlton JT. 1996. Pattern, process, and prediction in marine invasion ecology. *Biol. Conserv.* 78:97–106
36. Post JR, Sullivan M, Cox S, Lester NP, Walters CJ, et al. 2002. Canada's recreational fisheries: the invisible collapse? *Fisheries* 27:6–17
37. Schindler DW. 2001. The cumulative effects of climate warming and other human stresses on Canadian freshwaters in the new millennium. *Can. J. Fish. Aquat. Sci.* 58:18–29
38. Rahel FJ. 2000. Homogenization of fish faunas across the United States. *Science* 288:854–56
39. Lodge DM, Stein RA, Brown KM, Covich AP, Bronmark C, et al. 1998. Predicting impact of freshwater exotic species on native biodiversity: challenges in spatial scaling. *Australian J. Ecol.* 23:53–67
40. Mills EL, Leach JH, Carlton JT, Secor CL. 1994. Exotic species and the integrity of the Great Lakes. *BioScience* 44:666–76
41. Kaufman L. 1992. Catastrophic change in species-rich freshwater ecosystems. *BioScience* 42:846–58
42. Schindler DE, Kitchell JF, Ogutu-Ohwayo R. 1998. Ecological consequences of alternative gill net fisheries for Nile perch in Lake Victoria. *Conserv. Biol.* 12:56–64
43. Talhelm DR. 1988. *Economics of Great Lakes fisheries: a 1985 assessment.* Tech. Rep. Great Lakes Fish. Comm. Ann Arbor, MI
44. UN Food Agric. Organ. 2000. *The State of World Fisheries and Aquaculture 2000.* Rome: UN FAO. xiv + 142 pp.
45. Natl. Mar. Fish. Serv. 2002. *Annual report to Congress on the status of U.S. fisheries–2001.* US Dep. Commer., NOAA, Natl. Mar. Fish. Serv., Silver Spring, MD. http://www.nmfs.noaa.gov/sfa/reg_svcs/statusostocks/Status02.pdf
45a. Watson R, Pauly D. 2001. Systematic distortions in world fisheries catch trends. *Nature* 414:534–36
46. UN Food Agric. Organ. 2002. *FAO Yearbook of Fishery Statistics.* Vol. 91. Rome: UN FAO. 206 pp.
47. Pauly D, Christensen V, Dalsgaard J, Froese R, Torres F Jr. 1998. Fishing down marine food webs. *Science* 279:860–63
48. UN Food Agric. Organ. 2000. *Fishstat Plus: Universal Software for Fishery Statistical Time Series.* Version 2.3. Rome: UN FAO
49. Alverson DL, Freeberg MK, Murawski SA, Pope JG. 1994. *A global assessment of fisheries bycatch and discards.* UN FAO Fish. Tech. Pap. 339
50. Alverson DL. 1998. *Discarding Practices and Unobserved Fishing Mortality in Marine Fisheries: An Update.* Seattle: Wash. Sea Grant Program. 76 pp.
51. Hall MA, Alverson DL, Metuzals KI. 2000. By-Catch: Problems and Solutions. *Mar. Pollut. Bull.* 41:204–19
52. Hall MA. 1996. On bycatches. *Review of Fish Biology and Fisheries* 6:319–52
53. Isaksen B. 1997. The Norwegian approach to reduce bycatch and avoid discards. In *Technical Consultation of Reduction of Wastage in Fisheries*, ed. I Clucas, D James, pp. 89–93. Rome: UN FAO
54. Dayton PK, Thrush SF, Agardy MT, Hofman RJ. 1995. Environmental effects of

marine fishing. *Aquat. Conserv.: Mar. Freshw. Ecosyst.* 5:205–32
55. Jennings S, Kaiser MJ. 1998. The effects of fishing on marine ecosystems. *Adv. Mar. Biol.* 34:201–352
56. Koslow JA, Gowlett-Holmes K, Lowry JK, O'Hara T, Poore GCB, Williams A. 2001. Seamount benthic macrofauna off southern Tasmania: community structure and impacts of trawling. *Mar. Ecol.-Prog. Ser.* 213:111–25
57. Koenig CC, Coleman FC, Grimes CB, Fitzhugh GR, Scanlon KM, et al. 2000. Protection of fish spawning habitat for the conservation of warm-temperate reef-fish fisheries of shelf-edge reefs of Florida. *Bull. Mar. Sci.* 66:593–616
58. Friedlander AM, Boehlert GW, Field ME, Mason JE, Gardner JV, Dartnell P. 1999. Sidescan-sonar mapping of benthic trawl marks on the shelf and slope off Eureka, California. *Fish. Bull.* 97:786–801
59. Kaiser MJ, Edwards DB, Armstrong PJ, Radford K, Lough NEL, et al. 1998. Changes in megafaunal benthic communities in different habitats after trawling disturbance. *ICES J. Mar. Sci.* 55:353–61
60. Moran MJ, Stephenson PC. 2000. Effects of otter trawling on macrobenthos and management of demersal scalefish fisheries on the continental shelf of northwestern Australia. *ICES J. Mar. Sci.* 57:510–16
61. McConnaughey RA, Mier KL, Dew CB. 2000. An examination of chronic trawling effects on soft-bottom benthos of the eastern Bering Sea. *ICES J. Mar. Sci.* 57:1377–88
62. Prena J, Schwinghamer P, Rowell TW, Gordon DC, Gilkinson KD, et al. 1999. Experimental otter trawling on a sandy bottom ecosystem of the Grand Banks of Newfoundland: analysis of trawl bycatch and effects on epifauna. *Mar. Ecol.-Prog. Ser.* 181:107–24
63. Blaber SJM, Cyrus DP, Albaret JJ, Ching CV, Day JW, et al. 2000. Effects of fishing on the structure and functioning of estuarine and nearshore ecosystems. *ICES J. Mar. Sci.* 57:590–602
64. Kenchington ELR, Prena J, Gilkinson KD, Gordon DC, MacIsaac K, et al. 2001. Effects of experimental otter trawling on the macrofauna of a sandy bottom ecosystem on the Grand Banks of Newfoundland. *Can. J. Fish. Aquat. Sci.* 58:1043–57
65. Schwinghamer P, Gordon DC, Rowell TW, Prena J, McKeown DL, et al. 1998. Effects of experimental otter trawling on surficial sediment properties of a sandy-bottom ecosystem on the Grand Banks of Newfoundland. *Conserv. Biol.* 12:1215–22
66. Natl. Res. Counc. 2002. *Effects of trawling and dredging on seafloor habitat.* Washington, DC: Natl. Acad. 136 pp.
67. Carlton JT, Vermeij GJ, Lindberg DR, Carlton DA, Dudley EC. 1991. The first historical extinction of a marine invertebrate in an ocean basin: the demise of the eelgrass limpet *Lottia alveus*. *Biol. Bull.* 180:72–80
68. Roberts CM, Hawkins JP. 1999. Extinction risk in the sea. *Trends Ecol. Evol.* 14:241–46
69. Baum JK, Myers RA, Kehler DG, Worm B, Harley SJ, Doherty PA. 2003. Collapse and conservation of shark populations in the northwest Atlantic. *Science* 299:389–92
70. Brander K. 1981. Disappearance of common skate *Raia batis* from Irish Sea. *Nature* 290:48–49
71. Casey JM, Myers RA. 1998. Near extinction of a large widely distributed fish. *Science* 281:690–92
72. Greenstreet SPR, Hall SJ. 1996. Fishing and the ground-fish assemblage structure in the northwestern North Sea: an analysis of long-term and spatial trends. *J. Anim. Ecol.* 65:577–98
73. Pauly D, Christensen V, Froese R, Palomares ML. 2000. Fishing down aquatic food webs. *Am. Sci.* 88:46–51

74. Jennings S, Greenstreet SPR, Reynolds JD. 1999. Structural change in an exploited fish community: a consequence of differential fishing effects on species with contrasting life histories. *J. Anim. Ecol.* 68:617–27

75. Caddy JF, Csirke J, Garcia SM, Grainger RJR. 1998. How pervasive is "fishing down marine food webs"? *Science* 282:1383

76. Caddy JF, Garibaldi L. 2000. Apparent changes in the trophic composition of world marine harvests: the perspective from the FAO capture database. *Ocean Coast. Manag.* 43:615–55

77. Christensen V. 2000. Indicators for marine ecosystems affected by fisheries. *Mar. Freshw. Res.* 51:447–50

78. Pinnegar JK, Jennings S, O'Brien CM, Polunin NVC. 2002. Long-term changes in the trophic level of the Celtic Sea fish community and fish market price distribution. *J. Appl. Ecol.* 39:377–90

79. Pauly D, Palomares ML, Froese R, Saa P, Vakily M, et al. 2001. Fishing down Canadian aquatic food webs. *Can. J. Fish. Aquat. Sci.* 58:51–62

80. Caddy JF, Refk R, Do-Chi T. 1995. Productivity estimates for the Mediterranean: evidence of accelerating ecological change. *Ocean Coast. Manag.* 26:1–18

81. Milazzo M. 1998. *Subsidies in world fisheries: a reexamination.* Tech. Rep. World Bank Tech. Pap. No. 406, World Bank, Washington, DC

82. Organ. Econ. Co-op. Dev. 2000. *Transition to responsible fisheries: economics and policy implications.* Paris: OECD. 264 pp.

83. UN Food Agric. Organ. 2002. Number of fishers doubled since 1970. FAO Fish. Circ. 929. http://www.fao.org/fi/highligh/fisher/c929.asp

84. Iudicello S, Weber M, Wieland R. 1999. *Fish, Markets, and Fishermen: The Economics of Overfishing.* Washington, DC: Island. 192 pp.

85. Quinn TJ Jr, Deriso RB. 1999. *Quantitative Fish Dynamics.* New York: Oxford Univ. Press. 542 pp.

86. Hilborn R, Walters CJ. 1992. *Quantitative Fisheries Stock Assessment: Choice, Dynamics, and Uncertainty.* New York: Chapman & Hall. 570 pp.

87. Hilborn R. 2003. Are sustainable fisheries achievable? In *Marine Conservation Biology: The Science of Maintaining the Sea's Biodiversity*, ed. EA Norse, LB Crowder. Washington, DC: Island. In press

88. Larkin PA. 1977. An epitaph for the concept of maximum sustained yield. *Trans. Am. Fish. Soc.* 106:1–11

89. Caddy JF. 1998. *A short review of precautionary reference points and some proposals for their use in data-poor situations.* UN FAO Fish. Tech. Pap. 379

90. Pearse PH. 1982. *Turning the tide: a new policy for Canada's Pacific fisheries, final rep.* Comm. Pac. Fish. Policy, Vancouver, BC, Can.

91. Hilborn R, Parma A, Maunder M. 2002. Exploitation rate reference points for West Coast rockfish: Are they robust and are there better alternatives? *N. Am. J. Fish. Manag.* 22:365–75

92. Ricker WE. 1958. Maximum sustained yields from fluctuating environments and mixed stocks. *J. Fish. Res. Board Can.* 15:991–1006

93. Hightower JE. 1990. Multispecies harvesting policies for Washington-Oregon-California rockfish trawl fisheries. *Fish. Bull.* 88:645–56

94. Hilborn R, Punt AE. 2003. Beyond band-aids in fisheries management: fixing world fisheries. *Bull. Mar. Sci.* In press

95. Pauly D, Christensen V, Guénette S, Pitcher TJ, Sumaila UR, et al. 2002. Towards sustainability in world fisheries. *Nature* 418:689–95

96. Kirkwood GP. 1997. The revised management procedure of the International Whaling Commission. In *Global Trends: Fisheries Management.*, ed. MP Sissenwine. Bethesda, MD: Am. Fish. Soc. Symp. 20

97. Natl. Res. Counc. 1998. *Sustaining Marine Fisheries.* Washington, DC: Natl. Acad. 164 pp.
98. Pope JG. 1991. The ICES multispecies assessment. *ICES Mar. Sci. Symp.* 193:23–33
99. Christensen V. 1995. A model of trophic interactions in the North Sea in 1981, the year of the stomach. *Dana* 11:1–28
100. Polovina JJ. 1984. Model of a coral reef ecosystem I. The ECOPATH model and its application to French Frigate Shoals. *Coral Reefs* 3:1–11
101. Polovina JJ. 1984. An overview of the ECOPATH model. *Fishbyte* 2:5–7
102. Polovina JJ, Ow MD. 1983. *ECOPATH: a user's manual and program listings. Tech. Rep. H-83-23*, Natl. Mar. Fish. Serv., NOAA, Honolulu
103. Christensen V, Pauly D. 1992. ECOPATH II: a software for balancing steady-state ecosystem models and calculating network characteristics. *Ecol. Model.* 61:169–85
104. Pauly D, Christensen V, Walters CJ. 2000. Ecopath, ecosim, and ecospace as tools for evaluating the ecosystem impact of fisheries. *ICES J. Mar. Sci.* 57:697–706
105. Pauly D, Christensen V. 1995. Primary production required to sustain global fisheries. *Nature* 374:255–57
106. Hollowed AB, Bax N, Beamish R, Collie J, Fogarty M, et al. 2000. Are multispecies models an improvement on single-species models for measuring fishing impacts on marine ecosystems? *ICES J. Mar. Sci.* 57:707–19
107. Orensanz JM, Jamieson GS. 1998. The assessment and management of spatially structured stocks: an overview of the North Pacific Symposium on invertebrate stock assessment and management. See Ref. 164, pp. 441–60
108. Orensanz JM, Parma AM, Turk T, Valero JL. 2003. Dynamics, assessment, and management of exploited natural populations. In *Scallops: Biology, Ecology, and Aquaculture*, ed. SE Shumway. Amsterdam: Elsevier. In press
109. Castilla JC, Manriquez P, Alvarado J, Rosson A, Pino C, et al. 1998. Artisanal "caletas" as units of production and comanagers of benthic invertebrates in Chile. See Ref. 164, pp. 407–13
110. Castilla JC, Fernández M. 1998. Small-scale benthic fishes in Chile: on co-management and sustainable use of benthic invertebrates. *Ecol. Appl.* 8 (Suppl.): S124–32
111. Hilborn R. 1985. Fleet dynamics and individual variation: why some people catch more fish than others. *Can. J. Fish. Aquat. Sci.* 42:2–13
112. Wilen JE, Smith MD, Lockwood D, Botsford LW. 2002. Avoiding surprises: incorporating fisherman behavior into management models. *Bull. Mar. Sci.* 70:553–75
113. Gordon HS. 1954. Economic theory of a common property resources: the fishery. *J. Polit. Econ.* 62:124–42
114. Clark CW. 1985. *Bioeconomic Modelling and Fisheries Management.* New York: Wiley. 291 pp.
115. Hilborn R. 1990. Marine biota. In *The Earth as Transformed by Human Action*, ed. BL Turner III, pp. 371–86. Cambridge, UK: Cambridge Univ. Press
116. Natl. Res. Counc. 1999. *Sharing the fish: toward a national policy on individual fishing quotas.* Washington, DC: Natl. Acad. 422 pp.
117. H John Heinz III Cent. Sci. Econ. Environ. 2000. *Fishing Grounds: Defining a New Era for American Fisheries Management.* Washington, DC: Island. 241 pp.
118. Breen PA, Kendrick TH. 1997. A fisheries management success story: the Gisborne, New Zealand, fishery for red rock lobsters (*Jasus edwardsii*). *Mar. Freshw. Res.* 48:1103–10
119. Prince J, Walters CJ, Ruiz-Avila R, Sluczanowski P. 1998. Territorial user's rights and the Australian abalone (*Haliotis* sp.) fishery. See Ref. 164, pp. 367–75

120. Maunder MN, Starr PJ. 2002. Industry participation in stock assessment: the New Zealand SNA1 snapper (*Pagrus auratus*) fishery. *Mar. Policy* 26:481–92
121. Ostrom E. 1990. *Governing the Commons: The Evolution of Institutions for Collective Action.* Cambridge, UK: Cambridge Univ. Press. 280 pp.
122. Pew Oceans Comm. 2003. Managing marine fisheries in the United States. *Proc. Pew Oceans Comm. Workshop Mar. Fish. Manag., Seattle, 18–19 July 2001.* Arlington, VA: Pew Oceans Comm. 72 pp.
123. Hilborn R. 2002. The dark side of reference points. *Bull. Mar. Sci.* 70:403–8
124. Butterworth DS, Punt AE. 1999. Experiences in the evaluation and implementation of management procedures. *ICES J. Mar. Sci.* 56:985–98
125. Punt AE, Smith ADM, Cui G. 2001. Review of progress in the introduction of management strategy evaluation (MSE) approaches in Australia's South East Fishery. *Mar. Freshw. Res.* 52:719–26
126. Pearse PH. 1992. From open access to private property: recent innovations in fishing rights as instruments of fisheries policy. *Ocean Dev. Int. Law* 23:71–83
127. Macinko S, Bromley DW. 2002. *Who Owns America's Fisheries?* Washington, DC: Island. 41 pp.
128. Wertheimer AC, Swanson D. 2000. *The use of individual fishing quotas in the United States EEZ.* Presented at Use Prop. Rights Fish. Manag., FishRights99 Conf., Fremantle, West. Aust.
129. Sissenwine MP, Mace PM. 1992. ITQs in New Zealand: the era of fixed quota in perpetuity. *Fish. Bull.* 90:147–60
130. Orensanz JM, Hilborn R, Parma AM. 2000. Harvesting Methuselah's clams: is the geoduck fishery sustainable, or just apparently so? *Can. Stock Assess. Secr., Res. Doc.* 2000/175. 68 pp.
131. González E, Norambuena R, García M. 2001. Initial allocation of harvesting rights in the Chilean fishery for Patagonian toothfish. In *Case Studies on the Allocation of Transferable Quota Rights in Fisheries*, ed. R Shotton, pp. 305–21. Rome: UN FAO
132. Bray K. 2000. *A global review of illegal, unreported and unregulated (IUU) fishing. Tech. Rep. AUS:IUU/2000/6*, UN FAO, Roma
133. Tarr R. 2000. The South African abalone (Haliotis midae) fishery: a decade of challenges and change. See Ref. 165, pp. 32–40
134. Johannes RE. 2002. The renaissance of community-based marine resource management in Oceania. *Annu. Rev. Ecol. Syst.* 33:317–40
135. Turris BR. 1999. *A comparison of British Columbia's ITQ fisheries for groundfish trawl and sablefish: similar results from programmes with differing objectives, designs and processes.* Presented at FishRights99 Conf., Fremantle, West. Aust.
136. Garcia SM. 1994. The precautionary principle: its implications in capture fisheries management. *Ocean Coast. Manag.* 22:99–125
137. Partnersh. Interdiscip. Stud. Coast. Oceans. 2002. *Science of Marine Reserves*: http://www.piscoweb.org/outreach/pubs/reserves/booklet_final.pdf
138. Hilborn R, Maguire JJ, Parma AM, Rosenberg AA. 2001. The precautionary approach and risk management: Can they increase the probability of successes in fishery management? *Can. J. Fish. Aquat. Sci.* 58:99–107
139. Natl. Res. Counc. 2001. *Marine Protected Areas: Tools for Sustaining Ocean Ecosystems.* Washington, DC: Natl. Acad. 272 pp.
140. Halpern BS, Warner RR. 2002. Marine reserves have rapid and lasting effects. *Ecol. Lett.* 5:361–66
141. Roberts CM, Bohnsack JA, Gell F, Hawkins JP, Goodridge R. 2002. Marine reserves and fisheries management: response. *Science* 295:1234–35

142. Tupper MH, Wickstrom K, Hilborn R. 2002. Marine reserves and fisheries management. *Science* 295:1233
143. Anonymous. 2002. Measuring the effects of marine reserves on fisheries: the dilemmas of experimental programs. *MPA News* 4:1–3
144. Healey MC, Hennessey T. 1998. The paradox of fairness: the impact of escalating complexity on fishery management. *Mar. Policy* 22:109–18
145. Penn J, (ed.). 2002. *State of the Fisheries 2000/2001.* Fish. Res. Div., Dep. Fish. Perth, Aust. http://www.fish.wa.gov.au/sof/2000/sof20002001-00.pdf
146. Anonymous. 2000. *The Tasmanian Abalone Fishery. Revis. Policy Pap.*, Dep. Prim. Ind., Water Environ., Hobart, Tasman. Aust.
147. Francis RICC, Cordue PL, Haist V. 2002. *Review of the 2001 hoki stock assessment. NZ Fish. Assess. Rep 2002/42.* Natl. Inst. Water Atmos., Wellington, NZ
148. Breen PA, Kim SW, Starr PJ, Bentley N. 2002. *Assessment of the red rock lobsters (Jasus edwardsii) in area CRA 3 in 2001.* NZ Fish. Assess. Rep. 2002/27, Natl. Inst. Water Atmos., Wellington, NZ
149. Francis RICC. 2001. *Stock assessment for 2001 of orange roughy on the northeast Chatham Rise. Tech.*, WG-Deepwater-01/55. New Zealand Minist. Fish., Wellington, NZ
150. Clark W, Hare S. 2002. *Assessment of the Pacific halibut stock at the end of 2002.*, Int. Pac. Halibut Comm. Rep. Assess. Res. Act., Int. Pac. Halibut Comm., Seattle, WA http://www.iphc.washington.edu/halcom/research/sa/papers/sa02.pdf
151. Thompson G, Dorn M. 2002. *Assessment of the Pacific cod stock in the Eastern Bering Sea and Aleutian Islands area.* In *Stock Assess. Fish. Eval. Rep. Groundf. Resour. Bering Sea/Aleutian Islands Reg.* Sect. 1:33–120. North Pac. Fish. Mgmt. Council, Anchorage, AK
152. Heard W, Andersen A. 1999. *Alaska salmon in our living ocean. Rep. Status US Living Mar. Res., 1999. Tech. Memo. NMFS-F/SPO-41,* US Dep. Commer., NOAA, Washington, DC
153. Ianelli J, Barbeaux S, Honkalehto T, Walters G, Williamson N. 2002. *Eastern Bering Sea Walleye Pollock Stock Assessment.* See Ref. 151, Sec. 1:33–120
154. Barton J. 2002. Fisheries and fisheries management in Falkland Islands conservation zones. *Conser: Mar. Freshw. Ecosyst* 12:127–35
155. NAFO. 2003. *North Atlantic Fisheries Organization Statistical Information.* http://www.nafo.ca/activities/FRAMES/AcFrFish.html
156. ICES. 2001. *Current Stock Status.* Read on the web Jan. 2003. http://www.ices.dk/committe/acfm/comwork/report/2001/oct/cod-347d.pdf
157. Rowling KR, Makin DL. 2001. *Monitoring of the fishery for Gemfish Rexea solandri, 1996 to 2000. Aust. Fish. Manag. Agency Res. Proj. 99/337. Fish. Final Rep. Ser. 27,* New South Wales
158. Caton A, eds. 2002. *Fishery status reports 2000–2001: resource assessments of the Australian Commonwealth fisheries.* Dep. Agric. Fish., Bur. Rural Sci., Canberra, Aust. http://www.affa.gov.au/corporate_docs/publications/pdf/rural_science/fisheries/statusrep00/fsr00_01lr_2.pdf
159. Annala JH, Sullivan KJ, O'Brien CJ, Smith NWM, Varian SJAC. 2002. *Report from the fishery assessment plenary, May.* Wellington, NZ: Unpubl. rep. held in Natl. Inst. Water Atmos. library, Wellington
160. Muse B. 1998. *Management of the British Columbia abalone fishery. Alaska Commer. Fish. Entry Comm. Rep. CFEC 98-1N.* Juneau, AK. http://www.cfec.state.ak.us/research/divefish/abalone.pdf
161. Karpov K, Haaker P, Tanigushi I, Rogers-Bennett L. 2000. Serial depletion and collapses of the California abalone (Haliotis spp.) fishery. See Ref. 165, pp. 11–24
162. Woodby D, Larson R, Rumble J. 2000.

Decline of the Alaska abalone (Haliotis spp.) fishery and prospects for rebuilding the stock. See Ref. 165, pp. 25–31
163. Deleted in proof
164. Jamieson GS, Campbell A, eds. 1998. *Proc. North Pac. Symp. Invertebr. Stock Assess. Manag.* Mar. 6–10, 1995. *Can. Spec. Publ. Fish. Aquat. Sci. Rep. 125.* Natl. Res. Counc., Ottowa, Can.
165. Campbell A, ed. 2000. *Workshop on rebuilding abalone stocks in British Columbia.* Feb. 23–26, 1999, Nanaimo, BC. *Can. Spec. Publ. Fish. Aquat. Sci. Rep. 130.* Natl. Res. Counc., Ottowa, Can.

GREEN CHEMISTRY AND ENGINEERING: Drivers, Metrics, and Reduction to Practice

Anne E. Marteel,[1] Julian A. Davies,[1] Walter W. Olson,[2] and Martin A. Abraham[3]

Department of Chemistry,[1] Mechanical, Industrial, and Manufacturing Engineering,[2] and Chemical and Environmental Engineering,[3] University of Toledo, Toledo, Ohio 43606; email: annem1@bigplanet.com, jdavies@uoft02.utoledo.edu, wolson@eng.utoledo.edu, martin.abraham@utoledo.edu

Key Words industrial ecology, benign manufacturing, catalyst design, benign solvents

■ **Abstract** Green chemistry and engineering is the design of chemical manufacturing systems to minimize their adverse affects on the environment. Thus, a primary goal of green chemistry and engineering is to reduce the environmental impact of chemical processes and chemical manufacturing while simultaneously enhancing the overall process performance. Although it is beneficial to simply reduce the use of organic solvents in chemical processes, green chemistry and engineering goes further, in that it evaluates the entire manufacturing operation to identify techniques that can be applied to minimize the overall process hazard, while maintaining economic practicality. Evaluation of the environmental impacts of the manufacturing process requires a systems approach and appropriate metrics that permit quantitative assessment of environmental hazards. Thus, this chapter begins with a discussion of the drivers for green engineering and the metrics through which processes can be evaluated. Then, the hydroformylation process is used as a case study to illustrate the way in which green chemistry principles can be applied to real processes. Two elements are specifically highlighted: (*a*) the use of catalysts to facilitate active and selective chemistry and the immobilization of said catalysts within the reactor system, and (*b*) the development of processes based on benign reaction solvents, and the benefits that can accrue from simplified separations operations.

CONTENTS

GREEN CHEMISTRY: FUNDAMENTALS AND BASIS 402
  Drivers 404
  Metrics 410
APPLYING GREEN CHEMISTRY: A HYDROFORMYLATION CASE
  STUDY 413
  Multiphase Systems That Simplify Catalyst Recovery 415
  Catalyst Immobilization 417

Benign Solvents 418
SUSTAINABILITY ENGINEERING 420

GREEN CHEMISTRY: FUNDAMENTALS AND BASIS

One of the functions of the engineer is to develop processes to produce goods desired by the population. Environmental awareness in the general community has also increased. The last decade has heralded a paradigm shift in the way engineers view environmental propriety: Waste treatment is no longer a preferred means of dealing with process wastes. As stated in the Pollution Prevention Act of 1990, the option of first choice is to prevent the formation of waste at the source (1). It is unlikely that humankind will give up the products that have improved the quality of life. Thus, it is imperative that engineers learn how to evaluate the environmental impacts of a product and determine ways to minimize adverse environmental impacts in the concept and design stage.

Analysis of a process and evaluation of its environmental impact are truly engineering challenges across all engineering disciplines. Although chemical engineers may be adept at analyzing the chemical components of a waste stream, the mechanical engineer may have greater familiarity with manufacturing processes, while the civil engineer may possess greater skill at analyzing the ecological impacts of a waste stream. Clearly, each engineering discipline would approach the problem from a different viewpoint and would likely come to a different recommended solution. In an industrial operation, the clever manager would resolve this dilemma by assigning a team of engineers to evaluate the proposed process.

The strategy of green chemistry is the operation of chemical processes such that hazardous substances will not be used or generated (1). So, chemical operations should be designed or modified such that they are clean and sustainable while maintaining the current standard of living. Under green chemistry, the reduction of hazardous materials through careful selection of feedstocks and reagents as well as the use of alternative solvents is emphasized. Green chemistry should also include the use of catalysts to yield desired products in high selectivities.

According to the definition first provided by Anastas & Warner in 1998, "Green chemistry is the design of chemical products and processes that reduce or eliminate the use and generation of hazardous substances" (1). In a similar manner, the Green Engineering branch of the Environmental Protection Agency defines green engineering as "the design, commercialization, and use of processes and products, which are feasible and economical while minimizing the generation of pollution at the source and the risk to human health and the environment." Thus, green engineering focuses on achieving sustainability through the application of science and technology (2). Clearly, these two definitions describe two aspects of the same thing, with the chemist focused on the chemical process and the engineer focused on the manufacturing process. To paraphrase Professor Wei of Princeton University, chemical engineers need to focus on product engineering, not just process engineering (3). Regardless of the viewpoint, many of the same techniques are employed by chemists and chemical engineers to minimize the environmental impacts of manufacturing and of using chemical products.

Green chemistry principles are often applied to a single chemical reaction in a commercial chemical synthesis. However, the multiple steps in the synthetic scheme are related, and thus a change in one step will also impact other steps in the processes. Green engineering is even more dramatically impacted, because a change in the synthetic chemistry will require (as a minimum) modifications in the separations process and perhaps wholesale redevelopment of the chemical process. Thus, to truly determine the "greenness" of a proposed modification, it is necessary to look at the impacts of a proposed change on all steps in the process.

In the Pollution Prevention Act of 1990, the United States Congress established the U.S. governmental policy on pollution and the environment (4). It established a hierarchy (see Figure 1) with source reduction as the option of first choice in pollution prevention (P2). This hierarchy represents the shift in thinking that has occurred between the 1970s and now. End-of-pipe treatment solutions have been replaced with a goal of reduced waste generation, and where reduction is impossible, in-process or out-of-process recycling. As generally defined, P2 includes increased efficiency in the use of raw materials, energy, water, and other resources. This also includes protection of resources through conservation.

As part of P2, the idea of life cycle analysis (LCA) has emerged (4). An LCA consists of three parts. First, an inventory of raw materials, energy inputs, wastes, and emissions from the production of the first raw material to the final disposition of the product is created. Second, a statement of the environmental impact of each element of the inventory is prepared. This statement is used to produce the third part of the LCA, which is a strategy for reducing the overall impact of the process by targeting specific steps for improvement. Comparisons between existing

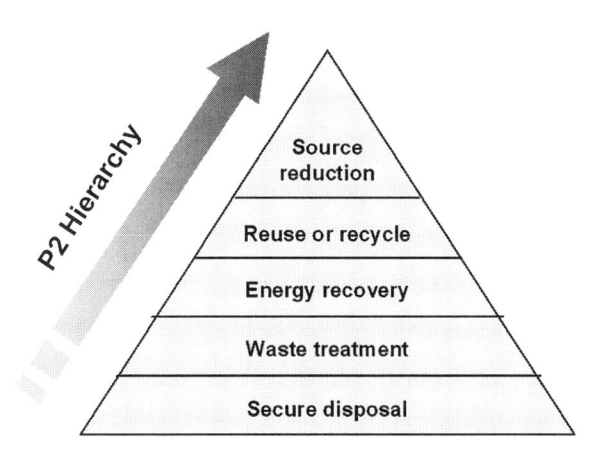

Figure 1 Pollution prevention hierarchy as outlined in Pollution Prevention Act of 1990.

hydroformylation processes and potential replacements could be performed using LCA. For example, an LCA on current hydroformylation processes might suggest the removal of organic solvents, but to do so would increase the energy inputs used from a coal-fired power plant, such that the overall environmental impact of the process would be increased. Then it may in fact be better overall to retain the current process.

P2 can be practiced on many scales. Three generally identified scales are: macroscale (industry wide), mesoscale (unit operation level), and microscale (reaction pathway level). An example of successful P2 at the mesoscale is the catalytic distillation process for production of methyl tertiary butyl ether (MTBE) using C_4 feedstocks and methanol (4). In this process, a reactor and two distillation towers are replaced by a single unit, which both produces MTBE and separates it from the unreacted feedstock. At the microscale, a new catalyst for polypropylene production, developed in the 1990s, reduced the production of nonlinear product by greater than 90% (4). This eliminated approximately 200 million lbs/yr of waste material that had previously been landfilled or burned.

Industrial use of green chemistry and engineering principles, or pollution prevention guidelines, requires some motivating force. In addition, it is necessary to know whether process changes that may be implemented actually have a positive impact. The following sections describe both the drivers and metrics needed for implementing potential changes to industrial processes.

Drivers

Although there has been much recent discussion of green chemistry, there has generally been very little emphasis on the benefits of green chemistry to industry. We all agree that irrational production of waste is generally undesirable, but it is a more difficult challenge to identify what level of waste production is acceptable within a process. In practical consideration, the acceptable level of waste production is based on the costs of modifying a process to implement green solutions relative to the expected increase in revenue that will be generated by this change. Should other factors be considered? How does one evaluate the cost of increasing CO_2 levels in the atmosphere, especially in light of the ongoing discussion as to its impacts on global climate change? Thus, a brief review of the impacts of green chemistry on industrial operations is presented herein.

During the industrial revolution, it was a common belief that the Earth's resources were essentially limitless and that its ability to assimilate waste products was also relatively unbounded. Thus, issues of pollution were not relevant. Today, we are much more aware of the natural resource limits that exist and that waste disposal inevitably adversely affects our ecosystems. Although the relationships that describe the impact of manufacturing on ecosystems are not yet fully understood, the reasons to practice green engineering in industry are substantial and include:

- Economic benefits
- Regulatory compliance

- Liability reduction
- Enhanced public image
- Federal and state grants
- Market incentives
- Reduced treatment costs
- Tax incentives
- Decreased worker exposure
- Decreased energy consumption
- Increased operating efficiencies
- Competitive advantage
- Reduced negative environmental impacts.

Environmental awareness has been steadily increasing throughout the latter half of the twentieth century. Previous industrial practices of burying wastes and forgetting about them have given way to waste treatment methods and, ultimately, pollution prevention. Today, industry is embracing concepts of green chemistry (5, 6) and responsible care (7) as the preferred means of meeting environmental targets.

The growth of industrial ecology parallels industrial awareness of not only the environmental benefits of green chemistry but also the economic, health, and safety implications. Industrial ecology takes a systems approach to manufacturing operations by evaluating the environmental impacts of a product over its life cycle (8). It implies that an industrial system can mimic a natural ecosystem and should act in harmony with nature (9). Thus, industrial ecology focuses on material and energy flows in an attempt to minimize the use of raw materials and the generation of waste products throughout the entire useful life of the manufactured product. The evaluation of a green product can often be enhanced by the use of the LCA (10).

Life cycle engineering provides a framework in which many of the green engineering concepts can be placed and can be represented as the three sides of a triangle, as shown in Figure 2. Life cycle inventory represents a rigorous accounting of the inputs and outputs associated with the process. The life cycle inventory can be related to the material and energy balances needed to determine the inputs and outputs from a process. Then, LCA reveals the trade-offs that are made between various stages of the manufacturing process. For example, if we consider the opportunities provided by the electric car, we quickly realize that the environmental implications of energy generation are merely shifted from the product use stage of the vehicle to the energy generation stage of a net energy production analysis. This also illustrates the importance of scoping and the poor quality of analysis that can result if the system boundaries are inadequately drawn. Life cycle impact analysis describes risk assessment, environmental hazards, and economics (which includes the issue of describing the loss of natural capital or the use of renewable resources). Product and process improvement provide the entry for discussion of design for recycling, opportunities for improved heat and mass

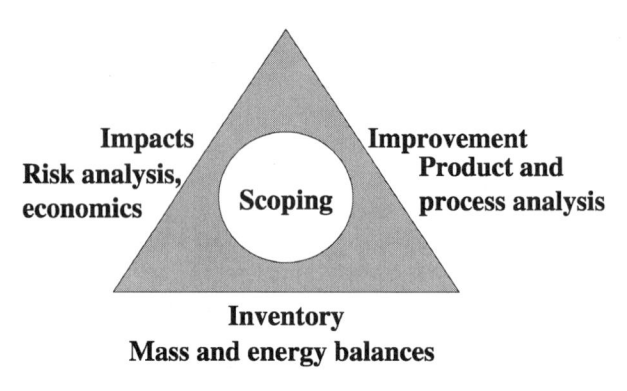

Figure 2 Diagram of the three legs of life cycle engineering, a paradigm basis for environmental decision making.

integration, and green chemistry. Finally, it is possible to extend this engineering analysis to nontechnical situations, leading to elements of industrial ecology and sustainable manufacturing.

Life Cycle Analysis (often called "Life Cycle *Assessment*" to emphasize limitations of a study) is the result of work initiated in the late 1980s and early 1990s by the Society of Environmental Toxicology and Chemistry (SETAC). The defining goals of LCA were embodied in the 1991 SETAC publication, *A Technical Framework for Life-Cycle Assessment* (11), and state, in part, "The life-cycle assessment is an objective process to evaluate the environmental burdens associated with a product, process, or activity by identifying and quantifying energy and material usage and environmental releases, to assess the impact of these energy and material uses on the environment, and to evaluate and implement opportunities to effect environmental improvements." Later, as practitioners began to understand the demands of an LCA, a fourth stage was added that should occur before the inventory stage: goal definition and scoping. The participants in the SETAC process clearly noted that the four stages were not conducted sequentially; rather, the LCA process involved feedback and interaction between the stages, as shown in Figure 3 (12).

As LCA continued to develop, quantitative methods were applied to the inventory stage. Developments in impact assessment and improvement assessment lagged. As of this date, most LCAs published are only results of the inventory stage or are more accurately referred to as Life Cycle Inventories (LCI). Inventory analysis is essentially a data collection activity. An LCI is based on performing mass and energy balances around the various phases of a product or process. The goal in an LCI is to track the material needs from extraction through disposal. However, this complete product cycle is sometimes truncated by scoping decisions and by streamlining based on time and cost considerations. An LCI contains an implicit assumption that the data will accurately reflect the relationships of inventories over all time. Another way of stating this is that LCI assumes that the systems acting on the material inventories are in a steady state. Considerable efforts have gone

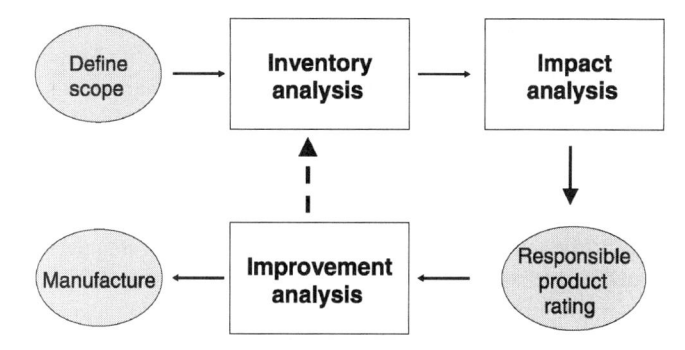

Figure 3 Schematic diagram showing the stages of a life cycle analysis [after (12)].

into the scoping and inventory analysis sections of LCA (13, 14) for a number of automotive components.

Environmental impact analysis requires relationships to be built between the inventories and their observed and known environmental effects. For many materials, data exist on the relationship between stressor effects and material concentrations. To make use of this data for impacts, one must know the concentration of the material in particular environmental systems (e.g., riparian or regional watersheds) over a certain period of time. The relationship needed for impact analysis is the relationship between a material concentration and time. Often the effect of a particular inventory item is not observed until sufficient time has passed between material extraction from a source until its usage or disposal. For example, the materials for an automobile take approximately one month to extract, refine, and manufacture (15). The automobile has a usage phase of an average of 8 to 10 years. Thus the total material impacts are not fully observed on manufacturing date because they include the CO_2 emissions that will be derived from driving the car over its life. However, LCI does not capture or analyze these delays. The result of failing to consider time is that evaluations of the use of materials for a given phase of the life cycle can be misleading.

The problem with time has been called the temporal problem of LCA. Advances in performing impact analysis using conventional risk assessment tools have been limited. Risk assessment requires that one understand the probability of certain events occurring and the fate and transport mechanisms. These depend on evaluations taken over time periods. As Owens stated, "The key LCA limitations in this respect are the loss of spatial, temporal, close response and threshold information" (15). It is difficult to consider how one might come to an environmental impact decision without considering time as a factor. The time problem of the LCA is manifested in several different ways. For example, Olson & Abraham (16) demonstrated the problems of competing cycles and feedback loops and the instabilities that can result from process changes designed to reduce overall environment impacts as materials usage is adjusted over time.

Consider, for example, the air emissions from the automobile. The total emissions can be distributed over the various life stages of the product using readily available data, as summarized in Table 1. Automotive companies recognize that the average life of the automobile in the United States is more than eight years and that models being produced today will not be presented to recyclers and dismantlers in significant numbers until year 2020. It is also well known that 87% of the major emissions from an automobile occurs as a result of the use phase of the LCI of the automobile (14), 12% occurs during the material production and manufacturing phases, and only 1% comes from the end-of-life stage.

Impact assessment and improvement papers that exist tend to be theoretical in nature with very few applications. Few present quantitative environmental impact data, although several papers claim that the LCI has led to significant improvements. Impacts, where reported, tend to be limited and incomplete. For example, Thiel (17) considered the impacts of aluminum and steel bumper carriers in an automobile. The author faithfully attempted to perform an LCA in accordance with the ISO 14040 standard series by including an impact assessment and an interpretation. He computed global warming potentials, acidification potentials, and eutrophication potentials. Yet other categories of impacts, such as human or aquatic toxicity, were ignored. Although the paper is informative and reflects current thinking of how to compare materials, it fails to provide information on where and when impact concentrations would occur and what the impact risks are. Thus the results are qualitative rather than quantitative. We are led to conclude that the impact analysis phase of LCA still requires considerable research and development.

One of the problems with performing impact analysis appears to be how to take the copious data provided by LCI and integrate time for making risk assessments. Cascio (18) highlighted the problem in his very complete reference on ISO 14000 by identifying it when proposing an environmental stressor method for impacts. However, he did not propose a solution to the problem. Owens (15), mentioned earlier, identified time as an impediment to applying risk analysis. Herrchen (19) noted the recent discussions of scientists concerning a "special need to consider temporal aspects in LCA of long lived products." She specifically acknowledged the failure of LCA factors to provide the means for computing loadings of emissions over time horizons. She stated but did not elaborate on the idea that time-based modeling is an essential solution to this problem.

Developments in measures to support corporate ecoefficiency include a recent "sustainability mapping tool" proposed by Grimberg & Greener of the Rocky Mountain Institute (20). This tool is a hierarchical evaluation of various corporate operational statistics in terms of their contribution (or, alternatively, their privation) to sustainability. At the lowest level, its questions address specific uses of materials, e.g., "What percent of miscellaneous materials (such as abrasives, chlorofluorocarbons, tires or toner cartridges) are recycled?" The answers to these questions are graded on a scale of 1 to 10 with 10 being the highest contribution to sustainability. At the next level, these values are aggregated into scores based on energy, building materials, purchasing, water usage, land usage, distribution,

TABLE 1 Life cycle inventory (LCI) of the generic vehicle

	Vehicle total (g)	Material production (g)	Manufacturing (g)	Operation (g)	Maintenance & repair (g)	End of life (g)
Carbon dioxide (CO_2, fossil)	59,092,200	4,439,850	2,562,160	51,331,400	615,481	14,327
Carbon monoxide (CO)	1,942,230	63,813	5,914	1,832,728	39,088	683
Hydrocarbons (except methane)	256,640	12,627	7,349	34,520	1,974	170
Methane (CH_4)	65,806	11,773	5,534	44,500	3,854	144
Nitrogen oxides (NO_X as NO_2)	254,193	12,871	8,295	229,465	2,755	806
Sulfur oxides (SO_X as SO_2)	133,326	30,491	14,917	83,180	4,424	315

and hazardous materials. The aggregated scores are then measures of the highest ecoefficiency levels, which include resource productivity, biomimicry, product to service, and investment in human capital.

Metrics

The introduction of the ISO 14000 standards in 1998 gave many businesses the impetus to begin evaluating their environmental performance and developing management plans in response to the perceived benefits of becoming ISO 14000 certified. The standard calls for managerial commitment, planning, implementation, measurement and evaluation, review, and improvement (21). As a result of changes in the environmental management structures, business concerns started to shift from response to government regulation to proactively seeking ways to improve environmental performance. In many cases, the corporations that instituted environmental management systems, such as those suggested within ISO 14000, found a positive impact on their corporate profit (22).

In order to determine whether an environmental benefit exists from the implementation of a process change, a means of measuring the environmental impact of a process is required. One of the challenges of any environmental analysis is the identification of a defining quantity for the environmental impact (23), whether it is within a single life stage of a manufactured product or it refers to chemical interactions in the environment. In general, the metrics are often process specific, and specific metrics that may apply within the chemical industry may not be as reasonable for the manufacturing sector. Although numerous environmental metrics have been proposed, the following discussion emphasizes those that are most appropriate for chemical operations.

The ability to monitor environmental performance has many advantages. Two of the most important questions can be answered when using environmental metrics. First, how am I doing? It is a simple question, but the answers achieved from using environmental metrics may be surprising. This leads to the next important question, i.e., what are the targets for improvement? Knowing specifically how much waste a company is producing and being able to pinpoint at which stage it is being created is a powerful concept. This allows management to focus on spending money to correct or improve a process to make it more efficient, rather than guessing which processes they think are inefficient. Other important reasons to include environmental metrics in management decisions include the following:

- Monitoring progress toward a goal over an extended time period
- Helping to fulfill regulatory compliance
- Gaining a competitive advantage over other companies by optimizing internal operations, which allows consumer demands to be met more effectively
- Improving corporate reputation for investors and insurers.

In order for any metric to be useful, certain criteria should be met. First, data must be available and applicable across a variety of systems, facilities, or locations.

Metrics should be simple to understand and user friendly. The data should not require large amounts of time to collect, and its collection should be cost effective as well. Companies should only keep track of those metrics that provide results they intend to use. The metrics need to be reproducible and allow for comparison of results. Often times the data needs to be normalized, which can be done through the use of ratios.

MATERIAL METRICS   One of the simplest metrics that is usually proposed is the proportion of material included in the product based on the amount of raw material consumed. This has been described as the mass index (24) or the material intensity (25) and can simply be calculated as

$$S = \frac{\text{mass in the product}}{\text{mass of the raw materials}}. \qquad 1.$$

As an alternative, one may consider the mass of material in the waste stream, and define the "E-factor" as the amount of material in the by-product relative to the amount in the product (26, 27). When either concept is reduced to an atomic level, the metric is generally described as "atom utilization" or "atom economy" (28), which simply relates the mass of atoms in the reaction products relative to the mass of atoms in the raw materials.

The challenge of comparing various elements of a process through different metrics has led to several techniques that combine environmental metrics into a single quantifiable number. One example is the potential environmental impact (PEI) used in the Waste Reduction (WAR) algorithm (29), which attempts to describe the significance of an environmental release in terms of its impact on the ecosystem. The WAR algorithm uses a specific measure of environmental impact; for example, the LD_{50} of a specific chemical normalizes this value and attempts to calculate the ecotoxicity of an entire chemical process (30). A series of PEI indices is calculated. The algorithm can also determine the impact of energy utilization by calculating the PEI of the effluents from the energy production processes and adding them to the PEI for the chemical process (31). In addition, the WAR algorithm can be applied to nonchemical processes, such as the service industry, depending on how one defines the various inputs and outputs of the process (32). Although the WAR algorithm can be used to evaluate the PEIs from candidate chemical processes for the selection of the most environmentally friendly process, the output of the calculation is a set of numbers with limited physical significance.

ENERGY METRICS   The production of energy remains one of the most significant processes in society today, and it still heavily relies on the use of nonrenewable hydrocarbon resources. Petroleum remains the primary energy source, related to the increase of automobile usage within the United States (see Figure 4, see color insert). However, if we look strictly at the electricity generation sector, coal is by far the dominant energy source, whereas the nonutility producers rely heavily on natural gas. Despite calls for greater use of renewable resources, their use as a fuel (on a percentage basis) has actually declined and makes up only 5% of energy use in the United States today.

A complete analysis of the impact of a process must include the environmental impact of the energy used within that process. As a result, another metric frequently used is the energy intensity (or efficiency) of the process. However, energy utilization is harder to measure than is material usage and often must be calculated for a process, rather than for a single chemical reaction. One appropriate measure is the energy usage (BTU or kJ) per amount of product in the exit stream (25), which can also be applied for a commercial chemical process (24). In some calculations, for example the sustainable process index (34), the energy requirement is simply converted to the amount of raw material consumed to produce the energy needed to operate the process. This conversion may be embedded within the calculation of the metric or may be a separate calculation that is combined into an overall measure further along the process.

Combination of energy and mass metrics can also be envisioned. For example, the thermodynamics community has turned to a new function termed "exergy," which attempts to characterize the combined energy and entropy affects of a process through rigorous thermodynamic variables. Generally speaking, the exergy of a material is the amount of useful work that can be derived from the material, and it is related to the material in relation to its place in the environment (35) or the entropy of the resulting product coupled with the energy required to produce that product from its component parts. In principle, exergy analysis provides a means of calculating the environmental impact of a process by evaluating the state of the raw materials and the undesired products (36), and it clearly combines both energy and material use into the calculation of environmental effectiveness. In practice however, exergy analysis must be integrated over the life cycle of the product to fully incorporate the environmental impacts of all of the life stages of a particular system (37).

SUSTAINABILITY METRICS   In recent years, sustainable development has been embraced as an underlying business practice. Sustainable development has many definitions, but each possesses the same basic theme that everyone accepts: providing for human needs without compromising the ability of future generations to meet their needs. Generally, sustainability can be described in terms of three simultaneous measures (38):

- economic indicators that track the costs and business aspects of the process,
- social indicators that track matters of human health and social welfare, and
- natural or ecological indicators that look at the depletion of natural capital through material and energy use or loss of biodiversity.

Another version of this same concept is ecoefficiency, which is described as business activities that create economic value while reducing ecological impact and resource usage. Ecoefficiency strives to create more value with less impact;

it enables more efficient production processes and the creation of better products and services. Thus, ecoefficiency is calculated as

ecoefficiency = economic indicator/environmental indicator

and incorporates two separate measures of performance; both of which must be measured separately and consistently.

Economic indicators must go beyond conventional financial reporting to describe the creation of wealth and its distribution and reinvestment for future growth. One example of an economic indicator is the value added by the operation. This is defined as the value of sales less the cost of goods, raw materials (including energy), and services purchased (39). Indicators of social performance reflect the company's attitude to treatment of its own employees, suppliers, contractors, and customers and also its impact on society. Examples of social performance indicators may include keeping track of promotion rates and lost time accident frequency (39).

Beyond these more conventional measures of performance, researchers are now defining sustainability metrics that attempt to combine measures of performance from each of the various dimensions of sustainability into a single parameter. As an example, Rees first introduced the concept of ecological footprint in 1996 as a measure of the amount of land area required to support the lifestyle of the average citizen; it takes into account the consumption of both natural resources and energy (40). In a similar fashion, Spangenberg (41) describes the "prism of sustainability" as a graphical tool that locates a process within a four-dimensional sustainability framework. Thus, the method of environmental space requires calculating the performance of a process separately for each dimension. Different choices of environmental performance metrics can be used depending on the system that is being evaluated. For example, in one study, urban sustainability was measured in terms of air quality (based on ground-level ozone), transportation (percentage of housing within 350 m of public transportation), urban ecology (availability of open space), and similar measures (42).

APPLYING GREEN CHEMISTRY: A HYDROFORMYLATION CASE STUDY

Although traditional manufactured goods (such as the automobile) have a significant environmental impact during the product use and disposal stages, chemical products generate a substantial portion of the hazardous materials that are present in the environment during the manufacturing stage. As a result, improvements in the chemical process through the implementation of green chemistry have the opportunity to impact the generation of hazardous materials during the manufacturing stage (43). According to the Vision 2020 report, "Catalysis-based chemical syntheses account for 60 percent of today's chemical products and 90 percent of current chemical processes." Thus, the following discussion of green chemistry concepts focuses on catalytic systems and, in particular, the design and development of catalysts to improve the yield or selectivity of the desired product or to minimize the need for catalyst recovery steps.

There is a tendency to focus on a single chemical reaction, but it is important to describe how changes in chemistry propagate throughout the chemical process. Modifications in a single reaction step can impact post-processing steps. For example, a change in the reaction solvent will impact not only the reactor design and product separation train, but it may also affect the energy usage required to achieve that separation and the heat exchanger design. An analysis of the environmental performance of the overall system must be completed to evaluate the benefits of a proposed process change (44), much like an LCA of a manufactured good must be completed to assess the improvements to its environmental performance brought about through a design change.

We have selected the hydroformylation reaction as a case study in which we describe the opportunities for green chemistry in reactive processes. Many of the concepts will be generally applicable to other reactive systems, although not all reactions will benefit equally from any proposed process change. In fact, a detailed analysis of the environmental implications through an appropriate process simulator (and metrics—such as the WAR algorithm described previously) should be completed in order to understand the benefits and drawbacks of any proposed change.

Hydroformylation is a particularly appropriate reaction to consider, because it accounts for the production of over 1 billion pounds of product per year, a large portion of which results from conversion of propene to butanal (45, 46). The resulting butanal is hydrogenated to 1-butanol and self-condensed, hydrogenated, and oxidized to give 2-ethylhexanol and 2-ethylhexanoic acid, which are used as solvents and for conversion to plasticizers. Hydroformylation of long-chain alkenes has significant impact on the production of fatty alcohols and esters for use in detergents, lubricants, and plasticizers. There is also a growing market for specialty chemicals produced via asymmetric hydroformylation of alkenes with applications of the resulting aldehydes in pharmaceuticals, fragrances, and pesticides production (47–49).

Commercial hydroformylation processes possess certain drawbacks that have been targeted for improvement. Originally developed by Union Carbide, the process was carried out in a homogeneous phase in which the catalyst was dissolved in the organic feed/product mixture. The Ruhrchemie and Rhone-Poulenc (RCH-RP) process, shown schematically in Figure 5*a* (see color insert) (50), was commercialized to eliminate the dependence on organic solvents and utilizes an aqueous system instead. This process has good catalyst stability, high yields, excellent energy integration, and good regioselectivities (normal:iso) as applied to propene and butene, but it cannot be extended to higher alkenes because of the very low solubility of the alkene in water.

There are several reasons for applying green chemical principles to the hydroformylation process.

- Simplifying the catalyst recovery step will reduce energy consumption in the process, the third level of pollution prevention. In addition, recycle of the catalyst could be made more effective.
- Catalyst immobilization would completely eliminate the need for catalyst recovery and reduce the amount of toxic material contained in the waste stream.
- Replacement of the organic solvent with a benign solvent would minimize toxic emissions and result in a source reduction, the highest level of pollution prevention at the top of the pyramid in Figure 1.

Each of these process modifications must be considered in terms of its implication to the overall process through appropriate use of life cycle and process analysis. The discussion below highlights some of the efforts that have been employed to improve the hydroformylation process that reduces the releases of hazardous materials to the environment and/or decreases energy consumption. Because the changes in the chemistry impact multiple steps in the process, multiple changes are often considered simultaneously.

Multiphase Systems That Simplify Catalyst Recovery

Successful operation of a homogeneously catalyzed process requires recovery and recycle of catalysts for economic operation. If one examines a detailed process flow sheet for hydroformylation following the RCH-RP process, it is found that half of the unit operations deal with separating the catalyst from the crude product stream. Water must be added to induce a phase separation and then must be recovered from the catalyst recycle stream before it is returned to the reactor. Thus, the catalyst recovery step is seen as a large consumer of energy (without increasing the product yield) and a contributor to the release of hazardous materials to the environment. Energy consumption can be substantially reduced if the catalyst recovery can be simplified; for example, using a phase separation carried out in a decanter, rather than through distillation or extraction processes. As a result, multiphase processes have been developed in which the catalyst is constrained in one phase and the reactants are located in a separate phase. The process schematic is then modified according to Figure 5*b* (see color insert). Optimization of the phase behavior is a thermodynamic task that provides maximum interfacial area within the reactor but ease and completeness of separation in the decanter.

Two-phase hydroformylation systems have been evaluated for their ability to simplify catalyst recovery while simultaneously facilitating the interaction of the catalyst and the substrate. In each case, a nonorganic phase is used to dissolve the catalyst, and the substrate acts as both an organic solvent and a reactant. This process concept provides some source reduction (because no additional organic solvents are employed in the catalyst recovery) and has substantial opportunity to reduce the overall energy consumption in the process. Examples based on biphasic aqueous, fluorous, and ionic liquid systems are described below.

Aqueous biphasic hydroformylation is dependent on mass transport and reaction conditions (temperature, partial pressures of gases, and stirring) as well as the type of substrate. The reaction usually takes place at the organic-aqueous interface. The more common, water-soluble, phosphine-based ligands are arylphosphines with polar functional groups ($-SO_3^-$, $-CO_2^-$, $-NR_3^+$) attached to the aryl rings (51). These types of ligands increased rates of hydroformylation for water-insoluble substrates. The addition of surfactants [also called amphiphiles or tensides (e.g., ammonium salts)] is useful when substrates are totally water insoluble (52). The cationic surfactant favored the formation of micelles (53), which promoted the substrate transfer to the interface between the aqueous and organic phases and coordination with the rhodium complexes.

In order to increase the surface area of the interface between the organic and aqueous phases, Arhancet and coworkers supported their aqueous phase catalyst throughout a high-surface area hydrophilic support (such as silica) (54). The water-soluble catalyst was dissolved in the thin aqueous layer on the surface of silica and remained near the surface of the support to form a heterogeneous system. The thickness of the water layer could be optimized to allow mobility of the complex and enable the reaction between the catalyst precursor and the olefinic substrate.

Along a similar line, dendrimeric catalyst systems are comprised of high molecular weight materials that may be dissolved in solution under reaction conditions (and thus appear to be homogeneous) but can easily be precipitated and separated following the reaction (55, 56). An active metal species and an appropriate ligand can be attached to the dendrimer to impart catalytic activity to the species. The dendrimers are highly branched and enable the formation of catalysts with a precise distribution of the catalytic sites, have tunable properties, and are easily separated from the reaction products by precipitation and microporous membrane filtration. The green aspect of this new type of support comes from the simple purification, vacuum filtration, and solvent washing that remove excess reagents and separate the dendrimers from the products.

The separation of homogeneous catalysts based on Ru^{2+}, Co^{2+}, or Mn^{2+} complexes requires a lot of energy and may involve the thermal decomposition of the catalyst. This problem can be solved via two-phase homogeneous fluorocarbon biphasic catalysis using a fluorocarbon solvent modified with long perfluoroalkyl chains as demonstrated by Horváth & Rabai (57). These systems employ a fluorous solvent in which the catalyst and reactant can be dissolved and a second phase in which the products are preferentially soluble. The two phases form a homogeneous phase at high temperature, whereas they are well separated at room temperature. This process is attractive in terms of separation of homogeneous catalysts or reagents, and because the fluorous solvents appear to be nontoxic, their use in reactions provides entry into the realm of green chemistry (58). Many reactions beside hydroformylation are compatible with the use of fluorous biphasic systems, including hydrogenation (59), hydride reduction (60), hydroboration (61), alkene epoxidation (62), and alkane and alkene functionalization (63).

Another solvent that permits two phase operations is the class of room temperature ionic liquids, which are conventionally defined as ionic salts that melt at a temperature below 100°C. Ionic liquids are generally considered to be environmentally friendly because they contain no vapor pressure, but other environmental implications of ionic liquids remain unknown. However, homogeneous catalysts may not be thermally stable during product recovery by distillation, and the presence of by-products with high-boiling points deactivates the catalyst. Nonvolatile ionic liquids, such as those based on the 1-butyl-3-methyl-imidazolium cation (BMIM), stabilize the catalysts during distillation, and the catalyst can be reused several times with no loss of activity (64–66). To minimize catalyst degradation due to heating, recovery of the product may be accomplished by extraction with water (67), ether (68), or supercritical carbon dioxide (scCO$_2$) (66, 69). Although traditional ionic liquids consist of halogen-containing anions, which include for example [AlCl$_4$]$^-$ and [PF$_6$]$^-$ (species that would generally not be considered environmentally friendly), new materials are now being developed based on organic anions, such as [n-C$_8$H$_{17}$OSO$_3$]$^-$ (70). This anion is halogen free and possesses strong hydrolysis stability, which circumvents the problem of halide waste.

Catalyst Immobilization

Heterogeneous catalysis involves supported catalysts, which completely eliminates the need for a separation and recovery step, as shown in Figure 5c (see color insert). In many cases, however, the decreased energy usage (because catalyst recovery is not required) and the reduction in source emissions are balanced by a reduced selectivity in the reaction. When this occurs, it is important to consider the overall environmental impacts of the process, rather than just evaluating the benefits obtained from the use of a heterogeneous catalyst. In addition, for a heterogeneous system, the catalyst must not leach into the solvent phase, and sufficient rates of transport must occur to allow the reagents to migrate to the active sites on the catalysts. Several examples of advances in the design of heterogeneous catalysts are detailed.

Polymer-supported catalysts have been used since the early 1960s but are still the subject of improvement and numerous publications. Much research has been devoted to the immobilization of metal complexes on organic polymers, such as cross-linked polystyrene (71). The advantages of a cross-linked polymer are the ability to modify the degree of cross-linking to tune the physical properties of the polymer and its easy functionalization. However, polymeric supports exhibit poor heat transfer ability and poor mechanical properties. They are also dependent on the reaction solvent because only some solvents cause the polymers to swell. Another problem is the leaching of metal from the polymer, which results in deactivation of the catalyst. These drawbacks can be partially eliminated if the catalyst precursors are covalently anchored on inorganic supports.

Silica, alumina, carbon nanotubes, and zeolites have been used as inorganic supports for catalyst precursors in hydroformylation (72). Silica supports are usually more mechanically stable and resistant against aging, solvents, and high temperatures than are organic polymeric supports. An alternative method to the impregnation technique is the use of sol-gel condensation methods to prepare the supports (73–75). The incorporation of the metal complex is achieved by stirring a mixture of the metal complex and the phosphinated support in aqueous ethanol under nitrogen. This is a waste-free one-pot synthesis in aqueous alcohol solution, which is a truly green process. This procedure enables a stronger coordination of the phosphine support to the metal complex, decreases considerably the leaching of metal during hydroformylation reaction in our case, and is consistent with the principles of green chemistry.

The green manufacture of catalysts for important organic reactions is based on the micelle-templated silicas and mesoporous high surface area support materials, which provide easy separation of the catalyst from organic components and high turnover numbers (76). The synthesis of micelle-templated silicas based on the neutral templating method offers many advantages, such as the simple washing for separation and the easy recovery and reuse of the template—truly a green mechanism. In 1992, Beck and coworkers at Mobil Corporation discovered a new family of silicate/aluminosilicate mesoporous molecular sieves M 41S with pore diameters varying between 2 and 50 nm (77). The synthesis of M 41S molecular sieves is based on surfactant/silicate solution chemistry. Contrary to the synthesis of zeolites, the template agent is not a single, solvated organic molecule or metal ion but is a surfactant with alkyl chain lengths varying from 8 (octyltrimethylammonium bromide) to 16 carbon atoms (cetyltrimethylammonium bromide). The dimensions of the carbon chain length determine the pore size of the mesoporous material. These supports offer thermal and chemical stability during reaction processes and enhanced accessibility and dispersion of active sites. The controlled pore size of these mesoporous materials is efficient for the control of molecular diffusion and product selectivity, which improves the performance of the MCM-supported catalysts and again reflects the principles of green chemistry (78, 79).

Benign Solvents

The first step in green chemistry is to eliminate waste at the source. Thus, the replacement of an organic solvent with a benign material represents a pollution prevention goal. This has already been done in the case of hydroformylation, which used water as a solvent in the commercial RCH-RP process. However, water is not a suitable solvent for higher alkenes because the low solubility leads to a reaction rate that is too slow to be economically viable. Thus, alternative solvents must be considered that provide a greater solubility for the reactants and catalysts.

One such example is supercritical carbon dioxide (scCO$_2$), an environmentally benign solvent that can be used as a replacement for many organic solvents. The beneficial properties of scCO$_2$ originate from the high diffusivity of solutes in the solvent combined with its low viscosity, which minimize gas-liquid mass transfer restrictions near the critical point (T$_c$ = 31.1°C and P$_c$ = 73.8 atm). Carbon

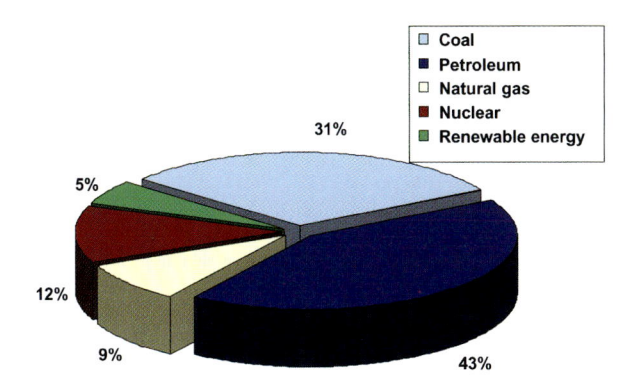

Figure 4 Distribution of energy production, which represents 66.9×10^{15} BTU in 2001 (33).

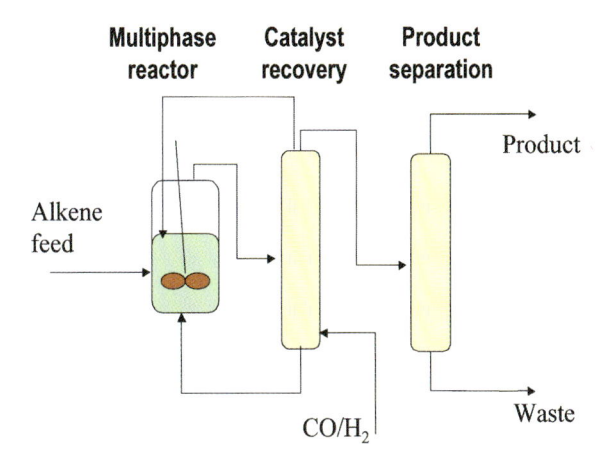

Figure 5a Schematic diagram of the hydroformylation process commercially utilized by Ruhrchemie and Rhone-Poulenc (RCH-RP).

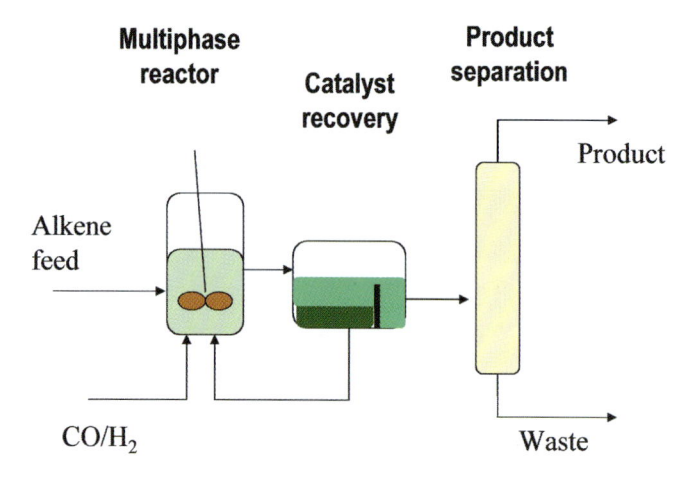

Figure 5b Schematic diagram of a modified hydroformylation process based on a biphasic reaction system.

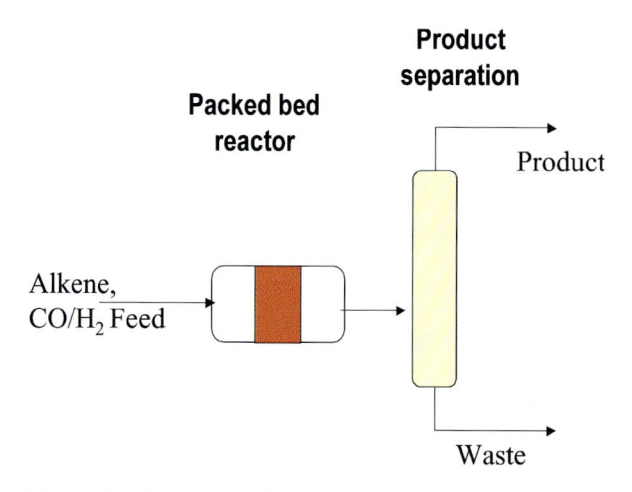

Figure 5c Schematic diagram of a modified hydroformylation process based on an immobilized catalyst.

GREEN CHEMISTRY   C-3

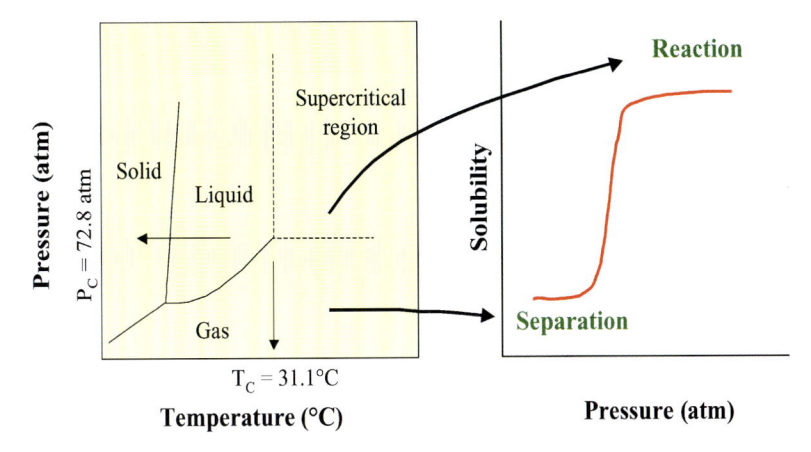

Figure 6 Schematic diagram illustrating the use of a supercritical fluid for a reaction and separation process.

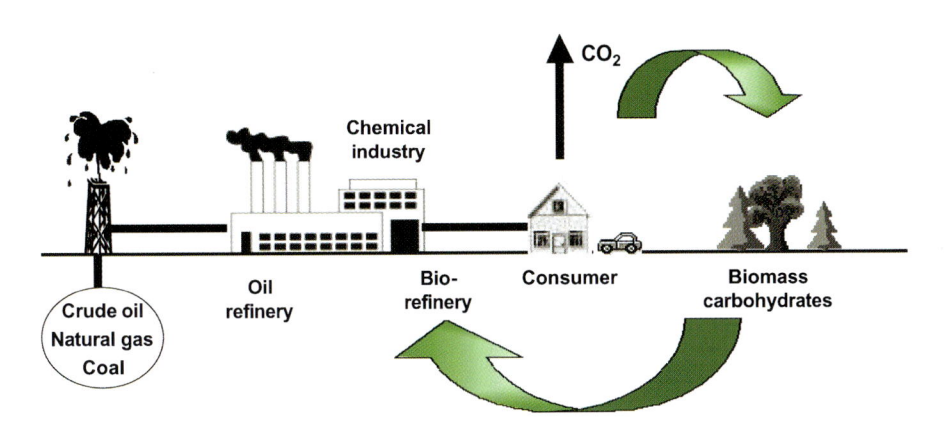

Figure 7 Sketch of the new economy based on biomass-derived chemicals [after (106)].

dioxide has been identified as a greenhouse gas, but its use as a solvent, as opposed to its production (e.g., by automobiles or in power generation), is considered to be environmentally benign. CO_2 is nontoxic, does not form air-polluting daughter products, and, additionally, is cheap and plentiful.

Numerous advantages are derived from the unique properties of supercritical CO_2. In homogeneous hydroformylation, control of the phase behavior, dissolution of the catalyst precursors, recovery of homogeneous catalysts by precipitation, and tunability of reaction rates and selectivities can be accomplished by applying small changes in temperature and pressure conditions. Solubility of the catalyst in $scCO_2$ is a critical parameter with homogeneous catalysts. To produce catalysts with sufficient solubility, different options are available. The more common approach is ligand modification. The addition of a cosolvent or, for charged complexes, the use of a suitable counter ion are other ways to enhance the solubility of catalysts.

Many catalytic reactions have been performed in $scCO_2$, such as hydrogenation of olefins, asymmetric hydrogenation of olefins and imines, hydroformylation of olefins and related carbonylation reactions, metal-catalyzed carbon-carbon bond formation, and oxidation reaction (80). Reviews have already been published by Jessop and coworkers on homogeneous catalysis in supercritical fluids (81). Important developments in homogeneous hydroformylation are now centered on the use of perfluoroalkyl-substituted arylphosphines as ligands for rhodium-catalyzed hydroformylation of higher alkenes (82, 83) and modified phosphite ligands to increase the activities and regioselectivities toward aldehyde production (84).

In heterogeneous hydroformylation, enhancement of the reaction rate, control of the selectivity, ease of product separation, catalyst regeneration, and longer catalyst lifetime are provided using $scCO_2$. Much of the behavior of the catalyst can be attributed to the methods used in its preparation. Dharmidhikari & Abraham prepared rhodium catalysts encapsulated in activated carbon and observed limited activity and deactivation due to slow adsorption of propene (85). In 2001, Snyder et al. used sol-gel-prepared functionalized silica supports for hydroformylation of propene in $scCO_2$ (86). The incipient wetness method was used to prepare the catalysts with [Rh(acac)$_3$] as the rhodium precursor. They demonstrated that the modification of the silica supports led to enhanced reaction rates but did not affect considerably the selectivity. Leaching was a serious problem as well as the rapid deactivation of the catalyst.

In 2000, Meehan and coworkers presented the results of hydroformylation of 1-octene in $scCO_2$ using a continuous process (87). It was the first time that such a heterogeneous system combining high activity and selectivity in a continuous flow reactor was described. In 2002, the hydroformylation of 1-hexene using silica-supported rhodium catalysts was performed in $scCO_2$ (73, 86). An increase in the pressure led to greater reactivity, but the regioselectivity was not substantially influenced at a constant conversion. The heterogeneously catalyzed hydroformylation of 1-hexene was also performed in liquid-phase toluene, and toluene expanded with CO_2 (75). Comparable reaction rates were obtained using $scCO_2$ and toluene expanded with CO_2 and was superior to the reaction rate obtained in liquid-phase toluene. The selectivity was the highest in $scCO_2$. The performance of the heterogeneous catalyst was also compared to that obtained with the homogeneous analog. The overall rate of aldehyde formation was the highest with the homogeneous catalyst in liquid-phase toluene. The initial regioselectivity was higher with the heterogeneous catalyst in $scCO_2$ but decreased over the course of the reaction. Overall, the performance of the heterogeneous catalyst in $scCO_2$ was superior to that obtained with the homogeneous analog in liquid toluene for hydroformylation of 1-hexene.

The use of $scCO_2$ as a reaction solvent not only allows for a reduction in source emissions, but it could also impact the energy requirements by simplifying the product separation train. Because of its tunable solvent properties, some product/reactant separations could be achievable by manipulating pressure (Figure 6, see color insert). For example, Poliakoff (87) reported a 90% recovery of substrate (1-octene) from reaction products (nonanals) by use of a two-stage depressurization.

In a commercial process, the $scCO_2$ stream could be reduced in pressure following the reactor to release the products, and a high pressure solvent/reactant stream could be recycled at lower compressor costs. For a process reacting at 2700 psig and separating at 2000 psig, the compression ratio is 1.35. A complete depressurization to atmospheric pressure would be possible (albeit not economical), but it would not be required. Overall, a decrease in fixed capital would be expected, even allowing for compression requirements, because at least one if not two extraction operations for catalyst recovery would be eliminated. Evaluation of the overall impacts of this process must include the energy consumption associated with solvent compression relative to the reduced energy consumption resulting from the simplified product separation.

SUSTAINABILITY ENGINEERING

Sustainability would be the ultimate achievement for the successful application of green chemistry. According to Collins, "The underlying theme and hope of green chemistry is that chemists can divert technology from paths that run nature down and exhaust its bounty to new courses that promote the vitality of nature and the sustainability of our civilization" (88). This philosophy, first formally proposed by the Brundtland Commission in 1987, states, "Sustainable Development meets the needs of the present without compromising the ability of future generations to meet their own needs" (89) and is now widely accepted.

Since the Brundtland report, a great amount of literature has been generated to define sustainability practices, measures, and accounting (90, 91). Using the concept of the triple bottom line, corporations have started to consider the interaction of economic, environmental, and social matters (92) when making business decisions. As a result, new engineering methods are being developed to account for depletion of natural capital and to measure the ecoefficiency of the design (93). Thus, a complete process design now incorporates the environmental implications of a product or process throughout its life cycle (94). Despite the assertion of business interest, and 16 years of intense effort since Brundtland, there are very few reports of successful application of sustainability in industry (95). However, the concepts of green chemistry and engineering have provided incremental progress toward the sustainability goal, as described in the following paragraphs.

One of the challenges of green chemistry is to provide renewable energy. Currently, the world operates predominantly on carbon extracted from the Earth's nonrenewable resources. Production of renewable energy includes opportunities such as wind and hydropower (96), which are potentially sustainable, but because of limitations in location and reliability, they have not become widely used. Recent interest has primarily involved the development of fuel cells and solar energy.

Fuel cells hold the promise for the generation of energy for both mobile and stationary usages, are 50% more efficient than the best current commercial alternatives for energy production, and produce largely inert by-products. Carrette et al. (97) provide an extensive overview of fuel cells. Current fuel cell research has emphasized developing efficient proton exchange membranes (PEM) that can operate in a wide range of environments and efficient generation of hydrogen for fuel. Other types of fuel cells, which include phosphoric acid (PAFC), molten carbonate (MCFC), and solid oxide (SOFC), have also been evaluated for specific opportunities, but they are more limited because of the inherent size of the system. Regardless, all fuel cells require a clean source of hydrogen.

In the near term (5–25 years), commercially available hydrocarbon resources will likely be used to generate hydrogen for fuel cell operations, with a gradual transition to hydrogen generation from bio-based fuels. Ghenciu (98) reviews the use of catalysts in the production of hydrogen for fuel cells, and Joensen & Rostrup-Nielsen (99) review the conversion of carbon-based fuels for fuel cell applications. Paglieri & Way (100) provide an extensive review of the use of palladium membranes for the purification of the gas product stream to produce a clean hydrogen product. Ultimately (>25 years), solar energy may be harnessed to produce hydrogen from water, and fuel cell technology may become a truly sustainable energy source.

Current commercial use of solar energy usually requires conversion to either thermal or electric energy, followed by storage in a chemical form. Würfel (101) discussed the thermodynamic limitations in converting solar energy, and Zalba et al. (102) reviewed chemical methods of storing thermal energy. Steinfeld (103) demonstrated a Zn/ZnO solar cell system for producing hydrogen. Green (104) discussed modern photovoltaic based on thin film silicon chemistries and the development of photovoltaic ceramics and nanostructured devices.

The development of renewable feedstocks, the second green chemistry challenge, has focused on the use of biomass. Biomass includes, but is not limited to, agricultural by-products, such as plant cellulose, and dairy wastes, such as cheese whey and cow manure. Biomass is highly available and renewable. The conversion of biomass into chemicals requires several steps (105). Danner & Braun (106) elucidate the opportunities for conversion of biomass and biomass wastes into chemicals, proposing a new economy in which biomass feedstocks replace petroleum (see Figure 7, see color insert). Conversion begins with the degradation of biomass into soluble fractions (hydrolysis), continues with primary conversion of soluble oligomeric mixtures into chemical precursors, and concludes with the upgrading of the precursor species into specific chemical products. As an example, starch can be converted to glucose, which is in turn transformed, either chemically or enzymatically, into a large spectrum of products that can be used as precursors to nutritive sweeteners, surfactants, pharmaceuticals, polymers, and other materials (107).

Strategies for the use of renewable materials include converting agricultural products into chemical precursors, generating energy, and creating structural materials. For example, Embree et al. (108) discuss the potential of creating oxygenated aromatic chemicals from lignin and plant tanin and identify a need for improvements in separation technology. A demonstration plant owned by the Biofine Corporation has been developed and operated to convert paper mill sludge, urban waste paper, agricultural residues, and cellulose fines from papermaking into levulinic acid (109). Conversion of biomass into hydrogen is also technically feasible (although not yet economically viable) and represents a minor extension of the conceptual biorefinery. MacKendry (110), in a three-part article, discusses the production of fuel feedstocks based on the gasification of biomass. Production of chemicals and energy may be combined, because energy can be produced as a by-product of chemical production, or vice versa (111), depending upon the conversion processes selected.

In the area of structural materials, Mohanty et al. (112) proposed the use of biocomposites based on biopolymers; these include cellulosic plastics, polylactides, starch plastics, polyhydroxyalkanoates (bacterial polyesters), and soy-based plastics. Alternatively, Hermann et al. (113) describe the incorporation of natural fibers into conventional polymeric composite materials. Recently, the Cargill-Dow process for the production of polylactide was described (114). It is instructive to note that the development of this process began in 1987 and was only recently commercialized, which indicates the length of time required for sustainable processes to emerge in the chemical industry.

Although there are very few specific examples of sustainability in industry, it is still too early to evaluate the success or failure of green chemistry and engineering in meeting sustainability goals. Mulholland et al. (115) point out that the chemical industry is working to reduce waste generation, minimize the impact of chemicals and chemical processes on the environment and the public, and minimize any hazards of chemical processes to the workers. In addition, innovative technologies have been developed that contribute to improving both the environmental and economic corporate bottom line (116). The development of innovative environmental catalysts can also be viewed as a crucial factor toward the development of a new sustainable industrial chemistry (117).

Green chemistry and engineering provide the technical basis for sustainability and are necessary (but not sufficient) for a sustainable society. Technical issues involving material and energy efficiency, ecosystem viability, and water conservation are being addressed by researchers, and solutions are slowly finding their way into industrial activity. Incremental change has occurred frequently, and occasionally, evolutionary change is seen. The development of new products and processes that are based on renewable resources are forthcoming, and new analysis tools to measure the environmental impact of a product or process are under development. Although there is substantial research activity in many areas that can impact the road to sustainability, there is no technology on the immediate horizon that will allow a prognostication of success.

The *Annual Review of Environment and Resources* is online at
http://environ.annualreviews.org

LITERATURE CITED

1. Anastas PT, Warner JC. 1998. *Green Chemistry Theory and Practice*, p 7. New York: Oxford Univ. Press. 152 pp.
2. Anastas PT, Zimmerman JB. 2003. Design through the 12 principles of green engineering. *Environ. Sci. Technol.* 37(5): A94–101
3. Wei J, Cussler EL. 2003. Chemical engineers are key to product engineering. *AIChE J.* 49(5):1072
4. Allen DT, Rosselot KS. 1997. *Pollution Prevention for Chemical Processes*. New York: Wiley. 434 pp.
5. Thornton J. 2001. Implementing green chemistry. An environmental policy for sustainability. *Pure Appl. Chem.* 73(8): 1231–36
6. Reinert KH. 2001. Integrating green chemistry and sustainability into a specialty chemical company. *Pure Appl. Chem.* 73(8):1269–72
7. Brandt C. 2002. Sustainable development and responsible care-chemical industry headed for a green future? *Chem. Unserer Zeit* 36(4):214–24
8. Graedel T. 1999. Green chemistry in an industrial ecology context. *Green Chem.* 1(5):126–28
9. Allen DT, Butner RS. 2002. Industrial ecology: a chemical engineering challenge. *Chem. Eng. Prog.* 98(11):40–45
10. Herrchen M, Klein W. 2000. Use of the life-cycle assessment (LCA) toolbox for an environmental evaluation of production processes. *Pure Appl. Chem.* 72(7):1247–52
11. Fava J, Denison R, Jones B, Curran M, Vigon B. 1991. *Technical Framework for Life Cycle Assessment*. Pensacola, FL: Soc. Environ. Toxicol. Chem.
12. Graedl TE, Allenby BR. 1995. *Industrial Ecology*. Englewood Cliffs, NJ: Prentice-Hall. 384 pp.
13. Keoleian GA, Kar K, Manion MM, Bulkley JW. 1997. *Industrial Ecology of the Automobile*. Warrendale, PA: Soc. Automot. Eng.
14. Sullivan JL, Williams RL, Yester S, Cobas-Flores E, Chubbs ST, Hentges SG, Pomper SD. 1998. *Life cycle assessment of a generic U.S. family sedan, overview of results USCAR AMP Project in SAE P-339*. Pap. SAE 982160. Presented at Total Life Cycle Conf. Proc., Warrendale, PA
15. Owens JW. 1997. Life cycle assessment in relation to risk assessment: an evolving perspective. *Risk Anal.* 17(3):359–66
16. Olson W, Abraham M. 2000. When is green really green? A pilot investigation of the time effects using LCA data. SAE 2000-01-1494/SAE P-353. *Proc. SAE Total Life Cycle Conf.*, pp. 213–23, Detroit, MI
17. Thiel C. 2000. *Comparative life cycle*

assessment of aluminum and steel bumper carriers. Presented at Total Life Cycle Conf., Detroit, MI
18. Cascio J, Baughn KT. 2000. Health safety, and ISO 14001. *Manuf. Eng.* 124(5):126–35
19. Herrchen M. 1998. Perspective of the systematic and extended use of temporal and spatial aspects of LCA of long lived products. *Chemosphere* 37(2):265–70
20. Grimberg KJ, Greener CS. 2003. Sustainability Mapping Tool. SAE 2003-01-0548/SAE SP-1788. *Proc. Sustain. Environ. Syst. Mater.*, pp. 1–44
21. Hersey K. 1998. A close look at ISO 14000. *Prof. Saf.* 43(7):26–29
22. Bhat VN. 1999. Does it pay to be green? *Int. J. Environ. Stud. A,B* 56(4):497–508
23. Eissen M, Metzger JO. 2001. Environmental performance metrics for daily use in synthetic chemistry. *Chem.-Eur. J.* 8(16):3580–85
24. Constable DJC, Curzons AD, dos Santos LMF, Green GR, Hannah RE. 2001. Green chemistry measures for process research and development. *Green Chem.* 3(1):7–9
25. Schwarz J, Beloff B, Beaver E. 2002. Use sustainability metrics to guide decision-making. *Chem. Eng. Prog.* 98(7):58–63
26. Sheldon RA. 1997. Catalysis: the key to waste minimization. *J. Chem. Technol. Biotechnol.* 68(4):381–88
27. Sheldon RA. 2000. Atom utilization, E factors and the catalytic solution. *C. R. Acad. Sci., Sér. II* 3:541–51
28. Trost BM. 1991. The atom economy: a search for synthetic efficiency. *Science* 254(5037):1471–77
29. Mallick SK, Cabezas H, Bare JC, Sikdar SK. 1996. A pollution prevention methodology for chemical process simulators. *Ind. Eng. Chem. Res.* 35(11):4128–38
30. Cabezas H, Bare JC, Mallick SK. 1997. Pollution prevention with chemical process simulators: the generalized waste reduction (WAR) algorithm. *Comput. Chem. Eng.* 21:S305–10
31. Young D, Scharp R, Cabezas H. 2000. The waste reduction (WAR) algorithm: environmental impacts, energy consumption, and engineering economics. *Waste Manag.* 20(8):605–15
32. Castillo EF, Mora M. 2000. Mathematical modelling as a tool for environmental evaluation of industrial sectors in Colombia. *Waste Manag.* 20(8):617–23
33. US Dep. Energy. *Energy Information Administration Home Page.* http://www.eia.doe.gov/
34. Narodoslawski N, Krotscheck C. 2000. Integrated ecological optimization of processes with the sustainable process index. *Waste Manag.* 20(8):599–603
35. Dewulf J, Van Langenhove H. 2002. Assessment of the sustainability of technology by means of a thermodynamically-based life cycle analysis. *Environ. Sci. Pollut. Res.* 9(4):267–73
36. Finnveden G, Ostlund P. 1997. Exergies of natural resources in life-cycle assessment and other applications. *Energy* 22(9):923–31
37. Bakshi BR. 2002. A thermodynamic framework for ecologically conscious process systems engineering. *Comput. Chem. Eng.* 26(2):269–82
38. Barrera-Roldan A, Saldivar-Valdes A. 2002. Proposal and application of a Sustainable Development Index. *Ecol. Indic.* 2:251–56
39. Sustain. Dev. Work. Group, Inst. Chem. Eng. 2001. *Sustainable Development Progress Metrics: Recommended for Use in the Process Industries*, Inst. Chem. Eng. Rugby, Warwickshire, UK, pp. 1–28
40. Palmer AR. 1999. Ecological footprints: evaluating sustainability. *Environ. Geosci.* 6(4):200–4
41. Spangenberg JJ. 2002. Environmental space and the prism of sustainability: frameworks for indicators measuring sustainable development. *Ecol. Indic.* 2:295–309
42. Shane AM, Graedel TE. 2000. Urban environmental sustainability metrics:

a provisional set. *J. Environ. Plan. Manag.* 43(5):643–63
43. Lankey RL, Anastas PT. 2002. Life-cycle approaches for assessing green chemistry technologies. *Ind. Eng. Chem. Res.* 41(18):4498–502
44. Graedel TE. 2001. Green chemistry as systems science. *Pure Appl. Chem.* 73(8): 1243–46
45. Reinius HK, Suomalainen P, Riihimaki H, Karvinen E, Pursiainen J, et al. 2001. o-Alkyl-substituted triphenyl phosphines: activity and regioselectivity in rhodium-catalyzed propene hydroformylation. *J. Catal.* 199(2):302–8
46. Karlsson M, Andersson C, Hjortkjaer J. 2001. Hydroformylation of propene and 1-hexene catalyzed by a α-zirconium phosphate supported rhodium-phosphine complex. *J. Mol. Catal. A-Chem.* 166(2): 337–43
47. Shibahara F, Nozaki K, Matsuo T, Hiyama T. 2002. Asymmetric hydroformylation with highly crosslinked polystyrene-supported (R,S)-BINAPHOS-Rh(I) complexes: the effect of immobilization position. *Bioorg. Med. Chem. Lett.* 12(14): 1825–27
48. Nozaki K, Shibahara F, Hiyama T. 2000. Vapor-phase asymmetric hydroformylation. *Chem. Lett.* (6):694–95
49. Lu S, Li X, Wang A. 2000. A new chiral diphosphine ligand and its asymmetric induction in catalytic hydroformylation of olefins. *Catal. Today* 63(2–4):531–36
50. van Leeuwen PWNM, Claver C. 2000. *Rhodium Catalyzed Hydroformylation*. Dordrecht, Ger.: Kluwer Acad.
51. Hanson BE. 1999. New directions in water soluble homogeneous catalysis. *Coord. Chem. Rev.* 185–186:795–807
52. Buhling A, Kamer PCJ, van Leeuwen PWNM. 1995. Rhodium-catalyzed hydroformylation of higher alkenes using amphiphilic ligands. *J. Mol. Catal. A-Chem.* 98(2):69–80
53. Chen H, Li YZ, Chen JR, Cheng PM, He YE, et al. 1999. Micellar effect in high olefin hydroformylation catalyzed by water-soluble rhodium complex. *J. Mol. Catal. A-Chem.* 149(1–2):1–6
54. Arhancet JP, Davis ME, Hanson BE. 1991. Supported aqueous-phase, rhodium hydroformylation catalysts. 2. Hydroformylation of linear, terminal and internal olefins. *J. Catal.* 129(1):100–5
55. Bourque SC, Alper H, Manzer LE, Arya P. 2000. Hydroformylation reactions using recyclable rhodium-complexed dendrimers on silica. *J. Am. Chem. Soc.* 122(5):956–57
56. de Groot D, Emmerink PG, Coucke C, Reek JNH, Kamer PCJ, et al. 2000. Rhodium catalysed hydroformylation using diphenylphosphine functionalised carbosilane dendrimers. *Inorg. Chem. Commun.* 3(12):711–13
57. Horváth IT, Rabai J. 1994. Facile catalyst separation without water-fluorous biphase hydroformylation of olefins. *Science* 266(5182):72–75
58. Fish RH. 1999. Fluorous biphasic catalysis: a new paradigm for the separation of homogeneous catalysts from their reaction substrates and products. *Chem.-Eur. J.* 5(6):1677–80
59. Rutherford D, Juliette JJJ, Rocaboy C, Horváth IT, Gladysz JA. 1998. Transition metal catalysis in fluorous media: application of a new immobilization principle to rhodium-catalyzed hydrogenation of alkenes. *Catal. Today* 42(4):381–88
60. Curran D, Hadida S. 1996. Tris(2-(perfluorohexyl)ethyl)tin hydride: a new fluorous reagent for use in traditional organic synthesis and liquid phase combinatorial synthesis. *J. Am. Chem. Soc.* 118(10):2531–32
61. Juliette JJJ, Rutherford D, Horváth IT, Gladysz JA. 1999. Transition metal catalysis in fluorous media: practical application of a new immobilization principle to rhodium-catalyzed hydroborations of alkenes and alkynes. *J. Am. Chem. Soc.* 121(12):2696–704
62. Pozzi G, Cinato F, Montanari F, Quici

S. 1998. Efficient aerobic epoxidation of alkenes in perfluorinated solvents catalysed by chiral (salen) Mn complexes. *Chem. Commun.* 8:877–78

63. Vincent JM, Rabion A, Yachandra VK, Fish RH. 1997. Fluorous biphasic catalysis: complexation of 1,4,7-[C$_8$F$_{17}$(CH$_2$)$_3$]$_3$-1,4,7-triazacyclononane with [M(C$_8$F$_{17}$(CH$_2$)$_2$CO$_2$)$_2$] (M = Mn, Co) to provide perfluoroheptane-soluble catalysis for alkane and alkene functionalization in the presence of t-BuOOH and O$_2$. *Angew. Chem.-Int. Ed. Engl.* 36(21):2346–49

64. Wasserscheid P, Waffenschmidt H. 2000. Ionic liquids in regioselective platinum-catalysed hydroformylation. *J. Mol. Catal. A-Chem.* 164(1–2):61–67

65. Wasserscheid P, Waffenschmidt H, Machnitzki P, Kottsieper KW, Stelzer O. 2001. Cationic phosphine ligands with phenylguanidinium modified xanthene moieties—a successful concept for highly regioselective, biphasic hydroformylation of oct-1-ene in hexafluorophosphate ionic liquids. *Chem. Commun.* 5:451–52

66. Sellin MF, Webb PB, Cole-Hamilton DJ. 2001. Continuous flow homogeneous catalysis: hydroformylation of alkenes in supercritical fluid-ionic liquid biphasic mixtures. *Chem. Commun.* 8:781–82

67. Huddleston J, Willauer H, Swatloski R, Visser A, Rogers R. 1998. Room temperature ionic liquids as novel media for 'clean' liquid-liquid extraction. *Chem. Commun.* 16:1765–66

68. Mizushima E, Hayashi T, Tanaka M. 2001. Palladium-catalysed carbonylation of aryl halides in ionic liquid media: high catalyst stability and significant rate-enhancement in alkoxycarbonylation. *Green Chem.* 3(2):76–79

69. Blanchard LA, Gu ZY, Brennecke JF. 2001. High-pressure phase behavior of ionic liquid/CO$_2$ systems. *J. Phys. Chem. B* 105(12):2437–44

70. Wasserscheid P, van Hal R, Bosman A. 2002. 1-n-Butyl-3-methylimidazolium ([bmim]) octylsulfate-an even 'greener' ionic liquid. *Green Chem.* 4(4):400–4

71. McNamara CA, Dixon MJ, Bradley M. 2002. Recoverable catalysts and reagents using recyclable polystyrene-based supports. *Chem. Rev.* 102(10):3275–99

72. Iwasawa Y. 1986. Inorganic oxide-attached metal catalysts. In *Tailored Metal Catalysts*, Vol. 1, ed. Y Iwasawa, pp. 1–85. Dordrecht, Ger.: Reidel

73. Tadd AR, Marteel A, Mason MR, Davies JA, Abraham MA. 2003. Hydroformylation of 1-hexene in scCO$_2$ using a heterogeneous rhodium catalyst. 1. Effect of process parameters. *J. Supercrit. Fluids* 25(2):183–95

74. Tadd AR, Marteel A, Mason MR, Davies JA, Abraham MA. 2002. Hydroformylation of 1-hexene in supercritical carbon dioxide using a heterogeneous rhodium catalyst. 2. Evaluation of reaction kinetics. *Ind. Eng. Chem. Res.* 41(18):4514–22

75. Hemminger O, Marteel A, Mason MR, Davies JA, Tadd AR, et al. 2002. Hydroformylation of 1-hexene in supercritical carbon dioxide using a heterogeneous rhodium catalyst. 3. Evaluation of solvent effects. *Green Chem.* 4(5):507–12

76. Clark JH. 2002. Solid acids for green chemistry. *Acc. Chem. Res.* 35(9):791–97

77. Beck JS, Vartuli JC, Roth WJ, Leonowicz ME, Kresge CT, et al. 1992. A new family of mesoporous molecular-sieves prepared with liquid-crystal templates. *J. Am. Chem. Soc.* 114(27):10834–43

78. Marteel AE, Davies JA, Mason MR, Tadd A, Tack T. 2002. *Development of heterogeneous catalysts for hydroformylation of 1-hexene in supercritical carbon dioxide.* Presented at Annu. Green Chem. Eng. Meet., 6th, Washington, DC

79. Marteel AE, Davies JA, Mason MR, Tack T, Bektesevic S, Abraham MA. 2003. Supported platinum/tin complexes as catalysts for hydroformylation of 1-hexene in supercritical carbon dioxide. *Catal. Commun.* 4(7):309–14

80. Ikariya T, Kayaki Y. 2000. Supercritical

fluids as reaction media for molecular catalysis. *Catal. Surv. Jpn.* 4(1):39–50
81. Jessop PG, Ikariya T, Noyori R. 1999. Homogeneous catalysis in supercritical fluids. *Chem. Rev.* 99(2):475–93
82. Kainz S, Koch D, Baumann W, Leitner W. 1997. Perfluoroalkyl-substituted arylphosphanes as ligands for homogeneous catalysis in supercritical carbon dioxide. *Angew. Chem.-Int. Ed. Engl.* 36(15):1628–30
83. Palo DR, Erkey C. 1999. Homogeneous hydroformylation of 1-octene in supercritical carbon dioxide with RhH(CO)(P(p-CF$_3$C$_6$H$_4$)$_3$)$_3$. *Ind. Eng. Chem. Res.* 38(5):2163–65
84. Sellin MF, Cole-Hamilton DJ. 2000. Hydroformylation reactions in supercritical carbon dioxide using insoluble metal complexes. *J. Chem. Soc.-Dalton Trans.* (11):1681–83
85. Dharmidhikari S, Abraham MA. 2000. Rhodium supported on activated carbon as a heterogeneous catalyst for hydroformylation of propylene in supercritical carbon dioxide. *J. Supercrit. Fluids* 18(1):1–10
86. Snyder G, Tadd A, Abraham MA. 2001. Evaluation of catalyst support effects during rhodium-catalyzed hydroformylation in supercritical CO$_2$. *Ind. Eng. Chem. Res.* 40(23):5317–25
87. Meehan NJ, Sandee AJ, Reek JNH, Kamer PCJ, van Leeuwen PWNM, Poliakoff M. 2000. Continuous, selective hydroformylation in supercritical carbon dioxide using an immobilised homogeneous catalyst. *Chem. Commun.* (16):1497–98
88. Collins T, Inst. Green Oxid. Chem. 2001. *Ethics: The Great Fields of Green Chemistry* http://www.chem.cmu.edu/groups/Collins/ethics/ethics06.html
89. World Comm. Environ. Dev. 1987. *Our Common Future.* New York: Oxford Univ. Press
90. Rounds KS, Cooper JS. 2002. Development of product design requirements using taxonomies of environmental issues. *Res. Eng. Design* 13:94–108
91. Epstein MJ, Wisner PS. 2001. Using a balanced scorecard to implement sustainability. *Environ. Qual. Manag.* 11(2):1–10
92. Elkington J. 1998. *Cannibals with Forks.* Stony Creek, CT: New Soc. 408 pp.
93. Hawken P, Lovins A, Lovins LH. 1999. *Natural Capitalism.* New York: Little, Brown. 396 pp.
94. Frankel C. 1998. *Earth's Company.* Stony Creek, CT: New Soc. 263 pp.
95. Fiksel J. 2001. Emergence of a sustainable business community. *Pure Appl. Chem.* 73:1265–68
96. Edinger R, Kaul S, 2000. Humankind's detour toward sustainability: past, present, and future of renewable energies and electric power generation. *Renew. Sustain. Energy Rev.* 3:295–313
97. Carette L, Friedrich KA, Stimming U. 2000. Fuel cells: principles, types, fuels, and applications. *ChemPhysChem* 1:162–93
98. Ghenciu AF. 2002. Review of fuel processing catalysts for hydrogen production in PEM fuel cell systems. *Curr. Opin. Solid State Mater. Sci.* 6:389–99
99. Joensen F, Rostrup-Nielsen JR. 2002. Conversion of hydrocarbons and alcohols for fuel cells *J. Power Sour.* 105:195–201
100. Paglieri SN, Way JD. 2002. Innovations in palladium membrane research. *Sep. Purif. Methods* 31:1–169
101. Würfel P. 2002. Thermodynamic limitations to solar energy conversion. *Physica E* 14:18–26
102. Zalba B, Marin JM, Cabeza LF, Mehling H. 2003. Review on thermal energy storage with phase change: materials, heat transfer analysis and applications. *Appl. Thermal Eng.* 23:251–83
103. Steinfeld A. 2002. Solar hydrogen production via a two-step water-splitting thermochemical cycle based on Zn/ZnO redox reactions. *Int. J. Hydrog. Energy* 27:611–19

104. Green MA. 2002. Photovoltaic principles. *Physica E* 14:11–17
105. Bozell JJ, Hoberg JO, Claffey D, Hames BR, Dimmel DR. 1998. New methodology for the production of chemicals from renewable feedstocks. In *Green Chemistry*, ed. PT Anastas, TC Williamson, pp. 27–45. New York: Oxford Univ. Press
106. Danner H, Braun R. 1999. Biotechnology for the production of commodity chemicals from biomass. *Chem. Soc. Rev.* 28:395–405
107. Abbadi A, Gotlieb KF, van Bekkum H. 1998. Study on solid acid catalyzed hydrolysis of maltose and related polysaccharides. *Starch-Starke* 50:23–28
108. Embree HD, Chen T, Payne GF. 2001. Oxygenated aromatic compounds from renewable resources: motivation, opportunities, and adsorptive separations. *Chem. Eng. J.* 84:133–47
109. Bozell JJ, Moens L, Elliott DC, Wang Y, Neuenscwander GG, Fitzpatrick SW. 2000. Production of levulinic acid and use as a platform chemical for derived products. *Resour. Conserv. Recycl.* 28:227–39
110. McKendry P. 2002. Energy production from biomass (part 1 to 3): overview of biomass. *Bioresour. Technol.* 83:37–46
111. Bridgwater AV. 2003. Renewable fuels and chemicals by thermal processing of biomass. *Chem. Eng. J.* 91:87–102
112. Mohanty AK, Misra M, Drzal LT. 2002. Sustainable bio-composites from renewable resources: opportunities and challenges in the green materials world. *J. Polym. Environ.* 10:19–26
113. Herrmann AS, Nickel J, Riedel U. 1998. Construction materials based upon biologically renewable resources—from components to finished parts. *Polym. Degrad. Stab.* 59:251–61
114. Vink ETH, Rabago KR, Glassner DA, Gruber PR. 2003. Applications of life cycle assessment to NatureWorks polylactide (PLA) production. *Polym. Degrad. Stab.* 80:403–19
115. Mulholland KL, Sylvester RW, Dyer JA. 2000. Sustainability: waste minimization, green chemistry and inherently safer processing. *Environ. Prog.* 19(4):260–68
116. Hjeresen DL, Kirchhoff MM, Lankey RL. 2002. Green chemistry: environment, economics, and competitiveness. *Corp. Environ. Strategy* 9(3):259–66
117. Centi G, Ciambelli P, Perathoner S, Russo P. 2002. Environmental catalysis: trends and outlook. *Catal. Today* 75(1–4):3–15

INTERNATIONAL ENVIRONMENTAL AGREEMENTS: A Survey of Their Features, Formation, and Effects

Ronald B. Mitchell
Department of Political Science, University of Oregon, Eugene, Oregon 97403-1284; email: rmitchel@oregon.uoregon.edu

Key Words negotiations, institutions, effectiveness, treaties, regimes, IEA, MEA, BEA

■ **Abstract** International environmental agreements (IEAs), legally binding intergovernmental efforts directed at reducing human impacts on the environment, are common features of global environmental governance. Using a clear definition allowed creation of a comprehensive database [available online at (31)] listing over 700 multilateral agreements (MEAs) and over 1000 bilateral agreements (BEAs), which included treaties, protocols, and amendments that address numerous pollutants; preservation of many species; and, increasingly, protection of various habitats. Research into the factors that explain the timing, content, and membership in environmental agreements clarifies that the interests and power of influential states create pressures for, or constraints on, progress in global environmental governance but that discourse, actors, and processes also play important roles. Variation in the effects of these agreements on environmental behaviors and outcomes often depends as much on characteristics of member countries, the international context, and the underlying environmental problem as on the differences in agreement design.

CONTENTS

INTRODUCTION	430
DEFINING INTERNATIONAL ENVIRONMENTAL AGREEMENTS	431
DESCRIBING THE POPULATION OF INTERNATIONAL ENVIRONMENTAL AGREEMENTS	434
Multilateral Agreements	434
Connections Among Multilateral Agreements: Lineages and Secretariats	435
Substantive and Temporal Patterns in Multilateral Agreements	437
Bilateral Agreements	438
NEGOTIATING INTERNATIONAL ENVIRONMENTAL AGREEMENTS: WHY WE HAVE THOSE WE HAVE	439
Interests, Power, and Discourse	439
Actors and Processes	442
MAKING INTERNATIONAL ENVIRONMENTAL AGREEMENTS EFFECTIVE: WHY SOME WORK AND OTHERS DO NOT	444

Identifying the Effects of Regimes 444
A Summary of the Effects of Environmental Agreements 446
The Determinants of Regime Effects 448
The Endogeneity Problem 452
CONCLUSION 453

INTRODUCTION

Since at least the late 1800s and with increasing regularity in the past half century, countries have negotiated hundreds of international legal agreements to address environmental problems they cannot resolve alone. Conventions addressing ozone depletion, climate change, and biodiversity are well-known, but governments have also concluded global, regional, and bilateral agreements to mitigate pollution of oceans, regional seas, rivers, and lakes; reduce over-exploitation of numerous species of fish, birds, and land and marine mammals; and slow the degradation of wetlands, deserts, and other habitats. This review surveys the landscape of such agreements, offering a precise definition of international environmental agreements (IEAs) to allow description of over 700 multilateral agreements (MEAs) of three or more member countries and more than 1000 bilateral treaties, conventions, protocols, and amendments (BEAs) designed to protect the environment.

After this survey, the review discusses the research on factors that influence the successful negotiation of IEAs. Why have countries quickly negotiated significant agreements to address some environmental problems while they have made few attempts, or have failed, to address others? An agreement's negotiation, timing, and content are functions of the perceived urgency and desirability of resolving the problem in a particular way, with those perceptions being functions, in turn, of material aspects of the problem's causes and consequences as well as political, economic, and social characteristics of the countries relevant to its resolution. Next, the review discusses research on the effects of IEAs, which has identified some that have had significant impacts on human behaviors and environmental quality and others that have had few such impacts. Scholars have examined only a small subset of extant IEAs, which precludes any general claims about their effectiveness. Research to date does suggest, however, that the ability of an IEA to induce positive changes depends less on ensuring that agreements contain particular rules or specific monitoring and enforcement provisions and more on ensuring that agreements contain provisions that are responsive to the type of environmental problem being addressed, the countries involved, and the exigencies of the international context in which they must operate.

Before proceeding, a caveat is in order: Although this review focuses on international environmental agreements, such arrangements are only one of the many environmental protection strategies currently in use. The United Nations (UN) has recently urged the supplementing of intergovernmental treaties with voluntary efforts, such as the "Global Compact" for "responsible corporate citizenship" and "type 2 partnerships" between governments and nongovernmental organizations

(NGOs) (1, 2). But many actors have not needed such encouragement and are taking individual and collaborative action at subnational, national, supranational, and transnational levels (3, 4–7). On climate change alone, corporations are trading CO_2 emissions, local governments are setting municipal emission targets, NGOs are developing carbon sequestration projects, and individuals are practicing energy conservation, in many cases long before actions by national governments. These and similar efforts are likely to contribute much to a global transition to sustainability and deserve considerable analytic attention (8). That said, the present review of legally binding intergovernmental efforts and research done on them sheds light on an important element of global efforts to better manage the relationship of humans to the natural environment.

DEFINING INTERNATIONAL ENVIRONMENTAL AGREEMENTS

Despite extensive public, legal, and social science interest in international environmental agreements, the empirical basis for claims regarding the number of such agreements and their characteristics remains weak. The web and most law libraries have numerous lists of international environmental laws. But comparing these lists reveals considerable variation in what each means by these terms. Many identify only selected, important, or major agreements or those related to a particular region or issue (9–17). Some combine binding (or *hard law*) treaties and conventions with nonbinding (or *soft law*) statements of principles, declarations, and resolutions (18). Most secretariats and even the UN-affiliated websites of the UN Environment Programme (UNEP), the UN Food and Agriculture Organization (FAO), and the UN International Maritime Organization (IMO) list only agreements negotiated under their auspices or that they administer (19–21). Governments usually list only those agreements to which they are a party (22, 23). Nominally comprehensive lists often overlook well-known environmental agreements, and almost none systematically identify the many protocols, amendments, and other modifications needed to reconstruct the historical development of international environmental law or its status at a particular point in time. Web-based lists are often not kept current (24, 25). Most do not provide users with (or worse, do not themselves use) systematic and explicit definitions and corresponding rules to include or exclude agreements. And many that do, including a particularly comprehensive list, include agreements that are not obviously environmental on the grounds that their environmental effects are hidden in the language of the agreement (26–28).

The variation in the coverage of international environmental law lists surely reflects (and may well serve) the purposes and audiences of those creating these lists but makes it difficult to address the seemingly straightforward task of accurately describing, let alone analyzing, the historical development and current status of the population of IEAs. Even the excellent ECOLEX database of environmental law developed by the World Conservation Union, UNEP, and FAO and the

Environmental Treaties and Resource Indicators database developed by Columbia's Center for International Earth Science Information Network have not produced definitive or complete lists of international environmental agreements (29, 30).

The present review seeks, in part, to remedy this state of affairs by proposing a clear, explicit definition of international environmental agreements that conforms reasonably well to common understandings of that phrase and using that definition to identify and describe the agreements that fit it [the list is available at (31)]. In this review, the definition of an *international environmental agreement* is an intergovernmental document intended as legally binding with a primary stated purpose of preventing or managing human impacts on natural resources. Providing a clear and explicit definition allows even readers who disagree with it to make sense of the discussion that follows and to identify whether the summary given here would need to be expanded or contracted to conform to their preferred definition.

What is an *agreement*? When used as part of the phrase international environmental agreement, the term usually corresponds closely to the 1969 Vienna Convention on the Law of Treaties' definition of a treaty, i.e., "an international agreement concluded between States in written form and governed by international law" in which states express a "consent to be bound" [Articles 2(1)(a) and 11 through 17] (32, p. 14). For most legal scholars, it is the consent to be bound that is crucial: Agreements are the documentation of legally binding arrangements among two or more states, regardless of whether they are designated as treaties, conventions, accords, or modifications of such arrangements (32).

The difficulty arises, of course, "not with the definition itself, but whether a particular instrument or transaction falls within the definition" (32, p. 14). I operationalized the definition to consist of:

1. instruments designated as convention, treaty, agreement, accord, or their non-English equivalents, and protocols and amendments to such instruments;
2. instruments, regardless of designation, establishing intergovernmental commissions;
3. instruments, regardless of designation, identified as binding by reliable sources (e.g., by a secretariat, UNEP, or published legal analysis); or
4. instruments, regardless of designation, whose texts fit accepted terminologies of legally binding agreements (32, p. 404).

I intentionally exclude intergovernmental soft law, such as action plans, agreed measures, codes of conduct, declarations, resolutions, and similar policies because they are not binding and also exclude the large number of European Union (EU) directives because they are distinct in several important ways from other international agreements (14, 33–35).

By clearly defining the term agreement, I seek to provide an accurate count and description of the range of distinct legally binding environmental commitments governments have made. A definition that includes protocols, amendments, and other binding modifications as well as the original agreements they modify will find more agreements than one that excludes such modifications. States generally employ original agreements when pursuing major new policy objectives, employ protocols for new but related policy directions, and employ amendments for relatively minor modifications to existing agreements. But there are many exceptions to this general rule. Therefore, to exclude modifications would understate the number of significant IEAs by ignoring commitments, such as the eight protocols to the Convention on Long-Range Transboundary Air Pollution (LRTAP), the Kyoto Protocol to the United Nations Framework Convention on Climate Change (UNFCCC), and the amendment to the International Convention for the Regulation of Whaling that halted commercial whaling. On the other hand, including all modifications overstates the number of significant IEAs by counting many minor, noncontroversial, or technical amendments. The approach taken here addresses these issues by using a broad definition that includes modifications while also distinguishing between the number of original agreements and the number of all legally binding agreements.

What is international? Although *international* can have broader meanings, when referring to IEAs, the term usually means intergovernmental. I operationalized this definition to include all agreements to which governments of two or more states have (or are allowed to) become parties but exclude instruments between single governments and either international organizations or NGOs and instruments between or among international organizations, corporations, or NGOs.

What is environmental? Environmental is the most difficult of the three elements of the phrase to define in a commonly accepted way. Most of the divergence noted among IEA compilations stems from environmental being "a term that everyone understands and no one is able to define" (36, p. 170; 37, p. 4). Indeed, two authors who analyzed UNEP's compilation of IEAs rejected eight as having "no significant environmental content" (38, p. 404). The definition used here seeks to categorize agreements in ways that correspond to most scholars' and practitioners' categorizations of environmental and nonenvironmental. The definition intentionally errs in being too broad (assuming those with narrower definitions can discard included agreements more readily then they can identify excluded ones) while trying to avoid including agreements most scholars and practitioners would not classify as environmental.

This review defines agreements as *environmental* if they seek, as a primary purpose, to manage or prevent human impacts on natural resources; plant and animal species (including in agriculture); the atmosphere; oceans; rivers; lakes; terrestrial habitats; and other elements of the natural world that provide ecosystem services (39). *Primary purpose* was operationalized by searching for terms corresponding to this conception in agreement titles, preambles, or articles specifically designating agreement goals [for search terms used, see (31)]. This excludes agreements addressing human health, conflict, cultural preservation, trade, oceans, outer space, nuclear radiation, transportation, weather, labor, and similar issues unless those agreements addressed environmental issues as a primary concern. The definition also excludes agreements whose effects are environmental, if that was not a primary purpose. A broader definition that includes agreements based on their having environmental effects, like that adopted by Burhenne, captures agreements on trade, regional economic integration, worker protection, and arms control (26). There may be considerable value in this expansive definition, but it (a) diverges significantly from common usage and (b) has the analytic drawback of requiring that agreement effects be identified before they can be categorized as environmental and, if used literally and consistently, of precluding analysis of why some environmental agreements fail (because those that have no environmental effects would be defined as not environmental). The more restrictive, purpose-based definition used here skirts these problems and also allows analysis of how, if at all, agreements intended to address environmental degradation differ from those intended to address other topics of international concern.

DESCRIBING THE POPULATION OF INTERNATIONAL ENVIRONMENTAL AGREEMENTS

What does the population of cases that meet this definition look like? This section provides a midterm report of initial, nondefinitive, descriptive statistics regarding this population of IEAs based on a recently developed database; the list of agreements composing the IEA database will be maintained and updated at Reference 31. An initial list of over 3500 unique instruments relevant to international environmental protection was compiled from over 30 print and electronic sources, and the websites of over 150 environmental treaty secretariats and 25 environment or foreign affairs ministries [sources are listed at (31)]. Careful application of the present inclusion rules, which was stricter than many contributing lists, eliminated approximately 675 documents as nonbinding, approximately 250 as nonintergovernmental, and approximately 1050 as nonenvironmental. The resulting list of IEAs seems likely to have identified an almost complete set of over 700 MEAs (between three or more governments) and a far less complete, but still large, subset of over 1000 BEAs (between two governments).

Multilateral Agreements

The list of IEAs allows relatively confident claims to be made about MEAs. At least 729 MEAs fit the IEA definition, far more than UNEP's 1996 listing of 216 or Burhenne's listing through 1998 of 474 (26, 40). This accounting is larger, in part, because it more systematically identifies protocols and amendments. Only half of the MEAs, 357, were original agreements, with 20 percent protocols and 30 percent amendments. Several MEAs were signed but never (or have not yet) entered into force, and over 50 have been replaced by other agreements or terminated. As implied by the discussion of original agreements and modifications above, this does not mean there are 700 fully distinct and separate multilateral commitments. Rather, it means that three or more governments have agreed on legally binding environmental commitments over 700 times; some are quite distinct from previous commitments, and others involve minor changes to previous commitments.

Connections Among Multilateral Agreements: Lineages and Secretariats

These 729 MEAs are not all independent but are linked to each other in various ways. Much recent scholarship has sought to capture these connections through the concept of international environmental regimes (41, 42). The term *regime* is usually defined broadly as "implicit or explicit principles, norms, rules, and decision-making procedures around which actors' expectations converge" (43, p. 2). This broad definition recognizes that state behaviors can be influenced by informal, nonbinding understandings as well as by formal legal agreements and that, even where legal agreements exist, the interpretation and implementation of those agreements and their impacts on state behavior often reflect numerous extra-legal factors related to ideas, norms, and the actors mobilized on the issue (44). This broad definition allows the *marine pollution protection regime* to be defined as including only those IMO conventions addressing global marine pollution or, alternatively, as including all international efforts addressing marine pollution, which include these IMO conventions but also include regional seas conventions, bilateral agreements, and related ministerial declarations. Although such breadth is useful for some analytic purposes, it would introduce unnecessary ambiguity into the present effort to clarify, classify, count, and describe IEAs.

Therefore, to group legally related agreements, the term *lineage* is used to refer to one or more legally linked instruments. A lineage is any set of agreements, protocols, and amendments that modify, extend, replace, or explicitly derive from one or more original agreements. For example, the marine pollution (MARPOL) lineage includes a 1954 agreement with 4 amendments replaced by a 1973 agreement and integral 1978 protocol that have been modified by another protocol and 36 amendments. Such lineages are distinct from but often form the basis of regimes. This definition groups the 729 MEAs into approximately 250 lineages. Over 40 percent of all agreements cluster into the largest twenty lineages, each of which has at least 8 instruments. Another 30 percent cluster in 50 lineages of 3 to 7 instruments each. The remaining 30 percent are split; 13 percent belong to 50 lineages that involve an initial agreement and a single modifying protocol or amendment, and 128 agreements (or 17 percent) have never been legally modified.

The larger lineages tend to consist of either frequently modified original agreements or sets of linked agreements. Rivaling the MARPOL lineage in number of agreements, the whaling lineage includes 2 early conventions and 4 protocols, the currently operative 1946 convention that replaced those, more than 50 annual binding amendments of the agreement's schedule of catch quotas, a 1956 protocol, a 1963 agreement on international observers, and several related bilateral agreements. The UN's Mediterranean Action Plan (MEDPLAN) generated an original agreement, eight protocols, and three amendments, and the 1979 LRTAP Convention has eight protocols covering various air pollutants. Members of the 1991 Convention Concerning the Protection of the Alps have negotiated 10 protocols in 10 years addressing, inter alia, sustainable development, nature protection, forestry, agriculture, tourism, soils, energy, and transportation. The 1979 Convention on the Conservation of Migratory Species of Wild Animals (CMS) has been amended three times, but it has also facilitated negotiation of six new agreements on seals, cetaceans, albatrosses and petrels, waterbirds, and bats (the last of which has been amended twice) and six nonbinding memorandums of understanding (MOUs) on other species.

Although multi-agreement lineages usually indicate considerable international activity on an issue, the absence of a long stream of legal instruments does not imply a lack of activity. Regimes need not develop only through binding agreements. Most fisheries set catch limits through resolutions, presumably to avoid ratification delays if such limits were made binding. Although the 1949 Convention for the Establishment of an Inter-American Tropical Tuna Commission has been legally modified only once, the Commission has adopted over 40 resolutions in the last 5 years alone, limiting, inter alia, catch, gear, bycatch, and fishing by nonparties. The 1971 Convention on Wetlands of International Importance has only one protocol and one amendment, but annual Conferences of the Parties have adopted numerous recommendations and worked closely with member states to improve protection of wetlands.

As already noted, an agreement's legal designation provides only limited insight into its substantive importance. The choice to establish a convention or treaty as a new original agreement, to negotiate a protocol, or to pass an amendment appears to be driven either by legal requirements in earlier agreements or facets of institutional culture. For example, most agreements admit new members without legal action, but new members have also been admitted through conventions, protocols, and amendments. Enforcement efforts have been codified both in original agreements and in protocols. By contrast, at least one very significant and controversial change, the commercial whaling moratorium, was adopted by amendment. The CMS agreement has used both binding agreements and nonbinding MOUs to protect endangered species. Notably, the two longest lineages (whaling with 70 instruments and MARPOL with 44) both rely on *tacit acceptance* procedures that allow particular types of amendments to enter into force on a given date unless a certain number of parties object rather than when a certain number of parties accept. Agreements that require explicit acceptance (with corresponding ratification delays) for an amendment to enter into force either deter otherwise desirable changes or channel reform efforts into mechanisms that are not legally binding.

Many IEAs that are not part of the same lineage are connected by having been negotiated under a common organization's auspices. Almost 200 agreements have been negotiated under the auspices of UN organizations. The UNEP Governing Council established a Regional Seas Programme in 1974 that has produced over 40 agreements covering 10 regional seas (15). The IMO has fostered not only 44 MARPOL agreements but 10 instruments on oil pollution compensation, 9 on dumping of wastes, and 6 on oil pollution accidents and response. The UN

Economic Commission for Europe facilitated nine LRTAP agreements but also five MEAs addressing transboundary environmental issues and numerous nonbinding regulations on motor vehicles (45). Fifteen agreements with 25 amendments have been concluded under the FAO Constitution (Article XIV), and numerous other IEAs have been concluded through the FAO's regional fisheries bodies and plant protection commissions (19, 46). The Council of Europe, the Benelux Economic Union, and the Association of Southeast Asian Nations (ASEAN) have also promoted development of various environmental agreements.

Most MEAs are managed through a policy-making body of member state representatives (e.g., a Conference of the Parties) and an administrative secretariat that coordinates the efforts of member states. Indeed, the primary goal of many agreements is to establish an organization to manage an environmental problem rather than to promulgate regulations that do so directly. Over 150 secretariats have been established to help manage agreements; some have large staffs actively engaged in formulating and implementing policies, yet others exist in name only [a list of these secretariats is available at (31)]. Many agreements also establish subsidiary bodies, such as the UNFCCC's Subsidiary Bodies for Implementation and for Scientific and Technological Advice or the International Whaling Commission's Scientific Committee.

Substantive and Temporal Patterns in Multilateral Agreements

Given the number of MEAs, it is not surprising that they cover a range of environmental problems. To categorize them involves, by necessity, creating groupings that reflect the perspective of the person categorizing and that cannot be mutually exclusive because many agreements address themselves to multiple environmental issues [for an alternative categorization, see (38)]. Thus, many individual agreements appear in multiple categories in the descriptive summary that follows. Almost half, 348, of all MEAs attempt to protect species or manage human impacts on those species. More than one third of the species-related instruments, 124, relate directly to fisheries and fish protection and management (with 72 original agreements and 52 protocols and amendments), and another 87 agreements, protocols, and amendments relate to other marine animals including whales, other cetaceans, turtles, and fur seals. Other species-specific agreements target polar bears, bats, vicuña (a South American camelid), birds, or wildlife generally. Over time, MEAs have come to focus more on pollution with a recent increase in agreements addressing habitat. Until 1972, less than 20 percent of MEAs, 39 of 221, were pollution related and 67 percent (149) were species related; since then, the adoption rate has been almost exactly even (199 on species, 203 on pollution). More than half of all pollution agreements, 126, address marine pollution, but many address lake and river pollution (a balance that is probably quite different among BEAs). Nuclear pollution from energy production and nuclear weapons has been explicitly addressed in 39 agreements. Although highly visible, MEAs addressing atmospheric pollutants have numbered only 20; these included climate change, acid rain, ozone protection, and air pollution from ships. Although habitat protection was addressed in agreements in 1900, 1933, and 1940, it has been an infrequent target of MEAs and constituted only about 3 percent of the total (22 agreements).

Although international environmental activity has increased recently, states began cooperating on what we would now consider environmental issues in the nineteenth century. By 1910, three agreements addressing the invasive species of *Phylloxera vastatrix* (a North American insect that devastated the French wine industry), five on European fisheries, two on transport of environmentally harmful materials on the Rhine, one on birds, and one on species and habitat conservation in Africa had been negotiated. Between 1911 and 1945, 21 MEAs were negotiated addressing protection of North Pacific fur seals and whales; fisheries in the Baltic and the Atlantic; and various agricultural issues (including formation of the FAO, locusts, and contagious animal diseases). A 1933 convention calling on governments to establish national parks listed more and less severely threatened species in separate annexes that foreshadowed the approach of the Convention on International Trade in Endangered Species (CITES) 40 years later. After World War II, MEAs were adopted with increasing speed. A prewar rate of an agreement every two years became a rate of seven agreements per year between 1946 and 1972, the year of the UN Conference on the Human Environment (UNCHE). That rate has continued to increase with 319 agreements completed in the 20 years from UNCHE to the 1992 UN Conference on Environment and Development (16 agreements per year), and 189 agreements completed from 1993 through 2002 (19 agreements per year).

Bilateral Agreements

Developing a comprehensive list of BEAs proves more difficult because they often are documented and known about only within the two signatory countries. Listings are generated less frequently than for multilaterals, often by foreign ministries that generally do not make them readily available, separate environmental from nonenvironmental agreements, or, understandably, reproduce them in languages other than those of the signatory states. Thus, a definitive description of BEAs, and hence of IEAs as a whole, must await a more concerted, resource-intensive effort than any yet undertaken. That said, the IEA database has made a significant effort in this direction that makes some description of the population of BEAs possible.

Although this project's IEA database focused initially on identifying multilaterals, it has since identified over 1040 BEAs. This number represents a lower bound of BEAs. An estimate for an upper bound can be arrived at by noting that BEAs exist in approximately a 3-to-1 ratio to MEAs in FAO's FAOLEX database and in work reported by Jacobson & Brown Weiss (47; 48, p. 1). Assuming this ratio holds for the population of IEAs, then the 700 MEAs identified here suggest an upper bound of 2100 BEAs, a number that could be refined through a more systematic accounting. Of the BEAs identified, only 100 (10 percent) are protocols or amendments, a much lower proportion than among MEAs; governments appear to replace BEAs more often than they modify them. Of the BEAs identified, about 30 percent address fisheries; 25 percent address freshwater management; 10 percent address environmental protection generally; and 10 percent address plant, animal, and agricultural issues. Time trends in BEAs parallel those of MEAs. Already by 1900, 29 had been negotiated, almost exclusively among European states to address river or fisheries management. The 74 BEAs signed from 1901 to 1945 (a rate of 1.5 per year) ramped up quickly to 227 being signed from 1946 to 1972 (8 per year), 389 from 1973 to 1992 (20 per year), and 314 from 1993 to 2002 (32 per year). Even this incomplete dataset of BEAs demonstrates that they play an important and increasing role in global environmental governance, one that has not yet received the same scholarly interest as, and seems likely to differ from, the role of MEAs.

NEGOTIATING INTERNATIONAL ENVIRONMENTAL AGREEMENTS: WHY WE HAVE THOSE WE HAVE

Investigating the causes of, and conditions that foster, negotiation of international agreements, including environmental ones, has been a major focus of international relations research for some time. This discussion switches to discussing environmental regimes to reflect the fact that research on their formation and research on their effects (described in the next section) generally are interested in understanding regimes in the broad sense defined above rather than in the narrower sense of formal legal agreements (49). Much research has focused on why the international community takes up (or ignores) a particular environmental issue at the time and in the form it does (50–55). Neither scientific nor public consensus about a problem's existence, importance, or causes nor efforts by those concerned about a problem are enough to produce international action. Indeed, there appear to be many necessary (or at least facilitative) conditions for the negotiation of IEAs but very few, if any, sufficient conditions. The timing and content of IEAs are influenced by the strength of states' interests in environmental protection relative to other concerns and their power to promote those interests, the knowledge and discourse that structure perceptions of environmental problems and their solutions, and the efforts of individuals and groups in proposing solutions and pressing governments to accept agreements that are on the table.

Interests, Power, and Discourse

Refining more general arguments from international relations, scholars of international environmental politics have sought to understand how the array of interests among states influences the ability to negotiate, and the design of, international agreements. They have proposed various typologies to explain why nations have formed regimes quickly in response to some environmental problems, more slowly in response to others, and not at all in response to yet others (42, 56–59). Despite differences, these typologies all see the ease or difficulty of regime formation as a function of conflicts between the political, economic, and environmental interests of relevant countries. In some environmental problems, the obstacles to agreement stem from a tragedy of the commons in which all countries have mixed motives, i.e., all want the problem resolved but none want to contribute to its resolution (60). Yet, the obstacles to agreement can be even greater in unidirectional or "upstream/downstream" problems in which upstream perpetrators lack any incentives to restrain their pollution levels, and downstream victims have no credible threats with which to induce such restraint (61). Likewise, problems involving fundamental conflicts over the environmental goal (as in current negotiations on whaling and climate change) tend to resist resolution more than those involving conflicts on the means of achieving a shared goal (as in negotiations to reduce acid precipitants through common targets or differentiated critical loads) (62).

These problem typologies help explain the content, as well as the likelihood, of agreement. In mixed motive problems, any agreement must address the ongoing incentives of members to cheat, i.e., the desire all members have to encourage others to contribute to the problem's remedy while, secretly, not contributing themselves. In contrast, agreements to harmonize environmental policies among states already committed to environmental protection (say, for domestic political reasons) need only identify the policies members should harmonize to, because the agreement is not addressing member's incentives to violate but only their need for a rule about how to comply (56, 63). Thus, agreements addressing overexploitation of fisheries (a mixed motive problem) usually have more stringent enforcement provisions than those among, for example, European states to harmonize national environmental policies to facilitate international trade. Further, agreements addressing mixed motive problems usually can rely on reciprocal behavioral commitments (e.g., all countries reducing pollution levels or fish harvests by specified amounts). Such commitments will not resolve upstream/downstream problems: Upstream countries do not benefit from downstream countries reducing their pollution and must be offered side payments or rewards to join and comply (61).

Features beyond the underlying politics of a problem also affect whether agreements are concluded. Highly visible, immediate, and dramatic environmental damage that actors in powerful states care about tend to receive international attention. Thus, marine pollution agreements have addressed oil pollution more often than less visible pollutants, such as chemicals, garbage, or sewage; the relative rarity of agreements on air pollution may reflect the diffuse, difficult to identify, and chronic nature of air pollution's effects. As the domestic policy literature notes, policy shifts more easily after accidents and crises or during moments of windows of opportunity (64, 65, 110–113). Although crises "are not driving forces like material conditions, interests, or ideas," they can prompt international action if deeper forces make conditions ripe (53, p. 77). Environmental disasters, such as the Chernobyl nuclear accident and chemical spills on the Rhine, raise public awareness of a problem, produce calls for action, and clear political "space for the consideration of new ideas on how to explain and solve problems" (66, p. 185). Scientific breakthroughs, like discovery of the stratospheric ozone hole, can serve a similar function (67; 68, p. 27; 69). And, when one country or region comes to see an environmental problem as a crisis, other countries also tend to see that problem in crisis terms, which makes international action easier than would have been possible even months before (54). However, the often chronic environmental problems of developing countries that have long ago been remedied in industrialized countries, such as poor water quality, often receive little international attention (70). Indeed, major oil spills off Europe and North America have often prompted negotiations on marine pollution, yet those off Africa and Latin America have not (71, 72).

Astute politicians and institutions, of course, do not wait for catalytic events but expend "political capital in an effort to persuade others to recognize [certain] issues as priority agenda items" (53, p. 7; 64). Scientists (and the "epistemic communities" they compose) clarify environmental impacts and propose solutions (73, p. 224). Although the legitimacy accorded to science gives global environmental assessments considerable influence, as evident with the Intergovernmental Panel on Climate Change's reports, many still "sink without a trace" (69). International organizations develop expertise and focus resources on certain issues, as with UNEP's Regional Seas efforts and IMO's efforts on marine pollution. And, often, international cooperation on one pollutant or species fosters cooperation in related areas. NGOs provide information, conduct research, and propose and evaluate policies, actions that introduce both ideas and political pressure into negotiations (74, 75). Corporations and other interest groups in agenda-setting states often internationalize domestic issues to avoid the costs of unilateral action by their governments (76). Although domestic political pressures can predispose certain governments to be leaders, leadership in any given case usually reflects an interplay between those pressures and characteristics of the environmental problem (53, p. 7; 54; 76).

Whether these factors produce agreement depends on how governments perceive their political interests and preferences. States become supportive "leaders" or oppositional "laggards" based on an interplay of the environmental "facts" (e.g., whether a state is upwind or downwind), the economic impacts of action and of inaction, and the way these factors are perceived by domestic political audiences (77, p. 78; 78). These basic preferences are influenced, in turn, by policy styles, party politics, bureaucratic structures, and transnational linkages (76, 79, 80). If interests and preferences vary from state to state, the constellations of interests among states also vary from environmental issue to environmental issue, with many involving multiple, overlapping types of problems. Thus, states concerned about a particular pollutant may face a tragedy of the commons problem among themselves and an upstream/downstream problem with polluting states that do not share their concern (62, 81).

State's goals for negotiations also influence how quickly they succeed. Framework conventions, cooperative research programs, or nonbinding resolutions may reflect universally low concern, an inability to resolve conflict between concerned and unconcerned states, or high concern but uncertainty about how best to address the problem. Disputes over the solutions proposed can cause as much resistance to agreement as disputes about whether the problem needs resolution. Even efforts that are relatively unambitious ecologically may be strongly opposed if they impose high costs on powerful states or influential economic actors. Thus, the climate convention has met considerable resistance because of the costs it requires states to incur, despite the fact that its emission targets fall far short of what climate experts consider necessary to avert climate change.

Although states have no obligation to join any agreement, membership is not always fully voluntary. A powerful state, or group of states, can impose regimes or make membership more attractive than non-membership (82, pp. 84–86; 83). Over the past quarter century, a combination of threats of American economic sanctions and public outcries have caused many whaling states, often reluctantly, to join the whaling convention, to reduce their opposition to a moratorium on commercial whaling, and to remain members of an agreement many view as increasingly ignoring their interests (84, 85). Power may reflect general economic or military power or more issue-specific power from the ability to influence outcomes if no agreement is reached or from voting and bargaining strength within a regime (86). Thus, China and India refused to join the ozone regime until industrialized states codified financial transfers (87). Brazil can block progress on tropical rainforest protection, as Botswana, Namibia, and Zimbabwe can on elephants. In contrast, if states responsible for a problem share a desire to resolve it, spontaneous patterns of social practice may make legal agreements unnecessary (82, pp. 84–86).

Although interests matter, IEAs are not simply aggregations of states' "well-developed conceptions of their own interests" (53, p. 97). Preferences can be unclear and unstable in environmental arenas in which knowledge is uncertain, issues are complex, and material interests are "weakly or ambiguously affected" (88, pp. 132–133). High levels of uncertainty can make interests and preferences hard to identify, sometimes hindering and sometimes facilitating agreement (63). Bargaining persuades as well as communicates interests, threats, and promises, and it alters perceived interests and whether and what type of regimes form (63). Framing a problem as global gives "every participant in the negotiation process real bargaining leverage" and veto power (53, p. 14). Framing the problem as regional may facilitate evolutionary progress, as evident in UNEP regional seas agreements and regional plant protection agreements. In short, how things are discussed, not just what is discussed, matters.

Actors and Processes

Within the constraints of interests, power, and discourse, actors and processes still influence when and what agreements get signed. Although different scholars have focused on states, secretariats, epistemic communities, NGOs, domestic political constituencies, and individual leaders, the similarities in their lists of how these different groups influence the negotiation process suggest functional distinctions may be more useful (75; 89; 90, p. 18; 91). Those who understand environmental trends and their causes can motivate negotiators by causing them to reestimate the costs of reaching, or failing to reach, agreement. When claims by other governments are suspect, policymakers often seek advice from scientists, international organizations, and NGOs they perceive as more impartial (75, p. 727; 90, p. 12). Indeed, many NGOs seek out resources and expertise to supplement traditional advocacy with impartial information provision. NGOs also provide negotiators insight into, and influence on, various constituencies' perceptions of environmental issues (74, p. 217).

At local, national, and international levels, NGOs, industry trade groups, and even scientists lobby, promote media coverage, campaign, protest, or engage in ecosabotage to raise issue salience. By providing information on the progress of international negotiations to constituencies, environmental NGOs and corporations create pressure to succeed in environmental negotiations (6, 7). States grant NGOs (e.g., the Earth Negotiations Bulletin) access to negotiations to get detailed daily reporting but accept, in exchange, dissemination of that reporting, which can increase public and NGO pressure for agreement (75, p. 730).

Agreement design is intimately connected with the negotiation progress. The desire to negotiate, sign, and ratify an agreement depends on the current terms of debate. States often reject substantive restrictions on their behavior only to sign framework conventions that require ongoing collective decisionmaking that is likely to produce similar, if not more stringent, restrictions. Incorporating financial mechanisms makes potential donors less likely to join but potential recipients more likely to join. Particular decision-making rules, proscriptions, prescriptions, implementation provisions, and withdrawal and renegotiation clauses can all become deal breakers or deal makers. This setting rewards "deft diplomats" who can "add and subtract issues to facilitate the bargaining process, craft the terms of negotiating texts, and broker the deals needed to achieve consensus" (53, p. 23). Although material resources are certainly helpful, high-ranking international, domestic, and nonstate representatives can foster agreement without such resources often simply by tabling compelling proposals (53, p. 23; 74; 75, p. 727; 91, p. 67).

Particularly when exogenous forces make reaching agreement difficult, maintaining political momentum becomes crucial (53, pp. 87; 88). Indeed, the many agreements in certain lineages noted above illustrates how secretariats or individual entrepreneurial leaders can develop, or keep alive, proposals and propose them when conditions become conducive (92). Thus, UNEP Executive Director, Mostafa Tolba, played a crucial role in fostering progress in the ozone negotiations by his careful drafting and introduction of texts at crucial points in the negotiating process (53, p. 119; 68, p. 26). Even the act of holding a meeting can promote agreement because ending the meeting without agreement is so often construed as failure.

As noted, protecting the international environment does not require international law. Indeed, circumventing the state may be quicker, easier, and more open to innovation (93). States sometimes act unilaterally to protect the global environment, funding environmental projects in other countries or sanctioning countries for violating domestic or international environmental standards (76, 94). NGOs and transnational issue networks can engage in world civic politics, using rhetorical persuasion to directly influence the values and behaviors of individuals and corporations (6, 7). Governments, NGOs, and trade groups (and partnerships among them) promote ecolabeling and voluntary codes of conduct, fund debt for nature swaps, and promote consumer boycotts and buy green campaigns that directly shape corporate incentives (6; 91, p. 66; 95–97).

MAKING INTERNATIONAL ENVIRONMENTAL AGREEMENTS EFFECTIVE: WHY SOME WORK AND OTHERS DO NOT

Ultimately, the value of IEAs is evident not in their negotiation but in their influence on human behaviors that harm the environment. Some environmental problems have improved since relevant IEAs were signed, but others have changed little or become worse. Global production of ozone depleting substances and European and North American emissions of acid precipitants have declined since treaties were signed while many marine ecosystems and fish stocks have deteriorated despite regional and global efforts. Yet, a simple interpretation of this variation (that the former agreements outperformed the latter) is likely to be wrong. It is tempting to interpret continuing environmental decline as failure and environmental improvement as success, to attribute improvements as caused by particular features of relevant agreements, and to promote those features as models for other environmental arenas. And these conclusions may be correct. But they often misinterpret the evidence. First, improvement is preferable to decline, but pressures for environmental degradation are often so strong that success may often only be evident in slower rates of degradation. Second, an IEA's influence requires comparing observed outcomes to what would have happened without the treaty rather than to what did happen before the treaty. Environmental quality and behavior are functions of numerous factors, and improvements often arise from fortuitous economic or technological changes unrelated to a treaty. Third, variation in effectiveness may reflect differences in the problems being addressed, the international context, or other factors that have little to do with the agreements themselves. Identical treaties would reduce ozone depletion and acid rain more than overfishing and marine pollution if the former proved more susceptible to regulation or had conditions that were more favorable than in the latter cases.

Work on the implementation, compliance, effects, and effectiveness of IEAs has been dominated by the study of regimes. During the 1990s, individuals and teams representing differing disciplines, countries, and theoretical approaches examined numerous cases to produce a remarkably coherent research program. By themselves, English-language edited volumes directly evaluating environmental regime effectiveness identify a plethora of factors and forces considered influential (41, 42, 94, 98–101).

Identifying the Effects of Regimes

Identifying an appropriate scale for evaluating regimes proves difficult because regime effects can be so varied. Most work on regime impacts has focused on whether regimes achieve their desired objectives in relatively direct ways. However, agreements can have indirect, nonobvious, and nonimmediate effects, such as when agreements improve scientific knowledge of a problem and thereby cause governments, corporate actors, and individuals to reassess their interests and adopt less environmentally harmful behaviors. They can have external effects in arenas beyond those targeted by the agreement (41). Indeed, any environmental agreement that causes environmental improvements will also cause corresponding economic changes. The ozone regime all but eliminated a flourishing chlorofluorocarbon (CFC) industry, and many IEAs that establish nature reserves or specially protected areas dramatically alter the lives of nearby residents. Effects can also be characterized as positive or negative (41, pp. 14, 15). Recent conflicts within CITES reflect, in part, concerns that a ban on ivory sales would have been negatively effective and undercut elephant protection by blocking revenues from ivory sales that range state governments could use to prevent poaching and preserve elephant habitat.

Starting with environmental quality, an agreement's explicit environmental goals serve as a useful metrics for evaluating how much a regime helped resolve "the problem that led to its formation" (102, p. 109; 103, p. 366). These environmental goals are useful metrics at times but are often unclear, are hortatory rather than realistic, or may change as scientific understanding improves (102, p. 109). Equally important, analysts may want to evaluate progress toward goals that differ from, or are more ambitious than, those held by the parties (81, 104). Thus, although the whaling convention sought "to provide for the proper conservation of whale stocks and thus make possible the orderly development of the whaling industry," some may want to know whether it has promoted a norm of a whale's right to life (105).

Much research to date has focused on changes in behavior rather than environmental improvements. This reflects a recognition that the latter requires the former and that our ability to estimate counterfactuals regarding environmental quality (a product of natural variation, human behavior, and myriad other factors) is even more limited than our ability to estimate counterfactuals regarding human behavior (41, 42, 101, 154). Legal compliance provides a useful initial metric but misses overcompliance and good faith noncompliance that also constitute evidence of regime influence (106). For example, LRTAP's influence was more evident in the otherwise-unlikely 10 percent reductions in Hungarian sulfur emissions than from Nordic reductions that far surpassed the 30 percent requirement but would have occurred anyway (78). The problem, of course, is that regimes may induce significant behavioral change that falls far short of the environmental goals of regime negotiators, let alone the goals held by interested scientists, analysts, or environmental advocates (81, p. 4).

Beyond identifying a scale for evaluation, the analyst must identify a reference point on the scale chosen. Two basic types of reference points have been identified: relative improvement and goal achievement (81, p. 5). The first compares observed outcomes to a no-agreement or no-regime baseline. The second compares them to the desired value, as defined by regime negotiators (goal achievement) or an independent analyst (collective optimum) (81, p. 6). These standards are complementary: The former, glass half full, criterion asks how far have we come; the latter, glass half empty, criterion asks how far have we yet to go. Several scholars have sought to combine these criteria in a measure of progress that calculates observed improvement from a no-regime baseline as a fraction of total possible improvement from that baseline, a strategy that moves us beyond claims that a regime made a difference toward claims that a regime achieved (or fell short of) its potential (81, 104).

Several additional aspects of regime effects research deserve comment. Research that compares one regime's performance to another's (rather than evaluating a single regime's performance) has begun but faces obstacles in convincingly accounting for differences in how hard problems are to resolve and comparing progress made in noncomparable realms (107). Questions of efficiency, cost-effectiveness, and equity also remain under studied. The plethora of claims regarding what features improve performance under what conditions have still to be carefully evaluated against the empirical evidence (81, p. 8; 102, p. 116; 103, p. 374). And efforts to answer these questions still rely excessively on case studies without sufficient use of other analytic techniques (108).

A Summary of the Effects of Environmental Agreements

A summary of existing analyses clarifies (a) that major obstacles exist to analyzing agreement effects accurately, (b) that only a relatively small subset of agreements have been analyzed, (c) that data exists on a significantly broader range of agreements, and (d) that more careful and systematic comparison of IEA effects is needed. Scholars have analyzed only a small fraction of extant IEAs, in part because the number of IEAs has been consistently underestimated but more because relevant data on behaviors or environmental quality are not readily available. First, finding effects data is difficult because, although some agreements have a single, unambiguous, and obvious behavioral indicator (e.g., the 1973 Agreement on the Conservation of Polar Bears or the 1976 Convention on the Protection of the Rhine Against Pollution by Chlorides), many others target multiple environmental problems (e.g., CITES addresses numerous species, and MARPOL addresses myriad ocean pollutants) or address behaviors that are not readily quantified (e.g., the Wetlands Convention requires countries to "promote the conservation [and] wise use of wetlands"). Second, agreements negotiated in the past 5–10 years are too recent to have had effects that can be evaluated. Third, data useful for distinguishing the influence of regimes from other factors often do not exist or exist but are not well known or readily available. In many cases, data collection begins only after agreements are signed, precluding pre-post analysis. In others, data is not systematically collected with the quality or precision needed. Data relevant to many older agreements may be buried as appendices in obscure reports that prove increasingly difficult to find in an electronic information age. Fourth, relevant data that do exist often are formatted in ways that discourage analysis. For example, FAO has an extensive database of fish catch (FISHSTAT) broken down by country, year, species, region where caught, and gear used (109). However, using that data to analyze any of the scores of extant fisheries agreements requires identifying which species were regulated in which regions in which years for which countries so that regulated catch can be compared to unregulated catch.

Despite these problems, available data would allow analysis of far more agreements than scholars usually assume. Many IEAs identified here probably do not have the quality and quantity of data needed to support rigorous analysis. But, several hundred agreements could be analyzed using data that exist or that could be developed readily by combining various data sources. FISHSTAT offers opportunities for evaluating the myriad fishery agreements and amendments and for comparing their binding requirements to their many nonbinding recommendations and regulations. Detailed multi-country, multi-year datasets also exist with data relevant to IEAs that address several endangered species, e.g., whales, polar bears, North Pacific fur seals, acid rain, and ozone depleting substances, and various marine and river pollutants. Useful datasets are often available from treaty secretariats; other international, governmental, and nongovernmental organizations; scientists; doctoral dissertations; and published sources. Careful combination and compilation of data from such sources as well as efforts to adopt techniques that would make better and more innovative use of the historical record could provide data useful to analyzing an even larger subset of all environmental agreements (110). Efforts to develop such datasets and analyze them using quantitative techniques have only recently begun (107).

A brief and incomplete summary gives some sense of how the effects of agreements, and assessments of those effects, vary. Most scholars credit the ozone agreements with rapidly reducing production and consumption of CFCs by industrialized countries, despite debate over whether this reflects regulatory, scientific, economic, or political dynamics and despite concern that the effects on developing countries may be less dramatic (87, 111, 112). A 1911 convention to protect fur seals is credited with dramatically reducing harvest and recovering seal stocks (113, 114). One recent analysis has argued that the whaling regime, until 1984, demonstrated "the impotence of ... IEAs" (115, p. 17); another has argued that the whaling regime has become "quite effective" recently (85, p. 380). Assessments of the LRTAP protocols and pollution of the Rhine suggest they had some influence on behaviors but that many environmental improvements could be better accounted for by factors other than the agreement (78, 116–120). The many MEDPLAN agreements are generally judged as having done little to reduce Mediterranean pollution (73, 121). There are so many fisheries regimes with such different regulatory approaches that, not surprisingly, some appear to have performed quite well, and others appear to have actually made matters worse (122–124). The reader of these and many other assessments is generally left with the sense that evaluating a single agreement well requires sensitivity to complexity and variation and that regimes often have effects that change over time due to institutional change,

change in exogenous factors, may influence one behavior or set of actors, but have no influence on other behaviors or actors (125).

This dynamic and multifaceted character of effects has been highlighted by projects that explicitly have tried to compare the effects of different regimes and the responses of different countries to different regimes (41, 42, 98, 101, 126, 154). A study led by Brown Weiss & Jacobson of five regimes concluded that the regimes related to ozone protection and ocean dumping of radioactive wastes (the London Dumping Convention) were more effective than those related to the 1972 World Heritage Convention and the 1982 International Tropical Timber Agreement (127, pp. 515, 516). Another study led by Miles & Underdal examined 14 regimes (each composed of multiple agreements) and found that more than half achieved significant or major behavioral improvements relative to the no-regime counterfactual during one or more time periods. They also found, however, that almost 60 percent were not particularly effective in "accomplishment of functionally optimal solutions" (128, p. 435). Like Brown Weiss & Jacobson, they deemed the regimes on ozone protection and ocean dumping of radioactive waste to be quite effective and had similar evaluations of the regional regimes protecting the North Sea from dumping by ships and aircraft and managing tuna fisheries in the Central and Southwest Pacific Ocean (42). They also found that the MEDPLAN, MARPOL, the whaling regime, and the 1980 Convention on the Conservation of Antarctic Marine Living Resources were not particularly effective at inducing behavioral change. Regimes related to LRTAP, protection of the North Sea from land-based pollution, and management of salmon in the North Pacific were found to have produced mixed results. Although both these studies judged CITES as being less effective than other agreements, several more detailed evaluations have judged its impacts quite favorably (128a, p. 26; 128b). The judgments made by these researchers, and particularly conflicting judgments such as those regarding CITES or the whaling regime, highlight (a) the difficulty of assessing agreement impacts, (b) the difficulty of comparing impacts, and (c) how much those impacts depend on the standard used by the analyst (117, p. 233). They also suggest that summary claims about regime effects may be less valuable than more nuanced claims about particular effects of interest during particular regime stages. That said, the literature as a whole suggests that some regimes fail quite miserably, others do reasonably well, but very few fully and permanently resolve the problems they address (128, p. 435).

The Determinants of Regime Effects

To say that IEA effects are evident in changes in behavior or environmental quality is not to say that they are the only sources of such changes. Any behavior that can be influenced by an agreement is also subject to many other influences. Changes in treaty-regulated behaviors are often due to factors other than the treaty. Even the strongest supporter of international environmental law would recognize that agreements, however well designed, are not always the cause of good outcomes.

The political science literature to date has focused on how regimes influence the environmental behaviors of states, but it could benefit by framing the question as what explains variation in the environmental behavior of states? This subtle shift directs our attention to the many nonlegal drivers of environmental behaviors that are often arrayed against international environmental agreements but sometimes facilitate their efforts. Environmental economists have done considerable research into factors that explain variation in pollution across countries, factors that have often been ignored when evaluating IEA effects (129). Including economic, technological, political, and other drivers of behavior as explanatory variables in an analysis allows their use as control variables and demonstrates that covariation between an IEA and some outcome persists even after controlling for other factors. This also allows assessment of whether an IEA's influence depends on, and is large or small relative to, these other influences. The plethora of factors hypothesized as driving environmental degradation can be categorized into four groups: characteristics of the country, the international context, the environmental problem, and the agreement (127). Cutting across these categories run distinctions between domestic and international factors and among economic, political, social, and demographic factors.

Both theoretical considerations and empirical evidence suggest that characteristics of the environmental problem explain the likely effects of an agreement on a given behavior but also explain variation in those behaviors (over time, across actors, and across problems) that have nothing to do with agreements (127, p. 521). At the simplest level, countries that are ecologically vulnerable and have low adjustment costs tend to be more responsive to agreements while those that are not affected ecologically or have high adjustment costs tend to be more recalcitrant (77). Problems whose resolution requires new behaviors tend to face violations owing to incentives and incapacity, whereas those that require restraint tend to face only violations owing to incentives. Environmental problems differ in how willing and able relevant actors are to alter their behavior and, hence, how difficult it will be to induce conformance with regime rules (42; 81, p. 1; 101; 102, p. 117). Market structures can reinforce or undercut regulatory efforts—the recovery of fur seals in response to the 1911 agreement owed much to the ease of monitoring that stemmed from London being the only major market for skins (113). Marine pollution agreements benefit from the incentives shipbuilders and ship insurers have to monitor and enforce them, but international endangered species agreements create shortages and price increases that encourage smuggling that undermines their effectiveness (71; 127, p. 521). The major threats to agreements that address tragedy of the commons situations involve efforts to cheat clandestinely; the success of such agreements often requires stringent compliance monitoring to identify cheating. The major threats to agreements that address upstream/downstream situations involve perpetrating states threatening victims with violations unless they receive more compensation for their cooperation; such extortion attempts are, by definition, public and so compliance monitoring is less crucial to these agreements (130).

Other important problem characteristics include the number of actors contributing to a problem, levels of uncertainty about the problem or its resolution, the role and position of corporations, and the concentration of the activity being regulated (127, figure 15.2). Variation in these factors can cause changes in behaviors independent of any agreement. New knowledge of a behavior's environmental impacts will, even without an agreement, reduce such behaviors if their damage imposes large and immediate costs on those engaged in the behavior or on others who have influence over those who engage in the behavior. Polluting behaviors often decline if environmentally friendly technologies become economically attractive, whereas extractive behaviors (e.g., fishing or whaling) tend to be less responsive to technological developments because environmental damage is more inherent to those behaviors. Social and cultural commitments to an activity and economic inertia can create resistance to change, as evident in the difficulty of reducing whaling by countries with cultural commitments to it, such as Norway, or reducing dependence on fossil fuels in most developed states.

Country characteristics explain why countries vary in their environmental degradation and in their responsiveness to agreements. Indeed, economic research has sought to explain pollution levels by reference to country characteristics, such as economic indicators, political and policy indicators, and demographic and social indicators (129, 131–133). Political scientists note the importance of relatively stable forces, such as history and culture, geographic size and heterogeneity, resource endowments, and the number of neighbors; more variable factors, such as level of development, type of government, the role of environmental parties, and attitudes and values; and quite immediate drivers, such as changes in administrative and financial capacity, leadership, NGO activities, and knowledge and information (127, p. 535; 134–137). These factors drive environmental behaviors independent of agreements but also influence the ability and willingness of states to implement international commitments. Marine pollution agreements had little influence on tanker owners and operators when their flag states were the only ones with enforcement rights; they became far more effective after amendments extended enforcement rights to port states that were both more concerned and more able to enforce them (71). Incapacity has been shown to be a major reason that many countries, particularly developing ones, fail to fulfill their environmental commitments (98, 127). And, incapacity problems are worse for agreements that must invoke positive expenditures of resources rather than simple requirements of restraint.

Characteristics of the international context tend to explain major shifts in environmental practices (127, p. 528). The end of the Cold War, the start of the war on terrorism, global economic booms or recessions, large-scale shifts toward democratic governance, and development of new technologies can alter how, and how much, countries protect the environment. Globalization can both encourage environmental protection and hasten environmental degradation (138). The increasing attention of global media and the public to environmental problems has led individuals, corporations, and countries to adopt behaviors and design technologies that produce less environmental harm. That attention is promoted by international conferences, such as the 1972 UN Conference on the Human Environment, the 1992 UN Conference on Environment and Development, and the 2002 World Summit on Sustainable Development, and by major scientific reports on such problems as climate change, biodiversity, or ozone loss (69). NGOs, such as Worldwide Fund for Nature and Greenpeace, and intergovernmental organizations, such as UNEP and the World Bank, have led countries to focus on environmental problems and provided financial and informational resources to address them. These forces also overlap and interplay with agreement features (139, 140). Indeed, although the increasing density of environmental agreements may foster the ability of each to achieve its objectives, there are competing views about whether integrating all environmental agreements into a global environmental organization would facilitate or impede environmental progress (141, 142).

Characteristics of the agreement constitute the influences on environmental behaviors of most interest (127, p. 523). Were realist theory always correct, then characteristics of the problem, countries, and international context would determine behavioral outcomes (143, 144). Institutionalists have shown, however, that regime design and problem-solving capacity also influence outcomes (81, p. 1; 145). Indeed, the time spent negotiating IEAs reflects the assumption that the outcomes achieved depend on agreement design, not just the exogenous factors just delineated. What follows attempts to make sense of the "plethora of propositions as to which types of institutions are likely to be more effective" (103, p. 374).

The social and political process of defining the problem, and the strategies and aggressiveness with which it is addressed, condition an agreement's effects because they determine the costs, obstacles, and resistance to achieving it (54, 146). Aggressive goals may motivate significant behavior change by those who try yet fail to meet them, or they may be ignored as unachievable (54, 147). More realistic goals may achieve visible results quickly but may provide few incentives for actors to do more. The means chosen also surely matter, but even simple questions, such as whether binding agreements induce more change than nonbinding resolutions, remain open (34). Clear regulatory rules may seem crucial to behavioral change, but we do not yet know how regulatory regimes compare to procedural regimes that facilitate recurring collective choice, programmatic regimes that pool resources toward collective goals, or generative regimes that develop new norms (53, p. 145; 102, p. 24). The conditions for success of regulatory regimes have been more fully specified, however, if only because their explicitness makes measuring their effects easier.

Regulatory regimes induce compliance through primary rule systems, information systems, and response systems (106). Effective regimes design these systems so they fit the environmental and behavioral demands of the problem. Regime designers must choose among behavioral prescriptions and proscriptions. Deciding which activity to regulate dictates which actors with what interests and capacities must change their behavior, how large and costly those changes will be, and whether other factors will reinforce or undercut compliance incentives. Designing more specific rules clarifies what is expected for those predisposed to comply and removes the opportunity to claim inadvertence or misinterpretation for those predisposed to violate (148). Even perceptions regarding the fairness of rules can influence their effects (127).

Regimes can increase their effects through choices regarding information systems. Regulating highly transparent activities or those that involve transactions between actors can reassure each actor that others are complying and allow them to protect their interests if they are not. Although most regimes rely on self-reporting systems, those that supply incentives and build the capacity to report appear to work better than others that sanction nonreporting or fail to address practical obstacles to reporting (149). Intrusive monitoring systems have been authorized in several environmental agreements, and rising environmental concern may make them more common.

A regime's influence also depends on how it responds to compliance and violation. In trade and arms control treaties, strategies of direct tit-for-tat reciprocity are likely to be both used and effective: Member states have incentives to raise tariffs on states that violate tariff rules and to build more missiles if other states violate a weapons limitation, and those responses, if carried out, are costly enough to deter many violations (150). In environmental realms, such strategies are less useful because regime supporters are generally unwilling to harm the environment in retaliation for a violation, and even if they did so, such actions would have little influence on those unconcerned about the environment. Recognizing this, many have stressed the need for treaties to couple economic sanctions with careful monitoring and verification mechanisms to trigger them (103, p. 363; 151; 152). Chayes & Chayes argue that such enforcement is less effective than compliance management using diplomacy, norms, and rewards (148). Empirical research has yet to resolve whether enforcement trumps management and, if so, under what conditions (152). Systems of implementation review, sunshine methods, eco-certification, and prior informed consent have also been used by various IEAs to induce behavior changes (127, 101). Norms unsupported by sanctions or rewards, e.g., the Wetland Convention's "wise use" requirement, can foster dialogue and discussion, which in turn may alter perceptions of (and engagement in) appropriate and inappropriate behaviors (153). Crucial questions remain regarding which of these (and other) strategies work best in which circumstances, once the analyst has controlled for characteristics of the issue area, international context, and actors.

The Endogeneity Problem

Evaluating IEA influence not only requires evaluating these competing explanations but poses a final, challenging endogeneity problem: The factors that drive environmental behaviors also determine the agreements that states negotiate as well as which states join agreements once they are concluded. Such factors offer a rival explanation for any purported IEA influence. Agreements are signed only by those states that are ready to limit environmental harm—and only when they are ready to do so. Therefore, by definition, but for reasons unrelated to IEAs, the activities of member states will differ both from their prior behavior and from that of nonmember states. Cases where different treaty provisions correlate with behaviors or environmental quality may be mere reflections of underlying differences in the problem being addressed or other factors. Thus, changes in economic interests may produce pressures to negotiate an agreement and to change behaviors. Highly interdependent (e.g., European) states may adopt more ambitious agreements and change their behavior more readily than less interdependent states. Empirical research on IEA effects faces several such obstacles that require careful theorizing and the use of analytic techniques that are available but are only beginning to be applied to the task.

CONCLUSION

If an IEA is defined as an intergovernmental document intended as legally binding (whether an original agreement or a modification thereto) with a primary stated purpose of managing or preventing human impacts on natural resources, over 700 multilateral IEAs can be identified. Although more difficult to identify, there are more than 1000 and perhaps as many as 2100 BEAs. MEAs break down into about 250 lineages of legally linked agreements, though almost 40 percent of agreements fall into only 20 distinct lineages with many other lineages consisting of only 1 or 2 agreements. Several IEAs were already signed by 1900, and agreement adoption has increased steadily to the point that currently an average of over 20 MEAs and 30 BEAs are signed each year. Among MEAs, an initial focus on species protection has increasingly been balanced by concern with pollutants and, more recently, with habitat protection.

Whether governments are willing to negotiate and join IEAs depends on a range of factors, including the magnitude, likelihood, and distribution of the consequences of an environmental problem; the environmental, economic, social, and political effects of taking or not taking action on the problem; the way those effects are distributed across countries; the way different sectors within those countries perceive the costs and benefits of those effects; each country's inclinations regarding whether and how to respond to such threats; and the general and issue-specific power countries have to promote or restrain international agreement. Crises involving environmental disasters or breakthroughs in scientific understanding can foster agreement where it might otherwise be unlikely. In understanding global efforts on climate change, regional efforts on air pollution and fisheries, or bilateral efforts on river and lake pollutants, these and related factors go far to explain both the positions of individual governments and the ebb and flow in the success and failure of negotiations.

Deciphering whether IEAs, once signed, change the behaviors of governments, corporations, and individuals in ways that improve the environment also poses challenging analytic tasks. The effects and effectiveness of most environmental agreements have yet to be carefully analyzed, but research to date has identified considerable variation in their effectiveness. Agreements on stratospheric ozone depletion, dumping of wastes in the North Sea, and dumping of radioactive wastes globally are some of those that have been judged as quite influential; those addressing the world's natural and cultural heritage, tropical timber, and many fisheries have usually been judged as less effective (42, 124, 154). But such judgments of these and other agreements depend considerably on the criteria used to evaluate effectiveness and on the analyst's skills in estimating what would have happened without the agreement. Research to date has demonstrated that, although the inclusion of specific design features in particular IEAs can sometimes make them more effective, whether any particular IEA design is effective also will depend on a wide range of other variables and parameters including characteristics of the countries involved, the environmental problem being addressed, and the international context (127).

Treaties, conventions, and other legal agreements among governments will be important features of global environmental governance for the foreseeable future. Policymakers will want to develop IEAs to address new environmental problems in the future and redesign existing IEAs that are performing poorly in the present. Scholars have begun to address these policy needs; they have shed light on the factors that foster and hinder intergovernmental negotiation and that lead some IEAs, once concluded, to perform well and others to perform poorly. But greater efforts to answer existing questions and pose new ones, to employ a broader range of methodologies, and to use evidence from more of the extant MEAs and BEAs than have been studied to date will allow researchers to advise policymakers more confidently and more effectively in the future.

ACKNOWLEDGMENTS

The author thanks William C. Clark, Peter H. Sand, and an anonymous reviewer for their helpful comments on an earlier draft of this article. William C. Clark, Robert O. Keohane, and Peter H. Sand have provided valuable advice throughout project development. This article benefited from excellent research assistance by Irina Parshikova, Kari Lundgren, Alexia dePottere-Smith, and Lindsey Schatzberg. The discussions of regime formation and effects build on an earlier version of this argument in Reference 49, which benefited from suggestions from Walter Carlsnaes, Peter Haas, David Patel, M.J. Peterson, Kal Raustiala, Thomas Risse, Beth Simmons, Detlef Sprinz, Paul Steinberg, Paul Wapner, and Oran Young. Research for this article was completed with generous support from a Sabbatical Fellowship in the Humanities and Social Sciences from the American Philosophical Society, a 2002 Summer Research Award from the University of Oregon, and Stanford University's Center for Environmental Science and Policy. All errors remain the responsibility of the author. The International Environmental Agreements database and links to all web-based sources cited in this review will be maintained at Reference 31.

The *Annual Review of Environment and Resources* is online at http://environ.annualreviews.org

LITERATURE CITED

1. UN Glob. Compact Netw. 2002. *The Global Compact.* http://www.unglobalcompact.org/
2. Kara J, Quarless D. 2002. *Guiding Principles for Partnerships for Sustainable Development ('Type 2 Outcomes') to be Elaborated by Interested Parties in the Context of the World Summit on Sustainable Development: Explanatory Note by the Vice-Chairs,* UN Comm. Sustain. Dev. New York. http://www.un.org/esa/sustdev/partnerships/guiding_principles7june2002
3. Nye JS, Donahue JD, eds. 2000. *Governance in a Globalizing World.* Washington, DC: Brookings Inst.
4. Keck ME, Sikkink K. 1998. *Activists Beyond Borders: Advocacy Networks in International Politics.* Ithaca: Cornell Univ. Press
5. Costanza R, Low BS, Ostrom E, Wilson J. 2001. *Institutions, Ecosystems, and Sustainability.* New York: Lewis
6. Wapner P. 1996. *Environmental Activism and World Civic Politics.* Albany, NY: State Univ. New York Press
7. Lipschutz RD, Mayer J. 1996. *Global Civil Society and Global Environmental Governance: The Politics of Nature From Place to Planet.* Albany, NY: State Univ. New York Press
8. Board Sustain. Dev. Policy Div., Natl. Res. Counc. 1999. *Our Common Journey: A Transition Toward Sustainability.* Washington, DC: Natl. Acad.
9. Kiss AC, eds. 1983. *Selected Multilateral Treaties in the Field of the Environment.* Vol. 1. Nairobi: UN Environ. Program.
10. Rummel-Bulska I, Osafo S, eds. 1991. *Selected Multilateral Treaties in the Field of the Environment.* Vol. 2. Nairobi: UN Environ. Program.
11. Hohmann H. 1992. *Basic Documents of International Environmental Law.* Boston: Graham & Trotman
12. Brown Weiss E, Magraw DB, Szasz PC. 1999. *International Environmental Law: Basic Instruments and References, 1992–1999.* Ardsley, NY: Transnational
12a. Sands P, Tarasofsky R. 1994. *Documents in International Environmental Law.* Manchester, UK: Manchester Univ. Press
13. Alder J, Lugten G, Kay R, Ferriss B. 2001. Compliance with international fisheries instruments in the North Atlantic. In *Fisheries Impacts on North Atlantic Ecosystems: Evaluations and Policy Exploration,* eds. T Pitcher, UR Sumaila, D Pauly, pp. 55–80. Vancouver: Fish. Cent., Univ. British Columbia
14. Burns W. 2002. *American Society of International Law Wildlife Interest Group Listing of Treaties and Soft Law Agreements.* http://eelink.net/~asilwildlife/treaties.shtml
15. UN Environ. Program. 2002. *Regional Seas Conventions and Protocols.* http://www.unep.ch/seas/main/hconlist.html
16. UN Environ. Program. 2002. *Legal Agreements Relating to the Marine Environment.* http://www.unep.ch/seas/main/hlegal.html
17. Hedley C. 2002. *Oceanlaw's Internet Guide to International Fisheries Law.* http://www.oceanlaw.net/
18. Molitor M, ed. 1991. *International*

Environmental Law: Primary Materials. Boston, MA: Kluwer Law Tax.
19. UN Food Agric. Organ. Legal Off. 2002. *Treaties Deposited With FAO.* http://www.fao.org/Legal/treaties/Treaty-e.htm
20. UN Environ. Program. Div. Environ. Conv. 2002. *Multilateral Environmental Agreements.* http://www.unep.ch/conventions/geclist.htm
21. Int. Marit. Organ. 2002. *Complete List of Conventions.* http://www.imo.org/Conventions/mainframe.asp?topic_id = 260
22. Can. Dep. Foreign Aff. Int. Trade. 2002. *Database of Canada's International Environmental Commitments.* http://pubx.dfait-maeci.gc.ca/A_Branch/AES/Env_commitments.nsf/Homepage/
23. Finn. Minist. Environ. 2002. *Finland's International Environmental Agreements.* http://www.vyh.fi/eng/intcoop/agreem/agree_t.htm
24. Pace Virtual Environ. Law Libr. 1997. *International Table of Contents.* http://www.pace.edu/lawschool/env/chronologicalorder.html
25. Fletcher Sch. Law Dipl. 2002. *Multilaterals Project: Multilateral Conventions.* http://fletcher.tufts.edu/multi/chrono.html
26. Burhenne WE, ed. 1974. *International Environmental Law: Multilateral Treaties.* Bonn: Kluwer Law Int.
27. Rüster B, Simma B, eds. 1975. *International Protection of the Environment: Treaties and Related Documents.* Dobbs Ferry, NY: Oceana
28. Rüster B, Simma B. 1990. *International Protection of the Environment, Second Series: Treaties and Related Documents.* Dobbs Ferry, NY: Oceana
29. ECOLEX. 2002. *Multilateral Treaties.* http://www.ecolex.org/
30. Cent. Int. Earth Sci. Inf. Netw. 2001. *ENTRI Treaty Texts: Menu of Treaty Texts.* http://sedac.ciesin.columbia.edu/entri/
31. Mitchell RB. 2003. *International Environmental Agreements Database.* http://darkwing.uoregon.edu/~rmitchel/iea/
32. Aust A. 2000. *Modern Treaty Law and Practice.* Cambridge, UK: Cambridge Univ. Press
33. Burhenne WE, Jahnke M. 1993. *International Environmental Soft Law: Collection of Relevant Instruments.* Dordrecht: M. Nijhoff
34. Brown Weiss E, ed. 1997. *International Compliance With Nonbinding Accords.* Washington, DC: Am. Soc. Int. Law
35. Abbott KW, Snidal D. 2000. Hard and soft law in international governance. *Int. Organ.* 54:421–56
36. Caldwell LK. 1980. *International Environmental Policy and Law.* Durham, NC: Duke Univ. Press
37. Birnie PW, Boyle AE. 2002. *International Law and the Environment.* Oxford: Oxford Univ. Press
38. Haas PM, Sundgren J. 1993. Evolving international environmental law: changing practices of national sovereignty. In *Global Accord: Environmental Challenges and International Responses*, ed. N Choucri, pp. 401–29. Cambridge, MA: MIT Press
39. Daily GC, ed. 1997. *Nature's Services: Societal Dependence on Natural Ecosystems.* Washington, DC: Island
40. UN Environ. Program. 1996. *Register of International Treaties and Other Agreements in the Field of the Environment.* Nairobi: UN Environ. Program.
41. Young OR, ed. 1999. *Effectiveness of International Environmental Regimes: Causal Connections and Behavioral Mechanisms.* Cambridge, MA: MIT Press
42. Miles EL, Underdal A, Andresen S, Wettestad J, Skjærseth JB, Carlin EM, eds. 2001. *Environmental Regime Effectiveness: Confronting Theory With Evidence.* Cambridge, MA: MIT Press
43. Krasner SD. 1983. Structural causes and regime consequences: regimes as

intervening variables. See Ref. 155, pp. 1–22
44. Lipson C. 1991. Why are some international agreements informal? *Int. Organ.* 45:495–538
45. UN Econ. Comm. Europe. 2002. *UN-ECE Environment and Human Settlements Division Home Page.* http://www.unece.org/env/
46. UN Food Agric. Organ. 2002. *FAO Regional Fisheries Bodies Home Page.* http://www.fao.org/fi/body/rfb/index.htm
47. UN Food Agric. Organ. 2002. *FAOLEX database.* http://faolex.fao.org/faolex/
48. Jacobson HK, Brown Weiss E. 1998. A framework for analysis. See Ref. 154, pp. 1–18
49. Mitchell RB. 2002. International environment. In *Handbook of International Relations,* ed. W Carlsnaes, T Risse, B Simmons, pp. 500–16. Thousand Oaks, CA: Sage
50. Young OR. 1989. The politics of international regime formation: managing natural resources and the environment. *Int. Organ.* 43:349–76
51. Lipschutz RD. 1991. Bargaining among nations: culture, history, and perceptions in regime formation. *Eval. Rev.* 15:46–74
52. Young OR, Osherenko G, eds. 1993. *Polar Politics: Creating International Environmental Regimes.* Ithaca: Cornell Univ. Press
53. Young OR. 1998. *Creating Regimes: Arctic Accords and International Governance.* Ithaca: Cornell Univ. Press
54. Soc. Learn. Group, eds. 2001. *Learning to Manage Global Environmental Risks.* Vol.1. *A Comparative History of Social Responses to Climate Change, Ozone Depletion and Acid Rain.* Cambridge: MIT Press
55. Soc. Learn. Group, ed. 2001. *Learning to Manage Global Environmental Risks.* Vol. 2. *A Functional Analysis of Social Responses to Climate Change, Ozone Depletion and Acid Rain.* Cambridge: MIT Press
56. Stein AA. 1983. Coordination and collaboration: regimes in an anarchic world. See Ref. 155, pp. 115–40
57. Martin LL. 1992. Interests, power, and multilateralism. *Int. Organ.* 46:765–92
58. Barkin JS, Shambaugh G, eds. 1999. *Anarchy and the Environment: The International Relations of Common Pool Resources.* Albany, NY: State Univ. New York Press
59. Wettestad J. 1999. *Designing Effective Environmental Regimes: The Key Conditions.* Cheltenham, UK: Edward Elgar
60. Hardin G. 1968. The tragedy of the commons. *Science* 162:1243–48
61. Mitchell RB, Keilbach P. 2001. Reciprocity, coercion, or exchange: symmetry, asymmetry and power in institutional design. *Int. Organ.* 55:891–917
62. Hasenclever A, Mayer P, Rittberger V. 1997. *Theories of International Regimes.* Cambridge, UK: Cambridge Univ. Press
63. Zürn M. 1998. The rise of international environmental politics: a review of current research. *World Polit.* 50:617–49
64. Kingdon JW. 1984. *Agendas, Alternatives, and Public Policies.* Boston, MA: Little, Brown
65. Sabatier PA, Jenkins-Smith HC, eds. 1993. *Policy Change and Learning: An Advocacy Coalition Approach.* Boulder, CO: Westview
66. Litfin KT. 1994. *Ozone Discourses: Science and Politics in Global Environmental Cooperation.* New York: Columbia Univ. Press
67. Benedick RE. 1998. *Ozone Diplomacy: New Directions in Safeguarding the Planet.* Cambridge, MA: Harvard Univ. Press
68. Keohane RO. 1996. Analyzing the effectiveness of international environmental institutions. See Ref. 94, pp. 3–27
69. Clark WC, Mitchell RB, Cash DW, Alcock F. 2002. *Information as influence: how institutions mediate the impact of*

scientific assessments on global environmental affairs. *Rep. Fac. Res. Work. Pap. RWP02-044*, Kennedy Sch. Gov., Harvard Univ., Cambridge, MA
70. Kammen DM, Dove MR. 1997. The virtues of mundane science. *Environment* 39:10–19
71. Mitchell RB. 1994. *Intentional Oil Pollution at Sea: Environmental Policy and Treaty Compliance*. Cambridge, MA: MIT Press
72. M'Gonigle RM, Zacher MW. 1979. *Pollution, Politics, and International Law: Tankers at Sea*. Berkeley, CA: Univ. of Calif. Press
73. Haas PM. 1990. *Saving the Mediterranean: The Politics of International Environmental Cooperation*. New York: Columbia Univ. Press
74. Princen T, Finger M. 1994. *Environmental NGOs in World Politics: Linking the Local and the Global*. New York: Routledge
75. Raustiala K. 1997. States, NGOs, and international environmental institutions. *Int. Stud. Q.* 41:719–40
76. DeSombre ER. 2000. *Domestic Sources of International Environmental Policy: Industry, Environmentalists, and U.S. Power*. Cambridge, MA: MIT Press
77. Sprinz D, Vaahtoranta T. 1994. The interest-based explanation of international environmental policy. *Int. Organ.* 48:77–105
78. Levy M. 1993. European acid rain: the power of tote-board diplomacy. See Ref. 98, pp. 75–132
79. O'Neill K. 2000. *Waste Trading Among Rich Nations*. Cambridge, MA: MIT Press
80. Schreurs MA, Economy E, eds. 1997. *The Internationalization of Environmental Protection*. Oxford: Oxford Univ. Press
81. Underdal A. 2001. One question, two answers. See Ref. 42, pp. 1–47
82. Young OR. 1989. *International Cooperation: Building Regimes for Natural Resources and the Environment*. Ithaca, NY: Cornell Univ. Press
83. Gruber L. 2000. *Ruling the World*. Princeton: Princeton Univ. Press
84. Caron DD. 1995. The International Whaling Commission and the North Atlantic Marine Mammal Commission: the institutional risks of coercion in consensual structures. *Am. J. Int. Law* 89:154–74
85. Andresen S. 2001. The International Whaling Commission (IWC): more failure than success? See Ref. 42, pp. 379–403
86. Keohane RO. 1986. Reciprocity in international relations. *Int. Organ.* 40:1–27
87. Parson EA. 2003. *Protecting the Ozone Layer: Science and Strategy*. Oxford: Oxford Univ. Press
88. Stokke OS. 1998. Understanding the formation of international environmental regimes: the discursive challenge. See Ref. 156, pp. 129–48
89. Sandford R. 1996. International environmental treaty secretariats: a case of neglected potential? *Environ. Impact Assess. Rev.* 16:3–12
90. Haas PM. 1992. Epistemic communities and international policy coordination. *Int. Organ.* 46:1–35
91. McCormick J. 1999. The role of environmental NGOs in international regimes. In *The Global Environment: Institutions, Law, and Policy*, ed. NJ Vig, RS Axelrod, pp. 52–71. Washington, DC: CQ Press
92. List M, Rittberger V. 1998. The role of intergovernmental organizations in the formation and evolution of international environmental regimes. See Ref. 156, pp. 67–81
93. Deudney D. 1990. The case against linking environmental degradation and national security. *Millennium* 19:461–76
94. Keohane RO, Levy MA, eds. 1996. *Institutions for Environmental Aid: Pitfalls and Promise*. Cambridge, MA: MIT Press

95. Jakobeit C. 1996. Nonstate actors leading the way: debt-for-nature swaps. See Ref. 94, pp. 127–66
96. Garcia-Johnson R. 2000. *Exporting Environmentalism: U.S. Multinational Chemical Corporations in Brazil and Mexico*. Cambridge, MA: MIT Press
97. Clapp J. 1998. The privatization of global environmental governance: ISO 14000 and the developing world. *Glob. Gov.* 4:295–316
98. Haas PM, Keohane RO, Levy MA, eds. 1993. *Institutions for the Earth: Sources of Effective International Environmental Protection*. Cambridge, MA: MIT Press
99. Cameron J, Werksman J, Roderick P, eds. 1996. *Improving Compliance With International Environmental Law*. London: Earthscan
100. Deleted in proof
101. Victor DG, Raustiala K, Skolnikoff EB, eds. 1998. *The Implementation and Effectiveness of International Environmental Commitments: Theory and Practice*. Cambridge, MA: MIT Press
102. Young OR. 1999. *Governance in World Affairs*. Ithaca, NY: Cornell Univ. Press
103. Bernauer T. 1995. The effect of international environmental institutions: how we might learn more. *Int. Organ.* 49:351–77
104. Helm C, Sprinz D. 2000. Measuring the effectiveness of international environmental regimes. *J. Confl. Resolut.* 44:630–52
105. D'Amato A, Chopra SK. 1991. Whales: their emerging right to life. *Am. J. Int. Law* 85:21–62
106. Mitchell RB. 1996. Compliance theory: an overview. See Ref. 99, pp. 3–28
107. Mitchell RB. 2002. A quantitative approach to evaluating international environmental regimes. *Glob. Environ. Polit.* 2:58–83
108. Sprinz D, Wolinsky Y, eds. 2004. *Methods of Inquiry in International Politics*. Ann Arbor: Univ. of Mich. Press. In press
109. UN Food Agric. Organ. 2002. *Fishery Software, FISHSTAT Plus: Universal Software for Fishery Statistical Time Series*. http://www.fao.org/fi/statist/FISOFT/FISHPLUS.asp
110. Jackson JBC, Kirby MX, Berger WH, Bjorndal KA, Botsford LW, et al. 2001. Historical overfishing and the recent collapse of coastal ecosystems. *Science* 293:629–37
111. Wettestad J. 2001. The Vienna Convention and Montreal Protocol on ozone-layer depletion. See Ref. 42, pp. 149–70
112. Greene O. 1998. The system for implementation review in the ozone regime. See Ref. 101, pp. 89–136
113. Gay JT. 1987. *American Fur Seal Diplomacy: The Alaskan Fur Seal Controversy*. New York: Peter Lang
114. Dorsey K. 1991. Putting a ceiling on sealing: conservation and cooperation in the international arena, 1909–1911. *Environ. Hist. Rev.* 15:27–45
115. Schneider V, Pearce D. 2002. What saved the whales? An economic analysis of 20th century whaling. Presented at New Zealand Assoc. Econ. Conf. 2002, Wellington
116. Wettestad J. 2001. The Convention on Long-Range Transboundary Air Pollution (CLRTAP). See Ref. 42, 197–221
117. Munton D, Soroos M, Nikitina E, Levy MA. 1999. Acid rain in Europe and North America. In *The Effectiveness of International Environmental Regimes: Causal Connections and Behavioral Mechanisms*, ed. OR Young, pp. 155–247. Cambridge, MA: MIT Press
118. Murdoch JC, Sandler T, Sargent K. 1997. A tale of two collectives: sulphur versus nitrogen oxides emission reduction in Europe. *Economica* 64:281–301
119. Bernauer T. 1995. The international financing of environmental protection: lessons from efforts to protect the River

Rhine against chloride pollution. *Environ. Polit.* 4:369–90
120. Bernauer T, Moser P. 1996. Reducing pollution of the Rhine River: the influence of international cooperation. *J. Environ. Dev.* 5:391–417
121. Skjærseth JB. 2001. The effectiveness of the Mediterranean Action Plan. See Ref. 42, pp. 311–30
122. Miles EL. 2001. The management of tuna fisheries in the west central and southwest Pacific. See Ref. 42, pp. 117–48
123. Stokke OS, Anderson LG, Mirovitskaya N. 1999. The Barents Sea fisheries. See Ref. 117, pp. 91–154
124. Peterson MJ. 1993. International fisheries management. See Ref. 98, pp. 249–308
125. Gehring T. 1994. *Dynamic International Regimes: Institutions for International Environmental Governance.* Frankfurt am Main: P. Lang
126. Breitmeier H. 1999. *International Regimes Database.* http://www.ifs.tu-darmstadt.de/pg/ird_home.htm
127. Jacobson HK, Brown Weiss E. 1998. Assessing the record and designing strategies to engage countries. See Ref. 154, pp. 511–54
128. Underdal A. 2001. Conclusions: patterns of regime effectiveness. See Ref. 42, pp. 433–65
128a. Sand PH. 1997. Commodity or taboo? International regulation of trade in endangered species. In *Green Globe Yearbook of International Co-operation on Environment and Development 1997*, ed. HO Bergesen, G Parmann, pp. 19–36. New York: Oxford Univ. Press
128b. Sand PH. 2001. A century of green lessons: the contribution of nature conservation regimes to global environmental governance. *Int. Environ. Agreements: Pol., Law Econ.* 1:33–72
129. Harbaugh W, Levinson A, Wilson D. 2000. *Re-examining the empirical evidence for an environmental Kuznets curve. Rep. 7711*, Natl. Bur. Econ. Res., Cambridge, MA
130. Darst RG. 2001. *Smokestack Diplomacy: Cooperation and Conflict in East-West Environmental Politics.* Cambridge, MA: MIT Press
131. Grossman GM, Krueger AB. 1995. Economic growth and the environment. *Q. J. Econ.* 110:353–77
132. Selden T, Song D. 1994. Environmental quality and development: Is there a Kuznets curve for air pollution emissions? *J. Environ. Econ. Manag.* 27:147–62
133. Anderson D, Cavendish W. 2001. Dynamic simulation and environmental policy analysis: beyond comparative statics and the environmental Kuznets curve. *Oxford Econ. Pap.* 53:721–46
134. Inglehart R. 1990. *Culture Shift in Advanced Industrial Society.* Princeton: Princeton Univ. Press
135. Dauvergne P. 1997. *Shadows in the Forest: Japan and the Politics of Timber in Southeast Asia.* Cambridge, MA: MIT Press
136. Ross ML. 2001. *Timber Booms and Institutional Breakdown in Southeast Asia.* Cambridge: Cambridge Univ. Press
137. Steinberg PF. 2001. *Environmental Leadership in Developing Countries: Transnational Relations and Biodiversity Policy in Costa Rica and Bolivia.* Cambridge, MA: MIT Press
138. Clark WC. 2000. Environmental globalization. See Ref. 3, pp. 86–108
139. Young OR. 2002. *The Institutional Dimensions of Environmental Change: Fit, Interplay, and Scale.* Cambridge, MA: MIT Press
140. Stokke OS. 2001. *Governing High Seas Fisheries: The Interplay of Global and Regional Regimes.* Oxford: Oxford Univ. Press
141. Biermann F. 2000. The case for a world environment organization. *Environment* 42:23–31
142. Juma C. 2000. The perils of centralizing

global environmental governance. *Environment* 42:44–45
143. Waltz K. 1979. *Theory of International Politics*. Reading, MA: Addison-Wesley
144. Strange S. 1983. Cave! Hic dragones: a critique of regime analysis. See Ref. 155, pp. 337–54
145. Mitchell RB. 1994. Regime design matters: intentional oil pollution and treaty compliance. *Int. Organ.* 48:425–58
146. Eijndhoven Jv, Clark WC, Jäger J. 2001. The long-term development of global environmental risk management: conclusions and implications for the future. See Ref. 55, pp. 181–97
147. Levy MA, Cavender-Bares J, Clark WC, Dinkelman G, Nikitina E, et al. 2001. Goal and strategy formulation in the management of global environmental risks. See Ref. 55, pp. 87–113
148. Chayes A, Chayes AH. 1995. *The New Sovereignty: Compliance With International Regulatory Agreements*. Cambridge, MA: Harvard Univ. Press
149. Mitchell RB. 1998. Sources of transparency: information systems in international regimes. *Int. Stud. Q.* 42:109–30
150. Axelrod R. 1984. *The Evolution of Cooperation*. New York: Basic Books
151. Wettestad J. 1995. Science, politics and institutional design: some initial notes on the Long-Range Transboundary Air Pollution Regime. *J. Environ. Dev.* 4:165–83
152. Downs GW, Rocke DM, Barsoom PN. 1996. Is the good news about compliance good news about cooperation? *Int. Organ.* 50:379–406
153. Finnemore M. 1996. *National Interests in International Society*. Ithaca: Cornell Univ. Press
154. Brown Weiss E, Jacobson HK, eds. 1988. *Engaging Countries: Strengthening Compliance With International Environmental Accords*. Cambridge, MA: MIT Press
155. Krasner SD, eds. 1983. *International Regimes*. Ithaca, NY: Cornell Univ. Press
156. Underdal A, eds. 1998. *The Politics of International Environmental Management*. Dordrecht: Kluwer Acad.

TRACKING MULTIPLE PATHWAYS OF HUMAN EXPOSURE TO PERSISTENT MULTIMEDIA POLLUTANTS: Regional, Continental, and Global-Scale Models

Thomas E. McKone[1] and Matthew MacLeod[2]

[1]*University of California, School of Public Health and Lawrence Berkeley National Laboratory, One Cyclotron Road, 90R-3058, Berkeley, California 94720; email: temckone@lbl.gov*
[2]*Lawrence Berkeley National Laboratory, One Cyclotron Road, 90R-3058, Berkeley, California 94720; email: mjmacleod@lbl.gov*

Key Words pollutant transport, mass-balance models, fugacity, model evaluation

■ **Abstract** Widespread observations of organic pollutant compounds in vegetation, soil, animals, and human tissue have motivated research on more accurate characterizations of chemical transport over regional, continental, and global scales. Efforts to assess human and ecosystem exposure to contaminants from multiple environmental media have been evolving over the last several decades. In this review, we summarize the development and evolution of the multimedia mass-balance approach to pollutant fate and exposure evaluation and illustrate some of the calculations used in multimedia assessments. The concepts that form the foundation of Mackay-type mass-balance compartment models are described, and the ongoing efforts to use multimedia models to quantify human exposures are discussed. A series of case studies of varying complexity are used to illustrate capabilities and limitations of selected multimedia approaches. We look to the future and consider current challenges and opportunities in the field of multimedia contaminant fate and exposure modeling.

CONTENTS

INTRODUCTION 464
    The History and Motivation for Multimedia Models 466
    A Brief Overview of Multimedia, Multipathway Modeling 467
    Overview of the Chapter 467
MULTIMEDIA CONTAMINANT FATE: THEORY AND MODELS 468
    Phase Equilibrium and Chemical Partitioning in Environmental Systems 468
    Fugacity and Fugacity Capacity 469
    Partitioning in a Closed System—Level I Models 470

Equilibrium Partitioning in an Open System—Level II Models 471
Nonequilibrium Partitioning in Open Systems—Level III Models 473
Dynamic, Open, and Nonequilibrium Systems—Level IV Models 475
MULTIPATHWAY EXPOSURE MODELS 475
Exposure Events 476
Cumulative Exposure Models 477
APPLICATIONS OF MULTIMEDIA FATE AND EXPOSURE MODELS 477
Generic Screening or Evaluative Models 478
Regional and Spatially Resolved Models 479
Assessing Exposures to Humans and Ecosystems 480
Sustainability and Life-Cycle Impact Assessment 482
MODEL EVALUATION STRATEGIES 482
Sensitivity and Uncertainty Analyses 483
Model Evaluation and Confidence Building 484
Discussion and Conclusions 486

INTRODUCTION

In the late-1950s, scientists began to recognize that certain chemical pollutants were capable of persisting in the environment for a long time, migrating between air, water, soils, and sediments, and accumulating to levels that could harm wildlife and humans. Carson brought this issue into the public eye in 1962 with her classic book *Silent Spring* (1), which described the potential environmental impacts of the insecticide DDT. Shortly thereafter, the discovery of polychlorinated biphenyls in fish throughout Sweden by Jensen (2) showed that industrial chemicals designed for use in closed systems were also entering the environment and accumulating to significant concentrations.

Prior to this time, the field of contaminant fate and exposure assessment was concentrated piecemeal on assessing chemical behavior in air, water, or soil, but this paradigm ran counter to the emerging realizations about the behavior of chemicals in the environment. A novel approach was required that described interactions between the seemingly distinct components of the ecosystem—the atmosphere, hydrosphere, lithosphere, and biosphere. In an effort to both articulate these issues and set new directions for environmental policy, the Council on Environmental Quality, which coordinates federal environmental initiatives in the United States, recommended in 1985 that long-term environmental research focus on 1. contaminant transfer rates among environmental media (i.e., soil, water, and air); 2. geohydrological processes at soil/water/air interfaces; 3. the role of biological, physical, and chemical processes in pollutant transport; and 4. the scientific basis for quantitative risk assessment (3). As illustrated in Figure 1, the multimedia approach requires comprehensive assessments that locate all points of chemical release to the environment, characterize mass-balance relationships, and track the contaminants through the entire environmental system to exposure of individuals or populations. A complete assessment of this type can be used to identify where in the chain of events control efforts would be most effective.

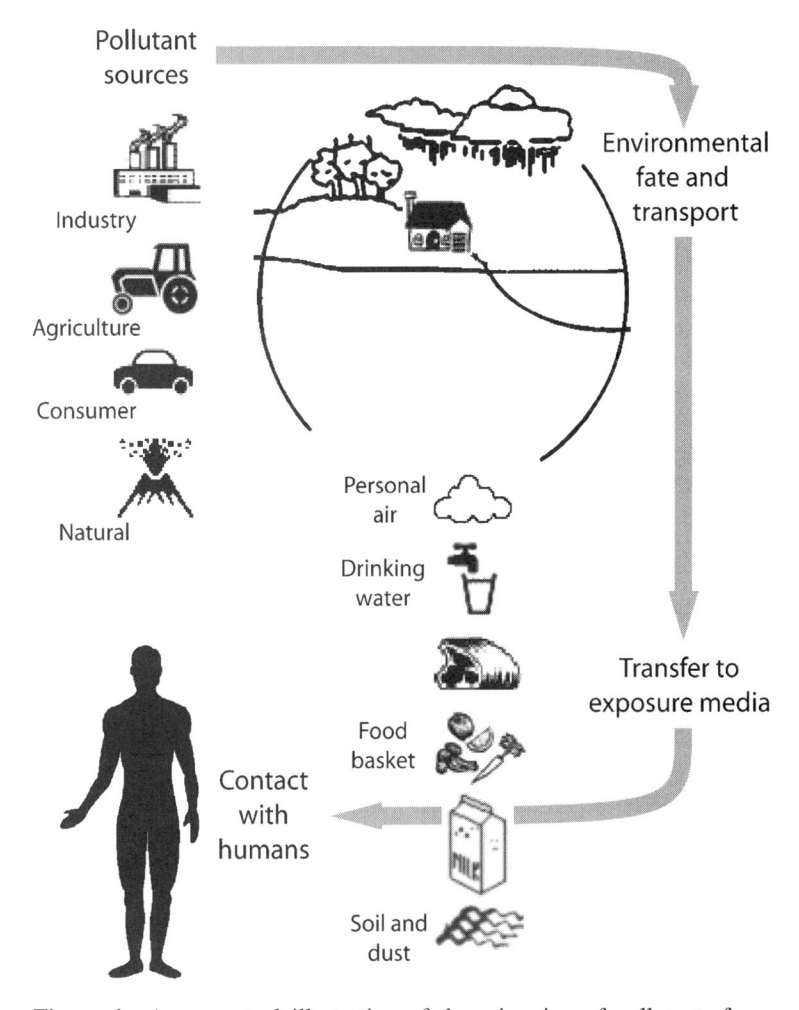

Figure 1 A conceptual illustration of the migration of pollutants from sources, through the multimedia environment and into exposure media, followed by contact with humans.

The emergence of the multimedia paradigm has focused attention on the long-term behavior and effects of chemicals released from modern industrial economies into the environment. Organic-chemical, inorganic-chemical, and radionuclide contamination of soils, the release of volatile and semivolatile organic compounds to air and to soil, and toxic-chemical runoff to surface water are all multimedia problems. Since 1985 an entire discipline of multimedia modeling of contaminants has evolved, and many useful techniques and modeling tools have been developed. Multimedia fate models are now widely applied for many types of environmental assessments. In this review, we document the development and application of multimedia models to questions about chemical transport and fate, cumulative exposure assessment, human and ecological health risk, and the behavior of persistent pollutants. We also explore questions about the models' reliability and how to address uncertainty in results and provide policy makers with useful guidance. These models have become widely accepted despite being impossible to validate in the conventional sense because of their inherent structure. We discuss reasons for this acceptance and suggest future research directions that will ensure the models remain useful conceptual and policy-making tools.

The History and Motivation for Multimedia Models

It is difficult to identify the true origin of multimedia models; however, it is clear that the need to assess human exposure to global fallout in the 1950s required considering transport through and among air, soil, surface water, vegetation, and food chains (4–9). Papers in the health physics and radioecology literature did not specifically refer to these models as multimedia, but they included many of the attributes that we now consider part of the multimedia-model genre. In the 1970s, growing concerns about the impacts of metal species such as lead, cadmium, mercury, and arsenic resulted in efforts to develop global and regional mass-balance models for these metals (10–12).

Regional/global mass-balance models for organic chemicals clearly emerged in the late 1970s with the publications of the first edition of *Chemodynamics* (13) and the seminal papers by Mackay describing the application of fugacity principles to environmental problems (14–16). In the early 1980s, Bennett (17–19) applied the source-to-dose methods of the health physics field to metals and organic chemicals with what he called the "exposure-commitment method," which was primarily an empirical model. By the late 1980s multimedia modeling had become more established and was the subject of several reviews, national workshops, and studies (20–24).

The most widely used multimedia models are the mass-conservative Mackay-type compartment models (14–16, 22, 24, 25). These models are most appropriate for treating transport and transformation of chemicals emanating from nonpoint sources over relatively long time and length scales at low concentrations.

An important extension of the multimedia paradigm was the introduction of comprehensive models that linked environmental contamination to multiple pathways for human or wildlife exposure. McKone & Layton (26) were among the first to link regional multimedia mass-balance models to deterministic multipathway exposure models to assess the health risks of the U.S. Army's program for managing the disposal of explosives and propellants. By the early 1990s, the paradigm was sufficiently well accepted by scientists and regulators that the California Environmental Protection Agency adopted a multimedia approach for setting clean-soil goals through its CalTOX program (27–31), and the European Union adopted a multimedia multipathway framework for chemical risk

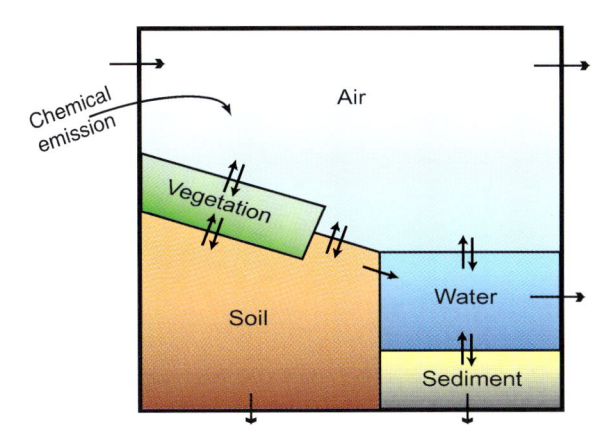

Figure 2 A conceptual multimedia environment. The arrows represent chemical transfer and transport pathways between the compartments.

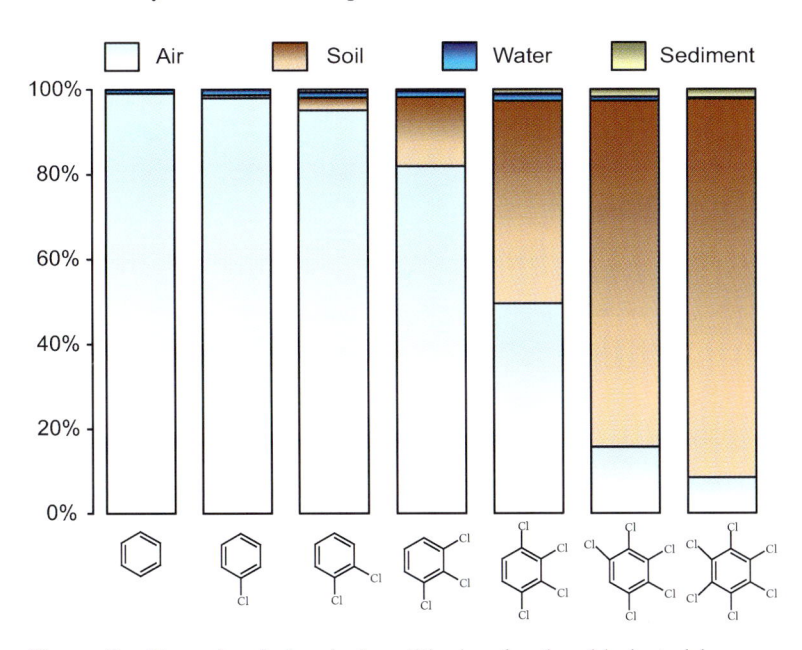

Figure 3 Example of chemical partitioning for the chlorinated benzene series.

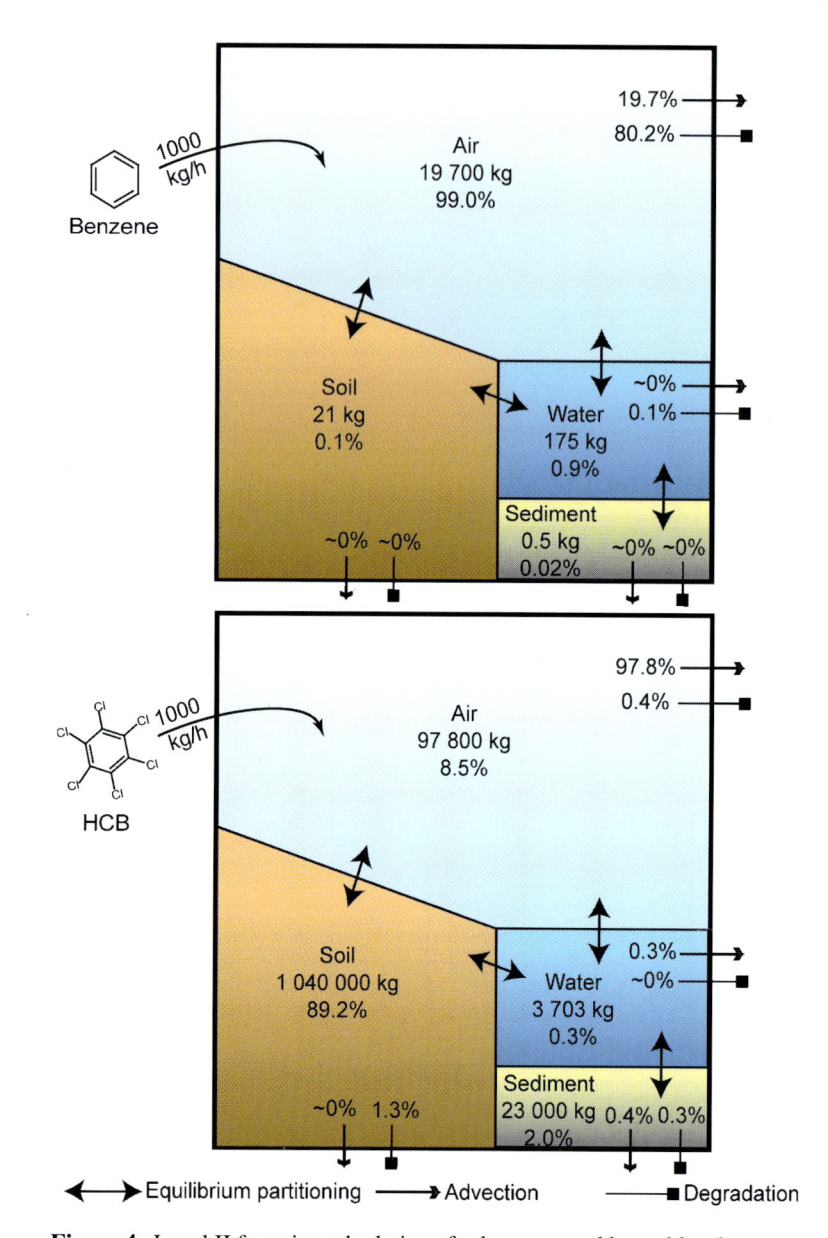

Figure 4 Level II fugacity calculations for benzene and hexachlorobenzene.

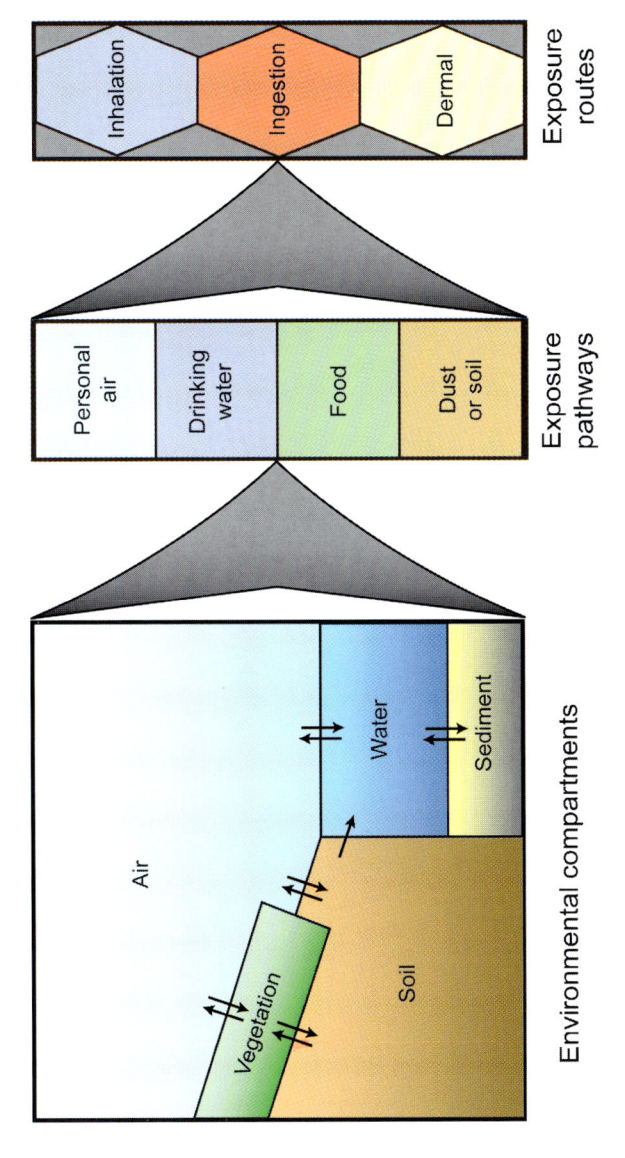

Figure 5 An illustration of the links between emissions, environmental media, and human contact.

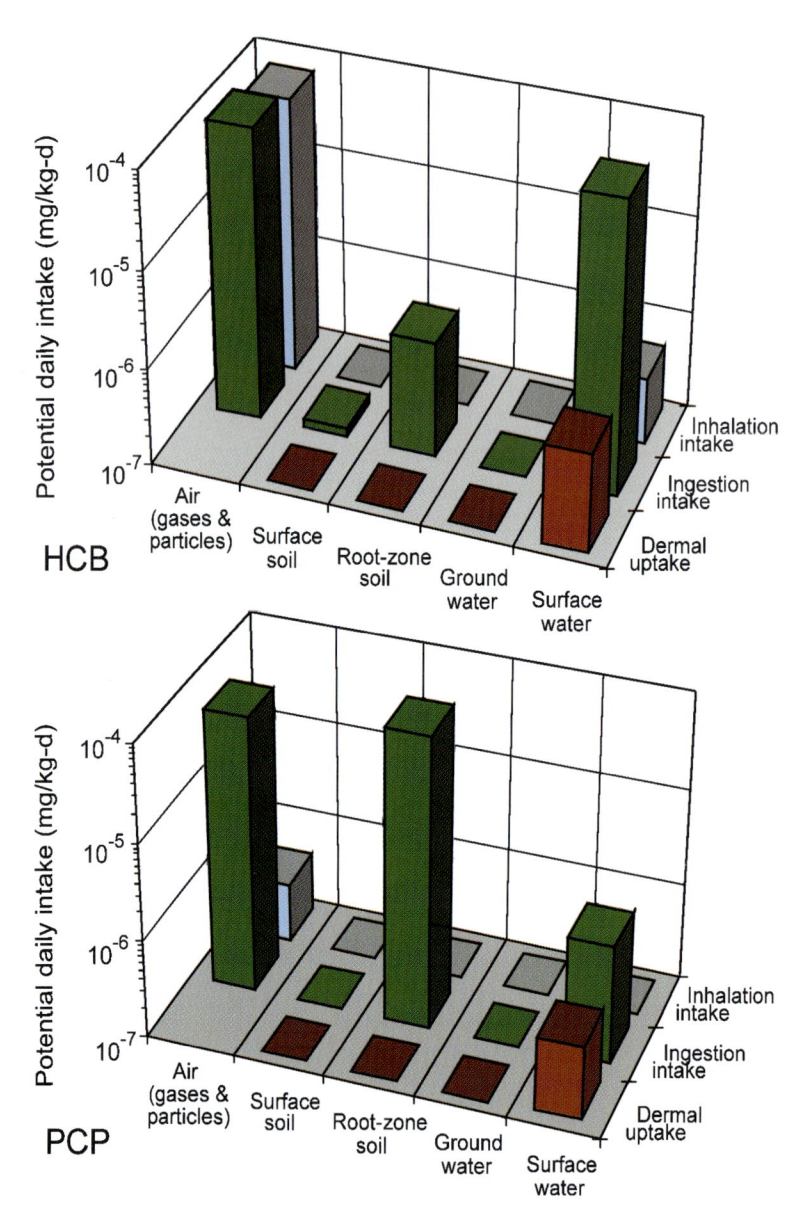

Figure 7 Classification of HCB and PCP intake by exposure route and environmental pathway in the example calculation.

assessment (32). The CalTOX model also introduced formal consideration of uncertainty and variability in multimedia models.

A Brief Overview of Multimedia, Multipathway Modeling

Multimedia fate and exposure models synthesize information about partitioning, reaction, and intermedia-transport properties of a chemical in a representative or generic environment with information about exposed humans or wildlife to assess impacts, such as health risk. The environment is treated as a set of compartments that are homogeneous subsystems exchanging water, nutrients, and chemical contaminants with other adjacent compartments. There are two basic features that make compartment models suitable for an integrated model of transport and transformation in multimedia environments: (a) Each compartment forms a unit in which one can balance gains and losses attributable to sources, transfers to and from other compartments, and chemical transformations, and (b) each compartment forms a unit in which chemical partitioning can be evaluated against equilibrium criteria.

A cumulative multipathway exposure assessment for humans relates contaminant concentrations in multiple environmental media to concentrations in the media with which a human population has contact (for example, personal air, tap water, foods, household dusts, and soils). The potential for harm is assessed either as the average daily intake or uptake rate or as time-averaged contact concentration.

Multimedia contaminant fate and exposure models have been useful to decision makers because these models provide an appropriate quantitative framework to evaluate our understanding of the complex interactions between chemicals and the environment. The greatest challenge for multimedia models is to provide useful information without creating overwhelming demands for input data and producing outputs that cannot be evaluated. The multimedia modeler must struggle to avoid making a model that has more detail than can be accommodated by existing theory and data while also including sufficient fidelity to the real system to make reliable classifications about the source-to-dose relationships of environmental chemicals.

Overview of the Chapter

The first section of this review focuses on the fundamental assumptions of compartment-based mass-balance models and their mathematical formulation. Simple examples illustrate multimedia fate calculations using the fugacity concept. In the next section, we describe multipathway exposure models used to calculate rates of exposure by humans or wildlife from measured or modeled contaminant concentrations. Finally, we describe and review efforts to combine the contaminant fate and exposure models to conduct source-to-dose calculations for multimedia environmental contaminants and discuss some of the philosophical and technical challenges currently facing model developers.

MULTIMEDIA CONTAMINANT FATE: THEORY AND MODELS

We present here an overview of mass-balance contaminant fate and transport calculations using the fugacity approach. The text by Mackay (25) provides a comprehensive discussion of this topic and is highly recommended for the interested reader. Additional information on many of the concepts discussed below and alternative formulations of mass-balance equations using rate constants and concentrations rather than the fugacity concept are available in Schwarzenbach et al. (33) and Thibodeaux (13).

Phase Equilibrium and Chemical Partitioning in Environmental Systems

In this section, we explore the philosophical approach used in developing multimedia contaminant fate models. The complexity of multimedia environments and our lack of data and knowledge limit our ability to quantify multimedia processes. As a result, the approach to model development is to simplify the chemical-environment system as much as possible and systematically build up a more detailed understanding of the system. At their core, all multimedia models of contaminant fate in the environment are based on a set of three postulates. The first two are axiomatic, and the third provides a convenient framework for avoiding being overwhelmed by the complexity and variability of the natural environment.

1. CONSERVATION OF MASS   This axiom provides the basis for writing mass-balance equations, which are indispensable tools in a wide range of engineering applications. Chemicals put into the environment will accumulate, particularly if removal processes are slow. Adoption of this postulate represents recognition that, although vast, the assimilative capacity of the environment for chemicals is finite.

2. CHEMICAL EQUILIBRIUM   According to the Second Law of Thermodynamics, chemicals are driven to disperse into the environment such that the chemical-environment system reaches thermodynamic equilibrium. In a closed system with multiple solvating phases at equilibrium a solute will be distributed in such a way that the system has reached a minimum of free energy. The change in free energy associated with movement of the solute from one region to another is directly proportional to the difference in chemical potential between the regions.

3. THE USE OF LINKED COMPARTMENTS   The environment can be usefully described as a set of linked compartments or boxes. In contrast to the axiomic laws above, this is clearly a gross simplification of the real system under study. The underlying assumption is that the overall fate of chemicals of interest is more strongly controlled by partitioning between the various phases available to the chemical than by spatial differences in properties within individual compartments

of the system. This postulate is consistent with a philosophical approach to model development that views a useful model as one that captures the characteristics of a system that are assumed to be important and omits those that are assumed to be extraneous.

With these three postulates as a foundation, multimedia mass-balance models describing the partitioning and ultimate fate of chemicals in the environment can be assembled. Figure 2 (see color insert) provides a simple generic example of a regional environment consisting of five discrete compartments. In order to formulate the equations that quantitatively describe the system illustrated in Figure 2, and recognizing the second postulate above, we introduce the fugacity concept.

Fugacity and Fugacity Capacity

Fugacity is a metric for quantifying chemical activity at low concentrations. Fugacity, f, can be viewed as the "escaping tendency" of a chemical in a phase, has dimensions of pressure, and is related to concentration, C, by a proportionality constant, fugacity capacity, Z:

$$C = Zf. \qquad 1.$$

In the International System (SI) of units, Z has units of mol m^{-3} Pa^{-1}. From the ideal gas law, it can be shown that Z for the vapor phase is $1/RT$ where R is the gas constant and T is absolute temperature.

Fugacity is a criterion of equilibrium. When a chemical reaches equilibrium distribution between two available phases, the fugacities of the chemical in the phases are equal. Equilibrium partitioning between two phases can also be described by a dimensionless partition coefficient K_{12}, which can be measured under laboratory conditions as the ratio of concentrations C_1 and C_2. Applying the relationship between concentration and fugacity, and recognizing that $f_1 = f_2$ at equilibrium:

$$K_{12} = \frac{C_1}{C_2} = \frac{fZ_1}{fZ_2} = \frac{Z_1}{Z_2}. \qquad 2.$$

Z can thus be determined experimentally for many phases by measuring partition coefficients between the phase of interest and a phase with known Z.

The environment shown in Figure 2 includes air, water, and soil and sediment particles. As shown in Table 1, Z values for these four phases can be derived from the Z value for air and appropriate partition coefficients measured in the laboratory. Several assumptions are required to arrive at these expressions; these include (*a*) that chemicals in the vapor phase obey the ideal gas law, (*b*) that chemicals in the aqueous phase form ideal dilute solutions, and (*c*) that octanol can be used as a surrogate to describe chemical partitioning to lipids and the organic carbon component of soil and sediments, as described by Karickhoff (34) and reviewed by Seth et al. (35).

TABLE 1 Fugacity capacities (Z values) for environmentally relevant phases

Phase	Definition of Z (mol/m³ Pa)	
Air	$Z_A = 1/(R \times T)$	$R = 8.314$ Pa × m³/mol × K T = temperature (K) H = Henry's Law constant (Pa × m³/mol)
Water	$Z_W = 1/H = C^S/P^S$	C^S = aqueous solubility (mol/m³) P^S = vapor pressure (Pa) y_S = fraction of organic carbon in soil k = Karickhoff constant = 0.41 L/kg
Soil solids	$Z_S = Z_W \times y_S \times k$ $\times K_{OW} \times \rho_S/1000$	K_{OW} = octanol-water partition coefficient ρ_S = density of soil (kg/L) 1000 converts L to m³
Sediment solids (x)	$Z_X = Z_W \times y_X \times k$ $\times K_{OW} \times \rho_X/1000$	y_X = fraction of organic carbon in sediment ρ_X = density of sediment (kg/L)

Partitioning in a Closed System—Level I Models

Treating the environment as an open or closed system and making different assumptions about compartment equilibria and temporal trends in concentration allow multimedia models of varying complexity to be assembled. Four levels of complexity suggested by Mackay (25) are summarized in Table 2. As one progresses from Level I to Level IV calculations, the fidelity of the calculation to the actual chemical-environment system increases, but it is at the cost of additional requirements for input data to describe both the environment and the chemical. At the lowest level of complexity, we model a closed system at equilibrium.

From the fugacity capacities in Table 1 and the law of conservation of mass, a simple fugacity calculation can be used to describe the equilibrium partitioning of a fixed number of moles (M) of chemical in a closed environmental system consisting of four compartments (which may be composed of several distinct phases) with defined volumes (V).

$$M = V_1 C_1 + V_2 C_2 + V_3 C_3 + V_4 C_4 = V_1 Z_1 f + V_2 Z_2 f + V_3 Z_3 f + V_4 Z_4 f$$
$$= f(V_1 Z_1 + V_2 Z_2 + V_3 Z_3 + V_4 Z_4). \qquad 3.$$

Where C is the concentration of chemical in each compartment, the prevailing fugacity of the chemical in the system can be calculated from the general equation:

$$f = \frac{M}{\sum V_i Z_i}. \qquad 4.$$

TABLE 2 Summary of fugacity calculations of different levels of complexity used to describe multimedia contaminant fate

Type of fugacity calculation	Key assumptions	Information garnered
Level I	Equilibrium partitioning Steady state Closed system	General partitioning tendencies for persistent chemicals
Level II	Equilibrium partitioning Steady state Open system	Estimate of overall persistence Important compartments for removal processes Relative importance of advection and degradation as removal pathways
Level III	Nonequilibrium Steady state Open system	Influence of mode of emission on fate and transport Refined assessment of overall persistence and loss pathways
Level IV	Nonequilibrium Dynamic Open system	Influence of mode of emission on fate and transport Time course of response of contaminant inventory by compartment to any time-varying condition

This simple equilibrium partitioning calculation is termed a Level I fugacity calculation (25). The results of the Level I calculation provide insight into the influence of chemical properties on environmental partitioning and a rapid assessment of the environmental media into which the chemical is likely to partition.

Figure 3 (see color insert) provides sample results from a Level I calculation for the homologous series of chlorinated benzenes as adapted from MacLeod & Mackay (36). Equilibrium partitioning of members of the series at each of the seven possible chlorination levels are plotted as a percentage in the air, water, soil, and sediment of a generic environment with properties similar to a jurisdictional region such as the state of Ohio or the country Greece.

As indicated in Figure 3, the less chlorinated congeners of the series of chlorinated benzenes partition almost exclusively to air. With increasing chlorination level, there is an increased tendency for chlorobenzenes to partition out of the atmosphere and into the organic carbon component of soils. This simple assessment of the equilibrium partitioning tendencies of chlorobenzenes is consistent with the observed environmental fate of these compounds (36).

Equilibrium Partitioning in an Open System—Level II Models

As illustrated above, Level I fugacity calculations provide an indication of the likely long-term partitioning of persistent contaminants in the environment, and they can be carried out with only a basic knowledge of chemical partitioning characteristics. However, in most cases it is desirable to describe the real environment-chemical system with more fidelity. At Level II complexity, sources are balanced with removal by chemical transformation and advection at the system boundaries, but the assumption of equilibrium partitioning among compartments is retained. In fugacity models, the rate of chemical transport and/or degradation is generally described using D values such that the product (Df) equals the removal rate in mol/h. D values therefore have SI units of mol/(Pa h) and are analogous to first-order rate constants. Because they are compartment models, multimedia models can account for area and volume sources but not point sources of pollution. In Level II models, sources are introduced as continuous inputs to one or more compartments.

TRANSFORMATION PROCESSES—CHEMICAL REMOVAL Chemical transformations may occur as a result of biotic or abiotic processes that include biotransformation, photolytic decomposition, hydrolytic transformation, and oxidation/reduction. These processes change the chemical identity of a compound and its fundamental properties, and thus its partitioning characteristics and behavior in the environment. The rate of transformation of contaminants in the environment ultimately determines their potential for persistence. For organic chemicals in particular, the United Nations Environment Program uses half-lives for transformation as criteria for classifying chemicals as persistent in the environment (37). Experimental methods (38) and estimation methods (39, 40) are available for specifying these fate processes in a variety of media. However, because transformation rates are highly variable and difficult to measure, they are among the most uncertain parameters used in multimedia models.

PHYSICAL DISPLACEMENT OF POLLUTANTS—ADVECTION In addition to transformation, Level II models account for physical displacement that removes chemicals at the boundaries of the environment being modeled. The Level II assumption of equilibrium makes assessment of displacement at compartment boundaries within the environmental system unnecessary. Physical displacement occurs by advection and turbulent diffusion. Advective removal refers to chemical displaced by entrainment in a moving medium, such as in a moving air mass, a flowing river, or in suspended sediments settling out of the water column to the bottom of a lake. Unlike degradation, chemicals that advect or diffuse out of the environmental system under consideration may return and, therefore, may not be permanently removed. In fact, for regions that are adjacent to relatively highly contaminated areas, advection into the region may be the dominant emission source term.

LEVEL II FUGACITY CALCULATIONS Degradation D values (D_R) can be calculated from an estimated pseudo first-order rate constant (k) for chemical transformation in the compartment of interest (i).

$$D_{Ri} = k_i V_i Z_i, \qquad 5.$$

where (V) is the volume of the environmental compartment. The rate constant k must be selected to represent the overall rate of degradation of the chemical, which as noted above may be taking place by several competing mechanisms.

Advection D values (D_A) are calculated as the product of the flow rate of the medium in which the chemical is entrained (G, m³/h) and its fugacity capacity.

$$D_{Ai} = G_i Z_i. \qquad 6.$$

The mass-balance condition at Level II is between sources of the chemical to the environment $(E, \text{mol/h})$ and removal processes. For a regional environment consisting of four compartments,

$$E = D_1 f + D_2 f + D_3 f + D_4 f, \qquad 7.$$

where D_i is the total D value for removal from a given compartment by chemical transformation and advection. The equilibrium assumption makes it possible to calculate a single fugacity for the system, which is the same in all compartments:

$$f = \frac{E}{\sum D_i} = \frac{E}{\sum (G_i + V_i k_i) Z_i}. \qquad 8.$$

Figure 4 (see color insert) shows Level II mass-balance diagrams for benzene and hexachlorobenzene in the generic evaluative environment used previously for the Level I calculations.

Hexachlorobenzene (HCB) is far less reactive in the environment than benzene, and it has a higher potential for persistence and transport out of the region of emission, as is evident in Figure 4. Whereas 80% of the removal of benzene from the environment is by transformation, specifically degradation in air, greater than 97% of removal of HCB is by advection in the atmosphere for the environmental system under consideration. The low rate of degradation and dominance of atmospheric transport as a removal process indicate that HCB is likely to travel long distances from areas of disposal or use and be present in remote environments, as is indeed observed (41).

Nonequilibrium Partitioning in Open Systems—Level III Models

A Level III fugacity model includes the rates of inter-media transport between environmental compartments. The mass-balance condition is applied to each environmental compartment. This requires quantification of diffusion and advection rates at the compartment boundaries. Although there is no requirement for equilibrium partitioning between adjacent compartments, it is still assumed that chemicals achieve equilibrium partitioning among the available phases within a compartment.

One of the major advantages of fugacity models is their ability to represent diffusive and advective transfer processes among environmental media of different composition. When the modeler relies on concentration-based algorithms, these mass-transfer calculations require the use of flux matching, careful unit conversions, and selection of appropriate partition factors at compartment boundaries. Because fugacity has the same units in all media, this difficulty is avoided in fugacity-based models.

DIFFUSIVE TRANSPORT AMONG COMPARTMENTS   In a fugacity model, the net diffusive flux, in mol/m^2-h, across the interfacial area separating compartments is:

$$flux = Y_{12}(f_1 - f_2), \qquad 9.$$

where Y_{12} is the fugacity mass-transfer coefficient across the boundary between compartments 1 and 2 with units mol/(m^2-Pa-h) and f_1 and f_2 are the fugacities of compartments 1 and 2. Equation 9 is analogous to the flow of electrons in a circuit in which $(f_1 - f_2)$ plays the role of a voltage difference, Y_{12} is a conductance, and the mass flux is the equivalent of electrical current. The fugacity mass-transfer coefficient depends on the mass-transfer coefficient on either side of the interface and the fugacity capacities of the two media that form the interface.

$$Y_{12} = \left(\frac{1}{Z_1 U_1} + \frac{1}{Z_2 U_2} \right)^{-1}, \qquad 10.$$

where U_1 and U_2 are the mass-transfer coefficients (m/h) in the boundary layers in compartments 1 and 2 and Z_1 and Z_2 are the fugacity capacities of compartments 1 and 2.

ADVECTIVE TRANSPORT AMONG COMPARTMENTS   The inter-compartment transfer of contaminants by advection is also modeled as a flux at the compartment boundary. To be consistent with the area normalized description of diffusion, this flux (mol/m^2-h) is modeled as the product of the velocity of the moving phase (m/h) and the contaminant concentration in that phase (mol/m^3).

$$\text{Advection flux} = \text{velocity} \times Z_{ik} f_i, \qquad 11.$$

where Z_{ik} and f_i represent the fugacity capacity of the moving phase and the fugacity of the chemical, respectively, in compartment i. For example, the flux of contaminant from air to surface soil through particle deposition is the product of the particle deposition velocity, v_d; the fugacity capacity of air particles, Z_{ap}; and the total fugacity of the bulk air compartment, f_a:

$$\text{Flux (air to ground-surface soil)} = v_d \times Z_{ap} \times f_a. \qquad 12.$$

Examples of inter-compartmental advection processes typically included in multimedia models are rainfall, deposition of atmospheric aerosol particles, resuspension of particles from soil, water-borne erosion of soil, runoff of precipitation, infiltration of water through soil, deposition of sediment particles in surface water, resuspension of sediment particles from the sediment layer, and surface water flows.

Once equations describing all inter-compartmental transfers of contaminants have been derived, mass-balance equations equating input and removal rates can be written for each compartment (i) of the environmental system.

$$E_i + \sum flow_{j \to i} = \sum flow_{i \to j} + \sum flow_{i \to \text{sink}}. \qquad 13.$$

On the left-hand side of Equation 13 are chemical inputs to compartment i by direct emission, E_i, and the total rate of inter-compartmental transfer to compartment i, $\Sigma flow_{j \to i}$. Removals from the compartment occur by inter-compartmental transfer ($\Sigma flow_{i \to j}$) and by advection out of the system or chemical transformation ($\Sigma flow_{i \to \text{sink}}$). For an environment consisting of n compartments, one can write n equations of this type and solve them algebraically to obtain the unknown fugacity of chemical in each compartment.

Dynamic, Open, and Nonequilibrium Systems—Level IV Models

By removing the assumption of steady-state conditions, we attain the Level IV system. Removal rates and rates of inter-media transport between environmental compartments are used to define a time-dependent description of mass distribution. The rate of chemical input to each compartment can be continuous or time varying. This makes assessment of transient effects possible, such as seasonal variations in emissions and/or climate and soil conditions.

MULTIPATHWAY EXPOSURE MODELS

Multimedia fate models provide additional insight into human and environmental impacts when exposure pathways are explicitly included in the model framework. Exposure assessment is the process of measuring or modeling the magnitude, frequency, and duration of contact between a potentially harmful agent and a target population, including the size and characteristics of that population (27, 42–46). In this section we describe a standard framework for organizing and calculating multipathway exposure to multimedia pollutants. Figure 5 (see color insert) illustrates how links between ambient environmental media and exposure media are included in an exposure model. Human exposures to pollutants released to the ambient environment result from contacts with contaminated air, water, soils, and food. Exposures may be dominated by contacts with a single medium or may reflect concurrent contacts with multiple exposure media. Here, we focus on models that describe the exposure of human individuals or populations to chemical agents dispersed in a multimedia environment.

An exposure assessment begins with exposure concentrations in contact media, which include the envelope of air surrounding the exposed person, the water and food ingested, and the layer of soil, water, or other substances that contacts the skin surface. The magnitude and relative contribution of each exposure pathway must be considered in order to assess total human exposure to a harmful substance and determine the best approach for more refined characterization of the exposure. For example, consider exposure of an individual to a semivolatile hazardous air pollutant that is released into air. In the atmosphere, the chemical will partition between the vapor phase and the condensed phase (the surface of airborne particles). Both the vapors and the particles containing the associated pollutant can be transported to the indoor or outdoor air surrounding a person, who may inhale the pollutant. However, the gas-phase and particle-phase pollutant may be transported with different efficiencies. The same pollutant could be transferred by deposition and runoff to surface water that provides drinking water to a population of individuals or transferred by deposition to vegetation that feeds the population or to the agricultural animals that supply meat and milk. Each of these scenarios represents a pathway from the air emission to contact with a human. Each pathway has an associated exposure surface and subsequent route of intake or uptake. The true potential for exposure cannot be quantified unless the pathways that account for a substantial fraction of the routes of intake and uptake for the receptor population are identified.

Exposure Events

The nature and magnitude of exposures to environmental contaminants depend largely on two things: (*a*) human factors and (*b*) the concentrations of contaminants in the exposure media. Human factors include all behavioral, sociological, and physiological characteristics of an individual that determine their contact rates with food, air, water, and soils. For example, about 35 percent of the U.S. population eats homegrown vegetables, which must be reflected in the treatment of this exposure pathway. Activity patterns, which are defined by allocation of an individual's time at different activities and locations, are also significant because they directly affect the magnitude of exposure to substances present in different indoor and outdoor environments.

Multimedia models that include multipathway exposures (such as the CalTOX model) use exposure events to construct cumulative intake from human factors and exposure concentrations. An *exposure event* occurs when human activities bring them into contact with an exposure medium within a specified microenvironment. Important attributes that define an exposure event are pollutant concentration in environmental media (i.e., ambient air, surface water, and soil), transport pathways from environmental media to exposure media, the duration of and number of exposure media contacts, and the timescale of interest for health effects. The timescale of possible health effects, i.e., whether chronic or acute, and the possibility of spatial and temporal variations in pollutant concentration are important considerations in compiling an exposure assessment. For some pollutants, such as criteria air pollutants, which have acute health effects associated with short-term exposure, the assessment must describe the number and duration of peak concentration events. Exposure events may need to be aggregated over periods as short as one hour or less. In contrast, for pollutants with chronic health impacts, it is more important to characterize long-term cumulative exposures over several years or decades.

The timescale and spatial scale of gradients in pollutant concentrations also provide critical insight into the resolution appropriate for modeling an exposure event. If a pollutant shows little spatial variation in concentration over a large region, even if there is time variation in the concentration, there is little need for including a number of geographic regions in the assessment. Similarly, for a pollutant whose concentration does not vary significantly in time, even if it shows large spatial variation, it may be possible to use longer timescales in an exposure assessment. The duration of the exposure event and the duration of human activities are also important considerations in the structure of the exposure-event model.

Cumulative Exposure Models

Multipathway exposure assessments use the intake or potential dose model that has been adapted from a general Environmental Protection Agency model (47). For each combination of environmental media and contact media, a transfer factor is calculated that defines the quantitative relationship between contaminant concentrations in the two media. These transfer factors are classified in terms of the route of exposure (inhalation, ingestion, and dermal) and the exposure medium/environmental medium link, for example, soil to house dust. There is thus a defining equation for each combination of environmental medium, exposure medium, and exposure route. These relationships are expressed in the CalTOX multimedia exposure model as an average daily potential dose rate (ADDpot), in mg/kg-d relative to a specified environmental medium concentration:

$$ADD_{pot} = C_{Env} \times \text{ITF} \times \frac{\text{CR}}{\text{BW}} \times \frac{\text{ED} \times \text{EF}}{\text{AT}}, \qquad 14.$$

where C_{Env} is the concentration in an environmental medium, mg/kg; ITF is the ratio of concentration in an exposure medium to concentration in environmental medium, unitless; CR is the contact rate with the exposure medium, kg/day; BW is the representative body weight, kg of the exposed individual or cohort; ED is the exposure duration, year; EF is exposure frequency, days/year; and AT is the averaging time for the exposure, days. AT is based on the timescale for health effects. For cancer as an endpoint, AT is lifetime; for other chronic agents it is less than lifetime, but often years.

APPLICATIONS OF MULTIMEDIA FATE AND EXPOSURE MODELS

Multimedia fate models are now widely used for screening-level chemical assessments, for setting goals for soil cleanup standards, for assessing the regional and global fate of persistent organic chemicals, and for life-cycle impact assessment.

In many of these applications the models are used for assessing environmental fate and potential human or ecological impacts. Emerging uses for these models include exposure tracking based on toxic release data and premanufacturing chemical classification. The U.S. Clear Air Act of 1990 and efforts in the European Union to conduct risk assessments for existing and new industrial chemicals have led to the development of specific application multimedia models. In this section, we provide an overview of some of the currently available multimedia fate and exposure models and examples of their applications.

Generic Screening or Evaluative Models

Many multimedia fate and exposure models are based on environmental parameters that are not representative of any specific geographical area. These generic models are used as a laboratory for evaluating the likely behavior of pollutants and how this relates to basic chemical properties. The focus is on comparative assessments of chemicals and interpreting how partitioning properties and degradability determine transport and fate processes. Early examples of evaluative regional fate models are the suite of fugacity models developed by Mackay in the early 1990s (22) and the Equilibrium Criterion or EQC model, which defined a standard four-compartment environment of air, water, soil, and sediment (48). Although these models were originally developed to track the fate of nonpolar, nondissociating organic compounds, their use has expanded to metals, inorganic species, surfactants, and polar organic chemicals.

Generic multipathway human-exposure models coupled with multimedia fate models have been developed in the United States and Europe. The California Environmental Protection Agency developed CalTOX for conducting generic assessments of chemical mobilization from hazardous waste sites and subsequent human exposure (28). In Europe, the Netherlands National Institute for Public Health and the Environment (RIVM) developed SimpleBox, a generic contaminant fate model based on concentrations and first-order rate constants but consistent with fugacity concepts (49, 50).

Recently, generic models of contaminant fate have been adapted to conduct rapid screening-level assessments of large numbers of chemicals for persistence (P) and potential for long-range transport (LRT). The P and LRT attributes have been identified as cause for global concern and have been used as a basis for international bans imposed on specific chemical compounds (51). Webster et al. (52) describe a generic Level III fugacity model for comparing chemicals in terms of persistence in the entire environment, rather than half-lives in individual media. Bennett et al. (53) and Pennington (54) proposed and applied similar models to calculate multimedia persistence. Generic models for assessing long-range transport potential have been developed by Bennett et al. (55), who introduced the concept of "characteristic travel distance" for multimedia chemicals, and by Beyer et al. (56). Faced with a proliferation of generic models for assessing P and LRT, Wania & Mackay (57) conducted a round-robin comparison of the models and found that, although the magnitude of P or LRT scores differed among the models, the relative ranking of a standard group of chemicals according to P or LRT was consistent.

Regional and Spatially Resolved Models

Multimedia models have evolved from evaluative models to regional mass-balance models, multi-region models, and global models. Regional multimedia mass balance models have the same framework as generic models but include geographical databases representing a specific political or ecological region. Multi-region models include more spatial resolution by linking several regional mass-balance models and have been applied on local, continental, and global scales.

REGIONAL-SCALE MASS-BALANCE MODELS   An advantage of regional models over evaluative models is that results can be directly compared with reported concentrations of contaminants in a specific area. For example, ChemCAN is a generic Level III fugacity model with the addition of a database of environmental parameters for 24 ecological regions of Canada (58). ChemCAN has been evaluated for a limited number of contaminants in the southern Ontario, Canada region (36) and also applied in Japan (59). The current version 4.0 of CalTOX includes a geographical database for several specific regions of California, 10 ecoregions of the United States, and political regions representing 48 of its states. The Simple-Box model was adapted into the EUSES framework (see below) and became a regional fate model for the European states. More recently regional-scale models that provide more detailed treatment of densely populated urban environments, forest canopy compartments, and coastal waters have been developed (60, 61).

Decision makers and model developers convened an international workshop in 1994 to assess the strengths and weaknesses of the available regional multimedia models and make recommendations about future research in regional environmental contaminant fate modeling (24). The workshop participants used simple model-comparison exercises to demonstrate the fundamental similarities between ChemCAN, CalTOX, SimpleBox, and HAZCHEM, an adaptation of ChemCAN applied to the European Member states (62). Among the recommendations from the workshop were more evaluation studies comparing model results against reported data on environmental concentrations, improved methodologies for conducting sensitivity and uncertainty analysis, and new model inter-comparison exercises when the science advances and models are refined.

MULTI-REGION MASS-BALANCE MODELS   The current set of regional multimedia fate models represent a region using a single set of environmental parameters representing the multiple environmental media. This limits their ability to track the movement of contaminants among different geographic regions. An emerging class of multimedia models includes spatial resolution by connecting a set of discrete regional fate models into a single larger model. The approach of linking different model units was first illustrated in contaminant fate models for river systems such as the Fraser River in British Columbia, Canada, (63) and the GREATER model for rivers in the European continent (64).

Regional models have also been linked to describe contaminant fate and transport on a continental-scale based on both air and water transport. The Berkeley-Trent North American contaminant fate model (BETR North America) includes 24 linked regions and an accompanying geographical information system (GIS) database of long-term flow patterns of air and water on the continental scale (65, 66). BETR North America has been applied to describe the entire use history and long-term fate of the persistent organochlorine pesticide toxaphene, including its atmospheric transport and deposition to the Laurentian Great Lakes (67). In another example of combining air- and water-shed transport, the generic CoZMo-POP framework has been adapted to describe contaminant fate in the Baltic Sea and its terrestrial drainage basin (68).

GLOBAL-SCALE MULTIMEDIA MODELS Wania & Mackay (69) introduced a multimedia global distribution model for persistent organic chemicals. They treated the global environment as nine connected climate zones and described contaminant fate in each zone with a fugacity mass-balance model. The model has been applied to describe the global fate and transport of the pesticide hexachlorocyclohexane (70) with a focus on transport and deposition to the Arctic.

Evaluative models of global contaminant fate have also been developed by Scheringer (71–74) to assess persistence and spatial range as endpoints in screening level assessments of environmental hazard for chemicals. These models are simpler than the Wania-Mackay global model and have proved useful in studies to determine how temperature gradients in the global environment affect the long-term fate of persistent contaminants.

Assessing Exposures to Humans and Ecosystems

In comparison to the proliferation of models of contaminant fate in the environment, there have been fewer efforts to develop source-to-dose relationships for humans using multimedia models coupled to multipathway exposure models. In the United States, CalTOX is an example of a model that evolved from an exposure model for hazardous sites into a comprehensive fate and human exposure model with integrated probabilistic assessment of uncertainty and variability (27, 75, 76). A predecessor to the CalTOX model called GEOTOX (26) provided an early example of linking regional multimedia mass-balance models to deterministic multipathway exposure models. In Europe, SimpleBox has been incorporated into a model framework for fate, exposure, and risk assessment of multiple chemicals. This system was first developed in the Netherlands as the Unified System for the Evaluation of Substances (USES) (77). The European community has adopted USES as a decision support framework and for conducting chemical risk assessments, the European Union System for the Evaluation of Substances (EU-SES).

EXAMPLE OF COMPARATIVE HUMAN-EXPOSURE ASSESSMENT   To illustrate the use of multimedia models for comparative exposure assessment, we apply the CalTOX model to two organic pollutants, hexachlorobenzene (HCB) and pentachlorophenol (PCP). CalTOX is used to estimate concentrations in the air (gas and particles), plants, soil (surface and vadose zones), and water compartments. Then the resulting potential multipathway human exposures are calculated using methods described above. This calculation is applied to a generic landscape of 1 million square kilometers, and the exposure calculations represent the general population, i.e., they do not account for workers who may be exposed to these chemicals occupationally. For each chemical, we model continuous releases for a period of 15 years. The illustrative multimedia releases used for both chemicals in these examples are 100,000 mol/d to air, 10,000 mol/d applied to the soil surface, and 1000 mol/d to surface water. The pollutants in this example are structurally similar but differ significantly in chemical properties and exposure pathways (Figure 6).

As demonstrated in earlier examples, HCB is a hydrophobic, persistent compound capable of long-range atmospheric transport on a global scale. HCB binds to soil and to suspended sediments in water and accumulates to some extent in the bottom sediments of lakes, rivers, and estuaries. It can bioaccumulate in fish, marine mammals, and birds, and it is also transferred into grasses, vegetables, and other plants. Like HCB, PCP is a manufactured chemical not found naturally in the environment. It is persistent in the environment and generally binds to soil particles, but its mobility in soils depends on the soil's acidity. PCP does not readily evaporate into the air and is not readily soluble in water. In soils and surface waters, microorganisms break down PCP into other compounds. PCP is subject to photolytic decomposition in surface water and air, but it still persists for hours or days in air, soils, and surface waters. It is present in fish, but tissue levels are usually low because PCP breaks down in the fish tissues.

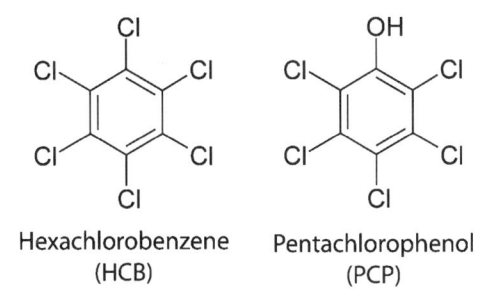

Figure 6 Chemical structures of HCB and PCP.

Figure 7 (see color insert) shows the relative contributions of different pathways to total HCB exposures calculated with CalTOX, compared to those for PCP. We see from this example that the human population is potentially exposed to HCB by a combination of ingestion and inhalation pathways with a minor contribution from dermal contact. Both pollutants can be transferred into foods from the atmosphere (by gaseous exchange and dry and wet deposition of particles), from soils (by uptake in the roots), and from surface water (by direct bioconcentration into aquatic organisms or by irrigation of crops). Detailed pathways analysis indicates exposure is due to eating low levels in contaminated terrestrial food products, eating contaminated fish, drinking milk or eating dairy products or meat from cattle grazing on contaminated pastures, drinking small amounts in contaminated water, breathing low levels in contaminated air, eating or touching contaminated soil, and absorbing small amounts from water while showering and bathing. Human populations are also exposed to PCP by eating contaminated food, such as fish and terrestrial food crops, and by dermal contact with soils and bathing water. PCP is relatively more efficiently transferred from soils into foods than HCB, as indicated by higher potential daily intake from foods grown on contaminated soils. Exposure due to inhalation of contaminated air is a significantly less important pathway than for HCB, as a result of the lower vapor pressure of PCP.

Sustainability and Life-Cycle Impact Assessment

The issues of long-term environmental sustainability, design for environment, and life-cycle impact assessment (LCIA) all require quantitative measures of hazard as weighting factors for pollutant releases. Because the scope of these issues does not allow for full-scale, site-specific risk assessments, analysts rely on generic and regional multimedia models as assessment tools. Generic versions of both CalTOX and USES have been used to conduct comparative assessments of fate and exposure in support of LCIA, sustainability, and comparative risk assessments (78, 79).

MODEL EVALUATION STRATEGIES

Multimedia fate and exposure models support decisions to tolerate, regulate, or monitor existing and new industrial and agricultural chemicals. In this role, fate/exposure models provide prospective analysis of future risk and retrospective analysis of the links between health outcomes and environmental releases. In using models to support regulation and monitoring policies, decision makers struggle with the questions of how likely they are to make unwarranted choices and what the associated health, economic, and political consequences of those choices are. To confront these questions, decision makers rely on modelers to quantify the reliability of their model predictions. Here we document current methods used to assess the performance of multimedia models. We describe the criteria for establishing model reliability and examine methods for model sensitivity and uncertainty analysis. Finally, a process for model evaluation suitable for multimedia fate models is suggested.

As is the case for all models, multimedia models have inherent capabilities and limitations. The limitations arise because models are simplifications of the real system that they describe, and all assessments using the models are based on imperfect knowledge of input parameters. Thus multimedia assessments have inherent uncertainty. This realization provides insight into how the models should be applied and helps decide whether and/or how to make the models more detailed. Confronting the uncertainties requires a model performance evaluation that estimates the degree of uncertainty in the assessment and illustrates the relative value of increasing model complexity by providing a more explicit representation of uncertainties or by assembling more data through field studies and experimental analysis.

Sensitivity and Uncertainty Analyses

Sensitivity and uncertainty analyses are powerful tools for assessing the performance and reliability of models. As applied to mathematical models, sensitivity analysis is quantification of changes in model results as a result of changes in individual model parameters. Uncertainty analysis is the determination of the variation or imprecision in the output function based on the collective variation of the model inputs. A full discussion of sensitivity and uncertainty analysis is provided in the texts by Morgan & Henrion (80) and the volume edited by Saltelli et al. (81). The goal of a sensitivity analysis is to rank input parameters, model algorithms, or model assumptions on the basis of their contribution to variance in the model output. Sensitivity analyses can be either local or global. A local sensitivity analysis is used to examine the effects of small changes in parameter values at some defined point in the range of outcome values. A global sensitivity analysis quantifies the effects of variation in parameters over their entire space of outcome values.

SENSITIVITY OF MULTIMEDIA MODELS   Eisenberg et al. (82), Eisenberg & McKone (83), and Hertwich et al. (84) have studied parameter variability and sensitivity in multimedia exposure models. For cumulative exposure assessments based on multimedia models, these studies indicate that output variance arises primarily from chemical-specific input parameters and secondarily from human-exposure factors. Landscape characteristics, such as climate, hydrologic conditions, and soil properties, are generally of minor importance. Among chemical properties, environmental half-lives are the most sensitive properties. Among exposure factors, food intakes are the most sensitive parameters for hydrophobic compounds, water ingestion for water-soluble compounds, and inhalation rates for volatile compounds.

SOURCES OF UNCERTAINTY   Uncertainty in model predictions arise from a number of sources: specification of the problem; formulation of the conceptual model; estimation of input values; and calculation, interpretation, and documentation of the results. Of these, only uncertainties due to estimation of input values (parameter uncertainty) can be quantified in a straightforward manner based on variance propagation techniques. Mis-specification of the problem and incorrect model formulation give rise to the wrong models. Having the wrong model results in errors that are potentially large, systematic, and often difficult to discover. As a result, the uncertainties resulting from these errors are potentially much larger and more difficult to characterize than parameter uncertainties. Efforts have been made to assess mis-specification and formulation errors using tools such as decision trees or based on elicitation of expert opinions [for example, the case study by Ragas et al. (85)].

UNCERTAINTY IMPORTANCE AND RANKING   A framework for the analysis of uncertainty in environmental models was developed by Morgan & Henrion (80) and Finkel (86) and has been applied by Hertwich et al. (87) to multimedia exposure models. This framework distinguishes among parameter uncertainty, model uncertainty, decision rule uncertainty, and natural variability in any of the parameters and calls for a separate treatment of the different types of uncertainty. More recently, Huijbregts et al. (88) have looked at geographical scenario uncertainty in generic fate and exposure factors. In evaluating parameter uncertainty and variability, Hertwich et al. (87) considered both uncertainty in chemical-specific input parameters as well as the variability in exposure factors and landscape parameters. They determined how the uncertainty and variability of these parameters impact estimates of potential dose for 236 different chemicals. The chemicals were grouped into five dominant exposure medium/route combinations (inhalation of ambient air; ingestion of water, meat, vegetation, or fish; and dermal contact with water). A Monte Carlo analysis was conducted for one representative chemical in each group. From this process, it was determined variance in calculated dose for a specific chemical is typically one to two orders of magnitude. For comparison, the point estimates in the potential dose for the full 236 chemical set spans 10 orders of magnitude. This demonstrates that in spite of the large uncertainties, the potential dose calculations for these chemicals offer a significant information gain relative to a simpler exposure index or the use of toxicity data alone.

Model Evaluation and Confidence Building

A widely held opinion is that the only reliable models are ones that have been validated. However, there continues to be wide disagreement and confusion in the scientific and regulatory communities about what it means to validate a model and if true validation is even possible. Recent papers have made convincing arguments that comparison of model output to observations, or one's view of reality, is not a sufficient measure of acceptability on its own to validate a model (89–93).

Hodges & Dewar (92) have proposed a classification scheme for models that distinguishes between those that can be validated and those that cannot. Models describing systems in which inputs and outputs are all directly and readily measurable and exhibit constancy in structure over time are the only ones that can be validated. Conditions not specified in the model must be constant within the limits of applicability of the model. Validity accrues when predictions made by the model are found accurate for conditions not originally considered when the model was constructed. In contrast, models that describe systems in which the structure is not constant in time or conditions not specified in the model are not constant can never be truly validated. These models cannot be validated, but as Hodges & Dewar point out (92), they are not useless. Some applications for non-validated models include assisting in decision making by stimulating intuition, illustrating an idea, summarizing data, or providing an incentive for improving data quality, and formulating hypotheses for subsequent testing.

Viewed in these terms, it is clear that multimedia models belong to a class of models that cannot be truly validated because the environmental systems and human activities described by these models comprise a system with operative processes that cannot be fully described, that does not exhibit constancy in structure in time, and has features that are not constant within its range of applicability. It is thus impossible to conduct the controlled experiments needed for true validation of multimedia models. For example, a multimedia contaminant fate model might be applied to predict the atmospheric concentration of benzene attributable to a specific source (for example, a refinery). However, this is not a general outcome that can be validated. For a given refinery in a given region, the model can be evaluated by shutting down the refinery and observing the resulting effect on benzene concentrations. However, acceptable model performance in the evaluation exercise does not necessarily mean that the model is generally applicable to describe the contribution of benzene emissions to total atmospheric concentrations of benzene for all refineries in all regions.

As has been pointed out by Oreskes et al. (89), models of this type are common in earth sciences, economics, and engineering as well as in the policy arena, but they cannot be fully verified or validated because descriptions of the operative processes are always incomplete. This limitation does not mean that multimedia models should be exempt from performance evaluation. On the contrary, the fact that the models cannot be validated requires a more thoughtful and systematic process for building confidence among model users. It is possible to build confidence in these models through a series of evaluation exercises, and they can be used to put bounds on the likely range of outcomes. The greater the number and the diversity of confirming observations that can be made, the more probable it is that the conceptualization embodied in the model is not flawed. Confirming observations do not demonstrate the veracity of the model, but they do support the probability that the model is useful and the hypotheses that it represents are not false. Although validity may not accrue with these evaluation exercises, user confidence will increase.

Confidence is further enhanced if the user can easily inspect or verify the operation of the algorithms and data transformations and determine whether the model is internally consistent and contains no logical flaws or technical errors, such as incorrect code implementation. Easy access to the raw data used as inputs, transformed data and the steps of data transformations used in the calculation, and the computer coded algorithms underlying these data transformations will thus enhance user confidence in the model. The availability of clear documentation for model structure and the possibility of performing calibration against an external standard (test data sets) or an internal standard (parallel algorithms to perform the same calculation) all increase user confidence in a model.

For multimedia models in particular, credibility is further enhanced by clearly quantifying the effects of variability and uncertainty in input parameters on model predictions. Communicating the uncertainties associated with contaminant fate and exposure assessments enhances their credibility by highlighting model inputs that control the outcome of the assessment for individual chemicals. Estimates of the uncertainty associated with specific model outputs can be used to inform the decision-making process and direct future refinements of the model or experimental studies to add additional information to the assessment.

Discussion and Conclusions

There is increasing international concern about the presence and possible accumulation of environmentally persistent chemical, physical, and biological pollutants that may threaten the sustainability of ecosystems and the health of humans. These contaminants are often traceable to human activities that support our modern lifestyle such as combustion for energy generation, construction practices, industrial processes, and agriculture activities. Many of the most persistent agents are not contained in a single environmental system, but they are multimedia pollutants that migrate in and between the air, water, soil, sediments, and biota of the environment. Environmentally persistent multimedia agents remind us that all pollutants are, to some extent, multimedia pollutants. These contaminants can accumulate in environmental media that lead to human exposure, e.g., air, indoor dusts, soils, and foodstuffs.

In this review, we described multimedia contaminant fate models at a range of complexity levels and multipathway human exposure models that work in concert with the fate models or with field monitoring data. These models have been useful conceptual tools for understanding the fate and transport processes that determine the behavior of contaminants in the environment, and how they may ultimately contact humans. From a policy perspective, these models can be used to inform decisions aimed at avoiding unacceptable detrimental impacts from development on both human health and ecosystems.

Multimedia models are impossible to truly validate, but they have established a high level of credibility because they are based on sound thermodynamic principles and they have been evaluated in a series of case studies. Our review highlights that there are many limitations on our ability to develop complex and reliable models of contaminant fate and exposure. The environment is incredibly intricate and conditions vary widely both spatially and temporally. Many of the contaminants that are released to the environment are poorly characterized. Properties that control their environmental fate and partitioning range over several orders of magnitude, and in some cases lie near the boundaries of measurable limits, which means there is considerable uncertainty about the nature of these chemicals even under controlled laboratory conditions. Thus, the multimedia modeler must struggle to avoid making a model that has more detail than can be supported by existing theory and data while also including sufficient fidelity to the real system to make reliable classifications about the source-to-dose relationships of environmental chemicals.

New and existing multimedia exposure models are taking on an increasingly important role in the regulatory environment, and as such, we need to ensure their credibility and adequacy. There is a need for novel strategies and tools that take advantage of new biomarker and exposure data to evaluate the performance of source-to-dose models. There is also a need for methods to use existing models to identify the type and quantity of information that would contribute to the greatest reduction in uncertainty in model outcomes. For example, none of the exposure models currently available provide an integrated simulation of major transport processes and indoor/outdoor relationships for toxic substances in air, water, food, and soil.

In looking to the future use of these models, we must address the trade-offs among complexity, reliability, and confidence. As these models evolve and proliferate, we must continue to evaluate their capabilities and limitations. There is an ongoing need to establish and improve upon the confidence placed in these models by decision makers. There is also the opportunity to build more complex and spatially explicit multimedia models. Are these two trends compatible? The increasing capability of personal computers makes possible more complex models, and some equate complexity with credibility. But often the opposite is the case—complexity makes the models much more difficult to verify and evaluate and makes it particularly difficult to assess data limitations. Future multimedia fate and exposure models will have to find an acceptable balance that increases the model's fidelity to the real environmental system through added complexity but retain the reliability and user confidence that have been established by the current generation of models.

ACKNOWLEDGMENTS

This work was supported by the U.S. Environmental Protection Agency National Exposure Research Laboratory through Interagency Agreement # DW-988-38190-01-0 and carried out at Lawrence Berkeley National Laboratory through the U.S. Department of Energy under Contract Grant No. DE-AC03-76SF00098. We thank Michael Sohn and Randy Maddalena whose careful review and thoughtful comments on earlier versions of this manuscript resulted in important and useful revisions.

LITERATURE CITED

1. Carson R. 1962. *Silent Spring*. Boston, MA: Houghton Mifflin
2. Jensen S. 1966. Report of a new chemical hazard. *New Sci.* 32:612
3. Counc. Environ. Qual. 1985. *Report on Long-Term Environmental Research and Development*, Exec. Off. Pres. US, CEQ, Washington, DC
4. Eisenbud M. 1963. *Environmental Radioactivity*. New York: McGraw-Hill
5. Eisenbud M. 1973. *Environmental Radioactivity*. New York: Academic. 2nd ed.
6. Eisenbud M. 1987. *Environmental Radioactivity from Natural, Industrial, and Military Sources*. New York: Academic. 3rd ed.
7. Ng YC. 1982. A review of transfer factors for assessing the dose from radionuclides in agricultural products. *Nuclear Saf.* 23:57–71
8. Whicker FW, Kirchner TB. 1987. Pathway: a dynamic food-chain model to predict radionuclide ingestion after fallout deposition. *Health Phys.* 52:717–37
9. UN Sci. Comm. Eff. At. Radiat. 1993. *Sources and effects of ionizing radiation: United Nations Scientific Committee on the effects of atomic radiation. UN UNSCEAR Rep Gen. Assem.*, New York
10. Garrels RM, Mackenzie FT, Hunt C. 1975. *Chemical Cycles and the Global Environment: Assessing Human Influences*. Los Altos, CA: Kaufmann
11. Nriagu JO. 1978. *The Biogeochemistry of Lead in the Environment*. New York: Elsevier/North-Holland Biomed.
12. Nriagu JO. 1979. *The Biogeochemistry of Mercury in the Environment*. New York: Elsevier/North-Holland Biomed.
13. Thibodeaux LJ. 1979. *Chemodynamics, Environmental Movement of Chemicals in Air, Water, and Soil*. New York: Wiley
14. Mackay D. 1979. Finding fugacity feasible. *Environ. Sci. Technol.* 13:1218–23
15. Mackay D, Paterson S. 1981. Calculating fugacity. *Environ. Sci. Technol.* 15:1006–14
16. Mackay D, Paterson S. 1982. Fugacity revisited—the fugacity approach to environmental transport. *Environ. Sci. Technol.* 16:A654–60
17. Bennett BG. 1981. The exposure commitment method in environmental pollutant assessment. *Environ. Monit. Assess.* 1:21–36
18. Bennett BG. 1982. Exposure of man to environmental nickel—an exposure commitment assessment. *Sci. Total Environ.* 22:203–12
19. Bennett BG. 1983. Exposure of man to environmental PCBs—an exposure commitment assessment. *Sci. Total Environ.* 29:101–11
20. Cohen Y. 1986. *Pollutants in a Multimedia Environment*. New York: Plenum
21. Allen DT, Cohen Y, Kaplan IR. 1989. *Intermedia Pollutant Transport: Modeling and Field Measurements*. New York: Plenum
22. Mackay D. 1991. *Multimedia Environmental Models: The Fugacity Approach*. Chelsea, MI: Lewis
23. Natl. Acad. Sci. 1994. *Science and Judgment in Risk Assessment*. Washington, DC: Natl. Res. Counc./Natl. Acad.
24. Cowan CE, Mackay D, Feijtel TCJ, Van De Meent D, Di Guardo A, et al. 1995. *The Multi-Media Fate Model: A Vital Tool for Predicting the Fate of Chemicals*. Pensacola, FL: Soc. Environ. Toxicol. Chem.
25. Mackay D. 2001. *Multimedia Environmental Models: The Fugacity Approach*. Chelsea, MI: Lewis. 2nd ed.

26. McKone TE, Layton DW. 1986. Screening the potential risk of toxic substances using a multimedia compartment model: estimation of human exposure. *Regul. Toxicol. Pharmacol.* 6:359–80
27. McKone TE, Daniels JI. 1991. Estimating human exposure through multiple pathways from air, water, and soil. *Regul. Toxicol. Pharmacol.* 13:36–61
28. McKone TE. 1993. *CalTOX, a multimedia total-exposure model for hazardous-wastes sites part I: executive summary.* Rep. UCRL-CR-111456PtI, Lawrence Livermore Natl. Lab., Livermore, CA
29. McKone TE. 1993. *CalTOX, a multimedia total-exposure model for hazardous-wastes sites part II: the dynamic multimedia transport and transformation model. Rep. UCRL-CR-111456PtII*, Lawrence Livermore Natl. Lab., Livermore, CA
30. McKone TE. 1993. *CalTOX, a multimedia total-exposure model for hazardous-wastes sites part III: the multiple-pathway exposure model. Rep. UCRL-CR-111456PtIII*, Lawrence Livermore Natl. Lab., Livermore, CA
31. Maddalena RL, McKone TE, Layton DW, Hsieh DPH. 1995. Comparison of multimedia transport and transformation models: regional fugacity model vs. CalTOX. *Chemosphere* 30:869–99
32. Natl. Inst. Public Health Environ. Prot. 1994. *Uniform system for the evaluation of substances (USES), version 1.0. Rep. VROM Distrib. 11144/150*, RIVM; Minist. Hous., Spat. Plan. Environ. (VROM); Minist. Welf., Health, Cult. Aff. (WVC), The Hague, Neth.
33. Schwarzenbach RP, Gschwend PM, Imboden DM. 1993. *Environmental Organic Chemistry.* New York: Wiley
34. Karickhoff SW. 1981. Semiempirical estimation of sorption of hydrophobic pollutants on natural sediments and soils. *Chemosphere* 10:833–46
35. Seth R, Mackay D, Muncke J. 1999. Estimating the organic carbon partition coefficient and its variability for hydrophobic chemicals. *Environ. Sci. Technol.* 33:2390–94
36. MacLeod M, Mackay D. 1999. An assessment of the environmental fate and exposure of benzene and the chlorobenzenes in Canada. *Chemosphere* 38:1777–96
37. UN Environ. Progamme. 2001. *Governments Give Green Light to Phase Out of World's Most Hazardous Chemicals. Stockholm Convention on Persistent Organic Pollutants* http://irptc.unep.ch/pops/POPs_Inc/press_releases/pressrel-01/pr5-01.htm
38. Howard PH. 1989. *Handbook of Environmental Fate and Exposure Data for Organic Chemicals.* Chelsea, MI: Lewis
39. Lyman WJ, Reehl WF, Rosenblatt DH. 1982. *Handbook of Chemical Property Estimation Methods.* New York, NY: McGraw-Hill
40. Mackay D, Boethling RS. 2000. *Handbook of Property Estimation Methods for Chemicals:Environmental and Health Sciences.* Boca Raton, FL: Lewis
41. Bailey RE. 2001. Global hexachlorobenzene emissions. *Chemosphere* 43:167–82
42. Natl. Acad. Sci. 1991a. *Frontiers in Assessing Human Exposure to Environmental Toxicants.* Washington, DC: Natl. Res. Counc./Natl. Acad.
43. Natl. Acad. Sci. 1991b. *Human Exposure Assessment for Airborne Pollutants: Advances and Opportunities*, Washington, DC: Natl. Res. Counc./Natl. Acad.
44. US Environ. Prot. Agency. 1992. Guidelines for exposure assessment: notice. *Fed. Regist.* 57:22888–938
45. Lioy P, Pellizzari E. 1996. Conceptual framework for designing a national survey of human exposure. *J. Expo. Anal. Environ. Epidemiol.* 5:425–44
46. Zartarian VG, Ott WR, Duan N. 1997. A quantitative definition of exposure and related concepts. *J. Expo. Anal. Environ. Epidemiol.* 7:411–37
47. US Environ. Prot. Agency. 1989. *Risk Assessment Guidance for Superfund Vol. I, Human Health Evaluation Manual (Part A). Rep. EPA/540/1-89/002*, EPA, Off.

Emerg. Remedial Response, Washington, DC

48. Mackay D, Di Guardo A, Paterson S, Cowan CE. 1996. Evaluating the environmental fate of a variety of types of chemicals using the EQC model. *Environ. Toxicol. Chem.* 15:1627–37

49. van de Meent D. 1996. *SimpleBox: a generic multimedia fate evaluation model. Rep. 672720 001*, Natl. Inst. Public Health Environ. Prot. (RIVM), Bilthoven, Neth.

50. Brandes LJ, Hollander HD, van de Meent D. 1996. *SimpleBox 2.0: a nested multimedia fate model for evaluating the environmental fate of chemicals. Rep. RIVM 719101029*, Natl. Inst. Public Health Environ. Prot. (RIVM), Bilthoven, Neth.

51. UN Environ. Programme. 1997. *Status Report on UNEP's and Other Related Activities on Persistent Organic Pollutants*. http://www.chem.unep.ch/pops/indxhtms/status.html

52. Webster E, Mackay D, Wania F. 1998. Evaluating environmental persistence. *Environ. Toxicol. Chem.* 17:2148–58

53. Bennett DH, Kastenberg WE, McKone TE. 1999. General formulation of characteristic time for persistent chemicals in a multimedia environment. *Environ. Sci. Technol.* 33:503–9

54. Pennington D. 2001. An evaluation of chemical persistence screening approaches. *Chemosphere* 44:1589–601

55. Bennett DH, McKone TE, Matthies M, Kastenberg WE. 1998. Evaluating the spatial range of persistent organic pollutants in a multi-media environment. *Environ. Sci. Technol.* 32:4023–30

56. Beyer A, Mackay D, Matthies M, Wania F, Webster E. 2000. Assessing long-range transport potential of persistent organic pollutants. *Environ. Sci. Technol.* 34:699–703

57. Wania F, Mackay D. 2000. *A comparison of overall persistence values and atmospheric travel distances calculated by various multimedia fate models. Rep. 2/2000*, Wania Environ. Chem. Corp., Toronto, ON. http://www.utsc.utoronto.ca/~wania/

58. Mackay D, Di Guardo A, Paterson S, Kicsi G, Cowan CE, Kane DM. 1996. Assessment of chemical fate in the environment using evaluative, regional and local-scale models: illustrative application to chlorobenzene and linear alkylbenzene sulfonates. *Environ. Toxicol. Chem.* 15:1638–48

59. Kawamoto K, MacLeod M, Mackay D. 2001. Evaluation and comparison of multimedia mass-balance models of chemical fate: application of EUSES and ChemCAN to 68 chemicals in Japan. *Chemosphere* 44:599–612

60. Priemer DA, Diamond ML. 2002. Application of the multimedia urban model to compare the fate of SOCs in an urban and forested watershed. *Environ. Sci. Technol.* 36:1004–23

61. Wania F, Persson J, Di Guardo A, McLachlan MS. 2000. *Cozmo-Pop. A fugacity-based multi-compartmental mass-balance model of the fate of persistent organic pollutants in the coastal zone. Rep. 1/2000*, Wania Group., Univ. Toronto., Can., http://www.utsc.utoronto.ca/~wania/

62. Eur. Cent. Ecotoxicol. Toxicol. Chem. 1994. *A Mathematical Model for Use in Risk Assessment of Substances. Rep. Special Rep. N. 8*, ECETOC, Brussels, Belg.

63. Gobas FAPC, Pasternak JP, Lien K, Duncan RK. 1998. Development and field validation of a multimedia exposure assessment model for waste load allocation in aquatic ecosystems: application to 2,3,7,8-tetrachlorodibenzo-P-dioxin and 2,3,7,8-tetrachlorodibenzofuran in the Frazer River watershed. *Environ. Sci. Technol.* 32:2442–49

64. Feijtel T, Boeije G, Matthies M, Young A, Morris G, et al. 1998. Development of a geography-referenced regional exposure assessment tool for European rivers—GREATER. *J. Hazard. Mater.* 61:359–65

65. MacLeod M, Woodfine DG, Mackay D, McKone T, Bennett D, Maddalena R.

2001. BETR North America: a regionally segmented multimedia contaminant fate model for North America. *Environ. Sci. Pollut. Res.* 8:156–63

66. Woodfine DG, MacLeod M, Mackay D, Brimacombe JR. 2001. Development of continental scale multimedia contaminant fate models: integrating GIS. *Environ. Sci. Pollut. Res.* 8:164–72

67. MacLeod M, Woodfine DG, Brimacombe J, Toose L, Mackay D. 2001. A dynamic mass budget for toxaphene in North America. *Environ. Toxicol. Chem.* 21:1628–37

68. Wania F, Persson J, Guardo AD, McLachlan M. 2000. *The POPcycling-Baltic model: a non-steady state multicompartment mass-balance model of the fate of persistent organic pollutants in the Baltic Sea environment. Rep. U-96069*, Nor. Inst. Air Res. (NILU), http://www.utsc.utoronto.ca/~wania/

69. Wania F, Mackay. D. 1995. A global distribution model for persistent organic chemicals. *Sci. Total Environ.* 160/161:211–32

70. Wania F, Mackay D. 1999. Global chemical fate of alpha-hexachlorocyclohexane. 2. Use of a global distribution model for mass balancing, source apportionment, and trend prediction. *Environ. Toxicol. Chem.* 18:1400–7

71. Scheringer M. 1996. Persistence and spatial range as endpoints of an exposure-based assessment of organic chemicals. *Environ. Sci. Technol.* 30:1652–59

72. Scheringer M. 1997. Characterization of the environmental distribution behavior of organic chemicals by means of persistence and spatial range. *Environ. Sci. Technol.* 31:2891–97

73. Scheringer M, Wegmann F, Fenner K, Hungerbuhler K. 2000. Investigation of the cold condensation of persistent organic pollutants with a global multimedia fate model. *Environ. Sci. Technol.* 34:1842–50

74. Scheringer M, Hungerbuhler K, Matthies M. 2001. The spatial scale of organic chemicals in multimedia fate modeling—recent developments and significance for chemical assessment. *Environ. Sci. Pollut. Res.* 8:150–55

75. McKone TE, Bogen KT. 1991. Predicting the uncertainties in risk assessment: a California groundwater case study. *Environ. Sci. Technol.* 25:1674–81

76. McKone TE. 1993b. The precision of QSAR methods for estimating intermedia transfer factors in exposure assessments. *SAR QSAR Environ. Res.* 1:41–51

77. Natl. Inst. Public Health Environ. 1999. *Uniform system for the evaluation of substances 3.0 (USES 3.0).* RIVM, Minist. Hous., Spat. Plan. Environ. (VROM), Minist. Health, Welf. Sports (VWS), Bithoven, Neth.

78. Huijbregts MAJ, Thissen U, Guinee JB, Jager T, Kalf D, et al. 2000. Priority assessment of toxic substances in life cycle assessment. Part I: calculation of toxicity potentials for 181 substances with the nested multi-media fate, exposure and effects model USES-LCA. *Chemosphere* 41:541–73

79. Hertwich EG, Mateles SF, Pease WS, McKone TE. 2001. Human toxicity potentials for life-cycle assessment and toxics release inventory risk screening. *Environ. Toxicol. Chem.* 20:928–39

80. Morgan GM, Henrion M. 1990. *Uncertainty: A Guide to Dealing with Uncertainty on Quantitative Risk and Policy Analysis.* Cambridge, UK: Cambridge Univ. Press

81. Saltelli A, Chan K, Scott EM, eds. 2000. *Sensitivity Analysis.* New York: Wiley

82. Eisenberg JNS, Bennett DH, McKone TE. 1998. Chemical dynamics of persistent organic pollutants: a sensitivity analysis relating soil concentration levels to atmospheric emissions. *Environ. Sci. Technol.* 32:115–23

83. Eisenberg JNS, McKone TE. 1998. Decision tree method for the classification of chemical pollutants: incorporation of across chemical variability and within chemical uncertainty. *Environ. Sci. Technol.* 32:3396–404

84. Hertwich EG, McKone TE, Pease WS. 1999. Parameter uncertainty and variability in evaluative fate and exposure models. *Risk Anal.* 19:1193–204
85. Ragas AMJ, Etienne RS, Willemsen FH, van de Meent D. 1999. Assessing model uncertainty for environmental decision making: a case study of the coherence of independently derived environmental quality objectives for air and water. *Environ. Toxicol. Chem.* 18:1856–67
86. Finkel AM. 1990. *Confronting Uncertainty in Risk Management—A Guide for Decision-Makers*. Washington, DC: Resourc. Future
87. Hertwich EG, McKone TE, Pease WS. 2000. A systematic uncertainty analysis of an evaluative fate and exposure model. *Risk Anal.* 20:439–54
88. Huijbregts MAJ, Guinee JB, Reijnders L. 2001. Priority assessment of toxic substances in life cycle assessment. III: Export of potential impact over time and space. *Chemosphere* 44:59–65
89. Oreskes N, Shraderfrechette K, Belitz K. 1994. Verification, validation, and confirmation of numerical-models in the earth-sciences. *Science* 263:641–46
90. Oreskes N, Belitz K, Shraderfrechette K. 1994. The meaning of models—response. *Science* 264:331
91. Oreskes N. 1998. Evaluation (not validation) of quantitative models. *Environ. Health Perspect.* 106:1453–60
92. Hodges JS, Dewar JA. 1992. *Is it you or your model talking: a framework for model validation. Rep. R-4114-AF/A/OSD*, Rand Publ., Santa Monica, CA
93. Beck MB, Ravetz JR, Mulkey LA, Barnwell TO. 1997. On the problem of model validation for predictive exposure assessment. *Stoch. Hydrol. Hydraul.* 11:229–54

GEOGRAPHIC INFORMATION SCIENCE AND SYSTEMS FOR ENVIRONMENTAL MANAGEMENT

Michael F. Goodchild

National Center for Geographic Information and Analysis, and Department of Geography, University of California, Santa Barbara, California 93106-4060; email: good@geog.ucsb.edu

Key Words geographic information system, representation, metadata, simulation modeling

■ **Abstract** The geographic context is essential both for environmental research and for policy-oriented environmental management. Geographic information systems are as a result increasingly important computing applications in this domain, and an understanding of the underlying principles of geographic information science is increasingly essential to sound scientific practice. The review begins by defining terms. Four major sections follow that discuss advances in GIS analysis and modeling, in the supply of geographic data for GIS, in software design, and in GIS representation. GIS-based modeling is constrained in part by architecture, but a number of recent products show promise, and GIS continues to support modeling through the coupling of software. The GIS data supply has benefited from a range of new satellite-based sensors and from developments in ground-based sensor networks. GIS software design is being revolutionized by two developments in the information technology mainstream: the trend to component-based software and object-oriented data modeling. Advances in GIS representation focus largely on time, the third spatial dimension, and uncertainty. References are provided to the more important and recent literature. The concluding section identifies three significant and current trends: toward increasing interoperability of data and services, increasing mobility of information technology, and increasing capabilities for dynamic simulation.

CONTENTS

1. INTRODUCTION 494
2. GIS ANALYSIS AND MODELING 497
   2.1. Types of Geographic Data 497
   2.2. Developments in GIS Analysis 500
   2.3. Developments in GIS Modeling 502
3. ADVANCES IN THE DATA SUPPLY 506
   3.1. New Sources of Imagery 506
   3.2. Sensors and Sensor Networks 507
   3.3. Archives and Digital Libraries 508
   3.4. Institutional Arrangements 510

    4. ADVANCES IN SOFTWARE 511
        4.1. Component-Based Software Design 511
        4.2. Schema Development 512
        4.3. The Grid 514
    5. ADVANCES IN GIS REPRESENTATION 514
        5.1. Uncertainty 515
    6. CONCLUSION 516

1. INTRODUCTION

We normally define the environment to include the surface and near-surface of the Earth; that is, the biosphere, the upper parts of the lithosphere, and the lower parts of the atmosphere. Some facts about this domain are universally true at any point in space and time: examples include general facts about the fluvial processes by which flowing water modifies landforms or general facts about the behaviors of certain species. The discovery of such general facts is of course the major focus of much scientific activity. But other facts are specific in space and often also specific in time. For example, the elevation of Mount Everest refers specifically to a small point on the Nepal-Tibet border and undergoes changes through time due to the continued uplift of the Himalayas (and also to improvements in measurement techniques). We commonly use the terms *geographic* and *geospatial* to describe collections of such facts about specific places in the environment, and *spatiotemporal* to describe collections of facts about specific places at specific times (*spatial* is commonly defined as a generalization of *geographic* to any space, which may include outer space or the space of the human body). Geographic facts are in themselves not as valuable and significant as general facts, but they are essential if general facts are to be extracted through the study of specific areas or applied in specific areas to provide the boundary conditions and parameters that are needed in order to forecast, to evaluate planning options, or to design new structures.

    Clearly a high proportion of the data needed for environmental management are geographic (for the purposes of this review the term will be used synonymously with geospatial and will include the possibility of temporal variation). Maps and atlases contain large quantities of geographic data, and geographic data can also be found scattered through books, journal articles, and many other media. Today, increasing quantities of geographic data take the form of electronic transactions, such as the locations telemetered from a collared mammal to a researcher studying its foraging habits and territorial behavior. Vast amounts of geographic data are now collected daily by imaging satellites and distributed via the Internet, and increasing amounts are collected by networks of ground-based sensors and through field observation.

    This review concerns two topics related to geographic data: geographic information science (GIScience), which is the research field that studies the general principles underlying the acquisition, management, processing, analysis, visualization, and storage of geographic data; and geographic information systems (GIS), which are computer software packages designed to carry out these activities. The history of GIS began in the 1960s with primitive efforts to use computers to process geographic data (1), and today a wide variety of packages are available from major commercial vendors, such as Intergraph (http://www.intergraph.com/), MapInfo (http://www.mapinfo.com/), and Environmental Systems Research Institute (ESRI) (http://www.esri.com/), and from academic groups, such as Clark Labs at Clark University (http://www.clarklabs.org/), developers of IDRISI. Figures 1*a* and 1*b* (see color insert) show screen shots of a popular GIS in use for analysis of atmospheric ozone and illustrate some of its major features.

Environmental management has been a prime motivator of developments in GIS, and a major area of application, throughout its history. The first GIS, the Canada Geographic Information System, was developed in the mid 1960s in order to handle the vast amount of mapped information collected by the Canada Land Inventory and from it to provide data to the Government of Canada on Canada's land resource, its utilization, and its management. The first commercially viable GIS, introduced in the early 1980s, found its initial customers among environmental management agencies and forestry companies. Environmental management continues to motivate developments in GIScience and their implementation in GIS. Geographic data and GIS are of such importance to the environmental disciplines that today we tend to think of them as indispensable parts of the research, teaching, and policy arenas. Abundant examples of GIS use in this context are available in textbooks, journals, conference proceedings, and on the World Wide Web (WWW).

The argument for geographic data and GIS, and more generally for taking a geographic or spatial perspective on the environment, is essentially twofold (2). First, our understanding of the environment is at least in part derived from studying it directly, rather than from replicating its behavior in the laboratory under controlled conditions. We draw inferences from the correlations we observe between different factors at a location, from the differences we observe when locations are compared, and from the context in which changes occur. All of these are supported by studying the environment in spatial and temporal detail. Scientific knowledge is of course most valuable when it is general, in other words when it is known to be true everywhere at all times. Thus the process of scientific knowledge creation is fundamentally a process of abstracting knowledge from space and time. The second argument for geographic data and GIS occurs when that general knowledge must be applied in making decisions or in developing policy. In this phase general knowledge must be recombined with the specifics of a place and time; general knowledge is expressed in the procedures and models implemented in the GIS, and the specifics of a location and time are expressed in the geographic data in the GIS database.

In recent years much interest has developed in the social context of GIS use. In the early years, when the cost of entry into GIS was much higher, access to it was largely restricted to large corporations and government agencies. But the steady fall in hardware and software costs over the past three decades has led to almost universal access, and community groups are now frequent users of GIS and rely on its capabilities to build arguments for and against local developments. The role of GIS in the decision making process is the focus of the growing research field of Public Participation GIS (3).

This review begins with an overview of recent literature in GIS applications to environment and resources, including advances in environmental modeling with GIS. This is followed in Section 3 by a review of advances in geographic data sources, which include the advent of several new and exciting passive and active sensors, growing interest in autonomous ground-based sensor networks, and the potential offered by mobile GIS functionality in the field. The mechanisms for disseminating the products of these sensors and systems remain fraught with difficulty, however, that stems from diverse practices in the design of online archives, lack of interoperability between systems, and the lack of effective search mechanisms over distributed data sources.

Recent advances in software engineering, which include the trend toward reusable components, are having profound effects on GIS and are reviewed in Section 4. It is now possible to combine components from a range of packages written to compliant standards; this avoids the traditional necessity to couple packages, a practice common in environmental modeling, when specialized modeling codes have frequently been coupled with GIS. These innovations offer advantages in a number of areas, including the design and development of spatial decision support systems, that is, systems designed to give decision makers the ability to evaluate decisions and scenarios. However, the infrastructure for sharing methods and models, expressed in digital form, lags far behind the infrastructure for sharing data, although arguably methods and models represent a higher form of scientific knowledge.

The history of GIScience began in the late 1980s as the widespread use of GIS began to draw attention to the need for a deeper understanding of fundamental principles and rejuvenated interest in older disciplines, such as cartography, surveying, and navigation (4–6). Recent advances have been made in understanding the importance of ontology, which is defined as the science of representation or the study of the things people choose to acquire information about. Ontology dominates the earliest stages of science, when researchers must decide what to describe, what to measure, and what to record in order to develop an understanding of an environmental system. Similarly, it dominates the design of GIS databases and ultimately constrains what one can do with the representation created in such a database. Ontological choices, or their more practical, everyday expression in the designs of databases, are thus fundamental to all science and particularly important in any science that is supported by information technology. Section 5 of the review discusses GIS representation, and it reviews recent research on alternative ontologies and on the potential of new developments in information science to support the integration of data produced by different researchers and disciplines into a seamless research environment. It also reviews recent work on uncertainty, which focuses on issues such as accuracy, and approaches to deal with areas of environmental science where definitions are inherently vague. The review ends with a brief summary of current trends in GIS and GIScience.

2. GIS ANALYSIS AND MODELING

2.1. Types of Geographic Data

In principle, a GIS can be designed to perform any conceivable operation on any type of geographic data. Like many other computer applications, its success depends on a fundamental economy of scale: Once the foundation has been built for managing geographic data, it is possible to extend the list of supported operations very quickly, at minimal cost. This same economy of scale underlies and explains the rich functionality of packages such as Excel, which performs a vast array of operations on data expressed in tables, or Word, which similarly performs almost any conceivable operation on text. GIS is simply the equivalent for geographic data.

However, this simple model fails in one crucial respect: There are many distinct types of geographic data. GIScientists distinguish between two fundamentally different conceptualizations of the geographic world (7–9). In the *continuous field* view, the surface of the Earth can be described by mapping a set of variables, each of which is a single-valued function of location, and perhaps time: $z = f(\mathbf{x})$, where $\mathbf{x}$ denotes location in space and time. Topography, for example, is often represented by mapping elevation as a function of the two horizontal dimensions and atmospheric pressure as a function of the three spatial dimensions and time. In addition to these examples of measurements on interval/ratio scales, the mapped variable can be nominal or categorical; for example, ownership is a single-valued function of the two horizontal dimensions, as is land cover class, or county name. Figure 2 shows topography that would normally be conceptualized as a continuous field of elevations.

In the second, or *discrete object* conceptualization, the Earth's surface is a space littered with objects. The objects may overlap, and there may be empty space between them. We often conceive of built environments in this manner, as spaces littered with buildings, streets, trees, vehicles, and other well-defined and discrete objects. Discrete objects are countable and readily identified, and those that are useful tend to be persistent through time. Figure 3 shows an example of phenomena that would likely be conceptualized as discrete objects: major water bodies, interstate highways, golf courses, and recreation areas in the Chicago area.

Both views are common in the environmental sciences, and they frequently interact. In ecology, for example, one might analyze the behavior of individual organisms, perhaps regarding distance between individuals as an important causal factor, which reflects a discrete object view. But at another, coarser scale, one might attempt to explain variation in the density of individuals in terms of variation in resources, by looking for correlations between continuous fields: The dependent variable, density, would be conceptualized as a field, as would the independent

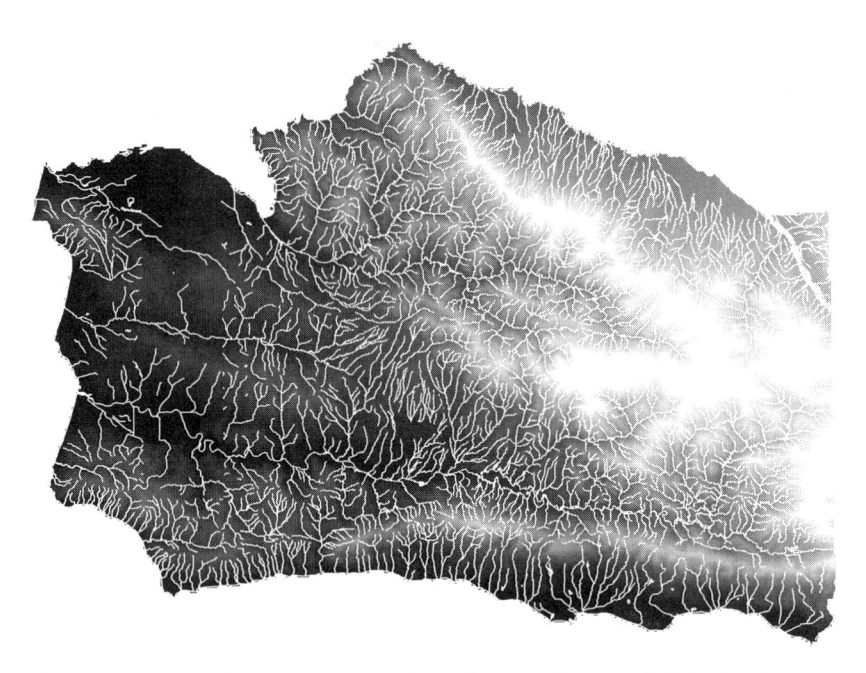

Figure 2 The mainland portion of Santa Barbara County, California, showing a continuous field of elevation (the *highest areas are white*), with superimposed streams.

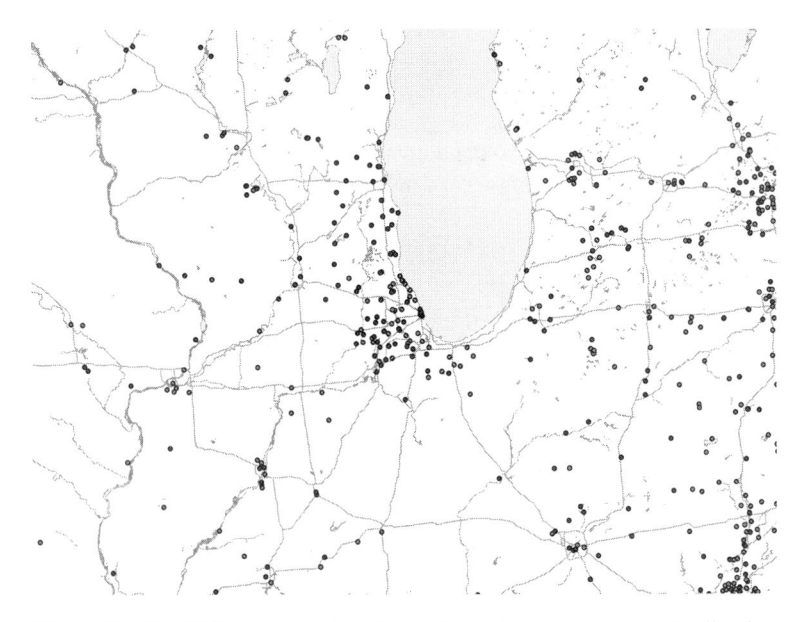

Figure 3 The Chicago area, showing various phenomena conceptualized as discrete objects: major water bodies, interstate highways, golf courses (*point symbols*), and recreation areas (*point symbols*).

variables. One might even try to model animal behavior as a discrete object responding to such continuous fields as habitat suitability or climate. Clearly a GIS that is intended for environmental applications must support both conceptualizations.

In practice, discrete objects are represented digitally by points, lines, areas, or volumes, as appropriate. Rivers might be represented as lines when they act as corridors or barriers and as areas or volumes when the interest is in the distribution of organisms within the river; the term *polymorphism* is used to describe such multiple, application-specific representations. Each feature has one or more attributes that describe its characteristics and one or more coordinates that describe its shape. The shapes of lines are commonly represented as sequences of points connected by straight lines, and areas as closed sequences (the terms *polyline* and *polygon* are used respectively).

Continuous fields present a more difficult representation problem, because in principle the function $z = f(\mathbf{x})$ can stand for an infinite amount of information, if the corresponding value of z must be independently measured and recorded at every point. In practice, any field representation must be an approximation for this reason, and six methods of approximation are commonly used in GIS (discussed here in the two-dimensional case):

- REGULARLY SPACED SAMPLE POINTS   Topography is most commonly represented in this form as a *digital elevation model.*

- IRREGULARLY SPACED SAMPLE POINTS   The continuous fields of meteorology, e.g., atmospheric temperature, pressure, and precipitation, are sampled at irregularly spaced measuring stations.

- RECTANGULAR CELLS   The continuous fields captured as remotely sensed images are represented as arrays of cells; each cell has as attribute the average spectral response across its extent.

- IRREGULAR POLYGONS   Nominal variables, such as land cover class, are most commonly represented as collections of nonoverlapping, space-exhausting areas, each with a single value that is assumed to apply homogeneously to its extent.

- TRIANGULAR MESH   Topographic surfaces are sometimes represented as meshes of irregular triangles (*triangulated irregular networks* or TINs), each with uniform slope and with continuity of value across triangle edges.

- DIGITIZED ISOLINES   Topographic surfaces are also sometimes represented as collections of lines, derived from the contours of the surface.

Of these six, the first two and the last are inherently different from the third, fourth, and fifth. While the latter three can be queried to obtain the value of the field at any location, the former three record values only at certain locations: points in the case of the first two and lines in the case of the last. One might term the latter set complete representations, and the former set incomplete representations, for this reason, though note that completeness does not imply perfect accuracy.

In order to support queries about the values of the field, or to support resampling, or various forms of visualization, an incomplete representation must be coupled with a method of *spatial interpolation*, defined as the means to estimate the field's value at locations where value is not recorded. A substantial number of methods of spatial interpolation are available (10–12), many of them implemented in GIS.

The representations of both discrete objects and continuous fields fall into two categories and are often described in these terms. Methods that record coordinates are termed *vector*, and they include all of the discrete object representations, plus the irregularly spaced sample points, irregular polygons, triangular mesh, and digitized isoline representations of fields. *Raster* methods, on the other hand, establish position implicitly through the ordering of the array and include the regularly spaced sample point and rectangular cell representations of continuous fields. For this reason, rasters are often loosely associated with continuous fields, and vectors with discrete objects, but the association is more likely to confuse than to illuminate.

Of the six methods, the last two are restricted to interval/ratio variables for obvious reasons. The third and fourth are used for both nominal and interval/ratio variables, although the first two might be used for both but are in practice used for interval/ratio variables.

These six are in principle not the only methods that might be used to represent fields, but they are the only methods widely implemented in GIS. In the scientific community more generally, much use is made of *finite-element* methods (FEM), which represent fields through polynomial functions over meshes that mix irregular triangles and quadrilaterals. FEM are commonly used in applications that require the solution of partial differential equations (PDEs), and there are many such applications in the Earth sciences, from tidal movements to atmospheric modeling. Links have often been made between FEM-based modeling software and GIS (13), but FEM has not been adopted as a basis for field representation in GIS, perhaps because of its greater mathematical complexity relative, say, to TINs.

Within this overall organization of geographic data it is possible to identify vast resources that are increasingly available over the Internet from archives, clearinghouses, and digital libraries and represent an investment over decades, and in some cases centuries, that certainly exceeds a trillion dollars worldwide. Most of this investment has been made by national governments through national mapping agencies and space agencies. But the commercial sector is growing rapidly, and geographic-data production is increasingly a function of local government and even individuals. Developments in the geographic data supply are reviewed in a subsequent section; the following sections discuss the uses of these data resources in analysis and modeling.

2.2. Developments in GIS Analysis

The set of possible forms of analysis and manipulation that is possible with GIS is vast, and much effort has gone into finding useful systems of organization that might help users to navigate the possibilities. Any GIS must of course support basic housekeeping operations, such as copying data sets between storage devices, transforming coordinates to different map projections, converting paper maps to digital databases, reformatting for use by other systems, editing, visualizing, and other routine functions. But the true power of GIS lies in its ability to search for patterns and anomalies, to summarize, to compare reality to the predictions of theories, or to reveal correlations. Tomlin (14) made one of the first successful efforts to codify analysis, identified four basic classes of operations, and defined an associated language that he termed cartographic modeling. The language, which bears some similarities to others defined in image processing (15), became the basis for command syntax in several GIS packages. But his work was limited to raster data, and efforts to extend it to vector data have thus far been unsuccessful.

Many texts on analysis of geographic data have adopted a codification based on data types. Bailey & Gatrell (16) divide techniques into those appropriate for sets of points, sets of areas, measures of interactions between objects, and analyses of continuous surfaces, for example, and similar approaches are used by Haining (17) and by O'Sullivan & Unwin (18).

Longley et al. (19) recently used a very different approach based on classifying techniques according to their conceptual frameworks:

- simple queries, which return results already existing in the database;
- measurements, which return measures of such properties as distance, length, area, or shape;
- transformations, which create new features from existing features;
- descriptive summaries, which compute summary statistics for entire collections of features;
- optimization, which results in designs that achieve user-defined objectives, such as the search for an optimum location; and
- hypothesis testing in which statistical methods are used to reason from a sample to a larger population.

Each of these categories might apply to any type of data, and to both discrete object and continuous field conceptualizations.

Today, GIS is used in a vast array of application domains, many of them strongly associated with the environment and with resources. Papers describing research that has made use of GIS to study problems in the environment and in resources appear in specialized journals, and several collections of papers have been published recently as books. GIS applications to environmental health have been described by Gatrell & Loytonen (20), Cromley & McLafferty (21), Briggs (22), and Lang (23). Haines-Young et al. (24) and Johnston (25) describe applications in landscape ecology. A forthcoming book by Bishop (26) contains solicited chapters describing the use of GIS in mountain geomorphology.

2.3. Developments in GIS Modeling

The term *modeling* is of course vastly overloaded with many nuances of meaning in different contexts. In GIS it has three important meanings, two of which are the focus of this section. First, modeling is used in the context of *data modeling*, or the process by which structures and templates are created that can be filled with measurements, observations, and other forms of data. The basics of data modeling for GIS were covered in a previous section at the conceptual level, and the more detailed physical levels of data modeling that include discussions of indexes and coding schemes are beyond the scope of this review.

In its second meaning, modeling refers to the use of GIS transformations and other procedures to create composite variables that have significance in some aspect of a GIS application. At a very primitive level the calculation of the Normalized Difference Vegetation Index (NDVI) (27) in remote sensing is an example of this kind of modeling; it takes inputs from two bands of a satellite-based sensor and computes the ratio of the difference to the sum to obtain a useful index of greenness. NDVI is often computed to show the march of the seasons across the midlatitudes as vegetation greens in the spring and decays in the fall. The Universal Soil Loss Equation (USLE) (28) is another example; it combines inputs representing various factors of importance in determining soil erosion and produces an index that is a useful estimate of soil loss. While the calculation of NDVI from raster image data is a straightforward arithmetic task, the calculation of USLE is more likely to involve the integration of field representations that use more than one of the six options listed above (perhaps elevation as a regular array of points or soil class as a collection of polygons) and hence to require a larger set of GIS functions, including raster-vector conversion. In summary, modeling in this second sense takes inputs and transforms them into outputs. All inputs and outputs are assumed to be valid at the same point in time, although the output may be used to estimate changes through time, as in the case of the USLE. This second meaning of modeling will be termed *static modeling* in this review.

The third meaning is strictly dynamic and will be termed *dynamic modeling*. Dynamic models are iterative; they take a set of initial conditions and apply transformations to obtain a series of predictions at time intervals stretching into the future. The transformations may be expressed in a number of forms, and this provides the basis for one system of classification of dynamic models. Some dynamic models implement the solution of PDEs to obtain predictions of future states of the modeled system; such models are particularly applicable in systems involving the behavior of fluids, such as water, ice, and the atmosphere. Underground flow through aquifers, for example, is often modeled through the solution of the Darcy flow equations (29). PDE-based models may be implemented through numerical operations on rasters, termed *finite-difference* methods, or through numerical operations on finite-element meshes, though as noted above FEM is normally implemented outside GIS. In both cases the mathematical expression of the model as a PDE must be approximated in its computational implementation through a series of operations on rasters or finite elements. For example, the mathematical concept of the derivative is implemented in finite-difference approximations as an arithmetic operation on small raster neighborhoods. In principle, then, PDEs could be implemented using the language of cartographic modeling discussed above, which includes all of the necessary operations.

In the discrete object domain, mathematical models address the interactions between objects, in the style of Newton's Law of Gravitation. Spatial interaction models attempt to replicate the interactions that exist between social entities, such as migration flows between states, flows of telephone traffic between cities, or flows of commuters between neighborhoods (30, 31). Flows are modeled as the product of factors relating to the origin's propensity to generate flow, the destination's propensity to attract it, and the role of intervening distance as an impediment. Spatial interaction models have found applications in resource management, in the modeling of population pressure on recreational resources, and in the analysis of tourist flows to destinations. Unlike PDEs, such models deal directly with objects and their digital representations, and they do not require the numerical approximations that occur when PDEs are transformed into finite-difference or finite-element models.

Other dynamic models lack the formal mathematical definition of PDEs and spatial interaction models; instead they define operations directly on digital representations. Such models are termed *computational*. Two important classes of computational models are *cellular automata* (CA) and *agent-based models* (ABM). In the former, the behavior of a system is modeled as a series of transition rules concerning the states of cells in a raster. For example, a number of research groups (32, 33) have developed CA models of urban growth; the models relate the transition of a cell from agriculture or open space to urban development as a function of the state of neighboring cells, as well as proximity to transportation, physical suitability for development, and other variables. ABM attempt to characterize the behavior of individuals and groups and the impacts of their decisions on their surroundings. ABM have also been applied to land use transition in rural areas (34).

Dynamic models that invoke continuous-field conceptualizations, either as inputs or outputs, must of necessity be scale dependent, because their predictions vary with the level of detail of the underlying field representations. Raster-based computational models give predictions that are specific to the physical dimensions of the raster. Scale-dependence in vector-based computational models is more difficult to characterize, however, because the concept of spatial resolution is not well defined for any of the vector-based field representations (irregular points, irregular polygons, TINs, and digitized isolines). Thus an important test of any computational model is its degree of sensitivity to scale change. CA models are among the most problematic in this sense; their definitions are scale-specific even though scale affects only the computational implementation of PDEs, not the PDEs themselves.

Static models are readily implemented in GIS, and a large number of such models have been operationalized, often as GIS scripts or extensions to standard GIS software. The concept of a script or macro, which allows the user to record and replay a sequence of commands, is common to many computer applications. In some cases, the recording occurs during the normal use of the software by user actions that start and stop the recording at appropriate points. In other cases, the script is written by the user in a language designed for the purpose, tested and executed later, and possibly shared with others. The popular GIS ArcView, for example, is supplied by its developer ESRI with a scripting language Avenue [Version 8 of ArcView replaces the vendor-specific Avenue with the Microsoft language Visual Basic. For an introduction to Avenue, see (35), and for Visual Basic, see (36)]. A large number of Avenue scripts have been coded or recorded and made available for standard environmental and resource applications (see http://arcscripts.esri.com/).

Dynamic models are much more difficult to implement in GIS scripting languages. GIS software was designed largely for transforming and analyzing data, rather than for the rapid iterations needed by dynamic models. Although it is possible to implement an iterative process, such as a CA model, in Avenue, the resulting performance is typically very disappointing to the point of being impractical. Instead, researchers have implemented dynamic models in other ways that avoid these performance issues. Three approaches are commonly identified; they are three forms of *coupling* of GIS and dynamic modeling (37).

First, *loose coupling* is defined as the implementation of dynamic models in two software packages, one designed purely for the modeling and the other the GIS. Data pass in both directions between the packages. Inputs often require reprojection, resampling, editing, and sometimes raster–vector conversion, and these operations are better performed in the GIS and passed to the dynamic model. During and after execution of the model, selected results are passed back to the GIS for display, further analysis, and archiving, again taking advantage of the existence of these functions in the GIS. This approach requires a degree of compatibility between the two packages, such that each can read and write the data formats of the other. When no common formats can be found, it is necessary to add a third package to do the necessary format conversions. The problem is exacerbated by the continuing insistence of some GIS vendors that their internal formats be proprietary.

Close coupling can be used when both packages are able to read and write the same formats and avoid the need for file transfer or conversion. Because of the proprietary nature of some GIS formats, this option is most likely to be available when using open-source GIS packages or GIS packages for which internal formats have been published.

Finally, *tight coupling* occurs when the dynamic model is written directly in the scripting language of the GIS. As noted above, this is uncommon because of the poor performance of many GIS products in these applications. But it is possible to achieve better performance if the GIS is designed from the start with dynamic modeling in mind. PCRaster (http://www.geog.uu.nl/pcraster/) is such a GIS, developed at the University of Utrecht for modeling dynamic environmental processes. It supports a scripting language developed by van Deursen (38) and others (39) that uses simple symbols to refer to entire raster representations; thus the command $A = B + C$ results in the cell-by-cell addition of two rasters, rather than the addition of two simple scalar quantities as in most programming languages. PCRaster has been applied to many physical processes, which range from erosion and mass wasting to groundwater flow. It is readily adapted to the CA models of urban growth mentioned above and to many other domains.

Underlying PCRaster is the notion that continuous fields can be manipulated and transformed through simple symbolic operations. Kemp (40, 41) and Vckovski (42) have argued that a symbolic representation of a field can be largely independent of the field's actual representation; for example, B might represent a raster, a TIN, or any of the other four field representations. Symbolic manipulation vastly simplifies the specification of GIS operations, because the addition of a TIN and a raster is expressed in the same way as the addition of two rasters, irrespective of the geometric relationship between the TIN triangles and the cells or of whether the cells in each raster coincide or have the same size. In this perspective, the operation of overlay, often considered the core operation of GIS analysis (1), becomes implicit and invisible to the user.

These concepts of coupling have been implemented in many examples of environmental modeling with GIS. The issues raised by such activities have been discussed in a series of conferences beginning in 1991 (the International Conference/Workshop on Integrating GIS and Environmental Modeling), in their published proceedings (43, 44; http://www.ncgia.ucsb.edu/conf/SANTA_FE_CD-ROM/main.html) and in other books (45–47). Models have been applied to processes in the atmosphere, to ecological systems, and hydrologic systems and to the couplings that exist between these systems.

Environmental modeling raises a number of important issues; many of them fall within the domain of GIScience. Scale has already been mentioned because it is desirable that models be as far as possible invariant under changes of scale. In practice, modelers attempt to implement models at the scales that are characteristic of the process of interest. At coarser scales the predictions will be inaccurate, and at finer scales, the model's operations will be to some degree redundant. Uncertainty is another fundamental issue. The inputs to any model are representations and as such cannot capture all of the detail that exists in the real world, so it is important to understand how uncertainties in inputs propagate through the model to become confidence limits on outputs, particularly if the model is highly nonlinear. There has been much interest in modeling uncertainty in geographic data in recent years, and Heuvelink provides an excellent summary of this work (48) and see Burrough & McDonnell (49). Uncertainty also exists in the model itself, its structure, and the values of its parameters, and hence it is common to include sensitivity analysis in the application of a model. The topic is addressed in greater detail in Section 5.1.

3. ADVANCES IN THE DATA SUPPLY

3.1. New Sources of Imagery

The past three decades have seen steady advances in the availability of data from satellites, and today remote sensing dominates all other sources of data for environmental management. Satellite orbits are independent of national borders; the data they produce are in principle cheap and readily available. A wide variety of types of sensors exists today, and the range of options is increasing steadily. Imaging sensors can also be mounted on aircraft, unmanned autonomous vehicles, and on the ground. All of these options are currently being pursued as sources of data for environmental management.

An important distinction should be made at the outset between two different types of application of imagery. *Mapping* applications, and those associated primarily with monitoring and management, make use of imagery to characterize the Earth's surface and to detect and map change in such variables as land cover class or in the positions of boundaries. Mapping applications rely heavily on human interpretation and on automated methods for classification. Imagery is widely used for this purpose in environmental management. *Measurement* applications, on the other hand, treat images as assemblages of signals that can be transformed into estimates of useful parameters, such as biomass density, leaf area, or sea surface temperature. These estimates are then used as input to dynamic models or as measurements of the rate of change of critical earth system parameters. Calculation of parameters from raw measurements often involves the type of static modeling discussed in the previous section.

Sensors and the imagery they produce can be characterized in many ways, and several excellent reviews of Earth imagery and its applications have appeared recently. Sensors can be passive, relying on the natural radiation that is reflected or emitted by the Earth's surface and the atmosphere; or they can be active, using radiation generated by the sensor itself. In the latter category are radar and laser sensors. The former have the ability to see through cloud, and interferometric radar is increasingly used as a source of precise measurements of topographic elevation (27). The airborne laser systems known as LiDAR are capable of providing even-higher-precision elevation measurements, to subcentimeter levels, and of acquiring three-dimensional information on vegetation and structures.

Sensors can also be characterized by their resolutions in the spatial, spectral, and temporal domains. Spatial resolution determines the level of detail that can be perceived on the Earth's surface, and today imagery is available from satellite sensors at submeter resolutions. Spectral resolution determines the amount of detail that can be extracted about the nature of the Earth's surface at any point. *Panchromatic* imagery integrates radiation into a single measurement, sensors such as Landsat's Thematic Mapper integrate parts of the visible and near-infrared spectrum into several distinct bands, and *hyperspectral* sensors, such as the Airborne Visible/Infra-Red Imaging Spectrometer (AVIRIS), divide the spectrum into large numbers of bands (224 in the case of AVIRIS). Finally, temporal resolution defines the frequency with which a sensor images any part of the Earth's surface and is normally expressed in days.

The number of sensors designed for applications in environmental management has multiplied dramatically in the past few years. Several new commercial sensors such as IKONOS and Quickbird have been launched and have pushed the lower limit of spatial resolution to below 1 m. This has opened new applications in such areas as the detailed mapping of land cover and high-precision mapping of infrastructure. Several nations, e.g., India, have recently entered the business of remote sensing and launched their own satellites for applications in environmental management. The Earth Observing System (EOS) series of satellites, designed by NASA for the measurement of parameters that are important in understanding the global environmental system, include the MODIS sensor on the TERRA platform, an increasingly popular source of essentially free data for the monitoring of environmental change. There is not sufficient space here to provide a complete review, but for examples, see (27, 47).

3.2. Sensors and Sensor Networks

In addition to sensors mounted on aircraft and satellites, environmental managers are just beginning to make use of various forms of ground-based sensors. The Global Positioning System (GPS) allows position on the Earth's surface to be measured using devices no larger than a hand calculator, to $+/-$ 10 m or better, and this has proven a boon to field-workers who need to find their positions and the positions of their measurements. Although GPS signals are obscured by tall buildings and heavy tree canopy, their accuracy has been substantially enhanced in the past few years with the removal of Selective Availability, the protocol that limited the accuracies obtainable by civilian receivers. Differential GPS, which works by comparing signals at field locations to those received by fixed receivers in known positions, allows locations to be determined to 1 m and often less.

Environmental management has benefited from the continuing reduction in size of many ground-based sensors, particularly of such properties as atmospheric temperature, pressure, and humidity; soil moisture content and pH; cloud cover; and canopy closure. With miniaturization has come a lowering of cost, improvements in telemetering, and the potential for installing semipermanent and dense networks of sensors (50). In the long term, there is interesting speculation about the potential of *digital dust*, ultra-miniature and extremely cheap sensors that may one day allow very dense networks of ground-based environmental sensing.

Sensor networks raise interesting questions of interoperability or the lack of it. A network of sensors measuring different parameters, manufactured by different companies to different specifications, must somehow be integrated if it is to be effective. Two systems are said to be interoperable if their outputs can be integrated and understood. The Open GIS Consortium (http://www.opengis.org/) is actively developing specifications for interoperable sensor networks; if these are successful, then manufacturers will be able to ensure interoperability through adherence to common, openly published specifications.

3.3. Archives and Digital Libraries

Our ability to acquire data is now so great that it commonly exceeds our ability both to distribute it and to make effective use of it. It is said that only a small fraction of all of the bits collected by remote sensing are ever examined in any detail, and an even smaller fraction ultimately leads to new science. The EOS satellites are sending data to Earth at rates on the order of a terabyte a day (1 terabyte = 10^{12} bytes, a quantity that would occupy a standard 56 k phone modem for approximately 4 years), yet few researchers have access to storage devices with anything approaching that capacity. Dissemination and use of this cornucopia of data require effective archiving, the ability for users to search across distributed archives for data of interest, and the tools needed to visualize and analyze the data. In recent years, an increasing proportion of the total being invested in satellite remote sensing programs has gone to the development of suitable dissemination systems.

A dissemination system has several essential components:

- A collection of archives, each with its own mechanism for search that allows users who visit the archive to find data sets meeting specific requirements (*visit* normally means remotely, via the Internet). Examples of such archives for geographic data are NASA's system of Distributed Active Archive Centers (http://nasadaacs.eos.nasa.gov/); the Federal Geographic Data Committee's National Geospatial Data Clearinghouse (http://www.fgdc.gov/); the Alexandria Digital Library (http://www.alexandria.ucsb.edu/); the Global Change Master Directory (http://gcmd.gsfc.nasa.gov/); and the EROS Data Center of the U.S. Geological Survey (http://edc.usgs.gov/).

- A set of recognized standard formats. Although it is unreasonable to expect everyone to adopt a single standard for geographic data, it is important that the number of choices be limited to a few, well-documented options.

- A standard for description of data sets, that is a standard for *metadata*. The Federal Geographic Data Committee's Content Standard for Digital Geospatial Metadata (CSDGM or the FGDC Standard; http://www.fgdc.gov/) is widely used, and several other standards are very similar, e.g., ISO 19115. Metadata are essential for search because they allows users to express needs in terms that are readily understood by archives.

Ideally, it would be possible for a user to search across any collection of archives simultaneously, provided each archive was sufficiently interoperable with the others. The library community Z39.50 standard supports this by establishing standard protocols. But the ideal, a search mechanism that works across the entire Internet to find any data sets that meet specified requirements, remains elusive (51). Unfortunately, current search engines, such as Google or Altavista, rely on keywords in text and are not effective over the much more specific domain of geographic data. Progress is being made, however, with the development of software agents that search over defined domains to recognize and open standard geographic data formats and to build custom catalogs (see, for example, MapFusion, a product of Global Geomatics Inc., http://www.globalgeo.com/).

Many geographic data sets are vast, and it is common for users to require only subsets. A standard Landsat image or scene, for example, covers an area of approximately 185 km on a side, and it is very unlikely that a study area would coincide exactly with the boundaries of one or more scenes. Downloading more data than are required can swamp limited bandwidth, especially for users confined to telephone-line connections. Recently, therefore, standards have been developed that allow users to request custom areas and require the archive to clip and edgematch data accordingly. These standards also place appropriate headers or wrappers on returned data, which allow the receiving system to open and process the data automatically without user intervention—for example by integrating the data with data from other archives and possibly by changing projection to the one in use at the client. The Open GIS Consortium's Web mapping specification (http://www.opengis.org/) is one example of this kind of standard and so is the Distributed Oceanographic Data System (DODS) (http://www.unidata.ucar.edu/packages/dods/), a protocol developed in the oceanographic community and now widely adopted in the Earth sciences. For an implementation see the ESRI Geography Network (http://www.geographynetwork.com/), which integrates fully with the company's GIS products and allows users in effect to treat distributed archives as the equivalent of a vastly enlarged hard drive.

Although much progress has been made in recent years in improving the ability of researchers and others working in the area of environmental management to discover and access data, there continue to be serious impediments to this process. As a result, it is common for the process of discovery and access to occupy substantial time, because of the need for extensive and lengthy human intervention. Although technologies similar to DODS, in principle, allow access to remote data sources at electronic speed, in practice data access and integration can be major deterrents to research. Some of the remaining problems include:

- The existence of multiple, incompatible standards that work against interoperability. Although standards exist in many domains of science and in many areas of management, they are often specific to disciplines, organizations, and projects. The techniques for translation between different standards are still rudimentary, and the problem is becoming more rather than less severe as the use of information technology expands and as new technologies are introduced.

- The lack of metadata for many datasets. Metadata are expensive and time-consuming to create, and the benefits are often regarded as too small to justify the investment.

- The lack of clear guidelines that would help a researcher in choosing between the vast number of possible WWW-based sources of data. Although many large archives exist and most possess excellent search tools, it is generally difficult for users to know which archives to search for given types of data because no overarching organization exists. In the absence of catalogs containing general descriptions of archive contents (or collection-level metadata) (52), searches must too often rely on personal knowledge, personal contacts, and time-consuming trial and error.

3.4. Institutional Arrangements

Several trends in recent years have made this situation more rather than less problematic. Until the 1980s, federal agencies were virtually the only sources of geographic data. Nearly all imagery and digitized maps originated with the agencies that could afford the massive investments needed for satellites, sensors, digitizers, data storage devices, and human interpretation and compilation of data. Today, however, the situation is dramatically different. Massive reductions by orders of magnitude in the costs of data collection systems have meant that virtually anyone can now be a collector and publisher of geographic data. Farmers investing in precision-agriculture systems now know more about microscale variation of soil properties than the responsible federal and state agencies; cities can create their own maps using GPS and imagery at low cost; and other countries and levels of government are now significant sources of digital geographic data.

Second, the ability of federal agencies to supply the rapidly increasing demand for geographic data has been severely curtailed by budget reductions and the inability of agencies to adapt to changing technology and new areas of application. In response to these and other trends, the National Research Council proposed the concept of a National Spatial Data Infrastructure (NSDI) (53). In essence, NSDI proposes to replace a centralized system of data creation and supply with a decentralized system in which spatially continuous coverage at uniform scale would be replaced by a patchwork, which varies in scale depending on local needs and is produced by a variety of local and federal agencies. For NSDI to work, there would have to be common standards and the technical means to work across boundaries in spite of scale changes and possible mismatches. Since the original proposal, much of NSDI has been put in place under the coordination of the FGDC and mandated by an executive order.

Unfortunately, the unified view promised by NSDI extends only over a subset of geographic data and addresses only a limited number of national needs. The imagery supply from such agencies as NASA marches to a different drummer and is managed to meet the needs of the earth system science research community, under the standards established by this community rather than as part of NSDI. Similarly the ecological community has established its own metadata standard, ecological metadata language (EML) (http://knb.ecoinformatics.org/software/eml/), that spans all types of data of interest to the ecological research community, including geographic data. Searches for geographic data of ecological relevance must therefore use at least two metadata formats: EML and FGDC/CSDGM.

One way to avoid basic incompatibilities between the standards of different communities with overlapping interests would be to use a lighter form of metadata that includes only the elements common to all searches. Domain-specific standards such as EML might be mapped to more general standards for broadly based searches and used only for relatively precise searches. The Dublin Core metadata standard (http://dublincore.org/) is an example of such a general-purpose approach that is easily mapped to the more-specialized and domain-specific standards.

4. ADVANCES IN SOFTWARE

Today, a vast array of software resources exist for environmental management. They range from core GIS products to spatial decision support systems, image processing systems, systems for achieving interoperability between data sources, and systems to support search and discovery of geographic data. Although each of these software domains is more or less specific to the needs of environmental management and geographic data, there exist many other types of software that are regularly used by environmental managers and researchers. Besides the basic suite of office products, these include statistical packages such as S, SPSS, or SAS; mathematical packages such as Mathlab; general modeling packages such as STELLA; and visualization packages such as AVS. In all of these cases, the software includes at least a rudimentary set of geographic data processing functions.

There is not sufficient space in this review to examine each of these areas separately; instead, the focus will be on changes that have occurred in software engineering and computing in general in the past few years and their likely impacts on the field of environmental management. These include component-based software design, support for schema development, and the effort to integrate WWW-based services known as the *Grid*.

4.1. Component-Based Software Design

Traditionally, GIS packages have been constructed as monolithic agglomerations of code, and some large commercial GISs have reached on the order of 10^6 lines of source code (a widely used software industry rule of thumb estimates that a professional programmer can produce 10 lines of fully debugged code per day; a large operating system will contain on the order of 10^7 lines of code). In the early 1980s, the GIS industry moved quickly to adopt standard relational database management systems, which obviated the need to write code to manage basic input and output operations and thus simplified the task somewhat. Standard graphics packages were also adopted at about this time and again simplified the task of managing display devices. But apart from these innovations, the task of constructing a GIS remained monolithic until well into the 1990s.

Recently, however, software developers have been able to take advantage of a new innovation in software engineering known as *component-based* design. In this paradigm, software is constructed as a collection of reusable modules, each designed to perform well-defined and simple tasks. A given application may require the use of only a small number of these, so the others can be left unloaded. Moreover, component-based design greatly simplifies the task of software management, because each component can be managed, updated, and replaced independently. Components from one package can be readily integrated with components from another and make it possible for applications to take advantage of the functions available in different packages simultaneously. Finally, in principle, it is possible for customers to purchase only the subset of components that they need, which makes it much easier for the vendor to customize products for particular niche markets.

Several standards for component-based software development have been established, of which perhaps the best-known is Microsoft's COM standard. Many major GIS products are now COM-compliant because they were extensively rewritten to take advantage of the new architecture; in some cases this was the first complete reengineering since the early 1980s. Ungerer & Goodchild (54) use a simple example of GIS analysis to show how the new approach can be used to build applications that span a popular GIS and a standard office product, Excel, by taking advantage of the geographic-data-processing power of the former and the table-processing power of the latter. They use the example of a simple areal interpolation (55), an operation that is conducted on a routine basis when the zones for which demographic data have been tabulated do not match the zones for which data are required.

The component-based approach is now widely used for GIS development. But an interesting question remains concerning the dynamic simulation models reviewed in Section 2.3. To date, the vast majority of such models have been constructed using monolithic approaches, with each model implemented in a separate and often very large agglomeration of software. The same is generally true of spatial-decision support systems (SDSS), which have by and large been built independently, from scratch for every application. There are obvious advantages to a modular approach that would recombine each model from generic components, because the cost and time of development of a new model or new SDSS would be greatly reduced. Densham (56) discusses the concept of a model-base management system, but to date such a system has proven remarkably difficult to operationalize [but see (57)]. The key issue is essentially one of granularity: What are the atomic pieces of a simulation model? Are they individual lines of code or something larger? Although these questions have been answered effectively for GIS analysis by the developers of component-based systems, the equivalent answers for dynamic modeling have proven much more elusive.

4.2. Schema Development

The relational database management systems that were widely adopted in the 1980s were based on a very simple model of data that could be readily applied to a very wide range of examples, which include geographic data. In the relational model (58), all data are assumed to relate to well-defined cases or instances and to describe those cases through a well-defined set of characteristics or attributes. In a GIS example, the cases might represent weather stations, and the attributes would be the weather measurements taken at each station. Data can be arrayed in a table with the cases in the rows and the attributes in the columns. The power of the relational model lies in its ability to manage data in multiple tables that describe different types of objects and their associated attributes and to link tables together through common keys. For example, one might record county as an attribute of each weather station and use this attribute as a common key to link the weather station data to data available for counties, such as agricultural production statistics. It is not uncommon for advanced GIS applications to involve tens or even hundreds of tables, each describing a different class of features on the Earth's surface.

The relational model dominated GIS thinking in the 1980s and most of the 1990s, and standard database management products such as Oracle, INFO, or Informix were widely used to manage data on a full range of GIS applications. But a sharp change occurred in the late 1990s that was driven in large part by two fundamental deficiencies of the relational model. First, since the earliest adoption of the model, it had been necessary to separate the tabular information about features and their attributes from the geometric information about feature form, because the latter could not be handled simply within the relational model. This led to an awkward hybrid structure (hence, for example, the dual name ARC/INFO for the leading ESRI GIS; see http://www.esri.com/) and meant that software developers could capitalize only partially on the benefits of database management. Second, the relational model had no way of representing the hierarchical relationships that exist between many types of geographic features. For example, there are hierarchical relationships between counties and states and between individual streams and watersheds.

In the late 1990s, the GIS industry began to shift to an *object-oriented* approach to data. Three principles underlie the approach. First, all objects are instances of more general classes, a principle that also underlies the relational model. Second, classes can have hierarchical relationships to more general classes and can share their properties. For example, the class cat could be regarded as a subclass of mammal; some of the characteristics of cats are also characteristic of all mammals, but others are specific to cats. This leads to a hierarchical approach to data in which subclasses inherit some of their properties from more general classes. At the top of the inheritance hierarchy are the types of features that are common to all GIS applications: points, lines, and areas.

Third, the object-oriented approach allows methods to be encapsulated with the classes of objects to which they apply. Common methods include the editing rules that are applied whenever the digital representations of features are modified or created; for example, all areas must have closed boundaries, or isolines must not cross each other.

The shift to object-oriented modeling has meant that GIS users can now take advantage of the many excellent tools that exist to support database design and development. These include Unified Modeling Language (UML) (59) and drawing packages, such as Microsoft Visio, that allow database designs to be laid out graphically and then automatically converted into collections of tables with appropriate links (60). One of the earliest areas of environmental management to take advantage of these capabilities has been hydrology. Maidment & Djokic (61) describe a comprehensive schema for hydrologic data that is readily incorporated into an object-oriented GIS. A number of similar schemas have now been developed through the efforts of different application communities (http://arconline. esri.com/datamodels.cfm).

4.3. The Grid

In recent years there has been much research and development effort devoted to a seamless, integrated approach to computing. Now that the vast majority of computers are connected through the Internet, it is argued, the opportunity exists to create a new kind of computing environment, a *cyberinfrastructure*, that will allow researchers and managers to work together in a more integrated way. Instead of needing to collect and integrate all data and software tools relevant to a particular project in the researcher's office computer, it would be possible in this new environment for researchers to access distributed data resources and distributed tools and to make use of them as if they were local.

Some of the tools needed to achieve this kind of integration were discussed above in the section on data access. Another type of support is under development in the form of services or processing capabilities that sites make available to remote users in much the same way that sites make data available to remote users. An example of such a service is a *gazetteer service*, which is defined as a remote capability to transform place-names into coordinates. Rather than having to provide this function locally through one's own GIS, as in the past, it is now possible to use the Alexandria Digital Library's gazetteer service (http://www.alexandria.ucsb.edu/) to do this remotely by sending a simple message to the service and receiving the results in return. Such services operate using protocols that allow the service to be fully automated and therefore to occur at electronic speed. It is likely that such services will grow very rapidly in the next few years and will replace large areas of processing that researchers now conduct locally.

5. ADVANCES IN GIS REPRESENTATION

The traditional representations used in GIS were discussed above in Section 2.1. This section focuses on recent research that has attempted to extend traditional representations and on the parallel question of uncertainty. In effect, a GIS representation is a set of rules for converting aspects of the real world into the language of computers, which is limited to a two-character alphabet. Standards such as MP3 provide these rules for other domains such as music; in GIS, raster and vector approaches provide two general classes of coding schemes, the specific details determined largely by the GIS developer.

Figure 1 (*a*) A screen shot of a GIS being used to analyze atmospheric ozone over Los Angeles. The map shows the monitoring stations (*white circles*), topography, and the interpolated surface of ozone concentration (*dark is highest*) using geostatistical interpolation (see Sections 2.1 and 5.1). (*b*) A cross-validation analysis of the interpolation, which compares measured values of ozone at each monitoring station to values interpolated from all other points.

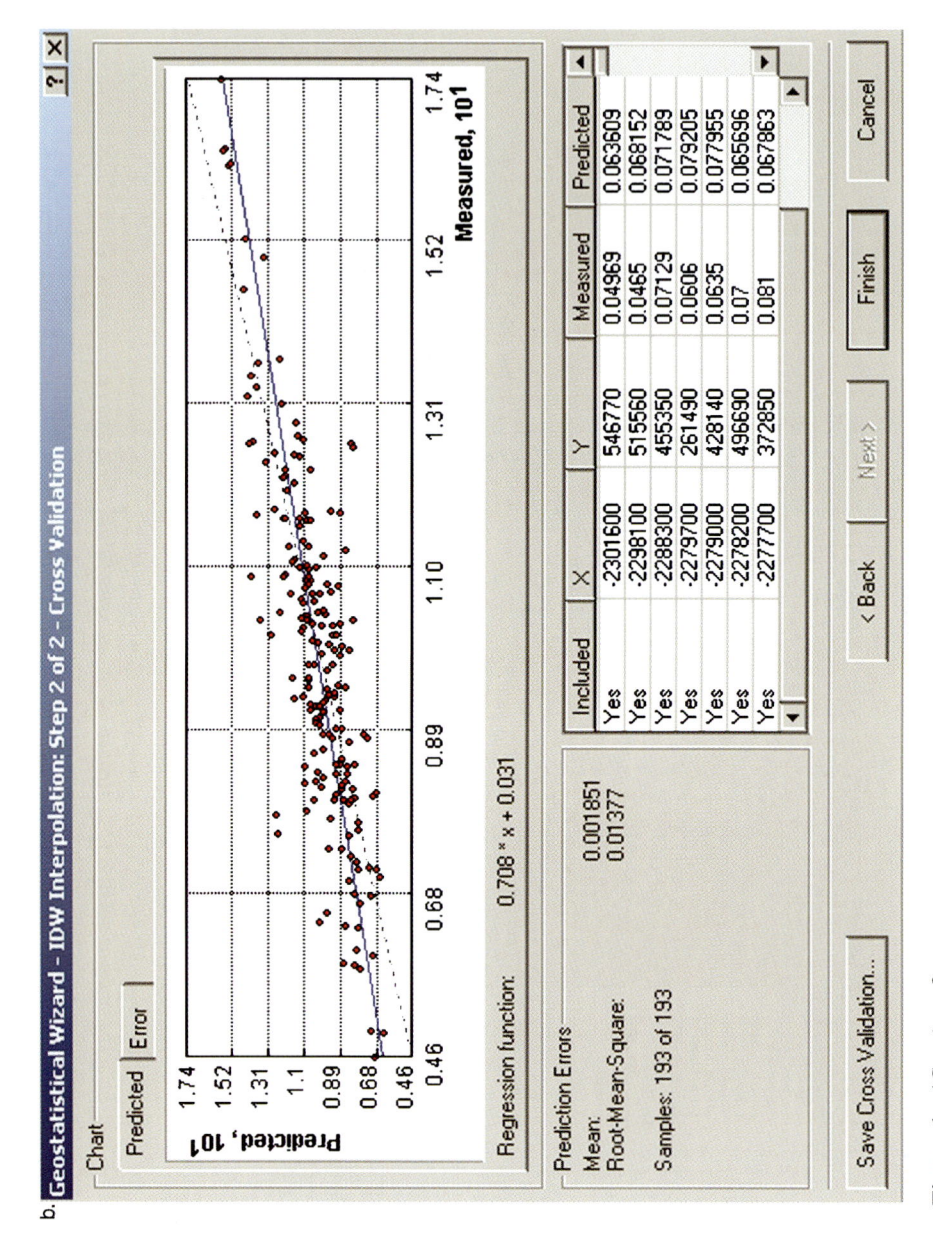

Figure 1 (*Continued*)

GIS inherits many of its core concepts from paper maps, and it is still common for GIS to be explained as a technology for capturing and processing the contents of maps. But maps impose many restrictions on geographic data that are not necessary in a digital environment (62). First and perhaps most important, maps must of necessity be static because once printed it is difficult to modify them, and it follows that maps tend therefore to capture only what is relatively static about the Earth's surface. The potential to incorporate time, to move from a spatial to a spatiotemporal basis for GIS, has stimulated much research over the years. Langran (63) reviewed early work on the topic, and Peuquet (64) provides a recent overview of the methodological basis of space and time. Today, GIS is increasingly used to store and analyze data on space-time tracks, on events occurring at specific points in space and time, and on changes through time detected by remote sensing.

A second constraint of paper maps is the inability to handle the third dimension effectively. In GIS, elevation is often treated as a function of the two horizontal dimensions, thus avoiding the need to move to a true three-dimensional approach. But applications in subsurface geology and hydrology, oceanography, and atmospheric science all require a full treatment of the third spatial dimension. Substantial effort has gone into integrating GIS with software for three-dimensional representation, but for most purposes GIS remains essentially a two-dimensional technology.

5.1. Uncertainty

The real geographic world is infinitely complex and reveals more and more detail apparently ad infinitum. In some cases the rate at which additional detail is revealed is predictable with remarkable precision, which led Mandelbrot (65) and others to propose the concept of *fractals* to describe the behavior of many real-world phenomena such as coastlines and topography. Today, fractal concepts are widely used to analyze geographic form and to create realistic simulations of natural landscapes, trees, and other structures (66).

It follows that no geographic representation can ever be complete, but it must instead approximate, generalize, or abstract a simpler version than exists in reality. The differences between a representation and the truth are crucial in many applications of GIS to environmental management, because they ultimately determine the uncertainty associated with predictions and decisions. Early research on this topic focused on the analysis of error by conventional methods (67). But error analysis assumes the existence of a truth, and it is clear that in many situations there is no easy way of defining the true value of an item of geographic information. For example, many if not all of the classifications used for mapping and characterizing soils, land cover, and vegetation are fundamentally vague, and there is no expectation that two independent observers would arrive at the same classification. Hence the term *uncertainty* is now more widely used to discuss the differences between GIS representations and the real world, and between one observer and another.

Extensive research on this topic began in the late 1980s (67), and very substantial progress has been made. Models now exist to characterize many forms of uncertainty and for all of the major types of geographic data. At this time, methods exist to propagate error and uncertainty from GIS inputs to outputs and hence to estimate confidence limits on GIS results. Much work has also gone into visualization of uncertainty. Major conferences have been held on the topic. Several focused on environmental management, and several collections have been published (68–71). Zhang & Goodchild (72) provide a recent review of uncertainty, and Hunsaker et al. (73) address issues of geographic data uncertainty in ecology. Scale, in the sense of spatial resolution, is treated in much of this literature within the framework of uncertainty, in the sense that finer resolution reduces uncertainty about the truth on the ground; a number of texts have addressed scale in GIS from this perspective (74, 75).

Much of this recent research makes use of the theoretical framework provided by *geostatistics*. In this framework a continuous field is conceptualized as a single realization of a stochastic process; multiple realizations might therefore represent the differences between repeated measurements, or repeated compilations of maps, or the uncertainties that exist about true values on the ground. Burrough & McDonnell (49) provide many examples of the use of geostatistical methods in environmental modeling using GIS, and for more comprehensive texts on geostatistics, see Goovaerts (10) or Isaaks & Srivastava (12). Geostatistical methods are now widely available in GIS software.

6. CONCLUSION

GIS is now widely accepted as an indispensible tool in environmental management. Although it is not the only computer application relevant to the field, or even the only one relevant to geographic data, it is without doubt the dominant application in the development of environmental policy and in environmental decision making. Many different GIS products exist from commercial vendors, and several have been developed by academics, some under the open-source paradigm that permits free use.

Given the limited space available, this review has provided little more than a high-level overview of some of the major issues and advances in the use of GIS for environmental management and in the underlying GIScience. The references will provide much more extensive and detailed sources of additional information.

Several trends are likely to impact the use of GIS in environmental management in the near future. One is continuing progress on interoperability and associated technologies, which will increasingly allow researchers and managers to access and use distributed data and services in what will eventually become a largely seamless and global computing environment. Another is mobility and the increasing ability to process and analyze information in the field, as it is collected. Field information technologies and field sensors have the potential to revolutionize the practice of environmental science and management and to make it possible to perform virtually all tasks in the field, in the presence of ground truth. Third, the growing sophistication and accuracy of environmental models and the increasing ability to use them and integrate them into different research and policy environments will mean that GIS use becomes more and more forward-looking and relevant to the broader objectives of policy, rather than the narrower objectives of inventory and description.

The *Annual Review of Environment and Resources* is online at
http://environ.annualreviews.org

LITERATURE CITED

1. Foresman TW, eds. 1998. *The History of Geographic Information Systems: Perspectives from the Pioneers*. Upper Saddle River, NJ: Prentice Hall
2. Goodchild MF, Anselin L, Appelbaum RP, Harthorn BH. 2000. Toward spatially integrated social science. *Int. Reg. Sci. Rev.* 23(2):139–59
3. Craig WJ, Harris TM, Weiner D, eds. 2002. *Community Participation and Geographic Information Systems*. London: Taylor & Francis
4. Goodchild MF. 1992. Geographical information science. *Int. J. Geogr. Inf. Syst.* 6(1):31–45
5. Wright DJ, Goodchild MF, Proctor JD. 1997. Demystifying the persistent ambiguity of GIS as 'tool' versus 'science.' *Ann. Assoc. Am. Geogr.* 87(2):346–62
6. Goodchild MF, Egenhofer MJ, Kemp KK, Mark DM, Sheppard E. 1999. Introduction to the Varenius project. *Int. J. Geogr. Inf. Sci.* 13(8):731–45
7. Couclelis H. 1992. People manipulate objects (but cultivate fields): beyond the raster-vector debate in GIS. In *Theories and Methods of Spatio-Temporal Reasoning in Geographic Space*, ed. AU Frank, I Campari, U Formentini, pp. 66–77. Berlin: Springer
8. Goodchild MF. 1992. Geographic data modeling. *Comput. Geosci.* 18(4):401–8
9. Worboys MF. 1995. *GIS: A Computing Perspective*. New York: Taylor & Francis
10. Goovaerts P. 1997. *Geostatistics for Natural Resources Evaluation*. New York: Oxford Univ. Press
11. Lam NS-N. 1983. Spatial interpolation methods: a review. *Am. Cartogr.* 10:129–49
12. Isaaks EH, Srivastava RM. 1989. *Applied Geostatistics*. New York: Oxford Univ. Press
13. Carey GF, ed. 1995. *Finite Element Modeling of Environmental Problems*. New York: Wiley
14. Tomlin CD. 1990. *Geographic Information Systems and Cartographic Modeling*. Englewood Cliffs, NJ: Prentice Hall
15. Serra JP. 1982. *Image Analysis and Mathematical Morphology*. New York: Academic
16. Bailey TC, Gatrell AC. 1995. *Interactive Spatial Data Analysis*. Harlow, Eng.: Longman
17. Haining RP. 1990. *Spatial Data Analysis in the Social and Environmental Sciences*. New York: Cambridge Univ. Press
18. O'Sullivan D, Unwin DJ. 2003. *Geographic Information Analysis*. New York: Wiley
19. Longley PA, Goodchild MF, Maguire DJ, Rhind DW. 2001. *Geographic Information Systems and Science*. New York: Wiley
20. Gatrell AC, Loytonen M, eds. 1998. *GIS and Health*. GISDATA Series 6. London: Taylor & Francis
21. Cromley EK, McLafferty SL. 2002. *GIS and Public Health*. New York: Guilford
22. Briggs DJ, ed. 2002. *GIS for emergency preparedness and health risk reduction*. Proc. NATO Adv. Study Inst. Dordrecht: Kluwer
23. Lang L. 2000. *GIS for Health Organizations*. Redlands, CA: ESRI Press

24. Haines-Young R, Green DR, Cousins S, eds. 1993. *Landscape Ecology and Geographic Information Systems*. New York: Taylor & Francis
25. Johnston, CA. 1998. *Geographic Information Systems in Ecology*. Oxford: Blackwell Sci.
26. Bishop M. 2003. *GIScience and Mountain Geomorphology*. New York: Springer Verlag
27. Campbell JB. 2002. *Introduction to Remote Sensing*. New York: Guilford. 3rd ed.
28. Wischmeier WH, Smith DD. 1965. *Predicting Rainfall-Erosion Losses from Cropland East of the Rocky Mountains: Guide for Selection of Practices for Soil and Water Conservation*. Agric. Handb. 282. Washington, DC: US Dep. Agric.
29. Darcy H. 1856. *Les Fontaines Publiques de la Ville de Dijon*. Paris: Dalmont
30. Haynes KE, Fotheringham AS. 1984. *Gravity and Spatial Interaction Models*. Beverly Hills, CA: Sage
31. Fotheringham AS, O'Kelly ME. 1989. *Spatial Interaction Models: Formulations and Applications*. Dordrecht: Kluwer Acad.
32. Torrens PM, O'Sullivan D. 2001. Cellular automata and urban simulation: where do we go from here? *Environ. Plan. B: Plan. Des.* 28:163–68
33. White R, Engelen G. 1997. Cellular automata as a basis for integrated dynamic regional modelling. *Environ. Plan. B: Plan. Des.* 24:235–46
34. Parker DC, Berger T, Manson SM, eds. 2002. *Meeting the challenge of complexity: Proc. Spec. Workshop Land Use/Land Cover Change, Irvine, CA, Oct. 4–7, 2001*. CIPEC Collab. Rep. CCR-3. Indiana Univ., Cent. Study of Instit., Popul., Environ. Change, Bloomington. http://www.csiss.org/events/other/agent-based/additional/proceedings.pdf
35. Razavi AH. 2002. *ArcView GIS Developer's Guide: Programming with Avenue*. Albany, NY: Onword. 4th ed.
36. Bradley JC, Millspaugh AC. 1999. *Programming in Visual Basic, Version 6.0*. Boston: Irwin/McGraw-Hill
37. Nyerges TL. 1993. Understanding the scope of GIS: its relationship to environmental modeling. In *Environmental Modeling with GIS*, ed. MF Goodchild, BO Parks, LT Steyaert, pp. 75–93. New York: Oxford Univ. Press
38. van Deursen WPA. 1995. *Geographical Information Systems and Dynamic Models: Development and Application of a Prototype Spatial Modelling Language*. Utrecht: Koninklijk Ned. Aardrijkskd. Genntschap/Fac. Ruimt. Wet. Univ. Utrecht
39. Wesseling CG, Karssenberg D, Burrough PA, van Deursen WPA. 1996. Integrating dynamic environmental models in GIS: the development of a dynamic modelling language. *Trans. GIS* 1(1):40–48
40. Kemp KK. 1997. Fields as a framework for integrating GIS and environmental process models. Part 1: representing spatial continuity. *Trans. GIS* 1(3):219–34
41. Kemp KK. 1997. Fields as a framework for integrating GIS and environmental process models. Part 2: Specifying field variables. *Trans. GIS* 1(3):235–46
42. Vckovski A. 1998. *Interoperable and Distributed Processing in GIS*. New York: Taylor & Francis
43. Goodchild MF, Parks BO, Steyaert LT, eds. 1993. *Environmental Modeling with GIS*. New York: Oxford Univ. Press
44. Goodchild MF, Steyaert LT, Parks BO, Johnston C, Maidment D, et al. 1996. *GIS and Environmental Modeling: Progress and Research Issues*. Fort Collins, CO: GIS World Books
45. Camara A. 2002. *Environmental Systems: A Multidimensional Approach*. New York: Oxford Univ. Press
46. Clarke KC, Parks BO, Crane MP, eds. 2002. *Geographic Information Systems and Environmental Modeling*. Upper Saddle River, NJ: Prentice Hall
47. Skidmore AK, Prins H. 2002. *Environmental Modelling with GIS and Remote Sensing*. New York: Taylor & Francis

48. Heuvelink GBM. 1998. *Error Propagation in Environmental Modelling with GIS*. New York: Taylor & Francis
49. Burrough PA, McDonnell RA. 1998. *Principles of Geographical Information Systems*. New York: Oxford Univ. Press
50. Natl. Res. Counc. 2001. *Embedded, Everywhere: A Research Agenda for Networked Systems of Embedded Computers*. Washington, DC: Natl. Acad.
51. Natl. Res. Counc. 1999. *Distributed Geolibraries: Spatial Information Resources*. Washington, DC: Natl. Acad.
52. Goodchild MF, Zhou J. 2003. Collection-level metadata. *Geoinformatica* 7(2):95–112
53. Natl. Res. Counc. 1993. *Toward a Coordinated Spatial Data Infrastructure for the Nation*. Washington, DC: Natl. Acad.
54. Ungerer MJ, Goodchild MF. 2002. Integrating spatial data analysis and GIS: a new implementation using the Component Object Model (COM). *Int. J. Geogr. Inf. Sci.* 16(1):41–54
55. Goodchild MF, Lam NS-N. 1980. Areal interpolation: a variant of the traditional spatial problem. *Geoprocessing* 1:297–312
56. Densham PJ. 1991. Spatial decision support systems. In *Geographical Information Systems: Principles and Applications*, ed. DJ Maguire, MF Goodchild, DW Rhind, pp. 403–12. Harlow, UK: Longman Sci. & Tech.
57. Bennett DA. 1997. A framework for the integration of geographical information systems and modelbase management. *Int. J. Geogr. Inf. Sci.* 11(4):337–57
58. Date CJ. 1975. *An Introduction to Database Systems*. Reading, MA: Addison-Wesley
59. Rumbaugh J, Jacobson I, Booch G. 1999. *The Unified Modeling Language Reference Manual*. Reading, MA: Addison-Wesley
60. Zeiler M. 1999. *Modeling Our World: The ESRI Guide to Geodatabase Design*. Redlands, CA: ESRI Press
61. Maidment D, Djokic D, eds. 2000. *Hydrologic and Hydraulic Modeling Support with Geographic Information Systems*. Redlands, CA: ESRI Press
62. Goodchild MF. 2000. Cartographic futures on a digital Earth. *Cartogr. Perspect.* 36:3–11
63. Langran G. 1992. *Time in Geographic Information Systems*. New York: Taylor & Francis
64. Peuquet DJ. 2002. *Representations of Space and Time*. New York: Guilford
65. Mandelbrot BB. 1983. *The Fractal Geometry of Nature*. San Francisco: Freeman
66. Barnsley MF. 1988. *Fractals Everywhere*. Boston: Academic
67. Goodchild MF, Gopal S, eds. 1989. *Accuracy of Spatial Databases*. New York: Taylor & Francis
68. Guptill SC, Morrison JL, eds. 1995. *Elements of Spatial Data Quality*. New York: Elsevier Sci.
69. Lowell K, Jaton A. 1999. *Spatial Accuracy Assessment: Land Information Uncertainty in Natural Resources*. Chelsea, MI: Ann Arbor
70. Mowrer HT, Congalton RG, eds. 2000. *Quantifying Spatial Uncertainty in Natural Resources: Theory and Applications for GIS and Remote Sensing*. Chelsea, MI: Ann Arbor
71. Shi W, Fisher PF, Goodchild MF, eds. 2002. *Spatial Data Quality*. New York: Taylor & Francis
72. Zhang J, Goodchild MF. 2002. *Uncertainty in Geographic Information*. New York: Taylor & Francis
73. Hunsaker CT, Goodchild MF, Friedl MA, Case EJ, eds. 2001. *Spatial Uncertainty in Ecology*. New York: Springer
74. Foody GM, Atkinson PM, eds. 2002. *Uncertainty in Remote Sensing and GIS*. New York: Wiley
75. Quattrochi DA, Goodchild MF, eds. 1997. *Scale in Remote Sensing and GIS*. Boca Raton, FL: Lewis

THE ROLE OF CARBON CYCLE OBSERVATIONS AND KNOWLEDGE IN CARBON MANAGEMENT

Lisa Dilling,[1] Scott C. Doney,[2] Jae Edmonds,[3] Kevin R. Gurney,[4] Robert Harriss,[1] David Schimel,[5] Britton Stephens,[6] and Gerald Stokes[3]

[1]*Environmental and Societal Impacts Group, National Center for Atmospheric Research, P.O. Box 3000, Boulder Colorado 80307; email: ldilling@ucar.edu, harriss@ucar.edu*
[2]*Marine Chemistry and Geochemistry, 360 Woods Hole Road, Woods Hole Oceanographic Institution, Woods Hole, Massachusetts 02543; email: sdoney@whoi.edu*
[3]*Pacific Northwest National Laboratory/Joint Global Change Research Institute at the University of Maryland, 8400 Baltimore Ave. Suite 201 College Park, Maryland 20740; email: jae@pnl.gov, stokes@pnl.gov*
[4]*Department of Atmospheric Science, Colorado State University, Fort Collins, Colorado 80523; email: keving@atmos.colostate.edu*
[5]*Climate and Global Dynamics Division, National Center for Atmospheric Research, P.O. Box 3000, Boulder, Colorado 80307; email: schimel@ucar.edu*
[6]*Atmospheric Technology Division, National Center for Atmospheric Research, P.O. Box 3000, Boulder, Colorado 80307; email: stephens@ucar.edu*

Key Words carbon sequestration, measurement techniques, climate, Kyoto protocol

■ **Abstract** Agriculture and industrial development have led to inadvertent changes in the natural carbon cycle. As a consequence, concentrations of carbon dioxide and other greenhouse gases have increased in the atmosphere and may lead to changes in climate. The current challenge facing society is to develop options for future management of the carbon cycle. A variety of approaches has been suggested: direct reduction of emissions, deliberate manipulation of the natural carbon cycle to enhance sequestration, and capture and isolation of carbon from fossil fuel use. Policy development to date has laid out some of the general principles to which carbon management should adhere. These are summarized as: how much carbon is stored, by what means, and for how long. To successfully manage carbon for climate purposes requires increased understanding of carbon cycle dynamics and improvement in the scientific capabilities available for measurement as well as for policy needs. The specific needs for scientific information to underpin carbon cycle management decisions are not yet broadly known. A stronger dialogue between decision makers and scientists must be developed to foster improved application of scientific knowledge to decisions. This review focuses on the current knowledge of the carbon cycle, carbon measurement capabilities (with an emphasis on the continental scale) and the relevance of carbon cycle science to carbon sequestration goals.

CONTENTS

```
INTRODUCTION ................................................. 522
CARBON MANAGEMENT POLICY PRINCIPLES ......................... 524
SEQUESTRATION AND DISPOSAL OPTIONS ........................... 526
  Terrestrial Sequestration .................................... 526
  Ocean Sequestration ......................................... 527
  Geologic Disposal ........................................... 528
SCIENTIFIC CAPABILITY FOR INFORMING CARBON
  SEQUESTRATION AND DISPOSAL POLICIES ......................... 528
  Quantification .............................................. 529
  Additionality and Separation ................................. 537
  Permanence .................................................. 541
  Environmental Effects and Linkages ........................... 542
  Predicting Future Atmospheric CO₂ Levels ..................... 543
AN EXAMPLE OF CARBON MANAGEMENT POLICY—LAND
  USE, LAND-USE CHANGE, AND FORESTRY IN THE KYOTO
  PROTOCOL ..................................................... 546
  Land Use, Land-Use Change, and Forestry Provisions ........... 546
CONCLUSIONS ................................................... 548
```

INTRODUCTION

Human combustion of fossil fuels and conversion of natural landscapes are commonly accepted to be the primary cause of the observed long-term increase in concentrations of atmospheric carbon dioxide (1). Carbon dioxide in the atmosphere acts as a greenhouse gas (GHG), and the human-induced increase from 280 to 370 ppm (parts per million) over the past 140 years is thought to have contributed to an average global temperature increase of $0.6 \pm 0.2°C$ as well as other changes in climate (2). Increasing concern that these changes might pose an unacceptable risk to human societies and the environment has prompted the international community, corporations, and local communities to consider options to mitigate further increases in atmospheric carbon dioxide (CO_2). Future atmospheric CO_2 trajectories can be slowed, and eventually reversed, in one of two ways: decreasing emissions due to fossil fuel combustion and land-use change or disposing and/or sequestering CO_2 to prevent it from accumulating in the atmosphere. Many of the latter approaches depend on successful manipulation of natural or managed systems that already are part of the active cycle of carbon exchanging throughout the earth system. Knowledge of the carbon cycle is therefore essential for successful application of deliberate carbon management strategies whether on land or in the ocean. Furthermore, quantification for policy verification and support may require advanced carbon cycle measurement capabilities, the details of which will depend on policy frameworks and protocols.

This review focuses on carbon cycle scientific knowledge and measurement capability for supporting carbon sequestration and disposal, only one aspect of carbon management. Other options for managing future atmospheric CO_2 increases, such as changes in energy systems, are equally critical and well described by Hoffert et al. and other reviews in this series (3, 4). As reviewed in the U.S. Department of Energy (DOE) "11-lab study," energy production and use can be managed to reduce carbon emissions by changing either the energy intensity or the carbon intensity of fuel used (5–7). Changing energy intensity involves improving the effectiveness of energy use in delivering gross domestic product (GDP) through end-use efficiency (fuel economy) or structural changes in the economy, and changing carbon intensity involves changing fuel to a less carbon intensive option (5, 7). Although the specification of a mitigation strategy can in principle be any mixture of effective technology, there is a preference for the strategy to be economically practical as well. The most comprehensive economic approaches are the economically efficient path approaches, first introduced by Wigley et al. (8). It is only when there is a cost for carbon that technologies, such as sequestration, capture and disposal, or perhaps even nonfossil derived hydrogen fuels, become an economically viable part of the mix. Economic drivers and cost incentives for climate and carbon management are being studied extensively and are not reviewed here [but see (9)].

Carbon sequestration and disposal have been seriously discussed as GHG management options for about a decade (10). Carbon sequestration and disposal remove carbon from the atmosphere by increasing the amount of carbon stored in biomass on land, in the ocean, or in geologic reservoirs. In order for these techniques to successfully meet climate policy goals, they must result in long-term, sustained net removal of CO_2 from the atmosphere through environmentally and economically acceptable means. Furthermore, the amount of carbon sequestered, environmental impact, and other parameters must be quantifiable in order for policy frameworks to be effective.

Development and application of policy in this area have relied on a number of carbon management principles, whose definition continues to be the subject of intense policy negotiations. The development and use of these principles imply an underpinning of a sophisticated understanding and application of carbon cycle science, which include observations, modeling, and fundamental knowledge. Here we evaluate the current capabilities and knowledge available from carbon cycle science to support the carbon management principles of quantification, additionality, separation, permanence, and environmental acceptability for the area of carbon sequestration and disposal. Additional steps will be needed to determine precisely what information policy makers need, if it is available and if it can be properly used.

In this review, we briefly describe the development of climate policy relevant to carbon management and outline the principles that have emerged from that process. We then describe several of the common sequestration and disposal approaches. The body of the review focuses on currently available scientific capabilities and knowledge as they apply to management principles for carbon sequestration and disposal.

Carbon cycle science provides only a part of the potential foundation necessary to the development of carbon management; technology, social science, economics, and political feasibility all play substantial roles as well. Nonetheless, we suggest that many assumptions of carbon management principles for sequestration depend on carbon cycle observations and knowledge and that these two areas of endeavor must therefore engage one another rigorously in the coming decade.

CARBON MANAGEMENT POLICY PRINCIPLES

The development of policy relevant to carbon cycle management has occurred primarily, but not exclusively, at the international level with the United Nations Framework Convention on Climate Change (UNFCCC) and its legally-binding instrument, the Kyoto Protocol (11). The Kyoto Protocol, constructed in 1997, has now been ratified (at which time, they become parties to the Protocol) by 101 nations, whose emissions are equivalent to 43.9% of the global emissions of quantified GHG in 1990. When the represented emissions reach the 55% mark, the Protocol will enter into force and thereby achieve its legally binding status for those nations that ratified it.

Because the Kyoto Protocol laid out relatively general guidance concerning how binding emission reductions were to be achieved, intense international negotiations occurred between 1997 and 2002. These resulted in the Marrakesh Accords, which contain far more detail on the broad issues outlined in the original Protocol and include description of emissions trading, funding, compliance, and carbon exchange with the biosphere (12). This last category of activity is referred within the negotiation process as land use, land-use change, and forestry (LULUCF), and later it included crop and rangeland management to emphasize the fact that carbon exchange with the biosphere includes both emissions and uptake. The biotic exchange reported must have occurred since 1990 and must be human induced. When biospheric or physical carbon uptake into the land or ocean from the atmosphere is greater than release over a region, it is defined as a "carbon sink." Other types of carbon sequestration activities beyond those defined as LULUCF are not included in the Kyoto framework but will be discussed in this review.

The introduction of carbon sinks as a climate mitigation tool during the Kyoto policy process has been controversial for a number of reasons. Some parties argued that nations should meet their targets by reducing fossil fuel emissions or else risk that the efforts would result in no appreciable change in overall GHG concentrations. Others argued that the policy benefited some nations over others, depending on the existing land-use characteristics and land-use history. But these arguments notwithstanding, the introduction of carbon sinks into the negotiating picture likely made it possible for the Kyoto Protocol to come into existence. Flexibility in implementation is often a key feature of international agreements, and the Kyoto Protocol was no exception (13).

Although the international Kyoto Protocol is certainly the most visible and extensive framework, numerous decision processes relevant to carbon management are underway at a variety of governmental scales and within private entities on a voluntary basis. For example, over 560 local municipal governments worldwide have passed resolutions to implement emission reductions measures through a variety of mechanisms suitable for their region (14). Multinational corporations, such as British Petroleum, have implemented their own internal emissions trading policies to gain experience in emissions trading and to help meet their internal emissions reduction goals (15). Privately- and publicly-funded field experiments, such as the International Energy Agency (IEA) Weyburn CO_2 Monitoring and Storage Project at the Weyburn oilfield in western Canada, are proceeding in anticipation of eventual international agreements on emissions reductions. These examples suggest that carbon management principles and policies are of much broader relevance than solely at the international negotiation level.

As currently framed, policies for carbon management depend on assigning credit for activities such as carbon sequestration or emissions reduction. The subtleties and criteria discussed for determining the value of carbon credits can be reduced to three main attributes: how much carbon is stored (or emissions prevented), by what mechanism, and for how long.

The following terms have emerged from consideration of LULUCF activities under the Kyoto framework but also have relevance for broader carbon management options. They provide an important set of carbon management principles because they have been guiding policy framing and activity implementation. Scientific knowledge and capability to underpin a subset of these principles in the implementation of carbon management will be elaborated in the analysis that follows. These principles will be defined for discussion purposes as:

Quantification refers to the ability to measure a parameter at the required scale, within the level of uncertainty to adequately meet policy goals.

Additionality is the carbon exchange through carbon management that must be in addition to what would have occurred in the absence of deliberate carbon management policy.

Separation means the carbon management activities due to planned direct, human-induced activity and distinguishable from natural occurrences. Therefore, biospheric carbon exchange due to mechanisms, such as CO_2 fertilization, unintentional nitrogen fertilization, and climate change, must be accounted for before credit is calculated.

Leakage refers to activities aimed at sequestering carbon but that fail because they simply displace biospheric emissions to a land area not included in the national accounting. For example, a project aimed at afforestation of a tropical pasture may result in deforestation elsewhere and negate the carbon gains within the project boundary. Leakage is not unique to LULUCF activities but can arise if industries shift GHG emitting production to parties that do not have emission limits.

Permanence has two distinct aspects; one relates to physical permanence and the other to institutional longevity. The first aspect acknowledges that carbon storage and exchange is a reversible process. Thus carbon sequestered during a commitment period may be emitted at a later time due to natural or human-induced processes. Similarly difficult is the notion of institutional permanence. Any accounting system will require an institutional longevity on the scale of biospheric timescales: decades to centuries.

Perverse incentive is one that rewards action that is actually detrimental to reducing emissions while perhaps fitting within the letter of the law. One example drawn from the current interpretation of the Kyoto Protocol is the possibility that parties using joint activity mechanisms may remove forest cover after 1990 but before the beginning of the first commitment period in 2008 followed by reforestation or afforestation activities. This would allow for the accrual of credits that are not true carbon removals when integrated over years prior to, and including, the first commitment period.

Transparency refers to the need for the activity accounting to be easily amenable to examination, verification, and validation. Much work has been performed in this regard by the Intergovernmental Panel on Climate Change (IPCC) and is embodied in the *Revised 1996 IPCC Guidelines for National Greenhouse Gas Inventories* (16) and subsequent work currently underway (17).

Verification refers to procedures that can be followed to establish the reliability of carbon exchange data. This will require independent estimation of the reported carbon exchange and implies two different methods.

SEQUESTRATION AND DISPOSAL OPTIONS

Several techniques for carbon sequestration and disposal are being considered, generally grouped by the part of the earth system that must be managed (3). For current purposes, the essential difference between sequestration and disposal is that *sequestration* enhances the uptake of carbon by the nonatmospheric components of the natural carbon cycle, and *disposal* places carbon or CO_2 in a location or state that prevents it from becoming part of the active carbon cycle. It should be noted that there is some debate about the specific nomenclature to be used, specifically disposal is sometimes referred to as storage. For policy purposes, capture and disposal is thought of as an emissions reduction strategy but sequestration is not; both strategies do ultimately lessen the atmospheric CO_2 content.

Terrestrial Sequestration

Much carbon is stored in natural and managed ecosystems on land. Terrestrial sequestration refers to the process of increasing carbon retained in soils or in standing biomass on a particular plot of land. Early estimates of the technical potential for global biospheric carbon sequestration commonly fall within a range of 1–2 GtC/year (18). In some regions, opportunities for land conversion, land restoration, and improved management could result in potential sequestration in specific agroecosystems (19–23). Potentially cost-effective activities for carbon sequestration in the forestry sector include increasing the area and productivity of forest lands, increasing agroforestry, and increasing the use of harvested materials in durable wood products or in biomass energy generation. It is clear from these and many other studies that the sequestration of carbon in forests, croplands, and rangelands should be seriously considered in the design of climate change mitigation strategies.

Terrestrial sequestration was the first sequestration method to be examined carefully as a carbon management option because of its inclusion in the Kyoto Protocol. Additionality, permanence, and other principles as they relate to terrestrial sequestration are discussed in detail below. Although not a part of the eventual Kyoto Protocol, maintenance of existing forests was intensely debated. It was rejected as a strategy in the current policy framing because it does not result in a net reduction of atmospheric CO_2. A role for maintenance of existing forests is still experimented with in voluntary carbon management strategies, such as those coordinated by environmental nonprofit groups.

Terrestrial sequestration has been suggested as a strategy for buying time to allow other, more permanent options to be implemented (24). Terrestrial sequestration is available for implementation immediately, for example, while development and implementation of carbon-free energy technologies is a longer-term enterprise. This suggests that near-term investment in biospheric carbon sequestration projects is not a substitute for significant attention to the development and implementation of carbon-free energy technologies but merely a complementary strategy (3). The U.S. Department of Energy sponsors an Internet resource on selected current research on carbon sequestration in terrestrial ecosystems at http://csite.esd.ornl.gov/.

Ocean Sequestration

The oceans are a large natural sink for excess CO_2. CO_2 exchanges at the air-sea interface, becomes dissolved, and then is transported in seawater through the thermohaline circulation. Carbon is also transported to depth by the sinking of phytoplankton and other organic material through the biological pump. Deliberate carbon sequestration has been conceived through two mechanisms that attempt to simulate these natural processes in the ocean. One method involves injecting CO_2 directly into the deep ocean, bypassing the mixed layer (25). The second is to add nutrients to the surface ocean to increase the rate of the biological pump. Opportunities for crediting carbon sequestered in the ocean are not yet available, but it is widely discussed as an option by researchers and entrepreneurs.

Deep-ocean injection would involve the transmission of a stream of liquid or gaseous CO_2 through a fixed or towed piping system down to depths in the ocean at which the CO_2 forms clathrates, semisolid substances. The clathrates would then slowly dissolve into the surrounding seawater and rapidly increase the local concentration for a period of time until stabilization occurs at a new higher dissolved concentration in a broader region. Pilot-scale experiments have been conducted to demonstrate the feasibility of this method (25). Long-term environmental effects have not yet been determined (26).

Ocean fertilization would involve adding a nutrient that is currently in short supply to the surface ocean, such as iron, to stimulate phytoplankton growth and thereby take up more CO_2 from the surrounding seawater into biomass (27). The approach then supposes that the excess biomass will sink out of the mixed layer of the ocean to the deep sea and effectively transfer the carbon from the atmosphere to the ocean. Field experiments have demonstrated that adding iron to the surface ocean in regions where it is lacking, such as the Equatorial Pacific and Southern Ocean, will indeed stimulate growth (27, 28). The fate of the stimulated biomass growth, that is whether it actually sinks out of the mixed layer to the deep ocean, has not yet been determined. This method has been criticized both for potential negative ecosystem effects and for concerns about its effectiveness (29, 30), although research is still underway to explore these issues (31).

Geologic Disposal

Geologic disposal is the process of placing CO_2 in a geological medium with the intent of retention for sufficiently long periods of time to assist in the stabilization of atmospheric concentrations (32). There are two different scenarios for disposal of carbon; one injects a dissolved gaseous form or a supercritical fluid into a confined geological medium, and the other reacts CO_2 with a mineral to form a new stable mineral form. The new mineral form is either created in situ, or the mineral reaction is used as a capture mechanism, and the resulting mineral is buried or used for some other purpose. In addition to a great deal of work conducted in DOE laboratories, academic institutions, private corporations, and two large academic-private partnerships have formed to research carbon sequestration and disposal and new energy technologies (33, 34).

SCIENTIFIC CAPABILITY FOR INFORMING CARBON SEQUESTRATION AND DISPOSAL POLICIES

All of the methods for carbon sequestration and disposal will need to adhere to the carbon management principles defined above in order to be successful, in particular: how much carbon is stored—quantification; by what means—additionality and separation; and for how long—permanence. In addition, any strategy will need to address environmental acceptability and economic feasibility. The scientific and social uncertainty underpinning future targets for atmospheric CO_2 levels discussed here is relevant to policy debates as well. Addressing the issues determining economic feasibility would require more space than we have in this review and are deferred to other reviews.

Quantification

Because carbon sequestration policy has thus far developed around the concept of meeting specific targets, quantification of carbon sequestration and emissions is of paramount concern. Whether to meet an absolute target set by a project, nation, or corporation or to ensure the value of traded carbon credits, methods must be established that are accepted and transparent. From a scientific point of view, the measurement system could be designed with attention to several attributes: quantity to be measured, accuracy and precision desired, cost, required spatial and temporal scales, targeted longevity of system, ease of use, and transparency to others. These requirements may change in relative importance when viewed from the policy maker's perspective.

CURRENT METHODS AND SCALING The current capability to quantify the amount of carbon stored or released from land or ocean depends on the scale at which the measurement is needed (both spatial and temporal). Often the quantity measured can only give information about carbon exchange or sequestration on a specific spatial scale, whether hundreds of kilometers or a few meters squared. Reconciling information gained at different scales is of intense interest in the scientific community, as elaborated below. Techniques do not easily scale up to extrapolate larger patterns or scale down to explain mechanisms at the local scale. This has implications for applying measurement techniques to specific policy needs.

For decision making purposes, information on carbon exchange will likely be needed at a variety of scales, from the global and national level to regional, state, and local levels, including the private sector. An enhanced dialogue between scientists and decision makers could aid in developing a mutual understanding of measurement capabilities and decision makers' constraints.

Global and continental scales For decades, observations at relatively few remote locations established the rate of the global average increase of CO_2 in the atmosphere (35–37). These observations provided the scientific confirmation that CO_2 was indeed increasing above the level expected by normal variability and spurred contemplation of policy measures. The continued operation, improvement, and expansion of these networks is critical for improving our understanding of the global carbon cycle and ensuring that the intended consequence of reducing the growth rate of atmospheric CO_2 is indeed happening (38).

Not all of the CO_2 released by human activity stays in the atmosphere. Approximately half of the excess CO_2 is absorbed by the land and ocean. On a global scale, determination of net carbon fluxes is challenging because they typically represent small differences between large gross fluxes. For example, the annual terrestrial and oceanic uptake of fossil fuel CO_2 emissions, presently on the order of 3.5 billion tons of carbon per year ($PgCyr^{-1}$), is small compared to the natural seasonal exchanges of roughly 60 $PgCyr^{-1}$ between the atmosphere and terrestrial biosphere and 90 PgCyr^{-1} between the atmosphere and oceans (39). The causes of these natural cycles, biological growth and decay, seasonal ocean heating and cooling, and large-scale ocean circulation, tend to be in approximate global balance such that the anthropogenic perturbation only becomes distinguishable on annual and longer timescales. Carbon cycle measurements are further complicated by large interannual variability in these natural processes, as shown in Figure 1 (see color insert).

The atmosphere also provides a way to measure integrated carbon exchange in the aggregate at very large scales, such as that of broad latitudinal zones. Spatial gradients in atmospheric CO_2 concentrations can be used to infer in a top-down sense the location of surface carbon sources and sinks using inverse modeling techniques (40, 41). Atmospheric inverse modeling maps the sum of anthropogenic uptake and any net pre-industrial carbon fluxes, such as those driven by the ocean thermohaline circulation and biological pump. Large-scale model estimates of broad latitudinal patterns are in general agreement in indicating a large sink ($\sim$3 PgCyr^{-1}) in northern midlatitudes, a moderate source ($\sim$1.5 PgCyr^{-1}) in the tropics, and a small sink ($\sim$1 PgCyr^{-1}) in the extratropical southern latitudes. (40, 42). Atmospheric ^{13}C and O_2/N_2 isotopic ratios and land and ocean constraints provide evidence that the northern midlatitude sink is primarily terrestrial in origin and that the tropical source is a mix of tropical ocean outgassing and biomass burning (42–46).

Recent expansion of the global atmospheric network has allowed a rich exploration of continental patterns of carbon sources and sinks using inversion techniques (41, 42, 45, 48–54). However, this move toward higher spatial resolution generally requires specification of additional information or "priors," and data and atmospheric model limitations prevent robust estimates on smaller scales. These limitations include sparse data, spatial and temporal mismatch between high-resolution measurements and coarse models, and systematic model errors. The largest model uncertainties are associated with representing seasonal covariation of atmospheric transport and biospheric carbon exchange (42, 55). To date, the attempts to differentiate surface carbon fluxes on a continental scale, such as Eurasia from North America or North America from the North Atlantic, have been somewhat consistent in similar time periods but have large uncertainties (for one regional example, see Table 1). To examine the causes of differences in atmospheric inversion results, a recent international model intercomparison (Transcom 3) divided the globe into 22 regions, compared 16 different transport models inverted using common data, and assumed prior fluxes and errors (42). The authors found uncertainties from $\pm$0.25 to $\pm$1.25 PgCyr^{-1}, depending on the region, resulting from differences in the transport models, model coarseness, and limited observational data in the tropics and over continents.

Additional challenges arise when applying atmospheric inverse techniques on smaller scales using continental data that is highly variable due to intense local sources and sinks. Although the amount of data is a major limitation, transport models typically employed in recent inverse studies are too coarse to use all of the available data, particularly that collected at high time resolution or over continents

TABLE 1 An example of continental and subcontinental carbon sink estimates: the carbon balance of either temperate North America or the United States (excluding fossil fuel emissions)

Method	Regional area	Time period	Magnitude (PgC/yr) (negative = uptake from atmosphere)	References
Atmospheric inverse				
(Fluxes estimated for all components and processes in a given region as viewed from the atmosphere)				
	United States (coterminous)	1981–1986	−0.2 ± 0.3	(51)
	United States (coterminous)	1980–1989	−0.4 to −1.5 ± 0.25	(53)
	North America (>15N; <70N)	1985–1995	−0.5 ± 0.6	(49)
	North America (>15N; <70N)	1985–1995	−0.7 ± 0.7	(50)
	North America (>15N)	1988–1992	−1.7 ± 0.5	(48)
	North America	1990–1995	−1.0 ± 1.2	(52)
	North America	1990–1994	−0.8 ± 0.6	(54)
	Temperate North America	1992–1996	−0.8 to −1.2 ± 0.4	(42)
Bottom-up				
(Fluxes estimated from individual components of terrestrial systems)				
Forests	United States (all 50)	na	−0.1	(70)
Forests	United States (coterminous)	na	−0.08	(72)
Forests	United States (coterminous)	1952–1992	−0.3	(77)
Agricultural soils	United States (all 50)	1980s	−0.1	(124)
Expanded inventory	United States (coterminous)	1980–1989	−0.3 to −0.6	(53)
Process-based				
(Contribution to total flux from various processes as estimated by models)				
Land-use change	United States (all 50)	1980s	−0.35	(124)
CO_2 and climate	United States (coterminous)	1980–1995	−0.08	(138)

where concentrations are more variable. Recent modeling work has shown that there is information about sources and sinks in such records (56). With considerably more data and significant improvements in transport models, one might expect inverse methods to be able to distinguish annual source and sink regions over land at the continental scales to within ±0.2–0.5 PgCyr^{-1} (57).

Local to regional scales Towers instrumented with eddy covariance instruments are very well suited for characterizing local exchange of trace gases including CO_2 between the atmosphere and biosphere over a range of timescales from diurnal to interannual (58). The growing network of eddy-flux towers provides key information on the response of the terrestrial biosphere across a multitude of biomes to meteorological and climate variability (59, 60). These instruments, however, are generally deployed on towers only a few meters above canopy height and thus provide fluxes from relatively small footprints (∼1 km^2). The heterogeneity between sites and the small spatial scale makes aggregation of data to quantify larger patterns of uptake or release difficult (61). In addition, complexities in the airflow patterns during low flux periods or nighttime flow, for example, have increased the uncertainty of calculating long-term uptake, especially in complex terrain (61, 62). A more troubling issue has to do with the potential for biased or unrepresentative site locations. For example, flux towers are rarely located in regions of active disturbance or complex terrain.

Several tall towers have also been instrumented for flux and concentration measurements at heights up to 500 meters above the ground (63). A number of ongoing studies highlight the ability of the tall-tower concentration measurements to constrain regional scale CO_2 fluxes (64). Methods are also being developed to combine surface concentration and flux measurements from shorter towers with boundary layer models to create so-called virtual tall towers (65).

Aircraft sampling can also bridge the spatial scale gap between eddy correlation flux towers and global atmospheric gas measurements. Weekly flask profiles for CO_2 and other gases, collected from light aircraft, extend the sampling above the boundary layer into the free troposphere and are now being made at over 20 sites worldwide. These measurements provide valuable additional data for inversion studies and strong tests for the representation of vertical mixing in transport models. Intensive airborne sampling campaigns from research aircraft have been carried out, and it is clear that such measurements can provide short-term estimates of regional scale CO_2 fluxes and high-resolution data for planning routine measurements (66–69).

Early attempts at direct estimation of terrestrial carbon budgets through biomass inventories focused on forests (70–73). All of the countries of Annex I (a set of nations that includes members of the European Community, the Russian Federation, eastern European countries, the United States, the United Kingdom, Australia, New Zealand, Japan, and Canada) of the Kyoto Protocol maintain continuous forest inventories (18). These inventories, generally conducted for timber and resource assessment purposes, can be used to infer changes in carbon stocks in timber over the time period of study. In general, forest inventories measure aboveground woody biomass, known as the stem wood volume, through either direct in situ observations or remote sensing. Wood volume is converted into equivalents of carbon specific to the forest type [e.g., (72)]. Carbon present in soils, leaf litter, and woody debris, as well as carbon in forest types not included in the definition of forests are not counted in most national forest inventories. Differences in how timberland is defined can also affect stock estimates. In addition, nations differ in how they assess their forests and in how all forests on private and public land are counted. Finally, most national forest inventories are conducted on a 10-year, or in rare cases 5-year, rotation cycle and therefore cannot assess changes on a shorter temporal scale than a decade. Some of the limitations of forest inventories have been pointed out in previous reviews in this series (74, 75). These methods remain somewhat uncertain, and efforts are increasing in many nations to improve capacity for full carbon accounting.

Agricultural lands, rangelands, grasslands, and lands in suburban mixed use are also not included as part of the forest inventories, although the U.S. Department of Agriculture maintains a separate crop yield and residue database. Wood products produced from harvested timber as well as agricultural products removed from a region for consumption elsewhere must also be counted in order to obtain a full carbon budget. Separate estimates have been conducted for many of these lands and biomass types in the United States and other nations in order to estimate a full carbon budget for continental regions (76, 77). As with forest inventories, inventories of other stocks and fluxes are subject to uncertainties and limitations to the ability to measure shorter-term intervals.

Ideally, aggregated data at the smaller scale should be consistent with independent estimates gathered with methods at the larger scale. It has been difficult to reconcile inventory-derived estimates showing little carbon uptake in temperate northern latitudes with atmospheric constraints suggesting large uptake (Table 1). One study recently attempted to reconcile atmospheric inversion-based estimates and land-based inventory approaches (53). Within the large uncertainty estimates for each approach, estimates for carbon uptake for the coterminous United States for the period of 1980–1989 were found to be consistent in the range of 0.3–0.58 PgC/yr. The study demonstrated the importance of vegetation processes other than forests as contributors to the U.S. carbon sink; a full 50% of fluxes were found to result from vegetation outside the forest sector, such as woody encroachment, which is primarily the expansion of scrubland. Several components of the land-based analysis are highly uncertain, as are the atmospheric inversion results. Also, not all of the terrestrial carbon storage estimated by atmospheric inversion studies is likely due to ecosystem processes. Fluxes from additional processes such as burial of carbon in reservoirs and sediments and export of carbon by rivers are included in atmospheric inversions, because the atmosphere integrates the results of all flux processes in the domain (78, 79).

Ocean measurements Somewhat paradoxically, ocean measurements can be used to address continental uptake issues (48, 80). The better the ocean uptake is defined on interannual to decadal scales, the better we can estimate the land by difference from the known fossil fuel emissions and atmospheric inventories. At the global scale, a major advance has been the development of accurate and precise analytical techniques for measuring dissolved inorganic carbon (DIC) in seawater sufficient to detect the anthropogenic uptake against the large natural background (81–84). Regional patterns of ocean carbon fluxes can be estimated from air-sea CO_2 partial pressure (ΔpCO_2) fields (85, 86) together with empirical parameterizations of gas-exchange rate as a function of wind speed [e.g., (87)]. A recent compilation of close to 1 million underway surface ΔpCO_2 data points collected over the last 40 years from research vessels and merchant ships of opportunity provides a good picture of the climatological seasonal cycle and the role of physical and biological processes (86). The resulting CO_2 flux maps are both an essential input to the atmospheric inversion models and an important check on the estimated global sources and sinks [e.g., (42)]. The atmospheric and ocean approaches agree reasonably well except for the Southern Ocean, where there are substantial ocean data gaps, especially in winter, as well as potential errors in atmospheric and oceanic transport models

(39). The coastal ocean is extremely variable in both space and time, with high frequency variations in surface water ΔpCO_2 and air-sea flux. The implications for the atmospheric CO_2 signal and high resolution atmospheric inversions are unclear. Finally, the river runoff of particulate and dissolved carbon in both organic and inorganic form is not negligible at roughly 0.8 $PgCyr^{-1}$ (79). Comprehensive strategies for ocean carbon observations have been developed that would bring together volunteer observing ship surface pCO_2 transects, hydrographic surveys, moorings, remote sensing data, and time-series stations (88) and anticipate the ability to constrain basin-scale annual-mean CO_2 fluxes to within 0.1–0.2 $PgCyr^{-1}$ (57).

Emission and carbon sequestration inventory Emissions inventories are another key set of data, now reported at the national level, that might also be valuable for carbon management if reported at different scales, such as the state level or county level. Emission inventories for CO_2, methane, and other GHGs are available for most nations and some regions and cities. The IPCC, IEA, and a variety of other organizations publish global inventories of CO_2 and other GHG emissions that are updated at regular intervals (2, 89). The IPCC has established a set of GHG reporting protocols for the estimation of GHG emissions (16). The sources of data for the inventories are developed in two ways. First the reported emissions can come from direct monitoring at the source, (e.g., stack monitors on chemical plants). Alternatively, activity measures can be made in which the primary data collected is the level of a particular activity, such as the tonnage of chemical manufactured. Then the level of activity is multiplied by an emission factor determined by other means, and that represents the amount of emission associated with the activity, such as the amount of CO_2 released during aluminum smelting (16, 91).

National data on specific components of carbon sequestration are also required to be reported by the UNFCCC along with emissions inventories. For example, the U.S. Environmental Protection Agent (EPA) estimated annual U.S. carbon sequestration for the year 2000 at 0.246 Pg carbon equivalent, a decline of approximately 17.7% from the estimated sequestration in 1990 (92). The EPA derives its estimates of carbon sequestration from changes in forest carbon stocks, changes in agricultural soil carbon stocks, changes in carbon stocks in urban trees, and changes in carbon stocks in landfilled yard trimmings. Many uncertainties remain in the accounting methodologies and conceptual framework for estimating carbon sequestration in vegetation, soils, and waste streams.

Remote sensing Remote sensing can provide high spatial and temporal coverage for some variables and thus can serve as a bridge between bottom-up local measurements and top-down atmospheric methods. Aboveground vegetation, ocean surface chlorophyll, and terrestrial and marine photosynthesis rates can be estimated using visible remote imagery combined with algorithms to convert remotely sensed parameters to biomass and carbon exchange (93, 94). In situ validation data is critical for developing and validating these algorithms. Satellite measurements cannot directly sense belowground biomass, a large component of carbon storage in terrestrial ecosystems, air-sea CO_2 fluxes, or key ocean properties, such as nutrients or DIC concentrations. In addition, carbon uptake is sensitive to a host of specific factors that cannot be easily detected from space; these include stand age, vegetation type, ecosystem health, plankton composition, and ocean circulation. Nevertheless, remote sensing is one of the few truly global tools available to characterize the carbon balance, and it has been used to document increased plant growth from observed climate variability (95–97). In addition, accurate measurements of atmospheric CO_2 concentrations from space would significantly advance our ability to constrain continental and regional CO_2 fluxes through inverse modeling (98). Existing satellite measurements of thermal emission can be used to estimate mid-troposphere CO_2 concentrations at a useful precision (99), and missions to measure total-column CO_2 from reflected near-IR are being planned (http://oco.jpl.nasa.gov/index.html).

Each of the techniques described above has unique advantages for yielding information on the carbon cycle, either for quantifying fluxes and budgets or elucidating process information. There is enormous power in combining these approaches by simultaneously assimilating all available information and measurements into a coherent, dynamically consistent picture of the carbon cycle (80, 100–102). Many regional field campaigns now being planned to focus on locating and quantifying carbon storage and determining mechanisms are following more integrated approaches (103–103e). The challenge remains to be able to effectively combine information from very different spatial and temporal scales in a rigorous and robust fashion. Data assimilation and multi-constraint analysis may offer a strategy for bridging scales and multiple data streams (104, 105).

MEASUREMENT FREQUENCY Simply documenting the amount of carbon present in a system at a given point in time is not equivalent to documenting the exchange of carbon with the atmosphere. The system must be monitored over time to measure changes at the timescale appropriate for the process. If the stocks change frequently on an annual basis, one must carefully consider when they are measured, so that short-term variations do not skew the reporting of a long-term trend. The same argument holds true for flux measurements. Flux measurements must be integrated over a long enough period such that variations in fluxes from the diurnal cycle, seasonal cycle, and episodic variability are considered. Ideally, the carbon balance of the land in question should be monitored for several annual cycles to ensure that variations in carbon uptake from year to year due to climate variability are taken into account. To reduce costs, some projects have taken the approach that only the pools of carbon that are likely to change much are monitored (18). However, this methodology may prove limiting in ecosystems that are less well known. Although much progress has been made on where carbon is stored within the components of managed and unmanaged ecosystems, it is still a subject of intense research (106). Techniques for nondestructive monitoring of some components such as soils are still needed.

CARBON ACCOUNTING   Opportunities for measurement are available at a variety of scales, but policy language may in fact further constrain the possibilities by allowing only certain activities or components to be counted towards carbon credits. This could greatly limit the usefulness of various techniques if they are not specific to the requirements of the policy prescription. For example, although atmospheric methods are able to integrate information over a large spatial scale, they generally cannot discriminate among the causes for the observed atmospheric response to carbon uptake. If policies count only forest activities as meritorious of credit, then a system over a mixed forest/grassland would need to separate out only the creditable biomass. An inventory method might provide much greater specificity, but it would be more labor intensive, would need more sampling sites to overcome heterogeneity of point measurements, and would be less able to integrate the combined effect of the full ecosystem components that are difficult to measure such as belowground biomass.

The *IPCC Special Report on Land Use, Land-Use Change and Forestry* (18) has reviewed several types of projects to date. So far, most projects have adopted a two-step approach to developing a baseline. The approach is a combination of predicting the likely fate of ecosystems within the project boundary and then estimating the resulting changes in carbon stocks that would occur without additional management (18). This is often done by a simple logical argument—what would have happened in the absence of climate policy—or by land-use models. After the baseline is established, quantification of carbon stocks occurs by comparison to control plots or proxy areas or by modeling. One way forward is to focus accounting efforts on projects that can be clearly identified as additional, for example, replanting forests on denuded land. In such cases, the carbon stored in the project can be easily inventoried.

Land itself is stationary, and therefore can be monitored consistently to document storage. But the products derived from the land are not. Movement of goods and products from agriculture and timber from the area of production to the area of consumption is not insignificant and must be counted to estimate accurate fluxes (53). Similarly, nonproduct related terrestrial carbon may be transported to rivers and through river flows to the coastal ocean, where it may decompose and be released back to the atmosphere (79, 107).

Accounting for carbon storage in the ocean would pose unique challenges. Monitoring of direct injection into the ocean can take place either at aboveground facilities if the injection point is located at the coast, by shipboard observation, or through undersea monitoring. Quantification of the amount of carbon injected as well as tracking of the resulting plume are required. Because of water movement, carbon sequestered at one location may be released to the atmosphere at a different location in another part of the world. This poses a challenge both for monitoring and for assigning credit or debit for the action. The long-term effectiveness of sequestration and fate of excess carbon fixed during ocean fertilization is still unknown (27, 30). Ocean sequestration is an area of intense study as well as commercial interest (25).

A system designed to monitor carbon sequestration, either that caused by natural or deliberate means, may ultimately need to be a compromise among various goals demanded by scientific rigor and practical expediency. The level of accuracy and precision of measurements is an area of potential trade-off and depends on the measurement itself. Often, for example, there is a trade-off between cost and accuracy or precision, because instruments available for a lower cost on the mass market may have different design criteria than those that a scientist might require for specialized experiments. It is unclear in many cases whether a few really good measurements or many lower quality measurements would be more useful. The longevity of the system, ease of use and maintenance, and autonomous operation all are critical elements that may be demanded for a low cost, ubiquitous carbon monitoring system (108).

Currently, the scale, frequency, precision, and accuracy at which decision makers might need carbon cycle information is not known well in the scientific community. Decision makers at many levels are moving forward with carbon management policies that will likely require scientific support for quantification at levels not currently feasible. For example, if the Russian Federation decided to undergo forestry related LULUCF activities to sequester carbon at the maximum rate allowed under the Marrakesh Accords, 17.7 MtCyr^{-1} (12), their total sink would be a factor of 30 smaller than the current uncertainty on an atmospheric inversion at this scale (42). The details of which carbon stock and what measurement scale are important for successful policy outcomes. Because the cultures of scientific endeavor and policy decisions are intentionally separated from each other, deliberate and sensitive mechanisms must be found to foster a two-way exchange of information on an ongoing basis.

Additionality and Separation

Additionality and separation are closely linked. Additionality states that changes in carbon storage must be in addition to what would have occurred otherwise, and separation states that credit can only be given for storage caused by direct, human-induced activity. These concepts are important for ensuring the effectiveness of carbon management for climate policy, because they prevent participants from claiming credit for carbon sequestration that would have happened anyway and thereby results in no net reduction of CO_2 in the atmosphere. The complexity of the carbon cycle and our lack of full knowledge of the human and natural processes that govern carbon exchange currently limit the ability of science to underpin policy in these areas.

It is not possible to trace the mechanistic origin of CO_2 in a system by direct observation except in a few cases using isotopes (18). In the natural system, carbon actively cycles between the atmosphere, ocean, and land on timescales from seconds to centuries. Processes operating at the interfaces, such as air-sea exchange, fire and disturbance on land, ecosystem growth patterns, and human land use, all act to moderate the amount of CO_2 in the atmosphere. A molecule that arrives in a plant whether by CO_2 fertilization or normal growth will look the same. Additionality and separation cannot therefore be directly quantified by measuring the properties of CO_2 or carbon itself. This is in sharp contrast to other chemical species released by human activity such as freons (chemicals formerly used in refrigerants and aerosol propellants), which were the target of other international negotiations, namely the Montreal Protocol.

The approach that must be followed for additionality and separation, therefore, is to identify and quantify mechanisms that are sequestering or releasing carbon. These mechanisms must be identified by indirect methods, such as modeling, comparison, and extrapolation of experimental and field results.

One step toward determining additionality is to first establish a baseline to which changes can be compared. The baseline is an accepted view of what the normal trajectory of carbon sequestration or release would be in a given plot of land or ocean parcel. For terrestrial sequestration, it is important to understand the land-use history, vegetation type, climate interactions, and other factors regulating carbon exchange at a given site in order to estimate what its carbon storage might have been in the absence of deliberate activity. There are several possibilities for defining a baseline, and they include changes that would result from a business as usual projection of an arbitrary year of activity levels, lack of active management, or not meeting performance benchmarks (18). One can also monitor a separate plot of land that has not been subject to deliberate sequestration activities as has been done in some pilot projects (109). All of the potential baseline definitions, however, suffer from similar sources of uncertainty—they are based on assumptions about the potential trajectory of the carbon exchange of a particular area.

Quantifying carbon storage in a single year without accompanying mechanistic information is not enough to set a baseline, because carbon storage can vary from year to year and decade to decade due to external factors such as climate variability (58) (Figure 1). This information is available for sites in some cases, but in regions where records are lacking, it is difficult to reconstruct. Often, models are used to project baselines into the future, but these also require data to be successful and can still be poor predictors of specific local change, because of unexpected social or policy changes (18). Lack of data in developing countries is especially acute in many areas of rapid environmental change.

Documenting separation requires identification of the mechanism causing the sequestration and determining that it is via deliberate actions (such as changes in land-use practices or pumping of carbon to the deep ocean) rather than indirect effects (such as passive recovery from land-use change or disturbance, CO_2 fertilization, nitrogen deposition, and climate variability). Separating the causes of carbon storage is very challenging, although elegant methods have been developed to extract the influence of various mechanisms with existing datasets in some cases [e.g., (110)]. Scientific knowledge of the mechanisms that drive carbon exchange is essential to informing separation.

Land-use change is a major factor contributing to both carbon emissions and carbon sequestration. Observation and modeling of land-use change is therefore an important component to establishing both additionality and separation. Significant progress is being made on observational methods for quantifying land-cover change (biophysical attributes of the Earth's surface) and land use (human purpose or intent applied to these attributes); these methods characterize the importance of these changes for carbon cycle dynamics and derive the causes of land-use and land-cover change from case studies. A recent meta analysis of 152 subnational cases of tropical deforestation has significantly advanced understanding of the causes of land-cover and land-use changes (111). Simple explanatory relationships relating land-cover and land-use change to population, affluence, technology, and/or infrastructure rarely provide an adequate understanding of land change. Land markets and policies respond to the interaction of local, regional, and global economic and institutional dynamics (112). The increasing quality and quantity of satellite observations is accelerating progress on cross-scale understanding of the status and trends of changes in land use and land cover. For example, National Land-Cover Data and associated derivative products are being produced that elucidate temporal and spatial patterns of recent changes in the U.S. landscape (113–115). The U.S. Geological Survey is compiling an overview of the land-use history of North America that is available at http://bioloby.usgs.gov/luhna/index.html. An especially important component of land-use and land-cover change in the United States is suburban and exurban development (116).

Climate variability is another strong influence on carbon uptake patterns that must be taken into account when establishing additionality and separation. The atmospheric growth rate of CO_2 varies from year to year by as much as 100%, which indicates strong variability in terrestrial carbon sinks, with weaker variability in ocean sinks (45, 117–127) (Figure 1). Explanations for the variability in terrestrial sinks are still being explored, but causes are likely due to factors associated with large-scale climate variability such as the El Niño/Southern Oscillation, droughts, fires, and insect outbreaks (127–129). Interannual variability of carbon fluxes also varies between regions. During certain periods of time, carbon sinks can be much stronger in a given region than in other regions, and trends in uptake do not always correlate in time between regions (130). Trends in terrestrial carbon uptake can also vary over decades, possibly due to climate or long-term changes in land use on the decadal scale, and effects may be separated from initial causes for many years (time lags) (59, 122, 126, 129). Thus, carbon exchange can vary significantly from year to year regardless of deliberate human actions engendered by policy, and measurement and crediting systems must take this into account.

Natural disturbance can also affect uptake rates of CO_2 in terrestrial ecosystems. In general, natural disturbances lead to short-term release of CO_2 from the terrestrial biosphere to the atmosphere, usually as a result of oxidation of organic matter through combustion or rapid decomposition (131). As ecosystems recover from disturbances over the long term, they will take up CO_2 from the atmosphere. Examples of natural disturbance include forest fires, insect infestation, and wind-driven blow-over events. These processes may be local in scale, but their frequencies may be linked to larger scale climate and lead to greater impact on the regional or global carbon balance. Disturbance processes are also often linked to each other. For example, the water table in Indonesia had been artificially lowered in forested lands as part of forest and agricultural management, making the 1998 El Niño-related fires much worse than they might otherwise have been (132, 133). Forests weakened by insect infestations are more susceptible to fire, and carbon release can be higher from those forests subject to this linked effect (134). In addition, droughts brought on in tropical regions by climate fluctuations such as El Niño can lead to increased susceptibility to fire and multiple regions can be affected (133, 135). Fires in the boreal region also may account for a large percentage of carbon release to the atmosphere (136). Fire suppression policies in the United States and elsewhere have likely contributed to the trend of an increasing forest carbon sink, although these stocks are also now more vulnerable to extreme conflagrations (137).

Other processes thought to influence the uptake of carbon in terrestrial systems at the present time are CO_2 fertilization, nitrogen deposition, and climate change itself. These processes would need to be accounted for if separation is a requirement for policy frameworks. Increased CO_2 can lead to increased plant growth and therefore carbon uptake, but the effect is thought to be minor compared with the effects of land-use change (109, 138, 139). Nitrogen deposition, and consequent potential stimulation of growth through increased nutrients, is also thought to only play a small role (110, 139). Changes in temperature and precipitation patterns can affect carbon storage, although vegetation responses to these patterns are not uniform and vary with geographic region and vegetation type (129). For example, a recent study showed a trend of increasing terrestrial carbon uptake due to increased precipitation over North America (140).

Models can be quite useful in simulating the effects of different mechanisms on carbon storage. For example, Houghton and colleagues (124) estimated contributions to the U.S. carbon budget from land-use change, such as cultivation and abandonment of agricultural lands, woody encroachment, fuel wood harvests, wildfire, fire suppression, and other disturbances. Houghton has also estimated global fluxes of carbon to the atmosphere by land-use change (124). Schimel and colleagues (138), in contrast, estimated carbon uptake in the coterminous United States from climate and CO_2 fertilization effects. Both of these approaches rely on models to estimate the extent of processes over the potential land area affected. It now appears that much of the documented forest carbon sink in the coterminous United States is due to regrowth on agricultural land and in areas harvested 20–100 years ago and forest management practices (plantations and fire suppression) that increase carbon stocks, rather than climate enhancement or CO_2 fertilization (53, 110, 138).

If additionality and separation are key components of future policy measures, cooperation with the scientific community will be essential to establish what types of parameters are feasibly measured or modeled. As reviewed by Houghton (139), all of the methods used to estimate terrestrial sinks have weaknesses, whether in their inability to attribute mechanisms, poor geographic resolution, or lack of precision. Therefore, it is extremely difficult to definitively separate the amount of carbon stored by deliberate mechanisms versus indirect ones, except in certain cases. Actions undertaken to store carbon are likely more easily monitored, such as changes in tillage practices, management of forests, and pumping carbon to the deep ocean or to deep aquifers. If further research shows that indirect effects on land are minor compared with land-use change and land management, as Caspersen et al. (110) suggest, separation may be easier to demonstrate (139). Furthermore, the concept of additionality can potentially result in perverse incentives if it discourages land managers from taking positive land management actions in the near term in the hope of gaining credit for those same steps at a future time (141).

Permanence

Because carbon is exchanged between terrestrial ecosystems, the atmosphere, and the ocean, carbon stored in one reservoir may not be retained in that reservoir indefinitely. Projects that aim to deliberately sequester carbon must therefore grapple with the issue of how long carbon can stay sequestered.

In land-use change projects, for example, any carbon stored in biomass or soil through deliberate sequestration practices could be lost to the atmosphere if that land is then disturbed through harvest of vegetation, fire, or other human or natural events. For example, a forest planted as a carbon mitigation strategy will only keep carbon out of the atmosphere as long as it is standing, and new forests must be continually planted over time to maintain carbon sequestration rates. Some have argued that permanence of land-use sequestration is difficult and perhaps unnecessary to gain benefit towards mitigation of CO_2 (24). This argument suggests that there is value to delaying emissions, thereby allowing policy and technological options to develop a more permanent solution. Policy analysts have devised several options for dealing with the issue of permanence in a policy framework; these include delayed credits, carbon insurance, land reserves, and expiring credits (142). These less permanent approaches take into account the likelihood of long-term stewardship of land for carbon sequestration purposes and the sovereignty of developing nations, which may find it unpalatable to commit to uses of their land in perpetuity (143).

Ocean sequestration faces similar issues of permanence, albeit at different timescales than terrestrial sequestration. Ocean water masses are constantly in motion. Water parcels containing higher amounts of carbon from direct injection or stimulated biomass production will not remain stationary. Even though the water parcels begin at great depth, for climate purposes it is important to know when that parcel of water will next contact the atmosphere. The average mixing time of the ocean is 1000 years (144), but some parcels of water will emerge to the surface much sooner and some later. When a parcel of water with a higher carbon concentration contacts the atmosphere, it will equilibrate, thereby releasing the stored carbon back to the atmosphere. The placement of injection sites will help to determine how long injected carbon remains sequestered. Modeling studies are useful in this regard, but there are still uncertainties in mesoscale dynamics that should be taken into account. For ocean fertilization, much work still needs to be done to determine where the excess CO_2 gets remineralized (i.e., at what depth) and when that water with enhanced CO_2 might next contact the atmosphere (31).

Geologic disposal is regarded as perhaps the most permanent option currently under consideration (32). For mineralization approaches on the surface, the measurement systems must be in place to assure that the storage or use of the mineralized product does not result in the eventual venting of the CO_2 to the atmosphere. For CO_2 that is kept in its gaseous or liquid form in underground geologic reservoirs, measurement systems must monitor and assure the integrity of the confining geological structures. Because the integrity of these structures will be important during the injection of the gas and to assure ongoing integrity of the reservoir, separate measurement systems may need to be developed in the near and long term.

Unique monitoring needs are required to sustain projects designed to be permanent. A system must be designed with a long-term strategy in mind. Issues that are common to long-term observational systems include preserving calibration between technique transitions, long-term support for measurements, and archiving and accessibility of data (108). In addition, measurements must be transparent to others, with a commonly accepted protocol, to enable long-term verification of carbon sequestration. Finally, carbon sequestration projects must be monitored for the long term to document potential unexpected changes in carbon storage or release. If, for example, under climate change ecosystems experience warmer and wetter conditions, rates of photosynthesis, respiration, and decomposition may change and result in undetermined changes in carbon exchange with the atmosphere. The direction of these changes is highly uncertain under current understanding. However, all mechanisms currently used to explain the present terrestrial carbon sink predict a saturation of the terrestrial sink sometime during the twenty-first century (2). Ocean circulation is also predicted to change as a result of climate change. Carbon sinks created deliberately under carbon management may or may not saturate; this depends on the mechanism used to create the sink.

Environmental Effects and Linkages

If manipulation of the natural carbon cycle is being considered as an option for carbon management, it is imperative to understand and monitor its impacts on other components of the earth system. The area of carbon sequestration is fairly new, and long-term studies are not yet available on environmental effects and potential unintended consequences. There have been some suggestions of potential benefits as well as negative impacts. The structure of food webs, nutrient cycles, biodiversity, indigenous livelihoods, nutritional content of food, ecosystem health, water quality, air quality, and vulnerability to disease all may potentially be affected by artificial manipulation of the carbon cycle. Public acceptance of carbon sequestration will likely depend on a thorough understanding of the environmental consequences.

Certain agricultural practices, such as reduced tillage, have the potential to be win-win situations for both carbon sequestration and soil quality, because they reduce surface water runoff, wind erosion, and enhancing wildlife habitat (76, 145–147). Similarly, restoration of degraded lands or use of degraded lands for carbon sequestration projects may have positive overall benefits. Reduced tillage may also have downsides with respect to environmental objectives, such as increased need for pesticide use (147). Emissions of other GHGs must be taken into account when estimating the climate effectiveness of tillage practices and other carbon sequestration options. For example, no-till systems do have a potential for slightly higher N_2O emissions than other systems, although no-till systems may have the lowest overall greenhouse warming potential (148). It has also been suggested that increasing forest cover may decrease albedo and result in a warming (149).

Potential cautions for carbon sequestration as a management option have been raised for environmental reasons, in particular biodiversity and ecosystem effects. Climate policy framing has explicitly stated that environmental sustainability is to be considered in climate mitigation solutions. In some cases, biodiversity can be improved through careful management of degraded lands (150). Caution must be exercised, however, that the maximization of carbon sequestration does not result in reduction of biodiversity, whether by expanding low diversity, mono-culture crops or by converting low biomass regions with high diversity, such as grasslands, to high biomass regions with low diversity, such as plantation forests.

Parallel cautions have been raised in the area of ocean sequestration. Concerns have been raised that large-scale manipulation of the ocean to store carbon through ocean fertilization may change ocean food webs, nutrient availability, and patterns of primary productivity (30). Research on environmental effects of ocean sequestration is only just beginning, and so unintended consequences on ocean systems are unknown at this time (25, 26). Some have suggested that the precautionary principle should be exercised in the management of the ocean for human needs, although this principle has not yet been extended to ocean sequestration (151). Use of the ocean poses additional legal and ethical issues, because there are vast regions that are not controlled by any state, and water masses move around the globe over time (152). This suggests that actions taken in one region of the ocean may well have impacts in other regions at later times.

It is clear that because the carbon cycle is linked to many other aspects of the earth system and human activity, decisions to manage the carbon cycle cannot be made in isolation. Carbon cycle information must therefore be considered as only one component of a broader, integrated discussion of carbon management in society.

Predicting Future Atmospheric CO_2 Levels

Some formulations of carbon policy depend partly on knowing what future levels of CO_2 might be under different scenarios. The ultimate goal of the UNFCCC, for example, is to "stabiliz[e] greenhouse gas concentrations in the atmosphere at a level that would prevent dangerous anthropogenic interference with the climate system" (4; Article 2). What constitutes "dangerous anthropogenic interference" is still being defined (153). Equally important to the success of these policy formulations is the ability to anticipate future atmospheric CO_2 concentrations. There is considerable uncertainty in discerning the natural and human-driven mechanisms that might control future CO_2 levels, and thus gauging the potential trajectory of atmospheric CO_2 is quite difficult. Knowledge of mechanisms not only informs how much carbon will be removed from the atmosphere but also provides insight into the potential success of carbon sequestration or emission reduction strategies. Surprises in the carbon cycle also have the potential to rapidly change carbon cycle exchange between the land, ocean, and atmosphere and therefore should be taken into account when considering policy options.

The methods used to generate scenarios of future CO_2 concentrations in the IPCC thus far have assumed a very simplistic concept of the natural carbon cycle and its interactions with human activity. CO_2 increases are projected without coupling between earth system responses and climate change. Climate model projections are done using even simpler conceptions of the carbon cycle in which, typically, monotonic concentration increases are used to project climate change (2). This simplification likely underestimates the sensitivity of the carbon cycle to climate change and human activity. The inclusion of nonlinear processes and feedbacks in models of the carbon cycle and/or climate system is a significant mathematical challenge. Yet, geological and historical records document phenomena in both natural and social systems that cannot be reproduced by existing models (154). Recent experiments have coupled active carbon cycle models to general circulation models and simulated impressive nonlinear feedbacks between the carbon cycle and climate. An experiment using the Hadley Centre model simulated a large pulse of CO_2 entering the atmosphere in the mid-twenty-first century, due to a dieback of tropical forests, but a similar simulation using a different model showed a much smaller effect (155, 156).

Currently, half of the CO_2 emitted by fossil fuel combustion and land-use change is taken up by the ocean and land (see Figure 1). It is unknown whether these mechanisms will continue to operate in the future at the same level. The types of mechanisms parameterized in models have a large impact on the sensitivity of the modeled future carbon cycle to climate change. For example, if the mechanism driving the current terrestrial carbon sink is recovery of forests from previous land use, it will have a different implication for future CO_2 levels than if the mechanism is CO_2 fertilization (157).

Climate model projections for this century suggest an ocean with warmer, more stratified surface waters and slower thermohaline circulation. All of this will contribute to reduced anthropogenic carbon uptake from the atmosphere, with the Southern Ocean being particularly sensitive. The response and feedbacks of ocean biology to climate and other global change perturbations is potentially large but not well understood in detail (158–160). In addition to the changes in ocean physics already mentioned, environmental factors such as aeolian deposition of trace metals

Figure 1 Interannual variations in global carbon fluxes for the past two decades. [U]pper red curve represents annual CO_2 inputs to the atmosphere from fossil-fuel [comb]ustion (91). The more variable orange curve represents the globally averaged [atmos]pheric CO_2 growth rate (171) after deseasonalizing and applying a 1-year run[ning] mean. The difference between these two curves represents the amount of CO_2 [taken] up by the land and ocean. The lower two curves are an estimate of the parti[tionin]g between these two fluxes, based on atmospheric ^{13}C and O_2 measurements [from] the Commonwealth Scientific and Industrial Research Organisation (CSIRO) [upda]te to (45) provided by R. Francey, personal communication]. The green curve [repre]sents CO_2 fluxes from the terrestrial biosphere to the air, and the blue curve [repres]ents CO_2 fluxes from the ocean to the air. The long-term average net flux [parti]tion comes from O_2 measurements; the shorter-term variations come from [the m]easurements. Graphically, the sum of the red, blue, and green curves should [appro]ximately total the orange curve. The decadal average land and ocean fluxes [from] the IPCC budget, also calculated from atmospheric O_2 measurements, are indi[cated] by the green and blue bars.

via dust, cloud cover and solar and UV irradiance, riverine and atmospheric nutrient deposition to the coastal ocean, and ocean carbonate chemistry are all sensitive to global change. Another carbon cycle surprise may await under the sea floor: geological data suggest that stocks of carbon in methane clathrates might have been released episodically in response to past climate warming (161, 162).

Emissions due to fossil fuel consumption are projected to play the dominant role in controlling atmospheric CO_2 in the twenty-first century (2). Indeed, "carbon cycle projections are more sensitive to uncertainties about carbon emissions than to uncertainties about the natural science of the carbon cycle" (163). Although several plausible scenarios have been developed as part of the IPCC process, predicting the evolution of society's relationship with energy and consumption of fossil fuel is highly uncertain. Increasing global anthropogenic CO_2 emissions throughout the twentieth century largely reflect the unprecedented rise of fossil fuel energy use by industrial nations (4). Historical variations in CO_2 emissions have been significantly influenced by political and institutional factors that changed short-term market behavior and long-term fuel choices (4). Projections of long-term future demand for fossil fuels have been unreliable (164). Econometric models typically rely on extrapolations from past experience and cannot anticipate surprises like the socially and politically driven oil price variations experienced over the past three decades (165).

Several examples of social phenomena that are poorly characterized in most emission scenarios are: (*a*) changes in the structure of production and work, (*b*) substitution of services for products, (*c*) changes in household composition and lifestyles, and (*d*) changes in nonenvironmental policies (166). The roles of population dynamics and technology as factors in CO_2 emissions have received the most attention to date. The dramatic reductions in fertility and the aging of populations taking place in many countries of the world could influence consumption patterns, political choices related to environmental issues, and the potential for the diffusion of innovative technologies. The impact of widespread adoption of information technology in business and society on CO_2 emissions is a recognized, albeit controversial, issue and an important research topic (167).

Urban planning and design has important implications for CO_2 emissions. For example, urban sprawl is closely associated with the growth in CO_2 emissions associated with the transportation sector. Cross-national studies have documented an inverse correlation between gasoline consumption and urban population densities. The DOE has supported the development of planning support materials that encourage mitigation of CO_2 emissions as a design objective for land-use planning and urban infrastructure development (168). Energy use is also influenced by a variety of other lifestyle characteristics (166). An enhanced program of research on how social, cultural, economic, and political factors influence consumer consumption patterns and emission dynamics will be crucial to improvements in scenario development and forecast methodologies for future carbon emissions.

There is significant uncertainty about the future trajectory of CO_2 levels in the atmosphere, in both the natural and human factors and policy responses that might

AN EXAMPLE OF CARBON MANAGEMENT POLICY—LAND USE, LAND-USE CHANGE, AND FORESTRY IN THE KYOTO PROTOCOL

Land Use, Land-Use Change, and Forestry Provisions

The key provisions within the Marrakesh Accords that define the categories and amounts allowed for Land Use, Land-Use Change, and Forestry (LULUCF) activities include four main elements (12):

- A set of principles to govern LULUCF activities
- A list of eligible LULUCF activities
- Common definitions necessary to define and employ the allowed LULUCF activities
- Methodological rules and guidelines that include a system of caps limiting the carbon credits available via LULUCF activities.

The principles reflect concerns that the use of LULUCF activities should not undermine the environmental integrity of the Protocol. They include, for example, the need for sound science and consistent methodologies, as well as the importance of conserving biodiversity. They also specify that naturally-occurring carbon uptake, which includes uptake as a consequence of indirect anthropogenic effects, should be excluded from the carbon accounting system and that any subsequent release of GHGs (both CO_2 and non-CO_2 such as methane, N_2O) must be promptly counted. The Subsidiary Body for Scientific and Technical Advice is the primarily conduit for official communication, such as scientific assessments and analyses of specific issues between the national negotiating bodies and the scientific community.

The list of eligible LULUCF activities is: afforestation, deforestation, reforestation, revegetation, forest management, cropland management, and grazing land management. Definitions for each of these allowed sequestration activities are provided in the Accords in addition to a single definition of a "forest." The forest definition allows for flexibility in terms of the minimum area of land considered, percent cover, and height at maturity. However, once chosen, a party must employ that definition for all LULUCF accounting in the first commitment period (2008 to 2012).

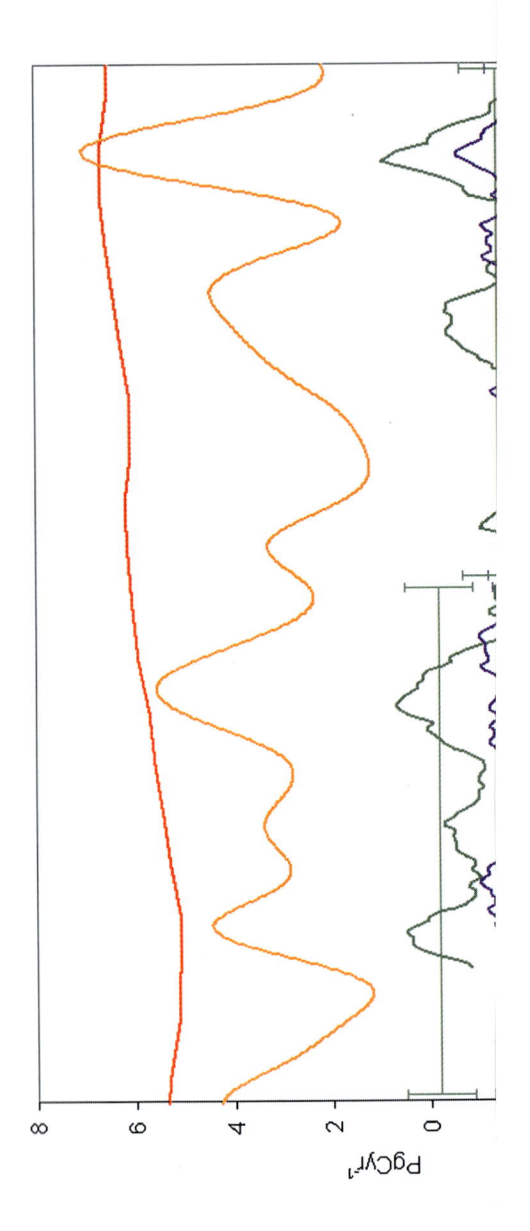

The amount of credit one can gain from the forest-related categories (afforestation, reforestation, deforestation, and forest management) is capped at an amount specified for those parties working under a GHG reduction target. Each party has some flexibility in how they use the forest-related cap through joint activities with other parties, through domestic action, or as an offset to domestic deforestation activities. The amount of LULUCF activity in the cropland management, grazing land management, and revegetation categories are unbounded.

For example, consider the emissions reduction target and a sequestration estimate for Canada. Canada has agreed to lower their emissions 6% below their base year amount of 167 Mt C eq/year (11). This implies that the average Canadian emissions during the first commitment period must come to roughly 157 Mt C eq/year or a reduction of about 10 Mt C eq/year. Emission projections in light of recent trends suggest that the business as usual Canadian emissions in the year 2010 would rise to roughly 197 Mt C eq/year. This suggests that were Canada to continue recent trends, their necessary reduction would be, at the most, 40 Mt C eq/year. Of course, the actual reduction will depend on their future emissions trajectory.

Estimates of Canadian sequestration potential combined with the negotiated caps for LULUCF activities suggest that Canada could accrue roughly 14 Mt C eq/year of credit through these mechanisms (K. Gurney, unpublished information). Relative to their negotiated target, these activities have the potential to meet or exceed their reduction. Relative to their likely emissions trajectory, these activities could make a substantial contribution.

This example highlights the first of a few challenges facing both the scientific and policy communities. Assuming one wanted to measure sequestration with an error of 50%, this would imply measurements that were accurate to less than 0.01 Gt C eq/year. This level of accuracy is well outside the anticipated capability of most current carbon accounting methods at the national or regional scale. Such accuracy is possible at the plot level, but the current disagreement between the various methods when aggregating to regional scales remains a barrier to confidence.

The example also emphasizes the need to both account for the politically eligible carbon credits and the complete carbon exchange. Separation can only be attempted at the plot or local scale, but consistency with regional scale estimates, where separation is not possible, is essential to build confidence in accounting estimates.

A further accounting distinction between the crop, grazing, and revegetation activities versus the forest-related activities is the time at which accounting is initiated (setting a baseline). For crop, grazing, and revegetation activities, the carbon credit or debit measured is the difference between total net emissions in the first commitment period (integral of 2008 to 2012) minus five times the net emissions in the base year (1990 for most parties). For forest-related activities, the carbon credit or debit is the difference in carbon stock between the end and beginning of the first commitment period, provided the activity for which one is accounting was begun on or after January 1, 1990.

A few other important details further guide the LULUCF accounting. First, once a land parcel is accounted for, it must remain in the accounting system indefinitely to address the issue of permanence. Accounting on a given land area begins at the onset of the activity or the beginning of the commitment period, whichever comes last. Finally, it is important to note in the context of measurement requirements and capabilities that the LULUCF accounting system specified in the Marrakesh Accords is not necessarily going to be utilized in future commitment periods. Given the ad hoc nature of the capped amounts on forest-related activities, future accounting may be substantially different.

The Marrakesh Accords represent significant progress in elaborating how and which LULUCF activities are to be included in the national carbon accounting under the Kyoto Protocol. However, difficult issues remain; many of which intersect current measurement and knowledge frontiers facing carbon cycle science. The challenge is to translate the various spatial and temporal scales represented in the scientific community's investigation of the carbon cycle into meaningful boundaries for specific LULUCF activities as defined above.

CONCLUSIONS

Knowledge of the carbon cycle has direct relevance to the success of carbon management policy as currently framed (169). The functioning of the carbon cycle must, therefore, be taken into account when designing and implementing policy to achieve the goal of reducing CO_2 and other GHGs to mitigate climate change. However, it has not yet been shown that the scientific process in carbon cycle research takes into account the specific needs of policy makers. As in other arenas where science is relevant to policy, some portion of the scientific portfolio must be posed in a framework that is policy relevant. Lessons from past interactions between science and policy have demonstrated that in the absence of a clearly established process with frequent feedbacks, scientific results may not be usable to answer the policy questions for which they are needed (170).

Measurement tools for carbon management are sophisticated but tend to be aimed at scientific objectives rather than policy implementation. For example, the atmospheric observing network has been designed to quantify global trends with precision; flux networks are focused on quantifying differences between different eco-climatic conditions, and inventory plots are designed to monitor economic potential and forest health. Linking these scale-specific approaches requires new, integrative experimental designs and analysis models. Costs of monitoring are currently high, because most techniques exist mainly in the research realm and do not enjoy economies of scale. Measurement and modeling uncertainties still limit progress in most components of the carbon cycle.

There may be a significant scale mismatch between currently available direct measurements and the needs of managers and policy makers. Direct measurements provide the strongest constraints at global to continental scales (atmospheric network), and at the plot scale (flux and process studies). Carbon flux estimates at intermediate scales (landscapes to the national scale) today must be converted and extrapolated using inventory methods and emission models. Many of the needs of decision makers for information on carbon management may fall within this intermediate scale. Systematic efforts to improve direct regional-scale measurement techniques, such as through tall tower and aircraft flux techniques, and also to via dust, cloud cover and solar and UV irradiance, riverine and atmospheric nutrient deposition to the coastal ocean, and ocean carbonate chemistry are all sensitive to global change. Another carbon cycle surprise may await under the sea floor: geological data suggest that stocks of carbon in methane clathrates might have been released episodically in response to past climate warming (161, 162).

Emissions due to fossil fuel consumption are projected to play the dominant role in controlling atmospheric CO_2 in the twenty-first century (2). Indeed, "carbon cycle projections are more sensitive to uncertainties about carbon emissions than to uncertainties about the natural science of the carbon cycle" (163). Although several plausible scenarios have been developed as part of the IPCC process, predicting the evolution of society's relationship with energy and consumption of fossil fuel is highly uncertain. Increasing global anthropogenic CO_2 emissions throughout the twentieth century largely reflect the unprecedented rise of fossil fuel energy use by industrial nations (4). Historical variations in CO_2 emissions have been significantly influenced by political and institutional factors that changed short-term market behavior and long-term fuel choices (4). Projections of long-term future demand for fossil fuels have been unreliable (164). Econometric models typically rely on extrapolations from past experience and cannot anticipate surprises like the socially and politically driven oil price variations experienced over the past three decades (165).

Several examples of social phenomena that are poorly characterized in most emission scenarios are: (*a*) changes in the structure of production and work, (*b*) substitution of services for products, (*c*) changes in household composition and lifestyles, and (*d*) changes in nonenvironmental policies (166). The roles of population dynamics and technology as factors in CO_2 emissions have received the most attention to date. The dramatic reductions in fertility and the aging of populations taking place in many countries of the world could influence consumption patterns, political choices related to environmental issues, and the potential for the diffusion of innovative technologies. The impact of widespread adoption of information technology in business and society on CO_2 emissions is a recognized, albeit controversial, issue and an important research topic (167).

Urban planning and design has important implications for CO_2 emissions. For example, urban sprawl is closely associated with the growth in CO_2 emissions associated with the transportation sector. Cross-national studies have documented an inverse correlation between gasoline consumption and urban population densities. The DOE has supported the development of planning support materials that encourage mitigation of CO_2 emissions as a design objective for land-use planning and urban infrastructure development (168). Energy use is also influenced by a variety of other lifestyle characteristics (166). An enhanced program of research on how social, cultural, economic, and political factors influence consumer consumption patterns and emission dynamics will be crucial to improvements in scenario development and forecast methodologies for future carbon emissions.

There is significant uncertainty about the future trajectory of CO_2 levels in the atmosphere, in both the natural and human factors and policy responses that might be adopted. If policy measures are formulated to aim for a specific level of CO_2 in the atmosphere, it will be important to know how uncertain future predictions are and where knowledge on mechanisms and interactions might make a difference to policy choices.

AN EXAMPLE OF CARBON MANAGEMENT POLICY—LAND USE, LAND-USE CHANGE, AND FORESTRY IN THE KYOTO PROTOCOL

Land Use, Land-Use Change, and Forestry Provisions

The key provisions within the Marrakesh Accords that define the categories and amounts allowed for Land Use, Land-Use Change, and Forestry (LULUCF) activities include four main elements (12):

- A set of principles to govern LULUCF activities
- A list of eligible LULUCF activities
- Common definitions necessary to define and employ the allowed LULUCF activities
- Methodological rules and guidelines that include a system of caps limiting the carbon credits available via LULUCF activities.

The principles reflect concerns that the use of LULUCF activities should not undermine the environmental integrity of the Protocol. They include, for example, the need for sound science and consistent methodologies, as well as the importance of conserving biodiversity. They also specify that naturally-occurring carbon uptake, which includes uptake as a consequence of indirect anthropogenic effects, should be excluded from the carbon accounting system and that any subsequent release of GHGs (both CO_2 and non-CO_2 such as methane, N_2O) must be promptly counted. The Subsidiary Body for Scientific and Technical Advice is the primarily conduit for official communication, such as scientific assessments and analyses of specific issues between the national negotiating bodies and the scientific community.

The list of eligible LULUCF activities is: afforestation, deforestation, reforestation, revegetation, forest management, cropland management, and grazing land management. Definitions for each of these allowed sequestration activities are provided in the Accords in addition to a single definition of a "forest." The forest definition allows for flexibility in terms of the minimum area of land considered, percent cover, and height at maturity. However, once chosen, a party must employ that definition for all LULUCF accounting in the first commitment period (2008 to 2012).

The amount of credit one can gain from the forest-related categories (afforestation, reforestation, deforestation, and forest management) is capped at an amount specified for those parties working under a GHG reduction target. Each party has

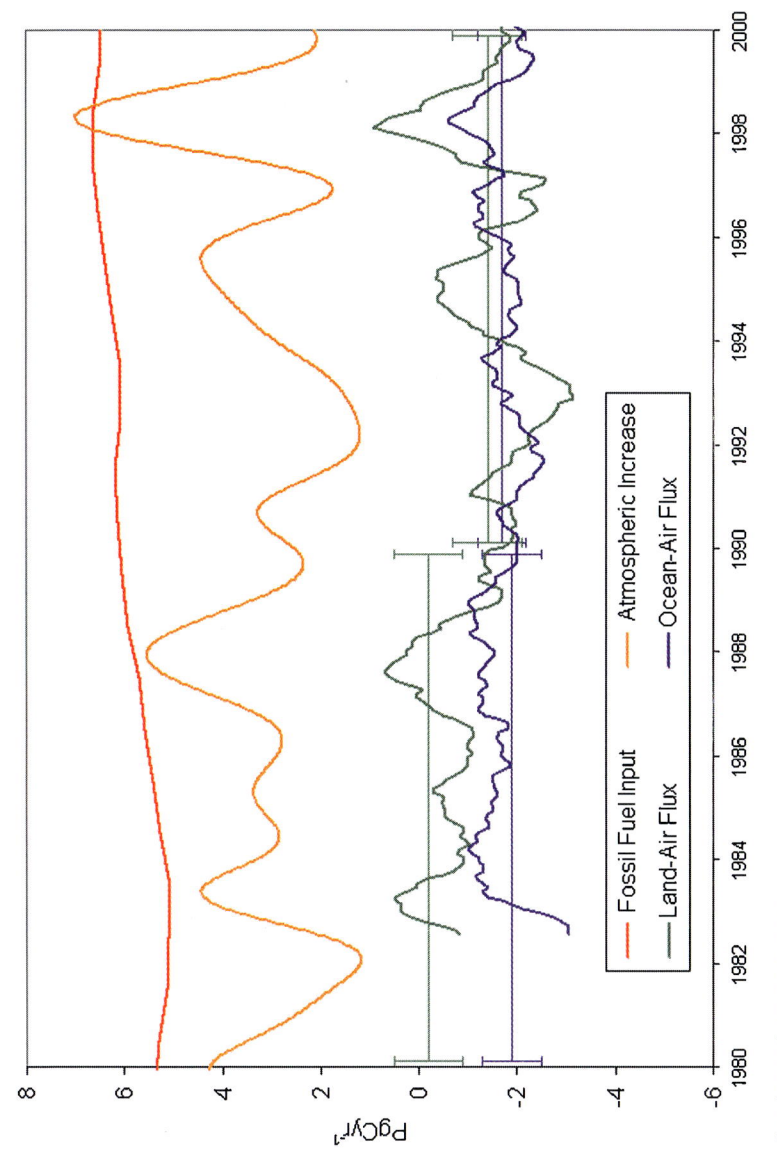

See legend on next page

Figure 1 Interannual variations in global carbon fluxes for the past two decades. The upper red curve represents annual CO_2 inputs to the atmosphere from fossil-fuel combustion (91). The more variable orange curve represents the globally averaged atmospheric CO_2 growth rate (171) after deseasonalizing and applying a 1-year running mean. The difference between these two curves represents the amount of CO_2 taken up by the land and ocean. The lower two curves are an estimate of the partitioning between these two fluxes, based on atmospheric ^{13}C and O_2 measurements from the Commonwealth Scientific and Industrial Research Organisation (CSIRO) [update to (45) provided by R. Francey, personal communication]. The green curve represents CO_2 fluxes from the terrestrial biosphere to the air, and the blue curve represents CO_2 fluxes from the ocean to the air. The long-term average net flux information comes from O_2 measurements; the shorter-term variations come from ^{13}C measurements. Graphically, the sum of the red, blue, and green curves should approximately total the orange curve. The decadal average land and ocean fluxes from the IPCC budget, also calculated from atmospheric O_2 measurements, are indicated by the green and blue bars.

evaluate sample designs, measurement approaches, and the validation of extrapolation techniques would aid in bridging this gap. Focused research efforts to understand the needs of decision makers and possible uses of carbon cycle science are also needed. One of the initial areas of focus may be to understand the scaling needs of decision makers at both the national and regional level. Attempts to upscale and downscale information may then be able to inform policy needs and aid in formulating realistic prescriptions.

Options to mitigate increasing CO_2 concentrations in the atmosphere are varied and wide-ranging. Those options that involve alteration of natural and managed ecosystems on land, or the ocean system, need to carefully consider the functioning of the carbon cycle in the coupled earth system, which includes human societies. Observed features of the carbon cycle, such as vulnerability of carbon stocks to exchange with other reservoirs, interannual and decadal variability, economic and environmental controls, and potential feedbacks with climate change, all affect the success of a carbon sequestration strategy.

Decisions on how to manage carbon will likely always be made to some degree under uncertainty. Even if the scientific uncertainty is reduced, the intended and unintended consequences will still be somewhat unpredictable. Research and understanding of decision making under uncertainty and decision making involving multiple stresses are critical to improving outcomes of decisions made to manage carbon in the environment.

This review focused on the connection between available carbon cycle science and implied needs from carbon sequestration principles. However, some of the greatest opportunities for mitigation of atmospheric CO_2 may lie in tackling the energy intensity and carbon intensity portions of the equation. Over the course of the twenty-first century, fossil fuel emissions are expected to be the dominant cause of increases in the atmospheric concentration of CO_2. Although major uncertainties exist in the functioning of the terrestrial and oceanic sinks, especially in the area of potential feedbacks, even these large uncertainties are smaller than the uncertainty of the future trajectory of fossil fuel and biomass burning (2). The human dimensions of the carbon cycle (i.e., energy supply and demand, consumption patterns, population growth, future development path of human societies, ability and willingness to adapt to change, and tolerance for risk) are extraordinarily difficult to predict.

Policy for carbon management must therefore be informed by carbon cycle science, and vice versa. Each endeavor has much to learn from the other. The challenge for this generation of policy negotiators and carbon cycle scientists is to forge an environment of communication in order to best implement rational policy that reaches the desired outcome without unacceptable negative consequences.

ACKNOWLEDGMENTS

The National Center for Atmospheric Research is supported by the National Science Foundation, WHOI contribution 10883.

The *Annual Review of Environment and Resources* is online at
http://environ.annualreviews.org

LITERATURE CITED

1. Keeling CD, Whorf TP. 2002. Atmospheric CO_2 records from sites in the SIO air sampling network. See Ref. 172. http://cdiac.esd.ornl.gov/trends/co2/siomlo.htm
2. Intergov. Panel Clim. Change. 2001. *Climate Change 2001: The Scientific Basis. Contribution of Working Group I to the Third Assessment Report of the Intergovernmental Panel on Climate Change.* ed. JT Houghton, Y Ding, DJ Griggs, M Noguer, PJ van der Linden, et al. Cambridge, UK/New York: Cambridge Univ. Press. 881 pp.
3. Hoffert MI, Caldeira K, Benford G, Criswell DR, Green C, et al. 2002. Advanced technology paths to global climate stability: energy for a greenhouse planet. *Science* 298:981–87
4. Smil V. 2000. Energy in the twentieth century: resources, conversions, costs, uses, and consequences. *Annu. Rev. Energy Environ.* 25:21–51
5. US Dep. Energy. 1997. *Technology Opportunities to Reduce Greenhouse Gas Emissions.* Washington DC: US DOE
6. Kaya Y. 1990. *Impact of carbon dioxide emission control on GNP growth: interpretation of proposed scenarios.* Presented at IPCC Energy Ind. Subgr., Response Strateg. Working Group, Paris
7. Brooks H. 1980. Technology, Evolution and Purpose. *Daedalus* 109:65–81
8. Wigley TML, Richels R, Edmonds JA. 1996. Economic and environmental choices in the stabilization of atmospheric CO_2 concentrations. *Nature* 319:240–43
9. Intergov. Panel Clim. Change. 2001. *Climate Change 2001: Mitigation—Contribution of Working Group III to the Third Assessment Report of the Intergovernmental Panel on Climate Change.* ed. B Metz, O Davidson, R Swart, J Pan. Cambridge, UK/New York: Cambridge Univ. Press. 752 pp.
10. U.S. Dep. Energy. 1999. *Carbon Sequestration Research and Development.* http://www.fe.doe.gov/coal_power/sequestration/reports/rd/index.shtml
11. UN Framew. Conv. Clim. Change. 1997. *Kyoto Protocol to the United Nations Framework Convention on Climate Change.* Presented at UN Framew. Conv. Clim. Change, FCCC/CP/1997/L.7/Add.1, 10 Dec. http://unfccc.int/resource/docs/convkp/conveng.pdf
12. UN Framew. Conv. Clim. Change. 2002. *Report of the conference of the parties on its seventh session.* Presented at UN Framew. Conv. Clim. Change, FCCC/CP/2001/13, Marrakesh, Oct. 29-Nov. 10, 2001
13. Grubb M, Yamin F. 2001. Climatic collapse at the Hague: what happened, why, and where do we go from here? *Int. Aff.* 77(2):261–76
14. Int. Counc. Local Environ. Initiat. 2003. *Cities for Climate Protection.* http://www.iclei.org/co2/
15. Br. Pet. 2002. *Emissions Trading.* http://www.bp.com/environ_social/environment/clim_change/emissions.asp
16. Intergov. Panel Clim. Change. 1997. *Greenhouse Gas Inventory Reference Manual: Revised 1996 IPCC Guidelines for National Greenhouse Gas Inventories.* Vols. 1–4. Paris: IPCC Secr. http://www.ipcc-nggip.iges.or.jp/public/gl/invs1.htm
17. Intergov. Panel Clim. Change. 2002. *Good Practice Guidance and Uncertainty Management in National Greenhouse Gas Inventories.* ed. J Penman, D

Kruger, I Galbally, T Hiraishi, B Nyenzi, et al. Kanagawa, Jpn.: Inst. Glob. Environ. Strateg. http://www.ipcc-nggip.iges.or.jp/public/gp/gpgaum.htm
18. Intergov. Panel Clim. Change. 2000. *IPCC Special Report on Land Use, Land-Use Change and Forestry*, ed. Watson RT, Noble IR, Bolin B, Ravindranath NH, Verardo DJ, Dokken DJ. Cambridge, UK/New York: Cambridge Univ. Press. 377 pp.
19. Bruce JP, Frome E, Haites H, Janzen R, Lal R, Paustian K. 1999. Carbon sequestration in soils. *J. Soil Water Conserv.* 54:382–89
20. Dumanski J, Desjardins RL, Tarnocai C, Monreal C, Gregorich EG, Kirkwood V, Campbell C. 1998. Possibilities for future carbon sequestration in Canadian agriculture in relation to land use. *Clim. Change* 40:81–103
21. Lal R, Kimble JM, Follett RF, Cole CV. 1998. *The Potential of U.S. Cropland to Sequester Carbon and Mitigate the Greenhouse Effect*. Chelsea, MI: Sleeping Bear
22. Paustian K, Andren O, Janzen HH, Lal R, Smith P, et al. 1997. Agricultural soils as a sink to mitigate CO_2 emissions. *Soil Use Manag.* 13:230–44
23. Turner DP, Koerper GP, Harmon ME, Lee JJ. 1995. Carbon sequestration by forests of the United States: current status and projections to the year 2040. *Tellus B* 47:232–39
24. Marland G, Fruit K, Sedjo R. 2001. Accounting for sequestered carbon: the question of permanence. *Environ. Sci. Policy* 4:259–68
25. Brewer PG, Friederich G, Peltzer ET, Orr Jr. FM. 1999. Direct experiments on the ocean disposal of fossil fuel CO_2. *Science* 284:943–45
26. Seibel BA, Walsh PJ. 2001. Potential impacts of CO_2 injection on deep-sea biota. *Science* 294:319–20
27. Coale KH, Johnson KS, Fitzwater SE, Gordon RM, Tanner S, et al. 1996. A massive phytoplankton bloom induced by an ecosystem-scale iron fertilization experiment in the equatorial Pacific Ocean. *Nature* 383:495–501
28. Boyd PW, Watson AJ, Law CS, Abraham ER, Trull T, et al. 2000. A mesoscale phytoplankton bloom in the polar Southern Ocean stimulated by iron fertilization. *Nature* 407:695–702
29. Joos F, Sarmiento JL, Siegenthaler U. 1991. Estimates of the effect of Southern Ocean iron fertilization on atmospheric CO_2 concentrations. *Nature* 349:772–74
30. Chisholm SW, Falkowski PG, Cullen JJ. 2001. Oceans: dis-crediting ocean fertilization. *Science* 294:309–10
31. Buesseler KO, Boyd PW. 2003. Will ocean fertilization work? *Science* 300:67–68
32. Holloway S. 2001. Storage of fossil fuel-derived carbon dioxide beneath the surface of the Earth. *Annu. Rev. Energy Environ.* 26:145–66
33. Princeton Univ. 2003. *Carbon Mitigation Initiative.* http://www.princeton.edu/~cmi/
34. Stanford Univ. 2002. *The Global Climate and Energy Project.* http://gcep.stanford.edu/
35. Keeling CD. 1960. The concentration and isotopic abundances of carbon dioxide in the atmosphere. *Tellus B* 12:200–3
36. Francey RJ, Steele LP, Langenfelds RL, Pak BC. 1999. High precision long-term monitoring of radiatively active and related trace gases at surface sites and from aircraft in the Southern Hemisphere atmosphere. *J. Atmos. Sci.* 56(2):279–85
37. Conway TJ, Tans P, Waterman LS, Thoning KW, Masarie KA, Gammon RH. 1988. Atmospheric carbon dioxide measurements in the remote global troposphere, 1981–84. *TellusB* 40:81–115
38. Francey RJ, Rayner PJ, Allison CE. 2001. Constraining the global carbon budget from global to regional scales—the measurement challenge. In *Global*

Biogeochemical Cycles in the Climate System, ed. E.-D. Schulze, pp. 245–52. San Diego, CA: Academic
39. Sarmiento JL, Gruber N. 2002. Sinks for anthropogenic carbon. *Phys. Today* 55:30–36
40. Tans PP, Fung I, Takahashi T. 1990. Observational constraints on the global atmospheric CO_2 budget. *Science* 247:1431–39
41. Enting IG, Trudinger CM, Francey RJ. 1995. A synthesis inversion of the concentration and d13C of atmospheric CO_2. *Tellus B* 47(1–2):35–52
42. Gurney KR, Law RM, Denning AS, Rayner PJ, Baker D, et al. 2002. Towards robust regional estimates of CO_2 sources and sinks using atmospheric transport models. *Nature* 415:626–30
43. Ciais P, Tans PP, Trolier M, White JWC, Francey RJ. 1995. A large Northern Hemisphere terrestrial CO_2 sink indicated by the $^{13}C/^{12}C$ ratio of atmospheric CO_2. *Science* 269:1098–102
44. Keeling RF, Piper SC, Heimann M. 1996. Global and hemispheric CO_2 sinks deduced from changes in atmospheric O_2 concentration. *Nature* 381:218–21
45. Rayner PJ, Enting IG, Francey RJ, Langenfelds RL. 1999. Reconstructing the recent carbon cycle from atmospheric CO_2, $\partial 13C$ and O_2/N_2 observations. *Tellus B* 51:213–32
46. Langenfelds RL, Francey RJ, Steele LP, Battle M, Keeling RF, Budd WF. 1999. Partitioning of the global fossil CO_2 sink using a 19-year trend in atmospheric O_2. *Geophys. Res. Lett.* 26(13):1897–1900
47. Deleted in proof
48. Fan S, Gloor M, Mahlman J, Pacala S, Sarmiento J, et al. 1998. A large terrestrial carbon sink in North America implied by atmospheric and oceanic carbon dioxide data. *Science* 282:442–46
49. Bousquet P, Ciais P, Peylin P, Ramonet M, Monfray P. 1999. Inverse modeling of annual atmospheric CO_2 sources and sinks 1. Method and control inversion. *J. Geophys. Res.* 104:26161–78
50. Bousquet P, Peylin P, Ciais P, Ramonet M, Monfray P. 1999. Inverse modeling of annual atmospheric CO_2 sources and sinks 2. Sensitivity study. *J. Geophys. Res.* 104:26179–93
51. Kaminski T, Heimann M, Giering R. 1999. A coarse grid three-dimensional global inverse model of the atmospheric transport. 2. Inversion of the transport of CO_2 in the 1980s. *J. Geophys. Res* 104:18555–81
52. Peylin P, Bousquet P, Ciais P, Monfray P. 1999. Differences of CO_2 flux estimates based on a time-independent versus a time-dependent inversion method. See Ref. 173, pp. 295–309
53. Pacala SW, Hurtt GC, Baker D, Peylin P, Houghton RA, et al. 2001. Consistent land- and atmosphere-based U.S. carbon sink estimates. *Science* 292:2316–20
54. Peylin P, Baker D, Sarmiento J, Ciais P, Bousquet P. 2002. Influence of transport uncertainty on annual mean and seasonal inversions of atmospheric CO_2 data. *J. Geophys. Res.* 107(D19):4385; 10.1029/2001JD000857
55. Denning AS, Fung IY, Randall DA. 1995. Latitudinal gradient of atmospheric CO_2 due to seasonal exchange with land biota. *Nature* 376:240–43
56. Law RM, Rayner PJ, Steele LP, Enting IG. 2003. Data and modelling requirements for CO_2 inversions using high-frequency data. *Tellus B* 55(2):512–21
57. Bender M, Doney S, Feely RA, Fung I, Gruber N, et al. 2002. *A Large-Scale CO_2 Observing Plan: In Situ Oceans and Atmosphere (LSCOP)*. Springfield, VA: Natl. Tech. Inf. Serv. http://www.ogp.noaa.gov/mpe/gcc/co2/observingplan/
58. Wofsy SC, Goulden ML, Munger JW, Fan SM, Bakwin PS, et al. 1993. Net exchange of CO_2 in a mid-latitude forest. *Science* 260:1314–17
59. Law BE, Falge E, Gu L, Baldocchi DD, Bakwin P, et al. 2002. Environmental

controls over carbon dioxide and water vapor exchange of terrestrial vegetation. *Agric. Forest. Met.* 113:97–120
60. Valentini R, Matteucci G, Dolman AJ, Schulze ED, Rebmann C, et al. 2000. Respiration as the main determinant of carbon balance in European forests. *Nature* 404:861–65
61. Massmann WJ, Lee X. 2002. Eddy covariance flux corrections and uncertainties in long-term studies of carbon and energy exchanges. *Agric. Forest Met.* 113:121–44
62. Baldocchi D, Finnigan J, Wilson K, Paw U KT, Falge E. 2000. On measuring net ecosystem carbon exchange over tall vegetation on complex terrain. *Bound.-Layer Meteorol.* 96:257–91
63. Bakwin PS, Tans PP, Zhao CL, Ussler W, Quesnell E. 1995. Measurements of carbon dioxide on a very tall tower. *Tellus B.* 47:535–49
64. AmeriFluxScience Meeting, 2002. Boulder, CO. http://cdiac.esd.ornl.gov/programs/ameriflux/science-meetings/boulder-oct2002/boulder.agenda.html or http://public.ornl.gov/ameriflux/Participants/Sites/Map/index.cfm
65. Davis KJ, Yi C, Berger BW, Kubesh RJ, Bakwin PS. 2000. Scalar budgets in the continental boundary layer. *Proc. 14th Symp. Bound. Layer Turbul., Aug. 7–11, Aspen, CO*, pp. 100–3. Washington DC: Am. Meteorol. Soc.
66. Lloyd J, Francey RJ, Mollicone D, Raupach MR, Sogachev A, et al. 2001. Vertical profiles, boundary layer budgets, and regional flux estimates for CO_2 and its $^{13}C/^{12}C$ ratio and for water vapor above a forest/bog mosaic in central Siberia. *Glob. Biogeochem. Cycles* 15(2):267–84
67. Chou WW, Wofsy SC, Harriss RC, Lin JC, Gerbig C, Sachse GW. 2002. Net fluxes of CO_2 in Amazonia derived from aircraft observations. *J. Geophys. Res.* 107(D22):4614; 10.1029/2001D001295
68. Harriss RC, Wofsy SC, Garstang M, Browell EV, Molion LCB, et al. 1988. The Amazon boundary layer experiment (ABLE 2A): dry season 1985. *J. Geophys. Res.* 93:1351–60
69. Stephens BB, Wofsy SC, Keeling RF, Tans PP, Potosnak MJ. 2002. The CO_2 budget and rectification airborne study: strategies for measuring rectifiers and regional fluxes. See Ref. 173, pp. 311–24
70. Birdsey RA. 1992. *Carbon storage and accumulation in United States forest ecosystems. Gen. Tech. Rep. WO-59.* US Dep. Agric., Washington, DC
71. Dixon RK, Brown S, Houghton RA, Solomon AM, Trexler MC, Wisniewski J. 1994. Carbon pools and flux of global forest ecosystems. *Science* 263:185–90
72. Turner DP, Koerper GJ, Harmon ME, Lee JJ. 1995. A carbon budget for forests of the coterminous United States. *Ecol. Appl.* 5:421–36
73. Brown SL, Schroeder PE. 1999. Spatial patterns of aboveground production and mortality of woody biomass for eastern US forests. *Ecol. Appl.* 9(3):968–80
74. Martin PH, Nabuurs GJ, Aubinet M, Karjalainen T, Vine EL, et al. 2001. Carbon sinks in temperate forests. *Annu. Rev. Energy Environ.* 26:435–65
75. Houghton RA, Ramakrishna K. 1999. A review of national emissions inventories from select non-annex I countries: implications for counting sources and sinks of carbon. *Annu. Rev. Energy Environ.* 24:571–605
76. Lal R. 2002. Soil carbon dynamics in cropland and rangeland. *Environ. Pollut.* 116:353–62
77. Birdsey RA, Heath LS. 1995. Carbon changes in U.S. forests. In *Productivity of America's forests and climate change, Gen. Tech. Rep. RM-271.* ed. LA Joyce, pp. 1–70. US For. Serv., Rocky Mt. For. Range Exp. Stn. Fort Collins, CO.
78. Stallard RF. 1998. Terrestrial sedimentation and the carbon cycle: coupling weathering and erosion to carbon burial. *Glob. Biogeochem. Cycles* 12:231–57
79. Aumont O, Orr JC, Monfray P, Ludwig

W, Amiotte-Suchet P, Probst JL. 2001. Riverine-driven interhemispheric transport of carbon *Glob. Biogeochem. Cycles* 15:393–405
80. Wofsy SC, Harriss RC. 2002. *The North American carbon program (NACP). Rep. NACP Comm. US Interag. Carbon Cycle Sci. Program.* US Glob. Change Res. Program, Washington, DC. http://www.esig.ucar.edu/nacp/index.html
81. Sabine CL, Key RM, Johnson KM, Millero FJ, Poisson A, et al. 1999. Anthropogenic CO_2 inventory of the Indian Ocean. *Glob. Biogeochem. Cycles* 13:179–98
82. Gruber N, Sarmiento JL, Stocker TF. 1996. An improved method for detecting anthropogenic CO_2 in the oceans. *Glob. Biogeochem. Cycles* 10:809–37
83. Quay PD, Sonnerup R, Westby T, Stutsman J, McNichol A. 2003. Changes of the $^{13}C/^{12}C$ of dissolved inorganic carbon in the ocean as a tracer of CO_2 uptake. *Glob. Biogeochem. Cycles* 17: No. 1; 10.1029/2001GB001817
84. McNeil BI, Matear RJ, Key RM, Bullister JL, Sarmiento JL. 2003. Anthropogenic CO_2 uptake by the ocean based on the global chlorofluorocarbon data set. *Science* 299:235–39
85. Takahashi T, Feely RA, Weiss RF, Wanninkhof RH, Chipman DW, et al. 1997. Global air-sea flux of CO_2, an estimate based on measurements of sea-air pCO_2 difference. *Proc. Natl. Acad. Sci. USA* 94:8292–99
86. Takahashi T, Sutherland SC, Sweeney C, Poisson A, Metzl N, et al. 2002. Global sea-air CO_2 flux based on climatological surface ocean pCO_2 and seasonal biological and temperature effects. *Deep-Sea Res. II* 49:1601–22
87. Wanninkhof RH. 1992. Relationship between gas exchange and wind speed over the ocean. *J. Geophys. Res.* 106:11761–74
88. Doney SC, Hood M. 2002. *A global ocean carbon observation system, a background report, Glob. Ocean Obs. Syst. Rep. 118,IOC/INF-1173*, pp. 1–55. UN Educ., Sci., Cult. Organ., Intergov. Oceanogr. Comm. Paris
89. US Energy Inf. Adm. 2002. *Emissions of Greenhouse Gases in the United States 2001.* DOE/EIA-0573. Washington, DC: US Dep. Energy
90. Deleted in proof
91. Marland G, Boden TA, Andres RJ. Fuel CO_2 emissions. In *Trends: A Compendium of Data on Global Change.* See Ref. 172. http://cdiac.esd.ornl.gov/trends/emis/em_cont.htm
92. US Environ. Prot. Agency. 2002. *Inventory of U.S. Greenhouse Gas Emissions and Sinks 1990–2000*, EPA-430-R-02-003. Washington, DC. http://yosemite.epa.gov/oar/globalwarming.nsf/content/ResourceCenterPublicationsGHGEmissionsUSEmissionsInventory 2002. html? OpenDocument
93. Tucker CJ, Sellers PJ. 1986. Satellite remote-sensing of primary production. *Int. J. Remote Sens.* 7:1395–416
94. McClain CR, Cleave ML, Feldman GC, Gregg WW, Hooker SB, Kuring N. 1998. Science quality SeaWiFS data for global biosphere research. *Sea Technol.* 39:10–14
95. Schimel DS. 1995. Terrestrial biogeochemical cycles-Global estimates with remote-sensing. *Remote Sens. Environ.* 51:49–56
96. Running SW, Loveland TR, Pierce LL, Nemani R, Hunt ER. 1995. A remote-sensing-based vegetation classification logic for global land-cover analysis. *Remote Sens. Environ.* 51:39–48
97. Myneni RB, Keeling CD, Tucker CJ, Asrar G, Nemani RR. 1997. Increased plant growth in the northern high latitudes from 1981 to 1991. *Nature* 386:698–702
98. Rayner PJ, O'Brien DM. 2001. The utility of remotely sensed CO_2 concentration data in surface source inversions. *Geophys. Res. Let.* 28:175–78

99. Engelen RJ, Denning AS, Gurney KR, Stephens GL. 2001. Global observations of the carbon budget 1. Expected satellite capabilities for emission spectroscopy in the EOS and NPOESS eras. *J. Geophys. Res.* 106(D17):20055–68
100. Running SW, Baldocchi DD, Turner DP, Gower ST, Bakwin PS, Hibbard KA. 1999. A global terrestrial monitoring network integrating tower fluxes, flask sampling, ecosystem modeling and EOS satellite data. *Remote Sens. Environ.* 70:108–27
101. Canadell JG, Mooney HA, Baldocchi DD, Berry JA, Ehleringer JR, et al. 2000. Carbon metabolism of the terrestrial biosphere: a multitechnique approach for improved understanding. *Ecosystems* 3:115–30
102. Wang YP, Barrett DJ. 2003. Estimating regional terrestrial carbon fluxes for the Australian continent using a multiple-constraint approach: I. Using remotely sensed data and ecological observations of net primary production. *Tellus B* 55(2):270–89
103. *CarboEurope*. http://www.bgc-jena.mpg.de/public/carboeur/index.html
103a. *Australia Carbon Dreaming*. http://globalcarbonproject.org/productsandresources/carbondreamingaustralia2
103b. *Large-Scale Biosphere-Atmosphere Experiment in Amazonia (LBA)*. http://daac.ornl.gov/lba_cptec/lba/indexi.htm
103c. *Canada's National Research Network for the Human Dimensions of Climate Change and Biosphere Greenhouse Gas Management*. http://www.sshrc.ca/web/apply/program_descriptions/biocap_e.asp
103d. *The North American Carbon Program (NACP)*. http://www.esig.ucar.edu/nacp/index.html
103e. *Fluxnet*. http://www-eosdis.ornl.gov/FLUXNET/
104. Kaminski T, Knorr W, Heimann M, Rayner P. 2002. Assimilating atmospheric data into a terrestrial biosphere model: a case study of the seasonal cycle. *Glob. Biogeochem. Cycles* 16(4):1066; doi:10.1029/2001GB001463
105. Vukicevic T, Braswell BH, Schimel D. 2001. A diagnostic study of temperature controls on global terrestrial carbon exchange. *Tellus B* 53(2):150–70
106. Schlesinger WH, Lichter J. 2001. Limited carbon storage in soil and litter of experimental forest plots under increased atmospheric CO_2. *Nature* 411:466–69
107. Richey JE, Melack JM, Aufdenkampe AK, Ballester VM, Hess LL. 2002. Outgassing from Amazonian rivers and wetlands as a large tropical source of atmospheric CO_2. *Nature* 416:617–20
108. Natl. Acad. Sci., Board Atmos. Sci. Clim., Clim. Res. Comm. 1999. *Adequacy of Climate Observing Systems*. Natl. Acad. Press, Washington, DC
109. Pinard MA, Putz F. 1997. Monitoring carbon sequestration benefits associated with reduced-impact logging project in Malaysia. *Mitig. Adapt. Strat. Glob. Change* 2:203–15
110. Caspersen JP, Pacala SW, Jenkins JC, Hurtt GC, Moorcroft PR, Birdsey RA. 2000. Contributions of land-use history to carbon accumulation in U.S. forests. *Science* 290:1148–51
111. Geist HJ, Lambin EF. 2001. *What drives tropical deforestation? A meta-analysis of proximate and underlying causes of deforestation based on subnational case study evidence*. Land Use Cover Change, LUCC Rep. Ser. 4. http://www.geo.ucl.ac.be/LUCC
112. Lambin EF, Turner BL, Helmut JG, Agbola SB, Angelsen A, et al. 2001. The causes of land-use and land-cover change: moving beyond the myths. *Glob. Environ. Change* 11:261–69
113. Vogelmann JE, Howard SM, Yang L, Larson CR, Wylie BK, Van Driel N. 2001. Completion of the 1990s National Land Cover Data Set for the conterminous United States from Landsat Thematic Mapper data and ancillary

data sources. *Photogramm. Eng. Remote Sens.* 67:650–52
114. Riiters KH, Wickham JD, Vogelmann JE, Jones KB. 2000. National land-cover pattern data. *Ecology* 81:604
115. US Geol. Surv. 2003. *National Land-Cover Data.* http://landcover.usgs.gov/nationallandcover.html
116. Heimlich RE, Anderson WD. 2001. *Development at the urban fringe and beyond: impacts on agricultural and rural land. Agric. Econ. Rep 803*, US Dep. Agric. Econ. Res. Serv. Springfield, VA: Natl. Tech. Inf. Serv. http://www.ers.usda.gov/publications/aer803/
117. Conway TJ, Tans PP, Waterman LS, Thoning KW. 1994. Evidence for interannual variability of the carbon cycle from the National Oceanic and Atmospheric Climate Monitoring and Diagnostics Laboratory global air sampling network. *J. Geophys. Res.* 99:22831–55
118. Houghton RA. 2000. Interannual variability in the global carbon cycle. *J. Geophys. Res.* 105:20121–30
119. Keeling CD, Whorf TP, Wahlen M, Vanderplicht J. 1995. Interannual extremes in the rate of rise of atmospheric carbon dioxide since 1980. *Nature* 375:666–70
120. Francey RJ, Tans PP, Allison CE, Enting IG, White JWC, Trolier M. 1995. Changes in oceanic and terrestrial carbon uptake since 1982. *Nature.* 373:326–30
121. Baker D. 2001. *Sources and sinks of atmospheric CO_2 estimated from batch least-squares inversions of CO_2 concentration measurements.* PhD thesis. Princeton Univ., 414 pp.
122. Battle M, Bender ML, Tans PP, White JWC, Ellis JT, et al. 2000. Global carbon sinks and their variability inferred from atmospheric O-2 and delta C-13. *Science* 287:2467–70
123. Feely RA, Boutin J, Cosca CE, Dandonneau Y, Etcheto J, et al. 2002. Seasonal and interannual variability of CO_2 in the equatorial Pacific. *Deep Sea Res. Part II* 49:2443–69
124. Houghton RA, Hackler JL, Lawrence KT. 1999. The U.S. carbon budget: contributions from land-use change. *Science* 285:574–78
125. Le Quéré C, Aumont O, Bopp L, Bousquet P, Ciais P, et al. 2003. Two decades of ocean CO_2 sink and variability. *Tellus B* 55(2):649–56
126. Trudinger CM, Enting IG, Francey RJ, Etheridge DM, Rayner PJ. 1999. Long-term variability in the global carbon cycle inferred from a high precision CO_2 and $\delta^{13}C$ ice core record. *Tellus B* 51(2):233–48
127. Langenfelds RL, Francey RJ, Pak BC, Steele LP, Lloyd J, Trudinger CM, Allison CE. 2002. Interannual growth rate variations of atmospheric CO_2 and its d13C, H2, CH4, and CO between 1992 and 1999 linked to biomass burning. *Glob. Biogeochem. Cycles* 16(3):1048;doi:10.1029/2001GB001466
128. Tian H, Melillo JM, Kicklighter DW, McGuire Ad, Helfrich III JVK, et al. 1998. Effect of interannual variability on carbon storage in Amazonian ecosystems. *Nature* 396:664–67
129. Schimel DS, House JI, Hibbard KA, Bousquet P, Ciais P, et al. 2001. Recent patterns and mechanisms of carbon exchange by terrestrial ecosytems. *Nature* 414:169–72
130. Bousquet P, Peylin P, Ciais P, Le Quéré C, Friedlingstein P, Tans PP. 2000. Regional changes in carbon dioxide fluxes of land and oceans since 1980. *Science* 290:1342–46
131. Wang Y, Amundson R, Trumbore S. 1999. The impact of land use change on C turnover in soils. *Glob. Biogeochem. Cycles* 13:47–57
132. Schimel D, Baker D. 2002. Carbon cycle: the wildfire factor. *Nature* 420:29–30
133. Page SE, Siegert F, Rieley JO, Boehm HDV, Jaya A, Limin S. 2002. The

amount of carbon released from peat and forest fires in Indonesia during 1997. *Nature* 420:61–65

134. Fleming RA, Candau JN, McAlpine RS. 2002. Landscape-scale analysis of interactions between insect defoliation and forest fire in central Canada. *Clim. Change* 55:251–72

135. Nepsted DC, Verissimo A, Alencar A, Nobre C, Lima E, et al. 1999. Large-scale impoverishment of Amazonian forests by logging and fire. *Nature* 398:505–8

136. Conard SG, Sukhinin AI, Stocks BJ, Cahoon DR, Davidenko EP, Ivanova GA. 2002. Determining effects of area burned and fire severity on carbon cycling and emissions in Siberia. *Clim. Change* 55:197–211

137. Tilman D, Reich P, Phillips H, Menton M, Patel A, et al. 2000. Fire suppression and ecosystem carbon storage. *Ecology* 81:2680–85

138. Schimel DS, Melillo J, Tian H, McGuire AD, Kicklighter D, et al. 2000. Contribution of increasing CO_2 and climate to carbon storage by ecosystems in the United States. *Science* 287:2004–6

139. Houghton RA. 2002. Magnitude, distribution and causes of terrestrial carbon sinks and some implications for policy. *Clim. Policy* 2:71–88

140. Nemani R, White M, Thornton P, Nishida K, Reddy S, et al. 2002. Recent trends in hydrologic balance have enhanced the terrestrial carbon sink in the United States, *Geophys. Res. Let.* 29:1468; doi:10.1029/2002GL014867

141. Subak S. 2002. Forest certification eligibility as a screen for CDM sinks projects. *Clim. Policy* 2:335–51

142. Subak S. 2003. Replacing carbon lost from forests: an assessment of insurance, reserves, and expiring credits. *Clim. Policy* In press. doi:10.1016/S1469-3062(03)00033-0

143. Schlamadinger B, Marland G. 2000. *Land use and global climate change: forests, land management and the Kyoto Protocol*. Rep. Pew Cent. Glob. Clim. Change, Arlington, VA. 54 pp. http://www.pewclimate.org/

144. Broecker WS. 1991. The great ocean conveyor. *Oceanography* 4:79–89

145. Burtraw D, Toman MA. 2001. "Ancillary benefits" of greenhouse gas mitigation policies. In *Climate Change Economics and Policy: An RFF Anthology*, ed. M. Toman. Washington, DC: Resour. Future. 288 pp.

146. Uri ND, Atwood JD, Sanabria J. 1998. The environmental benefits and costs of conservation tillage. *Sci. Total Environ.* 216:13–32

147. Marland G, McCarl BA, Schneider U. 2001. Soil carbon: policy and economics. *Clim. Change* 51:101–17

148. Robertson GP, Paul EA, Harwood RR. 2000. Greenhouse gases in intensive agriculture: contributions of individual gases to the radiative forcing of the atmosphere. *Science* 289:1922–25

149. Betts RA. 2000. Offset of the potential carbon sink from boreal forestation by decreases in surface albedo. *Nature* 408:187–90

150. Huston MA, Marland G. 2003. Carbon management and biodiversity. *J. Environ. Manag.* 67:77–86

151. MacDonald J. 1995. Appreciating the precautionary principle as an ethical solution in ocean management. *Ocean Dev. Int. Law* 26:255–86

152. Orbach M. 2003. Beyond the freedom of the seas. *Oceanography* 16:20–29

153. O'Neill BC, Oppenheimer M. 2002. Climate change: dangerous climate impacts and the Kyoto Protocol. *Science* 296:1971–72

154. Natl. Res. Counc./Comm. Abrupt Clim. Change. 2003. *Abrupt Climate Change: Inevitable Surprises*. Washington, DC: Natl. Acad. 244 pp.

155. Cox PM, Betts RA, Jones CD, Spall SA, Totterdell IJ. 2000. Acceleration

of global warming due to carbon-cycle feedbacks in a coupled climate model. *Nature* 408:184–87
156. Friedlingstein P, Bopp L, Ciais P, Dufresne JL, Fairhead L, et al. 2001. Positive feedback between future climate change and the carbon cycle. *Geophys. Res. Let.* 28: 1543–46
157. Hurtt GC, Pacala SW, Moorcroft PR, Caspersen J, Shevliakova E, et al. 2002. Projecting the future of the US carbon sink. *Proc. Nat. Acad. Sci. USA* 99: 1389–94
158. Sarmiento JL, Hughes TMC, Stouffer RJ, Manabe S. 1998. Simulated response of the ocean carbon cycle to anthropogenic climate warming. *Nature* 393: 245–49
159. Joos F, Plattner GK, Stocker TF, Marchal O, Schmittner A. 1999. Global warming and marine carbon cycle feedbacks on future atmospheric CO_2. *Science* 284:464–67
160. Boyd PW, Doney SC. 2002. Modelling regional responses by marine pelagic ecosystems to global climate change. *Geophys. Res. Lett.* 29(16):53.1–53.4; 10.1029/2001GL014130
161. Harvey LD, Huang Z. 1995. Evaluation of the potential impact of methane clathrate destabilization on future global warming. *J. Geophys. Res.* 100:2905–26
162. MacDonald GJ. 1990. Role of methane clathrates in past and future climates. *Clim. Change* 16:247–81
163. Natl. Res. Counc./Comm. Hum. Dimens. Glob. Change, Div. Behav. Soc. Sci. Educ. 2002. *Human Interactions with the Carbon Cycle: Summary of a Workshop*. Washington, DC: Natl. Acad. 41 pp.
164. Baumgartner T, Middtun A. 1987. *The Politics of Energy Forecasting*. London: Oxford Univ. Press
165. US Energy Inf. Adm. 2003. *World Oil Market and Oil Price Chronologies: 1970–2001*. http://www.eia.doe.gov/cabs/chron.html
166. Natl. Res. Counc./ Comm. Hum. Dimens. Glob. Change, Behav. Soc. Sci. Educ. 1997. *Environmentally Significant Consumption: Research Directions*. Washington, DC: Natl. Acad. 143 pp.
167. Lawrence Berkeley Natl. Lab. *Information Technology and Resource Use*. http://enduse.lbl.gov/Projects/InfoTech.html
168. US Dep. Energy/Cent. Excell. Sustain. Dev. 1996. *The Energy Yardstick: Using Places to Create More Sustainable Communities. Washington, DC*. http://www.sustainable.doe.gov
169. Steffen W, Noble I, Canadell J, Apps M, Schulze ED, et al. 1998. The terrestrial carbon cycle: implication for the Kyoto Protocol. *Science* 280:1293–94
170. Pielke RA Jr, Betsill MM. 1997. Policy for science for policy: a commentary on Lambright on ozone depletion and acid rain. *Res. Policy* 26:157–68
171. Clim. Monit. Diagn. Lab. 2002. *GLOBALVIEW-CO_2. Cooperative Atmospheric Data Integration Project-Carbon Dioxide*. CD-ROM, Natl. Ocean. Atmos. Adm., Boulder, CO
172. Carbon Dioxide Inf. Anal. Cent. *Trends: A Compendium of Data on Global Change*. Oak Ridge, TN: Oak Ridge Natl. Lab.
173. Kasibhatla P, Heimann M, Rayner P, Mahowald N, Prinn RG, Hartley DE, eds. *Inverse Methods in Global Biogeochemical Cycles*. Geophys. Monogr. Ser. 104. Washington, DC: Am. Geophys. Union. 324 pp.

CHARACTERIZING AND MEASURING SUSTAINABLE DEVELOPMENT

Thomas M. Parris[1] and Robert W. Kates[2]

[1]Research Scientist and Executive Director, Boston Office, ISciences, LLC, 685 Centre Street, Suite 207, Jamaica Plain, Massachusetts 02130; email: parris@isciences.com
[2]Independent Scholar, Trenton, Maine; email: rkates@acadia.net

Key Words sustainability, indicators, measurement, assessment

■ **Abstract** Sustainable development has broad appeal and little specificity, but some combination of development and environment as well as equity is found in many attempts to describe it. However, proponents of sustainable development differ in their emphases on what is to be sustained, what is to be developed, how to link environment and development, and for how long a time. Despite the persistent definitional ambiguities associated with sustainable development, much work (over 500 efforts) has been devoted to developing quantitative indicators of sustainable development. The emphasis on sustainability indicators has multiple motivations that include decision making and management, advocacy, participation and consensus building, and research and analysis. We select a dozen prominent examples and use this review to highlight their similarities and differences in definition of sustainable development, motivation, process, and technical methods. We conclude that there are no indicator sets that are universally accepted, backed by compelling theory, rigorous data collection and analysis, and influential in policy. This is due to the ambiguity of sustainable development, the plurality of purpose in characterizing and measuring sustainable development, and the confusion of terminology, data, and methods of measurement. A major step in reducing such confusion would be the acceptance of distinctions in terminology, data, and methods. Toward this end, we propose an analytical framework that clearly distinguishes among goals, indicators, targets, trends, driving forces, and policy responses. We also highlight the need for continued research on scale, aggregation, critical limits, and thresholds.

CONTENTS

1. INTRODUCTION 560
2. TWELVE SELECTED EFFORTS TO CHARACTERIZE
   AND MEASURE SUSTAINABLE DEVELOPMENT 562
   2.1. United Nations Commission on Sustainable Development 562
   2.2. Consultative Group on Sustainable Development Indicators 563
   2.3. Wellbeing Index 563
   2.4. Environmental Sustainability Index 563
   2.5. Global Scenario Group 564

2.6. Ecological Footprint 564
2.7. Genuine Progress Indicator 564
2.8. U.S. Interagency Working Group on Sustainable
     Development Indicators 565
2.9. Costa Rica System of Indicators for Sustainable Development 565
2.10. Boston Indicators Project 565
2.11. State Failure Task Force 566
2.12. Global Reporting Initiative 566
3. HOW IS SUSTAINABLE DEVELOPMENT DEFINED? 566
4. WHY CHARACTERIZE AND MEASURE
   SUSTAINABLE DEVELOPMENT? 569
5. HOW ARE GOALS, INDICATORS, AND TARGETS SELECTED? 572
6. HOW ARE INDICATORS CONSTRUCTED? 577
7. CONCLUSION 581

1. INTRODUCTION

The recent World Summit on Sustainable Development, although disappointing to many, did find that sustainable development is part of the mission of countless international organizations, national institutions, sustainable cities and locales, transnational corporations, and nongovernmental organizations (1–3). That the oxymoron-like character of sustainable development can be so inclusive must surely lie in its inherent ambiguity that seeks to finesse the real conflicts between economy and environment and between the present and the future. Some combination of development, environment and equity or economy, society, and environment are found in most attempts to describe it. However, proponents of sustainable development differ in their emphases on what is to be sustained, what is to be developed, how to link environment and development, and for how long a time.

To clarify the definitional ambiguities associated with sustainable development, we have found it useful to use the 2 × 3 taxonomy of the goals described in the extensive literature that defines or debates sustainable development shown in Table 1 (4). In the first column, under the heading "what is to be sustained," are three major categories: nature, life support systems, and community. A plurality of the literature seeks to emphasize sustaining life support systems in which nature or environment is a source of resources and services for the utilitarian life support of humankind (5, 6). In contrast, a significant portion of literature values nature for its intrinsic qualities and biodiversity rather than for its utilitarian qualities (7, 8). Finally, there are claims to sustain cultural diversity, livelihoods, groups, and places that constitute distinctive and threatened communities (9–11). Similarly, there are three quite distinct categories of what should be developed: people, economy, and society. The plurality of early literature focused on the economy, with its productive sectors providing both employment and desired consumption and wealth. In this literature, the economy provides the incentives and the means for investment as well as funds for environmental maintenance and restoration (12). Most recently the focus has shifted to people with an emphasis on human development, increased

TABLE 1 Taxonomy of sustainable development goals (4)

What is to be sustained	What is to be developed
Nature	People
Earth	Child survival
Biodiversity	Life expectancy
Ecosystems	Education
	Equity
	Equal opportunity
Life support	Economy
Ecosystem services	Wealth
Resources	Productive sectors
Environment	Consumption
Community	Society
Cultures	Institutions
Groups	Social capital
Places	States
	Regions

life expectancy, education, equity, and opportunity (13–15). Finally, there are also calls to develop society emphasizing the well-being and security of national states, regions, and institutions and the social capital of relationships and community ties (16–19).

In practice, groups and institutions tend to acknowledge the many multiple and conflicting objectives to be both sustained and developed but then adopt implicit objective functions that take the forms of such statements as sustain only, develop mostly, develop only but sustain somewhat, sustain, or develop—for favored objectives. Similarly, hard choices between sustainable development objectives can be avoided by adopting implicit time horizons. The Brundtland report itself chose a usefully ambiguous and now widely accepted time horizon as "now and in the future" (20). But in a future of a single generation, 25 years, almost any development appears sustainable. Over an infinite forever, none does because even the smallest growth extended indefinitely creates situations that seem surely unsustainable.

Despite the persistent definitional ambiguities associated with sustainable development, much work has been devoted to developing quantitative indicators of sustainable development. The *Compendium of Sustainable Development Indicator Initiatives* lists over 500 sustainability indicator efforts. Of this number, 67 are global in scope, 103 national in scope, 72 are state or provincial in scope, and 289 are local or metropolitan in scope (21). Several efforts have addressed criteria and methodology for constructing indicators; these efforts include work by the Scientific Committee on Problems of the Environment (22), the Balaton Group (23, 24), and others (25, 26). This literature is somewhat distinct from the theoretical and primarily economic treatment of the theory and norms of defining sustainable development (27–31).

The goal of this review is to assess the state of practice for characterizing and measuring sustainable development. Rather than attempt to exhaustively review the vast body of work in this field, we select a dozen prominent examples (introduced in Section 2) and use this review to highlight their similarities and differences by asking the following questions of each effort:

- Section 3—How is sustainable development defined?
- Section 4—Why characterize and measure sustainable development?
- Section 5—How are goals, indicators, and targets selected?
- Section 6—How are indicators constructed?

These comparisons suggest that there major sources of confusion in the field that inhibit future progress, and we conclude by offering our judgment of needed directions for the field.

2. TWELVE SELECTED EFFORTS TO CHARACTERIZE AND MEASURE SUSTAINABLE DEVELOPMENT

We selected our sample of a dozen efforts to characterize and measure sustainable development to be both representative of the field as a whole and to illustrate the diversity of approaches to definition, motivation, process, and technical methodology. We explicitly wished to include efforts ranging from global to national to local scales; governmental to nongovernmental sponsorship; and frameworks that focus on administrative units (e.g., countries) to frameworks that focus on specific actors (e.g., corporations). We did not consider efforts that primarily characterized themselves as state of the environment reports (32, 33). Pragmatic considerations also limited our pool of candidates to those efforts for which we could readily acquire sufficient documentation and background information to support our review. As a result, our sample over represents global scale and U.S.-based efforts.

2.1. United Nations Commission on Sustainable Development

The United Nations Commission on Sustainable Development (CSD) was created in 1992 under the auspices of the Economic and Social Council as a direct result of the United Nations Conference on Environment and Development. A major element of its work to date has focused on the development and testing of a suite of 58 indicators, whittled down from an initial list of 134 indicators, that cover social, environmental, economic, and institutional aspects of sustainable development (34). Although the original intent was to establish a common set of country-level indicators that could eventually be published as a comprehensive comparative time series dataset, recent CSD deliberations stressed that they are "intended only for use by countries at the national level on a voluntary basis, suited to country-specific conditions, and shall not lead to any type of conditionalities, including financial, technical and commercial" (35).

2.2. Consultative Group on Sustainable Development Indicators

The official work of the CSD has been complemented by several independent efforts. The Consultative Group on Sustainable Development Indicators (CGSDI), an international panel of a dozen experts in the field, was established in 1996 with funding from the Wallace Global Fund "to harmonize international work on indicators and to focus on the challenge of creating a single sustainability index." This work produced a "Dashboard of Sustainability," a set of 46 indicators organized into 4 clusters (environment, economy, society, and institutions) for over 100 countries. In parallel, the CGSDI developed a software package that allows users to select alternate methods for computing overall scores from the individual indicators and to graphically analyze the aggregated results (36).

2.3. Wellbeing Index

The World Conservation Union (IUCN) sponsored the development of the "Wellbeing Assessment" that was published in *The Wellbeing of Nations: A Country-by-Country Index of Quality of Life and the Environment* (37). The Wellbeing Index is a composite of 88 indicators for 180 countries. The indicators are aggregated into two subindexes (human wellbeing and ecosystem wellbeing). The human wellbeing index is in turn a composite of indices for health and population, wealth, knowledge and culture, community, and equity. The ecosystem wellbeing index is a composite of indices for land, water, air, species and genes, and resource use. In this scheme, the most sustainable countries include the northern European countries (Sweden, Finland, Norway, and Iceland), and the least sustainable countries are Uganda, Afghanistan, Syria, and Iraq. The United States ranks twenty-seventh, Hungary forty-fourth, and Brazil ninety-second out of 180 countries.

2.4. Environmental Sustainability Index

The World Economic Forum's Environmental Sustainability Index is also composite index derived from 68 indicators for 148 countries (38, 39). These indicators are aggregated into 5 components and 20 core indicators: environmental systems (air quality, water quantity, water quality, biodiversity, and land); reducing environmental stresses (air pollution, water stresses, ecosystem stresses, waste and consumption pressures, and population growth); reducing human vulnerability (basic human sustenance and environmental health); social and institutional capacity (science and technology, freedom to debate, environmental governance, private sector responsiveness, and ecoefficiency); and global stewardship (participation in international collaborative efforts to reduce greenhouse gas emissions and transboundary environmental pressures). At the extremes the Environmental

Sustainability Index agrees well with the Wellbeing Index. However, Hungary is ranked eleventh, Brazil is ranked twentieth, and the United States is ranked forty-fifth out of 148 countries, significantly different results than for the Wellbeing Index.

2.5. Global Scenario Group

The Global Scenario Group uses a set of 65 indicators describing aspects of international equity, national equity, hunger, energy use, water use, deforestation, carbon emissions, sulfur emissions, and toxic waste (40, 41). In contrast to the retrospective efforts above, these indicators are used characterize four alternative scenarios of future global responses to the sustainability challenge through 2050: *market forces*, *policy reform*, *fortress world*, and *the great transition*. In *market forces*, competitive, open, and integrated global markets drive world development. Social and environmental concerns are secondary. *Policy reform* assumes that comprehensive and coordinated government action is initiated for poverty reduction and environmental sustainability. *Fortress world* features an authoritarian response to the threat of breakdown, as the world divides into a kind of global apartheid with the elite in interconnected, protected enclaves, and an impoverished majority outside. The *great transition* validates global solidarity, cultural cross-fertilization, and economic connectedness while seeking a liberative, humanistic, and ecological transition.

2.6. Ecological Footprint

Redefining Progress produces two sustainability indices: ecological footprint and the genuine progress indicator. The Ecological Footprint is a global and country-by-country calculation of consumption and waste relative to the Earth's capacity to create new resources and absorb waste. It is constructed from impact measures for managing the use of croplands, grazing lands, forests, fisheries, infrastructure, and fossil fuels. These measures are then compared with the global stock of each resource. The result is a trend that steadily increases from 0.68 Earth consumed in 1961 to 1.22 in 1999, which indicates that consumption now exceeds the renewable supply of resources (42, 43).

2.7. Genuine Progress Indicator

The Genuine Progress Indicator (GPI) is a measure of the economic performance of the United States that includes the economic contributions of household and volunteer work while subtracting factors such as crime, pollution, and family breakdown. In contrast to gross domestic product per capita (GDP/capita), which steadily increased from 1959–1999, the GPI/capita peaked in the mid 1970s, then steadily declined through the early 1990s, and then increased though 1999 (44). The GPI is but one prominent example of effort to introduce economic externalities into systems of national accounts (12, 45–50).

2.8. U.S. Interagency Working Group on Sustainable Development Indicators

As another example of a national effort, we analyze the work of the U.S. Interagency Working Group on Sustainable Development Indicators (IWGSDI). It is a collection of 13 economic indicators, 16 environmental indicators, and 11 social indicators. No effort is made to construct composite indices of indicators. However, of the 40 indicators, 30 showed trends with clear impact relevant to sustainable development, and 17 of these 30 showed positive national trends (51).

2.9. Costa Rica System of Indicators for Sustainable Development

A third example of a national scale effort is Costa Rica's Sistema de Indicadores sobre Desarrollo Sostenable (System of Indicators for Sustainable Development) first published in 1998 (52). In contrast to the U.S. effort, Costa Rica uses the concept of sustainable development to organize the country's primary statistical abstract. The result is a compendium that currently contains 255 statistical tables organized into 3 broad categories: social (83 tables), economic (97 tables), and environmental (75 tables). The structure of the indicators varies from national time series (e.g., infant mortality, external debt, and energy intensity), to canton-by-canton and district-by-district comparisons of an aggregated social development index computed for 1999. There are also some efforts to situate Costa Rica in the international context using the Human Development Index (15), GDP/capita, inflation rates, prices of key commodities (petroleum, bananas, and coffee) and short term interest rates for U.S. dollars. As with other national statistical abstracts, the presentation is factual with virtually no commentary or overall assessment and spare use of graphics.

2.10. Boston Indicators Project

As an example of a community-based effort, we analyzed the work of the Boston Indicators Project (53). This effort assessed 159 indicators organized into 10 themes: civic health, culture, economy, education, environment, housing, health, safety, technology, and transportation. Figures are given by neighborhood, for Boston as a whole, and for the broader metropolitan area. Each theme includes narrative describing the historical context, regional context, citywide focus, neighborhood focus, and remaining challenges. As with the IWGSDI described above, no effort is made to construct composite indices. Other community-based indicator efforts include the Central Texas Sustainability Indicators Project (54), the Durban Metro State of the Environment and Development report (55), the Ghent Barometer of Sustainable Development (56), Hamilton Ontario's Vision 2020 (57), the Lancashire Green Audit (58), and Sustainable Seattle (59).

2.11. State Failure Task Force

The approaches described above define sustainability in terms of goals to be achieved. In contrast, several efforts take the converse approach by attempting to define indicators of the syndromes or nightmares we wish to avoid such as overuse of marginal lands (the "Sahel Syndrome"), damage of landscapes as the result of large scale projects (the "Aral Sea Syndrome"), or social-ecological degradation through uncontrolled urban growth (the "Favela Syndrome") (60, 61). An example of such efforts is the U.S. Central Intelligence Agency State Failure Task Force (16, 62–64). This group compiled a country-by-country historical record of 127 so-called state failures—revolutionary wars, ethnic wars, genocides or politicides, and adverse or disruptive regime crises—from 1956–1996. It then used data mining techniques such as stepwise multivariate regression and neural networks to inductively find indicators capable of predicting the onset of such events two years in advance. A pool of 75 indicators spanning social, economic, political, and environmental topics was considered. The best model on a global basis used indicators for infant mortality, trade openness [(imports + exports)/GDP], and the level of democracy. Countries with infant mortality above the median for a given year, trade openness below the median for a given year, and with partial democracies exhibited greater risk of failure. This simple model is able to predict approximately two thirds of the failure and nonfailure cases correctly.

2.12. Global Reporting Initiative

All of the above examples use pieces of territory (e.g., countries, counties, or cities) as their object of analysis. However, sustainability can be measured for other objects as well. For example, there is growing interest in rating the sustainability of companies. The most prominent of these efforts is the Global Reporting Initiative, an effort to establish globally applicable guidelines for reporting on the economic, environmental, and social performance initially for corporations and eventually for any business, governmental, or nongovernmental organization. These guidelines specify indicators for each of the three sectors that should be routinely reported by these organizations. The guidelines are now in use, in various degrees, by 156 companies, which include notables such as 3M, ABB, AT&T, Bristol-Myers Squibb, Danone, Dow, Ford, General Motors, and International Paper (65).

3. HOW IS SUSTAINABLE DEVELOPMENT DEFINED?

We use the taxonomy of the sustainable development goals described above to summarize the definitions of sustainability either explicitly or implicitly adopted by each of our selected efforts in Table 2 below and draw three conclusions. First, there is an extraordinarily broad list of items to be sustained and to be developed. This seems to be due both to the inherent ambiguity of sustainable development and to specifics of individual characterization and measurement efforts. Efforts that

TABLE 2 Definitions of sustainable development implicitly or explicitly adopted by selected indicator initiative

Indicator initiative	Implicit or explicit?	What is to be sustained?	What is to be developed?	For how long?
CSD	Implicit, but informed by Agenda 21	Climate, clean air, land productivity, ocean productivity, fresh water, biodiversity	Equity, health, education, housing, security, stabilized population	Sporadic references to 2015
CGSDI	Implicit, but informed by Agenda 21	Same as above	Equity, health, education, housing, security, stabilized population	Not stated, uses data for 1990 and 2000
Wellbeing Index	Explicit	"A condition in which the ecosystem maintains its diversity and quality—and thus its capacity to support people and the rest of life—and its potential to adapt to change and provide a wide change of choices and opportunities for the future"	"A condition in which all members of society are able to determine and meet their needs and have a large range of choices to meet their potential"	Not stated, uses most recent data as of 2001 and includes some indicators of recent change (e.g., inflation and deforestation)
Environmental Sustainability Index	Explicit	"Vital environmental systems are maintained at healthy levels, and to the extent to which levels are improving rather than deteriorating" [and] "levels of anthropogenic stress are low enough to engender no demonstrable harm to its environmental systems"	"People and social systems are not vulnerable (in the way of basic needs such as health and nutrition) to environmental disturbances; becoming less vulnerable is a sign that a society is on a track to greater sustainability" To have "in place institutions and underlying social patterns of skills, attitudes, and networks that foster effective responses to environmental challenges" Cooperation "with other countries to manage common environmental problems" and reduce "negative transboundary environmental impacts on other countries to levels that cause no serious harm"	Not stated, uses most recent data as of 2002 and includes some indicators of recent change (e.g., deforestation) or predicted change (e.g., population in 2025)

(*Continued*)

TABLE 2 (*Continued*)

Indicator initiative	Implicit or explicit?	What is to be sustained?	What is to be developed?	For how long?
Global Scenario Group	Explicit	"Preserving the essential health, services and beauties of the earth requires stabilizing the climate at safe levels, sustaining energy, materials and water resources, reducing toxic emissions and maintaining the world's ecosystems and habitats"	The ability to "meet human needs for food, water and health, and provide opportunities for education, employment and participation"	Through 2050
Ecological Footprint	Explicit	"The area of biologically productive land and water required to produce the resources consumed and to assimilate the wastes produced by humanity"	—	Not explicitly stated, computed annually from 1961–1999
Genuine Progress Indicator	Explicit	Clean air, land, and water	Economic performance, families, and security	Not stated, computed annually from 1950–2000
U.S. IWGSDI	Explicit	Environment, natural resources, and ecosystem services	Dignity, peace, equity, economy, employment, safety, health, and quality of life	Current and future generations
Costa Rica	Implicit	Ecosystem services, natural sources, and biodiversity	Economic and social development	Not stated, includes some time series dating back to 1950
Boston Indicators Project	Implicit	Open/green space, clean air, clean water, clean land, valued ecosystems, biodiversity, and aesthetics	Civil society, culture, economy, education, housing, health, safety, technology, and transportation	Not stated, uses most recent data as of 2000 and some indicators of recent change (e.g., change in poverty rates)
State Failure Task Force	Explicit	—	Intrastate peace/security	Two years
Global Reporting Initiative	Implicit	Reduced consumption of raw materials and reduced emissions of environmental contaminants from production or product use	Profitability, employment, diversity of workforce, dignity of workforce, health/safety of workforce, and health/safety/privacy of customers	Current reporting year

are defined by the need to establish a broad consensus among varied stakeholders have more difficulty being explicit about definitions than do the independent efforts. In the case of the CSD, the stakeholders are nations engaged in negotiations about how to compare their relative progress toward sustainable development. In the Boston case, the stakeholders are members of the community with varied opinions about policy and investment priorities for the future. In the case of the Global Reporting Initiative, the stakeholders are corporations, investors, and regulatory agencies that must agree on common principles and practices for evaluating the relative contributions of corporations toward or away from sustainability. In the context of such negotiation, it is not surprising that underlying definitional differences are downplayed in favor of reaching a common set of indicators, and in order to be inclusive, the range of indicators becomes very broad. In contrast, small self-appointed groups that share a common definition of sustainable development control their own efforts and can, therefore, be more explicit about their terms.

Second, few of the efforts are explicit about the time frame of sustainable development. When time frame is addressed at all, there is a clear bias toward the present or the near term. However, there are three exceptions worth noting. The Global Scenario Group attempts to quantify its scenarios through 2050, approximately two generations. The CSD also makes occasional reference to some of the human development targets established via international negotiations such as the World Summit on Social Development. These targets tend to be defined in terms of a single generation (15–25 years). Although the Ecological Footprint does not explicitly establish a time horizon, it does suggest that a global environmental footprint that is larger than the carrying capacity of the Earth cannot be indefinitely sustained. All of the remaining efforts focus on the present and, in some cases, the recent history leading up to the present. None of our examples approach sustainable development in terms of civilizations or millennia, though such sweeping approaches are occasionally found in the literature (66).

Third, the vast majority of the efforts are deductive, or top-down, in nature. They establish definitions of sustainability on the basis of first principles or negotiated consensus and then let these definitions drive their choice of indicators. Of our examples, only the State Failure Task Force uses an inductive, or bottom-up, approach in which significant indicators emerge from the analysis as powerful statistical predictors.

4. WHY CHARACTERIZE AND MEASURE SUSTAINABLE DEVELOPMENT?

Given the definitional ambiguity outlined above, why even bother to characterize and measure sustainable development? There are at least four major purposes: decision making and management, advocacy, participation and consensus building, and research and analysis. Table 3 summarizes the stated objectives of our dozen examples.

TABLE 3 Implicit and explicit motivations for characterizing and measuring sustainable development

Indicator initiative	Motivation
CSD	"Indicators can provide crucial guidance for decision-making in a variety of ways" Chapter 40 of Agenda 21 "calls on countries at the national level, as well as international, governmental and non-governmental organizations to develop and identify indicators of sustainable development that can provide a solid basis for decision-making at all levels" "Make indicators of sustainable development accessible to decision-makers at the national level, by defining them, elucidating their methodologies and providing training and other capacity building activities"
CGSDI	Not stated
Wellbeing Index	Provide "a clearly stated goal" Provide "a way of measuring progress toward the goal" Provide "an analytical tool for deciding priority actions" Provide "a process to keep the goal constantly in mind and to help people learn how to reach it"
Environmental Sustainability Index	"Assist the move toward a more analytically rigorous and data driven approach to environmental decision making" "Identification of issues where national performance is above or below expectations" "Priority-setting among policy areas within countries and regions" "Tracking of environmental trends" "Quantitative assessment of the success of policies and programs" "Investigation into interactions between environmental and economic performance and into the factors that influence environmental sustainability"
Global Scenario Group	"Offer guidance on how to act now to direct the flow of events towards desirable futures and away from undesirable ones" "Examine the prospects for world development in the twenty-first century" "Illuminate the vast range of possibilities in a structured way"
Ecological Footprint	"Help inform production choices." "Keep the market [as a whole] on an efficient path over time" Adjust market prices to include the costs borne by third parties "Provide indications of the consequences of the current distribution of resource access within and between generations from which, along with moral criteria, new distributions of rights might be made"
Genuine Progress Indicator	To replace Gross Domestic Product (GDP) as the primary scorecard of the nation's well-being for the general public, policymakers, and the media
U.S. IWGSDI	"Encourage a national dialogue that will ultimately result in a set of national indicators of sustainable development"
Costa Rica	To disseminate information that promotes the analysis of the sustainable development To serve as connection between producers and users of information To advance the development of sustainable development indicators
Boston Indicators Project	"Provide information to assist with community planning and problem-solving" "Help business, government, community, and civic leaders find effective points of intervention and collaboration" "Build relationships across traditional boundaries: sectors, races, neighborhoods, generations, levels of government, and between Boston and its metropolitan neighbors"

(Continued)

TABLE 3   (*Continued*)

Indicator initiative	Motivation
	"Tell the story of Boston's successes and challenges in ways obscured by conventional measures, so that problems can be assessed within the context of our social, economic and environmental assets"
	"Market Boston not only to newcomers but to Bostonians, who, with the help of the media, tend to see our glass as only half full when we compare ourselves with other cities and regions"
State Failure Task Force	"Develop a methodology [to] identify key factors and critical thresholds signaling a high risk of crisis in countries some two years in advance"
Global Reporting Initiative	To provide communities, investors, governments, and businesses timely, credible, and consistent information on an organization's economic, environmental, and social performance
	"Elevate sustainability reporting practices worldwide to a level equivalent to financial reporting"

Much of the literature in the field adopts the old axiom, "what gets measured, gets managed." For example, the Balaton Group states, "Intuitively we all use indicators to monitor complex systems we care about or need to control" (23). Thus the major role of indicators is to indicate progress toward or away from some common goals of sustainable development in order to advise the public, decision makers, and managers. This management control also implies the use of various policy responses, and indicators are to be used to identify opportunities for such responses, select priority actions, and evaluate their effectiveness. Examples of these motivations include the CSD statement that, "Indicators can provide crucial guidance for decision-making in a variety of ways" (34), the Global Scenario Group's goal of offering "guidance on how to act now to direct the flow of events towards desirable futures and away from undesirable ones" (67), and the Boston Indicators Project goal to "provide information to assist with community planning and problem-solving" (53).

Although it is true that characterization and measurement initiatives are almost always justified in terms of informed decision making,[1] it is important to recognize that there are other stated and unstated motives at work as well. Indeed, any effort to influence decision making involves value choices and hence is a form of advocacy. The fact that the concept of sustainable development has both broad political appeal and little specificity has created an environment that is particularly ripe for advocacy groups to leverage the political appeal by producing indices that define sustainable development in ways that advance their political agendas. This leads to considerable debate between advocacy groups regarding the relative merits of their respective indicator efforts. Indeed, the debate between the Friends of the Earth and the World Economic Forum is a good example of this

---

[1]Of our eleven examples, the only exception is Costa Rica where the stated purposes are presented purely in terms of information exchange and dissemination.

phenomenon (68). There is explicit acknowledgment of advocacy as partial motivation in the Wellbeing Index, the Environmental Sustainability Index, the Ecological Footprint, the Genuine Progress Indicator, the Boston Indicators Project, and the Global Reporting Initiative. While not explicitly stated, one can also assume that some degree of advocacy is also present in the motivation of the other efforts as well.

Sustainability indicators are also used as the focusing mechanism for participatory processes designed to broaden consensus on goals and for building working relationships across traditional political and institutional divides. This is most evident in the stated objectives of the IWGSDI and Boston Indicators Project. The IWGSDI is perhaps best understood as a negotiated consensus among the various agencies of the U.S. federal government. Similarly, the Boston Indicators Project can be viewed as a facilitated negotiation between the city government and the many interest groups within the city to build a vision for the future. Although the CSD does not explicitly state that consensus was a goal in and of itself, the extensive consultative processes employed by this effort suggest that this was indeed the case.

Sustainability indicators are also used to characterize the results of scenarios and modeling efforts and for research. The Global Scenario Group is a good example of how indicators are used to characterize scenarios and modeling efforts. Of our examples, only the State Failure Task Force has an explicit research agenda—to understand the correlations between sustainability indicators and a specific set of undesirable outcomes.

5. HOW ARE GOALS, INDICATORS, AND TARGETS SELECTED?

Characterizing and measuring sustainability involves making choices about how to define and quantify what is being developed, what is being sustained, and for how long. The goals, indicators and targets of sustainability that we review here are derivative of these choices. In our taxonomy, *goals* are broad, but specific qualitative statements about objectives chosen from the major categories of what to sustain and what to develop. Thus, a statement such as "we will spare no effort to free our fellow men, women and children from the abject and dehumanizing conditions of extreme poverty" as found in the United Nations Millennium Declaration is a human needs goal (13), and "stabilization of greenhouse gas concentrations in the atmosphere at a level that would prevent dangerous anthropogenic interference with the climate system" as found in the United Nations Framework Convention on Climate Change is a life support system goal (69). *Indicators* are quantitative measures selected to assess progress toward or away from a stated goal. For example, the Millennium Declaration uses the proportion of the world's people whose income is less than one dollar a day as basic indicator of extreme poverty (13). Similarly, indicators of greenhouse gas concentrations include measures of carbon dioxide and global warming potential in the atmosphere (70). *Targets* use indicators to make goals specific with endpoints and timetables, such as cutting the proportion of people living on less than one dollar a day in 2000 in half by 2015 (13) or reducing overall emissions of greenhouse gases by at least 5% below 1990 levels by 2008–2012 (70). Finally, *trends* are changes in the values of indicators over time, and *driving forces* and *policy responses* are processes that influence trends and our ability to meet agreed upon targets.

Many targets arise from consensus processes of selection and negotiation (71), but targets can also be chosen based on scientific theory and research. Thus the Global Scenario Group sought to establish targets based on consensus processes for social goals, such as reducing hunger, unsafe water, and illiteracy, by half in each generation until 2050. But in the absence of such consensus for many of the environmental goals, they selected targets based on existing scientific analysis of both what seems to be needed and what seems to be possible to do by 2050 (40, 41).

The distinction between indicators, driving forces, and policy responses is important. As defined above, indicators are limited to quantitative measures of progress toward or away from a stated goal. This definition of indicators explicitly excludes factors that influence progress and instead labels such factors as driving forces or policy responses. It also excludes measures of good intent, such as the existence of a national sustainability plan or membership in international organizations. We make these separations explicit because the widespread adoption of the "pressure-state-response" (72) and derivative frameworks (73) has resulted in a number of measurement efforts that lump indicators of desired outcomes with a smorgasbord of indicators of contestable cause and effect relationships (33). Thus, inputs in the form of driving forces, or more often as policy responses, substitute for the measurement of actual outcomes in achieving a goal. For example, the CSD includes an indicator for the presence of a national sustainable development strategy (34), the Wellbeing Index includes a measure for the number of Internet users per 10,000 population (37), and the Environmental Sustainability Index includes an indicator for the number of IUCN member organizations per million population (38).

As with any assessment effort, the process and methods with which various measurement efforts make choices about goals, indicators, and targets are closely related to their effectiveness in accomplishing their primary objectives (decision making and management, advocacy, participation and consensus building, and analysis and research). These processes and methods can be characterized by three attributes—salience, credibility, and legitimacy. *Salience* refers to relevance of the measurement system to decision makers, *credibility* refers to the scientific and technical adequacy of the measurement system, and *legitimacy* refers to the perception that the production of the measurement system is respectful of stakeholders' divergent values and beliefs, unbiased, and fair in its treatment of opposing views and interests (74–76). Table 4 briefly describes each of our examples using these three characteristics. Efforts to ensure any one of these attributes often result in the diminution of another. For example, the perceived lack of legitimacy and fears of policy misuse led the CSD to sharply curtail the scope of its work plan on sustainability indicators. It is also possible, however, that attempts to increase one

TABLE 4 Salience, credibility, and legitimacy in efforts to characterize and measure sustainable development

Indicator initiative	Salience	Credibility	Legitimacy
CSD	Mandate from Agenda 21 and Review at Rio+5 and World Summit on Sustainable Development	Effort primarily staffed by United Nations technocrats and in-depth consultations with selected countries via pilot process	Decision making by consensus of national delegates and in-depth consultations with selected countries via pilot process
CGSDI	Science-policy dialogue	Selective participation of experts on indicators	Self-appointed group of experts and informal consultations with others through workshops and meetings
Wellbeing Index	Author/publisher assessment and marketing by publisher	Credentials of author, publication in book form by respected publisher in field with backing by IUCN, and independent peer review conducted by publisher	Self-appointed expert
Environmental Sustainability Index	Association with World Economic Forum led to heightened press coverage	Credentials of lead authors, internal review process, publication by respected publisher in field, and independent review conducted by publisher	Self-appointed group of experts
Global Scenario Group	Producer/client relationships with the Commission on Sustainable Development, the United Nations Environment Programme, the U.S. National Academy of Sciences, the Organization for Economic Co-operation and Development, the Intergovernmental Panel on Climate Change, and the Millennium Ecosystem Assessment	Credentials of group members and authors and internal review process	Self-appointed group of experts with membership chosen to represent multiple disciplines and both developed and developing country perspectives

MEASURING SUSTAINABLE DEVELOPMENT 575

Ecological Footprint	Author assessment	Credentials of authors and publication of methods in Proceedings of the National Academy of Sciences	Self-appointed group of experts/advocates
Genuine Progress Indicator	Author assessment	Credentials of lead authors	Self-appointed group of experts/advocates
U.S. IWGSDI	Mandate from President's Commission on Sustainable Development	Credentials of working group members	Chartered working group with representation from many U.S. federal agencies
Costa Rica	Mandate from Agenda 21 (national commitment) and backing by minister of national planning and political economy	Credentials of production team	Core publication of government statistical agency
Boston Indicators Project	Backing by the mayor and the Boston Foundation provided leverage for press exposure	Credentials of lead authors and researchers and extensive review and comment process with participation by academic and practitioner experts	Blessing from popular mayor, and extensive consultation and review by stakeholders
State Failure Task Force	Series of analysis mandates from high-ranking policy makers	Credentials/expertise of task force members and limited publication of results, methods, and data	Group of experts appointed by U.S. federal government
Global Reporting Initiative	Growing list of major companies that publish reports that conform to the guidelines	Credentials of working group members	Steering committee representative of stakeholders and open process with multiple opportunities for stakeholder involvement

attribute can act in a complementary fashion. For example, the outreach efforts by the Boston Indicators Project incorporated a formal review process that also improved the technical credibility of the effort.

On the whole, efforts to ensure salience are rather weak. With the notable exceptions of the State Failure Task Force and the Global Reporting Initiative, none of our select efforts is closely linked to specific decision makers and decisions. In the case of the State Failure Task Force, the mechanism to ensure salience was a series of direct requests from high-ranking officials. In the case of the Global Reporting Initiative, salience is ensured by the economic clout of a diverse community of socially responsible investors that manages over $2 trillion (77). Although it is true that Boston and Costa Rican cases have general statements of support from key decision makers, they are not crafted in a manner that would directly influence any specific decisions. In cases such as the Wellbeing Index, Environmental Sustainability Index, and Ecological Footprint, salience relies upon the ability of their respective authors to assess the policy market for their publication and then use media exposure as their primary means to influence decision making. This observation is consistent with Mitra, who writes, "urban sustainability indicator programs are neither tied to, nor recognized by, local planning and government processes. As a volunteer effort operated parallel to city programs and not incorporated either as a process or used as a source of information, [these efforts] remain at the sidelines of the public policy debate. This often leads to a growing disinterest in continuing regular indicator analyses and updates" (78).

As with salience, many indicator efforts do little to ensure credibility. On the whole, there appears to be a belief that by drawing upon data from reliable sources with their own independent reservoirs of credibility, the effort as a whole will itself become technically credible. However, this does not lend credibility to the selection of indicators, any subsequent computations, or assessments of whether the condition is getting better or worse. Of our dozen efforts, only the Wellbeing Index, the Environmental Sustainability Index, the Ecological Footprint, and the Boston Indicators Project were subjected to formal independent reviews. Most of the efforts rely upon the credentials and expertise of selected participants to establish credibility. In some cases credibility has been enhanced by third-party publication. For example, the work of the Global Scenario Group was extensively used by the United Nations Environment Programme in its third Global Environment Outlook (32), the Wellbeing Index was published by Island Press, the Environmental Sustainability Index was published by Oxford University Press, and an article describing the methods of the Ecological Footprint was published in the *Proceedings of the National Academy of Sciences*.

As noted above, efforts that have primarily sought to establish a broader consensus placed greatest emphasis on mechanisms for establishing legitimacy. These mechanisms range from open and transparent processes with multiple opportunities for stakeholder involvement, as found in the Boston Indicators Project and Global Reporting Initiative, to formal systems of representation and decision making as found in the CSD. In contrast, efforts focused primarily on advocacy, such as the Ecological Footprint and the GPI, place less emphasis on ensuring legitimacy and rely on their own opinions to resolve any conflict. The middle ground is occupied by groups of experts, generally chosen to ensure either implicit or explicit representational goals. For example, the U.S. IWGSDI representation was chosen to establish a consensus among federal agencies; the Global Scenario Group representation was chosen to ensure a mix of disciplinary expertise and developed and developing country perspectives; and the State Failure Task Force was chosen to ensure a mix of disciplinary and theoretical approaches to the problem of violent intranational political conflict.

The contrast between the dominant stated goal, to inform decision making, and the relatively weak efforts to ensure salience, credibility, and legitimacy is striking and indicates a surprising degree of political naïveté among the sustainable development indicators community. Future work on indicators of sustainable development clearly needs to emphasize these concepts throughout the design and production of indicator systems. The approaches employed by the recently published *State of the Nation's Ecosystems* report may serve as an appropriate point of departure from past practice (33, 79).

6. HOW ARE INDICATORS CONSTRUCTED?

Numerous technical approaches have been employed in the development of characterizations and measurement systems for sustainability. Although most efforts are explicit about their own methods, the terminology is often inconsistent, and there is little discussion of the relative merits and drawbacks of alternate methods. The key methodological choices involve issues of data availability and use, spatial and temporal scale, selection of indicators, and the aggregation of indicators. We briefly summarize the methods employed by each of our examples in Table 5.

Almost all of the indicators used are derived from existing data sources. The nature of the data sets differs widely. They include indicators that have been routinely measured, reported, and assessed on a global basis sufficient to establish a long-term trend, indicators that are currently being measured and are likely to be so in the future, indicators that are not directly measured but only estimated through extensive modeling and extrapolation, and indicators that are not directly measured but are given rough contemporary estimates using proxies as available. Within each category, the quality also differs widely by virtue of what is being measured, where it is done, and the effort expended.

A second methodological choice of any measurement system involves issues of spatial and temporal scale. The first choice is the overall scope of the measurement system. All of our example efforts define scope in terms of contiguous geography (e.g., global, national, and metropolitan region). However, alternate scopes, such as land used for irrigated agriculture, are possible and may be more appropriate for certain types of analysis. Scale also has a temporal component that defines the period over which indicators will be reported. The Ecological Footprint, the Genuine

TABLE 5 Technical characteristics of indicators

Indicator initiative	Scale	Units of analysis	Selection criteria	Aggregation method
CSD	Global, present year	Country and year	Data availability and must meet specified scope and units of analysis	None
CGSDI	Global, present year	Country (most recent year available)	Data availability and must meet specified scope and units of analysis	Weighted index
Wellbeing Index	Global, present year	Country (most recent year available)	Data availability and must meet specified scope and units of analysis	Weighted index
Environmental Sustainability Index	Global, present year	Country (most recent year available)	Data availability and must meet specified scope and units of analysis	Weighted index
Global Scenario Group	Global, 1995 to 2050	Region and year	Data availability/model output and must meet specified scope and units of analysis	None
Ecological footprint	Global, 1961 to most recent year available	Country and year	Data availability, must support aggregation to a common scale, and must meet specified scope and units of analysis	Common scale

Genuine Progress Indicator	United States, 1950 to most recent year	Sectors	Data availability, must support aggregation to a common scale, and must meet specified scope and units of analysis	Common scale
U.S. IWGSDI	United States, 1790 to present (though most is focused on more recent periods)	Multiple	Data availability	None
Costa Rica	Costa Rica, 1950 to present (though most is focused on more recent periods)	Multiple	Data availability	None
Boston Indicators Project	Boston, 1980 to present (though most is focused on more recent periods)	Metropolitan region, Boston, neighborhoods	Data availability	None
State Failure Task Force	Global, 1955–present	Country and year	Data availability and must meet specified scope and units of analysis	Statistical model
Global Reporting Initiative	Global, current year	Corporate/ nongovernmental organization entities	Theoretical	None

Progress Indicator, the Global Scenario Group, and the State Failure Task Force explicitly define their temporal scope. Others, such as the CSD, CGSDI, Wellbeing Index, and Environmental Sustainability Index, are focused on producing values that reflect current conditions, but they do not describe trends over a period of time. The Boston, Costa Rica, and U.S. IWGSDI efforts let the availability of data define temporal scale. This latter approach results in scales that vary widely from indicator to indicator.

Scale also refers to the way in which the measurement system breaks down the overall scope of the effort into comparable units of analysis. Most of our selected efforts define these units geographically and nest the units within the larger scale of analysis. Thus, most of the global efforts use countries for their units of analysis. The one exception being the Global Scenario Group that uses 10 regions, each consisting of multiple countries, for its units of analysis. Of these global efforts, those that explicitly deal with time report trends for each country or region by year. However, the Global Scenario Group does not report its trends annually, rather it reports them for just 1995, 2025, and 2050. The Boston Indicators Project is unique in its explicit effort to report indicators for three distinct units of analysis—the greater metropolitan region, the city as a whole, and for each neighborhood within the city. It is important to note that units of analysis do not necessarily need to be defined in geographic terms. For example, the unit of analysis for the Global Reporting Initiative is the firm. Similarly, indicator efforts could be constructed in which the units of analysis are individuals (80), family units, political parties, climatic region, land cover type, or ecosystem type.

The selection of scale and comparative units of analysis are important for two reasons. The first relates to the intended audience of the effort. If the units of analysis do not correspond to the way in which the audience can effect change, there is little likelihood that the effort will have much salience. For example, if the intended audience is a national legislature, then an appropriate scope would be national with units of analysis that correspond to the constituencies of individual legislators. Alternatively, if the audience consists of park managers, then the scope would be the park as a whole, and an appropriate unit of analysis might be ecosystem type. The second reason is that alternate units of analysis result in different types of aggregation anomalies. This is best understood using the example electoral districting. Even though the voting age population in a given state has the same set of characteristics, the way in which the electoral districts are drawn within the state strongly influences the party, racial, and ethnic structure of the state legislature. It is striking that not one of our examples performs any kind of sensitivity analysis to see if their conclusions would be substantially different if they had used an alternate unit of analysis.

Once questions of scale are addressed, a next major technical distinction among measurement systems is the method by which indicators are selected and aggregated. Although all of the efforts are guided by some implicit or explicit definition of sustainable development, some are much more beholden to the ready availability of supporting data than others. Of our examples, the Boston, Costa Rica, and U.S. IWGSDI efforts are at the furthest end of this extreme because they report any data they could acquire that fit their broad definitions of sustainable development. The CGSDI, Wellbeing Index, Environmental Sustainability Index, Global Scenario Group, and State Failure Task Force are also largely driven by data availability, but they are more strongly focused in their search by guiding principals of sustainable development and the need to use indicators that conform to explicit definitions of scope and units of analysis. However, these efforts retain a significant amount of flexibility about indicators because they use subjective methods to compute an overall grade with no associated units. In contrast, efforts such as the Ecological Footprint and the GPI attempt to compute aggregate indices using scientific methods to establish equivalencies to a common unit of measure. These efforts are still limited by data availability, but their searches are more directly constrained by the underlying theoretical construct required to produce common scale indices. Other than bemoaning data gaps, none of our selected efforts makes explicit recommendations about additional data that should be acquired in the future to paint a more complete picture of sustainable development. This is in sharp contrast to a recent study of ecosystem health in the United States that specifically identified indicators that were needed but not currently available (33, 80).

7. CONCLUSION

In an emergent sustainability science, much work has been done on indicators of sustainable development. Perhaps more work has been done on this topic than on any of the other core questions of sustainability science (81). Yet to date, there are no indicator sets that are universally accepted, backed by compelling theory, rigorous data collection and analysis, and influential in policy (4). Why is this so? We offer three major reasons:

1. the ambiguity of sustainable development;
2. the plurality of purpose in characterizing and measuring sustainable development; and,
3. the confusion of terminology, data, and methods of measurement.

Although the definitional ambiguity of sustainable development persists, it is gradually being resolved. Increasingly, goals and targets for sustainable development are being adopted by global and local consensus. Thus, it is not semantic or philosophical clarification that is better at defining sustainable development, but normative judgments as to goals and targets reified in formal agreements, treaties, and declarations. These consensus goals and targets are converging on a minimal definition of sustainable development that includes meeting human needs, which reduces hunger and poverty, while preserving the life support systems of the planet (4, 72). However, these normative judgments are only a beginning. Additional research is required to scientifically identify needed goals and targets by identifying essential limits, boundaries, and thresholds in meeting human needs and preserving life support systems (82).

There is also a growing recognition that the plurality of purpose in characterizing and measuring sustainable development—decision making and management, advocacy, participation and consensus building, and research and analysis—each has its uses and serves different communities. However, these motives need to be clearly identified and stated. This would enable strategic design of procedural and technical methods in ways that would make explicit and optimize the trade-offs between salience, credibility, and legitimacy.

A major step in reducing the confusion of terminology would be the acceptance of the suggested distinctions between goals, indicators, targets, trends, driving forces, and policy responses. There is also a need to conduct research to evaluate the sensitivity of indicator systems to choices in scale, develop and refine methods for aggregating multiple indicators to a common scale, and identify critical limits and thresholds. In our judgment, a most pressing immediate need is for regular measurement of reporting of indicators that track progress toward or away from the growing sets of commonly accepted goals and targets. Elsewhere, we have attempted to design such a set using 14 such goals and targets of development and environment. We were generally successful in identifying a key single indicator for each goal by eliminating much of the repetitive use of similar indicators simply because data are available. However, several key indicators such as ocean biological community condition and land use/cover change are not available and require both further scientific work on creating common scale composite measures and then actually measuring them (72).

Much of the work on measuring sustainable development is driven by a desire to find a new universal indicator of progress akin to GDP or the Human Development Index. Indeed, many of the efforts include explicit references to the inadequacy of GDP as a measure of progress. In our opinion, it is unlikely that the community will soon be able to offer up an alternative to GDP that is as universally accepted, backed by compelling theory, rigorous data collection and analysis, and influential in policy. It must first resolve the persistent definitional ambiguity associated with the notion of sustainable development, the plurality of purpose in measurement, and the confusion of terminology, data, and methods. However, given the progress to date, it is clear that global and local measurement systems can and should serve as navigational aids for a sustainability transition. As we move forward, we must improve the integration of sustainable development theory with the practice of characterization and measurement and recognize that the process is as important as product. It is the process that establishes salience, credibility, and legitimacy and will ultimately lead us toward widespread consensus regarding measurable definitions of sustainable development. At the same time, pluralism is an important element of this process because it allows us to compare and contrast a plethora of approaches and then select the best attributes of each to pursue the next generation of research and application. This article provides a framework for making such comparisons and selections.

ACKNOWLEDGMENTS

The authors thank our colleagues in the Research and Assessment Systems for Sustainability Project (http://sust.harvard.edu/) for their encouragement and constructive criticism of earlier drafts of related papers. This paper is based on research supported (in part) by a grant from the National Science Foundation (award BCS-0004236) with contributions from the National Oceanic and Atmospheric Administration's Office of Global Programs for the Research and Assessment Systems for Sustainability Program and ISciences, L.L.C.

The *Annual Review of Environment and Resources* is online at
http://environ.annualreviews.org

LITERATURE CITED

1. Speth JG. 2003. Perspectives on the Johannesburg summit. *Environment* 45(1):24–29
2. Gutman P. 2003. What did WSSD accomplish? An NGO perspective. *Environment* 45(2):20–28
3. Schnoor J. 2003. Examining the world summit on sustainable development. *Environ. Sci. Technol.* 36(21):A429–30
4. Board Sustain. Dev. 1999. *Our Common Journey: A Transition Toward Sustainability*. Washington, DC: Natl. Acad.
5. Daily GC, eds. 1997. *Nature's Services: Societal Dependence on Natural Ecosystems*. Washington, DC: Island
6. Costanza R, D'Arge R 1997. The value of the world's ecosystems services and natural capital. *Nature* 387(6630):253–60
7. Sessions G, ed. 1994. *Deep Ecology for the Twenty-First Century*. Boston: Shambala
8. Swimme B, Berry T. 1994. *The Universe Story: From the Primordial Flaring Forth to the Ecozoic Era—A Celebration of the Unfolding of the Cosmos*. San Francisco, CA: Harper Collins
9. Muehlebach A. 2001. Making place at the United Nations: indigenous cultural politics at the U.N. working group on indigenous populations. *Cult. Anthropol.* 16(3): 415–48
10. World Comm. Cult. Dev. 1995. *Our Creative Diversity*. Paris, Fr.: UN Educ. Sci. Cult. Organ.
11. Martinez Cobo JR. 1987. *Study of the Problem of Discrimination Against Indigenous Populations*. New York: UN. Sub-comm. Prev. Discrim. Prot. Minor., E/CN.4/Sub.2/1986/7
12. Solow RM. 1993. An almost practical step toward sustainability. *Resourc. Policy.* 19(3):162–72
13. UN Gen. Assem. 2000. *United Nations Millennium Declaration*. New York: UN. A/RES/55/2
14. Int. Monet. Fund, Organ. Econ. Coop. Dev., UN, World Bank Group. 2000. *2000 A Better World for All: Progress Toward the International Development Goals*. Washington, DC: Commun. Dev.
15. UN Dev. Programme. 2002. *Human Development Report 2002*. New York: Oxford Univ. Press
16. Esty DC, Goldstone JA, Gurr TR, Harf B, Levy M, et al. 1998. *State failure task force rep.: phase II findings*. Sci. Appl. Int. Corp., McLean, VA

17. Putnam RD. 1995. Bowling alone: America's declining social capital. *J. Democr.* 6(1):65–70
18. Woolcock M. 1998. Social capital and economic development: toward a theoretical synthesis and policy framework. *Theory Soc.* 27(2):151–208
19. Varshney A. 2002. *Ethnic Conflict and Civic Life: Hindus and Muslims in India.* New Haven, CT: Yale Univ. Press
20. World Comm. Environ. Dev. 1987. *Our Common Future.* Oxford, UK: Oxford Univ. Press
21. Int. Inst. Sustain. Dev. 2000. *Compendium of Sustainable Development Indicator Initiatives* http://www.iisd.org/measure/compendium/
22. Moldan B, Billharz S, Matravers R, eds. 1997. *Sustainability Indicators: Report of the Project on Indicators of Sustainable Development.* New York: Wiley
23. Meadows D. 1998. *Indicators and Information Systems for Sustainable Development.* Hartland Four Corners, VT: Sustain. Inst.
24. Bossel H. 1999. *Indicators for Sustainable Development: Theory, Method, Applications.* Winnipeg, Can.: Int. Inst. Sustain. Dev.
25. Bell S, Morse S. 1999. *Sustainability Indicators: Measuring the Immeasurable.* London, UK: Earthscan
26. Farrell A, Hart M. 1998. What does sustainability really mean? *Environment* 44(9):4–9
27. Daly H, eds. 1973. *Toward a Steady-State Economy.* San Francisco, CA: Freeman
28. Page T. 1977. *Conservation and Economic Efficiency: An Approach to Materials Policy.* Baltimore, MD: Johns Hopkins Univ. Press
29. Neumayer E. 1999. *Weak Versus Strong Sustainability: Exploring the Limits of Two Opposing Paradigms.* Cheltenham, UK: Elgar
30. Dasgupta P. 2001. *Human Well-Being and the Natural Environment.* Oxford, UK: Oxford Univ. Press
31. Goodland H. 1995. The concept of sustainability. *Annu. Rev. Ecol. Syst.* 26:1–24
32. UN Environ. Programme. 2002. *Global Environmental Outlook 3.* London, UK: Earthscan
33. John Heinz H III Cent. Sci., Econ., Environ. 2002. *The State of the Nation's Ecosystems: Measuring the Lands, Waters, and Living Resources of the United States.* Oxford, UK: Cambridge Univ. Press. http://www.heinzctr.org/ecosystems
34. UN Div. Sustain. Dev. 2001. *Indicators of sustainable development: framework and methodologie.* Backgr. Pap. 3, 9th Sess. Comm. Sustain. Dev., New York, Apr. 16–27. DESA/DSD/2001/3. http://www.un.org/esa/sustdev/csd9/csd9_indi_bp3.pdf
35. UN Comm. Sustain. Dev. 2001. *Rep. 9th session. E/CN.17/2001/19.* UN, New York
36. Int. Inst. Sustain. Dev. 1999. *Consultative Group on Sustainable Development Indicators.* Winnipeg, Can.: IISD. http://iisd1.iisd.ca/cgsdi/
37. Prescott-Allen R. 2001. *The Wellbeing of Nations: A Country-by-Country Index of Quality of Life and the Environment.* Washington, DC: Island
38. World Econ. Forum. 2002. *2002 Environmental Sustainability Index.* Davos, Switz.: World Econ. Forum. http://www.ciesin.org/indicators/ESI/downloads.html
39. Esty DC, Cornelius PK. 2002. *Environmental Performance Measurement: The Global Report 2001–2002.* Oxford, UK: Oxford Univ. Press
40. Raskin P, Banuri T, Gallopín G, Gutman P, Hammond A, et al. 2002. *The Great Transition: The Promise and Lure of the Times Ahead.* Boston, MA: Stockh. Environ. Inst. http://www.tellus.org/seib/publications/Great_Transitions.pdf
41. Raskin P, Gallopin G, Gutman P, Hammond A, Swart R. 1998. *Bending the curve: toward global sustainability,* Polestar Rep. 8. Stockh. Environ. Inst., Boston, MA. http://www.tellus.org/seib/publications/bendingthecurve.pdf
42. Wackernagel M, Schulz NB, Deumling D,

Linares AC, Jenkins M, et al. 2002. Tracking the ecological overshoot of the human economy. *Proc. Natl. Acad. Sci. USA* 99(14):9266–71
43. Wackernagel M, Monfreda C, Deumling D. 2002. *Ecological Footprint of Nations: November 2002 Update*. Oakland, CA: Redefin. Prog.
44. Cobb C, Glickman M, Cheslog C. 2001. *The Genuine Progress Indicator: 2000 Update*. Oakland, CA: Redefin. Prog.
45. Cruz W, Repetto R. 1991. *Accounts Overdue: Natural Resource Depreciation in Costa Rica*. Washington, DC: Trop. Sci. Cent., World Resour. Inst.
46. Repetto R. 1992. Earth in the balance sheet: incorporating natural resources in national income accounts. *Environment* 34(7):12–24
47. UN Stat. Div., UN Environ. Programme. 2000. *Handbook of National Accounting: Integrated Environmental and Economic Accounting—An Operational Manual*. New York: UN. ST/ESA/STAT/SER.F/78
48. Kim S. 1994. *Pilot Compilation of the System of Integrated Environmental and Economic Accounts for Korea*. Seoul, Korea: Korea Environ. Inst.
49. Bartelmus P. 1998. *Green Accounting for a Sustainable Economy Policy Use and Analysis of Environmental Accounts in the Philippines*. Makati, Philipp.: Natl. Stat. Coord. Board
50. Panel Integr. Environ. Econ. Account. 1999. *Nature's Numbers: Expanding the National Economic Accounts to Include the Environment*. Washington DC: Natl. Acad.
51. US Interag. Working Group Sustain. Dev. Indic. 1998. *Sustainable Development in the United States: An Experimental Set of Indicators*. Washington, DC: IWGSDI, PR 42.8:SU 8/EX 7
52. Sist. Indicadores sobre Desarrollo Sosten. 1998. *Principales Indicadores de Costa Rica*. San José, Costa Rica: Minist. Planif. Nac. Política Econ. http://www.mideplan.go.cr/sides/
53. The Boston Indic. Proj. 2000. *The Wisdom of Our Choices: Boston's Indicators of Progress, Change and Sustainability 2000*. Boston, MA: Boston Found. http://www.tbf.org/boston/boston-L1.asp
54. Norton S, Crist Gross D, eds. 2002. *The central Texas indicators project: the 2002 rep.*, Cent. Texas Sustain. Indic. Proj., Austin, TX. http://www.centex-indicators.org/
55. City of Durban. 1999. *Durban Metro State of the Environment and Development*. http://www.ceroi.net/reports/durban/index.htm
56. Block T, Van Assche J. 2001. The co-design of indicators on urban sustainable development. Pap. 1st Int. Conf. Ecol. City, Virtual Forum, Barcelona, Jan.-Mar. http://cdonet.rug.ac.be/english/Urban_Sustainable_Development.pdf
57. Vision 2020 Indic. Proj. Team. 2001. *The City of Hamilton's sustainability indicators rep. 2000–2001: monitoring motion towards a sustainable community*. Plan. Dev. Dep., Hamilton, Ont., Can.
58. Lancashire Cty. Counc. 1997. *Lancashire green audit 2: a sustainability report*. Lancashire Cty. Counc., Preston, UK
59. Palmer K, ed. 1998. *Indicators of sustainable community 1998: a status report on long-term cultural, economic, and environmental health for Seattle/King County*, Sustain. Seattle, Seattle, WA
60. Schellnhuber HJ, Block A, Cassel-Gintz M, Kropp J, Lammel G, et al. 1997. Syndromes of global change. *GAIA—Ecol. Perspect. Sci., Humanit., Econ.* 6:19–34
61. Petschel-Held G, Block A, Cassel-Gintz M, Kropp J, Lüdeke MKB, et al. 1999. Syndromes of global change: a qualitative modeling approach to assist global environmental management. *Environ. Model. Assess.* 4:295–314
62. Esty DC, Goldstone JA, Gurr TR, Surko PT, Unger AN, Chen R. 1998. The state failure project: early warning research for US foreign policy planning. In *Preventive Measures: Building Risk Assessment and Crisis*

Early Warning Systems, ed. JL Davies, TR Gurr, pp. 27–38. Boulder, CO: Rowman & Littlefield
63. Esty DC, Goldstone JA, Gurr TR, Surko PT, Unger AN. 1995. *Work. Pap., state failure task force rep.* Sci. Appl. Int. Corp., McLean, VA
64. State Fail. Task Force. 1999. State failure task force rep., phase II findings, *Environ. Change Secur. Proj. Rep.* 5:49–72
65. Global Rep. Initiat. *Global Reporting Initiaitve.* http://www.globalreporting.org/
66. Diamond J. 1997. *Guns, Germs, and Steel: The Fate of Human Societies.* New York: Norton
67. Global Scenar. Group. *Global Scenario Group: An International Initiative to Examine Alternative Futures.* http://www.gsg.org/
68. Ecologist, Friends Earth. 2001. Keeping score. *Ecologist* 31(3):44–47
69. UN. 1992. *United Nations Framework Convention on Climate Change.* Rio de Janeiro, Brazil: UN
70. UN Framew. Conv. Clim. Change. 1997. *Kyoto Protocol to the United Nations Conference on Climate Change.* Kyoto, Japan: UNFCCC
71. Parris TM. 2003. Toward a sustainability transition: the international consensus. *Environment* 45(1):12–22
72. Organ. Econ. Co-op. Dev. 1991. *State of the Environment.* Paris, Fr.: OECD
73. UN Environ. Programme. 1997. *Global Environment Outlook.* New York: Oxford Univ. Press
74. Cash DW, Clark WC, Alcock F, Dickson NM, Eckley N, et al. 2003. Knowledge systems for sustainable development. *Proc. Natl. Acad. Sci. USA.* In press
75. Clark WC, Majone G. 1985. The critical appraisal of scientific inquiries with policy implications. *Sci., Technol., Hum. Values* 10:6–19
76. Clark W, Mitchell R, Cash DW, Alcock F. 2002. *Information as influence: How institutions mediate the impact of scientific assessments on global environmental affairs.* Fac. Res. Work. Pap. RWP02-044, Kennedy School Gov., Harvard Univ. http://ksgnotes1.harvard.edu/research/wpaper.nsf/rwp/RWP02-044/$File/rwp02_044_clark.pdf
77. Soc. Invest. Forum. 2001. *2001 report on socially responsible investing trends in the United States,* Soc. Invest. Forum, Washington, DC. http://www.socialinvest.org/areas/research/trends/SRI_Trends_Report_2001.pdf
78. Mitra A. 2003. *Painting the Town Green: The Use of Urban Sustainability Indicators in the United States of America.* London, UK: RICS Found.
79. O'Malley RO, Cavender-Bares K, Clark WC. 2003. Providing "better" data–not as simple as it might seem. *Environment* 45(4):8–18
80. Inglehart R, Aguir C, Ahmad AH, Aliev A, Alishauskiene R, et al. *World Values Surveys and European Values Surveys, 1981–1984, 1990–1993, and 1995–1997,* Inter-univ. Consort. Polit. Soc. Res., ICPSR Study 2790, Ann Arbor, MI. http://www.icpsr.umich.edu:8080/ICPSR-STUDY/02790.xml
81. Kates RW, Clark WC, Corell R, Hall M, Jaeger CC, et al. 2001. Sustainability science. *Science* 292:641–42
82. Schellnhuber HJ. 2002. *Scientifically Meaningful Limits or Boundaries.* http://sustainabilityscience.org/questions/limits.htm

JUST OIL? THE DISTRIBUTION OF ENVIRONMENTAL AND SOCIAL IMPACTS OF OIL PRODUCTION AND CONSUMPTION

Dara O'Rourke[1] and Sarah Connolly[2]

[1]Department of Environmental Science, Policy, and Management, 135 Giannini Hall, University of California, Berkeley, California 94720; email: orourke@nature.berkeley.edu
[2]Department of Urban Studies and Planning, Massachusetts Institute of Technology, 77 Massachusetts Avenue, Room 7-337, Cambridge, Massachusetts 02139; email: sarahc@mit.edu

Key Words petroleum, environmental justice, energy policy, health impacts

■ **Abstract** This review presents existing data and research on the global distribution of the impacts of oil production and consumption. The review describes and analyzes the environmental, social, and health impacts of oil extraction, transport, refining, and consumption, with a particular focus on the distribution of these burdens among socioeconomic and ethnic groups, communities, countries, and ecosystems. An environmental justice framework is used to analyze the processes influencing the distribution of harmful effects from oil production and use. A critical evaluation of current research and recommendations for future data collection and analysis on the distributional and procedural impacts of oil production and consumption conclude the review.

CONTENTS

I. INTRODUCTION 587
II. ENVIRONMENTAL JUSTICE FRAMEWORK 590
III. CONTROL OVER OIL 590
IV. IMPACTS OF EXPLORATION, DRILLING, AND EXTRACTION 593
V. IMPACTS OF OIL TRANSPORT 598
VI. IMPACTS OF OIL REFINING 603
VII. IMPACTS OF OIL CONSUMPTION 607
VIII. REGULATING THE OIL INDUSTRY 609
IX. CONCLUSIONS, FURTHER RESEARCH, AND POLICY
    IMPLICATIONS 612

I. INTRODUCTION

The National Energy Policy of the United States asserts that the country currently "faces the most serious energy shortage since the oil embargoes of the 1970s," which has been precipitated by "a fundamental imbalance between supply and demand" (1). The National Energy Policy Development Group (NEPDG), the panel convened by Vice-President Dick Cheney to develop the national energy policy, argues this crisis is driven by declining reserves in the United States and by "overly burdensome" and "often excessive and redundant" regulations that hinder new exploration and production of oil.

This panel asserts that the answer to today's oil problems lies in supporting more domestic oil exploration, increasing access to overseas oil, and developing more refining capacity in the United States. The NEPDG thus calls for (a) streamlined and more flexible regulation of oil exploration, production, and refining and (b) the opening of oil exploration in the National Petroleum Reserve-Alaska, the Outer Continental Shelf coastal regions, and the Arctic National Wildlife Refuge; it further recommends "an Executive Order to rationalize permitting for energy production . . . to expedite permits and other federal actions necessary for energy-related project approvals" (2).

President Bush has made this one of his top policy priorities, arguing that "It is in our nation's national interest that we develop more energy supplies at home" (3). Vice-President Cheney has added, "One of the things we need to do is to build more refineries" (4).

The administration is thus advancing energy policies that will significantly increase oil production and refining in the United States and that facilitate increased U.S. access to and investment in oil production and refining overseas. It is worth noting that the Bush administration is not the first to pursue increased access to oil as a matter of national interest. In January 1980, the Carter Doctrine identified the Persian Gulf as a "vital interest" of the country and declared that "an attempt by an outside force to gain control of the Persian Gulf region would be regarded as an assault on the vital interests of the United States." The Carter administration subsequently established a Rapid Deployment Force for use in the Middle East, deployed a permanent U.S. naval force in the Persian Gulf, and acquired new military bases in the region (5).

Although the case for the economic and political benefits of increased production and control over oil has been clearly articulated, the environmental, health, and social costs of increased oil flows are largely absent from government policy deliberations. And perhaps more importantly, the actual distribution of costs and benefits of increased oil production among countries, communities, and individuals is almost completely absent from public discourse.

Clearly, there are very real trade-offs resulting from increased oil production and consumption. But how well do policy makers and the public understand the costs and benefits of such a commitment to oil? What data are available to evaluate the impacts of oil production and consumption at different stages in the oil life cycle? What evidence and analysis are available to compare trade-offs in security, economic development benefits, energy dependence, environmental harm, health costs, and cultural consequences of increased oil production? The purpose of this review is to examine these trade-offs and to assess the distribution of economic, environmental, and health impacts of petroleum production and consumption.

Oil obviously provides significant benefits to society. Oil serves a wide diversity of purposes, which include transportation, heating, electricity, and industrial applications, and is an input into over 2000 end products (6). Oil is a high energy density abundant fuel, which is relatively easy to transport and store, and is extremely versatile in its end uses (7).

Oil is also the most valuable commodity in world trade. As Doyle (8) notes, "Roughly two billion dollars a day now change hands in worldwide petroleum transactions. It is the world's first trillion-dollar industry in terms of annual dollar sales." The oil industry is phenomenally profitable for some corporations and governments. Taxes from oil are a major source of income for some 90 governments. Petroleum is the largest single item in the balance of payments and exchanges between nations and a major factor in local level politics regarding development, jobs, health, and the environment. For many countries, oil is crucial to national economic viability, accounting for upwards of 80% of total national exports for Libya, Iran, Kuwait, Saudi Arabia, and Venezuela (9).

The global oil industry also provides significant jobs, profits, and taxes. As the International Labour Organisation (ILO) notes (6) the oil industry directly employs more than 2 million workers in production and refining. The ILO further estimates that each job in oil production or refining generates one to four indirect jobs in industries that either supply needed inputs or benefit from value added activities.

Interestingly, there are limited public data on the benefits of oil. Revenue and investment data from oil producing regions are sparse. This lack of transparency on oil's benefits has, in fact, motivated an international "Publish What You Pay" campaign (10) to require oil companies to disclose their payments to developing country governments for oil concessions. Dispersed information sources indicate that some countries, such as Ecuador and Angola, receive up to 50% of their revenue from oil taxes and profit sharing (11, 12).

Oil, also, obviously creates significant and varied negative impacts and costs to human health, cultures, and the environment. Thus, it is critical to evaluate the costs as well as the benefits of oil. Although the NEPDG report encourages more oil development, it provides little information on the negative consequences of this development. Instead, the report cites only technological advances that have minimized the impacts of oil exploration and refining.

Past analyses of the oil industry have fallen into several categories. First, there are a wide number of industry sources of data and analysis on the locations, production levels, technological challenges, and economics of oil production and refining (13, 14). There have also been a wide range of historical analyses of political and economic developments in the oil industry around the world (15–17). And more recently, there have emerged a growing number of exposes and reports on the environmental and social impacts of oil exporation, transport, and refining.

Unfortunately, there is no comprehensive source of data available to analyze the global distribution of impacts of oil production and consumption. A wide range of sources—government data, academic analyses, media coverage, nongovernmental organization (NGO) reports—must be consulted to evaluate the costs and benefits of oil.

II. ENVIRONMENTAL JUSTICE FRAMEWORK

This review presents existing data and analyses of the global distribution of the impacts of oil. Using an environmental justice framework (18, 19), we describe and evaluate the environmental, social, and health impacts of oil extraction, transport, refining, and consumption. This perspective seeks to provide a lens through which to examine the distributional and procedural impacts (and inequities) of oil extraction, transport, refining, and consumption among socioeconomic and ethnic groups, communities and countries, and ecosystems. Within this conceptualization, major concerns include the distribution of control over oil, the distribution of environmental and socioeconomic costs of oil, the hazards and risks from oil, and the procedures and politics surrounding the regulation of these risks.

The environmental justice framework stresses the need to evaluate power in driving the distribution of benefits and costs of industrial activities. In industries such as oil, it is not just ownership, as we will discuss below, but rather control over key stages of the oil chain that significantly influences who benefits and who pays the costs of oil development. Thus, we begin with an inquiry into current patterns of control over oil resources, infrastructure, and refining and follow with an assessment of the distribution of power and influence over government decisionmaking and regulation of the industry (Section III).

Next, we evaluate the distribution and regulation of environmental and health hazards from oil production and consumption. We are interested particularly in the distribution of risks and costs, both at the local and global level, of oil exploration, drilling, and extraction (Section IV), transport (Section V), refining (Section VI), and consumption (Section VII).

We also seek to analyze whether existing regulatory systems adequately protect impacted communities at each stage in the life cycle of oil. Extensive regulations govern oil exploration and refining. However, there is also wide variation in the implementation of these regulations, weak enforcement in many locales, and failures of regulation in certain arenas. We are thus interested in whether enforcement is effective at different stages in the oil supply chain and whether regulatory mechanisms are sufficient to motivate remediation and prevention of future impacts (Section VIII).

The review concludes with a critical evaluation of current research and data and with recommendations for further analysis of the distributional and procedural impacts of oil production and consumption.

III. CONTROL OVER OIL

Perhaps the most critical and historically contentious questions related to oil are simply who owns, controls, or has access to this resource? Control over reserves, production, distribution, and refining is critical to the distribution of benefits and costs of oil and to deeper global, economic, and political dynamics.

Approximately 90 countries produce oil, although a few major producers account for the bulk of world output. The Energy Information Agency estimates that the eleven Organization of Petroleum Exporting Countries (OPEC) members (Algeria, Indonesia, Iran, Iraq, Kuwait, Libya, Nigeria, Qatar, Saudi Arabia, the United Arab Emirates, and Venezuela) account for roughly 77% of the world's proven oil reserves and 40% of world oil production (20). The Persian Gulf contains approximately 680 billion barrels of proven oil reserves, which represents approximately 66% of the total world oil reserves (21). The Persian Gulf maintains 31% of the world total oil production capacity (just over 22 million barrels per day) (22).

In 2001, Persian Gulf countries had oil exports of approximately 16.8 million barrels per day of oil. As would be expected, Saudi Arabia exported the most oil of any country in 2001, with an estimated 7.4 million barrels per day (22). Major non-OPEC oil producing countries include the United States, Mexico, Denmark, Norway, the United Kingdom, the Russian Federation, China, and Vietnam.

Proven reserves—the most basic measure of who has the oil, and how much—have actually changed over the past 20 years. Proven reserves increased 54% between 1980 and 1990, largely due to improvements in exploration and drilling, but were then stagnant between 1990 and 2000 with an increase of only 1.4% globally (23). As would be expected, many countries' reserves are declining significantly. In the United States for instance, proven reserves declined from 36.5 billion barrels in 1980 to 30.1 billion barrels in 2000 (24). Table 1 presents basic information on oil reserves, production, and exports from leading oil producing nations.

While the physical location of oil does not change, systems of control over oil have changed significantly over the past two decades. In particular, there has been a

TABLE 1 World oil reserves, production, and exports in 2001 (25, 26)

Country	Total oil reserves (billion barrels)	Total oil production (million barrels per day)	Net oil exports (million barrels per day)
United States	22.0	9.02	0.9
Saudi Arabia	261.7	8.73	7.38
Russia	48.6	7.29	4.76
Iran	89.7	3.82	2.74
Mexico	28.3	3.59	1.65
Norway	9.4	3.41	3.22
China	24.0	3.30	0.1
Venezuela	76.9	3.07	2.60
Canada	6.6	2.80	1.8
United Kingdom	4.9	2.59	1.7
Iraq	112.5	2.45	2.00
United Arab Emirates	97.8	2.42	2.09
Nigeria	22.5	2.26	2.00
Kuwait	96.5	2.15	1.80

major restructuring and concentration of ownership in the global oil industry. This change in power and control has had significant implications for the distribution of benefits accruing to oil producers and refiners and for the distribution of costs to oil producing regions and consumers.

Historically, state-owned companies controlled most oil in the world. The four largest state oil companies, Saudi Aramco, Petroleos de Venezuela, Iran's NIOC, and Mexico's Pemex, produce 25% of the world's oil and hold 42% of the world's reserves (27). Physical ownership over oil, however, may not be as important as mechanisms of control and distribution. Access to and control over oil is as important today as actually owning it, and increasingly, private oil companies are exerting critical control over the industry. In this regard, privatization has progressed rapidly during the 1990s. In virtually every region of the world, an industry that was previously considered critical to economic and physical security and that was owned by the government has been partly or wholly sold to local and foreign private investors.

A recent wave of mergers, worth over $200 billion, has further changed the face of the industry during the 1990s (28). A top echelon of "super majors" has been created that far surpasses other publicly traded oil companies by any measure of size. "The scale of the super majors puts them on a par with the largest state companies. The four super majors—ExxonMobil, Royal Dutch/Shell, BP-Amoco, and Total Fina Elf—have a preponderance in the downstream, with about 32 percent of global product sales and 19 percent of refining capacity. This counterbalances to a large extent the dominant upstream positions of the four large state oil companies, Saudi Aramco, Petroleos de Venezuela, Iran's NIOC, and Mexico's Pemex. With the super majors and the largest state oil companies, the industry is now dominated by a handful of 10 or 12 giant concerns that dwarf those immediately beneath them" (27).

The recent concentration of the industry is particularly stark among firms operating in the United States. By 2001, five corporations (ExxonMobil, BP-Amoco-Arco, Chevron-Texaco, Phillips-Tosco, and Marathon) controlled 61% of the U.S. retail gas market, 47% of the U.S. oil refinery market, and 41% of U.S. oil exploration and production. These firms currently control 15% of world oil production—more than Saudi Arabia, Yemen, and Kuwait combined (29).

This change in control over oil extraction and distribution has had significant impacts on the very countries that own oil. The economic strength of a nation directly affects its ability to negotiate with the super majors and in turn to benefit from selling or leasing oil. Poor nations that are dependent on oil sales for key revenues are often adversely affected by their ownership of the resource (30). As Ross (12) has shown, poor countries that are oil dependent often have slower rates of economic development, higher levels of corruption, higher military spending, worse performance on reducing child malnutrition and adult illiteracy, and are more vulnerable to economic shocks.

There are also clear inequities in the distribution and consumption of oil. Advanced industrialized countries use orders of magnitude more oil than many

TABLE 2 World oil net importers in 2001 (25)

Country	Net oil imports (million barrels per day)
United States	10.8
Japan	5.4
Germany	2.7
South Korea	2.1
France	2.0
Italy	1.7
China	1.6
Spain	1.5
India	1.3

developing countries. Table 2 shows that the United States is by far the largest importer and consumer of oil in the world.

The United States imports almost 11 million barrels of oil per day. Interestingly, the United States currently only imports approximately 24% of its oil from the Persian Gulf; Canada is its top source of imported oil (15%), followed by Saudi Arabia (14%), Venezuela (14%), Mexico (12%), and Nigeria (6%) (31).

The United States is also the largest refiner of oil in the world, with overall refining capacity of approximately 16.6 million barrels per day. The average capacity of U.S. refineries increased from 70,000 barrels per day in 1985 to 115,000 barrels per day in 2001 (32). However, during this period, the number of U.S. refineries actually decreased by half from 324 to 143, further concentrating control in a handful of corporations and impacts in fewer communities. Russia, Japan, and China are the only other countries with refinery capacities exceeding 3 million barrels per day. Russia's refinery capacity stands at an estimated 5.4 million barrels per day, Japan's at 4.8 million, and China's at 4.5 million (25).

IV. IMPACTS OF EXPLORATION, DRILLING, AND EXTRACTION

Oil exploration, drilling, and extraction are the first phase—or what the industry calls the "upstream" phase—in the long life cycle of oil. There are currently approximately 40,000 oil fields in the world, (33) and there have been over 4000 new oil exploration licenses granted in the past 10 years (34). Increasingly complicated and expensive processes for locating oil deposits in remote and inhospitable locations, bringing the oil to the surface, and then getting it to a market have major environmental, cultural, and health impacts (35–37).

On- and off-shore exploration, drilling, and extraction activities are inherently invasive and affect ecosystems, human health, and local cultures. Oil companies combine the use of remote sensing and satellite mapping techniques with seismic testing to identify potential oil reserves. When reserves are identified remotely, companies build roads, platforms, and pipelines, bring in crews and vehicles, and drill exploratory test wells. Once oil is discovered, exploration activities are expanded for commercial-scale extraction, which requires more wells and infrastructure. Techniques for oil extraction include a range of drilling techniques and the use of subsurface explosives (including in a few historical cases the use of nuclear charges) (38).

The physical alteration of environments from exploration, drilling, and extraction can be greater than from a large oil spill. Major impacts include deforestation, ecosystem destruction, chemical contamination of land and water, long-term harm to animal populations (particularly migratory birds and marine mammals), human health and safety risks for neighboring communities and oil industry workers, and displacement of indigenous communities.

Exploration requires moving heavy equipment (mobile rigs for temporary drilling can weigh over 2 million pounds) into remote environments. Clearing land for roads and platforms can lead to deforestation and erosion (38). Drilling during both exploration and extraction phases uses significant quantities of water, which are contaminated through drilling and then discharged along with cuttings into the environment. These discharges result in chemical contamination of land and water from petroleum waste, drilling fluids, and by-products of drilling such as water, drill cuttings, and mud. As Epstein & Selber assert, "The general environmental effects of encroachment into natural habitats and the chronic effects of drilling and generating mud and discharge water on benthic (bottom-dwelling) populations, migratory bird populations and marine mammals constitute serious environmental concerns for these ecosystems" (38).

The oil and gas industry in the United States alone creates more solid and liquid waste than all other categories of municipal, agricultural, mining, and industrial wastes combined. Oil and gas drilling and pumping produce most of the sector's waste. Approximately 20% of nonhazardous waste produced in the United States every year comes from oil and gas exploration and production. However, the majority of production waste from the industry is the hazardous and toxic effluent known as *produced water*. Produced water is extracted from the ground along with oil and is often reinjected into wells under high pressure to force more oil to the surface. Produced water not reinjected is discharged into surface waters (8). As Doyle explains, this "produced water is at least four times saltier than ocean water and often contains 'industrial strength' quantities of toxins such as benzene, xylene, toluene, and ethylbenzene. Heavy metals such as barium, arsenic, cadmium, chromium, and mercury have also been found in produced water. Produced water can also be radioactive—in some cases, as much as 100 times more radioactive than the discharge of a nuclear power plant" (8).

In 1995, it was estimated that 15 billion barrels of produced water were extracted annually in the United States. Over 90% of onshore produced water is reinjected into wells (39). Reinjection is permissible under the Resource Conservation and Recovery Act (RCRA), because Congress conditionally exempted drilling fluids, produced waters, and other wastes from crude oil production (39).

Water used in oil production can also be contaminated by chemicals used during extraction. For example, the oil industry uses millions of tons of barium, a toxic heavy metal, in drilling fluids each year. Common components of drilling fluids can solubilize the barium, creating hazardous waste, which is often discharged into the environment from leaks of reinjected materials (8).

Exploration and extraction also produce voluminous amounts of solid wastes known as *drilling wastes* and *associated wastes*. In 1995, the U.S. sector produced 146 million barrels of drilling waste and 22 million barrels of associated wastes (39). Although associated wastes constitute a relatively small proportion of total wastes, they are most likely to contain a range of chemicals and naturally occurring materials that are of concern to health and safety. Each year 58% of associated wastes in the United States are reinjected, 9% are sent to commercial facilities, and 8% are disposed of through evaporation pits (39). In oil fields, virtually every stage in production has a waste pit. As Doyle notes, during drilling, "various muds, oily fluids, lubricants, and other chemicals are used to cool the drill bit, stabilize the walls of the bore hole, or liquefy earthen cuttings. These fluids and additives accumulate in large quantities during the drilling process, and are often stored or finally disposed in waste pits" (8). Exposed waste pits pose a danger not only to aquifers but also to animals and birds that mistake the pits for water holes and become coated with toxic wastes (8).

In addition to operational leaks, oil spills also occur during extraction. In 2002, the National Academy of Sciences estimated that 38,000 tons of petroleum hydrocarbons were released into the world's oceans each year during the 1990s as a result of oil and gas operations (40). On- and offshore oil production can also create significant air pollution. Emissions from drilling equipment, hydrocarbons escaping from wells, flaring of natural gas, and emissions from support vehicles can degrade local air quality (41).

Oil exploration, drilling, and extraction can also lead to a range of acute and chronic health impacts. These risks occur through exposure to naturally occurring radioactive materials brought to the surface during drilling, as well as through the bioaccumulation of oil, mercury, and other products in mammals and fish that humans consume (38). Noise, vibration, and exposure to toxic chemicals are also issues in upstream and downstream operations. Many of the substances used in daily extraction work cause adverse dermatologic and pulmonary reactions among workers. The most common dermatologic conditions are contact dermatitis and acne, but other conditions include keratotic facial and neck lesions, neoplastic change from exposure to oil and sunlight, and acquired perforating disease and calcinosis of the hands and fingers. Adverse pulmonary reactions to hard metal (a mixture of tungsten carbide and cobalt used for oil well drilling bits) include asthma, hypersensitivity pneumonitis, and interstitial pulmonary fibrosis (38).

The risk of explosions, injuries, and fatalities during exploration and extraction are also cause for concern. Virtually every segment of oil and gas production involves risk of fires and explosions, particularly offshore drilling operations that are vulnerable to blowouts. The handling of heavy pipes and other equipment also creates safety risks. Thus, oil workers around the world face significant occupational hazards. Oil exploration and drilling is the most dangerous sector of the oil industry. Recently, the oil and gas sector has experienced a series of major fires and explosions in both extraction installations and refineries. For example, in 1998 in Africa and the Middle East, there were 54 fatal incidents in onshore operations and 17 fatal incidents offshore (6).

Oil exploration often occurs in remote and harsh environments, such as deserts, jungles, the Arctic, and far offshore. Workers live in or near these harsh workplaces for long periods. These working conditions can create additional risk during transport, and stress from long shifts and social isolation.

There are no good international data or comprehensive analyses of the distribution of impacts from oil exploration, drilling, and extraction. However, a number of recent studies have shown that current oil exploration has a disproportionate impact on indigenous populations and sensitive, remote ecosystems (42). Kretzmann & Wright, for instance, report that indigenous groups in 6 continents and 39 countries "face an immediate to medium-term threat from new oil and gas exploration" (42). In the western Amazon alone, at least 50 indigenous groups, many of which are the world's last isolated indigenous peoples, live within oil and gas concessions that are under exploration or preproduction. These groups include the Tagaeri and Huaorani of Ecuador; the Mascho-Piro, Nahua, and Kugapakori of Peru; and the Nukak and U'Wa of Columbia. Beyond the Amazon, oil exploration, drilling, and extraction affect the Baka, Bakoli, and Ogoni of Central Africa; the Tavoyans, Mon, and Karen of Burma; the Eastern Khanty peoples of Western Siberia; and the Gwich'in of Alaska (42).

Oil production activities not only disrupt sensitive environments, but threaten the survival of indigenous populations that live in these ecosystems. Kretzmann & Wright argue that "territorial integrity and control are necessary for the cultural reproduction and ultimately the survival of Amazonian indigenous populations whose way of life and well being are closely tied to a thriving rainforest" (43). Throughout the Amazon basin, road building causes deforestation, which contributes to the loss of territory and displacement of native groups. The opening of access roads allows settlers with competing interests such as logging and mining to enter indigenous communities and colonize the areas (43). This colonization can also bring infectious diseases to previously unexposed native populations (38).

The contentious nature of these interactions can often lead to conflict over oil resources and infrastructure. At least four types of conflicts occur over oil: (a) conflict with indigenous groups over oil development; (b) civil unrest or war that uses disruption of oil operations as a tactic; (c) superpower geopolitics (e.g., control over Middle East oil reserves); and (d) terrorism targeting oil facilities. Table 3 summarizes examples of just one type of conflict, incursions into indigenous lands to control oil. Though by no means comprehensive, this table demonstrates the widespread impacts of oil development on indigenous peoples.

TABLE 3 Incursions into indigenous lands to control oil (44–46)

Location	Indigenous group	Companies and agencies involved
Alaska	Gwichin	BP Amoco
		ExxonMobil
		Chevron
		Phillips Petroleum
Australia	Aboriginal	Dept. of Mineral and Petroleum Resources
Bolivia	Chiquitano	Andean Development Corporation
	Ayoreo	British Gas
	Guaraní	Enron
	Weenhayek	Gas TransBoliviano SA
		Inter-American Development Bank
		Pan-American Energy
		Petrobras
		Repsol YPF
		Shell
		Transredes
		United States Overseas Private Investment Corporation
		World Bank
Brazil	Apurina	Brazilian National Development Bank
	Paumari	El Paso Energy
	Deni	GasPetro (Petrobras)
	Juma	Halliburton
Burma	Karen	Unocal
		Total Fina Elf
Colombia	Uwa	British Petroleum
		Occidental
		Shell
		AirScan
		Ecopetrol
Ecuador	Sarayacu Kichwa	Agip Oil
	Shuar	Alberta Energy
	Achuar	Burlington Resources
	Huaorani	ChevronTexaco
		Kerr McGee
		Occidental Petroleum
		Repsol-YPF
		Westdeutsche Landesbank
Indonesia	Aceh	Exxon
Nigeria	Ogoni	Shell
	Ijaw	Nigerian National Petroleum Company
Peru	Kirineri	Hunt Oil
	Nahua	Inter-American Development Bank
	Nanti	Shell
		United States Export-Import Bank

Migration of oil crews to new reserves also creates socioeconomic and human rights concerns, especially in the Middle East and other regions of the developing world, because poor and lower class populations move both by choice or are motivated (sometimes forcibly) to relocate to oil development centers. In Saudi Arabia, for example, 35% of the population is composed of immigrant workers. In addition, foreign workers account for 61% of the total workforce of Oman, 83% in Kuwait, and 91% in the United Arab Emirates (47).

This supply of cheap foreign labor, primarily from South Asia, is essential to the profitability of oil production in the Middle East. Countries, such as India, Pakistan, Nigeria, Egypt, Sudan, Bangladesh, Sri Lanka, Thailand, Indonesia, and the Philippines, provide both skilled and unskilled labor to the Middle East. In several Persian Gulf states, these temporary immigrant workers outnumber citizens by a factor of two to one or even three to one. Their presence in the region underscores the wealth disparity between those who bear the costs and those who benefit from oil production. Although the ruling classes in these kingdoms are among the richest people in the world, much of the citizenry does not benefit from the significant profits earned by the industry (48).

Even the most basic workplace rights and health and safety protections are abridged in some of the largest oil-producing countries. In Saudi Arabia, labor laws prohibit the right of workers to organize unions or bargain collectively and grant employers extensive control over foreign workers' movement. Human Rights Watch reports that many foreign workers suffer under oppressive working conditions and are denied legitimate claims to wages, benefits, and compensation (49).

V. IMPACTS OF OIL TRANSPORT

The current separation between the location of oil reserves and the location of oil consumption necessitates that crude oil be transported great distances to refineries and consumer markets. This has led to the development of increasingly complex transportation systems that allow oil to be delivered virtually anywhere in the world. Major oil routes now stretch from the Middle East to Japan, from South America to Europe, and from Africa to the United States. Transport of oil occurs via supertankers, barges, trucks, and pipelines. Oil tankers are currently the primary means of transportation, but oil is increasingly being transferred through pipelines. Today, oil makes up over half of the annual tonnage of all sea cargoes, and there are now more miles of oil pipelines in the world than railroads (50).

Transportation of oil results in regular oil spills throughout the world. Although large oil spills are well publicized, smaller but cumulatively significant spills from shipping, pipelines, and leaks often go undocumented. As Doyle explains, "oil transport—by pipelines, railcar, or truck—generates an unknown and untabulated amount of waste, including tank bottom sludges, contaminated water from storage tanks, oil/water separator sludge, solvent degreasers, used oil, contaminated product, product that does not meet specifications, lubricants, spent antifreeze, and clay filtration elements" (8).

Accidents occur along all segments of the transport system and at each point of transfer. Since the 1960s, large-scale oil spills have occurred almost every year. Transport by water is currently more likely to result in a spill than transport by pipeline. Ocean transport of crude oil and petroleum products accounted for 3000 gallons spilled per billion ton-miles in 1983 and nearly 8000 gallons per billion ton-miles in 1984. Pipeline spills contributed less than 100 gallons per billion ton-miles for both years (41).

In the past 20 years, there have been over 30 oil spills of 10 million gallons or more each. One to three spills of this size occur each year (50). In fact, a few very large spills are responsible for a high percentage of oil spilled annually. From 1990 to 1999 there were 346 spills over 7 tons, which totaled approximately 1.1 million tons, but 830,000 tons (75%) were spilled in just 10 incidents (just over 1% of incidents). Annual figures, therefore, can vary greatly depending on the number of large spills. For example, in 1999, 29,000 tons were spilled, but in 2001 only 8000 tons were spilled (51).

A key to the size of spills has been the trend in tanker construction toward massive ships. In the 1930s, large tankers carried about 20,000 tons of oil. By the early 1970s, tankers could carry 800,000 tons of oil. This increase in size (some tankers are over three football fields long) also increases the likelihood of accidents because supertankers are harder to maneuver (50). Table 4 highlights the largest oil spills on record.

To provide some perspective, the *Exxon-Valdez* spill, which released 12 million gallons of oil (53), was the largest U.S. spill recorded to date, but only the 28th largest oil spill in world history (38). The *Prestige* oil tanker that split in half off

TABLE 4 Ten largest oil spills in history ranked by volume (52)

Rank	Name	Year	Volume in gallons
1	Persian Gulf: tankers, pipelines and terminals, offshore Saudi Arabia	1991	240,000,000
2	Ixtoc I oil well, Ciudad del Carmen, Mexico	1979–1980	140,000,000
3	Nowruz Field, Persian Gulf	1983	80,000,000
3	Fergana oil well, Uzbekistan	1992	80,000,000
5	*Castillo de Bellver* tanker, offshore Cape Town, South Africa	1983	78,500,000
6	*Amoco Cadiz* tanker, offshore Brittany	1978	68,670,000
7	*Aegean Captain* tanker, offshore Tobago	1979	48,800,000
8	Production well D-103, Tripoli, Libya	1980	42,000,000
9	*Irenes Serenade* tanker, Pilos, Greece	1980	36,600,000
10	Kuwait storage tanks	1981	31,170,000

TABLE 5 Hot spots for tanker oil spills since 1960 (55)

Location of hot spot	Number of spills
Gulf of Mexico	267
Northeastern United States	140
Mediterranean Sea	127
Persian Gulf	108
North Sea	75
Japan	60
Baltic Sea	52
United Kingdom and English Channel	49
Malaysia and Singapore	39
West Coast of France/North and West Coasts of Spain	33
Korea	32

the coast of Spain in 2002, causing major ecological and economic damage, was carrying approximately 22 million gallons of oil.

Oil spills occur literally all around the world. The Oil Spill Intelligence Report has documented spills of at least 10,000 gallons in the waters of 112 nations since 1960. However, they also note that spills occur more frequently in certain areas (54). Table 5 shows a number of "hot spots" for oil spills from tankers.

In recent years there has been a steady increase in number of small spills while large-scale spills have stayed relatively constant. The cumulative impact of small spills of less than 100,000 gallons adds up to about 10 million gallons per year worldwide (50). Table 6 shows that the greatest quantity of oil from marine transport is actually released in the form of bilge and fuel oil. In fact, emissions of

TABLE 6 Sources of oil spills from marine transport, 1990 (56)

Emission source	Tons per year
Bilge and fuel oil	250,000
Tanker operations	160,000
Tanker accidents	110,000
Nontanker accidents	10,000
Marine terminal operations	30,000
Dry-docking and scrapping of ships	10,000
Total	570,000

bilge and fuel oil are equivalent to approximately five *Exxon-Valdez* spills per year. For many years, it has been common practice to dump oil-contaminated ballast water and tank washings directly into the sea. So while most of the large-scale spills result from grounded tankers or tanker collisions, the cumulative contamination from numerous relatively small accidents, leaks, and intentional discharges can actually surpass that of large spills from shipping (38).

Pipelines, which are highly prone to corrosion, are also a source of spills, leaks, and fires. Many pipelines are used long after their engineering life span (an estimated 15 years) (38). Using the U.S. Office of Pipeline Safety database, Nesmith & Haurwitz have estimated that 67 million gallons of crude oil, gasoline, and other petroleum products leaked from U.S. pipelines in the last decade. However, "there is consensus—among the industry, its regulators and its critics—that the database underrepresents the quantity of oil products that escapes from pipelines." The actual amount of leakage is potentially twice as high as the annual reported average (57). Even the U.S. government, in the National Energy Policy, acknowledges that inland oil spills are a major source of oil emissions and that these spills appear to be on the rise. As they report, "the federal government receives many more inland oil spill notifications (9,000 notifications a year in the early 1990s versus 10,000 to 12,000 a year in the late 1990s)" (2).

The main impacts of vessel oil spills obviously fall on marine ecosystems and coastal communities. A number of factors influence the scale of these impacts, including the size of the spill, the kind of oil, the season of the spill, and the vulnerability of local plants and animals (40). The spill size often determines the area affected, whether it reaches the shore, and how much of the shore it covers. The extent of contamination also depend on the nature of the coastal ecosystems and the types of birds and mammals affected (58). Some ecosystems, such as mangroves, salt marshes, coral reefs, and polar bear habitats, are particularly sensitive to oil spills and can take years to recover (59).

Oil spills also threaten human health through illness and injury during the spill, during cleanup, and through consumption of contaminated fish or shellfish. Drinking water supplies can also be contaminated through spills (50). But as Burger notes, "There are remarkably few studies of the health responses of local people exposed in the months following a spill" (50). In one study in Scotland following an oil spill, community members reported increased health problems, including increased psychiatric symptoms (50).

Oil spills can also have long-lasting economic consequences by damaging fisheries, excluding fisherfolk from fishing grounds, fouling fishing gear, and reducing fish stocks in succeeding years (50). Commercial fisheries can also be negatively impacted by the simple perception of tainted fish. Public concern about eating fish exposed to oil spills can damage the market for fish from an affected region. Even a few oiled fish can taint an entire region's catch. In the case of the *Exxon Valdez* oil spill in Alaska, closing the fisheries in Prince William Sound resulted in a season's loss of income for commercial fishermen and an estimated $135 million in lost revenues (50).

Subsistence communities are often even more severely harmed by oil spills. Unfortunately, there is no global database on impacts of oil releases on indigenous communities or sensitive ecosystems. Recent cases, however, highlight troubling impacts. The *Exxon Valdez* oil slick covered shorelines used by the Chugach people of Alaska for subsistence hunting, fishing, and gathering. Fifteen Aleut communities in Prince William Sound and the Gulf of Alaska were affected by the oil spill. Subsistence harvests came to a virtual halt after the oil spill. Communities decreased their harvests between 14% and 77% depending on whether they had access to oil-free upland species. One community on Chenaga Bay on the Prince William Sound reduced its harvest from 342 to 148 pounds per person per year. Another community in English Bay on the Kenai Peninsula reduced consumption from 289 to 141 pounds per person per year. The variety of species harvested also declined from 23 to 12 (50).

Oil pipelines have also caused disproportionate impacts on low-income and minority communities in the United States and been connected to human rights violations around the world. In the United States for example, the Pacific Pipeline, a project constructed by a consortium of Chevron, Unocal, and Texaco in the late 1990s, faced a lawsuit from the City of Los Angeles that alleged their routing of the pipeline constituted an environmental injustice. Pacific Pipeline is a 132-mile long heavy crude pipeline that transports 130,000 barrels per day of oil from Bakersfield, California, through the heart of Los Angeles, into the refinery district on the Pacific Coast (60). In transit through the City of Los Angeles, it bisects 75 neighborhoods. Analysis conducted by Impact Assessment Inc. for the City of Los Angeles demonstrated that 74 of the 75 communities had minority populations higher than the national average; 72 of the 75 had minority populations higher than the California average; 42 of the 75 had minority populations over 90% of the total tract population; all of the tracts had a higher percentage of non-English speakers than the national average; and 62 of 75 had per capita income lower than the national, state, county, and city levels (61).

Construction of oil pipelines in developing countries has also been associated with human rights abuses. The current debate regarding the construction of the Chad-Cameroon Pipeline highlights the potential for corruption and violations of human rights in such projects. The project, sponsored by an international consortium lead by ExxonMobil and ChevronTexaco involves the development of the Doba oil fields in southern Chad and the construction of a 1070-kilometer pipeline to an offshore oil-loading facility on Cameroon's Atlantic coast. Advocacy groups such as Rainforest Action Network (RAN) have raised concerns about increasing violence and human rights abuses, corruption, and devastation of the Bakola (or Pygmie) peoples who live along the pipeline. RAN notes that "both the US State Department and Amnesty International have documented serious human rights abuses by Chad and Cameroon governments, including extrajudicial killings, torture, abuse, rape, limiting freedom of the press and arresting opposition politicians and other civilians. Many believe that there has already been an increase in violence and human rights abuses in Chad as a result of the pipeline project" (62).

VI. IMPACTS OF OIL REFINING

Oil in its crude form has limited uses. It must be separated, converted, and refined into useful products such as gasoline, heating oil, jet fuel, and petrochemical feedstock. The basic oil refining process involves thermal "cracking" which applies both pressure and intense heat to crude oil in order to physically break large molecules into smaller ones to produce gasoline and distillate fuels. Any crude-oil constituents that are not converted into useful products during this process, or captured by pollution-control technologies, are released to the environment (63). Refineries produce huge volumes of air, water, solid, and hazardous waste, including toxic substances such as benzene, heavy metals, hydrogen sulfide, acid gases, mercury, and dioxin (64).

There is no single source of data on global refinery emissions or impacts. However, U.S. refinery emissions are reported by the Environmental Protection Agency (EPA) through the Sector Facility Indexing Project (SFIP) and the Toxic Release Inventory (TRI). Several independent studies have also examined refinery emissions in the United States (63, 65, 66). In the 1990s, the U.S. EPA targeted oil refineries as their top enforcement priority (64). According to the EPA, in 1999, 54% of refineries were in "significant non-compliance" (meaning they have committed persistent, serious violations) of the Clean Air Act; 22% were in significant noncompliance with the Clean Water Act; and 32% violated the Resource Recovery and Conservation Act (67).

The Emergency Planning and Community Right-to-Know Act of 1986 requires that manufacturing facilities above a certain size provide information about toxic chemical releases and offsite waste transfers to the national TRI. The oil refining sector, but not exploration or extraction, is required to report to the TRI. Each refining facility in the United States must report annual emissions of roughly 600 listed chemicals. Unfortunately, as Epstein et al. note, "Of the hundreds of toxic chemicals in crude oil and refinery products, only a few are typically reported to TRI. Many of those not included have similar structural, physical, and toxicological properties to those that are reported.... According to the Amoco Yorktown study, this refinery's TRI report forms cover only 9% of the total hydrocarbons released" (63).

Local environmental impacts from oil refineries result from toxic air and water emissions, accidental releases of chemicals, hazardous waste disposal, thermal pollution, and noise pollution. Analysis of the TRI data reveals that the petroleum refining industry releases 75% of its toxic emissions to the air, 24% to the water (including 20% to underground injection and 4% to surface waters), and 1% to the land (39). The primary hazardous air pollutants released by the industry are benzene, toluene, ethyl benzene, mixed xylenes, and n-heptane (39). The accumulation of refinery air emissions such as hydrocarbons, sulfur dioxide, and particulates in the atmosphere also contributes to acid rain (38). U.S. refineries are the second largest industrial source of sulfur dioxide, the third largest industrial source of nitrogen oxides, and the largest U.S. stationary source of volatile organic compounds (VOC) emissions, producing more than twice as many VOCs as the next sector, organic chemical plants. Refineries are also the fourth largest source of toxic air pollutants (65). Paul Templet, former head of the Louisiana Department of Environmental Quality and professor at Louisiana State University's Institute for Environmental Studies, has measured jobs and tax subsidies per pound of pollutants emitted and shown that petroleum refining produces 1048 pounds of pollution per job, as compared to 460 pounds of pollution per job for paper manufacturing, 222 pounds for plastics manufacturing, 61 pounds for tobacco production, and 28 pounds for food production (68).

The majority of refinery emissions actually occur through leaks rather than through regulated smokestacks or effluent pipes. In 1999, Congressman Henry A. Waxman commissioned an investigation into fugitive emissions from oil refineries by the minority staff of the House of Representatives Government Reform Committee. The study found that oil refineries significantly underreport leaks from valves to regulators and that these fugitive emissions add millions of pounds of pollutants to the atmosphere each year, including 80 million pounds of VOCs and 15 million pounds of toxic pollutants (65). Production pressures in the oil industry are such that it is more economical to allow fugitive emissions and to lose some oil than to close down leaky facilities for repair (8).

An EPA study of the Amoco oil refinery in Yorktown, Virginia, demonstrated that the cumulative effects of refinery leaks can lead to major impacts. Although only 0.3% by weight of crude oil by-products from the Amoco refinery was released into the environment, this led to over 11,000 gallons of oil components released (66). Because the oil refining industry in the United States processes more than 16 million barrels of crude oil each day, approximately 50,000 barrels of byproduct likely are released per day.

Refineries also use thousands of gallons of water per day for production and cooling processes. Treatment of liquid effluent does not entirely eliminate contaminants such as aromatic hydrocarbons (benzenes and napthenes) that enter waterways utilized by humans, fish, and wildlife (38). For example, one recent study of water pollution from oil refineries found significant levels of aromatic hydrocarbons that contributed to important differences in the diversity and abundance of fish between stations located up- and downstream from refineries (38). Thermal pollution from the release of refinery effluent, which is warmer than surrounding waters also disrupts marine ecosystems.

The operation of refineries results in fires, explosions, and chemical spills. In California, for example, refineries are responsible for over 90% of all accidental releases in the state. Hazardous-waste disposal from refinery facilities also threatens nearby communities. According to the EPA, oil refining is one of the top hazardous waste producing industries: "Disposal methods for toxic refinery wastes have tended to take advantage of wide open spaces instead of environmentally sound waste management techniques" (8). In fact, approximately two thirds of solid wastes from U.S. refineries are disposed of through burial in onsite reserve pits (39).

Wastes from oil refineries can create health risks to facility workers and surrounding communities. Workers are at risk of accidents involving fires, explosions, and chemical leaks and spills. Health hazards include exposure to heat, polluted air, noise, and hazardous materials, including asphalt, asbestos, aromatic hydrocarbons, arsenic, hexavalent chromium, nickel, carbon monoxide, coke dust, hydrogen sulfide, lead alkyls, natural gases, petroleum, phenol, and silica. Epstein & Selber (38) report a number of health impacts from exposure to these materials; these include the following:

1. severe burns or skin and eye irritation from high levels of benzene and hydrogen sulfide fumes, which may lead to dermatitis, bronchitis, and chemically induced pneumonia;

2. headaches and mental disturbances from carbon-monoxide exposures;

3. chronic lung disease from long-term exposures to coke dust, silica, and hydrogen sulfide;

4. psychosis and peripheral neuropathies from exposures to lead alkyls used as gasoline additives; and

5. increased cancer risks from exposures to carcinogenic materials such as benzene, xylene, arsenic, and hexavalent chromium.

Management of refineries and their impacts are also increasingly being outsourced to service companies. Conoco and ExxonMobil, for example, have contracted Philip Services to operate and maintain oil refineries, which minimizes the actual owners' liability and keeps contract employees' wages low. Contract workers are usually nonunion and often poorly trained; this results in more accidents and more risk to workers and surrounding communities.

Philip Services also operates landfills and other treatment, storage, and disposal (TSD) facilities for the oil industry and has disposed of waste materials at more than 200 third-party disposal facilities. Many of these sites have been declared superfund sites, although Philip's liability for cleanup of these sites is unknown. Even tracking Philip's current pollution record is difficult, given the loopholes in disclosure for TSD operations and as Philip has dozens of subsidiaries. In fact, in June 1999, Philip declared Chapter 11 reorganization.

Health impacts extend outside the walls of refineries, where studies have demonstrated the relationship between proximity of communities to refineries and cancer. For example, a 1994 analysis of 264 childhood leukemia clusters in the United Kingdom showed relative, nonrandom proximities to oil refineries (38). A similar study of all 22,458 children aged 0–15 years dying from leukemia or cancer in England, Wales, and Scotland between 1953 and 1980 found increased incidence of leukemia and other cancers near industrial facilities, particularly oil refineries, oil storage facilities, and railside oil distribution terminals (38).

A 1995 report by the Environmental Defense Fund, which used 1992 TRI data on the refining industry, developed a ranking of refineries throughout the United States. The study compared the pollution produced per barrel refined at each facility. Through this comparative analysis, it showed wide variation in emissions (and thus impacts) from facilities on local environments and human health. The report identified West Virginia, Kansas, Texas, Mississippi, and Wisconsin as the five worst states in terms of emissions per pound of product. Nevada, Georgia, New York, Alaska, and New Jersey were ranked as the five most efficient states (63).

The EPA SFIP brings together similar types of comparative environmental performance data on refineries. The SFIP reports production levels, compliance and inspection data, chemical releases and spills, and, interestingly, demographics of the surrounding population. By combining TRI data with inspection reports and demographic data, the SFIP is a unique resource for evaluating the distribution of impacts from oil refineries. These data show for instance that 56% of people living within three miles of refineries in the United States are minorities—almost double the national average.

Anecdotal evidence from areas surrounding particularly polluting refineries seems to confirm that low-income and communities of color are disproportionately affected by these facilities. For instance, predominantly African-American communities in Louisiana report long-term exposures to toxics and general disregard for health impacts from refineries located in the so-called Cancer Alley region along the Mississippi River. The residents of Saint Charles Parish in Louisiana provide graphic examples of these problems. At just one refinery, the Shell Norco facility, there have been repeated explosions that have claimed workers' and community members' lives, including a boy mowing a lawn and an older woman sleeping inside her house (personal interview with M. Richards member of Concerned Citizens of Norco, February 28, 2001). An explosion of a catalytic cracker at the refinery in 1988 resulted in the death of seven workers and the destruction of millions of dollars in property (69). In addition to these major events, numerous episodes of leaks, fires, tank car derailments, flares, and other problems have plagued the community. An entire website, funded by the Sierra Club Legal Defense Fund, has been established to track incidents of flaring in Norco (70).

Oil refining also has major impacts on poor communities in developing countries. In his recent book *Riding the Dragon* (71), Doyle documents environmental injustices observed at Shell's South African Petroleum Refinery (SAPREF) in Durban. Doyle's inventory of pollution concerns and major accidents at this one facility is staggering: underreporting of as much as 10 million pounds of sulfur dioxide per year; massive unreported oil leaks; explosions and fires releasing tons of hydrogen fluoride. More specific reports in 2001 include two fires, a chemical solvent spill, and a fuel spill all in January; a March leak of 25 tons of tetra-ethyl lead; a July underground pipeline leak of 1,000,000 liters of gas into the ground; a June failure of a refinery flare resulting in the release of unburned gases, including substantial amounts of hydrogen sulfide; a mid-August failure of the asphalt plant at the refinery; a September, marine fuel oil pipeline leak and about ten days later, another flare failure; and an October spill of 2000 liters of oil into Durban Harbor during a ship refueling operation.

Community organizing and monitoring in response to these events has led to documentation of emissions, contamination levels, and disease incidence in neighborhoods adjoining the SAPREF refinery. Residents have documented "very high benzene levels in the air—levels 30 times those permitted in the US.... In Durban, leukemia rates are 24 times the South African national average. Respiratory problems there are four times the national average" (71). Residents report ongoing acute health effects such as coughing, burning eyes, headache, dizziness, and nausea. They also complain about cases of severe asthma in the community, as well as cases of rare immune diseases, such as teenage lupus erythematosus and childhood kidney cancer.

Unfortunately, here again, no national or international agencies currently collect or publish data on community health impacts from oil activities. Data on mortalities from oil accidents are collected by different agencies depending on whether a worker or community member is killed and whether the accident is caused by a pipeline explosion, a refinery accident, or a tanker. The best data currently available, and even these are limited, cover workplace injuries and deaths in oil production and refining (72, 73). However, virtually no data are available on chronic health impacts among communities living close to refineries.

VII. IMPACTS OF OIL CONSUMPTION

The combustion of petroleum products contributes to numerous environmental impacts including air pollution, water pollution from gasoline and gasoline additives, and global warming. All three of these problems often disproportionately affect low-income, minority populations and developing nations.

Gasoline is composed of hydrocarbons, which as we have noted, include a number of carcinogenic compounds. In addition, substances, such as alkyl lead, oxygenates, and additional aromatic hydrocarbons (which include benzene, xylene, and toluene) are added to gasoline to improve its performance during combustion. The acute and chronic health effects from exposure to gasoline and its additives have been documented and include cancer, central nervous system toxicity, and poisoning from additives. These impacts tend to be concentrated particularly among lower-income populations that live closer to service stations, refineries, and transfer or storage facilities (38).

The combustion of oil results in six primary air pollutants: VOCs, oxides of nitrogen (which combine with VOCs to produce low-level ozone), carbon monoxide, particulate matter, oxides of sulfur, and lead. Although gasoline in the United States is now required to be unleaded, lead emissions from combustion of gasoline in the developing world are still common.

The International Center for Technology Assessment has quantified the externalized costs of using internal combustion engines with gasoline. According to their calculations, the unquantified environmental, health, and social costs of gasoline usage in the United States total between $231.7 and $942.9 billion per year. The cost of damage from automobile fumes is estimated to be between $39 and $600 billion per year. The estimate of the annual uncompensated health costs associated with auto emissions is $29.3 to $542.4 billion, which may be low given that auto pollution has been conclusively linked to increased health problems and mortality (74).

The environmental and health impacts of air pollution from gasoline combustion tend to occur disproportionately among low-income communities, communities of color, and poorer populations in developing nations. For example, although leaded gasoline is banned in the United States, its use is still widespread throughout the developing world where residents living in congested, high-traffic areas are exposed to lead emissions. In the United States, diesel emissions pose a similar risk to inner-city populations that face the highest level of exposure to diesel exhaust emissions from buses and trucks. Furthermore, "within cities, the highest density of buses and bus stations are found in the poorest neighborhoods, and poverty, race, and asthma rates are positively correlated" (38).

A study by Gotlieb et al. further demonstrates that asthma morbidity and mortality disproportionately impact minority populations, pointing out that in the early to mid-1980s the asthma mortality rate among black residents of the United States, aged 5 to 34 years, was three to five times as great as the rate among whites. This study, which was conducted in 1992, concluded that the asthma hospitalization rate in Boston was positively correlated with poverty rates and percentages of nonwhite residents and inversely correlated with income and educational levels. The asthma rate varied significantly within the city, from a low of 0.7/1000 persons in the Kenmore Square area to a high of 9.8/1000 in Roxbury (75).

It is now widely believed that human activities, primarily the burning of fossil fuels, are modifying natural atmospheric processes and contributing to global warming. Approximately three quarters of the anthropogenic emissions of carbon dioxide to the atmosphere have come from the combustion of fossil fuel (76). The Intergovernmental Panel on Climate Change has forecast major changes in ecological systems (and agricultural systems) and particularly stark impacts in some of the poorest countries in the world.

The United Nations Environment Program (UNEP) has also warned that the populations most vulnerable to climate changes are the landless, poor, and isolated. UNEP explains that "poor terms of trade, weak infrastructure, lack of access to technology and information, and armed conflict will make it more difficult for these people to cope with the agricultural consequences of climate change. Many of the world's poorest areas, dependent on isolated agricultural systems in semi-arid and arid regions, face the greatest risk. Many of these at-risk populations live in sub-Saharan Africa; South, East and Southeast Asia; tropical areas of Latin America; and some Pacific island nations" (77). It is also anticipated that low-lying islands may become totally uninhabitable, and entire populations will become environmental refugees (78). As some advocacy groups have argued, "On a global scale, climate change is likely to be the biggest environmental justice issue ever. The reason is simple: the poor are most vulnerable to the effects of climate change" (78).

The impacts of changes in global climatic patterns have already been witnessed throughout the developing world. Examples of devastating episodes include

Hurricane Mitch in Central America in 1998, which killed over 10,000 and created hundreds of thousands of environmental refugees; flooding in Bangladesh in 1998 that affected millions of people in one of the poorest nations on Earth; severe storms and flooding in Venezuela in 1999 that killed an estimated 20,000 and left 150,000 homeless; and extensive floods in Mozambique in 2000 and 2001 (38, 78).

VIII. REGULATING THE OIL INDUSTRY

The oil industry is regulated at each stage of its life cycle through a patchwork of environmental, health, and safety laws. The current U.S. administration and the oil industry itself have argued that the industry is actually "over-regulated" (1, 79). Environmental advocacy groups argue, conversely, that while the industry is subject to many formal regulations, the implementation of these regulations is often inadequate, particularly in poor communities and developing countries (8).

As each nation has its own regulations, it is not possible here to summarize global oil regulation. Instead, we focus on the regulatory framework of the United States and look in particular at the effectiveness of these regulations and their implementation.

The U.S. oil industry is regulated under a dispersed, fragmented, and sometimes overlapping set of statutes (39), which include the Federal Land Policy and Management Act; the Federal Oil and Gas Leasing Reform Act; the Outer Continental Shelf Lands Act; the National Environmental Policy Act; the Oil Pollution Act; the Clean Air Act's National Emission Standards for Hazardous Air Pollutants, National Ambient Air Quality Standards, New Source Review (NSR), and New Source Performance Standards; the Clean Water Act's National Pollutant Discharge Elimination System and Spill Prevention Control and Countermeasure Requirements; the Emergency Planning and Community Right-to-Know Act; and the Underground Injection Control program of the Safe Drinking Water Act.

Several states have also implemented local environmental standards for oil extraction and refining, which, in general, are stricter than federal standards. California, for instance, has implemented regulations for reformulated gasoline that are stricter than the Clean Air Act; an Air Quality Maintenance Plan which seeks to reduce emissions from stationary sources such as refineries; and comprehensive leak identification, maintenance, and inspection programs (80).

Both the production processes and the products of oil refining are regulated for their impacts. The formulation and composition of fuels is thus regulated to prevent environmental and health impacts (81). U.S. fuel regulation programs include the Oxygenated Fuels Program, the Highway Diesel Fuel Program, the Reformulated Fuels Program, and the Leaded Gasoline Removal Program.

Workplace hazards from oil production and refining are regulated by the Occupational Safety and Health Administration (OSHA). OSHA regulates occupational exposures to chemicals such as benzene, a common emission in petroleum refineries. OSHA has also developed safety management rules requiring refineries to conduct detailed reviews of their processes to determine workplace risk and injury potentials to workers (81).

Not withstanding this long list of statutes and agencies, the oil industry also benefits from a number of exemptions, or what their critics call loopholes, from federal environmental laws. A coalition of community groups in the United States recently complained that "despite a broad patchwork of regulations on refining operations, numerous loopholes allow refinery operators to skirt the law and operate their plants in a manner dangerous to public health" (82).

For instance, there is a "petroleum exclusion" exemption under the Comprehensive Environmental Response, Compensation, and Liability Act (81). Petroleum and the toxic components of crude oil, such as benzene, are exempted from classification as hazardous substances unless the concentration of these substances is increased by contamination or by addition after refining (39). The oil extraction industry is exempted from reporting toxic chemical releases to the TRI (39). Under the 1980 Amendments to the RCRA, Congress conditionally exempted drilling fluids, produced waters, and other wastes associated with exploration, development, or production (39). Oil exploration and production activities in offshore waters of Texas, Louisiana, Mississippi, and Alabama are exempt from Clean Air Act standards (39). Oil stripper wells are exempt from the Clean Water Act's standards. Crude oil gathering pipelines under six inches in diameter are exempt from the Hazardous Liquid Pipeline Safety Act. Oil barges are exempt from double hull requirements of the Oil Pollution Act (39).

The Bush Administration also recently loosened a major regulatory burden on oil refineries by rescinding "new source review" requirements when refineries upgrade technology or expand their capacity (83). By eliminating this regulatory requirement, oil refineries can now significantly expand capacity without applying for new permits or undergoing additional evaluations of Clean Air Act compliance. Environmental groups have criticized this change, arguing that the initiative "will allow virtually all pollution increases from old, high-polluting sources to go unregulated and public participation to be excluded" (84).

Another exemption in U.S. regulation relates to grandfathering of old refineries. Grandfathered plants, those built before environmental laws came into force, can operate without meeting current federal emissions standards (64). Accidental releases, upsets, and flaring, which the Waxman report documented, occur quite frequently at oil refineries; these allow significant emissions to go unregulated during nonpermitted events (64, 65). For example, the EPA has reported incidents of sulfur-dioxide releases through flaring in a single day that exceed annual permitted releases (65).

As we have noted, the EPA itself reports significant levels of noncompliance of the industry with air regulations, water standards, and solid waste regulations (85). But EPA enforcement resources have recently been cut back, thereby reducing the EPA's ability to police this noncompliance. The EPA's top enforcement officer recently resigned in frustration over the agency's reduction in inspections and fines. In an unusual public critique, he lamented, "We don't have an EPA anymore. We just have the White House and the energy lobby" (86).

Oil pipeline regulation is also limited in a number of regards. The U.S. government relies on an underfunded, understaffed agency, the Office of Pipeline Safety, to monitor over 2 million miles of oil and gas pipelines (enough to reach around the Earth 88 times). The agency has only 55 inspectors, and it rarely imposes fines for leaks, explosions, or even worker deaths. As Jim Hall, the former chairman of the National Transportation Safety Board, stated, "there is almost an absence of regulation" for oil pipelines (57).

The Office of Pipeline Safety reported annual leaks of approximately 6.7 million gallons of oil and gas per year during the 1990s, the equivalent of over one *Exxon Valdez* spill every two years. There were also 23 reported fatalities from pipeline accidents during the 1990s, which included several children (87). Because federal inspectors cannot monitor all 2.2 million miles of pipeline, the government asks industry to self-report pipeline problems. Unfortunately, industry metering systems are not accurate enough to detect most leaks or spills. This has led to the operation of leaking pipelines, unreported spills, and an increase in spills and incidents over the last 10 years (57). According to an audit conducted for the California State Assembly, actual pipeline spills outnumbered industry reported spills by ten to one (57).

As mentioned, levels of compliance and performance of oil refineries vary widely across the United States (63). Community groups have documented, largely through anecdotal reports, accompanying variations in regulatory enforcement. Some assert that Texas and Louisiana, the largest oil refining states, have the weakest enforcement agencies (64). California agencies appear to be stricter and more effective. A simple analysis of data from the EPA's SFIP shows that high minority communities (those communities with over 30% minority populations within 3 miles of a refinery) were subject to fewer inspections and enforcement actions than refineries in predominantly white communities. Figures 1 and 2 present simple trend lines of variations in inspections and enforcement actions with respect

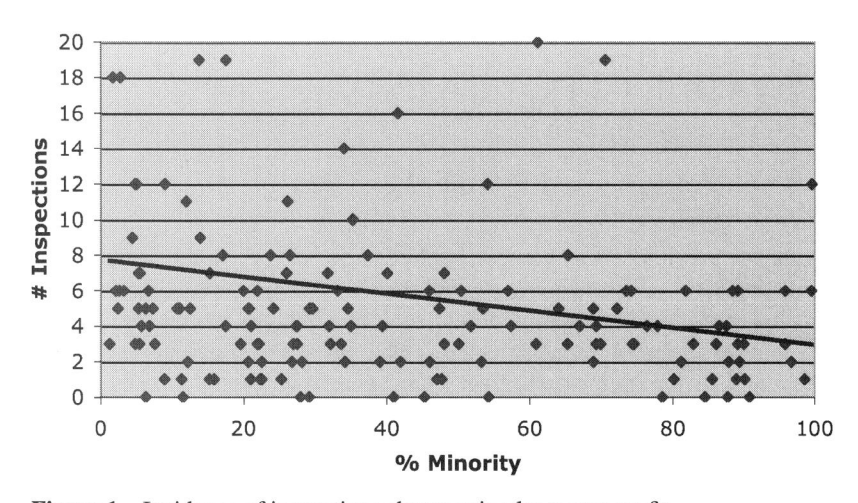

Figure 1 Incidence of inspections shown using least squares fit.

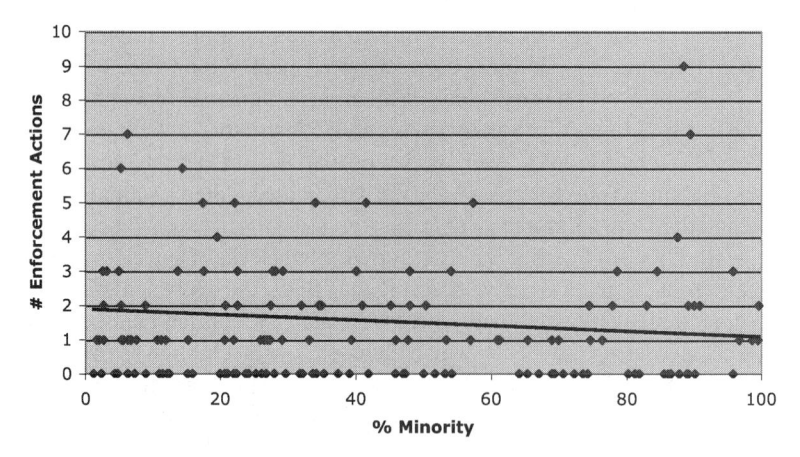

Figure 2 Incidence of enforcement.

to minority populations living in proximity to refineries in the United States. These data, while preliminary, seem to indicate a correlation between race and regulatory enforcement and, at a minimum, makes clear the need for further analysis of variations in the implementation of environmental regulations.

Environmental and health regulations in developing countries, although almost impossible to evaluate systematically, appear to be even weaker and more variable than U.S. regulations. A number of key oil-producing countries have either weak environmental laws, weak enforcement of these laws, or no environmental policies at all. The U.S. Energy Information Administration reports that "Nigeria does not have a pollution control policy" (88), and the laws that do exist are not enforced. Ecuador lacked environmental regulations until 1990, and dependence on oil revenue has since hindered environmental enforcement (11). Saudi Arabia did not have an environmental protection agency until 2001 (89).

IX. CONCLUSIONS, FURTHER RESEARCH, AND POLICY IMPLICATIONS

The impacts of oil production, transport, refining, and consumption are significant and widespread. From environmental impacts on fragile ecosystems, to cultural impacts on indigenous groups, health impacts on workers and communities, global climatic impacts, and military conflicts, oil is perhaps the single most controversial and influential commodity in the world. Our analysis of existing data has shown that oil's adverse impacts, which spread out virtually everywhere oil flows, appear to disproportionately affect groups such as indigenous communities, migrant workers, and poor communities living near refineries, pipelines, and gas stations. However, further research is needed to specify the distribution of environmental and social impacts from oil.

Although numerous studies have analyzed individual, discrete impacts of oil, little data or analysis is available assessing the overall distribution or cumulative impacts of oil. Current research and government data fail to evaluate the global distribution of benefits and costs from oil. It is virtually impossible to access even basic data on the spatial or demographic distribution of impacts from oil. One exception is the EPA's SFIP, which provides data on the demographics of populations living in proximity to oil refineries in the United States. But even these data are limited to simple measures of environmental performance of refineries.

Past studies have also failed to evaluate critical issues influencing the distribution of these impacts. Changing systems of control over the industry are particularly important in determining both who makes decisions over oil production, transport, and refining and who benefits from these decisions. The super-major oil corporations control an increasing percentage of oil extraction and refining and increasingly set the terms of oil's distribution and impacts. There is also very little information available to evaluate the implementation and effectiveness of government regulation of oil.

Thus, significant research is required to better measure and evaluate impacts of oil. There is a need for more and better data on environmental releases from oil extraction, transport, and refining. And there is a need for more and better analysis of the distribution of these impacts. Most governments currently rely on industry self-reporting of emissions, leaks, and accidents. Even in the United States, inspectors for key segments of the industry are scarce; ambient air sampling around facilities is limited; and monitoring of point sources, leaks, and accidents is minimal. Additionally, virtually no epidemiological or toxicological data are available on exposed communities, such as those living near refineries.

Greater public disclosure of data on the environmental, social, and financial impacts of oil exploration, production, and refining is also needed. Greater transparency regarding the performance of the oil industry would, at a minimum, help alert stakeholders to the true costs of oil consumption. A number of groups have called recently for reporting of oil revenues and payments to developing country governments and of the social and environmental impacts of these investments. Nongovernmental organizations and community groups around the world have also been calling for increased government inspections and enforcement authority over the oil industry. Even in the United States, exemptions and loopholes specific to the oil industry create a range of problems in environmental regulation. Finally, governments will have to engage and struggle with regulating oil companies if they are to seriously advance mechanisms to regulate global carbon emissions and mitigate climate impacts.

Oil is clearly at the center of current industrial development and economic activities. However, oil is also at the heart of some of the most troubling environmental, health, and social problems we face. How we manage both the benefits and costs of oil production and consumption will help determine the wealth, health, and safety of the planet. Understanding the distribution of impacts of oil and the effectiveness of current systems of regulation over these impacts is critical to advancing more democratic control over oil and to maximizing the benefits of oil while minimizing its adverse impacts. More open and robust debates in the United States and around the world regarding oil extraction, transport, refining, and consumption are critical to making our oil economy more just, equitable, and sustainable.

ACKNOWLEDGMENTS

The authors thank the Massachusetts Institute of Technology for financial support, George Draffan for research assistance, and Dan Kammen for helpful comments.

The *Annual Review of Environment and Resources* is online at
http://environ.annualreviews.org

LITERATURE CITED

1. Natl. Energy Policy Dev. Group. 2001. Overview. See Ref. 90, pp. viii–xv
2. Natl. Energy Policy Dev. Group. 2001. Protecting America's environment. See Ref. 90, pp. 3-1 to 3-14
3. Bush GW. 2001. *President Bush Calls for Action on Economy, Energy Remarks by the President to Business, Trade and Agriculture Leaders, October 26*. http://www.whitehouse.gov/news/releases/2001/10/20011026-9.html
4. Cheney R. 2001. *Town Hall Energy Meet., July 16*. http://www.whitehouse.gov/vicepresident/news-speeches/speeches/vp20010716-2.html
5. Klare M. 2001. *Resource Wars: The New Global Landscape of Global Conflict*, pp. 33, 60–61. New York: Metropolitan Books
6. Int. Labour Organ. 2002. *Oil and Gas Production; Oil Refining*. http://www.ilo.org/public/english/dialogue/sector/sectors/oilgas.htm
7. Youngquist W. 2000. *Alternative Energy Sources*. http://www.hubbertpeak.com/youngquist/altenergy.htm
8. Doyle J. 1994. *Crude Awakenings: The Oil Mess in America: Wasting Energy Jobs and the Environment*. Washington, DC: Friends Earth
9. Energy Intell. Group. 2003. *Polity Score and Reserves Table*. http://www.energyintel.com/grounds/tables.htm
10. Publish What You Pay Coalition. 2003. *Publish What You Pay Campaign*. http://www.publishwhatyoupay.org/
11. Trade Environ. Database. 2002. *Ecuador Oil Exports. The Mandala Project*. http://www.american.edu/TED/ECUADOR.htm
12. Ross M. 2001. *Extraction Sectors and the Poor*. Boston: Oxfam Am.
13. Anonymous. 2002. Worldwide Report. *Oil Gas J*. Dec. 23. 100(52):62–145
14. Pet. Econ. Ltd. 2002. Energy Map of the World. http://www.petroleum-economist.com
15. Yergin D. 1991. *The Prize: The Epic Quest for Oil, Money, and Power*. New York: Simon & Schuster
16. Sampson A. 1975. The Seven Sisters: *The Great Oil Companies and the World They Shaped*. New York: Viking
17. Clark JG. 1990. *The Political Economy of World Energy: A Twentieth Century Perspective*. Chapel Hill: Univ. North Carolina Press
18. Bullard R. 1994. Environmental justice for all. In *Unequal Protection: Environmental Justice and Communities of Color*, ed. RD Bullard, pp. 3–22. San Francisco: Sierra Club Books
19. Pulido L. 1996. A critical review of the methodology of environmental racism research. *Antipode* 28(2):142–59
20. Energy Inf. Adm. 2003. *Country Analysis*

Briefs: OPEC Fact Sheet. http://www.eia.doe.gov/emeu/cabs/opec.html
21. Standard & Poor's. 2002. Industry Surveys: Oil & Gas: Production & Marketing. April 4, p. 2. New York, NY
22. Energy Inf. Adm. 2002. *Country Analysis Briefs: Persian Gulf Oil and Gas Exports Fact Sheet.* http://www.eia.doe.gov/emeu/cabs/pgulf.html
23. Standard & Poor's. 2002. See Ref. 21, p. 3
24. BP-Amoco. 2002. *Statistical Review of World Energy.* http://www.bp.com/centres/energy2002/2001inreview.asp
25. Energy Inf. Adm. 2002. *Country Analysis Briefs: Non-OPEC Fact Sheet.* http://www.eia.doe.gov/emeu/cabs/nonopec.html
26. Energy Inf. Adm. 2002. *World Petroleum Supply and Disposition, 2000.* http://www.eia.doe.gov/emeu/iea/table31.html
27. Energy Intell. Group. 2003. *Ranking the World's Top Oil Companies, 2001: Fewer, Bigger, and Fiercely Competitive* (Abstr.). http://www.energyintel.com/ResDocDetail.asp?document_id=50195
28. Standard & Poor's. 2002. See Ref. 21, p. 9
29. Slocum T. 2001. *No Competition: Oil Industry Mergers Provide Higher Profits, Leave Consumers With Fewer Choices.* Public Citiz. http://www.citizen.org/documents/nocompetition.PDF
30. Karl TL. 1997. *The Paradox of Plenty: Oil Booms and Petro-States.* Berkeley: Univ. Calif. Press
31. Natl. Energy Policy Dev. Group. 2001. Strengthening Global Alliances. See Ref. 90, pp. 8-1 to 8-21
32. Standard & Poor's. 2002. See Ref. 21, p. 11
33. Mead W. 1993. Crude oil supply and demand. In *The Environment of Oil*, ed. RJ Gilbert, pp. 43–84. Boston: Kluwer Acad.
34. Petroconsultants UK Ltd. 1998. *World Petroleum Trends Rep.* Petroconsultants, London
35. Edoigiawerie C, Spickett J. 1995. The environmental impact of petroleum on the environment. *Afr. J. Health Sci.* 2(2):269–76
36. O'Connor O. 2000. *The Hidden Costs of Offshore Oil.* Living Oceans Soc., April/May. http://www.web.net/nben/envnews/media/00/offoil.htm
37. Pelley J. 2001. Will drilling for oil disrupt the Arctic National Wildlife Refuge? *Environ. Sci. Technol.* 35(11):240A–47A
38. Epstein PR, Selber J. 2002. *Oil: A Life Cycle Analysis of Its Health and Environmental Impacts.* Boston: Center Health Glob. Environ., Harv. Med. Sch.
39. US Environ. Prot. Agency Off. Compliance Enforc. 2000. *Profile of the Oil and Gas Extraction Industry.* Washington DC: GPO
40. Natl. Res. Counc. 2002. *Oil in the Sea III: Inputs, Fates, and Effects.* Washington, DC: Natl. Acad.
41. Caswell MF. 1993. Balancing energy and the environment. In *The Environment of Oil*, ed. RJ. Gilbert, pp. 179–214. Boston: Kluwer Acad.
42. Kretzmann S, Wright S. 1998. *Drilling to the Ends of the Earth: The Ecological, Social and Climate Imperative for Ending Oil Exploration.* Berkeley, CA: Rainfor. Action Netw. Proj. Undergr.
43. Kretzmann S, Wright S. 1997. *Human Rights and Environmental Operations Information on the Royal Dutch/Shell Group of Companies, 1996–1997.* Berkeley, CA: Rainfor. Action Netw. Proj. Undergr.
44. Amazon Watch. 2002. *Mega Projects.* http://www.amazonwatch.org
45. Hum. Rights Watch. 2002. *Corporations and Human Rights.* http://www.hrw.org/advocacy/corporations/
46. Project Undergr. 2002. *Oil Campaign.* http://www.moles.org/ProjectUnderground/oil/index.shtml
47. Model Arab Leag. 2002. *Codifying Immigrant Laborer Rights in the Arab World.* http://www.geocities.com/mtaerea1984/Pages/immigrant_labor.htm
48. South Asian Voice. 2001. *Understanding the Complexities and Contradictions of the Middle East Oil Wealth, Colonial and Neo-Colonial Intervention, and Cheap South Asian Labor.* http://india_resource.tripod.com/mideastoil.html

49. Hum. Rights Watch. 1999. *Saudi Arabia Human Rights Developments.* http://www.hrw.org/wr2k/Mena-08.htm
50. Burger J. 1997. *Oil Spills.* New Brunswick, NJ: Rutgers Univ. Press
51. Int. Tanker Own. Pollut. Fed. Ltd. 2002. *Past Spills Statistics.* http://www.itopf.com/stats.html
52. Welch J. 1994. International spill statistics: 1993. In *Oil Spill Intelligence Report.* Arlington, MA: Cutter Inf. Corp.
53. Earth Crash Earth Spirit. 2002. *Pollution: Oil Spill Central.* http://eces.org/ec/pollution/oilspills.shtml
54. Etkin DS. 1997. Oil Spills From Vessels (1960–1995): An International Historical Perspective. Cambridge, MA: Cutter Inf. Corp.
55. Natl. Ocean. Atmos. Adm./ Natl. Ocean Serv. 2002. *Oil Spills in History.* http://response.restoration.noaa.gov/faqs/history.html
56. Int. Counc. Local Environ. Initiat. 1993. *Oil Discharged into the Marine Environment from Maritime Transport.* http://www.iclei.org/efacts/oilspi1.gif
57. Nesmith J, Haurwitz RKM. 2001. Spills and explosions reveal lax regulation of powerful industry. *American-Statesman,* Austin, TX, July 22, p. A1
58. Boesch DF, Butler JN, Cacchione DA, Geraci JR, Neff JN, et al. 1987. An assessment of the long-term environmental effects of US offshore oil and gas development activities: future research needs. In *Long Term Environmental Effects of Offshore Oil and Gas Development,* ed. DF Boesch, NN Rabalais. London: Elsevier Appl. Sci.
59. IMO/FAO/UNESCO/WMO/WHO/IAEA/UN/UNEP. Jt. Group Experts Sci. Aspects Mar. Pollut. 1993. *Impact of Oil and Related Chemicals and Wastes on the Marine Environment, GESAMP Rep. Stud. 50.* London: Int. Marit. Organ.
60. Rooney Eng. Inc. 2000. *Pacific Pipeline System.* http://www.rooney-eng.com/ppsi.htm
61. Impact Assess. Inc. 1995. *Documentation in Support of Socioeconomic Review Comments to Draft Environmental Impact Statement/Subsequent Environmental Impact Report: Pacific Pipeline Project.* La Jolla, California
62. Rainfor. Action Netw. 2002. *The Chad/Cameroon Rainforest Oil Pipeline Case Study.* http://www.ran.org/ran_campaigns/citigroup/cs_chadcam.html
63. Epstein LN, Greetham S, Karuba A. 1995. *Ranking Refineries: What Do We Know About Oil Refinery Pollution from Right-to-Know Data?* Washington, DC: Environ. Def. Fund
64. Texas Sustain. Energy Econ. Dev. Coalit. 2001. *Crude Polluters: A Survey and Analysis of the US Refinery Sector and a Blueprint for Refinery Reform,* Austin: Texas SEED Coalit.
65. Minor. Staff, Spec. Investig. Div., Comm. Gov. Reform, US House. 1999. *Oil Refineries Fail to Report Millions of Pounds of Harmful Emissions.* Prep. for Represent. Henry A. Waxman. Nov. 10 http://www.house.gov/reform/min/pdfs/pdf_inves/pdf_enviro_oil_refine_rep.pdf
66. Kizior GJ. 1991. *Amoco/EPA Pollution Prevention Project: Solid Waste Sampling.* Naperville, IL: Amoco Oil Co. Environ. Eng. Res.
67. US Environ. Prot. Agency Off. Compliance Enforc. 1999. *Compliance and Enforcement Reports.* http://www.epa.gov/Compliance/resources/reports/planning/results/accomplishments/
68. Templet PH. 1993. The emissions-to-jobs ratio: a tool for evaluating pollution control programs. *Environ. Sci. Technol.* 27(5):810–12
69. Bell R. 1997. Shell official: '88 deal led to suit; residents unhappy with settlement, he says. *Times Picayune,* August 30, p. B1
70. Concerned Citiz. Norco Sierra Club. 2001. *FlareCam.* http://www.sierraclub.org/planet/200209.shell_victory
71. Doyle J. 2002. *Riding the Dragon: Royal*

Dutch Shell and the Fossil Fire. Boston: Environ. Health Fund.
72. Bur. Labor Stat. 2002. *Fatal Occupational Injuries by Industry*, 1996–2001. http://www.bls.gov/iif/oshwc/cfoi/cftb0155.pdf
73. Occup. Saf. Health Adm. 2003. *OSHA Priorities: Oil and Gas Well Drilling & Servicing.* http://www.osha.gov/oshinfo/priorities/oil.html
74. Int. Cent. Technol. Assess. 2002. *The Real Price Of Gasoline.* http://www.icta.org/projects/trans/rlprexsm.htm
75. Gottlieb DJ, Beiser AS, O'Connor GT. 1995. Poverty, race, and medication use are correlates of asthma hospitalization rates. *Chest* 108(1):28–35
76. Intergov. Panel Clim. Chang. 2001. *Climate Change 2001: The Scientific Basis*: *Summary for Policymakers.* http://www.ipcc.ch/pub/spm22-01.pdf
77. UN Environ. Program. 2001. *UNEP Climate Change Information Kit* http://www.unep.ch/conventions/info/ccinfokit/Infokitpercent20-percent202001.htm
78. Bruno K, Karliner J, Brotsky C. 1999. *Greenhouse Gangsters vs. Climate Justice.* San Francisco, CA: Transnatl. Res. Action Cent. http://www.corpwatch.org/upload/document/greenhousegangsters.pdf
79. Anonymous. *Refining damage mounts. Oil Gas J.* March 11. 100(10):19
80. Calif. Air Resour. Board. 2002. *California Air Pollution Control Laws.* http://www.arb.ca.gov/bluebook/bb02/toc.htm
81. US Environ. Prot. Agency Off. Compliance Enforc. 1995. *Profile of the Petroleum Refining Industry.* Washington, DC: GPO
82. Texas Sustain. Energy Econ. Dev. Coalit. 2001. See Ref. 103, p. 10
83. Stolberg S. 2002. Senators cross party lines on clean air. *New York Times.* January 22, p. A23
84. Environ. Def. 2002. *Fallout from EPA Rules Rollback.* Statement by Vickie Patton, sr. atty. Environ. Def. June 17. http://www.environmentaldefense.org/article.cfm?contentid=2132
85. US Environ. Prot. Agency Off. Compliance Assur. 1999. *Fiscal Year 1998 Accomplishments Report.* http://www.epa.gov/Compliance/resources/reports/planning/results/accomplishments/fy99accomplishment.pdf
86. Schaeffer E. 2002. *CBS News.* June 13
87. Off. Pipeline Saf. 2002. *Pipeline Statistics.* http://ops.dot.gov/stats.htm
88. Energy Inf. Adm. 2002. *Nigeria: Environmental Issues.* http://www.eia.doe.gov/emeu/cabs/nigenv.html
89. Energy Inf. Adm. 2002. *Saudi Arabia: Environmental Issues.* http://www.eia.doe.gov/emeu/cabs/saudenv.html
90. Natl. Energy Policy Dev. Group. 2001. *National Energy Policy.* Washington, DC: GPO

Subject Index

A
AAO
 See Antarctic Oscillation
ABC
 See Alternate base case analysis
ABM
 See Agent-based models
Absorbed photosynthetic active radiation, 178
Absorbed solar radiation, 178
Abundance of fish species off the northeastern Pacific Ocean over past 2200 years, reconstructed, 366
Actors
 in negotiating international environmental agreements, 442–44
Adaptive capacity
 loss of causing land-use change, 225
Additionality factors
 in carbon management, 525
 informing carbon sequestration and disposal policies, 537–41
ADE
 See Advection-diffusion equation
ADIFOR
 See Automatic Differentiation of Fortran
Advances in GIS representation, 514–16
 and uncertainty, 515–16
Advances in software, 511–14
 component-based software design, 511–12
 the grid, 514

schema development, 512–14
Advances in the data supply for environmental management, 506–11
 archives and digital libraries, 508–10
 institutional arrangements, 510–11
 new sources of imagery, 506–7
 sensors and sensor networks, 507–8
Advection
 physical displacement of pollutants by, 472
Advection-diffusion equation (ADE), 64–65, 85
Advective transport
 among compartments, 474
Aerosols
 uncertainties in model formulation for, 72
Agenda 21, 249, 271
Agent-based models (ABM), 503
 to understand land-use/cover changes, 229
Agreements
 defined, 432–34
Agricultural activity, 208–9
 driving extinction, 159–60
Agricultural area land cover and increase in world food production and agricultural inputs from 1961–1996, 211
 recent changes in, 211–12
Air quality modeling uncertainties in, 59–106

Airborne Visible/Infra-Red Imaging Spectrometer (AVIRIS), 506–7
Alaska
 opening oil exploration in, 588
ALE/GAGE/AGAGE
 See Atmospheric Lifetime Experiment/Global Atmospheric Gases Experiment/Advanced Global Atmospheric Gases Experiment network
Allocation of fish
 among users, 384–86
Alternate base case (ABC) analysis, 96–97
Alternative land use options in managed forests and arable lands
 U.S. potential for C-sequestration from adopting, 345
Altitude
 ozone and hydroxyl radical concentrations as functions of, 33
AMERIFLUX, 181–82
Amnesty International, 602
Analysis
 See Alternate base case analysis; Diagnostic analyses; Ecosystem analysis; Life cycle analysis; Process analysis techniques; Sensitivity analyses; Uncertainty analyses
Animal locomotion
 propagation by, 123–24

619

Antarctic Oscillation (AAO), 2–4
"Anthropocene Era," 138
AO
   See Arctic Oscillation
AOGCM
   See Atmosphere-ocean general circulation models
Arable land resources, 318–21
   alternative land use options in, 345
   estimating, 318–19
   preserving natural ecosystems, 320–21
   in sub-Saharan Africa and China, 319–20
"Aral Sea Syndrome," 566
Archives
   for environmental management, 508–10
Arctic National Wildlife Refuge
   opening oil exploration in, 588
Arctic Oscillation (AO), 2–4
ArcView GIS, 504
Arrhenius function, 179
Assessment of exposures to humans and ecosystems, 480–82
   comparative human exposure assessment, 481–82
Atmosphere-ocean general circulation models (AOGCM), 13–14
Atmospheric cleansing capacity, 29–57
   chemical composition of the atmosphere and major sources of its constituents, 31
   estimated global emission rates of tropospheric trace gases and amounts removed by reaction with OH, 32
   fundamental reactions, 33–39
   human influences, 39–45
   measuring the hydroxyl radical, 45–52
   ozone and hydroxyl radical concentrations as functions of latitude and altitude, 33
Atmospheric CO_2 concentration
   elevated, 189–91
   NPP comparisons for growth in enriched atmospheric CO_2, 190–91
Atmospheric deposition, 118–19
Atmospheric Lifetime Experiment/Global Atmospheric Gases Experiment/Advanced Global Atmospheric Gases Experiment (ALE/GAGE/AGAGE) network, 48–51
Atmospheric pollutants and the forest biological C cycle, 187–91
   atmospheric N deposition, 187–88
   climate warming, 188–89
   elevated atmospheric CO_2 concentration, 189–91
Atmospheric reactions, 33–39
   main chemical processes forming and removing stratospheric ozone, 38
   main tropospheric oxidation processes, 34
   in the stratosphere, 38–39
   in the troposphere, 33–38
Attitudes
   causing land-use change, 225
Australian extinctions, 153
Automatic Differentiation of Fortran (ADIFOR), 84
AVIRIS
   See Airborne Visible/Infra-Red Imaging Spectrometer

B

Balaton Group, 561, 571
Bayesian techniques, 86–87
BEAs
   See Bilateral agreements
Benign solvents
   in a hydroformylation case study, 418–20
Berkeley-Trent North American contaminant fate model (BETR North America), 480
BFM
   See Brute force method
Bilateral agreements (BEAs), 430, 438–39
Biodegradable wastes
   and not compromising the ability of future generations to meet their needs for sustainable development in urban areas, 253
Biodiversity, 137–67
   eco-geographic distribution, 148–52
   facets of, 138–39
   global magnitude of, 141–47
   loss of, 152–63
   novelties, 147
   patchy nature of threats to, 158
   potential magnitude of, 144
   through time, 140–41
Biogeochemical fluxes, 115
Biogeochemistry
   and the global carbon cycle, 19–21
Biological extinction

SUBJECT INDEX   621

major pulse of, 163
Biosphere
 defined, 108
 transport of energy, information, and material through, 107–35
Boston Indicators Project, 571–72, 576
 characterizing and measuring sustainable development, 565
Brassica oleracea, 146
Breeding to maintain yields against evolving sensitivity to pathogens, insect pests, and abiotic environmental conditions, 326
British Petroleum (BP-Amoco), 525, 592
Brundtland Commission, 249, 251, 420
Brute force method (BFM), 84
Bush, George W., 588, 610
Bykov's plant endemism plots, 144–45, 151

C

CA
 See Cellular automata
California
 indoor residential water use expected, from 1998–2020, 309
 urban improvements in water use, 309–10
California Department of Water Resources (CDWR), 279
California Environmental Protection Agency, 466, 478
CalTOX, 466–67, 478–82
Cambrian Period, 140
CAMS-OPI data, 7, 9
CAMx
 See Comprehensive Air

Quality Model extended version
Canada Land Inventory, 495
Carbon accounting, 536–37
Carbon cycle observations and knowledge in carbon management, 521–58
 and LULUCF in the Kyoto Protocol, 546–48
 sequestration and disposal options, 526–28
Carbon management policy principles, 524–26
 additionality, 525
 leakage, 525
 permanence, 525–26
 perverse incentive, 526
 quantification, 525
 separation, 525
 transparency, 526
 verification, 526
Carbon pools
 See Carbon sinks
Carbon sequestration, 343–49
 in forest products, 193–94
 inventorying, 534
 potential in vegetation and soil, 192–93
 soil quality and nitrogen requirements, 346–49
Carbon sequestration and disposal policies
 scientific capability for informing, 528–46
Carbon sequestration and greenhouse gas emissions, 343–46
 U.S. potential for C-sequestration from adopting alternative land use options in managed forests and arable lands, 345
Carbon sinks, 540
 estimates of continental and subcontinental, 531
 initial disturbance effects

on, 183–84
"Carrier"
 defined, 112
Carson, Rachel, 464
Carter Doctrine, 588
Catalyst immobilization in a hydroformylation case study, 417–18
Catalyst recovery
 multiphase systems that simplify, 415–17
Causes of land-use change
 changes in social organization, resource access, and attitudes, 225
 changing opportunities created by markets, 225
 empirical evidences on, 216–23
 a finite set of pathways of land-use change, 221–23
 fundamental high-level, 223–25
 general insights on sectoral causes of land-use change, 217–21
 loss of adaptive capacity and increased vulnerability, 225
 outside policy intervention, 225
 proximate versus underlying causes, 216–17
 resource scarcity, 225
 and their interactions, 223–28
 typology of, 224
CDWR
 See California Department of Water Resources
Cellular automata (CA), 503
Centrifugal force
 of Earth's spin, 119
CENTURY maize simulation model, 346
Cereal demand

and arable land resources, 318–21
carbon sequestration, greenhouse forcing, and soil quality, 343–49
meeting, while protecting natural resources and improving environmental quality, 315–58
nitrogen efficiency and trends in nitrogen fertilizer use, 330–43
projected changes in population, cereal demand, yields, area, and prices from 1995–2025, 318
yield potential and exploitable yield gaps, 321–30
Cereal production
global trends in, 317
CERES-Maize simulation model, 346
Cetaceans
Southern Hemisphere catches of different species, showing pattern of discovery, exploitation, and subsequent collapse of each species, 365
CFC
See Chloroflurocarbon industry
CGSDI
See Consultative Group on Sustainable Development Indicators
CH_3CCl_3 measurements
average OH concentrations estimated from, 50
Changes
in mean trophic level of global fisheries landings for marine and inland areas, 374
in N fertilizer requirements for the major cereals from 2000–2025, projected, 341
in population, cereal demand, yields, area, and prices from 1995–2025, projected, 318
Changes in the C cycle during succession, 184–87
age-related aboveground NPP decline for forest ecosystems in contrasting climates, 185
chronosequence of well-drained boreal black spruce, 186
Changes in water-use patterns, 298–310
cost-effectiveness of efficiency improvements, 303–8
urban improvements in California, 309–10
Characterization of sustainable development, 562–66
Boston Indicators Project, 565
Consultative Group on Sustainable Development Indicators, 563
Costa Rica Sistema de Indicadores sobre Desarrollo Sostenable, 565
Ecological Footprint, 564
Environmental Sustainability Index, 563–64
Genuine Progress Indicator, 564
Global Reporting Initiative, 566
Global Scenario Group, 564
State Failure Task Force, 566
United Nations Commission on Sustainable Development, 562–63
U.S. Interagency Working Group on Sustainable Development Indicators, 565
Wellbeing Index, 563
ChemCAN model, 479
Chemical composition of the atmosphere
and major sources of its constituents, 31
Chemical partitioning in environmental systems, 468–69
and chemical equilibrium, 468
and conservation of mass, 468
use of linked compartments, 468–69
Chemical processes
forming and removing stratospheric ozone, 38
Chemical removal transformation processes using, 472
Chemical structures
of HCB and PCP, 481
Chemical transport models (CTMs), 52
Chemistry
uncertainties in, 69–70
See also Green chemistry
Chemodynamics, 466
Cheney, Dick, 588
Chernobyl nuclear accident, 440
China
arable land resources, 319–20
GDP index and total water withdrawals, 301
Chloroflurocarbon (CFC) industry

SUBJECT INDEX 623

virtual elimination of, 445
Chronosequence studies, 184
　of well-drained boreal
　black spruce, 186
CIMMYT
　See International Maize
　and Wheat Improvement
　Center (CIMMYT)
Circulation system in oceans
　thermohaline, 120
CITES
　See Convention on
　International Trade in
　Endangered Species
Cities
　ecological footprints of,
　256–57
　implementing sustainable
　development in, 267–69
Civil unrest
　disrupting oil operations,
　596
Clark Labs, 495
Clean Air Act, 60, 478, 603,
　610
　Amendments to, 62
Clean Water Act, 603, 610
Cleansing capacity of the
　atmosphere, 29–57
　chemical composition of
　the atmosphere and major
　sources of its constituents,
　31
　estimated global emission
　rates of tropospheric trace
　gases and amounts
　removed by reaction with
　OH, 32
　fundamental reactions,
　33–39
　human influences, 39–45
　measuring the hydroxyl
　radical, 45–52
　ozone and hydroxyl radical
　concentrations as
　functions of latitude and
　altitude, 33

Climate change and its
　impacts, 1–28
　causes for changes in a
　modeling perspective,
　12–15
　climate variability, 3–9
　climatic impact of ENSO
　and PDO, 8–9
　the DOE PCM transient
　experiment, 15
　global-average surface
　temperature anomaly with
　respect to the 1951–1980
　climatology, 10
　impact of NAO on global
　climate variability, 7–8
　observed changes in the
　recent past, 10–12
　relationship with the
　leading modes, 9–15
Climate mode phenomena,
　3–7
　Antarctic Oscillation, 4
　Arctic Oscillation, 4
　biogeochemistry,
　disturbance, and the
　global carbon cycle,
　19–21
　and ecological impacts,
　16–21
　El Niño-Southern
　Oscillation, 5–7
　North Atlantic Oscillation,
　3–5
　Pacific Decadal
　Oscillation, 5–7
　population and
　reproductive responses,
　17–19
Climate Monitoring and
　Detection Laboratory
　(CMDL), 48
Climate system model
　(CSM), 13
Climate warming, 188–89
Climatic impacts on fish
　stocks, 364–67

　reconstructed abundance of
　fish species off the
　northeastern Pacific
　Ocean over past 2200
　years, 366
　Southern Hemisphere
　catches of different
　species of large cetaceans,
　365
Close coupling, 504
CMAQ
　See Community Multiscale
　Air Quality Model
CMDL
　See Climate Monitoring
　and Detection Laboratory
CMS
　See Convention on the
　Conservation of
　Migratory Species of
　Wild Animals
Coastal zones, 119–20
Co-occurrence
　of taxa, 139
Colluvial transport
　propagation through the
　action of gravity, 115–17
Colonization voyages, 153
"Communication"
　defined, 109
Community Multiscale Air
　Quality Model (CMAQ),
　96
Comparative human exposure
　assessment, 481–82
Compartments
　advective transport among,
　474
　diffusive transport among,
　474
　use of linked, 468–69
Compendium of Sustainable
　Development Indicator
　Initiatives, 561
Complex adaptive systems
　land-use change as an
　emergent property of, 227

Component-based software
  design, 511–12
Component models
  of a photochemical air
    quality modeling system,
    64
Comprehensive Air Quality
  Model extended version
  (CAMx), 96
Confidence building
  model evaluation and,
    484–86
Conflicts
  occurring over oil, 596
Conservation
  defined, 278–80
  of mass, 468
Consultative Group on
  Sustainable
  Development Indicators
  (CGSDI)
    characterizing and
      measuring sustainable
      development, 563
Consumptive use
  defined, 278
Continental scale in
  quantification, 529–31
  carbon sink estimates, 531
Continuous field view,
  497–98
Control over oil, 590–93
  incursions into indigenous
    lands for, 597
  world oil net importers in
    2001, 593
  world oil reserves,
    production, and exports in
    2001, 591
Convention for the
  Establishment of an
  Inter-American Tropical
  Tuna Commission, 436
Convention on International
  Trade in Endangered
  Species (CITES), 438,
  445–46, 448

Convention on Long-Range
  Transboundary Air
  Pollution (LRTAP), 433,
  435, 445
Convention on the
  Conservation of
  Antarctic Marine Living
  Resources, 448
Convention on the
  Conservation of
  Migratory Species of
  Wild Animals (CMS),
  436
Convention on Wetlands of
  International
  Importance, 436
Conversion of land cover
  versus modification,
  213–15
"Conveyor"
  defined, 112
Coriolis force, 120
Corroborative/alternative
  modeling, 94–98
  corroborative analyses,
    95–97
  potential uses within
    current regulatory
    context, 97–98
  subjective judgment,
    94–95
Cost-effectiveness of
  efficiency
    improvements, 303–8
  unaccounted for water, by
    country, 306–7
Costa Rica Sistema de
  Indicadores sobre
  Desarrollo Sostenible
    characterizing and
      measuring sustainable
      development, 565
Council on Environmental
  Quality, 464
Coupling, 504
CoZMoPOP model, 480
Credibility

  in efforts to characterize
    and measure sustainable
    development, 573–75
Cretaceous Period, 140
Crop species, 146
CSD
  See United Nations
  Commission on
  Sustainable Development
  (CSD)
CSM
  See Climate system model
CTMs
  See Chemical transport
  models
Cultural factors
  causing land-use change,
    220–21
Cultural needs
  for sustainable
    development in urban
    areas at the present, 252
Cumulative exposure models,
  477
Cyberinfrastructure, 514

D

Data
  inaccurate, 282
Data collection
  global and regional
    disparities in, 282
Data modeling, 502
DDT, 367, 464
Decoupled direct method
  (DDM), 84–85
Demand for water
  defined, 278
Demographic factors
  causing land-use change,
    218–19
Diagnostic analyses, 90–94
  future needs, 93–94
  limitations of available
    measurement data, 91
  processs analysis
    techniques, 91–92

techniques using extensive
    field measurements,
    92–93
DIC
    See Dissolved inorganic
    carbon
Diffuse radiation, 183
"Diffusion"
    defined, 113
Diffusive transport
    among compartments, 474
    propagation by random
    movements, 113
Digital dust, 507
Digital elevation model, 499
Digital libraries
    for environmental
    management, 508–10
Direct measurement of the
    hydroxyl radical, 45–48
    hourly average OH
    concentrations during
    spring and summer in
    MLOPEX, 46
    variation of daytime OH
    concentrations in
    POPCORN, 47
Disaggregation trends in
    cereal yields and
    nitrogen fertilizer use,
    336–40
    relationship between maize
    yield and N fertilizer rate,
    338
    relationships among rice
    yield, N fertilizer rate,
    and plant N accumulation,
    339
    relationships between yield
    of maize, rice, and wheat
    and average N rates
    applied, 337
Discarding
    in fishing, 370–72
Discourse
    in negotiating international
    environmental
    agreements, 439–42
Discrete object
    conceptualization,
    497–98
Disposal options, 526–28
    geologic disposal, 528
    See also Sequestration
    options
Dissolved inorganic carbon
    (DIC), 533, 535
Distribution
    of world's urban
    population by region,
    1950–2010, 246
Disturbances
    and the global carbon
    cycle, 19–21
Disturbances and forest
    biological C cycle,
    183–87
    changes in the C cycle
    during succession,
    184–87
    initial disturbance effects
    on C pools, 183–84
DOE PCM transient
    experiment, 15
Domestication
    and biodiversity, 139,
    146
Drilling
    associated wastes from,
    595
    impacts of, 593–98
Drivers
    of extinction, 159–60
Drivers of green chemistry,
    404–10
    life cycle inventory of the
    generic automobile,
    409
    stages of a life cycle
    analysis, 407
    three legs of life cycle
    engineering, 406
Dynamic systems
    Level IV models, 475

E

Earth Observing System
    (EOS) satellites, 507
Earth Summit, 249
Earth system science (ESS),
    124–25
Earth's spin
    centrifugal force of, 119
Eco-geographic distribution,
    148–52
    distribution of endemism,
    151–52
    the distribution of species,
    families, and orders,
    148–50
    population and genetic
    diversity distribution,
    150–51
ECOLEX database, 431
Ecological Footprint, 569,
    572, 576–77
    characterizing and
    measuring sustainable
    development, 564
Ecological footprints of
    cities, 256–57
Ecological influences
    vectors at a medial level of
    causation responsible for
    propagation in the
    biosphere, 112
Ecological metadata language
    (EML), 510
Economic factors
    causing land-use change,
    218
    needed for sustainable
    development in urban
    areas at the present, 252
Economic status
    of fisheries, 375
ECOPATH models, 380
Ecosystem analysis
    multispecies and, 379–80
Ecosystems
    assessing exposures to,
    480–82

status of fisheries and, 368–75
Effectiveness of international environmental agreements, 444–53
the determinants of regime effects, 448–52
the endogeneity problem, 452–53
identifying the effects of regimes, 444–46
Efficiency
cost-effectiveness of improvements in, 303–8
defined, 278–80
Electromagnetic radiation (EMR), 122–23
El Niño-Southern Oscillation (ENSO), 2, 5–13, 16–21, 539
climatic impact of, 8–9
Emergency Planning and Community Right-to-Know Act, 603
Emissions
inventorying, 534
projected change in various between 2000–2100 for various scenarios, 43
uncertainties in, 67–68
EML
See Ecological metadata language
Empirical orthogonal function (EOF) analysis, 3
EMR
See Electromagnetic radiation
Endemism, 144–46
Bykov's plant endemism plots, 144–45
defined, 139
distribution of, 151–52
Endogeneity
in land-cover change in tropical regions, 226–27
a problem in international environmental agreements, 452–53
Energy Information Agency, 590
Energy metrics
of green chemistry, 411–12
Enforcement in the oil industry
incidence of, 612
Engineering
green chemistry and, 401–28
Enriched atmospheric CO_2
NPP comparisons for growth in, 190–91
ENSO
See El Niño-Southern Oscillation
Environmental agreements
defined, 433–34
Environmental Defense Fund, 605
Environmental effects and linkages
informing carbon sequestration and disposal policies, 542–43
Environmental hazards
systems for managing liquid and solid wastes that reduce, 263
Environmental impacts of oil production and consumption, 587–617
control over oil, 590–93
impacts of exploration, drilling, and extraction, 593–98
impacts of oil consumption, 607–9
impacts of oil refining, 603–7
impacts of oil transport, 598–602
policy implications, 612–14
regulating the oil industry, 609–12
research needed, 612–14
Environmental justice framework, 590
Environmental needs
for sustainable development in urban areas at the present, 252
Environmental Protection Agency (EPA), 60, 477, 603–4, 606, 610
Green Engineering branch, 402
Environmental science
origins of, 124–25
Environmental Sustainability Index, 572–73, 576
characterizing and measuring sustainable development, 563–64
Environmental systems
phase equilibrium and chemical partitioning in, 468–69
Environmental Systems Research Institute (ESRI), 495, 504, 509
Environmental Treaties and Resource Indicators database, 431–32
Environmentally relevant phases
fugacity capacities for, 470
EOF
See Empirical orthogonal function analysis
EOS
See Earth Observing System satellites
EPA
See Environmental Protection Agency
Episodic land-cover changes versus progressive, 215–16
Equilibrium
chemical, 468

Equilibrium Criterion (EQC) model, 478
Equilibrium partitioning in an open system with Level II models, 471–73
  Level II fugacity calculations, 472–73
  physical displacement of pollutants by advection, 472
  transformation processes by chemical removal, 472
Equity
  in sustainable development, 260–63
ESRI
  See Environmental Systems Research Institute
ESS
  See Earth system science
Estimates of current water use, 282–92
Estimation
  of land reserves, 318–19
Estimation of current water use
  experience from the United States, 290–92
  global water use, 282–84
  national water use estimates of regional water use, 284–90
Estimation of trends in rice yield potential, 324–26
  breeding to maintain yields against evolving sensitivity to pathogens, insect pests, and abiotic environmental conditions, 326
  yield trend of cultivars and lines developed at the International Rice Research Institute, 325
Eukaryotic species, 141

remaining to be discovered, 147
Eulerian models, 65
EUROFLUX, 181
European Union, 478
European Union System for the Evaluation of Substances (EUSES), 481–82
  framework, 479
Evaluation of sustainable development in urban areas, 251–56
  meeting the needs of the present, 252
  not compromising the ability of future generations to meet their needs, 253
Evaluative models, 478–79
Exclusive Economic Zones (EEZ), 370
Exploitable yield gaps, 321–30
  are existing yield gaps large enough, 328–30
  definitions, 321
  importance of maintaining, 321–24
Exploitation
  driving extinction, 160
Exploration
  impacts of, 593–98
Exposure events, 476–77
Extinction
  change in mean trophic level of global fisheries landings for marine and inland areas, 374
  current and future rates of, 161–62
  drivers of, 159–60
  ecosystem impacts of, 373–75
  prehistoric and recent, 152–56
  rampant, 138

Extra-tidal currents, 120–21
Extraction
  impacts of, 593–98
ExxonMobil, 592
Exxon-Valdez oil spill, 599, 601–2, 611

F
FACE
  See Free-air CO_2 enrichment experiments
"Fair-trade" campaigns, 270
Families
  distribution of, 148–50
FAO
  See Food and Agriculture Organization
FAOLEX database, 438
Farm yields
  actual, defined, 322
FAST
  See Fourier amplitude sensitivity test method
"Favela Syndrome," 566
Feedback
  in land-cover change in tropical regions, 226–27
FEM
  See Finite-element methods
Field measurements
  diagnostic analysis techniques using extensive, 92–93
Finite-difference methods, 502
Finite-element methods (FEM), 500
Finite renewable resources
  and not compromising the ability of future generations to meet their needs for sustainable development in urban areas, 253
Finland

GDP index and total water withdrawals, 302
Fires, 184–87
"First contact" extinctions, 153
Fish species
 pollution, and the introduction of exotic, 367
Fisheries and ecosystems, 368–75
 discarding and waste, 370–72
 extinction and ecosystem impacts, 373–75
 habitat impacts of fishing, 372–73
 stock status, 368–70
 See also World fisheries
Fisheries management, 382–87
 allocating fish among users, 384–86
 failures of different stocks of the world, 390
 illegal fishing, 386–87
 institutional structure and governance, 382–84
 new solutions, 387
 the precautionary approach and marine protected areas, 387
 successes of different stocks of the world, 389
Fishing fleets
 the behavior of, 381–82
FISHSTAT, 447
Flows and movements as propagations, 108–12
 classes of entities conveyed by propagation, 111
 consequences, 112
 entities, 110–11
 initiating events or conditions, 109–10
 vectors, 111–12
 vectors at a medial level of causation responsible for propagating ecological influences in the biosphere, 112
Fluvial transport
 propagation by running waters, 114–15
Fluxes
 biogeochemical, 115
 defined, 109
 groundwater, 115
 measuring, 114
Fogging sampling techniques, 149
Food and Agriculture Organization (FAO), 209, 284, 319–20, 375, 431, 437–38
Food crops in sub-Saharan Africa
 rates of change in area, yield, and production, 320
Food production
 world increase from 1961–1996, 211
Forecasts concerning human influences, 42–45
 calculated changes in OH and ozone concentrations between 2000–2100, 44
 projected change in various emissions and gases between 2000–2100 for various scenarios, 43
Forecasts of future atmospheric CO_2 levels
 informing carbon sequestration and disposal policies, 543–46
Forecasts of future nitrogen fertilizer requirements, 340–42
 for the major cereals between 2000–2025, 341
Forecasts of water use, 292–96
 projections of global water use over time, 293
 summary of various global water forecasts, 294
Forest carbon cycle
 atmospheric pollutants and the forest biological C cycle, 187–91
 disturbances and forest biological C cycle, 183–87
 the forest C cycle and global change, 170–72
 greenhouse gas management and the role of forests, 192–95
 patterns and mechanisms of, 169–204
 research needed, 195–96
Forest-cover changes
 change estimates of humid tropical forest cover during 1990–1997, 210
 recent, 209–11
Forest ecosystem C cycle, 174–83
 net ecosystem production, 180–83
 net primary production, 176–79
 soil surface CO_2 flux, 179–80
 world forest summary estimates, 175
Forest fires, 184–87
Forest resources, 173–74
 forest land use change dynamics for tropical and nontropical regions, 173
Fortress world scenario, 564
Fossil fuel emissions
 offset by substituting wood/paper material, 194–95
Fourier amplitude sensitivity test (FAST) method, 85
Fractal calculations, 120

SUBJECT INDEX

Framework Convention on
  Climate Change, 193
Frameworks to understand
  land-use/cover changes,
    228–31
  agent-based perspective,
    229
  narrative perspective,
    230–31
  system perspective, 230
Free-air CO_2 enrichment
  (FACE) experiments,
    190–91
Freshwater withdrawals,
  285–89
Friends of the Earth, 571
Fugacity and fugacity
  capacity, 469–70
  for environmentally
    relevant phases, 470
Fugacity calculations
  of different levels of
    complexity used to
    describe multimedia
    contaminant fate, 471
  Level II, 472–73
Functional sensitivity
  analysis, 80–82
Future generations' needs for
  sustainable development
  in urban areas
    biodegradable wastes, 253
    finite renewable resources,
      253
    nonbiodegradable wastes,
      253
    nonrenewable resources,
      253
    not compromising, 253
    social/human capital,
      253
Future needs
  for diagnostic analyses,
    93–94
  for nitrogen fertilizer,
    projections of, 340–42
  for photochemical air
    quality modeling, 98–99
  of world fisheries, 390–91

G

Gap Inc., 270
Gases
  various, projected change
    between 2000–2100 for
    various scenarios, 43
  See also Greenhouse gas
    emissions
Gazetteer service, 514
Generic screening, 478–79
Genetic diversity, 142–44
  distribution of, 150–51
Genuine Progress Indicator
  (GPI), 572, 577
  characterizing and
    measuring sustainable
    development, 564
Geographic data types,
  497–500
  Chicago area showing
    various phenomena,
    498
  mainland portion of
    Santa Barbara County,
    California, 498
Geographic information
  system (GIS)
  advances in software,
    511–16
  advances in the data
    supply, 506–11
  GIS analysis and modeling,
    497–506
  and systems for
    environmental
    management, 493–519
  types of geographic data,
    497–500
Geologic disposal, 528
Geomorphology, 116
Geopolitics
  superpower, 596
GEOTOX, 480
GFM
  See Green's function
    method
GHG
  See Greenhouse gas
    emissions
GIS
  See Geographic
    information system
GIScience, 494–97
Glacial transport
  propagation by movement
    of ice masses, 117
Global Assessment of Land
  Degradation
    (GLASOD), 320
Global-average surface
  temperature anomaly
  with respect to the
    1951–1980 climatology,
    10
Global carbon cycle
  biogeochemistry,
    disturbance, and, 19–21
Global change
  the forest C cycle and,
    170–72
"Global Compact," 430
Global context
  for sustainability and
    development, 269–72
Global emission rates of
  tropospheric trace gases
  estimated, and amounts
    removed by reaction with
    OH, 32
Global fisheries landings
  change in mean trophic
    level for marine and
    inland areas, 374
Global goals
  enabling local action while
    meeting, 265–67
Global land-use/cover change
  historical changes in
    land-use/cover at a global
    scale, 208–9
  most rapid land-cover

changes of the last decades, 209–13
recent changes in agricultural area land cover, 211–12
recent changes in pastoral area land cover, 212
recent changes in urbanization, 212–13
recent estimates of, 208–13
recent forest-cover changes, 209–11
the still unmeasured land-cover changes, 213
Global Positioning System (GPS), 507
Global Reporting Initiative, 572, 576
characterizing and measuring sustainable development, 566
Global scale
of carbon sink estimates, 531
multimedia models, 480
in quantification, 529–31
transport at, 126
Global scale of biodiversity, 141–47
biodiversity novelties, 147
domesticated biodiversity, 146
endemism, 144–46
intraspecific diversity, 142–44
species diversity, 141–42
Global Scenario Group, 569, 571–73, 576–77
characterizing and measuring sustainable development, 564
Global systems
urban centers and, 259
Global trends
in cereal production and nitrogen fertilizer use, 334–36

Global water use, 282–84
over time, projections of, 293
summary of various forecasts, 294
water withdrawal and consumption estimates and projections, 283
Globalization, 450–51
causing land-use change, 221
Goals for sustainable development
selection of, 572–77
Government fisheries subsidies
from OECD countries in 1997, estimated, 376
GPI
See Genuine Progress Indicator
GPP
See Gross primary production
GPS
See Global Positioning System
Grain production
per capita, in relation to per capita water withdrawals, 298
Gravity, 120
"Great Fishing Experiment, The," 363
Great transition scenario, 564
GREATER model, 480
Green chemistry
applying, 413–20
drivers of, 404–10
and engineering, 401–28
fundamentals and basis, 402–13
a hydroformylation case study, 413–20
metrics, 410–13
pollution prevention hierarchy as outlined in

the Pollution Prevention Act of 1990, 403
and sustainability engineering, 420–23
Green consumerism, 269
Greenhouse gas emissions (GHG), 170, 187, 346–49, 522–25, 534, 546
carbon sequestration and, 343–46
reducing, 172, 192–93
Greenhouse gas management
carbon sequestration in forest products, 193–94
carbon sequestration potential in vegetation and soil, 192–93
offset fossil fuel emissions by substituting wood/paper material, 194–95
and the role of forests, 192–95
Greenpeace, 451
Green's function method (GFM), 85
Grid
for geographic information science applications, 514
Gross domestic product
per capita, in relation to per capita water withdrawals, 297
Gross primary production (GPP), 174, 181, 184
for forest biomes worldwide, 181
Groundfish
economic value of landings in Newfoundland from 1989–1996, 361
Groundwater fluxes, 115

H

Habitat loss
driving extinction, 161

impacts of fishing on,
372–73
Hadley Centre model, 544
Harpagornis moorei, 153
Harvesting
and sequential depletion,
363–64
Hazardous air pollutants,
603–4
Hazardous Liquid Pipeline
Safety Act, 610
HAZCHEM model, 479
HCB
See Hexachlorobenzene
Health needs
for sustainable
development in urban
areas at the present,
252
Heterozygosity
mean, 150
Hexachlorobenzene (HCB),
481–82
chemical structure of, 481
High-resolution Regional
Acid Deposition Model
(HR-RADM), 91–92
Historical perspective
in land-use/cover at a
global scale, 208–9
Historical perspective on
impacts of humans on
fish stocks, 363–68
climate, 364–67
harvesting and sequential
depletion, 363–64
inland fisheries, 367–68
pollution and introduction
of exotic species, 367
Historical world fisheries
catches, 369
Hong Kong
GDP and total water
withdrawals, 300
Hotspots, 151, 160
for tanker oil spills, 600
HR-RADM

See High-resolution
Regional Acid Deposition
Model
Human capital
and not compromising the
ability of future
generations to meet their
needs for sustainable
development in urban
areas, 253
Human Development Index,
565
Human exposure to persistent
multimedia pollutants
applications of multimedia
fate and exposure models,
477–82
history and motivation for
multimedia models,
466–67
migration of pollutants
from sources, through the
multimedia environment,
and into the human
exposure media, 465
model evaluation
strategies, 482–92
multimedia contaminant
fate, 468–75
multimedia and
multipathway modeling,
467
multipath exposure
models, 475–77
multiple pathways of,
463–92
regional, continental, and
global scale models,
463–92
Human influences
on the cleansing capacity
of the atmosphere, 39–45
effects of human-driven
changes in trace gas
emissions over time, 42
forecasts, 42–45
industrial revolution, 41–42

the natural atmosphere,
40–41
Human well-being and water
use, 296–98
China's GDP index and
total water withdrawals,
301
Finish GDP index and total
water withdrawals, 302
Hong Kong GDP and total
water withdrawals, 300
per capita grain production
in relation to per capita
water withdrawals, 298
per capita gross domestic
product in relation to per
capita water withdrawals,
297
Polish GDP in relation to
total water withdrawals in
Poland, 299
U.S. GNP index and total
water withdrawals, 301
water sales and population
for the Metropolitan
Water District of Southern
California, 299
Humans
alteration of transport
phenomena by, 124–26
assessing exposures to,
480–82
the ultimate animal
transport vector, 124
Humid tropical forest cover
change estimates during
1990–1997, 210
Hunting
subsistence, 160
Hydroformylation, 413–20
benign solvents, 418–20
catalyst immobilization,
417–18
multiphase systems that
simplify catalyst recovery,
415–17
Hydrology, 114–15

632 SUBJECT INDEX

groundwater, 115
Hydroxyl radical, 45–52
   comparing models and observations, 51–52
   direct measurement, 45–48
   indirect measurement, 48–51
Hyperspectral sensors, 506

I

ICES
   See International Council for the Exploration of the Sea
IDRISI, 495
IEAs
   See International environmental agreements
IGBP
   See International Geosphere Biosphere Program
IHDP
   See International Human Dimensions Programme on Global Environmental Change
IKONOS sensor, 507
Illegal fishing, 386–87
ILO
   See International Labour Organisation
Imagery
   for environmental management, new sources of, 506–7
IMO
   See International Maritime Organization
IMPACT
   See International Model for Policy Analysis of Agricultural Commodities and Trade
Impact Assessment Inc., 602
Impacts
   of climate change, 1–28

Impacts of exploration, drilling, and extraction, 593–98
   incursions into indigenous lands to control oil, 597
Impacts of oil transport, 598–602
   hotspots for tanker oil spills, 600
   largest oil spills in history ranked by volume, 599
   sources of oil spills from marine transport, 600
Incursions into indigenous lands to control oil, 597
India
   yield trends of wheat in, 329
Indicators of sustainable development
   construction of, 577–81
   selection of, 572–77
   technical characteristics of, 578–79
Indigenous groups
   and conflict over oil development, 596
Indigenous lands
   incursions into for control of oil, 597
Indirect measurement of the hydroxyl radical, 48–51
   average OH concentrations estimated from CH_3CCl_3 measurements, 50
Individual transferable quotas (ITQs), 385–86, 388
Industrial Revolution, 41–42
"Information transfer" defined, 109
Inland areas
   change in mean trophic level of global fisheries landings for, 374
Inland fisheries, 367–68

Inorganic nitrogen sources versus organic, 330–31
Inputs
   PAQSM, 66
   uncertainties in, 67–70
Inspections of the oil industry incidence of, 611
Institutional arrangements for environmental management data, 510–11
Institutional factors causing land-use change, 219–20
Integrated reaction rate/mass balance (IRR/MB), 92
Integrative frameworks
   to understand land-use/cover changes, 228–31
Interactions
   between causes of change, 225–26
Intercepted photosynthetic active radiation, 178
Intercepted solar radiation, 178
INTERCOM maize simulation model, 346
Interests
   in negotiating international environmental agreements, 439–42
Intergenerational equity
   in sustainable development, 260–63
Intergovernmental Panel on Climate Change (IPCC), 42–43, 441, 526, 544, 608
Intergraph, 495
International Center for Technology Assessment, 607
International Convention for the Regulation of Whaling, 433
International Council for the

Exploration of the Sea (ICES), 380
International Development Enterprises, 308
International Earth Science Information Network, 432
International environmental agreements (IEAs), 429–61
  bilateral, 438–39
  connections among multilateral agreements through lineages and secretariats, 435–37
  defining, 431–34
  describing the population of, 434–39
  making effective, 444–53
  multilateral, 434–35
  negotiating, 439–44
  substantive and temporal patterns in, 437–38
International Food Policy Research Institute, 319
International Geosphere Biosphere Program (IGBP), 173
  Land-Use and Land-Cover Change project of, 207
International Human Dimensions Programme on Global Environmental Change (IHDP), 207
International Labour Organisation (ILO), 589
International Maize and Wheat Improvement Center (CIMMYT), 328
International Maritime Organization (IMO), 431, 436, 441
International Model for Policy Analysis of Agricultural Commodities and Trade (IMPACT), 113, 318–19
International Rice Research Institute (IRRI), 323, 326
  yield trend of cultivars and lines developed at, 325
International Standards Organization (ISO), 269, 408, 410
International Tropical Timber Agreement, 448
International Whaling Commission, 437
Interspecies equity
  in sustainable development, 260–63
Intraspecific diversity, 142–44
Inventory
  of emissions and carbon sequestration, 534
Invertebrates
  threatened species of in 2002, 156
IPCC
  See Intergovernmental Panel on Climate Change
IPCC Special Report on Land Use, Land-Use Change and Forestry, 536
IRR/MB
  See Integrated reaction rate/mass balance
IRRI
  See International Rice Research Institute
ISO
  See International Standards Organization
Italian Alps
  rock falls in, 116
ITQs
  See Individual transferable quotas
IUCN
  See World Conservation Union (IUCN)
IWGSDI
  See U.S. Interagency Working Group on Sustainable Development Indicators (IWGSDI)

K

Kraft process, 195
Kyoto Protocol, 172, 192, 524–27, 532
  carbon management policy LULUCF in, 546–48

L

LAI
  See Leaf area index
Lake currents, 119–21
  extra-tidal currents, 120–21
  propagation by, 119–21
  tidal currents, 119–20
Land-cover change in tropical regions, 205–41
  the complex nature of land-cover changes, 213–16
  conversion versus modification in land cover, 213–15
  empirical evidences on the causes of land-use change, 216–23
  feedback and endogeneity, 226–27
  fundamental high-level causes of land-use change, 223–25
  integrative frameworks to understand land-use/cover changes, 228–31
  mode of interactions between causes of change, 225–26
  progressive versus episodic land-cover changes, 215–16
  recent estimates of global

634 SUBJECT INDEX

land-use/cover change, 208–13
  research needed, 231–32
  still unmeasured, 213
  synthesis of the causes of, 223–28
Land reserves
  estimating, 318–19
Land resources
  arable, 318–21
Land-use change
  as an emergent property of complex adaptive systems, 227
  and changes in social organization, resource access, and attitudes, 225
  and changing opportunities created by markets, 225
  fundamental high-level causes of, 223–25
  and loss of adaptive capacity and increased vulnerability, 225
  and outside policy intervention, 225
  and resource scarcity, 225
  typology of the causes of, 224
Land-Use and Land-Cover Change (LUCC) project, 207
Land use, land-use change, and forestry (LULUCF) activities, 524–25, 537, 546–48
Land-use transitions, 228
Landfills
  anaerobic conditions of, 193
Landsat's Thematic Mapper, 506
La Niña, 18
Latin hypercube sampling, 86
Latitude
  ozone and hydroxyl radical concentrations as functions of, 33
Latitudinal gradient, 148, 150, 152
LCA
  See Life cycle analysis
LCIA
  See Life-cycle impact assessment
Leaf area index (LAI), 177–79, 189
  for the dominant forest and woodland biomes in relation to precipitation, 177
Leakage
  in carbon management, 525
Legitimacy
  in efforts to characterize and measure sustainable development, 573–75
LEPA
  See Low-energy precision application
Level I models
  partitioning in a closed system, 470–71
Level II models
  equilibrium partitioning in an open system, 471–73
Level III models
  nonequilibrium partitioning in open systems, 473–75
Level IV models
  dynamic, open, and nonequilibrium systems, 475
LiDAR systems, 506
Life cycle analysis (LCA), 194, 403–8, 414
  stages of, 407
Life cycle engineering
  three legs of, 406
Life-cycle impact assessment (LCIA), 405
  sustainability and, 482
Life cycle inventory (LCI), 406–9
  of the generic automobile, 409
Light propagation
  propagation through the electromagnetic spectrum, 122–23
Light use efficiency (LUE), 178
Linked compartments
  use of, 468–69
Liquid wastes
  management systems that reduce environmental hazards of, 263
Local action
  enabling, while meeting national and global goals, 265–67
Local scale
  of quantification, 531–33
  transport at, 126
Loose coupling, 504
Loss of biodiversity, 152–63
  current and future rates of extinction, 161–62
  prehistoric and recent extinctions, 152–56
  recorded extinct species of vertebrates, invertebrates, and plants since 1500, 155
  threatened species, 156–61
  threats to populations, 162–63
Low-energy precision application (LEPA), 308
LRTAP
  See Convention on Long-Range Transboundary Air Pollution (LRTAP)
LUE
  See Light use efficiency
LULUCF

See Land use, land-use change, and forestry activities
Lyme disease
  vectors for, 124

M

Magnusson-Stevens Act, 383
Maize yield
  estimating trends in potential of, 327–28
  hypothetical relationship to N application rate, 348
  relationship to N fertilizer rate, 338
  relationship to plant N accumulation, and applied N when irrigated, 332–33
  simulation biomass models, 347
Managed forests
  alternative land use options in, 345
Managing liquid and solid wastes
  systems that reduce environmental hazards, 263
MapFusion, 509
MapInfo, 495
Marine areas
  change in mean trophic level of global fisheries landings for, 374
Marine pollution (MARPOL) protection regime, 435–36, 448
Marine protected areas (MPA)
  the precautionary approach, 387
Marine transport
  sources of oil spills from, 600
Market forces scenario, 564
Markets' changing opportunities
  causing land-use change, 225
MARPOL
  See Marine pollution protection regime
Marrakesh Accords, 524, 537, 546, 548
Mass-balance models
  multi-region, 479–80
  regional-scale, 479
Material metrics
  of green chemistry, 411
Mauna Loa Observatory Photochemistry Experiment (MLOPEX), 45–48
  hourly average OH concentrations during spring and summer in, 46
Maximum historical yield for major fisheries
  current yield divided by, 371–72
Maximum sustainable yield (MSY), 378
MCFC
  See Molten carbonate fuel cell
MEAs
  See Multilateral agreements
Measurement data available
  limiting diagnostic analyses, 91
Measurement frequency, 535
Measurement of sustainable development, 562–66
  Boston Indicators Project, 565
  Consultative Group on Sustainable Development Indicators, 563
  Costa Rica Sistema de Indicadores sobre Desarrollo Sostenible, 565
  Ecological Footprint, 564
  Environmental Sustainability Index, 563–64
  Genuine Progress Indicator, 564
  Global Reporting Initiative, 566
  Global Scenario Group, 564
  State Failure Task Force, 566
  United Nations Commission on Sustainable Development, 562–63
  U.S. Interagency Working Group on Sustainable Development Indicators, 565
  Wellbeing Index, 563
Mediterranean Action Plan (MEDPLAN), 435, 447–48
Meteorology, 36
  uncertainties in, 69
Metrics of green chemistry, 410–13
  energy metrics, 411–12
  material metrics, 411
  sustainability metrics, 412–13
Metropolitan Water District of Southern California
  water sales and population for, 299
Mexico
  yield trends of wheat in, 329
Microsoft Visio, 514
Mid-domain effect, 150
Migration of pollutants from sources
  through the multimedia environment and into the human exposure media, 465

Millennium Declaration, 572
Missoula Lake floods, 114
MLOPEX
    See Mauna Loa
    Observatory
    Photochemistry
    Experiment
Mobile Corporation, 418
Model evaluation strategies,
    482–92
    and confidence building,
        484–86
    sensitivity and uncertainty
        analyses, 483–84
Model formulation
    uncertainties in, 70–72
Model input uncertainties
    experts' estimates of, 74
Model uncertainty
    information
    importance and uses of,
        61–63
Modeling, 502
    cause for changes in
        perspective, 12–15
    multimedia and
        multipathway, 467
    uncertainties in use of, 73
Models
    of a PAQSM, 63–65
Models of pollution exposure,
    479–80
    global-scale multimedia
        models, 480
    multipath exposure,
        475–77
    multi-region mass-balance
        models, 479–80
    regional, continental, and
        global scale, 463–92
    regional-scale
        mass-balance models, 479
Moderate infrared
    spectrophotometer
    (MODIS)
    remotely-sensed imagery
        from, 173

Modification of land cover
    versus conversion, 213–15
MODIS sensor, 507
Molten carbonate fuel cell
    (MCFC), 421
Monte Carlo analysis, 86, 484
Montreal Protocol, 48, 538
Motivation
    implicit and explicit, for
        characterizing and
        measuring sustainable
        development, 570–71
    for multimedia models,
        466–67
MPA
    See Marine protected areas
MSVPA
    See Multispecies virtual
        population analysis
MSY
    See Maximum sustainable
        yield
Multilateral agreements
    (MEAs), 430, 434–35
    connections among
        lineages and secretariats,
        435–37
    substantive and temporal
        patterns in, 437–38
Multimedia contaminant fate,
    468–75
    dynamic, open, and
        nonequilibrium systems
        (Level IV models), 475
    equilibrium partitioning in
        an open system (Level II
        models), 471–73
    fugacity calculations of
        different levels of
        complexity used to
        describe, 471
    fugacity and fugacity
        capacity, 469–70
    nonequilibrium
        partitioning in open
        systems (Level III
        models), 473–75

    partitioning in a closed
        system (Level I models),
        470–71
    phase equilibrium and
        chemical partitioning in
        environmental systems,
        468–69
Multimedia fate and exposure
    model applications,
    477–82
    assessing exposures to
        humans and ecosystems,
        480–82
    generic screening or
        evaluative models,
        478–79
    regional and spatially
        resolved models, 479–80
    sustainability and life-cycle
        impact assessment, 482
Multimedia models
    sensitivity of, 483
Multi-model simulations, 170
Multipath exposure models,
    475–77
    cumulative, 477
    and exposure events,
        476–77
Multiphase systems
    simplifying catalyst
        recovery in
        hydroformylation, 415–17
Multi-region mass-balance
    models, 479–80
Multispecies and ecosystem
    analysis, 379–80
Multispecies virtual
    population analysis
    (MSVPA), 380

N
NAAQS
    See National Ambient Air
        Quality Standards
NAO
    See North Atlantic
        Oscillation

Narrative perspective
  to understand
  land-use/cover changes,
  230–31
NARSTO
  See North American
  Research Strategy for
  Tropospheric Ozone
National Academy of
  Sciences, 595
National Ambient Air Quality
  Standards (NAAQS),
  59–62, 74, 94
National Center for
  Atmospheric Research,
  96
National Corn Growers
  Association
  yield trends in contests
  sanctioned by, 328
National Energy Policy
  Development Group
  (NEPDG), 588
National Energy Policy
  (U.S.), 587, 601
National goals
  enabling local action while
  meeting, 265–67
National Land-Cover Data,
  539
National Oceanic and
  Atmospheric
  Administration (NOAA)
  Aeronomy Laboratory, 95
  Climate Monitoring and
  Detection Laboratory, 48
National Petroleum Reserve,
  588
National Research Council
  (NRC), 77, 290,
  510
National Spatial Data
  Infrastructure (NSDI),
  510
National water use estimates
  of regional water use,
  284–90
  freshwater withdrawal,
  285–89
National Water-Use
  Information Program,
  290
Natural atmosphere, 40–41
Natural ecosystems
  preserving, 320–21
Natural variability
  causing land-use change,
  217–18
NBP
  See Net biome production
NDVI
  See Normalized Difference
  Vegetation Index
Need for sustainable
  development in urban
  areas, 252
  economic, 252
  environmental, 252
  political, 252
  social, cultural, and health,
  252
Need for water
  defined, 278
Negotiation of international
  environmental
  agreements, 439–44
  actors and processes,
  442–44
  interests, power, and
  discourse, 439–42
NEP
  See Net ecosystem
  production
NEPDG
  See National Energy Policy
  Development Group
Net biome production (NBP),
  176, 187
Net ecosystem production
  (NEP), 172, 176,
  179–83, 185–87, 195
  contribution of root
  respiration to total soil
  surface CO_2 flux for
  forest biomes worldwide,
  181
  for forest biomes
  worldwide, 181
  variation for select forest
  biomes, 182
Net primary production
  (NPP), 172, 176–79,
  184–87, 189–90, 195
  decline in age-related,
  aboveground, for forest
  ecosystems in contrasting
  climates, 185
  leaf area index for the
  dominant forest and
  woodland biomes in
  relation to precipitation,
  177
  for major forest biomes
  and woodlands
  worldwide, 178
Netherlands National Institute
  for Public Health and the
  Environment (RIVM),
  478
Newfoundland cod
  catches since 1850, 361
NGOs
  See Nongovernmental
  organizations
NIOC (Iran), 592
Nitrogen deposition
  atmospheric, 187–88
Nitrogen rates applied
  relationship to maize, rice,
  and wheat yields, 337
Nitrogen requirements,
  346–49
Nitrogen use efficiency
  (NUE), 330–43
  at the field level, 331–34
  improving, 342–43
  inorganic versus organic
  nitrogen sources, 330–31
  relationships among grain
  yield, plant N
  accumulation, and applied

N in irrigated maize, 332–33
NOAA
  See National Oceanic and Atmospheric Administration
Nonbiodegradable wastes
  and not compromising the ability of future generations to meet their needs for sustainable development in urban areas, 253
Nonequilibrium partitioning
  in open systems in Level III models, 473–75
  advective transport among compartments, 474
  diffusive transport among compartments, 474
Nonequilibrium systems
  Level IV models, 475
Nongovernmental organizations (NGOs), 430–31, 433, 441–43, 451, 589
Nonrenewable resources
  and not compromising the ability of future generations to meet their needs for sustainable development in urban areas, 253
  and sinks, 257–59
Nontropical regions
  forest land use change dynamics for, 173
Normalized Difference Vegetation Index (NDVI), 502
North American Research Strategy for Tropospheric Ozone (NARSTO), 66, 75, 77
North Atlantic Oscillation (NAO), 2–5, 10–18
  impact on global climate variability, 7–8
NPP
  See Net primary production
NRC
  See National Research Council
NSDI
  See National Spatial Data Infrastructure
NUE
  See Nitrogen use efficiency
Numerical solution
  uncertainties in model formulation for, 72

O

Observational data
  uncertainties in, 68–69
Occupational Safety and Health Administration (OSHA), 609
Ocean-air interface, 114
Ocean currents, 119–21
  extra-tidal currents, 120–21
  propagation by, 119–21
  tidal currents, 119–20
Ocean measurements, 533–34
Ocean sequestration, 527–28
OECD
  See Organisation for Economic Co-operation and Development
Office of Pipeline Safety, 611
OH concentrations
  calculated changes in between 2000–2100, 44
Oil consumption
  impacts of, 607–9
Oil industry
  regulating, 609–12
Oil pipelines, 601
Oil Pollution Act, 610
Oil production, 592
Oil refining, 593
  impacts of, 603–7
  waste created in, 594–95
Oil Spill Intelligence Report, 600
Oil spills
  hazard of, 596
  hotspots for tanker, 600
  largest in history, ranked by volume, 599
  sources from marine transport, 600
Oil transactions
  dollar amount of worldwide, 589
Oil transport
  impacts of, 598–602
OPEC
  See Organization of Petroleum Exporting Countries
Open systems
  Level IV models, 475
Operational performance evaluation, 76–77
Orders
  distribution of, 148–50
Ordovician Period, 140
Organic nitrogen sources
  versus inorganic, 330–31
Organisation for Economic Co-operation and Development (OECD), 375–76
Organization of Petroleum Exporting Countries (OPEC), 591
OSHA
  See Occupational Safety and Health Administration
OTAG
  See Ozone Transport Assessment Group
Our Common Future, 249
Outer Continental Shelf
  coastal regions
  opening oil exploration in, 588
Outputs

PAQSM, 66–67
Oxidation processes
  main tropospheric, 34
Ozone, 172, 191
  calculated changes in
    concentrations of between
    2000–2100, 44
  chemical processes
    forming and removing
    stratospheric, 38
Ozone Transport Assessment
  Group (OTAG), 74

P

Pacific Decadal Oscillation
  (PDO), 2–12
  impact on global climate
    variability, 7–8
Pacific Fisheries Management
  Council (PFMC), 378
Pacific Pipeline, 602
PAFC
  See Phosphoric acid fuel
    cell
Panchromatic imagery, 506
"Paper" water, 279
PAQSMs
  See Photochemical air
    quality simulation models
PAR
  See Photosynthetic active
    radiation
Parallel Climate Model
  (PCM), 13
Parametric sensitivity
  analysis, 80–82
Particles
  velocity of fall of, 118
Partitioning in a closed
  system in Level I
    models, 470–71
  fugacity calculations of
    different levels of
    complexity used to
    describe multimedia
    contaminant fate, 471
Pastoral area land cover
  recent changes in, 212
Pathways of land-use change
  a finite set of, 221–23
PC
  See Principal component
    analysis
PCM
  See Parallel Climate Model
PCP
  See Pentachlorophenol
PDFs
  See Probability density
    functions
PDO
  See Pacific Decadal
    Oscillation
PEI
  See Potential
    environmental impact
PEM
  See Proton exchange
    membranes
Pemex (Mexico), 592
Pentachlorophenol (PCP),
  481–82
  chemical structure of, 481
Permanence factors
  in carbon management,
    525–26
  informing carbon
    sequestration and disposal
    policies, 541–42
Persian Gulf region
  initiative to gain control of,
    588
  significance of oil reserves
    in, 591
Perverse incentive
  in carbon management, 526
Petroleos de Venezuela, 592
PFMC
  See Pacific Fisheries
    Management Council
Phanerozoic Era, 138, 152
Phase equilibrium in
  environmental systems,
    468–69

chemical equilibrium, 468
conservation of mass, 468
use of linked
  compartments, 468–69
Phenolic glycoside, 191
Phosphoric acid fuel cell
  (PAFC), 421
Photochemical air quality
  simulation model
  (PAQSM) uncertainties,
    67–75
  comprehensive evaluation
    and analyses of, 79
  experts' estimates of, 74
  framework for analyses of,
    75–78
  importance and uses of
    model uncertainty
    information, 61–63
  in inputs, 67–70
  in model formulation,
    70–72
  regional, 59–106
  in use of modeling results,
    73
  variability, 72–73
Photochemical air quality
  simulation models
  (PAQSMs), 63–75
  component models of, 64
  corroborative/alternative
    modeling and subjective
    judgment, 94–98
  defined, 63–67
  diagnostic analyses, 90–94
  inputs, 66
  looking to the future,
    98–99
  models of, 63–65
  outputs, 66–67
  sensitivity analyses, 78–90
  types of, 65–66
Photochemistry of
  Plant-Emitted
  Compounds and OH
  Radicals in North
  Eastern Germany

Experiment (POPCORN), 45, 47–48
  variation of daytime OH concentrations in, 47
Photosynthetic active radiation (PAR), 176–78
  absorbed, 178
  intercepted, 178
Physical displacement of pollutants
  by advection, 472
Planetary winds, 120
Plants
  threatened species of in 2002, 156
Pleistocene Epoch, 117
Poland
  GDP in relation to total water withdrawals, 299
Policy interventions
  causing land-use change, 225
Policy principles in carbon management, 524–26
  additionality, 525
  leakage, 525
  permanence, 525–26
  perverse incentive, 526
  quantification, 525
  separation, 525
  transparency, 526
  verification, 526
Policy reform scenario, 564
Political needs
  for sustainable development in urban areas at the present, 252
Pollution
  and introduction of exotic species, 367
Pollution Prevention Act of 1990
  pollution prevention hierarchy as outlined in, 402–3
Polymorphism, 499
POPCORN
  See Photochemistry of Plant-Emitted Compounds and OH Radicals in North Eastern Germany Experiment
Populations
  distribution of, 150–51
  responses to climate change, 17–19
  threats to, 162–63
Populus tremuloides, 182
Potential environmental impact (PEI), 411
Potential for improving water-use efficiency, 298–310
  cost-effectiveness of efficiency improvements, 303–8
  urban improvements in California, 309–10
Power
  in negotiating international environmental agreements, 439–42
Predictions
  See Forecasts
Preservation
  of natural ecosystems, 320–21
Prestige oil tanker, 599–600
Principal component (PC) analysis, 3
Probability density functions (PDFs), 86
Procedural equity
  in sustainable development, 260–63
Proceedings of the National Academy of Sciences, 576
Process analysis techniques, 91–92
Processes
  in negotiating international environmental agreements, 442–44
Progressive land-cover changes
  versus episodic, 215–16
Projected change in various emissions and gases between 2000–2100 for various scenarios, 43
Projections
  See Forecasts
Prokaryotic species, 141
Propagation, 108–24
  by animal locomotion, 123–24
  by colluvial transport through the action of gravity, 115–17
  consequences, 112
  defined, 108–13
  diffusionary transport by random movements, 113
  entities, 110–11
  fluvial transport by running waters, 114–15
  glacial transport movement by ice masses, 117
  initiating events or conditions, 109–10
  by lake and ocean currents, 119–21
  by light through the electromagnetic spectrum, 122–23
  sedimentary, by particle settling in fluids, 117–19
  through acoustics, 123
  vectors, 111–12
  wind transport by currents of the atmosphere, 121–22
Proterozoic Eon, 117
Proton exchange membranes (PEM), 421
Proximal drivers
  of extinction, 159–60
Proximate causes
  of land-use change, 216–17

SUBJECT INDEX 641

Public Participation GIS, 496
Public transport
 improvements to, 263–64
"Pull-of-the-recent effect,"
 140

Q

Quantification, 529–37
 carbon accounting, 536–37
 in carbon management, 525
 current methods and
  scaling, 529–35
 emission and carbon
  sequestration inventory,
  534
 global and continental
  scales, 529–31
 informing carbon
  sequestration and disposal
  policies, 529–37
 local to regional scales,
  531–33
 measurement frequency,
  535
 ocean measurements,
  533–34
 remote sensing, 534–35
Quaternary Period, 152
Quickbird sensor, 507

R

Rainforest Action Network
 (RAN), 602
RAMS
 See Regional Atmospheric
  Modeling System
RAN
 See Rainforest Action
  Network
Rapid Deployment Force, 588
Raster methods, 500
RCH-RP
 See Ruhrchemie and
  Rhone-Poulenc process
RCRA
 See Resource Conservation
  and Recovery Act

Redefining Progress, 564
Rees, William, 257
Regime effects in
 international
 environmental
 agreements
 the determinants of,
  448–52
 identifying, 444–46
Regional Atmospheric
 Modeling System
 (RAMS), 96
Regional photochemical air
 quality modeling
 uncertainties in, 59–106
Regional-scale mass-balance
 models, 479
Regional scales
 of quantification, 531–33
Regional and spatially
 resolved models of
 pollution exposure,
 479–80
 global-scale multimedia
  models, 480
 multi-region mass-balance
  models, 479–80
 regional-scale
  mass-balance models, 479
Regional water use
 national estimates of,
  284–90
Regulation of the oil industry,
 609–12
 incidence of enforcement,
  612
 incidence of inspections,
  611
Regulatory context
 potential uses of
  corroborative/alternative
  modeling within, 97–98
Remote sensing, 319
 quantifying, 534–35
Removal processes
 uncertainties in model
  formulation for, 71–72

Renewable resources
 and not compromising the
  ability of future
  generations to meet their
  needs for sustainable
  development in urban
  areas, 253
Reproductive responses
 to climate change, 17–19
Research needed
 on the environmental
  impacts of oil production
  and consumption, 612–14
 in the forest carbon cycle,
  195–96
 into land-cover change in
  tropical regions, 231–32
Resolution
 uncertainties in, 70
Resource access
 causing land-use change,
  225
Resource Conservation and
 Recovery Act (RCRA),
 595, 610
Resource Recovery and
 Conservation Act, 603
Resource scarcity
 causing land-use change,
  225
Resources
 nonrenewable, 257–59
Revised 1996 IPCC
 Guidelines for National
 Greenhouse Gas
 Inventories, 526
Rhine river
 chemical spills on, 440
Rhizobium bacteria, 143
Rice producing countries
 yield trends in major,
  323
Rice yield
 estimating trends in
  potential for, 324–26
 relationship to N fertilizer
  rate and plant N

accumulation, 339
RIVM
  See Netherlands National Institute for Public Health and the Environment
Root respiration
  contribution to total soil surface CO_2 flux for forest biomes worldwide, 181
Royal Dutch/Shell, 592
Ruhrchemie and Rhone-Poulenc (RHC-RP) process, 414–15, 418

S

"Sahel Syndrome," 566
SAIMM
  See Systems Applications International Mesoscale Meteorological Model
Salience
  in efforts to characterize and measure sustainable development, 573–75
SARMAP
  See SJV/AUSPEX Regional Mapping of Air Pollution modeling system
Saudi Aramco, 592
Schema development, 512–14
Science of sustainable harvesting, 375–79
  estimated government fisheries subsidies from OECD countries in 1997, 376
  single-species sustainability, 377–79
Scientific capability for informing carbon sequestration and disposal policies, 528–46
  additionality and separation, 537–41
  environmental effects and linkages, 542–43
  permanence, 541–42
  predicting future atmospheric CO_2 levels, 543–46
  quantification, 529–37
Scientific Committee on Problems of the Environment, 561
SDSSs
  See Spatial-decision support systems
Sea level pressure (SLP), 3–4
Second Law of Thermodynamics, 468
Sector Facility Indexing Project (SFIP), 603, 606, 613
Sectoral causes of land-use change, 217–21
  cultural factors, 220–21
  demographic factors, 218–19
  economic and technological factors, 218
  general insights on, 217–21
  globalization, 221
  institutional factors, 219–20
  multiple causes, 217
  natural variability, 217–18
Sediment-water column boundary, 114
Sedimentation
  propagation by particle settling in fluids, 117–19
Sensitivity analyses, 78–90, 483–84
  applications, 87
  comprehensive evaluation and analyses of PAQSM uncertainties, 79
  functional, 80–82
  methods, 83–87
  parametric, 80–82
  selected sensitivity studies using PAQSM, 88–89
  sensitivity of multimedia models, 483
  sources of uncertainty, 483–84
  structural, 83
  uncertainty importance and ranking, 483–84
Sensors and sensor networks for environmental management, 507–8
Separation factors
  in carbon management, 525
  informing carbon sequestration and disposal policies, 537–41
Sequential depletion
  harvesting and, 363–64
Sequestration options, 526–28
  ocean sequestration, 527–28
  terrestrial sequestration, 526–27
SETAC
  See Society of Environmental Toxicology and Chemistry
Sewage farming, 265
SFIP
  See Sector Facility Indexing Project
Shellfish
  economic value of landings in Newfoundland from 1989–1996, 361
SHI
  See State Hydrologic Institute
"Shifting baseline syndrome," 364
Sierra Club Legal Defense Fund, 606
Silent Spring, 464
Silurian Period, 140

SUBJECT INDEX 643

SimpleBox model, 478–80
Single-species sustainability, 377–79
   relationship between spawning stock biomass and sustainable yield, 377
Sinks
   nonrenewable, 257–59
SIP
   See State Implementation Plan
SJV/AUSPEX Regional Mapping of Air Pollution (SARMAP) modeling system, 93
SJVAQS/AUSPEX program, 92
SLP
   See Sea level pressure
Snow-air interface, 114
SOC
   See Soil organic carbon
Social capital
   and not compromising the ability of future generations to meet their needs for sustainable development in urban areas, 253
Social impacts of oil production and consumption, 587–617
   control over oil, 590–93
   environmental justice framework, 590
   impacts of exploration, drilling, and extraction, 593–98
   impacts of oil consumption, 607–9
   impacts of oil refining, 603–7
   impacts of oil transport, 598–602
   policy implications, 612–14

   regulating the oil industry, 609–12
   research needed, 612–14
Social needs
   for sustainable development in urban areas at the present, 252
Social organization
   causing land-use change, 225
Social status
   of fisheries, 375
Society of Environmental Toxicology and Chemistry (SETAC), 406
Sociocultural changes, 113
SOFC
   See Solid oxide fuel cell
Soil
   carbon sequestration potential in, 192–93
Soil-air interface, 114
Soil organic carbon (SOC), 343–44, 347
Soil quality, 346–49
   hypothetical relationship between maize yield and N application rate, 348
   simulation models of maize biomass yield, 347
Soil-snow interface, 114
Soil surface CO_2 flux, 179–80
   annual soil surface CO_2 for major forest biomes and woodlands, 180
Solar radiation (SR)
   absorbed, 178
   intercepted, 178
Solid oxide fuel cell (SOFC), 421
Solid wastes
   management systems that reduce environmental hazards, 263

Sorensen's index, 149
Sound propagation through acoustics, 123
Spatial-decision support systems (SDSSs), 512
Spatial heterogeneity, 380
Spatial interpolation, 500
Spatially resolved models, 479–80
Spawning stock biomass
   relationship to sustainable yield, 377
Species
   bizarre, 147
   discoveries of new, 147
   distribution of, 148–50
   estimating total numbers of, 141–42, 149
   richness of, 148–49
Species diversity, 141–42
"Species half-life," 162
Species turnover, 149
State Failure Task Force, 569, 572, 576
   characterizing and measuring sustainable development, 566
State Hydrologic Institute (SHI), 283
State Implementation Plan (SIP), 61
State of the Nation's Ecosystems report, 577
Static modeling, 502
Stock status, 368–70
   current yield divided by maximum historical yield for major fisheries, 371–72
   historical world fisheries catches, 369
Stoke's Law relationships, 118, 121
Storm King Mountain
   wildfire on, 116

Stratosphere, 38–39
Stressfulness index, 93
Structural sensitivity analysis, 83
Subcontinental carbon sink estimates, 531
Subjective judgment
 corroborative/alternative modeling and, 94–95
Sub-Saharan Africa
 arable land resources, 319–20
 rates of change in area, yield, and production of major food crops in, 320
Subsistence hunting, 160
Substantive patterns
 in multilateral agreements, 437–38
Succession
 changes in the C cycle during, 184–87
Surface processes, 206
Sustainability
 and life-cycle impact assessment, 482
 single-species, 377–79
 of urban centers, 243–74
Sustainability engineering, 420–23
Sustainability metrics
 of green chemistry, 412–13
Sustainable development, 559–86
 and cities, controversies over, 249–51
 defined, 566–69
 implicit and explicit motivations for characterizing and measuring, 570–71
 indicator construction, 577–81
 need for characterizing and measuring, 569–72
 salience, credibility, and legitimacy in efforts to characterize and measure, 574–75
 selection of goals, indicators, and targets, 572–77
 taxonomy of goals for, 561
 twelve selected efforts to characterize and measure, 562–66
Sustainable development principles for urban authorities, 260–63
 intergenerational equity, 260–63
 interspecies equity, 260–63
 procedural equity, 260–63
 trans-boundary equity, 260–63
Sustainable harvesting, 375–79
 estimated government fisheries subsidies from OECD countries in 1997, 376
 single-species sustainability, 377–79
Sustainable yields
 relationship to spawning stock biomass, 377
Synergies that avoid conflict, 263–65
 improvements to public transport, 263–64
 systems for managing liquid and solid wastes that reduce environmental hazards, 263
System perspective
 to understand land-use/cover changes, 230
Systems Applications International Mesoscale Meteorological Model (SAIMM), 96

T
TAC
 See Total allowable catch
Targets for sustainable development
 selection of, 572–77
Taxa
 co-occurrence of, 139
 poorly studied, 154–56
Taxonomy
 of sustainable development goals, 561
Technical characteristics
 of indicators, 578–79
Technological factors
 causing land-use change, 218
Templet, Paul, 604
Temporal patterns
 in multilateral agreements, 437–38
Terrestrial sequestration, 526–27
Terrorism
 targeting oil facilities, 596
Thermohaline circulation system
 in oceans, 120
Threatened species, 156–61
 changes in number of species in different categories of threat, 157
 threatened species of vertebrates, invertebrates, and plants in 2002, 156
Threats to biodiversity
 patchy nature of, 158
Thresholds triggering concern, 92
Tidal currents, 119–20
Tight coupling, 504
TINs
 See Triangulated irregular networks
Tolba, Mostafa, 443
Total allowable catch (TAC), 385

Total Fina Elf, 592
Toxic Release Inventory
    (TRI), 603, 605, 610
Trace gas emissions
  effects of human-driven
    changes over time, 42
  estimated global emission
    rates of tropospheric, 32
Trans-boundary equity
  in sustainable
    development, 260–63
Transformation processes
  using chemical removal,
    472
Transparency
  in carbon management, 526
Transport of energy,
    information, and
    material through the
    biosphere, 107–35
  alteration of transport
    phenomena by humans,
    124–26
  flows and movements as
    propagations, 108–12
  kinds of propagations,
    113–24
  transport at the global and
    local scales, 126
  See also Public transport
Treatment, storage, and
    disposal (TSD) facilities,
    605
Trends in cereal production
  global, 317
Trends in nitrogen fertilizer
    use, 330–43
  disaggregating trends in
    cereal yields, 336–40
  global trends in cereal
    production, 334–36
  improving nitrogen use
    efficiency, 342–43
  inorganic versus organic
    nitrogen sources, 330–31
  nitrogen efficiency at the
    field level, 331–34

projection of future
    requirements, 340–42
Trends in rice yield potential
    estimating, 324–26
Trends in yield potential of
    maize and wheat
    estimating, 327–28
  yield trends in contests
    sanctioned by the
    National Corn Growers
    Association, 328
  yield trends of wheat in
    Mexico and India, 329
TRI
  See Toxic Release
    Inventory
Triangulated irregular
    networks (TINs), 499
Trifolium repens, 143
Tropical regions
  change estimates for forest
    cover during 1990–1997,
    210
  dynamics of land-use and
    land-cover change in,
    205–41
  forest land use change
    dynamics for, 173
Troposphere, 33–38
Tropospheric trace gases
  estimated global emission
    rates and amounts
    removed by reaction with
    OH, 32
TSD
  See Treatment, storage,
    and disposal facilities
Turbulence, 118
  uncertainties in model
    formulation for, 71
Typology
  of the causes of land-use
    change, 224

U

UAM-V
  See Variable Grid Urban

Airshed Model (UAM-V)
Ultimate drivers
  of extinction, 159–60
UML
  See Unified Modeling
    Language
Unaccounted for water
  by country, 306–7
Uncertainties in PAQSM
    inputs, 67–70
  chemistry, 69–70
  emissions, 67–68
  meteorology, 69
  observational data,
    68–69
  resolution, 70
Uncertainties in PAQSM
    model formulation,
    70–72
  for aerosols, 72
  for numerical solution,
    72
  for removal processes,
    71–72
  for turbulence, 71
Uncertainty
  and advances in GIS
    representation, 515–16
  in use of PAQSM modeling
    results, 73
Uncertainty analyses, 483–84
  defined, 75–76
  developing uncertainty
    information, 78
  framework for, 75–78
  operational performance
    evaluation, 76–77
  sensitivity of multimedia
    models, 483
  sources of uncertainty,
    483–84
  uncertainty importance and
    ranking, 483–84
UNCHE
  See United Nations
    Conference on the Human
    Environment

UNEP
  See United Nations Environmental Programme
UNFCCC
  See United Nations Framework Convention on Climate Change
Unified Modeling Language (UML), 513
Unified System for the Evaluation of Substances (USES), 480
Union Carbide, 414
United Nations
  Economic Commission for Europe, 436–37
  Food and Agriculture Organization, 209, 284, 319–20, 375, 431, 437–38
  International Maritime Organization, 431
  Mediterranean Action Plan, 435
  Millennium Declaration, 572
United Nations Commission on Sustainable Development (CSD), 571–73, 576
  characterizing and measuring sustainable development, 562–63
United Nations Conference on Environment and Development, 249, 262, 438, 451
United Nations Conference on the Human Environment (UNCHE), 438, 451
United Nations Environmental Programme (UNEP), 431, 436, 443, 451, 472, 576, 608
  Regional Seas efforts of, 441–42
United Nations Framework Convention on Climate Change (UNFCCC), 433, 524, 534, 543, 572
  Subsidiary Bodies for Implementation and for Scientific and Technological Advice, 437
United States
  estimates of current water use in, 290–92
  GNP index and total water withdrawals, 301
  total U.S. water withdrawals 1900–1995, 291
  U.S. population and per capita water withdrawals 1900–1995, 292
U.S. Army Corps of Engineers, 303
U.S. Department of Agriculture, 532
U.S. Department of Energy, 523, 527, 545
  Parallel Climate Model, 13
U.S. Energy Information Administration, 612
U.S. Geological Survey, 292, 539
U.S. Interagency Working Group on Sustainable Development Indicators (IWGSDI), 572, 577
  characterizing and measuring sustainable development, 565
U.S. State Department, 602
Unquantified or unquantifiable water uses and needs, 281–82
Urban authorities
  sustainable development principles for, 260–63
Urban centers
  and global systems, 259
Urban centers' sustainability, 243–74
  an urbanizing world, 245–49
  building synergies and avoiding conflicts, 263–65
  the controversies over sustainable development and cities, 249–51
  criteria for judging sustainable development in urban areas, 251–56
  ecological footprints of cities, 256–57
  enabling local action while meeting national and global goals, 265–67
  the global context for sustainability and development, 269–72
  implementing sustainable development in cities, 267–69
  nonrenewable resources and sinks, 257–59
  sustainable development and urban authorities, 260–63
  urban centers and global systems, 259
Urban water-use
  improvements in California, 309–10
  expected indoor residential water use from 1998–2020, 309
Urbanization
  recent changes in, 212–13
USES
  See Unified System for the Evaluation of Substances
USLE, 502

V

Variability
  PAQSM uncertainties, 72–73
Variable Grid Urban Airshed Model (UAM-V), 96
Variation
  in NEP for select forest biomes, 182
Vectors, 111–12
  defined, 111
  at a medial level of causation responsible for propagating ecological influences in the biosphere, 112
Vegetation
  carbon sequestration potential in, 192–93
Verification
  in carbon management, 526
Vertebrates
  threatened species of in 2002, 156
Vision 2020 report, 413
Vulnerability
  increased, causing land-use change, 225

W

Wallace Global Fund, 563
WAR
  See Waste Reduction algorithm
War
  disrupting oil operations, 596
Waste in fishing, 370–72
Waste Reduction (WAR) algorithm, 411
Water conservation
  defined, 280
Water-limited yield potential
  defined, 322
Water productivity
  defined, 280

Water use, 275–314
  changing water-use patterns, 298–310
  the connection between water use and human well-being, 296–98
  data problems, 281–82
  definitions of water use, conservation, and efficiency, 278–80
  estimates of current water use, 282–92
  forecasting water use, 292–96
  global and regional disparities in collection, 282
  how is water used, 280–82
  inaccurate data, 282
  needs versus wants for water, 277–78
  the potential for improving water-use efficiency, 298–310
  systematic collection of water use data, 281
  unquantified or unquantifiable water uses and needs, 281–82
Water-use efficiency
  defined, 280
Waxman, Henry A., 604
Wellbeing Index, 563, 572–73, 576
Wellbeing of Nations, The, 563
Wheat
  estimating trends in yield potential of, 327–28
Wind transport
  propagation by currents of the atmosphere, 121–22
Wisconsin glaciation, 152
Withdrawal
  defined, 278
World Bank, 451

World Checklist of Seed Plants, 142
World Commission on Environment and Development, 251
World Conservation Union (IUCN), 154, 156–60, 431, 563, 573
World Economic Forum, 563, 571
World fisheries, 359–98
  the behavior of fishing fleets, 381–82
  catches of Newfoundland cod since 1850, 361
  economic value of landings for groundfish and shellfish in Newfoundland from 1989–1996, 361
  fishery management of different stocks of the world, 389–90
  the future of world fisheries, 390–91
  historical perspective on impacts of humans on fish stocks, 363–68
  methods of fisheries management, 382–87
  multispecies and ecosystem analysis, 379–80
  the science of sustainable harvesting, 375–79
  social and economic status of fisheries, 375
  status of fisheries and ecosystems, 368–75
  what determines success and failure, 387–90
World food production
  increase from 1961–1996, 211
World forests
  summary estimates, 175
World Heritage Convention, 448

World oil
  net importers in 2001, 593
  reserves, production, and exports in 2001, 591
World Summit on Social Development, 569
World Summit on Sustainable Development, 451, 560
World urbanization, 245–49
  distribution of world's urban population by region, 1950–2010, 246
World Wide Web (WWW), 495

World's Water, The, 284
Worldwide Fund for Nature, 451
WWW
  See World Wide Web

Y

Yield potential, 321–30
  adequacy of existing yield gaps, 328–30
  defined, 322
  definitions, 321
  estimating trends in rice yield potential, 324–26
  estimating trends in yield potential of maize and wheat, 327–28
  importance of maintaining an exploitable yield gap, 321–24
  water-limited, defined, 322
  yield trends in major rice producing countries, 323
Yosemite Valley
  rock falls in, 116

Z

Zea diploperennis, 147

Cumulative Indexes

CONTRIBUTING AUTHORS, VOLUMES 19–28

A
Abraham MA, 28:401–28
Adelman MA, 22:13–46
Amann M, 25:339–75
Anderson D, 19:423–55;
  20:495–511, 562–73;
  22:187–215;
  27:271–308
Anderson J, 24:431–60
Atkinson GD, 19:457–74
Aubinet M, 26:435–65
Ausubel JH, 20:463–92
Azar C, 24:513–44

B
Bacon RW, 20:119–43;
  26:331–59
Baldwin SF, 26:391–434
Barkenbus JN,
  20:179–212
Barnes DF, 21:497–530
Battle M, 23:207–23
Baumol WJ, 20:71–81
Baxter L, 22:119–54
Beck PW, 24:113–37
Bender ML, 23:207–23
Besant-Jones J, 26:331–59
Blake DR, 25:685–740
Blanchard CL, 24:329–65
Blok K, 23:123–205
Bodansky DM, 20:425–61
Bormann FH, 21:1–29
Branch TA, 28:359–99
Broecker WS, 25:1–19
Brooks H, 26:28, 29–48
Brown MA, 23:287–385
Brown ML, 24:487–512
Brown N, 28:59–106
Brown RE, 27:119–58

Bukharin O, 21:467–96
Bullard CW,
  19:113–52
Bunn M, 22:403–86

C
Cairns J Jr, 21:167–89
Calwell C, 27:119–58
Cano-Ruiz JA,
  23:499–536
Carbonell R, 25:115–46
Carmichael G, 25:339–75
Cassman KG, 28:315–58
Cavanagh R, 20:519–25
Chapel SW, 22:155–85
Chaurey A, 27:309–48
Chávez O, 24:607–43
Chen Q, 25:567–600
Chertow MR, 25:313–37
Chow JC, 19:241–66
Chua S, 24:391–430
Cicchetti CJ, 20:512–18
Connolly S, 28:587–617
Connors SR, 25:147–97
Craig PP, 24:461–86;
  27:83–118
Cullicott C, 27:119–58

D
Daily GC, 21:125–44
Dargay J, 20:145–78
DeAngelo BJ, 22:75–118
Dearing A, 25:89–113
Davies JA, 28:401–28
de Beer J, 23:123–205
DeCicco J, 25:477–535
Decker EH, 25:685–740
De Laquil P III,
  21:371–402

Denison RA, 21:191–237
Dernbach J, 26:361–89
DeSimone JM, 25:115–46
Dilling L, 28:521–58
Dirzo R, 28:137–67
Dobermann A, 28:315–58
Doney SC, 28:521–58
Dowlatabadi H,
  24:513–44
Dracker R, 21:371–402
Drake EM, 21:145–66
Driese KL, 28:107–35
Dubourg WR, 19:457–74

E
Edmonds J, 24:487–512;
  28:521–58
Ehrenfeld J, 22:487–535
Ehrlich PR, 21:125–44
Elliott S, 25:685–740
Emanuel AE, 22:263–303
Erdal S, 25:765–802
Ernst B, 28:359–99
Eto JH, 27:119–58
Eyer JM, 21:347–70
Ezzati M, 27:233–70

F
Farhar BC, 19:211–39
Feinstein CD, 22:155–85
Fine J, 28:59–106
Fisher RK, 24:173–88
Fisher-Vanden K,
  22:589–628
Fisk WJ, 25:537–66
Floor WM, 21:497–530
Flynn J, 20:83–118
Foell W, 25:339–75
Forsberg C, 20:179–212

649

Friedmann R, 23:225–52
Fulkerson W, 24:487–512

G
Gadgil A, 23:253–86; 27:83–118
Galloway JN, 21:261–92
Gately D, 20:145–78
Geist HJ, 28:205–41
Geller H, 19:301–46
Gleick PH, 19:267–99; 28:275–314
Glicksman LR, 26:83–115
Goldemberg J, 23:1–23
Goldstein BD, 25:765–802
Goodchild MF, 28:493–519
Goody R, 27:1–20
Gopalakrishnan A, 27:369–95
Gower ST, 28:169–204
Graedel TE, 20:265–300; 21:69–98
Greden LV, 26:83–115
Green C, 25:339–75
Greene DL, 24:487–512; 25:477–535
Grubb M, 27:271–308
Grübler A, 24:545–69
Gurney KR, 28:521–58
Gutman PS, 19:189–210

H
Haddad BM, 22:357–401
Hadley S, 22:119–54
Hall SJ, 21:311–46
Håmsø B, 19:37–73
Harriss R, 28:521–58
Harte J, 22:75–118
He K, 27:397–431
Heath LS, 26:435–65
Heckman JR, 21:167–89
Held IM, 25:441–75
Hendriks C, 26:303–29
Henningsen J, 19:365–85
Hermann F, 20:233–64

Herzog HJ, 21:145–66
Hettelingh J-P, 25:339–75
Hilborn R, 28:359–99
Hirst E, 20:535–55; 22:119–54
Holdren JP, 22:403–86; 26:391–434
Holloway S, 26:145–66
Holzman LR, 19:347–64
Hordijk L, 25:339–75
Horgan SA, 21:347–70
Houghton RA, 21:293–310; 24:571–605
Huo H, 27:397–431

I
Iannucci JJ, 21:347–70

J
Jochem E, 19:365–85
Johnson T, 25:339–75
Joshi V, 25:741–63
Joskow PL, 20:526–34

K
Kammen DM, 27:233–70
Kandlikar M, 25:629–84
Karekezi S, 19:387–421
Karjalainen T, 26:435–65
Kates RW, 26:xiv, 1–26; 28:559–86
Kazimi MS, 24:139–71
Keeling CD, 23:25–82
Keeling RF, 23:207–23
Keith DW, 25:245–84
Khalil MAK, 24:645–61; 25:741–63
Kheshgi HS, 25:199–244
Kicklighter DW, 21:293–310
Kinsman J, 26:435–65
Kishore VVN, 25:741–63
Köhler J, 27:271–308
Koomey JG, 20:535–55; 23:287–385; 27:83–118, 119–58
Koplow D, 26:361–89

L
Lackner KS, 27:193–232
Laitner S, 27:119–58
Lambin EF, 28:205–41
Lashof DA, 22:75–118
Lee JJ, 26:167–200
Lepers E, 28:205–41
Levine MD, 23:287–385
Lew D, 27:309–48
Li J, 25:339–75
Lin J, 27:349–67
Linden HR, 21:31–67
Liverman DM, 24:607–43
Lukachko SP, 26:167–200
Lynd LR, 21:403–65

M
Macfarlane A, 26:201–35
MacLeod M, 28:463–92
Magnusson A, 28:359–99
Mahlman JD, 23:83–105
Malone TF, 20:1–29
March PA, 24:173–88
Marland G, 25:199–244
Marteel AE, 28:401–28
Martin N, 26:303–29
Martin PH, 26:435–65
Martinot E, 22:357–401; 27:309–48
Mashayekhi A, 19:37–73
Matos G, 23:107–22
Matson PA, 21:311–46
Mauzerall DL, 26:237–68
May AD, 21:239–60
McGowan JG, 25:147–97
McGranahan G, 28:243–74
McGuire AD, 21:293–310
McKone TE, 28:463–92
McMahon JE, 20:535–55
McNeill JA, 22:263–303
McRae GJ, 23:499–536
Melillo JM, 21:293–310
Miller AS, 19:347–64
Minte-Vera CV, 28:359–99
Mitchell C, 25:285–312
Mitchell JV, 24:83–111

Mitchell RB, 28:429–61
Mock JE, 22:305–56
Mödl A, 20:233–64
Mooney HA, 24:1–31
Moreira JR, 27:349–67
Morgenstern RD,
 24:431–60
Morris JG Jr, 24:367–90
Mosdale R, 24:281–328
Murtishaw S, 26:49–81

N
Nabuurs G-J, 26:435–65
Nadel S, 19:301–46;
 27:159–92
Nagpal T, 25:339–75
Nakićenović N,
 24:545–69
Nash CA, 21:239–60
Nash J, 22:487–535
Naylor RL, 21:99–123
Nichols AL, 20:556–61
Norford LK, 26:83–115

O
Ogden JM, 24:227–79
Olson WW, 28:401–28
Orans R, 22:155–85
O'Rourke D, 28:587–617
Ozawa Meida L, 26:303–29

P
Pacyna JM, 20:265–300
Parris TM, 28:559–86
Parson EA, 22:589–628
Patrick R, 22:1–11
Pearce D, 27:57–81
Pearce DW, 19:457–74
Peng C, 25:339–75
Price L, 26:117–43, 303–29
Prince RC, 25:199–244
Prinn RG, 28:29–57
Pu Y, 25:339–75

R
Rabl A, 25:601–27
Radermacher R, 19:113–52

Rajah N, 19:475–504
Ramachandran G, 25:629–84
Ramakrishna K,
 24:571–605
Ramankutty R, 25:339–75
Raven PH, 28:137–67
Ravindranath NH,
 23:387–437
Razavi H, 19:37–73
Reddy AKN, 27:23–56
Reiners WA, 28:107–35
Reynolds S, 28:59–106
Rind D, 22:47–74
Rochlin GI, 19:153–87
Rogner H-H, 22:217–62
Romm JP, 23:287–385
Rosenfeld AH, 23:287–385;
 24:33–82
Rosenzweig C, 22:47–74
Ross M, 19:75–112
Roth P, 28:59–106
Roth PM, 21:311–46
Rowland FS, 25:685–740
Russell A, 22:537–88
Russell M, 23:439–63
Ruth M, 26:117–43

S
Sagar AD, 25:377–439
Saleska SR, 22:75–118
Sànchez R, 24:607–43
San Martin RL,
 24:487–512
Sanstad AH, 20:535–55
Sathaye JA, 23:387–437
Satterthwaite D,
 28:243–74
Schafer A, 26:167–200
Scheuerell MD, 28:359–99
Schimel D, 28:1–28, 521–58
Schipper L, 20:325–86;
 26:49–81
Schock RN, 24:487–512
Schoenung SM, 21:347–70
Shah J, 25:339–75
Sheinbaum C, 23:225–52
Siddiqi TA, 20:213–32

Sinton JE, 22:357–401
Slovic P, 20:83–118
Smil V, 25:21–51, 53–88
Smith FA, 25:685–740
Smith KR, 25:741–63
Smith S, 19:475–504
Soden BJ, 25:441–75
Sørensen B, 20:387–424
Spadaro JV, 25:601–27
Spengler JD, 25:567–600
Srinivasan S, 24:281–328
Starr C, 20:31–44
Stephens B, 28:521–58
Stevens P, 24:281–328
Stieglitz M, 22:47–74
Stokes G, 28:521–58
Streets D, 25:339–75

T
Taylor DK, 25:115–46
Tester JW, 22:305–56
Themelis NJ, 23:465–97
Thomas VN, 20:301–24
Thornton J, 27:119–58
Ting M, 26:49–81
Todreas NE, 24:139–71
Toman MA, 24:431–60

U
Uma R, 25:741–63
Unander F, 26:49–81

V
Valero JL, 28:359–99
Varady RG, 24:607–43
Victor DG, 24:545–69
Vine EL, 26:435–65
von Meier A, 19:153–87
Vuilleumier L,
 28:59–106

W
Wagner L, 23:107–22
Waitz IA, 26:167–200
Wallace LA, 26:269–301
Walters DT, 28:315–58
Wamukonya N, 27:309–48

Wang G, 28:1–28
Wang X, 26:237–68
Watson JG, 19:241–66
Webber C, 27:119–58
Weinberg AM, 19:15–36
Wernick IK, 20:463–92; 23:465–97

White GF, 19:1–13
Worrell E, 23:123–205; 26:117–43, 303–29
Wright PM, 22:305–56
Wuebbles DJ, 20:45–70
Wyman CE, 24:189–226

Y

Yang C, 24:281–328
Yang H, 28:315–58

Z

Zhang J, 25:741–63
Zhang Q, 27:397–431

CHAPTER TITLES, VOLUMES 19–28

EARTH'S LIFE SUPPORT SYSTEMS

Climate

How Europe Convinced Itself that It Could Meet the Carbon Dioxide Stabilization Target	E Jochem, J Henningsen	19:365–85
Weighing Functions for Ozone Depletion and Greenhouse Gas Effects on Climate	DJ Wuebbles	20:45–70
The Emerging Climate Change Regime	DM Bodansky	20:425–61
The Role of Moisture Transport Between Ground and Atmosphere in Global Change	D Rind, C Rosenzweig, M Stieglitz	22:47–74
Terrestrial Ecosystem Feedbacks to Global Climate Change	DA Lashof, BJ DeAngelo, SR Saleska, J Harte	22:75–118
International Technology Transfer for Climate Change Mitigation and the Cases of Russia and China	E Martinot, JE Sinton, BM Haddad	22:357–401
Integrated Assessment Models of Global Climate Change	EA Parson, K Fisher-Vanden	22:589–628
Science and Nonscience Concerning Human-Caused Climate Warming	JD Mahlman	23:83–105
Climate Change Mitigation in the Energy and Forestry Sectors of Developing Countries	JA Sathaye, NH Ravindranath	23:387–437
Converging Paths Leading to the Role of the Oceans in Climate Change	WS Broecker	25:1–19
Geoengineering the Climate: History and Prospect	DW Keith	25:245–84
Water Vapor Feedback and Global Warming	IM Held, BJ Soden	25:441–75

Greenhouse Implications of Household Stoves: An Analysis for India	KR Smith, R Uma, VVN Kishore, J Zhang, V Joshi, MAK Khalil	25:741–63
Climate Change, Climate Modes, and Climate Impacts	G Wang, D Schimel	28:1–28

Atmosphere

Clear Sky Visibility as a Challenge for Society	JG Watson, JC Chow	19:241–66
Asia-Wide Emissions of Greenhouse Gases	TA Siddiqi	20:213–32
Anthropogenic Mobilization of Sulfur and Nitrogen: Immediate and Delayed Consequences	JN Galloway	21:261–92
NO_x Emissions from Soil: Implications for Air Quality Modeling in Agricultural Regions	SJ Hall, PA Matson, PM Roth	21:311–46
The O_2 Balance of the Atmosphere: A Tool for Studying the Fate of Fossil Fuel CO_2	ML Bender, M Battle, RF Keeling	23:207–23
Non-CO_2 Greenhouse Gases in the Atmosphere	MAK Khalil	24:645–61
The Causes and Consequences of Particulate Air Pollution in Urban India: A Synthesis of the Science	M Kandlikar, G Ramachandran	25:629–84
Observing and Thinking About the Atmosphere	R Goody	27:1–20
Urban Air Pollution in China: Current Status, Characteristics, and Progress	K He, H Huo, Q Zhang	27:397–431
The Cleansing Capacity of the Atmosphere	RG Prinn	28:29–57
Evaluating Uncertainties in Regional Photochemical Air Quality Modeling	J Fine, L Vuilleumier, S Reynolds, P Roth, N Brown	28:59–106

Marine and Terrestrial Ecosystems

Restoration Ecology: The State of an Emerging Field	J Cairns Jr, JR Heckman	21:167–89

Tropical Deforestation and the Global Carbon Budget	JM Melillo, RA Houghton, DW Kicklighter, AD McGuire	21:293–310
The Development of the Science of Aquatic Ecosystems	R Patrick	22:1–11
On the Road to Global Ecology	HA Mooney	24:1–31
Harmful Algal Blooms: An Emerging Public Health Problem with Possible Links to Human Stress on the Environment	JG Morris Jr.	24:367–90
Transport of Energy, Information, and Material Through the Biosphere	WA Reiners, KL Driese	28:107–35
Global State of Biodiversity and Loss	R Dirzo, PH Raven	28:137–67

Biogeochemistry

Phosphorus in the Environment: Natural Flows and Human Interferences	V Smil	25:53–88
Integrated Analysis for Acid Rain in Asia: Policy Implications and Results of RAINS-ASIA Model	J Shah, T Nagpal, T Johnson, M Amann, G Carmichael, W Foell, C Green, J-P Hettelingh, L Hordijk, J Li, C Peng, Y Pu, R Ramankutty, D Streets	25:339–75
Carbon Sinks in Temperate Forests	PH Martin, G-J Nabuurs, M Aubinet, T Karjalainen, EL Vine, J Kinsman, LS Heath	26:435–65
Carbonate Chemistry for Sequestering Fossil Carbon	KS Lackner	27:193–232
Patterns and Mechanisms of the Forest Carbon Cycle	ST Gower	28:169–204
The Role of Carbon Cycle Observations and Knowledge in Carbon Management	L Dilling, SC Doney, J Edmonds, KR Gurney, R Harriss, D Schimel, B Stephens, G Stokes	28:521–58

HUMAN USE OF ENVIRONMENT AND RESOURCES
Energy

From Technological Fixer to Think-Tanker	AM Weinberg	19:15–36
International Gas Trade: Potential Major Projects	B Håmsø, A Mashayekhi, H Razavi	19:37–73
Automobile Fuel Consumption and Emissions: Effects of Vehicle and Driving Characteristics	M Ross	19:75–112
New Technologies for Air Conditioning and Refrigeration	CW Bullard, R Radermacher	19:113–52
Nuclear Power Operations: A Cross-Cultural Perspective	GI Rochlin, A von Meier	19:153–87
Involuntary Resettlement in Hydropower Projects	PS Gutman	19:189–210
Trends in US Public Perceptions and Preferences on Energy and Environmental Policy	BC Farhar	19:211–39
Water and Energy	PH Gleick	19:267–99
Market Transformation Strategies to Promote End-Use Efficiency	H Geller, S Nadel	19:301–46
Products Liability and Associated Perceptions of Risk: Implications for Technological Innovation Related to Energy Efficiency and Environmental Quality	AS Miller, LR Holzman	19:347–64
Disseminating Renewable Energy Technologies in Sub-Saharan Africa	S Karekezi	19:387–421
A Personal History: Technology to Energy Strategy	C Starr	20:31–44
Yucca Mountain: A Crisis for Policy: Prospects for America's High-Level Nuclear Waste Program	J Flynn, P Slovic	20:83–118
The Response of World Energy and Oil Demand to Income Growth and Changes in Oil Prices	J Dargay, D Gately	20:145–78
Internationalizing Nuclear Safety: The Pursuit of Collective Responsibility	JN Barkenbus, C Forsberg	20:179–212
The Elimination of Lead in Gasoline	VN Thomas	20:301–24

Determinants of Automobile Use and Energy Consumption in OECD Countries	L Schipper	20:325–86
History of, and Recent Progress in, Wind-Energy Utilization	B Sørensen	20:387–424
Energy Efficiency and the Economists: The Case for a Policy Based on Economic Principles	D Anderson	20:495–511
Four Misconceptions About Demand-Side Management	CJ Cicchetti	20:512–18
Energy-Efficiency Solutions: What Commodity Prices Can't Deliver	R Cavanagh	20:519–25
Utility-Subsidized Energy-Efficiency Programs	PL Joskow	20:526–34
Energy Efficiency Policy and Market Failures	MD Levine, JG Koomey, JE McMahon, AH Sanstad, E Hirst	20:535–55
Demand-Side Management: An Nth-Best Solution?	AL Nichols	20:556–61
Roundtable on Energy Efficiency and the Economists—An Assessment	D Anderson	20:562–73
The Evolution of an Energy Contrarian	HR Linden	21:31–67
Carbon Dioxide Recovery and Disposal from Large Energy Systems	HJ Herzog, EM Drake	21:145–66
Energy Storage for a Competitive Power Market	SM Schoenung, JM Eyer, JJ Iannucci, SA Horgan	21:347–70
Progress Commercializing Solar-Electric Power Systems	R Dracker, P De Laquil III	21:371–402
Overview and Evaluation of Fuel Ethanol from Cellulosic Biomass: Technology, Economics, the Environment, and Policy	LR Lynd	21:403–65
Security of Fissile Materials in Russia	O Bukharin	21:467–96
My Education in Mineral (Especially Oil) Economics	MA Adelman	22:13–46
Transition-Cost Issues for US Electricity Utilities	E Hirst, L Baxter, S Hadley	22:119–54
The Distributed Utility: A New Electric Utility Planning and Pricing Paradigm	CD Feinstein, R Orans, SW Chapel	22:155–85

An Assessment of World Hydrocarbon Resources	H-H Rogner	22:217–62
Geothermal Energy from the Earth: Its Potential Impact as an Environmentally Sustainable Resource	JE Mock, JW Tester, PM Wright	22:305–56
Managing Military Uranium and Plutonium in the United States and the Former Soviet Union	M Bunn, JP Holdren	22:403–86
Mexican Electric End-Use Efficiency: Experiences to Date	R Friedmann, C Sheinbaum	23:225–52
The Art of Energy Efficiency: Protecting the Environment with Better Technology	AH Rosenfeld	24:33–82
Nuclear Energy in the Twenty-First Century: Examination of a Contentious Subject	PW Beck	24:113–37
Nuclear Power Economic Performance: Challenges and Opportunities	MS Kazimi, NE Todreas	24:139–71
It's Not Easy Being Green: Environmental Technologies Enhance Conventional Hydropower's Role in Sustainable Development	PA March, RK Fisher	24:173–88
Biomass Ethanol: Technical Progress, Opportunities, and Commerical Challenges	CE Wyman	24:189–226
Prospects for Building a Hydrogen Energy Infrastructure	JM Ogden	24:227–79
Fuel Cells: Reaching the Era of Clean and Efficient Power Generation in the Twenty-First Century	S Srinivasan, R Mosdale, P Stevens, C Yang	24:281–328
The Economics of "When" Flexibility in the Design of Greenhouse Gas Abatement Policies	MA Toman, RD Morgenstern, J Anderson	24:431–60
High-Level Nuclear Waste: The Status of Yucca Mountain	PP Craig	24:461–86
Energy in the Twentieth Century: Resources, Conversions, Costs, Uses, and Consequences	V Smil	25:21–51

Opportunities for Pollution Prevention and Energy Efficiency Enabled by the Carbon Dioxide Technology Platform	DK Taylor, R Carbonell, JM DeSimone	25:115–46
Windpower: A Turn of the Century Review	JG McGowan, SR Connors	25:147–97
The Potential of Biomass Fuels in the Context of Global Climate Change: Focus on Transportation Fuels	HS Kheshgi, RC Prince, G Marland	25:199–244
Engineering-Economic Analyses of Automotive Fuel Economy Potential in the United States	DL Greene, J DeCicco	25:477–535
Methyl tert-Butyl Ether as a Gasoline Oxygenate: Lessons for Environmental Public Policy	S Erdal, BD Goldstein	25:765–802
Indicators of Energy Use and Carbon Emissions: Explaining the Energy Economy Link	L Schipper, F Unander, S Murtishaw, M Ting	26:49–81
Energy Conservation in Chinese Residential Buildings: Progress and Opportunities in Design and Policy	LR Glicksman, LK Norford, LV Greden	26:83–115
Policy Modeling for Energy Efficiency Improvement in US Industry	E Worrell, L Price, M Ruth	26:117–43
Storage of Fossil Fuel-Derived Carbon Dioxide Beneath the Surface of the Earth	S Holloway	26:145–66
Historical and Future Trends in Aircraft Performance, Cost, and Emissions	JJ Lee, SP Lukachko, IA Waitz, A Schafer	26:167–200
Interim Storage of Spent Fuel in the United States	A Macfarlane	26:201–35
Global Electric Power Reform, Privatization, and Liberalization of the Electric Power Industry in Developing Countries	RW Bacon, J Besant-Jones	26:331–59

The PCAST Energy Studies: Toward a National Consensus on Energy Research, Development, Demonstration, and Deployment Policy	JP Holdren, SF Baldwin	26:391–434
The Evolution of an Energy Analyst: Some Personal Reflections	AKN Reddy	27:23–56
What Can History Teach Us? A Retrospective Examination of Long-Term Energy Forecasts for the United States	PP Craig, A Gadgil, JG Koomey	27:83–118
Appliance and Equipment Efficiency Standards	S Nadel	27:159–92
Household Energy, Indoor Air Pollution, and Health in Developing Countries: Knowledge Base for Effective Interventions	M Ezzati, DM Kammen	27:233–70
Renewable Energy Markets in Developing Countries	E Martinot, A Chaurey, D Lew, JR Moreira, N Wamukonya	27:309–48
Appliance Efficiency Standards and Labeling Programs in China	J Lin	27:349–67
Evolution of the Indian Nuclear Power Program	A Gopalakrishnan	27:369–95

Water

Drinking Water in Developing Countries	A Gadgil	23:253–86
Water Use	PH Gleick	28:275–314

Agriculture

Energy and Resource Constraints on Intensive Agricultural Production	RL Naylor	21:99–123
Protecting Agricultural Crops from the Effects of Tropospheric Ozone Exposure: Reconciling Science and Standard Setting in the United States, Europe, and Asia	DL Mauzerall, X Wang	26:237–68
Meeting Cereal Demand While Protecting Natural Resources and Improving Environmental Quality	KG Cassman, A Dobermann, DT Walters, H Yang	28:315–58

Settlements

Urban Congestion: A European Perspective on Theory and Practice	AD May, CA Nash	21:239–60
Energy and Material Flow Through the Urban Ecosystem	EH Decker, S Elliott, FA Smith, DR Blake, FS Rowland	25:685–740
Urban Centers: An Assessment of Sustainability	G McGranahan, D Satterthwaite	28:243–74

Industry and Manufacturing

Environmental Industries With Substantial Start-Up Costs as Contributors to Trade Competitiveness	WJ Baumol	20:71–81
National Materials Flows and the Environment	IK Wernick, JH Ausubel	20:463–92
On The Concept of Industrial Ecology	TE Graedel	21:69–98
Future Technologies for Energy-Efficient Iron and Steel Making	J de Beer, E Worrell, K Blok	23:123–205
Recycling Metals for the Environment	IK Wernick, NJ Themelis	23:465–97
Environmentally Conscious Chemical Process Design	JA Cano-Ruiz, GJ McRae	23:499–536
Industrial Symbiosis: Literature and Taxonomy	MR Chertow	25:313–37
Carbon Dioxide Emissions from the Global Cement Industry	E Worrell, L Price, N Martin, C Hendriks, L Ozawa Meida	26:303–29
Green Chemistry and Engineering: Drivers, Metrics, and Reduction to Practice	AE Marteel, JA Davies, WW Olson, MA Abraham	28:401–28

Living Resources

State of the World's Fisheries	R Hilborn, TA Branch, B Ernst, A Magnusson, CV Minte-Vera, MD Scheuerell, JL Valero	28:359–99

Land Use

Dynamics of Land-Use and Land-Cover Change in Tropical Regions	EF Lambin, HJ Geist, E Lepers	28:205–41

MANAGEMENT AND HUMAN DIMENSIONS
Governance

The Economics of Sustainable Development	DW Pearce, GD Atkinson, WR Dubourg	19:457–74
Using Taxes to Price Externalities: Experiences in Western Europe	N Rajah, S Smith	19:475–504
Privatization and Reform in the Global Electricity Supply Industry	RW Bacon	20:119–43
Rural Energy in Developing Countries: A Challenge for Economic Development	DF Barnes, WM Floor	21:497–530
Renewable Energy Technology and Policy for Development	D Anderson	22:187–215
Electric Power Quality	AE Emanuel, JA McNeill	22:263–303
From Physics to Development Strategies	J Goldemberg	23:1–23
Toward a Productive Divorce: Separating DOE Cleanups from Transition Assistance	M Russell	23:439–63
Economic Growth, Liberalization, and the Environment: A Review of the Economic Evidence	S Chua	24:391–430
Environmental Issues Along the United States-Mexico Border: Drivers of Change and Responses of Citizens and Institutions	DM Liverman, RG Varady, O Chávez, R Sánchez	24:607–43
Technologies Supportive of Sustainable Transportation	A Dearing	25:89–113
The England and Wales Non-Fossil Fuel Obligation: History and Lessons	C Mitchell	25:285–312
Federal Fossil Fuel Subsidies and Greenhouse Gas Emmissions: A Case Study of Increasing Transparency for Fiscal Policy	D Koplow, J Dernbach	26:361–89

International Environmental Agreements: A Survey of their Features, Formation, and Effects	RB Mitchell	28:429–61

Methods

Atmospheric Emissions Inventories: Status and Prospects	JM Pacyna, TE Graedel	20:265–300
Codes of Environmental Management Practice: Assessing their Potential as a Tool for Change	J Nash, J Ehrenfeld	22:487–535
Regional Photochemical Air Quality Modeling: Model Formulations, History, and State of the Science	A Russell	22:537–88
Engineering-Economic Studies of Energy Technologies to Reduce Greenhouse Gas Emissions: Opportunities and Challenges	MA Brown, MD Levine, JP Romm, AH Rosenfeld, JG Koomey	23:287–385
Methods for Attributing Ambient Air Pollutants to Emission Sources	CL Blanchard	24:329–65
A Review of Technical Change in Assessment of Climate Policy	C Azar, H Dowlatabadi	24:513–44
Modeling Technological Change: Implications for the Global Environment	A Grübler, N Nakićenović, DG Victor	24:545–69
An Intellectual History of Environmental Economics	D Pearce	27:57–81
Sorry, Wrong Number: The Use and Misuse of Numerical Facts in Analysis and Media Reporting of Energy Issues	JG Koomey, C Calwell, S Laitner, J Thornton, RE Brown, JH Eto, C Webber, C Cullicott	27:119–58
Induced Technical Change in Energy and Environmental Modeling: Analytic Approaches and Policy Implications	M Grubb, J Köhler, D Anderson	27:271–308

Geographic Information Science and Systems for Environmental Management	MF Goodchild	28:493–519

Observations, Monitoring, Indicators

International Environmental Labeling	A Mödl, F Hermann	20:233–64
Ecology: A Personal History	FH Bormann	21:1–29
Environmental Life-Cycle Comparisons of Recycling, Landfilling, and Incineration: A Review of Recent Studies	RA Denison	21:191–237
Rewards and Penalties of Monitoring the Earth	CD Keeling	23:25–82
A Review of National Emissions Inventories from Select Non-Annex I Countries: Implications for Counting Sources and Sinks of Carbon	RA Houghton, K Ramakrishna	24:571–605
Characterizing and Measuring Sustainable Development	TM Parris, RW Kates	28:559–86

Health and Well-Being

Global Change and Human Susceptibility to Disease	GC Daily, PR Ehrlich	21:125–44
Health and Productivity Gains From Better Indoor Environments and Their Relationship with Building Energy Efficiency	WJ Fisk	25:537–66
Indoor Air Quality Factors in Designing a Healthy Building	JD Spengler, Q(Yan) Chen	25:567–600
Public Health Impact of Air Pollution and Implications for the Energy System	A Rabl, JV Spadaro	25:601–27
Human Exposure to Volatile Organic Pollutants: Implications for Indoor Air Studies	LA Wallace	26:269–301
Tracking Multiple Pathways of Human Exposure to Persistent Multimedia Pollutants: Regional, Continental, and Global Scale Models	TE McKone, M MacLeod	28:463–92

Population and Consumption

Consumption of Materials in the United States, 1900–1995	G Matos, L Wagner	23:107–22

Capacity Development for the Environment: A View for the South, A View for the North	AD Sagar	25:377–439
Queries on the Human Use of the Earth	RW Kates	26:1–26
Just Oil? The Distribution of Environmental and Social Impacts of Oil Production and Consumption	D O'Rourke, S Connolly	28:587–617

Ethics, Values, Justice

Reflections on Changing Perceptions of the Earth	GF White	19:1–13
Reflections on the Human Prospect	TF Malone	20:1–29
Ethics and International Business	JV Mitchell	24:83–111
How Much Is Energy Research & Development Worth As Insurance?	RN Schock, W Fulkerson, ML Brown, RL San Martin, DL Greene, J Edmonds	24:487–512

EMERGING INTEGRATIVE THEMES

Cost-Effectiveness in Addressing the "CO_2 Problem," with Special Reference to the Investments of the Global Environment Facility	D Anderson	19:423–55
Autonomous Science and Socially Responsive Science: A Search for Resolution	H Brooks	26:29–48